OCT 1 9 2006

Mergent's
HANDBOOK OF NASDAQ STOCKS

PORT WASHINGTON PUBLIC LIBRARY
ONE LIBRARY DRIVE
PORT WASHINGTON, N.Y. 11050
TEL: 883-4400

Fall 2006

REFERENCE

INTRODUCTION

The Handbook of Nasdaq Stocks is a compact, easy-to-use reference for people who recognize that investing wisely in Nasdaq stocks can be a profitable endeavor. This valuable investment tool provides basic financial and business information on companies of high investor interest with common stocks listed primarily on The Nasdaq Stock Market. For information on companies not covered in the Nasdaq Handbook see Mergent Online, Mergent Manuals and Mergent Company Data on CD-ROM, which contain information on more than 15,000 companies.

The price charts, statistics, business descriptions and discussions of recent developments and prospects are presented in a format that provides investors with the necessary perspective when considering investment advice or suggestions. It also affords investors the opportunity to make investment decisions on their own.

Information is updated quarterly. Every effort is made to secure the most current operating results and dividend information available. In the case of year-end figures, preliminary results are included as they are received. Complete annual report information is shown in the following edition. The schedule below describes the publication dates and company reporting periods usually covered in each edition.

The Spring Edition covers quarterly reports and preliminary annual reports through December 31.

The Summer Edition covers quarterly reports and preliminary annual reports through March 31.

The Fall Edition covers quarterly reports and preliminary annual reports through June 30.

The Winter Edition covers quarterly reports and preliminary annual reports through September 30.

Note: For various reasons, some companies may not report in time to meet our publication deadlines. Company reports received close to press time are shown in the Addenda when space permits. The remainder of late reports are analyzed and published in the next edition of the Handbook.

The Handbook of Nasdaq Stocks also contains a number of special features. A guide on how to use the Handbook explains the various sections of a typical page, with illustrations and definitions of terms. For perspective on stock price movements, Nasdaq composite and industrial price charts are presented. In addition, there are rankings of Handbook companies that have demonstrated the best short-term and long-term price appreciation, as well as those with the highest revenues, net incomes, yields and returns on equity.

TABLE OF CONTENTS

Page

HOW TO USE THIS BOOK 4a

SPECIAL FEATURES
Price Score Leaders 10a
Rankings by Selected Investment Criteria 11a
Stocks with High and Low Price Earnings Multiples 12a
Low-Price Stocks 12a

CHARTS
NASDAQ - Composite 13a

ADDENDA
Companies Added and Dropped 14a
Nasdaq Dividend Achiever List 15a

EDITOR'S NOTE
To reflect the merger of the American Stock Exchange with Nasdaq, companies listed on the American Stock Exchange are included in *The Handbook of Nasdaq Stocks*.

COMPANY REPORTS   Arranged Alphabetically

HOW TO USE THIS BOOK

The presentation of historical data and analytical comments provides the answers to four basic questions for each company:

1. What does the company do? (See G.)
2. How has it done in the past? (See B, J.)
3. How is it doing now? (See C, D, H.)
4. How will it fare in the future? (See I.)

A. CAPSULE STOCK INFORMATION shows where the stock is traded and its symbol, a recent price and price/earnings ratio, plus the yield afforded by the indicated dividend based on a recent price. The indicated dividend is the current annualized dividend based on the most recent price. Some companies are designated as Dividend Achievers. Dividend Achievers have, by *Mergent's* criteria, increased their cash dividend payments for at least ten consecutive years, adjusting for splits. The number of years of consecutive increases is given for each Dividend Achiever.

B. LONG-TERM PRICE CHART illustrates the pattern of monthly stock price movements, fully adjusted for stock dividends and splits. The chart points out the degree of volatility in the price movement of the company's stock and what its long-term trend has been. It also shows how it has performed long-term relative to an initial investment in the S&P 500 Index equal to the price of the company's stock at the beginning of the period shown in the price chart. It indicates areas of price support and resistance, plus other technical points to be considered by the investor. The bars at the base of the long-term price chart indicate the monthly trading volume. Monthly trading volume offers the individual an opportunity to recognize at what periods stock accumulation occurs and what percent of a company's outstanding shares are traded.

PRICE SCORES – Above each company's price/volume chart are its *Mergent's Price Scores*. These are basic measures of the stock's performance. Each stock is measured against the New York Stock Exchange Composite Index.

A score of 100 indicates that the stock did as well as the New York Stock Exchange Composite Index during the time period. A score of less than 100 means that the stock did not do as well; a score of more than 100 means that the stock outperformed the NYSE Composite Index. All stock prices are adjusted for splits and stock dividends. The time periods measured for each company conclude with the date of the recent price shown in the top line of each company's profile.

The *7 YEAR PRICE SCORE* mirrors the common stock's price growth over the previous seven years. The higher the price score, the better the relative performance. It is based on the ratio of the latest 12-month average price to the current seven-year average. This ratio is then indexed against the same ratio for the market as a whole (the New York Stock Exchange Composite Index), which is taken as 100.

The *12 MONTH PRICE SCORE* is a similar measurement but for a shorter period of time. It is based on the ratio of the latest two-month average price to the current 12-month average. As was done for the Long-Term Price Score, this ratio is also indexed to the same ratio for the market as a whole.

C. INTERIM EARNINGS (Per Share) – Figures are reported before effect of extraordinary items, discontinued operations and cumulative effects of accounting changes. Each figure is for the quarterly period indicated. These figures are essentially as reported by the company, although all figures are adjusted for all stock dividends and splits.

4a

ILLUSTRATIVE, INC.

Exchange A	Symbol	Price	52Wk Range	Yield	P/E
NMS	ILLU	$27.04 (8/31/2006)	34.20-22.91	0.07	26.25

*7 Year Price Score 128.05 *NYSE Composite Index=100   *12 Month Price Score 91.29

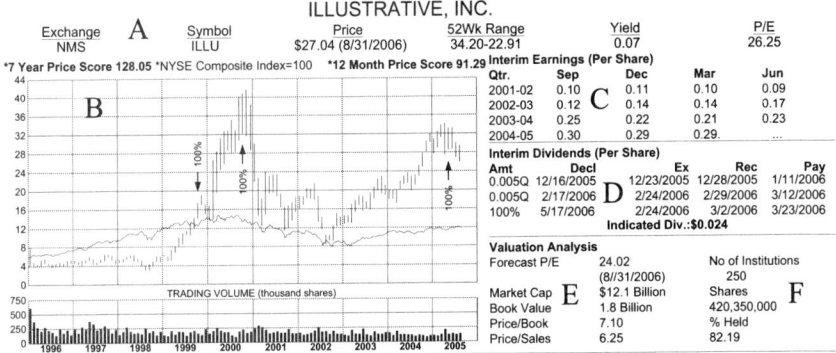

Interim Earnings (Per Share)

Qtr.	Sep	Dec	Mar	Jun
2001-02	0.10	0.11	0.10	0.09
2002-03	0.12 C	0.14	0.14	0.17
2003-04	0.25	0.22	0.21	0.23
2004-05	0.30	0.29	0.29.	...

Interim Dividends (Per Share)

Amt	Decl	Ex	Rec	Pay
0.005Q	12/16/2005	12/23/2005	12/28/2005	1/11/2006
0.005Q	2/17/2006 D	2/24/2006	2/29/2006	3/12/2006
100%	5/17/2006	2/24/2006	3/2/2006	3/23/2006

Indicated Div.:$0.024

Valuation Analysis

Forecast P/E	24.02	No of Institutions
	(8/31/2006)	250
Market Cap E	$12.1 Billion	Shares F
Book Value	1.8 Billion	420,350,000
Price/Book	7.10	% Held
Price/Sales	6.25	82.19

Business Summary: IT & Technology (MIC: 10.2 SIC: 7372 NAIC: 511210)   G
Illustrative offers a line of software and services for consumers, professionals and enterprises, in both public and private sectors. Co.'s digital imaging, design, and document technology platforms enable customers to create, manage and deliver content. Co. distributes its products through a network of distributors and dealers, value-added resellers, systems integrators, independent software vendors and original equipment manufacturers; direct to end users; and through Co.'s Web site. Co. also licenses its technology to major hardware manufacturers, software developers and service providers and offers integrated software services.

Recent Developments: H   For the quarter ended June 30 2006, net income was $149,778 thousand from net income of $109,401 thousand in the year-earlier quarter. Revenues were $496,029 thousand, up 21.0% from $410,085 thousand the year before. Operating income was $182,204 thousand versus an income of $141,839 thousand in the prior-year quarter, an increase of 28.5%. Total direct expense was $27,434 thousand versus $27,255 thousand in the prior-year quarter, an increase of 0.7%. Total indirect expense was $286,391 thousand versus $240,991 thousand in the prior-year quarter, an increase of 18.8%.

Prospects: I   Co.'s results are benefiting from solid demand for its core financial sofware products across all its major geographic markets. Consequently, for the third quarter ended Mar 31, 2006, Co. expects revenue of $430.0 million to $430.0 million, which represents 15.0% to 19.0% year-over-year growth, and earnings per share of $0.27 to $0.29. Also, Co. is targeting gross margin of about 85.0%, and operating margin of approximately 20.0% to 26.0%. Meanwhile, Co. continues to anticipate that its acquisition of FinSoftware, which was announced on May 31 2005, will close in October 2005.

Financial Data
(US$ in Thousands)

	6 Mos	3 Mos	06/30/2005	06/30/2004	06/30/2003	06/30/2002	06/30/2001	06/30/2000
Earnings Per Share J	1.03	0.96	0.91	0.55	0.40	0.41	0.56	0.46
Cash Flow Per Share	1.41	1.37	1.41	0.93	0.70	0.88	0.94	0.68
Tang Book Value Per Share	3.53	3.04	2.68	2.08	1.24	1.31	1.56	1.08
Dividends Per Share	0.025	0.025	0.025	0.025	0.025	0.025	0.025	0.025
Dividend Payout %	2.43	2.61	2.75	4.55	6.33	6.02	4.42	5.43
Income Statement								
Total Revenue	968,911	472,882	1,666,581	1,294,749	1,164,788	1,229,720	1,266,378	1,015,434
EBITDA	394,675	191,739	669,453	429,506	348,170	363,576	487,014	425,197
Depn & Amortn	30,082	14,954	60,808	49,014	63,481	56,645	43,275	50,770
Income Before Taxes	364,593	176,785	608,645	380,492	284,689	306,931	443,739	374,427
Income Taxes	62,921	24,891	158,247	114,148	93,290	101,287	155,931	136,676
Net Income	301,672	151,894	450,398	266,344	191,399	205,644	287,808	237,751
Average Shares	508,156	506,182	495,626	482,900	486,238	498,290	511,548	516,820
Balance Sheet								
Current Assets	1,999,568	1,699,939	1,551,029	1,329,028	814,172	767,364	877,912	623,015
Total Assets	2,421,216	2,122,810	1,958,632	1,555,045	1,051,610	930,623	1,069,416	803,859
Current Liabilities	517,924	484,188	451,408	436,530	377,289	313,651	314,605	267,629
Total Liabilities	551,313	498,245	535,155	454,245	377,289	313,651	316,872	291,650
Stockholders' Equity	1,869,903	1,624,565	1,423,477	1,100,800	674,321	616,972	752,544	512,209
Shares Outstanding	491,589	488,995	484,374	476,600	463,910	472,038	481,892	474,156
Statistical Record								
Return on Assets %	25.07	25.20	25.22	20.49	19.36	20.62	30.81	29.77
Return on Equity %	33.26	33.81	35.11	30.09	29.73	30.11	45.64	45.48
EBITDA Margin %	40.73	40.55	40.17	33.17	29.89	29.57	38.46	41.87
Net Margin %	31.14	32.12	27.03	20.57	16.43	16.72	22.73	23.41
Asset Turnover	0.87	0.90	0.93	1.00	1.18	1.23	1.36	1.27
Current Ratio	3.86	3.51	3.44	3.04	2.16	2.45	2.79	2.33
Price Range	34.20-19.85	32.45-17.20	31.48-17.20	22.91-12.40	21.49-8.35	38.34-11.42	41.63-13.77	19.14-4.67
P/E Ratio	33.20-19.27	33.81-17.91	34.59-18.90	41.66-22.55	53.72-20.88	93.52-27.85	74.33-24.58	41.61-10.16
Average Yield %	0.09	0.10	0.11	0.15	0.16	0.13	0.09	0.25

Address: 123 South Blvd., San Juan, CA 95102-1234 Telephone: 444-555-0000 K Fax: 444-555-0001	Web Site: www.illustrative.com Officers: Jack C. Warrick - Chmn. Chuck M. Norris - Vice Chmn.	Auditors: KPMG LLP Investor Contact: 444-555-0002 Transfer Agents: Computershare Investor Services LLC, Chicago, IL

5a

HOW TO USE THIS BOOK

D. INTERIM DIVIDENDS (Per Share) – The cash dividends are the actual dollar amounts declared by the company. No adjustments have been made for stock dividends and splits. **Ex-Dividend Date**: a stockholder must purchase the stock prior to this date in order to be entitled to the dividend. The **Record Date** indicates the date on which the shareholder had to have been a holder of record in order to qualify for the dividend. The **Payable Date** indicates the date the company paid or intends to pay the dividend. The cash amount shown in the first column is followed by a letter (example "Q" for quarterly) to indicate the frequency of the dividend. A notation of "Dividend payment suspended" indicates that dividend payments have been suspended within the most recent ten years.

Indicated Dividend This is the annualized amount (fully adjusted for splits) of the latest regular cash dividend. Companies with Dividend Reinvestment Plans are indicated here.

E. VALUATION ANALYSIS is a tool for evaluating a company's stock. Included are: Forecast Price/Earnings, Market Capitalization, Book Value, Price/Book and Price/Sales.

F. INSTITUTIONAL HOLDINGS – indicates the number of investment companies, insurance companies, mutual funds, bank trust and college endowment funds holding the stock and the total number of shares held as last reported.

G. BUSINESS SUMMARY explains what a company does in terms of the products or services it sells, its markets, and the position the company occupies in its industry. For a quick reference, included are the Company's Standard Industrial Classification (SIC), North American Industry Classification (NAIC) and Mergent's Industry Classification (MIC).

H. RECENT DEVELOPMENTS – This section captures what has happened in the most recent quarter for which results are available. It provides analysis of recently released sales and earnings figures, including special charges and credits, and may also include results by sector, expense trends and ratios, and other current information.

I. PROSPECTS – This section focuses on what is anticipated for the immediate future, as well as the outlook for the next few years, based on analysis by Mergent.

J. FINANCIAL DATA (fully adjusted for stock dividends and splits) is provided for at least the past seven fiscal years preceded by the most recent three-, six- and nine-month results if available.

Fiscal Years are the annual financial reporting periods as determined by each company. Annual prices and dividends are displayed based on the Company's fiscal year.

Per Share Data:

The Earnings Per Share figure is based on a trailing 12-month period. Earnings per share, and all per share figures, are adjusted for subsequent stock dividends and splits. Earnings per share reported after 12/15/97 are presented on a diluted basis, as described by Financial Accounting Standards Board Statement 128. Prior to that date, earnings per share are presented on a primary basis.

Cash Flow Per Share represents the annualized cash flow from operating activities (or for quarters, TTM cash flow from operating activities) divided by the average shares outstanding.

Tangible Book Value Per Share is calculated as stockholders equity (the value of common shares, paid-in capital and retained earnings) minus preferred stock and intangibles such as goodwill, patents and excess acquisition costs, divided by shares outstanding. It demonstrates the underlying cash value of each common share if the company were to be liquidated as of that date.

HOW TO USE THIS BOOK

Dividends Per Share is the total of cash payments made per share to shareholders for the trailing 12-month period.

Dividend Payout % is the proportion of earnings available for common stock that is paid to common shareholders in the form of cash dividends. It is significant because it indicates what percentage of earnings is being reinvested in the business for internal growth.

EDITOR'S NOTE: TTM net income is net income for the last 365 days (normally four reported quarters) ended on the quarterly balance sheet date. Where that last 365 days does not exactly equate to the last four reported quarters the net income for any included partial quarter is adjusted on a pro-rata basis.

INCOME STATEMENT, BALANCE SHEET AND STATISTICAL RECORD

Includes pertinent earnings and balance sheet information essential to analyzing a corporation's performance. The comparisons provide the necessary historical perspective to intelligently review the various operating and financial trends. Generic definitions follow.

Income Statement:

Total Revenues consists of all revenues from operations.

EBITDA represents earnings before, interest, taxes, depreciation and amortization, and special items.

Depreciation and Amortization includes all non-cash charges such as depletion and amortization as well as depreciation.

Income Before Taxes is the remaining income *after* deducting all costs, expenses, property charges, interest etc. but *before* deducting income taxes.

Income Taxes includes the amount charged against earnings to provide for current and deferred income taxes.

Net Income consists of all revenues less all expenses (operating and non-operating), and is presented before preference and common dividends.

Average Shares Outstanding is the weighted average number of shares including common equivalent shares outstanding during the year, as reported by the corporation and fully adjusted for all stock dividends and splits. The use of *average shares* minimizes the distortion in *earnings per share* which could result from issuance of a large amount of stock or the company's purchase of a large amount of its own stock during the year.

Balance Sheet:

Current Assets includes the short-term assets expected to be realized or consumed within one year. Normally includes cash and cash equivalents, short term investments, receivables, prepayments and inventories.

Total Assets represents all of the assets of the company, including tangible and intangible, and current and non-current.

Current Liabilities are all of the obligations of the company normally expected to be paid within one year. Includes bank overdrafts, short-term debt, payables and accruals.

Long-Term Obligations are the total long-term debts (due beyond one year) reported by the company, including bonds, capital lease obligations, notes, mortgages, debentures, etc.

Total Liabilities represents all liabilities of the company, whether current or non-current.

Stockholders' Equity is the sum of all capital stock accounts – paid in capital (including additional premium), retained earnings, and all other capital balances.

Shares Outstanding is the number of shares outstanding as of the date of the company's quarterly/annual report, exclusive of treasury stock and adjusted for subsequent stock dividends and splits.

Statistical Record:

Return on Assets % represents the ratio of annualized net income (or for Mos, TTM net income) to average total assets. This ratio represents how effectively assets are being used to produce a profit.

HOW TO USE THIS BOOK

Return on Equity % is the ratio of annualized net income (or for Mos, TTM net income) to average stockholders' equity, expressed as a percentage. This ratio illustrates how effectively the investment of the stockholders is being utilized to earn a profit.

EBITDA Margin % represents earnings before interest, taxes, depreciation and amortization as a percentage of total revenue.

Net Margin % is net income expressed as a percentage of total revenues.

Asset Turnover is annualized total revenue (or for Mos, TTM total revenue) divided by average total assets. A measure of efficiency for the use of assets.

Current Ratio represents current assets divided by current liabilities. The higher the figure the better the company is able to meet its current liabilities out of its current assets. A key measure of liquidity for industrial companies.

Debt to Equity is the ratio of long-term obligations to stockholders' equity.

Price Ranges are based on each Company's fiscal year. Where actual stock sales did not take place, a range of lowest bid and highest asked prices is shown.

Price/Earnings Ratio is shown as a range. The figures are calculated by dividing the stock's highest price for the year and its lowest price by the year's earnings per share. Growth stocks tend to command higher P/Es than cyclical stocks.

Average Yield % is the ratio of annual dividends to the real average of the prices over the fiscal year.

EDITOR'S NOTE: In order to preserve the historical relationships between prices, earnings and dividends, figures are not restated to reflect subsequent events. Figures are presented in U.S. dollars unless otherwise indicated.

K. ADDITIONAL INFORMATION on each stock includes the officers of the company, investor relations contact, address, telephone number, web site and transfer agents.

OTHER DEFINITIONS

Factors Pertaining Especially to Real Estate Investment Trusts

Property Income is income from property rental and other associated activities.

Non-Property Income includes interest income and other income not from property activities.

Factors Pertaining Especially to Utilities

Net Property, Plant & Equip is the cost of property, plant and equipment, less its accumulated depreciation.

PPE Turnover represents annualized total revenue (or for Mos, TTM total revenue) divided by average net property, plant and equipment.

Factors Pertaining Especially to Banks

Interest Income is all interest income, including income from loans and leases, securities and deposits.

Interest Expense is all interest expense, including from loans and leases, securities and deposits.

Net Interest Income is interest income less interest expense. This figure is presented before provision for losses.

Provision for Losses represents the amount charged against earnings to increase the provision made for losses on loans and leases.

Non-Interest Income is any income that is not interest-related. Such income could include trading revenue and gains on the sale of assets.

Non-Interest Expense is all expenses that are not interest-related, including employment costs, office costs, marketing costs, etc.

Net Loans & Leases includes all loans and leases net of provisions for losses. May include commercial, agricultural, real estate, consumer and foreign loans.

Total Deposits are all time and demand deposits entrusted to a bank.

HOW TO USE THIS BOOK

Net Interest Margin % is net interest income before provisions expressed as a percentage of total interest income. A key measure of bank profitability.

Efficiency Ratio % is non-interest expense expressed as a percentage of total revenue.

Loans to Deposits are net loans and leases divided by total deposits. A key measure of bank liquidity.

Factors Pertaining Especially to Insurance Companies

Premium Income is the amount of insurance premiums received from policyholders. This is the primary revenue source for insurance companies.

Benefits and Claims represents the payments made to policyholders under the terms of insurance contracts.

Loss Ratio % is benefits and claims expressed as a percentage of premium income. A key ratio of insurance company profitability.

ABBREVIATIONS AND SYMBOLS

A	Annual
ASE	American Stock Exchange
()	Deficit
(Div. Reinv. Plan)	Dividend Reinvestment Plan offered
E	Extra
M	Monthly
N/A	Not Applicable
N.M.	Not Meaningful
NYS	New York Stock Exchange
OTC	Over-The-Counter Market
Q	Quarterly
S	Semi-Annual
Sp	Special Dividend
U	Frequency Unknown

PRICE SCORE LEADERS

Rank	Company	Symbol	♦ 12-Month Score	♦ 7-Year Score
1	RSA Security Inc.	RSAS	155.8	71.9
2	Texas Reg. Bancshares, Inc.	TRBS	124.2	121.4
3	Atmel Corp.	ATML	121.2	43.5
4	Garmin Ltd.	GRMN	121.0	...
5	Spartan Stores Inc.	SPTN	120.9	...
6	Celgene Corp.	CELG	120.7	213.9
7	American Eagle Outfitters, Inc.	AEOS	119.9	141.3
8	Mentor Graphics Corp.	MENT	119.9	59.5
9	Cognizant Tech. Solutions Corp.	CTSH	115.5	205.1
10	Harleysville Group, Inc.	HGIC	115.4	97.7
11	ATI Technologies Inc.	ATYT	114.8	106.4
12	Andrx Corp.	ADRX	114.7	45.9
13	1st Source Corp.	SRCE	114.5	101.8
14	SEI Investments Co.	SEIC	113.0	100.1
15	Expeditors Intl. of Washington	EXPD	112.7	157.4
16	Sterling Bancshares, Inc.	SBIB	112.6	105.4
17	Polycom Inc.	PLCM	112.4	65.6
18	Rent-A-Center Inc.	RCII	112.1	89.4
19	Comcast Corp.	CMCS A	112.0	71.8
20	Emdeon Corp.	HLTH	111.6	69.0
21	Intuit Inc.	INTU	111.4	94.4
22	Swift Transportation Co., Inc.	SWFT	111.3	96.8
23	Lattice Semiconductor Corp.	LSCC	110.1	32.2
24	Pharmaceutical Product Dev. Inc.	PPDI	110.0	163.8
25	BEA Systems, Inc.	BEAS	109.8	44.7

Rank	Company	Symbol	♦ 7-Year Score	♦ 12-Month Score
1	Apple Computer, Inc.	AAPL	215.0	95.6
2	Celgene Corp.	CELG	213.9	120.7
3	Meridian Bioscience	VIVO	212.9	95.7
4	Cognizant Tech Sols.	CTSH	205.1	115.5
5	Raven Industries	RAVN	200.7	88.0
6	Urban Outfitters, Inc.	URBN	197.5	64.0
7	AutoDesk Inc.	ADSK	187.5	81.6
8	Express Scripts Inc.	ESRX	180.1	95.8
9	Amylin Pharmaceuticals, Inc.	AMLN	174.2	109.4
10	Gilead Sciences, Inc.	GILD	173.6	107.0
11	Badger Meter, Inc.	BMI	170.6	96.8
12	SanDisk Corp.	SNDK	170.6	84.8
13	Universal Forests Prod.	UFPI	167.1	87.1
14	Whole Foods Market	WFMI	165.3	82.5
15	Pharmaceutical Product Devel.	PPDI	163.8	110.0
16	Robinson (C.H.) Worldwide, Inc.	CHRW	162.1	109.7
17	Hunt (J.B.) Transport	JBHT	157.6	94.5
18	Expeditors Int'l of Wash., Inc.	EXPD	157.4	112.7
19	Activision, Inc.	ATVI	155.5	86.7
20	Starbucks Corp.	SBUX	154.7	100.2
21	People's Bank	PBCT	151.6	106.3
22	Corporate Executive Board Co.	EXBD	151.2	98.5
23	Research in Motion, Ltd.	RIMM	149.8	97.2
24	Idexx Laboratories, Inc.	IDXX	146.5	108.4
25	NVR Inc.	NVR	143.3	66.4

For an explanation of Mergent's Price Scores, please see page 4a.

10a

RANKINGS BY SELECTED INVESTMENT CRITERIA

25 Companies with High Revenues (Mil.)

Dell Inc	$55,908.0
Costco Wholesale Corp	52,935.2
Sears Holdings Corp.	49,124.0
Microsoft Corporation	44,282.0
Intel Corporation	38,826.0
Cisco Systems, Inc.	24,801.0
Comcast Corporation	22,255.0
Tech Data Corp.	20,482.9
Express Scripts	16,266.0
Staples Inc.	16,078.9
Flextronics International Ltd.	15,288.0
Oracle Corp.	14,380.0
PACCAR Inc.	14,057.4
Apple Computer, Inc.	13,931.0
Sun Microsystems Inc.	13,068.0
Amgen Inc.	12,430.0
Northwest Airlines Corp.	12,286.0
Sanmina-SCI Corporation	11,734.7
Amazon.com Inc.	8,490.0
Echostar Communications Corp.	8,425.5
Smurfit-Stone Container Corp.	8,396.0
Fifth Third Bancorp	7,495,0
Applied Materials, Inc.	6,991.8
Starbucks Corp.	6,369.3
SAFECO Corp.	6,351.1

25 Companies with High Net Income (Mil.)

Microsoft Corporation	$12,599.0
Intel Corporation	8,664.0
Cisco Systems, Inc.	5,741.0
Amgen Inc.	3,674.0
Dell Inc.	3,572.0
Oracle Corp.	3,381.0
Qualcomm, Inc.	2,143.0
Yahoo! Inc.	1,896.2
Fifth Third Bancorp	1,549.0
Echostar Communications Corp.	1,514.5
Apple Computer, Inc.	1,335.0
Applied Materials, Inc.	1,209.9
PACCAR Inc.	1,133.2
eBay Inc.	1,082.0
Teva Pharmaceutical Industries Ltd.	1,072.3
Costco Wholesale Corp.	1,063.1
Comcast Corp.	928.0
IAC/InterActive Corp.	876.2
Sears Holdings Corp.	858.0
Staples, Inc.	834.4
Gilead Sciences, Inc.	813.9
NVR Inc.	697.6
SAFECO Corporation	691.1
Adobe Systems, Inc.	602.8
Cincinnati Financial Corp.	602.0

25 Companies with High Yields

American Capital Strategies	8.6%
Capitol Federal Financial	5.9
FirstMerit Corp.	5.0
Corus Bankshares, Inc.	4.6
Huntington Bancshares, Inc.	4.2
MGE Energy Inc.	4.1
Fifth Third Bancorp	4.1
Susquehanna Bancshares, Inc.	3.9
Harleysville National Corp.	3.9
Otter Tail Corp.	3.8
Sky Financial Group	3.7
S & T Bancorp, Inc.	3.7
Chemical Financial Corp.	3.7
Washington Federal Inc.	3.7
Associated Banc-Corp	3.7
Park National Corp.	3.6
Fulton Financial Corp.	3.5
Wesbanco, Inc.	3.5
Republic Bancorp, Inc.	3.4
Popular Inc.	3.4
National Penn Bancshares, Inc.	3.3
First Indiana Corp.	3.3
First Charter Corp.	3.2
Independent Bank Corporation	3.2
Nash Finch Co.	3.2

25 Companies with High Return on Equity

Emmis Communications Corp.	98.8
NVR Inc.	92.3
Dell Inc.	66.2
Miller (Herman) Inc.	63.2
Apollo Group, Inc.	53.5
Autodesk Inc.	45.7
SEI Investments Co.	45.6
Imclone Systems Inc.	40.1
Adobe Systems, Inc.	36.8
Gilead Sciences, Inc.	33.2
Rent-A-Center Inc.	32.9
Raven Industries, Inc.	32.2
Novell, Inc.	32.1
Patterson-UTI Energy Inc.	31.4
QLogic Corp.	31.3
Paychex Inc.	30.6
Express Scripts Inc.	30.1
Performance Food Group Co.	30.0
PACCAR Inc.	29.6
Parametric Technology Corp.	29.5
Garmin Ltd.	29.3
Robinson (C.H.) Worldwide, Inc.	29.0
Microsoft Copr.	28.6
Cognizant Tech. Solutions	28.5
American Eagle Outfitters	27.8

STOCKS WITH HIGH AND LOW PRICE EARNINGS MULTIPLES

	High P/E		Low P/E
Celgene Corp.	451.11	Owens Corning	0.14
Biogen Idec Inc.	442.00	Emmis Communications Corp.	1.35
Quixote Corp.	338.40	NVR Inc.	5.05
Symantec Corp.	266.00	Nash Finch Co.	5.34
Andrx Corp.	183.38	Corus Bankshares, Inc.	7.47
Power-One, Inc.	169.75	National Penn Bancshares, Inc.	7.49
Lamar Advertising Co.	153.82	American Capital Strategies	7.62
Atmel Corp.	144.50	Ohio Casualty Corp.	7.70
Activision, Inc.	143.33	Cincinnati Financial Corp	8.37
Dentsply International, Inc.	112.34	Patterson-UTI Energy Inc.	8.40
Mentor Graphics Corp.	111.54	Imclone Systems Inc.	9.03
Sepracor Inc.	90.40	Pacific Sunwear of California, Inc.	9.09
Electronic Arts, Inc.	75.04	Wesco Financial Corp.	9.85
Amkor Technology Inc.	70.88	SAFECO Corporation	10.14
Advent Software, Inc.	69.68	PACCAR Inc.	10.45
Abraxis Bioscience Inc.	67.24	Harleysville Group, Inc.	11.01
Macrovision Corp.	59.69	QLogic Corp.	11.49
Affymetrix, Inc.	59.19	Popular Inc.	11.55
Comcast Corp.	58.40	First Indiana Corp.	12.16
RSA Security	58.02	Universal Forest Products Inc.	12.19
Red Hat Inc.	55.24	Associated Banc-Corp.	12.62
Silicon Laboratories Inc.	55.11	Pacific Capital Bancorp	12.65
Rambus Inc.	52.90	Independent Bank Corp.	12.68
Congnizant Tech. Solutions Corp.	51.40	Swift Transportation Co., Inc.	12.88
Cadence Design Systems Inc	51.38	MAF Bancorp, Inc.	13.10

LOW PRICE STOCKS

	Price		Price
Granite Broadcasting Corp.	0.12	PMC-Sierra Inc.	6.86
Federal-Mogul Corp.	0.36	Lattice Semiconductor Corp.	7.32
Northwest Airlines Corp.	0.54	Powerwave Technologies	7.58
Owens Corning	0.90	CompuWare Corp.	7.60
Charter Communications Inc.	1.39	Cobra Electronics Corp.	8.21
JDS Uniphase Corp.	2.27	UTStarcom Inc.	8.21
Credence Systems Corp.	2.53	Andrew Corp.	9.25
Applied Micro Circuits	2.73	Pathmark Stores, Inc.	9.71
Gemstar-TV Guide Intl.	3.22	Micrel, Inc.	10.02
Sanmina-SCI Corp	3.37	Wind River Systems, Inc.	10.17
Ciena Corp.	3.95	Tellabs, Inc.	10.19
Sirius Satellite Radio	4.08	JetBlue Airways Corp.	10.26
McData Corp.	4.18	Millennium Pharmaceuticals	10.84
Research Frontiers	4.20	Smurfit-Stone Container	11.39
Level 3 Communications, Inc.	4.43	Neurocrine Bio Sciences, Inc.	11.59
3Com Corp.	4.44	Flextronics International	11.79
TriQuint Semiconductor	4.93	Emdeon Corp.	11.85
Sun Microsystems	4.99	Corinthian Colleges, Inc.	12.12
LTX Corp	5.07	Foundry Networks Inc.	12.17
Amkor Technology Inc.	5.67	Emmis Communications Corp	12.23
Atmel Corp.	5.78	Activision, Inc.	12.90
Radio One, Inc.	6.18	Republic Bancorp, Inc.	12.93
RF Micro Devices	6.62	XM Satellite Radio Holdings Inc.	12.95
Novell, Inc.	6.68	Southwest Water Co.	12.97
Power-One, Inc.	6.79	Hudson City Bancorp	13.06

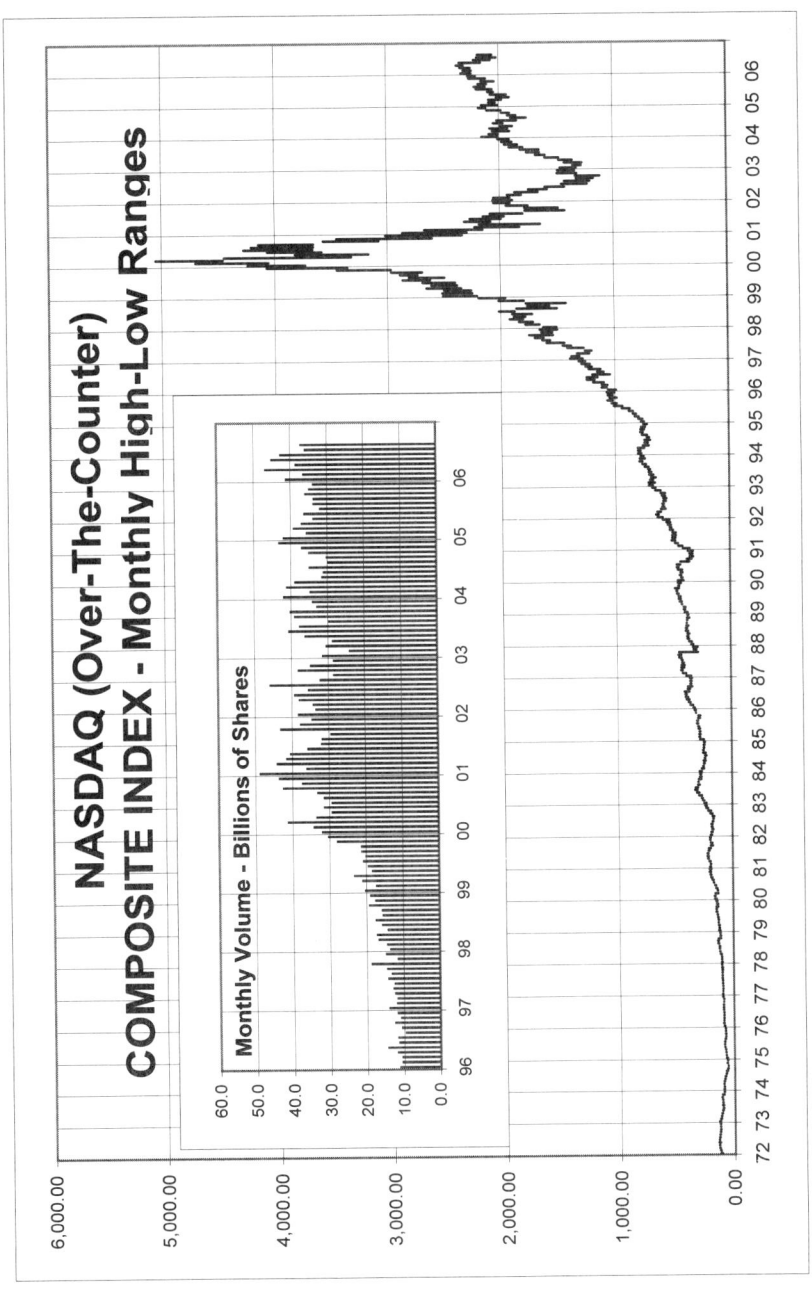

ADDENDA
COMPANIES ADDED AND DROPPED

Companies are removed for various reasons, such as listing on other exchanges, mergers, bankruptcies, lack of investor interest or company's failure to renew Corporate Visibility. Companies deleted from this edition:

Nextel Partners Inc.

The 2006 NASDAQ Dividend Achievers

Companies listed below qualified for the 2006 Edition of Mergent's Dividend Achievers. Also shown are total numbers of consecutive years of dividend growth.

Company Name	Years of Growth	Company Name	Years of Growth
1st Source Corp.	18	Matthews International Corp	11
Alfa Corp	20	McGrath RentCorp	15
Anchor BanCorp Wisconsin, Inc	12	Mercantile Bankshares Corp.	29
Applebee's International, Inc.	14	Meridian Bioscience Inc.	13
Arrow International, Inc.	13	MGE Energy Inc	30
Associated Banc-Corp.	35	Midland Co.	19
Badger Meter, Inc.	13	National Penn Bancshares, Inc.	27
BancFirst Corp.	12	Nordson Corp.	25
Capital City Bank Group, Inc.	12	Northern Trust Corp.	20
Chemical Financial Corp.	30	Old Second Bancorp., Inc.	11
Cincinnati Financial Corp.	45	Otter Tail Corp.	30
Cintas Corporation	23	Pacific Capital Bancorp	36
Commerce Bancshares, Inc.	37	Park National Corp.	18
Community Banks, Inc.	14	Paychex Inc	17
Community Trust Bancorp, Inc.	17	People's Bank	12
Compass Bancshares Inc.	24	Popular Inc.	13
Corus Bankshares, Inc.	19	Quixote Corp.	12
Courier Corp.	12	Raven Industries, Inc.	18
CVB Financial Corp.	15	Republic Bancorp, Inc.	13
DENTSPLY International, Inc.	11	Ross Stores, Inc.	11
Erie Indemnity Co.	10	S & T Bancorp, Inc.	16
Expeditors Intl of Washington	11	Sandy Spring Bancorp	10
Fifth Third Bancorp	33	SEI Investments Co.	14
First Busey Corp.	14	Sigma-Aldrich Corp.	24
First Charter Corp.	13	Sky Financial Group, Inc.	11
First Financial Holdings, Inc.	13	South Financial Group Inc	11
First Indiana Corp.	14	Southwest Bancorp, Inc.	11
First Midwest Bancorp, Inc.	13	Southwest Water Co.	10
First State Bancorporation	11	State Auto Financial Corp.	14
FirstMerit Corp	23	Sterling Bancshares, Inc.	12
Franklin Electric Co., Inc.	12	Sterling Financial Corp.	18
Fulton Financial Corp.	32	Suffolk Bancorp	16
Glacier Bancorp, Inc.	14	Susquehanna Bancshares, Inc	35
Greater Bay Bancorp	10	T Rowe Price Group Inc.	19
Harleysville Group, Inc.	19	Texas Regional Bancsha, Inc.	11
Harleysville National Corp.	19	Trustmark Corp.	32
IBERIABANK Corp	10	United Bankshares, Inc.	24
Independent Bank Corporation	17	Universal Forest Products Inc.	12
Jack Henry & Associates, Inc.	14	Washington Federal Inc.	22
Lancaster Colony Corp.	36	Wesbanco, Inc.	20
Linear Technology Corp.	13	Wesco Financial Corp.	34
LSI Industries Inc.	12	WestAmerica Bancorporation	16
MAF Bancorp, Inc.	11	Whitney Holding Corp.	12

ABRAXIS BIOSCIENCE INC

Exchange	Symbol	Price	52Wk Range	Yield	P/E
NMS	ABBI	$24.88 (8/31/2006)	48.27-19.99	N/A	67.24

*7 Year Price Score N/A   *NYSE Composite Index=100   *12 Month Price Score 65.36

Interim Earnings (Per Share)

Qtr.	Mar	Jun	Sep	Dec
2003	0.33	0.27	0.25	0.23
2004	0.16	0.13	0.19	0.30
2005	0.33	0.28	0.25	0.32
2006	0.37	(0.57)	...	...

Interim Dividends (Per Share)

Amt	Decl	Ex	Rec	Pay
50%	8/8/2003	9/3/2003	8/18/2003	9/2/2003

Valuation Analysis   **Institutional Holding**

Forecast P/E	N/A	No of Institutions	N/A
Market Cap	$4.0 Billion	Shares	
Book Value	985.2 Million	N/A	
Price/Book	4.01	% Held	
Price/Sales	6.84	N/A	

Business Summary: Pharmaceuticals (MIC: 9.1 SIC: 2834 NAIC: 325412)

Abraxis Bioscience is a pharmaceutical that develops, manufactures and markets injectable pharmaceutical products, primarily focused on the injectable oncology, anti-infective and critical care markets. Co.'s products are mainly used in hospitals, long-term care facilities, alternate care sites and clinics within North America. In addition, Co. holds the exclusive North American right to sell Abraxane®, a proprietary nanoparticle injectable oncology product that is a patented formulation of paclitaxel. Co. is organized along four key operating divisions: American Pharmaceutical Partners, Abraxis Oncology, Abraxis Research and Abraxis BioCapital.

Recent Developments: For the quarter ended June 30 2006, net loss amounted to $90.8 million versus net income of $20.4 million in the year-earlier quarter. Revenues were $160.7 million, up 29.1% from $124.5 million the year before. Operating loss was $107.8 million versus an income of $31.4 million in the prior-year quarter. Direct operating expenses rose 21.9% to $67.7 million from $55.5 million in the comparable period the year before. Indirect operating expenses increased 434.0% to $200.9 million from $37.6 million in the equivalent prior-year period.

Prospects: Co. believes that the underlying demand for its ABRAXANE® oncology product remains strong, and has revised its full-year 2006 ABRAXANE® sales guidance to between $170.0 million and $190.0 million. Going forward, Co. will continue to invest in a comprehensive development program for both its ABRAXANE® oncology product and hospital-based business. Specifically, Co. is continuing to study the use of ABRAXANE® in various oncology settings and is targeting six Investigational New Drug submissions over the next 12 to 18 months for new molecules which use the nab™ technology platform. Co. will also pursue strategic acquisitions and partnerships to boost its capabilities and product offerings.

Financial Data
(US$ in Thousands)

	6 Mos	3 Mos	12/31/2005	12/31/2004	12/31/2003	12/31/2002	12/31/2001	12/31/2000
Earnings Per Share	0.37	1.22	1.17	0.78	0.99	0.60	0.20	(0.29)
Cash Flow Per Share	2.16	1.86	0.92	0.67	0.83	0.52	0.31	0.55
Tang Book Value Per Share	N.M.	6.61	6.08	4.43	3.52	2.57	1.80	...
Income Statement								
Total Revenue	305,267	143,754	518,813	405,010	351,315	277,474	192,029	165,495
EBITDA	(78,099)	45,795	147,366	96,243	126,312	86,144	34,734	(4,485)
Depn & Amortn	20,126	4,520	15,900	9,200	9,002	9,980	9,352	7,761
Income Before Taxes	(95,885)	42,380	133,870	88,833	119,068	78,299	22,167	(13,797)
Income Taxes	(6,982)	14,833	47,458	32,140	47,375	33,100	9,539	(5,038)
Net Income	(88,903)	27,547	86,412	56,693	71,693	45,199	12,628	(8,759)
Average Shares	158,765	73,902	74,053	73,147	72,745	75,478	58,422	33,792
Balance Sheet								
Total Assets	1,717,609	550,835	513,382	373,333	303,785	220,976	239,787	122,823
Current Liabilities	212,101	67,260	70,958	57,809	55,680	40,268	98,860	35,526
Long-Term Obligations	175,500	...	...	...	...	...	...	14,938
Total Liabilities	732,389	68,889	72,587	60,642	57,724	40,268	109,717	84,124
Stockholders' Equity	985,220	481,946	440,795	312,691	246,061	180,708	130,070	38,699
Shares Outstanding	158,870	72,864	72,461	70,638	69,868	70,314	72,408	34,254
Statistical Record								
Return on Assets %	N.M.	18.33	19.49	16.70	27.32	19.62	6.97	N.M.
Return on Equity %	N.M.	21.61	22.94	20.24	33.60	29.09	14.96	N.M.
EBITDA Margin %	N.M.	31.86	28.40	23.76	35.95	31.05	18.09	N.M.
Net Margin %	N.M.	19.16	16.66	14.00	20.41	16.29	6.58	N.M.
Asset Turnover	0.53	1.11	1.17	1.19	1.34	1.20	1.06	1.46
Current Ratio	1.65	5.65	4.87	4.38	3.87	3.68	1.77	1.71
Debt to Equity	0.18	...	...	...	...	...	...	0.39
Price Range	48.27-23.45	58.14-27.93	58.14-32.66	47.04-21.68	39.32-11.02	15.72-5.51	14.20-12.51	...
P/E Ratio	130.46-63.38	47.66-22.89	49.69-27.91	60.31-27.79	39.72-11.13	26.20-9.18	71.00-62.53	...

Address: 1501 East Woodfield Road, Suite 300, Schaumburg, IL 60173-5787 Telephone: 847-969-2700	Web Site: www.abraxisbio.com Officers: Patrick Soon-Shiong M.D. - Chmn. Alan L. Heller - Pres., C.E.O.	Auditors: Ernst & Young, LLP

ACTIVISION, INC.

Exchange	Symbol	Price	52Wk Range	Yield	P/E
NMS	ATVI	$12.90 (8/31/2006)	17.42-10.72	N/A	143.33

*7 Year Price Score 155.48 *NYSE Composite Index=100 *12 Month Price Score 86.72

Interim Earnings (Per Share)

Qtr.	Jun	Sep	Dec	Mar
2003-04	0.01	(0.04)	0.30	0.03
2004-05	0.04	0.10	0.35	0.01
2005-06	(0.01)	(0.05)	0.23	(0.03)
2006-07	(0.06)	...	...	...

Interim Dividends (Per Share)

Amt	Decl	Ex	Rec	Pay
3-for-2	5/5/2003	6/9/2003	5/16/2003	6/6/2003
50%	2/12/2004	3/16/2004	2/23/2004	3/15/2004
4-for-3	2/23/2005	3/23/2005	3/7/2005	3/22/2005
33.33%	9/28/2005	10/25/2005	10/10/2005	10/24/2005

Valuation Analysis

		Institutional Holding	
Forecast P/E	27.50	No of Institutions	
	(9/9/2006)	260	
Market Cap	$3.6 Billion	Shares	
Book Value	1.2 Billion	255,761,872	
Price/Book	2.93	% Held	
Price/Sales	2.56	91.22	

Business Summary: IT & Technology (MIC: 10.2 SIC: 7372 NAIC: 511210)

Activision is an international publisher, developer and distributor of interactive software products. Co.'s products span across various genres such as action, adventure, strategy, and simulation. Co.'s products operate mainly on the Sony PlayStation 2, Nintendo GameCube, Microsoft Xbox and Microsoft Xbox 360 console systems, Nintendo Game Boy Advance, Sony PlayStation Portable and Nintendo Dual Screen hand-held devices and the personal computer. Co.'s target customer base ranges from casual players to game enthusiasts, children to adults, and mass-market consumers to 'value' buyers.

Recent Developments: For the quarter ended June 30 2006, net loss amounted to $17.8 million versus a net loss of $3.6 million in the year-earlier quarter. Revenues were $188.1 million, down 22.0% from $241.1 million the year before. Operating loss was $32.8 million versus a loss of $13.4 million in the prior-year quarter. Direct operating expenses declined 20.0% to $137.8 million from $172.3 million in the comparable period the year before. Indirect operating expenses increased 1.0% to $83.1 million from $82.3 million in the equivalent prior-year period.

Prospects: Co.'s anticipated fiscal 2007 releases will include brands backed by intellectual property and/or highly anticipated motion picture releases. Co. has a long-term relationship with Marvel Entertainment, Inc. through an exclusive licensing agreement for the Spider-Man and X-Men franchises through 2017, granting it the exclusive rights to develop and publish video games based on Marvel's comic book franchises Spider-Man and X-Men. Additionally, through Co.'s licensing agreement with Spider-Man Merchandising, LP, it will be developing and publishing video games based on Columbia Pictures/Marvel Entertainment, Inc.'s feature film "Spider-Man 3," which is expected to be released in May 2007.

Financial Data
(US$ in Thousands)

	3 Mos	03/31/2006	03/31/2005	03/31/2004	03/31/2003	03/31/2002	03/31/2001	03/31/2000
Earnings Per Share	0.09	0.14	0.50	0.30	0.24	0.22	0.13	(0.23)
Cash Flow Per Share	0.14	0.31	0.86	0.28	0.35	0.55	0.55	0.52
Tang Book Value Per Share	3.45	3.69	3.64	2.91	1.90	1.68	0.95	0.71
Income Statement								
Total Revenue	188,069	1,468,000	1,405,857	947,656	864,116	786,434	620,183	572,205
EBITDA	(2,020)	210,054	330,442	207,147	215,702	151,793	107,737	85,844
Depn & Amortn	30,764	187,800	145,400	97,900	112,295	68,673	75,193	124,580
Income Before Taxes	(24,511)	48,587	197,663	115,992	103,407	83,120	32,544	(38,736)
Income Taxes	(6,685)	6,688	59,328	38,277	37,227	30,882	12,037	(4,648)
Net Income	(17,826)	41,899	138,335	77,715	66,180	52,238	20,507	(34,088)
Average Shares	278,335	299,437	278,859	257,587	276,414	237,819	164,399	148,145
Balance Sheet								
Total Assets	1,437,402	1,419,523	1,306,963	968,817	704,816	556,887	359,957	309,737
Current Liabilities	161,608	192,163	207,051	136,079	104,405	123,674	115,250	103,948
Long-Term Obligations	...	...	...	...	2,671	3,122	63,401	73,778
Total Liabilities	202,568	193,939	207,051	136,079	107,076	126,796	178,651	177,728
Stockholders' Equity	1,234,834	1,225,584	1,099,912	832,738	597,740	430,091	181,306	132,009
Shares Outstanding	280,315	277,020	268,040	244,144	240,224	226,822	163,694	155,929
Statistical Record								
Return on Assets %	2.05	3.07	12.16	9.26	10.49	11.40	6.12	N.M.
Return on Equity %	2.36	3.60	14.32	10.84	12.88	17.09	13.09	N.M.
EBITDA Margin %	N.M.	14.31	23.50	21.92	24.96	19.30	17.37	15.00
Net Margin %	N.M.	2.85	9.84	8.20	7.66	6.64	3.31	N.M.
Asset Turnover	1.05	1.08	1.24	1.13	1.37	1.72	1.85	1.92
Current Ratio	6.58	5.81	5.42	5.97	5.05	3.69	2.59	2.54
Debt to Equity	...	...	...	...	N.M.	0.01	0.35	0.56
Price Range	17.42-10.75	17.42-10.85	13.88-7.12	8.90-3.42	8.66-3.18	8.07-3.72	4.13-0.94	2.96-1.72
P/E Ratio	193.56-119.44	124.43-77.46	27.77-14.23	29.66-11.39	36.10-13.24	36.70-16.89	31.73-7.25	...

Address: 3100 Ocean Park Boulevard, Santa Monica, CA 90405 Telephone: 310-255-2000 Fax: 310-255-2100	Web Site: www.activision.com Officers: Robert A. Kotick - Chmn., C.E.O. Brian G. Kelly - Co-Chmn.	Auditors: PricewaterhouseCoopers LLP Investor Contact: 310-255-2000

ACXIOM CORP.

Exchange	Symbol	Price	52Wk Range	Yield	P/E
NMS	ACXM	$24.29 (8/31/2006)	26.46-18.63	0.82	28.58

*7 Year Price Score 90.22   *NYSE Composite Index=100   *12 Month Price Score 100.76

Interim Earnings (Per Share)

Qtr.	Jun	Sep	Dec	Mar
2003-04	0.13	0.13	0.22	0.17
2004-05	0.14	0.20	0.24	0.16
2005-06	0.07	0.08	0.31	0.26
2006-07	0.20	...	...	...

Interim Dividends (Per Share)

Amt	Decl	Ex	Rec	Pay
0.05Q	11/2/2005	11/9/2005	11/14/2005	12/5/2005
0.05Q	2/9/2006	2/15/2006	2/20/2006	3/13/2006
0.05Q	5/31/2006	6/8/2006	6/12/2006	7/3/2006
0.05Q	8/3/2006	8/10/2006	8/14/2006	9/12/2006

Indicated Div: $0.20

Valuation Analysis	**Institutional Holding**
Forecast P/E	19.45	No of Institutions
	(9/9/2006)	182
Market Cap	$2.1 Billion	Shares
Book Value	720.6 Million	65,063,896
Price/Book	2.97	% Held
Price/Sales	1.57	73.88

Business Summary: IT & Technology (MIC: 10.2 SIC: 7374 NAIC: 518210)
Acxiom provides customer and information management services for various companies worldwide. Co. operates through two business segments: U.S. Services and Data, and International Services and Data. Both of the segments include consulting, database and data warehousing, list processing services, data content and software products. U.S. Services and Data provides services that integrate and manage customer, consumer and business data using its information management skills and technology, as well as its InfoBase data products. International Services and Data provides customer data, data management, risk management and business process outsourcing services to clients across the globe.

Recent Developments: For the quarter ended June 30 2006, net income increased 168.2% to $17.8 million from $6.6 million in the year-earlier quarter. Revenues were $336.7 million, up 8.5% from $310.3 million the year before. Operating income was $36.3 million versus $15.0 million in the prior-year quarter, an increase of 142.5%. Direct operating expenses rose 1.0% to $245.6 million from $243.2 million in the comparable period the year before. Indirect operating expenses increased 5.2% to $54.7 million from $52.1 million in the equivalent prior-year period.

Prospects: Co.'s near-term outlook appears encouraging, reflecting top- and bottom-line growth. Specifically, Co.'s results are benefiting from an increase in both its services and data revenues. Meanwhile, Co. has recently completed construction on an additional 30,000 square foot data center in Little Rock, AR, which is expected to be occupied in the second quarter of fiscal 2007. For fiscal year ending Mar 31 2007, Co. continues to expect U.S. revenue growth of 7.0% to 10.0%, as well as U.S. operating margins of between 14.0% and 15.0%. International revenue growth is expected to range from 0% to 5.0%, while international margins are anticipated to be between 2.0% and 4.0%.

Financial Data

(US$ in Thousands)	3 Mos	03/31/2006	03/31/2005	03/31/2004	03/31/2003	03/31/2002	03/31/2001	03/31/2000
Earnings Per Share	0.85	0.71	0.74	0.64	0.24	(0.36)	0.07	1.00
Cash Flow Per Share	3.07	3.18	2.85	3.03	2.87	1.70	0.54	1.23
Tang Book Value Per Share	0.31	0.37	2.58	0.96	1.30	1.20	2.35	4.37
Dividends Per Share	0.200	0.200	0.170	0.040	...	...	...	...
Dividend Payout %	23.53	28.17	22.97	6.25	...	...	...	...
Income Statement								
Total Revenue	336,705	1,332,568	1,223,042	1,010,822	958,222	866,110	1,009,887	964,460
EBITDA	36,962	364,225	320,512	236,801	204,753	101,400	218,638	254,638
Depn & Amortn	...	231,137	195,120	150,241	154,902	123,394	120,793	86,529
Income Before Taxes	29,193	104,344	106,201	67,293	28,088	(50,526)	71,332	144,577
Income Taxes	11,385	40,216	36,483	8,949	6,321	(19,833)	27,465	54,214
Net Income	17,808	64,128	69,718	58,344	21,767	(31,964)	6,379	90,363
Average Shares	90,423	90,289	99,446	97,237	90,542	88,478	92,494	94,640
Balance Sheet								
Total Assets	1,545,047	1,540,498	1,399,879	1,215,784	1,093,246	1,156,834	1,232,725	1,105,296
Current Liabilities	371,913	379,990	364,262	296,103	171,665	177,670	214,320	180,008
Long-Term Obligations	374,846	376,415	141,704	293,457	289,677	396,850	369,172	289,234
Total Liabilities	824,494	834,321	585,045	628,568	530,690	645,903	616,277	517,566
Stockholders' Equity	720,553	706,177	814,834	587,216	562,556	510,931	616,448	587,730
Shares Outstanding	87,972	88,148	95,213	85,936	90,149	87,337	90,029	87,837
Statistical Record								
Return on Assets %	4.90	4.36	5.33	5.04	1.93	N.M.	0.55	9.08
Return on Equity %	10.81	8.43	9.95	10.12	4.06	N.M.	1.06	19.24
EBITDA Margin %	10.98	27.33	26.21	23.43	21.37	11.71	21.65	26.40
Net Margin %	5.29	4.81	5.70	5.77	2.27	N.M.	0.63	9.37
Asset Turnover	0.89	0.91	0.94	0.87	0.85	0.72	0.86	0.97
Current Ratio	0.91	0.89	0.92	0.97	1.68	2.03	1.64	1.89
Debt to Equity	0.52	0.53	0.17	0.50	0.51	0.78	0.60	0.49
Price Range	26.46-18.63	26.46-16.75	26.94-20.65	21.96-12.96	19.38-12.25	19.87-7.85	44.17-20.19	35.38-14.75
P/E Ratio	31.13-21.92	37.27-23.59	36.41-27.91	34.31-20.25	80.75-51.04	...	631.03-288.39	35.38-14.75
Average Yield %	0.88	0.93	0.72	0.24	...	...	...	...

Address: 1 Information Way, P.O. Box 8180, Little Rock, AR 72203-8180	Web Site: www.acxiom.com	Auditors: KPMG LLP
Telephone: 501-342-1000	Officers: Charles D. Morgan - Chmn., Company Leader Rodger S. Kline - Chief Fin.& Admin. Leader	Investor Contact: 501-342-1000
Fax: 501-342-3925		

ADC TELECOMMUNICATIONS INC

Exchange	Symbol	Price	52Wk Range	Yield	P/E
NMS	ADCT	$13.65 (8/31/2006)	27.15-11.98	N/A	47.07

*7 Year Price Score 31.24   *NYSE Composite Index=100   *12 Month Price Score 65.79

Interim Earnings (Per Share)

Qtr.	Jan	Apr	Jul	Oct
2002-03	(0.35)	(0.28)	(0.14)	0.07
2003-04	0.00	(0.21)	(0.14)	0.49
2004-05	0.42	0.27	0.20	0.02
2005-06	(0.02)	0.19	0.10	...

Interim Dividends (Per Share)
No Dividends Paid

Valuation Analysis

Forecast P/E	15.74		Institutional Holding
	(9/9/2006)		No of Institutions 222
Market Cap	$1.6 Billion		Shares
Book Value	827.8 Million		92,795,440
Price/Book	1.93		% Held
Price/Sales	1.24		79.16

Business Summary: Communications (MIC: 10.1 SIC: 3661 NAIC: 334210)
ADC Telecommunications is a global provider of communications network infrastructure services. Co. provides connections for communications networks over copper, fiber, coaxial and wireless media that enable the use of high-speed Internet, data, video and voice services by residences, businesses and mobile communications subscribers. Co.'s products include fiber optic, copper and coaxial based frames, cabinets, cables, connectors, cards and other physical components that enable the delivery of communications for wireline, wireless, cable, and broadcast networks. Co.'s products also include network access devices such as high-bit-rate digital subscriber line and wireless coverage applications.

Recent Developments: For the quarter ended July 28 2006, income from continuing operations decreased 38.1% to $23.2 million from $37.5 million in the year-earlier quarter. Net income decreased 52.7% to $11.3 million from $23.9 million in the year-earlier quarter. Revenues were $343.6 million, up 11.9% from $307.0 million the year before. Operating income was $24.0 million versus $35.9 million in the prior-year quarter, a decrease of 33.1%. Direct operating expenses rose 22.1% to $231.4 million from $189.5 million in the comparable period the year before. Indirect operating expenses increased 8.1% to $88.2 million from $81.6 million in the equivalent prior-year period.

Prospects: On Aug 9 2006, Co. announced that it has entered into an agreement with Andrew Corp. to terminate its pending acquisition of Andrew. To effect the mutual termination, Andrew agreed to pay Co. $10.0 million. Andrew also agreed to pay Co. another $65.0 million in the event that Andrew effects a business combination transaction in one year. Meanwhile, Co. continues to execute its position as a global supplier of network infrastructure services through a combination of business development initiatives, new product developments and execution in its core business. As such, Co. expects sales of $1.27 billion to $1.29 billion and earnings of $0.51 to $0.56 per diluted share in fiscal 2006.

Financial Data
(US$ in Thousands)

	9 Mos	6 Mos	3 Mos	10/31/2005	10/31/2004	10/31/2003	10/31/2002	10/31/2001
Earnings Per Share	0.29	0.39	0.47	0.91	0.14	(0.70)	(10.08)	(11.48)
Cash Flow Per Share	0.88	0.90	0.52	0.51	0.03	0.34	0.53	0.84
Tang Book Value Per Share	3.76	3.57	3.28	3.16	3.34	5.45	6.38	14.85
Income Statement								
Total Revenue	974,500	647,400	280,200	1,169,200	784,300	773,200	1,047,700	2,402,800
EBITDA	101,800	55,400	14,200	152,800	71,200	(29,200)	(785,900)	(1,720,700)
Depn & Amortn	50,300	33,700	16,600	67,200	41,700	59,200	104,700	197,800
Income Before Taxes	54,000	24,300	(1,100)	92,700	33,200	(82,100)	(882,200)	(1,920,700)
Income Taxes	7,000	3,900	1,300	7,200	1,900	(5,400)	262,800	(633,000)
Net Income	32,300	21,000	(1,800)	110,700	16,400	(76,700)	(1,145,000)	(1,287,700)
Average Shares	117,400	117,900	116,700	131,100	116,014	114,771	113,657	112,428
Balance Sheet								
Total Assets	1,574,200	1,568,500	1,514,700	1,535,000	1,428,100	1,296,900	1,144,200	2,499,700
Current Liabilities	263,500	275,300	250,800	286,600	302,000	265,800	397,800	599,400
Long-Term Obligations	400,000	400,000	400,000	400,000	400,000	400,000	10,800	3,000
Total Liabilities	746,400	757,200	731,700	761,100	768,800	669,200	412,000	606,300
Stockholders' Equity	827,800	811,300	783,000	773,900	659,300	627,700	732,200	1,893,400
Shares Outstanding	117,200	117,200	117,000	116,500	115,728	115,228	114,228	113,142
Statistical Record								
Return on Assets %	2.17	3.01	3.87	7.47	1.20	N.M.	N.M.	N.M.
Return on Equity %	4.17	5.92	7.62	15.45	2.54	N.M.	N.M.	N.M.
EBITDA Margin %	10.45	8.56	5.07	13.07	9.08	N.M.	N.M.	N.M.
Net Margin %	3.31	3.24	N.M.	9.47	2.09	N.M.	N.M.	N.M.
Asset Turnover	0.84	0.83	0.82	0.79	0.57	0.63	0.58	0.74
Current Ratio	3.57	3.34	3.36	2.98	2.77	3.79	1.73	2.18
Debt to Equity	0.48	0.49	0.51	0.52	0.61	0.64	0.01	0.61
Price Range	27.15-11.98	27.15-15.40	26.39-13.16	26.39-13.16	22.46-12.39	21.84-11.06	39.76-7.28	185.06-21.07
P/E Ratio	93.62-41.31	69.62-39.49	56.15-28.00	29.00-14.46	189.00-88.50	...	...	...

Address: 13625 Technology Drive, Eden Prairie, MN 55344-2252
Telephone: 952-938-8080
Fax: 952-917-1717

Web Site: www.adc.com
Officers: Robert E. Switz Jr. - Pres., C.E.O. Gokul V. Hemmady - V.P., C.F.O.

Auditors: Ernst & Young LLP
Investor Contact: 952-917-0590

ADOBE SYSTEMS, INC.

Exchange	Symbol	Price	52Wk Range	Yield	P/E
NMS	ADBE	$32.44 (8/31/2006)	40.51-26.47	N/A	33.44

*7 Year Price Score 115.97 *NYSE Composite Index=100   *12 Month Price Score 86.64

Interim Earnings (Per Share)

Qtr.	Feb	May	Aug	Nov
2002-03	0.12	0.14	0.14	0.17
2003-04	0.25	0.22	0.21	0.23
2004-05	0.30	0.29	0.29	0.31
2005-06	0.17	0.20	...	...

Interim Dividends (Per Share)

Amt	Decl	Ex	Rec	Pay
0.006Q	9/17/2004	9/24/2004	9/28/2004	10/12/2004
0.006Q	12/16/2004	12/23/2004	12/28/2004	1/11/2005
0.006Q	3/17/2005	3/24/2005	3/29/2005	4/12/2005
100%	3/17/2005	5/24/2005	5/2/2005	5/23/2005

Valuation Analysis   **Institutional Holding**

Forecast P/E	26.03	No of Institutions
	(9/9/2006)	556
Market Cap	$18.8 Billion	Shares
Book Value	4.8 Billion	514,148,192
Price/Book	3.94	% Held
Price/Sales	8.19	88.77

Business Summary: IT & Technology (MIC: 10.2 SIC: 7372 NAIC: 511210)

Adobe Systems is an international software company that offers a line of creative, business and mobile software and services used by high-end consumers, creative professionals, designers, knowledge workers, original equipment manufacturers (OEM), developers and enterprises for creating, managing, delivering and engaging with compelling content and experiences across multiple operating systems, devices and media. Co. distributes its products through a network of distributors and dealers, value-added resellers (VARs), systems integrators, independent software vendors (ISVs) and OEMs, direct to end users, and through its own Web site at www.adobe.com.

Recent Developments: For the quarter ended June 2 2006, net income decreased 17.8% to $123.1 million from $149.8 million in the year-earlier quarter. Revenues were $635.5 million, up 28.1% from $496.0 million the year before. Operating income was $147.9 million versus $182.2 million in the prior-year quarter, a decrease of 18.8%. Direct operating expenses rose 139.1% to $65.6 million from $27.4 million in the comparable period the year before. Indirect operating expenses increased 47.3% to $421.9 million from $286.4 million in the equivalent prior-year period.

Prospects: Despite exhibiting revenue that is slightly below its targeted range, Co. is encouraged by its ability to deliver on its earnings targets during the second quarter of fiscal 2006. Going forward, Co. remains optimistic by its growth prospects as the momentum of digital content continue to accelerate. As such, Co. expects revenue of $580.0 million to $610.0 million and earnings of $0.13 to $0.16 per share for the third quarter of fiscal 2006. However, for the fiscal year 2006, Co. projects revenue of $2.54 billion to $2.60 billion and earnings per share (EPS) of $0.70 to $0.76, down from its prior target for revenue of $2.70 billion and earnings per share of between $0.74 and $0.82.

Financial Data
(US$ in Thousands)

	6 Mos	3 Mos	12/02/2005	12/03/2004	11/28/2003	11/29/2002	11/30/2001	12/01/2000
Earnings Per Share	0.97	1.06	1.19	0.91	0.55	0.40	0.41	0.56
Cash Flow Per Share	1.37	1.25	1.49	1.41	0.93	0.70	0.88	0.94
Tang Book Value Per Share	3.51	3.86	3.54	2.68	2.08	1.24	1.31	1.56
Dividends Per Share	...	0.006	0.013	0.025	0.025	0.025	0.025	0.025
Dividend Payout %	...	0.59	1.05	2.75	4.55	6.33	6.02	4.42
Income Statement								
Total Revenue	1,290,934	655,478	1,966,321	1,666,581	1,294,749	1,164,788	1,229,720	1,266,378
EBITDA	455,115	218,040	830,111	669,453	429,506	348,170	363,576	487,014
Depn & Amortn	146,361	73,783	64,335	60,808	49,014	63,481	56,645	43,275
Income Before Taxes	308,754	144,257	765,776	608,645	380,492	284,689	306,931	443,739
Income Taxes	80,585	39,185	162,937	158,247	114,148	93,290	101,287	155,931
Net Income	228,169	105,072	602,839	450,398	266,344	191,399	205,644	287,808
Average Shares	613,804	621,839	508,070	495,626	482,900	486,238	498,290	511,548
Balance Sheet								
Total Assets	5,501,486	5,801,733	2,440,315	1,958,632	1,555,045	1,051,610	930,623	1,069,416
Current Liabilities	574,281	571,297	480,395	451,408	436,530	377,289	313,651	314,605
Total Liabilities	732,879	725,121	575,989	535,155	454,245	377,289	313,651	316,872
Stockholders' Equity	4,768,607	5,076,612	1,864,326	1,423,477	1,100,800	674,321	616,972	752,544
Shares Outstanding	579,179	598,719	488,729	484,374	476,600	463,910	472,038	481,892
Statistical Record								
Return on Assets %	13.40	14.07	27.48	25.22	20.49	19.36	20.62	30.81
Return on Equity %	16.00	16.64	36.77	35.11	30.09	29.73	30.11	45.64
EBITDA Margin %	35.25	33.26	42.22	40.17	33.17	29.89	29.57	38.46
Net Margin %	17.67	16.03	30.66	27.03	20.57	16.43	16.72	22.73
Asset Turnover	0.58	0.54	0.90	0.93	1.00	1.18	1.23	1.36
Current Ratio	4.05	4.54	4.18	3.44	3.04	2.16	2.45	2.79
Price Range	40.51-25.91	40.51-25.91	34.97-25.91	31.48-17.20	22.91-12.40	21.49-8.35	38.34-11.42	41.63-13.77
P/E Ratio	41.76-26.71	38.22-24.44	29.39-21.77	34.59-18.90	41.66-22.55	53.72-20.88	93.52-27.85	74.33-24.58
Average Yield %	...	0.02	0.04	0.11	0.15	0.16	0.13	0.09

Address: 345 Park Avenue, San Jose, CA 95110-2704
Telephone: 408-536-6000
Fax: 408-536-6799

Web Site: www.adobe.com
Officers: John E. Warnock - Chmn. Charles M. Geschke - Chmn.

Auditors: KPMG LLP
Investor Contact: 408-536-4416
Transfer Agents: Computershare Investor Services LLC, Chicago, IL

ADTRAN, INC.

Exchange	Symbol	Price	52Wk Range	Yield	P/E
NMS	ADTN	$24.87 (8/31/2006)	32.95-20.26	1.45	18.98

*7 Year Price Score 99.34 *NYSE Composite Index=100 *12 Month Price Score 80.34

Interim Earnings (Per Share)

Qtr.	Mar	Jun	Sep	Dec
2003	0.12	0.14	0.19	0.32
2004	0.25	0.26	0.23	0.19
2005	0.20	0.27	0.42	0.41
2006	0.21	0.27	...	...

Interim Dividends (Per Share)

Amt	Decl	Ex	Rec	Pay
0.09Q	10/17/2005	11/2/2005	11/4/2005	11/17/2005
0.09Q	1/23/2006	2/3/2006	2/7/2006	2/17/2006
0.09Q	4/17/2006	5/2/2006	5/4/2006	5/18/2006
0.09Q	7/17/2006	8/2/2006	8/4/2006	8/18/2006

Indicated Div: $0.36

Valuation Analysis   **Institutional Holding**
Forecast P/E   19.92   No of Institutions
                  (9/9/2006)   192
Market Cap $1.8 Billion   Shares
Book Value   488.4 Million   56,393,188
Price/Book   3.74   % Held
Price/Sales   3.51   77.51

Business Summary: Communications (MIC: 10.1 SIC: 3661 NAIC: 334210)
ADTRAN develops products and services that facilitate access to communications networks. Co.'s equipment is used by service providers to deliver broadband data, voice, video, and Internet services to business and residential subscribers. Businesses, schools, and government agencies use Co.'s products to connect facilities, remote offices, and mobile workers, enabling corporate information services, Internet access, telecommuting, and videoconferencing within their organizations. Co.'s product portfolio consists of more than 1,400 different high-speed network access devices used primarily in the "last mile," or local loop, of the network, and in local area networks on customers' premises.

Recent Developments: For the quarter ended June 30 2006, net income increased 0.5% to $20.8 million from $20.7 million in the year-earlier quarter. Revenues were $122.3 million, up 2.9% from $118.9 million the year before. Operating income was $28.5 million versus $28.9 million in the prior-year quarter, a decrease of 1.3%. Direct operating expenses rose 1.1% to $49.9 million from $49.3 million in the comparable period the year before. Indirect operating expenses increased 8.0% to $43.9 million from $40.7 million in the equivalent prior-year period.

Prospects: Results are benefiting from the sales increase of Co.'s Systems products, primarily attributable to higher Broadband Access, Optical Access and NetVanta® routers and switches, offset partially by a decline in its GR303 concentrators and narrowband system revenues. Meanwhile, Co.'s gross profit is also increasing due to favorable product mix, continuing improvements in manufacturing efficiencies and product cost reductions, offset partially by the charge for stock-based compensation expense. Looking ahead, Co. is optimistic and believes that its business outlook remains positive as it continues to build momentum in its primary growth areas.

Financial Data

(US$ in Thousands)	6 Mos	3 Mos	12/31/2005	12/31/2004	12/31/2003	12/31/2002	12/31/2001	12/31/2000
Earnings Per Share	1.31	1.31	1.30	0.93	0.76	0.29	0.20	1.35
Cash Flow Per Share	1.72	1.67	1.70	1.09	1.11	1.23	1.07	(0.15)
Tang Book Value Per Share	6.65	7.25	6.82	6.11	6.23	5.17	5.05	4.99
Dividends Per Share	0.360	0.350	0.340	0.320	1.150	...	...	...
Dividend Payout %	27.48	26.72	26.15	34.41	151.32	...	...	...
Income Statement								
Total Revenue	230,944	108,648	513,215	454,517	396,676	345,725	387,081	462,949
EBITDA	57,590	25,331	169,108	127,931	106,611	42,041	34,528	189,230
Depn & Amortn	5,494	2,737	13,199	15,373	15,247	16,406	16,799	13,419
Income Before Taxes	57,740	25,458	153,374	110,016	88,830	32,177	23,737	183,034
Income Taxes	20,671	9,203	52,224	34,875	27,315	7,401	6,409	62,231
Net Income	37,069	16,255	101,150	75,141	61,515	24,776	17,329	120,802
Average Shares	77,284	78,909	77,966	80,985	80,739	85,998	87,021	89,334
Balance Sheet								
Total Assets	594,511	661,972	652,618	559,942	593,900	521,213	522,537	546,336
Current Liabilities	49,947	47,114	51,049	36,015	40,309	32,045	26,625	46,408
Long-Term Obligations	50,000	50,000	50,000	50,000	50,000	50,000	50,000	50,000
Total Liabilities	106,090	105,400	110,447	93,305	100,079	86,001	84,909	111,751
Stockholders' Equity	488,421	556,572	542,171	466,637	493,821	435,212	437,628	434,425
Shares Outstanding	73,443	76,725	79,536	76,414	79,294	84,110	86,703	87,105
Statistical Record								
Return on Assets %	17.50	16.86	16.68	12.99	11.03	4.75	3.24	21.85
Return on Equity %	21.33	20.22	20.05	15.60	13.24	5.68	3.97	28.87
EBITDA Margin %	24.94	23.31	32.95	28.15	26.88	12.16	8.92	40.87
Net Margin %	16.05	14.96	19.71	16.53	15.51	7.17	4.48	26.09
Asset Turnover	0.89	0.85	0.85	0.79	0.71	0.66	0.72	0.84
Current Ratio	6.42	8.33	7.74	8.40	6.46	7.35	9.16	6.55
Debt to Equity	0.10	0.09	0.09	0.11	0.10	0.11	0.11	0.12
Price Range	32.95-21.79	32.95-17.27	32.95-15.76	37.18-18.23	37.48-14.78	17.13-7.50	15.00-9.00	39.84-8.50
P/E Ratio	25.15-16.63	25.15-13.18	25.35-12.12	39.98-19.60	49.32-19.45	59.07-25.88	75.00-45.00	29.51-6.30
Average Yield %	1.29	1.29	1.39	1.19	4.54	...	...	...

Address: 901 Explorer Blvd., Huntsville, AL 35806-2807 Telephone: 256-963-8000 Fax: 256-963-8004	Web Site: www.adtran.com Officers: Mark C. Smith - Chmn., C.E.O. Howard A. Thrailkill - Pres., C.O.O.	Auditors: PricewaterhouseCoopers LLP

ADVENT SOFTWARE, INC.

Exchange	Symbol	Price	52Wk Range	Yield	P/E
NMS	ADVS	$32.75 (8/31/2006)	37.14-25.05	N/A	69.68

*7 Year Price Score 76.87 *NYSE Composite Index=100 *12 Month Price Score 104.52

Interim Earnings (Per Share)

Qtr.	Mar	Jun	Sep	Dec
2003	(0.23)	(0.30)	(0.17)	(2.30)
2004	(0.03)	(0.25)	(0.16)	(0.05)
2005	0.02	0.10	0.19	0.12
2006	0.11	0.05	...	...

Interim Dividends (Per Share)
No Dividends Paid

Valuation Analysis **Institutional Holding**

Forecast P/E	67.85	No of Institutions
	(9/9/2006)	135
Market Cap	$921.6 Million	Shares
Book Value	178.7 Million	27,033,652
Price/Book	5.16	% Held
Price/Sales	5.24	96.07

Business Summary: IT & Technology (MIC: 10.2 SIC: 7371 NAIC: 541511)
Advent Software offers integrated software products for automating and integrating data and work flows across investment management organizations, as well as the information flows between the investment management organization and external parties. Co.'s Advent Investment Management segment develops, markets and sells stand-alone and client/server software products, data interfaces and related maintenance and services that automate, integrate and support certain functions of investment management organizations. Co.'s MicroEdge segment is engaged in the sale of software and services for grant management, matching gifts and volunteer tracking for the grantmaking community worldwide.

Recent Developments: For the quarter ended June 30 2006, net income decreased 59.3% to $1.6 million from $3.9 million in the year-earlier quarter. Revenues were $44.4 million, up 8.4% from $40.9 million the year before. Operating income was $497,000 versus a loss of $658,000 in the prior-year quarter. Direct operating expenses rose 8.0% to $14.0 million from $13.0 million in the comparable period the year before. Indirect operating expenses increased 4.3% to $29.9 million from $28.6 million in the equivalent prior-year period.

Prospects: Co. is optimistic regarding the potential market viability of its Advent Portfolio Exchange® and Geneva® systems, based on the robust demand for these installations during the second quarter of 2006. Moreover, such growth has enabled Co. to expand its customer base while investing for further growth and managing its costs, all of which is slated towards strengthening its capability to provide software and services to the investment management industry. Looking ahead, Co. projects revenues to be in the range of $44.0 million to $46.0 million for the third quarter of 2006, while its revenue guidance remains at the $180.0 million to $185.0 million range for the full-year 2006.

Financial Data
(US$ in Thousands)

	6 Mos	3 Mos	12/31/2005	12/31/2004	12/31/2003	12/31/2002	12/31/2001	12/31/2000
Earnings Per Share	0.47	0.52	0.44	(0.49)	(3.00)	(0.57)	0.89	0.75
Cash Flow Per Share	1.49	1.32	1.18	0.76	0.22	0.89	1.34	1.23
Tang Book Value Per Share	2.67	3.81	4.46	4.63	4.90	8.06	11.88	6.87
Income Statement								
Total Revenue	88,016	43,656	168,701	149,990	137,159	159,436	170,215	134,931
EBITDA	10,846	5,935	29,840	5,627	(14,971)	(4,058)	58,107	45,211
Depn & Amortn	6,903	3,540	15,300	21,851	23,160	19,142	10,434	6,161
Income Before Taxes	3,943	2,395	14,540	(16,224)	(38,131)	(23,200)	47,673	39,050
Income Taxes	(1,062)	(1,007)	405	20	59,412	(3,964)	16,208	13,276
Net Income	5,005	3,402	14,135	(16,244)	(97,543)	(19,236)	31,465	25,774
Average Shares	31,332	31,819	32,474	32,944	32,473	33,659	35,383	34,237
Balance Sheet								
Total Assets	283,859	317,089	340,575	354,577	344,946	432,736	453,675	245,701
Current Liabilities	94,960	88,309	92,222	80,121	61,337	53,902	47,602	34,869
Total Liabilities	105,178	98,545	98,596	88,902	66,487	59,381	49,286	36,100
Stockholders' Equity	178,681	218,544	241,979	265,675	278,459	373,355	404,389	209,601
Shares Outstanding	28,140	30,203	31,147	32,733	32,938	32,853	34,043	30,498
Statistical Record								
Return on Assets %	5.08	5.32	4.07	N.M.	N.M.	N.M.	9.00	11.77
Return on Equity %	7.55	7.53	5.57	N.M.	N.M.	N.M.	10.25	13.88
EBITDA Margin %	12.32	13.59	17.69	3.75	N.M.	N.M.	34.14	33.51
Net Margin %	5.69	7.79	8.38	N.M.	N.M.	N.M.	18.49	19.10
Asset Turnover	0.59	0.55	0.49	0.43	0.35	0.36	0.49	0.62
Current Ratio	1.56	2.08	2.27	2.61	3.08	3.99	7.54	5.62
Price Range	36.33-20.26	32.91-16.95	32.91-16.60	21.90-14.91	19.07-11.63	62.17-9.91	67.93-30.89	75.50-30.94
P/E Ratio	77.30-43.11	63.29-32.60	74.80-37.73	...	...	...	76.33-34.71	100.67-41.25

Address: 301 Brannan Street, San Francisco, CA 94107
Telephone: 415-543-7696
Fax: 415-543-5070

Web Site: www.advent.com
Officers: John H. Scully - Chmn. Stephanie G. DiMarco - Pres., C.E.O.

Auditors: PricewaterhouseCoopers LLP
Investor Contact: 800-727-0605

AFFYMETRIX, INC.

Exchange	Symbol	Price	52Wk Range	Yield	P/E
NMS	AFFX	$21.31 (8/31/2006)	52.37-18.81	N/A	59.19

*7 Year Price Score 71.43 *NYSE Composite Index=100 *12 Month Price Score 60.00

Interim Earnings (Per Share)

Qtr.	Mar	Jun	Sep	Dec
2003	(0.22)	0.09	0.10	0.27
2004	(0.03)	0.11	0.24	0.41
2005	0.24	0.12	0.13	0.35
2006	0.03	(0.15)	...	...

Interim Dividends (Per Share)
No Dividends Paid

Valuation Analysis | Institutional Holding
Forecast P/E	3108.98	No of Institutions
(9/9/2006)		190
Market Cap	$1.4 Billion	Shares
Book Value	533.5 Million	68,200,296
Price/Book	2.70	% Held
Price/Sales	3.99	N/A

Business Summary: Biotechnology (MIC: 9.2 SIC: 3826 NAIC: 334516)
Affymetrix develops, manufactures, sells and services consumables and systems for genetic analysis in the life sciences and clinical healthcare. Co.'s GeneChip® microarray platform includes: disposable deoxyribonucleic acid probe arrays (chips) consisting of nucleic acid sequences set out in an ordered, high density pattern, certain reagents for use with the probe arrays, a scanner and other instruments used to process the probe arrays, and software to analyze and manage genomic or genetic information obtained from the probe arrays. Co. also provides microarray technology that includes licenses for fabricating, scanning, collecting and analyzing results from complementary technologies.

Recent Developments: For the quarter ended June 30 2006, net loss amounted to $10.1 million versus net income of $8.3 million in the year-earlier quarter. Revenues were $80.1 million, down 4.7% from $84.1 million the year before. Operating loss was $9.1 million versus an income of $8.5 million in the prior-year quarter. Direct operating expenses rose 26.9% to $28.1 million from $22.2 million in the comparable period the year before. Indirect operating expenses increased 14.4% to $61.1 million from $53.4 million in the equivalent prior-year period.

Prospects: On June 27 2006, Co. announced that it has granted Epigenomics AG non-exclusive access to its microarray technology to develop and sell microarray-based in-vitro diagnostic tests for oncology and other indications. For 2006, Co. expects lower instrument sales as it finishes its instrument upgrade cycle. Nevertheless, Co. remains focused on growing its business and increasing its operational profitability. Co. also expects lower gross margins as it continues to expand its manufacturing capacity to support its anticipated sales growth in consumables, and plans to increase the prices for its 500K genotyping product, in line with its plans to launch this product onto one chip in 2006.

Financial Data
(US$ in Thousands)

	6 Mos	3 Mos	12/31/2005	12/31/2004	12/31/2003	12/31/2002	12/31/2001	12/31/2000
Earnings Per Share	0.36	0.63	0.84	0.74	0.24	(0.03)	(0.58)	(0.98)
Cash Flow Per Share	0.72	0.61	1.01	0.81	1.53	0.54	(0.47)	(0.38)
Tang Book Value Per Share	5.17	5.12	4.97	2.70	2.00	1.59	1.56	1.93
Income Statement								
Total Revenue	166,457	86,391	367,602	345,962	300,796	289,874	224,874	200,830
EBITDA	11,156	8,372	91,933	87,385	60,869	48,731	7,515	(43,064)
Depn & Amortn	15,263	7,060	27,780	25,349	26,663	29,930	42,035	10,326
Income Before Taxes	(4,931)	888	62,608	50,934	16,848	(929)	(34,520)	(53,390)
Income Taxes	3,298	(937)	5,092	3,326	2,563	701	300	600
Net Income	(8,229)	1,825	57,516	47,608	14,285	(1,630)	(33,121)	(53,990)
Average Shares	67,313	68,680	70,586	66,878	60,583	58,018	57,382	55,035
Balance Sheet								
Total Assets	767,894	753,914	766,823	499,771	700,164	601,403	580,015	620,780
Current Liabilities	101,091	89,631	107,195	96,739	368,523	86,245	73,005	90,590
Long-Term Obligations	120,000	120,000	120,000	120,000	120,000	368,900	375,000	380,060
Total Liabilities	234,359	224,900	246,985	250,584	535,109	466,467	451,005	473,650
Stockholders' Equity	533,535	529,014	519,838	249,187	165,055	134,936	129,010	147,130
Shares Outstanding	67,677	67,459	67,220	61,588	59,454	58,504	58,007	57,143
Statistical Record								
Return on Assets %	3.83	6.71	9.08	7.91	2.20	N.M.	N.M.	N.M.
Return on Equity %	5.91	10.48	14.96	22.92	9.52	N.M.	N.M.	N.M.
EBITDA Margin %	6.70	9.69	25.01	25.26	20.24	16.81	3.34	N.M.
Net Margin %	N.M.	2.11	15.65	13.76	4.75	N.M.	N.M.	N.M.
Asset Turnover	0.55	0.57	0.58	0.58	0.46	0.49	0.37	0.43
Current Ratio	4.03	4.52	4.22	3.34	1.52	5.31	6.11	5.62
Debt to Equity	0.22	0.23	0.23	0.48	0.73	2.73	2.91	2.58
Price Range	59.25-25.60	59.25-30.31	59.25-33.94	37.46-23.74	29.75-16.58	39.94-14.60	72.88-14.50	160.25-45.53
P/E Ratio	164.58-71.11	94.05-48.11	70.54-40.40	50.62-32.08	123.96-69.08	...	...	...

Address: 3380 Central Expressway, Santa Clara, CA 95051
Telephone: 408-731-5000
Fax: 408-481-9442

Web Site: www.affymetrix.com
Officers: Stephen P.A. Fodor - Chmn., C.E.O. Susan E. Siegel - Pres.

Auditors: Ernst & Young LLP
Investor Contact: 408-731-5000

ALEXANDER & BALDWIN, INC.

Exchange	Symbol	Price	52Wk Range	Yield	P/E
NMS	ALEX	$43.86 (8/31/2006)	55.40-39.82	2.28	15.34

*7 Year Price Score 122.41 *NYSE Composite Index=100 *12 Month Price Score 85.13

Interim Earnings (Per Share)

Qtr.	Mar	Jun	Sep	Dec
2003	0.42	0.56	0.52	0.44
2004	0.63	0.70	0.58	0.42
2005	0.86	0.66	0.81	0.53
2006	0.84	0.68	...	...

Interim Dividends (Per Share)

Amt	Decl	Ex	Rec	Pay
0.225Q	10/28/2005	11/8/2005	11/10/2005	12/1/2005
0.225Q	1/26/2006	2/15/2006	2/17/2006	3/2/2006
0.25Q	4/27/2006	5/9/2006	5/11/2006	6/1/2006
0.25Q	6/22/2006	8/1/2006	8/3/2006	9/7/2006

Indicated Div: $1.00

Valuation Analysis

Forecast P/E	16.63 (9/9/2006)	
Market Cap	$1.9 Billion	
Book Value	988.0 Million	
Price/Book	1.91	
Price/Sales	1.16	

Institutional Holding

No of Institutions	181
Shares	34,044,604
% Held	79.05

Business Summary: Shipping (MIC: 15.3 SIC: 4499 NAIC: 483113)

Alexander & Baldwin is a holding company, engaged in a variety of businesses with most of its operations centered in Hawaii. Through its subsidiaries, Matson Navigation Company Inc. and Matson Integrated Logistics Inc., Co. is engaged in ocean transportation, related shoreside operations as well as its intermodal, truck brokerage and logistics services. Co.'s real-estate operations are conducted through subsidiary, A&B Properties Inc. In addition, Co. is in the food products business through its subsidiaries, Hawaiian Commercial & Sugar Company and Kauai Coffee Company Inc.

Recent Developments: For the quarter ended June 30 2006, income from continuing operations decreased 28.8% to $20.5 million from $28.8 million in the year-earlier quarter. Net income increased 2.7% to $30.2 million from $29.4 million in the year-earlier quarter. Revenues were $418.2 million, up 6.9% from $391.2 million the year before. Operating income was $34.2 million versus $47.5 million in the prior-year quarter, a decrease of 28.0%. Direct operating expenses rose 12.9% to $347.7 million from $308.1 million in the comparable period the year before. Indirect operating expenses increased 2.0% to $36.3 million from $35.6 million in the equivalent prior-year period.

Prospects: Co.'s prospects remain promising. In the Real-Estate segment, Co. anticipates that it will attain its long-term objective of 13.0% to 15.0% in annual growth for full-year 2006, based on robust occupancy across its Hawaii and Mainland U.S. properties. Meanwhile, Co. is progressing towards the trans-Pacific expansion within its Ocean Transportation segment through the transition from its Matson's APL Alliance to its new Guam and China services. In this respect, Co. expects earnings for its Ocean Transportation segment in the second half of 2006 will correspond to its earnings level during the second half of 2005.

Financial Data
(US$ in Thousands)

	6 Mos	3 Mos	12/31/2005	12/31/2004	12/31/2003	12/31/2002	12/31/2001	12/31/2000
Earnings Per Share	2.86	2.84	2.86	2.33	1.94	1.41	2.72	2.21
Cash Flow Per Share	4.30	6.20	6.38	4.05	3.27	1.36	3.72	2.54
Tang Book Value Per Share	22.94	23.69	23.05	20.88	19.22	17.54	17.53	17.19
Dividends Per Share	0.925	0.900	0.900	0.900	0.900	0.900	0.900	0.900
Dividend Payout %	32.34	31.69	31.47	38.63	46.39	63.83	33.09	40.72
Income Statement								
Total Revenue	779,500	362,200	1,607,000	1,494,000	1,233,000	1,088,885	1,190,073	1,068,646
EBITDA	78,200	46,100	277,000	248,000	194,000	150,629	281,296	219,271
Depn & Amortn	...	...	84,000	80,000	73,000	70,717	75,433	72,304
Income Before Taxes	76,900	45,100	185,000	159,000	109,000	68,232	187,205	122,715
Income Taxes	28,700	17,200	69,000	60,000	40,000	21,734	67,392	44,391
Net Income	67,600	37,400	126,000	101,000	81,000	58,156	110,628	90,574
Average Shares	44,300	44,300	44,000	43,200	41,900	41,008	40,535	40,898
Balance Sheet								
Total Assets	2,157,000	2,127,000	2,071,000	1,778,000	1,760,000	1,597,569	1,544,419	1,666,012
Current Liabilities	267,000	255,000	254,000	235,000	183,000	151,087	195,569	153,006
Long-Term Obligations	353,000	294,000	296,000	214,000	330,000	247,789	207,378	330,766
Total Liabilities	1,169,000	1,079,000	1,057,000	874,000	949,000	873,921	833,752	972,361
Stockholders' Equity	988,000	1,048,000	1,014,000	904,000	811,000	723,648	710,667	693,651
Shares Outstanding	43,067	44,236	44,000	43,300	42,200	41,268	40,529	40,353
Statistical Record								
Return on Assets %	6.10	6.37	6.55	5.69	4.82	3.70	6.89	5.60
Return on Equity %	13.02	12.63	13.14	11.75	10.56	8.11	15.76	13.24
EBITDA Margin %	10.03	12.73	17.24	16.60	15.73	13.83	23.64	20.52
Net Margin %	8.67	10.33	7.84	6.76	6.57	5.34	9.30	8.48
Asset Turnover	0.79	0.81	0.84	0.84	0.73	0.69	0.74	0.66
Current Ratio	1.11	1.29	1.19	1.23	1.35	1.55	1.12	1.37
Debt to Equity	0.36	0.28	0.29	0.24	0.41	0.34	0.29	0.48
Price Range	55.40-41.15	55.40-37.64	55.40-37.64	44.74-29.56	34.56-23.82	29.15-20.90	28.94-20.81	28.06-18.50
P/E Ratio	19.37-14.39	19.51-13.25	19.37-13.16	19.20-12.69	17.81-12.28	20.67-14.82	10.64-7.65	12.70-8.37
Average Yield %	1.87	1.86	1.91	2.62	3.22	3.59	3.69	3.86

| **Address:** 822 Bishop Street, Honolulu, HI 96813-3924
Telephone: 808-525-6611
Fax: 808-525-6652 | **Web Site:** www.alexanderbaldwin.com
Officers: Charles M. Stockholm - Chmn. W. Allen Doane - Pres., C.E.O. | **Auditors:** Deloitte & Touche LLP
Investor Contact: 808-525-8422
Transfer Agents: Mellon Investor Services LLC, San Francisco, CA & Ridgefield Park, NJ |

ALFA CORP

Exchange	Symbol	Price	52Wk Range	Yield	P/E	Div Acheiver
NMS	ALFA	$16.90 (8/31/2006)	17.92-15.18	2.60	14.44	20 Years

*7 Year Price Score 105.30 *NYSE Composite Index=100 *12 Month Price Score 95.51

Interim Earnings (Per Share)

Qtr.	Mar	Jun	Sep	Dec
2003	0.23	0.24	0.23	0.27
2004	0.32	0.26	0.26	0.28
2005	0.27	0.35	0.31	0.30
2006	0.25	0.31	...	...

Interim Dividends (Per Share)

Amt	Decl	Ex	Rec	Pay
0.10Q	10/31/2005	11/10/2005	11/15/2005	12/1/2005
0.10Q	1/23/2006	2/13/2006	2/15/2006	3/1/2006
0.11Q	4/25/2006	5/11/2006	5/15/2006	6/1/2006
0.11Q	7/24/2006	8/11/2006	8/15/2006	9/1/2006

Indicated Div: $0.44 (Div. Reinv. Plan)

Valuation Analysis   Institutional Holding
Forecast P/E   13.60   No of Institutions
            (9/9/2006)   66
Market Cap $1.4 Billion   Shares
Book Value   761.8 Million   8,494,335
Price/Book   1.78   % Held
Price/Sales   1.73   10.58

Business Summary: Insurance (MIC: 8.2 SIC: 6331 NAIC: 524126)
Alfa is a financial services holding company that offers property casualty insurance, life insurance and financial services products through its wholly-owned subsidiaries. Co. is affiliated with Alfa Mutual Insurance Company, Alfa Mutual Fire Insurance Company, and Alfa Mutual General Insurance Company. At Dec 31 2005, Co.'s insurance subsidiaries wrote life insurance in Alabama, Georgia and Mississippi and property casualty insurance in Georgia, Mississippi, Missouri, Indiana, Ohio, Virginia, Tennessee, Arkansas, Kentucky, and Florida. Co.'s noninsurance subsidiaries are engaged in consumer financing, commercial leasing, agency operations and benefits administration.

Recent Developments: For the quarter ended June 30 2006, net income decreased 10.7% to $25.5 million from $28.6 million in the year-earlier quarter. Revenues were $195.4 million, up 5.2% from $185.7 million the year before. Net premiums earned were $170.9 million versus $156.1 million in the prior-year quarter, an increase of 9.5%. Net investment income fell 26.6% to $16.8 million from $22.9 million a year ago.

Prospects: Co. is benefiting from higher property casualty insurance premiums, particularly in its Alfa Vision Insurance Corporation (AVIC), Alfa Insurance Corporation (AIC) and Alfa General Insurance Corporation (AGI) subsidiaries, driven by increases in its overall productions and personal lines attributable to improved homeowner and manufactured homebuilding premiums. Co. is also benefiting from higher life insurance premiums, due to an increase in term life premiums. Meanwhile, Co. has taken appropriate measures to ensure that its fraudulent transactions has been remedied, while it continues to seek for rate changes from insurance regulators in order to meet strategic business objectives.

Financial Data
(US$ in Thousands)

	6 Mos	3 Mos	12/31/2005	12/31/2004	12/31/2003	12/31/2002	12/31/2001	12/31/2000
Earnings Per Share	1.17	1.21	1.23	1.11	0.98	0.90	0.88	0.85
Cash Flow Per Share	1.89	1.77	1.64	1.84	1.27	1.36	1.31	1.52
Tang Book Value Per Share	9.22	9.20	9.14	8.66	7.96	7.09	6.50	6.05
Dividends Per Share	0.410	0.400	0.388	0.343	0.315	0.297	0.282	0.255
Dividend Payout %	35.04	33.06	31.50	30.86	32.14	33.06	32.10	30.00
Income Statement								
Premium Income	339,848	168,994	633,072	561,356	525,229	491,105	452,869	429,197
Total Revenue	395,841	200,467	756,905	660,368	618,047	587,548	546,296	510,313
Benefits & Claims	228,131	118,820	432,856	389,969	364,533	346,456	312,944	295,881
Income Before Taxes	62,607	27,770	137,862	120,629	106,597	99,345	98,094	94,746
Income Taxes	16,962	7,632	38,828	31,184	28,128	27,637	28,133	27,925
Net Income	45,646	20,137	99,034	89,445	78,469	71,708	69,506	66,821
Average Shares	81,179	81,122	80,712	80,489	80,390	79,546	78,963	78,814
Balance Sheet								
Total Assets	2,450,745	2,447,204	2,381,874	2,222,698	2,045,075	1,884,055	1,697,604	1,546,303
Total Liabilities	1,688,958	1,686,350	1,625,882	1,531,245	1,406,562	1,317,957	1,188,493	1,072,742
Stockholders' Equity	761,787	760,855	755,992	691,452	638,512	566,098	509,112	473,561
Shares Outstanding	80,273	80,325	80,284	79,833	80,217	79,278	78,359	78,297
Statistical Record								
Return on Assets %	3.94	4.13	4.30	4.18	3.99	4.00	4.29	4.63
Return on Equity %	12.66	13.37	13.68	13.41	13.03	13.34	14.15	15.11
Loss Ratio %	67.13	70.31	68.37	69.47	69.40	70.55	69.10	68.94
Net Margin %	11.53	10.05	13.08	13.54	12.70	12.20	12.72	13.09
Price Range	17.92-14.57	17.92-12.82	17.92-12.82	15.60-12.86	13.50-10.92	16.05-10.75	12.35-9.06	9.69-7.31
P/E Ratio	15.32-12.45	14.81-10.60	14.57-10.42	14.05-11.59	13.78-11.14	17.83-11.94	14.03-10.30	11.40-8.60
Average Yield %	2.50	2.51	2.52	2.47	2.50	2.31	2.69	2.93

Address: 2108 East South Boulevard, Montgomery, AL 36116-2015	Web Site: www.alfains.com	Auditors: KPMG LLP
Telephone: 334-288-3900	Officers: Jerry A. Newby - Chmn., Pres. C. Lee Ellis - Exec. V.P., Oper., Treas.	Investor Contact: 334-288-3900
Fax: 334-288-0905		Transfer Agents: American Stock Transfer and Trust Co., New York, NY

ALTERA CORP.

Exchange	Symbol	Price	52Wk Range	Yield	P/E
NMS	ALTR	$20.23 (8/31/2006)	22.03-15.76	N/A	27.34

*7 Year Price Score 64.51 *NYSE Composite Index=100 *12 Month Price Score 90.22

Interim Earnings (Per Share)

Qtr.	Mar	Jun	Sep	Dec
2001	0.16	(0.23)	0.05	(0.09)
2002	0.05	0.06	0.06	0.07
2003	0.08	0.09	0.11	0.12
2004	0.15	0.20	0.22	0.15
2005	0.17	0.18	0.21	0.19

Interim Dividends (Per Share)
No Dividends Paid

Valuation Analysis

		Institutional Holding	
Forecast P/E	23.81	No of Institutions	
	(9/9/2006)	298	
Market Cap	$7.3 Billion	Shares	
Book Value	1.3 Billion	322,380,160	
Price/Book	5.75	% Held	
Price/Sales	6.47	89.73	

Business Summary: IT & Technology (MIC: 10.2 SIC: 3674 NAIC: 334413)
Altera designs, manufactures, and markets programmable logic devices, or PLDs; HardCopy® devices; pre-defined design building blocks known as intellectual property, or IP, cores; and associated development tools. Co.'s PLDs, which consist of field-programmable gate arrays, or FPGAs, and complex programmable logic devices are semiconductor integrated circuits that are manufactured as standard chips that Co.'s customers program to perform desired logic functions within their electronic systems. Co.'s HardCopy devices enable its customers to move from a high-density FPGA to a low-cost, high-volume, non-programmable implementation of their designs.

Recent Developments: For the year ended Dec 30 2005, net income increased 1.4% to $278.8 million from $275.1 million in the prior year. Revenues were $1.12 billion, up 10.6% from $1.02 billion the year before. Operating income was $322.2 million versus $314.9 million in the prior year, an increase of 2.3%. Direct operating expenses rose 18.0% to $365.9 million from $310.2 million in the comparable period the year before. Indirect operating expenses increased 11.3% to $435.6 million from $391.3 million in the equivalent prior-year period.

Prospects: Top-line growth is being driven primarily by increased sales of Co.'s new products, primarily its Statix and Cyclone families. Separately, Co. anticipates its capital expenditures will increase in 2006 as it launches a program to replace its enterprise resource planning system (ERP). Total planned expenditures are estimated to be $25.0 million in 2006 and Co. expects to install and have the system operational in 2007. Meanwhile, Co. is projecting first-quarter 2006 sales growth in the range of 4.0% to 7.0% sequentially, while gross margins are expected to be in the range of 65.0% to 67.5% of sales.

Financial Data
(US$ in Thousands)

	12/30/2005	12/31/2004	12/31/2003	12/31/2002	12/31/2001	12/31/2000	12/31/1999	12/31/1998
Earnings Per Share	0.74	0.72	0.40	0.23	(0.10)	1.19	0.54	0.39
Cash Flow Per Share	1.12	0.84	0.86	0.65	(0.31)	1.38	1.02	0.72
Tang Book Value Per Share	3.52	3.42	2.93	2.95	2.89	3.21	2.81	2.26
Income Statement								
Total Revenue	1,123,739	1,016,364	827,207	711,684	839,376	1,376,815	836,623	654,342
EBITDA	386,436	361,183	268,376	183,194	59,844	795,243	372,493	280,583
Depn & Amortn	29,400	30,400	55,875	59,866	72,847	49,829	29,416	30,038
Income Before Taxes	357,036	330,783	212,501	123,328	(13,003)	745,414	343,077	244,183
Income Taxes	78,207	55,672	57,376	32,065	26,779	247,107	111,499	79,356
Net Income	278,829	275,111	155,125	91,263	(39,782)	496,907	223,994	154,387
Average Shares	376,192	382,473	389,753	391,708	386,097	416,629	414,928	406,356
Balance Sheet								
Total Assets	1,822,781	1,746,666	1,487,606	1,371,737	1,361,427	2,004,134	1,439,599	1,093,331
Current Liabilities	554,701	468,042	385,202	240,501	246,927	756,204	321,526	211,610
Long-Term Obligations	3,871	...	...	...	...	...	...	...
Total Liabilities	558,572	468,042	385,202	240,501	246,927	756,204	321,526	211,610
Stockholders' Equity	1,264,209	1,278,624	1,102,404	1,131,236	1,114,500	1,247,930	1,118,073	881,721
Shares Outstanding	359,419	373,759	376,080	383,504	386,301	389,265	397,260	390,540
Statistical Record								
Return on Assets %	15.67	16.97	10.85	6.68	N.M.	28.78	17.69	15.09
Return on Equity %	21.99	23.05	13.89	8.13	N.M.	41.89	22.40	21.77
EBITDA Margin %	34.39	35.54	32.44	25.74	7.13	57.76	44.52	42.88
Net Margin %	24.81	27.07	18.75	12.82	N.M.	36.09	26.77	23.59
Asset Turnover	0.63	0.63	0.58	0.52	0.50	0.80	0.66	0.64
Current Ratio	2.70	3.28	3.30	4.89	4.57	2.34	3.44	3.78
Price Range	22.88-16.28	26.82-17.75	25.36-10.84	25.48-8.67	34.31-15.38	64.81-23.94	33.88-12.15	15.22-7.20
P/E Ratio	30.92-22.00	37.25-24.65	63.40-27.10	110.78-37.50	...	54.46-20.12	62.73-22.51	39.02-18.87

Address: 101 Innovation Dr., San Jose, CA 95134	Web Site: www.altera.com
Telephone: 408-544-7000	Officers: John P. Daane - Chmn., Pres., C.E.O. Robert W. Reed - Vice-Chmn.
Fax: 408-428-0163	
	Auditors: PricewaterhouseCoopers LLP
	Investor Contact: 408-544-7000
	Transfer Agents: EquiServe Trust Company, Kansas City, MO

AMAZON.COM INC.

Exchange	Symbol	Price	52Wk Range	Yield	P/E
NMS	AMZN	$30.83 (8/31/2006)	49.50-26.07	N/A	44.04

*7 Year Price Score 88.32 *NYSE Composite Index=100 *12 Month Price Score 75.86

Interim Earnings (Per Share)

Qtr.	Mar	Jun	Sep	Dec
2003	(0.03)	(0.11)	0.04	0.18
2004	0.26	0.18	0.13	0.82
2005	0.18	0.12	0.07	0.46
2006	0.12	0.05	...	...

Interim Dividends (Per Share)
No Dividends Paid

Valuation Analysis **Institutional Holding**

Forecast P/E	57.17	No of Institutions
(9/9/2006)		285
Market Cap	$12.9 Billion	Shares
Book Value	383.0 Million	305,072,096
Price/Book	33.73	% Held
Price/Sales	1.40	72.82

Business Summary: Retail - Miscellaneous (MIC: 5.11 SIC: 5961 NAIC: 454111)

Amazon.com operates retail websites. Co. has two main segments: North America, which includes www.amazon.com and www.amazon.ca; and International, which includes www.amazon.co.uk, www.amazon.de, www.amazon.fr, www.amazon.co.jp and www.joyo.com. In addition, Co. operates other websites, including www.a9.com and www.alexa.com that enable search and navigation; www.imdb.com, a movie database, and Amazon Mechanical Turk at www.mturk.com, which provides a Web service for computers to integrate a network of humans directly into their processes. Co.'s websites enable it to sell various products across dozens of product categories, such as books, music and musical instrument, software, and beauty.

Recent Developments: For the quarter ended June 30 2006, net income decreased 57.7% to $22.0 million from $52.0 million in the year-earlier quarter. Revenues were $2.14 billion, up 22.0% from $1.75 billion the year before. Operating income was $47.0 million versus $104.0 million in the prior-year quarter, a decrease of 54.8%. Direct operating expenses rose 25.1% to $1.63 billion from $1.30 billion in the comparable period the year before. Indirect operating expenses increased 33.5% to $462.0 million from $346.0 million in the equivalent prior-year period.

Prospects: Co.'s results reflect strong top-line growth, notably in North America, due to increased sales fueled by its Amazon Prime, lower prices for its customers, free shipping offers, and increased selection in its product categories. Going forward, Co. will focus on investing in its Amazon Prime membership program, while executing its future technology initiatives, which will position it to move into the seller platforms, web services and digital. For the second half of 2006, Co. expects a decrease in its year-over-year growth rates in technology spending. For fiscal 2006, Co. anticipates net sales of $10.15 billion to $10.65 billion, and operating income of $310.0 million to $440.0 million.

Financial Data
(US$ in Thousands)

	6 Mos	3 Mos	12/31/2005	12/31/2004	12/31/2003	12/31/2002	12/31/2001	12/31/2000
Earnings Per Share	0.70	0.77	0.84	1.39	0.08	(0.39)	(1.56)	(4.02)
Cash Flow Per Share	1.46	1.74	1.78	1.39	0.99	0.46	(0.33)	(0.37)
Tang Book Value Per Share	0.45	0.31	0.21	...	...	...	...	...
Income Statement								
Total Revenue	4,418,000	2,279,000	8,490,000	6,921,124	5,263,699	3,932,936	3,122,433	2,761,983
EBITDA	244,000	142,000	448,000	403,738	...	...	...	...
Depn & Amortn	83,000	40,000	(28,000)	(31,162)	72,752	21,213	134,571	322,818
Income Before Taxes	150,000	96,000	428,000	355,870	...	...	...	...
Income Taxes	77,000	45,000	95,000	(232,581)	...	...	...	...
Net Income	73,000	51,000	359,000	588,451	35,282	(149,132)	(567,277)	(1,411,273)
Average Shares	426,000	426,000	426,000	424,757	419,352	378,363	364,211	350,873
Balance Sheet								
Total Assets	3,165,000	2,990,000	3,696,000	3,248,508	2,162,033	1,990,449	1,637,547	2,135,169
Current Liabilities	1,458,000	1,407,000	1,929,000	1,620,400	1,252,701	1,065,958	921,414	974,956
Long-Term Obligations	1,324,000	1,259,000	1,521,000	1,847,397	1,925,373	2,277,305	2,156,133	2,127,464
Total Liabilities	2,782,000	2,666,000	3,450,000	3,475,719	3,198,140	3,343,263	3,077,547	3,102,420
Stockholders' Equity	383,000	324,000	246,000	(227,211)	(1,036,107)	(1,352,814)	(1,440,000)	(967,251)
Shares Outstanding	419,000	417,000	416,000	409,711	403,354	387,906	373,218	357,140
Statistical Record								
Return on Assets %	10.48	12.16	10.34	21.69	1.70	N.M.	N.M.	N.M.
Return on Equity %	189.34	409.88	3,821.38	...	...	...	...	...
EBITDA Margin %	5.52	6.23	5.28	5.83	...	...	...	...
Net Margin %	1.65	2.24	4.23	8.50	0.67	N.M.	N.M.	N.M.
Asset Turnover	3.21	3.25	2.45	2.55	2.54	2.17	1.66	1.20
Current Ratio	1.53	1.55	1.52	1.57	1.45	1.52	1.31	1.40
Debt to Equity	3.46	3.89	6.18	...	...	...	...	...
Price Range	49.50-31.61	49.50-31.72	49.50-31.72	57.17-33.83	59.91-18.89	24.25-9.13	21.88-5.97	89.38-15.19
P/E Ratio	70.71-45.16	64.29-41.19	58.93-37.76	41.14-24.34	748.88-236.13	...	...	...

Address: 1200 12th Avenue South, Suite 1200, Seattle, WA 98144-2734 **Telephone:** 206-266-1000 **Fax:** 206-266-1821	**Web Site:** www.amazon.com **Officers:** Jeffrey P. Bezos - Chmn., Pres., C.E.O. Thomas J. Szkutak - Sr. V.P., C.F.O.	**Auditors:** Ernst & Young LLP **Investor Contact:** 206-266-2171

AMERICAN CAPITAL STRATEGIES LTD.

Exchange	Symbol	Price	52Wk Range	Yield	P/E
NMS	ACAS	$38.73 (8/31/2006)	39.00-32.56	8.57	7.62

*7 Year Price Score 101.78 *NYSE Composite Index=100 *12 Month Price Score 96.82

Interim Earnings (Per Share)

Qtr.	Mar	Jun	Sep	Dec
2003	(0.02)	0.48	0.48	1.17
2004	0.51	1.22	0.74	1.15
2005	1.22	0.82	0.90	0.68
2006	1.34	2.16	...	...

Interim Dividends (Per Share)

Amt	Decl	Ex	Rec	Pay
0.03Q	12/15/2005	12/29/2005	12/30/2005	1/18/2006
0.80Q	2/14/2006	2/24/2006	2/28/2006	4/3/2006
0.82Q	5/2/2006	5/25/2006	5/30/2006	7/5/2006
0.83Q	8/1/2006	9/1/2006	9/6/2006	10/2/2006

Indicated Div: $3.32

Valuation Analysis

		Institutional Holding	
Forecast P/E	N/A	No of Institutions	223
Market Cap	$5.4 Billion	Shares	45,953,084
Book Value	3.8 Billion	% Held	32.32
Price/Book	1.40		
Price/Sales	7.60		

Business Summary: Finance Intermediaries & Services (MIC: 8.7 SIC: 6726 NAIC: 525990)
American Capital Strategies is a buyout and mezzanine fund which provides investment capital to middle market companies. Co. invests primarily in senior and mezzanine (subordinated) debt and equity of companies in need of capital for buyouts, growth, acquisitions and recapitalizations. Co. is an investor in and sponsor of management and employee buyouts, invest in private equity sponsored buyouts and provides capital directly to early stage and mature private and small public companies. Through its asset management business, Co. is also a manager of debt and equity investments in private companies. As of Dec 31 2005, the total portfolio value of Co.'s investments was $5.1 million.

Recent Developments: For the quarter ended June 30 2006, net income increased 265.9% to $290.3 million from $79.3 million in the year-earlier quarter. Revenues were $212.0 million, up 61.0% from $131.7 million the year before.

Prospects: Co.'s results continue to exhibit robust growth on its earnings return on equity as well as book value. Moreover, Co. continues to note strong investment opportunities, driven by its significant market coverage and capabilities. Going forward, Co. believes that its investment volume will retain its continuing strength throughout the second half of 2006. Separately, on Aug 1 2006, Co. announced the sale of its portfolio company KAC Holdings Inc. to Illinois Tool Works Inc., from which Co. realized a gain of $47.0 million and recognized total proceeds of $89.0 million upon the exit, earning a 53.0% compounded annual rate of return on its investment over the life of its investment.

Financial Data
(US$ in Thousands)

	6 Mos	3 Mos	12/31/2005	12/31/2004	12/31/2003	12/31/2002	12/31/2001	12/31/2000
Earnings Per Share	5.08	3.74	3.60	3.63	2.15	0.50	0.58	(0.19)
Cash Flow Per Share	2.54	2.46	3.04	2.58	2.15	1.84	1.15	1.48
Tang Book Value Per Share	27.63	25.30	24.37	21.11	17.83	15.82	16.84	15.90
Dividends Per Share	3.220	3.150	3.080	2.910	2.790	2.570	2.300	2.170
Dividend Payout %	63.39	84.22	85.56	80.17	129.77	514.00	396.55	...
Income Statement								
Total Revenue	385,213	173,178	554,500	336,082	206,280	147,022	104,237	62,728
Income Taxes	...	...	12,504	2,130	...	...	...	...
Net Income	452,398	162,054	364,909	281,445	117,984	20,061	18,605	(4,373)
Average Shares	134,189	121,086	101,376	77,638	54,996	39,880	32,001	22,748
Balance Sheet								
Total Assets	7,408,622	5,800,142	5,449,109	3,491,427	2,041,724	1,318,523	904,184	614,644
Total Liabilities	3,574,021	2,679,192	2,551,472	1,619,001	865,809	630,864	263,919	169,477
Stockholders' Equity	3,834,601	3,120,950	2,897,637	1,872,426	1,175,915	687,659	640,265	445,167
Shares Outstanding	138,808	123,364	118,913	88,705	65,949	43,469	38,017	28,003
Statistical Record								
Return on Assets %	10.67	8.63	8.16	10.15	7.02	1.81	2.45	N.M.
Return on Equity %	20.76	16.26	15.30	18.42	12.66	3.02	3.43	N.M.
Price Range	39.50-32.56	39.50-31.08	39.50-31.02	34.70-25.27	29.73-21.59	32.45-16.34	29.86-21.88	26.00-20.38
P/E Ratio	7.78-6.41	10.56-8.31	10.97-8.62	9.56-6.96	13.83-10.04	64.90-32.68	51.48-37.72	...
Average Yield %	8.92	8.74	8.68	9.53	10.95	10.14	8.66	9.35

Address: 2 Bethesda Metro Center, 14th Floor, Bethesda, MD 20814 **Telephone:** 301-951-6122 **Fax:** 301-654-6714	**Web Site:** www.american-capital.com **Officers:** Malon Wilkus - Chmn., Pres., C.E.O. John R. Erickson - Exec. V.P., C.F.O.	**Auditors:** ERNST & YOUNG LLP **Investor Contact:** 301-951-6122

AMERICAN EAGLE OUTFITTERS, INC.

Exchange	Symbol	Price	52Wk Range	Yield	P/E
NMS	AEOS	$38.61 (8/31/2006)	38.61-20.00	1.17	18.74

*7 Year Price Score 141.30 *NYSE Composite Index=100 *12 Month Price Score 119.93

Interim Earnings (Per Share)
Qtr.	Apr	Jul	Oct	Jan
2003-04	0.04	0.06	0.07	0.25
2004-05	0.17	0.20	0.39	0.67
2005-06	0.35	0.37	0.47	0.70
2006-07	0.42	0.47	...	...

Interim Dividends (Per Share)
Amt	Decl	Ex	Rec	Pay
0.075Q	11/17/2005	12/21/2005	12/23/2005	1/6/2006
0.075Q	3/2/2006	3/22/2006	3/24/2006	4/7/2006
0.113Q	6/14/2006	6/22/2006	6/26/2006	7/7/2006
0.113Q	8/16/2006	9/20/2006	9/22/2006	10/6/2006

Indicated Div: $0.45

Valuation Analysis
		Institutional Holding	
Forecast P/E	15.60	No of Institutions	
	(9/9/2006)	281	
Market Cap	$5.8 Billion	Shares	114,844,848
Book Value	1.3 Billion	% Held	77.45
Price/Book	4.46		
Price/Sales	2.33		

Business Summary: Retail - Apparel and Accessory Stores (MIC: 5.8 SIC: 5651 NAIC: 448140)
American Eagle Outfitters is a retailer that designs, markets and sells its own brand of clothing targeting 15 to 25 year-olds, providing merchandise at affordable prices. Co. also distributes merchandise via its e-commerce operation, ae.com, which provides additional sizes, colors and styles of AE merchandise and ships around the world. Co.'s collection includes standards like jeans and graphic t-shirts as well as accessories, outerwear, footwear, basics and swimwear under its American Eagle Outfitters®, American Eagle® and AE® brand names. As of Jan 28 2006, Co. operated 869 American Eagle Outfitters stores in the U.S. and Canada.

Recent Developments: For the quarter ended July 29 2006, income from continuing operations increased 24.2% to $72.1 million from $58.0 million in the year-earlier quarter. Net income increased 24.3% to $72.1 million from $58.0 million in the year-earlier quarter. Revenues were $602.3 million, up 16.8% from $515.9 million the year before. Operating income was $109.3 million versus $85.6 million in the prior-year quarter, an increase of 27.6%. Direct operating expenses rose 13.9% to $327.8 million from $287.9 million in the comparable period the year before. Indirect operating expenses increased 16.1% to $165.3 million from $142.4 million in the equivalent prior-year period.

Prospects: On June 28 2006, Co. completed its acquisition of an existing building and adjacent land in Pittsburgh's SouthSide Works urban redevelopment district for approximately $22.0 million. The acquired property, which will become Co.'s new corporate headquarters, is expected to be occupied in spring 2007. Meanwhile, Co. continues to progress towards its real estate expansion plans and remains on-track to complete 46 new AE store openings and 66 renovations in fiscal 2006. In addition, Co. expects to have a total of about 20 MARTIN + OSA stores opened by the end of fiscal 2007. For the fiscal third quarter ended Oct 2006, Co. is raising its earnings guidance to $0.56 to $0.58 per share.

Financial Data
(US$ in Thousands)	6 Mos	3 Mos	01/28/2006	01/29/2005	01/31/2004	02/01/2003	02/02/2002	02/03/2001
Earnings Per Share	2.06	1.96	1.89	1.42	0.41	0.61	0.71	0.65
Cash Flow Per Share	4.65	3.42	3.18	2.55	1.34	0.73	1.23	1.06
Tang Book Value Per Share	8.59	8.15	7.74	6.40	4.46	3.90	3.32	2.46
Dividends Per Share	0.338	0.300	0.275	0.060	...	...	...	...
Dividend Payout %	16.35	15.28	14.55	4.23				
Income Statement								
Total Revenue	1,124,754	522,428	2,309,371	1,881,241	1,519,968	1,463,141	1,371,899	1,093,477
EBITDA	265,521	125,595	551,545	435,108	162,866	194,274	211,120	176,000
Depn & Amortn	40,938	19,233	74,578	68,273	56,281	50,661	41,875	23,200
Income Before Taxes	224,583	106,362	476,967	366,835	106,585	143,613	169,245	152,800
Income Taxes	88,328	42,206	183,256	142,603	46,585	54,878	63,750	59,042
Net Income	136,255	64,156	294,163	213,343	60,000	88,735	105,495	93,758
Average Shares	152,807	152,258	155,354	150,244	144,414	145,566	147,594	144,264
Balance Sheet								
Total Assets	1,736,566	1,617,258	1,605,649	1,293,659	865,071	741,339	672,721	543,046
Current Liabilities	338,626	294,559	361,623	253,265	189,035	141,586	149,942	149,147
Long-Term Obligations	...	...	...	...	13,874	16,356	19,361	24,889
Total Liabilities	443,178	394,159	450,097	330,173	221,401	163,857	170,669	175,351
Stockholders' Equity	1,293,388	1,223,099	1,155,552	963,486	643,670	577,482	502,052	367,695
Shares Outstanding	149,395	148,934	147,931	149,000	142,000	142,000	143,812	140,000
Statistical Record								
Return on Assets %	19.86	20.42	20.35	19.82	7.49	12.58	17.40	20.55
Return on Equity %	26.16	26.61	27.84	26.62	9.85	16.48	24.33	29.18
EBITDA Margin %	23.61	24.04	23.88	23.13	10.72	13.28	15.39	16.10
Net Margin %	12.11	12.28	12.74	11.34	3.95	6.06	7.69	8.57
Asset Turnover	1.55	1.60	1.60	1.75	1.90	2.08	2.26	2.40
Current Ratio	3.44	3.61	2.99	3.27	2.78	3.02	2.52	2.14
Debt to Equity	...	...	...	...	0.02	0.03	0.04	0.07
Price Range	35.65-20.00	33.48-20.00	33.48-20.00	25.24-9.55	11.21-6.78	14.50-5.14	20.64-8.79	19.29-3.96
P/E Ratio	17.31-9.71	17.08-10.20	17.71-10.58	17.77-6.73	27.34-16.53	23.77-8.43	29.07-12.37	29.68-6.09
Average Yield %	1.22	1.11	1.03	0.36	...	...	...	...

Address: 150 Thorn Hill Drive, Warrendale, PA 15086-7528
Telephone: 724-776-4857
Fax: 724-776-6160

Web Site: www.ae.com
Officers: Jay L. Schottenstein - Chmn. Roger S. Markfield - Vice-Chmn., Pres.

Auditors: ERNST & YOUNG LLP
Investor Contact: 724-776-4857
Transfer Agents: National City Bank, Cleveland, OH

AMERICAN NATIONAL INSURANCE CO. (GALVESTON, TX)

Exchange	Symbol	Price	52Wk Range	Yield	P/E
NMS	ANAT	$115.04 (8/31/2006)	129.72-110.55	2.61	15.14

*7 Year Price Score 106.52 *NYSE Composite Index=100 *12 Month Price Score 97.95

Interim Earnings (Per Share)

Qtr.	Mar	Jun	Sep	Dec
2003			6.87	
2004	2.44	2.42	1.77	3.01
2005	3.42	2.10	2.04	1.34
2006	2.11	...	...	...

Interim Dividends (Per Share)

Amt	Decl	Ex	Rec	Pay
0.75Q	10/27/2005	11/30/2005	12/2/2005	12/16/2005
0.75Q	2/23/2006	3/1/2006	3/3/2006	3/17/2006
0.75Q	4/28/2006	5/31/2006	6/2/2006	6/16/2006
0.75Q	7/27/2006	8/30/2006	9/1/2006	9/15/2006

Indicated Div: $3.00

Valuation Analysis
Forecast P/E N/A

Institutional Holding
No of Institutions 91
Shares 15,267,698
% Held 57.66

Market Cap $3.0 Billion
Book Value 3.4 Billion
Price/Book 0.90
Price/Sales 1.00

Business Summary: Insurance (MIC: 8.2 SIC: 6311 NAIC: 524113)
American National Insurance is engaged in operating in the insurance industry. Operating on a multiple product line basis, Co. offers a broad line of insurance. In addition, through non-insurance subsidiaries, Co. offers mutual funds and invests in real estate. Business is conducted in all states and the District of Columbia, as well as Puerto Rico, Guam and American Samoa. Through a subsidiary, Co. also conducts business in Mexico. Various distribution systems are utilized, including home service, multiple line, group brokerage, credit, independent third party marketing organizations and direct sales to the public.

Recent Developments: For the quarter ended Mar 31 2006, net income decreased 38.1% to $56.2 million from $90.9 million in the year-earlier quarter. Revenues were $748.8 million, down 1.1% from $756.8 million the year before. Net premiums earned were $484.9 million versus $502.0 million in the prior-year quarter, a decrease of 3.4%.

Prospects: Notwithstanding the recent decrease in income from the property and casualty lines compared with the corresponding prior-year period, Co.'s prospects appear satisfactory. Notably, Co.'s Multiple Line property and casualty operations first quarter combined ratio for 2006 was affected by catastrophe losses from storms in the Midwest states and above average non-catastrophe storm losses, resulting in a combined ratio of 94.1%. According to Co., as a result of very low catastrophe activity, the first quarter 2005 property and casualty combined ratio was 82.6%.

Financial Data
(US$ in Thousands)

	3 Mos	12/31/2005	12/31/2004	12/31/2003	12/31/2002	12/31/2001	12/31/2000	12/31/1999
Earnings Per Share	7.60	8.87	9.63	6.87	0.64	2.45	5.29	10.07
Cash Flow Per Share	...	16.88	25.17	14.22	11.61	12.70	7.36	6.52
Tang Book Value Per Share	...	127.57	124.46	117.52	108.53	110.89	114.19	115.68
Dividends Per Share	2.980	2.970	2.960	2.960	2.960	2.930	2.860	2.780
Dividend Payout %	39.21	33.48	30.74	43.09	462.50	119.59	54.06	27.61
Income Statement								
Premium Income	484,899	2,116,055	2,029,429	1,965,782	1,747,194	1,546,003	1,292,026	1,230,936
Total Revenue	748,817	3,045,474	2,879,336	2,684,506	2,241,343	2,134,381	1,834,481	1,889,614
Benefits & Claims	367,048	1,557,395	1,406,689	1,372,939	1,320,425	1,202,901	963,468	866,142
Income Before Taxes	94,204	342,869	375,006	271,725	26,835	105,119	206,942	388,681
Income Taxes	38,002	106,990	119,413	89,560	9,980	40,188	66,768	122,068
Net Income	56,202	235,879	255,593	182,165	16,855	64,931	140,174	266,613
Average Shares	...	26,589	26,552	26,479	26,479	26,479	26,479	26,479
Balance Sheet								
Total Assets	17,561,221	17,516,881	16,570,827	15,140,234	12,139,172	11,258,137	9,270,387	9,090,526
Total Liabilities	14,169,264	14,138,834	13,275,069	12,028,212	9,265,443	8,321,798	6,246,730	6,027,380
Stockholders' Equity	3,391,557	3,378,047	3,295,758	3,112,022	2,873,729	2,936,339	3,023,657	3,063,146
Shares Outstanding	...	26,479	26,479	26,479	26,479	26,479	26,479	26,479
Statistical Record								
Return on Assets %	1.17	1.38	1.61	1.34	0.14	0.63	1.52	2.98
Return on Equity %	6.01	7.07	7.96	6.09	0.58	2.18	4.59	8.92
Loss Ratio %	75.70	73.60	69.31	69.84	75.57	77.81	74.57	70.36
Net Margin %	7.51	7.75	8.88	6.79	0.75	3.04	7.64	14.11
Price Range	122.97-98.65	122.97-98.65	105.80-84.48	89.48-75.36	101.38-66.34	84.10-66.56	73.00-49.56	89.38-61.38
P/E Ratio	16.18-12.98	13.86-11.12	10.99-8.77	13.02-10.97	158.41-103.66	34.33-27.17	13.80-9.37	8.88-6.09
Average Yield %	2.60	2.64	3.10	3.54	3.43	3.84	4.71	3.91

Address: One Moody Plaza, Galveston, TX 77550-7999
Telephone: 409-763-4661
Fax: 409-766-6502

Web Site: www.anico.com
Officers: Robert L. Moody - Chmn., C.E.O. G.
Richard Ferdinandtsen - Pres., C.O.O.

Auditors: KPMG LLP
Investor Contact: 409-766-6447
Transfer Agents: Mellon Investor Services LLC, Ridgefield Park, NJ

AMERICAN POWER CONVERSION CORP.

Exchange	Symbol	Price	52Wk Range	Yield	P/E
NMS	APCC	$17.57 (8/31/2006)	26.71-16.39	2.28	33.15

*7 Year Price Score 87.93 *NYSE Composite Index=100 *12 Month Price Score 79.89

Interim Earnings (Per Share)

Qtr.	Mar	Jun	Sep	Dec
2003			0.88	
2004	0.17	0.13	0.34	0.27
2005	0.18	0.21	0.24	0.09
2006	0.07	0.13	...	...

Interim Dividends (Per Share)

Amt	Decl	Ex	Rec	Pay
0.10Q	11/2/2005	11/17/2005	11/21/2005	12/14/2005
0.10Q	2/1/2006	2/15/2006	2/20/2006	3/15/2006
0.10Q	5/12/2006	5/24/2006	5/26/2006	6/14/2006
0.10Q	8/15/2006	8/24/2006	8/28/2006	9/13/2006

Indicated Div: $0.40

Valuation Analysis

		Institutional Holding	
Forecast P/E	27.84	No of Institutions	
	(9/9/2006)	306	
Market Cap	$3.3 Billion	Shares	
Book Value	1.5 Billion	143,802,512	
Price/Book	2.18	% Held	
Price/Sales	1.57	75.49	

Business Summary: Electrical (MIC: 11.14 SIC: 3629 NAIC: 335999)

American Power Conversion and its subsidiaries design, develop, manufacture, and market power protection and management products for computer, communications and electronic applications worldwide. Co.'s products include uninterruptible power supply products (UPSs), electrical surge protection devices, power conditioning products, cooling equipment, and associated software, services, and accessories. These products are primarily used with sensitive electronic devices which rely on electric utility power. Co.'s principal markets are in North America, Europe, and the Far East.

Recent Developments: For the quarter ended June 25 2006, net income decreased 41.0% to $24.7 million from $41.9 million in the year-earlier quarter. Revenues were $560.0 million, up 16.5% from $480.6 million the year before. Operating income was $27.0 million versus $49.9 million in the prior-year quarter, a decrease of 46.0%. Direct operating expenses rose 22.8% to $371.4 million from $302.3 million in the comparable period the year before. Indirect operating expenses increased 26.0% to $161.7 million from $128.4 million in the equivalent prior-year period.

Prospects: Co. continues to experience strong demand across geographies and its major operating segments, which extends its double digit year-over-year revenue growth trend. Meanwhile, through the streamlining of operations, supply chain initiatives and pricing actions, Co. is taking steps to improve its gross margin while maintaining investments in innovation, sales and marketing programs to drive awareness and adoption of Co.'s network-critical physical infrastructure application globally. However, Co. still expects overall gross margins to be hampered on a year-over-year basis by rising operational costs, and a shift in product mix toward the faster-growing, lower-margin Large Systems products.

Financial Data
(US$ in Thousands)

	6 Mos	3 Mos	12/31/2005	12/31/2004	12/31/2003	12/31/2002	12/31/2001	12/31/2000
Earnings Per Share	0.53	0.61	0.72	0.90	0.88	0.42	0.58	0.83
Cash Flow Per Share	0.32	0.52	0.82	0.72	0.61	1.60	0.60	0.09
Tang Book Value Per Share	7.81	7.91	8.11	7.58	7.28	6.34	5.67	5.00
Dividends Per Share	0.400	0.400	0.400	0.360	0.160	...	...	...
Dividend Payout %	75.14	65.35	55.56	40.00	18.18	...	...	...
Income Statement								
Total Revenue	1,038,778	478,793	1,979,532	1,699,877	1,464,798	1,300,025	1,433,312	1,483,563
EBITDA	78,162	32,649	259,922	262,647	286,555	213,358	214,489	274,254
Depn & Amortn	27,580	13,946	51,080	48,487	47,450	51,522	55,936	40,943
Income Before Taxes	50,582	18,703	208,842	214,160	239,105	161,836	158,553	233,311
Income Taxes	11,381	4,208	64,761	32,705	62,167	45,314	45,188	67,660
Net Income	39,201	14,495	144,081	181,455	176,938	82,022	113,365	165,651
Average Shares	194,342	197,305	199,798	201,658	201,517	196,993	196,793	200,156
Balance Sheet								
Total Assets	1,962,391	2,010,076	2,075,462	1,843,872	1,805,966	1,604,580	1,420,772	1,317,105
Current Liabilities	418,999	424,212	420,802	326,164	280,726	277,440	183,078	206,119
Total Liabilities	430,343	435,592	435,713	341,613	295,083	292,528	199,384	219,924
Stockholders' Equity	1,532,048	1,574,484	1,639,749	1,502,259	1,510,883	1,312,052	1,221,388	1,097,181
Shares Outstanding	190,179	192,697	195,778	192,137	199,732	196,246	195,775	194,821
Statistical Record								
Return on Assets %	5.44	6.32	7.35	9.92	10.38	5.42	8.28	13.63
Return on Equity %	6.80	7.92	9.17	12.01	12.54	6.48	9.78	16.53
EBITDA Margin %	7.52	6.82	13.13	15.45	19.56	16.41	14.96	18.49
Net Margin %	3.77	3.03	7.28	10.67	12.08	6.31	7.91	11.17
Asset Turnover	1.10	1.06	1.01	0.93	0.86	0.86	1.05	1.22
Current Ratio	3.99	4.08	4.30	4.92	5.34	4.60	5.83	4.68
Price Range	28.33-18.51	28.33-20.04	28.33-20.15	27.37-14.92	24.50-13.84	16.33-9.33	19.12-10.55	47.63-9.94
P/E Ratio	53.45-34.92	46.44-32.85	39.35-27.99	30.41-16.58	27.84-15.73	38.88-22.21	32.97-18.19	57.38-11.97
Average Yield %	1.75	1.67	1.67	1.79	0.92	...	...	...

Address: 132 Fairgrounds Road, West Kingston, RI 02892
Telephone: 401-789-5735
Fax: 401-789-3710

Web Site: www.apc.com
Officers: Rodger B. Dowdell Jr. - Chmn., Pres., C.E.O. Richard J. Thompson - Sr. V.P., Fin., C.F.O.

Auditors: KPMG LLP
Investor Contact: 800-788-2208xt2994

AMGEN INC

Exchange	Symbol	Price	52Wk Range	Yield	P/E
NMS	AMGN	$68.03 (8/31/2006)	86.17-63.92	N/A	29.97

*7 Year Price Score 95.87 *NYSE Composite Index=100 *12 Month Price Score 89.72

Interim Earnings (Per Share)

Qtr.	Mar	Jun	Sep	Dec
2003	0.37	0.45	0.46	0.41
2004	0.52	0.57	0.18	0.53
2005	0.67	0.82	0.77	0.67
2006	0.82	0.01	...	...

Interim Dividends (Per Share)
No Dividends Paid

Valuation Analysis	**Institutional Holding**
Forecast P/E 18.12 (9/9/2006)	No of Institutions 1165
Market Cap $79.6 Billion	Shares 853,552,704
Book Value 16.8 Billion	% Held 72.38
Price/Book 4.73
Price/Sales 6.01

Business Summary: Biotechnology (MIC: 9.2 SIC: 2836 NAIC: 325414)
Amgen develops, manufactures, and markets human therapeutics based on advances in cellular and molecular biology. Principle products include EPOGEN®, Aranesp®, Neulasta®, NEUPOGEN®, and ENBREL®, which is marketed under a co-promotion agreement with Wyeth in the U.S. and Canada. EPOGEN® and Aranesp® stimulate the production of red blood cells to treat anemia. Neulasta® and NEUPOGEN® selectively stimulate the production of neutrophils, one type of white blood cell that helps the body fight infections. ENBREL® blocks the biologic activity of tumor necrosis factor, a substance induced in response to inflammatory and immunological responses, such as rheumatoid arthritis and psoriasis.

Recent Developments: For the quarter ended June 30 2006, net income decreased 98.6% to $14.0 million from $1.03 billion in the year-earlier quarter. Revenues were $3.60 billion, up 13.6% from $3.17 billion the year before. Operating income was $295.0 million versus $1.29 billion in the prior-year quarter, a decrease of 77.2%. Direct operating expenses declined 7.0% to $493.0 million from $530.0 million in the comparable period the year before. Indirect operating expenses increased 108.7% to $2.82 billion from $1.35 billion in the equivalent prior-year period.

Prospects: Co. expects Aranesp®, ENBREL, and Neulasta® to continue to drive sales growth in the near term. Co. also remains focused on growing its operating segments, including increasing its penetration in the therapeutic areas in which its products are used. For full year 2006, Co. expects revenue to be $14.00 billion to $14.30 billion. Separately, Co. expects to obtain approval for Vectibix™ in 3rd line metastatic colorectal cancer in the U.S. later in 2006, with launch of Vectibix™ by the end of 2006. In addition, outside the U.S., marketing applications have been submitted to the European Medicines Agency, Health Canada, Australia and Switzerland.

Financial Data
(US$ in Thousands)

	6 Mos	3 Mos	12/31/2005	12/31/2004	12/31/2003	12/31/2002	12/31/2001	12/31/2000
Earnings Per Share	2.27	3.08	2.93	1.81	1.69	(1.21)	1.03	1.05
Cash Flow Per Share	4.39	4.14	3.97	2.90	2.77	1.95	1.42	1.58
Tang Book Value Per Share	1.42	2.76	5.08	4.08	4.06	2.80	4.99	4.16
Income Statement								
Total Revenue	6,821,000	3,217,000	12,430,000	10,550,000	8,356,000	5,523,000	4,015,700	3,629,400
EBITDA	2,106,000	1,533,000	5,808,000	4,167,000	3,891,100	(193,000)	1,965,800	1,902,000
Depn & Amortn	476,000	219,000	841,000	734,000	686,500	447,300	265,900	211,800
Income Before Taxes	1,630,000	1,314,000	4,868,000	3,395,000	3,173,100	(684,500)	1,686,300	1,674,300
Income Taxes	615,000	313,000	1,194,000	1,032,000	913,600	707,400	566,600	535,800
Net Income	1,015,000	1,001,000	3,674,000	2,363,000	2,259,500	(1,391,900)	1,119,700	1,138,500
Average Shares	1,185,000	1,218,000	1,258,000	1,320,000	1,346,000	1,153,500	1,084,400	1,084,700
Balance Sheet								
Total Assets	31,288,000	31,315,000	29,297,000	29,221,000	26,176,500	24,456,300	6,443,100	5,399,600
Current Liabilities	5,913,000	5,383,000	3,595,000	4,157,000	2,246,300	1,529,200	1,002,900	862,100
Long-Term Obligations	7,232,000	7,198,000	3,957,000	3,937,000	3,079,500	3,047,700	223,000	223,000
Total Liabilities	14,449,000	13,924,000	8,846,000	9,516,000	6,787,400	6,170,300	1,225,900	1,085,100
Stockholders' Equity	16,839,000	17,391,000	20,451,000	19,705,000	19,389,100	18,286,000	5,217,200	4,314,500
Shares Outstanding	1,170,000	1,178,000	1,224,000	1,260,000	1,283,700	1,289,100	1,045,800	1,037,400
Statistical Record								
Return on Assets %	9.46	13.01	12.56	8.51	8.93	N.M.	18.91	23.96
Return on Equity %	15.41	20.98	18.30	12.06	11.99	N.M.	23.49	30.95
EBITDA Margin %	30.88	47.65	46.73	39.50	46.57	N.M.	48.95	52.41
Net Margin %	14.88	31.12	29.56	22.40	27.04	N.M.	27.88	31.37
Asset Turnover	0.45	0.44	0.42	0.38	0.33	0.36	0.68	0.76
Current Ratio	1.61	2.07	2.57	2.21	3.30	4.19	3.85	3.41
Debt to Equity	0.43	0.41	0.19	0.20	0.16	0.17	0.04	0.05
Price Range	86.17-60.46	86.17-57.20	86.17-57.20	66.23-52.70	71.54-48.34	62.48-31.07	74.19-51.51	78.00-51.31
P/E Ratio	37.96-26.63	27.98-18.57	29.41-19.52	36.59-29.12	42.33-28.60	...	72.03-50.01	74.29-48.87

Address: One Amgen Center Drive, Thousand Oaks, CA 91320-1799
Telephone: 805-447-1000
Fax: 805-447-1010

Web Site: www.amgen.com
Officers: Kevin W. Sharer - Chmn., Pres., C.E.O.
Dennis M. Fenton Ph.D. - Exec. V.P., Oper., Compliance Officer

Auditors: to Ernst & Young LLP
Investor Contact: 805-447-4634
Transfer Agents: American Stock Transfer & Trust Company

AMKOR TECHNOLOGY INC.

Exchange	Symbol	Price	52Wk Range	Yield	P/E
NMS	AMKR	$5.67 (8/31/2006)	12.87-3.66	N/A	70.88

*7 Year Price Score 39.94 *NYSE Composite Index=100 *12 Month Price Score 92.29

Interim Earnings (Per Share)

Qtr.	Mar	Jun	Sep	Dec
2003	0.09	(0.31)	0.09	0.13
2004	0.06	0.06	(0.13)	(0.20)
2005	(0.68)	(0.30)	(0.11)	0.30
2006	0.19	...	...	...

Interim Dividends (Per Share)
No Dividends Paid

Valuation Analysis

		Institutional Holding	
Forecast P/E	5.94	No of Institutions	
	(9/9/2006)	134	
Market Cap	$1.0 Billion	Shares	
Book Value	260.4 Million	72,492,816	
Price/Book	3.85	% Held	
Price/Sales	0.43	40.96	

Business Summary: IT & Technology (MIC: 10.2 SIC: 3674 NAIC: 334413)
Amkor Technology is a subcontractor of semiconductor packaging and test services. The packaging process creates an electrical interconnect between the semiconductor chip and the system board. In packaging, the fabricated semiconductor wafers are cut into individual chips which are attached to a substrate and then encased in a protective material to provide optimal electrical connectivity and thermal performance. The packaged chips are then tested using sophisticated equipment to ensure that each packaged chip meets its design specifications. Co. maintains production capabilities in China, Korea, Japan, the Philippines, Singapore, Taiwan and the U.S.

Recent Developments: For the first quarter ended Mar 31 2006, net income amounted to $34.7 million compared with a net loss of $119.1 million in the equivalent year-earlier quarter. Revenues were $645.1 million, up 54.5% from $417.5 million the year before. Operating income was $84.3 million versus a loss of $76.0 million in the prior-year quarter. Direct operating expenses rose 31.0% to $490.1 million from $374.1 million in the comparable period the year before. Indirect operating expenses decreased 40.8% to $70.7 million from $119.4 million in the equivalent prior-year period.

Prospects: Looking ahead, Co.'s customers' forecasts suggest modest growth in the second quarter and continued growth in the third quarter of 2006. As a result, for the second quarter of 2006, Co. expects net income of $0.24 to $0.28 per diluted share, and sales to be 2.0% to 4.0% above sales in the first quarter of 2006. In addition, Co. estimates gross margin to be in a range of 25.0% to 26.0%. Also, Co. expects the tight supply throughout the semiconductor industry, and a more restricted behavior towards capacity expansion, will restrain production and dampen the amplitude of industry cyclicality. A less volatile business environment should enable Co. to improve long-term results.

Financial Data

(US$ in Thousands)	3 Mos	12/31/2005	12/31/2004	12/31/2003	12/31/2002	12/31/2001	12/31/2000	12/31/1999
Earnings Per Share	0.08	(0.78)	(0.21)	0.01	(5.04)	(2.87)	1.02	0.63
Cash Flow Per Share	1.27	0.55	1.23	1.06	1.08	1.02	2.56	2.46
Tang Book Value Per Share	N.M.	N.M.	N.M.	N.M.	N.M.	1.93	3.79	3.85
Income Statement								
Total Revenue	645,089	2,099,949	1,901,279	1,603,768	1,639,707	1,517,862	2,387,294	1,909,972
EBITDA	147,406	278,306	357,443	333,253	(69,754)	199,197	650,178	330,984
Depn & Amortn	66,061	257,321	229,979	238,275	333,596	465,083	332,909	180,332
Income Before Taxes	38,400	(144,887)	(21,438)	(45,303)	(550,847)	(429,950)	197,429	105,288
Income Taxes	3,612	(5,551)	15,192	(233)	65,815	(81,691)	22,285	26,600
Net Income	34,673	(136,889)	(37,536)	2,198	(826,759)	(450,861)	154,153	76,719
Average Shares	191,015	176,385	175,342	167,142	164,124	157,111	153,223	135,067
Balance Sheet								
Total Assets	3,009,903	2,955,091	2,965,368	2,571,874	2,557,984	3,223,518	3,393,284	1,755,089
Current Liabilities	816,506	634,732	439,030	439,851	511,121	371,334	446,431	312,898
Long-Term Obligations	1,778,801	1,956,347	2,040,813	1,650,707	1,737,690	1,771,453	...	687,456
Total Liabilities	2,745,883	2,726,840	2,589,160	2,169,532	2,316,472	2,206,864	2,078,450	1,017,348
Stockholders' Equity	260,398	224,301	369,529	401,004	231,367	1,008,717	1,314,834	737,741
Shares Outstanding	176,905	176,733	175,718	174,508	165,156	161,782	152,118	131,010
Statistical Record								
Return on Assets %	0.57	N.M.	N.M.	0.09	N.M.	N.M.	5.97	5.56
Return on Equity %	6.64	N.M.	N.M.	0.70	N.M.	N.M.	14.98	12.49
EBITDA Margin %	22.85	13.25	18.80	20.78	N.M.	13.12	27.23	17.33
Net Margin %	5.37	N.M.	N.M.	0.14	N.M.	N.M.	6.46	4.02
Asset Turnover	0.79	0.71	0.68	0.63	0.57	0.46	0.92	1.38
Current Ratio	0.97	1.21	1.79	1.77	1.36	1.43	1.23	1.62
Debt to Equity	6.83	8.72	5.52	4.12	7.51	1.76	...	0.93
Price Range	9.74-2.94	6.68-2.94	20.93-3.34	21.40-4.11	24.25-1.20	25.00-9.42	64.56-12.00	28.25-7.31
P/E Ratio	121.75-36.75	...	...	N.M.	...	...	63.30-11.76	44.84-11.61

Address: 1900 S. Price Road, Chandler, AZ 85248 Telephone: 480-821-5000 Fax: 480-821-8267	Web Site: www.amkor.com Officers: James J. Kim - Chmn., C.E.O. John N. Boruch - Pres., C.O.O.	Auditors: PricewaterhouseCoopers LLP Investor Contact: 480-821-5000 Transfer Agents: Computershare Investors Service

AMYLIN PHARMACEUTICALS, INC.

Exchange	Symbol	Price	52Wk Range	Yield	P/E
NMS	AMLN	$45.33 (8/31/2006)	51.21-30.02	N/A	N/A

*7 Year Price Score 174.17 *NYSE Composite Index=100 *12 Month Price Score 109.36

Interim Earnings (Per Share)

Qtr.	Mar	Jun	Sep	Dec
2003	(0.34)	(0.40)	(0.40)	(0.18)
2004	(0.40)	(0.42)	(0.36)	(0.49)
2005	(0.43)	(0.26)	(0.65)	(0.62)
2006	(0.61)	(0.38)	...	...

Interim Dividends (Per Share)
No Dividends Paid

Valuation Analysis

		Institutional Holding	
Forecast P/E	N/A	No of Institutions	
	(9/9/2006)	235	
Market Cap	$5.6 Billion	Shares	
Book Value	512.0 Million	122,401,296	
Price/Book	10.96	% Held	
Price/Sales	19.36	98.71	

Business Summary: Pharmaceuticals (MIC: 9.1 SIC: 2834 NAIC: 325412)
Amylin Pharmaceuticals is a biopharmaceutical company engaged in the discovery, development and commercialization of innovative medicines to improve the lives of people with diabetes, obesity and cardiovascular disease. Co. have two approved products, BYETTA® (exenatide) injection and SYMLIN® (pramlintide acetate) injection, both of which were commercially launched in the U.S. during the second quarter of 2005. Co. have a field force in excess of 400 people dedicated to marketing BYETTA and SYMLIN in the U.S., which includes its specialty and primary care sales forces, a managed care and government affairs organization, a medical science organization, and diabetes care specialists.

Recent Developments: For the quarter ended June 30 2006, net loss amounted to $46.4 million versus a net loss of $26.6 million in the year-earlier quarter. Revenues were $118.1 million, up 152.6% from $46.8 million the year before. Operating loss was $53.8 million versus a loss of $26.6 million in the prior-year quarter. Direct operating expenses rose 864.8% to $14.7 million from $1.5 million in the comparable period the year before. Indirect operating expenses increased 118.9% to $157.3 million from $71.8 million in the equivalent prior-year period.

Prospects: Co.'s results are being restrained by lower revenues from increased research and development expenses, and higher selling, general and administrative expenses. Meanwhile, Co. plans to increase its supply of BYETTA in the third quarter of 2006, so as to accelerate medical education activities and expand its field force. Moreover, Co. is working with Alkermes and Parsons Corporation to establish a manufacturing facility for the commercial production of exenatide long-acting release formulation, and expects to complete in stages through 2008 at a cost of $150.0 million. Also, Co expects to complete a Phase 2 clinical study of AC2592, for the treatment of congestive heart failure, in 2006.

Financial Data
(US$ in Thousands)

	6 Mos	3 Mos	12/31/2005	12/31/2004	12/31/2003	12/31/2002	12/31/2001	12/31/2000
Earnings Per Share	(2.26)	(2.14)	(1.96)	(1.67)	(1.33)	(1.39)	(1.09)	(0.71)
Cash Flow Per Share	(1.51)	(1.79)	(1.72)	(1.73)	(1.55)	(0.26)	(1.03)	(0.58)
Tang Book Value Per Share	4.14	0.28	0.63	...	0.68	0.15	...	0.49
Income Statement								
Total Revenue	200,495	82,346	140,474	34,268	85,652	13,395	...	...
Depn & Amortn	6,737	3,278	10,487	7,307	5,136	3,384	2,689	3,105
Net Income	(114,295)	(67,901)	(206,832)	(157,157)	(122,808)	(109,787)	(71,972)	(44,043)
Average Shares	122,675	111,285	105,532	94,054	92,396	79,106	65,927	61,644
Balance Sheet								
Total Assets	1,044,546	540,426	568,046	357,800	311,045	168,545	63,527	90,635
Current Liabilities	134,012	109,467	99,670	41,937	45,404	68,013	8,937	7,246
Long-Term Obligations	375,000	375,000	387,454	382,290	177,196	62,947	58,073	52,103
Total Liabilities	532,504	508,840	498,782	445,170	247,829	156,247	67,010	59,349
Stockholders' Equity	512,042	31,586	69,264	(87,370)	63,216	12,298	(3,483)	31,286
Shares Outstanding	123,817	111,843	110,531	94,489	93,625	81,979	67,554	63,383
Statistical Record								
Asset Turnover	0.38	0.42	0.30	0.10	0.36	0.12	...	...
Current Ratio	7.21	4.39	5.17	7.73	6.36	2.36	6.28	11.82
Debt to Equity	0.73	11.87	5.59	...	2.80	5.12	...	1.67
Price Range	49.37-18.54	48.95-14.65	41.43-14.65	25.86-16.85	30.22-14.05	18.80-7.49	14.72-4.94	18.25-7.13

Address: 9373 Towne Centre Drive, Suite 110, San Diego, CA 92121
Telephone: 858-552-2200
Fax: 858-552-2212

Web Site: www.amylin.com
Officers: Joseph C. Cook Jr. - Chmn. Ginger L. Graham - Pres., C.E.O.

Auditors: Ernst & Young LLP

ANCHOR BANCORP WISCONSIN, INC

Exchange	Symbol	Price	52Wk Range	Yield	P/E	Div Acheiver
NMS	ABCW	$29.22 (8/31/2006)	32.78-28.42	2.33	14.61	12 Years

*7 Year Price Score 108.41 *NYSE Composite Index=100 *12 Month Price Score 95.07

Interim Earnings (Per Share)

Qtr.	Jun	Sep	Dec	Mar
2003-04	0.59	0.48	0.43	0.52
2004-05	0.46	0.46	0.47	0.71
2005-06	0.52	0.48	0.50	0.53
2006-07	0.49	...	...	...

Interim Dividends (Per Share)

Amt	Decl	Ex	Rec	Pay
0.16Q	10/21/2005	10/28/2005	11/1/2005	11/15/2005
0.16Q	1/20/2006	1/27/2006	1/31/2006	2/15/2006
0.16Q	4/19/2006	4/26/2006	4/28/2006	5/15/2006
0.17Q	7/21/2006	7/28/2006	8/1/2006	8/15/2006

Indicated Div: $0.68

Valuation Analysis   **Institutional Holding**

Forecast P/E	13.33	No of Institutions
	(9/9/2006)	103
Market Cap	$640.0 Million	Shares
Book Value	326.5 Million	9,894,697
Price/Book	1.96	% Held
Price/Sales	2.06	45.12

Business Summary: Trusts & Holding Entities (MIC: 8.9 SIC: 6036 NAIC: 522120)

Anchor BanCorp Wisconsin is a bank holding company. Through its subsidiary, AnchorBank, fsb (the Bank), Co. is engaged in the provision of checking, savings, money market accounts, mortgages, home equity and other consumer loans, student loans, credit cards, annuities and related consumer financial services; banking services to businesses; investments services; credit life and disability insurance; holding and development of foreclosed properties; and management of investment portfolio. Co. also invests in real estate partnerships and real estate held for development and sale. As of Mar 31 2006, the Bank had 60 branch offices with assets of $4.28 billion and total deposits of $3.04 billion.

Recent Developments: For the quarter ended June 30 2006, net income decreased 7.9% to $10.6 million from $11.6 million in the year-earlier quarter. Net interest income increased 2.2% to $32.8 million from $32.1 million in the year-earlier quarter. Provision for loan losses was $1.2 million versus $265,000 in the prior-year quarter, an increase of 354.7%. Non-interest income fell 29.1% to $13.3 million from $18.8 million, while non-interest expense declined 12.0% to $26.4 million.

Prospects: Co. attributes its lower earnings largely to a decrease in non-interest income as a result of a decline in its real estate investment partnership revenue, partially offset by the decreases in its non-interest expense and minority interest income of real estate partnership operations. Also, Co.'s net interest margin declined due to higher yields on interest earnings assets as its interest rate spread is being pressured by the rising interest rate environment. On the brighter side, Co. is benefiting from strong loan growth, as evidenced by the solid gains in interest income on loans attributable to an increase in its average balance of loans, along with an increase in deposits.

Financial Data
(US$ in Thousands)

	3 Mos	03/31/2006	03/31/2005	03/31/2004	03/31/2003	03/31/2002	03/31/2001	03/31/2000
Earnings Per Share	2.00	2.03	2.10	2.02	2.02	1.55	1.16	0.78
Cash Flow Per Share	3.15	2.13	2.86	3.84	2.41	(1.43)	2.41	0.97
Tang Book Value Per Share	14.00	13.78	13.03	12.27	11.40	11.12	9.63	9.02
Dividends Per Share	0.640	0.615	0.485	0.430	0.362	0.323	0.295	0.250
Dividend Payout %	32.00	30.30	23.10	21.29	17.95	20.81	25.43	32.05
Income Statement								
Interest Income	66,266	238,550	199,979	190,262	209,605	225,701	228,647	202,065
Interest Expense	33,421	105,846	79,276	79,907	92,856	128,454	148,096	119,393
Net Interest Income	32,845	132,704	120,703	110,355	116,749	97,247	80,551	82,672
Provision for Losses	1,205	3,900	1,579	1,950	1,800	2,485	945	1,306
Non-Interest Income	13,307	66,976	134,864	82,076	32,753	21,615	13,503	13,717
Non-Interest Expense	26,439	118,447	162,575	113,641	68,004	59,531	51,450	59,985
Income Before Taxes	18,070	75,610	77,867	76,840	79,698	56,846	41,659	35,098
Income Taxes	7,423	30,927	29,532	29,471	30,135	20,479	14,682	15,596
Net Income	10,647	44,683	48,335	47,369	49,563	36,367	26,977	19,502
Average Shares	21,791	22,026	23,011	23,399	24,592	23,462	23,207	25,159
Balance Sheet								
Net Loans & Leases	3,713,863	3,614,265	3,414,608	3,066,812	2,770,988	2,627,248	2,414,976	2,302,721
Total Assets	4,356,921	4,275,140	4,050,456	3,810,986	3,538,621	3,507,076	3,127,474	2,911,152
Total Deposits	3,177,220	3,040,217	2,873,533	2,602,954	2,574,188	2,553,987	2,119,320	1,897,369
Total Liabilities	4,022,622	3,947,118	3,729,976	3,502,147	3,245,617	3,229,564	2,907,862	2,693,937
Stockholders' Equity	326,495	321,025	310,678	301,548	293,004	277,512	219,612	217,215
Shares Outstanding	21,902	21,854	22,319	22,954	23,942	24,950	22,814	24,088
Statistical Record								
Return on Assets %	1.03	1.07	1.23	1.29	1.41	1.10	0.89	0.77
Return on Equity %	13.64	14.15	15.79	15.89	17.37	14.63	12.35	10.82
Net Interest Margin %	49.57	55.63	60.36	58.00	55.70	43.09	35.23	40.91
Efficiency Ratio %	33.23	38.77	48.55	41.73	28.06	24.07	21.25	27.80
Loans to Deposits	1.17	1.19	1.19	1.18	1.08	1.03	1.14	1.21
Price Range	32.78-28.43	32.78-26.32	29.61-24.00	27.10-21.95	24.25-17.99	21.64-13.13	16.75-12.88	20.00-12.75
P/E Ratio	16.39-14.22	16.15-12.97	14.10-11.43	13.42-10.87	12.00-8.91	13.96-8.47	14.44-11.10	25.64-16.35
Average Yield %	2.11	2.05	1.82	1.74	1.69	1.94	1.92	1.54

| Address: 25 West Main Street, Madison, WI 53703
Telephone: 608-252-8700
Fax: 608-252-8783 | Web Site: www.anchorbank.com
Officers: Douglas J. Timmerman - Chmn., Pres., C.E.O. Michael W. Helser - C.F.O., Treas. | Auditors: McGladrey & Pullen, LLP
Investor Contact: 608-252-1810
Transfer Agents: American Stock Transfer & Trust Company, New York, NY |

ANDREW CORP.

Exchange	Symbol	Price	52Wk Range	Yield	P/E
NMS	ANDW	$9.25 (8/31/2006)	13.74-7.42	N/A	46.25

*7 Year Price Score 55.79 *NYSE Composite Index=100 *12 Month Price Score 76.77

Interim Earnings (Per Share)

Qtr.	Dec	Mar	Jun	Sep
2002-03	0.06	(0.03)	0.08	(0.02)
2003-04	0.02	0.06	0.11	0.00
2004-05	0.09	0.02	0.08	0.05
2005-06	0.09	0.02	0.04	...

Interim Dividends (Per Share)
No Dividends Paid

Valuation Analysis

		Institutional Holding	
Forecast P/E	22.49	No of Institutions	
	(9/9/2006)	240	
Market Cap	$1.5 Billion	Shares	
Book Value	1.6 Billion	145,337,232	
Price/Book	0.93	% Held	
Price/Sales	0.72	91.03	

Business Summary: Metal Works (MIC: 11.3 SIC: 3357 NAIC: 331491)
Andrew is a supplier of communications products and systems to the wireless subsystem infrastructure market. Co. produces products which are based on the radio frequency (RF) path. Co.'s products are used in the infrastructure for traditional wireless networks, third generation (3G) technologies, voice, data, video and Internet services, as well as applications for microwave and satellite communications and other specialized applications. Co. operated its business in the following five segments: Antenna and Cable Products, Base Station Subsystems, Network Solutions, Wireless Innovations and Satellite Communications.

Recent Developments: For the quarter ended June 30 2006, net income decreased 46.4% to $7.0 million from $13.0 million in the year-earlier quarter. Revenues were $550.7 million, up 13.0% from $487.2 million the year before. Operating income was $18.0 million versus $23.8 million in the prior-year quarter, a decrease of 24.4%. Direct operating expenses rose 14.6% to $429.1 million from $374.3 million in the comparable period the year before. Indirect operating expenses increased 16.3% to $103.6 million from $89.1 million in the equivalent prior-year period.

Prospects: Co.'s outlook appears favorable, reflecting positive global demand trends for the wireless infrastructure industry. For the fourth fiscal quarter ending Sep 2006, Co. expects sales to range from $540.0 million to $570.0 million due primarily to higher Wireless Infrastructure sales and the inclusion of sales from its Apr 2006 acquisition of Precision Antennas Ltd. Accordingly, Co. projects earnings per share of $0.10 to $0.13, including intangible amortization expenses but excluding any potential restructuring charges and a gain of about $9.0 million related to the completed sale of the first of two parcels of land that comprise its Orland Park, IL, manufacturing facility.

Financial Data

(US$ in Thousands)	9 Mos	6 Mos	3 Mos	09/30/2005	09/30/2004	09/30/2003	09/30/2002	09/30/2001
Earnings Per Share	0.20	0.24	0.24	0.24	0.20	0.08	(0.30)	0.76
Cash Flow Per Share	0.51	0.58	0.66	0.55	0.29	0.57	1.78	1.97
Tang Book Value Per Share	4.06	4.02	3.93	3.93	3.64	3.16	4.09	6.85
Income Statement								
Total Revenue	1,547,040	996,352	514,699	1,961,234	1,838,749	1,014,486	864,801	1,049,495
EBITDA	103,314	67,059	40,378	157,051	164,182	101,756	70,848	149,772
Depn & Amortn	57,876	37,740	18,960	84,000	103,443	74,404	56,316	54,383
Income Before Taxes	37,884	23,643	18,530	63,179	48,923	23,326	13,070	90,621
Income Taxes	12,509	5,231	3,687	24,321	15,938	4,622	2,578	28,999
Net Income	25,375	18,412	14,843	38,858	32,985	15,520	(26,379)	61,622
Average Shares	160,357	160,260	178,140	161,953	160,258	109,866	87,295	81,542
Balance Sheet								
Total Assets	2,381,264	2,308,166	2,285,122	2,311,027	2,240,945	2,073,233	1,123,666	857,732
Current Liabilities	482,421	431,952	427,105	435,616	378,839	273,958	236,570	179,428
Long-Term Obligations	268,617	268,258	269,071	275,604	284,844	301,364	13,391	39,905
Total Liabilities	800,558	750,086	745,871	760,475	718,071	649,263	278,422	257,082
Stockholders' Equity	1,580,706	1,558,080	1,539,251	1,550,552	1,522,874	1,423,970	845,244	600,650
Shares Outstanding	159,660	159,651	159,321	160,919	160,866	158,292	98,217	81,530
Statistical Record								
Return on Assets %	1.42	1.70	1.70	1.71	1.52	0.97	N.M.	7.36
Return on Equity %	2.12	2.52	2.50	2.53	2.23	1.37	N.M.	10.78
EBITDA Margin %	6.68	6.73	7.84	8.01	8.93	10.03	8.19	14.27
Net Margin %	1.64	1.85	2.88	1.98	1.79	1.53	N.M.	5.87
Asset Turnover	0.88	0.87	0.88	0.86	0.85	0.63	0.87	1.25
Current Ratio	2.30	2.46	2.47	2.47	2.62	3.25	2.02	3.10
Debt to Equity	0.17	0.17	0.17	0.18	0.19	0.21	0.02	0.07
Price Range	13.93-8.75	13.93-10.21	13.93-10.21	15.33-10.67	21.26-9.40	14.17-5.50	24.43-6.50	27.13-13.31
P/E Ratio	69.65-43.75	58.04-42.54	58.04-42.54	63.88-44.46	106.30-47.00	177.13-68.75	...	35.69-17.52

Address: 10500 West 153rd Street, Orland Park, IL 60462
Telephone: 708-349-3300
Fax: 708-349-5943

Web Site: www.andrew.com
Officers: Charles R. Nicholas - Chmn. Ralph E. Faison - Pres., C.E.O.

Auditors: Ernst & Young LLP
Investor Contact: 800-232-6767

ANDRX CORP (DE)

Exchange	Symbol	Price	52Wk Range	Yield	P/E
NMS	ADRX	$23.84 (8/31/2006)	23.99-14.63	N/A	183.38

*7 Year Price Score 45.93   *NYSE Composite Index=100   *12 Month Price Score 114.71

Interim Earnings (Per Share)

Qtr.	Mar	Jun	Sep	Dec
2003	0.09	0.20	0.16	0.21
2004	0.36	0.09	0.16	0.28
2005	0.48	0.11	0.15	0.11
2006	(0.15)	0.02	...	...

Interim Dividends (Per Share)
No Dividends Paid

Valuation Analysis / Institutional Holding

Forecast P/E	N/A	No of Institutions	168
Market Cap	$1.8 Billion	Shares	51,541,912
Book Value	771.9 Million	% Held	69.83
Price/Book	2.28		
Price/Sales	1.76		

Business Summary: Pharmaceuticals (MIC: 9.1 SIC: 2834 NAIC: 325412)

Andrx is a pharmaceutical company. Co. develops and commercializes generic versions of controlled-release pharmaceutical products using its proprietary controlled-release drug delivery technologies. Co. also develops and commercializes oral contraceptives and selective immediate-release products. In addition, Co. distributes pharmaceutical products, primarily generics, which have been commercialized by others, as well as its own, primarily to independent and chain pharmacies and physicians' offices. Moreover, Co. develops and manufactures pharmaceutical products for other pharmaceutical companies, including combination products and controlled-release formulations.

Recent Developments: For the quarter ended June 30 2006, net income decreased 82.0% to $1.4 million from $8.0 million in the year-earlier quarter. Revenues were $254.8 million, down 2.7% from $261.7 million the year before. Operating loss was $2.4 million versus an income of $10.4 million in the prior-year quarter. Direct operating expenses rose 1.7% to $203.1 million from $199.6 million in the comparable the year before. Indirect operating expenses increased 4.5% to $54.0 million from $51.7 million in the equivalent prior-year period.

Prospects: On Jul 10 2006, Co. and Watson Pharmaceuticals, Inc. announced that they have entered into an amendment to their Mar 12 2006 definitive agreement, in which Co. agreed to be acquired by Watson. The amendment extends the deadline for the closing of the transaction from Sep 12 2006 to Nov 13 2006, subject to certain conditions. In view of that, Co. anticipates that the transaction will close in the third or fourth quarter of 2006. Separately, Co. continues to progress toward improving its compliance with Good Manufacturing Practices (cGMP). Accordingly, Co. continues to work with consultants in order to improve its pharmaceutical operations going forward.

Financial Data
(US$ in Thousands)

	6 Mos	3 Mos	12/31/2005	12/31/2004	12/31/2003	12/31/2002	12/31/2001	12/31/2000
Earnings Per Share	0.13	0.22	0.85	0.89	0.66	(1.22)	1.01	0.95
Cash Flow Per Share	0.45	0.61	1.70	1.20	1.99	(0.57)	0.36	0.68
Tang Book Value Per Share	10.30	10.25	10.39	9.38	7.95	7.16	7.60	6.62
Income Statement								
Total Revenue	496,180	241,429	1,042,025	1,145,087	1,046,338	770,980	749,041	519,960
EBITDA	(10,496)	(16,097)	47,233	127,137	109,144	(135,496)	79,584	95,700
Depn & Amortn	13,585	6,231	35,530	34,568	30,537	22,367	22,039	9,570
Income Before Taxes	(16,208)	(18,435)	20,894	94,062	78,208	(152,643)	68,931	98,402
Income Taxes	(5,644)	(6,434)	(41,572)	28,403	30,031	(60,826)	31,385	39,870
Net Income	(9,869)	(11,306)	62,466	65,659	48,177	(91,817)	37,546	58,532
Average Shares	74,476	73,662	73,640	73,530	72,655	77,619	78,045	85,658
Balance Sheet								
Total Assets	1,120,249	1,089,507	1,170,916	989,713	958,446	789,479	789,214	667,956
Current Liabilities	213,022	181,140	260,810	245,373	294,003	208,058	136,238	108,159
Long-Term Obligations	...	...	...	...	12,609	...	...	...
Total Liabilities	348,366	321,314	394,006	290,952	335,545	223,772	141,320	108,159
Stockholders' Equity	771,883	768,193	776,910	698,761	622,901	565,707	647,894	559,797
Shares Outstanding	73,881	73,775	73,567	72,924	72,331	71,504	77,226	84,514
Statistical Record								
Return on Assets %	0.84	1.47	5.78	6.72	5.51	N.M.	5.15	11.38
Return on Equity %	1.22	2.10	8.47	9.91	8.11	N.M.	6.22	14.95
EBITDA Margin %	N.M.	N.M.	4.53	11.10	10.43	N.M.	10.62	18.41
Net Margin %	N.M.	N.M.	5.99	5.73	4.60	N.M.	5.01	11.26
Asset Turnover	0.91	0.93	0.96	1.17	1.20	0.98	1.03	1.01
Current Ratio	3.79	4.00	2.88	2.28	2.21	2.35	4.28	5.19
Debt to Equity	...	...	...	...	0.02	...	...	...
Price Range	23.87-14.63	23.87-14.63	23.81-14.63	30.38-16.59	24.04-7.89	70.92-12.00	77.00-39.31	95.38-20.19
P/E Ratio	183.62-112.54	108.50-66.50	28.01-17.21	34.13-18.64	36.42-11.95		76.24-38.92	100.39-21.25

Address: 4955 Orange Drive, Davie, FL 33314
Telephone: 954-584-0300
Fax: 954-217-4327

Web Site: www.andrx.com
Officers: Angelo C. Malahias - Pres. Thomas P. Rice - C.E.O.

Auditors: ERNST & YOUNG LLP
Investor Contact: 954-217-4344

APOLLO GROUP, INC.

Exchange	Symbol	Price	52Wk Range	Yield	P/E
NMS	APOL	$50.21 (8/31/2006)	78.66-43.12	N/A	19.77

*7 Year Price Score 97.79 *NYSE Composite Index=100 *12 Month Price Score 81.61

Interim Earnings (Per Share)

Qtr.	Nov	Feb	May	Aug
2002-03	0.30	0.24	0.39	0.36
2003-04	0.44	0.35	0.56	(0.58)
2004-05	0.58	0.47	0.77	0.58
2005-06	0.73	0.46	...	...

Interim Dividends (Per Share)

Amt	Decl	Ex	Rec	Pay
50%	1/10/2001	2/6/2001	1/22/2001	2/5/2001
50%	4/5/2002	4/26/2002	4/15/2002	4/25/2002

Valuation Analysis

		Institutional Holding	
Forecast P/E	18.53	No of Institutions	
	(9/9/2006)	321	
Market Cap	$8.7 Billion	Shares	
Book Value	441.4 Million	146,709,728	
Price/Book	19.64	% Held	
Price/Sales	3.60	85.15	

Business Summary: Vocational Education Services (MIC: 6.2 SIC: 8299 NAIC: 611430)
Apollo Group provides higher education to working adults through its wholly-owned subsidiaries. The University of Phoenix, Inc. maintains 63 local campuses and 112 learning centers in 34 states, Puerto Rico, Alberta, and British Columbia and also offers its educational programs worldwide through its computerized educational delivery system. Western International University, Inc. offers undergraduate and graduate degree programs at local campuses in Arizona and through joint ventures in China and India. Institute for Professional Development provides program development and management consulting services to regionally accredited private colleges and universities (client institutions).

Recent Developments: For the second quarter ended Feb 28 2006, net income decreased 7.4% to $80.6 million compared with $87.1 million in the equivalent year-earlier quarter. Revenues were $569.6 million, up 12.6% from $505.7 million the year before. Operating income was $129.5 million versus $139.5 million in the prior-year quarter, a decrease of 7.2%. Direct operating expenses rose 16.6% to $258.4 million from $221.6 million in the comparable period the year before. Indirect operating expenses increased 25.7% to $181.6 million from $144.5 million in the equivalent prior-year period.

Prospects: Co.'s top line results are benefiting from an increase in tuition and other net revenues, resulting from higher average daily student enrollments, as well as tuition price increases. Going forward, Co. expects tuition and other net revenues at University of Phoenix to increase as a percentage of total revenues during the third quarter of fiscal 2006, as Axia College is transferred from Western International University to University of Phoenix. Co. also remains focused on investing in its core working adults business, growing its echo boomer business, and leveraging its strategic relationship with advertising.com, to drive revenue growth in the second half of 2006 and beyond.

Financial Data
(US$ in Thousands)

	6 Mos	3 Mos	08/31/2005	08/31/2004	08/31/2003	08/31/2002	08/31/2001	08/31/2000
Earnings Per Share	2.54	2.55	2.39	0.77	1.30	0.87	0.60	0.41
Cash Flow Per Share	3.80	3.62	3.09	2.91	1.96	1.51	0.96	0.69
Tang Book Value Per Share	2.34	3.08	3.73	4.89	5.17	3.52	2.41	1.32
Income Statement								
Total Revenue	1,198,435	628,884	2,251,472	1,798,423	1,339,517	1,009,455	769,474	609,997
EBITDA	381,115	232,352	787,926	505,805	432,756	292,474	192,373	141,445
Depn & Amortn	32,773	17,050	58,084	49,317	45,497	38,622	31,370	27,368
Income Before Taxes	348,342	215,302	729,842	456,488	401,804	265,924	175,109	120,305
Income Taxes	136,933	84,528	285,111	178,714	154,794	104,774	67,292	49,114
Net Income	211,409	130,774	444,731	277,774	247,010	161,150	107,817	71,191
Average Shares	175,235	180,331	186,015	178,897	177,637	175,697	173,998	172,415
Balance Sheet								
Total Assets	1,055,152	1,232,501	1,302,945	1,452,273	1,378,204	979,642	680,343	404,790
Current Liabilities	528,838	572,497	517,972	465,438	335,223	264,314	182,200	131,089
Total Liabilities	613,734	653,972	596,071	495,132	351,279	280,649	198,458	143,582
Stockholders' Equity	441,418	578,529	706,874	957,141	1,026,925	698,993	481,885	261,208
Shares Outstanding	172,682	175,743	179,661	188,044	191,422	187,961	184,435	169,257
Statistical Record								
Return on Assets %	40.46	36.95	32.28	19.57	20.95	19.42	19.87	18.85
Return on Equity %	82.78	69.16	53.45	27.92	28.62	27.29	29.02	28.84
EBITDA Margin %	31.80	36.95	35.00	28.12	32.31	28.97	25.00	23.19
Net Margin %	17.64	20.79	19.75	15.45	18.44	15.96	14.01	11.67
Asset Turnover	2.12	1.86	1.63	1.27	1.14	1.22	1.42	1.62
Current Ratio	1.12	1.35	1.61	1.84	2.83	2.76	2.67	1.88
Price Range	81.21-49.38	85.33-58.87	85.33-62.96	97.93-60.90	66.09-38.11	42.18-23.33	30.16-14.84	18.47-8.36
P/E Ratio	31.97-19.44	33.46-23.09	35.70-26.34	127.18-79.09	50.84-29.32	48.48-26.82	50.27-24.73	45.05-20.39

Address: 4615 East Elwood Street, Phoenix, AZ 85040 **Telephone:** 480-966-5394 **Fax:** 480-929-7499	**Web Site:** www.apollogrp.edu **Officers:** Todd S. Nelson - Chmn., Pres., C.E.O. Peter V. Sperling - Sr. V.P.	**Auditors:** Deloitte & Touche LLP **Investor Contact:** 800-990-APOL **Transfer Agents:** EquiServe Trust N.A. Providence, RI

APPLE COMPUTER, INC.

Exchange	Symbol	Price	52Wk Range	Yield	P/E
NMS	AAPL	$67.85 (8/31/2006)	85.59-46.22	0.18	34.44

*7 Year Price Score 215.01 *NYSE Composite Index=100 *12 Month Price Score 95.63

Interim Earnings (Per Share)

Qtr.	Dec	Mar	Jun	Sep
2002-03	(0.01)	0.02	0.03	0.06
2003-04	0.09	0.06	0.08	0.13
2004-05	0.35	0.34	0.37	0.50
2005-06	0.65	0.47	...	...

Interim Dividends (Per Share)

Amt	Decl	Ex	Rec	Pay
2-for-1	2/11/2005	2/28/2005	2/18/2005	2/28/2005

Indicated Div: $0.12

Valuation Analysis

		Institutional Holding	
Forecast P/E	34.02	No of Institutions	
	(9/9/2006)	704	
Market Cap	$57.6 Billion	Shares	
Book Value	8.7 Billion	575,859,328	
Price/Book	6.64	% Held	
Price/Sales	3.37	77.88	

Business Summary: IT & Technology (MIC: 10.2 SIC: 3571 NAIC: 334111)

Apple Computer designs, manufactures, and markets personal computers and related software, services, peripherals, and networking solutions. Co. also designs, develops, and markets a line of portable digital music players along with related accessories and services including the online distribution of third-party music, audio books, music videos, short films, and television shows. Co.'s products and services include the Macintosh line of desktop and notebook computers, the iPod digital music player, the Xserve G5 server and Xserve RAID storage products, a portfolio of consumer and professional software applications, the Mac OS X operating system and the iTunes Music Store.

Recent Developments: For the quarter ended Apr 1 2006, net income increased 41.4% to $410.0 million from $290.0 million in the year-earlier quarter. Revenues were $4.36 billion, up 34.4% from $3.24 billion the year before. Operating income was $529.0 million versus $402.0 million in the prior-year quarter, an increase of 31.6%. Direct operating expenses rose 34.6% to $3.06 billion from $2.28 billion in the comparable period the year before. Indirect operating expenses increased 35.7% to $768.0 million from $566.0 million in the equivalent prior-year period.

Prospects: Looking forward to its fiscal fourth quarter ended Sep 2006, Co. expects revenue of approximately $4.50 billion to $4.60 billion, and earnings per diluted share of about $0.46 to $0.48, including an estimated $0.03 per share expense effect from non-cash stock-based compensation. Separately, Co.'s total capital expenditures were $275.0 million during the first six months of 2006, $82.0 million of which were for retail store facilities and equipment related to its Retail segment. Co. anticipates it will utilize approximately $700.0 million for capital expenditures during 2006, about $210.0 million of which is expected to be utilized for expansion of its Retail segment.

Financial Data
(US$ in Thousands)

	6 Mos	3 Mos	09/24/2005	09/25/2004	09/27/2003	09/28/2002	09/29/2001	09/30/2000
Earnings Per Share	1.97	1.84	1.56	0.35	0.10	0.09	(0.04)	1.09
Cash Flow Per Share	1.61	2.42	3.14	1.26	0.40	0.13	0.27	1.25
Tang Book Value Per Share	10.06	9.76	8.78	6.33	5.61	5.54	5.59	6.00
Income Statement								
Total Revenue	10,108,000	5,749,000	13,931,000	8,279,000	6,207,000	5,742,000	5,363,000	7,983,000
EBITDA	1,363,000	795,000	1,632,000	322,000	92,000	205,000	50,000	1,176,000
Depn & Amortn	102,000	52,000	...	...	...	118,000	102,000	84,000
Income Before Taxes	1,436,000	831,000	1,815,000	383,000	92,000	87,000	(52,000)	1,092,000
Income Taxes	461,000	266,000	480,000	107,000	24,000	22,000	(15,000)	306,000
Net Income	975,000	565,000	1,335,000	276,000	69,000	65,000	(25,000)	786,000
Average Shares	878,537	874,207	856,780	774,622	726,932	723,570	691,226	720,648
Balance Sheet								
Total Assets	13,911,000	14,181,000	11,551,000	8,050,000	6,815,000	6,298,000	6,021,000	6,803,000
Current Liabilities	4,456,000	5,060,000	3,484,000	2,680,000	2,357,000	1,658,000	1,518,000	1,933,000
Long-Term Obligations	...	...	...	...	...	316,000	317,000	300,000
Total Liabilities	5,229,000	5,801,000	4,085,000	2,974,000	2,592,000	2,203,000	2,101,000	2,696,000
Stockholders' Equity	8,682,000	8,380,000	7,466,000	5,076,000	4,223,000	4,095,000	3,920,000	4,107,000
Shares Outstanding	849,188	845,617	835,019	782,887	733,453	717,917	701,843	671,353
Statistical Record								
Return on Assets %	14.19	13.47	13.66	3.72	1.06	1.06	N.M.	12.93
Return on Equity %	22.62	22.38	21.35	5.95	1.66	1.63	N.M.	21.45
EBITDA Margin %	13.48	13.83	11.71	3.89	1.48	3.57	0.93	14.73
Net Margin %	9.65	9.83	9.58	3.33	1.11	1.13	N.M.	9.85
Asset Turnover	1.42	1.36	1.43	1.12	0.95	0.93	0.84	1.31
Current Ratio	2.53	2.40	2.96	2.63	2.50	3.25	3.39	2.81
Debt to Equity	...	...	...	...	...	0.08	0.08	0.07
Price Range	85.59-34.21	74.98-31.63	53.20-18.77	19.00-9.85	11.55-6.56	13.06-7.00	13.30-7.00	36.05-12.88
P/E Ratio	43.45-17.32	40.75-17.20	34.10-12.03	54.30-28.14	115.50-65.60	145.06-77.72	...	33.07-11.81

Address: 1 Infinite Loop, Cupertino, CA 95014
Telephone: 408-996-1010
Fax: 408-974-2483

Web Site: www.apple.com
Officers: Steven P. Jobs - C.E.O. Timothy D. Cook - C.O.O.

Auditors: KPMG LLP
Investor Contact: 877-438-2775
Transfer Agents: ComputerShare Investor Services, Chicago, IL

APPLEBEE'S INTERNATIONAL, INC.

Exchange	Symbol	Price	52Wk Range	Yield	P/E	Div Achiever
NMS	APPB	$20.75 (8/31/2006)	25.53-17.35	0.96	17.58	14 Years

*7 Year Price Score 98.21 *NYSE Composite Index=100 *12 Month Price Score 83.99

Interim Earnings (Per Share)

Qtr.	Mar	Jun	Sep	Dec
2003	0.29	0.24	0.30	0.27
2004	0.35	0.34	0.34	0.31
2005	0.38	0.34	0.28	0.27
2006	0.36	0.27	...	...

Interim Dividends (Per Share)

Amt	Decl	Ex	Rec	Pay
0.047A	12/12/2003	12/23/2003	12/26/2003	1/23/2004
50%	5/13/2004	6/16/2004	5/28/2004	6/15/2004
0.06A	12/10/2004	12/21/2004	12/24/2004	1/21/2005
0.20A	10/26/2005	12/21/2005	12/23/2005	1/23/2006

Indicated Div: $0.20

Valuation Analysis

Forecast P/E	17.86 (9/9/2006)
Market Cap	$1.5 Billion
Book Value	468.2 Million
Price/Book	3.30
Price/Sales	1.20

Institutional Holding

No of Institutions	196
Shares	63,361,700
% Held	85.13

Business Summary: Food (MIC: 4.1 SIC: 5812 NAIC: 722110)

Applebee's International develops, franchises and operates casual dining restaurants under the name "Applebee's Neighborhood Grill & Bar®" (Applebee's). Co. also offers its customers the convenience of carry-out service. In addition, Co.'s restaurants are located in 49 U.S. states and 14 countries outside of the U.S. As of Dec 25 2005, Co. had a total of 1,804 Applebee's restaurants, by which its franchisees operated 1,318 of these restaurants and 486 restaurants were company-operated. Also, as of Dec 25 2005, Co. had a total number of approximately 32,260 full and part-time associates.

Recent Developments: For the quarter ended June 25 2006, net income decreased 25.8% to $20.4 million from $27.5 million in the year-earlier quarter. Revenues were $331.0 million, up 7.9% from $306.6 million the year before. Operating income was $34.4 million versus $41.6 million in the prior-year quarter, a decrease of 17.3%. Direct operating expenses rose 10.3% to $260.6 million from $236.2 million in the comparable period the year before. Indirect operating expenses increased 25.0% to $36.0 million from $28.8 million in the equivalent prior-year period.

Prospects: Going forward, Co. remains with its focus on enhancing its brand appeal through the addition of over 20 new or improved menu items by the end of 2006, as an attempt to address the challenges experience in the recent consumer spending environment. For the remainder of fiscal year 2006, Co. expects to open approximately 125 new restaurants, with approximately 6 company-restaurants and 20 to 25 franchise-restaurants are expected to open in the third quarter of 2006. Meanwhile, Co. anticipates system-wide comparable sales to be in a range from flat to down 2.0% and earnings of $1.12 to $1.22 per diluted share for the full-fiscal year 2006.

Financial Data
(US$ in Thousands)

	6 Mos	3 Mos	12/25/2005	12/26/2004	12/28/2003	12/29/2002	12/30/2001	12/31/2000
Earnings Per Share	1.18	1.25	1.27	1.33	1.09	0.97	0.76	0.71
Cash Flow Per Share	2.43	2.68	2.82	2.34	2.13	1.63	1.27	1.23
Tang Book Value Per Share	4.33	4.05	3.50	4.51	4.21	3.64	2.92	2.30
Dividends Per Share	0.200	0.200	0.200	0.060	0.047	0.040	0.036	0.033
Dividend Payout %	16.90	15.95	15.75	4.51	4.27	4.11	4.71	4.58
Income Statement								
Total Revenue	675,252	344,279	1,216,650	1,111,634	990,138	826,796	744,344	690,152
EBITDA	109,842	65,219	216,552	216,835	188,706	167,990	149,612	146,118
Depn & Amortn	32,141	21,775	55,458	46,714	40,788	35,686	38,279	36,876
Income Before Taxes	72,162	40,890	156,504	168,495	146,185	130,136	103,877	99,938
Income Taxes	24,607	13,739	54,702	57,630	52,627	47,109	38,227	36,777
Net Income	47,555	27,151	101,802	110,865	93,558	83,027	64,401	63,161
Average Shares	75,083	75,281	80,010	83,600	85,408	85,383	85,315	88,755
Balance Sheet								
Total Assets	892,754	888,130	878,588	754,431	644,001	566,114	500,411	471,707
Current Liabilities	137,495	142,651	197,674	151,698	149,332	115,186	97,746	93,835
Long-Term Obligations	197,066	207,534	180,208	35,472	20,670	52,186	74,525	90,461
Total Liabilities	424,580	439,595	465,978	257,704	184,269	173,533	175,228	189,989
Stockholders' Equity	468,174	448,535	412,610	496,727	459,732	392,581	325,183	281,718
Shares Outstanding	74,370	74,461	74,198	81,128	82,789	83,082	83,722	85,116
Statistical Record								
Return on Assets %	10.55	11.74	12.50	15.90	15.51	15.61	13.29	13.60
Return on Equity %	18.61	20.15	22.45	23.25	22.01	23.20	21.28	23.20
EBITDA Margin %	16.27	18.94	17.80	19.51	19.06	20.32	20.10	21.17
Net Margin %	7.04	7.89	8.37	9.97	9.45	10.04	8.65	9.15
Asset Turnover	1.50	1.51	1.49	1.59	1.64	1.55	1.54	1.49
Current Ratio	0.56	0.56	0.46	0.66	0.58	0.60	0.70	0.57
Debt to Equity	0.42	0.46	0.44	0.07	0.04	0.13	0.23	0.32
Price Range	26.76-19.49	28.30-20.06	28.91-20.06	28.39-22.79	26.59-15.39	18.18-13.09	16.24-8.50	11.07-6.56
P/E Ratio	22.68-16.52	22.64-16.05	22.76-15.80	21.35-17.14	24.40-14.12	18.74-13.49	21.37-11.18	15.60-9.23
Average Yield %	0.87	0.83	0.79	0.24	0.23	0.25	0.29	0.39

Address: 4551 W. 107th Street, Overland Park, KS 66207
Telephone: 913-967-4000
Fax: 913-341-1694

Web Site: www.applebees.com
Officers: Lloyd L. Hill - Chmn., Pres., C.E.O. Steven K. Lumpkin - Exec. V.P., C.F.O., Treas.

Auditors: Deloitte & Touche LLP
Investor Contact: 913-967-4109
Transfer Agents: American Stock Transfer & Trust Co, New York, NY

APPLIED MATERIALS, INC.

Exchange	Symbol	Price	52Wk Range	Yield	P/E
NMS	AMAT	$16.90 (8/31/2006)	20.82-14.76	1.18	20.36

*7 Year Price Score 65.09 *NYSE Composite Index=100 *12 Month Price Score 87.83

Interim Earnings (Per Share)

Qtr.	Jan	Apr	Jul	Oct
2002-03	(0.04)	(0.04)	(0.02)	0.01
2003-04	0.05	0.22	0.26	0.26
2004-05	0.17	0.18	0.23	0.15
2005-06	0.09	0.26	0.33	...

Interim Dividends (Per Share)

Amt	Decl	Ex	Rec	Pay
0.03Q	9/16/2005	11/15/2005	11/17/2005	12/8/2005
0.03Q	12/15/2005	2/14/2006	2/16/2006	3/9/2006
0.05Q	3/22/2006	5/16/2006	5/18/2006	6/8/2006
0.05Q	6/14/2006	8/15/2006	8/17/2006	9/7/2006

Indicated Div: $0.20

Valuation Analysis

		Institutional Holding	
Forecast P/E	15.63	No of Institutions	
	(9/9/2006)	663	
Market Cap	$25.9 Billion	Shares	
Book Value	8.7 Billion	1,135,271,936	
Price/Book	2.99	% Held	
Price/Sales	3.10	72.60	

Business Summary: IT & Technology (MIC: 10.2 SIC: 3674 NAIC: 334413)

Applied Materials develops, manufactures, markets and services integrated circuit fabrication equipment for the worldwide semiconductor and semiconductor-related industry. Most of Co.'s products are single-wafer systems with multiple process chambers attached to a base platform, by which each wafer is processed separately in its own environment, allowing precise process control, while the system's multiple chambers enable simultaneous, high productivity manufacturing. Co. sells most of its single-wafer, multi-chamber systems on four basic platforms; namely the Centura®, the Endura®, the Producer® and the Vantage®.

Recent Developments: For the quarter ended July 31 2006, net income increased 38.5% to $512.0 million from $369.6 million in the year-earlier quarter. Revenues were $2.54 billion, up 55.9% from $1.63 billion the year before. Operating income was $680.8 million versus $302.7 million in the prior-year quarter, an increase of 124.9%. Direct operating expenses rose 44.3% to $1.32 billion from $914.8 million in the comparable period the year before. Indirect operating expenses increased 30.9% to $542.6 million from $414.4 million in the equivalent prior-year period.

Prospects: On Jul 20 2006, Co. and Dainippon Screen Mfg. Co. Ltd. (Screen) completed the formation of Tokyo-based Sokudo Co. Ltd. (Sokudo), a joint-venture in which Co. holds a 48.0% ownership while Screen owns the remaining 52.0%. Specifically, Co. has contributed approximately $151.0 million to Sokudo and, along with Screen, is transferring its technology and resources to the new company. Going forward, the formation of Sokudo bodes well with Co.'s long-term growth strategy of entering into new areas with significant growth potential, as the new company will result in the creation of significantly improved track product that will enhance Co.'s expanding portfolio of lithography-enabling products.

Financial Data

(US$ in Thousands)	9 Mos	6 Mos	3 Mos	10/30/2005	10/31/2004	10/26/2003	10/27/2002	10/28/2001
Earnings Per Share	0.83	0.73	0.65	0.73	0.78	(0.09)	0.16	0.30
Cash Flow Per Share	0.95	0.92	0.89	0.76	0.95	0.48	0.30	0.98
Tang Book Value Per Share	5.15	5.24	5.19	5.30	5.33	4.62	4.87	4.66
Dividends Per Share	0.140	0.120	0.090	0.060	...	...	...	...
Dividend Payout %	16.87	16.39	13.81	8.22				
Income Statement								
Total Revenue	6,648,721	4,105,278	1,857,592	6,991,823	8,013,053	4,477,291	5,062,312	7,343,248
EBITDA	1,583,176	840,524	213,615	1,748,549	2,120,650	70,609	597,484	1,317,117
Depn & Amortn	197,385	135,514	69,676	300,584	356,985	384,391	387,526	386,971
Income Before Taxes	1,506,902	784,391	183,925	1,581,569	1,829,250	(211,556)	340,511	1,103,802
Income Taxes	439,268	228,797	41,145	371,669	477,947	(62,409)	71,507	328,574
Net Income	1,067,634	555,594	142,780	1,209,900	1,351,303	(149,147)	269,004	507,829
Average Shares	1,562,615	1,586,404	1,608,165	1,657,493	1,721,645	1,659,557	1,701,557	1,694,658
Balance Sheet								
Total Assets	11,773,857	11,451,756	11,209,908	11,269,157	12,093,445	10,311,622	10,224,765	9,828,510
Current Liabilities	2,431,807	2,187,529	1,878,503	1,765,414	2,287,981	1,640,877	1,501,456	1,532,816
Long-Term Obligations	406,970	406,905	407,380	407,380	410,436	456,422	573,853	564,805
Total Liabilities	3,107,913	2,833,086	2,542,329	2,340,608	2,831,418	2,243,588	2,205,116	2,221,773
Stockholders' Equity	8,665,944	8,618,670	8,667,579	8,928,549	9,262,027	8,068,034	8,019,649	7,606,737
Shares Outstanding	1,533,915	1,563,791	1,586,574	1,606,694	1,680,264	1,677,400	1,648,028	1,631,540
Statistical Record								
Return on Assets %	11.24	10.06	9.16	10.39	11.87	N.M.	2.69	5.00
Return on Equity %	14.82	13.20	11.88	13.34	15.34	N.M.	3.45	6.92
EBITDA Margin %	23.81	20.47	11.50	25.01	26.46	1.58	11.80	17.94
Net Margin %	16.06	13.53	7.69	17.30	16.86	N.M.	5.31	6.92
Asset Turnover	0.72	0.64	0.61	0.60	0.70	0.44	0.51	0.72
Current Ratio	3.05	3.35	5.08	5.35	4.49	5.10	5.38	5.08
Debt to Equity	0.05	0.05	0.05	0.05	0.04	0.06	0.07	0.07
Price Range	20.82-14.76	20.82-15.08	20.82-14.50	18.58-14.50	25.61-15.61	22.21-11.67	27.76-10.35	29.36-13.75
P/E Ratio	25.08-17.78	28.52-20.66	32.03-22.31	25.45-19.86	32.83-20.01	...	173.50-64.69	97.88-45.83
Average Yield %	0.79	0.68	0.52	0.36	...	...	...	...

Address: 3050 Bowers Avenue, P.O. Box 58039, Santa Clara, CA 95052-8039
Telephone: 408-727-5555
Fax: 408-727-9943

Web Site: www.appliedmaterials.com
Officers: James C. Morgan - Chmn. Michael R. Splinter - Pres., C.E.O.

Auditors: KPMG LLP
Investor Contact: 800-882-0373
Transfer Agents: ComputerShare Investor Services, Chicago, IL

APPLIED MICRO CIRCUITS CORP.

Exchange	Symbol	Price	52Wk Range	Yield	P/E
NMS	AMCC	$2.73 (8/31/2006)	4.14-2.15	N/A	N/A

*7 Year Price Score 14.55 *NYSE Composite Index=100 *12 Month Price Score 81.37

Interim Earnings (Per Share)

Qtr.	Jun	Sep	Dec	Mar
2002-03	(1.35)	(0.24)	(0.13)	(0.75)
2003-04	(0.18)	(0.08)	(0.09)	0.00
2004-05	(0.07)	(0.06)	(0.27)	(0.02)
2005-06	(0.01)	(0.02)	0.00	...

Interim Dividends (Per Share)
No Dividends Paid

Valuation Analysis

		Institutional Holding	
Forecast P/E	22.08	No of Institutions	
	(9/9/2006)	195	
Market Cap	$800.7 Million	Shares	
Book Value	910.9 Million	188,149,728	
Price/Book	0.88	% Held	
Price/Sales	3.09	63.93	

Business Summary: IT & Technology (MIC: 10.2 SIC: 3674 NAIC: 334413)

Applied Micro Circuits designs, develops and manufactures high-performance, high-bandwidth silicon integrated circuit products for wide area networks. Co. uses a combination of digital, mixed-signal and high-frequency analog design expertise as well as system-level knowledge and multiple silicon process technologies to offer integrated circuit products that enable the transport of voice and data over wide area networks. Co.'s system products portfolio includes routers, optical and digital cross connects, next-generation voice and media gateways and add/drop multiplexers.

Recent Developments: For the quarter ended Dec 31 2005, net income amounted to $584,000 versus a net loss of $81.9 million in the year-earlier quarter. Revenues were $65.2 million, up 6.8% from $61.1 million the year before. Operating loss was $5.7 million versus a loss of $84.1 million in the prior-year quarter. Direct operating expenses declined 0.5% to $30.0 million from $30.2 million in the comparable period the year before. Indirect operating expenses decreased 64.5% to $40.9 million from $115.1 million in the equivalent prior-year period.

Prospects: Despite declining revenues from its storage and communications businesses, primarily due to product transitions and revenue decreases in earlier non-core products, Co. is anticipating robust revenue growth in its Embedded Products business going forward. However, due to product revenue transitions, Co.'s environment for revenue growth remains challenging but nonetheless is improving, thus it is continuing to focus on controlling its operating expenses to help boost bottom-line results. Additionally, Co. is entering the fourth quarter with improved backlog position and overall, expects to continue to make progress.

Financial Data (US$ in Thousands)	9 Mos	6 Mos	3 Mos	03/31/2005	03/31/2004	03/31/2003	03/31/2002	03/31/2001
Earnings Per Share	(0.05)	(0.32)	(0.36)	(0.41)	(0.34)	(2.47)	(12.08)	(1.63)
Cash Flow Per Share	0.01	(0.07)	(0.12)	(0.04)	(0.14)	(0.16)	(0.12)	0.75
Tang Book Value Per Share	1.34	1.37	1.40	1.44	2.83	3.57	3.93	4.10
Income Statement								
Total Revenue	194,851	129,608	64,673	253,756	131,177	101,591	152,840	435,543
EBITDA	4,879	2,057	2,518	(94,815)	(111,182)	(652,962)	(3,406,326)	(115,588)
Depn & Amortn	27,611	19,807	10,135	48,396	30,478	38,069	327,770	377,157
Income Before Taxes	(11,008)	(10,277)	(4,028)	(124,512)	(106,653)	(643,312)	(3,686,619)	(437,296)
Income Taxes	(964)	351	176	2,861	(1,776)	...	(80,929)	(1,081)
Net Income	(10,044)	(10,628)	(4,204)	(127,373)	(104,877)	(745,541)	(3,605,690)	(436,215)
Average Shares	299,049	305,476	306,327	309,456	306,476	301,252	298,502	267,363
Balance Sheet								
Total Assets	972,367	994,821	1,009,839	1,102,395	1,188,103	1,224,557	1,829,193	5,453,278
Current Liabilities	61,440	58,116	53,445	125,197	67,556	52,369	56,797	92,871
Long-Term Obligations	...	...	...	...	...	...	1,145	2,266
Total Liabilities	61,440	58,116	53,445	125,197	67,556	52,369	57,942	215,177
Stockholders' Equity	910,927	936,705	956,394	977,198	1,120,547	1,172,188	1,771,251	5,238,101
Shares Outstanding	293,284	302,694	305,402	308,328	310,985	303,751	300,468	299,822
Statistical Record								
EBITDA Margin %	2.50	1.59	3.89	N.M.	N.M.	N.M.	N.M.	N.M.
Asset Turnover	0.25	0.24	0.23	0.22	0.11	0.07	0.04	0.13
Current Ratio	6.65	7.39	8.14	4.17	13.46	20.50	19.67	14.01
Price Range	4.25-2.40	4.25-2.52	5.32-2.52	6.28-2.93	8.98-3.26	8.79-2.49	30.00-6.29	107.00-16.50

Address: 6290 Sequence Drive, San Diego, CA 92121-4358 **Telephone:** 858-450-9333 **Fax:** 858-450-9885	**Web Site:** www.amcc.com **Officers:** Roger A. Smullen Sr. - Vice-Chmn. Kambiz Hooshmand - Pres., C.E.O.	**Auditors:** Ernst & Young LLP **Investor Contact:** 858-535-4217 **Transfer Agents:** Computershare Investor Services

ARROW INTERNATIONAL, INC.

Exchange	Symbol	Price	52Wk Range	Yield	P/E	Div Acheiver
NMS	ARRO	$32.31 (8/31/2006)	34.70-27.50	2.10	33.66	13 Years

*7 Year Price Score 104.51 *NYSE Composite Index=100 *12 Month Price Score 99.14

Interim Earnings (Per Share)

Qtr.	Nov	Feb	May	Aug
2002-03	0.26	0.27	0.33	0.18
2003-04	0.33	0.35	0.26	0.32
2004-05	0.30	0.12	0.35	0.11
2005-06	0.26	0.28	0.31	...

Interim Dividends (Per Share)

Amt	Decl	Ex	Rec	Pay
0.15Q	11/9/2005	11/23/2005	11/28/2005	12/12/2005
0.17Q	2/13/2006	2/23/2006	2/27/2006	3/13/2006
0.17Q	5/15/2006	5/25/2006	5/30/2006	6/12/2006
0.17Q	8/14/2006	8/24/2006	8/28/2006	9/11/2006

Indicated Div: $0.68

Valuation Analysis
Forecast P/E 25.61 (9/9/2006)
Market Cap $1.4 Billion
Book Value 506.1 Million
Price/Book 2.86
Price/Sales 3.10

Institutional Holding
No of Institutions 102
Shares 22,933,132
% Held 51.12

Business Summary: Medical Instruments & Equipment (MIC: 9.6 SIC: 3841 NAIC: 339112)

Arrow International develops, manufactures and markets a range of disposable catheters, heart assist devices and related products for critical and cardiac care. Co.'s critical care products are used primarily for central vascular access in the administration of fluids, drugs and blood products, patient monitoring and diagnostic purposes. These products include Arrow-Howes™ Multi-Lumen Catheter, percutaneous sheath introducers, FlexTip Plus™ epidural catheters, Percutaneous Thrombolytic Devices, custom tubing sets and the HemoSonic™. Co.'s cardiac care products include cardiac assist products such as intra-aortic balloon (IAB), pumps and catheters.

Recent Developments: For the quarter ended May 31 2006, net income decreased 12.2% to $13.9 million from $15.8 million in the year-earlier quarter. Revenues were $122.3 million, up 3.5% from $118.1 million the year before. Operating income was $19.3 million versus $23.7 million in the prior-year quarter, a decrease of 18.6%. Direct operating expenses rose 9.8% to $63.0 million from $57.4 million in the comparable period the year before. Indirect operating expenses increased 8.1% to $39.9 million from $36.9 million in the equivalent prior-year period.

Prospects: Going forward, Co. is very optimistic regarding further market acceptance for its new Maximal Barrier Central Venous Access Kit, based on growing sales of the product since its launch in January 2006. Moreover, Co.'s European market continues to exhibit solid growth, bolstered by its recent acquisition of certain assets from its United Kingdom (UK) distributor, Kimal PLC. It is expected that this acquisition will increase Co.'s sales by approximately $2.0 million for fiscal year 2006. As such, Co. is targeting net sales to range from $476.0 million to $480.0 million and earnings of $1.24 to $1.26 per diluted share for the full-fiscal year 2006.

Financial Data
(US$ in Thousands)

	9 Mos	6 Mos	3 Mos	08/31/2005	08/31/2004	08/31/2003	08/31/2002	08/31/2001
Earnings Per Share	0.96	1.00	0.84	0.88	1.26	1.04	0.89	1.05
Cash Flow Per Share	1.58	1.53	1.57	1.78	2.11	1.82	1.78	0.97
Tang Book Value Per Share	9.25	9.16	8.92	8.79	8.30	8.04	7.32	6.43
Dividends Per Share	0.640	0.620	0.600	0.540	0.350	0.195	0.138	0.128
Dividend Payout %	66.67	62.00	71.43	61.36	27.78	18.75	15.45	12.14
Income Statement								
Total Revenue	352,405	230,148	113,644	454,296	433,134	380,376	340,759	334,042
EBITDA	74,453	48,171	23,533	75,210	106,916	88,941	79,862	94,063
Depn & Amortn	19,835	13,075	6,437	21,508	23,778	23,226	21,693	22,696
Income Before Taxes	56,677	36,243	17,525	54,824	82,877	66,918	57,777	69,470
Income Taxes	18,314	11,779	5,695	15,311	26,935	21,248	18,777	22,925
Net Income	38,363	24,464	11,830	39,513	55,942	45,670	39,000	46,545
Average Shares	45,281	45,275	45,167	45,007	44,301	43,773	44,211	44,240
Balance Sheet								
Total Assets	643,927	617,728	605,828	600,490	549,208	493,897	425,680	417,710
Current Liabilities	113,247	97,889	94,988	91,853	80,474	77,966	50,425	78,424
Long-Term Obligations	...	...	...	...	...	3,735	300	600
Total Liabilities	137,861	123,786	122,066	121,983	102,877	103,251	65,324	91,621
Stockholders' Equity	506,066	493,942	483,762	478,507	446,331	390,646	360,356	326,089
Shares Outstanding	44,844	44,775	44,682	44,617	43,774	43,285	43,941	44,002
Statistical Record								
Return on Assets %	7.01	7.47	6.44	6.87	10.70	9.93	9.25	11.59
Return on Equity %	8.77	9.33	8.02	8.54	13.33	12.16	11.36	15.23
EBITDA Margin %	21.13	20.93	20.71	16.56	24.68	23.38	23.44	28.16
Net Margin %	10.89	10.63	10.41	8.70	12.92	12.01	11.45	13.93
Asset Turnover	0.75	0.76	0.77	0.79	0.83	0.83	0.81	0.83
Current Ratio	3.10	3.53	3.51	3.60	3.60	3.10	4.46	2.60
Debt to Equity	...	...	...	...	...	0.01	N.M.	N.M.
Price Range	33.80-27.50	36.02-27.50	36.02-27.50	36.02-27.21	32.72-22.43	25.80-15.75	24.20-16.93	20.16-17.06
P/E Ratio	35.21-28.65	36.02-27.50	42.88-32.74	40.93-30.92	25.97-17.80	24.81-15.14	27.19-19.02	19.20-16.25
Average Yield %	2.08	1.97	1.89	1.72	1.27	0.95	0.68	0.68

Address: 2400 Bernville Road, Reading, PA 19605
Telephone: 610-378-0131
Fax: 610-374-5360

Web Site: www.arrowintl.com
Officers: Carl G. Anderson Jr. - Chmn, C.E.O. James T. Hatlan - Sr. V.P., Manufacturing

Auditors: PricewaterhouseCoopers LLP
Investor Contact: 610-320-3917
Transfer Agents: Registrar and Transfer Company, Cranford, NJ

ASSOCIATED BANC-CORP.

Exchange	Symbol	Price	52Wk Range	Yield	P/E	Div Acheiver
NMS	ASBC	$31.54 (8/31/2006)	34.83-29.09	3.68	12.62	35 Years

*7 Year Price Score 104.03 *NYSE Composite Index=100 *12 Month Price Score 93.55

Interim Earnings (Per Share)

Qtr.	Mar	Jun	Sep	Dec
2003	0.51	0.51	0.53	0.50
2004	0.53	0.58	0.57	0.57
2005	0.59	0.57	0.63	0.64
2006	0.60	0.63	...	...

Interim Dividends (Per Share)

Amt	Decl	Ex	Rec	Pay
0.27Q	10/26/2005	11/3/2005	11/7/2005	11/15/2005
0.27Q	1/25/2006	2/2/2006	2/6/2006	2/15/2006
0.29Q	4/20/2006	5/4/2006	5/8/2006	5/15/2006
0.29Q	7/26/2006	8/4/2006	8/8/2006	8/15/2006

Indicated Div: $1.16 (Div. Reinv. Plan)

Valuation Analysis   **Institutional Holding**

Forecast P/E	13.00 (9/9/2006)	No of Institutions	220
Market Cap	$4.2 Billion	Shares	59,975,116
Book Value	2.3 Billion	% Held	45.36
Price/Book	1.84		
Price/Sales	2.76		

Business Summary: Commercial Banking (MIC: 8.1 SIC: 6022 NAIC: 522110)

Associated Banc-Corp. is a bank holding company. Through its banking subsidiaries and various nonbanking subsidiaries, Co. provides a range of banking and nonbanking products and services to individuals and businesses in the communities it serves. Co.'s banking and wealth management activities are conducted mainly in Wisconsin, Minnesota, and Illinois, and are primarily delivered through branch facilities in this tri-state area, as well as supplemented through loan production offices, supermarket branches, a customer service call center and 24-hour phone-banking services, an interstate ATM network, and internet banking services. As of Dec 31 2005, Co. had total assets of $22.10 billion.

Recent Developments: For the quarter ended June 30 2006, net income increased 12.9% to $83.5 million from $74.0 million in the year-earlier quarter. Net interest income increased 1.0% to $168.4 million from $166.7 million in the year-earlier quarter. Provision for loan losses was unchanged at $3.7 million versus the prior-year quarter. Non-interest income rose 25.1% to $77.2 million from $61.7 million, while non-interest expense advanced 7.2% to $124.7 million.

Prospects: Co.'s growth prospects appear to be strong. Co.'s acquisition of State Financial Services Corporation (State Financial) in October 2005 is primarily driving the growth in its net interest income, aided by its organic growth and corporate initiatives exhibited throughout the first half of 2006. Similarly, the State Financial acquisition is positively affecting several key components within Co.'s balance sheet. For instance, Co.'s assets growth is fueled primarily by the increases in loans deriving from the acquisition, coupled with its initiative in October 2005 to reduce its wholesale funding as an attempt to counteract the flat yield curve and competitive pricing pressures.

Financial Data
(US$ in Thousands)

	6 Mos	3 Mos	12/31/2005	12/31/2004	12/31/2003	12/31/2002	12/31/2001	12/31/2000
Earnings Per Share	2.50	2.44	2.43	2.25	2.05	1.86	1.64	1.49
Cash Flow Per Share	3.09	2.71	2.59	3.37	4.49	2.67	(0.00)	1.68
Tang Book Value Per Share	9.69	9.46	9.78	9.39	9.64	9.14	10.92	8.88
Dividends Per Share	1.100	1.080	1.060	0.977	0.887	0.808	0.739	0.671
Dividend Payout %	44.00	44.26	43.62	43.41	43.32	43.43	45.19	45.01
Income Statement								
Interest Income	631,840	310,543	1,094,025	767,122	727,364	792,106	880,622	931,157
Interest Expense	296,572	143,674	421,770	214,495	216,602	290,840	458,637	547,590
Net Interest Income	335,268	166,869	672,255	552,627	510,762	501,266	421,985	383,567
Provision for Losses	8,151	4,465	13,019	14,668	46,813	50,699	28,210	20,206
Non-Interest Income	147,981	70,773	291,086	210,247	246,435	220,308	195,603	184,196
Non-Interest Expense	248,131	123,471	480,463	377,869	388,668	374,549	338,369	317,736
Income Before Taxes	226,967	109,706	469,859	370,337	321,716	296,326	251,009	229,821
Income Taxes	61,711	27,999	149,698	112,051	93,059	85,607	71,487	61,838
Net Income	165,256	81,707	320,161	258,286	228,657	210,719	179,522	167,983
Average Shares	133,441	136,404	131,931	115,025	111,760	113,239	109,751	112,876
Balance Sheet								
Net Loans & Leases	15,202,219	15,335,779	15,003,060	13,692,125	10,114,188	10,140,684	8,891,660	8,793,147
Total Assets	21,128,354	21,518,860	22,100,082	20,520,136	15,247,894	15,043,275	13,604,374	13,128,394
Total Deposits	13,646,408	13,616,870	13,573,089	12,786,239	9,792,843	9,458,490	8,612,611	9,291,646
Total Liabilities	18,853,494	19,274,165	19,775,104	18,502,717	13,899,467	13,771,092	12,533,958	12,159,698
Stockholders' Equity	2,274,860	2,244,695	2,324,978	2,017,419	1,348,427	1,272,183	1,070,416	968,696
Shares Outstanding	132,411	132,327	135,674	129,770	110,040	111,420	98,003	109,091
Statistical Record								
Return on Assets %	1.59	1.54	1.50	1.44	1.51	1.47	1.34	1.31
Return on Equity %	15.56	15.20	14.75	15.31	17.45	17.99	17.61	17.84
Net Interest Margin %	52.41	53.73	61.45	72.04	70.22	63.28	47.92	41.19
Efficiency Ratio %	31.28	32.38	34.69	38.66	39.91	37.00	31.44	28.49
Loans to Deposits	1.11	1.13	1.07	1.03	1.11	1.11	1.03	0.95
Price Range	34.83-29.09	34.83-29.09	34.74-29.09	34.85-27.09	28.75-21.43	25.50-18.13	22.37-18.03	18.87-12.29
P/E Ratio	13.93-11.64	14.27-11.92	14.30-11.97	15.49-12.04	14.03-10.46	13.71-9.75	13.64-10.99	12.66-8.25
Average Yield %	3.34	3.31	3.28	3.22	3.57	3.57	3.57	4.44

Address: 1200 Hansen Road, Green Bay, WI 54304 **Telephone:** 920-491-7000	**Web Site:** www.associatedbank.com **Officers:** Robert C. Gallagher - Chmn. John C. Seramur - Vice-Chmn.
Auditors: KPMG LLP **Investor Contact:** 920-491-7120 **Transfer Agents:** National City Bank, Cleveland, OH	

ATI TECHNOLOGIES INC.

Exchange	Symbol	Price	52Wk Range	Yield	P/E
NMS	ATYT	$21.48 (8/31/2006)	21.50-12.18	N/A	N/A

*7 Year Price Score 106.44 *NYSE Composite Index=100 *12 Month Price Score 114.79 **Interim Earnings (Per Share)**

Qtr.	Nov	Feb	May	Aug
2002-03	0.02	(0.04)	0.05	0.10
2003-04	0.19	0.19	0.19	0.24
2004-05	0.25	0.22	0.00	(0.40)
2005-06	0.03	0.13	...	...

Interim Dividends (Per Share)

Amt	Decl	Ex	Rec	Pay

Valuation Analysis **Institutional Holding**

Forecast P/E	43.70	No of Institutions
	(9/12/2006)	171
Market Cap	$5.4 Billion	Shares
Book Value	1.1 Billion	155,484,560
Price/Book	4.97	% Held
Price/Sales	2.41	61.30

Business Summary: IT & Technology (MIC: 10.2 SIC: 3572 NAIC: 334112)

ATI Technologies is a provider of graphics processors and technologies. Co. is engaged in the design, manufacturing and selling of innovative 3D graphics and digital media silicon solutions. Co. markets its products to original equipment manufacturers, system builders, distributors and retailers in North America, Europe and the Asia-Pacific region.

Recent Developments: For the quarter ended May 31 2006, net income was $31.9 million compared with a net loss of $400,000 in the equivalent period of the previous year. Revenues increased 23.0% to $652.3 million from $530.2 million in the year-earlier quarter. Gross margin advanced 27.3% to $196.6 million from $154.4 million in the prior-year period. Research and development expense rose 3.4% to $91.5 million from $88.5 milion in the previous year. Operating expenses climbed 8.0% to $169.6 million from $157.1 million the year before. Income from operations was $27.0 million versus a loss of $2.6 million in 2005.

Prospects: On Jul 24 2006, Co. announced that it plans to be acquired by AMD in a transaction valued at approximately C$5.40 billion. Under the terms of the transaction, AMD will acquire all of the outstanding common shares of Co. for a combination of $4.20 billion in cash and 57.0 million shares of Co.'s common stock, based on the number of shares of Co.'s common stock outstanding at Jul 21 2006. The transaction in expected to be completed in the fourth quarter of 2006. Meanwhile, given the anticipated near-term PC market conditions, revenues for the fourth quarter of fiscal 2006 are expected to be between $620.0 million and $660.0 million.

Financial Data (US$ in Thousands)	6 Mos	3 Mos	08/31/2005	08/31/2004	08/31/2003	08/31/2002	08/31/2001	08/31/2000
Earnings Per Share	(0.24)	(0.15)	0.07	0.80	0.14	0.20	(0.23)	(0.32)
Cash Flow Per Share	0.06	0.25	0.41	0.75	0.44	0.24	0.44	...
Tang Book Value Per Share	3.54	3.29	3.21	3.00	2.07	1.85	1.71	1.55
Income Statement								
Total Revenue	1,263,065	590,703	2,222,509	1,996,717	1,385,293	1,021,722	1,037,809	1,372,043
EBITDA	72,547	20,424	71,329	278,712	83,574	80,825	63,532	3,765
Depn & Amortn	19,228	9,991	31,575	26,031	34,705	120,422	135,462	56,709
Income Before Taxes	52,298	9,920	37,658	250,623	46,970	(40,256)	(73,110)	(53,048)
Income Taxes	10,529	2,294	20,729	45,824	11,741	7,209	(18,905)	16,286
Net Income	34,143	7,626	16,929	204,799	35,229	(47,465)	(54,205)	(69,334)
Average Shares	258,158	256,568	258,314	256,208	244,353	234,895	230,879	215,124
Balance Sheet								
Current Assets	1,481,081	1,331,589	1,350,931	1,199,376	797,256	601,295	475,639	531,723
Total Assets	1,890,570	1,734,242	1,743,491	1,513,486	1,116,058	915,055	848,890	1,015,011
Current Liabilities	757,718	663,246	691,382	504,657	366,968	239,642	152,079	240,637
Long-Term Obligations	29,150	29,108	29,110	28,053	28,073	15,798	...	...
Total Liabilities	795,606	701,631	729,353	568,798	416,449	268,028	167,255	249,737
Stockholders' Equity	1,094,964	1,032,611	1,014,138	944,688	699,609	647,027	681,635	765,274
Shares Outstanding	253,474	251,700	251,473	249,287	241,742	236,870	232,118	229,436
Statistical Record								
Return on Assets %	N.M.	N.M.	1.04	15.53	3.47	N.M.	N.M.	N.M.
Return on Equity %	N.M.	N.M.	1.73	24.84	5.23	N.M.	N.M.	N.M.
EBITDA Margin %	5.74	3.46	3.21	13.96	6.03	7.91	6.12	0.27
Net Margin %	2.70	1.29	0.76	10.26	2.54	N.M.	N.M.	N.M.
Asset Turnover	1.23	1.29	1.36	1.51	1.36	1.16	1.11	1.73
Current Ratio	1.95	2.01	1.95	2.38	2.17	2.51	3.13	2.21
Debt to Equity	0.03	0.03	0.03	0.03	0.04	0.02	...	...
Price Range	18.02-11.34	20.21-11.34	20.39-11.34	18.86-13.59	15.10-3.79	15.37-5.51	11.07-3.84	21.75-8.34
P/E Ratio	...	...	291.29-162.00	23.57-16.99	107.86-27.07	76.85-27.55	...	...

Address: 1 Commerce Valley Drive East, Markham, L3T 7X6
Telephone: 905-882-2600
Fax: 905-882-2620

Web Site: www.ati.com
Officers: K. Y. Ho - Chmn, David E. Orton - Pres., C.E.O.

Auditors: KPMG LLP
Transfer Agents: CIBC Mellon Trust Company, Toronto, Ontario, Canada

ATMEL CORP.

Exchange	Symbol	Price	52Wk Range	Yield	P/E
NMS	ATML	$5.78 (8/31/2006)	5.86-1.98	N/A	144.50

*7 Year Price Score 43.48 *NYSE Composite Index=100 *12 Month Price Score 121.23

Interim Earnings (Per Share)

Qtr.	Mar	Jun	Sep	Dec
2003	(0.11)	(0.09)	(0.07)	0.03
2004	0.02	0.02	(0.04)	(0.02)
2005	(0.09)	(0.09)	0.00	0.11
2006	0.02	...	...	...

Interim Dividends (Per Share)
No Dividends Paid

Valuation Analysis

Forecast P/E	33.53		No of Institutions
	(9/12/2006)		182
Market Cap	$2.8 Billion		Shares
Book Value	981.1 Million		251,346,048
Price/Book	2.87		% Held
Price/Sales	1.66		51.63

Business Summary: IT & Technology (MIC: 10.2 SIC: 3674 NAIC: 334413)

Atmel designs and manufactures semiconductor integrated circuit products. The application specific integrated circuits (ASICs) segment develops semicustom gate arrays, cell-based integrated circuits, custom ASICs and smart cards to meet the requirements of customer-specific applications. The microcontrollers segment develops proprietary and standard microcontrollers and military and aerospace application specific products. The nonvolatile memory segment develops erasable and electrically erasable programmable read-only memories and Flash memories. The radio frequency (RF) and automotive segment develops RF and analog circuits for the telecommunications, automotive and industrial markets.

Recent Developments: For the quarter ended Mar 31 2006, net income amounted to $9.6 million versus a net loss of $43.0 million in the year-earlier quarter. Revenues were $436.8 million, up 4.1% from $419.8 million the year before. Operating income was $23.6 million versus a loss of $34.0 million in the prior-year quarter. Direct operating expenses declined 11.3% to $295.1 million from $332.8 million in the comparable period the year before. Indirect operating expenses decreased 2.5% to $118.1 million from $121.0 million in the equivalent prior-year period.

Prospects: Top-line results are primarily reflecting robust growth in Co.'s Microcontroller segment, driven by substantially higher AVR unit shipments. In particular, Co. noted the continuing market acceptance for its proprietary AVR® microcontroller following the recent introduction of its new 32-bit and picoPower® AVR architecture, by which has resulted in further allocation of its fabrication capacity to meet the increased demand. Going forward into the second quarter of fiscal year 2006, Co. anticipates revenues should grow between the 1.0% and 3.0% range on a sequential basis, while its gross margins should be in the range of 31.0% to 33.0%.

Financial Data
(US$ in Thousands)

	3 Mos	12/31/2005	12/31/2004	12/31/2003	12/31/2002	12/31/2001	12/31/2000	12/31/1999
Earnings Per Share	0.04	(0.07)	(0.01)	(0.25)	(1.37)	(0.90)	0.55	0.13
Cash Flow Per Share	0.49	0.42	0.48	0.55	0.42	0.64	1.53	0.67
Tang Book Value Per Share	2.02	1.92	2.28	2.08	2.08	3.19	4.10	1.98
Income Statement								
Total Revenue	436,784	1,675,715	1,649,722	1,330,635	1,193,814	1,472,268	2,012,672	1,330,161
EBITDA	83,264	279,623	351,102	174,962	(247,928)	(172,706)	724,629	379,480
Depn & Amortn	59,825	290,617	298,426	279,013	253,588	302,016	255,215	200,879
Income Before Taxes	17,240	(40,588)	25,697	(104,051)	(551,567)	(531,393)	415,586	128,821
Income Taxes	7,606	(7,690)	28,131	13,945	90,229	(113,045)	149,610	46,374
Net Income	9,634	(32,898)	(2,434)	(117,996)	(641,796)	(418,348)	265,976	53,379
Average Shares	490,819	481,534	476,063	469,869	466,949	464,575	491,989	414,644
Balance Sheet								
Total Assets	1,961,175	1,927,345	2,323,523	2,154,690	2,302,559	3,024,197	3,824,887	2,014,910
Current Liabilities	626,032	614,968	613,689	551,186	707,447	734,753	1,189,371	551,812
Long-Term Obligations	117,172	133,479	323,950	358,031	453,509	693,212	668,503	654,033
Total Liabilities	980,042	987,054	1,211,927	1,136,573	1,333,416	1,537,670	1,930,030	1,213,431
Stockholders' Equity	981,133	940,291	1,111,596	1,018,117	969,143	1,486,527	1,894,857	801,479
Shares Outstanding	486,498	483,366	477,926	473,047	465,630	466,059	462,473	404,178
Statistical Record								
Return on Assets %	0.94	N.M.	N.M.	N.M.	N.M.	N.M.	9.08	2.68
Return on Equity %	1.98	N.M.	N.M.	N.M.	N.M.	N.M.	19.67	6.96
EBITDA Margin %	19.06	16.69	21.28	13.15	N.M.	N.M.	36.00	28.53
Net Margin %	2.21	N.M.	N.M.	N.M.	N.M.	N.M.	13.22	4.01
Asset Turnover	0.81	0.79	0.73	0.60	0.45	0.43	0.69	0.67
Current Ratio	1.70	1.62	1.75	1.76	1.45	1.62	1.51	1.88
Debt to Equity	0.12	0.14	0.29	0.35	0.47	0.47	0.35	0.82
Price Range	5.05-1.98	3.92-1.98	7.87-2.99	6.85-1.47	10.85-0.70	17.94-5.50	29.75-9.66	15.19-3.52
P/E Ratio	126.25-49.50	...	...	...	...	...	54.09-17.56	116.83-27.04

Address: 2325 Orchard Parkway, San Jose, CA 95131
Telephone: 408-441-0311
Fax: 408-487-2600

Web Site: www.atmel.com
Officers: George Perlegos - Chmn., Pres., C.E.O. Gust Perlegos - Exec. V.P., Office of the Pres.

Auditors: PricewaterhouseCoopers LLP
Investor Contact: 408-487-2780
Transfer Agents: American Stock Transfer & Trust, New York, NY

AUTODESK INC.

Exchange	Symbol	Price	52Wk Range	Yield	P/E
NMS	ADSK	$34.76 (8/31/2006)	47.60-30.06	N/A	28.49

*7 Year Price Score 187.47 *NYSE Composite Index=100 *12 Month Price Score 81.56

Interim Earnings (Per Share)

Qtr.	Apr	Jul	Oct	Jan
2003-04	0.04	0.14	0.10	0.25
2004-05	0.18	0.16	0.30	0.27
2005-06	0.31	0.30	0.38	0.34
2006-07	0.20	...	...	...

Interim Dividends (Per Share)

Amt	Decl	Ex	Rec	Pay
0.015Q	9/9/2004	9/22/2004	9/24/2004	10/8/2004
100%	11/18/2004	12/21/2004	12/6/2004	12/20/2004
0.015Q	12/10/2004	12/22/2004	12/27/2004	1/7/2005
0.015Q	3/10/2005	3/22/2005	3/25/2005	4/8/2005

Valuation Analysis

Forecast P/E	19.14 (9/9/2006)
Market Cap	$8.1 Billion
Book Value	846.3 Million
Price/Book	9.52
Price/Sales	5.02

Institutional Holding

No of Institutions	368
Shares	196,833,296
% Held	84.95

Business Summary: IT & Technology (MIC: 10.2 SIC: 7372 NAIC: 511210)

Autodesk is a design software and services company, which operates through two segments: Design Solutions Segment; and Media and Entertainment Segment. Through these segments, Co. provides products to customers in the building, manufacturing, infrastructure and digital media markets that enable them to create, manage and share their data and designs digitally; as well as a range of discipline-specific design and documentation tools that include its AutoCAD based vertical products and its 3D design products. Co.'s products are sold in over 160 countries, both directly and through its network of approximately 1,700 resellers and distributors.

Recent Developments: For the quarter ended Apr 30 2006, net income decreased 36.2% to $48.5 million from $76.1 million in the year-earlier quarter. Revenues were $436.0 million, up 22.8% from $355.1 million the year before. Operating income was $59.3 million versus $90.6 million in the prior-year quarter, a decrease of 34.6%. Direct operating expenses rose 14.7% to $49.9 million from $43.5 million in the comparable period the year before. Indirect operating expenses increased 47.9% to $326.8 million from $221.0 million in the equivalent prior-year period.

Prospects: Co. is experiencing solid growth across its portfolio of businesses, primarily attributable to revenue growth generated by its new seats and emerging businesses. Moreover, Co.'s 3D products continue to increase their market penetration, particularly for its Revit family of products. Looking ahead, Co. expects net revenues for the second quarter of fiscal 2007 to range from $440.0 million to $450.0 million and earnings of $0.26 and $0.28 per diluted share. For full-fiscal year 2007, Co.'s net revenues are expected to be in the range of $1.81 billion to $1.85 billion, while earnings are expected to be between $1.07 and $1.15 per diluted share.

Financial Data
(US$ in Thousands)

	3 Mos	01/31/2006	01/31/2005	01/31/2004	01/31/2003	01/31/2002	01/31/2001	01/31/2000
Earnings Per Share	1.22	1.33	0.90	0.52	0.14	0.40	0.40	0.04
Cash Flow Per Share	1.92	1.81	1.64	0.99	0.38	0.97	0.86	0.43
Tang Book Value Per Share	1.90	1.84	2.07	1.98	1.71	2.11	1.78	2.10
Dividends Per Share	...	0.015	0.060	0.060	0.060	0.060	0.060	0.060
Dividend Payout %	...	1.13	6.67	11.54	42.86	15.00	15.09	150.00
Income Statement								
Total Revenue	436,000	1,523,200	1,233,767	951,643	824,945	947,491	936,324	820,182
EBITDA	75,300	426,700	298,277	158,018	87,310	189,600	229,906	103,668
Depn & Amortn	12,500	43,700	51,949	34,822	48,844	62,907	68,844	79,748
Income Before Taxes	62,800	383,000	246,328	123,196	38,466	126,693	161,062	23,920
Income Taxes	14,300	54,100	24,820	2,880	6,562	35,169	51,540	14,112
Net Income	48,500	328,900	221,508	120,316	31,904	90,313	93,233	9,808
Average Shares	244,700	247,500	246,977	231,304	229,550	224,550	234,056	245,624
Balance Sheet								
Total Assets	1,439,600	1,360,800	1,142,204	1,017,160	883,650	902,444	807,759	907,326
Current Liabilities	520,000	506,900	477,468	384,922	310,028	370,651	333,913	299,392
Total Liabilities	593,300	569,500	494,126	395,517	314,442	373,130	348,085	305,027
Stockholders' Equity	846,300	791,300	648,078	621,643	569,208	529,314	459,674	602,299
Shares Outstanding	231,700	229,600	227,611	223,440	224,528	222,574	218,856	236,964
Statistical Record								
Return on Assets %	23.03	26.28	20.46	12.66	3.57	10.56	10.84	1.23
Return on Equity %	38.70	45.70	34.80	20.21	5.81	18.26	17.51	1.85
EBITDA Margin %	17.27	28.01	24.18	16.60	10.58	20.01	24.55	12.64
Net Margin %	11.12	21.59	17.95	12.64	3.87	9.53	9.96	1.20
Asset Turnover	1.23	1.22	1.14	1.00	0.92	1.11	1.09	1.02
Current Ratio	1.51	1.46	1.64	1.55	1.45	1.52	1.47	1.82
Price Range	47.60-32.12	47.60-28.53	38.57-12.55	13.28-6.64	11.68-5.45	10.39-6.30	13.72-4.98	10.97-4.28
P/E Ratio	39.02-26.33	35.79-21.45	42.86-13.94	25.53-12.78	83.39-38.93	25.98-15.74	34.30-12.46	274.22-107.03
Average Yield %	...	0.04	0.27	0.67	0.78	0.67	0.75	0.84

Address: 111 McInnis Parkway, San Rafael, CA 94903
Telephone: 415-507-5000
Fax: 415-507-5100

Web Site: www.autodesk.com
Officers: Carol A. Bartz - Chmn., Pres., C.E.O.
George M. Bado - Sr. V.P., Worldwide Sales, Consulting

Auditors: ERNST & YOUNG LLP
Investor Contact: 415-507-6705

AVOCENT CORP

Exchange	Symbol	Price	52Wk Range	Yield	P/E
NMS	AVCT	$30.23 (8/31/2006)	34.64-22.09	N/A	24.18

*7 Year Price Score 78.51   *NYSE Composite Index=100   *12 Month Price Score 87.56

Interim Earnings (Per Share)

Qtr.	Mar	Jun	Sep	Dec
2003	0.17	0.16	0.28	0.20
2004	0.17	(0.27)	0.21	0.24
2005	0.04	0.22	0.33	0.38
2006	0.26	0.28	...	...

Interim Dividends (Per Share)
No Dividends Paid

Valuation Analysis

		Institutional Holding	
Forecast P/E	15.22	No of Institutions	
	(9/9/2006)	182	
Market Cap	$1.4 Billion	Shares	
Book Value	648.0 Million	46,629,740	
Price/Book	2.10	% Held	
Price/Sales	3.26	N/A	

Business Summary: Office Equipment Supplies (MIC: 11.12 SIC: 3577 NAIC: 334119)

Avocent designs, manufactures, licenses, and sells products and technologies that provide connectivity and centralized management of information technology (IT) infrastructure. Co. provides connectivity and management products and technologies that centralize control of servers, desktop computers, serial devices, wireless devices, mobile devices, and network appliances, thus increasing the efficiency of IT personnel. Server manufacturers resell private-labeled Avocent KVM (keyboard, video, and mouse) switches and embedded technology in their systems, and companies large and small depend on Co.'s products and technologies for managing their growing IT infrastructure.

Recent Developments: For the quarter ended June 30 2006, net income increased 22.4% to $13.6 million from $11.1 million in the year-earlier quarter. Revenues were $118.0 million, up 31.8% from $89.5 million the year before. Operating income was $17.2 million versus $7.8 million in the prior-year quarter, an increase of 120.8%. Direct operating expenses rose 26.9% to $46.6 million from $36.7 million in the comparable period the year before. Indirect operating expenses increased 20.4% to $54.2 million from $45.0 million in the equivalent prior-year period.

Prospects: Co.'s earnings reflect higher sales, margins growth and cost reductions implemented in the second half of 2005. Meanwhile, Co. is on track with its Cyclades integration efforts and expects to realize additional operational efficiencies during the next two quarters. Moreover, Co. has agreed to acquire LANDesk Group Limited, a privately held company in Salt Lake City, UT, which will significantly expand its product lines to include software for the centralized management and protection of information technology assets. The transaction is expected to close in the third quarter of 2006. Hence, for the third quarter of 2006, Co. expects revenues of bewteen $138.0 million and $144.0 million.

Financial Data
(US$ in Thousands)

	6 Mos	3 Mos	12/31/2005	12/31/2004	12/31/2003	12/31/2002	12/31/2001	12/31/2000
Earnings Per Share	1.25	1.19	0.96	0.36	0.81	0.24	(7.22)	(3.92)
Cash Flow Per Share	1.49	1.58	1.44	1.56	1.79	1.58	1.64	0.57
Tang Book Value Per Share	5.83	6.91	8.80	8.15	7.80	5.78	5.14	4.80
Income Statement								
Total Revenue	212,517	94,512	369,888	365,255	304,238	260,600	255,911	222,372
EBITDA	48,381	22,070	92,632	60,993	79,710	41,790	(185,825)	(51,386)
Depn & Amortn	11,326	4,141	25,546	30,501	26,664	26,550	137,588	64,617
Income Before Taxes	36,909	17,929	67,086	30,492	53,046	15,240	(323,413)	(116,003)
Income Taxes	10,395	4,996	18,737	12,452	14,499	4,502	(2,947)	14,553
Net Income	26,514	12,933	48,349	18,040	38,547	10,738	(320,466)	(130,556)
Average Shares	48,709	50,109	50,254	50,530	47,693	45,549	44,374	33,266
Balance Sheet								
Total Assets	748,361	829,895	773,751	770,781	660,763	568,607	547,198	815,889
Current Liabilities	70,035	83,001	53,747	46,629	42,722	34,722	36,537	27,967
Long-Term Obligations	12,005	...	...	...	...	...	...	...
Total Liabilities	100,373	104,775	58,429	57,484	53,606	50,935	60,590	55,709
Stockholders' Equity	647,988	725,120	715,322	713,297	607,157	517,672	486,608	760,180
Shares Outstanding	45,036	48,927	48,837	50,232	47,350	45,210	44,650	43,820
Statistical Record								
Return on Assets %	8.35	7.52	6.26	2.51	6.27	1.92	N.M.	N.M.
Return on Equity %	9.30	8.33	6.77	2.72	6.85	2.14	N.M.	N.M.
EBITDA Margin %	22.77	23.35	25.04	16.70	26.20	16.04	N.M.	N.M.
Net Margin %	12.48	13.68	13.07	4.94	12.67	4.12	N.M.	N.M.
Asset Turnover	0.56	0.49	0.48	0.51	0.49	0.47	0.38	0.48
Current Ratio	4.17	4.15	7.41	7.18	7.00	6.94	7.07	8.70
Debt to Equity	0.02	...	...	...	...	...	...	...
Price Range	35.11-22.09	35.11-23.16	40.61-23.16	41.82-25.91	38.88-21.79	27.30-12.15	38.38-13.05	70.94-24.00
P/E Ratio	28.09-17.67	29.50-19.46	42.30-24.13	116.17-71.97	48.00-26.90	113.75-50.63	...	...

Address: 4991 Corporate Dr., Huntsville, AL 35805 **Telephone:** 256-430-4000	**Web Site:** www.avocent.com **Officers:** John R. Cooper - Chmn., Pres., C.E.O. Douglas E. Pritchett - Exec. V.P., Global Mktg.	**Auditors:** PricewaterhouseCoopers LLP **Investor Contact:** 256-430-4000 **Transfer Agents:** American Stock Transfer & Trust Company, New York, NY

BADGER METER, INC.

Exchange	Symbol	Price	52Wk Range	Yield	P/E	Div Acheiver
ASE	BMI	$26.17 (8/31/2006)	32.50-16.50	1.22	27.26	13 Years

*7 Year Price Score 170.60 *NYSE Composite Index=100 *12 Month Price Score 96.75

Interim Earnings (Per Share)

Qtr.	Mar	Jun	Sep	Dec
2003	0.05	0.20	0.20	0.12
2004	0.18	0.22	0.25	0.06
2005	0.26	0.29	0.27	0.12
2006	0.29	0.28	...	...

Interim Dividends (Per Share)

Amt	Decl	Ex	Rec	Pay
0.075Q	2/17/2006	2/24/2006	2/28/2006	3/15/2006
0.075Q	4/28/2006	5/30/2006	6/1/2006	6/15/2006
100%	4/28/2006	6/16/2006	6/1/2006	6/15/2006
0.08Q	8/11/2006	8/30/2006	9/1/2006	9/15/2006

Indicated Div: $0.32

Valuation Analysis   **Institutional Holding**

Forecast P/E	22.99	No of Institutions
	(9/9/2006)	62
Market Cap	$368.3 Million	Shares
Book Value	83.4 Million	7,072,224
Price/Book	4.42	% Held
Price/Sales	1.61	50.25

Business Summary: Instruments and Related Products (MIC: 11.15 SIC: 3824 NAIC: 334514)

Badger Meter is a marketer and manufacturer of products using flow measurement and control technologies developed both internally and with other technology companies. Co.'s product lines are within two general categories: utility and industrial. The utility category is comprised of two product lines, residential and commercial water meters (with various Automatic-Meter-Reading technology systems), as well as its own proprietary product, Orion®. Co.'s industrial product lines include automotive fluid meters and systems, small precision valves, electromagnetic meters, impeller flow meters and industrial process meters (all with related accessories and instrumentation).

Recent Developments: For the quarter ended June 30 2006, net income decreased 2.6% to $4.0 million from $4.2 million in the year-earlier quarter. Revenues were $62.4 million, up 8.7% from $57.4 million the year before. Operating income was $7.7 million versus $7.5 million in the prior-year quarter, an increase of 2.6%. Direct operating expenses rose 11.9% to $41.8 million from $37.3 million in the comparable period the year before. Indirect operating expenses increased 2.5% to $12.9 million from $12.6 million in the equivalent prior-year period.

Prospects: Co.'s near-term outlook appears to be slightly mixed. On one hand, Co.'s earnings growth will continue to be interrupted by the effect of higher copper costs, by which Co. expects will be mitigated by its implementation of price increases in the third quarter of 2006. Conversely, Co. remains optimistic regarding continued growth in its sales for the second half of 2006, given the robust sales of its Orion®-proprietary mobile radio frequency Automatic-Meter-Reading system and its commercial products for the utility market. Furthermore, Co. expects its new facility in Mexico, scheduled to be operational by the end of 2006, will improve its manufacturing efficiency while reducing its costs.

Financial Data

(US$ in Thousands)	6 Mos	3 Mos	12/31/2005	12/31/2004	12/31/2003	12/31/2002	12/31/2001	12/31/2000
Earnings Per Share	0.96	0.98	0.94	0.71	0.57	0.55	0.26	0.50
Cash Flow Per Share	0.75	1.25	1.36	0.42	1.09	0.97	0.68	1.00
Tang Book Value Per Share	5.36	5.08	4.80	4.15	3.55	3.20	3.32	3.29
Dividends Per Share	0.300	0.295	0.290	0.275	0.265	0.255	0.250	0.215
Dividend Payout %	31.09	30.02	30.69	38.73	46.09	46.36	97.09	43.00
Income Statement								
Total Revenue	123,241	61,036	216,654	205,010	183,989	167,317	138,537	146,389
EBITDA	19,020	9,562	30,765	26,832	22,920	21,266	13,192	19,006
Depn & Amortn	3,642	1,879	6,359	7,245	7,832	7,980	6,801	6,073
Income Before Taxes	14,577	7,294	22,798	17,980	13,351	11,437	5,010	10,727
Income Taxes	6,297	3,063	9,545	8,347	5,774	4,166	1,646	3,786
Net Income	8,280	4,231	13,253	9,633	7,577	7,271	3,364	6,941
Average Shares	14,381	14,302	14,022	13,614	13,196	13,216	13,100	13,880
Balance Sheet								
Total Assets	159,874	153,711	145,867	142,961	133,851	126,463	98,836	98,710
Current Liabilities	52,027	41,871	39,586	45,247	37,052	48,555	23,782	37,695
Long-Term Obligations	6,966	15,675	15,360	14,819	24,450	13,046	20,498	5,944
Total Liabilities	76,491	75,324	72,451	78,895	78,680	78,368	55,834	55,391
Stockholders' Equity	83,383	78,387	73,416	64,066	55,171	48,095	43,002	43,319
Shares Outstanding	14,073	13,888	13,696	13,444	13,169	12,882	12,718	12,828
Statistical Record								
Return on Assets %	9.02	9.30	9.18	6.94	5.82	6.45	3.41	6.86
Return on Equity %	18.20	19.31	19.28	16.11	14.67	15.96	7.79	16.04
EBITDA Margin %	15.41	15.67	14.20	13.09	12.46	12.71	9.52	12.98
Net Margin %	6.71	6.93	6.12	4.70	4.12	4.35	2.43	4.74
Asset Turnover	1.49	1.49	1.50	1.48	1.41	1.49	1.40	1.45
Current Ratio	1.62	1.92	1.83	1.58	1.70	1.14	1.87	1.18
Debt to Equity	0.08	0.20	0.21	0.23	0.44	0.27	0.48	0.14
Price Range	32.50-16.50	29.17-13.06	25.52-13.06	15.62-8.59	9.94-6.44	8.47-5.58	8.00-5.00	9.19-5.75
P/E Ratio	33.85-17.19	29.77-13.33	27.14-13.89	21.99-12.09	17.43-11.29	15.41-10.14	30.77-19.23	18.38-11.50
Average Yield %	1.27	1.39	1.57	2.50	3.30	3.50	3.85	2.96

Address: 4545 W. Brown Deer Road, Milwaukee, WI 53223
Telephone: 414-355-0400
Fax: 414-355-7499

Web Site: www.badgermeter.com
Officers: James L. Forbes - Chmn. Richard A. Meeusen - Pres., C.E.O.

Auditors: Ernst & Young LLP
Investor Contact: 414-371-5702
Transfer Agents: American Stock Transfer

BANCFIRST CORP. (OKLAHOMA CITY, OKLA)

Exchange	Symbol	Price	52Wk Range	Yield	P/E	Div Acheiver
NMS	BANF	$47.37 (8/31/2006)	48.45-39.19	1.52	17.29	12 Years

*7 Year Price Score 128.01 *NYSE Composite Index=100 *12 Month Price Score 105.12

Interim Earnings (Per Share)
Qtr.	Mar	Jun	Sep	Dec
2003	0.54	0.51	0.47	0.49
2004	0.52	0.54	0.58	0.69
2005	0.68	0.70	0.57	0.72
2006	0.68	0.76	...	...

Interim Dividends (Per Share)
Amt	Decl	Ex	Rec	Pay
100%	1/26/2006	3/2/2006	2/16/2006	3/1/2006
0.16Q	2/23/2006	3/29/2006	3/31/2006	4/17/2006
0.16Q	5/25/2006	7/17/2006	6/30/2006	7/17/2006
0.18Q	8/24/2006	9/27/2006	9/30/2006	10/16/2006

Indicated Div: $0.72

Valuation Analysis
Forecast P/E	15.53 (9/9/2006)
Market Cap	$744.5 Million
Book Value	320.4 Million
Price/Book	2.32
Price/Sales	3.00

Institutional Holding
No of Institutions	79
Shares	3,881,274
% Held	24.69

Business Summary: Commercial Banking (MIC: 8.1 SIC: 6021 NAIC: 522110)

BancFirst is a bank holding company that provides a range of commercial banking services to retail customers and small to medium-sized businesses both in the non-metropolitan trade centers of Oklahoma and the metropolitan markets of Oklahoma City, Tulsa, Lawton, Muskogee, Norman and Shawnee. Retail and commercial banking services include commercial, real estate, agricultural and consumer lending; depository and funds transfer services; collections; safe deposit boxes; cash management services; retail brokerage services; and other services tailored for both individual and corporate customers. As of Dec 31 2005, total assets were $3.22 billion and deposits amounted to $2.80 billion.

Recent Developments: For the quarter ended June 30 2006, net income increased 9.0% to $12.2 million from $11.2 million in the year-earlier quarter. Net interest income increased 8.5% to $35.8 million from $32.9 million in the year-earlier quarter. Provision for loan losses was $917,000 versus $1.3 million in the prior-year quarter, a decrease of 29.6%. Non-interest income rose 7.0% to $14.7 million from $13.8 million, while non-interest expense advanced 8.4% to $30.8 million.

Prospects: Co.'s near-term outlook appears optimistic, reflecting an increase in its net interest income, attributable to improved loans and earning assets supported by favorable growth in its deposits from customer relationships. Moreover, Co. is experiencing non-interest income growth, driven by increases in revenues from trust services, transaction accounts and electronic banking services. Separately, on Aug 3 2006, Co. has completed its acquisition of First Bartlesville Bank, which has assets of approximately $47.0 million. As a result, the bank will operate as First Bartlesville Bank pending its incorporation into Co.'s system, which is expected to occur in the fourth quarter of 2006.

Financial Data
(US$ in Thousands)	6 Mos	3 Mos	12/31/2005	12/31/2004	12/31/2003	12/31/2002	12/31/2001	12/31/2000
Earnings Per Share	2.74	2.68	2.68	2.33	2.00	2.03	1.67	1.60
Cash Flow Per Share	3.50	1.72	3.60	8.57	2.02	2.58	2.14	1.91
Tang Book Value Per Share	17.95	17.35	16.87	15.38	14.26	14.12	12.17	10.59
Dividends Per Share	0.640	0.620	0.600	0.530	0.470	0.400	0.360	0.330
Dividend Payout %	23.36	23.13	22.39	22.80	23.50	19.70	21.56	20.69
Income Statement								
Interest Income	101,643	49,286	171,706	144,765	141,032	157,139	182,643	182,389
Interest Expense	31,289	14,685	40,255	27,519	31,915	47,809	77,711	80,054
Net Interest Income	70,354	34,601	131,451	117,246	109,117	109,330	104,932	102,335
Provision for Losses	1,598	681	4,607	2,699	3,722	5,276	1,780	4,045
Non-Interest Income	28,141	13,409	54,284	51,855	48,820	45,212	36,908	29,902
Non-Interest Expense	61,118	30,292	117,165	108,744	105,382	98,380	96,620	87,724
Income Before Taxes	35,779	17,037	63,963	57,658	48,833	50,886	43,440	40,468
Income Taxes	12,689	6,156	21,128	20,482	16,951	17,324	15,479	14,251
Net Income	23,090	10,881	42,835	37,176	31,882	33,562	27,961	26,217
Average Shares	16,080	16,045	16,000	15,991	15,945	16,520	16,742	16,448
Balance Sheet								
Net Loans & Leases	2,311,732	2,278,528	2,289,909	2,067,769	1,921,075	1,790,495	1,692,902	1,640,958
Total Assets	3,389,689	3,357,717	3,223,030	3,046,977	2,921,369	2,796,862	2,757,045	2,570,255
Total Deposits	2,954,960	2,934,980	2,804,519	2,657,434	2,585,690	2,428,648	2,401,328	2,267,397
Total Liabilities	3,069,259	3,047,019	2,920,681	2,769,480	2,665,997	2,545,354	2,533,877	2,373,297
Stockholders' Equity	320,430	310,698	302,349	277,497	255,372	251,508	223,168	196,958
Shares Outstanding	15,716	15,687	15,637	15,681	15,645	16,273	16,520	16,224
Statistical Record								
Return on Assets %	1.36	1.33	1.37	1.24	1.12	1.21	1.05	1.07
Return on Equity %	14.38	14.56	14.77	13.92	12.58	14.14	13.31	14.46
Net Interest Margin %	68.29	70.20	76.56	80.99	77.37	69.58	57.45	56.11
Efficiency Ratio %	45.95	48.32	51.85	55.31	55.51	48.62	44.01	41.32
Loans to Deposits	0.78	0.78	0.82	0.78	0.74	0.74	0.70	0.72
Price Range	46.42-39.19	45.22-31.80	45.22-31.80	39.79-27.50	29.90-21.43	25.87-17.23	21.63-16.88	20.13-12.44
P/E Ratio	16.94-14.30	16.87-11.86	16.87-11.86	17.08-11.80	14.95-10.71	12.74-8.49	12.95-10.10	12.58-7.77
Average Yield %	1.50	1.52	1.52	1.74	1.83	1.83	1.86	2.11

Address: 101 North Broadway, Oklahoma City, OK 73102-8401 **Telephone:** 405-270-1086 **Fax:** 405-270-1089	**Web Site:** www.bancfirst.com **Officers:** H. E. Rainbolt - Chmn. James R. Daniel - Vice-Chmn.	**Auditors:** Grant Thornton LLP **Investor Contact:** 405-270-1044 **Transfer Agents:** BancFirst Trust and Investment Management, Oklahoma City, OK

BEA SYSTEMS, INC.

Exchange	Symbol	Price	52Wk Range	Yield	P/E
NMS	BEAS	$13.73 (8/31/2006)	13.99-8.25	N/A	38.14

*7 Year Price Score 44.71   *NYSE Composite Index=100   *12 Month Price Score 109.75

Interim Earnings (Per Share)

Qtr.	Apr	Jul	Oct	Jan
2003-04	0.06	0.06	0.07	0.09
2004-05	0.06	0.07	0.08	0.11
2005-06	0.08	0.09	0.09	0.09
2006-07	0.09	...	...	...

Interim Dividends (Per Share)
No Dividends Paid

Valuation Analysis

		Institutional Holding	
Forecast P/E	23.52	No of Institutions	
	(9/9/2006)	256	
Market Cap	$5.4 Billion	Shares	
Book Value	1.2 Billion	308,586,944	
Price/Book	4.45	% Held	
Price/Sales	4.34	78.72	

Business Summary: IT & Technology (MIC: 10.2 SIC: 7371 NAIC: 541511)

BEA Systems is a provider of enterprise application infrastructure software and related services. Customers use Co.'s products as a deployment platform for Internet-based applications and as a means for enterprise application integration among mainframe, client/server and Internet-based applications. Co.'s products serve as a platform, integration tool or portal framework for applications such as billing, provisioning, customer service, electronic funds transfers, ATM networks, securities trading and settlement, online banking, Internet sales, inventory management, supply chain management, enterprise resource planning, scheduling, logistics, and hotel, airline and car rental reservations.

Recent Developments: For the quarter ended Apr 30 2006, net income increased 3.4% to $35.3 million from $34.1 million in the year-earlier quarter. Revenues were $323.2 million, up 14.7% from $281.7 million the year before. Operating income was $33.6 million versus $48.5 million in the prior-year quarter, a decrease of 30.7%. Direct operating expenses rose 26.7% to $78.8 million from $62.2 million in the comparable period the year before. Indirect operating expenses increased 23.3% to $210.8 million from $171.0 million in the equivalent prior-year period.

Prospects: Co.'s top-line results are being supported by increased demand for its core WebLogic products and the introduction of AquaLogic, which includes the AquaLogic Service Bus and products acquired through Plumtree Software Inc. in Oct 2005 and Fuego Inc. in Feb 2006. Going forward, Co.'s strategy is to focus on expanding and refreshing its existing application infrastructure products; expanding its service infrastructure products; and broadening its application infrastructure products into targeted emerging use cases. Additionally, Co. will continue to grow its business through opportunistic acquisitions, primarily focused on adding features or products that complement or expand its products.

Financial Data
(US$ in Thousands)

	3 Mos	01/31/2006	01/31/2005	01/31/2004	01/31/2003	01/31/2002	01/31/2001	01/31/2000
Earnings Per Share	0.36	0.36	0.32	0.28	0.20	(0.09)	0.04	(0.06)
Cash Flow Per Share	0.80	0.73	0.66	0.53	0.48	0.57	0.60	0.31
Tang Book Value Per Share	2.33	2.30	2.42	2.20	1.81	1.49	1.06	0.67
Income Statement								
Total Revenue	323,236	1,199,845	1,080,094	1,012,492	934,058	975,893	819,760	464,410
EBITDA	50,061	279,455	249,105	246,754	180,768	45,048	85,970	71,960
Depn & Amortn	5,819	31,958	31,898	50,714	38,859	27,057	15,598	57,200
Income Before Taxes	49,225	215,425	187,223	169,534	119,823	(4,268)	47,462	(5,657)
Income Taxes	13,971	72,682	56,167	50,860	35,947	31,410	30,380	13,917
Net Income	35,254	142,743	131,056	118,674	83,876	(35,678)	17,082	(19,574)
Average Shares	401,300	397,850	415,873	421,050	418,540	396,498	412,700	310,817
Balance Sheet								
Total Assets	2,327,156	2,475,531	2,348,394	2,220,189	1,809,959	1,659,951	1,592,336	1,258,841
Current Liabilities	889,227	1,136,623	532,191	502,857	445,581	428,517	389,900	235,533
Long-Term Obligations	227,622	227,388	780,194	741,639	550,000	550,000	561,421	578,489
Total Liabilities	1,118,142	1,365,294	1,315,227	1,250,051	1,004,010	986,035	986,332	814,022
Stockholders' Equity	1,209,014	1,110,237	1,033,167	970,138	805,949	673,916	606,004	444,819
Shares Outstanding	392,002	385,943	398,091	408,390	405,751	403,860	390,196	361,864
Statistical Record								
Return on Assets %	6.18	5.92	5.72	5.89	4.83	N.M.	1.19	N.M.
Return on Equity %	12.91	13.32	13.05	13.36	11.34	N.M.	3.24	N.M.
EBITDA Margin %	15.49	23.29	23.06	24.37	19.35	4.62	10.49	15.49
Net Margin %	10.91	11.90	12.13	11.72	8.98	N.M.	2.08	N.M.
Asset Turnover	0.53	0.50	0.47	0.50	0.54	0.60	0.57	0.56
Current Ratio	1.80	1.59	3.59	3.52	3.42	2.95	3.10	4.12
Debt to Equity	0.19	0.20	0.76	0.76	0.68	0.82	0.93	1.30
Price Range	13.99-7.05	10.71-6.85	14.14-5.96	15.09-9.24	18.13-4.95	67.19-9.28	86.19-29.50	46.00-3.47
P/E Ratio	38.86-19.58	29.75-19.03	44.19-18.63	53.89-33.00	90.65-24.75	...	N.M.	...

Address: 2315 North First Street, San Jose, CA 95131
Telephone: 408-570-8000
Fax: 408-570-8901

Web Site: www.bea.com
Officers: Alfred S. Chuang - Chmn., Pres., C.E.O.
Mark P. Dentinger - Exec. V.P., C.F.O.

Auditors: Ernst & Young LLP
Investor Contact: 408-570-8293
Transfer Agents: EquiServe, Boston, MA

BED, BATH & BEYOND, INC.

Exchange	Symbol	Price	52Wk Range	Yield	P/E
NMS	BBBY	$33.73 (8/31/2006)	43.33-31.42	N/A	17.39

*7 Year Price Score 91.66 *NYSE Composite Index=100 *12 Month Price Score 87.70

Interim Earnings (Per Share)

Qtr.	May	Aug	Nov	Feb
2003-04	0.19	0.32	0.33	0.47
2004-05	0.27	0.39	0.40	0.59
2005-06	0.33	0.47	0.45	0.67
2006-07	0.35	...	...	...

Interim Dividends (Per Share)
No Dividends Paid

Valuation Analysis	**Institutional Holding**
Forecast P/E	13.80	No of Institutions
	(9/9/2006)	544
Market Cap	$9.5 Billion	Shares
Book Value	2.4 Billion	227,216,112
Price/Book	3.99	% Held
Price/Sales	1.59	80.51

Business Summary: Retail - Miscellaneous (MIC: 5.11 SIC: 5999 NAIC: 453998)

Bed Bath and Beyond is a nationwide chain of retail stores, operating under the names Bed Bath and Beyond (BBB), Christmas Tree Shops (CTS) and Harmon. Co. sells an assortment of merchandise principally including domestics merchandise and home furnishings as well as food, giftware and health and beauty care items. As of Feb 25 2006, Co. had a total of 809 stores located in 46 U.S. states, the District of Columbia and Puerto Rico and ranged in size from approximately 5,000 to 100,000 square feet, but were primarily between 20,000 square feet and 50,000 square feet.

Recent Developments: For the quarter ended May 27 2006, net income increased 1.5% to $100.4 million from $98.9 million in the year-earlier quarter. Revenues were $1.40 billion, up 12.2% from $1.24 billion the year before. Operating income was $148.8 million versus $150.9 million in the prior-year quarter, a decrease of 1.4%. Direct operating expenses rose 11.4% to $805.9 million from $723.6 million in the comparable period the year before. Indirect operating expenses increased 19.3% to $441.3 million from $369.9 million in the equivalent prior-year period.

Prospects: Co. is experiencing robust growth in its consolidated net sales, attributable primarily to its continuing store expansion program, coupled with an increase in its comparable store sales due to several factors such as the continued consumer acceptance of its merchandise offerings as well as its solid focus on customer service. Going forward into fiscal year 2006, Co. expects to open approximately 75 to 80 stores within both new and existing markets. In addition, Co. intends to continue the expansion as well as integration of its Christmas Tree Shops (CTS) and Harmon concepts, which include the opening of six CTS stores throughout the year.

Financial Data (US$ in Thousands)	3 Mos	02/25/2006	02/26/2005	02/28/2004	03/01/2003	03/02/2002	03/03/2001	02/26/2000
Earnings Per Share	1.94	1.92	1.65	1.31	1.00	0.74	0.59	0.46
Cash Flow Per Share	2.34	2.25	2.06	1.85	1.44	1.17	0.69	0.49
Tang Book Value Per Share	8.45	8.05	6.99	6.14	4.93	3.75	2.84	1.99
Income Statement								
Total Revenue	1,395,963	5,809,562	5,147,678	4,477,981	3,665,164	2,927,962	2,396,655	1,877,966
EBITDA	180,562	993,454	891,562	725,173	555,867	408,647	319,488	240,965
Depn & Amortn	31,812	114,283	99,148	85,830	75,810	62,547	46,650	31,625
Income Before Taxes	158,409	915,091	811,187	649,545	491,348	357,072	281,839	215,130
Income Taxes	57,978	342,244	306,223	250,075	189,169	137,473	109,917	83,901
Net Income	100,431	572,847	504,964	399,470	302,179	219,599	171,922	131,229
Average Shares	285,153	298,973	306,642	304,690	301,147	298,667	292,876	288,234
Balance Sheet								
Total Assets	3,532,759	3,382,140	3,199,979	2,865,023	2,188,842	1,647,517	1,195,725	865,800
Current Liabilities	1,010,561	989,546	873,593	769,534	680,171	511,278	353,189	286,783
Total Liabilities	1,148,288	1,119,690	996,217	874,203	736,921	553,167	378,707	306,755
Stockholders' Equity	2,384,471	2,262,450	2,203,762	1,990,820	1,451,921	1,094,350	817,018	559,045
Shares Outstanding	282,226	280,990	294,063	300,278	294,430	291,441	287,890	280,812
Statistical Record								
Return on Assets %	16.67	17.45	16.70	15.85	15.80	15.49	16.41	17.56
Return on Equity %	24.46	25.72	24.14	23.27	23.80	23.04	24.58	27.13
EBITDA Margin %	12.93	17.10	17.32	16.19	15.17	13.96	13.33	12.83
Net Margin %	7.19	9.86	9.81	8.92	8.24	7.50	7.17	6.99
Asset Turnover	1.73	1.77	1.70	1.78	1.92	2.07	2.29	2.51
Current Ratio	2.15	2.09	2.40	2.56	2.34	2.40	2.51	2.26
Price Range	46.84-35.22	46.84-35.50	44.09-33.89	43.80-30.30	37.74-26.95	35.22-20.38	27.06-11.38	19.47-11.97
P/E Ratio	24.14-18.15	24.40-18.49	26.72-20.54	33.44-23.13	37.74-26.95	47.59-27.54	45.87-19.28	42.32-26.02

Address: 650 Liberty Avenue, Union, NJ 07083
Telephone: 908-688-0888
Fax: 908-810-8813

Web Site: www.bedbathandbeyond.com
Officers: Warren Eisenberg - Co-Chmn. Leonard Feinstein - Co-Chmn.

Auditors: KPMG LLP
Investor Contact: 908-668-0888
Transfer Agents: American Stock Transfer & Trust Company

BIOGEN IDEC INC

Exchange	Symbol	Price	52Wk Range	Yield	P/E
NMS	BIIB	$44.20 (8/31/2006)	50.10-35.94	N/A	442.00

*7 Year Price Score 77.10 *NYSE Composite Index=100 *12 Month Price Score 95.90

Interim Earnings (Per Share)

Qtr.	Mar	Jun	Sep	Dec
2003	0.24	0.17	0.26	(5.59)
2004	(0.12)	0.00	0.10	0.08
2005	0.12	0.10	0.08	0.16
2006	0.36	(0.50)	...	...

Interim Dividends (Per Share)

Amt	Decl	Ex	Rec	Pay
200%	11/30/2000	1/18/2001	12/26/2000	1/17/2001

Valuation Analysis

		Institutional Holding	
Forecast P/E	21.53	No of Institutions	
	(9/9/2006)	408	
Market Cap	$15.2 Billion	Shares	
Book Value	7.0 Billion	286,935,424	
Price/Book	2.17	% Held	
Price/Sales	6.07	83.51	

Business Summary: Biotechnology (MIC: 9.2 SIC: 2836 NAIC: 325414)

Biogen Idec develops, manufactures and commercializes oncology and immunology therapies. Products include: Avonex® (Interferon beta-1a) for the treatment of relapsing multiple sclerosis (MS); Rituxan® (rituximab) and Zevalin® (ibritumomab tiuxetan), which treat certain B-cell non-Hodgkin's lymphomas; TYSABRI® (natalizumab) to treat relapsing forms of MS to reduce the frequency of clinical relapses; and Amevive® (alefacept), for the treatment of adult patients with moderate-to-severe chronic plaque psoriasis who are candidates for systemic therapy or phototherapy. Co. receives revenues from royalties on sales by its licensees of a number of products covered under patents that it controls.

Recent Developments: For the quarter ended June 30 2006, net loss amounted to $170.6 million versus net income of $34.5 million in the year-earlier quarter. Revenues were $660.0 million, up 9.0% from $605.6 million the year before. Operating loss was $122.0 million versus an income of $46.3 million in the prior-year quarter. Direct operating expenses rose 9.7% to $78.0 million from $71.1 million in the comparable period the year before. Indirect operating expenses increased 44.2% to $704.1 million from $488.2 million in the equivalent prior-year period.

Prospects: On May 31 2006, Co. announced that it has signed a definitive agreement to acquire Fumapharm AG, a pharmaceutical company that develops therapeutics derived from fumaric acid esters. This transaction, which is expected to close within the next two months, supports Co.'s goal of developing therapeutics for patients with multiple sclerosis (MS) and psoriasis, as well as the expansion of its European operations. Upon completion, Co. will acquire all of the issued and outstanding shares of the capital stock of Fumapharm and will take over manufacture and sale of FUMADERM® product for the treatment of psoriasis in Germany through Fumapharm's existing network.

Financial Data
(US$ in Thousands)

	6 Mos	3 Mos	12/31/2005	12/31/2004	12/31/2003	12/31/2002	12/31/2001	12/31/2000
Earnings Per Share	0.10	0.70	0.47	0.07	(4.92)	0.85	0.59	0.30
Cash Flow Per Share	2.30	2.45	2.65	2.17	1.23	1.17	1.02	0.46
Tang Book Value Per Share	8.72	9.04	8.24	7.27	6.90	7.29	6.26	4.73
Income Statement								
Total Revenue	1,271,216	611,175	2,422,500	2,211,562	679,183	404,222	272,677	154,682
EBITDA	241,175	291,620	641,196	465,443	(839,172)	224,032	137,443	60,598
Depn & Amortn	198,922	123,230	438,105	439,677	59,880	10,156	6,306	4,739
Income Before Taxes	91,445	191,654	256,195	64,093	(880,624)	231,522	161,604	69,347
Income Taxes	142,868	72,464	95,484	39,007	(5,527)	83,432	59,945	11,939
Net Income	(47,644)	122,969	160,711	25,086	(875,097)	148,090	101,659	48,145
Average Shares	342,375	345,815	346,163	343,475	177,982	179,634	181,481	159,310
Balance Sheet								
Total Assets	8,340,162	8,524,226	8,366,947	9,165,758	9,503,945	2,059,689	1,141,216	856,406
Current Liabilities	499,982	520,797	583,026	1,260,748	404,825	56,225	35,289	23,045
Long-Term Obligations	44,526	43,978	43,444	101,879	887,270	866,205	135,977	128,888
Total Liabilities	1,331,571	1,381,384	1,461,071	2,339,357	2,450,617	949,999	184,737	161,787
Stockholders' Equity	7,008,591	7,142,842	6,905,876	6,826,401	7,053,328	1,109,690	956,479	694,619
Shares Outstanding	343,593	343,862	339,961	327,934	328,201	152,182	152,775	146,866
Statistical Record								
Return on Assets %	0.42	2.73	1.83	0.27	N.M.	9.25	10.18	8.25
Return on Equity %	0.51	3.45	2.34	0.36	N.M.	14.33	12.31	11.24
EBITDA Margin %	18.97	47.71	26.47	21.05	N.M.	55.42	50.41	39.18
Net Margin %	N.M.	20.12	6.63	1.13	N.M.	36.64	37.28	31.13
Asset Turnover	0.30	0.28	0.28	0.24	0.12	0.25	0.27	0.27
Current Ratio	2.90	3.06	2.78	1.53	4.54	17.39	19.84	27.39
Debt to Equity	0.01	0.01	0.01	0.01	0.13	0.78	0.14	0.19
Price Range	50.10-34.08	50.10-33.35	67.80-33.35	67.92-36.70	41.57-28.09	70.96-30.15	74.57-35.69	75.08-19.13
P/E Ratio	501.00-340.80	71.57-47.64	144.26-70.96	970.29-524.29	...	83.48-35.47	126.39-60.49	250.28-63.75

Address: 14 Cambridge Center, Cambridge, MA 02142 Telephone: 617-679-2000 Fax: 617-679-2617	Web Site: www.idecpharm.com Officers: William H. Rastetter Ph.D. - Chmn. James C. Mullen - Pres., C.E.O.	Auditors: PricewaterhouseCoopers LLP Transfer Agents: EquiServe Trust Company, Providence, RI

BIOMET, INC.

Exchange	Symbol	Price	52Wk Range	Yield	P/E
NMS	BMET	$32.71 (8/31/2006)	38.87-30.35	0.92	20.07

*7 Year Price Score 91.71   *NYSE Composite Index=100   *12 Month Price Score 89.89

Interim Earnings (Per Share)

Qtr.	Aug	Nov	Feb	May
2001-02	0.21	0.23	0.23	0.22
2002-03	0.25	0.27	0.28	0.30
2003-04	0.30	0.32	0.34	0.32
2004-05	0.24	0.36	0.38	0.41
2005-06	0.40	0.41	0.43	0.40

Interim Dividends (Per Share)

Amt	Decl	Ex	Rec	Pay
0.15A	7/2/2003	7/9/2003	7/11/2003	7/18/2003
0.20A	6/25/2004	7/14/2004	7/16/2004	7/23/2004
0.25A	6/30/2005	7/13/2005	7/15/2005	7/22/2005
0.30A	6/28/2006	7/12/2006	7/14/2006	7/21/2006

Indicated Div: $0.30

Valuation Analysis

Forecast P/E	15.34 (9/9/2006)
Market Cap	$8.0 Billion
Book Value	1.7 Billion
Price/Book	4.67
Price/Sales	3.96

Institutional Holding

No of Institutions	507
Shares	163,409,888
% Held	66.74

Business Summary: Medical Instruments & Equipment (MIC: 9.6 SIC: 3842 NAIC: 339113)
Biomet and its subsidiaries design, manufacture and market products used primarily by musculoskeletal medical specialists in both surgical and nonsurgical therapy. Co.'s product portfolio includes reconstructive and fixation devices, electrical bone growth stimulators, orthopedic support devices, operating room supplies, general surgical instruments, arthroscopy products, spinal products, bone cements and accessories, bone substitute materials, craniomaxillofacial implants and instruments, and dental reconstructive implants and associated instrumentation.

Recent Developments: For the year ended May 31 2006, net income increased 15.5% to $406.1 million from $351.6 million in the prior year. Revenues were $2.03 billion, up 7.8% from $1.88 billion the year before. Operating income was $608.3 million versus $546.9 million in the prior year, an increase of 11.2%. Direct operating expenses rose 9.2% to $582.1 million from $533.1 million in the comparable period the year before. Indirect operating expenses increased 4.4% to $835.3 million from $800.0 million in the equivalent prior-year period.

Prospects: Co.'s national branding campaign is contributing to the increase in its operating expenses. Nevertheless, Co. expects its investments towards the program should aid in reducing expenses associated with the campaign going forward. Meanwhile, Co. continues to experience robust growth in its orthopedic reconstructive devices, dental reconstructive implants and internal fixation devices. Also, Co. noted improvements in its electrical stimulation device sales as well as an accelerated growth in its spinal hardware and orthobiologic products for the spine. For the fourth quarter of fiscal 2006, Co. expects sales of $530.0 million to $540.0 million and earnings of $0.45 to $0.46 per share.

Financial Data
(US$ in Thousands)

	05/31/2006	05/31/2005	05/31/2004	05/31/2003	05/31/2002	05/31/2001	05/31/2000	05/31/1999
Earnings Per Share	1.63	1.38	1.27	1.10	0.88	0.73	0.65	0.46
Cash Flow Per Share	1.67	1.63	1.51	1.20	0.69	0.71	0.50	0.59
Tang Book Value Per Share	4.88	4.16	4.44	4.46	3.96	3.73	3.28	2.84
Dividends Per Share	0.250	0.200	0.150	0.100	0.090	0.071	0.062	0.053
Dividend Payout %	15.34	14.49	11.81	9.09	10.23	9.74	9.52	11.65
Income Statement								
Total Revenue	2,025,739	1,879,950	1,615,253	1,390,300	1,191,902	1,030,663	920,582	757,414
EBITDA	704,752	628,163	571,801	501,799	427,322	357,610	323,651	216,972
Depn & Amortn	82,177	69,602	59,468	45,659	47,827	42,824	39,766	29,512
Income Before Taxes	611,201	549,700	508,796	451,743	376,115	310,676	280,692	186,346
Income Taxes	205,057	198,084	176,098	156,961	127,665	105,906	99,738	62,527
Net Income	406,144	351,616	325,627	286,701	239,740	197,546	173,771	116,361
Average Shares	248,430	254,148	257,204	261,394	271,247	270,746	267,241	255,109
Balance Sheet								
Total Assets	2,263,922	2,096,577	1,787,697	1,672,169	1,521,723	1,489,311	1,218,448	1,067,956
Current Liabilities	520,432	501,391	313,402	266,654	237,699	241,822	181,443	201,430
Total Liabilities	547,423	532,646	339,487	274,147	241,437	248,028	187,252	211,319
Stockholders' Equity	1,716,499	1,563,931	1,448,210	1,286,134	1,176,479	1,146,186	943,323	775,947
Shares Outstanding	244,976	249,879	254,262	257,489	263,651	269,124	266,479	253,300
Statistical Record								
Return on Assets %	18.63	18.10	18.77	17.95	15.92	14.59	15.16	12.14
Return on Equity %	24.76	23.35	23.75	23.28	20.64	18.91	20.16	16.12
EBITDA Margin %	34.79	33.41	35.40	36.09	35.85	34.70	35.16	28.65
Net Margin %	20.05	18.70	20.16	20.62	20.11	19.17	18.88	15.36
Asset Turnover	0.93	0.97	0.93	0.87	0.79	0.76	0.80	0.79
Current Ratio	2.53	2.34	3.56	4.17	4.01	4.00	4.35	3.38
Price Range	38.91-32.89	49.41-35.33	41.30-27.51	33.50-22.76	33.66-25.29	30.39-15.19	19.75-11.14	20.03-11.94
P/E Ratio	23.87-20.18	35.80-25.60	32.52-21.66	30.45-20.69	38.25-28.74	41.63-20.81	30.38-17.14	43.54-25.97
Average Yield %	0.69	0.46	0.43	0.35	0.30	0.30	0.40	0.34

Address: 56 East Bell Drive, Warsaw, IN 46582 **Telephone:** 574-267-6639 **Fax:** 574-267-8137	**Web Site:** www.biomet.com **Officers:** Niles L. Noblitt - Chmn. Jerry L. Ferguson - Vice-Chmn.	**Auditors:** Ernst & Young LLP **Transfer Agents:** American Stock Transfer & Trust Company, New York, NY

BOB EVANS FARMS, INC.

Exchange	Symbol	Price	52Wk Range	Yield	P/E
NMS	BOBE	$28.34 (8/31/2006)	30.93-21.58	1.98	16.87

*7 Year Price Score 89.88   *NYSE Composite Index=100   *12 Month Price Score 101.90

Interim Earnings (Per Share)

Qtr.	Jul	Oct	Jan	Apr
2003-04	0.55	0.51	0.44	0.54
2004-05	0.40	0.30	0.19	0.16
2005-06	0.20	0.37	0.39	0.56
2006-07	0.36	...	...	...

Interim Dividends (Per Share)

Amt	Decl	Ex	Rec	Pay
0.12Q	11/8/2005	11/16/2005	11/18/2005	12/1/2005
0.12Q	2/10/2006	2/15/2006	2/17/2006	3/1/2006
0.12Q	5/8/2006	5/17/2006	5/19/2006	6/1/2006
0.14Q	8/14/2006	8/17/2006	8/21/2006	9/1/2006

Indicated Div: $0.56

Valuation Analysis

		Institutional Holding	
Forecast P/E	15.71	No of Institutions	
	(9/9/2006)	159	
Market Cap	$1.0 Billion	Shares	
Book Value	718.3 Million	27,604,808	
Price/Book	1.44	% Held	
Price/Sales	0.65	76.11	

Business Summary: Hospitality & Tourism (MIC: 5.1 SIC: 5812 NAIC: 722110)

Bob Evans Farms is a full-service restaurant company and a producer of pork sausage and complementary, homestyle, convenience food items. As of Apr 28 2006, Co. owned and operated 580 Bob Evans Restaurants and 7 Bob Evans Restaurants & General Stores located in 19 states and 102 Mimi's Cafés located in 17 states. Through two restaurant concepts, Co. serves a variety of breakfast, lunch and dinner items in family-friendly settings. In addition to restaurant operations, Co. offers a line of pork sausage, bacon and ham products and approximately 50 complementary, convenience food items through more than 18,700 grocery stores in 35 states.

Recent Developments: For the quarter ended July 28 2006, net income increased 82.8% to $13.1 million from $7.2 million in the year-earlier quarter. Revenues were $403.4 million, up 2.0% from $395.6 million the year before. Operating income was $22.0 million versus $14.0 million in the prior-year quarter, an increase of 57.0%. Direct operating expenses declined 3.5% to $114.6 million from $118.7 million in the comparable period the year before. Indirect operating expenses increased 1.5% to $266.8 million from $262.9 million in the equivalent prior-year period.

Prospects: In the near term, Co. intends to focus on improving same-store sales and profitability at Bob Evans Restaurants. Accordingly, Co. has recently introduced two product lines, three varieties each of its new Country Benedicts and its new Knife & Fork Sandwiches. These products should help drive stronger sales, particularly as Co. increases marketing support for its Knife & Fork Sandwiches. In addition, Co. is curtailing its investment in new Bob Evans Restaurant locations pending an improvement in projected returns, while continuing to invest in new Mimi's Cafes. As a result, for fiscal 2007 ending Apr 2007, Co. expects to open about 10 new Bob Evans Restaurants and 14 Mimi's Cafes.

Financial Data
(US$ in Thousands)

	3 Mos	04/28/2006	04/29/2005	04/30/2004	04/25/2003	04/26/2002	04/27/2001	04/28/2000
Earnings Per Share	1.68	1.52	1.04	2.03	2.10	1.91	1.44	1.38
Cash Flow Per Share	3.92	4.17	3.69	3.85	4.13	3.86	3.19	2.46
Tang Book Value Per Share	16.58	16.38	15.20	17.84	16.21	14.73	12.92	11.86
Dividends Per Share	0.480	0.480	0.480	0.470	0.430	0.380	0.360	0.360
Dividend Payout %	28.53	31.58	46.15	23.15	20.48	19.90	25.00	26.09
Income Statement								
Total Revenue	403,373	1,584,819	1,460,195	1,197,997	1,091,337	1,061,846	1,023,814	964,623
EBITDA	40,288	157,613	133,741	163,407	161,283	145,837	123,258	121,967
Depn & Amortn	18,302	72,256	66,835	50,106	44,150	41,974	39,772	36,480
Income Before Taxes	19,503	73,712	57,672	111,990	115,503	100,836	78,714	83,954
Income Taxes	6,417	18,938	20,704	39,955	40,426	33,154	27,943	31,061
Net Income	13,086	54,774	36,968	72,035	75,077	67,682	50,771	52,893
Average Shares	36,467	35,944	35,644	35,513	35,813	35,490	35,284	38,366
Balance Sheet								
Total Assets	1,209,264	1,209,183	1,183,986	868,233	784,591	721,973	678,715	624,441
Current Liabilities	175,532	159,485	188,628	145,847	141,549	130,496	158,125	175,721
Long-Term Obligations	175,333	206,333	210,333	24,333	28,333	32,333	36,000	431
Total Liabilities	491,000	504,727	531,155	238,070	223,672	200,608	221,620	195,651
Stockholders' Equity	718,264	704,456	652,831	630,163	560,919	521,365	457,095	428,790
Shares Outstanding	36,432	36,033	35,403	35,240	34,494	35,294	34,803	35,457
Statistical Record								
Return on Assets %	5.05	4.59	3.61	8.58	9.99	9.69	7.81	8.73
Return on Equity %	8.84	8.09	5.78	11.90	13.91	13.87	11.49	11.80
EBITDA Margin %	9.99	9.95	9.16	13.64	14.78	13.73	12.04	12.64
Net Margin %	3.24	3.46	2.53	6.01	6.88	6.37	4.96	5.48
Asset Turnover	1.33	1.33	1.43	1.43	1.45	1.52	1.58	1.59
Current Ratio	0.50	0.52	0.30	0.33	0.34	0.34	0.28	0.26
Debt to Equity	0.24	0.29	0.32	0.04	0.05	0.06	0.08	N.M.
Price Range	30.93-21.58	30.93-20.40	31.28-20.31	34.08-23.26	32.87-21.22	31.18-15.69	21.38-12.56	22.06-12.06
P/E Ratio	18.41-12.85	20.35-13.42	30.08-19.53	16.79-11.46	15.65-10.10	16.32-8.21	14.84-8.72	15.99-8.74
Average Yield %	1.83	1.93	1.90	1.59	1.68	1.70	2.05	2.14

Address: 3776 South High Street, Columbus, OH 43207
Telephone: 614-491-2225
Fax: 614-492-4949

Web Site: www.bobevans.com; www.mimiscafe.com
Officers: Robert E. H. Rabold - Chmn. Larry C. Corbin - Interim Pres., C.E.O.

Auditors: ERNST & YOUNG LLP
Investor Contact: 614-492-4920
Transfer Agents: Bob Evans Farms, Inc., Columbus, OH

BOK FINANCIAL CORP.

Exchange	Symbol	Price	52Wk Range	Yield	P/E
NMS	BOKF	$52.00 (8/31/2006)	53.32-43.58	1.15	16.72

*7 Year Price Score 115.77 *NYSE Composite Index=100 *12 Month Price Score 104.87

Interim Earnings (Per Share)

Qtr.	Mar	Jun	Sep	Dec
2003	0.69	0.62	0.58	0.52
2004	0.58	0.68	0.72	0.69
2005	0.78	0.75	0.76	0.72
2006	0.81	0.82	...	...

Interim Dividends (Per Share)

Amt	Decl	Ex	Rec	Pay
0.10Q	10/25/2005	11/9/2005	11/14/2005	11/30/2005
0.10Q	1/31/2006	2/9/2006	2/13/2006	2/28/2006
0.15Q	4/25/2006	5/10/2006	5/12/2006	5/31/2006
0.15Q	7/25/2006	8/10/2006	8/14/2006	8/31/2006

Indicated Div: $0.60

Valuation Analysis

		Institutional Holding	
Forecast P/E	15.42	No of Institutions	
	(9/9/2006)	102	
Market Cap	$3.5 Billion	Shares	11,687,996
Book Value	1.6 Billion	% Held	17.48
Price/Book	2.20		
Price/Sales	2.82		

Business Summary: Commercial Banking (MIC: 8.1 SIC: 6021 NAIC: 522110)

Bok Financial is a financial holding company whose primary focus is to provide a range of financial products and services, including loans and deposits, cash management services, fiduciary services, mortgage banking and brokerage and trading services to middle-market businesses, financial institutions and consumers. Commercial banking is a major part of the Co.'s business. Co. operates five principal lines of business: Oklahoma corporate banking, Oklahoma consumer banking, mortgage banking, wealth management and regional banking. As of Dec 31 2005, 43.0% of the revenues have come from commissions and fees.

Recent Developments: For the quarter ended June 30 2006, net income increased 9.0% to $55.0 million from $50.5 million in the year-earlier quarter. Net interest income increased 7.6% to $121.1 million from $112.5 million in the year-earlier quarter. Provision for loan losses was $3.8 million versus $2.0 million in the prior-year quarter, an increase of 88.3%. Non-interest income fell 3.9% to $90.9 million from $94.6 million, while non-interest expense declined 3.1% to $122.1 million.

Prospects: Co.'s is experiencing growth in net interest revenue, driven by solid loan growth. In addition, Co.'s net interest margins continues to improve modestly due to growth in earning assets and deposits, partially offset by asset spread compression. Separately, on Aug 11 2006, Co. announced that its subsidiary, Bank of Arizona, opened its East Valley Business Banking Office to service the growing business needs of the Tempe, Mesa, Chandler and Gilbert business markets. Bank of Arizona also announced plans to continue expanding in the Phoenix area by moving its business banking office to a new full-service branch. Co. expects the new 5,500 square-foot branch to be completed in 12 to 15 months.

Financial Data
(US$ in Thousands)

	6 Mos	3 Mos	12/31/2005	12/31/2004	12/31/2003	12/31/2002	12/31/2001	12/31/2000
Earnings Per Share	3.11	3.04	3.01	2.68	2.38	2.34	1.84	1.60
Cash Flow Per Share	2.99	3.05	3.29	4.35	4.81	4.38	5.05	3.32
Tang Book Value Per Share	18.70	18.47	18.32	18.68	15.77	14.69	10.63	8.73
Dividends Per Share	0.450	0.400	0.300	...	...	...	...	...
Dividend Payout %	14.47	13.16	9.97	...	...	...	...	...
Income Statement								
Interest Income	464,025	223,585	769,934	614,284	565,173	574,913	654,633	638,730
Interest Expense	225,593	106,259	320,593	191,041	175,144	206,712	327,859	369,843
Net Interest Income	238,432	117,326	449,341	423,243	390,029	368,201	326,774	268,887
Provision for Losses	7,195	3,400	12,441	20,439	35,636	33,730	37,610	17,204
Non-Interest Income	180,317	89,437	346,946	308,890	302,992	323,997	259,276	198,903
Non-Interest Expense	239,506	117,399	469,106	441,224	410,111	425,637	368,762	302,815
Income Before Taxes	172,048	85,984	314,740	270,470	247,274	232,831	179,678	147,771
Income Taxes	62,316	31,236	113,235	91,447	88,914	82,422	63,612	47,631
Net Income	109,732	54,748	201,505	179,023	158,360	150,409	116,302	100,140
Average Shares	67,317	67,260	67,047	66,732	66,509	64,329	63,309	62,565
Balance Sheet								
Net Loans & Leases	9,689,943	9,097,816	9,036,102	7,820,349	7,355,250	6,784,913	6,193,473	5,435,207
Total Assets	16,924,085	16,300,769	16,252,907	14,395,414	13,581,743	12,245,045	11,130,388	9,748,334
Total Deposits	11,306,785	11,308,246	11,375,318	9,674,398	9,219,863	8,128,525	6,905,744	6,046,005
Total Liabilities	15,341,075	14,735,334	14,713,753	12,996,920	12,353,113	11,151,488	10,301,905	9,044,758
Stockholders' Equity	1,583,010	1,565,435	1,539,154	1,398,494	1,228,630	1,093,557	828,483	703,576
Shares Outstanding	66,840	66,883	66,702	59,422	58,923	58,420	54,313	55,395
Statistical Record								
Return on Assets %	1.27	1.31	1.31	1.28	1.23	1.29	1.11	1.10
Return on Equity %	13.62	13.70	13.72	13.59	13.64	15.65	15.18	15.84
Net Interest Margin %	50.37	52.47	58.36	68.90	69.01	64.04	49.92	42.10
Efficiency Ratio %	36.86	37.50	42.00	47.79	47.24	47.35	40.35	36.15
Loans to Deposits	0.86	0.80	0.79	0.81	0.80	0.83	0.90	0.90
Price Range	49.75-43.58	49.31-40.26	49.31-39.79	49.18-37.29	39.83-29.22	34.42-25.76	29.97-18.94	18.88-13.60
P/E Ratio	16.00-14.01	16.22-13.24	16.38-13.22	18.35-13.91	16.73-12.28	14.71-11.01	16.29-10.29	11.80-8.50
Average Yield %	0.96	0.88	0.67	...	...	...	...	...

Address: Bank Of Oklahoma Tower, P.O. Box 2300, Tulsa, OK 74192
Telephone: 918-588-6000
Fax: 918-588-6300

Web Site: www.bokf.com
Officers: George B. Kaiser - Chmn. Stanley A. Lybarger - Pres., C.E.O.

Auditors: Ernst & Young, LLP
Investor Contact: 918-588-6717
Transfer Agents: SunTrust Bank

BROADCOM CORP.

Exchange	Symbol	Price	52Wk Range	Yield	P/E
NMS	BRCM	$29.39 (8/31/2006)	48.84-22.02	N/A	35.84

*7 Year Price Score 69.74   *NYSE Composite Index=100   *12 Month Price Score 74.20

Interim Earnings (Per Share)

Qtr.	Mar	Jun	Sep	Dec
2003	(0.17)	(2.05)	(0.01)	0.05
2004	0.08	0.12	0.09	0.14
2005	0.13	0.03	0.23	0.34
2006	0.22	...	...	...

Interim Dividends (Per Share)
No Dividends Paid

Valuation Analysis   **Institutional Holding**

Forecast P/E	21.34	No of Institutions	
	(9/9/2006)	465	
Market Cap	$16.0 Billion	Shares	
Book Value	3.7 Billion	386,422,848	
Price/Book	4.37	% Held	
Price/Sales	5.30	70.86	

Business Summary: IT & Technology (MIC: 10.2 SIC: 3674 NAIC: 334413)

Broadcom is a provider of wired and wireless broadband communications semiconductors. Co.'s products are designed to enable the convergence of high-speed data, high definition video, voice and audio at home, in the office and on the go. Co.'s portfolio includes products for digital cable, satellite and Internet Protocol set-top boxes; high definition television; cable and DSL modems and residential gateways; high-speed transmission and switching for local, metropolitan, wide area and storage networking; home and wireless networking; cellular and terrestrial wireless communications; VoIP and telephony systems; broadband network and security processors; and SystemI/ Otm server devices.

Recent Developments: For the quarter ended Mar 31 2006, net income increased 95.0% to $134.9 million from $69.2 million in the year-earlier quarter. Revenues were $900.6 million, up 63.7% from $550.3 million the year before. Operating income was $112.8 million versus $72.4 million in the prior-year quarter, an increase of 55.7%. Direct operating expenses rose 62.6% to $432.8 million from $266.1 million in the comparable period the year before. Indirect operating expenses increased 67.6% to $355.1 million from $211.8 million in the equivalent prior-year period.

Prospects: For second quarter 2006, Co. expects total net revenue to grow by about 3.0% to 5.0% over the prior quarter. However, gross margin may decline due to unfavorable factors including potential fluctuations in silicon wafer costs and assembly, competitive pricing programs, packaging and testing costs, and future changes in product mix. Going forward, Co. expects research and development cost to continue to increase due to the growth and diversification of the markets it serves, changes in its compensation policies, new product opportunities, and any expansion into new market technologies. Co. remains committed to extending its reach into the wired and wireless communications markets it operates.

Financial Data
(US$ in Thousands)

	3 Mos	12/31/2005	12/31/2004	12/31/2003	12/31/2002	12/31/2001	12/31/2000	12/31/1999
Earnings Per Share	0.82	0.73	0.42	(2.19)	(5.57)	(7.19)	(2.09)	0.24
Cash Flow Per Share	0.98	0.88	1.04	0.07	(0.17)	0.13	0.61	0.22
Tang Book Value Per Share	4.48	3.79	2.60	1.43	0.94	2.19	3.31	1.59
Income Statement								
Total Revenue	900,647	2,670,788	2,400,610	1,610,095	1,082,948	961,821	1,096,160	518,183
EBITDA	129,773	408,829	371,032	(850,618)	(1,804,037)	(1,932,809)	(526,777)	137,194
Depn & Amortn	15,252	68,527	91,690	90,948	147,128	888,987	164,998	17,872
Income Before Taxes	138,259	391,509	294,352	(934,738)	(1,938,982)	(2,798,777)	(691,775)	119,322
Income Taxes	3,373	(20,220)	75,607	25,127	297,594	(56,729)	(3,953)	36,035
Net Income	134,886	411,729	218,745	(959,865)	(2,236,576)	(2,742,048)	(687,822)	83,287
Average Shares	602,776	560,946	523,555	438,013	401,985	381,031	330,151	348,427
Balance Sheet								
Total Assets	4,323,482	3,752,199	2,885,839	2,017,622	2,216,153	3,623,298	4,677,822	585,309
Current Liabilities	646,285	594,622	497,100	503,576	534,017	411,882	202,562	86,062
Long-Term Obligations	...	...	...	...	1,212	4,006	...	548
Total Liabilities	655,312	606,760	519,853	527,817	571,632	415,888	202,562	86,610
Stockholders' Equity	3,668,170	3,145,439	2,365,986	1,489,805	1,644,521	3,207,410	4,475,260	498,699
Shares Outstanding	545,300	524,320	495,762	459,033	416,705	396,756	366,482	313,896
Statistical Record								
Return on Assets %	12.99	12.41	8.90	N.M.	N.M.	N.M.	N.M.	20.25
Return on Equity %	15.52	14.94	11.32	N.M.	N.M.	N.M.	N.M.	23.49
EBITDA Margin %	14.41	15.31	15.46	N.M.	N.M.	N.M.	N.M.	26.48
Net Margin %	14.98	15.42	9.11	N.M.	N.M.	N.M.	N.M.	16.07
Asset Turnover	0.82	0.80	0.98	0.76	0.37	0.23	0.42	1.26
Current Ratio	4.34	3.93	3.19	1.98	1.35	1.64	4.32	4.55
Price Range	48.84-18.32	33.00-18.32	31.07-17.01	24.88-8.23	34.29-6.47	88.96-12.51	182.42-51.67	91.67-16.69
P/E Ratio	59.56-22.34	45.21-25.10	73.97-40.51	...	...	...	...	... 381.94-69.53

Address: 16215 Alton Parkway, Irvine, CA 92618-3616
Telephone: 949-450-8700
Fax: 949-450-8710

Web Site: www.broadcom.com
Officers: Henry Samueli Ph.D - Chmn., Chief Tech. Officer Scott A. McGregor - Pres., C.E.O.

Auditors: Ernst & Young LLP
Investor Contact: 949-.92-6.5663
Transfer Agents: U.S.Stock Transfer Corporation

CABOT MICROELECTRONICS CORP

Exchange	Symbol	Price	52Wk Range	Yield	P/E
NMS	CCMP	$31.44 (8/31/2006)	38.25-25.84	N/A	23.29

*7 Year Price Score N/A   *NYSE Composite Index=100   *12 Month Price Score 92.49

Interim Earnings (Per Share)

Qtr.	Dec	Mar	Jun	Sep
2002-03	0.38	0.37	0.40	0.39
2003-04	0.46	0.39	0.49	0.53
2004-05	0.40	0.25	0.34	0.34
2005-06	0.39	0.22	0.40	...

Interim Dividends (Per Share)
No Dividends Paid

Valuation Analysis

Forecast P/E	21.38
	(9/9/2006)
Market Cap	$761.0 Million
Book Value	364.9 Million
Price/Book	2.09
Price/Sales	2.47

Institutional Holding

No of Institutions	161
Shares	29,081,296
% Held	N/A

Business Summary: Stone, Clay, Glass, and Concrete Products (MIC: 11.2 SIC: 3291 NAIC: 327910)

Cabot Microelectronics supplies high-performance polishing slurries used in the manufacture of integrated circuit (IC) devices, in a process called chemical mechanical planarization (CMP), which is used by IC device manufacturers to planarize or flatten many of the multiple layers of material that are built upon silicon wafers in the production of advanced ICs. This enables IC device manufacturers to produce smaller, faster and more complex IC devices with fewer defects. In addition, Co. produces CMP slurries for polishing certain components in hard disk drives, specifically rigid disk substrates and magnetic heads.

Recent Developments: For the quarter ended June 30 2006, net income increased 17.3% to $9.8 million from $8.3 million in the year-earlier quarter. Revenues were $84.9 million, up 30.6% from $65.0 million the year before. Operating income was $13.8 million versus $10.6 million in the prior-year period, an increase of 29.8%. Direct operating expenses rose 31.6% to $44.5 million from $33.8 million in the comparable period the year before. Indirect operating expenses increased 29.4% to $26.7 million from $20.6 million in the equivalent prior-year period.

Prospects: On June 15 2006, Co. announced that it has agreed to acquire most of the assets of QED Technologies, Inc. and certain related proprietary technology and intellectual property for between $19.0 million to $23.5 million, to boost its capabilities and expand into new markets under its Engineered Surface Finishes initiative. The purchase should be mildly dilutive to earnings per share over the next two years and accretive thereafter. Also, on Jul 5 2006, Co. announced that it has entered into a patent assignment agreement with International Business Machines Corp. (IBM) to acquire a number of IBM's patents and associated rights related to chemical mechanical planarization slurry technology.

Financial Data
(US$ in Thousands)

	9 Mos	6 Mos	3 Mos	09/30/2005	09/30/2004	09/30/2003	09/30/2002	09/30/2001
Earnings Per Share	1.35	1.29	1.32	1.32	1.88	1.53	1.66	1.72
Cash Flow Per Share	2.05	2.30	2.05	1.95	2.59	1.95	2.21	2.63
Tang Book Value Per Share	14.99	14.39	14.13	13.83	12.75	10.92	8.71	6.80
Income Statement								
Total Revenue	233,813	148,877	81,488	270,484	309,433	251,665	235,165	227,192
EBITDA	48,130	29,566	17,813	62,848	87,459	71,799	72,735	71,275
Depn & Amortn	14,996	9,800	4,832	19,072	17,611	15,732	12,012	7,787
Income Before Taxes	36,563	22,038	14,054	46,523	69,848	56,067	60,723	63,488
Income Taxes	11,773	7,030	4,483	14,050	23,120	18,334	20,038	21,586
Net Income	24,790	15,008	9,571	32,473	46,728	37,733	40,685	41,902
Average Shares	24,204	24,233	24,363	24,612	24,882	24,664	24,565	24,327
Balance Sheet								
Total Assets	403,016	387,496	392,709	386,763	363,291	315,617	258,385	196,681
Current Liabilities	31,355	28,258	36,422	35,622	32,375	28,916	30,571	26,366
Long-Term Obligations	4,680	4,937	5,188	5,436	6,385	7,452	12,365	3,500
Total Liabilities	38,132	37,010	47,382	47,679	47,669	43,844	44,879	30,394
Stockholders' Equity	364,884	350,486	345,327	339,084	315,622	271,773	213,506	166,287
Shares Outstanding	24,204	24,204	24,298	24,424	24,613	24,712	24,254	24,079
Statistical Record								
Return on Assets %	8.52	8.33	8.40	8.66	13.73	13.15	...	25.18
Return on Equity %	9.45	9.25	9.54	9.92	15.87	15.55	...	30.60
EBITDA Margin %	20.58	19.86	21.86	23.24	28.26	28.53	30.93	31.37
Net Margin %	10.60	10.08	11.75	12.01	15.10	14.99	17.30	18.44
Asset Turnover	0.79	0.76	0.74	0.72	0.91	0.88	...	1.37
Current Ratio	8.24	8.77	6.95	6.90	7.09	6.19	4.03	3.66
Debt to Equity	0.01	0.01	0.02	0.02	0.02	0.03	0.06	0.02
Price Range	38.25-25.84	37.14-27.39	40.07-27.39	40.80-27.39	61.61-26.86	67.00-33.25	86.54-34.75	99.38-36.63
P/E Ratio	28.33-19.14	28.79-21.23	30.36-20.75	30.91-20.75	32.77-14.29	43.79-21.73	52.13-20.93	57.78-21.29

Address: 870 North Commons Drive, Aurora, IL 60504
Telephone: 630-375-6631
Fax: 630-499-2666

Web Site: www.cabotcmp.com
Officers: William P. Noglows - Chmn., Pres., C.E.O.
William S. Johnson - V.P., C.F.O., Treas.

Auditors: PricewaterhouseCoopers LLP
Investor Contact: 630-499-2600
Transfer Agents: Fleet National Bank c/o EquiServe, LP, Providence, RI

CADENCE DESIGN SYSTEMS INC

Exchange	Symbol	Price	52Wk Range	Yield	P/E
NMS	CDNS	$16.44 (8/31/2006)	19.47-15.00	N/A	51.38

*7 Year Price Score 80.34 *NYSE Composite Index=100 *12 Month Price Score 92.20

Interim Earnings (Per Share)

Qtr.	Mar	Jun	Sep	Dec
2003	(0.07)	(0.03)	(0.06)	0.09
2004	(0.03)	0.01	0.07	0.20
2005	0.00	0.00	0.07	0.08
2006	0.07	0.10	...	...

Interim Dividends (Per Share)
No Dividends Paid

Valuation Analysis

		Institutional Holding	
Forecast P/E	15.71	No of Institutions	
	(9/9/2006)	254	
Market Cap	$4.6 Billion	Shares	
Book Value	1.9 Billion	259,833,392	
Price/Book	2.45	% Held	
Price/Sales	3.28	92.61	

Business Summary: IT & Technology (MIC: 10.2 SIC: 7372 NAIC: 511210)
Cadence Design Systems licenses electronic design automation (EDA) software, sells or leases EDA hardware technology and and intellectual property and provides design and methodology services throughout the world to help manage and accelerate electronic product development processes. Co.'s products and services are used by electronics companies to design and develop complex integrated circuits (ICs), IC packages and printed circuit boards, and commercial electronic systems. Co. combines its design technologies into "platforms" for four major design activities: functional verification, digital IC design, custom IC design and system interconnect.

Recent Developments: For the quarter ended July 1 2006, net income increased to $30.4 million from $483,000 in the year-earlier quarter. Revenues were $358.5 million, up 11.7% from $320.9 million the year before. Operating income was $42.3 million versus $186.0 million in the prior-year quarter, an increase of. Direct operating expenses declined 0.3% to $59.8 million from $60.0 million in the comparable period the year before. Indirect operating expenses decreased 1.7% to $256.4 million from $260.7 million in the equivalent prior-year period.

Prospects: Co.'s prospects appear encouraging, bolstered by recent solid top-line growth. Specifically, Co.'s results are benefiting from higher product revenue and maintenance revenue, due to an increase in revenue from licenses for its Functional Verification and Digital Integrated Circuits Design products. For the second quarter of fiscal 2006, Co. is expecting total revenue in the range of $350.0 million to $360.0 million, and earnings per diluted share in the range of $0.12 to $0.14. Concurrently, for fiscal 2006, Co. is targeting total revenue in the range of $1.43 billion to $1.48 billion, and earnings per diluted share in the range of $0.45 to $0.53.

Financial Data

(US$ in Thousands)	6 Mos	3 Mos	12/31/2005	01/01/2005	01/03/2004	12/28/2002	12/29/2001	12/30/2000
Earnings Per Share	0.32	0.22	0.16	0.25	(0.07)	0.27	0.55	0.19
Cash Flow Per Share	1.37	1.43	1.53	1.38	0.63	1.35	1.02	0.58
Tang Book Value Per Share	1.69	1.75	1.60	1.83	1.41	2.88	2.78	2.35
Income Statement								
Total Revenue	686,727	328,214	1,329,192	1,197,480	1,119,484	1,293,067	1,430,440	1,279,550
EBITDA	158,341	72,966	303,040	297,663	203,741	403,312	468,697	272,646
Depn & Amortn	79,544	40,942	184,717	210,613	232,732	242,543	230,434	206,810
Income Before Taxes	91,646	37,929	128,483	86,437	(30,565)	157,966	242,148	67,996
Income Taxes	39,857	16,568	79,140	11,963	(12,999)	86,017	100,861	18,019
Net Income	52,167	21,779	49,343	74,474	(17,566)	71,949	141,287	49,977
Average Shares	317,000	315,354	314,383	305,774	266,794	267,500	257,660	262,696
Balance Sheet								
Total Assets	3,404,102	3,381,830	3,401,312	2,989,839	2,817,902	2,438,261	1,730,030	1,477,321
Current Liabilities	609,235	555,799	605,851	548,958	481,928	511,890	472,391	491,574
Long-Term Obligations	474,000	511,000	548,000	420,000	420,061	52,659	1,476	3,298
Total Liabilities	1,521,126	1,494,159	1,556,608	1,289,869	1,245,621	778,956	608,683	567,856
Stockholders' Equity	1,882,976	1,887,671	1,844,704	1,699,970	1,572,281	1,659,305	1,121,347	909,465
Shares Outstanding	280,565	282,505	280,956	271,563	268,442	269,688	249,904	243,662
Statistical Record								
Return on Assets %	3.09	2.20	1.55	2.57	N.M.	3.46	8.83	3.41
Return on Equity %	5.47	3.86	2.79	4.56	N.M.	5.19	13.95	5.29
EBITDA Margin %	23.06	22.23	22.80	24.86	18.20	31.19	32.77	21.31
Net Margin %	7.60	6.64	3.71	6.22	N.M.	5.56	9.88	3.91
Asset Turnover	0.43	0.43	0.42	0.41	0.42	0.62	0.89	0.87
Current Ratio	2.07	2.25	2.11	1.95	1.75	1.48	1.34	1.13
Debt to Equity	0.25	0.27	0.30	0.25	0.27	0.03	N.M.	N.M.
Price Range	19.47-13.75	18.50-13.50	18.30-12.96	19.40-11.55	18.32-9.24	24.12-8.95	32.31-15.48	28.69-13.50
P/E Ratio	60.84-42.97	84.09-61.36	114.38-81.00	77.60-46.20	...	89.33-33.15	58.75-28.15	150.99-71.05

Address: 2655 Seely Avenue, Building 5, San Jose, CA 95134
Telephone: 408-943-1234
Fax: 408-943-0513

Web Site: www.cadence.com
Officers: Michael J. Fister - Pres., C.E.O., Dir. Kevin Bushby - Exec. V.P., Worldwide Field Opers.

Auditors: KPMG LLP
Investor Contact: 408-236-5972
Transfer Agents: Mellon Investor Services, South Hackensack, NJ

CALIFORNIA FIRST NATIONAL BANCORP

Exchange	Symbol	Price	52Wk Range	Yield	P/E
NMS	CFNB	$15.42 (8/31/2006)	16.00-12.25	2.85	17.33

*7 Year Price Score 92.43 *NYSE Composite Index=100 *12 Month Price Score 104.52

Interim Earnings (Per Share)

Qtr.	Sep	Dec	Mar	Jun
2002-03	0.27	0.26	0.21	0.23
2003-04	0.21	0.22	0.25	0.21
2004-05	0.14	0.18	0.17	0.23
2005-06	0.21	0.21	0.24	...

Interim Dividends (Per Share)

Amt	Decl	Ex	Rec	Pay
0.10Q	12/9/2005	12/21/2005	12/23/2005	1/6/2006
0.11Q	1/25/2006	3/22/2006	3/24/2006	4/7/2006
0.11Q	6/9/2006	6/21/2006	6/23/2006	7/7/2006
0.11Q	9/8/2006	9/20/2006	9/22/2006	10/6/2006

Indicated Div: $0.44

Valuation Analysis

Forecast P/E	N/A
Market Cap	$172.0 Million
Book Value	191.4 Million
Price/Book	0.90
Price/Sales	4.47

Institutional Holding

No of Institutions	18
Shares	1,567,906
% Held	14.05

Business Summary: Commercial Banking (MIC: 8.1 SIC: 6712 NAIC: 551111)

California First National Bancorp is a bank holding company with assets of $278.8 million and total deposits of $59.5 million as of June 30 2005. Through its subsidiaries, Co. provides banking and leasing services. Co. leases high-technology and other capital assets to customers located throughout the United States. Co. is also engaged in the re-marketing of leased assets at lease expiration. Co.'s banking subsidiary, California First National Bank gathers deposits using the telephone, the Internet, and direct mail from a centralized location and leases capital assets to businesses and organizations and provides business loans to fund the purchase of assets leased by third parties.

Recent Developments: For the quarter ended Mar 31 2006, net income increased 39.5% to $2.8 million from $2.0 million in the year-earlier quarter. Revenues were $10.0 million, up 14.5% from $8.7 million the year before.

Prospects: Co.'s near-term outlook appears encouraging. For instance, Co. is experiencing robust bottom-line growth, as a result of higher net direct finance and interest income after provision for lease losses together with a decrease in selling, general and administrative expenses. In addition, Co.'s results are benefiting from an increase in the average investment in capital leases held in its portfolio and a slight increase in average yields earned. Also, Co. is seeing an improvement in its interest income, driven by an increase in interest rates together with slightly higher average investment balances.

Financial Data
(US$ in Thousands)

	9 Mos	6 Mos	3 Mos	06/30/2005	06/30/2004	06/30/2003	06/30/2002	06/30/2001
Earnings Per Share	0.89	0.82	0.79	0.72	0.88	0.96	1.29	1.39
Cash Flow Per Share	(0.89)	1.31	1.24	0.85	0.07	1.34	2.40	...
Tang Book Value Per Share	17.16	17.08	16.96	16.84	18.47	18.04	17.12	15.97
Dividends Per Share	0.410	0.400	2.300	2.300	0.400	0.160	0.160	0.160
Dividend Payout %	46.07	48.78	291.14	319.44	45.45	16.67	12.40	11.51
Income Statement								
Total Revenue	28,437	18,722	9,634	34,537	35,800	35,892	44,284	65,736
Income Before Taxes	12,157	7,906	3,985	13,080	15,949	17,448	24,072	25,775
Income Taxes	4,711	3,063	1,544	4,905	6,140	6,717	9,268	9,923
Net Income	7,446	4,843	2,441	8,175	9,809	10,731	14,804	15,852
Average Shares	11,457	11,428	11,381	11,340	11,190	11,223	11,434	11,422
Balance Sheet								
Total Assets	300,893	285,399	277,520	278,819	274,545	278,691	308,641	336,666
Total Liabilities	109,524	95,612	89,075	91,883	70,696	81,414	117,250	157,413
Stockholders' Equity	191,369	189,787	188,445	186,936	203,849	197,277	191,391	179,253
Shares Outstanding	11,154	11,113	11,113	11,098	11,038	10,933	11,179	11,227
Statistical Record								
Return on Assets %	3.54	3.41	3.22	2.95	3.54	3.65	4.59	...
Return on Equity %	5.41	5.00	4.59	4.18	4.88	5.52	7.99	...
Price Range	14.46-9.95	13.99-9.95	14.96-9.95	14.96-9.95	14.88-9.49	17.03-8.20	16.08-10.55	14.50-5.63
P/E Ratio	16.25-11.18	17.06-12.13	18.94-12.59	20.78-13.82	16.91-10.78	17.74-8.54	12.47-8.18	10.43-4.05
Average Yield %	3.25	3.22	18.59	18.50	3.29	1.35	1.31	1.64

Address: 18201 Von Karman Avenue, Suite 800, Irvine, CA 92612 **Telephone:** 949-255-0500 **Fax:** 949-255-0501	**Web Site:** www.calfirstbancorp.com **Officers:** Patrick E. Paddon - Pres., C.E.O. Glen T. Tsuma - V.P., C.O.O., Treas.	**Auditors:** PricewaterhouseCoopers LLP **Investor Contact:** 714-436-6540 **Transfer Agents:** Mellon Investor Services LLC

CAPITAL CITY BANK GROUP, INC.

Exchange	Symbol	Price	52Wk Range	Yield	P/E	Div Acheiver
NMS	CCBG	$32.15 (8/31/2006)	39.30-29.91	2.02	18.91	12 Years

*7 Year Price Score 113.70 *NYSE Composite Index=100 *12 Month Price Score 90.15

Interim Earnings (Per Share)

Qtr.	Mar	Jun	Sep	Dec
2003	0.38	0.39	0.38	0.37
2004	0.30	0.38	0.66	0.41
2005	0.36	0.44	0.46	0.40
2006	0.40	0.44	...	...

Interim Dividends (Per Share)

Amt	Decl	Ex	Rec	Pay
0.163Q	11/22/2005	12/1/2005	12/5/2005	12/19/2005
0.163Q	2/23/2006	3/2/2006	3/6/2006	3/20/2006
0.163Q	5/25/2006	6/1/2006	6/5/2006	6/19/2006
0.163Q	8/24/2006	8/31/2006	9/5/2006	9/19/2006

Indicated Div: $0.65

Valuation Analysis
Forecast P/E 17.86 (9/9/2006)
Market Cap $595.8 Million
Book Value 311.7 Million
Price/Book 1.91
Price/Sales 2.84

Institutional Holding
No of Institutions 41
Shares 3,296,991
% Held 17.79

Business Summary: Commercial Banking (MIC: 8.1 SIC: 6022 NAIC: 522110)
Capital City Bank Group is a financial holding company. Through its bank subsidiaries, Co. provides a range of banking services including traditional deposit and credit services, asset management, trust, mortgage banking, bank cards, data processing, and securities brokerage services through 69 banking offices and four mortgage lending offices in Florida, Georgia and Alabama. Co. also provides data processing services to financial institutions, government agencies and commercial clients located throughout North Florida and South Georgia. As of Dec 31 2005, Co. had total assets of $2.63 billion and total deposits of $2.08 billion.

Recent Developments: For the quarter ended June 30 2006, net income increased 5.7% to $8.3 million from $7.9 million in the year-earlier quarter. Net interest income increased 11.3% to $30.2 million from $27.1 million in the year-earlier quarter. Provision for loan losses was $121,000 versus $388,000 in the prior-year quarter, a decrease of 68.8%. Non-interest income rose 16.3% to $14.0 million from $12.0 million, while non-interest expense advanced 16.8% to $31.1 million.

Prospects: Co. is experiencing favorable results in both its core and fee-based businesses. Particularly, Co.'s short duration asset portfolios are responding positively to rising interest rates, thus leading to net interest margin improvement. Also, Co. is benefiting from the higher interest rate environment and favorable pricing variances, as well as favorable credit quality. However, the lack of recent loan growth, coupled with higher non-interest expenses, tempers Co.'s near term outlook. Meanwhile, Co. stated that it continues to evaluate expansion opportunities. During the second half of 2006, Co. plans to open three new offices in existing markets.

Financial Data (US$ in Thousands)	6 Mos	3 Mos	12/31/2005	12/31/2004	12/31/2003	12/31/2002	12/31/2001	12/31/2000
Earnings Per Share	1.70	1.70	1.66	1.74	1.52	1.39	1.02	1.14
Cash Flow Per Share	2.60	2.68	2.42	2.62	2.29	2.30	2.02	1.68
Tang Book Value Per Share	11.03	10.83	10.48	9.97	10.70	9.55	8.39	7.93
Dividends Per Share	0.639	0.629	0.619	0.584	0.525	0.402	0.381	0.349
Dividend Payout %	37.62	37.00	37.26	33.49	34.53	28.92	37.42	30.62
Income Statement								
Interest Income	80,781	39,412	140,053	101,525	99,487	106,095	118,983	109,334
Interest Expense	21,464	10,282	30,063	15,441	14,839	22,503	48,249	46,234
Net Interest Income	59,317	29,130	109,990	86,084	84,648	83,592	70,734	63,100
Provision for Losses	788	667	2,507	2,141	3,436	3,297	3,983	3,120
Non-Interest Income	27,048	13,045	49,198	50,553	41,939	37,176	32,037	26,769
Non-Interest Expense	61,162	30,092	109,814	89,226	84,378	81,698	72,804	59,147
Income Before Taxes	24,415	11,416	46,867	45,270	38,773	35,773	25,984	27,602
Income Taxes	8,679	3,995	16,586	15,899	13,580	12,691	9,118	9,449
Net Income	15,736	7,421	30,281	29,371	25,193	23,082	16,866	18,153
Average Shares	18,652	18,665	18,281	16,810	16,563	16,592	16,615	15,960
Balance Sheet								
Net Loans & Leases	2,035,596	2,037,377	2,050,084	1,812,788	1,329,203	1,272,726	1,231,255	1,041,268
Total Assets	2,697,486	2,674,719	2,625,462	2,364,013	1,846,502	1,824,771	1,821,423	1,527,460
Total Deposits	2,153,859	2,109,156	2,079,346	1,894,886	1,474,205	1,434,200	1,550,101	1,268,367
Total Liabilities	2,385,742	2,363,656	2,319,686	2,107,213	1,643,693	1,638,240	1,649,640	1,379,853
Stockholders' Equity	311,744	311,063	305,776	256,800	202,809	186,531	171,783	147,607
Shares Outstanding	18,530	18,666	18,631	17,694	16,545	16,495	16,629	15,794
Statistical Record								
Return on Assets %	1.19	1.25	1.21	1.39	1.37	1.27	1.01	1.22
Return on Equity %	10.47	10.97	10.77	12.75	12.94	12.88	10.56	12.94
Net Interest Margin %	72.97	73.91	78.53	84.79	85.08	78.79	59.45	57.71
Efficiency Ratio %	56.11	57.37	58.03	58.67	59.66	57.02	48.21	43.46
Loans to Deposits	0.95	0.97	0.99	0.96	0.90	0.89	0.79	0.82
Price Range	39.30-29.91	39.30-28.17	39.30-28.17	36.79-27.59	37.24-21.80	25.27-14.72	16.64-12.76	16.28-11.04
P/E Ratio	23.12-17.59	23.12-16.57	23.67-16.97	21.14-15.86	24.50-14.34	18.18-10.59	16.31-12.51	14.28-9.68
Average Yield %	1.83	1.81	1.82	1.81	1.84	2.09	2.55	2.71

Address: 217 North Monroe Street, Tallahassee, FL 32301
Telephone: 850-671-0300
Fax: 850-224-3097
Web Site: www.mycapitalcitybank.com
Officers: William G. Smith Jr. - Chmn., Pres., C.E.O. J. Kimbrough Davis - Exec. V.P., C.F.O.
Auditors: KPMG LLP
Investor Contact: 850-671-0316

CAPITOL FEDERAL FINANCIAL

Exchange	Symbol	Price	52Wk Range	Yield	P/E
NMS	CFFN	$33.94 (8/31/2006)	34.88-31.63	5.89	48.49

*7 Year Price Score 104.13 *NYSE Composite Index=100 *12 Month Price Score 99.40

Interim Earnings (Per Share)

Qtr.	Dec	Mar	Jun	Sep
2002-03	0.40	0.17	0.11	0.04
2003-04	0.06	0.13	0.13	(1.80)
2004-05	0.25	0.24	0.22	0.18
2005-06	0.18	0.19	0.15	...

Interim Dividends (Per Share)

Amt	Decl	Ex	Rec	Pay
0.30Q	11/9/2005	11/16/2005	11/18/2005	12/2/2005
0.50Q	1/24/2006	2/1/2006	2/3/2006	2/17/2006
0.50Q	4/26/2006	5/3/2006	5/5/2006	5/19/2006
0.50Q	7/26/2006	8/2/2006	8/4/2006	8/18/2006

Indicated Div: $2.00

Valuation Analysis

		Institutional Holding	
Forecast P/E	51.42	No of Institutions	
	(9/9/2006)	77	
Market Cap	$2.5 Billion	Shares	5,312,881
Book Value	860.0 Million	% Held	7.17
Price/Book	2.92		
Price/Sales	5.85		

Business Summary: Other Depository Banking (MIC: 8.5 SIC: 6035 NAIC: 522120)

Capitol Federal Financial is a holding company. Through its subsidiary, Capitol Federal Savings Bank (the Bank), Co. provides retail banking services primarily the entire metropolitan areas of Topeka, Wichita, Lawrence, Manhattan, Emporia and Salina, Kansas and a portion of the metropolitan area of greater Kansas City. The Bank emphasizes mortgage lending, primarily originating and purchasing one-to four-family mortgage loans and providing personal retail financial services. As of Sept 30 2005, Co. had total assets of $8.41 billion and total deposits of $3.96 billion.

Recent Developments: For the quarter ended June 30 2006, net income decreased 30.0% to $11.3 million from $16.2 million in the year-earlier quarter. Net interest income decreased 20.6% to $30.8 million from $38.8 million in the year-earlier quarter. Non-interest income was unchanged at $6.1 million, while non-interest expense declined 3.2% to $18.2 million.

Prospects: Due to the continued narrowing of the spread in interest rates between terms to maturity, the treasury yield curve continued to flatten during the quarter ended Dec 31 2005, which has contributed to net interest margin compression. Co. noted that if interest rates on treasury securities with terms to maturity of less than or equal to two years continue to rise through the first half of 2006, and interest rates for terms longer than two years do not rise significantly, it will result in a reduced net interest margin in fiscal year 2006 versus fiscal year 2005. This is due to Co.'s interest-bearing liabilities resetting to current market rates faster than its interest-earning assets.

Financial Data
(US$ in Thousands)

	9 Mos	6 Mos	3 Mos	09/30/2005	09/30/2004	09/30/2003	09/30/2002	09/30/2001
Earnings Per Share	0.70	0.77	0.82	0.89	(1.48)	0.72	1.22	0.99
Cash Flow Per Share	1.20	1.23	1.40	1.44	1.32	3.25	(0.34)	1.24
Tang Book Value Per Share	11.61	11.62	11.61	11.61	11.21	13.24	13.39	13.04
Dividends Per Share	2.300	2.800	2.800	2.500	2.810	2.120	0.740	0.570
Dividend Payout %	328.57	363.64	341.46	280.90	...	294.44	60.66	57.58
Income Statement								
Interest Income	306,245	203,818	101,860	400,107	384,833	441,536	557,132	580,740
Interest Expense	207,810	136,147	68,004	244,201	268,642	326,848	370,743	410,458
Net Interest Income	98,435	67,671	33,856	155,906	116,191	114,688	186,389	170,282
Provision for Losses	170	130	268	215	64	...	184	75
Non-Interest Income	17,941	11,872	5,850	23,348	23,585	43,162	29,444	16,337
Non-Interest Expense	53,717	35,543	17,600	73,664	309,038	72,560	68,613	63,193
Income Before Taxes	62,489	43,870	21,838	105,375	(169,326)	85,290	147,036	123,351
Income Taxes	24,283	16,970	8,525	40,316	(63,051)	33,259	57,444	45,572
Net Income	38,206	26,900	13,313	65,059	(106,275)	52,031	89,592	77,779
Average Shares	72,753	72,922	72,971	73,081	71,599	72,392	73,579	78,943
Balance Sheet								
Net Loans & Leases	5,564,502	5,522,825	5,565,077	5,464,130	4,747,228	4,307,440	4,867,569	5,416,507
Total Assets	8,117,173	8,252,195	8,318,836	8,409,687	8,541,036	8,582,544	8,781,127	8,635,443
Total Deposits	3,895,869	4,015,128	3,937,237	3,960,297	4,127,472	4,237,889	4,391,874	4,285,835
Total Liabilities	7,257,141	7,390,382	7,456,598	7,544,624	7,708,622	7,606,099	7,793,697	7,587,181
Stockholders' Equity	860,032	861,813	862,238	865,063	832,414	976,445	987,430	1,048,262
Shares Outstanding	74,059	74,143	74,236	74,286	73,990	73,309	73,553	80,409
Statistical Record								
Return on Assets %	0.62	0.67	0.71	0.77	N.M.	0.60	1.03	0.92
Return on Equity %	5.92	6.50	7.00	7.67	N.M.	5.30	8.80	7.65
Net Interest Margin %	30.04	33.17	33.24	38.97	30.19	25.97	33.46	29.32
Efficiency Ratio %	16.75	16.62	16.34	17.40	75.67	14.97	11.70	10.58
Loans to Deposits	1.43	1.38	1.41	1.38	1.15	1.02	1.11	1.26
Price Range	36.50-31.63	36.50-31.63	37.16-32.84	37.16-32.18	39.19-29.31	32.04-20.37	27.91-19.30	19.74-13.75
P/E Ratio	52.14-45.19	47.40-41.08	45.32-40.05	41.75-36.16	...	44.50-28.29	22.88-15.82	19.94-13.89
Average Yield %	6.85	8.28	8.10	7.21	8.35	7.35	3.16	3.42

Address: 700 Kansas Avenue, Topeka, KS 66603 **Telephone:** 785-235-1341	**Web Site:** www.capfed.com **Officers:** John C. Dicus - Chmn. John B. Dicus - Pres., C.E.O.	**Auditors:** Deloitte & Touche LLP **Investor Contact:** 785-270-6055 **Transfer Agents:** American Stock Transfer & Trust Company, New York, NY

CAREER EDUCATION CORP

Exchange	Symbol	Price	52Wk Range	Yield	P/E
NMS	CECO	$19.15 (8/31/2006)	41.70-17.80	N/A	15.20

*7 Year Price Score 103.57 *NYSE Composite Index=100 *12 Month Price Score 75.69

Interim Earnings (Per Share)

Qtr.	Mar	Jun	Sep	Dec
2003	0.20	0.20	0.26	0.53
2004	0.40	0.38	0.41	0.53
2005	0.53	0.50	0.53	0.69
2006	0.53	(0.49)	...	...

Interim Dividends (Per Share)

Amt	Decl	Ex	Rec	Pay
2-for-1	9/17/2001	10/1/2001	9/17/2001	9/28/2001
100%	7/22/2003	8/25/2003	8/5/2003	8/22/2003

Valuation Analysis   **Institutional Holding**

Forecast P/E	11.64	No of Institutions
(9/9/2006)	235	
Market Cap	$1.8 Billion	Shares
Book Value	934.5 Million	98,323,184
Price/Book	1.94	% Held
Price/Sales	0.89	94.71

Business Summary: Schools and Universities (MIC: 6.1 SIC: 8221 NAIC: 611310)
Career Education is a provider of private, for-profit, postsecondary education. As of Dec 31 2005, Co. had 86 campuses, including two online campuses, located throughout the U.S. and in France, Canada, and the U.K. Co.'s College, Schools and Universities (CSU) segment represents an aggregation of its on-ground schools that provide educational services primarily in a classroom or laboratory setting. Co.'s Online Education Group (OEG) segment represents an aggregation of the online campuses of American InterContinental University, American InterContinental University Online, as well as Colorado Technical University, Colorado Technical University Online and Stonecliffe College Online.

Recent Developments: For the quarter ended June 30 2006, loss from continuing operations was $47.5 million compared with income of $52.8 million in the year-earlier quarter. Net loss amounted to $47.5 million versus net income of $52.8 million in the year-earlier quarter. Revenues were $486.8 million, down 2.1% from $497.5 million the year before. Operating loss was $33.8 million versus an income of $81.8 million in the prior-year quarter. Direct operating expenses rose 2.0% to $156.5 million from $153.5 million in the comparable period the year before. Indirect operating expenses increased 38.8% to $364.1 million from $262.2 million in the equivalent year-earlier period.

Prospects: Co.'s near-term outlook appears constructive as it continues to concentrate on its short-term strategic initiatives designed to stabilize its business and its schools' student populations, as well as establish a sound platform for sustainable long-term growth. The initiatives include Co.'s continuing focus to identify strategies to improve student lead management, enrollment rates, and show rates such as pre-orientation programs that have been implemented at a majority of its schools to prepare students and reinforce their enrollment decision, strategies to improve admissions representative quality and performance, and an increased focus on marketing its programs to local markets.

Financial Data (US$ in Thousands)	6 Mos	3 Mos	12/31/2005	12/31/2004	12/31/2003	12/31/2002	12/31/2001	12/31/2000
Earnings Per Share	1.26	2.25	2.26	1.71	1.19	0.71	0.42	0.28
Cash Flow Per Share	3.37	3.96	3.75	3.69	2.42	1.17	0.59	0.34
Tang Book Value Per Share	5.80	6.18	5.68	4.88	2.70	2.10	1.14	1.32
Income Statement								
Total Revenue	1,015,415	528,630	2,034,555	1,728,532	1,188,609	751,008	529,240	325,293
EBITDA	89,821	101,248	451,877	353,335	244,462	149,282	101,314	59,974
Depn & Amortn	42,951	21,009	78,720	57,816	44,177	33,636	30,818	20,594
Income Before Taxes	55,160	84,185	383,283	295,669	199,444	114,360	69,737	39,506
Income Taxes	49,970	31,486	143,347	116,050	80,276	46,888	31,382	17,322
Net Income	5,190	52,699	233,878	179,619	119,168	67,472	38,355	21,406
Average Shares	96,989	100,220	103,383	105,004	100,522	95,094	90,780	77,560
Balance Sheet								
Total Assets	1,360,705	1,562,537	1,506,105	1,387,012	1,119,150	586,136	490,789	280,699
Current Liabilities	275,290	340,933	326,754	320,656	306,621	160,208	120,373	56,914
Long-Term Obligations	17,499	16,673	16,358	21,591	25,453	2,686	45,553	14,626
Total Liabilities	426,216	490,436	469,858	402,181	371,330	180,439	184,384	79,806
Stockholders' Equity	934,489	1,072,101	1,036,247	984,831	747,820	405,697	306,405	200,893
Shares Outstanding	94,695	97,571	98,112	102,537	100,194	92,059	89,395	81,294
Statistical Record								
Return on Assets %	9.10	15.29	16.17	14.30	13.98	12.53	9.94	8.69
Return on Equity %	12.82	21.82	23.14	20.68	20.66	18.95	15.12	13.57
EBITDA Margin %	8.85	19.15	22.21	20.44	20.57	19.88	19.14	18.44
Net Margin %	0.51	9.97	11.50	10.39	10.03	8.98	7.25	6.58
Asset Turnover	1.43	1.36	1.41	1.38	1.39	1.39	1.37	1.32
Current Ratio	1.93	1.91	1.77	1.60	1.10	0.93	1.08	1.52
Debt to Equity	0.02	0.02	0.02	0.02	0.03	0.01	0.15	0.07
Price Range	41.70-29.57	41.11-29.02	42.05-29.02	70.66-26.75	55.11-19.08	26.20-15.10	18.05-7.95	11.13-3.50
P/E Ratio	33.10-23.47	18.27-12.90	18.61-12.84	41.32-15.64	46.31-16.03	36.89-21.27	42.98-18.94	39.73-12.50

Address: 2895 Greenspoint Parkway, Suite 600, Hoffman Estates, IL 60195
Telephone: 847-781-3600
Fax: 847-781-3610

Web Site: www.careered.com
Officers: John M. Larson - Chmn., Pres., C.E.O. Patrick K. Pesch - Exec. V.P., C.F.O., Treas.

Auditors: ERNST & YOUNG LLP
Investor Contact: 847-585-3899

CBRL GROUP INC

Exchange	Symbol	Price	52Wk Range	Yield	P/E
NMS	CBRL	$37.84 (8/31/2006)	47.00-32.41	1.37	16.24

*7 Year Price Score 105.08 *NYSE Composite Index=100 *12 Month Price Score 88.08

Interim Earnings (Per Share)

Qtr.	Oct	Jan	Apr	Jul
2002-03	0.45	0.48	0.46	0.70
2003-04	0.56	0.57	0.52	0.60
2004-05	0.61	0.63	0.52	0.73
2005-06	0.51	0.61	0.47	...

Interim Dividends (Per Share)

Amt	Decl	Ex	Rec	Pay
0.13Q	9/22/2005	10/12/2005	10/14/2005	11/8/2005
0.13Q	11/22/2005	1/11/2006	1/13/2006	2/8/2006
0.13Q	3/17/2006	4/11/2006	4/14/2006	5/8/2006
0.13Q	5/25/2006	7/12/2006	7/14/2006	8/8/2006

Indicated Div: $0.52

Valuation Analysis

Forecast P/E	15.17 (9/9/2006)
Market Cap	$1.8 Billion
Book Value	270.9 Million
Price/Book	6.66
Price/Sales	0.68

Institutional Holding

No of Institutions	209
Shares	41,668,336
% Held	N/A

Business Summary: Hospitality & Tourism (MIC: 5.1 SIC: 5812 NAIC: 722110)

CBRL Group is a holding company. Through its subsidiaries, Co. is engaged in the operation and development of the Cracker Barrel Old Country Store® ("Cracker Barrel") and Logan's Roadhouse® ("Logan's") restaurant and retail concepts. Cracker Barrel stores are intended to appeal to both the traveler and the local customer. Logan's restaurants feature steaks, seafood, ribs and chicken dishes among other items served in a distinctive atmosphere. As or Sept 23, 2005, Cracker Barrel, operated 534 full-service "country store" restaurants and gift shops, in 41 states; and Logan's Roadhouse, Inc. operated 127 Logan's restaurants in 16 states.

Recent Developments: For the quarter ended Apr 28 2006, net income decreased 9.8% to $24.0 million from $26.6 million in the year-earlier quarter. Revenues were $644.2 million, up 2.6% from $628.0 million the year before. Operating income was $38.8 million versus $42.8 million in the prior-year quarter, a decrease of 9.4%. Direct operating expenses declined 0.9% to $201.8 million from $203.7 million in the comparable period the year before. Indirect operating expenses increased 5.8% to $403.6 million from $381.5 million in the equivalent prior-year period.

Prospects: Co.'s outlook remains clouded by lackluster comparable store restaurant sales trends, as well as uncertain consumer sentiment owing to pressures from winter heating costs and rising interest rates. Thus, Co. estimates that its fiscal second quarter ended Jan 27 2006 and full fiscal year 2006 total revenues could grow between 3.0% and 6.0% above last year. Looking ahead to full fiscal year 2006, Co. estimates net income could range from $2.30 to $2.45 per diluted share, including the effect of stock options expense. For the full year of fiscal 2006, Co. anticipates opening 20 new Cracker Barrel stores, 20 to 22 new Logan's company-owned units, and two new Logan's franchised units.

Financial Data
(US$ in Thousands)

	9 Mos	6 Mos	3 Mos	07/29/2005	07/30/2004	08/01/2003	08/02/2002	08/03/2001
Earnings Per Share	2.33	2.38	2.40	2.45	2.25	2.09	1.64	0.87
Cash Flow Per Share	3.70	4.74	5.58	5.87	4.11	4.90	3.54	2.59
Tang Book Value Per Share	3.72	17.89	17.17	16.65	16.14	14.66	13.73	13.69
Dividends Per Share	0.510	0.500	0.490	0.590	0.330	0.020	0.020	0.020
Dividend Payout %	21.93	21.04	20.44	24.08	14.67	0.96	1.22	2.30
Income Statement								
Total Revenue	1,971,913	1,327,713	633,357	2,567,548	2,380,947	2,198,182	2,066,892	1,963,692
EBITDA	183,052	125,609	59,015	269,483	249,004	238,457	212,059	161,598
Depn & Amortn	53,512	34,878	17,186	67,321	63,868	64,376	62,759	64,902
Income Before Taxes	122,142	86,027	39,331	193,565	176,697	165,262	142,531	84,464
Income Taxes	41,651	29,508	13,609	66,925	63,435	58,733	50,742	35,283
Net Income	80,491	56,519	25,722	126,640	113,262	106,529	91,789	49,181
Average Shares	52,523	51,843	51,836	53,382	50,369	50,998	56,090	56,799
Balance Sheet								
Total Assets	1,586,307	1,565,607	1,583,937	1,533,272	1,434,862	1,326,323	1,263,737	1,212,872
Current Liabilities	252,819	257,549	292,602	295,345	246,782	246,714	233,075	197,249
Long-Term Obligations	194,998	208,563	236,140	212,218	185,138	186,730	194,476	125,000
Total Liabilities	1,315,359	627,889	687,830	663,284	554,615	531,427	480,743	366,764
Stockholders' Equity	270,948	937,718	896,107	869,988	880,247	794,896	782,994	846,108
Shares Outstanding	47,661	47,165	46,726	46,619	48,769	47,872	50,272	55,026
Statistical Record								
Return on Assets %	7.68	7.99	8.01	8.56	8.23	8.25	7.43	3.80
Return on Equity %	21.12	13.42	13.84	14.51	13.56	13.54	11.30	5.78
EBITDA Margin %	9.28	9.46	9.32	10.50	10.46	10.85	10.26	8.23
Net Margin %	4.08	4.26	4.06	4.93	4.76	4.85	4.44	2.50
Asset Turnover	1.71	1.73	1.69	1.73	1.73	1.70	1.67	1.52
Current Ratio	0.76	0.73	0.76	0.64	0.82	0.71	0.74	0.79
Debt to Equity	0.72	0.22	0.26	0.24	0.21	0.23	0.25	0.15
Price Range	47.00-33.25	44.36-33.25	44.10-33.25	44.10-30.21	41.63-30.78	39.80-20.52	33.76-18.70	24.13-12.06
P/E Ratio	20.17-14.27	18.64-13.97	18.38-13.85	18.00-12.33	18.50-13.68	19.04-9.82	20.59-11.40	27.73-13.86
Average Yield %	1.31	1.30	1.24	1.52	0.90	0.07	0.07	0.11

Address: 305 Hartmann Drive, P.O. Box 787, Lebanon, TN 37088-0787 **Telephone:** 615-443-9869 **Fax:** 615-443-6780	**Web Site:** www.cbrlgroup.com **Officers:** Michael A. Woodhouse - Chmn., Pres., C.E.O. Lawrence E. White - Sr. V.P., Fin., C.F.O.	**Auditors:** Deloitte & Touche LLP **Transfer Agents:** SunTrust Bank, Atlanta, Ga

CELGENE CORP.

Exchange	Symbol	Price	52Wk Range	Yield	P/E
NMS	CELG	$40.69 (8/31/2006)	48.91-22.95	N/A	452.11

*7 Year Price Score 213.92 *NYSE Composite Index=100 *12 Month Price Score 120.74

Interim Earnings (Per Share)

Qtr.	Mar	Jun	Sep	Dec
2003	0.00	0.01	0.01	0.01
2004	0.03	0.04	0.06	0.04
2005	0.13	0.03	0.00	0.01
2006	0.04	0.03	...	...

Interim Dividends (Per Share)

Amt	Decl	Ex	Rec	Pay
100%	9/9/2004	10/25/2004	10/15/2004	10/22/2004
100%	12/27/2005	2/27/2006	2/17/2006	2/24/2006

Valuation Analysis　　**Institutional Holding**

Forecast P/E	87.55	No of Institutions
	(9/9/2006)	346
Market Cap	$14.3 Billion	Shares
Book Value	745.6 Million	284,952,512
Price/Book	19.12	% Held
Price/Sales	21.67	81.24

Business Summary: Biotechnology (MIC: 9.2 SIC: 8731 NAIC: 541710)

Celgene is an integrated biopharmaceutical company which is engaged primarily in the discovery, development and commercialization of therapies designed to treat cancer and inflammatory diseases through gene and protein regulation. Co.'s commercial stage programs include pharmaceutical sales of THALOMID® and ALKERAN®, a licensing agreement with Novartis Pharma AG for Focalin® and the Ritalin® family of drugs, which are used in the treatment of attention deficit disorder/attention deficit hyperactivity disorder. Co.'s wholly owned subsidiary, Celgene Cellular Therapeutics, is engaged in the development of stem cell therapies and biomaterials derived from human placental tissue.

Recent Developments: For the quarter ended June 30 2006, net income decreased 11.4% to $9.6 million from $10.8 million in the year-earlier quarter. Revenues were $197.2 million, up 35.4% from $145.7 million the year before. Operating income was $30.6 million versus $37.1 million in the prior-year quarter, a decrease of 17.6%. Direct operating expenses rose 47.3% to $26.8 million from $18.2 million in the comparable period the year before. Indirect operating expenses increased 54.7% to $139.8 million from $90.4 million in the equivalent prior-year period.

Prospects: On June 29 2006, the U.S. Food and Drug Administration granted approval for Co.'s Supplemental New Drug Application for REVLIMID in combination with dexamethasone as an additional indication for the treatment of patients with multiple myeloma who have received at least one prior therapy. Going forward, Co. will strive to maximize REVLIMID's full commercial and clinical potential. Meanwhile, Co. has increased reseach and development investments in multiple Phase II and Phase III programs evaluating REVLIMID across a broad range of hematological cancers with unmet medical needs including: multiple myeloma, myelodysplastic syndromes, chronic lymphocyte leukemia and non-Hodgkin's lymphoma.

Financial Data
(US$ in Thousands)

	6 Mos	3 Mos	12/31/2005	12/31/2004	12/31/2003	12/31/2002	12/31/2001	12/31/2000
Earnings Per Share	0.09	0.09	0.18	0.16	0.04	(0.32)	(0.01)	(0.06)
Cash Flow Per Share	(0.05)	0.18	0.12	0.47	0.06	(0.12)	(0.01)	(0.01)
Tang Book Value Per Share	1.75	1.70	1.48	0.97	0.92	0.84	1.03	1.00
Income Statement								
Total Revenue	379,080	181,841	536,941	377,502	271,475	135,746	114,243	84,250
EBITDA	83,995	39,310	112,254	87,048	29,970	(95,521)	1,274	(12,035)
Depn & Amortn	11,861	5,879	18,545	14,326	10,824	5,549	5,327	4,697
Income Before Taxes	67,409	31,066	84,212	63,171	13,479	(101,097)	(4,136)	(18,813)
Income Taxes	41,777	15,042	20,556	10,415	718	(98)	(1,230)	(1,808)
Net Income	25,632	16,024	63,656	52,756	13,511	(100,000)	(1,912)	(16,284)
Average Shares	370,360	400,699	390,585	345,710	341,592	309,348	300,432	266,392
Balance Sheet								
Total Assets	1,372,683	1,319,786	1,246,637	1,107,293	791,336	327,287	353,982	346,726
Current Liabilities	145,913	123,562	135,637	141,415	71,794	44,286	29,968	33,783
Long-Term Obligations	399,967	399,975	399,984	400,004	400,016	40	11,760	12,347
Total Liabilities	627,052	601,202	610,862	629,849	481,282	50,589	43,557	51,193
Stockholders' Equity	745,631	718,584	635,775	477,444	310,054	276,698	310,425	295,533
Shares Outstanding	350,361	346,363	342,171	330,137	325,644	320,706	302,299	295,999
Statistical Record								
Return on Assets %	2.39	2.57	5.41	5.54	2.42	N.M.	N.M.	N.M.
Return on Equity %	4.63	5.02	11.44	13.36	4.61	N.M.	N.M.	N.M.
EBITDA Margin %	22.16	21.62	20.91	23.06	11.04	N.M.	1.12	N.M.
Net Margin %	6.76	8.81	11.86	13.98	4.98	N.M.	N.M.	N.M.
Asset Turnover	0.52	0.50	0.46	0.40	0.49	0.40	0.33	0.44
Current Ratio	7.39	8.42	7.17	6.01	10.17	6.69	11.23	9.83
Debt to Equity	0.54	0.56	0.63	0.84	1.29	N.M.	0.04	0.04
Price Range	47.43-20.11	44.22-16.85	32.42-12.59	16.05-9.80	11.91-5.25	7.98-2.88	9.57-3.80	18.69-4.73
P/E Ratio	527.00-223.44	491.33-187.22	180.14-69.92	100.28-61.27	297.75-131.19	...	...	...

Address: 86 Morris Avenue, Summit, NJ 07901　Telephone: 732-271-1001	Web Site: www.celgene.com　Officers: John W. Jackson - Chmn., C.E.O. Sol J. Barer Ph.D. - Pres., C.O.O.	Auditors: KPMG LLP

C D W CORP

Exchange	Symbol	Price	52Wk Range	Yield	P/E
NMS	CDWC	$58.30 (8/31/2006)	61.46-50.57	0.89	17.15

*7 Year Price Score 89.26   *NYSE Composite Index=100   *12 Month Price Score 95.98

Interim Earnings (Per Share)
Qtr.	Mar	Jun	Sep	Dec
2003	0.49	0.51	0.52	0.51
2004	0.63	0.67	0.76	0.73
2005	0.72	0.80	0.88	0.86
2006	0.75	0.91	...	...

Interim Dividends (Per Share)
Amt	Decl	Ex	Rec	Pay
0.30A	7/23/2003	9/10/2003	9/12/2003	9/26/2003
0.36A	5/20/2004	6/14/2004	6/16/2004	6/30/2004
0.43A	5/11/2005	6/14/2005	6/16/2005	6/30/2005
0.52A	5/17/2006	6/14/2006	6/16/2006	6/30/2006

Indicated Div: $0.52

Valuation Analysis
Forecast P/E	N/A
Market Cap	$4.6 Billion
Book Value	1.2 Billion
Price/Book	3.73
Price/Sales	0.70

Institutional Holding
No of Institutions	253
Shares	62,593,544
% Held	80.32

Business Summary: Retail - Miscellaneous (MIC: 5.11 SIC: 5961 NAIC: 454111)
CDW is a direct marketer of multi-brand information technology products and services in the U.S. Co.'s offering includes hardware and peripherals, software, accessories and other products. Co. offers customers a range of technology products from brands including Adobe, APC, Apple, Cisco, Hewlett-Packard, IBM, Lenovo, Microsoft, Sony, Symantec, Toshiba and ViewSonic, among others. Co. also provides value-added services and web-based tools to its customers, including the ability to custom configure multi-branded solutions, manage software licenses through Co.'s Software License Tracker tool, track tagged assets through its IT Asset Management Tracking Database and generate online quotes.

Recent Developments: For the quarter ended June 30 2006, net income increased 9.0% to $73.1 million from $67.1 million in the year-earlier quarter. Revenues were $1.63 billion, up 6.1% from $1.54 billion the year before. Operating income was $107.8 million versus $102.5 million in the prior-year quarter, an increase of 5.2%. Direct operating expenses rose 5.2% to $1.37 billion from $1.30 billion in the comparable period the year before. Indirect operating expenses increased 15.7% to $156.2 million from $135.0 million in the equivalent prior-year period.

Prospects: Results are benefiting from strong sales growth from both of its corporate sector and public sector businesses. In addition, Co. is seeing an increase in its gross profit margin due primarily to higher net service contract and commission revenue, a climb in the level of vendor incentives, and a favorable comparison of delivery charges due to more limited delivery promotions. However, Co.'s selling and administrative expenses are increasing due primarily to high payroll costs as a result of the continuing investment in its sales force, increases in administrative areas to support a larger and growing business as well as growth in sales commission expense.

Financial Data
(US$ in Thousands)

	6 Mos	3 Mos	12/31/2005	12/31/2004	12/31/2003	12/31/2002	12/31/2001	12/31/2000
Earnings Per Share	3.40	3.29	3.26	2.79	2.03	2.10	1.89	1.79
Cash Flow Per Share	3.24	2.88	3.74	2.20	1.51	2.73	3.52	1.63
Tang Book Value Per Share	15.64	15.87	15.81	14.91	12.73	11.01	9.10	7.27
Dividends Per Share	0.520	0.430	0.430	0.360	0.300	...	...	...
Dividend Payout %	15.29	13.07	13.19	12.90	14.78	...	...	...
Income Statement								
Total Revenue	3,222,087	1,588,629	6,291,845	5,737,774	4,664,616	4,264,579	3,961,545	3,842,452
EBITDA	213,718	99,863	439,243	408,282	298,505	312,912	282,541	266,466
Depn & Amortn	12,690	6,579	21,440	17,390	16,166	16,263	15,202	7,548
Income Before Taxes	211,727	98,491	432,958	399,860	289,564	306,197	279,976	268,657
Income Taxes	76,938	36,813	160,866	158,415	114,378	120,948	111,290	106,388
Net Income	134,789	61,678	272,092	241,445	175,186	185,249	168,686	162,269
Average Shares	80,564	81,973	83,566	86,552	86,175	88,296	89,136	90,860
Balance Sheet								
Total Assets	1,655,711	1,728,994	1,649,056	1,520,935	1,311,632	1,095,664	937,029	748,437
Current Liabilities	412,081	447,368	367,761	279,518	248,463	171,594	158,372	112,186
Total Liabilities	434,219	472,367	384,491	279,518	250,448	171,594	158,372	112,186
Stockholders' Equity	1,221,492	1,256,627	1,264,565	1,241,417	1,061,184	924,070	778,657	636,251
Shares Outstanding	78,118	79,185	79,964	83,284	83,342	83,961	85,573	87,465
Statistical Record								
Return on Assets %	17.30	16.42	17.17	17.00	14.55	18.23	20.02	25.80
Return on Equity %	23.49	22.30	21.72	20.91	17.65	21.76	23.84	31.51
EBITDA Margin %	6.63	6.29	6.98	7.12	6.40	7.34	7.13	6.93
Net Margin %	4.18	3.88	4.32	4.21	3.76	4.34	4.26	4.22
Asset Turnover	4.04	3.86	3.97	4.04	3.88	4.20	4.70	6.11
Current Ratio	3.57	3.44	4.08	4.97	5.94	5.39	6.01	
Price Range	63.90-52.76	63.90-52.88	66.35-52.88	74.34-56.51	62.90-38.50	59.39-40.73	56.00-26.81	83.50-23.35
P/E Ratio	18.79-15.52	19.42-16.07	20.35-16.22	26.65-20.25	30.99-18.97	28.28-19.40	29.63-14.19	46.65-13.06
Average Yield %	0.90	0.74	0.73	0.56	0.61	...	...	...

Address: 200 N. Milwaukee Ave., Vernon Hills, IL 60061 **Telephone:** 847-465-6000 **Fax:** 847-465-7700	**Web Site:** www.cdw.com **Officers:** John A. Edwardson - Chmn., C.E.O. Harry J. Harczak Jr. - Exec. V.P., Sales

Auditors: PricewaterhouseCoopers LLP
Investor Contact: 847-419-8234

CEPHALON, INC.

Exchange	Symbol	Price	52Wk Range	Yield	P/E
NMS	CEPH	$57.02 (8/31/2006)	82.49-40.52	N/A	34.98

*7 Year Price Score 93.29 *NYSE Composite Index=100 *12 Month Price Score 100.66

Interim Earnings (Per Share)

Qtr.	Mar	Jun	Sep	Dec
2003	0.21	0.38	0.31	0.53
2004	0.37	(0.12)	(2.94)	1.40
2005	0.44	(4.29)	0.50	0.32
2006	0.05	0.76	...	...

Interim Dividends (Per Share)

No Dividends Paid

Valuation Analysis   Institutional Holding

Forecast P/E	15.64	No of Institutions
	(9/9/2006)	258
Market Cap	$3.4 Billion	Shares
Book Value	853.4 Million	82,301,688
Price/Book	4.03	% Held
Price/Sales	2.39	N/A

Business Summary: Pharmaceuticals (MIC: 9.1 SIC: 2834 NAIC: 325412)

Cephalon is an international biopharmaceutical company focused on the discovery, development and marketing of products to treat sleep disorders, neurological disorders, cancer and pain. In addition to an active research and development program, Co. domestically markets, Provigil® tablets for treating excessive daytime sleepiness associated with narcolepsy, Actiq® for the management of breakthrough cancer pain in opioid tolerant patients and Gabitril® for the treatment of partial seizures associated with epilepsy. In the U.K., Co. markets Provigil and other products, including Tegretol®, a treatment for epilepsy and Ritalin®, a treatment for attention deficit hyperactivity disorder.

Recent Developments: For the quarter ended June 30 2006, net income amounted to $50.4 million versus a net loss of $249.0 million in the year-earlier quarter. Revenues were $440.1 million, up 53.9% from $286.0 million the year before. Operating income was $81.9 million versus a loss of $244.0 million in the prior-year quarter. Direct operating expenses rose 94.1% to $68.6 million from $35.4 million in the comparable period the year before. Indirect operating expenses decreased 41.4% to $289.6 million from $494.6 million in the equivalent prior-year period.

Prospects: On May 1 2006, Co. received an approvable letter from the FDA for NUVIGIL™ (armodafinil) Tablets, following its submission for a New Drug Application in March 2005 seeking to market NUVIGIL for the treatment of excessive sleepiness. However, FDA approval of NUVIGIL is contingent upon finalizing the product label. Separately, on Apr 13 2006, FDA approved VIVITROL™, Co.'s proprietary extended-release medication for the treatment of alcohol dependence, of which is expected to be launched in late June 2006. For full-year 2006, Co. is raising its sales guidance to a range of $1.48 billion to $1.53 billion as well as its basic income per common share guidance to range from $3.90 to $4.10.

Financial Data
(US$ in Thousands)

	6 Mos	3 Mos	12/31/2005	12/31/2004	12/31/2003	12/31/2002	12/31/2001	12/31/2000
Earnings Per Share	1.63	(3.42)	(3.01)	(1.31)	1.44	2.79	(1.27)	(2.70)
Cash Flow Per Share	3.78	2.13	3.20	3.15	3.60	1.86	0.25	(2.60)
Tang Book Value Per Share	N.M.	N.M.	N.M.	0.14	2.61	N.M.	N.M.	0.69
Income Statement								
Total Revenue	797,054	356,943	1,211,892	1,015,425	714,807	506,897	266,643	111,790
EBITDA	148,006	33,202	(121,677)	44,807	200,658	133,081	...	...
Depn & Amortn	62,451	29,367	124,377	67,291	52,737	46,528	14,434	3,945
Income Before Taxes	86,474	4,341	(245,118)	(28,184)	130,314	62,433	...	...
Income Taxes	32,490	774	(70,164)	45,629	46,456	(112,629)	...	...
Net Income	53,984	3,567	(174,954)	(73,813)	83,858	171,528	(61,148)	(110,241)
Average Shares	66,654	73,508	58,051	56,489	64,072	67,442	48,292	40,893
Balance Sheet								
Total Assets	2,966,399	2,935,341	2,819,206	2,440,176	2,381,656	1,689,090	1,389,087	308,435
Current Liabilities	1,208,168	2,002,021	1,278,603	216,311	137,688	119,647	106,930	80,767
Long-Term Obligations	762,535	12,331	763,097	1,284,410	1,409,417	860,897	866,589	55,138
Total Liabilities	2,112,999	2,178,470	2,207,035	1,610,132	1,611,286	1,046,505	990,356	143,242
Stockholders' Equity	853,400	756,871	612,171	830,044	770,370	642,585	398,731	165,193
Shares Outstanding	60,361	60,357	58,072	57,640	55,533	55,152	54,685	42,340
Statistical Record								
Return on Assets %	3.40	N.M.	N.M.	N.M.	4.12	11.14	N.M.	N.M.
Return on Equity %	14.36	N.M.	N.M.	N.M.	11.87	32.94	N.M.	N.M.
EBITDA Margin %	18.57	9.30	N.M.	4.41	28.07	26.25	...	...
Net Margin %	6.77	1.00	N.M.	N.M.	11.73	33.84	N.M.	N.M.
Asset Turnover	0.48	0.48	0.46	0.42	0.35	0.33	0.31	0.41
Current Ratio	0.90	0.58	0.82	5.46	9.95	6.57	6.87	1.75
Debt to Equity	0.89	0.02	1.25	1.55	1.83	1.34	2.17	0.33
Price Range	82.49-38.47	82.49-37.88	65.28-37.88	60.59-42.01	53.31-37.34	77.36-36.81	77.58-41.13	80.00-32.63
P/E Ratio	50.61-23.60	...	...	...	...	37.02-25.93	27.73-13.19	...

Address: 41 Moores Road, Frazier, PA 19355
Telephone: 610-344-0200
Fax: 610-344-0065

Web Site: www.cephalon.com
Officers: Frank Baldino Jr. - Chmn., C.E.O. Peter E. Grebow Ph. D. - Exec. V.P., Worldwide Technical Opers.

Auditors: PricewaterhouseCoopers LLP
Investor Contact: 610-738-6376
Transfer Agents: StockTrans, Inc., Ardmore, PA

CHARTER COMMUNICATIONS INC

Exchange	Symbol	Price	52Wk Range	Yield	P/E
NMS	CHTR	$1.39 (8/31/2006)	1.71-0.94	N/A	N/A

*7 Year Price Score N/A *NYSE Composite Index=100 *12 Month Price Score 98.73

Interim Earnings (Per Share)

Qtr.	Mar	Jun	Sep	Dec
2003	(0.62)	(0.13)	0.07	(0.20)
2004	(1.00)	(1.39)	(10.89)	(1.09)
2005	(1.16)	(1.18)	0.09	(1.07)
2006	(1.45)	(1.20)	...	...

Interim Dividends (Per Share)
No Dividends Paid

Valuation Analysis
		Institutional Holding	
Forecast P/E	N/A	No of Institutions	117
	(9/9/2006)	Shares	292,977,120
Market Cap	$609.5 Million	% Held	66.81
Book Value	N/A		
Price/Book	N/A		
Price/Sales	0.11		

Business Summary: Media (MIC: 13.1 SIC: 4841 NAIC: 517510)
Charter Communications is a broadband communications company. Through its broadband network of coaxial and fiber optic cable, Co. offers traditional cable video programming, including analog and digital; high-speed cable Internet access; advanced broadband cable services, such as video on demand, high definition television service and interactive television; and, in some of its markets, Co. offers telephone service. At Dec 31 2005, Co. served approximately 5.9 million analog video customers, of which approximately 2.8 million were also digital video customers.

Recent Developments: For the quarter ended June 30 2006, loss from continuing operations was $402.0 million compared with a loss of $359.0 million in the year-earlier quarter. Net loss amounted to $382.0 million versus a net loss of $355.0 million in the year-earlier quarter. Revenues were $1.38 billion, up 9.2% from $1.27 billion the year before. Operating income was $146.0 million versus $100.0 million in the prior-year quarter, an increase of 46.0%. Direct operating expenses rose 11.9% to $611.0 million from $546.0 million in the comparable period the year before. Indirect operating expenses increased 1.0% to $626.0 million from $620.0 million in the equivalent prior-year period.

Prospects: Going forward, Co. plans to focus on disciplined, targeted marketing and operational execution aimed at generating profitable revenue growth. Separately, on Jul 3 2006, Co. announced completion of the sales of various assets to Cebridge Acquisition Co., LLC and New Wave Communications for total proceeds of approximately $896.0 million, subject to post-closing adjustments. The transactions include certain cable television systems in West Virginia and Virginia, sold to Cebridge, and in Illinois and Kentucky, sold to New Wave. These sales reflect Co.'s strategy to divest geographically non-strategic assets aimed at enhancing overall operating efficiency, while also increasing its liquidity.

Financial Data (US$ in Thousands)	6 Mos	3 Mos	12/31/2005	12/31/2004	12/31/2003	12/31/2002	12/31/2001	12/31/2000
Earnings Per Share	(3.63)	(3.61)	(3.13)	(14.47)	(0.82)	(8.55)	(4.37)	(3.67)
Cash Flow Per Share	0.89	1.00	0.84	1.57	2.60	2.54	1.92	5.00
Income Statement								
Total Revenue	2,703,000	1,374,000	5,254,000	4,977,000	4,819,000	4,566,000	3,953,132	3,249,222
EBITDA	826,000	376,000	2,436,000	(514,000)	2,688,000	175,000	1,665,940	1,469,919
Depn & Amortn	698,000	358,000	1,499,000	1,495,000	1,479,000	1,437,000	3,010,068	2,473,082
Income Before Taxes	(815,000)	(450,000)	(852,000)	(3,679,000)	(348,000)	(2,768,000)	(2,655,916)	(2,054,945)
Income Taxes	60,000	9,000	115,000	(103,000)	(110,000)	(520,000)	...	...
Net Income	(841,000)	(459,000)	(967,000)	(4,341,000)	(238,000)	(2,514,000)	(1,177,677)	(828,650)
Average Shares	317,646	317,413	310,159	300,291	294,597	294,440	269,594	225,697
Balance Sheet								
Total Assets	16,145,000	16,203,000	16,431,000	17,673,000	21,364,000	22,384,000	24,961,824	23,043,566
Current Liabilities	1,240,000	1,304,000	1,191,000	1,217,000	1,235,000	1,405,000	1,374,994	1,367,234
Long-Term Obligations	19,913,000	19,573,000	19,437,000	19,464,000	18,647,000	18,671,000	16,342,873	13,060,455
Total Liabilities	21,907,000	21,586,000	21,351,000	22,079,000	21,539,000	22,343,000	22,100,032	19,920,362
Stockholders' Equity	(5,762,000)	(5,383,000)	(4,920,000)	(4,406,000)	(175,000)	41,000	2,861,792	3,123,204
Shares Outstanding	438,524	438,487	416,254	305,253	295,088	294,670	294,550	233,850
Statistical Record								
EBITDA Margin %	30.56	27.37	46.36	N.M.	55.78	3.83	42.14	45.24
Asset Turnover	0.33	0.32	0.31	0.25	0.22	0.19	0.16	0.15
Current Ratio	0.88	0.79	0.27	0.76	0.28	0.45	0.27	0.32
Debt to Equity	...	...	...	...	...	455.39	5.71	4.18
Price Range	1.71-0.94	1.71-0.90	2.30-0.90	5.43-2.03	5.23-0.78	16.60-0.79	24.35-12.00	23.31-10.56

Address: 12405 Powerscourt Drive, St. Louis, MO 63131
Telephone: 314-965-0555
Web Site: www.charter.com
Officers: Paul G. Allen - Chmn. Carl E. Vogel - Pres., C.E.O.
Auditors: KPMG LLP
Investor Contact: 314-543-2459

CHECK POINT SOFTWARE TECHNOLOGIES, LTD. (ISRAEL)

Exchange	Symbol	Price	52Wk Range	Yield	P/E
NMS	CHKP	$18.59 (8/31/2006)	24.38-16.47	N/A	N/A

*7 Year Price Score 49.79 *NYSE Composite Index=100 *12 Month Price Score 83.48

Interim Earnings (Per Share)

Qtr.	Mar	Jun	Sep	Dec
2004			0.95	
2005			1.27	
2006	0.25	0.27	...	...

Interim Dividends (Per Share)

Amt	Decl	Ex	Rec	Pay
2-for-1	12/20/1999	1/31/2000	1/23/2000	1/28/2000
100%	6/30/2000	7/26/2000	7/14/2000	7/25/2000
50%	1/18/2001	2/13/2001	2/1/2001	2/12/2001

Valuation Analysis | **Institutional Holding**
Forecast P/E | 13.90 | No of Institutions
 | (9/9/2006) | N/A
Market Cap | $4.5 Billion | Shares
Book Value | 1.8 Billion | N/A
Price/Book | 2.56 | % Held
Price/Sales | 7.84 | N/A

Business Summary: IT & Technology (MIC: 10.2 SIC: 5045 NAIC: 423430)

Check Point Software Technologies is engaged in developing, marketing and supporting Internet security solutions for enterprise networks and service providers. Co. operates in one reportable segment which is sales of its network security products, packaged and marketed mostly under the VPN-1 product family and related software subscription, support technical services and training program. Co. sells its software products worldwide through multiple distribution channels ("channel partners") including distributors, resellers, system integrators, Original Equipment Manufacturers ("OEMs") and Managed Security service Providers ("MSPs").

Recent Developments: For the quarter ended June 30 2006, net income decreased 15.7% to $65.7 million compared with $78.0 million in the corresponding period of the previous year. Revenues fell 3.4% to $138.9 million from $144.6 million in the year-earlier quarter. Product and license revenues declined 6.2% to $122.0 million from $117.3 million, while services revenues increased 17.1% to $16.9 million from $14.4 million the year before. Operating expenses jumped 17.7% to $74.9 million from $63.7 million in 2005. Operating income dropped 20.9% to $64.0 million versus $80.9 million in the prior-year period.

Prospects: During the quarter, Co. continued to generate solid financial results that were in line with its projections. Meawhile, Co. will look to continue executing its product target for 2006 by enhancing its product offering with its new perimeter security product lines, VPN-1 Power and VPN-1 UTM. Also, Co. introduced the latest version of the NGX security platform in the second quarter, which should further its strategy for a unified security architecture. Going forward, Co. remains focused on providing security services and executing on its business objectives.

Financial Data
(US$ in Thousands)

	12/31/2005	12/31/2004	12/31/2003	12/31/2002	12/31/2001	12/31/2000	12/31/1999	12/31/1998
Earnings Per Share	1.27	0.95	0.96	1.00	1.25	0.84	0.39	0.20
Cash Flow Per Share	1.46	1.20	1.17	1.16	...	...	...	...
Tang Book Value Per Share	6.47	5.76	5.86	4.83	3.77	1.56	0.55	0.54
Income Statement								
Total Revenue	579,350	515,360	432,572	426,989	527,643	425,283	219,567	141,941
EBITDA	402,283	328,043	322,872	319,281	381,523	258,444	109,885	73,824
Depn & Amortn	16,418	23,047	23,682	14,955	...	...	...	...
Income Before Taxes	385,865	304,996	299,190	304,326	381,523	258,444	109,885	73,824
Income Taxes	66,181	56,603	55,311	49,246	59,603	37,231	14,104	3,947
Net Income	319,684	248,393	243,879	255,080	321,920	221,213	95,781	69,877
Average Shares	251,747	260,608	255,083	254,772	258,075	393,772	554,526	348,255
Balance Sheet								
Total Assets	2,092,495	1,917,891	1,713,665	1,425,611	1,142,908	777,639	394,346	212,235
Current Liabilities	307,859	279,046	245,234	232,789	225,384	227,190	101,212	35,471
Total Liabilities	316,774	287,067	252,120	238,569	227,180	228,356	101,838	36,528
Stockholders' Equity	1,775,721	1,630,824	1,461,545	1,187,042	915,728	549,283	292,508	175,707
Shares Outstanding	244,309	248,217	249,276	245,908	242,824	353,197	529,796	326,504
Statistical Record								
Return on Assets %	15.94	13.64	15.54	19.86	33.52	37.65	31.58	41.58
Return on Equity %	18.77	16.02	18.42	24.26	43.95	52.41	40.91	50.66
EBITDA Margin %	69.44	63.65	74.64	74.77	72.31	60.77	50.05	52.01
Net Margin %	55.18	48.20	56.38	59.74	61.01	52.02	43.62	49.23
Asset Turnover	0.29	0.28	0.28	0.33	0.55	0.72	0.72	0.84
Current Ratio	4.85	3.84	5.01	3.76	2.58	2.38	2.96	3.28
Price Range	24.95-19.67	26.99-16.57	21.27-12.97	47.20-12.11	110.58-20.70	113.33-30.54	34.85-4.46	7.96-2.17
P/E Ratio	19.65-15.49	28.41-17.44	22.16-13.51	47.20-12.11	88.47-16.56	134.92-36.35	89.37-11.43	39.79-10.83

Address: 3A Jabotinsky Street, Ramat-Gan, 52520
Telephone: 375-345-55
Fax: 357-592-56

Web Site: www.checkpoint.com
Officers: Gil Shwed - Chmn., C.E.O. Marius Nacht - Vice Chmn., Sr. V. P.

Auditors: Kost, Forer & Gabbay
Investor Contact: 650-628-2000
Transfer Agents: American Stock Transfer & Trust Company, New York, NY

CHECKFREE CORP

Exchange	Symbol	Price	52Wk Range	Yield	P/E
NMS	CKFR	$35.80 (8/31/2006)	56.50-33.66	N/A	30.86

*7 Year Price Score 105.12 *NYSE Composite Index=100 *12 Month Price Score 89.40

Interim Earnings (Per Share)

Qtr.	Sep	Dec	Mar	Jun
2002-03	(0.18)	(0.13)	(0.09)	(0.19)
2003-04	(0.07)	(0.01)	0.08	0.12
2004-05	0.07	0.14	0.17	0.12
2005-06	0.28	0.36	0.40	...

Interim Dividends (Per Share)

No Dividends Paid

Valuation Analysis

		Institutional Holding	
Forecast P/E	19.37	No of Institutions	
	(9/9/2006)	259	
Market Cap	$3.3 Billion	Shares	
Book Value	1.5 Billion	82,933,664	
Price/Book	2.22	% Held	
Price/Sales	3.79	90.75	

Business Summary: Miscellaneous Business Services (MIC: 12.8 SIC: 7389 NAIC: 541519)

CheckFree is a provider of financial electronic commerce products and services. Through its Electronic Commerce division, Co. enables consumers to receive and pay bills. For the year ended June 30 2005, Co. processed approximately 905.0 million transactions, and delivered approximately 140.0 million electronic bills. Through its Investment Services division, Co. provides a range of portfolio management services to financial institutions, including broker dealers, money managers and investment advisors. Co.'s Software division provides financial software, maintenance, support and professional services.

Recent Developments: For the quarter ended Mar 31 2006, income from continuing operations increased 109.6% to $32.2 million from $15.4 million in the year-earlier quarter. Net income increased 141.3% to $37.7 million from $15.6 million in the year-earlier quarter. Revenues were $226.9 million, up 19.9% from $189.2 million the year before. Operating income was $48.9 million versus $21.4 million in the prior-year quarter, an increase of 128.1%. Direct operating expenses rose 25.7% to $91.4 million from $72.7 million in the comparable period the year before. Indirect operating expenses decreased 8.8% to $86.7 million from $95.1 million in the equivalent prior-year period.

Prospects: Co.'s results are benefiting from solid top-line growth in its Software unit, Electronic Commerce unit and CheckFree Investment Services unit. Based on solid year-to-date results, Co. has raised its fourth quarter fiscal 2006 ending Jun 30 2006 revenue guidance to a range from $226.0 million to $231.0 million. For full fiscal 2006, Co. expects earnings to be in the range of $1.34 to $1.37 and free cash flow to be about $175.0 million. Meanwhile, the expirations of its five-year agreements with Microsoft and FDC will continue to impact year-over-year revenue growth in fiscal 2007, and expecting its consolidated operating margin to be around the mid- to upper-20% range in the near-term.

Financial Data
(US$ in Thousands)

	9 Mos	6 Mos	3 Mos	06/30/2005	06/30/2004	06/30/2003	06/30/2002	06/30/2001
Earnings Per Share	1.16	0.93	0.71	0.50	0.11	(0.59)	(5.04)	(4.49)
Cash Flow Per Share	2.41	2.30	2.41	2.27	1.90	1.78	0.52	(0.00)
Tang Book Value Per Share	6.09	6.41	5.98	5.49	4.23	3.60	1.81	0.40
Income Statement								
Total Revenue	654,464	431,697	215,757	757,832	606,464	551,646	490,477	433,320
EBITDA	216,566	147,502	75,928	240,723	196,779	149,890	(99,954)	(53,263)
Depn & Amortn	78,238	55,809	35,680	176,598	177,582	226,638	435,565	427,495
Income Before Taxes	146,711	97,065	42,704	71,841	11,730	(82,396)	(539,821)	(478,497)
Income Taxes	55,180	36,943	16,347	25,040	1,195	(33,106)	(98,871)	(115,362)
Net Income	97,778	60,122	26,357	46,801	10,535	(52,184)	(440,950)	(363,135)
Average Shares	94,199	93,589	92,818	92,914	91,864	88,807	87,452	80,863
Balance Sheet								
Total Assets	1,738,263	1,702,761	1,637,368	1,569,916	1,548,932	1,587,270	1,637,477	2,183,953
Current Liabilities	233,130	249,321	229,032	198,821	202,441	110,282	112,427	128,615
Long-Term Obligations	25,376	25,253	25,685	25,389	25,504	176,692	175,316	176,541
Total Liabilities	265,046	280,802	262,797	233,501	249,750	319,121	331,816	451,767
Stockholders' Equity	1,473,217	1,421,959	1,374,571	1,336,415	1,299,182	1,268,149	1,305,661	1,732,186
Shares Outstanding	91,308	90,982	90,670	90,257	90,164	89,266	88,085	86,928
Statistical Record								
Return on Assets %	6.61	5.38	4.23	3.00	0.67	N.M.	N.M.	N.M.
Return on Equity %	7.76	6.37	4.99	3.55	0.82	N.M.	N.M.	N.M.
EBITDA Margin %	33.09	34.17	35.19	31.76	32.45	27.17	N.M.	N.M.
Net Margin %	14.94	13.93	12.22	6.18	1.74	N.M.	N.M.	N.M.
Asset Turnover	0.52	0.51	0.50	0.49	0.39	0.34	0.26	0.30
Current Ratio	2.55	2.60	2.66	2.70	2.30	3.76	2.79	2.11
Debt to Equity	0.02	0.02	0.02	0.02	0.02	0.14	0.13	0.10
Price Range	53.99-32.93	49.09-32.93	41.96-27.67	41.96-24.81	34.18-19.81	29.00-7.46	35.20-11.11	70.88-24.38
P/E Ratio	46.54-28.39	52.78-35.41	59.10-38.97	83.92-49.62	310.73-180.09	...	...	...

Address: 4411 East Jones Bridge Road, Norcross, GA 30092 Telephone: 678-375-3000	Web Site: www.checkfree.com Officers: Peter J. Kight - Chmn., C.E.O. Mark A. Johnson - Vice-Chmn.	Auditors: Deloitte & Touche LLP Investor Contact: 678-375-1278 Transfer Agents: Wells Fargo Shareowner Services, South St. Paul, MN

CHEESECAKE FACTORY INC. (THE)

Exchange	Symbol	Price	52Wk Range	Yield	P/E
NMS	CAKE	$24.89 (8/31/2006)	38.48-21.93	N/A	23.26

*7 Year Price Score 109.31 *NYSE Composite Index=100 *12 Month Price Score 72.57

Interim Earnings (Per Share)

Qtr.	Mar	Jun	Sep	Dec
2003	0.17	0.20	0.19	0.20
2004	0.21	0.23	0.16	0.25
2005	0.24	0.29	0.27	0.29
2006	0.24	...	...	...

Interim Dividends (Per Share)

Amt	Decl	Ex	Rec	Pay
50%	5/12/2000	6/9/2000	5/24/2000	6/8/2000
50%	5/24/2001	6/19/2001	6/4/2001	6/18/2001
50%	11/9/2004	12/9/2004	11/23/2004	12/8/2004

Valuation Analysis

Forecast P/E	23.22 (9/9/2006)
Market Cap	$2.0 Billion
Book Value	677.7 Million
Price/Book	2.90
Price/Sales	1.64

Institutional Holding

No of Institutions	237
Shares	72,601,800
% Held	91.80

Business Summary: Hospitality & Tourism (MIC: 5.1 SIC: 5812 NAIC: 722110)

The Cheesecake Factory owns and operates full-service, casual dining restaurants and distributes cheesecakes and other baked desserts. As of Feb 21 2006, Co. operated 103 full-service, casual dining restaurants under The Cheesecake Factory® mark in 29 states and the District of Columbia. Co. also operated seven full-service, casual dining restaurants under the Grand Lux Cafe® mark in Sunrise, FL; Garden City, NY; Houston, TX; Dallas, TX; Chicago, IL; Los Angeles, CA and Las Vegas, NV; and one self-service, limited menu "express" foodservice operation under The Cheesecake Factory Express® mark inside the DisneyQuest® family entertainment center in Orlando, FL.

Recent Developments: For the quarter ended Apr 4 2006, net income increased 1.6% to $19.3 million from $19.0 million in the year-earlier quarter. Revenues were $306.4 million, up 14.2% from $268.2 million the year before. Operating income was $25.7 million versus $28.1 million in the prior-year quarter, a decrease of 8.6%. Direct operating expenses rose 11.7% to $76.9 million from $68.9 million in the comparable period the year before. Indirect operating expenses increased 19.0% to $203.7 million from $171.2 million in the equivalent prior-year period.

Prospects: Co.'s results are being supported by comparable sales gains at its Cheesecake Factory restaurants and Grand Lux Cafes. Looking ahead, Co. intends to continue to develop its restaurants in high profile locations within densely populated areas in both existing and new markets. In fiscal 2006, Co. anticipates opening as many as 21 new restaurants, including up to three Grand Lux Cafes, and expects to achieve about 20.0% square footage growth. However, since many of these openings are late in the year, Co. will not realize its full benefit until fiscal 2007. Co. also expects fiscal 2006 bakery sales to other foodservice operators, retailers and distributors to rise between 8.0% and 10.0%.

Financial Data
(US$ in Thousands)

	3 Mos	01/03/2006	12/28/2004	12/30/2003	12/31/2002	01/01/2002	01/02/2001	12/28/1999
Earnings Per Share	1.07	1.09	0.84	0.75	0.64	0.53	0.43	0.31
Cash Flow Per Share	2.06	2.08	1.94	1.55	1.27	1.07	0.80	0.56
Tang Book Value Per Share	8.53	8.18	6.94	5.95	5.04	4.01	3.38	2.67
Income Statement								
Total Revenue	306,366	1,177,643	969,232	773,835	651,970	539,130	438,281	347,482
EBITDA	39,775	174,874	135,790	113,622	95,290	74,550	59,380	42,330
Depn & Amortn	12,393	45,135	35,943	27,960	22,855	17,457	13,682	10,913
Income Before Taxes	28,906	133,657	102,081	89,128	76,320	61,421	50,358	34,224
Income Taxes	9,638	46,111	35,543	31,292	27,245	22,112	18,257	12,492
Net Income	19,268	87,546	66,538	57,836	49,075	39,309	32,101	21,732
Average Shares	80,540	80,176	79,395	77,772	76,737	74,845	75,287	71,512
Balance Sheet								
Total Assets	948,424	925,922	758,717	584,808	463,842	356,927	288,392	221,785
Current Liabilities	115,387	129,892	109,846	81,554	61,993	57,107	43,127	32,936
Total Liabilities	270,691	278,222	215,865	126,906	84,278	67,456	47,556	36,212
Stockholders' Equity	677,733	647,700	542,852	457,902	379,564	289,471	240,836	185,573
Shares Outstanding	79,087	78,831	77,933	76,573	74,922	71,639	70,696	68,883
Statistical Record								
Return on Assets %	9.99	10.23	9.93	11.06	11.99	12.22	12.38	10.70
Return on Equity %	13.90	14.47	13.33	13.85	14.71	14.87	14.81	12.60
EBITDA Margin %	12.98	14.85	14.01	14.68	14.62	13.83	13.55	12.18
Net Margin %	6.29	7.43	6.87	7.47	7.53	7.29	7.32	6.25
Asset Turnover	1.39	1.38	1.45	1.48	1.59	1.68	1.69	1.71
Current Ratio	1.82	1.33	1.04	1.42	1.18	1.02	1.92	2.08
Price Range	38.48-29.80	38.30-29.80	33.49-25.45	29.79-18.55	28.29-16.97	23.85-13.77	21.36-8.42	9.78-5.80
P/E Ratio	35.96-27.85	35.14-27.34	39.87-30.30	39.72-24.74	44.20-26.51	45.01-25.97	49.68-19.57	31.54-18.70

Address: 26901 Malibu Hills Road, Calabasas Hills, CA 91301
Telephone: 818-871-3000
Fax: 818-880-6501

Web Site: www.thecheesecakefactory.com
Officers: David Overton - Chmn., C.E.O. Gerald W. Deitchle - Pres.

Auditors: PricewaterhouseCoopers LLP
Investor Contact: 818-871-3000

CHEMICAL FINANCIAL CORP.

Exchange	Symbol	Price	52Wk Range	Yield	P/E	Div Acheiver
NMS	CHFC	$29.52 (8/31/2006)	34.48-28.73	3.73	14.76	30 Years

*7 Year Price Score 87.05 *NYSE Composite Index=100 *12 Month Price Score 92.55

Interim Earnings (Per Share)
Qtr.	Mar	Jun	Sep	Dec
2003	0.56	0.55	0.58	0.54
2004	0.56	0.55	0.56	0.57
2005	0.53	0.53	0.54	0.50
2006	0.47	0.49	...	...

Interim Dividends (Per Share)
Amt	Decl	Ex	Rec	Pay
0.265Q	10/18/2005	11/30/2005	12/2/2005	12/16/2005
0.275Q	12/12/2005	3/1/2006	3/3/2006	3/17/2006
0.275Q	4/18/2006	5/31/2006	6/2/2006	6/16/2006
0.275Q	7/19/2006	8/30/2006	9/1/2006	9/15/2006

Indicated Div: $1.10 (Div. Reinv. Plan)

Valuation Analysis | Institutional Holding
Forecast P/E	14.92	No of Institutions	
	(9/9/2006)	76	
Market Cap	$732.6 Million	Shares	8,429,410
Book Value	499.8 Million	% Held	34.00
Price/Book	1.47		
Price/Sales	2.96		

Business Summary: Commercial Banking (MIC: 8.1 SIC: 6022 NAIC: 522110)

Chemical Financial is a multibank holding company with total assets of $3.75 billion as of Dec 31 2005. Through Chemical Bank, Co. offers commercial banking and fiduciary products and services, including checking accounts, savings and individual retirement accounts, time deposit instruments, electronically accessed banking products, residential and commercial real estate financing, commercial lending, consumer financing, debit cards, safe deposit services, automated teller machines, access to insurance and investment products, money transfer services and trust services. As of Dec 31 2005, Co. had 132 banking offices and one loan production office across 32 counties of Michigan.

Recent Developments: For the quarter ended June 30 2006, net income decreased 7.5% to $12.2 million from $13.2 million in the year-earlier quarter. Net interest income decreased 6.9% to $33.2 million from $35.7 million in the year-earlier quarter. Provision for loan losses was $400,000 versus $730,000 in the prior-year quarter, a decrease of 45.2%. Non-interest income rose 7.8% to $10.5 million from $9.8 million, while non-interest expense advanced 1.3% to $25.1 million.

Prospects: Co.'s near-term outlook appears to be cautiously optimistic. Co.'s financial results continue to be restrained by rising interest rates, a trend which is believed to continue for the remainder of 2006. Nevertheless, Co. is encouraged by its prospects towards further growth and improved operating capabilities, driven by the recent initiation of its strategic restructuring plan. Furthermore, Co. is moving forward with its system-wide sales and service training program to improve sales, cross-sales as well as customer development and retention across its 123 branch office network.

Financial Data
(US$ in Thousands)	6 Mos	3 Mos	12/31/2005	12/31/2004	12/31/2003	12/31/2002	12/31/2001	12/31/2000
Earnings Per Share	2.00	2.04	2.10	2.25	2.24	2.20	1.71	1.78
Cash Flow Per Share	2.33	2.59	2.67	3.22	4.21	3.86	0.10	2.08
Tang Book Value Per Share	17.31	17.28	17.13	16.31	15.25	15.68	13.97	17.41
Dividends Per Share	1.080	1.070	1.060	1.010	0.952	0.871	0.829	0.760
Dividend Payout %	54.00	52.45	50.48	44.87	42.55	39.58	48.37	42.72
Income Statement								
Interest Income	105,668	52,277	199,304	189,250	185,037	211,044	219,250	131,085
Interest Expense	38,860	18,686	57,453	41,616	45,265	65,352	89,182	54,035
Net Interest Income	66,808	33,591	141,851	147,634	139,772	145,692	130,068	77,050
Provision for Losses	860	460	4,285	3,819	2,834	3,765	2,004	487
Non-Interest Income	20,350	9,832	39,220	39,329	39,094	34,534	31,873	17,364
Non-Interest Expense	50,197	25,121	98,463	98,469	91,923	93,526	94,597	50,860
Income Before Taxes	36,101	17,842	78,323	84,675	84,109	82,935	65,340	43,067
Income Taxes	11,975	5,945	25,445	27,993	28,393	27,990	22,617	14,061
Net Income	24,126	11,897	52,878	56,682	55,716	54,945	42,723	29,006
Average Shares	25,010	25,141	25,193	25,217	24,943	24,929	24,876	16,303
Balance Sheet								
Net Loans & Leases	2,731,036	2,663,699	2,676,066	2,551,419	2,448,096	2,044,514	2,151,547	1,067,636
Total Assets	3,730,642	3,738,079	3,749,316	3,764,125	3,708,888	3,568,893	3,488,306	1,973,424
Total Deposits	2,791,353	2,866,139	2,819,880	2,863,473	2,967,236	2,847,272	2,789,524	1,606,217
Total Liabilities	3,230,854	3,233,558	3,248,251	3,279,289	3,250,839	3,138,554	3,098,850	1,704,695
Stockholders' Equity	499,788	504,521	501,065	484,836	458,049	430,339	389,456	268,729
Shares Outstanding	24,817	25,101	25,079	25,169	24,991	24,868	24,821	15,439
Statistical Record								
Return on Assets %	1.35	1.36	1.41	1.51	1.53	1.56	1.56	1.50
Return on Equity %	10.11	10.35	10.73	11.99	12.54	13.40	12.98	11.16
Net Interest Margin %	62.21	64.26	71.17	78.01	75.54	69.03	59.32	58.78
Efficiency Ratio %	39.24	40.45	41.28	43.08	41.01	38.08	37.67	34.26
Loans to Deposits	0.98	0.93	0.95	0.89	0.83	0.72	0.77	0.66
Price Range	35.25-28.75	35.25-28.97	40.88-28.97	41.11-31.51	36.10-25.27	34.43-24.22	28.79-17.52	27.53-17.80
P/E Ratio	17.63-14.38	17.28-14.20	19.46-13.80	18.27-14.01	16.12-11.28	15.65-11.01	16.84-10.24	15.47-10.00
Average Yield %	3.40	3.33	3.22	2.92	3.19	3.15	3.48	3.41

Address: 333 East Main Street, Midland, MI 48640-0569	**Web Site:** www.chemicalbankmi.com
Telephone: 989-839-5350	**Officers:** Frank P. Popoff - Chmn. David B. Ramaker - Pres., C.E.O.
Fax: 989-839-5255	
	Auditors: Ernst & Young LLP
	Investor Contact: 989-839-5350
	Transfer Agents: Computershare Investor Services, LLC, Chicago, IL

CIENA CORP

Exchange	Symbol	Price	52Wk Range	Yield	P/E
NMS	CIEN	$3.95 (8/31/2006)	5.41-2.12	N/A	N/A

*7 Year Price Score 13.81 *NYSE Composite Index=100 *12 Month Price Score 105.29

Interim Earnings (Per Share)

Qtr.	Jan	Apr	Jul	Oct
2002-03	(0.25)	(0.17)	(0.20)	(0.25)
2003-04	(0.16)	(0.16)	(0.25)	(0.93)
2004-05	(0.10)	(0.13)	(0.09)	(0.44)
2005-06	(0.01)	0.00	(0.01)	...

Interim Dividends (Per Share)
No Dividends Paid

Valuation Analysis

		Institutional Holding	
Forecast P/E	179.50	No of Institutions	
	(9/9/2006)	263	
Market Cap	$2.3 Billion	Shares	
Book Value	729.9 Million	404,159,232	
Price/Book	3.20	% Held	
Price/Sales	4.47	68.77	

Business Summary: Communications (MIC: 10.1 SIC: 3669 NAIC: 334290)

Ciena is engaged in supplying communications networking equipment, software and services to telecommunications service providers, cable operators, governments and enterprises. Co.'s product and service offerings include broadband access, multiservice optical access, metro transport and switching, multiservice edge switching and routing, core transport and switching, network management, and global network services. Co. operates its business through four separate business segments: the Transport and Switching Group (TSG), the Data Networking Group (DNG), the Broadband Access Group (BBG) and Global Network Services (GNS).

Recent Developments: For the quarter ended July 31 2006, net loss amounted to $4.3 million versus a net loss of $51.0 million in the year-earlier quarter. Revenues were $152.5 million, up 38.0% from $110.5 million the year before. Operating loss was $12.8 million versus a loss of $53.5 million in the prior-year quarter. Direct operating expenses rose 11.0% to $80.8 million from $72.9 million in the comparable period the year before. Indirect operating expenses decreased 7.3% to $84.5 million from $91.1 million in the equivalent prior-year period.

Prospects: Co. is experiencing positive indicators in overall market demand for services related to Internet Protocol service delivery. Overall, revenue growth is being driven by customers' making network investments to address capacity needs, higher broadband usage and network traffic from a broader mix of services. Thus, Co. expects revenue for its fiscal fourth quarter ending Oct 2006 to grow sequentially by up to 5.0%. Separately, Co. noted that it has encountered increased competition, particularly for long-haul and metro transport products. This competition has come from larger, incumbent competitors as well as smaller, start-up companies and low-cost networking equipment producers in China.

Financial Data
(US$ in Thousands)

	9 Mos	6 Mos	3 Mos	10/31/2005	10/31/2004	10/31/2003	10/31/2002	10/31/2001
Earnings Per Share	(0.46)	(0.54)	(0.67)	(0.76)	(1.51)	(0.87)	(4.37)	(5.75)
Cash Flow Per Share	(0.12)	(0.16)	(0.20)	(0.22)	(0.47)	(0.54)	(0.07)	0.50
Tang Book Value Per Share	0.68	0.66	0.67	0.66	0.94	1.87	2.89	5.80
Income Statement								
Total Revenue	404,104	251,605	120,430	427,257	298,707	283,136	361,155	1,603,229
EBITDA	43,538	30,507	13,812	(332,921)	(654,609)	(255,226)	(1,310,405)	(1,393,057)
Depn & Amortn	37,019	26,171	13,751	76,028	106,921	93,704	131,020	283,081
Income Before Taxes	(11,497)	(7,532)	(5,992)	(434,379)	(788,343)	(385,261)	(1,486,764)	(1,706,729)
Income Taxes	989	669	299	1,320	1,121	1,256	110,735	87,333
Net Income	(12,486)	(8,201)	(6,291)	(435,699)	(789,464)	(386,517)	(1,597,499)	(1,794,062)
Average Shares	589,381	584,625	580,771	575,187	521,454	446,696	365,202	311,815
Balance Sheet								
Total Assets	1,830,539	1,820,138	1,544,891	1,675,229	2,137,054	2,378,165	2,751,022	3,317,301
Current Liabilities	173,662	175,685	174,272	178,464	158,579	186,199	223,818	254,382
Long-Term Obligations	877,142	879,182	581,196	648,752	690,000	730,428	843,616	863,883
Total Liabilities	1,100,666	1,095,360	808,285	939,862	982,632	1,047,348	1,223,753	1,188,319
Stockholders' Equity	729,873	724,778	736,606	735,367	1,154,422	1,330,817	1,527,269	2,128,982
Shares Outstanding	590,932	587,644	581,581	580,340	571,656	473,214	432,842	328,022
Statistical Record								
EBITDA Margin %	10.77	12.12	11.47	N.M.	N.M.	N.M.	N.M.	N.M.
Asset Turnover	0.28	0.25	0.25	0.22	0.13	0.11	0.12	0.74
Current Ratio	7.18	7.32	5.59	6.17	6.81	6.60	7.32	8.61
Debt to Equity	1.20	1.21	0.79	0.88	0.60	0.55	0.55	0.41
Price Range	5.41-2.05	5.41-2.05	4.00-1.69	3.45-1.69	7.97-1.71	7.50-3.50	21.16-2.45	117.50-9.51

Address: 1201 Winterson Road, Linthicum, MD 21090-2205
Telephone: 410-865-8500
Web Site: www.ciena.com
Officers: Patrick H. Nettles Ph. D. - Exec. Chmn. Gary B. Smith - Pres., C.E.O.
Auditors: PricewaterhouseCoopers LLP
Investor Contact: 410-865-8500
Transfer Agents: EquiServe Trust Company, Providence, RI

CINCINNATI FINANCIAL CORP.

Exchange	Symbol	Price	52Wk Range	Yield	P/E	Div Acheiver
NMS	CINF	$46.70 (8/31/2006)	47.95-40.29	2.87	8.37	45 Years

*7 Year Price Score 94.68 *NYSE Composite Index=100 *12 Month Price Score 103.36

Interim Earnings (Per Share)

Qtr.	Mar	Jun	Sep	Dec
2003	0.32	0.47	0.58	0.73
2004	0.82	0.87	0.50	1.09
2005	0.81	0.89	0.66	1.03
2006	3.13	0.76	...	...

Interim Dividends (Per Share)

Amt	Decl	Ex	Rec	Pay
0.305Q	11/21/2005	12/21/2005	12/23/2005	1/17/2006
0.335Q	2/3/2006	3/22/2006	3/24/2006	4/14/2006
0.335Q	5/26/2006	6/21/2006	6/23/2006	7/14/2006
0.335Q	8/14/2006	9/20/2006	9/22/2006	10/16/2006

Indicated Div: $1.34 (Div. Reinv. Plan)

Valuation Analysis

Forecast P/E	15.60
	(9/9/2006)
Market Cap	$8.1 Billion
Book Value	6.1 Billion
Price/Book	1.33
Price/Sales	1.80

Institutional Holding

No of Institutions	308
Shares	88,675,016
% Held	51.19

Business Summary: Insurance (MIC: 8.2 SIC: 6331 NAIC: 524126)

Cincinnati Financial is a holding company. Through a select group of independent insurance agencies in 32 U.S. states, Co. primarily markets commercial lines and personal lines property casualty insurance products. In addition, Co. provides fully-owns three subsidiaries: The Cincinnati Insurance Company; CFC Investment Company which provides leasing and financing services; and CinFin Capital Management Company, which provides asset management services to institutions, corporations and individuals. As of Dec 31 2005, Co. had 3,983 associates, with approximately 2,800 headquarters associates providing support to approximately 1,150 field associates.

Recent Developments: For the quarter ended June 30 2006, net income decreased 16.5% to $132.0 million from $158.0 million in the year-earlier quarter. Revenues were $981.0 million, up 4.4% from $940.0 million the year before. Net premiums earned were $822.0 million versus $794.0 million in the prior-year quarter, an increase of 3.5%. Net investment income rose 10.9% to $143.0 million from $129.0 million a year ago.

Prospects: Despite higher catastrophe losses and flat performance within its personal lines premiums during the first half of 2006, Co. is encouraged by the continued robust performance within its commercial lines insurance business as well as its solid investment income growth. Going forward, Co. expects its property casualty written premiums to grow by at least 2.0% for full-year 2006, with growth in its commercial lines to significantly offset the expected decline in its personal lines. Moreover, Co.'s investment income growth is targeted at the 8.0% to 8.5% range for the year. Meanwhile, Co. intends to further expand its products and services by targeting 55 to 60 new agency appointments in 2006.

Financial Data
(US$ in Thousands)

	6 Mos	3 Mos	12/31/2005	12/31/2004	12/31/2003	12/31/2002	12/31/2001	12/31/2000
Earnings Per Share	5.58	5.71	3.40	3.28	2.10	1.32	1.08	0.66
Cash Flow Per Share	4.11	5.69	4.60	4.65	4.61	3.74	3.04	2.01
Tang Book Value Per Share	35.06	35.86	34.98	35.64	35.17	31.34	33.58	33.80
Dividends Per Share	1.280	1.250	1.205	1.035	0.907	0.807	0.762	0.689
Dividend Payout %	22.94	21.89	35.46	31.60	43.29	60.96	70.59	104.11
Income Statement								
Premium Income	1,627,000	804,000	3,164,000	3,020,000	2,748,000	2,478,000	2,152,000	1,906,922
Total Revenue	2,588,000	1,607,000	3,767,000	3,614,000	3,181,000	2,843,000	2,561,000	2,330,994
Benefits & Claims	1,047,000	501,000	1,911,000	1,846,000	1,887,000	1,826,000	1,663,000	1,581,123
Income Before Taxes	1,009,000	834,000	823,000	800,000	480,000	279,000	221,000	108,664
Income Taxes	325,000	282,000	221,000	216,000	106,000	41,000	28,000	(9,701)
Net Income	684,000	552,000	602,000	584,000	374,000	238,000	193,000	118,365
Average Shares	175,022	176,127	177,116	178,376	178,292	179,920	178,605	180,722
Balance Sheet								
Total Assets	16,936,000	16,763,000	16,003,000	16,107,000	15,509,000	14,059,000	13,959,000	13,287,091
Total Liabilities	10,871,000	10,559,000	9,917,000	9,858,000	9,305,000	8,461,000	7,961,000	7,292,096
Stockholders' Equity	6,065,000	6,204,000	6,086,000	6,249,000	6,204,000	5,598,000	5,998,000	5,994,995
Shares Outstanding	173,000	173,000	174,000	175,350	176,400	178,605	178,605	177,382
Statistical Record								
Return on Assets %	5.97	6.20	3.75	3.68	2.53	1.70	1.42	0.96
Return on Equity %	16.14	16.54	9.76	9.35	6.34	4.10	3.22	2.07
Loss Ratio %	64.35	62.31	60.40	61.13	68.67	73.69	77.28	82.91
Net Margin %	26.43	34.35	15.98	16.16	11.76	8.37	7.54	5.08
Price Range	47.01-39.56	45.68-38.62	45.68-38.62	43.34-36.95	37.91-30.52	42.67-29.65	38.73-32.03	38.89-24.21
P/E Ratio	8.42-7.09	8.00-6.76	13.44-11.36	13.21-11.27	18.05-14.53	32.32-22.46	35.86-29.66	58.92-36.68
Average Yield %	2.95	2.96	2.88	2.60	2.60	2.21	2.16	2.13

Address: 6200 S. Gilmore Road, Fairfield, OH 45014-5141
Telephone: 513-870-2000
Fax: 513-870-2066

Web Site: www.cinfin.com
Officers: John J. Schiff Jr. - Chmn., Pres., C.E.O. James E. Benoski - Vice-Chmn., Chief Insurance Officer

Auditors: Deloitte & Touche LLP
Investor Contact: 513-870-2639
Transfer Agents: Cincinnati Financial Corporation, Fairfield, OH

CINTAS CORPORATION

Exchange	Symbol	Price	52Wk Range	Yield	P/E	Div Acheiver
NMS	CTAS	$37.03 (8/31/2006)	45.26-34.92	0.95	19.09	23 Years

*7 Year Price Score 76.96 *NYSE Composite Index=100 *12 Month Price Score 87.87

Interim Earnings (Per Share)

Qtr.	Aug	Nov	Feb	May
2001-02	0.33	0.34	0.32	0.37
2002-03	0.36	0.37	0.34	0.38
2003-04	0.37	0.40	0.39	0.42
2004-05	0.42	0.43	0.41	0.48
2005-06	0.47	0.46	0.46	0.55

Interim Dividends (Per Share)

Amt	Decl	Ex	Rec	Pay
0.27A	1/24/2003	2/5/2003	2/7/2003	3/14/2003
0.29A	1/27/2004	2/6/2004	2/10/2004	3/16/2004
0.32A	1/28/2005	2/4/2005	2/8/2005	3/15/2005
0.35A	1/24/2006	2/3/2006	2/7/2006	3/14/2006

Indicated Div: $0.35

Valuation Analysis

Forecast P/E	15.25 (9/9/2006)
Market Cap	$6.0 Billion
Book Value	2.1 Billion
Price/Book	2.89
Price/Sales	1.78

Institutional Holding

No of Institutions	348
Shares	107,293,832
% Held	66.78

Business Summary: Apparel (MIC: 4.4 SIC: 2326 NAIC: 315225)

Cintas is engaged in providing highly specialized products and services to businesses of all types throughout the United States and Canada. Co. is a provider of corporate identity uniforms through rental and sales programs, as well as a significant provider of related business services, including entrance mats, restroom products and services, first aid, safety and fire protection products and services, document shredding and storage, branded promotional products and flame resistant clothing. Co. classifies its businesses into two operating segments: Rentals and Other Services.

Recent Developments: For the year ended May 31 2006, net income increased 8.9% to $327.2 million from $300.5 million in the prior year. Revenues were $3.40 billion, up 11.0% from $3.07 billion the year before. Direct operating expenses rose 10.6% to $1.95 billion from $1.76 billion in the comparable period the year before. Indirect operating expenses increased 12.7% to $933.0 million from $827.8 million in the equivalent prior-year period.

Prospects: In spite of the business interruption that results from the hurricanes in the Gulf Coast region and escalating energy prices, Co. is experiencing robust increases in its recent results, with all of its business services exhibiting positive growth. Going forward, Co. anticipates cost pressures from energy prices will continue despite the recent mild decline in gasoline prices. Therefore, Co. is projecting earnings in the range of $1.93 to $2.00 per diluted share for full-year fiscal 2006, while reiterating its present revenue guidance of between $3.35 billion and $3.45 billion.

Financial Data
(US$ in Thousands)

	05/31/2006	05/31/2005	05/31/2004	05/31/2003	05/31/2002	05/31/2001	05/31/2000	05/31/1999
Earnings Per Share	1.94	1.74	1.58	1.45	1.36	1.30	1.14	0.82
Cash Flow Per Share	2.75	2.41	2.97	1.94	2.22	1.46	1.54	1.23
Tang Book Value Per Share	4.57	6.16	5.41	4.48	4.39	7.27	6.20	5.24
Dividends Per Share	0.350	0.320	0.290	0.270	0.250	0.220	0.187	0.147
Dividend Payout %	18.04	18.39	18.35	18.62	18.38	16.92	16.37	17.89
Income Statement								
Total Revenue	3,403,608	3,067,283	2,814,059	2,686,585	2,271,052	2,160,700	1,901,991	1,751,568
EBITDA	682,468	625,168	575,339	538,820	491,610	468,543	411,272	314,222
Depn & Amortn	160,653	148,175	143,259	143,061	120,025	112,089	99,513	90,228
Income Before Taxes	521,815	476,993	432,080	395,759	371,585	356,454	311,759	223,994
Income Taxes	194,637	176,475	159,875	146,506	137,334	134,003	118,372	85,055
Net Income	327,178	300,518	272,205	249,253	234,251	222,451	193,387	138,939
Average Shares	168,545	172,649	172,372	172,037	172,244	171,629	169,987	169,341
Balance Sheet								
Total Assets	3,425,237	3,059,744	2,810,297	2,582,946	2,519,234	1,752,224	1,581,342	1,407,818
Current Liabilities	411,828	356,481	325,686	304,839	312,634	250,903	235,392	212,097
Long-Term Obligations	794,454	465,291	473,685	534,763	703,250	220,940	254,378	283,581
Total Liabilities	1,337,274	955,609	922,328	936,614	1,095,475	520,909	538,466	536,395
Stockholders' Equity	2,087,963	2,104,135	1,887,969	1,646,332	1,423,759	1,231,315	1,042,876	871,423
Shares Outstanding	163,181	170,658	171,377	170,599	169,930	169,370	168,281	166,423
Statistical Record								
Return on Assets %	10.09	10.24	10.07	9.77	10.97	13.35	12.90	11.46
Return on Equity %	15.61	15.06	15.36	16.24	17.65	19.56	20.15	18.21
EBITDA Margin %	20.05	20.38	20.45	20.06	21.65	21.68	21.62	17.94
Net Margin %	9.61	9.80	9.67	9.28	10.31	10.30	10.17	7.93
Asset Turnover	1.05	1.05	1.04	1.05	1.06	1.30	1.27	1.44
Current Ratio	2.86	3.27	3.18	2.88	2.73	3.27	3.06	2.99
Debt to Equity	0.38	0.22	0.25	0.32	0.49	0.18	0.24	0.33
Price Range	45.32-37.56	47.86-38.21	50.21-34.93	52.21-30.90	56.28-37.92	53.56-34.00	45.19-24.25	51.67-27.17
P/E Ratio	23.36-19.36	27.51-21.96	31.78-22.11	36.01-21.31	41.38-27.88	41.20-26.15	39.64-21.27	63.01-33.13
Average Yield %	0.84	0.74	0.68	0.64	0.53	0.50	0.51	0.37

Address: 6800 Cintas Boulevard, P.O. Box 625737, Cincinnati, OH 45262-5737
Telephone: 513-459-1200
Fax: 513-573-4030

Web Site: www.cintas.com
Officers: Richard T. Farmer - Chmn. Robert J. Kohlhepp - Vice-Chmn.

Auditors: Ernst & Young LLP
Investor Contact: 513-459-1200
Transfer Agents: Computershare Investor Services LLC, Chicago, IL

CISCO SYSTEMS, INC.

Exchange	Symbol	Price	52Wk Range	Yield	P/E
NMS	CSCO	$21.99 (8/31/2006)	21.99-16.93	N/A	24.99

*7 Year Price Score 59.40 *NYSE Composite Index=100 *12 Month Price Score 97.94

Interim Earnings (Per Share)

Qtr.	Oct	Jan	Apr	Jul
2002-03	0.08	0.14	0.14	0.14
2003-04	0.15	0.10	0.17	0.19
2004-05	0.21	0.21	0.21	0.24
2005-06	0.20	0.22	0.22	...

Interim Dividends (Per Share)
No Dividends Paid

Valuation Analysis **Institutional Holding**

Forecast P/E	21.54	No of Institutions
	(9/9/2006)	1238
Market Cap	$135.5 Billion	Shares
Book Value	24.6 Billion	3,981,408,768
Price/Book	5.51	% Held
Price/Sales	4.99	65.22

Business Summary: Information Technologies & Communications (MIC: 10 SIC: 3669 NAIC: 334290)
Cisco Systems manufactures and sells networking as well as communications products and services. Co. provides a line of products for transporting data, voice and video within buildings, across campuses and around the world. Co. conducts its business globally through four geographical segments: the Americas; Europe, the Middle East, and Africa (EMEA); Asia Pacific; and Japan. As of Jul 30 2005, Co.'s worldwide sales and marketing organization consisted of approximately 14,000 individuals, with field sales offices in more than 60 countries, selling its products and services both directly and through various channels with support from its sales force.

Recent Developments: For the quarter ended Apr 29 2006, net income decreased 0.4% to $1.40 billion from $1.41 billion in the year-earlier quarter. Revenues were $7.32 billion, up 18.3% from $6.19 billion the year before. Operating income was $1.65 billion versus $1.82 billion in the prior-year quarter, a decrease of 9.1%. Direct operating expenses rose 26.5% to $2.60 billion from $2.05 billion in the comparable period the year before. Indirect operating expenses increased 32.6% to $3.07 billion from $2.32 billion in the equivalent prior-year period.

Prospects: Co.'s near-term outlook remains solid, despite anticipating ongoing price-focused competition particularly from China. For 2006, Co. will continue to focus its resources on commercial market segment, additional sales coverage, advanced technologies and evolving support model as well as its Emerging Markets plattform. Separately, on Apr 5 2006, Co. acquired SyPixx Networks, Inc. (SyPixx) a provider of network-centric video surveillance software and hardware for a purchase price of $51.0 million in cash and options, based on its prior agreement in March 2006. As a result, SyPixx's video surveillance products will be part of Co.'s new business unit within its Emerging Market Technologies Group.

Financial Data
(US$ in Thousands)

	9 Mos	6 Mos	3 Mos	07/30/2005	07/31/2004	07/26/2003	07/27/2002	07/28/2001
Earnings Per Share	0.88	0.87	0.86	0.87	0.62	0.50	0.25	(0.14)
Cash Flow Per Share	1.30	1.24	1.20	1.17	1.02	0.74	0.90	0.89
Tang Book Value Per Share	2.12	2.77	2.51	2.74	3.16	3.35	3.33	3.07
Income Statement								
Total Revenue	20,500,000	13,178,000	6,550,000	24,801,000	22,045,000	18,878,000	18,915,000	22,293,000
EBITDA	5,879,000	3,865,000	1,863,000	8,493,000	7,923,000	5,944,000	4,667,000	1,362,000
Depn & Amortn	856,000	512,000	258,000	1,009,000	1,443,000	1,591,000	1,957,000	2,236,000
Income Before Taxes	5,487,000	3,675,000	1,759,000	8,036,000	6,992,000	5,013,000	2,710,000	(874,000)
Income Taxes	1,451,000	1,039,000	498,000	2,295,000	2,024,000	1,435,000	817,000	140,000
Net Income	4,036,000	2,636,000	1,261,000	5,741,000	4,401,000	3,578,000	1,893,000	(1,014,000)
Average Shares	6,288,999	6,247,999	6,339,999	6,612,001	7,057,001	7,223,001	7,447,001	7,196,001
Balance Sheet								
Total Assets	43,082,000	33,652,000	31,755,000	33,883,000	35,594,000	37,107,000	37,795,000	35,238,000
Current Liabilities	10,430,000	9,521,000	9,236,000	9,511,000	8,703,000	8,294,000	8,375,000	8,096,000
Long-Term Obligations	6,346,000	...	...	...	...	...	...	...
Total Liabilities	18,459,000	10,684,000	10,314,000	10,699,000	9,678,000	9,068,000	9,124,000	8,118,000
Stockholders' Equity	24,615,000	22,964,000	21,437,000	23,174,000	25,826,000	28,029,000	28,656,000	27,120,000
Shares Outstanding	6,163,999	6,151,999	6,153,999	6,330,999	6,735,001	6,998,001	7,303,001	7,324,001
Statistical Record								
Return on Assets %	14.51	16.59	17.02	16.57	11.91	9.58	5.20	N.M.
Return on Equity %	23.12	23.96	24.43	23.50	16.08	12.66	6.81	N.M.
EBITDA Margin %	28.68	29.33	28.44	34.24	35.94	31.49	24.67	6.11
Net Margin %	19.69	20.00	19.25	23.15	19.96	18.95	10.01	N.M.
Asset Turnover	0.70	0.77	0.77	0.72	0.60	0.51	0.52	0.66
Current Ratio	2.44	2.27	2.14	1.37	1.65	1.62	2.08	1.59
Debt to Equity	0.26	...	...	...	...	...	...	...
Price Range	21.97-16.93	20.17-16.93	20.17-16.93	21.24-17.02	29.13-17.53	19.08-8.60	21.79-11.24	68.63-13.69
P/E Ratio	24.97-19.24	23.18-19.46	23.45-19.69	24.41-19.56	46.98-28.27	38.16-17.20	87.16-44.96	...

Address: 170 West Tasman Drive, San Jose, CA 95134-1706
Telephone: 408-526-4000
Fax: 408-526-4100
Web Site: www.cisco.com
Officers: John P. Morgridge - Chmn. Donald T. Valentine - Vice-Chmn.
Auditors: PricewaterhouseCoopers LLP
Investor Contact: 408-525-4856

CITRIX SYSTEMS, INC.

Exchange	Symbol	Price	52Wk Range	Yield	P/E
NMS	CTXS	$30.71 (8/31/2006)	45.16-23.66	N/A	29.82

*7 Year Price Score 98.85 *NYSE Composite Index=100 *12 Month Price Score 99.10

Interim Earnings (Per Share)

Qtr.	Mar	Jun	Sep	Dec
2003	0.18	0.17	0.18	0.21
2004	0.05	0.18	0.22	0.29
2005	0.22	0.16	0.23	0.32
2006	0.24	0.24	...	...

Interim Dividends (Per Share)
No Dividends Paid

Valuation Analysis

		Institutional Holding	
Forecast P/E	23.29	No of Institutions	
	(9/9/2006)	320	
Market Cap	$5.7 Billion	Shares	
Book Value	1.5 Billion	145,193,856	
Price/Book	3.73	% Held	
Price/Sales	5.49	78.99	

Business Summary: IT & Technology (MIC: 10.2 SIC: 7372 NAIC: 511210)

Citrix Systems is a supplier of access infrastructure software and services that enable enterprise-wide deployment, management and access of applications and information, including those designed for Microsoft® Windows® and UNIX® operating systems, Web-based information systems, as well as Web-based desktop access. Co.'s MetaFrame® products provide secure access to Windows-based, Web-based and UNIX applications regardless of the user's location, network connection or type of client hardware platforms. Co.'s Citrix® Online products include GoToAssist™ for technical support; GoToMyPC®, for remote access of desktop resources; and GoToMeeting™ for online conferencing and sharing of resources.

Recent Developments: For the quarter ended June 30 2006, net income increased 66.6% to $46.5 million from $27.9 million in the year-earlier quarter. Revenues were $275.5 million, up 30.4% from $211.2 million the year before. Operating income was $51.2 million versus $49.1 million in the prior-year quarter, an increase of 4.3%. Direct operating expenses rose 112.2% to $24.1 million from $11.4 million in the comparable period the year before. Indirect operating expenses increased 32.7% to $200.2 million from $150.8 million in the equivalent prior-year period.

Prospects: For full year 2006, Co. projects net revenue of $1.11 billion to $1.12 billion, and earnings of $1.00 to $1.05 per diluted share. Subsequently, on Aug 7 2006, Co. signed a definitive agreement to acquire Orbital Data Corp., a provider of services that optimize the delivery of applications over wide area networks, for about $50.0 million. The transaction, which is expected to close in 2006 third quarter, should add about $2.0 million in revenue and $0.04 to earnings per diluted share during the second half of 2006. In addition, Co. expects the transaction to add $10.0 million to $12.0 million in revenue and to be $0.06 to $0.07 dilutive to earnings per share in 2007.

Financial Data
(US$ in Thousands)

	6 Mos	3 Mos	12/31/2005	12/31/2004	12/31/2003	12/31/2002	12/31/2001	12/31/2000
Earnings Per Share	1.03	0.95	0.93	0.75	0.74	0.52	0.54	0.47
Cash Flow Per Share	1.69	1.77	1.70	1.57	1.55	1.05	1.24	1.31
Tang Book Value Per Share	4.30	3.37	2.68	2.80	3.24	2.57	2.48	2.94
Income Statement								
Total Revenue	535,466	259,998	908,722	741,157	588,625	527,448	591,629	470,446
EBITDA	133,733	78,824	254,511	188,057	192,183	141,815	210,686	202,254
Depn & Amortn	30,425	26,803	50,388	33,531	34,336	41,438	79,588	50,248
Income Before Taxes	120,701	59,185	225,508	164,433	160,687	113,157	152,551	135,017
Income Taxes	29,572	14,506	59,168	32,887	33,744	19,237	47,291	40,505
Net Income	91,129	44,679	166,340	131,546	126,943	93,920	105,260	94,512
Average Shares	191,500	186,013	178,036	174,734	171,447	179,359	194,498	199,731
Balance Sheet								
Total Assets	1,991,933	1,776,859	1,681,656	1,286,084	1,344,939	1,161,531	1,208,230	1,112,573
Current Liabilities	450,460	429,170	426,076	342,159	626,004	188,889	192,501	159,387
Long-Term Obligations	...	...	31,000	...	...	333,549	346,214	330,497
Total Liabilities	472,467	448,782	478,176	361,179	638,141	530,466	544,346	503,966
Stockholders' Equity	1,519,466	1,328,077	1,203,480	924,905	706,798	614,590	647,330	592,875
Shares Outstanding	184,312	179,987	176,608	170,383	164,472	168,136	185,177	184,055
Statistical Record								
Return on Assets %	11.32	11.25	11.21	9.97	10.13	7.93	9.07	8.77
Return on Equity %	15.23	15.24	15.63	16.08	19.21	14.89	16.97	16.74
EBITDA Margin %	24.98	30.32	28.01	25.37	32.65	26.89	35.61	42.99
Net Margin %	17.02	17.18	18.30	17.75	21.57	17.81	17.79	20.09
Asset Turnover	0.61	0.63	0.61	0.56	0.47	0.45	0.51	0.44
Current Ratio	1.92	1.82	1.70	1.25	1.29	1.99	1.80	3.68
Debt to Equity	...	...	0.03	...	...	0.54	0.53	0.56
Price Range	45.16-21.40	37.90-21.34	29.24-21.07	25.82-15.09	26.94-10.98	23.98-5.00	36.69-17.31	118.56-14.31
P/E Ratio	43.84-20.78	39.89-22.46	31.44-22.66	34.43-20.12	36.41-14.84	46.12-9.62	67.94-32.06	252.26-30.45

Address: 851 West Cypress Creek Road, Fort Lauderdale, FL 33309
Telephone: 954-267-3000
Fax: 954-341-6880

Web Site: www.citrix.com
Officers: Stephen M. Dow - Chmn. Mark B. Templeton - Pres., C.E.O.

Auditors: Ernst & Young LLP

COBRA ELECTRONICS CORP.

Exchange	Symbol	Price	52Wk Range	Yield	P/E
NMS	COBR	$8.21 (8/31/2006)	14.76-7.64	N/A	30.41

*7 Year Price Score 112.46 *NYSE Composite Index=100 *12 Month Price Score 85.28

Interim Earnings (Per Share)

Qtr.	Mar	Jun	Sep	Dec
2003	(0.07)	0.06	0.06	0.23
2004	(0.08)	0.08	0.09	0.28
2005	0.86	0.11	0.29	0.55
2006	(0.17)	(0.40)	...	...

Interim Dividends (Per Share)

No Dividends Paid

Valuation Analysis   **Institutional Holding**

Forecast P/E	N/A	No of Institutions
		30
Market Cap	$53.3 Million	Shares
Book Value	67.5 Million	2,207,186
Price/Book	0.79	% Held
Price/Sales	0.37	34.01

Business Summary: Communications (MIC: 10.1 SIC: 3663 NAIC: 334220)
Cobra Electronics is a manufacturer of two-way mobile communication products operating in the consumer electronics industry. Principal products include: microTALK GMRS, PMR two-way radios; 9 Band™, 10 Band™, 11 Band™ and 12 Band™ radar detectors with exclusive Strobe Alert™ technology; Citizens Band radios, including those with exclusive SoundTracker® and NightWatch™ technologies; HighGear™ accessories; GPS hand-held receivers; Marine VHF radios and chartplotters; and NAV ONE™ mobile navigation devices.

Recent Developments: For the quarter ended June 30 2006, net loss amounted to $2.7 million versus net income of $723,000 in the year-earlier quarter. Revenues were $39.6 million, up 17.6% from $33.7 million the year before. Operating loss was $3.9 million versus an income of $878,000 in the prior-year quarter. Direct operating expenses rose 41.3% to $35.4 million from $25.1 million in the comparable period the year before. Indirect operating expenses increased 5.0% to $8.1 million from $7.7 million in the equivalent prior-year period.

Prospects: Co.'s near term outlook appears mixed. On the positive side, Co. is forecasting that net sales in 2006 will exceed those of 2005. Sales gains are expected to be driven by mobile navigation, including sales of Co.'s newest product, the NavOne 2500, which is scheduled to ship to customers in Sep 2006. However, Co. stated that it expects earnings to decline from last year, absent the non-recurring events from last year and the asset write downs taken in second quarter of 2006. The decline in earnings reflects some delays in the introduction of certain higher margin products as well as substantial airfreight expenses likely to be incurred to ensure that inventory levels are maintained.

Financial Data (US$ in Thousands)	6 Mos	3 Mos	12/31/2005	12/31/2004	12/31/2003	12/31/2002	12/31/2001	12/31/2000
Earnings Per Share	0.27	0.78	1.81	0.36	0.28	0.26	0.73	1.12
Cash Flow Per Share	(0.12)	(1.08)	(0.82)	0.44	0.86	3.08	0.27	(0.92)
Tang Book Value Per Share	9.19	9.20	9.58	8.06	8.99	8.77	8.56	7.89
Dividends Per Share	0.160	...	...	...	...	...	...	...
Dividend Payout %	59.26	...	...	...	...	...	...	...
Income Statement								
Total Revenue	64,893	25,307	133,084	122,877	114,811	135,840	154,121	144,565
EBITDA	(3,181)	(1,740)	18,427	7,356	6,037	6,032	11,279	13,968
Depn & Amortn	2,648	...	4,844	3,369	2,732	2,738	2,213	1,758
Income Before Taxes	(5,706)	(1,662)	13,583	3,877	3,143	3,066	8,279	11,321
Income Taxes	(1,892)	(535)	1,599	1,496	1,302	1,346	3,594	4,132
Net Income	(3,814)	(1,127)	11,984	2,381	1,841	1,720	4,685	7,189
Average Shares	6,753	6,778	6,609	6,603	6,495	6,505	6,402	6,394
Balance Sheet								
Total Assets	86,608	91,048	92,922	82,494	76,233	75,182	89,592	77,905
Current Liabilities	12,528	13,635	13,531	13,198	10,005	11,445	12,529	26,311
Long-Term Obligations	...	...	...	...	...	...	15,378	...
Total Liabilities	19,074	20,895	20,670	22,367	18,532	18,903	35,620	29,279
Stockholders' Equity	67,534	70,153	72,252	60,127	57,701	56,279	53,972	48,626
Shares Outstanding	6,489	6,489	6,489	6,444	6,419	6,419	6,303	6,166
Statistical Record								
Return on Assets %	2.05	5.88	13.66	2.99	2.43	2.09	5.59	10.43
Return on Equity %	2.66	7.65	18.11	4.03	3.23	3.12	9.13	15.90
EBITDA Margin %	N.M.	N.M.	13.85	5.99	5.26	4.44	7.32	9.66
Net Margin %	N.M.	N.M.	9.00	1.94	1.60	1.27	3.04	4.97
Asset Turnover	1.67	1.57	1.52	1.54	1.52	1.65	1.84	2.10
Current Ratio	5.42	5.13	5.28	4.58	5.64	5.15	5.97	2.37
Debt to Equity	...	...	...	...	...	...	0.28	...
Price Range	14.76-7.00	14.76-7.00	14.76-7.00	10.05-6.16	7.55-5.88	9.25-5.86	10.00-5.01	8.00-4.25
P/E Ratio	54.67-25.93	18.92-8.97	8.15-3.87	27.92-17.11	26.96-21.00	35.58-22.54	13.70-6.86	7.14-3.79
Average Yield %	1.57	...	...	...	...	...	...	...

Address: 6500 West Cortland Street, Chicago, IL 60707
Telephone: 773-889-8870
Fax: 773-889-1678
Web Site: www.cobra.com
Officers: Carl Korn - Chmn. James R. Bazet - Pres., C.E.O.
Auditors: Grant Thornton LLP
Investor Contact: 773-804-6281
Transfer Agents: American Stock Transfer & Trust Co.

COGNIZANT TECHNOLOGY SOLUTIONS CORP.

Exchange	Symbol	Price	52Wk Range	Yield	P/E
NMS	CTSH	$69.91 (8/31/2006)	71.20-43.00	N/A	51.40

*7 Year Price Score 205.08 *NYSE Composite Index=100 *12 Month Price Score 115.50

Interim Earnings (Per Share)

Qtr.	Mar	Jun	Sep	Dec
2003	0.07	0.10	0.12	0.13
2004	0.14	0.17	0.18	0.21
2005	0.22	0.25	0.28	0.39
2006	0.32	0.37	...	...

Interim Dividends (Per Share)

Amt	Decl	Ex	Rec	Pay
200%	3/5/2003	4/2/2003	3/19/2003	4/1/2003
100%	4/12/2004	6/18/2004	5/27/2004	6/17/2004

Valuation Analysis

Forecast P/E 47.23 (9/9/2006)
Market Cap $9.8 Billion
Book Value 874.2 Million
Price/Book 11.27
Price/Sales 8.84

Institutional Holding

No of Institutions 349
Shares 127,874,656
% Held 90.75

Business Summary: IT & Technology (MIC: 10.2 SIC: 7371 NAIC: 541511)

Cognizant Technology Solutions is a provider of custom information technology (IT) consulting and technology services companies located in North America, Europe and Asia. Co. provides technology strategy consulting, development of complex systems, enterprise software package implementation and maintenance, data warehousing and business intelligence, application testing, application maintenance, infrastructure management, and vertically-oriented business process outsourcing. Co. provides its services using an integrated on-site/offshore business model that combines technical and account management teams located on-site at customer location and offshore at development centers.

Recent Developments: For the quarter ended June 30 2006, net income increased 52.8% to $55.1 million from $36.0 million in the year-earlier quarter. Revenues were $336.8 million, up 59.1% from $211.7 million the year before. Operating income was $60.7 million versus $42.4 million in the prior-year quarter, an increase of 43.2%. Direct operating expenses rose 59.9% to $188.3 million from $117.8 million in the comparable period the year before. Indirect operating expenses increased 70.3% to $87.8 million from $51.6 million in the equivalent prior-year period.

Prospects: Co.'s results are reflecting robust revenue growth across all business lines, indicating strong ongoing demand for its broad range of services particularly enterprise resource planning and customer relationship management, enhanced systems development, testing, data warehousing as well as infrastructure management. Moreover, Co. is encouraged by the significant growth rate exhibited in Europe during the second quarter of 2006. Looking ahead, Co. anticipates revenue of at least $363.0 million and earnings of approximately $0.38 per diluted share for the third quarter of 2006. For fiscal 2006, Co. expects revenue of at least $1.37 billion and earnings of at least $1.45 per diluted share.

Financial Data
(US$ in Thousands)

	6 Mos	3 Mos	12/31/2005	12/31/2004	12/31/2003	12/31/2002	12/31/2001	12/31/2000
Earnings Per Share	1.36	1.24	1.13	0.70	0.42	0.27	0.18	0.14
Cash Flow Per Share	1.26	1.12	1.17	0.97	0.64	0.48	0.28	0.27
Tang Book Value Per Share	5.96	5.41	4.88	3.22	1.97	1.24	0.84	0.58
Income Statement								
Total Revenue	622,315	285,479	885,830	586,673	368,231	229,086	177,778	137,031
EBITDA	130,125	60,145	197,690	134,153	82,039	51,125	39,265	30,105
Depn & Amortn	14,831	7,030	21,400	16,447	11,936	7,842	6,367	4,507
Income Before Taxes	122,584	56,552	185,272	122,095	72,231	45,091	35,399	28,247
Income Taxes	20,349	9,388	19,006	21,852	14,866	10,529	13,239	10,564
Net Income	102,235	47,164	166,266	100,243	57,365	34,562	22,160	17,683
Average Shares	150,493	149,354	146,895	142,556	135,814	127,386	122,226	121,536
Balance Sheet								
Total Assets	1,046,066	934,327	869,893	572,745	360,589	231,473	144,983	109,540
Current Liabilities	169,320	138,874	155,748	115,060	62,636	41,487	21,698	26,722
Total Liabilities	171,873	141,176	155,748	119,216	86,519	65,992	46,191	43,424
Stockholders' Equity	874,193	793,151	714,145	453,529	274,070	165,481	98,792	66,116
Shares Outstanding	140,886	140,377	139,346	134,177	128,674	122,520	116,130	111,912
Statistical Record								
Return on Assets %	23.19	23.58	23.05	21.42	19.38	18.36	17.41	19.75
Return on Equity %	27.86	27.91	28.48	27.48	26.10	26.16	26.88	31.61
EBITDA Margin %	20.91	21.07	22.32	22.87	22.28	22.32	22.09	21.97
Net Margin %	16.43	16.52	18.77	17.09	15.58	15.09	12.46	12.90
Asset Turnover	1.29	1.29	1.23	1.25	1.24	1.22	1.40	1.53
Current Ratio	4.79	5.11	4.26	3.95	4.45	4.24	5.41	3.30
Price Range	69.01-43.00	60.16-39.94	52.25-35.86	42.77-20.37	24.20-8.74	12.61-5.50	8.38-3.33	11.65-5.15
P/E Ratio	50.74-31.62	48.52-32.21	46.24-31.73	61.10-29.10	57.62-20.82	46.70-20.38	46.53-18.52	83.18-36.71

Address: 500 Glenpointe Centre West, Teaneck, NJ 07666
Telephone: 201-801-0233
Fax: 201-801-0243

Web Site: www.cognizant.com
Officers: John E. Klein - Chmn. Lakshmi Narayanan - Pres., C.E.O.

Auditors: PricewaterhouseCoopers LLP
Transfer Agents: American Stock Transfer & Trust Co.

COLUMBIA SPORTSWEAR CO.

Exchange	Symbol	Price	52Wk Range	Yield	P/E
NMS	COLM	$48.82 (8/31/2006)	57.31-42.07	N/A	14.53

*7 Year Price Score 95.40 *NYSE Composite Index=100 *12 Month Price Score 96.75

Interim Earnings (Per Share)

Qtr.	Mar	Jun	Sep	Dec
2003	0.37	0.23	1.56	0.79
2004	0.49	0.26	1.68	0.98
2005	0.52	0.16	1.74	0.97
2006	0.52	0.13	...	...

Interim Dividends (Per Share)

Amt	Decl	Ex	Rec	Pay
3-for-2	5/2/2001	6/5/2001	5/17/2001	6/4/2001

Valuation Analysis

Forecast P/E	15.29
	(9/9/2006)
Market Cap	$1.7 Billion
Book Value	716.4 Million
Price/Book	2.43
Price/Sales	1.45

Institutional Holding

No of Institutions	122
Shares	14,650,204
% Held	41.06

Business Summary: Apparel (MIC: 4.4 SIC: 2329 NAIC: 315299)

Columbia Sportswear is engaged in the design, manufacture, marketing and distribution of active outdoor apparel, including outerwear, sportswear, footwear, equipment and related accessories. Co. also licenses its brands in 13 product categories, including casual and outdoor socks, base layer thermal underwear, packs and adventure travel bags, belts and personal leather goods for men, leather outerwear, outdoor tools, camping gear, home furnishings, insulated coolers and containers, fishing and hunting waders, eyewear, watches and shoe and apparel care. As of Dec 31 2005, Co.'s products were sold to approximately 12,000 retailers throughout the world.

Recent Developments: For the quarter ended June 30 2006, net income decreased 23.4% to $4.8 million from $6.3 million in the year-earlier quarter. Revenues were $211.6 million, up 13.6% from $186.2 million the year before. Operating income was $5.5 million versus $8.3 million in the prior-year quarter, a decrease of 34.5%. Direct operating expenses rose 15.5% to $130.1 million from $112.7 million in the comparable period the year before. Indirect operating expenses increased 16.5% to $76.0 million from $65.2 million in the equivalent prior-year period.

Prospects: Results are benefiting from sales increases driven by growth in demand for Co.'s apparel products in the international markets and strong shipments of footwear products domestically. Consequently, Co. anticipates third-quarter 2006 revenue growth of 11.0% to 12.0%, with a net income decline of approximately 12.0%, including approximately $2.0 million in after-tax stock-based compensation expense, compared with the same period of 2005. For full-year 2006, Co. projects net sales growth of approximately 11.0% compared with 2005, and diluted earnings per share of approximately $3.22, including $0.20 in stock-based compensation expense.

Financial Data
(US$ in Thousands)

	6 Mos	3 Mos	12/31/2005	12/31/2004	12/31/2003	12/31/2002	12/31/2001	12/31/2000
Earnings Per Share	3.36	3.39	3.36	3.40	2.96	2.56	2.23	1.48
Cash Flow Per Share	4.02	3.80	3.51	2.32	3.03	4.27	1.75	1.35
Tang Book Value Per Share	19.62	20.36	19.81	18.57	15.62	11.72	9.00	6.46
Income Statement								
Total Revenue	471,764	260,211	1,155,791	1,095,307	951,786	816,319	779,581	614,825
EBITDA	45,169	33,803	209,512	230,056	213,254	183,042	165,604	110,723
Depn & Amortn	11,883	5,980	23,546	18,628	23,065	19,367	17,423	14,330
Income Before Taxes	37,099	29,721	190,855	214,921	190,669	164,029	145,613	92,155
Income Taxes	12,799	10,254	60,119	76,297	70,548	61,511	56,789	33,544
Net Income	24,300	19,467	130,736	138,624	120,121	102,518	88,824	58,611
Average Shares	36,965	37,339	38,943	40,812	40,591	40,063	39,840	39,607
Balance Sheet								
Total Assets	916,082	934,925	970,778	949,444	783,766	592,817	474,967	375,086
Current Liabilities	183,299	149,733	212,313	146,896	118,886	98,849	95,802	97,636
Long-Term Obligations	...	...	7,414	12,636	16,335	20,636	25,047	26,000
Total Liabilities	199,663	165,510	227,988	169,194	142,937	120,098	121,578	126,097
Stockholders' Equity	716,419	769,415	742,790	780,250	640,829	472,719	353,389	248,989
Shares Outstanding	35,620	36,925	36,863	40,126	40,253	39,737	39,282	38,564
Statistical Record								
Return on Assets %	14.44	13.62	13.62	15.95	17.45	19.20	20.90	17.19
Return on Equity %	18.22	16.42	17.17	19.46	21.57	24.82	29.49	26.98
EBITDA Margin %	9.57	12.99	18.13	21.00	22.41	22.42	21.24	18.01
Net Margin %	5.15	7.48	11.31	12.66	12.62	12.56	11.39	9.53
Asset Turnover	1.36	1.24	1.20	1.26	1.38	1.53	1.83	1.80
Current Ratio	3.55	4.60	3.61	5.15	5.22	4.66	3.83	2.96
Debt to Equity	...	...	0.01	0.02	0.03	0.04	0.07	0.10
Price Range	57.31-42.07	54.54-42.07	59.61-42.07	60.93-50.52	59.28-32.80	47.55-28.79	50.99-20.21	36.00-11.83
P/E Ratio	17.06-12.52	16.09-12.41	17.74-12.52	17.92-14.86	20.03-11.08	18.57-11.25	22.87-9.06	24.32-8.00

Address: 14375 NW Science Park Drive, Portland, OR 97229-5418
Telephone: 503-985-4000
Fax: 503-985-5800

Web Site: www.columbia.com
Officers: Gertrude Boyle - Chmn. Timothy P. Boyle - Pres., C.E.O.

Auditors: Deloitte & Touche LLP
Investor Contact: 800-547-8066
Transfer Agents: Mellon Investor Services LLC, Ridgefield Park, NJ

COMCAST CORP

Exchange	Symbol	Price	52Wk Range	Yield	P/E
NMS	CMCS A	$35.04 (8/31/2006)	35.47-25.92	N/A	58.40

*7 Year Price Score 71.76 *NYSE Composite Index=100 *12 Month Price Score 112.00

Interim Earnings (Per Share)

Qtr.	Mar	Jun	Sep	Dec
2003	(0.13)	(0.01)	1.41	0.17
2004	0.03	0.12	0.10	0.19
2005	0.06	0.19	0.10	0.06
2006	0.22	0.22	...	...

Interim Dividends (Per Share)
No Dividends Paid

Valuation Analysis / Institutional Holding

Forecast P/E	41.87	No of Institutions
	(9/9/2006)	651
Market Cap	$73.3 Billion	Shares
Book Value	39.9 Billion	991,098,368
Price/Book	1.84	% Held
Price/Sales	3.13	72.56

Business Summary: Media (MIC: 13.1 SIC: 4841 NAIC: 561499)

Comcast is engaged in the development, management and operation of broadband cable systems. Co. manages its operations through two reportable segments "Cable" and "Content". Co.'s Cable segment develops, manages and operates its broadband cable systems, including video, high-speed Internet and phone services. Co.'s Content segment includes its six national cable networks: E! Entertainment Television, Style Network, The Golf Channel, OLN, G4 and AZN Television. As of Dec 31 2005, Co.'s cable operations served more than 21 million video subscribers.

Recent Developments: For the quarter ended June 30 2006, net income increased 7.0% to $460.0 million from $430.0 million in the year-earlier quarter. Revenues were $6.23 billion, up 11.3% from $5.60 billion the year before. Operating income was $1.23 billion versus $1.05 billion in the prior-year quarter, an increase of 17.3%. Indirect operating expenses increased 9.9% to $5.00 billion from $4.55 billion in the equivalent prior-year period.

Prospects: Co.'s results are being driven by continued growth in the cable system assets of its digital cable and high-speed Internet services, and rate increases in its video services. For 2006, excluding pending transactions with Adelphia and Time Warner, Co. now anticipates cable revenue growth between 10.0% and 11.0% compared with its previous guidance of 9.0% to 10.0%. Revenue generating unit (RGU) additions are expected to increase about 20.0% above previous guidance of at least 3.5 million additions or approximately 60.0% above 2005 RGU additions of 2.6 million. Full year 2006 consolidated revenue is projected to grow between 10.0% and 11.0% versus Co.'s previous guidance of 9.0% to 10.0%.

Financial Data
(US$ in Thousands)

	6 Mos	3 Mos	12/31/2005	12/31/2004	12/31/2003	12/31/2002	12/31/2001	12/31/2000
Earnings Per Share	0.60	0.57	0.42	0.43	1.44	(0.25)	0.63	2.13
Cash Flow Per Share	2.67	2.49	2.24	2.64	1.27	2.70	1.66	...
Income Statement								
Total Revenue	12,129,000	5,901,000	22,255,000	20,307,000	18,348,000	12,460,000	9,836,000	8,357,000
EBITDA	4,784,000	2,267,000	8,479,000	8,309,000	6,319,000	2,986,000	5,004,000	6,912,000
Depn & Amortn	2,354,000	1,151,000	4,803,000	4,623,000	4,438,000	2,032,000	3,416,000	2,619,000
Income Before Taxes	1,458,000	640,000	1,880,000	1,810,000	(137,000)	70,000	854,000	3,565,000
Income Taxes	526,000	164,000	933,000	826,000	(16,000)	134,000	470,000	1,429,000
Net Income	926,000	466,000	928,000	970,000	3,240,000	(274,000)	609,000	2,021,000
Average Shares	2,123,000	2,142,000	2,208,000	2,250,000	2,256,000	1,110,000	965,000	949,000
Balance Sheet								
Total Assets	103,088,000	102,982,000	103,146,000	104,694,000	109,159,000	113,105,000	38,261,000	...
Current Liabilities	5,764,000	5,700,000	6,269,000	8,635,000	9,654,000	15,383,000	3,223,000	...
Long-Term Obligations	23,360,000	23,249,000	21,682,000	20,093,000	23,835,000	27,957,000	11,742,000	...
Total Liabilities	62,509,000	62,294,000	62,270,000	62,804,000	67,205,000	72,102,000	22,908,000	...
Stockholders' Equity	39,907,000	40,026,000	40,219,000	41,422,000	41,662,000	38,329,000	14,473,000	...
Shares Outstanding	2,092,795	2,103,412	2,138,619	2,212,070	2,251,408	2,248,161	935,760	...
Statistical Record								
Return on Assets %	1.23	1.21	0.89	0.90	2.92	N.M.	...	...
Return on Equity %	3.15	3.07	2.27	2.33	8.10	N.M.	...	...
EBITDA Margin %	39.44	38.42	38.10	40.92	34.44	23.96	50.87	82.71
Net Margin %	7.63	7.90	4.17	4.78	17.66	N.M.	6.19	24.18
Asset Turnover	0.22	0.22	0.21	0.19	0.17	0.16	...	...
Current Ratio	0.61	0.70	0.41	0.41	0.56	0.46	1.45	...
Debt to Equity	0.59	0.58	0.54	0.49	0.57	0.73	0.81	...
Price Range	33.52-25.92	33.78-25.92	34.30-25.92	36.13-26.48	34.54-23.57	37.13-17.40	45.25-32.79	51.44-29.75
P/E Ratio	55.87-43.20	59.26-45.47	81.67-61.71	84.02-61.58	23.99-16.37	...	71.83-52.05	24.15-13.97

Address: 1500 Market Street, Philadelphia, PA 19102-2148
Telephone: 215-665-1700

Web Site: www.comcast.com
Officers: Brian L. Roberts - Chmn., Pres. C.E.O.
Julian A. Brodsky - Vice-Chmn.

Auditors: Deloitte & Touche LLP
Investor Contact: 215-981-7537
Transfer Agents: Computershare Trust Co., N.A., Providence, RI

COMMERCE BANCSHARES, INC.

Exchange	Symbol	Price	52Wk Range	Yield	P/E	Div Acheiver
NMS	CBSH	$50.12 (8/31/2006)	53.29-47.57	1.96	15.19	37 Years

*7 Year Price Score 109.69 *NYSE Composite Index=100 *12 Month Price Score 95.71

Interim Earnings (Per Share)
Qtr.	Mar	Jun	Sep	Dec
2003	0.60	0.65	0.72	0.71
2004	0.68	0.72	0.84	0.71
2005	0.70	0.76	0.90	0.81
2006	0.78	0.82	...	...

Interim Dividends (Per Share)
Amt	Decl	Ex	Rec	Pay
0.229Q	10/21/2005	11/25/2005	11/29/2005	12/13/2005
0.245Q	2/17/2006	3/7/2006	3/9/2006	3/28/2006
0.245Q	4/19/2006	6/5/2006	6/7/2006	6/27/2006
0.245Q	7/28/2006	9/11/2006	9/13/2006	9/27/2006

Indicated Div: $0.98 (Div. Reinv. Plan)

Valuation Analysis
Forecast P/E	19.85 (9/9/2006)
Market Cap	$3.3 Billion
Book Value	1.3 Billion
Price/Book	2.50
Price/Sales	3.00

Institutional Holding
No of Institutions	173
Shares	28,271,788
% Held	42.63

Business Summary: Commercial Banking (MIC: 8.1 SIC: 6022 NAIC: 522110)

Commerce Bancshares is a bank holding company. Co. conducts its principal activities through its banking and non-banking subsidiaries from approximately 340 locations throughout Missouri, Illinois and Kansas. Co. owns three national banking associations, which are headquartered in Missouri, Kansas and Nebraska. The Nebraska bank is limited to the issuance of credit cards. Co.'s principal activities include retail and commercial banking, investment management, securities brokerage, mortgage banking, credit related insurance, venture capital and real estate activities. As of Dec 31 2005, Co. had total assets of $13.89 billion and total deposits of $10.85 billion.

Recent Developments: For the quarter ended June 30 2006, net income increased 1.8% to $55.3 million from $54.4 million in the year-earlier quarter. Net interest income decreased 0.7% to $126.5 million from $127.4 million in the year-earlier quarter. Provision for loan losses was $5.7 million versus $5.5 million in the prior-year quarter, an increase of 3.1%. Non-interest income rose 7.6% to $91.5 million from $85.0 million, while non-interest expense advanced 5.3% to $129.6 million.

Prospects: Co.'s near-term outlook appears to be promising. Co.'s results are benefiting from overall revenue growth, coupled with positive expense control and lower levels of loan losses. Moreover, the increase in Co.'s net interest income is being derived from improvement in the mix of assets on its balance sheet. Notably, the growth in Co.'s loans is primarily attributable to the increase in its business and construction loan portfolios, reflecting new business particularly in regional markets, as well as increased borrowings by existing customers. In addition, such growth is aided by a combination of Co.'s deposit growth and a reduction in its investment securities portfolio.

Financial Data
(US$ in Thousands)

	6 Mos	3 Mos	12/31/2005	12/31/2004	12/31/2003	12/31/2002	12/31/2001	12/31/2000
Earnings Per Share	3.30	3.24	3.16	2.95	2.68	2.50	2.25	2.16
Cash Flow Per Share	5.53	4.86	4.22	3.59	3.53	3.33	3.42	2.89
Tang Book Value Per Share	19.32	18.99	19.05	19.20	18.69	17.63	15.36	13.59
Dividends Per Share	0.947	0.931	0.914	0.834	0.674	0.535	0.501	0.463
Dividend Payout %	28.68	28.68	28.93	28.26	25.18	21.42	22.33	21.39
Income Statement								
Interest Income	387,877	188,627	697,566	610,090	617,410	652,553	750,962	812,168
Interest Expense	137,663	64,892	195,864	112,759	115,018	152,588	283,052	331,515
Net Interest Income	250,214	123,735	501,702	497,331	502,392	499,965	467,910	480,653
Provision for Losses	10,104	4,432	28,785	30,351	40,676	34,108	36,423	35,159
Non-Interest Income	180,911	89,448	341,199	326,931	301,667	280,572	277,512	252,808
Non-Interest Expense	259,511	129,961	496,522	482,769	472,144	452,927	439,638	430,381
Income Before Taxes	161,510	78,790	317,594	311,142	291,239	293,502	269,361	267,921
Income Taxes	53,233	25,846	94,347	90,801	84,715	94,004	87,387	89,347
Net Income	108,277	52,944	223,247	220,341	206,524	199,498	181,974	178,574
Average Shares	67,460	67,927	70,561	74,619	77,298	79,920	81,101	82,517
Balance Sheet								
Net Loans & Leases	9,251,447	9,009,771	8,770,736	8,172,965	8,007,458	7,745,326	7,508,509	7,778,220
Total Assets	14,273,397	13,731,122	13,885,545	14,250,368	14,287,164	13,308,415	12,902,806	11,115,117
Total Deposits	11,042,345	11,154,356	10,851,813	10,434,309	10,206,208	9,913,311	10,031,966	9,081,738
Total Liabilities	12,942,002	12,412,877	12,547,707	12,823,488	12,836,210	11,892,078	11,630,323	9,971,362
Stockholders' Equity	1,331,395	1,318,245	1,337,838	1,426,880	1,450,954	1,416,337	1,272,483	1,143,755
Shares Outstanding	66,400	66,864	67,693	71,754	74,934	77,679	79,539	79,866
Statistical Record								
Return on Assets %	1.60	1.63	1.59	1.54	1.50	1.52	1.52	1.58
Return on Equity %	16.79	16.83	16.15	15.27	14.41	14.84	15.06	16.02
Net Interest Margin %	63.48	65.60	71.92	81.52	81.37	76.62	62.31	59.18
Efficiency Ratio %	44.56	46.74	47.80	51.52	51.37	48.54	42.75	40.41
Loans to Deposits	0.84	0.81	0.81	0.78	0.78	0.78	0.75	0.86
Price Range	53.29-47.57	53.29-44.36	53.29-44.36	47.81-39.96	44.70-30.61	38.25-28.59	33.84-26.04	33.30-20.05
P/E Ratio	16.15-14.42	16.45-13.69	16.86-14.04	16.21-13.55	16.68-11.42	15.30-11.44	15.04-11.58	15.42-9.28
Average Yield %	1.86	1.87	1.89	1.92	1.85	1.55	1.69	1.83

Address: 1000 Walnut, Kansas City, MO 64106 **Telephone:** 816-234-2000 **Fax:** 816-234-2369	**Web Site:** www.commercebank.com **Officers:** David W. Kemper - Chmn., Pres., C.E.O. Johnathan M. Kemper - Vice-Chmn.	**Auditors:** KPMG LLP **Investor Contact:** 800-892-7100 **Transfer Agents:** EquiServe Trust Company, N.A, Jersey City, NJ

COMMUNITY BANKS, INC. (PA)

Exchange	Symbol	Price	52Wk Range	Yield	P/E	Div Achiever
NMS	CMTY	$26.12 (8/31/2006)	28.42-23.90	3.06	14.59	14 Years

*7 Year Price Score 99.97   *NYSE Composite Index=100   *12 Month Price Score 94.30

Interim Earnings (Per Share)
Qtr.	Mar	Jun	Sep	Dec
2003	0.39	0.38	0.39	0.39
2004	0.39	0.41	0.43	0.42
2005	0.42	(0.09)	0.42	0.50
2006	0.44	0.44	...	...

Interim Dividends (Per Share)
Amt	Decl	Ex	Rec	Pay
0.19Q	2/14/2006	3/16/2006	3/20/2006	4/3/2006
5%	2/14/2006	4/11/2006	4/14/2006	4/28/2006
0.20Q	5/9/2006	6/15/2006	6/19/2006	7/3/2006
0.20Q	8/1/2006	9/14/2006	9/18/2006	10/2/2006

Indicated Div: $0.80

Valuation Analysis
Forecast P/E 14.08 (9/9/2006)
Market Cap $612.6 Million
Book Value 465.8 Million
Price/Book 1.32
Price/Sales 2.82

Institutional Holding
No of Institutions 55
Shares 4,051,422
% Held 17.27

Business Summary: Commercial Banking (MIC: 8.1 SIC: 6021 NAIC: 522110)
Community Banks is a financial holding company whose wholly-owned subsidiaries include CommunityBanks, CommunityBanks Investments, Inc., and Community Banks Life Insurance Company. Co. operates 71 branch banking offices located in Adams, Berks, Chester, Cumberland, Dauphin, Lancaster, Luzerne, Northumberland, Schuylkill, Snyder, and York Counties in Pennsylvania, and Carroll County in Maryland. Co. provides a range of services including secured and unsecured commercial loans, residential and commercial mortgages and various forms of consumer lending. Deposit services include checking, savings, time and money market deposits. As of Dec 31 2005, Co. had total assets of $3.33 billion.

Recent Developments: For the quarter ended June 30 2006, net income amounted to $10.5 million versus a net loss of $1.1 million in the year-earlier quarter. Net interest income increased 81.1% to $27.0 million from $14.9 million in the year-earlier quarter. Provision for loan losses was $650,000 versus $750,000 in the prior-year quarter, a decrease of 13.3%. Non-interest income rose 52.6% to $8.5 million from $5.6 million, while non-interest expense declined 2.1% to $20.7 million.

Prospects: On June 19 2006, Co. announced that its subsidiary, CommunityBanks, has reached a definitive agreement with Omega Financial Corporation to acquire Sentry Trust Company (Sentry), located in Chambersburg, PA. Pending necessary approvals, the transaction is expected to be consummated in the third quarter of 2006. Co. expects this acquisition to add depth to its trust administration services and provide it with the capability to offer fiduciary services to the growing Cumberland Valley. In addition, Sentry complements Co.'s banking expansion into Chambersburg.

Financial Data
(US$ in Thousands)

	6 Mos	3 Mos	12/31/2005	12/31/2004	12/31/2003	12/31/2002	12/31/2001	12/31/2000
Earnings Per Share	1.79	1.27	1.35	1.65	1.55	1.40	1.09	1.23
Cash Flow Per Share	1.93	1.64	1.24	2.32	2.79	1.20	1.35	0.69
Tang Book Value Per Share	8.83	9.12	9.04	11.86	10.80	10.02	8.97	8.47
Dividends Per Share	0.762	0.743	0.714	0.640	0.597	0.520	0.461	0.419
Dividend Payout %	42.46	58.56	52.82	38.84	38.52	37.02	42.10	34.18
Income Statement								
Interest Income	95,827	46,889	142,293	99,799	94,865	96,700	98,075	79,578
Interest Expense	41,956	20,025	59,648	43,242	42,329	46,212	52,140	41,720
Net Interest Income	53,871	26,864	82,645	56,557	52,536	50,488	45,935	37,858
Provision for Losses	1,150	500	2,300	3,100	2,500	3,350	5,080	2,308
Non-Interest Income	16,927	8,384	26,437	23,213	20,441	13,975	12,141	7,363
Non-Interest Expense	41,231	20,533	75,069	49,993	45,718	39,300	36,521	25,774
Income Before Taxes	28,417	14,215	31,713	26,677	24,759	21,813	16,475	17,139
Income Taxes	7,344	3,646	6,072	4,879	4,359	3,367	2,879	4,288
Net Income	21,073	10,569	25,641	21,798	20,400	18,446	13,596	12,851
Average Shares	23,858	24,212	18,975	13,203	13,121	13,116	12,461	12,232
Balance Sheet								
Net Loans & Leases	2,320,889	2,263,510	2,211,532	1,201,530	1,065,433	892,225	845,146	684,044
Total Assets	3,385,599	3,421,562	3,332,430	1,954,799	1,860,130	1,679,898	1,509,734	1,121,372
Total Deposits	2,406,551	2,373,865	2,294,367	1,305,537	1,230,685	1,132,913	1,003,225	779,246
Total Liabilities	2,919,839	2,945,975	2,855,757	1,802,458	1,716,724	1,550,736	1,398,485	1,034,229
Stockholders' Equity	465,760	475,587	476,673	152,341	143,406	129,162	111,249	87,143
Shares Outstanding	23,455	23,831	24,060	12,847	12,841	12,713	12,292	10,268
Statistical Record								
Return on Assets %	1.58	1.13	0.97	1.14	1.15	1.16	1.03	1.22
Return on Equity %	13.68	9.79	8.15	14.70	14.97	15.35	13.71	16.20
Net Interest Margin %	55.19	57.29	58.08	56.67	55.38	52.21	46.84	47.57
Efficiency Ratio %	36.01	37.15	44.49	40.64	39.65	35.51	33.14	29.65
Loans to Deposits	0.96	0.95	0.96	0.92	0.87	0.79	0.84	0.88
Price Range	28.42-23.90	28.42-21.94	28.42-21.94	32.88-24.14	30.61-19.84	21.38-16.87	20.46-13.39	15.18-10.45
P/E Ratio	15.88-13.35	22.38-17.28	21.05-16.25	19.93-14.63	19.75-12.80	15.27-12.05	18.77-12.28	12.34-8.49
Average Yield %	2.87	2.86	2.80	2.30	2.54	2.71	2.78	3.19

Address: 750 East Park Dr., Harrisburg, PA 17111 Telephone: 717-920-1698 Fax: 717-692-2972	Web Site: www.communitybanks.com Officers: Eddie L. Dunklebarger - Chmn., Pres., C.E.O. Donald F. Holt - Exec. V.P., Fin., C.F.O.	Auditors: Beard Miller Company LLP

COMMUNITY TRUST BANCORP, INC.

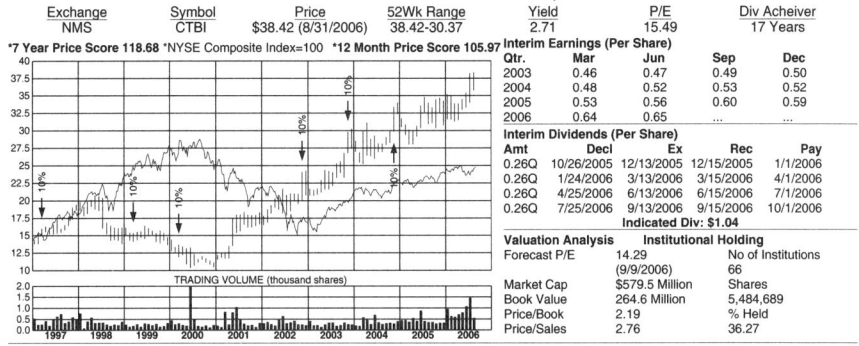

Exchange	Symbol	Price	52Wk Range	Yield	P/E	Div Acheiver
NMS	CTBI	$38.42 (8/31/2006)	38.42-30.37	2.71	15.49	17 Years

*7 Year Price Score 118.68 *NYSE Composite Index=100 *12 Month Price Score 105.97

Interim Earnings (Per Share)

Qtr.	Mar	Jun	Sep	Dec
2003	0.46	0.47	0.49	0.50
2004	0.48	0.52	0.53	0.52
2005	0.53	0.56	0.60	0.59
2006	0.64	0.65	...	...

Interim Dividends (Per Share)

Amt	Decl	Ex	Rec	Pay
0.26Q	10/26/2005	12/13/2005	12/15/2005	1/1/2006
0.26Q	1/24/2006	3/13/2006	3/15/2006	4/1/2006
0.26Q	4/25/2006	6/13/2006	6/15/2006	7/1/2006
0.26Q	7/25/2006	9/13/2006	9/15/2006	10/1/2006

Indicated Div: $1.04

Valuation Analysis   **Institutional Holding**

Forecast P/E	14.29	No of Institutions
	(9/9/2006)	66
Market Cap	$579.5 Million	Shares
Book Value	264.6 Million	5,484,689
Price/Book	2.19	% Held
Price/Sales	2.76	36.27

Business Summary: Commercial Banking (MIC: 8.1 SIC: 6021 NAIC: 522110)

Community Trust Bancorp is a bank holding company that owns all the capital stock of one commercial bank and one trust company, serving small and mid-sized communities in eastern, northeast, central, and south central Kentucky and southern West Virginia. The commercial bank is Community Trust Bank, Inc. The trust company, Community Trust and Investment Company, has offices in Lexington, Pikeville, Ashland, Middlesboro, and Versailles, KY. Through its subsidiaries, Co. engages in a range of commercial and personal banking and trust activities. Lending activities include making commercial, construction, mortgage, and personal loans. At Dec 31 2005, Co. had total assets of $2.85 billion.

Recent Developments: For the quarter ended June 30 2006, net income increased 16.7% to $9.9 million from $8.5 million in the year-earlier quarter. Net interest income increased 8.3% to $26.8 million from $24.8 million in the year-earlier quarter. Provision for loan losses was $1.4 million versus $1.7 million in the prior-year quarter, a decrease of 20.6%. Non-interest income fell 4.7% to $8.4 million from $8.9 million, while non-interest expense advanced 0.9% to $19.9 million.

Prospects: Co. attributes its recent bottom-line growth to increased net interest income, which is being driven by higher net interest margin. In addition, Co.'s loan portfolio remains solid, benefiting from loan growth in three of its major loan categories which includes, commercial, consumer and residential real estate, partially offset by a slight decrease in consumer portfolio. Furthermore, Co. continues to experience decreasing provision for loan losses, as a result of the improvement in credit quality trends and a reduction in overall losses. Meanwhile, Co. noted that its total assets at Jun 30 2006 were $3.00 billion, compared to $2.80 billion from a year earlier.

Financial Data
(US$ in Thousands)

	6 Mos	3 Mos	12/31/2005	12/31/2004	12/31/2003	12/31/2002	12/31/2001	12/31/2000
Earnings Per Share	2.48	2.39	2.27	2.05	1.92	1.81	1.45	1.40
Cash Flow Per Share	3.35	3.09	3.06	8.08	15.36	13.15	9.40	4.55
Tang Book Value Per Share	13.14	12.87	12.48	11.64	10.63	9.70	8.36	8.06
Dividends Per Share	1.020	1.000	0.980	0.867	0.746	0.647	0.609	0.572
Dividend Payout %	41.13	41.84	43.17	42.31	38.91	35.74	41.97	40.74
Income Statement								
Interest Income	90,726	43,967	160,162	130,401	128,514	146,550	176,835	175,749
Interest Expense	37,934	17,991	56,957	37,189	43,895	57,293	93,717	91,515
Net Interest Income	52,792	25,976	103,205	93,212	84,619	89,257	83,118	84,234
Provision for Losses	1,350	...	8,285	8,648	9,332	10,086	9,185	9,217
Non-Interest Income	16,568	8,124	33,467	33,917	36,372	27,928	23,774	19,526
Non-Interest Expense	39,944	20,077	78,569	74,595	70,735	67,341	64,938	61,927
Income Before Taxes	28,066	14,023	49,818	43,886	40,924	39,758	32,769	32,616
Income Taxes	8,406	4,255	15,406	12,936	12,033	12,158	10,497	10,270
Net Income	19,660	9,768	34,412	30,950	28,891	27,600	22,272	22,346
Average Shares	15,274	15,252	15,139	15,082	15,044	15,255	15,396	15,911
Balance Sheet								
Net Loans & Leases	2,111,003	2,073,112	2,077,838	1,875,502	1,711,607	1,611,336	1,687,424	1,668,639
Total Assets	2,965,211	2,967,793	2,849,213	2,709,094	2,474,039	2,487,911	2,503,905	2,261,975
Total Deposits	2,290,466	2,309,791	2,246,551	2,140,418	2,067,615	2,127,716	2,155,772	1,943,916
Total Liabilities	2,700,651	2,707,961	2,595,268	2,472,925	2,252,646	2,278,492	2,312,299	2,080,071
Stockholders' Equity	264,560	259,832	253,945	236,169	221,393	209,419	191,606	181,904
Shares Outstanding	15,082	15,015	14,997	14,845	14,807	14,941	15,207	15,573
Statistical Record								
Return on Assets %	1.30	1.26	1.24	1.19	1.16	1.11	0.93	1.00
Return on Equity %	14.77	14.55	14.04	13.49	13.41	13.76	11.93	12.58
Net Interest Margin %	57.35	59.08	64.44	71.48	65.84	60.91	47.00	47.93
Efficiency Ratio %	35.99	38.54	40.58	45.40	42.90	38.60	32.37	31.71
Loans to Deposits	0.92	0.90	0.92	0.88	0.83	0.76	0.78	0.86
Price Range	35.40-30.37	35.18-28.06	34.79-28.00	34.00-25.25	30.27-20.73	24.30-16.46	18.41-11.55	14.43-10.38
P/E Ratio	14.27-12.25	14.72-11.74	15.33-12.33	16.59-12.31	15.77-10.80	13.42-9.09	12.69-7.97	10.31-7.41
Average Yield %	3.10	3.12	3.11	3.04	3.15	3.28	3.95	4.76

Address: 346 North Mayo Trail, Pikeville, KY 41501-2947 **Telephone:** 606-432-1414 **Fax:** 606-437-3345	**Web Site:** www.ctbi.com **Officers:** Burlin Coleman - Chmn. Jean R. Hale - Vice-Chmn., Pres., C.E.O.	**Auditors:** Deloitte & Touche LLP **Investor Contact:** 606-432-1414 **Transfer Agents:** Community Trust Bancorp, Inc., Pikeville, KY

COMPASS BANCSHARES INC.

Exchange	Symbol	Price	52Wk Range	Yield	P/E	Div Acheiver
NMS	CBSS	$58.00 (8/31/2006)	59.86-43.64	2.69	17.47	24 Years

*7 Year Price Score 118.33 *NYSE Composite Index=100 *12 Month Price Score 108.91

Interim Earnings (Per Share)

Qtr.	Mar	Jun	Sep	Dec
2003	0.64	0.68	0.68	0.69
2004	0.69	0.73	0.75	0.78
2005	0.78	0.81	0.83	0.76
2006	0.85	0.88	...	...

Interim Dividends (Per Share)

Amt	Decl	Ex	Rec	Pay
0.35Q	11/14/2005	12/13/2005	12/15/2005	1/2/2006
0.39Q	2/21/2006	3/13/2006	3/15/2006	4/3/2006
0.39Q	5/23/2006	6/13/2006	6/15/2006	7/3/2006
0.39Q	8/28/2006	9/13/2006	9/15/2006	10/2/2006

Indicated Div: $1.56 (Div. Reinv. Plan)

Valuation Analysis **Institutional Holding**
Forecast P/E 16.13 No of Institutions
(9/9/2006) 275
Market Cap $7.5 Billion Shares
Book Value 2.6 Billion 54,070,460
Price/Book 2.88 % Held
Price/Sales 3.03 41.79

Business Summary: Commercial Banking (MIC: 8.1 SIC: 6021 NAIC: 522110)

Compass Bancshares is a bank holding company headquartered in Birmingham, AL, with total assets of $30.80 billion as of Dec 31 2005. Co.'s Compass Bank conducts a general commercial banking and trust business at 384 banking centers, including 139 in Texas, 90 in Alabama, 71 in Arizona, 42 in Florida, 32 in Colorado, and 10 in New Mexico. In addition, Compass Bank operates loan production offices in Georgia, Illinois and Maryland. Compass Bank performs a range of banking services, including receiving demand and time deposits, making personal and commercial loans and furnishing personal and commercial checking accounts.

Recent Developments: For the quarter ended June 30 2006, net income increased 8.9% to $115.4 million from $106.0 million in the year-earlier quarter. Net interest income increased 21.7% to $287.7 million from $236.5 million in the year-earlier quarter. Provision for loan losses was $27.3 million versus $27.8 million in the prior-year quarter, a decrease of 1.7%. Non-interest income rose 3.4% to $181.4 million from $175.4 million, while non-interest expense advanced 19.4% to $265.9 million.

Prospects: Nothwithstanding the challenges of a flat yield curve, as well as the pressure of rising funding costs and uncertainty over interest rates, Co.'s near term outlook appears promising. Co.'s results are being fueled by an increase in revenue, as both net interest income and non-interest income are exhibiting solid gains. Moreover, solid growth in both Co.'s earning assets and average deposits is reflective of its focus on generating significant loans as well as on the continued growth of its lower-cost transaction account deposits. With respect to these factors, Co. is cautiously optimistic regarding its outlook for the remainder of 2006.

Financial Data
(US$ in Thousands)

	6 Mos	3 Mos	12/31/2005	12/31/2004	12/31/2003	12/31/2002	12/31/2001	12/31/2000
Earnings Per Share	3.32	3.25	3.18	2.95	2.69	2.42	2.11	2.00
Cash Flow Per Share	4.81	5.13	4.95	4.19	3.28	4.21	3.24	1.76
Tang Book Value Per Share	14.93	14.57	15.54	14.14	12.93	13.06	13.53	12.24
Dividends Per Share	1.480	1.440	1.400	1.250	1.120	1.000	0.920	0.880
Dividend Payout %	44.58	44.31	44.03	42.37	41.64	41.32	43.60	44.00
Income Statement								
Interest Income	961,661	450,198	1,545,152	1,273,526	1,277,287	1,386,923	1,517,721	1,432,844
Interest Expense	413,718	189,937	576,173	361,698	367,757	462,068	691,862	752,044
Net Interest Income	547,943	260,261	968,979	911,828	909,530	924,855	825,859	680,800
Provision for Losses	44,434	17,112	117,818	105,658	119,681	136,331	106,241	53,539
Non-Interest Income	346,710	165,344	658,678	617,590	526,184	441,063	376,378	298,904
Non-Interest Expense	510,220	244,370	901,803	868,478	797,883	752,429	685,770	569,589
Income Before Taxes	339,999	164,123	608,036	555,282	518,150	477,158	410,226	356,576
Income Taxes	116,719	56,214	206,206	185,498	176,282	162,759	139,829	115,985
Net Income	223,280	107,909	401,830	369,784	341,868	314,399	270,397	240,591
Average Shares	131,395	126,793	126,423	125,416	127,186	129,850	129,138	120,454
Balance Sheet								
Net Loans & Leases	23,942,972	23,025,657	21,105,042	18,598,583	17,120,920	16,248,490	13,515,893	11,340,877
Total Assets	33,613,492	32,782,179	30,798,232	28,184,628	26,963,113	23,884,709	23,015,000	19,992,244
Total Deposits	22,837,259	22,128,509	20,384,115	17,039,151	15,687,823	15,135,387	13,735,245	14,033,244
Total Liabilities	31,007,980	30,224,239	28,562,203	26,139,375	25,091,230	21,953,207	21,299,359	18,511,780
Stockholders' Equity	2,605,512	2,557,940	2,236,029	2,045,253	1,871,883	1,931,502	1,715,641	1,480,462
Shares Outstanding	129,319	129,059	123,538	123,264	122,086	126,116	126,800	120,972
Statistical Record								
Return on Assets %	1.34	1.33	1.36	1.34	1.34	1.34	1.26	1.26
Return on Equity %	17.72	17.71	18.77	18.83	17.98	17.24	16.92	17.93
Net Interest Margin %	56.25	57.81	62.71	71.60	71.21	66.68	54.41	47.51
Efficiency Ratio %	38.37	39.70	40.92	45.92	44.24	41.16	36.21	32.89
Loans to Deposits	1.05	1.04	1.04	1.09	1.09	1.07	0.98	0.81
Price Range	56.40-43.64	51.68-42.88	49.68-42.88	48.67-37.77	39.59-29.99	35.87-26.18	29.08-19.13	24.28-15.75
P/E Ratio	16.99-13.14	15.90-13.19	15.62-13.48	16.50-12.80	14.72-11.15	14.82-10.82	13.78-9.06	12.14-7.88
Average Yield %	2.98	3.05	3.02	2.91	3.23	3.16	3.74	4.64

Address: 15 South 20th Street, Birmingham, AL 35203 Telephone: 205-297-3000 Fax: 205-933-3043	Web Site: www.compassbank.com Officers: D. Paul Jones Jr. - Chmn., C.E.O. Garrett R. Hegel - C.F.O.	Auditors: PricewaterhouseCoopers LLP Investor Contact: 205-297-3331 Transfer Agents: Continental Stock Transfer & Trust Company, New York, NY

COMPUWARE CORP.

Exchange	Symbol	Price	52Wk Range	Yield	P/E
NMS	CPWR	$7.60 (8/31/2006)	9.84-6.12	N/A	19.49

*7 Year Price Score 67.68 *NYSE Composite Index=100 *12 Month Price Score 82.64

Interim Earnings (Per Share)

Qtr.	Jun	Sep	Dec	Mar
2003-04	0.01	(0.02)	0.06	0.09
2004-05	0.00	0.02	0.11	0.07
2005-06	0.06	0.06	0.10	0.15
2006-07	0.08	...	...	...

Interim Dividends (Per Share)
No Dividends Paid

Valuation Analysis

		Institutional Holding	
Forecast P/E	15.96	No of Institutions	241
	(9/9/2006)		
Market Cap	$2.8 Billion	Shares	278,643,008
Book Value	1.6 Billion	% Held	74.80
Price/Book	1.79		
Price/Sales	2.35		

Business Summary: IT & Technology (MIC: 10.2 SIC: 7372 NAIC: 511210)

Compuware is engaged in the development, marketing and support of an integrated set of systems software products designed to improve the productivity of information technology (IT) organizations in application development, application delivery, application service management and IT portfolio management. In addition, Co.'s professional services include business systems analysis, design, communication, programming and implementation as well as software conversion and systems planning and consulting. Co.'s two business segments; products and professional services, are offered across an array of technologies, including mainframe and distributed systems platforms.

Recent Developments: For the quarter ended June 30 2006, net income increased 19.1% from $24.6 million in the year-earlier quarter. Revenues were $296.3 million, down 0.3% from $297.3 million the year before. Operating income was $32.9 million versus $29.5 million in the prior-year quarter, an increase of 11.6%. Direct operating expenses rose 2.0% to $114.2 million from $111.9 million in the comparable period the year before. Indirect operating expenses decreased 4.3% to $149.2 million from $155.9 million in the equivalent prior-year period.

Prospects: Co.'s results are benefiting from higher software product revenue, due to license revenue growth related to its Vantage product line resulting from increased customer demand for performance related software, offset by lower revenues from Co.'s professional services due to cost reduction initiatives adopted by certain domestic customers within the automotive sector. Going forward, Co. will focus on growing revenue and profit margins by enhancing and promoting its existing product lines, expanding its product and service offerings through key acquisitions, developing strategic partnerships in order to provide clients with its product applications and managing its costs.

Financial Data
(US$ in Thousands)

	3 Mos	03/31/2006	03/31/2005	03/31/2004	03/31/2003	03/31/2002	03/31/2001	03/31/2000
Earnings Per Share	0.39	0.37	0.20	0.13	0.27	(0.66)	0.32	0.91
Cash Flow Per Share	0.65	0.60	0.63	0.67	1.00	1.04	0.92	0.46
Tang Book Value Per Share	3.18	3.17	3.01	3.00	2.78	2.42	1.78	1.23
Income Statement								
Total Revenue	296,318	1,205,361	1,231,839	1,264,647	1,375,340	1,728,547	2,010,050	2,230,628
EBITDA	57,156	205,948	162,613	111,192	210,023	(152,631)	295,732	633,286
Depn & Amortn	13,393	50,193	56,388	55,175	53,808	98,216	103,663	71,510
Income Before Taxes	43,763	191,460	106,225	56,017	156,215	(250,847)	192,069	561,776
Income Taxes	14,442	48,500	29,743	6,185	53,113	(5,592)	72,986	209,800
Net Income	29,321	142,960	76,482	49,832	103,102	(245,255)	119,083	351,976
Average Shares	377,527	387,569	388,501	384,608	378,440	371,786	372,809	384,691
Balance Sheet								
Total Assets	2,492,273	2,510,968	2,478,218	2,234,081	2,122,685	1,993,938	2,279,374	2,415,907
Current Liabilities	543,877	545,407	578,196	493,064	469,165	556,147	568,834	596,057
Long-Term Obligations	...	...	...	...	...	...	140,000	450,000
Total Liabilities	906,462	931,469	962,063	820,490	790,994	804,087	902,002	1,212,035
Stockholders' Equity	1,585,811	1,579,499	1,516,155	1,413,591	1,331,691	1,189,851	1,377,372	1,203,872
Shares Outstanding	372,520	377,903	388,403	385,343	382,367	375,820	369,816	361,621
Statistical Record								
Return on Assets %	5.98	5.73	3.25	2.28	5.01	N.M.	5.07	17.15
Return on Equity %	9.46	9.24	5.22	3.62	8.18	N.M.	9.23	30.74
EBITDA Margin %	19.29	17.09	13.20	8.79	15.27	N.M.	14.71	28.39
Net Margin %	9.90	11.86	6.21	3.94	7.50	N.M.	5.92	15.78
Asset Turnover	0.49	0.48	0.52	0.58	0.67	0.81	0.86	1.09
Current Ratio	2.63	2.65	2.35	2.32	2.24	1.91	1.76	1.66
Debt to Equity	...	...	...	...	...	...	0.10	0.37
Price Range	9.84-6.64	9.84-5.93	8.73-4.44	8.39-3.39	12.20-2.56	14.28-7.71	21.38-5.91	39.06-17.81
P/E Ratio	25.23-17.03	26.59-16.03	43.65-22.20	64.54-26.08	45.19-9.48	...	66.80-18.46	42.93-19.57

Address: One Campus Maritus, Detroit, MI 48226-5099
Telephone: 313-227-7300
Fax: 313-227-7555

Web Site: www.compuware.com
Officers: Peter Karmanos Jr. - Chmn., C.E.O. Robert C. Paul Covisint - C.E.O., Pres.

Auditors: Deloitte & Touche LLP
Investor Contact: 248-737-7345
Transfer Agents: EquiServe Trust Company N.A., Kansas City, MO

COMVERSE TECHNOLOGY, INC.

Exchange	Symbol	Price	52Wk Range	Yield	P/E
NMS	CMVT	$20.90 (8/31/2006)	29.24-17.34	N/A	38.00

*7 Year Price Score 55.34 *NYSE Composite Index=100 *12 Month Price Score 77.91

Interim Earnings (Per Share)

Qtr.	Apr	Jul	Oct	Jan
2002-03	(0.13)	0.02	(0.43)	(0.16)
2003-04	(0.03)	(0.01)	(0.02)	0.02
2004-05	0.03	0.06	0.08	0.10
2005-06	0.11	0.16	0.18	...

Interim Dividends (Per Share)
No Dividends Paid

Valuation Analysis

		Institutional Holding	
Forecast P/E	23.27	No of Institutions	
	(9/9/2006)	311	
Market Cap	$4.2 Billion	Shares	
Book Value	1.9 Billion	193,265,120	
Price/Book	2.18	% Held	
Price/Sales	3.78	95.67	

Business Summary: Communications (MIC: 10.1 SIC: 3661 NAIC: 334210)

Comverse Technology designs, develops, manufactures, markets and supports systems and software for multimedia communications and information processing applications. Through Comverse, Inc., Co. provides services products that enable telecommunications service providers to offer a variety of revenue and traffic generating services accessible to large numbers of simultaneous users. Through Verint Systems Inc., Co. provides analytic software-based solutions for communications interception, digital video security and surveillance, and enterprise business intelligence. Through Ulticom, Inc., Co. provides service enabling signaling software for wireline, wireless and Internet communications.

Recent Developments: For the quarter ended Oct 31 2005, net income increased 140.0% to $38.3 million from $16.0 million in the year-earlier quarter. Revenues were $299.0 million, up 21.8% from $245.5 million the year before. Operating income was $27.6 million versus $14.1 million in the prior-year quarter, an increase of 95.5%. Direct operating expenses rose 24.9% to $121.1 million from $96.9 million in the comparable period the year before. Indirect operating expenses increased 11.8% to $150.3 million from $134.4 million in the equivalent prior-year period.

Prospects: On Dec 12 2005, Co. announced that it has completed its acquisition of the GSS division and certain related assets of CSG Systems International, Inc. for approximately $249.0 million in cash, subject to certain post closing adjustments. The combination of GSS, a provider in software-based billing applications, with Co.'s Real-Time Billing group is expected to expand significantly Co.'s addressable market, and enhance its leadership position in the emerging converged billing market, serving wireless, wireline, cable, satellite, and Internet-based service providers.

Financial Data

(US$ in Thousands)	9 Mos	6 Mos	3 Mos	01/31/2005	01/31/2004	01/31/2003	01/31/2002	01/31/2001
Earnings Per Share	0.55	0.45	0.35	0.28	(0.03)	(0.69)	0.29	1.39
Cash Flow Per Share	0.54	0.43	0.64	0.60	0.68	0.52	0.79	1.51
Tang Book Value Per Share	9.59	9.40	9.19	8.93	8.43	8.25	8.68	7.33
Income Statement								
Total Revenue	857,602	558,636	272,801	959,442	765,892	735,889	1,270,218	1,225,058
EBITDA	176,266	78,590	33,207	153,878	87,331	(58,829)	122,879	321,159
Depn & Amortn	46,990	...	...	66,742	71,771	67,355	63,824	53,196
Income Before Taxes	129,276	78,590	33,207	83,156	8,580	(126,184)	59,055	267,963
Income Taxes	17,581	11,180	4,953	13,214	8,206	3,294	4,436	18,827
Net Income	97,370	59,075	24,261	57,330	(5,386)	(129,478)	54,619	249,136
Average Shares	215,983	214,081	213,065	204,804	190,351	187,212	186,434	189,964
Balance Sheet								
Total Assets	3,128,841	3,052,425	2,997,295	2,925,286	2,728,042	2,403,659	2,704,163	2,625,264
Current Liabilities	520,063	500,927	515,659	487,299	321,007	360,351	366,853	415,306
Long-Term Obligations	419,834	419,907	419,942	420,000	544,723	390,838	600,000	900,000
Total Liabilities	975,219	955,884	955,774	935,432	894,018	770,419	1,026,452	1,335,634
Stockholders' Equity	1,936,265	1,888,447	1,840,636	1,794,029	1,672,546	1,549,692	1,616,408	1,236,165
Shares Outstanding	201,861	200,925	200,223	198,878	194,549	187,754	186,248	168,643
Statistical Record								
Return on Assets %	3.95	3.28	2.61	2.02	N.M.	N.M.	2.05	12.49
Return on Equity %	6.41	5.33	4.21	3.30	N.M.	N.M.	3.83	25.52
EBITDA Margin %	20.55	14.07	12.17	16.04	11.40	N.M.	9.67	26.22
Net Margin %	11.35	10.57	8.89	5.98	N.M.	N.M.	4.30	20.34
Asset Turnover	0.37	0.36	0.35	0.34	0.30	0.29	0.48	0.61
Current Ratio	5.45	5.52	5.26	5.39	7.67	5.90	6.53	5.48
Debt to Equity	0.22	0.22	0.23	0.23	0.33	0.25	0.37	0.73
Price Range	27.77-20.59	25.58-15.48	25.58-15.48	25.03-15.48	19.95-8.82	21.37-6.82	113.31-15.90	121.63-65.25
P/E Ratio	50.49-37.44	56.84-34.40	73.09-44.23	89.39-55.29	...	...	390.73-54.83	87.50-46.94

Address: 170 Crossways Park Drive, Woodbury, NY 11797 Telephone: 516-677-7200 Fax: 516-677-7355	Web Site: www.comverse.com Officers: Kobi Alexander - Chmn., C.E.O. Itsik Danziger - Pres.	Auditors: Deloitte & Touche LLP Investor Contact: 516-677-7200

CONMED CORP.

Exchange	Symbol	Price	52Wk Range	Yield	P/E
NMS	CNMD	$20.49 (8/31/2006)	30.25-18.09	N/A	32.52

*7 Year Price Score 86.05 *NYSE Composite Index=100 *12 Month Price Score 87.66

Interim Earnings (Per Share)

Qtr.	Mar	Jun	Sep	Dec
2003	0.50	0.09	0.33	0.44
2004	0.40	0.41	0.06	0.25
2005	0.36	0.35	0.26	0.10
2006	0.15	0.12	...	...

Interim Dividends (Per Share)

Amt	Decl	Ex	Rec	Pay
50%	8/9/2001	9/10/2001	8/21/2001	9/7/2001

Valuation Analysis

Forecast P/E	24.36
	(9/9/2006)
Market Cap	$571.2 Million
Book Value	457.1 Million
Price/Book	1.25
Price/Sales	0.91

Institutional Holding

No of Institutions	106
Shares	27,461,976
% Held	98.48

Business Summary: Medical Instruments & Equipment (MIC: 9.6 SIC: 3845 NAIC: 334510)

Conmed is a medical technology company with an emphasis on surgical devices and equipment for minimally invasive procedures and monitoring. Co.'s products serve the clinical areas of arthroscopy, powered surgical instruments, electrosurgery, cardiac monitoring disposables, endosurgery and endoscopic technologies. They are used by surgeons and physicians in a variety of specialties including orthopedics, general surgery, gynecology, neurosurgery, and gastroenterology. Co. manufactures substantially all of its products and assembles them from components it produces.

Recent Developments: For the quarter ended June 30 2006, net income decreased 67.5% to $3.4 million from $10.5 million in the year-earlier quarter. Revenues were $163.5 million, up 3.3% from $158.3 million the year before. Operating income was $10.6 million versus $19.6 million in the prior-year quarter, a decrease of 46.1%. Direct operating expenses rose 12.5% to $85.7 million from $76.2 million in the comparable period the year before. Indirect operating expenses increased 7.5% to $67.2 million from $62.5 million in the equivalent prior-year period.

Prospects: Co. is experiencing sales growth, particularly from its capital equipment business due to increases in video imaging products and electrosurgical generator sales. In addition, Co. is also benefiting from the continuing trend for higher growth in international markets. Going forward, Co.'s long-term growth strategy includes continuing innovation and commercialization of new proprietary products and processes. For the third quarter of 2006, Co. expects revenues to range from $152.0 million to $157.0 million. Co. also anticipates achieving 5.0% organic sales growth for 2006 versus 2005 and continues to project that its operating margin in 2007 should improve to approximately 14.0% of sales.

Financial Data
(US$ in Thousands)

	6 Mos	3 Mos	12/31/2005	12/31/2004	12/31/2003	12/31/2002	12/31/2001	12/31/2000
Earnings Per Share	0.63	0.86	1.08	1.11	1.10	1.23	1.00	0.83
Cash Flow Per Share	1.43	1.50	1.45	2.53	2.01	1.64	3.21	1.56
Income Statement								
Total Revenue	321,939	158,466	617,305	558,388	497,130	453,062	428,722	392,230
EBITDA	35,692	18,459	94,534	90,029	98,912	101,719	99,106	93,951
Depn & Amortn	14,670	7,328	30,786	27,693	27,035	22,370	30,148	29,487
Income Before Taxes	11,481	6,265	48,170	49,562	53,009	54,836	38,134	30,178
Income Taxes	3,727	1,925	16,176	16,097	20,927	19,741	13,728	10,864
Net Income	7,754	4,340	31,994	33,465	32,082	34,151	24,406	19,314
Average Shares	28,266	28,358	29,736	30,105	29,256	27,827	24,401	23,271
Balance Sheet								
Total Assets	907,578	907,065	903,783	872,825	805,058	742,140	701,608	679,571
Current Liabilities	62,040	64,494	62,132	63,061	54,855	57,974	119,837	78,276
Long-Term Obligations	296,902	297,423	302,643	290,485	260,448	254,756	262,500	342,680
Total Liabilities	450,521	451,366	450,777	424,842	371,568	355,201	417,974	448,968
Stockholders' Equity	457,057	455,699	453,006	447,983	433,490	386,939	283,634	230,603
Shares Outstanding	27,877	28,086	28,192	28,979	29,103	28,808	25,261	22,990
Statistical Record								
Return on Assets %	2.05	2.86	3.60	3.98	4.15	4.73	3.53	2.87
Return on Equity %	3.96	5.55	7.10	7.57	7.82	10.19	9.49	8.72
EBITDA Margin %	11.09	11.65	15.31	16.12	19.90	22.45	23.12	23.95
Net Margin %	2.41	2.74	5.18	5.99	6.45	7.54	5.69	4.92
Asset Turnover	0.69	0.69	0.69	0.66	0.64	0.63	0.62	0.58
Current Ratio	4.12	4.03	4.11	3.54	3.67	3.34	1.37	2.45
Debt to Equity	0.65	0.65	0.67	0.65	0.60	0.66	0.93	1.49
Price Range	31.81-18.09	32.58-18.09	32.58-22.55	30.89-20.73	24.30-13.95	27.00-15.60	21.21-10.83	20.50-8.08
P/E Ratio	50.49-28.71	37.88-21.03	30.17-20.88	27.83-18.68	22.09-12.68	21.95-12.68	21.21-10.83	24.70-9.74

Address: 525 French Road, Utica, NY 13502
Telephone: 315-797-8375
Fax: 315-797-0321

Web Site: www.conmed.com
Officers: Eugene R. Corasanti - Chmn., C.E.O. Joseph J. Corasanti - Pres., C.O.O.

Auditors: PricewaterhouseCoopers LLP
Investor Contact: 315-797-8375

COPART, INC.

Exchange	Symbol	Price	52Wk Range	Yield	P/E
NMS	CPRT	$28.07 (8/31/2006)	28.11-22.55	N/A	28.94

*7 Year Price Score 118.69 *NYSE Composite Index=100 *12 Month Price Score 102.68

Interim Earnings (Per Share)

Qtr.	Oct	Jan	Apr	Jul
2002-03	0.16	0.15	0.17	0.15
2003-04	0.17	0.19	0.27	0.24
2004-05	0.24	0.25	0.33	0.27
2005-06	0.25	0.08	0.37	...

Interim Dividends (Per Share)

Amt	Decl	Ex	Rec	Pay
3-for-2	12/12/2001	1/22/2002	1/4/2002	1/21/2002

Valuation Analysis

Forecast P/E	22.90 (9/9/2006)
Market Cap	$2.5 Billion
Book Value	775.0 Million
Price/Book	3.27
Price/Sales	5.01

Institutional Holding

No of Institutions	174
Shares	60,577,472
% Held	67.03

Business Summary: Retail - Automotive (MIC: 5.7 SIC: 5599 NAIC: 441229)

Copart is engaged as a provider of salvage vehicle auction services in U.S. Co. provides vehicle suppliers, primarily insurance companies, with a range of services to process and sell salvage vehicles over the Internet through its Virtual Bidding Second Generation Internet auction-style sales technology. Co. sells principally to licensed vehicle dismantlers, rebuilders, repair licensees, used vehicle dealers and exporters. Co. provides vehicle suppliers a range of services that expedite each stage of the salvage vehicle sales process and minimize administrative and processing costs.

Recent Developments: For the quarter ended Apr 30 2006, income from continuing operations increased 8.0% to $33.2 million from $30.7 million in the year-earlier quarter. Net income increased 12.3% to $34.7 million from $30.9 million in the year-earlier quarter. Revenues were $149.5 million, up 17.0% from $127.8 million the year before. Operating income was $53.4 million versus $47.5 million in the prior-year quarter, an increase of 12.4%. Direct operating expenses rose 16.3% to $80.0 million from $68.8 million in the comparable period the year before. Indirect operating expenses increased 40.3% to $16.1 million from $11.5 million in the equivalent prior-year period.

Prospects: Co.'s top-line results reflect increased vehicle sales volume, coupled with increased revenue per transaction driven by higher auction proceeds per vehicle, due largely to its Virtual Bidding Second Generation Internet auction style sales technology. However, these growths are being offset by incremental costs incurred from the effects of hurricanes Katrina and Rita. Looking ahead, Co. expects the majority of its unsold salvage vehicles received as a result of the hurricanes to be sold primarily in the next two quarters. Moreover, Co. noted that the processing of the hurricane vehicles has had and may continue to have a negative effect on gross and operating margin percentages going forward.

Financial Data (US$ in Thousands)	9 Mos	6 Mos	3 Mos	07/31/2005	07/31/2004	07/31/2003	07/31/2002	07/31/2001
Earnings Per Share	0.97	0.93	1.10	1.10	0.87	0.62	0.63	0.51
Cash Flow Per Share	1.38	1.27	1.49	1.51	1.28	0.87	0.92	0.69
Tang Book Value Per Share	7.31	6.91	6.79	6.54	5.40	4.55	4.06	3.06
Income Statement								
Total Revenue	391,351	241,839	119,025	457,111	400,796	347,423	316,456	253,889
EBITDA	146,356	86,371	42,161	191,512	159,599	118,082	108,136	84,390
Depn & Amortn	22,920	14,817	7,292	31,300	30,808	25,545	16,308	14,350
Income Before Taxes	128,821	75,135	36,648	165,069	130,297	94,167	93,658	71,044
Income Taxes	46,950	26,441	13,835	62,953	51,076	36,945	36,268	28,359
Net Income	65,374	30,667	22,813	102,116	79,220	57,222	57,389	42,685
Average Shares	92,884	92,636	92,730	92,984	91,537	93,017	91,251	84,614
Balance Sheet								
Total Assets	869,863	828,368	834,562	793,528	673,023	587,100	535,848	316,635
Current Liabilities	93,683	89,579	98,311	80,111	63,223	54,184	47,046	41,108
Long-Term Obligations	...	...	...	...	9	16	85	409
Total Liabilities	94,857	90,752	99,405	84,149	70,760	61,461	49,631	47,482
Stockholders' Equity	775,006	737,616	735,157	709,379	602,263	525,640	486,217	269,152
Shares Outstanding	90,350	90,235	90,446	90,337	90,075	89,883	92,239	88,000
Statistical Record								
Return on Assets %	11.02	11.09	13.26	13.93	12.54	10.19	13.46	14.75
Return on Equity %	12.40	12.47	15.03	15.57	14.01	11.31	15.20	17.46
EBITDA Margin %	37.40	35.71	35.42	41.90	39.82	33.99	34.17	33.24
Net Margin %	16.70	12.68	19.17	22.34	19.77	16.47	18.13	16.81
Asset Turnover	0.62	0.62	0.61	0.62	0.63	0.62	0.74	0.88
Current Ratio	4.35	4.26	3.95	4.70	4.64	4.17	4.80	2.69
Price Range	27.71-22.04	25.90-21.39	26.88-19.11	26.88-17.85	26.73-8.43	14.75-7.06	25.67-12.14	20.07-8.33
P/E Ratio	28.57-22.72	27.85-23.00	24.44-17.37	24.44-16.23	30.72-9.69	23.79-11.39	40.74-19.27	39.35-16.34

Address: 4665 Business Center Drive, Fairfield, CA 94534 **Telephone:** 707-639-5000 **Fax:** 707-639-5196	**Web Site:** www.copart.com **Officers:** Willis J. Johnson - Chmn., C.E.O. A. Jayson Adair - Pres.	**Auditors:** KPMG LLP **Transfer Agents:** The First National Bank of Boston

CORINTHIAN COLLEGES, INC.

Exchange	Symbol	Price	52Wk Range	Yield	P/E
NMS	COCO	$12.12 (8/31/2006)	15.00-11.73	N/A	35.65

*7 Year Price Score 72.66   *NYSE Composite Index=100   *12 Month Price Score 96.98

Interim Earnings (Per Share)

Qtr.	Sep	Dec	Mar	Jun
2002-03	0.15	0.17	0.20	0.20
2003-04	0.20	0.23	0.23	0.20
2004-05	0.20	0.22	0.24	(0.03)
2005-06	0.08	0.12	0.17	...

Interim Dividends (Per Share)

Amt	Decl	Ex	Rec	Pay
100%	4/25/2002	5/28/2002	5/9/2002	5/24/2002
100%	2/18/2004	3/24/2004	3/4/2004	3/23/2004

Valuation Analysis

Forecast P/E 19.13 (9/9/2006)
Market Cap $1.0 Billion
Book Value 383.7 Million
Price/Book 2.72
Price/Sales 1.08

Institutional Holding

No of Institutions 179
Shares 97,518,720
% Held N/A

Business Summary: Schools and Universities (MIC: 6.1 SIC: 8221 NAIC: 611310)
Corinthian Colleges is a for-profit, post-secondary education company in the United States, with more than 66,100 students enrolled as of June 30, 2005. As of June 30, 2005, Co. operated 94 colleges in 24 states and 34 colleges and 14 corporate training centers in 7 Canadian provinces, and served the large and growing segment of the population seeking to acquire career-oriented education.

Recent Developments: For the quarter ended Mar 31 2006, net income decreased 32.3% to $14.7 million from $21.6 million in the year-earlier quarter. Revenues were $250.3 million, down 1.0% from $252.8 million the year before. Operating income was $19.8 million versus $36.2 million in the prior-year quarter, a decrease of 45.3%. Direct operating expenses rose 2.3% to $137.3 million from $134.3 million in the comparable period the year before. Indirect operating expenses increased 13.0% to $93.1 million from $82.4 million in the equivalent prior-year period.

Prospects: Co. continues its emphasize on regenerating its enrollment growth to address the decline in its new students starts due to low conversion rates in some of its key source channels, the teach-out of its New Orleans campus due to hurricane damage and the deceleration of enrollment at its three Georgia Medical Institute schools currently under accreditation scrutiny. Meanwhile, the improvement in Co.'s operating margin is attributable to its effective management of variable expenses such as marketing and bad debt during the third quarter of fiscal 2006. Looking ahead, Co. expects earnings to be between $0.13 and $0.15 per diluted share for the fourth quarter ending June 30 2006.

Financial Data
(US$ in Thousands)

	9 Mos	6 Mos	3 Mos	06/30/2005	06/30/2004	06/30/2003	06/30/2002	06/30/2001
Earnings Per Share	0.34	0.41	0.51	0.63	0.87	0.71	0.44	0.29
Cash Flow Per Share	1.53	1.56	1.32	1.41	1.28	0.82	0.71	0.26
Tang Book Value Per Share	1.57	1.62	1.74	1.65	1.19	1.12	1.09	0.72
Income Statement								
Total Revenue	731,014	480,761	236,294	963,565	804,283	517,293	338,146	244,163
EBITDA	79,548	48,402	21,349	130,163	158,077	122,267	70,018	45,611
Depn & Amortn	29,192	19,283	9,566	36,148	22,947	12,575	6,653	4,860
Income Before Taxes	51,853	29,953	12,095	93,245	133,288	109,349	64,903	42,829
Income Taxes	19,093	11,852	4,717	34,822	51,649	43,412	25,955	17,098
Net Income	32,760	18,101	7,378	58,423	81,639	65,937	38,948	25,731
Average Shares	87,790	92,005	92,870	92,760	94,014	92,056	89,388	86,924
Balance Sheet								
Total Assets	646,057	671,073	695,097	674,572	552,993	329,398	207,806	138,636
Current Liabilities	156,398	167,965	144,262	139,707	102,245	66,657	49,063	28,434
Long-Term Obligations	45,287	51,547	69,313	66,441	58,772	13,970	1,515	2,138
Total Liabilities	262,364	279,393	272,772	263,747	195,038	95,057	56,752	33,073
Stockholders' Equity	383,693	391,680	422,325	410,825	357,955	234,341	151,054	105,563
Shares Outstanding	86,069	88,000	91,405	91,202	90,305	87,644	85,908	84,892
Statistical Record								
Return on Assets %	4.57	5.82	7.41	9.52	18.45	24.55	22.48	22.00
Return on Equity %	7.36	9.49	11.89	15.20	27.49	34.22	30.35	29.48
EBITDA Margin %	10.88	10.07	9.03	13.51	19.65	23.64	20.71	18.68
Net Margin %	4.48	3.77	3.12	6.06	10.15	12.75	11.52	10.54
Asset Turnover	1.47	1.50	1.51	1.57	1.82	1.93	1.95	2.09
Current Ratio	1.30	1.38	1.70	1.65	1.61	1.63	2.22	2.40
Debt to Equity	0.12	0.13	0.16	0.16	0.16	0.06	0.01	0.02
Price Range	17.24-11.73	19.69-11.77	19.72-12.56	24.74-10.29	35.81-22.51	24.94-11.93	16.95-6.29	12.34-2.93
P/E Ratio	50.71-34.50	48.02-28.71	38.67-24.63	39.27-16.33	41.16-25.87	35.13-16.80	38.51-14.30	42.55-10.10

Address: 6 Hutton Centre Drive, Suite 400, Santa Ana, CA 92707-5764 **Telephone:** 714-427-3000	**Web Site:** www.cci.edu **Officers:** David G. Moore - Chmn. Jack D. Massimino - Pres., C.E.O.	**Auditors:** Ernst & Young LLP **Investor Contact:** 714-424-2678 **Transfer Agents:** U.S. Stock Transfer, Glendale, CA

CORPORATE EXECUTIVE BOARD CO.

Exchange	Symbol	Price	52Wk Range	Yield	P/E
NMS	EXBD	$87.64 (8/31/2006)	112.43-75.40	1.37	47.63

*7 Year Price Score 151.16 *NYSE Composite Index=100 *12 Month Price Score 98.48

Interim Earnings (Per Share)

Qtr.	Mar	Jun	Sep	Dec
2003	0.22	0.25	0.14	0.32
2004	0.31	0.32	0.30	0.42
2005	0.42	0.41	0.47	0.52
2006	0.42	0.43	...	...

Interim Dividends (Per Share)

Amt	Decl	Ex	Rec	Pay
0.10Q	11/4/2005	12/13/2005	12/15/2005	12/30/2005
0.30Q	2/7/2006	3/8/2006	3/10/2006	3/31/2006
0.30Q	5/4/2006	6/13/2006	6/15/2006	6/30/2006
0.30Q	8/4/2006	9/13/2006	9/15/2006	9/29/2006

Indicated Div: $1.20

Valuation Analysis

Forecast P/E	44.54
	(9/9/2006)
Market Cap	$3.5 Billion
Book Value	398.4 Million
Price/Book	8.86
Price/Sales	8.61

Institutional Holding

No of Institutions	252
Shares	39,364,924
% Held	97.77

Business Summary: Accounting & Management Consulting Services (MIC: 12.2 SIC: 8742 NAIC: 541611)

Corporate Executive Board is a provider of best practices research and analysis focusing on corporate strategy, operations and general management issues. As of Dec 31 2005, Co. provided its services to a membership of more than 2,800 corporations. Co.'s services are provided primarily on an annual subscription basis and include best practices research studies, executive education seminars, customized research briefs, Web-based access to the program's content database and decision support tools. Co.'s research programs focus on separate business areas, such as human resources, research and development, information technology, sales and marketing, finance, and operations and procurement.

Recent Developments: For the quarter ended June 30 2006, net income increased 4.2% to $17.8 million from $17.0 million in the year-earlier quarter. Revenues were $111.7 million, up 27.8% from $87.4 million the year before. Operating income was $22.8 million versus $22.5 million in the prior-year quarter, an increase of 1.2%. Direct operating expenses rose 29.8% to $39.1 million from $30.1 million in the comparable period the year before. Indirect operating expenses increased 43.3% to $49.8 million from $34.8 million in the equivalent prior-year period.

Prospects: Co.'s top line results are being driven by cross-selling of additional subscriptions to existing members. Other factors cited by Co. contributing to the recent increase in revenues included the addition of new members and the introduction of new research programs. Looking ahead, Co. is increasing its target for annual revenue growth to a minimum of 27.0%. For full-year 2006, Co. anticipates diluted earnings to be $1.91 per share. For the second half of 2006, Co. expects earnings per diluted share of $0.50 for the third quarter and $0.56 for the fourth quarter.

Financial Data
(US$ in Thousands)

	6 Mos	3 Mos	12/31/2005	12/31/2004	12/31/2003	12/31/2002	12/31/2001	12/31/2000
Earnings Per Share	1.84	1.82	1.83	1.34	0.93	0.79	0.59	0.43
Cash Flow Per Share	3.93	4.48	4.59	3.11	2.40	2.12	1.55	1.31
Tang Book Value Per Share	9.69	9.92	9.55	8.41	6.49	5.74	4.13	2.11
Dividends Per Share	0.800	0.600	0.400	0.300	...	...	...	...
Dividend Payout %	43.48	32.97	21.86	22.39	...	...	...	...
Income Statement								
Total Revenue	216,731	105,069	362,226	280,724	210,211	162,357	128,112	95,491
EBITDA	60,210	29,642	122,780	89,344	71,944	55,133	39,533	27,032
Depn & Amortn	3,492	1,807	9,170	8,959	7,949	6,962	4,644	2,573
Income Before Taxes	56,718	27,835	113,610	80,385	63,995	48,171	34,889	24,459
Income Taxes	21,836	10,716	38,550	26,729	28,307	18,570	13,257	9,539
Net Income	34,882	17,119	75,060	53,656	35,688	29,601	21,632	14,920
Average Shares	41,233	41,065	41,092	39,925	38,577	37,671	36,465	34,638
Balance Sheet								
Total Assets	717,129	729,819	726,995	578,451	423,482	359,581	257,518	152,494
Current Liabilities	304,486	316,078	332,012	241,157	178,396	143,624	111,753	85,536
Total Liabilities	318,691	324,704	341,581	250,990	181,489	146,224	113,534	86,933
Stockholders' Equity	398,438	405,115	385,414	327,461	241,993	213,357	143,984	65,561
Shares Outstanding	40,263	40,014	39,482	38,930	37,283	37,182	34,898	31,144
Statistical Record								
Return on Assets %	11.26	11.08	11.50	10.68	...	9.59	10.55	12.70
Return on Equity %	19.31	19.05	21.06	18.79	...	16.57	20.65	38.95
EBITDA Margin %	27.78	28.21	33.90	31.83	34.22	33.96	30.86	28.31
Net Margin %	16.09	16.29	20.72	19.11	16.98	18.23	16.89	15.62
Asset Turnover	0.61	0.57	0.55	0.56	...	0.53	0.62	0.81
Current Ratio	1.54	1.55	1.74	1.26	1.33	1.23	1.37	0.88
Price Range	112.43-75.40	102.25-63.28	91.47-62.00	69.06-45.10	51.30-29.25	40.08-24.30	43.50-23.52	47.00-20.88
P/E Ratio	61.10-40.98	56.18-34.77	49.98-33.88	51.53-33.66	55.16-31.45	50.73-30.76	73.73-39.86	109.30-48.55
Average Yield %	0.89	0.74	0.54	0.54	...	...	...	...

Address: 2000 Pennsylvania Avenue, NW, Suite 6000, Washington, DC 20006 Telephone: 202-777-5000 Fax: 202-777-5920	Web Site: www.executiveboard.com Officers: James J. McGonigle - Chmn., C.E.O. Timothy R. Yost - C.F.O.	Auditors: Ernst & Young LLP

CORUS BANKSHARES, INC.

Exchange	Symbol	Price	52Wk Range	Yield	P/E	Div Acheiver
NMS	CORS	$21.81 (8/31/2006)	33.47-20.19	4.59	7.47	19 Years

*7 Year Price Score 139.91 *NYSE Composite Index=100 *12 Month Price Score 79.52

Interim Earnings (Per Share)

Qtr.	Mar	Jun	Sep	Dec
2003	0.22	0.23	0.28	0.30
2004	0.31	0.42	0.49	0.47
2005	0.48	0.54	0.69	0.67
2006	0.75	0.82	...	...

Interim Dividends (Per Share)

Amt	Decl	Ex	Rec	Pay
0.20Q	2/14/2006	3/22/2006	3/24/2006	4/10/2006
100%	4/18/2006	5/19/2006	5/1/2006	5/18/2006
0.20Q	4/18/2006	6/23/2006	6/27/2006	7/10/2006
0.25Q	8/29/2006	9/25/2006	9/27/2006	10/10/2006

Indicated Div: $1.00

Valuation Analysis
Forecast P/E 6.40 (9/9/2006)
Market Cap $1.2 Billion
Book Value 762.4 Million
Price/Book 1.60
Price/Sales 1.96

Institutional Holding
No of Institutions 144
Shares 38,928,924
% Held 69.54

Business Summary: Commercial Banking (MIC: 8.1 SIC: 6022 NAIC: 522110)

Corus Bankshares is a bank holding company with total assets of $8.46 billion and total deposits of $7.28 billion as of Dec 31 2005. Co. provides consumer and corporate banking products and services through its wholly-owned banking subsidiary, Corus Bank, N.A. The two main business activities for Co. are commercial real estate lending and deposit gathering. The third, and smaller, business is servicing the check cashing industry. The bank has eleven retail branches in the Chicago metropolitan area and offers general banking services such as checking, savings, money market and time deposit accounts, as well as safe deposit boxes and a variety of additional services.

Recent Developments: For the quarter ended June 30 2006, net income increased 53.2% to $47.8 million from $31.2 million in the year-earlier quarter. Net interest income increased 48.8% to $85.9 million from $57.7 million in the year-earlier quarter. Non-interest income fell 36.5% to $3.2 million from $5.0 million, while non-interest expense advanced 9.8% to $16.5 million.

Prospects: Co.'s outlook appears positive, reflecting solid bottom-line growth. Specifically, Co.'s results are benefiting from higher net interest income, which is being driven by growth in average loans outstanding. In addition, Co.'s deposit growth continues to be strong. The growth is being supported by increases in retail certificates of deposit and is the direct result of Co.'s national marketing of selected deposit accounts to both individuals and businesses at market-leading rates. Meanwhile, Co. continues to expect to close its acquisition of Amsouth Bancorporation, announced in May 2006, during the fourth quarter of 2006.

Financial Data
(US$ in Thousands)

	6 Mos	3 Mos	12/31/2005	12/31/2004	12/31/2003	12/31/2002	12/31/2001	12/31/2000
Earnings Per Share	2.92	2.64	2.38	1.70	1.02	0.86	0.95	1.31
Cash Flow Per Share	1.41	1.86	1.63	1.44	1.00	0.99	0.76	0.64
Tang Book Value Per Share	13.54	12.93	12.27	10.70	9.66	8.46	7.88	7.02
Dividends Per Share	0.750	0.725	0.700	0.625	0.415	0.159	0.154	0.149
Dividend Payout %	25.68	27.46	29.41	36.76	40.69	18.41	16.23	11.38
Income Statement								
Interest Income	348,584	166,817	446,949	222,059	170,239	152,878	188,630	223,676
Interest Expense	178,843	83,002	197,291	70,595	46,812	54,591	80,921	102,625
Net Interest Income	169,741	83,815	249,658	151,464	123,427	98,287	107,709	121,051
Provision for Losses	3,000	3,000	6,000	...	...	...	...	...
Non-Interest Income	5,968	2,797	15,258	14,066	14,554	15,821	17,881	36,416
Non-Interest Expense	33,655	17,195	61,322	56,273	52,533	47,472	51,100	52,908
Income Before Taxes	139,054	66,417	210,285	146,606	87,814	73,894	82,325	113,657
Income Taxes	47,904	23,028	73,056	48,667	29,404	24,580	28,142	38,903
Net Income	91,150	43,389	137,229	97,939	58,410	49,314	54,183	74,754
Average Shares	58,035	58,018	57,710	57,636	57,406	57,180	57,236	57,208
Balance Sheet								
Net Loans & Leases	4,457,047	4,642,891	4,484,771	2,760,946	2,397,323	1,705,340	1,434,788	1,512,279
Total Assets	9,571,933	9,232,474	8,458,740	5,017,787	3,643,830	2,617,050	2,659,322	2,598,467
Total Deposits	8,312,927	7,995,867	7,275,346	4,100,152	2,846,402	2,059,773	2,121,456	2,107,630
Total Liabilities	8,809,546	8,505,698	7,768,965	4,418,196	3,097,650	2,135,009	2,208,436	2,196,114
Stockholders' Equity	762,387	726,776	689,775	599,591	546,180	482,041	450,886	402,353
Shares Outstanding	55,978	55,865	55,849	55,591	56,073	56,476	56,638	56,572
Statistical Record								
Return on Assets %	2.10	2.06	2.04	2.26	1.87	1.87	2.06	2.99
Return on Equity %	24.24	22.91	21.29	17.05	11.36	10.57	12.70	20.42
Net Interest Margin %	47.27	50.24	55.86	68.21	72.50	64.29	57.10	54.12
Efficiency Ratio %	8.90	10.14	13.27	23.83	28.43	28.14	24.74	20.34
Loans to Deposits	0.54	0.58	0.62	0.67	0.84	0.83	0.68	0.72
Price Range	33.47-24.45	32.51-22.82	32.32-21.65	25.09-15.51	16.05-9.86	13.35-9.74	15.29-10.13	12.47-5.11
P/E Ratio	11.46-8.37	12.31-8.64	13.58-9.09	14.76-9.12	15.73-9.67	15.52-11.33	16.09-10.66	9.52-3.90
Average Yield %	2.56	2.56	2.60	3.02	3.32	1.37	1.25	1.97

Address: 3959 N. Lincoln Avenue, Chicago, IL 60613-2431
Telephone: 773-832-3088
Fax: 773-549-0734

Web Site: www.corusbank.com
Officers: Joseph C. Glickman - Chmn. Robert J. Glickman - Pres., C.E.O.

Auditors: Ernst & Young LLP
Investor Contact: 773-832-3088
Transfer Agents: Mellon Investor Services, LLC, Ridgefield Park, NJ

COSTCO WHOLESALE CORP

Exchange	Symbol	Price	52Wk Range	Yield	P/E
NMS	COST	$46.79 (8/31/2006)	57.58-41.36	1.11	20.34

*7 Year Price Score 99.33 *NYSE Composite Index=100 *12 Month Price Score 99.84

Interim Earnings (Per Share)

Qtr.	Nov	Feb	May	Aug
2002-03	0.31	0.39	0.33	0.51
2003-04	0.34	0.48	0.42	0.62
2004-05	0.40	0.62	0.43	0.73
2005-06	0.45	0.62	0.49	...

Interim Dividends (Per Share)

Amt	Decl	Ex	Rec	Pay
0.115Q	11/7/2005	11/16/2005	11/18/2005	12/2/2005
0.115Q	1/26/2006	2/7/2006	2/9/2006	2/24/2006
0.13Q	4/25/2006	5/8/2006	5/10/2006	5/26/2006
0.13Q	7/18/2006	7/28/2006	8/1/2006	8/25/2006

Indicated Div: $0.52

Valuation Analysis **Institutional Holding**

Forecast P/E	20.70	No of Institutions
	(9/9/2006)	604
Market Cap	$22.0 Billion	Shares
Book Value	9.2 Billion	371,871,712
Price/Book	2.38	% Held
Price/Sales	0.38	79.46

Business Summary: Retail - General (MIC: 5.2 SIC: 5331 NAIC: 452990)

Costco operates membership warehouses based on the concept that offering members very low prices on a limited selection of nationally branded and selected private label products in a wide range of merchandise categories will produce high sales volumes and rapid inventory turnover. As of Aug 28 2005, Co. operated 460 warehouse clubs: 338 in the United States (in 37 states and Puerto Rico); 65 in Canada (in 9 Canadian provinces); 16 in the United Kingdom (13 in England; 3 in Scotland); five in Korea; four in Taiwan; five Japan; and 27 in Mexico (through a 50%-owned joint venture). Merchandise offered by Co. includes food, sundries, hardlines softlines and other.

Recent Developments: For the quarter ended May 7 2006, net income increased 12.3% to $235.6 million from $209.8 million in the year-earlier quarter. Revenues were $13.27 billion, up 10.6% from $12.00 billion the year before. Operating income was $354.7 million versus $316.1 million in the prior-year quarter, an increase of 12.2%. Direct operating expenses rose 10.8% to $11.64 billion from $10.50 billion in the comparable period the year before. Indirect operating expenses increased 9.0% to $1.28 billion from $1.18 billion in the equivalent prior-year period.

Prospects: Top-line results are benefiting from an increase in Co.'s comparable warehouse sales as well as the opening of 18 net new warehouses since the end of the second quarter of fiscal 2005. Co. anticipates spending between $1.10 billion and $1.30 billion during fiscal 2006 in the U.S. and Canada for real estate, construction, remodeling and equipment for its warehouse clubs and related operations, along with approximately $100.0 million to $150.0 million for its international expansion, primarily in the U.K., Asia and Mexico. During the remainder of fiscal 2006, Co. expects to open an additional 16 to 18 new warehouse clubs as part of its expansion plans.

Financial Data
(US$ in Thousands)

	9 Mos	6 Mos	3 Mos	08/28/2005	08/29/2004	08/31/2003	09/01/2002	09/02/2001
Earnings Per Share	2.30	2.24	2.23	2.18	1.85	1.53	1.48	1.29
Cash Flow Per Share	3.74	4.18	3.97	3.77	4.58	3.31	2.25	2.30
Tang Book Value Per Share	19.66	19.30	19.06	18.80	16.48	14.33	12.51	10.81
Dividends Per Share	0.345	0.460	0.445	0.430	0.200	...	...	...
Dividend Payout %	15.03	20.56	19.91	19.72	10.81	...	...	...
Income Statement								
Total Revenue	40,255,104	26,981,929	12,927,353	52,935,228	48,106,992	42,545,552	38,762,499	34,797,037
EBITDA	1,542,762	1,041,973	465,635	1,979,352	1,846,459	1,586,455	1,509,061	1,336,802
Depn & Amortn	336,728	224,397	114,600	477,868	440,721	391,302	341,781	301,297
Income Before Taxes	1,196,708	810,929	347,311	1,548,962	1,400,624	1,158,233	1,138,184	1,003,481
Income Taxes	449,092	298,908	131,493	485,870	518,231	437,233	438,201	401,392
Net Income	747,616	512,021	215,818	1,063,092	882,393	721,000	699,983	602,089
Average Shares	480,533	482,127	486,367	492,035	482,459	479,326	479,262	475,827
Balance Sheet								
Total Assets	17,284,327	17,175,566	17,382,220	16,513,642	15,092,548	13,191,688	11,620,263	10,089,786
Current Liabilities	7,492,306	7,250,021	7,454,831	6,608,974	6,170,550	5,011,107	4,449,733	4,112,189
Long-Term Obligations	229,931	536,998	546,820	710,675	993,746	1,289,649	1,210,638	859,393
Total Liabilities	7,983,484	8,048,368	8,255,657	7,573,919	7,408,472	6,510,591	5,806,296	5,091,016
Stockholders' Equity	9,238,621	9,066,017	9,067,032	8,881,109	7,624,810	6,554,980	5,694,237	4,882,940
Shares Outstanding	469,802	469,635	475,828	472,480	462,637	457,479	455,325	451,754
Statistical Record								
Return on Assets %	6.49	6.42	6.44	6.75	6.26	5.83	6.47	6.45
Return on Equity %	12.21	12.22	12.60	12.92	12.48	11.80	13.27	13.24
EBITDA Margin %	3.83	3.86	3.60	3.74	3.84	3.73	3.89	3.84
Net Margin %	1.86	1.90	1.67	2.01	1.83	1.69	1.81	1.73
Asset Turnover	3.35	3.32	3.22	3.36	3.41	3.44	3.58	3.73
Current Ratio	1.11	1.17	1.19	1.22	1.18	1.14	1.04	0.94
Debt to Equity	0.02	0.06	0.06	0.08	0.13	0.20	0.21	0.18
Price Range	56.70-41.36	51.00-40.17	50.14-40.17	49.74-39.99	42.89-30.71	37.43-27.24	46.32-31.22	46.25-30.63
P/E Ratio	24.65-17.98	22.77-17.93	22.48-18.01	22.82-18.34	23.18-16.60	24.46-17.80	31.30-21.09	35.85-23.74
Average Yield %	0.72	1.00	0.98	0.95	0.54	...	...	...

Address: 999 Lake Drive, Issaquah, WA 98027 **Telephone:** 425-313-8100 **Fax:** 425-313-8103	**Web Site:** www.costco.com **Officers:** Jeffrey H. Brotman - Chmn. James D. Sinegal - Pres., C.E.O.	**Auditors:** KPMG LLP **Investor Contact:** 425-313-8203 **Transfer Agents:** Mellon Investor Services, L.L.C., South Hackensack, New Jersey

COURIER CORP.

Exchange	Symbol	Price	52Wk Range	Yield	P/E	Div Acheiver
NMS	CRRC	$36.84 (8/31/2006)	44.90-32.71	1.30	20.02	12 Years

*7 Year Price Score 139.19 *NYSE Composite Index=100 *12 Month Price Score 94.03

Interim Earnings (Per Share)

Qtr.	Dec	Mar	Jun	Sep
2002-03	0.37	0.31	0.39	0.57
2003-04	0.32	0.31	0.42	0.61
2004-05	0.33	0.33	0.47	0.64
2005-06	0.36	0.35	0.48	...

Interim Dividends (Per Share)

Amt	Decl	Ex	Rec	Pay
0.12Q	11/3/2005	11/9/2005	11/14/2005	11/25/2005
0.12Q	1/18/2006	2/8/2006	2/10/2006	2/24/2006
0.12Q	4/13/2006	5/3/2006	5/5/2006	5/26/2006
0.12Q	7/13/2006	8/2/2006	8/4/2006	8/25/2006

Indicated Div: $0.48

Valuation Analysis
Forecast P/E 18.71 (9/9/2006)
Market Cap $456.0 Million
Book Value 168.8 Million
Price/Book 2.70
Price/Sales 1.83

Institutional Holding
No of Institutions 59
Shares 6,251,041
% Held 50.50

Business Summary: Printing (MIC: 13.4 SIC: 2732 NAIC: 323117)
Courier is engaged in book manufacturing and specialty publishing. Co.'s book manufacturing segment provides services from prepress and production through storage and distribution. Co.'s principal book manufacturing markets are religious, educational and specialty trade books. Co.'s specialty publishing segment consists of Dover Publications, Inc. and Research & Education Association, Inc. (REA). Dover publishes over 30 specialty categories ranging from literature and poetry classics to paper dolls, and from music scores to clip art. REA publishes test preparation and study-guide books and software for high school, college and graduate students and professionals.

Recent Developments: For the quarter ended June 24 2006, net income increased 9.1% to $6.1 million from $5.5 million in the year-earlier quarter. Revenues were $70.4 million, up 19.9% from $58.8 million the year before. Direct operating expenses rose 22.8% to $48.3 million from $39.3 million in the comparable period the year before. Indirect operating expenses increased 18.1% to $12.7 million from $10.8 million in the equivalent prior-year period.

Prospects: Going forward, Co.'s Apr 2006 Creative Homeowner acquisition is expected to add a sizable volume of book manufacturing business as existing third-party contracts expire. In addition, Co.'s effort at its Dover Publications and Research & Education Association subsidiaries is gaining traction with improved programs and products, as well as favorable relationships with book retailers. In its book manufacturing segment, Co.'s investments are providing better options for its publishing customers to capitalize on growing demand for enhanced four-color books. Hence, for fiscal 2006, Co. expects sales of $269.0 million to $273.0 million and net income per diluted share of $1.94 to $2.00.

Financial Data
(US$ in Thousands)

	9 Mos	6 Mos	3 Mos	09/24/2005	09/25/2004	09/27/2003	09/28/2002	09/29/2001
Earnings Per Share	1.84	1.82	1.81	1.77	1.67	1.65	1.35	1.13
Cash Flow Per Share	3.21	2.82	3.15	2.89	2.38	2.65	2.51	2.48
Tang Book Value Per Share	8.06	10.12	9.84	9.96	8.45	7.61	6.00	4.77
Dividends Per Share	0.460	0.440	0.387	0.333	0.233	0.200	0.178	0.160
Dividend Payout %	25.07	24.13	21.40	18.83	14.00	12.10	13.16	14.17
Income Statement								
Total Revenue	185,635	115,211	57,684	227,039	211,179	202,002	202,184	211,943
EBITDA	34,094	20,952	10,369	45,508	42,457	39,376	35,278	33,729
Depn & Amortn	10,857	7,101	3,370	11,660	10,929	9,798	10,687	11,796
Income Before Taxes	23,237	13,851	6,999	34,236	31,551	29,526	24,111	20,034
Income Taxes	8,301	4,971	2,512	12,102	11,011	10,254	7,936	6,817
Net Income	14,936	8,880	4,487	22,134	20,540	20,120	16,175	13,217
Average Shares	12,607	12,581	12,551	12,490	12,331	12,180	11,988	11,695
Balance Sheet								
Total Assets	230,276	200,268	199,363	196,965	175,199	151,101	131,658	133,615
Current Liabilities	33,120	26,190	29,347	30,662	29,363	26,813	27,755	31,029
Long-Term Obligations	17,218	383	404	425	510	593	674	16,501
Total Liabilities	61,462	36,580	39,432	41,031	40,209	35,681	35,739	53,290
Stockholders' Equity	168,814	163,688	159,931	155,934	134,990	115,420	95,919	80,325
Shares Outstanding	12,378	12,348	12,321	12,313	12,046	11,896	11,733	11,502
Statistical Record								
Return on Assets %	11.13	12.11	12.09	11.93	12.62	14.27	12.23	9.61
Return on Equity %	14.52	14.90	15.07	15.26	16.45	19.09	18.41	17.90
EBITDA Margin %	18.37	18.19	17.98	20.04	20.10	19.49	17.45	15.91
Net Margin %	8.05	7.71	7.78	9.75	9.73	9.96	8.00	6.24
Asset Turnover	1.21	1.27	1.26	1.22	1.30	1.43	1.53	1.54
Current Ratio	2.35	3.12	2.81	3.18	2.96	2.90	2.22	1.92
Debt to Equity	0.10	N.M.	N.M.	N.M.	N.M.	0.01	0.01	0.21
Price Range	44.90-32.71	42.15-31.24	41.96-31.24	41.96-27.55	30.41-22.63	24.89-15.74	19.78-9.33	12.73-8.00
P/E Ratio	24.40-17.78	23.16-17.16	23.18-17.26	23.71-15.56	18.21-13.55	15.08-9.54	14.65-6.91	11.27-7.08
Average Yield %	1.21	1.21	1.09	0.96	0.86	0.95	1.11	1.62

Address: 15 Wellman Avenue, North Chelmsford, MA 01863
Telephone: 978-251-6000
Fax: 978-251-8228

Web Site: www.courier.com
Officers: James F. Conway III - Chmn., Pres., C.E.O.
George Q. Nichols - Corp. Sr. V.P.

Auditors: Deloitte & Touche LLP
Transfer Agents: EquiServe Trust Company, N.A.

CREDENCE SYSTEMS CORP.

Exchange	Symbol	Price	52Wk Range	Yield	P/E
NMS	CMOS	$2.53 (8/31/2006)	9.30-1.83	N/A	N/A

*7 Year Price Price Score 30.20 *NYSE Composite Index=100 *12 Month Price Score 40.43

Interim Earnings (Per Share)

Qtr.	Jan	Apr	Jul	Oct
2002-03	(0.49)	(0.46)	(0.50)	(0.34)
2003-04	(0.18)	0.06	(0.42)	(0.30)
2004-05	(0.41)	(0.21)	(0.43)	(0.29)
2005-06	(0.04)	(0.14)	...	...

Interim Dividends (Per Share)
No Dividends Paid

Valuation Analysis

Forecast P/E	N/A	Institutional Holding
	(9/9/2006)	No of Institutions 155
Market Cap	$253.0 Million	Shares
Book Value	671.6 Million	93,262,016
Price/Book	0.38	% Held
Price/Sales	0.53	93.24

Business Summary: Instruments and Related Products (MIC: 11.15 SIC: 3825 NAIC: 334515)

Credence Systems is engaged in designing, manufacturing, selling and servicing engineering validation test equipment, diagnostics and failure analysis products and automatic test equipment (ATE) used for testing semiconductor integrated circuits (ICs). Co. also develops, licenses and distributes software products that provide automation applications in the IC design and test flow fields. Co. serves a spectrum of the semiconductor industry's testing needs through a range of products that test digital logic, mixed-signal, system-on-a-chip, radio frequency and non-volatile memory semiconductors.

Recent Developments: For the second quarter ended Apr 30 2006, net loss amounted to $14.2 million compared with a net loss of $19.5 million in the equivalent year-earlier quarter. Revenues were $124.8 million, up 22.4% from $101.9 million the year before. Operating loss was $12.8 million versus a loss of $18.2 million in the prior-year quarter. Direct operating expenses rose 37.3% to $80.8 million from $58.8 million in the comparable period the year before. Indirect operating expenses decreased 7.4% to $56.8 million from $61.4 million in the equivalent prior-year period.

Prospects: Co.'s operating results are being tempered by a continuing weakness in its memory business, which required it to revalue its Kalos 2 inventory. Also, the recent decision by an integrated device manufacturer to decrease capital spending has caused Co. to reassess the viability of its memory product. As a result, Co. is stopping further memory product development, and is redirecting its resources in its digital and mixed-signal business, which should accelerate development programs for the consumer-mobile market. For the third quarter of fiscal 2006, Co. expects net sales to be $125.0 million to $129.0 million, with a loss per share of $0.09 to $0.11.

Financial Data (US$ in Thousands)	6 Mos	3 Mos	10/31/2005	10/31/2004	10/31/2003	10/31/2002	10/31/2001	10/31/2000
Earnings Per Share	(0.83)	(0.90)	(1.28)	(0.88)	(1.80)	(2.81)	(1.65)	2.65
Cash Flow Per Share	(0.12)	(0.31)	(0.06)	(0.23)	(1.06)	(0.46)	(1.15)	1.47
Tang Book Value Per Share	1.60	1.65	1.62	2.91	5.67	7.55	9.76	11.65
Income Statement								
Total Revenue	242,935	118,168	429,320	439,803	182,414	164,209	301,718	679,738
EBITDA	10,534	10,364	(36,242)	(4,233)	(77,906)	(125,533)	(115,651)	240,301
Depn & Amortn	26,477	12,938	71,852	56,293	39,985	50,405	59,276	34,621
Income Before Taxes	(15,543)	(2,415)	(108,543)	(60,415)	(112,059)	(163,632)	(155,587)	223,891
Income Taxes	2,734	1,631	11,389	3,989	1,006	7,227	(56,905)	83,468
Net Income	(18,277)	(4,046)	(119,932)	(64,478)	(113,112)	(170,481)	(98,676)	140,382
Average Shares	99,886	99,492	93,864	73,058	62,737	60,570	59,818	54,176
Balance Sheet								
Total Assets	1,004,582	1,032,072	1,046,305	1,173,106	698,493	582,249	757,419	879,237
Current Liabilities	133,674	151,075	163,985	179,995	82,979	61,410	70,398	148,355
Long-Term Obligations	180,000	180,000	180,000	180,000	181,058	...	...	...
Total Liabilities	332,981	351,367	364,276	384,898	267,866	63,012	76,479	157,010
Stockholders' Equity	671,601	680,705	682,029	788,208	430,627	519,237	680,940	722,227
Shares Outstanding	100,018	99,867	99,448	85,284	63,805	60,914	61,426	53,664
Statistical Record								
Return on Assets %	N.M.	N.M.	N.M.	N.M.	N.M.	N.M.	N.M.	22.96
Return on Equity %	N.M.	N.M.	N.M.	N.M.	N.M.	N.M.	N.M.	30.99
EBITDA Margin %	4.34	8.77	N.M.	N.M.	N.M.	N.M.	N.M.	35.35
Net Margin %	N.M.	N.M.	N.M.	N.M.	N.M.	N.M.	N.M.	20.65
Asset Turnover	0.46	0.42	0.39	0.47	0.28	0.25	0.37	1.11
Current Ratio	2.58	2.39	2.26	2.65	5.43	4.81	5.60	3.71
Debt to Equity	0.27	0.26	0.26	0.23	0.42	...	...	...
Price Range	10.94-5.83	10.94-5.83	10.94-5.83	17.05-6.43	16.59-6.44	24.64-6.30	29.50-11.26	74.59-16.13
P/E Ratio	...	...	...	...	...	...	...	28.15-6.08

Address: 1421 California Circle, Milpitas, CA 95035
Telephone: 408-635-4300
Fax: 408-635-4985

Web Site: www.credence.com
Officers: David A. Ranhoff - Pres., C.E.O., C.O.O.
John R. Detwiler - Sr. V.P., C.F.O., Sec.

Auditors: Ernst & Young LLP
Transfer Agents: ComputerShare Investor Services, Providence, RI

CREE, INC.

Exchange	Symbol	Price	52Wk Range	Yield	P/E
NMS	CREE	$18.62 (8/31/2006)	35.00-17.73	N/A	19.00

*7 Year Price Score 74.74 *NYSE Composite Index=100 *12 Month Price Score 73.96

Interim Earnings (Per Share)

Qtr.	Sep	Dec	Mar	Jun
2001-02	0.09	(0.24)	(0.94)	(0.31)
2002-03	0.05	0.12	0.14	0.17
2003-04	0.12	0.17	0.20	0.28
2004-05	0.32	0.32	0.27	0.27
2005-06	0.28	0.23	0.31	0.17

Interim Dividends (Per Share)

Amt	Decl	Ex	Rec	Pay
2-for-1	7/13/1999	8/2/1999	7/26/1999	7/30/1999
2-for-1	10/31/2000	12/11/2000	12/1/2000	12/8/2000

Valuation Analysis

Forecast P/E	21.55
	(9/9/2006)
Market Cap	$1.4 Billion
Book Value	827.6 Million
Price/Book	1.74
Price/Sales	3.40

Institutional Holding

No of Institutions	195
Shares	69,714,184
% Held	90.26

Business Summary: IT & Technology (MIC: 10.2 SIC: 3674 NAIC: 334413)

Cree develops and manufactures semiconductor materials and devices based on silicon carbide (SiC), gallium nitride (GaN), and related compounds. Co.'s SiC and GaN materials technologies are the basis for many of the devices that Co. develops and produces. The physical and electronic properties of SiC and GaN offer technical advantages over traditional silicon, gallium arsenide (GaAs), sapphire and other materials used for certain electronic applications. Co. currently focuses its expertise in SiC and GaN on light emitting diodes (LEDs), including high power packaged LEDs and high-power products, including power switching, radio frequency and microwave devices.

Recent Developments: For the year ended June 25 2006, income from continuing operations decreased 25.0% to $80.0 million from $106.6 million a year earlier. Net income decreased 15.9% to $76.7 million from $91.1 million in the prior year. Revenues were $423.0 million, up 10.0% from $384.5 million the year before. Operating income was $98.8 million versus $139.1 million in the prior year, a decrease of 28.9%. Direct operating expenses rose 28.3% to $222.1 million from $173.0 million in the comparable period the year before. Indirect operating expenses increased 41.1% to $102.1 million from $72.3 million in the equivalent prior-year period.

Prospects: Co. remains optimistic regarding the opportunities associated with its LED chips and SiC materials technology to broaden its product line, with anticipated growth in these markets due to global demand for more energy-efficient and environmentally focused technology. Specifically, Co. plans to expand the product offerings of its XLampfamily of LED-based products by incorporating its new EZBright power chips. Also, Co. plans to lower product costs by starting the conversion to four-inch wafer production, along with higher production at its subcontractors. For the first quarter of fiscal 2007, Co. expects revenue of $102.0 million to $106.0 million with earnings of $0.14 to $0.17 per share.

Financial Data
(US$ in Thousands)

	06/25/2006	06/26/2005	06/27/2004	06/29/2003	06/30/2002	06/24/2001	06/25/2000	06/27/1999
Earnings Per Share	0.98	1.18	0.77	0.48	(1.40)	0.37	0.44	0.23
Cash Flow Per Share	1.99	2.35	2.06	1.23	0.53	1.04	0.96	0.37
Tang Book Value Per Share	10.32	9.05	7.64	7.13	6.57	6.89	6.52	2.19
Income Statement								
Total Revenue	422,952	389,064	306,870	229,822	155,434	177,227	108,562	60,050
EBITDA	173,851	190,356	135,462	85,146	(96,633)	61,197	48,354	22,081
Depn & Amortn	74,381	69,743	55,954	42,099	39,489	26,679	10,948	5,499
Income Before Taxes	112,363	126,000	83,593	47,164	(130,414)	50,186	46,806	17,642
Income Taxes	32,404	34,857	25,633	12,263	(28,691)	22,343	16,286	4,940
Net Income	76,673	91,143	57,960	34,901	(101,723)	27,843	30,520	12,702
Average Shares	78,207	77,172	75,745	75,303	72,718	75,735	70,434	56,864
Balance Sheet								
Total Assets	900,200	777,408	628,000	563,694	504,195	615,123	486,202	144,217
Current Liabilities	37,390	36,036	44,982	28,292	22,054	21,738	23,062	9,545
Total Liabilities	72,587	64,490	48,868	28,323	22,091	26,026	23,062	14,195
Stockholders' Equity	827,613	712,918	579,132	535,371	482,104	589,097	463,140	130,022
Shares Outstanding	77,227	75,568	73,245	74,127	72,729	72,907	70,696	58,516
Statistical Record								
Return on Assets %	9.17	13.01	9.75	6.55	N.M.	5.07	9.71	11.74
Return on Equity %	9.98	14.15	10.43	6.88	N.M.	5.31	10.32	13.78
EBITDA Margin %	41.10	48.93	44.14	37.05	N.M.	34.53	44.54	36.77
Net Margin %	18.13	23.43	18.89	15.19	N.M.	15.71	28.11	21.15
Asset Turnover	0.51	0.56	0.52	0.43	0.27	0.32	0.35	0.56
Current Ratio	10.07	7.81	5.22	7.40	7.89	12.23	12.53	7.71
Price Range	35.00-22.00	41.99-18.28	28.74-11.84	25.84-10.21	32.45-10.59	80.81-12.26	99.09-11.78	18.13-2.69
P/E Ratio	35.71-22.45	35.58-15.49	37.32-15.38	53.83-21.27	...	218.41-33.14	225.21-26.78	78.80-11.68

Address: 4600 Silicon Drive, Durham, NC 27703
Telephone: 919-313-5300
Fax: 919-361-5452

Web Site: www.cree.com
Officers: Charles M. Swoboda - Chmn., Pres., C.E.O. Cynthia B. Merrell - C.F.O., Chief Acctg. Officer, Treas.

Auditors: Ernst & Young LLP
Investor Contact: 919-313-5300
Transfer Agents: American Stock Transfer & Trust Company, New York, NY

CSG SYSTEMS INTERNATIONAL INC.

Exchange	Symbol	Price	52Wk Range	Yield	P/E
NMS	CSGS	$26.92 (8/31/2006)	27.30-20.09	N/A	19.23

*7 Year Price Score 69.09   *NYSE Composite Index=100   *12 Month Price Score 106.53

Interim Earnings (Per Share)

Qtr.	Mar	Jun	Sep	Dec
2003	0.17	0.23	(1.04)	0.13
2004	0.21	0.15	0.32	0.24
2005	0.17	0.17	0.28	0.46
2006	0.33	0.33	...	...

Interim Dividends (Per Share)

No Dividends Paid

Valuation Analysis

		Institutional Holding	
Forecast P/E	19.41	No of Institutions	
	(9/9/2006)	159	
Market Cap	$1.3 Billion	Shares	
Book Value	317.3 Million	51,020,544	
Price/Book	4.05	% Held	
Price/Sales	3.47	N/A	

Business Summary: Miscellaneous Business Services (MIC: 12.8 SIC: 7374 NAIC: 518210)

CSG Systems International is a provider of outsourced billing, customer care and print and mail applications and services supporting the North American converged broadband and direct broadcast satellite (DBS) markets. Co.'s processing, software, and professional services allows clients to automate their customer care and billing functions, including set-up and activation of customer accounts, sales support, order processing, invoice calculation, production and mailing of invoices, management reporting, electronic presentment and payment of invoices, as well as deployment and management of the client's field technicians.

Recent Developments: For the quarter ended June 30 2006, income from continuing operations increased 2.4% to $15.6 million from $15.2 million in the year-earlier quarter. Net income increased 82.6% to $15.6 million from $8.5 million in the year-earlier quarter. Revenues were $95.1 million, down 1.9% from $96.9 million the year before. Operating income was $21.8 million versus $24.8 million in the prior-year quarter, a decrease of 12.0%. Direct operating expenses rose 0.4% to $46.9 million from $46.7 million in the comparable period the year before. Indirect operating expenses increased 3.8% to $26.4 million from $25.4 million in the equivalent prior-year period.

Prospects: Going forward, Co. continues to execute on several financial objectives, which include focusing on its core strengths and creating a long-term sustainable and profitable business. Moreover, Co. continues to migrate customer accounts to its Advanced Convergent Platform, while helping its clients to rollout new advanced service offerings. This, in turn, will allow Co.'s clients to introduce new services and drive revenues. As a result, Co. is raising the lower end of its 2006 revenue guidance and anticipates revenue of $377.0 million to $381.0 million. In addition, Co. believes that its 2006 income from continuing operations will now range between $1.34 and $1.38 per diluted share.

Financial Data (US$ in Thousands)	6 Mos	3 Mos	12/31/2005	12/31/2004	12/31/2003	12/31/2002	12/31/2001	12/31/2000
Earnings Per Share	1.40	1.24	1.09	0.92	(0.51)	0.85	2.08	1.60
Cash Flow Per Share	2.17	2.25	2.14	2.36	1.17	1.69	3.40	1.28
Tang Book Value Per Share	5.52	5.13	5.35	0.29	N.M.	N.M.	3.16	2.52
Income Statement								
Total Revenue	188,013	92,960	377,317	529,746	439,660	610,932	476,908	398,895
EBITDA	67,065	32,916	115,259	120,091	6,501	138,705	206,560	164,640
Depn & Amortn	13,177	6,100	38,820	42,401	41,681	39,034	24,546	19,390
Income Before Taxes	50,100	24,931	72,961	69,206	(48,460)	87,544	183,442	145,203
Income Taxes	19,029	9,465	26,219	22,022	(22,183)	42,926	69,521	54,734
Net Income	31,071	15,466	53,229	47,184	(26,277)	44,618	113,921	90,469
Average Shares	47,121	47,409	48,571	51,223	51,432	52,525	54,639	56,680
Balance Sheet								
Total Assets	642,661	632,828	638,376	710,407	724,775	731,317	374,046	332,089
Current Liabilities	84,121	86,736	94,762	162,012	240,395	184,454	123,710	107,637
Long-Term Obligations	230,000	230,000	230,000	230,000	183,788	253,630	...	32,820
Total Liabilities	325,312	328,823	340,046	402,337	433,990	449,212	123,998	140,920
Stockholders' Equity	317,349	304,005	298,330	308,070	290,785	282,105	250,048	191,169
Shares Outstanding	47,751	47,953	47,886	51,016	53,788	51,726	52,663	52,530
Statistical Record								
Return on Assets %	10.06	9.08	7.89	6.56	N.M.	8.07	32.27	29.72
Return on Equity %	22.17	19.99	17.56	15.72	N.M.	16.77	51.64	58.58
EBITDA Margin %	35.67	35.41	30.55	22.67	1.48	22.70	43.31	41.27
Net Margin %	16.53	16.64	14.11	8.91	N.M.	7.30	23.89	22.68
Asset Turnover	0.55	0.63	0.56	0.74	0.60	1.11	1.35	1.31
Current Ratio	6.32	5.97	5.65	2.07	1.29	1.65	1.65	1.76
Debt to Equity	0.72	0.76	0.77	0.75	0.63	0.90	...	0.17
Price Range	25.90-16.87	24.59-15.87	24.59-15.87	21.07-12.49	16.84-8.40	40.91-8.98	63.30-30.76	73.69-27.94
P/E Ratio	18.50-12.05	19.83-12.80	22.56-14.56	22.90-13.58	...	48.13-10.56	30.43-14.79	46.05-17.46

Address: 7887 East Belleview Ave., Suite 1000, Englewood, CO 80111 **Telephone:** 303-796-2850 **Fax:** 303-796-2881	**Web Site:** www.csgsys.com **Officers:** Hank Bonde - Pres., C.O.O. Peter E. Kalan - Exec. V.P., Fin., C.F.O.	**Auditors:** KPMG LLP **Investor Contact:** 303-804-4065 **Transfer Agents:** BankBoston, N.A., Boston, MA

CVB FINANCIAL CORP.

Exchange	Symbol	Price	52Wk Range	Yield	P/E	Div Acheiver
NMS	CVBF	$14.94 (8/31/2006)	17.16-13.90	2.41	15.89	15 Years

*7 Year Price Score 115.82 *NYSE Composite Index=100 *12 Month Price Score 90.12

Interim Earnings (Per Share)
Qtr.	Mar	Jun	Sep	Dec
2003	0.17	0.16	0.17	0.18
2004	0.13	0.23	0.22	0.22
2005	0.23	0.22	0.24	0.21
2006	0.24	0.25	...	...

Interim Dividends (Per Share)
Amt	Decl	Ex	Rec	Pay
5-for-4	12/21/2005	1/27/2006	1/10/2006	1/26/2006
0.09Q	12/21/2005	1/9/2006	1/11/2006	1/26/2006
0.09Q	3/15/2006	3/27/2006	3/29/2006	4/12/2006
0.09Q	6/21/2006	7/3/2006	7/6/2006	7/20/2006

Indicated Div: $0.36

Valuation Analysis
		Institutional Holding	
Forecast P/E	14.56	No of Institutions	
	(9/9/2006)	83	
Market Cap	$1.1 Billion	Shares	
Book Value	338.3 Million	14,768,901	
Price/Book	3.38	% Held	
Price/Sales	3.68	19.29	

Business Summary: Commercial Banking (MIC: 8.1 SIC: 6022 NAIC: 522110)
CVB Financial is a bank holding company, with assets of $5.42 billion and deposits of $3.42 billion as of Dec 31 2005. Co.'s Citizens Business Bank, operates 40 business financial centers serving customers in the Inland Empire, San Gabriel Valley, Orange County, Madera County, Fresno County, Tulare County, and Kern County areas of California. Co. provides traditional banking activities, including the acceptance of deposits and the lending and investing of money through the operations of the Bank. The Bank also provides trust services to its customers. The bank's subsidiary, Golden West Enterprises, Inc., provides automobile and equipment leasing, and brokers mortgage loans.

Recent Developments: For the quarter ended June 30 2006, net income increased 8.2% to $18.9 million from $17.5 million in the year-earlier quarter. Net interest income increased 3.0% to $43.2 million from $41.9 million in the year-earlier quarter. Non-interest income rose 11.0% to $8.1 million from $7.3 million, while non-interest expense advanced 5.2% to $24.3 million.

Prospects: Co.'s results are benefiting from an increase in interest income due primarily to the growth in average earning assets, as well as higher interest rates. However, these positive factors have been partially offset by an increase in interest expense and higher provision for credit losses. Nonetheless, Co. indicated that the credit quality of its loan portfolio is favorable, while the decline in net interest margin is being mitigated by strong growth in its balance sheet. Furthermore, Co. is benefiting from construction growth in Southern California, as it provide construction loans to builders. The job market also continues to appear strong in the Central Valley and Inland Empire.

Financial Data
(US$ in Thousands)

	6 Mos	3 Mos	12/31/2005	12/31/2004	12/31/2003	12/31/2002	12/31/2001	12/31/2000
Earnings Per Share	0.94	0.92	0.91	0.80	0.69	0.65	0.53	0.46
Cash Flow Per Share	1.64	1.75	1.16	1.00	0.96	0.82	0.54	0.58
Tang Book Value Per Share	3.86	3.87	3.90	3.85	3.44	3.26	2.87	2.44
Dividends Per Share	0.358	0.356	0.352	0.314	0.279	0.256	0.205	0.162
Dividend Payout %	38.01	38.78	38.68	39.25	40.43	39.64	38.94	35.48
Income Statement								
Interest Income	149,033	72,132	248,488	197,702	166,346	154,323	155,877	150,867
Interest Expense	62,047	28,307	77,436	46,517	37,053	40,439	52,806	56,760
Net Interest Income	86,986	43,825	171,052	151,185	129,293	113,884	103,071	94,107
Provision for Losses	1,150	250	...	...	...	...	1,750	2,800
Non-Interest Income	15,820	7,729	27,505	27,907	29,989	29,018	22,192	19,023
Non-Interest Expense	47,729	23,470	91,593	89,722	77,794	66,056	60,155	56,345
Income Before Taxes	53,927	27,834	106,964	89,370	81,488	76,846	63,358	53,985
Income Taxes	16,770	9,594	36,346	27,884	28,656	27,101	23,300	19,302
Net Income	37,157	18,240	70,618	61,486	52,832	49,745	40,058	34,683
Average Shares	77,185	77,081	77,193	76,598	76,734	76,618	76,086	75,641
Balance Sheet								
Net Loans & Leases	2,813,525	2,693,543	2,640,659	2,117,580	1,738,659	1,424,343	1,167,071	1,032,341
Total Assets	5,952,419	5,527,914	5,422,971	4,511,011	3,854,349	3,123,411	2,514,102	2,307,996
Total Deposits	3,592,853	3,476,681	3,424,046	2,875,039	2,660,510	2,309,964	1,876,959	1,595,030
Total Liabilities	5,614,165	5,188,349	5,080,094	4,193,528	3,567,628	2,863,590	2,293,354	2,119,366
Stockholders' Equity	338,254	339,565	342,877	317,483	286,721	259,821	220,748	188,630
Shares Outstanding	76,500	76,479	76,430	75,832	75,452	74,822	74,727	74,280
Statistical Record								
Return on Assets %	1.35	1.37	1.42	1.47	1.51	1.76	1.66	1.60
Return on Equity %	21.51	21.44	21.39	20.30	19.33	20.70	19.57	21.00
Net Interest Margin %	56.13	60.76	68.84	76.47	77.73	73.80	66.12	62.38
Efficiency Ratio %	28.54	29.39	33.19	39.77	39.62	36.03	33.78	33.17
Loans to Deposits	0.78	0.77	0.77	0.74	0.65	0.62	0.62	0.65
Price Range	17.52-13.90	17.52-13.60	17.52-13.60	17.87-12.10	12.88-10.68	12.44-8.01	9.14-5.40	6.74-4.57
P/E Ratio	18.64-14.78	19.04-14.78	19.25-14.95	22.34-15.13	18.66-15.48	19.13-12.32	17.25-10.19	14.64-9.93
Average Yield %	2.28	2.29	2.26	2.10	2.37	2.50	2.82	2.86

Address: 701 North Haven Avenue, Suite 350, Ontario, CA 91764
Telephone: 909-980-4030
Fax: 909-481-2130

Web Address: www.cbbank.com
Officers: George A. Borba - Chmn. D. Linn Wiley - Pres., C.E.O.

Auditors: McGladrey & Pullen, LLP
Investor Contact: 909-980-4030
Transfer Agents: U.S. Stock Transfer Corporation, Glendale, CA

CYTYC CORP.

Exchange	Symbol	Price	52Wk Range	Yield	P/E
NMS	CYTC	$23.89 (8/31/2006)	30.11-22.96	N/A	22.97

*7 Year Price Score 112.16 *NYSE Composite Index=100 *12 Month Price Score 88.28

Interim Earnings (Per Share)

Qtr.	Mar	Jun	Sep	Dec
2003	0.17	0.16	0.17	0.18
2004	0.01	0.19	0.21	0.21
2005	0.18	0.23	0.26	0.27
2006	0.24	0.24	...	...

Interim Dividends (Per Share)

Amt	Decl	Ex	Rec	Pay
200%	1/31/2001	3/5/2001	2/16/2001	3/2/2001

Valuation Analysis

Forecast P/E	21.65 (9/9/2006)
Market Cap	$2.7 Billion
Book Value	645.5 Million
Price/Book	4.20
Price/Sales	4.83

Institutional Holding

No of Institutions	236
Shares	101,648,272
% Held	90.34

Business Summary: Instruments and Related Products (MIC: 11.15 SIC: 3826 NAIC: 334516)

Cytyc is a women's health company that designs, develops, manufactures and markets products that cover a range of women's health applications, including cervical cancer screening, treatment of excessive menstrual bleeding, radiation treatment of early-stage breast cancer and breast cancer risk assessment. Co. operates in three segments: domestic diagnostic products segment, which develops and markets the ThinPrep System; domestic surgical products segment, which manufactures the NovaSure System, the MammoSite Radiation Therapy System and the GliaSite Radiation Therapy System; and international segment, which markets its diagnostic and surgical products outside of the U.S.

Recent Developments: For the quarter ended June 30 2006, net income increased 13.0% to $31.7 million from $28.0 million in the year-earlier quarter. Revenues were $150.4 million, up 20.0% from $125.4 million the year before. Operating income was $49.9 million versus $46.1 million in the prior-year quarter, an increase of 8.1%. Direct operating expenses rose 26.6% to $33.1 million from $26.1 million in the comparable period the year before. Indirect operating expenses increased 26.9% to $67.5 million from $53.2 million in the equivalent prior-year period.

Prospects: Co.'s top-line results are being driven primarily by robust domestic sales of its NovaSure® Endometrial Ablation product and continued strong performance of its diagnostics business. Moreover, Co.'s results are benefiting from an increase in its MammoSite® Radiation Therapy System sales. Meanwhile, Co. is seeing higher sales in its international business, due in part to the ongoing expansion of its ThinPrep business and NovaSure growth in the U.K. and Canada. Going forward, Co.'s core research and development strategy is to enhance its existing product lines, while continuing to develop additional medical diagnostic and surgical devices and therapeutic applications for women's health.

Financial Data
(US$ in Thousands)

	6 Mos	3 Mos	12/31/2005	12/31/2004	12/31/2003	12/31/2002	12/31/2001	12/31/2000
Earnings Per Share	1.04	1.00	0.94	0.63	0.68	0.39	0.10	0.32
Cash Flow Per Share	1.45	1.56	1.55	1.23	0.74	0.82	0.79	0.23
Tang Book Value Per Share	0.62	0.71	0.40	0.87	2.25	1.90	1.95	1.30
Income Statement								
Total Revenue	290,937	140,540	508,251	393,593	303,060	236,493	220,993	142,065
EBITDA	112,647	54,234	208,207	150,924	132,305	82,674	39,647	39,207
Depn & Amortn	16,587	8,029	25,601	17,569	8,747	8,922	7,351	4,925
Income Before Taxes	96,132	46,243	178,718	130,397	125,983	77,257	37,708	39,016
Income Taxes	35,088	16,879	65,232	56,809	49,763	29,363	25,073	853
Net Income	61,044	29,364	113,486	73,588	76,220	47,894	12,635	38,163
Average Shares	123,582	125,877	125,446	121,922	112,807	122,782	120,776	117,960
Balance Sheet								
Total Assets	1,031,405	1,050,554	1,039,879	809,350	390,900	361,626	386,760	170,886
Current Liabilities	54,034	58,916	89,183	42,585	32,920	36,585	35,615	23,840
Total Liabilities	385,908	390,406	411,528	321,905	37,269	36,898	36,452	23,840
Stockholders' Equity	645,497	660,148	628,351	487,445	353,631	324,728	350,308	147,046
Shares Outstanding	113,377	115,347	115,273	113,428	109,581	113,555	121,355	113,039
Statistical Record								
Return on Assets %	13.19	12.65	12.27	12.23	20.26	12.80	4.53	26.88
Return on Equity %	21.87	20.74	20.34	17.45	22.47	14.19	5.08	31.45
EBITDA Margin %	38.72	38.59	40.97	38.35	43.66	34.96	17.94	27.60
Net Margin %	20.98	20.89	22.33	18.70	25.15	20.25	5.72	26.86
Asset Turnover	0.59	0.56	0.55	0.65	0.81	0.63	0.79	1.00
Current Ratio	5.92	5.84	3.78	7.53	7.37	5.76	6.06	5.92
Price Range	30.11-21.50	30.11-21.20	29.22-21.20	28.62-13.79	15.55-9.39	27.52-6.88	29.52-13.88	22.42-9.17
P/E Ratio	28.95-20.67	30.11-21.20	31.09-22.55	45.43-21.89	22.87-13.81	70.56-17.64	295.20-138.75	70.05-28.65

Address: 85 Swanson Road, Boxborough, MA 01719
Telephone: 978-263-8000
Fax: 978-635-1033

Web Site: www.cytyc.com
Officers: Patrick J. Sullivan - Chmn., Pres., C.E.O. C. William McDaniel - Vice-Chmn.

Auditors: Deloitte & Touche LLP
Investor Contact: 978-263-8000

DELL INC

Exchange	Symbol	Price	52Wk Range	Yield	P/E
NMS	DELL	$22.55 (8/31/2006)	35.60-19.91	N/A	16.22

*7 Year Price Score 70.05 *NYSE Composite Index=100 *12 Month Price Score 75.85

Interim Earnings (Per Share)

Qtr.	Apr	Jul	Oct	Jan
2003-04	0.23	0.24	0.26	0.29
2004-05	0.28	0.31	0.33	0.26
2005-06	0.37	0.41	0.25	0.43
2006-07	0.33	...	...	...

Interim Dividends (Per Share)
No Dividends Paid

Valuation Analysis

		Institutional Holding	
Forecast P/E	N/A	No of Institutions	890
Market Cap	$51.4 Billion	Shares	
Book Value	3.4 Billion		1,473,417,216
Price/Book	15.24	% Held	
Price/Sales	0.92		64.86

Business Summary: IT & Technology (MIC: 10.2 SIC: 3571 NAIC: 334111)

Dell designs, develops, manufactures, markets, sells, and supports a range of computer systems and services that are customized to customer requirements, which include enterprise systems, client systems, printing and imaging systems, software and peripherals and global services. Co.'s range of computer systems include Dell XPS™, Dimension™, and OptiPlex™ desktop computers, Inspiron™ and Latitude™ notebook computers, Dell Precision™ mobile workstation, PowerEdge™ and PowerConnect™ networking products, Dell Axim™ handhelds as well as printers, monitors, plasma and LCD televisions, projectors and numerous third-party printers, software, digital cameras and other products.

Recent Developments: For the quarter ended May 5 2006, net income decreased 18.4% to $762.0 million from $934.0 million in the year-earlier quarter. Revenues were $14.22 billion, up 6.2% from $13.39 billion the year before. Operating income was $949.0 million versus $1.17 billion in the prior-year quarter, a decrease of 19.2%. Direct operating expenses rose 7.8% to $11.74 billion from $10.90 billion in the comparable period the year before. Indirect operating expenses increased 15.6% to $1.52 billion from $1.32 billion in the equivalent prior-year period.

Prospects: Co.'s prospects upon continuing its global growth within the upcoming three to five years appears to be viable. Results are significantly benefiting from Co.'s expansion of business outside the U.S., as demonstrated by the opening of its second manufacturing operation in Xiamen, China on May 30 2006. In addition, Co. is experiencing overall growth across its portfolio of products, particularly in Enhanced Services. Meanwhile, Co. is accelerating its plans to drive $3.00 billion of cost improvement in fiscal year 2007, primarily towards reduction in structural material, component, transformational as well as improved warranty costs.

Financial Data
(US$ in Thousands)

	3 Mos	02/03/2006	01/28/2005	01/30/2004	01/31/2003	02/01/2002	02/02/2001	01/28/2000
Earnings Per Share	1.39	1.46	1.18	1.01	0.80	0.46	0.79	0.61
Cash Flow Per Share	2.01	1.98	2.12	1.43	1.37	1.46	1.60	1.55
Tang Book Value Per Share	1.48	1.77	2.61	2.46	1.89	1.80	2.16	2.06
Income Statement								
Total Revenue	14,216,000	55,908,000	49,205,000	41,444,000	35,404,000	31,168,000	31,888,000	25,265,000
EBITDA	1,105,000	4,995,000	4,795,000	4,001,000	3,255,000	1,970,000	3,434,000	2,607,000
Depn & Amortn	106,000	393,000	334,000	263,000	211,000	239,000	240,000	156,000
Income Before Taxes	999,000	4,574,000	4,445,000	3,724,000	3,027,000	1,731,000	3,194,000	2,451,000
Income Taxes	237,000	1,002,000	1,402,000	1,079,000	905,000	485,000	958,000	785,000
Net Income	762,000	3,572,000	3,043,000	2,645,000	2,122,000	1,246,000	2,177,000	1,666,000
Average Shares	2,318,000	2,449,000	2,568,000	2,619,000	2,644,000	2,726,000	2,746,000	2,728,000
Balance Sheet								
Total Assets	22,871,000	23,109,000	23,215,000	19,311,000	15,470,000	13,535,000	13,435,000	11,471,000
Current Liabilities	16,320,000	15,927,000	14,136,000	10,896,000	8,933,000	7,519,000	6,543,000	5,192,000
Long-Term Obligations	503,000	504,000	505,000	505,000	506,000	520,000	509,000	508,000
Total Liabilities	19,497,000	18,980,000	16,730,000	13,031,000	10,597,000	8,841,000	7,813,000	6,163,000
Stockholders' Equity	3,374,000	4,129,000	6,485,000	6,280,000	4,873,000	4,694,000	5,622,000	5,308,000
Shares Outstanding	2,280,000	2,330,000	2,485,000	2,556,000	2,579,000	2,602,000	2,601,000	2,575,000
Statistical Record								
Return on Assets %	14.63	15.17	14.35	15.25	14.67	9.27	17.20	18.21
Return on Equity %	74.08	66.22	47.81	47.56	44.48	24.22	39.19	43.80
EBITDA Margin %	7.77	8.93	9.74	9.65	9.19	6.32	10.77	10.32
Net Margin %	5.36	6.39	6.18	6.38	5.99	4.00	6.83	6.59
Asset Turnover	2.45	2.37	2.32	2.39	2.45	2.32	2.52	2.76
Current Ratio	1.07	1.11	1.20	0.98	1.00	1.05	1.45	1.48
Debt to Equity	0.15	0.12	0.08	0.08	0.10	0.11	0.09	0.10
Price Range	41.54-25.32	41.76-29.00	42.38-31.20	36.98-22.86	30.94-22.33	30.49-16.63	58.13-16.63	54.31-33.06
P/E Ratio	29.88-18.22	28.60-19.86	35.92-26.44	36.61-22.63	38.68-27.91	66.28-36.15	73.58-21.04	89.04-54.20

Address: One Dell Way, Round Rock, TX 78682
Telephone: 512-338-4400
Fax: 512-283-6161

Web Site: www.dell.com
Officers: Michael S. Dell - Chmn. Kevin B. Rollins - Pres., C.E.O.

Auditors: PricewaterhouseCoopers LLP
Investor Contact: 512-338-4400
Transfer Agents: American Stock Transfer and Trust Company

DENTSPLY INTERNATIONAL, INC.

Exchange	Symbol	Price	52Wk Range	Yield	P/E	Div Acheiver
NMS	XRAY	$32.58 (8/31/2006)	33.17-25.55	0.43	112.34	11 Years

*7 Year Price Score 117.08 *NYSE Composite Index=100 *12 Month Price Score 106.26

Interim Earnings (Per Share)

Qtr.	Mar	Jun	Sep	Dec
2003	0.24	0.28	0.26	0.31
2004	0.55	0.30	0.28	0.41
2005	0.30	0.35	(0.39)	(0.01)
2006	0.31	0.37	...	...

Interim Dividends (Per Share)

Amt	Decl	Ex	Rec	Pay
0.035Q	2/14/2006	3/23/2006	3/27/2006	4/6/2006
0.035Q	5/10/2006	6/22/2006	6/26/2006	7/6/2006
100%	5/10/2006	7/18/2006	6/26/2006	7/17/2006
0.035Q	7/25/2006	9/27/2006	9/29/2006	10/10/2006
Indicated Div: $0.14				

Valuation Analysis

Forecast P/E	22.30 (9/9/2006)
Market Cap	$5.0 Billion
Book Value	1.3 Billion
Price/Book	4.03
Price/Sales	2.85

Institutional Holding

No of Institutions	353
Shares	119,547,808
% Held	77.72

Business Summary: Medical Instruments & Equipment (MIC: 9.6 SIC: 3843 NAIC: 339114)

DENTSPLY International is a worldwide designer, developer, manufacturer and marketer of a range of products for the dental market. Co.'s dental products are classified through three key categories: dental consumables, dental laboratory products and specialty dental products. These products are distributed worldwide under several brand names and trademarks such as AQUASIL™, BIOPURE™, CAVITRON®, DENTSPLY®, ELEPHANT®, FRIADENT®, GAC ORTHOWORKS™, IN-OVATION™, MIDWEST®, NUPRO®, ORAQIX®, PROFILE®, RINN®, SEAL & PROTECT™, THERMAFIL®, XENO® and XYLOCAINE®. Additionally, Co. conducts its business in over 120 foreign countries, primarily through its foreign subsidiaries.

Recent Developments: For the quarter ended June 30 2006, net income increased 2.5% to $59.3 million from $57.9 million in the year-earlier quarter. Revenues were $472.4 million, up 6.2% from $444.8 million the year before. Operating income was $86.6 million versus $81.1 million in the prior-year quarter, an increase of 6.7%. Direct operating expenses rose 5.9% to $230.3 million from $217.6 million in the comparable period the year before. Indirect operating expenses increased 6.4% to $155.6 million from $146.1 million in the equivalent prior-year period.

Prospects: Going forward, Co. is optimistic regarding its ability in adhering to its long-term overall internal growth rate of 4.0% to 6.0%, given by the continued strength demonstrated during the first half of 2006. As such, Co. expects to increase its internal investment in growth initiatives throughout the upcoming quarters, which include the continuing enhancement and further launching of new products. In this respect, Co. expects to attain its target of launching between 20 and 25 new products in 2006. Meanwhile, Co. is increasing its earnings guidance for full-year 2006 to be in the range of $1.40 to $1.44 per diluted share.

Financial Data
(US$ in Thousands)

	6 Mos	3 Mos	12/31/2005	12/31/2004	12/31/2003	12/31/2002	12/31/2001	12/31/2000
Earnings Per Share	0.29	0.28	0.28	1.54	1.08	0.93	0.77	0.64
Cash Flow Per Share	1.66	1.39	1.46	1.90	1.64	1.11	1.36	0.93
Tang Book Value Per Share	1.34	1.87	1.52	1.18	N.M.	N.M.	N.M.	1.13
Dividends Per Share	0.135	0.130	0.125	0.109	0.099	0.092	0.092	0.085
Dividend Payout %	46.55	47.27	44.64	7.04	9.12	9.95	11.90	13.28
Income Statement								
Total Revenue	903,440	430,996	1,715,135	1,694,232	1,570,925	1,513,742	1,129,094	889,796
EBITDA	179,546	82,617	130,366	343,080	321,062	292,229	260,035	202,446
Depn & Amortn	23,397	12,095	50,560	49,296	45,661	43,859	54,334	41,359
Income Before Taxes	157,275	71,209	71,038	274,155	251,196	220,985	185,127	151,796
Income Taxes	47,955	21,205	25,625	63,869	81,343	73,033	63,631	50,780
Net Income	109,320	50,004	45,413	253,165	174,183	147,952	121,496	101,016
Average Shares	159,834	161,060	162,016	164,028	161,294	159,988	157,950	157,119
Balance Sheet								
Total Assets	2,566,713	2,442,154	2,407,329	2,798,145	2,445,587	2,087,033	1,798,151	866,615
Current Liabilities	716,176	778,267	741,234	404,607	337,684	365,745	358,517	168,138
Long-Term Obligations	413,307	186,861	270,104	779,940	790,202	769,823	723,524	109,500
Total Liabilities	1,316,103	1,132,495	1,165,561	1,353,572	1,323,100	1,249,846	1,188,195	341,684
Stockholders' Equity	1,250,397	1,309,476	1,241,580	1,443,973	1,122,069	835,928	609,519	520,370
Shares Outstanding	154,500	158,400	157,800	161,200	158,600	156,800	155,800	155,100
Statistical Record								
Return on Assets %	1.86	1.80	1.74	9.63	7.69	7.62	9.12	11.67
Return on Equity %	3.65	3.38	3.38	19.68	17.79	20.47	21.51	20.37
EBITDA Margin %	19.87	19.17	7.60	20.25	20.44	19.31	23.03	22.75
Net Margin %	12.10	11.60	2.65	14.94	11.09	9.77	10.76	11.35
Asset Turnover	0.69	0.68	0.66	0.64	0.69	0.78	0.85	1.03
Current Ratio	1.62	1.37	1.39	2.61	2.15	1.48	1.35	1.94
Debt to Equity	0.33	0.14	0.22	0.54	0.70	0.92	1.19	0.21
Price Range	31.11-25.55	29.11-25.55	28.98-25.55	28.24-20.98	23.59-16.35	21.45-15.64	16.92-11.27	14.21-7.77
P/E Ratio	107.28-88.10	103.98-91.25	103.52-91.25	18.34-13.63	21.85-15.14	23.06-16.81	21.97-14.64	22.20-12.14
Average Yield %	0.48	0.47	0.46	0.44	0.49	0.50	0.65	0.82

Address: 221 West Philadelphia Street, York, PA 17405-0872
Telephone: 717-845-7511
Fax: 717-854-2343
Web Site: www.dentsply.com
Officers: Gary K. Kunkle Jr. - Chmn., C.E.O. Thomas L. Whiting - Pres., C.O.O.
Auditors: PricewaterhouseCoopers LLP
Investor Contact: 717-849-4370
Transfer Agents: Wachovia Bank, N.A.

DOLLAR TREE STORES INC.

Exchange	Symbol	Price	52Wk Range	Yield	P/E
NMS	DLTR	$28.78 (8/31/2006)	29.62-20.75	N/A	17.13

*7 Year Price Score 69.97   *NYSE Composite Index=100   *12 Month Price Score 104.29

Interim Earnings (Per Share)

Qtr.	Apr	Jul	Oct	Jan
2003-04	0.29	0.25	0.31	0.69
2004-05	0.31	0.26	0.28	0.73
2005-06	0.26	0.25	0.29	0.80
2006-07	0.31	0.28	...	...

Interim Dividends (Per Share)
No Dividends Paid

Valuation Analysis | **Institutional Holding**
Forecast P/E | 14.40 | No of Institutions
 | (9/9/2006) | 236
Market Cap | $2.9 Billion | Shares
Book Value | 1.1 Billion | 102,845,816
Price/Book | 2.64 | % Held
Price/Sales | 0.81 | 98.36

Business Summary: Retail - General (MIC: 5.2 SIC: 5331 NAIC: 452990)
Dollar Tree Stores is an operator of discount variety stores offering merchandise at the fixed price of $1.00. Co.'s merchandise mix consists of consumable merchandise such as candy and food, health and beauty care, and household consumables; variety merchandise such as toys, durable housewares, gifts, party goods, greeting cards, hardware and other items; and seasonal goods that include Easter, Halloween and Christmas merchandise, along with summer toys as well as lawn and garden merchandise. As of Jan 28 2006, Co. operated 2,914 single-price point stores under the names of Dollar Tree, Dollar Bills and Dollar Express throughout 48 U.S. states.

Recent Developments: For the quarter ended July 29 2006, net income increased 6.2% to $29.0 million from $27.3 million in the year-earlier quarter. Revenues were $883.6 million, up 14.9% from $769.0 million the year before. Operating income was $48.0 million versus $46.6 million in the prior-year quarter, an increase of 3.0%. Direct operating expenses rose 16.3% to $590.3 million from $507.5 million in the comparable period the year before. Indirect operating expenses increased 14.1% to $245.3 million from $214.9 million in the equivalent prior-year period.

Prospects: Co.'s results are reflecting an increase in comparable store net sales, driven by its initiatives in 2005 which include expansion of payment modes accepted by its stores, as well as the launch of freezers and coolers to more of its stores. Simultaneously, these initiatives have also contributed towards mitigating the effect of higher fuel costs experienced by Co.'s customers. Looking ahead, Co. estimates sales to be in the range of $895.0 million to $915.0 million and earnings of $0.30 to $0.32 per diluted share for the third fiscal quarter of 2006. For full-fiscal year 2006, Co. expects sales of $3.90 billion to $3.96 billion and earnings of $1.74 to $1.82 per diluted share.

Financial Data (US$ in Thousands)	6 Mos	3 Mos	01/28/2006	01/29/2005	01/31/2004	02/01/2003	12/31/2002	12/31/2001
Earnings Per Share	1.68	1.65	1.60	1.58	1.54	(0.09)	1.35	1.09
Cash Flow Per Share	3.88	3.87	3.38	2.45	2.05	(2.40)	1.82	1.59
Tang Book Value Per Share	9.49	9.72	9.79	9.16	7.81	7.07	7.16	5.45
Income Statement								
Total Revenue	1,740,100	856,500	3,393,924	3,126,009	2,799,872	160,789	2,329,188	1,987,271
EBITDA	175,500	89,700	423,956	423,899	395,981	(972)	324,067	255,905
Depn & Amortn	74,100	36,300	140,717	129,291	101,495	7,217	71,615	53,763
Income Before Taxes	98,900	52,600	275,218	288,170	288,752	(8,519)	251,459	200,251
Income Taxes	37,000	19,700	101,300	107,920	111,169	(3,279)	96,812	77,170
Net Income	61,900	32,900	173,918	180,250	177,583	(10,525)	154,647	123,081
Average Shares	104,100	106,800	108,759	113,986	115,581	114,661	114,547	112,990
Balance Sheet								
Total Assets	1,775,300	1,837,800	1,798,400	1,792,672	1,480,306	1,304,239	1,116,377	902,048
Current Liabilities	340,900	344,500	295,456	294,355	265,102	267,060	206,511	201,022
Long-Term Obligations	250,000	250,000	250,611	250,534	154,827	163,911	23,647	33,506
Total Liabilities	661,500	670,400	626,125	628,460	465,784	458,420	260,973	250,312
Stockholders' Equity	1,113,800	1,167,400	1,172,275	1,164,212	1,014,522	845,819	855,404	651,736
Shares Outstanding	102,000	105,200	106,552	113,020	114,083	114,231	114,186	112,505
Statistical Record								
Return on Assets %	10.41	10.09	9.71	11.04	12.79	N.M.	15.32	14.93
Return on Equity %	16.26	15.93	14.93	16.59	19.14	N.M.	20.52	21.03
EBITDA Margin %	10.09	10.47	12.49	13.56	14.14	N.M.	13.91	12.88
Net Margin %	3.56	3.84	5.12	5.77	6.34	N.M.	6.64	6.19
Asset Turnover	2.10	1.99	1.90	1.92	2.02	1.52	2.31	2.41
Current Ratio	2.57	2.75	3.19	3.29	2.73	2.88	3.47	2.79
Debt to Equity	0.22	0.21	0.21	0.22	0.15	0.19	0.03	0.05
Price Range	28.57-20.75	28.57-20.75	28.80-20.75	33.71-22.46	39.29-18.40	27.42-21.77	40.27-19.55	34.54-15.81
P/E Ratio	17.01-12.35	17.32-12.58	18.00-12.97	21.34-14.22	25.51-11.95	...	29.83-14.48	31.69-14.51

Address: 500 Volvo Parkway, Chesapeake, VA 23320
Telephone: 757-321-5000

Web Site: www.DollarTree.com
Officers: Macon F. Brock Jr. - Chmn. Bob Sasser - Pres., C.E.O.

Auditors: KPMG LLP
Investor Contact: 757-321-5000
Transfer Agents: National City Bank, Cleveland, OH

EBAY INC.

Exchange	Symbol	Price	52Wk Range	Yield	P/E
NMS	EBAY	$27.82 (8/31/2006)	46.77-22.99	N/A	38.64

*7 Year Price Score 114.68 *NYSE Composite Index=100 *12 Month Price Score 68.70

Interim Earnings (Per Share)

Qtr.	Mar	Jun	Sep	Dec
2003	0.08	0.07	0.08	0.11
2004	0.15	0.14	0.14	0.15
2005	0.19	0.21	0.18	0.20
2006	0.17	0.17	...	...

Interim Dividends (Per Share)

Amt	Decl	Ex	Rec	Pay
2-for-1	7/24/2003	8/29/2003	8/4/2003	8/28/2003
2-for-1	1/19/2005	2/17/2005	1/31/2005	2/16/2005

Valuation Analysis

		Institutional Holding	
Forecast P/E	32.39	No of Institutions	
	(9/9/2006)	631	
Market Cap	$39.4 Billion	Shares	
Book Value	11.3 Billion	922,197,760	
Price/Book	3.49	% Held	
Price/Sales	7.52	65.15	

Business Summary: Miscellaneous Business Services (MIC: 12.8 SIC: 7389 NAIC: 518111)
eBay provides online marketplaces for the sale of goods and services, online payments services and online communication offerings. Co. has three primary businesses; the eBay Marketplaces that enable online commerce in a range of formats, including the traditional auction platform, and other online platforms, such as Rent.com; the Payments, which consists of Co.'s PayPal business, enables individuals or businesses to send and receive payments online; and Co.'s Communications that consist of Co.'s Skype business that allows Voice over Internet Protocol calls between Skype users, and provides Skype users low-cost connectivity to traditional fixed-line and mobile telephones.

Recent Developments: For the quarter ended June 30 2006, net income decreased 14.3% to $250.0 million from $291.6 million in the year-earlier quarter. Revenues were $1.41 billion, up 29.9% from $1.09 billion the year before. Operating income was $311.4 million versus $379.0 million in the prior-year quarter, a decrease of 17.8%. Direct operating expenses rose 52.5% to $292.5 million from $191.8 million in the comparable period the year before. Indirect operating expenses increased 56.5% to $806.9 million from $515.5 million in the equivalent prior-year period.

Prospects: Looking ahead, Co. expects net revenues in 2006 will be driven primarily by increased transaction revenues across its U.S. Marketplaces, International Marketplaces, Payments and Communications segments. Accordingly, Co. will continue to invest in the areas of global expansion for its eBay Marketplaces, Payments and Communications businesses, as well as customer support, site operations, marketing and various corporate infrastructure areas. For full-year 2006, Co. expects total net revenues of $5.70 billion to $5.90 billion, and earnings per diluted share of $0.69 to $0.72, including the estimated effect of stock-based compensation from the adoption of FAS 123R of about $0.16 to $0.17.

Financial Data
(US$ in Thousands)

	6 Mos	3 Mos	12/31/2005	12/31/2004	12/31/2003	12/31/2002	12/31/2001	12/31/2000
Earnings Per Share	0.72	0.76	0.78	0.57	0.34	0.21	0.08	0.04
Cash Flow Per Share	1.50	1.49	1.48	0.97	0.68	0.42	0.23	0.10
Tang Book Value Per Share	2.95	2.58	2.21	2.73	2.24	1.46	1.11	0.94
Income Statement								
Total Revenue	2,801,203	1,390,419	4,552,401	3,271,309	2,165,096	1,214,100	748,821	431,424
EBITDA	951,140	471,670	1,929,855	1,390,809	824,814	476,201	252,435	119,381
Depn & Amortn	265,712	123,286	377,000	253,700	159,000	76,576	86,641	38,050
Income Before Taxes	683,752	347,637	1,549,377	1,128,230	661,500	398,133	162,943	77,957
Income Taxes	185,474	99,354	467,285	343,885	206,738	145,946	80,009	32,725
Net Income	498,276	248,282	1,082,043	778,223	441,771	249,891	90,448	48,294
Average Shares	1,435,757	1,437,581	1,393,875	1,367,720	1,313,314	1,171,280	1,122,380	1,121,384
Balance Sheet								
Total Assets	13,250,251	12,568,535	11,788,986	7,991,051	5,820,134	4,124,444	1,678,529	1,182,403
Current Liabilities	1,719,405	1,681,508	1,484,935	1,084,870	647,276	386,224	180,139	137,442
Long-Term Obligations	...	...	...	75	124,476	13,798	12,008	11,404
Total Liabilities	1,966,779	1,941,735	1,741,005	1,262,710	923,892	567,971	249,391	168,643
Stockholders' Equity	11,283,472	10,626,800	10,047,981	6,728,341	4,896,242	3,556,473	1,429,138	1,013,760
Shares Outstanding	1,415,197	1,409,069	1,404,183	1,338,608	1,298,586	1,245,108	1,109,036	1,077,000
Statistical Record								
Return on Assets %	9.27	10.15	10.94	11.24	8.88	8.61	6.32	4.49
Return on Equity %	10.95	12.03	12.90	13.35	10.45	10.02	7.40	5.16
EBITDA Margin %	33.95	33.92	42.39	42.52	38.10	39.22	33.71	27.67
Net Margin %	17.79	17.86	23.77	23.79	20.40	20.58	12.08	11.19
Asset Turnover	0.47	0.46	0.46	0.47	0.44	0.42	0.52	0.40
Current Ratio	2.64	2.32	2.14	2.68	3.32	3.80	4.91	4.91
Debt to Equity	...	...	...	N.M.	0.03	N.M.	0.01	0.01
Price Range	46.77-28.25	46.77-31.14	58.17-31.14	58.88-31.50	32.31-16.95	17.69-12.28	17.76-7.55	30.47-6.98
P/E Ratio	64.96-39.24	61.54-40.97	74.58-39.92	103.31-55.26	95.01-49.87	84.23-58.46	222.00-94.34	761.72-174.61

Address: 2145 Hamilton Avenue, San Jose, CA 95125	Web Site: www.ebay.com	Auditors: PricewaterhouseCoopers LLP
Telephone: 408-376-7400	Officers: Pierre M. Omidyar - Chmn. Margaret C. Whitman - Pres., C.E.O.	

ECHOSTAR COMMUNICATIONS CORP.

Exchange	Symbol	Price	52Wk Range	Yield	P/E
NMS	DISH	$31.75 (8/31/2006)	35.44-24.52	N/A	21.60

*7 Year Price Score 75.02 *NYSE Composite Index=100 *12 Month Price Score 108.79

Interim Earnings (Per Share)

Qtr.	Mar	Jun	Sep	Dec
2003	0.12	0.26	0.07	0.01
2004	(0.09)	0.18	0.22	0.15
2005	0.69	1.79	0.46	0.30
2006	0.33	0.38	...	...

Interim Dividends (Per Share)

Amt	Decl	Ex	Rec	Pay
1.00U	11/9/2004	12/6/2004	12/8/2004	12/14/2004

Valuation Analysis **Institutional Holding**

Forecast P/E	23.15	No of Institutions
	(9/9/2006)	238
Market Cap	$14.1 Billion	Shares
Book Value	N/A	179,285,344
Price/Book	N/A	% Held
Price/Sales	1.56	40.31

Business Summary: Media (MIC: 13.1 SIC: 4841 NAIC: 517510)

EchoStar Communications is a holding company. Its subsidiaries operate two interrelated business units. The DISH Network provides a direct broadcast satellite (DBS) subscription television service in the United States. EchoStar Technologies (ETC) designs and develops DBS set-top boxes, antennae and other digital equipment for the DISH Network. Also, ETC designs, develops and distributes similar equipment for international satellite service providers. As of Dec 31 2005, the DISH Network had about 12.0 million subscribers. Co. has 14 owned or leased in-orbit satellites for more than 2,300 video and audio channels to consumers in the U.S. Co. offers over 115 foreign-language channels.

Recent Developments: For the quarter ended June 30 2006, net income decreased 80.3% to $168.8 million from $855.5 million in the year-earlier quarter. Revenues were $2.46 billion, up 17.3% from $2.10 billion the year before. Operating income was $349.6 million versus $333.4 million in the prior-year quarter, an increase of 4.9%. Direct operating expenses rose 15.3% to $1.62 billion from $1.41 billion in the comparable period the year before. Indirect operating expenses increased 36.9% to $486.4 million from $355.3 million in the equivalent prior-year period.

Prospects: Co. is experiencing growth in gross new subscribers for its DISH Network, mainly due to an increase in gross activations pursuant to its partnership with AT&T, Inc., and to a lesser extent, through an increase in gross activations through its other agency relationships. Meanwhile, Co. continues to explore growth opportunities with attractive margins in the lower end of the market. Looking ahead, Co. will continue to evaluate additional ways to further grow its business strategically, including exploring improved mobile video and data distribution technologies. Co. also believes that its PocketDISH as well as other similar products will offer market video profitability going forward.

Financial Data (US$ in Thousands)	6 Mos	3 Mos	12/31/2005	12/31/2004	12/31/2003	12/31/2002	12/31/2001	12/31/2000
Earnings Per Share	1.47	2.88	3.22	0.46	0.46	(0.92)	(0.45)	(1.32)
Cash Flow Per Share	4.63	4.34	3.92	2.15	1.19	0.14	1.03	(0.25)
Dividends Per Share	...	...	...	1.000	...	...	...	...
Dividend Payout %	...	...	...	217.39	...	...	...	...
Income Statement								
Total Revenue	4,748,395	2,289,706	8,425,501	7,151,216	5,739,296	4,820,825	4,001,138	2,715,220
EBITDA	1,204,179	586,804	2,174,309	1,226,224	1,134,820	(54,266)	347,491	(240,537)
Depn & Amortn	527,338	248,348	836,892	536,401	408,506	384,864	287,841	191,862
Income Before Taxes	488,744	230,818	1,007,091	226,378	238,882	(809,106)	(214,044)	(620,656)
Income Taxes	172,684	83,537	(507,449)	11,609	14,376	72,544	1,454	555
Net Income	316,060	147,281	1,514,540	214,769	224,506	(881,650)	(215,498)	(621,211)
Average Shares	453,126	445,613	484,131	467,598	488,314	480,429	477,172	471,023
Balance Sheet								
Total Assets	9,104,609	8,934,670	7,410,210	6,029,277	7,585,018	6,260,585	6,519,686	4,665,950
Current Liabilities	2,374,145	2,385,849	2,150,071	2,071,865	2,972,284	1,645,219	1,488,367	1,223,057
Long-Term Obligations	7,241,967	7,239,218	5,898,831	5,757,826	5,499,327	5,733,621	5,706,480	4,014,812
Total Liabilities	9,616,112	9,625,067	8,276,834	8,107,489	8,617,542	7,466,223	7,297,458	5,294,218
Stockholders' Equity	(511,503)	(690,397)	(866,624)	(2,078,212)	(1,032,524)	(1,205,638)	(777,772)	(628,268)
Shares Outstanding	444,704	444,418	443,904	455,670	478,805	480,974	479,450	474,184
Statistical Record								
Return on Assets %	8.03	17.33	22.54	3.15	3.24	N.M.	N.M.	N.M.
EBITDA Margin %	25.36	25.63	25.81	17.15	19.77	N.M.	8.68	N.M.
Net Margin %	6.66	6.43	17.98	3.00	3.91	N.M.	N.M.	N.M.
Asset Turnover	1.11	1.12	1.25	1.05	0.83	0.75	0.72	0.63
Current Ratio	1.67	1.60	1.11	1.02	1.54	2.02	2.36	1.68
Price Range	32.25-24.52	32.11-24.52	33.25-24.52	39.33-27.26	40.53-22.26	29.45-14.16	38.51-20.47	79.00-22.75
P/E Ratio	21.94-16.68	11.15-8.51	10.33-7.61	85.50-59.26	88.11-48.39	...	...	...
Average Yield %	...	...	...	3.07	...	...	...	...

Address: 9601 South Meridian Boulevard, Englewood, CO 80112 **Telephone:** 303-723-1000 **Fax:** 303-723-1499	**Web Site:** www.echostar.com **Officers:** Charles W. Ergen - Chmn., C.E.O. Carl Vogel - Vice-Chmn.	**Auditors:** KPMG LLP **Investor Contact:** 303-723-2201 **Transfer Agents:** Computershare Investor Services, Golden, Co

ELECTRONIC ARTS, INC.

Exchange	Symbol	Price	52Wk Range	Yield	P/E
NMS	ERTS	$51.03 (8/31/2006)	61.89-40.88	N/A	75.04

*7 Year Price Score 111.22 *NYSE Composite Index=100 *12 Month Price Score 87.48

Interim Earnings (Per Share)

Qtr.	Jun	Sep	Dec	Mar
2003-04	0.06	0.25	1.26	0.28
2004-05	0.08	0.31	1.18	0.02
2005-06	(0.19)	0.16	0.83	(0.05)
2006-07	(0.26)	...	...	...

Interim Dividends (Per Share)

Amt	Decl	Ex	Rec	Pay
2-for-1	8/14/2000	9/11/2000	8/25/2000	9/8/2000
2-for-1	...	11/18/2003	11/3/2003	11/17/2003

Valuation Analysis

		Institutional Holding	
Forecast P/E	46.66	No of Institutions	
	(9/9/2006)	468	
Market Cap	$15.6 Billion	Shares	
Book Value	3.4 Billion	283,390,368	
Price/Book	4.55	% Held	
Price/Sales	5.21	92.41	

Business Summary: IT & Technology (MIC: 10.2 SIC: 7372 NAIC: 511210)
Electronic Arts develops, markets, publishes and distributes interactive software games that are playable by consumers on home video game consoles (such as the Sony PlayStation® 2, Microsoft Xbox®, and Xbox 360™, and Nintendo GameCube™), personal computers, mobile platforms (including cellular handsets and hand-held game players such as the Nintendo DS™ and the PlayStation® Portable "PSP™") and online, over the Internet and other proprietary online networks. Some of Co.'s games are based on content that Co. licenses from others (e.g., Madden NFL Football), and some of Co.'s games are based on its own wholly-owned intellectual property (e.g., The Sims™, Need for Speed™ and BLACK™).

Recent Developments: For the quarter ended June 30 2006, net loss amounted to $81.0 million versus a net loss of $58.0 million in the year-earlier quarter. Revenues were $413.0 million, up 13.2% from $365.0 million the year before. Operating loss was $119.0 million versus a loss of $96.0 million in the prior-year quarter. Direct operating expenses rose 11.3% to $168.0 million from $151.0 million in the comparable period the year before. Indirect operating expenses increased 17.4% to $364.0 million from $310.0 million in the equivalent prior-year period.

Prospects: Co. believes that it is well-positioned for the opportunities ahead in transitioning to new-generation consoles, as it is on schedule with support for the launch of PlayStation 3, and has increased its developments efforts for its Nintendo DS and Wii. Moreover, Co. expects sales of games for cellular to grow significantly in fiscal 2007, due to its recent acquisition of JAMDAT Mobile Inc. For the second quarter of fiscal 2007, Co. expects net revenue to range from $635.0 million to $685.0 million, and loss per share to be $0.28 to $0.22 per share. For full fiscal 2007, Co. anticipates net revenue of $2.80 billion to $3.00 billion, and a loss of $0.30 per diluted share to breakeven.

Financial Data
(US$ in Thousands)

	3 Mos	03/31/2006	03/31/2005	03/31/2004	03/31/2003	03/31/2002	03/31/2001	03/31/2000
Earnings Per Share	0.68	0.75	1.59	1.87	1.09	0.35	(0.04)	0.44
Cash Flow Per Share	1.92	1.96	2.08	2.26	2.53	1.04	0.74	0.18
Tang Book Value Per Share	8.38	8.29	10.66	8.52	5.81	2.91	3.19	2.86
Income Statement								
Total Revenue	413,000	2,951,000	3,129,000	2,957,141	2,482,244	1,724,675	1,322,273	1,420,011
EBITDA	(69,000)	400,000	797,000	874,073	553,088	259,188	65,171	216,539
Depn & Amortn	29,000	86,000	72,000	77,513	91,639	110,901	78,601	46,725
Income Before Taxes	(98,000)	389,000	725,000	796,560	461,449	148,287	(13,430)	169,814
Income Taxes	(17,000)	147,000	221,000	219,268	143,049	45,969	(4,163)	52,642
Net Income	(81,000)	236,000	504,000	577,292	317,097	101,509	(11,082)	116,751
Average Shares	306,000	314,000	318,000	308,233	292,892	286,284	264,112	265,484
Balance Sheet								
Total Assets	4,193,000	4,386,000	4,370,000	3,400,611	2,359,533	1,699,374	1,378,918	1,192,312
Current Liabilities	675,000	869,000	828,000	722,253	570,876	452,982	340,026	265,302
Total Liabilities	751,000	966,000	861,000	722,253	574,794	456,080	344,571	268,919
Stockholders' Equity	3,429,000	3,408,000	3,498,000	2,678,358	1,784,739	1,243,294	1,034,347	923,393
Shares Outstanding	306,000	304,994	310,440	301,532	288,716	389,245	281,428	281,738
Statistical Record								
Return on Assets %	5.25	5.39	12.97	19.99	15.62	6.60	N.M.	11.12
Return on Equity %	6.46	6.83	16.32	25.80	20.94	8.91	N.M.	14.68
EBITDA Margin %	N.M.	13.55	25.47	29.56	22.28	15.03	4.93	15.25
Net Margin %	N.M.	8.00	16.11	19.52	12.77	5.89	N.M.	8.22
Asset Turnover	0.74	0.67	0.81	1.02	1.22	1.12	1.03	1.35
Current Ratio	4.17	3.47	4.48	4.03	3.35	2.54	2.41	2.66
Price Range	61.90-40.88	61.90-49.34	69.46-44.00	53.87-28.57	36.07-23.98	33.02-21.39	28.06-13.30	30.25-11.45
P/E Ratio	91.03-60.12	82.53-65.92	43.69-27.67	28.81-15.28	33.09-22.00	94.34-61.11	...	68.75-26.03

Address: 209 Redwood Shores Parkway, Redwood City, CA 94065 **Telephone:** 650-628-1500	**Web Site:** www.ea.com **Officers:** Lawrence F. Probst III - Chmn., C.E.O. Warren C. Jenson - Exec. V.P., C.F.O., Chief Admin. Officer
Auditors: KPMG LLP **Investor Contact:** 415-571-7171 **Transfer Agents:** Wells Fargo Bank, N.A.	

EMDEON CORP

Exchange	Symbol	Price	52Wk Range	Yield	P/E
NMS	HLTH	$11.85 (8/31/2006)	12.54-7.52	N/A	42.32

*7 Year Price Score 68.98 *NYSE Composite Index=100 *12 Month Price Score 111.58

Interim Earnings (Per Share)

Qtr.	Mar	Jun	Sep	Dec
2003	(0.02)	(0.09)	0.02	0.03
2004	0.02	0.02	0.02	0.06
2005	0.03	0.05	0.04	0.10
2006	0.06	0.08	...	...

Interim Dividends (Per Share)
No Dividends Paid

Valuation Analysis / Institutional Holding

Forecast P/E	13.85	No of Institutions	197
	(9/9/2006)		
Market Cap	$3.3 Billion	Shares	198,340,816
Book Value	1.1 Billion	% Held	71.89
Price/Book	3.00		
Price/Sales	2.43		

Business Summary: IT & Technology (MIC: 10.2 SIC: 7374 NAIC: 518210)

Emdeon is a provider of business, technology and information solutions that support both the financial and clinical aspects of healthcare delivery. Co. automates business and administrative functions for healthcare payers and providers such as patient billing, and communications through its Business Services segment. Co.'s Practice Services segment develops and markets IT systems for healthcare providers and related services. WebMD provides health information to consumers, physicians and healthcare professionals, employers and health plans through online portals and health-focused publications. Porex develops porous plastic products for healthcare, industrial and consumer applications.

Recent Developments: For the quarter ended June 30 2006, net income increased 43.4% to $23.2 million from $16.2 million in the year-earlier quarter. Revenues were $354.9 million, up 10.0% from $322.6 million the year before. Direct operating expenses rose 8.4% to $197.1 million from $182.0 million in the comparable period the year before. Indirect operating expenses increased 7.7% to $129.1 million from $119.8 million in the equivalent prior-year period.

Prospects: On Aug 8 2006, Co. entered into a definitive agreement to divest its Practice Services segment to Sage Software Inc., a subsidiary of The Sage Group plc, for $565.0 million in cash. The divestiture, which is expected to close in September 2006, represents a part of Co.'s process to seek strategic alternatives for both its Practice Services and Business Services segments. In this regard, Co. intends to finalize the respective evaluation process of its Business Services segment potentially by late August or early September 2006. For full-year 2006, Co. projects revenue to be in the range of $1.43 billion to $1.45 billion and net income of $0.30 to $0.33 per diluted share.

Financial Data
(US$ in Thousands)

	6 Mos	3 Mos	12/31/2005	12/31/2004	12/31/2003	12/31/2002	12/31/2001	12/31/2000
Earnings Per Share	0.28	0.25	0.21	0.12	(0.05)	(0.16)	(19.18)	(12.61)
Cash Flow Per Share	0.75	0.64	0.47	0.28	0.27	0.31	(0.40)	(1.88)
Tang Book Value Per Share	N.M.	N.M.	N.M.	N.M.	0.49	1.48	1.86	1.72
Income Statement								
Total Revenue	694,000	339,119	1,276,879	1,160,351	963,980	925,877	706,595	517,153
EBITDA	89,090	40,292	70,859	47,755	15,304	(69,317)	(6,718,775)	...
Depn & Amortn	39,770	19,656	2,541	2,975	2,246	1,109	...	...
Income Before Taxes	48,815	20,364	73,525	44,244	20,745	(59,704)	(6,689,669)	...
Income Taxes	9,996	4,562	(357)	4,910	4,140	(10,002)	...	...
Net Income	39,612	16,431	72,974	39,334	(17,006)	(49,702)	(6,684,318)	(3,085,608)
Average Shares	296,722	295,492	352,852	333,343	325,811	304,167	348,569	244,388
Balance Sheet								
Total Assets	2,204,440	2,162,310	2,195,683	2,302,224	2,135,306	1,766,248	1,556,338	8,455,631
Current Liabilities	299,195	308,409	313,832	328,427	305,528	311,819	306,358	338,386
Long-Term Obligations	650,000	650,000	665,353	649,999	649,999	300,119	...	...
Total Liabilities	965,141	973,781	979,185	1,078,008	956,709	612,447	317,566	363,646
Stockholders' Equity	1,086,838	1,041,933	1,074,736	1,224,216	1,178,597	1,153,801	1,238,772	8,091,985
Shares Outstanding	275,508	273,370	278,327	313,191	308,174	300,406	310,864	356,070
Statistical Record								
Return on Assets %	3.91	3.58	3.24	1.77	N.M.	N.M.	N.M.	N.M.
Return on Equity %	6.70	6.95	6.35	3.27	N.M.	N.M.	N.M.	N.M.
EBITDA Margin %	12.84	11.88	5.55	4.12	1.59	N.M.	N.M.	...
Net Margin %	5.71	4.85	5.72	3.39	N.M.	N.M.	N.M.	N.M.
Asset Turnover	0.61	0.59	0.57	0.52	0.49	0.56	0.14	0.08
Current Ratio	2.27	2.14	2.26	1.15	1.66	1.38	2.41	2.79
Debt to Equity	0.60	0.62	0.62	0.53	0.55	0.26	...	...
Price Range	12.41-7.52	11.53-7.52	11.53-7.44	10.17-6.57	12.38-7.68	8.90-4.40	10.13-3.24	71.06-5.50
P/E Ratio	44.32-26.86	46.12-30.08	54.90-35.43	84.75-54.75	...	...	...	...

Address: 669 River Drive, Center 2, Elmwood Park, NJ 07407-1361
Telephone: 201-703-3400
Fax: 201-703-3401
Web Site: www.webmd.com
Officers: Martin J. Wygod - Chmn. Kevin Cameron - C.E.O.
Auditors: Ernst & Young LLP
Investor Contact: 201-703-3415
Transfer Agents: American Stock Transfer Trust Company, New York, NY

EMMIS COMMUNICATIONS CORP.

Exchange	Symbol	Price	52Wk Range	Yield	P/E
NMS	EMMS	$12.23 (8/31/2006)	23.96-11.15	N/A	1.35

*7 Year Price Score 57.71   *NYSE Composite Index=100   *12 Month Price Score 78.09

Interim Earnings (Per Share)

Qtr.	May	Aug	Nov	Feb
2003-04	0.01	0.14	0.16	(0.43)
2004-05	(1.36)	0.23	0.31	(4.77)
2005-06	0.14	0.15	5.30	3.42
2006-07	0.17	...	...	...

Interim Dividends (Per Share)
No Dividends Paid

Valuation Analysis

		Institutional Holding	
Forecast P/E	49.38	No of Institutions	
	(9/9/2006)	125	
Market Cap	$454.8 Million	Shares	
Book Value	282.5 Million		35,325,616
Price/Book	1.61	% Held	
Price/Sales	1.19		94.86

Business Summary: Media (MIC: 13.1 SIC: 4832 NAIC: 515112)

Emmis Communications is a diversified media company, primarily focused on radio broadcasting. Co. owns and operates seven FM radio stations serving three key markets - New York, Los Angeles and Chicago. In addition, Co. owns and operates fifteen FM and two AM radio stations in Phoenix, St. Louis, Austin (Co. has a 50.1% controlling interest in its radio stations located there), Indianapolis and Terre Haute, IN. Co. also operates an international radio business, with a network of radio stations in Belgium, Slovakia, Hungary and Bulgaria. Additionally, Co. publishes several city and regional magazines and operates three television stations in New Orleans, Honolulu and Orlando, respectively.

Recent Developments: For the quarter ended May 31 2006, loss from continuing operations was $269,000 compared with income of $4.3 million in the year-earlier quarter. Net income decreased 16.6% to $8.7 million from $10.4 million in the year-earlier quarter. Revenues were $89.8 million, down 2.8% from $92.4 million the year before. Operating income was $16.0 million versus $19.2 million in the prior-year quarter, a decrease of 16.7%. Indirect operating expenses increased 0.8% to $73.8 million from $73.2 million in the equivalent prior-year period.

Prospects: On May 8 2006, Co. announced that ECC Acquisition, Inc. has made a non-binding proposal to acquire its outstanding shares for $15.25 per share. Also on May 8 2006, Co. announced that it has agreed to sell WKCF-TV, its WB/CW affiliate in Orlando, to Hearts-Argyle Television, Inc. for $217.5 million. Co. expects the transaction to close within three to six months. Meanwhile, on Jul 12 2006, Co. announced that it has completed the sale of its KKFR-FM (Power 92.3) radio station in Phoenix to Bonneville International Corp. and Bonneville Holding Co. for $77.5 million, and will use the net proceeds of about $76.3 million to repay outstanding debt.

Financial Data
(US$ in Thousands)

	3 Mos	02/28/2006	02/28/2005	02/29/2004	02/28/2003	02/28/2002	02/28/2001	02/29/2000
Earnings Per Share	9.04	8.13	(5.58)	(0.12)	(3.27)	(1.54)	0.10	(0.09)
Cash Flow Per Share	1.55	1.61	2.19	2.15	1.79	1.47	2.09	0.73
Income Statement								
Total Revenue	89,787	387,381	618,460	591,868	562,363	533,780	470,618	325,265
EBITDA	17,167	50,409	123,062	212,118	225,119	189,786	198,284	114,668
Depn & Amortn	3,678	20,023	81,680	101,435	93,970	149,333	94,454	53,818
Income Before Taxes	927	(36,668)	(25,276)	24,725	27,314	(88,647)	31,386	8,864
Income Taxes	25	(15,455)	15,941	12,450	13,265	(25,623)	17,650	6,875
Net Income	8,654	357,771	(304,368)	2,256	(164,468)	(64,108)	13,736	(33)
Average Shares	37,129	42,876	56,128	55,066	53,014	47,334	46,869	36,156
Balance Sheet								
Total Assets	1,377,707	1,512,701	1,823,035	2,300,569	2,116,413	2,510,069	2,506,872	1,327,306
Current Liabilities	77,312	221,903	115,941	118,892	131,657	255,341	117,151	84,442
Long-Term Obligations	653,192	667,944	1,179,236	1,267,477	1,207,876	1,350,456	1,393,684	314,607
Total Liabilities	951,417	1,097,222	1,370,443	1,551,623	1,411,708	1,774,512	1,699,401	550,939
Stockholders' Equity	282,540	271,729	452,592	748,946	704,705	735,557	807,471	776,367
Shares Outstanding	37,191	37,044	56,472	55,728	53,885	48,011	47,130	45,971
Statistical Record								
Return on Assets %	22.17	21.45	N.M.	0.10	N.M.	N.M.	0.72	N.M.
Return on Equity %	95.26	98.79	N.M.	0.31	N.M.	N.M.	1.73	N.M.
EBITDA Margin %	19.12	13.01	19.90	35.84	40.03	35.56	42.13	35.25
Net Margin %	9.64	92.36	N.M.	0.38	N.M.	N.M.	2.92	N.M.
Asset Turnover	0.24	0.23	0.30	0.27	0.24	0.21	0.25	0.28
Current Ratio	1.72	1.15	1.42	1.45	1.21	1.03	1.84	1.33
Debt to Equity	2.31	2.46	2.61	1.69	1.71	1.84	1.73	0.41
Price Range	23.96-12.13	23.96-15.38	25.80-17.18	28.05-15.12	31.42-12.41	33.29-12.99	48.00-18.69	62.32-20.16
P/E Ratio	2.65-1.34	2.95-1.89	...	...	...	...	480.00-186.88	...

Address: One Emmis Plaza, 40 Monument Circle, Suite 700, Indianapolis, IN 46204
Telephone: 317-266-0100
Fax: 317-631-3750

Web Site: www.emmis.com
Officers: Jeffrey H. Smulyan - Chmn., Pres. Walter Z. Berger - Exec. V.P., C.F.O., Treas.

Auditors: ERNST & YOUNG LLP

ENDO PHARMACEUTICALS HOLDINGS INC

Exchange	Symbol	Price	52Wk Range	Yield	P/E
NMS	ENDP	$33.00 (8/31/2006)	34.32-24.75	N/A	20.25

*7 Year Price Score N/A *NYSE Composite Index=100 *12 Month Price Score 104.72

Interim Earnings (Per Share)

Qtr.	Mar	Jun	Sep	Dec
2003	0.12	0.34	0.30	(0.24)
2004	0.31	0.24	0.31	0.22
2005	0.10	0.37	0.50	0.55
2006	0.15	0.43	...	...

Interim Dividends (Per Share)
No Dividends Paid

Valuation Analysis
Forecast P/E	20.18 (9/9/2006)
Market Cap	$4.4 Billion
Book Value	972.4 Million
Price/Book	4.52
Price/Sales	4.78

Institutional Holding
No of Institutions	239
Shares	121,911,856
% Held	91.50

Business Summary: Pharmaceuticals (MIC: 9.1 SIC: 2834 NAIC: 325412)

Endo Pharmaceuticals Holdings, through its wholly owned subsidiary, Endo Pharmaceuticals Inc., is engaged in the sales, marketing, research and development of branded and generic pharmaceutical products used primarily to treat and manage pain. Co.'s portfolio of branded products includes brand names such as Lidoderm®, Percocet®, Percodan®, Frova®, and DepoDur™. Co. markets its branded pharmaceutical products to high-prescribing physicians in pain management, neurology, surgery, anesthesiology, oncology and primary care. In addition, Co.'s sales force also targets retail pharmacies and other healthcare professionals throughout the U.S.

Recent Developments: For the quarter ended June 30 2006, net income increased 17.5% to $57.6 million from $49.0 million in the year-earlier quarter. Revenues were $228.0 million, up 16.1% from $196.4 million the year before. Operating income was $89.2 million versus $77.1 million in the prior-year quarter, an increase of 15.7%. Direct operating expenses rose 19.3% to $50.4 million from $42.3 million in the comparable period the year before. Indirect operating expenses increased 14.8% to $88.4 million from $77.0 million in the equivalent prior-year period.

Prospects: For the rest of 2006, Co. will continue to advance its development pipeline primarily in the pain management area, with significant emphasis on its Rapinyl™ for treating cancer pain; the topical ketoprofen patch, which relieves pain and inflammation associated with soft-tissue injuries; and the transdermal sufentanil patch, which provides relief of chronic pain. For full-year 2006, Co. continues to expect net sales of $880.0 million to $910.0 million due primarily to the expected growth in the net sales of its Lidoderm®, for the treatment of the pain of post-herpetic neuralgia; and the launch of its Opana® ER and Opana® products, which treats moderate-to-severe acute and chronic pain.

Financial Data
(US$ in Thousands)

	6 Mos	3 Mos	12/31/2005	12/31/2004	12/31/2003	12/31/2002	12/31/2001	12/31/2000
Earnings Per Share	1.63	1.57	1.52	1.08	0.53	0.30	(0.40)	(1.97)
Cash Flow Per Share	3.48	3.16	2.15	1.30	1.70	1.07	0.88	0.44
Tang Book Value Per Share	5.09	4.68	4.24	2.71	2.61	1.32	0.98	N.M.
Income Statement								
Total Revenue	433,063	205,043	820,164	615,100	595,608	398,973	251,979	197,429
EBITDA	124,752	31,081	329,129	239,955	115,926	68,817	24,939	(119,044)
Depn & Amortn	8,499	4,058	15,880	11,020	6,670	3,532	52,837	28,858
Income Before Taxes	126,474	31,586	324,244	231,096	108,998	60,894	(38,860)	(163,021)
Income Taxes	48,300	11,048	121,949	87,787	39,208	30,081	(3,753)	(6,181)
Net Income	78,174	20,538	202,295	143,309	69,790	30,813	(36,542)	(156,840)
Average Shares	133,936	133,790	133,289	132,718	132,439	102,126	91,505	79,454
Balance Sheet								
Total Assets	1,395,266	1,342,983	1,371,678	947,491	753,880	512,972	470,995	467,840
Current Liabilities	403,492	413,027	509,513	273,248	185,674	152,429	175,666	100,225
Long-Term Obligations	...	...	...	...	...	...	...	162,154
Total Liabilities	422,845	431,657	528,308	291,541	186,263	160,280	175,873	269,667
Stockholders' Equity	972,421	911,326	843,370	655,950	567,617	352,692	295,122	198,173
Shares Outstanding	133,114	132,963	132,800	131,856	131,769	102,064	102,063	89,138
Statistical Record								
Return on Assets %	17.78	18.20	17.45	16.80	11.02	6.26	N.M.	N.M.
Return on Equity %	25.66	26.42	26.98	23.36	15.17	9.51	N.M.	N.M.
EBITDA Margin %	28.81	15.16	40.13	39.01	19.46	17.25	9.90	N.M.
Net Margin %	18.05	10.02	24.67	23.30	11.72	7.72	N.M.	N.M.
Asset Turnover	0.75	0.77	0.71	0.72	0.94	0.81	0.54	0.49
Current Ratio	2.49	2.31	1.95	2.08	2.55	1.69	1.37	1.73
Debt to Equity	...	...	...	...	...	...	...	0.82
Price Range	33.43-24.75	33.43-19.07	31.17-19.07	26.65-16.24	23.35-7.70	13.10-5.69	12.09-5.19	12.25-5.13
P/E Ratio	20.51-15.18	21.29-12.15	20.51-12.55	24.68-15.04	44.06-14.53	43.67-18.97	...	...

Address: 100 Painters Drive, Chadds Ford, PA 19317 **Telephone:** 610-558-9800	**Web Site:** **Officers:** Carol A. Ammon - Chmn. Peter A. Lankau - Pres., C.E.O.	**Auditors:** Deloitte & Touche LLP

ERIE INDEMNITY CO.

Exchange	Symbol	Price	52Wk Range	Yield	P/E	Div Acheiver
NMS	ERIE	$51.04 (8/31/2006)	53.71-48.58	2.82	17.01	10 Years

*7 Year Price Score 100.78 *NYSE Composite Index=100 *12 Month Price Score 94.23

Interim Earnings (Per Share)

Qtr.	Mar	Jun	Sep	Dec
2003	0.65	0.77	0.79	0.60
2004	0.70	0.81	0.83	0.87
2005	0.83	1.10	0.76	0.65
2006	0.73	0.86	...	...

Interim Dividends (Per Share)

Amt	Decl	Ex	Rec	Pay
0.36Q	12/13/2005	1/3/2006	1/5/2006	1/20/2006
0.36Q	2/21/2006	4/3/2006	4/5/2006	4/20/2006
0.36Q	4/18/2006	7/3/2006	7/6/2006	7/20/2006
0.36Q	7/25/2006	10/3/2006	10/5/2006	10/20/2006

Indicated Div: $1.44

Valuation Analysis **Institutional Holding**

Forecast P/E	16.98	No of Institutions
	(9/9/2006)	100
Market Cap	$3.0 Billion	Shares
Book Value	1.1 Billion	23,819,888
Price/Book	2.64	% Held
Price/Sales	2.68	41.09

Business Summary: Insurance (MIC: 8.2 SIC: 6411 NAIC: 524126)

Erie Indemnity operates mainly as the management services company that provides sales, underwriting and policy issuance services to the policyholders of Erie Insurance Exchange (the Exchange). Co. also operates as a property/casualty insurer through its wholly-owned subsidiaries, Erie Insurance Company, Erie Insurance Property and Casualty Company, and Erie Insurance Company of New York. The Exchange and its property/casualty subsidiary, Flagship City Insurance Company, and Co.'s three property/casualty subsidiaries write personal and commercial lines property and casualty coverages exclusively through 7,800 independent agents as of Dec 31 2005 and pool their underwriting results.

Recent Developments: For the quarter ended June 30 2006, net income decreased 26.1% to $56.3 million from $76.2 million in the year-earlier quarter. Revenues were $325.6 million, down 5.8% from $345.7 million the year before. Net premiums earned were $53.8 million versus $54.2 million in the prior-year quarter, a decrease of 0.6%.

Prospects: Co. continues to expand its agency force and expects 125 new agency appointments in 2006. Also, Co. expects to stimulate policy growth by implementing bonuses to eligible agents for each new private passenger auto policy issued. For the balance of 2006, Co. estimates that pricing actions approved, contemplated or filed and awaiting approval through 2006 could reduce written premium for its Property and Casualty Group by $65.0 million. As such, the total reduction in written premium from rating actions for 2006 is estimated to be $118.7 million. Meanwhile, on May 31 2006, Co. and Erie Insurance Exchange completed their acquisition of Erie Family Life Insurance Co.

Financial Data (US$ in Thousands)	6 Mos	3 Mos	12/31/2005	12/31/2004	12/31/2003	12/31/2002	12/31/2001	12/31/2000
Earnings Per Share	3.00	3.24	3.34	3.21	2.81	2.42	1.71	2.12
Cash Flow Per Share	4.93	4.07	4.83	3.46	3.17	2.64	2.08	1.88
Tang Book Value Per Share	19.33	20.84	20.90	20.11	18.16	15.42	13.55	12.16
Dividends Per Share	1.370	1.335	1.300	0.645	0.975	0.680	0.610	0.540
Dividend Payout %	45.67	41.20	38.92	20.09	34.70	28.10	35.67	25.47
Income Statement								
Premium Income	107,852	54,026	215,824	208,202	191,592	163,958	137,648	123,708
Total Revenue	627,239	301,646	1,124,950	1,123,144	1,048,788	963,387	799,861	698,016
Benefits & Claims	68,688	30,053	140,385	153,220	152,984	139,225	117,201	99,564
Income Before Taxes	158,878	73,938	339,456	326,347	295,053	255,401	182,876	223,938
Income Taxes	55,092	25,077	111,733	105,140	102,237	84,886	60,615	71,545
Net Income	105,721	49,466	231,104	226,413	199,725	172,126	122,261	152,393
Average Shares	65,554	67,505	69,293	70,492	70,997	71,081	71,342	71,954
Balance Sheet								
Total Assets	2,909,847	3,006,215	3,101,261	2,979,744	2,754,607	2,357,676	1,935,566	1,680,599
Total Liabilities	1,786,300	1,747,346	1,822,659	1,712,863	1,590,437	1,370,304	1,070,311	901,584
Stockholders' Equity	1,123,547	1,258,869	1,278,602	1,266,881	1,164,170	987,372	865,255	779,015
Shares Outstanding	58,125	60,393	61,165	62,995	64,092	64,037	63,836	64,056
Statistical Record								
Return on Assets %	6.78	7.45	7.60	7.88	7.81	8.02	6.76	9.50
Return on Equity %	16.67	17.63	18.16	18.58	18.57	18.58	14.87	20.58
Loss Ratio %	63.69	55.63	65.05	73.59	79.85	84.92	85.15	80.48
Net Margin %	16.85	16.40	20.54	20.16	19.04	17.87	15.29	21.83
Price Range	54.66-50.13	54.83-50.15	54.83-50.15	53.00-41.75	43.24-34.10	45.49-35.90	40.63-26.50	32.50-24.00
P/E Ratio	18.22-16.71	16.92-15.48	16.42-15.01	16.51-13.01	15.39-12.14	18.80-14.83	23.76-15.50	15.33-11.32
Average Yield %	2.61	2.54	2.47	1.35	2.49	1.67	1.82	1.84

Address: 100 Erie Insurance Place, Erie, PA 16530
Telephone: 814-870-2000
Fax: 814-870-4040

Web Site: www.erieinsurance.com
Officers: F. William Hirt - Chmn. Jeffrey A. Ludrof - Pres., C.E.O.

Auditors: Ernst & Young LLP

EXPEDITORS INTERNATIONAL OF WASHINGTON, INC.

Exchange	Symbol	Price	52Wk Range	Yield	P/E	Div Acheiver
NMS	EXPD	$39.81 (8/31/2006)	58.28-26.93	0.55	19.14	11 Years

*7 Year Price Score 157.41 *NYSE Composite Index=100 *12 Month Price Score 112.75

Interim Earnings (Per Share)

Qtr.	Mar	Jun	Sep	Dec
2003	0.12	0.13	0.15	0.72
2004	0.14	0.17	0.20	0.90
2005	0.17	0.20	0.25	1.34
2006	0.23	0.25	...	...

Interim Dividends (Per Share)

Amt	Decl	Ex	Rec	Pay
0.075S	5/9/2005	5/27/2005	6/1/2005	6/15/2005
0.075S	11/7/2005	11/29/2005	12/1/2005	12/15/2005
0.11S	5/3/2006	5/30/2006	6/1/2006	6/15/2006
100%	5/3/2006	6/26/2006	6/9/2006	6/23/2006

Indicated Div: $0.22

Valuation Analysis

Forecast P/E	36.55 (9/9/2006)
Market Cap	$8.5 Billion
Book Value	969.6 Million
Price/Book	8.76
Price/Sales	1.97

Institutional Holding

No of Institutions	323
Shares	200,193,168
% Held	93.86

Business Summary: Misc. Transportation Services (MIC: 15.4 SIC: 4731 NAIC: 541614)
Expeditors International of Washington is engaged in the business of providing global logistics services. Co. offers its customers an international network supporting the movement and strategic positioning of goods. Co.'s services include the consolidation or forwarding of air and ocean freight. Co. also provides additional services including distribution management, vendor consolidation, cargo insurance, purchase order management and customized logistics information. As of May 4 2005, Co. had 159 full-service offices, 53 satellite locations and seven international service centers located on six continents.

Recent Developments: For the quarter ended June 30 2006, net income increased 53.5% to $56.3 million from $36.7 million in the year-earlier quarter. Revenues were $1.13 billion, up 21.7% from $928.0 million the year before. Operating income was $88.8 million versus $58.7 million in the prior-year quarter, an increase of 51.2%. Direct operating expenses rose 20.3% to $730.8 million from $607.5 million in the comparable period the year before. Indirect operating expenses increased 18.3% to $309.8 million from $261.7 million in the equivalent prior-year period.

Prospects: Co.'s near-term outlook appears optimistic, reflecting solid top- and bottom-line growth. The growth is being driven by an improvement in net revenues from its airfreight, ocean freight and ocean services, and customs brokerage and other services units. Meanwhile, Co. routinely invests in technology, office furniture and equipment and leasehold improvements. Notably, in the second quarter of 2006, Co. made capital expenditures of $100.0 million as compared with $14.0 million for the same period in 2005. For full year 2006, Co. expects total capital expenditures to be $165.0 million, including ongoing capital expenditures, and additional real estate acquisitions and developments.

Financial Data (US$ in Thousands)	6 Mos	3 Mos	12/31/2005	12/31/2004	12/31/2003	12/31/2002	12/31/2001	12/31/2000
Earnings Per Share	2.08	2.02	1.96	1.41	1.12	1.03	0.89	0.76
Cash Flow Per Share	1.55	1.51	2.62	1.81	1.09	1.12	1.61	1.51
Tang Book Value Per Share	4.47	4.49	8.41	7.40	5.96	4.98	4.02	3.52
Dividends Per Share	0.185	0.150	0.150	0.110	0.080	0.060	0.050	0.035
Dividend Payout %	8.92	7.41	7.65	7.80	7.14	5.83	5.65	4.61
Income Statement								
Total Revenue	2,153,916	1,024,592	3,901,781	3,317,499	2,624,941	2,296,903	1,652,633	1,695,181
EBITDA	193,015	95,121	341,362	271,933	217,122	195,544	170,232	150,854
Depn & Amortn	16,679	8,053	32,310	27,978	25,816	23,675	24,618	23,401
Income Before Taxes	184,963	91,315	320,154	249,580	195,642	177,990	154,294	133,348
Income Taxes	72,555	37,052	94,624	88,415	71,142	65,461	57,051	50,313
Net Income	108,681	52,352	218,634	156,126	121,952	112,529	97,243	83,035
Average Shares	224,374	222,560	111,633	110,817	109,001	108,881	109,741	109,358
Balance Sheet								
Total Assets	1,715,550	1,656,210	1,566,044	1,364,053	1,040,847	879,948	688,437	661,740
Total Liabilities	745,949	681,896	638,440	549,177	392,122	356,136	273,814	299,956
Stockholders' Equity	969,601	974,314	913,721	807,404	645,501	523,812	414,623	361,784
Shares Outstanding	213,258	213,311	106,613	106,643	105,056	104,220	103,223	102,902
Statistical Record								
Return on Assets %	15.64	15.34	14.92	12.95	12.70	14.35	14.40	14.11
Return on Equity %	27.19	25.83	25.41	21.43	20.86	23.98	25.05	25.71
EBITDA Margin %	8.96	9.28	8.75	8.20	8.27	8.51	10.30	8.90
Net Margin %	5.05	5.11	5.60	4.71	4.65	4.90	5.88	4.90
Asset Turnover	2.75	2.70	2.66	2.75	2.73	2.93	2.45	2.88
Price Range	56.01-24.91	43.52-23.86	36.26-23.86	28.86-17.88	20.14-14.95	17.14-12.70	16.32-10.81	14.72-8.16
P/E Ratio	26.93-11.97	21.54-11.81	18.50-12.18	20.46-12.68	17.98-13.35	16.64-12.33	18.34-12.15	19.37-10.73
Average Yield %	0.51	0.49	0.53	0.48	0.45	0.41	0.37	0.31

Address: 1015 Third Avenue, 12th Floor, Seattle, WA 98104 **Telephone:** 206-674-3400 **Fax:** 206-674-3459	**Web Site:** www.expditors.com **Officers:** Peter J. Rose - Chmn., C.E.O. Glenn M. Alger - Pres., C.O.O.
Auditors: KPMG LLP **Investor Contact:** 206-674-3427 **Transfer Agents:** EquiServe Trust Company	

EXPRESS SCRIPTS INC

Exchange	Symbol	Price	52Wk Range	Yield	P/E
NMS	ESRX	$84.08 (8/31/2006)	93.91-56.98	N/A	29.19

*7 Year Price Score 180.07 *NYSE Composite Index=100 *12 Month Price Score 95.80

Interim Earnings (Per Share)

Qtr.	Mar	Jun	Sep	Dec
2003	0.37	0.37	0.41	0.44
2004	0.45	0.41	0.40	0.53
2005	0.57	0.68	0.68	0.75
2006	0.70	0.75	...	...

Interim Dividends (Per Share)

Amt	Decl	Ex	Rec	Pay
100%	5/23/2001	6/25/2001	6/8/2001	6/22/2001
100%	5/25/2005	6/27/2005	6/10/2005	6/24/2005

Valuation Analysis   **Institutional Holding**

Forecast P/E	24.99	No of Institutions
	(9/9/2006)	458
Market Cap	$11.6 Billion	Shares
Book Value	1.0 Billion	124,218,208
Price/Book	11.21	% Held
Price/Sales	0.67	90.18

Business Summary: Insurance (MIC: 8.2 SIC: 5912 NAIC: 446110)

Express Scripts is a pharmacy benefit management (PBM) company that provides pharmacy benefit management services, including retail drug card programs, home delivery pharmacy services, Specialty services, drug formulary management programs and other clinical management programs for client groups that include health maintenance organizations (HMOs), health insurers, third-party administrators, employers, union-sponsored benefit plans and government health programs. Co.'s PBM services involve the management of outpatient prescription drug usage to foster better and more cost-effective pharmaceutical care through the application of managed care principles and information technology.

Recent Developments: For the quarter ended June 30 2006, net income increased 5.7% to $107.8 million from $102.0 million in the year-earlier quarter. Revenues were $4.45 billion, up 12.9% from $3.94 billion the year before. Operating income was $192.5 million versus $148.4 million in the prior-year quarter, an increase of 29.7%. Direct operating expenses rose 11.5% to $4.09 billion from $3.67 billion in the comparable period the year before. Indirect operating expenses increased 33.3% to $171.1 million from $128.4 million in the equivalent prior-year period.

Prospects: Co.'s investments in its specialty infrastructure, including the closure of unprofitable infusion sites, along with system and other integration activities should allow it to capitalize on the growth opportunities in the specialty market. Accordingly, Co. believes that its margins will be enhanced as it continues to upsell specialty services to its pharmacy benefit management (PBM) clients and PBM services to its specialty clients. Looking ahead, Co. is raising its 2006 earnings guidance to a range of $3.16 to $3.28 per diluted share as a result of the favorable outcome of its formulary strategy, as well as continued growth in generic utilization, specialty pharmacy and home delivery.

Financial Data
(US$ in Thousands)

	6 Mos	3 Mos	12/31/2005	12/31/2004	12/31/2003	12/31/2002	12/31/2001	12/31/2000
Earnings Per Share	2.88	2.81	2.68	1.79	1.58	1.27	0.78	(0.06)
Cash Flow Per Share	4.75	4.75	5.39	3.24	2.94	2.74	1.80	1.61
Income Statement								
Total Revenue	8,896,700	4,444,600	16,266,000	15,114,728	13,294,517	12,260,634	9,328,782	6,786,864
EBITDA	427,100	208,800	737,000	574,378	508,629	458,975	325,916	113,620
Depn & Amortn	51,900	25,800	96,000	85,900	65,300	91,798	90,573	78,615
Income Before Taxes	340,000	167,500	615,000	450,643	405,302	329,658	208,244	(4,468)
Income Taxes	127,500	62,800	215,000	172,436	154,674	125,795	83,172	3,553
Net Income	212,500	104,700	400,000	278,207	249,600	202,836	124,700	(9,126)
Average Shares	143,400	149,100	149,000	155,032	157,856	159,334	159,654	152,784
Balance Sheet								
Total Assets	5,053,400	5,430,800	5,493,000	3,600,086	3,409,174	3,206,992	2,500,245	2,276,644
Current Liabilities	2,177,800	2,216,900	2,394,000	1,813,411	1,626,408	1,543,757	1,245,617	1,115,944
Long-Term Obligations	1,605,400	1,360,500	1,401,000	412,057	455,018	562,556	346,119	396,441
Total Liabilities	4,020,000	3,814,200	4,028,000	2,403,772	2,215,181	2,204,137	1,668,248	1,571,400
Stockholders' Equity	1,033,400	1,616,600	1,465,000	1,196,314	1,193,993	1,002,855	831,997	705,244
Shares Outstanding	137,749	147,028	145,993	147,716	155,144	155,742	156,062	156,176
Statistical Record								
Return on Assets %	9.56	9.18	8.80	7.92	7.55	7.11	5.22	N.M.
Return on Equity %	34.71	28.69	30.06	23.21	22.72	22.11	16.22	N.M.
EBITDA Margin %	4.80	4.70	4.53	3.80	3.83	3.74	3.49	1.67
Net Margin %	2.39	2.36	2.46	1.84	1.88	1.65	1.34	N.M.
Asset Turnover	3.91	3.69	3.58	4.30	4.02	4.30	3.91	2.84
Current Ratio	0.84	1.00	0.94	0.80	0.96	0.90	0.97	0.89
Debt to Equity	1.55	0.84	0.96	0.34	0.38	0.56	0.42	0.56
Price Range	93.91-47.78	93.91-42.35	89.56-36.62	39.91-29.73	37.61-23.72	32.53-21.09	30.31-18.00	26.36-7.45
P/E Ratio	32.61-16.66	33.42-15.07	33.42-13.66	22.29-16.61	23.80-15.01	25.61-16.60	38.85-23.08	...

Address: 13900 Riverport Drive, Maryland Heights, MO 63043
Telephone: 314-770-1666
Fax: 314-770-2378

Web Site: www.express-scripts.com
Officers: Barrett A. Toan - Chmn. George Paz - Pres., C.E.O., C.F.O.

Auditors: PricewaterhouseCoopers LLP
Investor Contact: 800-332-5455x64205
Transfer Agents: American Stock Transfer & Trust Company, New York, NY

FASTENAL CO.

Exchange	Symbol	Price	52Wk Range	Yield	P/E
NMS	FAST	$36.68 (8/31/2006)	48.84-29.38	1.09	29.82

*7 Year Price Score 142.05 *NYSE Composite Index=100 *12 Month Price Score 90.17

Interim Earnings (Per Share)

Qtr.	Mar	Jun	Sep	Dec
2003	0.13	0.14	0.16	0.13
2004	0.19	0.23	0.23	0.22
2005	0.25	0.29	0.30	0.26
2006	0.32	0.34	...	...

Interim Dividends (Per Share)

Amt	Decl	Ex	Rec	Pay
0.155S	7/12/2005	8/18/2005	8/22/2005	9/2/2005
2-for-1	10/11/2005	11/14/2005	10/31/2005	11/10/2005
0.20S	1/19/2006	2/15/2006	2/20/2006	3/3/2006
0.20S	7/11/2006	8/17/2006	8/21/2006	9/1/2006

Indicated Div: $0.40

Valuation Analysis

Forecast P/E	27.11 (9/9/2006)
Market Cap	$5.5 Billion
Book Value	850.3 Million
Price/Book	6.51
Price/Sales	3.30

Institutional Holding

No of Institutions	299
Shares	106,236,576
% Held	70.39

Business Summary: Retail - Hardware (MIC: 5.6 SIC: 5251 NAIC: 444130)

Fastenal sells thousands of different types of threaded fasteners and other industrial and construction supplies through 1,533 Company operated Fastenal stores, as of Dec 31 2004, located in the U.S., Canada, Puerto Rico, Mexico and Singapore. Threaded fasteners include products such as nuts, bolts, screws, studs, and related washers. Co. also sells other industrial and construction supplies, such as paints, various pins, machinery keys, concrete anchors, batteries, sealants, metal framing systems, wire rope, stainless strut, private label stud anchors, rivets and related accessories.

Recent Developments: For the quarter ended June 30 2006, net income increased 15.4% to $51.5 million from $44.6 million in the year-earlier quarter. Revenues were $458.8 million, up 19.7% from $383.3 million the year before. Operating income was $82.8 million versus $71.7 million in the prior-year quarter, an increase of 15.4%. Direct expenses rose 19.4% to $229.8 million from $192.5 million in the comparable period the year before. Indirect operating expenses increased 22.8% to $146.2 million from $119.1 million in the equivalent prior-year period.

Prospects: Results are being fueled by continued solid sales growth rates, reflecting a continuation of the strong environments that Co. experienced in 2004 and 2005. Gross profit margins also improved due to Co.'s freight model initiative, representing its focused effort to haul a higher percentage of its products utilizing its trucking network, combined with its improved direct sourcing operations. Going forward, Co. aims to continue opening about 13.0% to 18.0% new stores each year and hence, expects to open about 228 to 316 new stores in 2006. Further, Co. expects to complete the conversion of its last 55 stores to its advanced standard inventory stocking model (CSP2) during the rest of 2006.

Financial Data
(US$ in Thousands)

	6 Mos	3 Mos	12/31/2005	12/31/2004	12/31/2003	12/31/2002	12/31/2001	12/31/2000
Earnings Per Share	1.23	1.18	1.10	0.86	0.56	0.50	0.46	0.53
Cash Flow Per Share	0.85	0.91	0.81	0.38	0.60	0.12	0.60	0.25
Tang Book Value Per Share	5.63	5.31	5.19	4.51	3.80	3.29	2.80	2.37
Dividends Per Share	0.355	0.355	0.310	0.200	0.105	0.025	0.022	0.020
Dividend Payout %	28.98	30.08	28.18	23.26	18.92	5.00	4.86	3.76
Income Statement								
Total Revenue	890,520	431,703	1,523,333	1,238,492	994,928	905,438	818,283	745,740
EBITDA	174,844	84,549	296,937	230,867	155,648	136,243	126,359	141,372
Depn & Amortn	15,095	7,609	29,073	23,710	20,511	17,012	14,967	11,977
Income Before Taxes	160,547	77,328	269,056	208,336	136,336	121,207	113,634	131,430
Income Taxes	61,180	29,474	102,242	77,347	52,216	46,381	43,522	50,700
Net Income	99,367	47,854	166,814	130,989	84,120	75,542	70,112	80,730
Average Shares	151,402	151,390	151,508	151,972	151,784	151,754	151,756	151,754
Balance Sheet								
Total Assets	980,533	953,372	890,035	770,234	651,543	559,008	475,244	402,464
Current Liabilities	113,250	135,919	91,538	71,183	60,941	47,064	40,651	36,579
Total Liabilities	130,279	152,004	106,486	85,865	74,803	59,137	50,356	43,206
Stockholders' Equity	850,254	801,368	783,549	684,369	576,740	499,871	424,888	359,258
Shares Outstanding	150,993	151,054	151,055	151,754	151,754	151,754	151,754	151,754
Statistical Record								
Return on Assets %	20.49	20.17	20.09	18.38	13.90	14.61	15.98	22.33
Return on Equity %	23.49	23.72	22.73	20.72	15.63	16.34	17.88	25.11
EBITDA Margin %	19.63	19.58	19.49	18.64	15.64	15.05	15.44	18.96
Net Margin %	11.16	11.08	10.95	10.58	8.45	8.34	8.57	10.83
Asset Turnover	1.86	1.82	1.84	1.74	1.64	1.75	1.86	2.06
Current Ratio	6.39	5.15	7.09	7.56	7.45	8.42	8.41	8.02
Price Range	48.84-29.38	47.39-25.57	41.65-25.57	31.93-22.34	25.29-13.96	21.58-13.63	17.86-11.83	17.78-8.92
P/E Ratio	39.71-23.89	40.16-21.67	37.86-23.24	37.12-25.98	45.16-24.92	43.16-27.26	38.82-25.71	33.55-16.83
Average Yield %	0.92	1.03	0.98	0.72	0.56	0.14	0.15	0.15

Address: 2001 Theurer Boulevard, Winona, MN 55987-1500
Telephone: 507-454-5374
Fax: 507-453-8049

Web Site: www.fastenal.com
Officers: Robert A. Kierlin - Chmn. Willard D. Overton - Pres., C.E.O.

Auditors: KPMG LLP
Transfer Agents: Wells Fargo Bank Minnesota, National Association

FEDERAL-MOGUL CORP.

Exchange	Symbol	Price	52Wk Range	Yield	P/E
OTC	FDML Q	$0.36 (8/31/2006)	0.65-0.26	N/A	N/A

*7 Year Price Score N/A *NYSE Composite Index=100 *12 Month Price Score 91.22

Interim Earnings (Per Share)

Qtr.	Mar	Jun	Sep	Dec
2003	(0.39)	(0.06)	(0.34)	(1.38)
2004	(0.23)	(0.10)	(0.39)	(3.10)
2005	(0.54)	(0.13)	(0.79)	(2.29)
2006	(0.77)	(0.19)	...	...

Interim Dividends (Per Share)
No Dividends Paid

Valuation Analysis
		Institutional Holding	
Forecast P/E	N/A	No of Institutions	5
Market Cap	$32.3 Million	Shares	2,281,900
Book Value	N/A	% Held	2.55
Price/Book	N/A		
Price/Sales	0.01		

Business Summary: Automotive (MIC: 15.1 SIC: 3714 NAIC: 336399)
Federal-Mogul is a supplier of vehicular parts, components, modules and systems to customers in the automotive, small engine, heavy-duty and industrial markets. Co. offers a diverse array of products for original equipment and parts replacement applications, including engine bearings, pistons, piston pins, rings, cylinder liners, valve train and transmission products, connecting rods, sealing systems, element resistant systems protection sleeving products, electrical connectors and sockets, and disc pads. Co., which operates in 31 countries, conducts its operations through five primary segments: Powertrain, Sealing Systems and Systems Protection, Friction, Aftermarket and Corporate.

Recent Developments: For the quarter ended June 30 2006, net loss amounted to $16.8 million versus a net loss of $11.6 million in the year-earlier quarter. Revenues were $1.63 billion, down 2.0% from $1.67 billion the year before. Direct operating expenses declined 3.4% to $1.33 billion from $1.37 billion in the comparable period the year before. Indirect operating expenses increased 1.6% to $234.9 million from $231.1 million in the equivalent prior-year period.

Prospects: Co.'s outlook appears mixed. For instance, Co. is experiencing a decrease in its net sales, due largely to the unfavorable currency effect. Moreover, production volumes in Co.'s existing markets and customers served are largely flat year-over-year, with increased demand for existing European Powertrain applications being offset by a reduction in global demand for replacement engine parts. Meanwhile, gross margin is being positively affected by productivity improvements, as well as improvements generated on raw material costs. Going forward, Co. remains focused on the implementation of its global profitable growth strategy.

Financial Data
(US$ in Thousands)

	6 Mos	3 Mos	12/31/2005	12/31/2004	12/31/2003	12/31/2002	12/31/2001	12/31/2000
Earnings Per Share	(4.04)	(3.98)	(3.75)	(3.83)	(2.17)	(19.62)	(13.27)	(4.02)
Cash Flow Per Share	4.21	4.30	3.57	5.32	3.66	3.09	0.47	(2.19)
Dividends Per Share	...	...	...	...	...	...	...	0.010
Income Statement								
Total Revenue	3,231,900	1,600,300	6,286,000	6,174,100	5,546,000	5,422,400	5,457,000	6,013,200
EBITDA	215,700	79,000	273,100	247,800	272,300	279,700	(205,700)	397,100
Depn & Amortn	159,400	78,800	344,200	335,700	307,100	277,100	373,700	374,400
Income Before Taxes	(27,000)	(38,800)	(202,700)	(189,400)	(133,000)	(120,200)	(854,200)	(262,300)
Income Taxes	58,200	29,600	131,500	136,100	52,500	90,800	219,500	19,200
Net Income	(85,200)	(68,400)	(334,200)	(334,000)	(189,500)	(1,628,900)	(1,001,500)	(281,500)
Average Shares	89,100	89,100	89,100	87,300	87,100	83,000	75,600	70,500
Balance Sheet								
Total Assets	8,045,900	7,766,300	7,735,100	8,265,200	8,116,700	7,913,300	9,053,200	10,255,000
Current Liabilities	1,824,400	1,730,600	1,664,600	1,450,800	1,018,800	1,423,800	982,300	1,703,800
Long-Term Obligations	81,900	7,600	8,100	10,100	331,200	14,300	266,700	3,559,700
Total Liabilities	10,546,400	10,260,600	10,168,100	10,190,900	9,493,600	9,316,900	8,634,200	8,704,800
Stockholders' Equity	(2,500,500)	(2,494,300)	(2,433,000)	(1,925,700)	(1,376,900)	(1,403,600)	419,000	1,550,200
Shares Outstanding	89,609	94,482	89,098	89,057	87,131	87,131	82,369	70,619
Statistical Record								
EBITDA Margin %	6.67	4.94	4.34	4.01	4.91	5.16	N.M.	6.60
Asset Turnover	0.78	0.79	0.79	0.75	0.69	0.64	0.57	0.59
Current Ratio	1.86	1.87	1.88	2.02	2.49	1.66	2.29	1.25
Debt to Equity	...	...	...	...	...	...	0.64	2.30
Price Range	0.86-0.26	0.89-0.30	0.89-0.30	0.49-0.16	...	...	...	...

Address: 26555 Northwestern Highway, Southfield, MI 48034
Telephone: 248-354-7700
Fax: 248-354-8950

Web Site: www.federal-mogul.com
Officers: Robert S. Miller Jr. - Chmn. Jose Maria Alapont - Pres., C.E.O.

Auditors: Ernst & Young LLP
Transfer Agents: The Bank of New York, New York, NY

FIFTH THIRD BANCORP (CINCINNATI, OH)

Exchange	Symbol	Price	52Wk Range	Yield	P/E	Div Acheiver
NMS	FITB	$39.34 (8/31/2006)	42.15-35.23	4.07	14.90	33 Years

*7 Year Price Score 60.69 *NYSE Composite Index=100 *12 Month Price Score 96.13

Interim Earnings (Per Share)

Qtr.	Mar	Jun	Sep	Dec
2003	0.72	0.75	0.76	0.80
2004	0.75	0.79	0.83	0.31
2005	0.72	0.75	0.71	0.59
2006	0.65	0.69	...	...

Interim Dividends (Per Share)

Amt	Decl	Ex	Rec	Pay
0.38Q	9/20/2005	9/28/2005	9/30/2005	10/18/2005
0.38Q	12/20/2005	12/29/2005	12/30/2005	1/17/2006
0.38Q	3/28/2006	3/30/2006	3/31/2006	4/18/2006
0.40Q	6/20/2006	6/28/2006	6/30/2006	7/20/2006

Indicated Div: $1.60 (Div. Reinv. Plan)

Valuation Analysis

		Institutional Holding	
Forecast P/E	14.33	No of Institutions	480
	(9/9/2006)	Shares	375,386,272
Market Cap	$21.9 Billion	% Held	67.29
Book Value	9.6 Billion		
Price/Book	2.30		
Price/Sales	2.73		

Business Summary: Commercial Banking (MIC: 8.1 SIC: 6022 NAIC: 522110)

Fifth Third Bancorp is a bank holding company. Co.'s subsidiaries engage in commercial and retail banking, electronic payment processing services and investment advisory services. Co. provides financial products and services to the retail, commercial, governmental, educational and medical sectors, including checking, savings and money market accounts, and credit products. As of Dec 31 2005, Co. had $105.23 billion in assets and $67.43 billion in deposits and operated 19 affiliates with 1,119 banking centers located throughout Ohio, Kentucky, Indiana, Michigan, Illinois, Florida, Tennessee, West Virginia, Pennsylvania and Missouri.

Recent Developments: For the quarter ended June 30 2006, net income decreased 8.4% to $382.0 million from $417.0 million in the year-earlier quarter. Net interest income decreased 5.3% to $710.0 million from $750.0 million in the year-earlier quarter. Provision for loan losses was $71.0 million versus $60.0 million in the prior-year quarter, an increase of 18.3%. Non-interest income rose 3.1% to $655.0 million from $635.0 million, while non-interest expense advanced 4.3% to $759.0 million.

Prospects: Going forward, Co. will focus on maintaining its loan growth trends and growing core deposit balances to more effectively fund future loan growth and improve net interest margin trends. Co. will also continue to focus on improving execution in retail brokerage and growing its institutional money management business by improving penetration and cross-sell in its large middle market commercial customer base. Overall, Co. remains focused on investing in certain high opportunity markets, including the expected addition of approximately 50 net new banking centers in 2006, in order to provide better services to its customers as well as to drive deposit and loan growth.

Financial Data
(US$ in Thousands)

	6 Mos	3 Mos	12/31/2005	12/31/2004	12/31/2003	12/31/2002	12/31/2001	12/31/2000
Earnings Per Share	2.64	2.70	2.77	2.68	3.03	2.76	1.86	1.83
Cash Flow Per Share	7.72	9.04	7.56	6.23	14.19	3.84	1.66	1.70
Tang Book Value Per Share	11.97	11.88	11.91	13.33	12.92	12.65	13.09	10.50
Dividends Per Share	1.540	1.490	1.460	1.310	1.130	0.980	0.830	0.700
Dividend Payout %	58.33	55.19	52.71	48.88	37.29	35.51	44.62	38.25
Income Statement								
Interest Income	2,876,000	1,398,000	4,995,000	4,114,000	3,991,000	4,129,000	4,709,000	3,263,000
Interest Expense	1,455,000	687,000	2,030,000	1,102,000	1,086,000	1,429,000	2,276,000	1,793,000
Net Interest Income	1,421,000	711,000	2,965,000	3,012,000	2,905,000	2,700,000	2,433,000	1,470,000
Provision for Losses	149,000	78,000	330,000	268,000	399,000	246,000	236,000	89,000
Non-Interest Income	1,272,000	617,000	2,500,000	2,465,000	2,483,000	2,194,000	1,797,000	1,013,000
Non-Interest Expense	1,490,000	731,000	2,927,000	2,972,000	2,442,000	2,216,000	2,341,000	1,119,000
Income Before Taxes	1,054,000	519,000	2,208,000	2,237,000	2,547,000	2,432,000	1,653,000	1,275,000
Income Taxes	312,000	160,000	659,000	712,000	805,000	759,000	550,000	412,000
Net Income	746,000	363,000	1,549,000	1,525,000	1,755,000	1,635,000	1,094,000	863,000
Average Shares	557,000	557,000	558,000	568,000	580,000	592,020	591,316	475,978
Balance Sheet								
Net Loans & Leases	71,824,000	70,673,000	69,181,000	59,095,000	51,538,000	45,245,000	40,924,000	25,569,000
Total Assets	106,111,000	105,044,000	105,225,000	94,456,000	91,143,000	80,894,000	71,026,000	45,857,000
Total Deposits	70,523,000	69,010,000	67,434,000	58,226,000	57,095,000	52,208,000	45,854,000	30,948,000
Total Liabilities	96,555,000	95,575,000	95,779,000	85,532,000	82,618,000	71,958,000	62,966,000	40,966,000
Stockholders' Equity	9,556,000	9,469,000	9,446,000	8,924,000	8,525,000	8,475,000	7,639,000	4,891,000
Shares Outstanding	557,894	556,500	555,623	557,648	566,685	574,355	582,674	465,651
Statistical Record								
Return on Assets %	1.41	1.45	1.55	1.64	2.04	2.15	1.87	1.97
Return on Equity %	15.57	16.42	16.86	17.43	20.65	20.29	17.46	19.19
Net Interest Margin %	48.07	50.86	59.36	73.21	72.79	65.39	51.67	45.05
Efficiency Ratio %	35.60	36.28	39.05	45.17	37.72	35.05	35.98	26.17
Loans to Deposits	1.02	1.02	1.03	1.01	0.90	0.87	0.89	0.83
Price Range	43.48-35.23	44.40-35.23	48.09-35.23	59.90-45.78	61.81-47.73	69.40-55.86	64.43-47.19	60.50-30.00
P/E Ratio	16.47-13.34	16.44-13.05	17.36-12.72	22.35-17.08	20.40-15.75	25.14-20.24	34.64-25.37	33.06-16.39
Average Yield %	3.90	3.68	3.46	2.49	2.03	1.54	1.44	1.54

Address: 38 Fountain Square Plaza, Cincinnati, OH 45263 Telephone: 513-534-5300 Fax: 513-579-6246	Web Site: www.53.com Officers: George A. Schaefer Jr. - Pres., C.E.O. Paul L. Reynolds - Exec. V.P., Gen. Couns., Sec.	Auditors: Deloitte & Touche LLP Investor Contact: 513-534-6936 Transfer Agents: Fifth Third Bank, Cincinnati, OH

FIRST BUSEY CORP.

Exchange	Symbol	Price	52Wk Range	Yield	P/E	Div Acheiver
NMS	BUSE	$21.55 (8/31/2006)	21.55-18.06	2.97	16.33	14 Years

*7 Year Price Score 99.33 *NYSE Composite Index=100 *12 Month Price Score 99.33

Interim Earnings (Per Share)

Qtr.	Mar	Jun	Sep	Dec
2003	0.23	0.26	0.26	0.21
2004	0.26	0.27	0.28	0.28
2005	0.32	0.31	0.36	0.31
2006	0.32	0.33	...	...

Interim Dividends (Per Share)

Amt	Decl	Ex	Rec	Pay
0.14Q	10/3/2005	10/14/2005	10/18/2005	10/21/2005
0.16Q	1/3/2006	1/12/2006	1/17/2006	1/20/2006
0.16Q	4/3/2006	4/13/2006	4/18/2006	4/21/2006
0.16Q	7/3/2006	7/14/2006	7/18/2006	7/21/2006

Indicated Div: $0.64

Valuation Analysis

Forecast P/E	15.36 (9/9/2006)
Market Cap	$462.1 Million
Book Value	173.9 Million
Price/Book	2.66
Price/Sales	2.94

Institutional Holding

No of Institutions	35
Shares	2,214,770
% Held	10.33

Business Summary: Commercial Banking (MIC: 8.1 SIC: 6022 NAIC: 522110)

First Busey is a financial holding company. Co. operates three wholly-owned banking subsidiaries, Busey Bank, First Capital Bank and Busey Bank Florida, with operations in Illinois, Indiana and Florida. Through these subsidiaries, Co. offers a range of banking services, including commercial, financial, agricultural and real estate loans, and retail banking services, including demand and savings deposits, loans, money transfers, safe deposit services, IRA, Keogh and other fiduciary services, automated banking and automated fund transfers. As of Dec 31 2005, Co.'s total assets were $2.26 billion and total deposits were $1.81 billion.

Recent Developments: For the quarter ended June 30 2006, net income increased 12.1% to $7.0 million from $6.3 million in the year-earlier quarter. Net interest income increased 12.3% to $19.3 million from $17.1 million in the year-earlier quarter. Provision for loan losses was $300,000 versus $1.4 million in the prior-year quarter, a decrease of 78.9%. Non-interest income rose 15.8% to $6.9 million from $6.0 million, while non-interest expense advanced 21.7% to $14.8 million.

Prospects: Co.'s bottom line results are being driven by growth in net interest income and non-interest income, partially offset by an increase in interest expense, reflecting the combination of growth in deposits and long-term debt and a market driven increase in deposit and borrowing rates. Specifically, growth in net interest income is primarily due to loan growth combined with higher yields on investment securities and outstanding loans. Meanwhile, growth in non-interest income is driven by growth in customer service fees, trust fees and net security gains.

Financial Data
(US$ in Thousands)

	6 Mos	3 Mos	12/31/2005	12/31/2004	12/31/2003	12/31/2002	12/31/2001	12/31/2000
Earnings Per Share	1.32	1.30	1.29	1.09	0.97	0.87	0.77	0.69
Cash Flow Per Share	1.65	1.39	1.46	2.42	2.68	(0.70)	0.11	1.11
Tang Book Value Per Share	5.37	5.50	5.14	5.01	5.64	5.17	4.64	3.97
Dividends Per Share	0.600	0.580	0.560	0.510	0.453	0.400	0.347	0.320
Dividend Payout %	45.45	44.62	43.41	46.79	46.90	45.80	45.22	46.60
Income Statement								
Interest Income	68,851	33,160	116,304	85,919	73,849	76,085	89,985	93,242
Interest Expense	31,102	14,662	45,342	30,041	25,618	30,494	46,435	50,476
Net Interest Income	37,749	18,498	70,962	55,878	48,231	45,591	43,550	42,766
Provision for Losses	700	400	3,490	2,905	3,058	3,125	2,020	2,515
Non-Interest Income	13,077	6,173	23,537	23,790	24,685	22,537	21,460	18,288
Non-Interest Expense	28,930	14,143	51,115	43,085	39,969	38,926	38,974	37,249
Income Before Taxes	21,196	10,128	39,894	33,678	29,889	26,077	24,016	21,290
Income Taxes	7,294	3,261	12,960	11,224	10,025	8,173	8,363	7,237
Net Income	13,902	6,867	26,934	22,454	19,864	17,904	15,653	14,053
Average Shares	21,433	21,460	20,918	20,511	20,534	20,425	20,432	20,404
Balance Sheet								
Net Loans & Leases	1,816,051	1,737,004	1,714,235	1,447,109	1,145,639	1,024,822	942,534	966,609
Total Assets	2,342,375	2,273,066	2,263,422	1,964,441	1,522,084	1,435,578	1,300,689	1,355,044
Total Deposits	1,862,201	1,825,727	1,809,399	1,558,822	1,256,595	1,213,605	1,105,999	1,148,787
Total Liabilities	2,168,469	2,101,513	2,093,708	1,825,569	1,396,907	1,320,415	1,194,899	1,262,719
Stockholders' Equity	173,906	171,553	169,714	138,872	125,177	115,163	105,790	92,325
Shares Outstanding	21,444	20,477	21,504	20,608	20,516	20,352	20,516	20,176
Statistical Record								
Return on Assets %	1.28	1.28	1.27	1.28	1.34	1.31	1.18	1.08
Return on Equity %	17.64	17.57	17.46	16.96	16.53	16.21	15.80	16.05
Net Interest Margin %	53.94	55.78	61.01	65.04	65.31	59.92	48.40	45.87
Efficiency Ratio %	34.72	35.96	36.55	39.27	40.56	39.47	34.97	33.40
Loans to Deposits	0.98	0.95	0.95	0.93	0.91	0.84	0.85	0.84
Price Range	21.23-18.06	21.23-18.06	21.23-18.06	21.53-17.83	18.81-14.93	15.78-13.04	14.67-11.88	15.33-10.96
P/E Ratio	16.08-13.68	16.33-13.89	16.46-14.00	19.75-16.36	19.40-15.40	18.14-14.99	19.05-15.42	22.22-15.88
Average Yield %	2.98	2.93	2.83	2.71	2.70	2.77	2.60	2.49

Address: 201 West Main Street, Urbana, IL 61801 Telephone: 217-365-4556	Web Site: www.busey.com Officers: Douglas C. Mills - Chmn., Pres., C.E.O. Barbara J. Jones - C.F.O.	Auditors: McGladrey & Pullen, LLP Transfer Agents: First Busey Corporation

FIRST CHARTER CORP.

Exchange	Symbol	Price	52Wk Range	Yield	P/E	Div Acheiver
NMS	FCTR	$24.29 (8/31/2006)	26.66-22.34	3.21	28.58	13 Years

*7 Year Price Score 100.24 *NYSE Composite Index=100 *12 Month Price Score 95.74

Interim Earnings (Per Share)

Qtr.	Mar	Jun	Sep	Dec
2003	0.33	(0.14)	0.30	(0.02)
2004	0.31	0.34	0.38	0.36
2005	0.34	0.37	0.39	(0.28)
2006	0.37	0.37	...	...

Interim Dividends (Per Share)

Amt	Decl	Ex	Rec	Pay
0.19Q	7/27/2005	9/14/2005	9/16/2005	10/17/2005
0.19Q	10/19/2005	12/14/2005	12/16/2005	1/20/2006
0.19Q	3/9/2006	3/28/2006	3/30/2006	4/21/2006
0.195Q	6/28/2006	7/7/2006	7/11/2006	7/21/2006

Indicated Div: $0.78 (Div. Reinv. Plan)

Valuation Analysis

Forecast P/E	15.26 (9/9/2006)
Market Cap	$755.9 Million
Book Value	336.9 Million
Price/Book	2.24
Price/Sales	2.57

Institutional Holding

No of Institutions	65
Shares	7,737,928
% Held	24.81

Business Summary: Commercial Banking (MIC: 8.1 SIC: 6021 NAIC: 522110)

First Charter is a regional financial services company with assets of $4.23 billion as of Dec 31 2005. Co. is the holding company for First Charter Bank, which operates 55 financial centers and four insurance offices, as well as 137 ATMs (automated teller machines) throughout North Carolina. The Bank also operates loan origination offices in Asheville, NC and Reston, VA. Co. provides businesses and individuals with a broad range of financial services, including banking, financial planning, funds management, investments, insurance, mortgages and employee benefit programs.

Recent Developments: For the quarter ended June 30 2006, net income increased 2.4% to $11.5 million from $11.3 million in the year-earlier quarter. Net interest income increased 4.3% to $32.6 million from $31.3 million in the year-earlier quarter. Provision for loan losses was $880,000 versus $2.9 million in the prior-year quarter, a decrease of 69.4%. Non-interest income fell 0.4% to $17.2 million from $17.3 million, while non-interest expense advanced 7.1% to $31.4 million.

Prospects: On June 1 2006, Co. and GBC Bancorp, Inc. announced that they have signed a definitive agreement to merge. Under the terms of the merger, Co. will issue a combination of common stock and cash for the outstanding common shares of GBC. The Merger requires 70.0% of the shares of GBC common stock to be exchanged for Co.'s common stock, with the remainder of the consideration being cash. Upon closing, GBC shareholders will receive an aggregate of 2,975,000 Co.'s shares and about $30.6 million in cash, representing an approximate transaction value of $102.0 million, based on an estimated value of its common stock of $24 per share. The merger is expected to close during 2006 fourth quarter.

Financial Data

(US$ in Thousands)	6 Mos	3 Mos	12/31/2005	12/31/2004	12/31/2003	12/31/2002	12/31/2001	12/31/2000
Earnings Per Share	0.85	0.85	0.82	1.40	0.47	1.30	1.12	0.79
Cash Flow Per Share	1.31	1.53	1.26	1.07	(3.61)	1.20	1.43	2.65
Tang Book Value Per Share	10.12	10.07	9.82	9.70	10.08	10.80	10.06	9.79
Dividends Per Share	0.765	0.760	0.760	0.750	0.740	0.730	0.720	0.700
Dividend Payout %	90.00	89.41	92.68	53.57	157.45	56.15	64.29	88.61
Income Statement								
Interest Income	123,388	59,646	224,605	187,303	178,292	196,388	215,276	216,244
Interest Expense	58,651	27,556	99,722	64,293	70,490	83,227	109,912	108,314
Net Interest Income	64,737	32,090	124,883	123,010	107,802	113,161	105,364	107,930
Provision for Losses	2,399	1,519	9,343	8,425	27,518	8,270	4,465	7,615
Non-Interest Income	35,481	18,241	50,213	60,896	64,180	47,631	38,773	30,565
Non-Interest Expense	62,948	31,512	131,222	111,017	127,032	97,772	87,579	92,727
Income Before Taxes	34,871	17,300	34,531	64,464	17,432	54,750	52,093	38,153
Income Taxes	11,881	5,856	9,220	22,022	3,286	14,947	16,768	13,312
Net Income	22,990	11,444	25,311	42,442	14,146	39,803	35,325	24,841
Average Shares	31,339	31,153	30,784	30,277	30,007	30,702	31,660	31,580
Balance Sheet								
Net Loans & Leases	3,042,768	2,981,458	2,917,020	2,412,529	2,227,030	2,045,266	1,929,052	2,128,960
Total Assets	4,363,274	4,283,356	4,232,420	4,431,605	4,206,693	3,745,949	3,332,737	2,932,199
Total Deposits	2,988,802	2,800,346	2,799,479	2,609,846	2,427,897	2,322,647	2,162,945	1,998,234
Total Liabilities	4,026,339	3,949,729	3,908,825	4,116,918	3,907,254	3,421,263	3,023,396	2,622,912
Stockholders' Equity	336,935	333,627	323,595	314,687	299,439	324,686	309,341	309,287
Shares Outstanding	31,120	30,974	30,736	30,054	29,720	30,069	30,742	31,601
Statistical Record								
Return on Assets %	0.59	0.60	0.58	0.98	0.36	1.12	1.13	1.03
Return on Equity %	8.04	8.19	7.93	13.78	4.53	12.56	11.42	9.23
Net Interest Margin %	51.22	53.80	55.60	65.67	60.46	57.62	48.94	49.91
Efficiency Ratio %	38.82	40.46	47.75	44.73	52.39	40.07	34.47	37.57
Loans to Deposits	1.02	1.06	1.04	0.92	0.92	0.88	0.89	1.07
Price Range	26.66-21.97	26.66-20.85	26.66-20.85	28.11-19.52	21.20-16.69	20.57-15.33	18.75-13.44	17.50-12.50
P/E Ratio	31.36-25.85	31.36-24.53	32.51-25.43	20.08-13.94	45.11-35.51	15.82-11.79	16.74-12.00	22.15-15.82
Average Yield %	3.15	3.21	3.23	3.32	3.92	4.11	4.37	4.78

Address: 10200 David Taylor Drive, Charlotte, NC 28262	**Web Site:** www.firstcharter.com	**Auditors:** KPMG LLP
Telephone: 704-688-4300	**Officers:** J. Roy Davis Jr. - Chmn. Michael R. Coltrane - Vice-Chmn.	**Investor Contact:** 800-422-4650
		Transfer Agents: Registrar & Transfer Company, Cranford, NJ

FIRST FINANCIAL HOLDINGS, INC.

Exchange	Symbol	Price	52Wk Range	Yield	P/E	Div Achiever
NMS	FFCH	$34.54 (8/31/2006)	34.55-28.06	2.78	15.22	13 Years

*7 Year Price Score 97.78 *NYSE Composite Index=100 *12 Month Price Score 102.12

Interim Earnings (Per Share)

Qtr.	Dec	Mar	Jun	Sep
2002-03	0.50	0.54	0.50	0.53
2003-04	0.41	0.50	0.52	0.50
2004-05	0.47	0.56	0.49	0.57
2005-06	0.50	0.61	0.59	...

Interim Dividends (Per Share)

Amt	Decl	Ex	Rec	Pay
0.24Q	10/28/2005	11/8/2005	11/11/2005	11/25/2005
0.24Q	1/27/2006	2/8/2006	2/10/2006	2/24/2006
0.24Q	4/28/2006	5/10/2006	5/12/2006	5/26/2006
0.24Q	7/28/2006	8/9/2006	8/11/2006	8/25/2006

Indicated Div: $0.96 (Div. Reinv. Plan)

Valuation Analysis

		Institutional Holding	
Forecast P/E	14.79	No of Institutions	60
	(9/9/2006)		
Market Cap	$414.5 Million	Shares	3,830,421
Book Value	176.8 Million	% Held	31.92
Price/Book	2.34		
Price/Sales	2.08		

Business Summary: Other Depository Banking (MIC: 8.5 SIC: 6035 NAIC: 522120)

First Financial Holdings is a savings and loan holding company. Co. is originates first mortgage loans on residential properties, makes construction, consumer, non-residential mortgage and commercial business loans, invests in mortgage-backed securities, federal government and agency obligations, money market obligations, certain corporate obligations, full-service brokerage activities, property, casualty, life and health insurance sales, third party administrative services, trust and fiduciary services, reinsurance of private mortgage insurance and premium finance activities. As of Sept 30 2005, Co. had total assets of $2.50 billion and total deposits of $1.70 billion.

Recent Developments: For the quarter ended June 30 2006, net income increased 16.6% to $7.2 million from $6.2 million in the year-earlier quarter. Net interest income increased 5.1% to $20.2 million from $19.3 million in the year-earlier quarter. Provision for loan losses was $1.4 million versus $1.0 million in the prior-year quarter, an increase of 39.9%. Non-interest income rose 29.7% to $14.1 million from $10.9 million, while non-interest expense advanced 11.0% to $21.8 million.

Prospects: Co.'s results are being driven by solid growth in its advice businesses comprising insurance, brokerage and trust, combined with robust loan performance particularly in its commercial and consumer loans. Going forward, Co. continues to accelerate its in-store banking program through commitments to open two additional in-store offices in fiscal 2007. Separately, on Jun 29 2006, Co. announced that it has acquired Employer Benefits Strategies Inc., an independent insurance agency based in Summerville, SC. The acquisition is in line with Co.'s strategy to expand the employee benefits efforts of its insurance offerings.

Financial Data
(US$ in Thousands)

	9 Mos	6 Mos	3 Mos	09/30/2005	09/30/2004	09/30/2003	09/30/2002	09/30/2001
Earnings Per Share	2.27	2.17	2.12	2.09	1.92	2.07	2.04	1.64
Cash Flow Per Share	4.78	3.45	3.63	3.82	1.26	4.37	0.04	2.40
Tang Book Value Per Share	12.83	12.57	12.31	12.23	11.60	13.02	12.55	11.71
Dividends Per Share	0.950	0.940	0.930	0.920	0.880	0.760	0.680	0.620
Dividend Payout %	41.85	43.32	43.87	44.02	45.83	36.71	33.33	37.80
Income Statement								
Interest Income	110,670	72,018	35,235	130,776	126,593	134,381	154,026	173,277
Interest Expense	51,593	33,180	15,823	54,318	49,991	55,921	71,342	102,908
Net Interest Income	59,077	38,838	19,412	76,458	76,602	78,460	82,684	70,369
Provision for Losses	3,622	2,209	900	4,826	5,675	6,235	5,888	4,975
Non-Interest Income	40,852	26,719	12,516	49,245	42,175	40,965	30,959	24,918
Non-Interest Expense	64,195	42,364	21,540	80,052	74,764	70,781	63,944	55,143
Income Before Taxes	32,112	20,984	9,488	40,825	38,338	42,409	43,811	35,169
Income Taxes	11,401	7,452	3,365	14,600	13,784	15,198	15,659	12,610
Net Income	20,711	13,532	6,123	26,225	24,554	27,211	28,152	22,559
Average Shares	12,163	12,189	12,230	12,528	12,818	13,173	13,832	13,733
Balance Sheet								
Net Loans & Leases	2,037,695	1,978,837	1,923,132	1,878,730	1,813,531	1,781,881	1,924,828	1,905,333
Total Assets	2,651,694	2,591,097	2,566,331	2,522,405	2,442,313	2,322,882	2,264,674	2,325,664
Total Deposits	1,812,002	1,804,780	1,691,172	1,657,072	1,520,817	1,481,651	1,440,271	1,395,785
Total Liabilities	2,474,909	2,417,166	2,395,522	2,351,276	2,277,126	2,159,876	2,099,026	2,168,771
Stockholders' Equity	176,785	173,931	170,809	171,129	165,187	163,006	165,648	156,893
Shares Outstanding	11,999	12,024	12,020	12,115	12,303	12,522	13,195	13,395
Statistical Record								
Return on Assets %	1.07	1.06	1.05	1.06	1.03	1.19	1.23	0.98
Return on Equity %	15.93	15.54	15.63	15.60	14.92	16.56	17.46	15.31
Net Interest Margin %	52.36	52.81	55.09	58.46	60.51	58.39	53.68	40.61
Efficiency Ratio %	41.36	40.84	45.11	44.47	44.30	40.37	34.57	27.82
Loans to Deposits	1.12	1.10	1.14	1.13	1.19	1.20	1.34	1.37
Price Range	32.64-28.06	32.55-25.55	32.96-25.55	33.70-25.55	33.10-27.05	30.96-23.70	32.74-22.04	26.00-15.13
P/E Ratio	14.38-12.36	15.00-11.77	15.55-12.05	16.12-12.22	17.24-14.09	14.96-11.45	16.05-10.80	15.85-9.22
Average Yield %	3.08	3.14	3.16	3.10	2.95	2.84	2.51	3.07

Address: 34 Broad Street, Charleston, SC 29401 **Telephone:** 843-529-5933 **Fax:** 843-529-5929	**Web Site:** www.firstfinancialholdings.com **Officers:** A. Thomas Hood - Pres., C.E.O. Susan E. Baham - Exec. V.P., C.F.O.	**Auditors:** KPMG LLP **Investor Contact:** 843-529-5933 **Transfer Agents:** Register & Transfer Company, Cranford, NJ

FIRST INDIANA CORP.

Exchange	Symbol	Price	52Wk Range	Yield	P/E	Div Achiever
NMS	FINB	$24.45 (8/31/2006)	29.08-23.90	3.27	12.16	14 Years

*7 Year Price Score 124.66 *NYSE Composite Index=100 *12 Month Price Score 91.12

Interim Earnings (Per Share)

Qtr.	Mar	Jun	Sep	Dec
2003	0.24	(0.09)	(0.13)	0.10
2004	0.27	0.26	(0.06)	0.28
2005	0.32	0.36	0.38	0.38
2006	0.85	0.40	...	...

Interim Dividends (Per Share)

Amt	Decl	Ex	Rec	Pay
25%	1/18/2006	2/28/2006	2/13/2006	2/27/2006
0.20Q	1/18/2006	3/2/2006	3/6/2006	3/15/2006
0.20Q	4/19/2006	6/2/2006	6/6/2006	6/15/2006
0.20Q	7/19/2006	9/8/2006	9/6/2006	9/15/2006

Indicated Div: $0.80 (Div. Reinv. Plan)

Valuation Analysis

Forecast P/E	15.32 (9/9/2006)
Market Cap	$408.2 Million
Book Value	174.2 Million
Price/Book	2.34
Price/Sales	2.76

Institutional Holding

No of Institutions	78
Shares	6,303,916
% Held	37.77

Business Summary: Other Depository Banking (MIC: 8.5 SIC: 6035 NAIC: 522120)

First Indiana is a financial holding company. Through its community bank subsidiary, First Indiana Bank, N.A., Co. offers a full range of banking services to businesses and individuals in central Indiana. Co. attracts deposits and originates commercial and consumer loans and offers cash management services. Additionally, Co. originates home equity loans on a national basis through a network of agents and brokers. These loans are primarily sold to investors. As of Dec 31 2005, Co. had total assets of $1.97 billion and operated 30 banking centers and 3 loan origination offices.

Recent Developments: For the quarter ended June 30 2006, income from continuing operations increased 9.4% to $6.7 million from $6.1 million in the year-earlier quarter. Net income increased 6.7% to $6.7 million from $6.3 million in the year-earlier quarter. Net interest income increased 2.9% to $17.7 million from $17.2 million in the year-earlier quarter. Credit for loan losses was $1.4 million versus $650,000 in the prior-year quarter, an increase of 107.7%. Non-interest income fell 11.8% to $7.3 million from $8.3 million, while non-interest expense declined 5.2% to $15.5 million.

Prospects: Co.'s earnings improvement is being contributed by a modest increase in net interest income. Increased earnings assets are largely due to Co.'s higher loan balances outstanding, with particularly strength in its business loan category due to the deliberate and continuing shift in the mix of loans in its portfolios to emphasize credits that match its targeted risk profile and the expansion of the business loan portfolio through its business development programs. However, Co. is experiencing a decline in net interest margin in the increasing interest rate environment, as its customers continue to manage their funds more aggressively, choosing higher cost, more rate sensitive products.

Financial Data
(US$ in Thousands)

	6 Mos	3 Mos	12/31/2005	12/31/2004	12/31/2003	12/31/2002	12/31/2001	12/31/2000
Earnings Per Share	2.01	1.97	1.44	0.74	0.13	1.07	1.00	1.24
Cash Flow Per Share	2.58	2.11	2.60	10.59	0.99	1.30	1.80	0.53
Tang Book Value Per Share	8.41	8.40	8.25	7.60	8.30	10.72	10.15	9.50
Dividends Per Share	0.720	0.664	0.608	0.540	0.528	0.512	0.410	0.358
Dividend Payout %	35.82	33.71	42.22	72.58	412.50	47.76	40.96	28.87
Income Statement								
Interest Income	62,179	30,131	107,180	101,644	114,330	125,923	157,128	172,810
Interest Expense	26,584	12,277	38,070	32,203	37,430	52,143	83,079	95,042
Net Interest Income	35,595	17,854	69,110	69,441	76,900	73,780	74,049	77,768
Provision for Losses	(1,600)	(250)	(3,200)	11,550	38,974	20,756	15,228	9,756
Non-Interest Income	14,718	7,440	29,318	40,435	49,563	46,765	43,963	25,638
Non-Interest Expense	31,645	16,172	63,061	71,478	83,637	66,502	70,501	53,728
Income Before Taxes	20,268	9,372	38,567	26,848	3,852	33,287	32,283	39,922
Income Taxes	7,655	3,462	14,067	9,665	1,323	12,107	12,274	15,105
Net Income	21,266	14,563	25,271	14,678	2,529	21,180	20,009	24,817
Average Shares	16,911	17,193	17,549	19,735	19,650	19,761	19,998	19,996
Balance Sheet								
Net Loans & Leases	1,624,406	1,529,221	1,528,018	1,447,018	1,761,794	1,793,164	1,719,351	1,750,848
Total Assets	2,088,700	2,035,657	1,966,356	1,898,263	2,193,137	2,125,214	2,046,657	2,085,948
Total Deposits	1,579,074	1,503,081	1,449,276	1,370,697	1,489,972	1,339,204	1,379,478	1,399,983
Total Liabilities	1,914,540	1,859,916	1,790,914	1,726,120	1,984,243	1,904,003	1,837,626	1,887,136
Stockholders' Equity	174,160	175,741	175,442	172,143	208,894	221,211	209,031	198,812
Shares Outstanding	16,694	16,888	17,163	17,528	19,433	19,425	19,304	19,467
Statistical Record								
Return on Assets %	1.73	1.77	1.31	0.72	0.12	1.02	0.97	1.22
Return on Equity %	19.75	19.61	14.54	7.68	1.18	9.85	9.81	13.17
Net Interest Margin %	55.36	59.25	64.48	68.32	67.26	58.59	47.13	45.00
Efficiency Ratio %	39.35	43.04	46.20	50.31	51.03	38.51	35.06	27.07
Loans to Deposits	1.03	1.02	1.05	1.06	1.18	1.34	1.25	1.25
Price Range	29.08-23.25	29.08-18.95	29.08-16.87	19.00-14.21	16.31-12.24	17.97-13.00	17.18-12.90	16.68-10.76
P/E Ratio	14.47-11.57	14.76-9.62	20.19-11.72	25.68-19.20	125.48-94.15	16.79-12.15	17.18-12.90	13.45-8.68
Average Yield %	2.69	2.68	2.58	3.34	3.67	3.39	2.64	2.78

Address: 135 North Pennsylvania Street, Indianapolis, IN 46204 **Telephone:** 317-269-1200 **Fax:** 317-269-1341	**Web Site:** www.firstindiana.com **Officers:** Marni M. McKinney - Chmn., C.E.O. Robert H. Warrington - Pres.	**Auditors:** KPMG LLP **Investor Contact:** 317-472-2184 **Transfer Agents:** National City, Corporate Trust Operations, Cleveland, OH

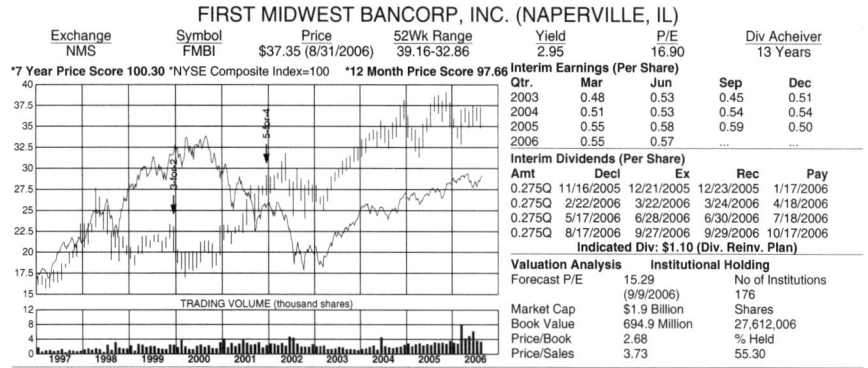

FIRST MIDWEST BANCORP, INC. (NAPERVILLE, IL)

Exchange	Symbol	Price	52Wk Range	Yield	P/E	Div Acheiver
NMS	FMBI	$37.35 (8/31/2006)	39.16-32.86	2.95	16.90	13 Years

*7 Year Price Score 100.30 *NYSE Composite Index=100 *12 Month Price Score 97.66

Interim Earnings (Per Share)

Qtr.	Mar	Jun	Sep	Dec
2003	0.48	0.53	0.45	0.51
2004	0.51	0.53	0.54	0.54
2005	0.55	0.58	0.59	0.50
2006	0.55	0.57	...	...

Interim Dividends (Per Share)

Amt	Decl	Ex	Rec	Pay
0.275Q	11/16/2005	12/21/2005	12/23/2005	1/17/2006
0.275Q	2/22/2006	3/22/2006	3/24/2006	4/18/2006
0.275Q	5/17/2006	6/28/2006	6/30/2006	7/18/2006
0.275Q	8/17/2006	9/27/2006	9/29/2006	10/17/2006

Indicated Div: $1.10 (Div. Reinv. Plan)

Valuation Analysis **Institutional Holding**

Forecast P/E	15.29	No of Institutions
	(9/9/2006)	176
Market Cap	$1.9 Billion	Shares
Book Value	694.9 Million	27,612,006
Price/Book	2.68	% Held
Price/Sales	3.73	55.30

Business Summary: Commercial Banking (MIC: 8.1 SIC: 6021 NAIC: 522110)

First Midwest Bancorp is a bank-holding company of with total assets of $7.21 billion and total deposits of $5.15 billion as of Dec 31 2005. Through its primary bank subsidiary, The First Midwest Bank (the Bank), Co. is engaged in commercial and retail banking and offers a range of lending, depository, and related financial services such as trust and investment management services, cash management services, safe deposit box operations, and other banking services for consumer, commercial and industrial and governmental customers. As of Dec 31 2005, the Bank had 68 banking offices primarily in suburban metropolitan Chicago.

Recent Developments: For the quarter ended June 30 2006, net income increased 8.4% to $28.7 million from $26.5 million in the year-earlier quarter. Net interest income increased 11.0% to $66.0 million from $59.4 million in the year-earlier quarter. Provision for loan losses was $2.1 million versus $1.8 million in the prior-year quarter, an increase of 14.4%. Non-interest income rose 28.4% to $25.3 million from $19.7 million, while non-interest expense advanced 26.1% to $52.0 million.

Prospects: Co.'s solid results are reflecting continued strong growth in its corporate loans, led by significantly improved performance in its middle-market, real-estate commercial and real-estate construction lending. In addition, Co.'s retail progress remains favorable as more new core deposit accounts have been opened throughout the first half of 2006. Meanwhile, Co. is progressing towards the integration of its recent Bank Calumet acquisition, which translates its focus on maximizing the sales and marketing prospects within the Northwest Indiana marketplace. Given such performance, Co. expects to attain earnings in the range of $2.38 to $2.44 per diluted share for the full-year 2006.

Financial Data
(US$ in Thousands)

	6 Mos	3 Mos	12/31/2005	12/31/2004	12/31/2003	12/31/2002	12/31/2001	12/31/2000
Earnings Per Share	2.21	2.22	2.21	2.12	1.97	1.86	1.63	1.46
Cash Flow Per Share	2.08	1.67	2.71	3.19	2.67	2.74	1.74	1.49
Tang Book Value Per Share	7.93	7.89	9.87	9.45	9.09	10.07	9.18	8.75
Dividends Per Share	1.075	1.050	1.015	0.900	0.790	0.700	0.650	0.592
Dividend Payout %	48.64	47.30	45.93	42.45	40.10	37.63	39.88	40.44
Income Statement								
Interest Income	224,575	101,525	366,700	315,342	291,067	329,664	385,218	421,517
Interest Expense	101,152	44,060	130,850	86,478	81,313	110,910	180,838	231,906
Net Interest Income	123,423	57,465	235,850	228,864	209,754	218,754	204,380	189,611
Provision for Losses	3,649	1,590	8,930	12,923	10,805	15,410	19,084	9,094
Non-Interest Income	46,639	21,372	74,612	79,381	74,170	66,991	68,866	63,198
Non-Interest Expense	95,702	43,712	165,703	163,338	149,452	148,052	145,356	144,416
Income Before Taxes	70,711	33,535	135,829	131,984	123,667	122,283	108,806	99,299
Income Taxes	16,208	7,767	34,452	32,848	30,889	32,133	26,668	23,759
Net Income	54,503	25,768	101,377	99,136	92,778	90,150	82,138	75,540
Average Shares	50,244	46,879	45,893	46,860	46,982	48,415	50,401	51,603
Balance Sheet								
Net Loans & Leases	4,978,986	4,979,815	4,249,798	4,078,560	4,003,378	3,358,917	3,324,561	3,188,103
Total Assets	8,692,828	8,715,524	7,210,151	6,863,381	6,906,658	5,980,533	5,667,919	5,906,484
Total Deposits	6,258,185	6,050,839	5,147,832	4,905,378	4,815,108	4,172,954	4,193,921	4,252,205
Total Liabilities	7,997,890	8,027,040	6,666,083	6,331,343	6,384,118	5,488,580	5,220,652	5,459,761
Stockholders' Equity	694,938	688,484	544,068	532,038	522,540	491,953	447,267	446,723
Shares Outstanding	49,925	49,866	45,387	46,065	46,581	47,206	48,725	51,082
Statistical Record								
Return on Assets %	1.32	1.30	1.44	1.44	1.44	1.55	1.42	1.32
Return on Equity %	16.91	16.88	18.84	18.75	18.29	19.20	18.38	18.46
Net Interest Margin %	53.60	56.60	64.32	72.58	72.06	66.36	53.06	44.98
Efficiency Ratio %	35.05	35.57	37.55	41.38	40.92	37.33	32.01	29.79
Loans to Deposits	0.80	0.82	0.83	0.83	0.83	0.80	0.79	0.75
Price Range	39.16-32.86	39.16-31.30	39.16-31.30	38.19-31.38	32.57-25.08	31.85-24.02	29.19-20.95	23.20-17.00
P/E Ratio	17.72-14.87	17.64-14.10	17.72-14.16	18.01-14.80	16.53-12.73	17.12-12.91	17.91-12.85	15.89-11.64
Average Yield %	2.95	2.93	2.86	2.62	2.73	2.48	2.64	3.02

| **Address:** 300 Park Blvd., Suite 400, P.O. Box 459, Itasca, IL 60143-9768
Telephone: 630-875-7450
Fax: 630-357-3577 | **Web Site:** www.firstmidwest.com
Officers: Robert P. O'Meara - Chmn. John M. O'Meara - Pres., C.E.O. | **Auditors:** Ernst & Young LLP
Investor Contact: 630-875-7345
Transfer Agents: Mellon Investor Services, Ridgefield Park, NJ |

1ST SOURCE CORP.

Exchange	Symbol	Price	52Wk Range	Yield	P/E	Div Acheiver
NMS	SRCE	$29.95 (8/31/2006)	31.01-19.42	1.87	17.72	18 Years

*7 Year Price Score 101.83 *NYSE Composite Index=100 *12 Month Price Score 114.50

Interim Earnings (Per Share)

Qtr.	Mar	Jun	Sep	Dec
2003	0.19	0.20	0.20	0.24
2004	0.22	0.38	0.15	0.34
2005	0.30	0.35	0.41	0.39
2006	0.44	0.45	...	...

Interim Dividends (Per Share)

Amt	Decl	Ex	Rec	Pay
0.127Q	1/26/2006	2/2/2006	2/6/2006	2/15/2006
0.127Q	4/27/2006	5/4/2006	5/8/2006	5/15/2006
10%	7/27/2006	8/3/2006	8/7/2006	8/15/2006
0.14Q	7/27/2006	8/4/2006	8/8/2006	8/15/2006

Indicated Div: $0.56

Valuation Analysis

Forecast P/E	N/A
Market Cap	$681.4 Million
Book Value	352.3 Million
Price/Book	1.93
Price/Sales	2.64

Institutional Holding

No of Institutions	60
Shares	14,968,052
% Held	66.54

Business Summary: Commercial Banking (MIC: 8.1 SIC: 6022 NAIC: 522110)

1st Source is a registered bank holding company. As of Dec 31 2005, Co. had total assets of $3.51 billion and total deposits of $2.75 billion. Through its subsidiary, 1st Source Bank, Co. provides consumer and commercial banking services to individual and business customers through 64 banking locations in the northern Indiana and southwestern Michigan regional market area. Co. also competes for business nationwide by offering specialized financing services for used private and cargo aircraft, automobiles for leasing and rental agencies, medium and heavy duty trucks, construction and environmental equipment.

Recent Developments: For the quarter ended June 30 2006, net income increased 24.9% to $10.3 million from $8.2 million in the year-earlier quarter. Net interest income increased 12.2% to $27.1 million from $24.2 million in the year-earlier quarter. Credit for loan losses was $1.7 million versus $3.4 million in the prior-year quarter, a decrease of 51.0%. Non-interest income rose 22.9% to $18.9 million from $15.4 million, while non-interest expense advanced 5.7% to $32.4 million.

Prospects: Co. is benefiting from an improvement in its net interest margin, led by the growth in loans and leases and yields on the loan and lease portfolios. In addition, Co. is seeing its non-interest income growth being driven by a gain on sale of mortgage servicing rights, along with an increase in equipment rental income and service charges on deposit accounts. Also, Co.'s credit quality remains solid, reflecting in part an increase in net recoveries. However, Co. expects its net interest margin to continue to be pressured by the challenging interest rate environment. Going forward, Co. remains focused on executing its long range plans, including the investment in new systems and facilities.

Financial Data
(US$ in Thousands)

	6 Mos	3 Mos	12/31/2005	12/31/2004	12/31/2003	12/31/2002	12/31/2001	12/31/2000
Earnings Per Share	1.69	1.59	1.46	1.08	0.83	0.43	1.65	1.63
Cash Flow Per Share	3.74	3.08	2.17	2.85	8.66	3.59	3.68	2.85
Tang Book Value Per Share	13.98	13.53	15.03	14.16	13.65	13.28	13.26	12.48
Dividends Per Share	0.482	0.464	0.445	0.382	0.336	0.327	0.319	0.304
Dividend Payout %	28.57	29.14	30.43	35.29	40.66	76.60	19.31	18.69
Income Statement								
Interest Income	97,177	46,396	168,532	151,437	162,322	199,503	242,183	235,392
Interest Expense	44,933	21,297	70,104	52,749	59,070	80,817	123,397	130,425
Net Interest Income	52,244	25,099	98,428	98,688	103,252	118,686	118,786	104,967
Provision for Losses	(1,971)	(300)	(5,855)	229	17,361	39,657	28,623	14,877
Non-Interest Income	35,839	16,922	68,533	62,733	80,196	73,117	92,836	73,914
Non-Interest Expense	61,792	29,406	123,439	127,091	138,904	137,735	121,232	104,003
Income Before Taxes	30,495	14,998	49,377	34,101	27,183	11,405	61,767	60,001
Income Taxes	10,285	5,065	15,626	9,136	8,029	1,366	21,059	20,030
Net Income	20,210	9,933	33,751	24,965	19,154	10,039	38,498	37,573
Average Shares	22,810	22,959	23,052	23,083	23,265	23,441	23,287	23,080
Balance Sheet								
Net Loans & Leases	2,555,955	2,420,407	2,404,734	2,216,496	2,160,955	2,266,874	2,477,740	2,264,418
Total Assets	3,608,526	3,459,910	3,511,277	3,563,715	3,330,153	3,407,468	3,562,691	3,182,181
Total Deposits	2,814,609	2,678,421	2,745,587	2,807,003	2,487,215	2,712,905	2,882,806	2,462,724
Total Liabilities	3,256,214	3,112,560	3,165,701	3,237,115	3,015,462	3,098,039	3,211,751	2,866,859
Stockholders' Equity	352,312	347,350	345,576	326,600	314,691	309,429	306,190	270,572
Shares Outstanding	22,751	22,788	22,996	23,062	23,058	23,306	23,094	21,686
Statistical Record								
Return on Assets %	1.10	1.08	0.95	0.72	0.57	0.29	1.14	1.24
Return on Equity %	11.31	10.90	10.04	7.76	6.14	3.26	13.35	14.71
Net Interest Margin %	53.46	54.10	58.40	65.17	63.61	59.49	49.05	44.59
Efficiency Ratio %	46.47	46.44	52.07	59.34	57.28	50.52	36.19	33.62
Loans to Deposits	0.91	0.90	0.88	0.79	0.87	0.84	0.86	0.92
Price Range	30.75-19.42	27.25-17.88	23.64-17.88	25.39-18.91	20.36-11.55	24.25-9.96	25.45-15.53	20.61-12.94
P/E Ratio	18.20-11.49	17.14-11.25	16.19-12.25	23.51-17.51	24.53-13.91	56.41-23.15	15.43-9.41	12.65-7.94
Average Yield %	2.05	2.11	2.12	1.74	2.09	1.82	1.71	1.91

Address: 100 North Michigan Street, South Bend, IN 46601	**Web Site:** www.1stsource.com
Telephone: 574-235-2000	**Officers:** Christopher J. Murphy III - Chmn., Pres., C.E.O. Wellington D. Jones III - Exec. V.P.
Auditors: Ernst & Young LLP	
Investor Contact: 574-235-2702	
Transfer Agents: 1st Source Bank, South Bend, IN	

FIRST STATE BANCORPORATION

Exchange	Symbol	Price	52Wk Range	Yield	P/E	Div Acheiver
NMS	FSNM	$25.59 (8/31/2006)	27.31-20.67	1.25	19.10	11 Years

*7 Year Price Score 142.00 *NYSE Composite Index=100 *12 Month Price Score 97.44

Interim Earnings (Per Share)

Qtr.	Mar	Jun	Sep	Dec
2003	0.23	0.25	0.27	0.23
2004	0.23	0.22	0.27	0.28
2005	0.28	0.32	0.39	0.38
2006	0.24	0.33	...	...

Interim Dividends (Per Share)

Amt	Decl	Ex	Rec	Pay
0.07Q	10/21/2005	11/7/2005	11/9/2005	12/7/2005
0.08Q	1/20/2006	2/6/2006	2/8/2006	3/8/2006
0.08Q	4/28/2006	5/8/2006	5/10/2006	6/7/2006
0.08Q	7/21/2006	8/7/2006	8/9/2006	9/6/2006

Indicated Div: $0.32

Valuation Analysis
- Forecast P/E: N/A
- Market Cap: $450.0 Million
- Book Value: 216.9 Million
- Price/Book: 2.07
- Price/Sales: 2.65

Institutional Holding
- No of Institutions: 97
- Shares: 12,138,827
- % Held: 69.06

Business Summary: Commercial Banking (MIC: 8.1 SIC: 6029 NAIC: 522110)

First State Bancorporation is a New Mexico-based bank holding company. Through its subsidiary bank, First State Bank N.M., Co. offers a range of financial services to commercial and individual customers, including checking accounts, short and medium term loans, revolving credit facilities, inventory and accounts receivable financing, equipment financing, residential and small commercial construction lending, residential mortgage loans, installment and personal loans, safe deposit services, and credit cards. At Dec 31 2005, Co. operated 31 branch offices in New Mexico, Colorado and Utah. At Dec 31 2005, Co. had total assets of $2.16 billion and total deposits of $1.51 billion.

Recent Developments: For the quarter ended June 30 2006, net income increased 21.5% to $6.0 million from $4.9 million in the year-earlier quarter. Net interest income increased 40.4% to $28.9 million from $20.5 million in the year-earlier quarter. Provision for loan losses was $1.4 million versus $1.7 million in the prior-year quarter, a decrease of 20.0%. Non-interest income rose 17.2% to $4.9 million from $4.2 million, while non-interest expense advanced 49.9% to $22.9 million.

Prospects: Co.'s outlook appears constructive, reflecting recent strong loan growth. Also, Co. is benefiting from the expansion of net interest margin due to its recent acquisitions, the rate increases made by the Federal Reserve Bank, as well as its asset sensitive position. Meanwhile, Co. expects the amortization of the purchase accounting adjustments related to its acquisitions of Access and New Mexico Financial Corp. to positively affect its net interest margin over the remainder of 2006 by approximately 7 to 9 basis points. Co. believes that the competitive environment for deposits will significantly determine the effect on the net interest margin of changes in interest rates.

Financial Data
(US$ in Thousands)

	6 Mos	3 Mos	12/31/2005	12/31/2004	12/31/2003	12/31/2002	12/31/2001	12/31/2000
Earnings Per Share	1.34	1.33	1.36	0.99	0.97	0.83	0.81	0.72
Cash Flow Per Share	2.20	1.90	2.04	1.07	2.59	1.12	0.45	0.28
Tang Book Value Per Share	7.97	7.73	7.60	6.60	5.87	5.05	5.93	5.20
Dividends Per Share	0.300	0.290	0.280	0.235	0.215	0.195	0.170	0.135
Dividend Payout %	22.39	21.80	20.59	23.74	22.05	23.49	21.12	18.62
Income Statement								
Interest Income	86,083	41,412	121,957	93,442	83,713	62,448	55,713	52,152
Interest Expense	29,983	14,162	37,712	23,875	22,629	18,384	20,478	20,198
Net Interest Income	56,100	27,250	84,245	69,567	61,084	44,064	35,235	31,953
Provision for Losses	4,109	2,729	3,920	4,500	5,543	2,589	2,386	2,475
Non-Interest Income	9,214	4,340	16,451	14,191	14,521	12,698	9,414	7,782
Non-Interest Expense	45,022	22,089	63,590	55,043	47,242	38,584	29,600	26,180
Income Before Taxes	16,183	6,772	33,186	23,780	22,820	15,589	12,663	11,080
Income Taxes	5,873	2,450	11,788	8,555	7,969	5,631	4,521	3,849
Net Income	10,310	4,322	21,398	15,225	14,851	9,958	8,142	7,232
Average Shares	17,910	17,802	15,689	15,443	15,196	11,995	10,098	9,993
Balance Sheet								
Net Loans & Leases	1,897,009	1,813,090	1,508,514	1,362,464	1,217,364	1,005,187	541,515	453,776
Total Assets	2,606,176	2,492,276	2,157,571	1,815,510	1,646,739	1,386,870	827,921	652,729
Total Deposits	2,078,998	1,965,705	1,510,007	1,401,303	1,195,875	1,079,684	685,022	528,408
Total Liabilities	2,389,222	2,279,391	1,997,392	1,671,201	1,514,298	1,269,402	769,577	601,411
Stockholders' Equity	216,944	212,885	160,179	144,309	132,441	117,468	58,345	51,318
Shares Outstanding	17,584	17,577	15,394	15,324	15,209	14,655	9,771	9,786
Statistical Record								
Return on Assets %	0.97	0.98	1.08	0.88	0.98	0.90	1.10	1.18
Return on Equity %	12.21	11.94	14.06	10.97	11.89	11.33	14.85	15.06
Net Interest Margin %	64.58	65.80	69.08	74.45	72.97	70.56	63.24	61.27
Efficiency Ratio %	46.29	48.28	45.94	51.14	48.09	51.35	45.45	43.68
Loans to Deposits	0.91	0.92	1.00	0.97	1.02	0.93	0.79	0.86
Price Range	27.31-18.69	27.23-16.85	25.79-16.85	19.25-14.51	17.99-10.70	13.90-9.26	10.74-6.63	7.13-5.13
P/E Ratio	20.38-13.95	20.47-12.67	18.96-12.39	19.45-14.66	18.55-11.03	16.75-11.15	13.27-8.18	9.90-7.12
Average Yield %	1.27	1.31	1.38	1.46	1.57	1.66	1.98	2.17

Address: 7900 Jefferson N.E., Albuquerque, NM 87109
Telephone: 505-241-7500
Fax: 505-241-7124

Web Site: www.fsbnm.com
Officers: Michael R. Stanford - Pres., C.E.O. H. Patrick Dee - Exec. V.P., C.O.O., Treas., Sec.

Auditors: KPMG LLP
Investor Contact: 505-241-7500

FIRSTMERIT CORP

Exchange	Symbol	Price	52Wk Range	Yield	P/E	Div Acheiver
NMS	FMER	$23.01 (8/31/2006)	28.14-20.94	5.04	15.44	23 Years

*7 Year Price Score 80.70 *NYSE Composite Index=100 *12 Month Price Score 87.11

Interim Earnings (Per Share)

Qtr.	Mar	Jun	Sep	Dec
2003	0.45	0.44	0.46	0.07
2004	0.15	0.36	0.37	0.33
2005	0.36	0.43	0.43	0.34
2006	0.37	0.35	...	...

Interim Dividends (Per Share)

Amt	Decl	Ex	Rec	Pay
0.28Q	11/17/2005	11/23/2005	11/28/2005	12/19/2005
0.28Q	2/16/2006	2/23/2006	2/27/2006	3/20/2006
0.28Q	5/18/2006	5/25/2006	5/30/2006	6/19/2006
0.29Q	8/17/2006	8/24/2006	8/28/2006	9/18/2006

Indicated Div: $1.16

Valuation Analysis
Forecast P/E 14.66 (9/9/2006)
Market Cap $1.8 Billion
Book Value 870.7 Million
Price/Book 2.11
Price/Sales 2.41

Institutional Holding
No of Institutions 159
Shares 35,960,872
% Held 44.92

Business Summary: Commercial Banking (MIC: 8.1 SIC: 6021 NAIC: 522110)
FirstMerit is a bank-holding company with total assets of $10.16 billion and total deposits of $7.23 billion as of Dec 31 2005. Through its banking subsidiary, FirstMerit Bank, N.A. (FirstMerit Bank), Co. operates primarily as a regional banking organization, providing a range of banking, fiduciary, financial, insurance and investment services to corporate, institutional and individual customers throughout northern and central Ohio, as well as western Pennsylvania. As of Dec 31 2005, FirstMerit Bank operated a network of 161 full-service banking offices and 176 automated teller machines.

Recent Developments: For the quarter ended June 30 2006, net income decreased 23.5% to $27.7 million from $36.1 million in the year-earlier quarter. Net interest income decreased 2.3% to $85.7 million from $87.8 million in the year-earlier quarter. Provision for loan losses was $13.2 million versus $6.0 million in the prior-year quarter, an increase of 120.3%. Non-interest income rose 4.0% to $52.1 million from $50.1 million, while non-interest expense advanced 7.3% to $85.2 million.

Prospects: Co.'s outlook appears mixed. On the positive side, Co.'s recent net interest margin has shown improvement amidst a challenging interest rate environment. Also, Co. is experiencing moderate loan growth, driven by its commercial loan portfolio. However, Co. noted that it continues to be affected by lower demand for credit in its region. Meanwhile, Co.'s trend of improving its charge-off levels has been hindered by costs related to a credit relationship during the second quarter of 2006. Nevertheless, Co. believes that such costs are non-recurring and therefore, expects to return to its trend of lower charge-off levels for the remainder of 2006.

Financial Data
(US$ in Thousands)

	6 Mos	3 Mos	12/31/2005	12/31/2004	12/31/2003	12/31/2002	12/31/2001	12/31/2000
Earnings Per Share	1.49	1.57	1.56	1.21	1.42	1.81	1.35	1.80
Cash Flow Per Share	2.36	2.97	2.21	2.19	3.63	10.73	5.80	0.02
Tang Book Value Per Share	9.10	9.12	9.48	9.95	9.94	9.68	9.06	10.48
Dividends Per Share	1.120	1.110	1.100	1.060	1.020	0.980	0.930	0.860
Dividend Payout %	75.17	70.70	70.51	87.60	71.83	54.14	68.89	47.78
Income Statement								
Interest Income	291,342	143,072	541,446	497,395	567,269	648,013	726,899	791,495
Interest Expense	119,639	57,099	192,451	146,590	173,656	226,417	335,443	415,251
Net Interest Income	171,703	85,973	348,995	350,805	393,613	421,596	391,456	376,244
Provision for Losses	19,265	6,106	43,820	73,923	102,211	98,628	61,807	32,708
Non-Interest Income	97,475	45,397	190,466	174,285	210,146	186,402	182,419	163,891
Non-Interest Expense	167,117	81,899	313,508	311,929	326,952	287,030	328,597	275,192
Income Before Taxes	82,796	43,365	182,133	139,238	174,596	222,340	183,471	232,235
Income Taxes	25,171	13,401	51,650	36,024	52,939	67,974	60,867	72,448
Net Income	57,625	29,964	130,483	103,214	120,969	154,366	116,305	159,787
Average Shares	80,203	80,648	83,844	84,995	84,929	85,317	86,288	88,861
Balance Sheet								
Net Loans & Leases	6,717,042	6,584,513	6,590,582	6,335,787	6,454,046	7,091,515	7,262,085	7,128,800
Total Assets	10,254,773	10,100,717	10,161,317	10,122,627	10,473,635	10,688,206	10,193,374	10,215,203
Total Deposits	7,402,239	7,510,562	7,233,652	7,365,447	7,502,784	7,711,259	7,539,400	7,614,932
Total Liabilities	9,384,075	9,230,165	9,223,737	9,141,370	9,486,460	9,723,549	9,282,567	9,300,314
Stockholders' Equity	870,698	870,552	937,580	981,257	987,175	964,657	910,807	914,889
Shares Outstanding	80,005	79,768	83,843	84,190	84,724	84,505	84,991	87,032
Statistical Record								
Return on Assets %	1.19	1.28	1.29	1.00	1.14	1.48	1.14	1.57
Return on Equity %	13.20	14.35	13.60	10.46	12.40	16.46	12.74	18.23
Net Interest Margin %	57.82	60.09	64.46	70.53	69.39	65.06	53.85	47.54
Efficiency Ratio %	42.53	43.45	42.83	46.44	42.06	34.40	36.14	28.80
Loans to Deposits	0.91	0.88	0.91	0.86	0.86	0.92	0.96	0.94
Price Range	28.89-20.94	28.89-23.91	28.89-24.36	28.74-23.23	27.81-18.16	29.49-18.89	27.94-21.10	27.63-13.50
P/E Ratio	19.39-14.05	18.40-15.23	18.52-15.62	23.75-19.20	19.58-12.79	16.29-10.44	20.70-15.63	15.35-7.50
Average Yield %	4.37	4.23	4.13	4.08	4.42	3.87	3.71	4.24

Address: III Cascade Plaza, 7th Floor, Akron, OH 44308-1103
Telephone: 330-996-6300
Fax: 330-253-1849

Web Site: www.firstmerit.com
Officers: John R. Cochran - Chmn., C.E.O. Sid A. Bostic - Pres., C.O.O.

Auditors: PricewaterhouseCoopers LLP
Investor Contact: 330-996-6300
Transfer Agents: American Stock Transfer & Trust Co., New York, NY

FISERV, INC.

Exchange	Symbol	Price	52Wk Range	Yield	P/E
NMS	FISV	$44.16 (8/31/2006)	46.52-40.66	N/A	16.36

*7 Year Price Score 96.45 *NYSE Composite Index=100 *12 Month Price Score 97.34

Interim Earnings (Per Share)

Qtr.	Mar	Jun	Sep	Dec
2003	0.38	0.40	0.41	0.42
2004	0.47	0.48	0.47	0.49
2005	0.71	0.59	0.60	0.80
2006	0.64	0.66	...	...

Interim Dividends (Per Share)
No Dividends Paid

Valuation Analysis	**Institutional Holding**
Forecast P/E 17.14	No of Institutions
(9/9/2006)	462
Market Cap $7.7 Billion	Shares
Book Value 2.4 Billion	137,994,544
Price/Book 3.22	% Held
Price/Sales 1.80	79.20

Business Summary: IT & Technology (MIC: 10.2 SIC: 7374 NAIC: 518210)

Fiserv provides integrated information management systems and services to the financial and health benefits industries, including transaction processing, outsourcing, business process outsourcing and software and systems solutions. At Dec 31 2005, Co. served more than 17,000 clients globally, including banks, credit unions, financial planners and investment advisers, insurance companies and agents, self-insured employers, leasing companies, lenders, savings institutions and retailers/merchants. Co. operates centers in the U.S. for full-service financial data processing, software system development, item processing and check imaging, technology support and related product businesses.

Recent Developments: For the quarter ended June 30 2006, income from continuing operations decreased 2.6% to $111.0 million from $114.0 million in the year-earlier quarter. Net income increased 3.2% to $117.7 million from $114.0 million in the year-earlier quarter. Revenues were $1.09 billion, up 9.7% from $996.4 million the year before. Operating income was $184.2 million versus $187.2 million in the prior-year quarter, a decrease of 1.6%. Direct operating expenses rose 12.1% to $765.8 million from $682.9 million in the comparable period the year before. Indirect operating expenses increased 13.4% to $143.2 million from $126.3 million in the equivalent prior-year period.

Prospects: Co.'s outlook appears positive. For instance, Co. has recently signed multi-year agreements with three new clients to provide pharmacy benefit and administration services, which should generate incremental, full-year revenue of $190.0 million to $230.0 million going forward. Also, on Jul 17 2006, Co. announced that it has acquired The Jerome Group LLC, a direct marketing firm and digital print provider, which will become part of its Personix division of Fiserv Output Solutions. For full-year 2006, Co. has raised its continuing operations earnings guidance to $2.48 to $2.54 per share, primarily as a result of a one-time tax benefit realized in the second quarter of $0.02 per share.

Financial Data

(US$ in Thousands)	6 Mos	3 Mos	12/31/2005	12/31/2004	12/31/2003	12/31/2002	12/31/2001	12/31/2000
Earnings Per Share	2.70	2.63	2.70	1.91	1.61	1.37	1.09	0.93
Cash Flow Per Share	3.60	3.64	3.16	3.57	2.68	3.01	2.37	3.15
Tang Book Value Per Share	N.M.	N.M.	N.M.	0.96	N.M.	0.81	2.09	1.71
Income Statement								
Total Revenue	2,189,865	1,096,668	4,059,478	3,729,746	3,033,670	2,568,887	1,890,467	1,653,606
EBITDA	470,043	240,319	1,011,397	844,923	703,759	586,573	506,797	470,966
Depn & Amortn	92,901	47,366	179,179	185,363	171,791	141,110	147,696	148,842
Income Before Taxes	362,262	186,847	817,951	641,366	516,413	436,290	347,028	300,035
Income Taxes	135,071	70,636	306,594	246,468	201,401	170,153	138,811	123,014
Net Income	233,880	116,211	516,438	377,642	315,012	266,137	208,217	177,021
Average Shares	177,551	181,783	190,967	197,287	195,937	194,951	191,584	189,804
Balance Sheet								
Total Assets	6,471,208	6,089,155	6,039,516	8,383,349	7,214,175	6,438,705	5,322,242	5,586,320
Current Liabilities	3,124,221	2,778,909	2,978,391	2,901,133	4,315,251	4,128,212	3,374,323	3,999,290
Long-Term Obligations	783,095	757,935	595,385	505,327	699,116	482,824	343,093	334,958
Total Liabilities	4,075,708	3,706,019	3,573,776	5,818,927	5,014,367	4,611,036	3,717,416	4,334,248
Stockholders' Equity	2,395,500	2,383,136	2,465,740	2,564,422	2,199,808	1,827,669	1,604,826	1,252,072
Shares Outstanding	174,691	177,083	181,754	194,248	194,260	191,645	190,281	185,708
Statistical Record								
Return on Assets %	8.00	7.85	7.16	4.83	4.61	4.53	3.82	3.24
Return on Equity %	20.05	19.88	20.53	15.81	15.64	15.51	14.58	15.07
EBITDA Margin %	21.46	21.91	24.91	22.65	23.20	22.83	26.81	28.48
Net Margin %	10.68	10.60	12.72	10.13	10.38	10.36	11.01	10.71
Asset Turnover	0.69	0.67	0.56	0.48	0.44	0.44	0.35	0.30
Current Ratio	0.24	0.27	0.28	0.36	0.62	0.59	0.59	1.04
Debt to Equity	0.33	0.32	0.24	0.20	0.32	0.26	0.21	0.27
Price Range	46.81-40.66	46.81-39.32	46.81-36.95	40.85-32.44	40.20-27.57	46.60-22.60	44.39-29.58	41.42-17.71
P/E Ratio	17.34-15.06	17.80-14.95	17.34-13.69	21.39-16.98	24.97-17.12	34.01-16.50	40.72-27.14	44.53-19.04

Address: 255 Fiserv Drive, Brookfield, WI 53045
Telephone: 262-879-5000
Fax: 262-879-5013

Web Site: www.fiserv.com
Officers: Donald F. Dillon - Chmn. Leslie M. Muma - Pres., C.E.O.

Auditors: Deloitte & Touche LLP
Investor Contact: 262-879-5000
Transfer Agents: EquiServe Trust Company

FLEXTRONICS INTERNATIONAL LTD. (SINGAPORE)

Exchange	Symbol	Price	52Wk Range	Yield	P/E
NMS	FLEX	$11.79 (8/31/2006)	13.84-9.20	N/A	40.21

*7 Year Price Score 50.17 *NYSE Composite Index=100 *12 Month Price Score 98.69 **Interim Earnings (Per Share)**

Qtr.	Jun	Sep	Dec	Mar
2004-05	0.13	0.16	0.17	0.12
2005-06	0.10	0.00	0.07	0.07
2006-07	0.14	...	...	...

Interim Dividends (Per Share)

Amt	Decl	Ex	Rec	Pay
2-for-1	12/2/1999	12/23/1999	12/8/1999	12/22/1999
100%	7/26/2000	10/17/2000	9/22/2000	10/16/2000

Valuation Analysis

Forecast P/E	12.28
	(9/9/2006)
Market Cap	$6.8 Billion
Book Value	5.4 Billion
Price/Book	1.27
Price/Sales	0.45

Institutional Holding

No of Institutions	N/A
Shares	N/A
% Held	N/A

Business Summary: Electrical (MIC: 11.14 SIC: 3679 NAIC: 334419)

Flextronics International is a provider of design and electronics manufacturing services to original equipment manufacturers in markets such as: Computing, which includes products such as desktop, handheld and notebook computers; Mobile communication devices, which includes GSM handsets; Consumer digital devices, which includes products such as set top boxes, home entertainment equipment; Industrial, Semiconductor and White Goods, which includes products such as home appliances, industrial meters; Automotive, Marine and Aerospace, which includes products such as navigation instruments; Infrastructure, which includes products such as cable modems, cellular base stations; and Medical devices.

Recent Developments: For the three months ended June 30 2006, income was $75.7 million, before a gain of $8.8 million from discontinued operations, compared with income of $56.8 million, before a gain of $1.9 million from discontinued operations, in the corresponding quarter of the previous year. Results for 2005 included pre-tax restructuring and other charges of $5.1 million. Net sales climbed 6.2% to $4.06 billion from $3.82 billion in the prior-year period. Gross profit increased 6.1% to $236.0 million from $222.3 million the year before. Operating income jumped 32.5% to $116.9 million from $88.2 million in 2005.

Prospects: Co. is experiencing a reacclaceration of significant growth in its core EMS business, includes design, vertically-integrated manufacturing services, components and logistics. Also, Co. is please with results in terms of incremental business wins from both new and existing customers. Meanwhile, Co. expects revenue from continuing operations is expected to grow 250% to 30.0% on a year-over-year basis to a range of $4.70 billion to $4.90 billion. Furthermore, Co. expects earnings to increase 10.0% to 25.0% from $0.19 per diluted share. Moreover, Co. has increased its revenue growth rate expectations for fiscal 2007 to approximately 25.0%.

Financial Data
(US$ in Thousands)

	03/31/2006	03/31/2005	03/31/2004	03/31/2003	03/31/2002	03/31/2001	03/31/2000	03/31/1999
Earnings Per Share	0.24	0.58	(0.67)	(0.16)	(0.31)	(1.01)	0.51	0.32
Cash Flow Per Share	0.96	1.31	0.36	1.18	1.75	(1.06)	...	...
Tang Book Value Per Share	4.43	3.03	3.11	4.52	5.69	6.33	6.06	2.13
Income Statement								
Total Revenue	15,287,976	15,908,223	14,530,416	13,378,699	13,104,847	12,109,699	4,307,193	1,807,628
EBITDA	555,564	650,579	242,679	271,847	241,029	(33,319)	143,204	62,922
Depn & Amortn	390,828	373,670	662,798	419,086	483,631	518,985	6,782	3,622
Income Before Taxes	164,736	276,909	(420,119)	(147,239)	(242,602)	(552,304)	136,422	59,300
Income Taxes	54,218	(62,962)	(67,741)	(63,786)	(88,854)	(106,285)	15,507	7,770
Net Income	141,162	339,871	(352,378)	(83,453)	(153,748)	(445,019)	120,915	51,530
Average Shares	600,604	585,499	525,318	517,198	489,553	441,991	236,548	194,110
Balance Sheet								
Total Assets	10,958,407	11,007,572	9,583,937	8,394,104	8,644,699	7,571,655	3,087,082	1,094,379
Current Liabilities	3,958,304	3,880,194	3,376,917	2,581,019	3,158,304	2,541,306	1,255,604	412,887
Long-Term Obligations	1,488,975	1,709,643	1,624,261	1,049,853	863,293	917,313	214,727	197,179
Total Liabilities	5,603,760	5,783,524	5,216,724	3,852,084	4,189,203	3,541,294	1,493,840	628,128
Stockholders' Equity	5,354,647	5,224,048	4,367,213	4,542,020	4,455,496	4,030,361	1,593,242	466,251
Shares Outstanding	578,161	568,329	529,944	520,228	513,011	481,531	251,395	200,394
Statistical Record								
Return on Assets %	1.29	3.30	N.M.	N.M.	N.M.	N.M.	5.77	5.61
Return on Equity %	2.67	7.09	N.M.	N.M.	N.M.	N.M.	11.71	15.13
EBITDA Margin %	3.63	4.09	1.67	2.03	1.84	N.M.	3.32	3.48
Net Margin %	0.92	2.14	N.M.	N.M.	N.M.	N.M.	2.81	2.85
Asset Turnover	1.39	1.55	1.61	1.57	1.62	2.27	2.05	1.97
Current Ratio	1.24	1.23	1.26	1.35	1.44	1.75	1.83	1.58
Debt to Equity	0.28	0.33	0.37	0.23	0.19	0.23	0.13	0.42
Price Range	14.25-9.20	18.85-10.08	19.31-8.27	18.95-5.87	33.01-13.00	44.13-15.00	39.06-10.56	12.75-2.83
P/E Ratio	59.38-38.33	32.50-17.38	...	...	...	...	76.59-20.71	39.84-8.84

Address: One Marina Boulevard,, #28-00, 018989	Web Site: www.flextronics.com	Auditors: Deloitte & Touche LLP
Telephone: 689-071-88	Officers: Richard L. Sharp - Chmn. Michael M. McNamara - C.E.O.	Investor Contact: 408-576-7722
		Transfer Agents: EquiServe Trust Company, NA, Providence, RI, United States

FOUNDRY NETWORKS INC

Exchange	Symbol	Price	52Wk Range	Yield	P/E
NMS	FDRY	$12.17 (8/31/2006)	18.16-9.07	N/A	31.21

*7 Year Price Score 37.40 *NYSE Composite Index=100 *12 Month Price Score 76.72

Interim Earnings (Per Share)

Qtr.	Mar	Jun	Sep	Dec
2003	0.11	0.13	0.15	0.17
2004	0.14	0.11	(0.03)	0.12
2005	0.07	0.07	0.11	0.14
2006	0.07	...	...	...

Interim Dividends (Per Share)
No Dividends Paid

Valuation Analysis

		Institutional Holding	
Forecast P/E	25.87	No of Institutions	
	(9/9/2006)	201	
Market Cap	$1.8 Billion	Shares	
Book Value	851.6 Million	114,851,464	
Price/Book	2.07	% Held	
Price/Sales	4.07	78.83	

Business Summary: Office Equipment Supplies (MIC: 11.12 SIC: 3577 NAIC: 334119)

Foundry Networks designs, develops, manufactures, markets and sells a range of data networking products, including Ethernet Layer 2 and Layer 3 switches, Metro routers, and Internet traffic management products. Co.'s enterprise products include FastIron®, FastIron Edge®, IronPoint™, BigIron®, ServerIron®, EdgeIron™, and AccessIron™ product lines. Co.'s enterprise products, combined with its network management and security, are designed to meet the needs for wireless access, wiring closet, data center, wide area networks (WAN) access and campus applications. For service providers, Co. offers its high-performance BigIron switches, NetIron® Metro routers, and ServerIron Web switches.

Recent Developments: For the quarter ended Mar 31 2006, net income increased 10.2% to $11.0 million from $9.9 million in the year-earlier quarter. Revenues were $114.0 million, up 34.7% from $84.6 million the year before. Operating income was $11.0 million versus $10.5 million in the prior-year quarter, an increase of 4.0%. Direct operating expenses rose 39.3% to $44.5 million from $31.9 million in the comparable period the year before. Indirect operating expenses increased 38.9% to $58.6 million from $42.2 million in the equivalent prior-year period.

Prospects: Co.'s top- and bottom-line results are being positively affected by improved productivity of its recent sales force additions, as well as increased sales of its newly introduced products. In particular, the increase in sales is due to increased sales of its XMR MPLS router and its Metro router from service providers and large enterprise customers. Co. is also benefiting from increased demand of its BigIron RX family of Layer 2/3 switches in the enterprise and service provider markets. Looking ahead to the second quarter of 2006, Co. plans to continue to expand its product portfolio by introducing several significant new platforms addressing the enterprise and service provider markets.

Financial Data (US$ in Thousands)	3 Mos	12/31/2005	12/31/2004	12/31/2003	12/31/2002	12/31/2001	12/31/2000	12/31/1999
Earnings Per Share	0.39	0.39	0.34	0.55	0.18	0.02	0.69	0.20
Cash Flow Per Share	0.68	0.79	0.60	0.92	0.41	0.28	...	...
Tang Book Value Per Share	5.89	5.64	5.15	4.49	3.28	3.03	2.92	1.59
Income Statement								
Total Revenue	114,001	403,856	409,104	399,628	300,742	311,176	377,156	133,522
EBITDA	20,519	93,674	80,672	117,621	33,178	2,475	138,459	40,644
Depn & Amortn	2,617	9,124	7,439	5,564	6,007	6,566	7,563	9,908
Income Before Taxes	17,902	84,550	73,233	117,225	32,196	4,655	142,131	32,622
Income Taxes	6,948	28,537	25,266	42,143	9,659	1,769	54,010	9,750
Net Income	10,954	56,013	47,967	75,082	22,537	2,886	88,121	22,872
Average Shares	149,208	143,323	143,118	135,631	123,780	125,521	127,131	114,835
Balance Sheet								
Total Assets	981,577	921,924	811,192	658,144	451,535	412,138	398,466	213,498
Current Liabilities	107,259	104,076	87,241	67,649	53,436	50,306	53,450	31,894
Total Liabilities	129,966	125,904	104,854	67,649	53,436	50,306	53,450	31,894
Stockholders' Equity	851,611	796,020	706,338	590,495	398,099	361,832	345,016	181,604
Shares Outstanding	144,706	141,149	137,225	131,622	121,328	119,298	118,076	114,189
Statistical Record								
Return on Assets %	6.31	6.46	6.51	13.53	5.22	0.71	...	...
Return on Equity %	7.23	7.46	7.38	15.19	5.93	0.82	...	...
EBITDA Margin %	18.00	23.19	19.72	29.43	11.03	0.80	36.71	30.44
Net Margin %	9.61	13.87	11.72	18.79	7.49	0.93	23.36	17.13
Asset Turnover	0.48	0.47	0.56	0.72	0.70	0.77	...	...
Current Ratio	7.23	6.92	6.95	7.24	8.31	8.04	7.36	6.66
Price Range	18.16-8.12	14.61-8.12	33.75-8.50	27.68-7.04	10.23-4.44	23.50-5.80	207.56-13.00	161.19-63.00
P/E Ratio	46.56-20.82	37.46-20.82	99.26-25.00	50.33-12.80	56.83-24.67	N.M.	300.82-18.84	805.94-315.00

Address: 2100 Gold Street, P.O. Box 649100, San Jose, CA 95164-9100
Telephone: 408-586-1700
Fax: 408-586-1900

Web Site: www.foundrynetworks.com
Officers: Bobby R. Johnson Jr. - Chmn., Pres., C.E.O.
Woody L. Akin - Sr. V.P., Worldwide Sales

Auditors: Ernst & Young LLP
Investor Contact: 415-296-7383
Transfer Agents: U.S. Stock Transfer Corporation

FRANKLIN ELECTRIC CO., INC.

Exchange	Symbol	Price	52Wk Range	Yield	P/E	Div Acheiver
NMS	FELE	$48.21 (8/31/2006)	62.08-39.01	0.91	21.24	12 Years

*7 Year Price Score 130.76 *NYSE Composite Index=100 *12 Month Price Score 100.05

Interim Earnings (Per Share)

Qtr.	Mar	Jun	Sep	Dec
2003	0.18	0.41	0.47	0.47
2004	0.23	0.48	0.48	0.47
2005	0.25	0.59	0.57	0.57
2006	0.42	0.70	...	...

Interim Dividends (Per Share)

Amt	Decl	Ex	Rec	Pay
0.10Q	10/21/2005	11/1/2005	11/3/2005	11/17/2005
0.10Q	1/31/2006	2/7/2006	2/9/2006	2/23/2006
0.11Q	4/27/2006	5/9/2006	5/11/2006	5/25/2006
0.11Q	7/21/2006	8/1/2006	8/3/2006	8/17/2006

Indicated Div: $0.44

Valuation Analysis

Forecast P/E	18.63
	(9/9/2006)
Market Cap	$1.1 Billion
Book Value	309.6 Million
Price/Book	3.57
Price/Sales	2.17

Institutional Holding

No of Institutions	110
Shares	14,245,349
% Held	62.09

Business Summary: Purpose Machinery (MIC: 11.13 SIC: 3561 NAIC: 333911)

Franklin Electric is engaged in the design, manufacture and distribution of groundwater and fuel pumping systems, as well as submersible motors, drives, controls and monitoring devices. Co.'s products are sold in North America, Europe, Middle East, South Africa, Australia, Mexico, Japan, China and other world markets. In addition, Co.'s products are sold by its sales force, manufacturing representatives and repair shops. As of Dec 31 2005, Co.'s primary properties within and outside the U.S. constituted a total of 161.3 acres of land, encompassing approximately 2,129,000 in square footage.

Recent Developments: For the quarter ended July 1 2006, net income increased 21.4% to $16.4 million from $13.5 million in the year-earlier quarter. Revenues were $162.7 million, up 31.7% from $123.5 million the year before. Operating income was $26.1 million versus $20.9 million in the prior-year quarter, an increase of 24.8%. Direct operating expenses rose 32.6% to $108.9 million from $82.1 million in the comparable period the year before. Indirect operating expenses increased 34.9% to $27.6 million from $20.5 million in the equivalent prior-year period.

Prospects: On June 7 2006, Co. announced the implementation of sales price increases in the market across many of its product lines to be effective in the third quarter of 2006, as an attempt to mitigate the accelerated rise in raw material cost, particularly in copper. Notwithstanding, Co.'s near-term outlook remains solid, as its operating results are bolstered by strong growth of its pump and control systems products, coupled with its ongoing manufacturing migration to low-cost regions. Meanwhile, Co. is moving towards the integration of its Little Giant Pump Company acquisition in April 2006, which is projected to strengthen its position within the global water-pumping equipment supply industry.

Financial Data

(US$ in Thousands)	6 Mos	3 Mos	12/31/2005	01/01/2005	01/03/2004	12/28/2002	12/29/2001	12/30/2000
Earnings Per Share	2.27	2.15	1.98	1.65	1.52	1.42	1.20	0.98
Cash Flow Per Share	3.12	2.83	3.35	2.62	2.14	2.69	1.84	0.86
Tang Book Value Per Share	7.32	9.89	9.32	8.03	6.26	5.28	5.10	4.56
Dividends Per Share	0.410	0.400	0.380	0.310	0.275	0.255	0.235	0.215
Dividend Payout %	18.09	18.58	19.19	18.79	18.03	18.02	19.67	21.99
Income Statement								
Total Revenue	273,649	110,980	439,559	404,305	359,502	354,872	322,908	325,731
EBITDA	50,504	19,452	86,830	74,665	66,182	64,672	57,238	47,859
Depn & Amortn	8,452	4,075	14,971	15,143	13,748	12,878	12,660	10,839
Income Before Taxes	40,783	15,184	71,093	59,034	51,327	50,477	43,385	35,909
Income Taxes	14,642	5,485	25,084	20,951	16,847	18,273	16,235	13,683
Net Income	26,141	9,699	46,009	38,083	34,480	32,204	27,150	22,226
Average Shares	23,400	23,100	23,200	23,100	22,626	22,732	22,740	22,736
Balance Sheet								
Total Assets	491,333	384,404	379,762	333,473	281,971	258,583	195,643	197,179
Current Liabilities	83,055	53,851	64,022	54,445	45,401	50,247	40,425	47,064
Long-Term Obligations	62,434	12,350	12,324	13,752	14,960	25,946	14,465	15,874
Total Liabilities	181,772	102,099	112,200	99,140	89,033	105,445	72,374	81,181
Stockholders' Equity	309,561	282,305	267,562	234,333	192,938	153,138	123,269	115,998
Shares Outstanding	22,943	22,646	22,485	22,041	21,828	21,648	21,336	22,016
Statistical Record								
Return on Assets %	12.78	13.95	12.94	12.41	12.55	14.22	13.86	11.94
Return on Equity %	19.43	19.20	18.38	17.88	19.60	23.37	22.76	21.00
EBITDA Margin %	18.46	17.53	19.75	18.47	18.41	18.22	17.73	14.69
Net Margin %	9.55	8.74	10.47	9.42	9.59	9.07	8.41	6.82
Asset Turnover	1.23	1.31	1.24	1.32	1.31	1.57	1.65	1.75
Current Ratio	2.64	3.86	3.17	3.05	2.82	2.25	2.71	2.17
Debt to Equity	0.20	0.04	0.05	0.06	0.08	0.17	0.12	0.14
Price Range	62.08-37.76	55.39-34.93	44.70-34.93	43.30-29.57	32.50-23.14	29.50-19.98	21.02-16.00	18.19-14.36
P/E Ratio	27.35-16.63	25.76-16.25	22.58-17.64	26.24-17.92	21.38-15.22	20.77-14.07	17.52-13.33	18.56-14.65
Average Yield %	0.89	0.96	0.94	0.87	0.98	1.08	1.30	1.28

Address: 400 East Spring Street, Bluffton, IN 46714-3798 **Telephone:** 260-824-2900 **Fax:** 260-824-2909	**Web Site:** www.franklin-electric.com **Officers:** R. Scott Trumbull - Chmn., C.E.O. Gregg C. Sengstack - Sr. V.P., Int'l, Fueling Group	**Auditors:** Deloitte & Touche LLP **Investor Contact:** 260-824-2900 **Transfer Agents:** Illinois Stock Transfer Company, Chicago, IL

FULTON FINANCIAL CORP. (PA)

Exchange	Symbol	Price	52Wk Range	Yield	P/E	Div Acheiver
NMS	FULT	$16.70 (8/31/2006)	17.29-15.00	3.53	16.06	32 Years

*7 Year Price Score 94.93 *NYSE Composite Index=100 *12 Month Price Score 97.95

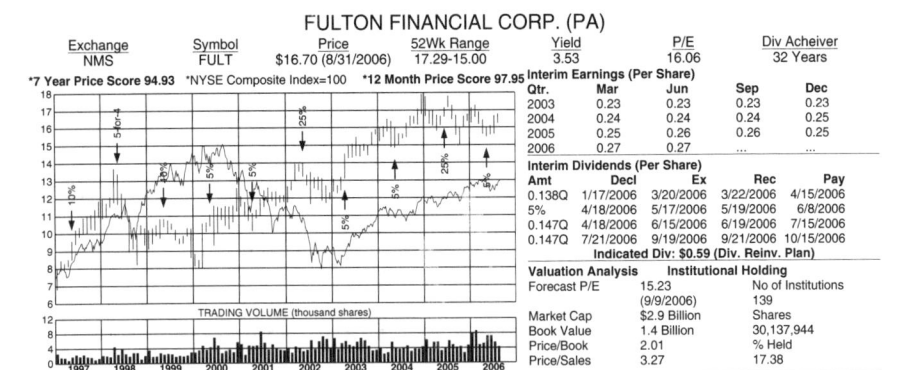

Interim Earnings (Per Share)

Qtr.	Mar	Jun	Sep	Dec
2003	0.23	0.23	0.23	0.23
2004	0.24	0.24	0.24	0.25
2005	0.25	0.26	0.26	0.25
2006	0.27	0.27	...	...

Interim Dividends (Per Share)

Amt	Decl	Ex	Rec	Pay
0.138Q	1/17/2006	3/20/2006	3/22/2006	4/15/2006
5%	4/18/2006	5/17/2006	5/19/2006	6/8/2006
0.147Q	4/18/2006	6/15/2006	6/19/2006	7/15/2006
0.147Q	7/21/2006	9/19/2006	9/21/2006	10/15/2006

Indicated Div: $0.59 (Div. Reinv. Plan)

Valuation Analysis
Forecast P/E 15.23 (9/9/2006)
Market Cap $2.9 Billion
Book Value 1.4 Billion
Price/Book 2.01
Price/Sales 3.27

Institutional Holding
No of Institutions 139
Shares 30,137,944
% Held 17.38

Business Summary: Commercial Banking (MIC: 8.1 SIC: 6021 NAIC: 522110)
Fulton Financial is a multi-bank financial holding company that provides a range of banking and financial services to businesses and consumers through its wholly owned banking subsidiaries: Fulton Bank, Lebanon Valley Farmers Bank, Swineford National Bank, Lafayette Ambassador Bank, FNB Bank N.A., Hagerstown Trust, Delaware National Bank, The Bank, The Peoples Bank of Elkton, Skylands Community Bank, Premier Bank, Resource Bank, First Washington State Bank and Somerset Valley Bank as well as its financial services subsidiaries. Co. operates throughout central and eastern Pennsylvania, Maryland, Delaware, New Jersey and Virginia. As of Dec 31 2005, Co. had total assets of $12.40 billion.

Recent Developments: For the quarter ended June 30 2006, net income increased 12.3% to $46.7 million from $41.6 million in the year-earlier quarter. Net interest income increased 22.9% to $122.9 million from $99.9 million in the year-earlier quarter. Provision for loan losses was $875,000 versus $725,000 in the prior-year quarter, an increase of 20.7%. Non-interest income fell 6.0% to $36.0 million from $38.3 million, while non-interest expense advanced 16.1% to $90.8 million.

Prospects: Co.'s outlook appears positive, bolstered by contributions deriving from its recent acquisitions. For instance, Co.'s loan growth is primarily benefiting from its acquisitions of Somerset Valley Bank and The Columbia Bank in July 2005 and February 2006, respectively. Organically, Co.'s loan growth is augmented by increases in its deposits, particularly in certificates of deposit. Going forward, Co. will continue to focus on generating growth through its acquisition strategy, which will allow its existing products and services to be marketed in new key areas with strong market demographics.

Financial Data
(US$ in Thousands)

	6 Mos	3 Mos	12/31/2005	12/31/2004	12/31/2003	12/31/2002	12/31/2001	12/31/2000
Earnings Per Share	1.04	1.03	1.00	0.97	0.93	0.89	0.76	0.76
Cash Flow Per Share	1.05	1.20	0.89	0.93	1.28	0.64	0.70	0.88
Tang Book Value Per Share	4.48	4.71	5.06	5.17	5.49	5.41	4.94	4.97
Dividends Per Share	0.562	0.552	0.540	0.493	0.452	0.405	0.366	0.328
Dividend Payout %	53.77	53.53	54.00	50.97	48.66	45.43	48.35	42.95
Income Statement								
Interest Income	405,858	192,652	625,797	493,643	435,531	469,288	518,178	462,581
Interest Expense	167,964	77,609	213,219	135,994	131,094	158,219	227,962	210,481
Net Interest Income	237,894	115,043	412,578	357,649	304,437	311,069	290,216	252,100
Provision for Losses	1,875	1,000	3,120	4,717	9,705	11,900	14,585	8,645
Non-Interest Income	72,609	36,607	144,268	138,864	136,987	115,783	100,994	69,611
Non-Interest Expense	178,809	88,016	316,291	273,615	234,176	225,536	216,669	165,022
Income Before Taxes	129,819	62,634	237,435	218,181	197,543	189,416	159,956	148,044
Income Taxes	39,239	18,755	71,361	65,264	59,363	56,468	46,367	44,240
Net Income	90,580	43,879	166,074	152,917	138,180	132,948	113,589	103,804
Average Shares	175,484	164,920	166,260	158,341	148,490	149,491	150,402	136,087
Balance Sheet								
Net Loans & Leases	9,945,413	9,612,515	8,331,881	7,494,920	6,082,294	5,245,148	5,301,148	4,806,498
Total Assets	14,561,545	14,174,485	12,401,555	11,158,351	9,767,288	8,387,778	7,770,711	6,571,155
Total Deposits	10,146,652	9,953,846	8,804,839	7,895,524	6,751,783	6,245,528	5,986,804	4,934,405
Total Liabilities	13,121,357	12,726,146	11,118,584	9,916,061	8,820,352	7,524,036	6,959,257	5,891,819
Stockholders' Equity	1,440,188	1,448,339	1,282,971	1,242,290	946,936	863,742	811,454	679,336
Shares Outstanding	173,300	165,700	164,850	164,981	149,388	146,294	149,405	136,554
Statistical Record								
Return on Assets %	1.33	1.32	1.41	1.46	1.52	1.65	1.58	1.64
Return on Equity %	13.18	12.56	13.15	13.93	15.26	15.87	15.24	16.00
Net Interest Margin %	57.62	59.72	65.93	72.45	69.90	66.29	56.01	54.50
Efficiency Ratio %	36.43	38.39	41.07	43.26	40.90	38.55	34.99	31.01
Loans to Deposits	0.98	0.97	0.95	0.95	0.90	0.84	0.89	0.97
Price Range	17.81-15.00	17.81-15.00	17.81-15.00	17.90-14.84	15.89-12.20	14.02-11.64	12.61-10.14	12.57-7.99
P/E Ratio	17.12-14.42	17.29-14.56	17.81-15.00	18.45-15.30	17.09-13.12	15.75-13.08	16.59-13.34	16.54-10.52
Average Yield %	3.44	3.34	3.26	3.09	3.16	3.15	3.14	3.18

Address: One Penn Square, P.O. Box 4887, Lancaster, PA 17604 **Telephone:** 717-291-2411 **Fax:** 717-291-2695	**Web Site:** www.fult.com **Officers:** Rufus A. Fulton Jr. - Chmn., C.E.O. R. Scott Smith Jr. - Pres., C.O.O.	**Auditors:** KPMG LLP **Investor Contact:** 717-291-2739 **Transfer Agents:** Stock Transfer Department, Lancaster, PA

GARMIN LTD.

Exchange	Symbol	Price	52Wk Range	Yield	P/E
NMS	GRMN	$46.76 (8/31/2006)	53.77-27.32	1.07	12.71

*7 Year Price Score N/A *NYSE Composite Index=100 *12 Month Price Score 121.00

Interim Earnings (Per Share)

Qtr.	Mar	Jun	Sep	Dec
2004	0.32	0.52	0.62	0.44
2005	0.44	0.68	0.95	0.81
2006	0.80	1.12	...	...

Interim Dividends (Per Share)

Amt	Decl	Ex	Rec	Pay
0.25A	7/28/2004	11/29/2004	12/1/2004	12/15/2004
0.25A	7/27/2005	11/29/2005	12/1/2005	12/15/2005
0.50A	5/3/2006	11/29/2006	12/1/2006	12/15/2006
2-for-1	7/21/2006	8/16/2006	8/2/2006	8/15/2006

Indicated Div: $0.50

Valuation Analysis

		Institutional Holding	
Forecast P/E	21.19	No of Institutions	
	(9/9/2006)	N/A	
Market Cap	$10.1 Billion	Shares	
Book Value	1.2 Billion	N/A	
Price/Book	8.73	% Held	
Price/Sales	9.83	N/A	

Business Summary: Instruments and Related Products (MIC: 11.15 SIC: 3812 NAIC: 334511)

Garmin is a worldwide provider of navigation, communications and information devices, most of which are enabled by Global Positioning System ("GPS") technology. Co. designs, develops, manufactures and markets a diverse family of hand-held, portable and fixed-mount GPS-enabled products and other navigation, communications and information products for the general aviation and consumer markets. Each of Co.'s GPS products utilizes its proprietary integrated circuit and receiver designs to collect, calculate and display location, direction, speed and other information in forms optimized for specific uses.

Recent Developments: For the 13 weeks ended Jul 1 2006, net income advanced 66.2% to $123.3 million compared with $74.2 million in the corresponding period of the previous year. Net sales soared 63.5% to $432.5 million from $264.5 million in the prior-year quarter. Gross profit jumped 54.5% to $216.3 million from $140.0 million, but slipped as a percentage of net sales to 50.0% from 52.9%. Total operating expenses climbed 60.5% to $81.7 million from $50.9 million in the year-earlier period. Operating income improved 51.1% to $134.6 million versus $89.1 million the year before.

Prospects: Co. is pleased with the delivery of its 15 newest products. These products, which include many automotive/mobile and marine products, are being well received by the market. Co. continues to experience strong sales of both new and existing automotive/mobile and look forward to additional new product introductions. Meanwhile, Co.'s response to its marine products is positive, although success in this segment is being somewhat dampened by poor weather and higher fuel prices experienced by its marine customers. Moreover, Co. expects revenue to exceed $1.60 billion for full-year 2006, and earnings per share to exceed $3.90.

Financial Data
(US$ in Thousands)

	12/31/2005	12/25/2004	12/27/2003	12/28/2002	12/29/2001	12/30/2000	12/25/1999	12/26/1998
Earnings Per Share	1.43	0.94	0.82	0.66	0.53	0.53	0.32	0.17
Cash Flow Per Share	1.12	0.97	0.81	0.82	0.60	...	0.22	0.19
Tang Book Value Per Share	5.19	4.09	3.27	2.68	2.03	1.67	0.97	1.22
Dividends Per Share	0.250	0.250	0.250	...	...	0.145	0.065	0.060
Dividend Payout %	17.54	26.46	30.49	...	...	27.62	20.31	34.29
Income Statement								
Total Revenue	1,027,773	762,549	572,989	465,144	369,119	345,741	232,586	169,030
EBITDA	396,658	280,429	239,108	193,728	153,913	136,284	85,954	48,891
Depn & Amortn	43,596	34,599	20,104	16,131	10,868	...	5,572	4,338
Income Before Taxes	372,600	255,211	225,943	182,734	152,035	140,922	84,132	47,520
Income Taxes	61,381	49,511	47,309	39,937	38,587	35,259	19,965	12,354
Net Income	311,219	205,700	178,634	142,797	113,448	105,663	64,167	35,166
Average Shares	218,236	218,060	217,804	216,402	216,894	201,012	200,000	199,248
Balance Sheet								
Total Assets	1,362,235	1,117,391	856,945	698,115	532,155	463,347	254,645	174,532
Current Liabilities	195,485	176,267	104,434	73,405	49,028	42,041	32,241	29,247
Long-Term Obligations	...	...	...	20,000	28,011	46,359	27,715	9,345
Total Liabilities	204,971	181,534	107,255	95,616	78,186	98,108	60,046	38,592
Stockholders' Equity	1,157,264	935,857	749,690	602,499	453,969	365,239	194,599	135,940
Shares Outstanding	216,134	216,654	216,332	215,839	215,549	216,484	200,000	111,111
Statistical Record								
Return on Assets %	24.70	20.89	23.04	23.28	22.85	28.96	29.98	...
Return on Equity %	29.26	24.47	26.49	27.11	27.77	37.14	38.93	...
EBITDA Margin %	38.59	36.78	41.73	41.65	41.70	39.42	36.96	28.92
Net Margin %	30.28	26.98	31.18	30.70	30.73	30.56	27.59	20.80
Asset Turnover	0.82	0.77	0.74	0.76	0.74	0.95	1.09	...
Current Ratio	4.10	3.61	5.17	6.34	7.19	9.23	6.14	4.97
Debt to Equity	...	...	...	0.03	0.06	0.13	0.14	0.07
Price Range	35.20-19.75	30.43-14.22	28.00-14.04	15.16-9.00	12.56-7.20	10.59-9.09	...	...
P/E Ratio	24.62-13.81	32.37-15.12	34.15-17.12	22.98-13.64	23.70-13.58	19.99-17.16	...	...
Average Yield %	0.94	1.15	1.21	...	...	1.49	...	...

Address: PO Box 30464 SMB, 5th Floor, Harbour Place, 103 South Church Street, Grand Cayman **Telephone:** 946-520-3	Web Site: www.garmin.com Officers: Min H. Kao - Chmn., C.E.O. Kevin S. Rauckman - C.F.O., Treas.	Auditors: Ernst & Young LLP

GEMSTAR-TV GUIDE INTERNATIONAL INC

Exchange	Symbol	Price	52Wk Range	Yield	P/E
NMS	GMST	$3.22 (8/31/2006)	3.62-2.40	N/A	16.10

*7 Year Price Score 12.16 *NYSE Composite Index=100 *12 Month Price Score 96.47

Interim Earnings (Per Share)

Qtr.	Mar	Jun	Sep	Dec
2003	(0.11)	(0.06)	(0.04)	(1.20)
2004	(0.09)	0.10	(0.23)	(0.05)
2005	(0.01)	(0.01)	0.12	0.03
2006	0.02	0.03	...	...

Interim Dividends (Per Share)
No Dividends Paid

Valuation Analysis

		Institutional Holding	
Forecast P/E	39.00	No of Institutions	
	(9/9/2006)	130	
Market Cap	$1.4 Billion	Shares	
Book Value	397.9 Million	179,880,240	
Price/Book	3.45	% Held	
Price/Sales	2.59	42.21	

Business Summary: Media & Entertainment (MIC: 13 SIC: 2721 NAIC: 511120)

Gemstar-TV Guide International is a media, entertainment and technology company that develops, licenses, markets and distributes technologies, products and services targeted at the television guidance and home entertainment needs of television viewers worldwide. Co.'s Publishing Segment comprises TV Guide magazine, TV Guide Online (www.tvguide.com) and TV Guide Data Solutions. Co.'s Cable and Satellite Segment includes the operations of TV Guide Channel, TV Guide Interactive, TVG Network, TV Guide Spot and TV Guide Mobile. Co.'s Consumer Electronics (CE) Licensing Segment licenses its proprietary technologies and services to the CE manufacturing industry.

Recent Developments: For the quarter ended June 30 2006, income from continuing operations was $14.6 million compared with a loss of $7.3 million in the year-earlier quarter. Net income amounted to $14.6 million versus a net loss of $5.1 million in the year-earlier quarter. Revenues were $133.3 million, down 15.8% from $158.3 million the year before. Operating income was $15.2 million versus $2.7 million in the prior-year quarter, an increase of 452.8%. Direct operating expenses declined 24.9% to $100.9 million from $134.3 million in the comparable period the year before. Indirect operating expenses decreased 18.8% to $17.3 million from $21.3 million in the equivalent prior-year period.

Prospects: Going forward, Co. intends to continue its strategy of pursuing various strategic initiatives slated towards strengthening its position in the consumer market for video guidance across multiple platforms. For instance, on June 21 2006, Co. acquired the web site www.jumptheshark.com and related assets from Jump the Shark Inc., by which Co. will develop and promote the acquired website into its new online community section. It is expected that the acquisition of the Jump the Shark website will further bolster Co.'s site by way of enhancing its key program listings, expert recommendations, movie reviews as well as entertainment news and information.

Financial Data
(US$ in Thousands)

	6 Mos	3 Mos	12/31/2005	12/31/2004	12/31/2003	12/31/2002	12/31/2001	12/31/2000
Earnings Per Share	0.20	0.16	0.13	(0.22)	(1.41)	(15.64)	(1.45)	(0.64)
Cash Flow Per Share	(0.03)	(0.16)	(0.29)	0.91	0.01	0.26	0.45	0.53
Income Statement								
Total Revenue	277,321	144,032	604,192	732,300	878,652	1,001,391	1,368,170	731,109
EBITDA	39,718	15,817	(5,189)	(42,031)	(454,876)	(2,458,048)	286,465	238,897
Depn & Amortn	16,567	7,961	30,140	40,548	172,940	356,354	962,722	443,312
Income Before Taxes	34,929	13,025	(19,785)	(76,874)	(633,980)	(2,824,241)	(703,555)	(229,198)
Income Taxes	11,728	4,459	(40,395)	(7,925)	(56,582)	(589,103)	(106,033)	(16,084)
Net Income	23,201	8,566	54,815	(94,461)	(577,398)	(6,423,175)	(599,622)	(213,114)
Average Shares	426,256	426,213	426,240	422,723	410,265	410,610	412,389	334,804
Balance Sheet								
Total Assets	1,223,397	1,218,128	1,259,682	1,362,373	1,334,169	2,089,174	9,686,641	10,789,477
Current Liabilities	310,602	306,342	339,126	396,339	464,177	619,111	608,925	560,984
Long-Term Obligations	12,419	12,569	12,715	13,274	138,736	163,861	271,029	586,485
Total Liabilities	825,543	836,000	886,476	1,051,581	958,196	1,194,704	2,135,503	2,733,514
Stockholders' Equity	397,854	382,128	373,206	310,792	375,973	894,470	7,551,138	8,055,963
Shares Outstanding	426,199	426,184	426,162	424,063	417,845	408,156	414,748	410,960
Statistical Record								
Return on Assets %	6.84	5.31	4.18	N.M.	N.M.	N.M.	N.M.	N.M.
Return on Equity %	24.67	19.44	16.03	N.M.	N.M.	N.M.	N.M.	N.M.
EBITDA Margin %	14.32	10.98	N.M.	N.M.	N.M.	N.M.	20.94	32.68
Net Margin %	8.37	5.95	9.07	N.M.	N.M.	N.M.	N.M.	N.M.
Asset Turnover	0.42	0.45	0.46	0.54	0.51	0.17	0.13	0.08
Current Ratio	2.17	2.15	2.04	1.99	1.03	1.00	1.38	1.69
Debt to Equity	0.03	0.03	0.03	0.04	0.37	0.18	0.04	0.07
Price Range	3.76-2.40	4.46-2.40	6.00-2.40	8.00-4.06	5.90-2.80	28.04-2.52	56.94-17.28	101.38-34.50
P/E Ratio	18.80-12.00	27.88-15.00	46.15-18.46	...	...	...	...	...

Address: 6922 Hollywood Boulevard, 12th Floor, Los Angeles, CA 90028
Telephone: 323-817-4600
Fax: 323-817-4623

Web Site: www.gemstar-tvguideinternational.com
Officers: Jeff Shell - C.E.O. Stephen H. Kay - Exec. V.P., Gen. Couns.

Auditors: Ernst & Young LLP
Investor Contact: 323-817-4600

GENTEX CORP.

Exchange	Symbol	Price	52Wk Range	Yield	P/E
NMS	GNTX	$14.48 (8/31/2006)	20.68-12.94	2.62	20.11

*7 Year Price Price Score 84.15   *NYSE Composite Index=100   *12 Month Price Score 82.20

Interim Earnings (Per Share)

Qtr.	Mar	Jun	Sep	Dec
2003	0.17	0.17	0.17	0.18
2004	0.19	0.19	0.16	0.19
2005	0.17	0.17	0.18	0.19
2006	0.17	0.18	...	...

Interim Dividends (Per Share)

Amt	Decl	Ex	Rec	Pay
0.09Q	11/30/2005	1/4/2006	1/6/2006	1/20/2006
0.09Q	3/2/2006	4/5/2006	4/7/2006	4/21/2006
0.09Q	5/25/2006	7/5/2006	7/7/2006	7/21/2006
0.095Q	8/14/2006	10/4/2006	10/6/2006	10/20/2006

Indicated Div: $0.38

Valuation Analysis   **Institutional Holding**

Forecast P/E	20.70	No of Institutions
	(9/9/2006)	214
Market Cap	$2.1 Billion	Shares
Book Value	729.8 Million	123,535,912
Price/Book	2.91	% Held
Price/Sales	3.81	84.14

Business Summary: Automotive (MIC: 15.1 SIC: 3714 NAIC: 336399)

Gentex designs, develops, manufactures and markets proprietary products employing electro-optic technology: automatic-dimming rearview mirrors for the automotive industry and fire protection products primarily for the commercial building industry. Co.'s auto-dimming mirrors gradually darkens to the degree necessary to eliminate rearview glare from following vehicle headlights through the use of electrochromic technology and the glare-sensing capabilities of its Motorized Mirror. Co. manufactures about 60 models of smoke alarms and detectors, combined with over 160 models of signaling appliances. All of the smoke detectors/alarms operate on a photoelectric principle to detect smoke.

Recent Developments: For the quarter ended June 30 2006, net income increased 4.6% to $27.2 million from $26.0 million in the year-earlier quarter. Revenues were $142.4 million, up 7.6% from $132.4 million the year before. Operating income was $33.4 million versus $33.8 million in the prior-year quarter, a decrease of 1.0%. Direct operating expenses rose 10.5% to $91.5 million from $82.8 million in the comparable period the year before. Indirect operating expenses increased 10.5% to $17.5 million from $15.8 million in the equivalent prior-year period.

Prospects: Co.'s near-term prospects appear uncertain as oil prices and higher interest rates continue to hamper the sales of vehicles, especially in the mid- and full-sized truck or SUV segments, in addition to the uncertainty associated with customer changeover plant shutdowns and new vehicle and/or product launches. Co. also continues to experience pricing pressures from automotive customers that will continue to affect its margins, thus preventing it from offsetting the price reductions with yield improvements, engineering and purchasing cost reductions, and increases in unit sales volume. However, Co. still expects unit shipment growth of about 5.0% to 10.0% for full-year 2006.

Financial Data
(US$ in Thousands)

	6 Mos	3 Mos	12/31/2005	12/31/2004	12/31/2003	12/31/2002	12/31/2001	12/31/2000
Earnings Per Share	0.72	0.71	0.70	0.72	0.69	0.56	0.43	0.47
Cash Flow Per Share	0.84	0.79	0.81	0.85	0.76	0.79	0.54	0.53
Tang Book Value Per Share	4.97	5.32	5.39	5.03	4.50	3.76	3.19	2.71
Dividends Per Share	0.355	0.350	0.345	0.310	0.075	...	...	...
Dividend Payout %	49.31	49.30	49.29	43.06	10.95	...	...	...
Income Statement								
Total Revenue	281,412	139,021	536,484	505,666	469,019	395,258	310,305	297,421
EBITDA	92,590	45,388	185,348	189,047	179,709	146,787	112,751	116,665
Depn & Amortn	14,220	7,117	25,453	23,315	21,544	19,714	16,134	12,142
Income Before Taxes	78,370	38,271	159,895	165,733	158,164	127,073	96,618	104,523
Income Taxes	24,763	11,900	50,367	53,076	51,403	41,302	31,401	33,979
Net Income	53,607	26,371	109,528	112,657	106,761	85,771	65,217	70,544
Average Shares	151,044	155,751	157,030	156,721	155,368	153,204	151,743	151,036
Balance Sheet								
Total Assets	824,494	915,009	922,646	856,859	762,530	609,173	506,823	428,129
Current Liabilities	72,813	72,988	58,088	50,856	50,480	29,060	20,985	19,691
Total Liabilities	94,711	96,844	81,050	73,579	68,886	35,532	27,822	26,025
Stockholders' Equity	729,782	818,165	841,595	783,280	693,643	573,640	479,001	402,104
Shares Outstanding	146,828	153,758	156,043	155,733	154,081	152,442	150,343	148,582
Statistical Record								
Return on Assets %	12.85	12.18	12.31	13.88	15.57	15.37	13.95	18.37
Return on Equity %	14.37	13.62	13.48	15.21	16.85	16.30	14.80	19.56
EBITDA Margin %	32.90	32.65	34.55	37.39	38.32	37.14	36.34	39.23
Net Margin %	19.05	18.97	20.42	22.28	22.76	21.70	21.02	23.72
Asset Turnover	0.64	0.61	0.60	0.62	0.68	0.71	0.66	0.77
Current Ratio	6.95	8.22	10.66	11.65	9.61	9.53	12.38	9.68
Price Range	20.68-13.73	20.68-15.39	20.27-15.39	23.23-15.69	22.39-12.03	16.60-12.09	16.89-9.55	19.34-8.28
P/E Ratio	28.72-19.07	29.13-21.68	28.96-21.99	32.26-21.78	32.44-17.43	29.64-21.60	39.27-22.22	41.16-17.62
Average Yield %	2.07	1.97	1.97	1.64	0.45	...	...	...

Address: 600 N. Centennial Street, Zeeland, MI 49464 **Telephone:** 616-772-1800 **Fax:** 616-772-7348	**Web Site:** www.gentex.com **Officers:** Fred T. Bauer - Chmn., C.E.O. Garth Deur - Exec. V.P.	**Auditors:** Ernst & Young LLP **Investor Contact:** 616-772-1800

GENZYME CORP.

Exchange	Symbol	Price	52Wk Range	Yield	P/E
NMS	GENZ	$66.23 (8/31/2006)	77.53-55.00	N/A	39.42

*7 Year Price Score 117.08 *NYSE Composite Index=100 *12 Month Price Score 94.09

Interim Earnings (Per Share)

Qtr.	Mar	Jun	Sep	Dec
2003	0.28	0.32	(0.43)	0.25
2004	0.29	0.34	0.42	(0.68)
2005	0.36	0.46	0.43	0.39
2006	0.37	0.49	...	...

Interim Dividends (Per Share)
No Dividends Paid

Valuation Analysis
Forecast P/E	23.88	Institutional Holding	
	(9/9/2006)	No of Institutions	486
Market Cap	$17.3 Billion	Shares	229,584,224
Book Value	5.6 Billion	% Held	87.84
Price/Book	3.07		
Price/Sales	5.85		

Business Summary: Biotechnology (MIC: 9.2 SIC: 2836 NAIC: 325414)

Genzyme is a global biotechnology company. Co.'s Renal unit develops, manufactures and distributes products that treat patients suffering from renal diseases, including chronic renal failure. The Therapeutics unit develops, manufactures and distributes therapeutic products. The Transplant unit develops, manufactures and distributes therapeutic products that address pre-transplantation, prevention and treatment of acute rejection in organ transplantation. Biosurgery develops, manufactures and distributes biotherapeutics and biomaterial products. Diagnostics/Genetics develops, manufactures and distributes raw materials and in vitro diagnostics products, and provides testing services.

Recent Developments: For the quarter ended June 30 2006, net income increased 8.8% to $134.5 million from $123.6 million in the year-earlier quarter. Revenues were $793.4 million, up 18.7% from $668.1 million the year before. Operating income was $112.7 million versus $164.7 million in the prior-year quarter, a decrease of 31.5%. Direct operating expenses rose 27.6% to $185.3 million from $145.3 million in the comparable period the year before. Indirect operating expenses increased 38.3% to $495.3 million from $358.2 million in the equivalent prior-year period.

Prospects: Going forward, Co. expects sales of Renagel® and Hectorol®, which treats renal diseases, to increase driven by growing patient access to its products and the continued support from nephrologists worldwide; while sales of Myozyme®, which treats Pompe disease, should increase as patients shift from clinical trials or expanded access programs and as new patients are identified. Meanwhile, marketing applications for Myozyme® have been submitted in Japan and Canada and Co. expects to file for approval in several other countries in 2006. For full 2006, Co. reaffirms its revenue guidance of $3.10 billion to $3.30 billion and earnings guidance of $1.78 to $1.88 per diluted share.

Financial Data (US$ in Thousands)	6 Mos	3 Mos	12/31/2005	12/31/2004	12/31/2003	12/31/2002	12/31/2001	12/31/2000
Earnings Per Share	1.68	1.65	1.65	0.37	0.42	(0.81)	...	...
Cash Flow Per Share	2.85	2.74	2.87	2.52	1.77	1.03	...	...
Tang Book Value Per Share	10.01	8.86	7.99	8.11	6.32	5.04	4.09	2.61
Income Statement								
Total Revenue	1,524,198	730,842	2,734,842	2,201,145	1,713,871	1,329,472	1,223,630	903,320
EBITDA	514,671	233,172	933,189	470,996	192,114	265,363	97,799	68,685
Depn & Amortn	165,356	82,391	284,652	205,073	160,459	134,000	179,009	60,437
Income Before Taxes	340,842	146,343	628,919	227,696	5,055	104,211	(118,343)	(7,462)
Income Taxes	105,371	45,369	187,430	141,169	72,647	19,015	(2,020)	55,478
Net Income	235,471	100,974	441,489	86,527	(67,592)	(13,074)	(112,156)	(62,940)
Average Shares	276,312	276,809	272,224	234,318	225,419	219,388	211,176	179,366
Balance Sheet								
Total Assets	7,372,871	7,027,926	6,878,865	6,069,421	5,004,528	4,083,049	3,935,745	3,318,100
Current Liabilities	616,632	515,895	550,023	624,398	392,025	607,800	282,990	241,099
Long-Term Obligations	813,493	814,741	815,652	810,991	1,415,349	600,038	844,809	665,240
Total Liabilities	1,728,223	1,675,417	1,728,998	1,689,265	2,068,116	1,385,202	1,326,556	1,142,959
Stockholders' Equity	5,644,648	5,352,509	5,149,867	4,380,156	2,936,412	2,697,847	2,609,189	2,175,141
Shares Outstanding	261,375	260,344	259,151	249,018	224,610	272,088	269,389	243,485
Statistical Record								
Return on Assets %	6.53	6.81	6.82	1.56	N.M.	N.M.	N.M.	N.M.
Return on Equity %	8.85	9.05	9.27	2.36	N.M.	N.M.	N.M.	N.M.
EBITDA Margin %	33.77	31.90	34.12	21.40	11.21	19.96	7.99	7.60
Net Margin %	15.45	13.82	16.14	3.93	N.M.	N.M.	N.M.	N.M.
Asset Turnover	0.42	0.43	0.42	0.40	0.38	0.33	0.34	0.35
Current Ratio	3.33	3.48	3.03	2.62	3.37	1.96	3.00	3.32
Debt to Equity	0.14	0.15	0.16	0.19	0.48	0.22	0.32	0.31
Price Range	77.53-55.00	77.53-55.99	77.53-55.26	58.16-41.00	52.32-28.82	59.86-16.88	61.00-37.97	51.50-20.38
P/E Ratio	46.15-32.74	46.99-33.93	46.99-33.49	157.19-110.81	124.57-68.62	...	...	...

Address: 500 Kendall St., Cambridge, MA 02142
Telephone: 617-252-7500
Fax: 617-252-7600

Web Site: www.genzyme.com
Officers: Henri A. Termeer - Chmn., Pres., C.E.O. Michael S. Wyzga - Exec. V.P., Fin., C.F.O., Chief Acctg. Officer

Auditors: PricewaterhouseCoopers LLP
Investor Contact: 180-043-61443

GILEAD SCIENCES, INC.

Exchange	Symbol	Price	52Wk Range	Yield	P/E
NMS	GILD	$63.40 (8/31/2006)	65.16-42.59	N/A	30.48

*7 Year Price Score 173.59 *NYSE Composite Index=100 *12 Month Price Score 107.01

Interim Earnings (Per Share)

Qtr.	Mar	Jun	Sep	Dec
2003	(1.11)	0.23	0.17	0.48
2004	0.25	0.24	0.25	0.25
2005	0.34	0.41	0.38	0.59
2006	0.55	0.56	...	...

Interim Dividends (Per Share)

Amt	Decl	Ex	Rec	Pay
2-for-1	1/19/2001	2/22/2001	2/2/2001	2/21/2001
2-for-1	1/30/2002	3/8/2002	2/14/2002	3/7/2002
2-for-1	7/28/2004	9/7/2004	8/12/2004	9/3/2004

Valuation Analysis

Forecast P/E	27.17	Institutional Holding
	(9/9/2006)	No of Institutions 567
Market Cap	$28.9 Billion	Shares 398,615,808
Book Value	3.2 Billion	% Held 87.25
Price/Book	9.05	
Price/Sales	11.66	

Business Summary: Biotechnology (MIC: 9.2 SIC: 2836 NAIC: 325414)

Gilead Sciences is a biopharmaceutical company engaged in the development of humanized antibodies to prevent or treat various disease conditions. Co. has antibodies under development for autoimmune and inflammatory conditions, asthma and cancer. Co. also holds fundamental patents for its antibody humanization technology. Co. markets Viread, Emtriva, and Truvada for the treatment of human immunodeficiency virus; Hepsera for the treatment of chronic hepatitis B; AmBisome for the treatment of fungal infection and Vistide for the treatment of cytomegalovirus. Co. receives royalties on sales of Tamiflu and Macugen.

Recent Developments: For the quarter ended June 30 2006, net income increased 35.3% to $265.2 million from $196.0 million in the year-earlier quarter. Revenues were $685.3 million, up 38.4% from $495.3 million the year before. Operating income was $365.3 million versus $277.5 million in the prior-year quarter, an increase of 31.6%. Direct operating expenses rose 23.1% to $77.9 million from $63.3 million in the comparable period the year before. Indirect operating expenses increased 56.7% to $242.1 million from $154.5 million in the equivalent prior-year period.

Prospects: Co.'s strong product sales continues to be driven by its HIV product franchise, including the continued robust sale of Truvada® and Viread®, as well as of Hepsera® for the treatment of chronic Hepatitis B. Meanwhile, Co. is making significant progress in the development of its oral HIV integrase inhibitor, GS 9137, releasing results from its Phase I/II study of the drug and commencing a Phase II program to evaluate the safety and efficacy of this product candidate. Separately, on Apr 27 2006, Co. has filed a New Drug Application to the U.S FDA for the approval of a once-daily single tablet regimen of Truvada® and Sustiva® for the treatment of HIV.

Financial Data
(US$ in Thousands)

	6 Mos	3 Mos	12/31/2005	12/31/2004	12/31/2003	12/31/2002	12/31/2001	12/31/2000
Earnings Per Share	2.08	1.93	1.72	0.99	(0.18)	0.17	0.13	(0.16)
Cash Flow Per Share	1.50	1.54	1.57	1.18	0.58	0.19	(0.23)	(0.10)
Tang Book Value Per Share	7.01	7.32	6.59	4.17	2.35	1.45	1.17	0.93
Income Statement								
Total Revenue	1,378,180	692,878	2,028,400	1,324,621	867,864	466,790	233,769	195,555
EBITDA	828,923	412,414	1,198,011	688,175	(124,777)	101,678	86,118	(22,676)
Depn & Amortn	23,833	11,243	35,777	24,408	20,859	14,428	14,691	12,008
Income Before Taxes	796,159	397,447	1,161,792	656,422	(167,533)	73,397	57,447	(39,049)
Income Taxes	268,305	134,743	347,878	207,051	(95,530)	1,300	4,135	1,199
Net Income	527,854	262,704	813,914	449,371	(72,003)	72,097	52,271	(56,776)
Average Shares	476,217	481,802	474,284	464,246	402,210	412,954	404,642	364,200
Balance Sheet								
Total Assets	5,179,648	4,036,534	3,764,651	2,155,963	1,554,722	1,288,183	794,786	678,099
Current Liabilities	507,968	421,903	455,338	253,453	185,895	104,892	80,117	58,238
Long-Term Obligations	1,439,417	184,382	240,650	234	345,323	595,273	250,389	252,238
Total Liabilities	1,981,734	648,121	736,873	285,091	551,748	716,842	342,349	326,975
Stockholders' Equity	3,197,914	3,388,413	3,027,778	1,870,872	1,002,974	571,341	452,437	351,124
Shares Outstanding	456,276	462,850	459,726	448,822	426,506	395,190	386,082	377,150
Statistical Record								
Return on Assets %	25.13	28.71	27.49	24.15	N.M.	6.92	7.10	N.M.
Return on Equity %	35.37	33.73	33.23	31.19	N.M.	14.08	13.01	N.M.
EBITDA Margin %	60.15	59.52	59.06	51.95	N.M.	21.78	36.84	N.M.
Net Margin %	38.30	37.91	40.13	33.92	N.M.	15.45	22.36	N.M.
Asset Turnover	0.63	0.72	0.69	0.71	0.61	0.45	0.32	0.35
Current Ratio	4.91	8.00	6.79	7.30	6.81	11.29	8.83	10.20
Debt to Equity	0.45	0.05	0.08	N.M.	0.34	1.04	0.55	0.72
Price Range	65.16-40.99	63.74-35.20	55.63-31.04	39.04-25.88	34.99-16.15	19.86-13.28	18.05-6.76	14.52-5.43
P/E Ratio	31.33-19.71	33.03-18.24	32.34-18.05	39.43-26.14	...	116.79-78.09	138.87-51.98	...

Address: 333 Lakeside Drive, Foster City, CA 94404 **Telephone:** 650-574-3000 **Fax:** 650-578-9264	**Web Site:** www.gilead.com **Officers:** James M. Denny - Chmn. John C. Martin - Pres., C.E.O.	**Auditors:** ERNST & YOUNG LLP **Investor Contact:** 650-574-3000 **Transfer Agents:** Mellon Investor Services LLC, South Hackensack, NJ

GLACIER BANCORP, INC.

Exchange	Symbol	Price	52Wk Range	Yield	P/E	Div Achiever
NMS	GBCI	$32.48 (8/31/2006)	33.27-28.13	1.97	18.88	14 Years

*7 Year Price Score 142.85 *NYSE Composite Index=100 *12 Month Price Score 97.23

Interim Earnings (Per Share)

Qtr.	Mar	Jun	Sep	Dec
2003	0.32	0.33	0.31	0.31
2004	0.34	0.34	0.38	0.37
2005	0.37	0.41	0.42	0.43
2006	0.42	0.45	...	...

Interim Dividends (Per Share)

Amt	Decl	Ex	Rec	Pay
0.15Q	9/28/2005	10/6/2005	10/11/2005	10/20/2005
0.16Q	12/28/2005	1/6/2006	1/10/2006	1/19/2006
0.16Q	3/29/2006	4/7/2006	4/11/2006	4/20/2006
0.16Q	6/28/2006	7/7/2006	7/11/2006	7/20/2006

Indicated Div: $0.64 (Div. Reinv. Plan)

Valuation Analysis

Forecast P/E	17.23 (9/9/2006)
Market Cap	$1.1 Billion
Book Value	352.8 Million
Price/Book	2.99
Price/Sales	3.95

Institutional Holding

No of Institutions	106
Shares	16,624,958
% Held	51.22

Business Summary: Other Depository Banking (MIC: 8.5 SIC: 6035 NAIC: 522120)

Glacier Bancorp is a regional multi-bank holding company providing commercial banking services from 71 banking offices in Montana, Idaho, Wyoming, Utah and Washington. Co. offers a range of banking products and services, including transaction and savings deposits, commercial, consumer, and real estate loans, mortgage origination services, and retail brokerage services. Co. serves individuals, small to medium-sized businesses, community organizations and public entities. As of Dec 31 2005, Co. had total assets of $3.71 billion and total deposits of $2.53 billion.

Recent Developments: For the quarter ended June 30 2006, net income increased 12.0% to $14.7 million from $13.1 million in the year-earlier quarter. Net interest income increased 17.3% to $37.6 million from $32.1 million in the year-earlier quarter. Provision for loan losses was $1.4 million versus $1.6 million in the prior-year quarter, a decrease of 12.7%. Non-interest income rose 12.0% to $12.9 million from $11.5 million, while non-interest expense advanced 19.9% to $27.0 million.

Prospects: On May 31 2006, Co. entered into a definitive agreement to acquire First National Bank of Morgan for $20.0 million, which represents its first whole-bank acquisition and charter in Utah. The purchase expands Co.'s focused community banking strategy in Utah and should be immediately accretive to its earnings. Meanwhile, Co. continues to assess acquisition opportunities and seek out banks to boost its performance and profitability. Accordingly, Co. plans to open eight new offices along with significant expansion to eight existing facilities in 2006. Thus, Co. expects some pressure on its short term earnings, but expects the new offices to expand its presence in key markets going forward.

Financial Data
(US$ in Thousands)

	6 Mos	3 Mos	12/31/2005	12/31/2004	12/31/2003	12/31/2002	12/31/2001	12/31/2000
Earnings Per Share	1.72	1.68	1.64	1.43	1.24	1.08	0.78	0.70
Cash Flow Per Share	2.43	2.69	2.46	2.28	3.16	0.56	(1.04)	1.94
Tang Book Value Per Share	8.22	7.97	7.65	7.43	6.45	5.80	4.66	4.66
Dividends Per Share	0.620	0.604	0.580	0.534	0.459	0.372	0.349	0.360
Dividend Payout %	36.05	35.95	35.37	37.32	36.97	34.43	44.78	51.09
Income Statement								
Interest Income	115,885	55,952	189,985	147,285	130,830	133,989	137,920	78,837
Interest Expense	41,951	19,644	59,978	39,892	38,478	47,522	65,546	37,357
Net Interest Income	73,934	36,308	130,007	107,393	92,352	86,467	72,374	41,480
Provision for Losses	2,520	1,165	6,023	4,195	3,809	5,745	4,525	1,864
Non-Interest Income	24,054	11,156	44,626	34,565	33,562	25,917	23,251	13,294
Non-Interest Expense	52,777	25,827	90,926	72,133	65,944	57,813	57,385	31,327
Income Before Taxes	42,691	20,472	77,684	65,630	56,161	48,826	33,715	21,583
Income Taxes	14,396	6,843	25,311	21,014	18,153	16,424	12,026	7,580
Net Income	28,295	13,629	52,373	44,616	38,008	32,402	21,689	14,003
Average Shares	32,897	32,826	31,892	31,144	30,656	29,982	27,742	19,841
Balance Sheet								
Net Loans & Leases	2,630,254	2,502,279	2,374,647	1,687,329	1,413,392	1,248,666	1,294,924	726,503
Total Assets	3,913,382	3,800,158	3,706,344	3,010,737	2,739,633	2,281,344	2,085,747	1,056,712
Total Deposits	2,692,769	2,693,399	2,534,712	1,729,708	1,597,625	1,459,923	1,446,064	720,570
Total Liabilities	3,560,552	3,455,767	3,373,105	2,740,553	2,501,794	2,069,095	1,908,764	958,599
Stockholders' Equity	352,830	344,391	333,239	270,184	237,839	212,249	176,983	98,113
Shares Outstanding	32,439	32,314	32,172	30,686	30,254	29,709	29,002	19,674
Statistical Record								
Return on Assets %	1.51	1.53	1.56	1.55	1.51	1.48	1.38	1.44
Return on Equity %	17.23	17.64	17.36	17.52	16.89	16.65	15.77	15.79
Net Interest Margin %	62.78	64.89	68.43	72.92	70.59	64.53	52.48	52.61
Efficiency Ratio %	37.00	38.49	38.76	39.67	40.11	36.15	35.61	34.00
Loans to Deposits	0.98	0.93	0.94	0.98	0.88	0.86	0.90	1.01
Price Range	33.27-26.13	33.27-21.16	33.27-21.16	28.35-18.89	21.11-13.71	14.40-11.12	12.22-7.31	8.53-6.40
P/E Ratio	19.34-15.19	19.80-12.60	20.29-12.90	19.83-13.21	17.02-11.05	13.33-10.30	15.66-9.37	12.18-9.14
Average Yield %	2.06	2.12	2.14	2.38	2.73	2.88	3.55	4.92

Address: 49 Commons Loop, Kalispell, MT 59901-2679
Telephone: 406-756-4200
Fax: 406-756-3518

Web Site: www.glacierbancorp.com
Officers: John S. MacMillan - Chmn. Michael J. Blodnick - Pres., C.E.O.

Auditors: KPMG LLP
Transfer Agents: TrustCorp, Great Falls, MT

GRANITE BROADCASTING CORP

Exchange	Symbol	Price	52Wk Range	Yield	P/E
OTC	GBTV K	$0.12 (8/31/2006)	0.45-0.11	N/A	N/A

*7 Year Price Score N/A   *NYSE Composite Index=100   *12 Month Price Score 70.76

Interim Earnings (Per Share)

Qtr.	Mar	Jun	Sep	Dec
2003	(0.82)	(0.70)	(0.76)	(0.87)
2004	(0.90)	(0.81)	(1.03)	(1.56)
2005	(1.00)	(0.83)	(1.00)	(2.25)
2006	(0.79)	(1.58)	...	...

Interim Dividends (Per Share)
No Dividends Paid

Valuation Analysis

		Institutional Holding	
Forecast P/E	N/A	No of Institutions	2
Market Cap	$2.3 Million	Shares	14,900
Book Value	N/A	% Held	0.08
Price/Book	N/A		
Price/Sales	0.02		

Business Summary: Media & Entertainment (MIC: 13 SIC: 4833 NAIC: 515120)
Granite Broadcasting is a television broadcasting company, focused on developing and operating small to middle-market television broadcast stations in the U.S. As of Dec 31 2005, Co. owned and operated six middle-market stations and provided advertising, sales, promotion and administrative services, and selected programming to two additional stations owned by Malara Broadcast Group, all of which were affiliated with either the ABC, NBC or CBS television networks. The stations that Co. owns and the stations to which it provides services under local services agreements operate in geographically diverse markets including California, New York, Michigan, Indiana, Minnesota and Illinois.

Recent Developments: For the quarter ended June 30 2006, loss from continuing operations was $32.4 million compared with a loss of $15.0 million in the year-earlier quarter. Net loss amounted to $31.4 million versus a net loss of $16.2 million in the year-earlier quarter. Revenues were $26.9 million, up 0.8% from $26.7 million the year before. Operating income was $2.0 million versus $3.3 million in the prior-year quarter, a decrease of 39.4%. Direct operating expenses declined 2.3% to $10.0 million from $10.2 million in the comparable period the year before. Indirect operating expenses increased 13.1% to $14.9 million from $13.2 million in the equivalent prior-year period.

Prospects: On Jul 18 2006, Co. terminated the previous agreements to sell its television stations KBWB Channel 20 in San Francisco, CA and WMYD Channel 20 in Detroit, MI to affiliates of DS Audible LLC. In this regard, Co. had the right to terminate these agreements, which were subjected to both sales occurring, if the sales did not close by June 30 2006. Thenceforth, Co. will retain its WMYD station, which will become an affiliate of My Network TV in September 2006 while continuing to market its KBWB station to interested parties. As such, Co. expects to report low double-digit net revenue growth for full-year 2006 that reflect the inclusion of WBNG into its operations for the first half of 2006.

Financial Data
(US$ in Thousands)

	6 Mos	3 Mos	12/31/2005	12/31/2004	12/31/2003	12/31/2002	12/31/2001	12/31/2000
Earnings Per Share	(5.62)	(4.87)	(5.08)	(4.30)	(3.15)	(4.13)	(5.89)	(3.10)
Cash Flow Per Share	(0.18)	(1.26)	(1.17)	(0.96)	(1.09)	(3.92)	(3.07)	0.07
Income Statement								
Total Revenue	51,677	21,006	86,160	113,765	108,544	135,344	113,075	140,070
EBITDA	(4,322)	(3,729)	(7,109)	(38,104)	(12,724)	211,874	(15,598)	22,475
Depn & Amortn	4,860	2,450	12,928	14,323	16,261	24,882	32,812	32,589
Income Before Taxes	(33,744)	(18,569)	(66,026)	(95,004)	(63,978)	140,149	(102,283)	(42,097)
Income Taxes	15,648	(142)	(695)	(11,714)	(17,030)	60,243	(26,745)	(10,876)
Net Income	(46,973)	(15,619)	(99,380)	(83,290)	(46,946)	(79,629)	(76,745)	(27,509)
Average Shares	19,802	19,694	19,558	19,365	18,990	19,098	18,568	18,203
Balance Sheet								
Total Assets	388,532	375,776	405,837	429,929	519,023	475,164	731,097	732,091
Current Liabilities	76,250	66,651	84,290	40,838	41,195	43,090	39,845	40,290
Long-Term Obligations	428,209	428,271	428,871	400,791	400,087	312,791	401,206	311,391
Total Liabilities	866,492	822,441	836,915	762,019	768,455	663,522	829,241	724,276
Stockholders' Equity	(477,961)	(446,665)	(431,077)	(332,090)	(249,430)	(188,358)	(98,142)	7,816
Shares Outstanding	19,956	19,756	19,578	19,382	19,012	18,760	18,626	18,179
Statistical Record								
EBITDA Margin %	N.M.	N.M.	N.M.	N.M.	N.M.	156.54	N.M.	16.05
Asset Turnover	0.22	0.23	0.21	0.24	0.22	0.22	0.15	0.19
Current Ratio	1.40	2.31	2.15	2.52	3.62	2.49	2.69	2.12
Debt to Equity	...	...	...	...	...	...	...	39.84
Price Range	0.45-0.11	0.45-0.11	0.45-0.15	0.50-0.13	...	...	...	...

Address: 767 Third Avenue, 34th Floor, New York, NY 10017 **Telephone:** 212-826-2530 **Fax:** 212-826-2858	**Web Site:** www.granitetv.com **Officers:** W. Don Cornwell - Chmn., C.E.O. Stuart J. Beck - Pres., Sec.	**Auditors:** Ernst & Young LLP **Investor Contact:** 212-826-2530

GREATER BAY BANCORP

Exchange	Symbol	Price	52Wk Range	Yield	P/E	Div Achiever
NMS	GBBK	$28.47 (8/31/2006)	30.73-22.73	2.21	15.47	10 Years

*7 Year Price Score 84.50 *NYSE Composite Index=100 *12 Month Price Score 102.17

Interim Earnings (Per Share)

Qtr.	Mar	Jun	Sep	Dec
2003	0.45	0.41	0.39	0.36
2004	0.43	0.43	0.40	0.24
2005	0.34	0.38	0.44	0.48
2006	0.46	0.46	...	...

Interim Dividends (Per Share)

Amt	Decl	Ex	Rec	Pay
0.15Q	9/28/2005	10/5/2005	10/7/2005	10/17/2005
0.15Q	12/21/2005	12/29/2005	1/3/2006	1/16/2006
0.158Q	3/29/2006	4/7/2006	4/11/2006	4/17/2006
0.158Q	6/28/2006	7/6/2006	7/10/2006	7/17/2006

Indicated Div: $0.63

Valuation Analysis

Forecast P/E	15.83 (9/9/2006)
Market Cap	$1.4 Billion
Book Value	814.7 Million
Price/Book	1.78
Price/Sales	2.27

Institutional Holding

No of Institutions	162
Shares	33,181,520
% Held	65.12

Business Summary: Commercial Banking (MIC: 8.1 SIC: 6021 NAIC: 522110)

Greater Bay Bancorp, with assets of $7.12 billion as of Dec 31 2005, is a financial holding company with one bank subsidiary, Greater Bay Bank, National Association, and one commercial insurance brokerage subsidiary, ABD Insurance and Financial Services. Co. provides a range of commercial banking and financial services to small- and medium-sized businesses, property managers, business executives, real estate developers, professionals and other individuals. Co. operates community banking offices throughout the San Francisco Bay area. ABD provides commercial insurance brokerage, employee benefits consulting and risk management services to business clients throughout the United States.

Recent Developments: For the quarter ended June 30 2006, net income increased 10.8% to $25.1 million from $22.7 million in the year-earlier quarter. Net interest income increased 0.6% to $65.8 million from $65.4 million in the year-earlier quarter. Credit for loan losses was $1.9 million versus a provision for loan losses of $2.3 million in the prior-year quarter. Non-interest income rose 4.7% to $56.8 million from $54.2 million, while non-interest expense advanced 4.1% to $84.5 million.

Prospects: Looking ahead to full year 2006, based on expectations of moderate economic growth in its primary market area, coupled with a planned increase in its lending and relationship management staff, Co. expects core loan portfolio growth in the mid to high single digit range. In addition, Co. estimates core deposit totals to remain flat for the balance of 2006 relative to the quarter end balance as of June 30 2006. Accordingly, for full year 2006, Co. anticipates its net interest margin to fluctuate in the 4.2% to 4.3% range. Furthermore, Co. projects net charge-offs from 15 basis points to 25 basis points of average loans outstanding for full year 2006.

Financial Data

(US$ in Thousands)	6 Mos	3 Mos	12/31/2005	12/31/2004	12/31/2003	12/31/2002	12/31/2001	12/31/2000
Earnings Per Share	1.84	1.76	1.64	1.50	1.62	2.30	1.57	1.35
Cash Flow Per Share	2.04	2.31	2.56	1.78	3.15	2.23	2.60	2.79
Tang Book Value Per Share	8.29	7.95	7.61	7.96	8.25	7.92	9.31	7.69
Dividends Per Share	0.608	0.600	0.600	0.570	0.540	0.490	0.430	0.350
Dividend Payout %	33.02	34.09	36.59	38.00	33.33	21.30	27.39	25.93
Income Statement								
Interest Income	212,075	103,754	390,783	376,499	407,719	505,412	507,241	368,363
Interest Expense	79,621	37,134	123,573	90,876	109,838	159,418	186,232	136,400
Net Interest Income	132,454	66,620	267,210	285,623	297,881	345,994	321,009	231,963
Provision for Losses	(7,890)	(6,004)	(13,269)	5,521	28,195	59,776	54,727	28,096
Non-Interest Income	116,803	60,033	211,932	186,585	171,542	155,510	44,842	45,525
Non-Interest Expense	176,600	92,114	336,061	314,315	292,208	245,401	204,840	152,714
Income Before Taxes	80,547	40,543	156,350	152,372	149,020	196,327	106,284	96,678
Income Taxes	29,658	14,772	59,123	59,453	57,017	72,053	26,468	38,138
Net Income	51,019	25,901	97,227	92,919	92,003	124,274	79,816	58,540
Average Shares	51,173	52,727	55,058	57,881	52,993	54,135	50,940	43,505
Balance Sheet								
Net Loans & Leases	4,702,924	4,655,156	4,645,810	4,361,603	4,411,639	4,661,547	4,370,977	3,517,408
Total Assets	7,369,654	7,108,506	7,120,969	6,932,057	7,601,423	8,075,727	7,877,054	5,130,378
Total Deposits	5,022,233	5,108,761	5,058,539	5,102,839	5,312,667	5,272,273	4,990,071	4,165,061
Total Liabilities	6,542,161	6,302,186	6,332,259	6,156,370	6,835,604	7,379,018	7,180,370	4,708,513
Stockholders' Equity	814,713	793,581	776,011	763,066	750,517	681,059	463,684	322,365
Shares Outstanding	50,916	50,288	49,906	51,179	52,529	51,577	49,831	41,929
Statistical Record								
Return on Assets %	1.47	1.49	1.38	1.28	1.17	1.56	1.23	1.51
Return on Equity %	13.59	13.56	12.63	12.24	12.85	21.71	20.31	24.17
Net Interest Margin %	60.78	64.21	68.38	75.86	73.06	68.46	63.29	62.97
Efficiency Ratio %	51.18	56.24	55.76	55.82	50.44	37.13	37.10	36.90
Loans to Deposits	0.94	0.91	0.92	0.85	0.83	0.88	0.88	0.84
Price Range	30.73-22.73	27.94-22.55	28.73-22.55	31.82-25.07	29.34-12.94	37.11-14.11	42.88-19.98	43.31-18.03
P/E Ratio	16.70-12.35	15.88-12.81	17.52-13.75	21.21-16.71	18.11-7.99	16.13-6.13	27.31-12.73	32.08-13.36
Average Yield %	2.28	2.38	2.33	2.00	2.67	1.90	1.59	1.34

| **Address:** 1900 University Ave., 6th Fl, EastPalo Alto, CA 94303
Telephone: 650-813-8200
Fax: 650-494-9190 | **Web Site:** www.gbbk.com
Officers: Byron A. Scordelis - Pres., C.E.O. Steven C. Smith - Exec. V.P., C.F.O., Chief Admin. Officer | **Auditors:** PricewaterhouseCoopers LLP
Transfer Agents: Wells Fargo Shareowners Services, South St. Paul, MN |

HARLEYSVILLE GROUP, INC. (PA)

Exchange	Symbol	Price	52Wk Range	Yield	P/E	Div Acheiver
NMS	HGIC	$35.99 (8/31/2006)	35.99-21.87	2.11	11.01	19 Years

*7 Year Price Score 97.74 *NYSE Composite Index=100 *12 Month Price Score 115.38

Interim Earnings (Per Share)

Qtr.	Mar	Jun	Sep	Dec
2003	(0.11)	0.33	(1.16)	(0.66)
2004	0.55	0.32	0.29	0.38
2005	0.39	0.48	0.54	0.60
2006	0.70	1.43	...	...

Interim Dividends (Per Share)

Amt	Decl	Ex	Rec	Pay
0.175Q	11/8/2005	12/13/2005	12/15/2005	12/30/2005
0.175Q	2/22/2006	3/13/2006	3/15/2006	3/30/2006
0.175Q	6/6/2006	6/13/2006	6/15/2006	6/30/2006
0.19Q	8/8/2006	9/13/2006	9/15/2006	9/29/2006

Indicated Div: $0.76 (Div. Reinv. Plan)

Valuation Analysis

		Institutional Holding	
Forecast P/E	13.45	No of Institutions	87
	(9/9/2006)	Shares	10,599,143
Market Cap	$1.1 Billion	% Held	34.06
Book Value	634.3 Million		
Price/Book	1.76		
Price/Sales	1.12		

Business Summary: Insurance (MIC: 8.2 SIC: 6331 NAIC: 524126)
Harleysville Group is an insurance holding company that engages, through its subsidiaries, in the property and casualty insurance business on a regional basis. Co. and Harleysville Mutual Insurance Company, which owned about 56% of Co.'s outstanding shares as of Dec 31 2005, operate together as a network of regional insurance companies that underwrite an array of personal and commercial coverages. The personal lines of insurance include both auto and homeowners, and the commercial lines include auto, commercial multi-peril and workers compensation. These insurance coverages are marketed primarily in the Eastern and Midwestern U.S. through about 1,600 insurance agencies.

Recent Developments: For the quarter ended June 30 2006, net income increased 207.9% to $44.7 million from $14.5 million in the year-earlier quarter. Revenues were $276.5 million, up 16.8% from $236.7 million the year before. Net premiums earned were $209.3 million versus $209.9 million in the prior-year quarter, a decrease of 0.3%. Net investment income rose 10.0% to $24.8 million from $22.6 million a year ago.

Prospects: Co.'s near-term outlook appears optimistic, reflecting steady improvement in its statutory combined ratio as well as a significant increase in its operating earnings. For the second half of 2006, Co.'s focus will continue to be on the basics of its business in order to generate additional improvement in its operations and realize its goals for 2006. In addition, Co. will maintain its discipline, despite the existing soft market, as it focuses on its goals of attaining a long-term underwriting profit and an operating return on equity of at least 12.0%. Furthermore, Co. will continue to work closely with its agency force in order to realize these objectives.

Financial Data
(US$ in Thousands)

	6 Mos	3 Mos	12/31/2005	12/31/2004	12/31/2003	12/31/2002	12/31/2001	12/31/2000
Earnings Per Share	3.27	2.32	2.01	1.55	(1.59)	1.53	1.46	1.67
Cash Flow Per Share	5.55	6.15	5.44	3.84	4.49	3.81	1.56	0.13
Tang Book Value Per Share	20.44	20.36	20.07	19.47	19.16	21.13	20.05	19.54
Dividends Per Share	0.700	0.695	0.690	0.680	0.670	0.630	0.580	0.550
Dividend Payout %	21.41	29.96	34.33	43.87	...	41.18	39.73	32.93
Income Statement								
Premium Income	417,665	208,345	841,567	837,665	823,407	764,636	729,889	688,330
Total Revenue	516,075	239,537	948,340	953,392	924,965	847,736	827,751	802,571
Benefits & Claims	271,038	135,989	567,396	605,660	727,875	521,617	519,822	492,801
Income Before Taxes	93,615	28,228	78,921	55,637	(89,450)	56,482	51,800	57,705
Income Taxes	28,177	7,520	17,490	8,759	(41,821)	10,227	8,307	9,013
Net Income	66,380	21,650	61,431	46,878	(47,629)	46,255	43,493	48,692
Average Shares	31,298	31,065	30,585	30,154	29,985	30,295	29,818	29,136
Balance Sheet								
Total Assets	2,902,123	2,874,375	2,905,266	2,718,063	2,680,389	2,311,524	2,045,290	2,021,862
Total Liabilities	2,267,861	2,247,654	2,290,883	2,130,139	2,107,642	1,679,412	1,454,992	1,455,281
Stockholders' Equity	634,262	626,721	614,383	587,924	572,747	632,112	590,298	566,581
Shares Outstanding	31,029	30,785	30,610	30,191	29,900	29,917	29,444	29,001
Statistical Record								
Return on Assets %	3.59	2.55	2.18	1.73	N.M.	2.12	2.14	2.40
Return on Equity %	16.40	11.78	10.22	8.06	N.M.	7.57	7.52	8.88
Loss Ratio %	64.89	65.27	67.42	72.30	88.40	68.22	71.22	71.59
Net Margin %	12.86	9.04	6.48	4.92	(5.15)	5.46	5.25	6.07
Price Range	31.72-20.78	30.01-18.90	27.80-18.90	24.96-17.84	27.50-18.99	31.44-19.90	30.00-20.40	29.81-11.81
P/E Ratio	9.70-6.35	12.94-8.15	13.83-9.40	16.10-11.51	...	20.55-13.01	20.55-13.97	17.85-7.07
Average Yield %	2.70	2.93	3.08	3.37	2.86	2.43	2.28	3.09

Address: 355 Maple Avenue, Harleysville, PA 19438-2297 **Telephone:** 215-256-5000 **Fax:** 215-256-5340	**Web Site:** www.harleysvillegroup.com **Officers:** William W. Scranton III - Chmn. Michael L. Browne - Pres., C.E.O.	**Auditors:** KPMG LLP **Investor Contact:** 215-256-5151 **Transfer Agents:** Mellon Investor Services, Ridgefield Park, NJ

HARLEYSVILLE NATIONAL CORP.

Exchange	Symbol	Price	52Wk Range	Yield	P/E	Div Achiever
NMS	HNBC	$20.67 (8/31/2006)	24.90-18.06	3.87	15.90	19 Years

*7 Year Price Score 93.92 *NYSE Composite Index=100 *12 Month Price Score 94.71

Interim Earnings (Per Share)

Qtr.	Mar	Jun	Sep	Dec
2003	0.30	0.32	0.32	0.29
2004	0.31	0.32	0.34	0.34
2005	0.31	0.33	0.34	0.33
2006	0.30	0.31	...	...

Interim Dividends (Per Share)

Amt	Decl	Ex	Rec	Pay
0.181Q	2/9/2006	2/24/2006	2/28/2006	3/15/2006
0.181Q	5/11/2006	5/26/2006	5/31/2006	6/15/2006
0.19Q	8/10/2006	8/29/2006	8/31/2006	9/15/2006
5%	8/10/2006	8/30/2006	9/1/2006	9/15/2006

Indicated Div: $0.80 (Div. Reinv. Plan)

Valuation Analysis
Forecast P/E   N/A
Market Cap $599.5 Million
Book Value   277.7 Million
Price/Book   2.16
Price/Sales   3.00

Institutional Holding
No of Institutions 59
Shares   5,537,907
% Held   19.08

Business Summary: Commercial Banking (MIC: 8.1 SIC: 6021 NAIC: 522110)

Harleysville National is the bank holding company for Harleysville National Bank and Trust Company. Co., through its subsidiary, provides a range of banking services including loans and deposits, investment management and trust and investment advisory services to individual and corporate customers located in eastern Pennsylvania. Co. also engages in the full-service commercial banking and trust business. As of Dec 31 2005, Co. had 45 branch offices located in Montgomery, Bucks, Chester, Berks, Carbon, Wayne, Monroe, Lehigh and Northampton counties, PA. At Dec 31 2005, Co. had total assets of $3.12 billion.

Recent Developments: For the quarter ended June 30 2006, net income decreased 4.2% to $9.3 million from $9.7 million in the year-earlier quarter. Net interest income decreased 2.6% to $21.3 million from $21.8 million in the year-earlier quarter. Provision for loan losses was $900,000 versus $650,000 in the prior-year quarter, an increase of 38.5%. Non-interest income rose 29.3% to $10.0 million from $7.8 million, while non-interest expense advanced 5.2% to $17.8 million.

Prospects: Co.'s net interest margin is being challenged by the rising interest rate environment, as deposit and short-term borrowing rates rise faster than loan rates. Nonetheless, Co. is encouraged by the significant improvement in its fee-based businesses within its wealth management division. Additionally, Co. is seeing promising growth in its core loan and deposit products, mainly in its real estate loan category and time deposits category, respectively. Separately, on Jul 26 2006, Co. entered into an agreement for the sale of its Honesdale branch located in Wayne County, PA to the First National Community Bank. The sale should allow Co. to better focus on expanding within its core markets.

Financial Data
(US$ in Thousands)

	6 Mos	3 Mos	12/31/2005	12/31/2004	12/31/2003	12/31/2002	12/31/2001	12/31/2000
Earnings Per Share	1.30	1.31	1.31	1.31	1.24	1.15	1.01	0.91
Cash Flow Per Share	1.25	0.98	1.24	1.74	1.72	1.17	1.54	1.24
Tang Book Value Per Share	7.85	7.94	8.25	8.07	8.23	7.49	6.77	6.11
Dividends Per Share	0.753	0.736	0.718	0.649	0.565	0.487	0.428	0.372
Dividend Payout %	58.16	56.26	54.62	49.67	45.42	42.23	42.21	40.92
Income Statement								
Interest Income	86,319	42,096	151,739	127,729	119,200	132,630	138,679	131,811
Interest Expense	43,572	20,625	64,618	42,638	40,079	52,610	64,937	65,774
Net Interest Income	42,747	21,471	87,121	85,091	79,121	80,020	73,742	66,037
Provision for Losses	2,100	1,200	3,401	2,555	3,200	4,370	3,930	2,312
Non-Interest Income	18,953	8,933	29,990	28,158	27,638	22,523	22,225	12,206
Non-Interest Expense	34,900	17,125	62,479	59,561	59,629	56,297	55,043	44,677
Income Before Taxes	24,700	12,079	51,231	51,133	43,930	41,876	36,994	31,254
Income Taxes	6,464	3,128	12,403	12,566	8,597	8,949	8,174	5,650
Net Income	18,236	8,951	38,828	38,567	35,333	32,927	28,820	25,604
Average Shares	29,351	29,379	29,490	29,465	28,505	28,507	28,505	28,197
Balance Sheet								
Net Loans & Leases	2,010,049	1,981,025	1,963,600	1,826,111	1,391,638	1,316,102	1,301,051	1,196,845
Total Assets	3,217,018	3,201,693	3,117,359	3,024,515	2,510,939	2,490,864	2,208,971	1,935,213
Total Deposits	2,479,658	2,425,673	2,365,457	2,212,563	1,979,081	1,979,822	1,746,862	1,489,050
Total Liabilities	2,939,281	2,921,704	2,844,127	2,753,983	2,283,886	2,284,658	2,019,622	1,761,677
Stockholders' Equity	277,737	279,989	273,232	270,532	227,053	206,206	189,349	173,536
Shares Outstanding	29,001	28,954	28,807	28,970	27,603	27,534	27,779	28,136
Statistical Record								
Return on Assets %	1.22	1.24	1.26	1.39	1.41	1.40	1.39	1.43
Return on Equity %	13.81	14.07	14.28	15.46	16.31	16.65	15.88	16.84
Net Interest Margin %	48.11	51.00	57.42	66.62	66.38	60.33	53.17	50.10
Efficiency Ratio %	32.77	33.56	34.38	38.21	40.61	36.28	34.21	31.02
Loans to Deposits	0.81	0.82	0.83	0.83	0.70	0.66	0.74	0.80
Price Range	24.90-18.06	24.90-17.83	24.13-17.83	26.93-19.26	28.05-16.46	18.53-14.53	17.07-7.49	11.41-7.44
P/E Ratio	19.16-13.89	19.01-13.61	18.42-13.61	20.55-14.71	22.62-13.28	16.11-12.64	16.90-7.41	12.54-8.18
Average Yield %	3.73	3.61	3.48	2.81	2.78	2.95	3.11	3.99

Address: 483 Main Street, P.O. Box 195, Harleysville, PA 19438
Telephone: 215-256-8851

Web Site: www.hncbank.com
Officers: Walter E. Daller Jr. - Chmn. Gregg J. Wagner - Pres., C.E.O.

Auditors: Grant Thornton LLP
Investor Contact: 888-462-2100
Transfer Agents: American Stock Transfer & Trust Company, New York, NY

HUDSON CITY BANCORP, INC.

Exchange	Symbol	Price	52Wk Range	Yield	P/E
NMS	HCBK	$13.06 (8/31/2006)	14.00-11.30	2.30	24.64

*7 Year Price Score 136.58 *NYSE Composite Index=100 *12 Month Price Score 100.09

Interim Earnings (Per Share)
Qtr.	Mar	Jun	Sep	Dec
2003	0.09	0.09	0.08	0.09
2004	0.09	0.10	0.11	0.11
2005	0.11	0.11	0.13	0.14
2006	0.13	0.13	...	...

Interim Dividends (Per Share)
Amt	Decl	Ex	Rec	Pay
0.07Q	10/18/2005	11/2/2005	11/4/2005	12/1/2005
0.075Q	1/17/2006	2/1/2006	2/3/2006	3/1/2006
0.075Q	4/18/2006	5/3/2006	5/5/2006	6/1/2006
0.075Q	7/19/2006	8/2/2006	8/4/2006	9/1/2006

Indicated Div: $0.30

Valuation Analysis
Forecast P/E	24.94 (9/9/2006)
Market Cap	$7.5 Billion
Book Value	5.0 Billion
Price/Book	1.49
Price/Sales	5.35

Institutional Holding
No of Institutions	243
Shares	315,732,608
% Held	N/A

Business Summary: Other Depository Banking (MIC: 8.5 SIC: 6036 NAIC: 522120)

Hudson City Bancorp is a holding company. Co.'s subsidiary, Hudson City Savings Bank, is a community- and customer-oriented retail savings bank offering traditional deposit products, residential real estate mortgage loans and consumer loans. In addition, Co. purchases mortgages, mortgage-backed securities, securities issued by the U.S. government and government-sponsored agencies and other investments. As of Dec 31 2005, Co. had 84 branches located in 15 counties throughout the State of New Jersey, four branch offices located in Suffolk County, NY and two branch offices in Richmond County (Staten Island), NY. As of Dec 31 2005, Co. had total assets of $28.08 billion.

Recent Developments: For the quarter ended June 30 2006, net income increased 13.8% to $73.2 million from $64.3 million in the year-earlier quarter. Net interest income increased 16.6% to $153.6 million from $131.7 million in the year-earlier quarter. Non-interest income rose 16.9% to $1.5 million from $1.2 million, while non-interest expense advanced 27.3% to $38.5 million.

Prospects: Co. intends to grow its assets during the second half of 2006 primarily the origination and purchase of mortgage loans, while purchasing investment and mortgage-backed securities as a supplement to its investments in mortgage loans. Also, Co. plans that approximately half of the growth in interest-earning assets will be short-term or variable-rate in nature, in order to assist in the management of its interest rate risk. Meanwhile, Co. intends to grow customer deposits by offering products at competitive but prudent rates and by opening new branch offices. Separately, on Jul 14 2006, Co. announced that it has completed its $265.0 million acquisition of Sound Federal Bancorp Inc.

Financial Data
(US$ in Thousands)

	6 Mos	3 Mos	12/31/2005	12/31/2004	12/31/2003	12/31/2002	12/31/2001	12/31/2000
Earnings Per Share	0.53	0.51	0.48	0.40	0.35	0.32	0.21	0.16
Cash Flow Per Share	0.40	0.55	0.50	0.51	0.42	0.36	0.26	0.17
Tang Book Value Per Share	8.75	8.80	8.83	2.35	2.18	2.14	2.03	2.11
Dividends Per Share	0.290	0.281	0.268	0.218	0.162	0.108	0.073	0.045
Dividend Payout %	54.72	55.00	55.81	54.26	46.85	34.16	34.81	27.88

Income Statement

Interest Income	743,828	359,688	1,178,908	915,058	777,328	784,217	690,498	614,041
Interest Expense	432,560	202,009	616,774	430,066	376,354	395,774	403,427	360,039
Net Interest Income	311,268	157,679	562,134	484,992	400,974	388,443	287,071	254,002
Provision for Losses	...	...	65	790	900	1,500	1,875	2,130
Non-Interest Income	2,719	1,264	8,007	16,557	29,664	8,013	4,694	4,541
Non-Interest Expense	76,800	38,285	127,703	118,348	102,527	93,541	81,824	78,997
Income Before Taxes	237,187	120,658	442,373	382,411	327,211	301,415	208,066	177,416
Income Taxes	88,791	45,430	166,318	143,145	119,801	109,382	73,517	62,590
Net Income	148,396	75,228	276,055	239,266	207,410	192,033	134,549	114,826
Average Shares	552,077	561,308	581,063	593,000	601,681	609,157	637,953	705,119

Balance Sheet

Net Loans & Leases	16,954,111	16,012,234	15,036,709	11,327,647	8,766,264	6,931,891	5,932,101	4,841,041
Total Assets	31,329,322	29,675,576	28,075,353	20,145,981	17,033,360	14,144,604	11,426,768	9,380,373
Total Deposits	11,613,829	11,521,708	11,383,300	11,477,300	10,453,780	9,138,629	7,912,762	6,604,121
Total Liabilities	26,330,667	24,563,137	22,873,877	18,743,097	15,703,994	12,828,521	10,138,032	7,915,804
Stockholders' Equity	4,998,655	5,112,439	5,201,476	1,402,884	1,329,366	1,316,083	1,288,736	1,464,569
Shares Outstanding	571,475	581,199	588,905	596,784	608,614	615,466	635,805	694,806

Statistical Record

Return on Assets %	1.04	1.14	1.14	1.28	1.33	1.50	1.29	1.28
Return on Equity %	5.70	8.83	8.36	17.47	15.68	14.74	9.77	7.78
Net Interest Margin %	39.98	43.84	47.68	53.00	51.58	49.53	41.57	41.37
Efficiency Ratio %	9.99	10.61	10.76	12.70	12.70	11.81	11.77	12.77
Loans to Deposits	1.46	1.39	1.32	0.99	0.84	0.76	0.75	0.73
Price Range	14.00-11.30	13.50-10.17	12.55-10.17	12.60-10.21	11.93-5.81	6.54-4.11	4.12-2.86	3.16-1.98
P/E Ratio	26.42-21.32	26.47-19.94	26.15-21.18	31.51-25.53	34.09-16.60	20.45-12.83	19.60-13.60	19.74-12.37
Average Yield %	2.32	2.37	2.34	1.93	1.96	1.96	2.10	1.77

Address: West 80 Century Road, Paramus, NJ 07652 **Telephone:** 201-967-1900 **Fax:** 201-967-0559	**Auditors:** KPMG LLP **Investor Contact:** 201-967-8290 **Transfer Agents:** Mellon Investor Services LLC, Ridgefield Park, NJ
Web Site: www.HudsonCitySavingsBank.com **Officers:** Leonard S. Gudelski - Chmn. Ronald E. Hermance Jr. - Pres., C.E.O.	

HUNT (J.B.) TRANSPORT SERVICES, INC.

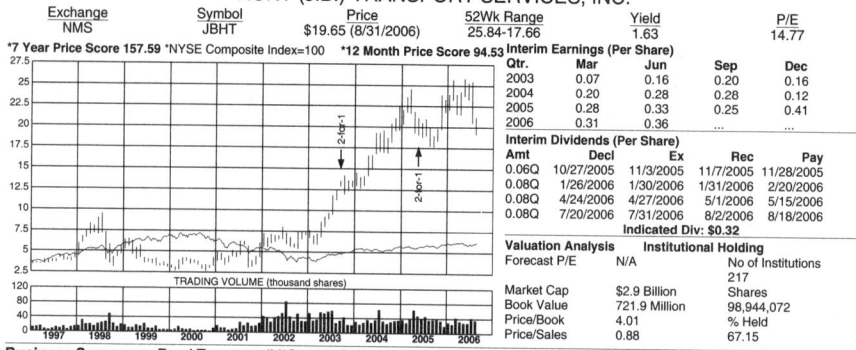

Exchange	Symbol	Price	52Wk Range	Yield	P/E
NMS	JBHT	$19.65 (8/31/2006)	25.84-17.66	1.63	14.77

*7 Year Price Score 157.59 *NYSE Composite Index=100 *12 Month Price Score 94.53

Interim Earnings (Per Share)

Qtr.	Mar	Jun	Sep	Dec
2003	0.07	0.16	0.20	0.16
2004	0.20	0.28	0.28	0.12
2005	0.28	0.33	0.25	0.41
2006	0.31	0.36	...	...

Interim Dividends (Per Share)

Amt	Decl	Ex	Rec	Pay
0.06Q	10/27/2005	11/3/2005	11/7/2005	11/28/2005
0.08Q	1/26/2006	1/30/2006	1/31/2006	2/20/2006
0.08Q	4/24/2006	4/27/2006	5/1/2006	5/15/2006
0.08Q	7/20/2006	7/31/2006	8/2/2006	8/18/2006

Indicated Div: $0.32

Valuation Analysis

Forecast P/E N/A
Market Cap $2.9 Billion
Book Value 721.9 Million
Price/Book 4.01
Price/Sales 0.88

Institutional Holding

No of Institutions 217
Shares 98,944,072
% Held 67.15

Business Summary: Road Transport (MIC: 15.2 SIC: 4213 NAIC: 484121)

J.B. Hunt Transport Services is holding company that, together with its wholly owned subsidiaries and associated companies, provides a wide range of transportation services to a diverse group of customers throughout the U.S. continental, Canada and Mexico. Co.'s service offerings include transportation of full truckload containerizable freight, which Co. directly transports utilizing company-controlled revenue equipment and company drivers or independent contractors. Co. also provides customized freight movement, revenue equipment, labor and systems services that are tailored to meet individual customers' requirements and typically involve long-term contracts.

Recent Developments: For the quarter ended June 30 2006, net income increased 1.3% to $55.3 million from $54.6 million in the year-earlier quarter. Revenues were $838.3 million, up 10.4% from $759.2 million the year before. Operating income was $95.4 million versus $93.0 million in the prior-year quarter, an increase of 2.6%. Direct operating expenses rose 16.4% to $435.4 million from $374.0 million in the comparable period the year before. Indirect operating expenses increased 5.2% to $307.4 million from $292.2 million in the equivalent prior-year period.

Prospects: Co.'s outlook appears favorable, reflecting recent improved operating results across all three of its business segments. Specifically, Co. is seeing an increase in its operating revenue primarily attributable to growth in its fleet of trucks, containers and trailers to support its additional Intermodal and Dedicated Contract Services businesses. During the second quarter of 2006, Co. added a total of 150 trucks to its fleet, bringing the net increase in total trucks for 2006 to 232 incremental units compared with the same period last year. Meanwhile, Co. noted that cost increases continue to be covered by higher freight rates across all of its business segments.

Financial Data
(US$ in Thousands)

	6 Mos	3 Mos	12/31/2005	12/31/2004	12/31/2003	12/31/2002	12/31/2001	12/31/2000
Earnings Per Share	1.33	1.30	1.28	0.88	0.58	0.33	0.23	0.26
Cash Flow Per Share	2.91	2.71	2.11	2.43	2.09	1.15	1.20	0.88
Tang Book Value Per Share	4.90	5.57	5.31	5.29	4.39	3.75	3.18	3.04
Dividends Per Share	0.280	0.260	0.240	0.045	...	...	...	0.013
Dividend Payout %	21.05	20.00	18.75	5.14	...	...	...	4.90
Income Statement								
Total Revenue	1,618,154	779,900	3,127,899	2,786,154	2,433,469	2,247,886	2,100,305	2,160,447
EBITDA	262,626	124,331	502,225	457,596	335,280	245,583	213,137	202,634
Depn & Amortn	88,050	43,530	163,034	149,843	150,339	145,973	143,011	134,446
Income Before Taxes	171,006	80,295	333,626	302,279	167,729	74,847	43,082	42,441
Income Taxes	66,692	31,315	126,315	156,023	72,270	23,031	10,137	6,366
Net Income	104,314	48,980	207,311	146,256	95,459	51,816	32,945	36,075
Average Shares	154,619	158,245	162,559	166,936	163,708	156,168	144,796	141,668
Balance Sheet								
Total Assets	1,544,524	1,522,901	1,548,874	1,491,706	1,347,071	1,318,728	1,260,298	1,231,921
Long-Term Obligations	177,000	47,400	124,000	...	...	218,967	353,607	300,388
Total Liabilities	822,632	662,430	731,849	630,756	643,935	728,241	801,981	803,918
Stockholders' Equity	721,892	860,471	817,025	860,950	703,136	590,487	458,317	428,003
Shares Outstanding	147,356	154,407	153,813	162,786	160,220	157,270	143,915	140,857
Statistical Record								
Return on Assets %	13.92	13.91	13.64	10.28	7.16	4.02	2.64	3.05
Return on Equity %	26.90	25.14	24.71	18.65	14.76	9.88	7.43	8.68
EBITDA Margin %	16.23	15.94	16.06	16.42	13.78	10.93	10.15	9.38
Net Margin %	6.45	6.28	6.63	5.25	3.92	2.31	1.57	1.67
Asset Turnover	2.18	2.13	2.06	1.96	1.84	1.74	1.69	1.83
Price Range	25.84-17.66	25.74-17.66	24.60-17.66	22.50-12.71	14.20-5.89	8.05-5.39	6.29-3.09	4.30-2.66
P/E Ratio	19.43-13.28	19.80-13.58	19.22-13.80	25.57-14.44	24.48-10.15	24.39-16.35	27.34-13.45	16.53-10.22
Average Yield %	1.28	1.24	1.16	0.26	...	...	...	0.36

Address: 615 J.B. Hunt Corporate Drive, Lowell, AR 72745
Telephone: 501-820-0000
Fax: 479-820-8397

Web Site: www.jbhunt.com
Officers: Wayne Garrison - Chmn. J. Byan Hunt Jr. - Sr. Chmn.

Auditors: Ernst & Young LLP
Investor Contact: 479-820-8110
Transfer Agents: EquiServe Trust Company

HUNTINGTON BANCSHARES, INC

Exchange	Symbol	Price	52Wk Range	Yield	P/E
NMS	HBAN	$23.92 (8/31/2006)	24.73-21.19	4.18	13.14

*7 Year Price Score 92.54   *NYSE Composite Index=100   *12 Month Price Score 99.05

Interim Earnings (Per Share)

Qtr.	Mar	Jun	Sep	Dec
2003	0.38	0.42	0.39	0.40
2004	0.45	0.47	0.40	0.39
2005	0.41	0.45	0.47	0.44
2006	0.45	0.46	...	...

Interim Dividends (Per Share)

Amt	Decl	Ex	Rec	Pay
0.215Q	10/18/2005	12/14/2005	12/16/2005	1/3/2006
0.25Q	1/18/2006	3/15/2006	3/17/2006	4/3/2006
0.25Q	4/20/2006	6/14/2006	6/16/2006	7/3/2006
0.25Q	7/18/2006	9/13/2006	9/15/2006	10/2/2006

Indicated Div: $1.00

Valuation Analysis
Forecast P/E 13.11 (9/9/2006)
Market Cap $5.7 Billion
Book Value 2.9 Billion
Price/Book 1.93
Price/Sales 2.29

Institutional Holding
No of Institutions 270
Shares 102,228,680
% Held 43.04

Business Summary: Commercial Banking (MIC: 8.1 SIC: 6021 NAIC: 522110)
Huntington Bancshares is a multi-state bank holding company with total assets of $32.76 billion and total deposits of $22.41 billion as of Dec 31 2005. Co.'s subsidiaries are engaged in full-service commercial and consumer banking, mortgage banking, automobile financing, equipment leasing, investment management, trust services, discount brokerage services, underwriting credit life and disability insurance, and selling other insurance and financial products and services. As of Dec 31 2005, Co. had 344 domestic banking offices located in Florida, Indiana, Kentucky, Michigan, Ohio and West Virginia. Co. also has international offices located in the Cayman Islands and Hong Kong.

Recent Developments: For the quarter ended June 30 2006, net income increased 4.9% to $111.6 million from $106.4 million in the year-earlier quarter. Net interest income increased 8.4% to $262.2 million from $241.9 million in the year-earlier quarter. Provision for loan losses was $15.7 million versus $12.9 million in the prior-year quarter, an increase of 22.1%. Non-interest income rose 4.4% to $163.0 million from $156.2 million, while non-interest expense advanced 1.7% to $252.4 million.

Prospects: Co.'s near-term prospects appear constructive, reflecting solid improvement in its commercial loan pipeline. Accordingly, Co. believes that its commercial loan growth will improve going forward. Meanwhile, Co. continues to experience increases in retail banking households, as well as commercial and small business relationships. For the full year of 2006, Co. is expecting earnings to be in the range of $1.78 to $1.84 per share. Separately, on Mar 1 2006, Co. announced that it has completed its acquisition of Unizan Financial Corp. in a transaction valued at approximately $610.0 million.

Financial Data
(US$ in Thousands)

	6 Mos	3 Mos	12/31/2005	12/31/2004	12/31/2003	12/31/2002	12/31/2001	12/31/2000
Earnings Per Share	1.82	1.81	1.77	1.71	1.61	1.49	0.71	1.32
Cash Flow Per Share	2.82	1.26	2.93	2.29	5.83	2.79	0.56	2.31
Tang Book Value Per Share	9.70	9.95	10.44	10.02	8.99	8.95	6.77	9.43
Dividends Per Share	0.930	0.895	0.845	0.750	0.670	0.640	0.720	0.764
Dividend Payout %	51.10	49.45	47.74	43.86	41.61	42.95	101.41	57.85
Income Statement								
Interest Income	986,690	464,787	1,641,765	1,347,315	1,305,756	1,531,585	1,939,519	2,108,505
Interest Expense	480,815	221,107	679,354	435,941	456,770	547,783	943,337	1,166,073
Net Interest Income	505,875	243,680	962,411	911,374	848,986	983,802	996,182	942,432
Provision for Losses	35,285	19,540	81,299	55,062	163,993	227,340	308,793	90,479
Non-Interest Income	322,553	159,534	632,282	818,598	1,069,153	684,811	509,480	493,559
Non-Interest Expense	490,774	238,415	969,820	1,122,244	1,214,909	852,048	1,023,587	885,617
Income Before Taxes	302,369	145,259	543,574	552,666	523,987	589,225	173,282	459,895
Income Taxes	86,309	40,803	131,483	153,741	138,294	226,000	(5,239)	131,449
Net Income	216,060	104,456	412,091	398,925	372,363	363,225	178,521	328,446
Average Shares	244,538	234,371	233,475	233,856	231,582	244,012	251,715	249,570
Balance Sheet								
Net Loans & Leases	26,067,064	25,861,750	24,203,819	23,289,066	20,739,864	20,587,530	21,191,301	20,312,311
Total Assets	36,265,777	35,665,909	32,764,805	32,565,497	30,483,804	27,578,710	28,500,159	28,599,377
Total Deposits	24,592,932	24,555,163	22,409,675	20,768,161	18,487,395	17,499,326	20,187,304	19,777,245
Total Liabilities	33,326,621	32,585,729	30,207,304	30,027,859	28,208,802	25,274,875	26,083,719	26,233,330
Stockholders' Equity	2,939,156	3,080,180	2,557,501	2,537,638	2,275,002	2,303,831	2,416,440	2,366,047
Shares Outstanding	237,361	245,183	224,106	231,605	229,008	232,878	251,193	250,859
Statistical Record								
Return on Assets %	1.23	1.24	1.26	1.26	1.28	1.30	0.63	1.14
Return on Equity %	15.27	14.82	16.18	16.53	16.26	15.39	7.47	14.40
Net Interest Margin %	50.24	52.43	58.62	67.64	65.02	64.23	51.36	44.70
Efficiency Ratio %	36.84	38.19	42.65	51.81	51.16	38.44	41.80	34.04
Loans to Deposits	1.06	1.05	1.08	1.12	1.12	1.18	1.05	1.03
Price Range	25.40-21.19	25.40-21.19	25.40-21.19	25.17-21.06	22.50-17.99	20.94-16.20	19.14-12.94	21.70-12.81
P/E Ratio	13.96-11.64	14.03-11.71	14.35-11.97	14.72-12.32	13.98-11.17	14.05-10.87	26.96-18.22	16.44-9.71
Average Yield %	3.92	3.77	3.57	3.23	3.33	3.35	4.50	4.54

Address: 41 South High Street, Columbus, OH 43287
Telephone: 614-480-8300
Fax: 614-480-3761

Web Site: www.huntington.com
Officers: Thomas E. Hoaglin - Chmn., Pres., C.E.O.
Michael J. McMennamin - Vice-Chmn., Treas.

Auditors: Deloitte & Touche LLP
Investor Contact: 614-480-5676
Transfer Agents: ComputerShare Investor Services, Chicago, IL

IAC/INTERACTIVECORP

Exchange	Symbol	Price	52Wk Range	Yield	P/E
NMS	IACI	$28.48 (8/31/2006)	31.24-23.62	N/A	34.73

*7 Year Price Score 77.38 *NYSE Composite Index=100 *12 Month Price Score 92.71

Interim Earnings (Per Share)

Qtr.	Mar	Jun	Sep	Dec
2003	(0.46)	0.32	0.04	0.48
2004	0.10	0.18	0.24	(0.14)
2005	0.18	1.78	0.19	0.32
2006	0.14	0.17	...	...

Interim Dividends (Per Share)
No Dividends Paid

Valuation Analysis
Forecast P/E   N/A
Market Cap $8.8 Billion
Book Value   8.9 Billion
Price/Book   0.99
Price/Sales   1.39

Institutional Holding
No of Institutions   307
Shares   233,290,336
% Held   78.21

Business Summary: Media (MIC: 13.1 SIC: 4833 NAIC: 454111)

IAC InterActiveCorp operates a diversified portfolio of specialized and global brands in the following sectors: Retailing, which includes the U.S. and International reporting segments; Services, which includes the Ticketing, Lending, Real Estate, Teleservices and Home Services reporting segments; Media & Advertising; and Membership & Subscriptions, which includes the Vacations, Personals and Discounts reporting segments.

Recent Developments: For the quarter ended June 30 2006, income from continuing operations decreased 85.5% to $59.1 million from $408.7 million in the year-earlier quarter. Net income decreased 91.3% to $53.8 million from $621.4 million in the year-earlier quarter. Revenues were $1.61 billion, up 17.5% from $1.37 billion the year before. Operating income was $81.2 million versus $65.6 million in the prior-year quarter, an increase of 23.8%. Direct operating expenses rose 11.1% to $856.2 million from $770.4 million in the comparable period the year before. Indirect operating expenses increased 26.0% to $674.9 million from $535.8 million in the equivalent prior-year period.

Prospects: Co.'s operating outlook appears to be positive, given favorable top-line growth exhibited across all its business sectors. In particular, Co. is experiencing a significant growth in its Media & Advertising sector, primarily attributable to the inclusion of its 2005 acquisition of IAC Search & Media as well as an increase in traffic at its Citysearch website, which favorably affected its pay-for-performance revenue. Meanwhile, Co.'s Services sector has improved substantially, as a result of growth at its Ticketmaster web-based business, due to higher domestic concert and sporting event ticket sales and international expansion.

Financial Data
(US$ in Thousands)

	6 Mos	3 Mos	12/31/2005	12/31/2004	12/31/2003	12/31/2002	12/31/2001	12/31/2000
Earnings Per Share	0.82	2.43	2.46	0.40	0.46	9.08	1.20	(0.82)
Cash Flow Per Share	0.44	0.81	2.07	3.65	4.35	3.48	3.58	2.07
Tang Book Value Per Share	0.26	1.25	1.01	2.40	1.75	3.00	N.M.	N.M.
Income Statement								
Total Revenue	3,159,673	1,550,578	5,753,671	6,192,680	6,328,118	4,621,224	5,284,807	4,601,492
EBITDA	321,383	150,628	1,263,931	801,356	620,439	300,633	1,557,939	1,514,476
Depn & Amortn	145,450	72,013	335,676	526,971	440,957	323,402	1,376,337	1,408,853
Income Before Taxes	183,380	82,419	991,685	378,670	262,391	47,028	133,164	71,405
Income Taxes	77,176	34,376	391,069	179,186	70,691	5,572	108,877	112,869
Net Income	100,991	47,183	876,150	164,861	167,396	1,953,103	383,608	(147,983)
Average Shares	324,297	337,315	356,618	371,211	321,665	213,158	187,050	179,844
Balance Sheet								
Total Assets	13,429,928	13,743,974	13,917,765	22,398,865	21,586,588	15,663,113	11,703,052	10,473,870
Current Liabilities	2,201,827	2,144,709	2,232,997	2,645,715	1,878,181	1,541,456	1,595,296	1,173,247
Long-Term Obligations	858,063	881,978	959,410	796,715	1,120,097	1,211,145	544,667	552,501
Total Liabilities	4,505,601	4,471,432	4,686,937	7,793,561	7,171,003	7,731,650	7,757,551	7,033,999
Stockholders' Equity	8,924,327	9,272,542	9,230,828	14,605,304	14,415,585	7,931,463	3,945,501	3,439,871
Shares Outstanding	310,303	319,041	317,821	348,824	347,826	225,164	188,868	184,234
Statistical Record								
Return on Assets %	1.61	4.60	4.83	0.75	0.90	14.27	3.46	N.M.
Return on Equity %	2.45	7.13	7.35	1.13	1.50	32.89	10.39	N.M.
EBITDA Margin %	10.17	9.71	21.97	12.94	9.80	6.51	29.48	32.91
Net Margin %	3.20	3.04	15.23	2.66	2.65	42.26	7.26	N.M.
Asset Turnover	0.36	0.36	0.32	0.28	0.34	0.34	0.48	0.47
Current Ratio	1.66	1.83	1.79	1.85	2.24	3.00	1.87	1.51
Debt to Equity	0.10	0.10	0.10	0.05	0.08	0.15	0.14	0.16
Price Range	31.24-23.62	31.24-23.76	30.68-23.42	38.74-21.30	47.47-23.31	37.04-18.02	31.14-18.38	31.48-18.67
P/E Ratio	38.10-28.80	12.86-9.78	12.47-9.52	96.85-53.26	103.20-50.68	4.08-1.98	25.95-15.32	...

Address: 152 West 57th Street, New York, NY 10019
Telephone: 212-314-7300
Fax: 212-314-7399

Web Site: www.iac.com
Officers: Barry Diller - Chmn., C.E.O. Victor A. Kaufman - Vice-Chmn.

Auditors: Ernst & Young LLP, IACís
Investor Contact: 212-314-7300
Transfer Agents: The Bank of New York

IBERIABANK CORP

Exchange	Symbol	Price	52Wk Range	Yield	P/E	Div Acheiver
NMS	IBKC	$58.30 (8/31/2006)	61.41-48.19	2.06	24.81	10 Years

*7 Year Price Score 129.53 *NYSE Composite Index=100 *12 Month Price Score 101.89

Interim Earnings (Per Share)

Qtr.	Mar	Jun	Sep	Dec
2003	0.66	0.68	0.69	0.70
2004	0.72	0.70	0.78	0.81
2005	0.75	0.82	(0.15)	0.80
2006	0.81	0.89	...	...

Interim Dividends (Per Share)

Amt	Decl	Ex	Rec	Pay
0.26Q	9/19/2005	9/28/2005	9/30/2005	10/19/2005
0.28Q	11/22/2005	12/28/2005	12/30/2005	1/19/2006
0.28Q	3/23/2006	3/29/2006	3/31/2006	4/20/2006
0.30Q	6/20/2006	6/28/2006	6/30/2006	7/17/2006

Indicated Div: $1.20

Valuation Analysis
Forecast P/E 16.71 (9/9/2006)
Market Cap $563.4 Million
Book Value 266.4 Million
Price/Book 2.12
Price/Sales 3.26

Institutional Holding
No of Institutions 82
Shares 5,258,368
% Held 54.38

Business Summary: Commercial Banking (MIC: 8.1 SIC: 6022 NAIC: 522110)

IBERIABANK is the bank holding company for IBERIABANK, a Louisiana chartered commercial bank. The Bank operates 44 full service offices in its market areas, including New Orleans, Baton Rouge, Shreveport, Monroe, and the Acadiana region of Louisiana. Co. provides a variety of financial services to individuals and businesses throughout its service area. Primary deposit products are checking, savings and certificate of deposit accounts and primary lending products are consumer, commercial and mortgage loans. Co. also offers discount brokerage services and insurance services to its clients. At Dec 31 2005, Co. had total assets of $2.85 billion and total deposits of $2.24 billion.

Recent Developments: For the quarter ended June 30 2006, net income increased 8.9% to $8.9 million from $8.1 million in the year-earlier quarter. Net interest income increased 7.0% to $22.8 million from $21.3 million in the year-earlier quarter. Credit for loan losses was $1.9 million versus a provision for loan losses of $630,000 in the prior-year quarter. Non-interest income fell 22.0% to $5.3 million from $6.7 million, while non-interest expense advanced 8.8% to $17.5 million.

Prospects: On Jul 27 2006, Co. announced signing of a definitive agreement to acquire Pocahontas Bancorp Inc. (Pocahontas) of Jonesboro, AR for a purchase price of $76.3 million. At June 30 2006, Pocahontas's had total assets of $733.0 million, including loans totaling $429.0 million and deposits of $535.0 million. Under the terms of the agreement, shareholders of Pocahontas will receive 0.2781 share of Co.'s common stock per outstanding share of Pocahontas common stock. Co. expects this acquisition to further expand its presence into Northeast Arkansas. This transaction is expected to be completed prior to year-end 2006, subject to regulatory and Pocahontas shareholder approval.

Financial Data (US$ in Thousands)	6 Mos	3 Mos	12/31/2005	12/31/2004	12/31/2003	12/31/2002	12/31/2001	12/31/2000
Earnings Per Share	2.35	2.28	2.24	3.01	2.74	2.42	1.89	1.70
Cash Flow Per Share	4.66	3.76	4.57	3.97	4.79	5.19	0.24	3.15
Tang Book Value Per Share	17.92	18.09	17.85	18.06	16.15	14.59	13.20	11.28
Dividends Per Share	1.120	1.060	1.004	0.848	0.720	0.608	0.560	0.528
Dividend Payout %	47.66	46.49	44.82	28.19	26.32	25.17	29.66	31.13
Income Statement								
Interest Income	77,380	37,588	135,329	108,610	96,562	87,552	100,368	104,046
Interest Expense	32,205	15,168	50,531	33,982	28,929	27,958	46,018	52,730
Net Interest Income	45,175	22,420	84,798	74,628	67,633	59,594	54,350	51,316
Provision for Losses	(1,467)	435	17,069	4,041	6,300	6,197	5,046	3,861
Non-Interest Income	11,525	6,266	26,141	23,217	23,064	17,866	15,144	12,738
Non-Interest Expense	34,577	17,114	64,438	54,897	50,629	44,032	41,711	39,704
Income Before Taxes	23,590	11,137	29,432	38,907	33,768	27,231	22,737	20,489
Income Taxes	6,689	3,091	7,432	11,568	10,216	8,778	8,229	7,514
Net Income	16,901	8,046	22,000	27,339	23,552	18,453	14,508	12,975
Average Shares	9,939	9,884	9,812	9,092	8,606	7,649	7,678	7,641
Balance Sheet								
Net Loans & Leases	1,996,717	1,917,523	1,880,434	1,630,510	1,394,119	1,031,391	944,898	930,286
Total Assets	2,977,609	2,926,353	2,852,592	2,448,602	2,115,811	1,570,588	1,426,825	1,396,162
Total Deposits	2,368,894	2,326,058	2,242,956	1,773,489	1,589,106	1,242,232	1,237,394	1,143,187
Total Liabilities	2,711,227	2,657,857	2,589,023	2,228,440	1,920,642	1,430,990	1,292,408	1,269,120
Stockholders' Equity	266,382	268,496	263,569	220,162	195,169	139,598	134,417	127,042
Shares Outstanding	9,664	9,692	9,548	8,605	8,398	7,141	7,485	7,823
Statistical Record								
Return on Assets %	0.83	0.80	0.83	1.19	1.28	1.23	1.03	0.94
Return on Equity %	8.85	8.52	9.10	13.13	14.07	13.47	11.10	10.60
Net Interest Margin %	57.04	59.65	62.66	68.71	70.04	68.07	54.15	49.32
Efficiency Ratio %	38.67	39.02	39.91	41.64	42.32	41.77	36.11	34.00
Loans to Deposits	0.84	0.82	0.84	0.92	0.88	0.83	0.76	0.81
Price Range	61.41-48.19	59.06-44.26	56.20-44.26	53.68-42.93	48.16-30.45	32.80-21.88	24.10-16.20	17.40-9.05
P/E Ratio	26.13-20.51	25.90-19.41	25.09-19.76	17.83-14.26	17.58-11.11	13.55-9.04	12.75-8.57	10.24-5.32
Average Yield %	2.04	2.04	2.00	1.80	1.89	2.09	2.63	4.15

Address: 200 West Congress Street, Lafayette, LA 70501 Telephone: 337-521-4003	Web Site: www.iberiabank.com Officers: William H. Fenstermaker - Chmn. Darryl G. Byrd - Pres., C.E.O.	Auditors: Castaing, Hussey & Lolan, LLI

ICOS CORP.

Exchange	Symbol	Price	52Wk Range	Yield	P/E
NMS	ICOS	$24.58 (8/31/2006)	30.18-19.24	N/A	N/A

*7 Year Price Score 56.23 *NYSE Composite Index=100 *12 Month Price Score 90.08

Interim Earnings (Per Share)

Qtr.	Mar	Jun	Sep	Dec
2003	(0.65)	(0.19)	(0.63)	(0.55)
2004	(1.36)	(0.82)	(0.42)	(0.53)
2005	(0.73)	(0.35)	(0.18)	0.09
2006	(0.01)	0.09	...	...

Interim Dividends (Per Share)
No Dividends Paid

Valuation Analysis

		Institutional Holding	
Forecast P/E	124.81	No of Institutions	
	(9/9/2006)	129	
Market Cap	$1.6 Billion	Shares	
Book Value	N/A		47,352,624
Price/Book	N/A	% Held	
Price/Sales	20.94		72.35

Business Summary: Pharmaceuticals (MIC: 9.1 SIC: 2834 NAIC: 325412)

ICOS is a biotechnology company experienced with protein-based and small molecule therapeutics. Through Lilly ICOS LLC (Lilly ICOS), a joint venture with Eli Lilly and Company, Co. is marketing Cialis® (tadalafil) for the treatment of erectile dysfunction. Lilly ICOS is also evaluating tadalafil as a potential treatment in benign prostatic hyperplasia (BPH), hypertension and pulmonary arterial hypertension (PAH). Additionally, Co. is working to develop and commercialize potential treatments for other serious unmet medical conditions such as cancer and inflammatory diseases.

Recent Developments: For the quarter ended June 30 2006, net income amounted to $6.1 million versus a net loss of $22.6 million in the year-earlier quarter. Revenues were $18.5 million, up 2.5% from $18.1 million the year before. Operating income was $6.4 million versus a loss of $22.6 million in the prior-year quarter. Indirect operating expenses decreased 70.2% to $12.2 million from $40.7 million in the equivalent prior-year period.

Prospects: Co.'s prospects appear constructive. For instance, Co.'s Lilly ICOS joint venture has submitted a regulatory filing seeking marketing approval of Cialis® once-a-day dosing to treat erectile dysfunction in Europe and a licensing application for once-a-day dosing in Canada, and plans to file a new drug application for once-a-day dosing in the U.S in late 2006. If approved, the once-a-day dosages could be launched in late 2007. For full 2006, Co. expects net income of $265.0 million and $280.0 million for its Lilly ICOS joint venture and worldwide Cialis® net product sales of $920.0 million to $950.0 million. Thus, Co. has raised its net income guidance to $6.0 million to $15.0 million.

Financial Data

(US$ in Thousands)	6 Mos	3 Mos	12/31/2005	12/31/2004	12/31/2003	12/31/2002	12/31/2001	12/31/2000
Earnings Per Share	(0.01)	(0.45)	(1.17)	(3.13)	(2.01)	(2.64)	(1.48)	(2.11)
Cash Flow Per Share	(0.17)	(0.72)	(1.19)	(0.85)	(1.14)	(0.67)	(0.11)	(0.94)
Tang Book Value Per Share	...	...	...	0.10	3.16	5.11	7.59	4.03
Income Statement								
Total Revenue	37,275	18,727	71,410	74,608	75,104	92,877	93,369	90,733
EBITDA	13,341	...	(59,017)	(180,794)	(110,290)	...	...	(72,743)
Depn & Amortn	4,135	2,105	9,008	10,630	12,251	11,842	7,088	(37,952)
Income Before Taxes	5,797	...	(74,842)	(198,248)	(126,119)	...	...	(34,791)
Income Taxes	375	...	...	...	(612)	...	...	...
Net Income	5,422	(653)	(74,842)	(198,248)	(125,507)	(161,617)	(80,173)	(97,866)
Average Shares	65,034	64,320	63,996	63,435	62,561	61,304	54,073	46,343
Balance Sheet								
Total Assets	266,135	248,496	241,767	324,981	524,854	385,660	507,587	268,174
Current Liabilities	23,404	20,760	22,387	39,803	47,275	53,302	43,540	54,182
Long-Term Obligations	278,650	278,650	278,650	278,650	278,650	...	...	...
Total Liabilities	302,054	299,410	301,037	318,453	325,925	68,028	53,837	57,079
Stockholders' Equity	(35,919)	(50,914)	(59,270)	6,528	198,929	317,632	453,750	211,095
Shares Outstanding	65,453	65,289	65,046	63,633	63,013	62,104	59,744	52,382
Statistical Record								
EBITDA Margin %	35.79	...	N.M.	N.M.	N.M.	...	...	N.M.
Net Margin %	14.55	N.M.	N.M.	N.M.	N.M.	N.M.	N.M.	N.M.
Asset Turnover	0.30	0.29	0.25	0.18	0.16	0.21	0.24	0.48
Current Ratio	5.95	6.82	6.46	6.18	9.42	4.05	9.76	4.59
Debt to Equity	...	...	...	42.69	1.40	...	...	...
Price Range	30.18-19.24	30.18-20.32	30.18-20.32	44.40-21.12	47.08-15.91	57.44-13.84	69.34-40.00	59.56-27.06

Address: 22021-20th Avenue S.E., Bothell, WA 98021
Telephone: 425-485-1900
Fax: 425-485-1911

Web Site: www.icos.com
Officers: Paul N. Clark - Chmn., Pres., C.E.O. Gary L. Wilcox Ph.D. - Exec. V.P., Oper.

Auditors: KPMG LLP
Investor Contact: 425-485-1900

IDEXX LABORATORIES, INC.

Exchange	Symbol	Price	52Wk Range	Yield	P/E
NMS	IDXX	$92.01 (8/31/2006)	92.01-62.54	N/A	36.22

*7 Year Price Score 146.49 *NYSE Composite Index=100 *12 Month Price Score 108.39

Interim Earnings (Per Share)

Qtr.	Mar	Jun	Sep	Dec
2003	0.34	0.47	0.44	0.34
2004	0.49	0.66	0.56	0.49
2005	0.51	0.59	0.61	0.60
2006	0.55	0.78	...	...

Interim Dividends (Per Share)
No Dividends Paid

Valuation Analysis

		Institutional Holding	
Forecast P/E	35.08	No of Institutions	214
	(9/9/2006)	Shares	29,531,730
Market Cap	$2.9 Billion	% Held	94.82
Book Value	357.0 Million		
Price/Book	8.04		
Price/Sales	4.19		

Business Summary: Biotechnology (MIC: 9.2 SIC: 2835 NAIC: 325412)
Idexx Laboratories develops, manufactures and distributes products and provides services for the veterinary and food and water testing markets. Co.'s products and services include point-of-care veterinary diagnostic products; laboratory and consulting services used by veterinarians; veterinary pharmaceutical products; information products and services and digital radiography systems for veterinarians; and diagnostic and health monitoring products and services for production animals. Additionally, Co. produces products that test water for certain microbiological contaminants and products that test milk for antibiotic residues.

Recent Developments: For the quarter ended June 30 2006, net income increased 29.3% to $25.8 million from $19.9 million in the year-earlier quarter. Revenues were $191.4 million, up 19.1% from $160.6 million the year before. Operating income was $37.0 million versus $28.9 million in the prior-year quarter, an increase of 28.2%. Direct operating expenses rose 15.3% to $92.3 million from $80.1 million in the comparable period the year before. Indirect operating expenses increased 20.0% to $62.0 million from $51.7 million in the equivalent prior-year period.

Prospects: Co.'s outlook appears positive as it begins to benefit from its investment in sales and marketing, innovation and quality, as well as from the robust market environment for its businesses worldwide. Co. is also seeing improved gross profit due to lower cost of instruments and consumables, relatively favorable pricing in certain businesses, as well as higher relative sales of higher margin products. Accordingly, for full-year 2006, Co. has raised its revenue to a range of $730.0 million to $734.0 million, up from $704.0 million to $712.0 million; and its diluted earnings per share to a range of $2.64 and $2.70, up from $2.44 to $2.52, including $0.04 of certain income tax benefits.

Financial Data
(US$ in Thousands)

	6 Mos	3 Mos	12/31/2005	12/31/2004	12/31/2003	12/31/2002	12/31/2001	12/31/2000
Earnings Per Share	2.54	2.35	2.30	2.19	1.59	1.30	1.09	1.02
Cash Flow Per Share	3.92	3.56	3.58	2.78	3.42	3.07	1.39	0.81
Tang Book Value Per Share	7.18	7.71	7.86	8.25	10.14	8.46	8.94	7.88
Income Statement								
Total Revenue	359,528	168,164	638,095	549,181	475,992	412,670	386,081	367,432
EBITDA	78,210	33,633	139,700	126,462	99,284	85,939	78,781	72,732
Depn & Amortn	14,209	6,658	24,369	18,427	18,897	20,124	22,229	19,481
Income Before Taxes	65,364	27,744	118,472	111,103	83,254	68,770	58,781	58,247
Income Taxes	21,463	9,584	40,670	33,165	26,278	23,381	21,161	21,615
Net Income	44,053	18,273	78,254	78,332	57,090	45,389	37,620	36,632
Average Shares	33,014	33,418	34,055	35,800	35,931	35,043	34,640	36,081
Balance Sheet								
Total Assets	501,378	475,242	490,676	514,237	521,875	416,652	373,107	335,796
Current Liabilities	123,321	98,368	106,566	99,952	100,736	75,679	71,377	74,049
Long-Term Obligations	6,795	...	...	519	...	...	...	...
Total Liabilities	144,344	111,995	121,366	116,185	107,797	75,679	71,377	74,049
Stockholders' Equity	357,034	363,059	369,010	397,660	413,292	340,973	301,730	261,747
Shares Outstanding	31,186	31,617	31,820	33,092	34,679	33,681	33,740	33,231
Statistical Record								
Return on Assets %	16.91	16.37	15.57	15.08	12.17	11.49	10.61	10.50
Return on Equity %	22.60	21.01	20.41	19.27	15.14	14.12	13.35	13.38
EBITDA Margin %	21.75	20.00	21.89	23.03	20.86	20.83	20.41	19.79
Net Margin %	12.25	10.87	12.26	14.26	11.99	11.00	9.74	9.97
Asset Turnover	1.37	1.36	1.27	1.06	1.01	1.05	1.09	1.05
Current Ratio	2.20	2.86	2.81	3.02	3.68	3.82	3.30	2.91
Debt to Equity	0.02	...	...	N.M.	...	...	...	...
Price Range	86.36-61.63	86.36-53.50	74.16-52.90	67.62-45.76	48.55-32.06	36.55-23.98	31.25-19.13	29.56-14.63
P/E Ratio	34.00-24.26	36.75-22.77	32.24-23.00	30.88-20.89	30.53-20.16	28.12-18.45	28.67-17.55	28.98-14.34

Address: One Idexx Drive, Westbrook, ME 04092-2041
Telephone: 207-856-0300
Fax: 207-856-0346

Web Site: www.idexx.com
Officers: Jonathan W. Ayers - Chmn., Pres., C.E.O. William C. Wallen Ph.D. - Sr. V.P., Chief Scientific Officer

Auditors: PricewaterhouseCoopers LLP
Investor Contact: 207-856-8155

IMCLONE SYSTEMS INC.

Exchange	Symbol	Price	52Wk Range	Yield	P/E
NMS	IMCL	$29.90 (8/31/2006)	42.29-28.05	N/A	9.03

*7 Year Price Score 76.35 *NYSE Composite Index=100 *12 Month Price Score 93.78

Interim Earnings (Per Share)

Qtr.	Mar	Jun	Sep	Dec
2003	(0.47)	(0.47)	(0.22)	(0.36)
2004	0.76	0.29	0.45	(0.14)
2005	0.33	0.30	0.35	0.03
2006	2.51	0.42	...	...

Interim Dividends (Per Share)
No Dividends Paid

Valuation Analysis

		Institutional Holding	
Forecast P/E	10.59	No of Institutions	
	(9/9/2006)	161	
Market Cap	$2.5 Billion	Shares	
Book Value	582.7 Million	70,015,368	
Price/Book	4.32	% Held	
Price/Sales	4.19	83.14	

Business Summary: Biotechnology (MIC: 9.2 SIC: 2836 NAIC: 325414)

Imclone Systems is a biopharmaceutical company engaged in the development of a portfolio of targeted biologic treatments designed to address the medical needs of patients with cancer. Co. is focused on two strategies for treating cancer, growth factor blockers and angiogenesis inhibitors. Co.'s commercially available product, ERBITUX® (Cetuximab), binds specifically to the epidermal growth factor receptor (EGFR, HER1, c-ErbB-1) on both normal and tumor cells, and competitively inhibits the binding of the epidermal growth factor (EGF) and other ligands, such as transforming growth factor-alpha. ERBITUX® is used primarily as part of the treatment of a certain type of head and neck cancer.

Recent Developments: For the quarter ended June 30 2006, net income increased 42.9% to $37.2 million from $26.0 million in the year-earlier quarter. Revenues were $149.9 million, up 62.2% from $92.4 million the year before. Operating income was $39.1 million versus $21.1 million in the prior-year quarter, an increase of 85.3%. Direct operating expenses rose to $26.9 million from $1.1 million in the comparable period the year before. Indirect operating expenses increased 19.5% to $83.9 million from $70.2 million in the equivalent prior-year period.

Prospects: On Jul 20 2006, Co. announced the amending and supplementing of its 1998 development and license agreement with Merck KGaA. Accordingly, Co. has consented to Merck's sublicense of certain intellectual property rights relating to the development and commercialization of matuzumab, its anti-EGFR antibody, to Takeda Pharmaceutical Company. Consequently, Merck agreed to pay Co. EUR 2.5 million upon execution of the agreements and a further EUR 5.0 million upon Co.'s written consent to the sublicense. Merck also agreed to raise its fixed royalty to 9.5% for all sales of ERBITUX®, a treatment for patients with EGFR-expressing, metastatic colorectal cancer, outside the U.S. and Canada.

Financial Data
(US$ in Thousands)

	6 Mos	3 Mos	12/31/2005	12/31/2004	12/31/2003	12/31/2002	12/31/2001	12/31/2000
Earnings Per Share	3.31	3.19	1.01	1.33	(1.52)	(2.15)	(1.47)	(1.22)
Cash Flow Per Share	2.15	2.57	(0.77)	3.21	(1.26)	(0.06)	1.01	(0.49)
Tang Book Value Per Share	6.93	6.25	3.02	2.14	...	...	...	0.64
Income Statement								
Total Revenue	394,987	245,131	383,673	388,690	80,830	60,005	33,219	1,413
EBITDA	199,107	147,584	83,706	141,566	(94,064)	(141,563)	...	...
Depn & Amortn	16,429	3,996	16,940	16,169	13,187	11,783	7,412	3,936
Income Before Taxes	196,688	149,290	88,074	131,014	(112,011)	(157,224)	...	...
Income Taxes	(70,112)	(80,301)	1,578	17,361	491	725	...	...
Net Income	266,800	229,591	86,496	113,653	(112,502)	(157,949)	(102,229)	(70,351)
Average Shares	92,184	91,817	92,183	91,193	74,250	73,408	69,429	63,030
Balance Sheet								
Total Assets	1,727,873	1,712,505	1,343,415	1,434,776	381,595	484,506	474,202	371,491
Current Liabilities	256,175	279,653	242,119	303,690	125,785	145,941	54,284	85,371
Long-Term Obligations	600,000	600,000	600,000	600,000	240,033	240,033	242,200	242,200
Total Liabilities	1,145,159	1,187,513	1,091,011	1,255,938	652,188	670,135	479,376	328,059
Stockholders' Equity	582,714	524,992	252,404	178,838	(270,593)	(185,629)	(5,174)	43,432
Shares Outstanding	84,141	84,001	83,407	83,056	75,106	73,650	73,159	65,767
Statistical Record								
Return on Assets %	19.22	18.76	6.23	12.48	N.M.	N.M.	N.M.	N.M.
Return on Equity %	72.30	78.47	40.11	...	...	...	N.M.	N.M.
EBITDA Margin %	50.41	60.21	21.82	36.42	N.M.	N.M.	...	...
Net Margin %	67.55	93.66	22.54	29.24	N.M.	N.M.	N.M.	N.M.
Asset Turnover	0.39	0.35	0.28	0.43	0.19	0.13	0.08	0.01
Current Ratio	4.53	4.18	3.75	3.50	0.97	1.95	6.44	3.60
Debt to Equity	1.03	1.14	2.38	3.35	...	...	...	5.58
Price Range	42.29-28.65	39.00-28.65	46.12-28.65	86.79-34.00	48.13-9.00	46.46-6.11	73.83-26.06	84.56-18.38
P/E Ratio	12.78-8.65	12.23-8.98	45.66-28.37	65.26-25.56	...	...	...	...

Address: 180 Varick Street, New York, NY 10014
Telephone: 212-645-1405
Fax: 212-645-2054

Web Site: www.imclone.com
Officers: David M. Kies - Chmn. David Sidransky M.D. - Vice-Chmn.

Auditors: KPMG LLP
Investor Contact: 212-645-1405

INDEPENDENT BANK CORPORATION (IONIA, MI)

Exchange	Symbol	Price	52Wk Range	Yield	P/E	Div Acheiver
NMS	IBCP	$25.10 (8/31/2006)	28.47-24.03	3.19	12.68	17 Years

*7 Year Price Score 114.59 *NYSE Composite Index=100 *12 Month Price Score 92.40

Interim Earnings (Per Share)

Qtr.	Mar	Jun	Sep	Dec
2003	0.40	0.41	0.46	0.42
2004	0.38	0.40	0.44	0.45
2005	0.47	0.51	0.50	0.49
2006	0.53	0.46	...	...

Interim Dividends (Per Share)

Amt	Decl	Ex	Rec	Pay
0.19Q	2/6/2006	4/3/2006	4/5/2006	4/28/2006
0.19Q	5/23/2006	6/30/2006	7/5/2006	7/31/2006
5%	8/1/2006	8/31/2006	9/5/2006	9/29/2006
0.20Q	8/1/2006	10/3/2006	10/5/2006	10/31/2006

Indicated Div: $0.80 (Div. Reinv. Plan)

Valuation Analysis
Forecast P/E N/A
Market Cap $576.2 Million
Book Value 256.5 Million
Price/Book 2.25
Price/Sales 2.17

Institutional Holding
No of Institutions 89
Shares 8,526,402
% Held 37.14

Business Summary: Commercial Banking (MIC: 8.1 SIC: 6022 NAIC: 522110)

Independent Bank is a bank holding company. Co.'s commercial banking activities include providing checking and savings accounts, commercial lending, direct and indirect consumer financing, mortgage lending, insurance premium and automobile warranty financing and safe deposit box services. Co. also offers title insurance services and provides investment and insurance services through a third party agreement with PrimeVest Financial Services, Inc. Co.'s principal markets are the rural and suburban communities across lower Michigan. As of Dec 31 2005, Co. had four main offices, 89 branches, 4 drive-thru facilities and 18 loan production offices. At Dec 31 2005, total assets were $3.36 billion.

Recent Developments: For the quarter ended June 30 2006, net income decreased 12.6% to $10.6 million from $12.1 million in the year-earlier quarter. Net interest income decreased 3.0% to $33.4 million from $34.4 million in the year-earlier quarter. Provision for loan losses was $2.7 million versus $2.5 million in the prior-year quarter, an increase of 7.2%. Non-interest income fell 4.1% to $10.8 million from $11.3 million, while non-interest expense advanced 2.7% to $26.8 million.

Prospects: Co.'s results are being hurt by the flat yield curve and competition for deposits and loans which continues to pressure its net interest margin. Notably, Co. is experiencing a decline in net interest income in its insurance premium finance segment as growth in the balance of its finance receivables more than offset by a significant decline in margins. Nevertheless, Co. believes that the margins in its insurance premium finance segment will stabilize once the Federal interest rate tightening cycle ends. Moreover, Co. will focus on cost reductions which should further decrease its non-interest expenses annually, while seeking for other areas for revenue enhancements or cost reductions.

Financial Data
(US$ in Thousands)

	6 Mos	3 Mos	12/31/2005	12/31/2004	12/31/2003	12/31/2002	12/31/2001	12/31/2000
Earnings Per Share	1.98	2.03	1.97	1.67	1.70	1.30	1.05	0.84
Cash Flow Per Share	2.09	2.15	2.07	2.85	6.46	(0.66)	(0.91)	1.31
Tang Book Value Per Share	8.33	7.99	7.86	6.99	6.40	6.39	5.82	5.79
Dividends Per Share	0.743	0.707	0.680	0.444	0.653	0.377	0.314	0.280
Dividend Payout %	37.50	34.78	34.48	26.63	38.50	28.93	30.00	33.25
Income Statement								
Interest Income	114,309	55,857	204,924	162,547	139,366	129,815	141,359	138,415
Interest Expense	47,345	22,295	68,555	45,014	44,113	48,008	62,460	67,865
Net Interest Income	66,964	33,562	136,369	117,533	95,253	81,807	78,899	70,550
Provision for Losses	4,297	1,586	8,071	4,309	4,032	3,562	3,737	3,287
Non-Interest Income	23,383	12,312	42,245	37,798	42,604	30,911	27,085	18,961
Non-Interest Expense	55,862	28,790	105,424	98,668	82,506	68,293	68,526	58,949
Income Before Taxes	30,188	15,498	65,119	52,354	51,319	40,863	33,721	27,275
Income Taxes	7,243	3,155	18,207	13,796	13,727	11,396	9,288	7,266
Net Income	22,945	12,343	46,912	38,558	37,592	29,467	24,398	20,009
Average Shares	23,321	23,329	23,797	23,042	22,115	22,619	23,345	23,732
Balance Sheet								
Net Loans & Leases	2,628,557	2,591,452	2,532,726	2,200,553	1,649,665	1,364,737	1,368,517	1,365,682
Total Assets	3,442,721	3,402,774	3,355,848	3,094,027	2,358,557	2,057,562	1,888,457	1,783,791
Total Deposits	2,710,336	2,690,977	2,641,057	2,176,947	1,702,806	1,535,603	1,387,367	1,389,900
Total Liabilities	3,186,207	3,154,007	3,107,589	2,863,735	2,196,341	1,919,515	1,756,554	1,655,455
Stockholders' Equity	256,514	248,767	248,259	230,292	162,216	138,047	131,903	128,336
Shares Outstanding	22,955	22,810	23,090	23,367	21,574	21,613	22,662	22,175
Statistical Record								
Return on Assets %	1.39	1.46	1.45	1.41	1.70	1.49	1.33	1.14
Return on Equity %	18.55	19.66	19.61	19.59	25.04	21.83	18.75	16.49
Net Interest Margin %	57.14	60.09	66.55	72.31	68.35	63.02	55.81	50.97
Efficiency Ratio %	38.74	42.23	42.65	49.25	45.34	42.49	40.68	37.46
Loans to Deposits	0.97	0.96	0.96	1.01	0.97	0.89	0.99	0.98
Price Range	28.47-24.42	28.47-24.46	28.56-24.46	27.76-21.64	27.66-16.09	18.43-13.63	15.18-9.29	9.85-5.13
P/E Ratio	14.38-12.33	14.02-12.05	14.50-12.42	16.62-12.96	16.27-9.46	14.18-10.48	14.46-8.84	11.72-6.11
Average Yield %	2.80	2.66	2.53	1.82	3.05	2.32	2.58	3.94

Address: 230 West Main Street, P.O. Box 491, Ionia, MI 48846 **Telephone:** 616-527-9450 **Fax:** 616-527-8791	**Web Site:** www.ibcp.com **Officers:** Charles C. Van Loan - Chmn. Michael M. Magee Jr. - Pres., C.E.O.	**Auditors:** Crowe Chizek and Company LLC **Investor Contact:** 616-527-9450 **Transfer Agents:** EquiServe Trust Company, N.A., Providence, RI

INTEGRATED DEVICE TECHNOLOGY, INC.

Exchange	Symbol	Price	52Wk Range	Yield	P/E
NMS	IDTI	$17.23 (8/31/2006)	17.28-9.32	N/A	N/A

*7 Year Price Score 47.90 *NYSE Composite Index=100 *12 Month Price Score 109.61

Interim Earnings (Per Share)

Qtr.	Jun	Sep	Dec	Mar
2003-04	(0.05)	0.01	0.02	0.07
2004-05	(0.05)	0.08	0.03	0.05
2005-06	0.06	(0.16)	(0.21)	(0.14)
2006-07	(0.01)	...	...	...

Interim Dividends (Per Share)
No Dividends Paid

Valuation Analysis

		Institutional Holding	
Forecast P/E	15.76	No of Institutions	
	(9/9/2006)	223	
Market Cap	$3.4 Billion	Shares	
Book Value	1.9 Billion	190,059,952	
Price/Book	1.83	% Held	
Price/Sales	5.53	95.21	

Business Summary: IT & Technology (MIC: 10.2 SIC: 3674 NAIC: 334413)

Integrated Device Technology is engaged in designing, developing, manufacturing, and marketing semiconductor products for the advanced communications, computing and consumer industries. Co.'s communications products target markets including the core, metro, access, enterprise, small office/home office (SOHO), data center and wireless markets. Co.'s computing products are designed specifically for personal computing (PC) and server applications and the consumer products are optimized for gaming consoles, set-top boxes, digital TV and smart phones.

Recent Developments: For the quarter ended July 2 2006, net loss amounted to $1.6 million versus net income of $6.6 million in the year-earlier quarter. Revenues were $185.5 million, up 97.7% from $93.8 million the year before. Operating loss was $3.3 million versus a loss of $3.8 million in the prior-year quarter. Direct operating expenses rose 98.1% to $101.3 million from $51.1 million in the comparable period the year before. Indirect operating expenses increased 88.3% to $87.6 million from $46.5 million in the equivalent prior-year period.

Prospects: Co.'s solid revenue growth reflects continuing product momentum across its computing and communication end markets due to its aggressive buildup of its memory buffer products combined with strength in its communications' sub segments. This is despite a softer-than-seasonal market for Co.'s personal computer clock business. Similarly, Co. noted that strong profit growth resulting from the combination of top line growth and cost and expense management are allowing it to achieve its operating margin target range by at least one year ahead of its plans.

Financial Data
(US$ in Thousands)

	3 Mos	04/02/2006	04/03/2005	03/28/2004	03/30/2003	03/31/2002	04/01/2001	04/02/2000
Earnings Per Share	(0.52)	(0.52)	0.12	0.06	(2.68)	(0.44)	3.76	1.32
Cash Flow Per Share	0.70	0.78	0.75	0.75	0.11	(0.27)	4.63	2.63
Tang Book Value Per Share	2.38	2.12	6.61	6.90	6.86	9.55	11.10	7.12
Income Statement								
Total Revenue	185,536	527,778	390,640	345,443	343,878	379,817	991,789	701,722
EBITDA	45,532	88,434	60,710	59,012	(118,319)	48,601	557,269	240,498
Depn & Amortn	45,543	185,980	59,397	52,543	82,306	96,320	90,914	89,045
Income Before Taxes	(90)	(84,109)	13,353	6,125	(201,139)	(48,957)	463,221	137,486
Income Taxes	1,474	(2,401)	20	(271)	76,757	(2,765)	48,018	6,875
Net Income	(1,564)	(81,708)	13,333	6,396	(277,896)	(46,192)	415,203	130,611
Average Shares	198,706	157,345	108,204	108,526	103,520	104,560	110,287	99,002
Balance Sheet								
Total Assets	2,057,028	2,037,691	902,140	905,553	881,312	1,225,819	1,470,401	1,162,182
Current Liabilities	153,105	147,638	99,425	105,678	98,845	119,889	254,486	186,886
Long-Term Obligations	...	...	...	15,651	23,775	51,221	76,018	271,722
Total Liabilities	182,344	179,492	115,024	121,329	122,620	171,110	330,504	481,031
Stockholders' Equity	1,874,684	1,858,199	787,116	784,224	758,692	1,054,709	1,139,897	681,151
Shares Outstanding	199,083	198,388	106,136	105,957	103,693	104,396	102,658	95,667
Statistical Record								
Return on Assets %	N.M.	N.M.	1.45	0.72	N.M.	N.M.	31.63	13.99
Return on Equity %	N.M.	N.M.	1.67	0.83	N.M.	N.M.	45.73	26.93
EBITDA Margin %	24.54	16.76	15.54	17.08	N.M.	12.80	56.19	34.27
Net Margin %	N.M.	N.M.	3.41	1.85	N.M.	N.M.	41.86	18.61
Asset Turnover	0.42	0.36	0.43	0.39	0.33	0.28	0.76	0.75
Current Ratio	3.47	3.18	6.87	6.68	6.73	7.40	3.75	4.55
Debt to Equity	...	...	...	0.02	0.03	0.05	0.07	0.40
Price Range	16.06-9.32	15.52-9.32	16.74-9.23	20.96-7.94	34.53-6.90	50.24-17.80	103.33-27.81	43.81-6.13
P/E Ratio	...	...	139.50-76.92	349.33-132.33	...	...	27.48-7.40	33.19-4.64

Address: 6024 Silver Creek Valley Road, Santa Clara, CA 95138
Telephone: 408-284-8200
Fax: 408-284-3572

Web Site: www.idt.com
Officers: Kenneth Kannappan - Chmn. Gregory S. Lang - Pres., C.E.O.

Auditors: PricewaterhouseCoopers LLP
Investor Contact: 408-654-6420

INTEL CORP

Exchange	Symbol	Price	52Wk Range	Yield	P/E
NMS	INTC	$19.57 (8/31/2006)	27.43-16.86	2.04	17.79

*7 Year Price Score 57.78 *NYSE Composite Index=100 *12 Month Price Score 83.52

Interim Earnings (Per Share)

Qtr.	Mar	Jun	Sep	Dec
2003	0.14	0.14	0.25	0.32
2004	0.26	0.27	0.30	0.34
2005	0.35	0.33	0.32	0.40
2006	0.23	0.15	...	...

Interim Dividends (Per Share)

Amt	Decl	Ex	Rec	Pay
0.08Q	9/15/2005	11/3/2005	11/7/2005	12/1/2005
0.10Q	1/19/2006	2/3/2006	2/7/2006	3/1/2006
0.10Q	3/22/2006	5/3/2006	5/7/2006	6/1/2006
0.10Q	7/13/2006	8/3/2006	8/7/2006	9/1/2006

Indicated Div: $0.40

Valuation Analysis
Forecast P/E 24.64 (9/9/2006)
Market Cap $112.9 Billion
Book Value 34.8 Billion
Price/Book 3.24
Price/Sales 3.03

Institutional Holding
No of Institutions 1245
Shares 3,135,353,344
% Held 54.36

Business Summary: IT & Technology (MIC: 10.2 SIC: 3674 NAIC: 334413)

Intel is engaged in the manufacture of semiconductor chip, developing advanced integrated digital technology platforms for the computing and communications industries. Co.'s products include chips, boards and other semiconductor components that are the building blocks integral to computers, servers, as well as networking and communications products. Co.'s component-level products consist of integrated circuits used to process information. Co.'s operating segments are: the Digital Enterprise Group, the Mobility Group, the Flash Memory Group, the Digital Home Group, the Digital Health Group, and the Channel Platforms Group.

Recent Developments: For the quarter ended July 1 2006, net income decreased 56.6% to $885.0 million from $2.04 billion in the year-earlier quarter. Revenues were $8.01 billion, down 13.2% from $9.23 billion the year before. Operating income was $1.07 billion versus $2.65 billion in the prior-year quarter, a decrease of 59.5%. Direct operating expenses declined 4.7% to $3.84 billion from $4.03 billion in the comparable period the year before. Indirect operating expenses increased 21.3% to $3.10 billion from $2.55 billion in the equivalent prior-year period.

Prospects: On June 27 2006, Co. signed an agreement to sell its communications and application processor business to Marvell Technology Group, Ltd. for $600.0 million plus the assumption of certain liabilities. The sale will enable Co. to focus its investments on its core businesses, including its Intel Architecture-based processors and emerging technologies for mobile computing, such as Wi-Fi and WiMAX broadband wireless technologies. The transaction is expected to close in the fourth quarter of 2006. For the third quarter of 2006, Co. expects revenue to be between $8.30 billion and $8.90 billion. Accordingly, Co. expects sequential revenue growth of 7.5% in the fourth quarter of 2006.

Financial Data
(US$ in Thousands)

	6 Mos	3 Mos	12/31/2005	12/25/2004	12/27/2003	12/28/2002	12/29/2001	12/30/2000
Earnings Per Share	1.10	1.28	1.40	1.16	0.85	0.46	0.19	1.51
Cash Flow Per Share	2.03	2.26	2.39	2.06	1.77	1.38	1.29	1.88
Tang Book Value Per Share	5.36	5.25	5.46	5.57	5.26	4.74	4.59	4.67
Dividends Per Share	0.360	0.340	0.320	0.160	0.080	0.080	0.080	0.070
Dividend Payout %	32.62	26.49	22.86	13.79	9.41	17.39	42.11	4.64
Income Statement								
Total Revenue	16,949,000	8,940,000	38,826,000	34,209,000	30,141,000	26,764,000	26,539,000	33,726,000
EBITDA	5,249,000	2,926,000	16,523,000	14,935,000	12,208,000	9,214,000	8,652,000	19,976,000
Depn & Amortn	2,428,000	1,213,000	4,471,000	4,769,000	4,952,000	5,224,000	6,469,000	4,835,000
Income Before Taxes	3,127,000	1,874,000	12,610,000	10,417,000	7,442,000	4,204,000	2,183,000	15,141,000
Income Taxes	885,000	517,000	3,946,000	2,901,000	1,801,000	1,087,000	892,000	4,606,000
Net Income	2,242,000	1,357,000	8,664,000	7,516,000	5,641,000	3,117,000	1,291,000	10,535,000
Average Shares	5,867,999	5,953,999	6,177,999	6,494,001	6,621,001	6,759,001	6,879,001	6,986,001
Balance Sheet								
Total Assets	46,088,000	47,194,000	48,314,000	48,143,000	47,143,000	44,224,000	44,395,000	47,945,000
Current Liabilities	8,422,000	9,843,000	9,234,000	8,006,000	6,879,000	6,595,000	6,570,000	8,650,000
Long-Term Obligations	2,054,000	2,040,000	2,106,000	703,000	936,000	929,000	1,050,000	707,000
Total Liabilities	11,292,000	12,836,000	12,132,000	9,564,000	9,297,000	8,756,000	8,565,000	10,623,000
Stockholders' Equity	34,796,000	34,358,000	36,182,000	38,579,000	37,846,000	35,468,000	35,830,000	37,322,000
Shares Outstanding	5,766,999	5,807,999	5,918,999	6,252,999	6,487,001	6,575,001	6,690,001	6,721,001
Statistical Record								
Return on Assets %	14.50	16.60	17.67	15.82	12.38	7.05	2.80	22.58
Return on Equity %	18.54	21.83	22.80	19.72	15.43	8.77	3.54	29.67
EBITDA Margin %	30.97	32.73	42.56	43.66	40.50	34.43	32.60	59.23
Net Margin %	13.23	15.18	22.31	21.97	18.72	11.65	4.86	31.24
Asset Turnover	0.80	0.81	0.79	0.72	0.66	0.61	0.58	0.72
Current Ratio	1.99	1.83	2.30	3.00	3.33	2.87	2.68	2.45
Debt to Equity	0.06	0.06	0.06	0.02	0.02	0.03	0.03	0.02
Price Range	28.71-16.86	28.71-19.46	28.71-21.99	34.24-19.68	34.12-15.05	35.79-13.22	37.81-19.30	74.87-30.06
P/E Ratio	26.10-15.33	22.43-15.20	20.51-15.71	29.52-16.97	40.14-17.71	77.80-28.74	199.01-101.58	49.59-19.91
Average Yield %	1.58	1.39	1.29	0.62	0.34	0.34	0.27	0.13

Address: 2200 Mission College Boulevard, Santa Clara, CA 95054-1549 **Telephone:** 408-765-8080 **Fax:** 408-765-2633	**Web Site:** www.intel.com **Officers:** Andrew S. Grove - Chmn. Craig R. Barrett - C.E.O.	**Auditors:** Ernst & Young LLP **Investor Contact:** 408-765-1679 **Transfer Agents:** Computershare Investor Services

INTERNATIONAL BANCSHARES CORP.

Exchange	Symbol	Price	52Wk Range	Yield	P/E
NMS	IBOC	$28.51 (8/31/2006)	30.34-27.48	2.46	14.33

*7 Year Price Score 106.35 *NYSE Composite Index=100 *12 Month Price Score 95.16

Interim Earnings (Per Share)

Qtr.	Mar	Jun	Sep	Dec
2003	0.51	0.46	0.55	0.46
2004	0.43	0.42	0.51	0.51
2005	0.58	0.52	0.55	0.53
2006	0.37	0.54	...	...

Interim Dividends (Per Share)

Amt	Decl	Ex	Rec	Pay
0.256S	4/1/2005	4/13/2005	4/15/2005	4/29/2005
25%	4/1/2005	6/1/2005	5/2/2005	5/31/2005
0.256S	10/3/2005	10/12/2005	10/14/2005	11/1/2005
0.28S	4/3/2006	4/12/2006	4/17/2006	5/1/2006

Indicated Div: $0.70

Valuation Analysis
Forecast P/E N/A
Market Cap $1.8 Billion
Book Value 784.7 Million
Price/Book 2.29
Price/Sales 2.46

Institutional Holding
No of Institutions 96
Shares 11,425,151
% Held 18.14

Business Summary: Commercial Banking (MIC: 8.1 SIC: 6022 NAIC: 522110)
International Bancshares is a financial holding company serving more than 200 main banking and branch facilities located in more than 80 communities in South, Central and Southeast Texas and the State of Oklahoma. Co., through its subsidiaries, is primarily engaged in the business of banking, including the acceptance of checking and savings deposits and the making of commercial, real estate, personal, home improvement, automobile and other installment and term loans. As of Dec 31 2005, Co. had total assets of $10.39 billion and total deposits of $6.66 billion.

Recent Developments: For the quarter ended June 30 2006, net income increased 3.9% to $34.7 million from $33.4 million in the year-earlier quarter. Net interest income decreased 7.6% to $72.0 million from $78.0 million in the year-earlier quarter. Provision for loan losses was $82,000 versus $221,000 in the prior-year quarter, a decrease of 62.9%. Non-interest income rose 26.0% to $47.0 million from $37.3 million, while non-interest expense advanced 4.2% to $67.7 million.

Prospects: Co.'s increasing non-banking service charges, commissions and fees reflect additional income being recognized by its investment services unit. The increase is due to fair value adjustments being recorded by its investment services unit and higher income being recognized on an equity investment held by its lead bank subsidiary. Looking ahead, Co. appears well positioned to benefit from its role as a facilitator of trade along the U.S. border with Mexico. Co. noted that it does a large amount of business with customers domiciled in Mexico. Accordingly, deposits from persons and entities domiciled in Mexico comprise a large and stable portion of the deposit base of Co.'s bank subsidiaries.

Financial Data
(US$ in Thousands)

	6 Mos	3 Mos	12/31/2005	12/31/2004	12/31/2003	12/31/2002	12/31/2001	12/31/2000
Earnings Per Share	1.99	1.97	2.18	1.88	1.98	1.58	1.27	1.13
Cash Flow Per Share	2.97	3.03	3.31	2.54	2.41	2.16	1.37	1.44
Tang Book Value Per Share	7.28	7.51	7.29	6.60	8.33	7.74	6.24	5.55
Dividends Per Share	0.536	0.512	0.512	0.512	0.432	0.283	0.262	0.257
Dividend Payout %	26.93	25.99	23.49	27.23	21.85	17.92	20.71	22.66
Income Statement								
Interest Income	291,692	142,317	508,705	352,378	318,051	353,928	394,419	421,627
Interest Expense	145,329	68,004	206,830	108,602	94,725	116,415	200,808	251,756
Net Interest Income	146,363	74,313	301,875	243,776	223,326	237,513	193,611	169,871
Provision for Losses	679	597	960	6,500	8,291	8,541	8,631	6,824
Non-Interest Income	87,639	40,618	167,222	134,816	127,273	85,645	75,524	57,501
Non-Interest Expense	146,578	78,857	255,988	195,180	159,754	154,843	135,441	111,957
Income Before Taxes	86,745	35,477	212,149	176,912	182,554	159,774	125,063	108,591
Income Taxes	28,112	11,502	71,370	57,880	60,426	54,013	41,721	33,417
Net Income	58,633	23,975	140,779	119,032	122,128	100,631	83,342	75,174
Average Shares	63,742	64,170	64,485	63,380	61,670	63,857	65,785	66,221
Balance Sheet								
Net Loans & Leases	4,751,792	4,574,058	4,547,896	4,804,069	2,700,354	2,725,349	2,608,467	2,212,467
Total Assets	10,649,121	10,482,202	10,391,853	9,917,951	6,578,310	6,495,635	6,381,401	5,860,714
Total Deposits	6,650,356	6,778,354	6,656,426	6,571,104	4,435,699	4,239,899	4,332,834	3,744,598
Total Liabilities	9,864,415	9,679,970	9,598,986	9,164,861	6,000,927	5,948,371	5,884,373	5,443,822
Stockholders' Equity	784,706	802,232	792,867	753,090	577,383	547,264	497,028	416,892
Shares Outstanding	63,001	63,272	63,728	63,526	60,477	61,054	64,021	65,128
Statistical Record								
Return on Assets %	1.23	1.22	1.39	1.44	1.87	1.56	1.36	1.33
Return on Equity %	16.41	16.27	18.21	17.84	21.72	19.27	18.24	19.46
Net Interest Margin %	48.23	52.22	59.34	69.18	70.22	67.11	49.09	40.29
Efficiency Ratio %	34.48	43.11	37.87	40.06	35.87	35.23	28.82	23.37
Loans to Deposits	0.71	0.67	0.68	0.73	0.61	0.64	0.60	0.59
Price Range	30.49-27.48	30.49-27.20	31.57-27.20	35.33-26.37	30.40-18.43	21.99-17.06	17.99-10.42	11.74-9.76
P/E Ratio	15.32-13.81	15.48-13.81	14.48-12.48	18.79-14.03	15.35-9.31	13.92-10.80	14.16-8.21	10.38-8.64
Average Yield %	1.83	1.75	1.73	1.61	1.77	1.46	1.85	2.39

Address: 1200 San Bernardo Avenue, Laredo, TX 78042-1359 Telephone: 956-722-7611	Web Site: www.ibc.com Officers: Dennis E. Nixon - Chmn., Pres., C.E.O. Eduardo J. Farias - Exec. V.P.	Auditors: KPMG LLP

INTERNATIONAL SPEEDWAY CORP

Exchange	Symbol	Price	52Wk Range	Yield	P/E
NMS	ISCA	$48.40 (8/31/2006)	56.07-43.97	0.17	15.46

*7 Year Price Score 87.67 *NYSE Composite Index=100 *12 Month Price Score 91.07

Interim Earnings (Per Share)

Qtr.	Feb	May	Aug	Nov
2002-03	0.48	0.24	0.68	0.59
2003-04	0.52	0.11	1.28	1.02
2004-05	0.77	0.50	0.69	1.03
2005-06	0.83	0.58	...	...

Interim Dividends (Per Share)

Amt	Decl	Ex	Rec	Pay
0.06A	4/11/2003	5/28/2003	5/31/2003	6/30/2003
0.06A	...	5/26/2004	5/31/2004	6/30/2004
0.06A	4/6/2005	5/26/2005	5/31/2005	6/30/2005
0.08A	4/13/2006	5/26/2006	5/31/2006	6/30/2006

Indicated Div: $0.08

Valuation Analysis

Forecast P/E 15.14 (9/9/2006)
Market Cap $2.6 Billion
Book Value 1.1 Billion
Price/Book 2.32
Price/Sales 3.35

Institutional Holding

No of Institutions 192
Shares 26,364,008
% Held 49.39

Business Summary: Sporting & Recreational (MIC: 13.5 SIC: 7948 NAIC: 711212)

International Speedway is a promoter of motorsports entertainment activities. As of Dec 31 2005, Co. owned and/or operated eleven motorsports facilities: Daytona International Speedway in Florida; Talladega Superspeedway in Alabama; Michigan International Speedway in Michigan; Richmond International Raceway in Virginia; California Speedway in California; Kansas Speedway in Kansas; Phoenix International Raceway in Arizona; Homestead-Miami Speedway in Florida; Martinsville Speedway in Virginia; Darlington Raceway in South Carolina; and Watkins Glen International in New York. In 2005, these facilities promoted over 100 motorsports racing events.

Recent Developments: For the quarter ended May 31 2006, income from continuing operations increased 15.8% to $30.7 million from $26.5 million in the year-earlier quarter. Net income increased 15.8% to $30.7 million from $26.5 million in the year-earlier quarter. Revenues were $172.1 million, up 9.3% from $157.4 million the year before. Operating income was $52.2 million versus $46.9 million in the prior-year quarter, an increase of 11.3%. Direct operating expenses rose 4.7% to $78.4 million from $74.9 million in the comparable period the year before. Indirect operating expenses increased 16.3% to $41.5 million from $35.7 million in the equivalent prior-year period.

Prospects: On Mar 29 2006, Co. announced that its subsidiary Daytona International Speedway, LLC has extended its lease agreement with the Daytona Beach Racing and Recreational Facilities District through Nov 7 2054, which will result in annual lease-related expenses of approximately $800,000 throughout fiscal years 2007 to 2054. Meanwhile, Co. continues to benefit from higher broadcast rights fees for its NASCAR NEXTEL Cup and Busch series, higher corporate sponsorship and hospitality revenues as well as other motorsports-related revenue. Looking ahead, Co. is maintaining its full-year 2006 revenues expectation of $780.0 million to $800.0 million and earnings of $3.20 to $3.30 per diluted share.

Financial Data
(US$ in Thousands)

	6 Mos	3 Mos	11/30/2005	11/30/2004	11/30/2003	11/30/2002	11/30/2001	11/30/2000
Earnings Per Share	3.13	3.05	2.99	2.94	1.98	(7.74)	1.65	0.95
Cash Flow Per Share	3.35	2.86	2.76	4.25	3.67	3.37	3.03	2.64
Tang Book Value Per Share	16.22	15.73	14.83	11.89	11.91	9.96	6.76	4.86
Dividends Per Share	0.080	0.060	0.060	0.060	0.060	0.060	0.060	0.060
Dividend Payout %	2.56	1.97	2.01	2.04	3.03	...	3.64	6.32
Income Statement								
Total Revenue	366,016	193,934	740,129	647,848	575,745	550,552	528,510	440,430
EBITDA	154,763	90,190	322,196	273,855	240,383	240,111	231,101	169,798
Depn & Amortn	28,807	14,224	53,415	47,671	46,160	43,971	57,729	53,740
Income Before Taxes	121,077	72,832	260,948	208,514	172,865	173,074	150,313	91,834
Income Taxes	46,219	28,701	101,876	82,218	67,417	66,803	62,680	41,408
Net Income	74,740	44,053	159,361	156,318	105,448	(410,978)	87,633	50,426
Average Shares	53,266	53,249	53,240	53,182	53,133	53,101	53,076	53,049
Balance Sheet								
Total Assets	1,969,791	1,976,935	1,797,069	1,619,510	1,303,792	1,155,971	1,702,146	1,665,438
Current Liabilities	274,913	262,276	182,491	191,196	376,505	136,503	135,866	140,551
Long-Term Obligations	368,241	418,314	368,387	369,315	75,168	309,606	402,477	470,551
Total Liabilities	858,201	892,263	757,114	737,772	577,327	533,646	666,724	714,567
Stockholders' Equity	1,111,590	1,084,672	1,039,955	881,738	726,465	622,325	1,035,422	950,871
Shares Outstanding	53,177	53,144	53,322	53,268	53,217	53,186	53,163	53,145
Statistical Record								
Return on Assets %	8.97	8.78	9.33	10.67	8.57	N.M.	5.20	3.08
Return on Equity %	16.18	16.17	16.59	19.39	15.64	N.M.	8.82	5.43
EBITDA Margin %	42.28	46.51	43.53	42.27	41.75	43.61	43.73	38.55
Net Margin %	20.42	22.72	21.53	24.13	18.32	N.M.	16.58	11.45
Asset Turnover	0.41	0.41	0.43	0.44	0.47	0.39	0.31	0.27
Current Ratio	0.81	0.95	1.08	1.78	0.72	1.09	0.79	0.62
Debt to Equity	0.33	0.39	0.35	0.42	0.10	0.50	0.39	0.49
Price Range	59.30-44.10	59.30-44.10	59.30-48.89	54.53-41.09	46.15-35.82	45.86-34.13	47.26-33.27	66.00-30.50
P/E Ratio	18.95-14.09	19.44-14.46	19.83-16.35	18.55-13.98	23.31-18.09	...	28.64-20.16	69.47-32.11
Average Yield %	0.15	0.11	0.11	0.13	0.15	0.15	0.15	0.14

Address: 1801 West International Speedway Boulevard, Daytona Beach, FL 32114 **Telephone:** 386-254-2700 **Fax:** 386-257-0281	**Web Site:** www.iscmotorsports.com **Officers:** William C. France - Chmn. James C. France - Vice Chmn., C.E.O.	**Auditors:** Ernst & Young LLP **Transfer Agents:** SunTrust Bank, Central Florida, NA, Atlanta, GA

INTERSIL CORP.

Exchange	Symbol	Price	52Wk Range	Yield	P/E
NMS	ISIL	$25.33 (8/31/2006)	30.70-20.09	0.79	27.84

*7 Year Price Score N/A *NYSE Composite Index=100 *12 Month Price Score 88.30

Interim Earnings (Per Share)

Qtr.	Mar	Jun	Sep	Dec
2003	0.10	(0.01)	0.06	0.16
2004	0.19	0.19	(0.21)	0.10
2005	0.09	0.12	0.19	0.20
2006	0.22	0.30	...	...

Interim Dividends (Per Share)

Amt	Decl	Ex	Rec	Pay
0.05Q	11/2/2005	11/8/2005	11/11/2005	11/22/2005
0.05Q	1/25/2006	2/9/2006	2/8/2006	2/17/2006
0.05Q	4/20/2006	5/8/2006	5/10/2006	5/20/2006
0.05Q	8/7/2006	8/8/2006	8/8/2006	8/18/2006

Indicated Div: $0.20

Valuation Analysis

		Institutional Holding	
Forecast P/E	20.62 (9/9/2006)	No of Institutions	242
Market Cap	$3.6 Billion	Shares	137,590,736
Book Value	2.5 Billion	% Held	97.99
Price/Book	1.44		
Price/Sales	5.08		

Business Summary: IT & Technology (MIC: 10.2 SIC: 3674 NAIC: 334413)

Intersil is a global desgner and manufacturer of analog integrated circuits (ICs). Co.'s high-end consumer segment products are used in DVD recorders, LCD televisions and cell phones. Co.'s industrial products segment includes operational amplifiers, bridge driver power management products, and other standard analog products targeting the medical imaging, energy management and factory automation markets. Co.'s communications segment products are targeted to applications in the DSL, home gateway, satellite and VOIP markets. Co.'s computing segment produces desktop, server and notebook power management products, including core power devices and other power management integrated circuits.

Recent Developments: For the quarter ended June 30 2006, net income increased 148.0% to $43.0 million from $17.3 million in the year-earlier quarter. Revenues were $187.6 million, up 34.9% from $139.1 million the year before. Operating income was $35.6 million versus $18.0 million in the prior-year quarter, an increase of 98.0%. Direct operating expenses rose 29.0% to $80.3 million from $62.2 million in the comparable period the year before. Indirect operating expenses increased 21.8% to $71.7 million from $58.9 million in the equivalent prior-year period.

Prospects: Co.'s results are being led by solid revenue growth, notably in its high end consumer market from its product proliferation in handhelds and displays, and a seasonal increase in demand for optical storage products. Co. is also benefiting from revenue growth in its communication and industrial markets, driven by continued healthy seasonal demand and the ramp up of many 2005 and 2006 design wins. Going forward into the third quarter of 2006, Co. expects revenue to grow about 3.0% to 5.0% from its second quarter revenue of $187.6 million, while earnings per share is expected at about $0.25 as it remains cautious regarding the softness in its computing and several consumer related products.

Financial Data
(US$ in Thousands)

	6 Mos	3 Mos	12/30/2005	12/31/2004	01/02/2004	01/03/2003	12/28/2001	12/29/2000
Earnings Per Share	0.91	0.73	0.59	0.28	0.32	(0.63)	0.37	0.07
Cash Flow Per Share	1.38	1.22	1.08	0.70	0.52	0.79	0.27	0.45
Tang Book Value Per Share	7.20	6.97	6.85	6.68	8.33	6.56	7.64	6.68
Dividends Per Share	0.190	0.180	0.170	0.130	0.030	...	...	...
Dividend Payout %	20.85	24.62	28.81	46.43	9.38	...	...	...
Income Statement								
Total Revenue	366,564	178,932	600,255	535,775	507,684	649,718	481,066	435,452
EBITDA	86,681	44,701	134,637	56,287	120,181	56,153	168,157	76,994
Depn & Amortn	16,551	8,320	34,497	36,297	49,783	53,477	72,288	35,745
Income Before Taxes	84,069	43,173	119,106	33,217	79,356	13,944	114,479	43,856
Income Taxes	8,704	10,793	32,284	(7,136)	20,899	18,914	62,405	30,759
Net Income	75,365	32,380	85,877	40,681	45,837	(4,970)	39,889	7,009
Average Shares	144,066	145,000	145,200	143,600	141,300	125,600	108,900	101,000
Balance Sheet								
Total Assets	2,623,973	2,593,723	2,583,717	2,587,570	2,454,745	2,368,454	1,200,233	1,229,768
Current Liabilities	155,262	151,147	154,110	148,167	202,628	165,783	136,491	118,134
Long-Term Obligations	...	...	...	...	...	...	...	64,966
Total Liabilities	155,262	151,147	154,110	148,167	202,628	165,783	142,985	218,732
Stockholders' Equity	2,468,711	2,442,576	2,429,607	2,439,403	2,252,117	2,202,671	1,057,248	1,011,036
Shares Outstanding	140,617	141,077	141,051	143,769	139,331	136,927	106,847	105,306
Statistical Record								
Return on Assets %	5.06	4.08	3.33	1.62	1.91	N.M.	3.29	0.52
Return on Equity %	5.37	4.33	3.54	1.74	2.06	N.M.	3.87	1.02
EBITDA Margin %	23.65	24.98	22.43	10.51	23.67	8.64	34.96	17.68
Net Margin %	20.56	18.10	14.31	7.59	9.03	N.M.	8.29	1.61
Asset Turnover	0.27	0.25	0.23	0.21	0.21	0.36	0.40	0.33
Current Ratio	6.05	5.96	5.10	5.10	5.11	5.11	5.62	5.43
Debt to Equity	...	...	...	...	...	...	...	0.06
Price Range	30.70-18.77	30.31-15.55	26.67-13.82	29.29-15.20	29.91-13.87	37.21-11.25	42.36-13.88	67.00-19.06
P/E Ratio	33.74-20.63	41.52-21.30	45.20-23.42	104.61-54.29	93.47-43.34	...	114.49-37.50	957.14-272.32
Average Yield %	0.77	0.80	0.87	0.66	0.14	...	...	...

Address: 1001 Murphy Ranch Road, Milpitas, CA 95035 **Telephone:** 949-341-7062 **Fax:** 949-341-7053	**Web Site:** www.intersil.com **Officers:** Gregory L. Williams - Chmn. Richard M. Beyer - Pres., C.E.O.
Auditors: Ernst & Young LLP **Investor Contact:** 949-341-7062 **Transfer Agents:** American Stock Transfer & Trust Co.	

INTUIT INC

Exchange	Symbol	Price	52Wk Range	Yield	P/E
NMS	INTU	$30.26 (8/31/2006)	31.53-21.34	N/A	25.86

*7 Year Price Score 94.40 *NYSE Composite Index=100 *12 Month Price Score 111.39

Interim Earnings (Per Share)

Qtr.	Oct	Jan	Apr	Jul
2002-03	(0.13)	0.30	0.70	(0.05)
2003-04	(0.14)	0.36	0.67	(0.10)
2004-05	(0.12)	0.39	0.81	(0.04)
2005-06	(0.13)	0.51	0.84	...

Interim Dividends (Per Share)
No Dividends Paid

Valuation Analysis
Forecast P/E 30.32 (9/9/2006)
Market Cap $10.3 Billion
Book Value 1.7 Billion
Price/Book 6.18
Price/Sales 4.58

Institutional Holding
No of Institutions 359
Shares 283,887,584
% Held 83.08

Business Summary: IT & Technology (MIC: 10.2 SIC: 7372 NAIC: 511210)
Intuit is a provider of business and financial management products and services. Co.'s Small Business portfolio consists of its QuickBooks-Related segment, which includes QuickBooks accounting and business management software, and Intuit-Branded Small Business products and services. Co.'s Tax portfolio is comprised of its Consumer Tax segment, which includes TurboTax consumer tax return preparation products and services, and its Professional Tax segment, including its Lacerte and ProSeries professional tax products and services. Co.'s Other portfolio consists primarily of its Quicken personal finance products and services and its businesses in Canada and the U.K.

Recent Developments: For the quarter ended Apr 30 2006, income from continuing operations increased 0.2% to $298.6 million from $298.1 million in the year-earlier quarter. Net income decreased 0.6% to $298.6 million compared with $300.5 million in the corresponding prior-year quarter. Revenues were $952.6 million, up 14.1% from $834.9 million the year before. Operating income was $480.1 million versus $422.2 million in the prior-year period, an increase of 13.7%. Direct operating expenses rose 5.5% to $110.2 million from $104.5 million in the comparable period the year before. Indirect operating expenses increased 17.6% to $362.3 million from $308.1 million in the equivalent prior-year period.

Prospects: On May 19 2006, Sage Software, a subsidiary of The Sage Group plc, announced that it has completed the acquisition of the Master Builder product and business from Co. Meanwhile, Co.'s revenue growth is being driven by a robust Consumer Tax season, coupled with improved performance from QuickBooks. For the fourth quarter of fiscal 2006, Co. expects revenue of $310.0 million to $330.0 million, and a diluted loss per share of $0.24 to $0.22, an increase from its previous guidance due to tax liabilities arising from the sale of its Master Builder business. For fiscal year 2006, Co. expects revenue to be $2.31 billion to $2.33 billion, and diluted earnings per share of $2.20 to $2.22.

Financial Data
(US$ in Thousands)

	9 Mos	6 Mos	3 Mos	07/31/2005	07/31/2004	07/31/2003	07/31/2002	07/31/2001
Earnings Per Share	1.17	1.14	1.01	1.01	0.79	0.81	0.32	(0.20)
Cash Flow Per Share	1.84	1.58	1.70	1.62	1.47	1.39	0.85	0.56
Tang Book Value Per Share	3.16	2.75	2.60	3.11	2.75	3.13	3.93	4.15
Income Statement								
Total Revenue	1,999,378	1,046,775	304,071	2,037,703	1,867,663	1,650,743	1,358,348	1,261,461
EBITDA	711,529	202,400	(62,831)	664,150	549,942	483,087	157,249	(21,651)
Depn & Amortn	86,481	57,829	29,219	108,093	97,042	90,249	72,310	74,891
Income Before Taxes	644,148	155,271	(92,050)	556,057	452,900	392,838	84,939	(96,542)
Income Taxes	247,864	57,635	(34,439)	181,074	135,870	129,636	15,179	(229)
Net Income	435,817	137,169	(45,804)	381,627	317,030	343,034	140,160	(82,793)
Average Shares	355,918	363,582	354,812	376,796	400,162	421,910	435,794	415,918
Balance Sheet								
Total Assets	2,958,786	2,694,275	2,442,366	2,716,451	2,696,178	2,790,267	2,963,026	2,961,736
Current Liabilities	1,270,142	1,123,858	924,829	1,003,404	857,365	796,165	732,777	787,962
Long-Term Obligations	1,652	2,338	3,019	15,075	16,394	29,265	14,610	12,413
Total Liabilities	1,285,851	1,140,373	941,743	1,020,952	873,759	825,430	747,387	800,410
Stockholders' Equity	1,672,935	1,553,902	1,500,623	1,695,499	1,822,419	1,964,837	2,215,639	2,161,326
Shares Outstanding	341,695	347,653	353,891	358,540	380,182	398,944	422,328	421,052
Statistical Record								
Return on Assets %	13.89	15.27	15.60	14.10	11.53	11.92	4.73	N.M.
Return on Equity %	23.67	25.56	24.28	21.70	16.70	16.41	6.40	N.M.
EBITDA Margin %	35.59	19.34	N.M.	32.59	29.45	29.26	11.58	N.M.
Net Margin %	21.80	13.10	N.M.	18.73	16.97	20.78	10.32	N.M.
Asset Turnover	0.75	0.79	0.85	0.75	0.68	0.57	0.46	0.43
Current Ratio	1.56	1.53	1.45	1.61	1.77	2.10	2.72	2.73
Debt to Equity	N.M.	N.M.	N.M.	0.01	0.01	0.01	0.01	0.01
Price Range	28.43-20.57	27.79-18.85	24.50-18.85	24.50-18.51	26.57-17.93	27.39-17.40	25.05-14.54	34.50-11.72
P/E Ratio	24.30-17.58	24.37-16.54	24.25-18.67	24.25-18.33	33.63-22.70	33.81-21.48	78.27-45.44	...

Address: 2700 Coast Avenue, Mountain View, CA 94043	**Web Site:** www.intuit.com	**Auditors:** Ernst & Young LLP
Telephone: 650-944-6000	**Officers:** William V. Campbell - Chmn. Stephen M. Bennett - Pres., C.E.O.	**Investor Contact:** 650-944-5436
Fax: 650-944-3060		**Transfer Agents:** American Stock Transfer & Trust Company, New York, NY

INVESTORS FINANCIAL SERVICES CORP.

Exchange	Symbol	Price	52Wk Range	Yield	P/E
NMS	IFIN	$46.36 (8/31/2006)	50.85-31.02	0.19	19.81

*7 Year Price Score 100.45 *NYSE Composite Index=100 *12 Month Price Score 102.44

Interim Earnings (Per Share)

Qtr.	Mar	Jun	Sep	Dec
2003	0.08	0.42	0.40	0.48
2004	0.52	0.52	0.53	0.52
2005	0.60	0.64	0.53	0.60
2006	0.56	0.65	...	...

Interim Dividends (Per Share)

Amt	Decl	Ex	Rec	Pay
0.02Q	10/19/2005	10/27/2005	10/31/2005	11/15/2005
0.022Q	1/20/2006	1/27/2006	1/31/2006	2/15/2006
0.022Q	4/12/2006	4/26/2006	4/28/2006	5/15/2006
0.022Q	7/13/2006	7/27/2006	7/31/2006	8/15/2006

Indicated Div: $0.09

Valuation Analysis

Forecast P/E 19.62 (9/9/2006)
Market Cap $3.1 Billion
Book Value 869.2 Million
Price/Book 3.52
Price/Sales 2.76

Institutional Holding

No of Institutions 231
Shares 70,042,784
% Held N/A

Business Summary: Wealth Management (MIC: 8.8 SIC: 6282 NAIC: 523930)

Investors Financial Services is a bank holding company that provides asset administration services for the financial services industry through its wholly-owned subsidiary, Investors Bank & Trust Company®. Co.'s services include middle office outsourcing, global custody, multicurrency accounting, fund administration, securities lending, foreign exchange, cash management, performance measurement, institutional transfer agency, investment advisory services, lines of credit and brokerage and transition management services. As of Dec 31 2005, Co. provided services for approximately $1.800 trillion in net assets, including approximately $0.300 trillion of foreign net assets.

Recent Developments: For the quarter ended June 30 2006, net income increased 0.4% to $44.3 million from $44.1 million in the year-earlier quarter. Revenues were $307.0 million, up 29.7% from $236.8 million the year before. Direct operating expenses rose 50.4% to $99.4 million from $66.1 million in the comparable period the year before. Indirect operating expenses increased 31.5% to $148.9 million from $113.2 million in the equivalent prior-year period.

Prospects: Co.'s operating results are primarily reflecting higher contributions from its core services such as middle office outsourcing, global custody, multicurrency accounting and mutual fund administration. Also, Co. is encouraged by robust revenue growth in its value-added services that include foreign exchange, securities lending, cash management and investment advisory services. As such, Co. will maintain its target towards further growth by utilizing its resources in additional personnel, technology and office space in both the U.S. and Europe. For 2006, Co.'s net operating revenue is expected to grow by 12.0% to 15.0%, while earnings are projected to range from $2.40 to $2.45 per share.

Financial Data
(US$ in Thousands)

	6 Mos	3 Mos	12/31/2005	12/31/2004	12/31/2003	12/31/2002	12/31/2001	12/31/2000
Earnings Per Share	2.34	2.33	2.37	2.09	1.38	1.04	0.77	0.54
Cash Flow Per Share	2.92	3.67	3.22	3.34	2.43	0.94	0.88	0.70
Tang Book Value Per Share	11.96	11.67	11.01	9.51	7.05	5.60	4.11	2.42
Dividends Per Share	0.085	0.083	0.080	0.070	0.060	0.050	0.040	0.030
Dividend Payout %	3.63	3.54	3.38	3.35	4.35	4.81	5.23	5.56
Income Statement								
Interest Income	272,358	134,437	447,705	313,149	246,063	247,847	252,054	181,745
Interest Expense	190,472	91,116	277,280	125,469	93,180	104,369	142,773	122,927
Net Interest Income	81,886	43,321	170,425	187,680	152,883	143,478	109,281	58,818
Non-Interest Income	318,595	149,467	525,537	425,491	336,193	294,116	243,263	162,041
Non-Interest Expense	284,609	135,684	460,109	398,383	344,921	336,667	277,952	169,040
Income Before Taxes	115,872	57,104	235,853	214,788	144,155	100,927	74,592	51,819
Income Taxes	34,170	19,701	76,035	72,826	52,395	30,400	22,804	16,655
Net Income	81,702	37,403	159,818	141,962	91,760	68,946	50,200	33,576
Average Shares	67,723	67,224	67,473	67,916	66,475	66,371	65,736	62,062
Balance Sheet								
Net Loans & Leases	335,697	307,921	402,370	134,530	199,530	143,737	232,113	129,269
Total Assets	12,367,469	12,426,804	12,096,393	11,167,825	9,224,572	7,214,777	5,298,645	3,811,115
Total Deposits	5,919,293	5,424,691	4,992,590	5,396,382	4,207,118	3,332,918	2,278,877	2,331,884
Total Liabilities	11,498,288	11,606,605	11,323,535	10,455,563	8,683,737	6,748,518	4,931,593	3,608,061
Stockholders' Equity	869,181	820,199	772,858	712,262	540,835	442,956	342,778	178,808
Shares Outstanding	65,984	63,406	62,927	66,522	65,410	64,764	63,942	59,825
Statistical Record								
Return on Assets %	1.26	1.29	1.37	1.39	1.12	1.10	1.10	1.05
Return on Equity %	18.81	20.02	21.52	22.60	18.65	17.55	19.25	21.22
Net Interest Margin %	27.96	32.22	38.07	59.93	62.13	57.89	43.36	32.36
Efficiency Ratio %	48.50	47.79	47.28	53.93	59.24	62.12	56.12	49.17
Loans to Deposits	0.06	0.06	0.08	0.02	0.05	0.04	0.10	0.06
Price Range	50.85-31.02	50.61-31.02	53.21-31.02	49.98-35.19	38.78-20.90	38.99-20.06	43.00-25.00	47.63-9.38
P/E Ratio	21.73-13.26	21.72-13.31	22.45-13.09	23.91-16.84	28.10-15.14	37.50-19.29	55.84-32.47	88.19-17.38
Average Yield %	0.21	0.21	0.20	0.16	0.21	0.15	0.12	0.13

Address: 200 Clarendon Street, P.O. Box 9130, Boston, MA 02116
Telephone: 617-937-6700

Web Site: www.investorsbnk.com
Officers: Kevin J. Sheehan - Chmn., C.E.O. Michael F. Rogers - Pres.

Auditors: Deloitte & Touche LLP
Transfer Agents: EquiServe

INVITROGEN CORP.

Exchange	Symbol	Price	52Wk Range	Yield	P/E
NMS	IVGN	$60.85 (8/31/2006)	84.73-55.88	N/A	31.37

*7 Year Price Score 91.93 *NYSE Composite Index=100 *12 Month Price Score 89.22

Interim Earnings (Per Share)

Qtr.	Mar	Jun	Sep	Dec
2003	0.34	0.34	0.26	0.23
2004	0.20	0.36	0.52	0.54
2005	0.82	0.27	0.42	0.81
2006	0.35	0.36	...	...

Interim Dividends (Per Share)
No Dividends Paid

Valuation Analysis **Institutional Holding**

Forecast P/E	18.75	No of Institutions
	(9/9/2006)	289
Market Cap	$3.2 Billion	Shares
Book Value	2.2 Billion	54,247,884
Price/Book	1.50	% Held
Price/Sales	2.62	92.24

Business Summary: Biotechnology (MIC: 9.2 SIC: 2836 NAIC: 541710)

Invitrogen develops, manufactures and markets research tools in reagent, kit and high-throughput applications forms to customers engaged in life sciences research, drug discovery, diagnostics and the commercial manufacture of biological products. In addition, Co. supplies sera, cell and tissue culture media and reagents used in life sciences research, as well as in processes to grow cells in the laboratory and produce pharmaceuticals and other high valued proteins. Co. conducts its business through two principal product segments: BioDiscovery and BioProduction. Co. markets its products directly and through distributors or agents worldwide.

Recent Developments: For the quarter ended June 30 2006, net income increased 32.0% to $19.7 million from $14.9 million in the year-earlier quarter. Revenues were $313.6 million, up 2.3% from $306.5 million the year before. Operating income was $25.8 million versus $22.9 million in the prior-year quarter, an increase of 12.6%. Direct operating expenses declined 4.2% to $123.1 million from $128.4 million in the comparable period the year before. Indirect operating expenses increased 6.2% to $164.8 million from $155.1 million in the equivalent prior-year period.

Prospects: For full-year 2006, Co. projects overall revenue growth of 5.0% to 9.0%. Co. expects to see continued productivity gains in its sales and marketing expenditures as it adds product specialists to support its existing customer account managers, allowing it to increase the effectiveness of its direct selling organization as it expands its product portfolio. Meanwhile, Co. will continue to implement programs and actions to improve its efficiency in the general and administrative area, particularly in the areas of process improvement and automation. Also, Co. expects to continue to invest in targeted research and development efforts as it expands its capabilities to accelerate innovation.

Financial Data (US$ in Thousands)	6 Mos	3 Mos	12/31/2005	12/31/2004	12/31/2003	12/31/2002	12/31/2001	12/31/2000
Earnings Per Share	1.94	1.85	2.33	1.63	1.17	0.90	(2.81)	(1.80)
Cash Flow Per Share	4.34	5.27	5.92	4.88	3.34	2.35	2.34	(2.48)
Tang Book Value Per Share	N.M.	N.M.	N.M.	0.94	6.98	10.61	9.24	5.87
Income Statement								
Total Revenue	622,641	309,004	1,198,452	1,023,851	777,738	648,597	629,290	246,195
EBITDA	135,118	69,247	340,969	275,337	200,220	155,549	140,650	27,476
Depn & Amortn	77,780	39,732	157,609	147,029	110,617	87,667	286,952	91,819
Income Before Taxes	55,253	27,612	173,830	121,376	85,068	71,176	(137,281)	(54,536)
Income Taxes	16,355	8,394	41,784	32,551	24,329	22,207	9,338	(514)
Net Income	38,898	19,218	132,046	88,825	60,130	47,667	(147,666)	(54,326)
Average Shares	54,824	54,822	60,014	60,396	51,353	52,963	52,549	30,156
Balance Sheet								
Total Assets	3,887,409	3,850,500	3,877,049	3,614,335	3,165,689	2,614,966	2,667,212	2,369,215
Current Liabilities	412,936	440,546	511,577	196,185	125,693	140,955	126,582	153,028
Long-Term Obligations	1,151,896	1,151,902	1,151,923	1,300,000	1,022,500	674,533	676,030	179,203
Total Liabilities	1,724,671	1,758,399	1,835,255	1,701,084	1,358,842	968,853	993,727	585,879
Stockholders' Equity	2,162,738	2,092,101	2,041,794	1,913,251	1,806,847	1,642,610	1,671,078	1,778,397
Shares Outstanding	53,371	53,194	52,958	51,443	51,394	49,972	53,000	51,914
Statistical Record								
Return on Assets %	2.78	2.78	3.53	2.61	2.08	1.80	N.M.	N.M.
Return on Equity %	5.24	5.14	6.68	4.76	3.49	2.88	N.M.	N.M.
EBITDA Margin %	21.70	22.41	28.45	26.89	25.74	23.98	22.35	11.16
Net Margin %	6.25	6.22	11.02	8.68	7.73	7.35	N.M.	N.M.
Asset Turnover	0.32	0.33	0.32	0.30	0.27	0.25	0.25	0.20
Current Ratio	2.84	2.56	2.25	6.79	10.24	6.87	9.52	4.39
Debt to Equity	0.53	0.55	0.56	0.68	0.57	0.41	0.40	0.10
Price Range	88.27-61.76	88.27-61.76	88.27-61.76	81.92-46.93	70.76-28.28	61.93-26.73	81.95-47.90	97.06-39.88
P/E Ratio	45.50-31.84	47.71-33.38	37.88-26.51	50.26-28.79	60.48-24.17	68.81-29.70	...	...

Address: 1600 Faraday Avenue, Carlsbad, CA 92008 **Telephone:** 760-603-7200 **Fax:** 760-603-7201	**Web Site:** www.invitrogen.com **Officers:** Gregory T. Lucier - Chmn., Pres., C.E.O. Claude D. Benchimol Ph.D. - Sr. V.P., R&D	**Auditors:** Ernst & Young LLP

JACK HENRY & ASSOCIATES, INC.

Exchange	Symbol	Price	52Wk Range	Yield	P/E	Div Achiever
NMS	JKHY	$19.16 (8/31/2006)	23.67-17.29	1.15	20.83	14 Years

*7 Year Price Score 82.89 *NYSE Composite Index=100 *12 Month Price Score 91.19

Interim Earnings (Per Share)

Qtr.	Sep	Dec	Mar	Jun
2002-03	0.13	0.13	0.14	0.15
2003-04	0.15	0.16	0.18	0.19
2004-05	0.18	0.19	0.21	0.23
2005-06	0.21	0.23	0.25	...

Interim Dividends (Per Share)

Amt	Decl	Ex	Rec	Pay
0.045Q	11/2/2005	11/14/2005	11/16/2005	12/2/2005
0.055Q	1/30/2006	2/14/2006	2/16/2006	3/2/2006
0.055Q	5/8/2006	5/11/2006	5/15/2006	5/31/2006
0.055Q	8/28/2006	9/6/2006	9/8/2006	9/22/2006

Indicated Div: $0.22 (Div. Reinv. Plan)

Valuation Analysis

Forecast P/E	17.75
	(9/9/2006)
Market Cap	$1.8 Billion
Book Value	579.9 Million
Price/Book	3.06
Price/Sales	3.10

Institutional Holding

No of Institutions	180
Shares	63,443,740
% Held	68.46

Business Summary: IT & Technology (MIC: 10.2 SIC: 7373 NAIC: 541512)

Jack Henry & Associates is a provider of integrated computer systems providing data processing and management information to banks, credit unions and credit unions, other financial and non-financial institutions in U.S. Co. performs data conversion and hardware and software installation for the implementation of its systems and applications. Co. also provides continuing customer support services. For Co.'s customers who prefer not to acquire hardware and software, Co. provides outsourcing services through six data centers and twenty-two item-processing centers. Co. develops software applications designed primarily for use on hardware supporting IBM and UNIX/NT operating systems.

Recent Developments: For the quarter ended Mar 31 2006, net income increased 20.7% to $23.5 million from $19.4 million in the year-earlier quarter. Revenues were $145.5 million, up 8.3% from $134.4 million the year before. Operating income was $34.7 million versus $31.0 million in the prior-year quarter, an increase of 11.9%. Direct operating expenses rose 6.1% to $81.8 million from $77.1 million in the comparable period the year before. Indirect operating expenses increased 10.3% to $29.0 million from $26.3 million in the equivalent prior-year period.

Prospects: Revenue growth in bank systems and services is due to increasing support and service revenue from maintenance for in-house and outsourced customers, plus the ongoing steady increase in ATM and debit card processing activity. Co. expects this to continue as it further improves its processes and continues to create demand and value for its customers. Meanwhile, license revenue is increasing and hardware revenue decreasing mainly due to sales mix and products being delivered. Also, revenue in Co.'s credit union system and services segment is increasing in the support and service component from maintenance for in-house and outsourced customers, along with ATM and debit card processing activity.

Financial Data
(US$ in Thousands)

	9 Mos	6 Mos	3 Mos	06/30/2005	06/30/2004	06/30/2003	06/30/2002	06/30/2001
Earnings Per Share	0.92	0.88	0.84	0.81	0.68	0.55	0.62	0.61
Cash Flow Per Share	1.27	1.33	1.40	1.19	1.26	1.13	1.01	0.84
Tang Book Value Per Share	2.79	2.49	2.58	2.45	3.06	2.78	2.54	2.20
Dividends Per Share	0.190	0.180	0.175	0.170	0.150	0.140	0.130	0.110
Dividend Payout %	20.65	20.45	20.83	20.99	22.06	25.45	20.97	18.03
Income Statement								
Total Revenue	429,895	284,400	136,983	535,863	467,415	404,627	396,657	345,468
EBITDA	131,865	85,921	41,214	157,980	132,346	107,465	114,116	108,345
Depn & Amortn	32,532	21,310	10,653	38,911	33,540	30,194	27,470	21,888
Income Before Taxes	100,029	65,172	30,829	119,843	99,705	77,791	88,473	86,923
Income Taxes	35,511	24,114	11,407	44,342	37,390	28,394	31,408	31,292
Net Income	64,518	41,058	19,422	75,501	62,315	49,397	57,065	55,631
Average Shares	94,390	93,637	93,998	92,998	91,859	89,270	92,367	91,344
Balance Sheet								
Total Assets	769,374	765,878	738,306	814,153	653,614	548,575	486,142	433,121
Current Liabilities	125,736	160,385	156,903	246,583	173,240	146,780	112,656	107,018
Long-Term Obligations	...	...	...	...	...	...	...	228
Total Liabilities	189,476	218,516	207,393	296,999	210,696	183,352	145,403	130,617
Stockholders' Equity	579,898	547,362	530,913	517,154	442,918	365,223	340,739	302,504
Shares Outstanding	92,476	91,451	91,500	91,497	90,204	88,156	88,950	88,846
Statistical Record								
Return on Assets %	12.06	11.52	11.41	10.29	10.34	9.55	12.42	14.75
Return on Equity %	15.93	15.96	15.81	15.73	15.38	13.99	17.74	24.34
EBITDA Margin %	30.67	30.21	30.09	29.48	28.31	26.56	28.77	31.36
Net Margin %	15.01	14.44	14.18	14.09	13.33	12.21	14.39	16.10
Asset Turnover	0.80	0.78	0.80	0.73	0.78	0.78	0.86	0.92
Current Ratio	1.38	1.12	1.17	1.06	1.50	1.48	1.60	1.61
Price Range	22.90-17.15	21.76-17.15	21.76-17.15	21.76-17.15	21.97-16.53	17.79-8.31	31.51-16.09	31.47-18.88
P/E Ratio	24.89-18.64	24.73-19.49	25.90-20.42	26.86-21.17	32.31-24.31	32.35-15.11	50.82-25.95	51.59-30.94
Average Yield %	0.98	0.95	0.91	0.89	0.79	1.07	0.56	0.45

Address: 663 Highway 60, P.O. Box 807, Monett, MO 65708 Telephone: 417-235-6652 Fax: 417-235-4281	Web Site: www.jackhenry.com Officers: Michael E. Henry - Chmn. John W. Henry - Vice-Chmn., Sr. V.P.	Auditors: Deloitte & Touche LLP Investor Contact: 417-235-6652 Transfer Agents: Boston Equiserve, Boston, MA

JDS UNIPHASE CORP

Exchange	Symbol	Price	52Wk Range	Yield	P/E
NMS	JDSU	$2.27 (8/31/2006)	4.18-1.53	N/A	N/A

*7 Year Price Score 10.19   *NYSE Composite Index=100   *12 Month Price Score 83.03

Interim Earnings (Per Share)

Qtr.	Sep	Dec	Mar	Jun
2002-03	(0.37)	(0.15)	(0.10)	(0.04)
2003-04	(0.02)	(0.04)	(0.01)	(0.01)
2004-05	(0.02)	(0.03)	(0.03)	(0.10)
2005-06	(0.04)	(0.03)	0.00	...

Interim Dividends (Per Share)
No Dividends Paid

Valuation Analysis / Institutional Holding

Forecast P/E	70.33	No of Institutions
	(9/9/2006)	354
Market Cap	$3.8 Billion	Shares
Book Value	1.6 Billion	774,641,408
Price/Book	2.36	% Held
Price/Sales	3.62	45.98

Business Summary: IT & Technology (MIC: 10.2 SIC: 3674 NAIC: 334413)

JDS Uniphase designs and manufactures products for fiberoptic communications, as well as for the industrial, commercial and consumer markets. Co.'s communications products, which include components, modules and subsystems, are used by communications equipment providers for telecommunications, data communications, and cable television networks. These products include transmitters, receivers, amplifiers, dispersion compensators, multiplexers and demultiplexers, add/drop modules, switches, optical performance monitors and couplers, splitters and circulators. Co. also provides test and measurement equipment used to assess performance of optical components.

Recent Developments: For the quarter ended Mar 31 2006, net income amounted to $3.7 million versus a net loss of $38.6 million in the year-earlier quarter. Revenues were $314.9 million, up 89.4% from $166.3 million the year before. Operating loss was $39.2 million versus a loss of $44.6 million in the prior-year quarter. Direct operating expenses rose 40.9% to $199.4 million from $141.5 million in the comparable period the year before. Indirect operating expenses increased 122.9% to $154.7 million from $69.4 million in the equivalent prior-year period.

Prospects: Results continue to be positively affected by Co.'s ongoing manufacturing consolidation and cost reduction programs. In addition, Co. is experiencing double-digit revenue growth in both its Optical Communications as well as its Communications Test and Measurement segments. Looking ahead to the fourth quarter of fiscal 2006, Co. expects revenue to be between $302.0 million and $322.0 million. Separately, on Apr 13 2006, Co. announced that it has entered into an agreement to acquire Test-Um Inc., a provider of home networking test instruments for the FTTx (Fiber-to-the-x) and digital cable markets. The acquisition is expected to be completed by the end of June 2006.

Financial Data
(US$ in Thousands)

	9 Mos	6 Mos	3 Mos	06/30/2005	06/30/2004	06/30/2003	06/30/2002	06/30/2001
Earnings Per Share	(0.17)	(0.20)	(0.20)	(0.18)	(0.08)	(0.66)	(6.50)	(51.40)
Cash Flow Per Share	(0.06)	(0.06)	(0.08)	(0.10)	(0.09)	(0.15)	0.06	0.05
Tang Book Value Per Share	0.35	0.32	0.34	0.72	0.89	0.99	1.43	2.78
Income Statement								
Total Revenue	886,100	571,200	258,300	712,200	635,900	675,900	1,098,200	3,232,800
EBITDA	(11,100)	(41,700)	(32,500)	(193,300)	(72,500)	(841,100)	(6,855,700)	(50,999,900)
Depn & Amortn	85,400	61,400	29,000	61,300	55,900	79,200	1,645,300	5,542,400
Income Before Taxes	(96,500)	(103,100)	(61,500)	(254,600)	(128,400)	(920,300)	(8,501,000)	(56,493,800)
Income Taxes	8,900	6,000	5,500	6,700	(15,800)	13,500	237,300	(371,900)
Net Income	(105,400)	(109,100)	(67,000)	(261,300)	(115,500)	(933,800)	(8,738,300)	(56,121,900)
Average Shares	1,698,000	1,655,700	1,581,300	1,445,400	1,436,700	1,419,700	1,344,300	1,091,900
Balance Sheet								
Total Assets	2,602,800	2,611,400	2,545,100	2,080,400	2,421,500	2,137,800	3,004,500	12,245,400
Current Liabilities	356,400	399,900	328,900	239,800	350,300	422,800	482,500	848,500
Long-Term Obligations	468,400	467,800	467,200	466,900	464,000	...	5,500	12,800
Total Liabilities	979,700	1,020,500	964,100	750,700	850,400	466,700	533,100	1,538,900
Stockholders' Equity	1,623,100	1,590,900	1,581,000	1,329,700	1,571,100	1,671,100	2,471,400	10,706,500
Shares Outstanding	1,684,005	1,675,192	1,652,410	1,448,291	1,440,404	1,431,324	1,370,482	1,318,246
Statistical Record								
Asset Turnover	0.44	0.37	0.32	0.32	0.28	0.26	0.14	0.17
Current Ratio	3.72	3.31	3.91	6.62	5.33	3.58	3.85	3.58
Debt to Equity	0.29	0.29	0.30	0.35	0.30	...	N.M.	N.M.
Price Range	4.18-1.36	3.17-1.36	3.56-1.36	3.79-1.36	5.73-2.85	4.28-1.62	12.96-2.29	135.94-10.00

Address: 1768 Automation Parkway, San Jose, CA 95131
Telephone: 408-546-5000
Fax: 408-546-4300

Web Site: www.jdsu.com
Officers: Martin A. Kaplan - Chmn. Kevin J. Kennedy Ph.D - C.E.O.

Auditors: Ernst & Young LLP
Investor Contact: 408-546-5000

JETBLUE AIRWAYS CORP

Exchange	Symbol	Price	52Wk Range	Yield	P/E
NMS	JBLU	$10.26 (8/31/2006)	15.69-8.95	N/A	N/A

*7 Year Price Score N/A *NYSE Composite Index=100 *12 Month Price Score 90.82

Interim Earnings (Per Share)

Qtr.	Mar	Jun	Sep	Dec
2003	0.11	0.24	0.17	0.12
2004	0.09	0.13	0.05	0.01
2005	0.04	0.07	0.01	(0.26)
2006	(0.18)	0.08	...	...

Interim Dividends (Per Share)

Amt	Decl	Ex	Rec	Pay
3-for-2	10/24/2002	12/13/2002	12/2/2002	12/12/2002
3-for-2	10/7/2003	11/21/2003	11/10/2003	11/20/2003
3-for-2	10/20/2005	12/27/2005	12/12/2005	12/23/2005

Valuation Analysis

		Institutional Holding	
Forecast P/E	N/A	No of Institutions	188
Market Cap	$1.8 Billion	Shares	181,573,216
Book Value	918.0 Million	% Held	N/A
Price/Book	1.96		
Price/Sales	0.90		

Business Summary: Aviation (MIC: 1.1 SIC: 4512 NAIC: 481111)

JetBlue Airways is a low-cost passenger airline that provides customer service primarily on point-to-point routes. Co. leases all of its facilities at each of the airports it serves. Co.'s service facilities which include ticket counter and gate space, operations support area and baggage service offices, generally have a term ranging from less than one year to five years. As of Feb 14 2006, Co. operated a total of 369 daily flights encompassing 34 destinations in 15 U.S. states, Puerto Rico, the Dominican Republic and The Bahamas. Also, as of Feb 14 2006, Co. operated a fleet consisting of 87 Airbus A320 and nine EMBRAER 190 aircraft.

Recent Developments: For the quarter ended June 30 2006, net income increased 7.7% to $14.0 million from $13.0 million in the year-earlier quarter. Revenues were $612.0 million, up 42.7% from $429.0 million the year before. Operating income was $47.0 million versus $40.0 million in the prior-year quarter, an increase of 17.5%. Direct operating expenses rose 59.4% to $314.0 million from $197.0 million in the comparable period the year before. Indirect operating expenses increased 30.7% to $251.0 million from $192.0 million in the equivalent prior-year period.

Prospects: Going forward, Co. will continue to execute its Return to Profitability plan which focuses on a combination of right-sizing capacity, optimizing revenue sources and introducing new revenue initiatives as well as cost reductions. For instance, Co. will focus more on its capacity additions for short- and medium-haul markets as it targets operating capacity to increase by 20.0% to 22.0% for full-year 2006. In this respect, Co. anticipates the addition of 10 new Airbus A320 aircraft and 10 new EMBRAER 190 aircraft to its operating fleet during the remainder of 2006. As such, it is expected that these initiatives will yield approximately $60.0 million in net revenue and expense savings.

Financial Data
(US$ in Thousands)

	6 Mos	3 Mos	12/31/2005	12/31/2004	12/31/2003	12/31/2002	12/31/2001	12/31/2000
Earnings Per Share	(0.35)	(0.36)	(0.13)	0.29	0.65	0.37	0.34	(7.90)
Cash Flow Per Share	0.86	1.07	1.06	1.28	1.96	...	15.11	0.63
Tang Book Value Per Share	5.02	4.89	5.03	4.49	3.98	2.41	...	...
Income Statement								
Total Revenue	1,102,000	490,000	1,701,000	1,265,972	998,351	635,191	320,414	104,618
EBITDA	118,000	19,000	184,000	198,846	249,998	137,630	58,421	(14,666)
Depn & Amortn	73,000	34,000	117,000	77,420	50,865	26,922	10,417	3,995
Income Before Taxes	(22,000)	(47,000)	(24,000)	76,822	175,439	95,024	41,915	(21,569)
Income Taxes	(4,000)	(15,000)	(4,000)	29,355	71,541	40,116	3,378	(239)
Net Income	(18,000)	(32,000)	(20,000)	47,467	103,898	54,908	38,537	(21,330)
Average Shares	180,841	173,246	159,889	166,213	161,311	...	12,633	4,484
Balance Sheet								
Total Assets	4,306,000	4,068,000	3,892,000	2,798,644	2,185,757	1,378,923	673,773	344,128
Current Liabilities	842,000	797,000	676,000	485,998	369,619	269,664	194,126	91,024
Long-Term Obligations	2,287,000	2,154,000	2,103,000	1,395,939	1,011,610	639,498	290,665	137,110
Total Liabilities	3,388,000	3,179,000	2,981,000	2,042,444	1,514,621	964,250	495,499	234,729
Stockholders' Equity	918,000	889,000	911,000	756,200	671,136	414,673	(32,167)	(54,153)
Shares Outstanding	175,473	173,708	172,621	156,354	153,103	143,456	14,728	14,650
Statistical Record								
Return on Assets %	N.M.	N.M.	N.M.	1.90	5.83	5.35	7.57	...
Return on Equity %	N.M.	N.M.	N.M.	6.63	19.14	28.71	...	...
EBITDA Margin %	10.71	3.88	10.82	15.71	25.04	21.67	18.23	N.M.
Net Margin %	N.M.	N.M.	N.M.	3.75	10.41	8.64	12.03	N.M.
Asset Turnover	0.52	0.50	0.51	0.51	0.56	0.62	0.63	...
Current Ratio	0.74	0.77	0.94	1.06	1.75	1.05	0.74	0.66
Debt to Equity	2.49	2.42	2.31	1.85	1.51	1.54	...	...
Price Range	15.69-8.95	15.69-9.72	15.69-11.52	20.23-13.59	31.23-10.59	16.15-8.93	...	...
P/E Ratio	...	...	...	69.75-46.87	48.04-16.29	43.64-24.14	...	...

Address: 118-29 Queens Boulevard, Forest Hills, NY 11375
Telephone: 718-286-7900

Web Site: www.jetblue.com
Officers: David Neeleman - Chmn., C.E.O. David Barger - Pres., C.O.O.

Auditors: Ernst & Young LLP

JUNIPER NETWORKS INC

Exchange	Symbol	Price	52Wk Range	Yield	P/E
NMS	JNPR	$14.66 (8/31/2006)	24.60-12.20	N/A	24.85

*7 Year Price Score 38.57 *NYSE Composite Index=100 *12 Month Price Score 71.93

Interim Earnings (Per Share)

Qtr.	Mar	Jun	Sep	Dec
2003	0.01	0.03	0.02	0.04
2004	0.08	(0.02)	0.09	0.11
2005	0.13	0.15	0.14	0.17
2006	0.13	...	...	...

Interim Dividends (Per Share)
No Dividends Paid

Valuation Analysis
Forecast P/E	19.43
	(9/9/2006)
Market Cap	$8.3 Billion
Book Value	6.9 Billion
Price/Book	1.20
Price/Sales	3.80

Institutional Holding
No of Institutions	312
Shares	434,635,232
% Held	76.82

Business Summary: Office Equipment Supplies (MIC: 11.12 SIC: 3577 NAIC: 334119)
Juniper Networks designs and sells products that provide customers Internet Protocol network infrastructure applications. Co.'s applications are incorporated into the global web of interconnected public and private networks across a range of media, including voice, video and data, that travel to and from end users around the world. Co.'s infrastructure applications allow service providers and other network-intensive businesses to support and deliver services and applications on an efficient and low cost integrated network. Co.'s customers include service providers, government organizations, cable operators, mobile operators, research and education institutions and network businesses.

Recent Developments: For the quarter ended Mar 31 2006, net income increased 0.4% to $75.8 million from $75.4 million in the year-earlier quarter. Revenues were $566.7 million, up 26.2% from $449.1 million the year before. Operating income was $90.9 million versus $100.9 million in the prior-year quarter, a decrease of 9.9%. Direct operating expenses rose 28.7% to $184.9 million from $143.7 million in the comparable period the year before. Indirect operating expenses increased 42.2% to $290.8 million from $204.5 million in the equivalent prior-year period.

Prospects: Results are benefiting from increased acceptance of Co.'s products from both its enterprise and service provider clients. Going forward, Co. will intensify its focus on execution in order to capitalize in an environment that positively aligns its capabilities with the market requirements, as exemplified by its recently-outlined Application Acceleration Strategy. This strategy defines new capabilities designed to address challenges related to limited bandwidth, latency, application contention and system-wide management in the distributed and extended enterprise, while further establishing Co.'s DX and WX/WXC product lines to be employed across a suite of application acceleration platforms.

Financial Data

(US$ in Thousands)	3 Mos	12/31/2005	12/31/2004	12/31/2003	12/31/2002	12/31/2001	12/31/2000	12/31/1999
Earnings Per Share	0.59	0.59	0.25	0.10	(0.34)	(0.00)	0.43	(0.05)
Cash Flow Per Share	1.05	1.16	0.89	0.47	0.01	0.92	0.88	0.11
Tang Book Value Per Share	3.13	3.04	2.89	1.48	1.18	2.36	1.87	1.47
Income Statement								
Total Revenue	566,714	2,063,957	1,336,019	701,393	546,547	887,022	673,501	102,606
EBITDA	152,432	640,999	322,040	123,692	(52,902)	56,765	215,984	(4,381)
Depn & Amortn	41,828	138,800	97,643	64,698	63,047	73,598	21,895	10,239
Income Before Taxes	110,604	502,199	219,018	58,994	(115,150)	16,537	230,372	(6,609)
Income Taxes	34,841	148,170	83,272	19,795	4,500	29,954	82,456	2,425
Net Income	75,763	354,029	135,746	39,199	(119,650)	(13,417)	147,916	(9,034)
Average Shares	603,589	598,907	542,625	403,072	350,695	319,378	347,858	189,322
Balance Sheet								
Total Assets	8,035,764	8,026,599	6,999,714	2,411,097	2,614,669	2,389,588	2,103,129	513,378
Current Liabilities	631,376	627,400	502,837	290,813	242,024	242,219	216,408	55,663
Long-Term Obligations	399,942	399,959	400,000	557,841	942,114	1,150,000	1,156,719	...
Total Liabilities	1,116,165	1,126,889	1,006,977	848,654	1,184,138	1,392,219	1,373,127	55,663
Stockholders' Equity	6,919,599	6,899,710	5,992,737	1,562,443	1,430,531	997,369	730,002	457,715
Shares Outstanding	565,750	568,243	540,526	390,272	374,331	329,146	318,085	311,877
Statistical Record								
Return on Assets %	4.66	4.71	2.88	1.56	N.M.	N.M.	11.28	N.M.
Return on Equity %	5.43	5.49	3.58	2.62	N.M.	N.M.	24.84	N.M.
EBITDA Margin %	26.90	31.06	24.10	17.64	N.M.	6.40	32.07	N.M.
Net Margin %	13.37	17.15	10.16	5.59	N.M.	N.M.	21.96	N.M.
Asset Turnover	0.29	0.27	0.28	0.28	0.22	0.39	0.51	0.37
Current Ratio	2.94	2.90	2.81	2.38	2.81	4.65	6.23	6.79
Debt to Equity	0.06	0.06	0.07	0.36	0.66	1.15	1.58	...
Price Range	27.12-17.06	27.19-19.75	30.39-18.68	19.01-6.80	21.99-4.43	136.63-9.29	243.00-51.29	59.08-16.48
P/E Ratio	45.97-28.92	46.08-33.47	121.56-74.72	190.10-68.00	...	...	565.12-119.28	...

Address: 1194 N. Mathilda Ave., Sunnyvale, CA 94089
Telephone: 408-745-2000
Fax: 408-745-2100

Web Site: www.juniper.net
Officers: Scott Kriens - Chmn., Pres., C.E.O. Pradeep Sindhu - Vice-Chmn, Chief Tech. Officer

Auditors: Ernst & Young LLP
Investor Contact: 408-745-2371

KELLY SERVICES, INC.

Exchange	Symbol	Price	52Wk Range	Yield	P/E
NMS	KELY A	$27.31 (8/31/2006)	30.80-25.76	1.83	20.85

*7 Year Price Score 85.00 *NYSE Composite Index=100 *12 Month Price Score 95.86

Interim Earnings (Per Share)

Qtr.	Mar	Jun	Sep	Dec
2003	0.01	0.04	0.04	0.05
2004	0.03	0.14	0.21	0.24
2005	0.11	0.26	0.35	0.37
2006	0.24	0.35	...	...

Interim Dividends (Per Share)

Amt	Decl	Ex	Rec	Pay
0.10Q	11/3/2005	11/10/2005	11/15/2005	12/2/2005
0.10Q	2/8/2006	2/16/2006	2/21/2006	3/3/2006
0.10Q	5/10/2006	5/19/2006	5/23/2006	6/2/2006
0.125Q	8/8/2006	8/18/2006	8/22/2006	9/1/2006

Indicated Div: $0.50

Valuation Analysis
Forecast P/E 16.96 (9/9/2006)
Market Cap $983.0 Million
Book Value 708.2 Million
Price/Book 1.39
Price/Sales 0.18

Institutional Holding
No of Institutions 116
Shares 29,097,140
% Held 89.45

Business Summary: Human Resources Services (MIC: 12.6 SIC: 7363 NAIC: 561320)

Kelly Services is a worldwide staffing provider, by which it assigns professional and technical employees in the fields of finance and accounting, education, engineering, information technology, legal, science, health and home care. Co. also offers staff management systems for its customers including staff leasing, outsourcing, consulting, recruitment and vendor management services. Co. serves customers throughout the U.S., the Americas, Europe, and the Asia-Pacific region. As of Jan 1 2006, Co. provided employment for more than 700,000 employees to a variety of customers worldwide.

Recent Developments: For the quarter ended July 2 2006, net income increased 35.8% to $12.7 million from $9.3 million in the year-earlier quarter. Revenues were $1.42 billion, up 8.0% from $1.31 billion the year before. Operating income was $21.3 million versus $13.6 million in the prior-year quarter, an increase of 56.7%. Direct operating expenses rose 8.1% to $1.19 billion from $1.10 billion in the comparable period the year before. Indirect operating expenses increased 4.2% to $208.9 million from $200.5 million in the equivalent prior-year period.

Prospects: Notwithstanding the recent general slowing of the U.S. economy, Co. remains confident that the balance of 2006 will be a period of moderate economic expansion, providing for continued job creation and sustainable demand for temporary staffing. Noticeably, Co.'s results continues to demonstrate solid growth in its earnings, attributable to robust sales combined with improved operating efficiency across its business segments. Looking ahead, Co. expects earnings to be in the range of $0.43 to $0.48 per share for the third quarter of 2006. For full-year 2006, Co. remains with its earnings guidance of between $1.50 and $1.60 per share.

Financial Data (US$ in Thousands)	6 Mos	3 Mos	01/01/2006	01/02/2005	12/28/2003	12/29/2002	12/30/2001	12/30/2000
Earnings Per Share	1.31	1.22	1.09	0.62	0.14	0.52	0.46	2.43
Cash Flow Per Share	1.41	0.75	0.58	1.66	0.87	2.52	4.04	2.50
Tang Book Value Per Share	17.01	16.68	16.30	15.76	15.18	15.17	16.93	17.44
Dividends Per Share	0.400	0.400	0.400	0.400	0.400	0.400	0.850	0.990
Dividend Payout %	30.47	32.75	36.70	64.52	285.71	76.92	184.78	40.74
Income Statement								
Total Revenue	2,776,498	1,360,089	5,289,825	4,984,051	4,325,155	4,323,470	4,256,892	4,487,291
EBITDA	55,659	23,766	98,367	79,630	56,532	75,820	72,363	185,150
Depn & Amortn	20,610	10,329	42,215	44,137	47,795	45,428	44,396	39,465
Income Before Taxes	35,268	13,477	55,965	34,632	8,660	30,754	27,586	145,276
Income Taxes	14,037	4,919	16,702	12,502	3,550	12,185	11,037	58,100
Net Income	21,231	8,558	39,263	22,130	5,110	18,569	16,549	87,176
Average Shares	36,198	36,076	35,949	35,461	35,355	35,900	35,930	35,843
Balance Sheet								
Total Assets	1,377,530	1,337,276	1,312,857	1,247,368	1,137,737	1,072,133	1,039,381	1,089,576
Current Liabilities	539,831	521,596	520,915	483,618	417,316	367,194	348,189	466,107
Total Liabilities	669,319	648,856	640,814	593,058	524,104	453,069	432,226	466,107
Stockholders' Equity	708,211	688,420	672,043	654,310	613,633	619,064	607,155	623,469
Shares Outstanding	35,992	35,914	35,823	35,503	34,772	35,529	35,867	35,739
Statistical Record								
Return on Assets %	3.57	3.38	3.08	1.83	0.46	1.76	1.55	8.26
Return on Equity %	6.99	6.57	5.94	3.43	0.83	3.04	2.69	14.54
EBITDA Margin %	2.00	1.75	1.86	1.60	1.31	1.75	1.70	4.13
Net Margin %	0.76	0.63	0.74	0.44	0.12	0.43	0.39	1.94
Asset Turnover	4.17	4.17	4.14	4.11	3.93	4.11	4.00	4.25
Current Ratio	1.84	1.84	1.82	1.84	1.90	1.96	1.92	1.62
Price Range	30.80-25.76	30.80-25.76	30.80-25.76	31.41-25.35	29.38-19.12	29.24-18.02	29.25-17.85	28.75-20.94
P/E Ratio	23.51-19.66	25.25-21.11	28.26-23.92	50.66-40.89	209.86-136.57	56.23-34.65	63.59-38.80	11.83-8.62
Average Yield %	1.44	1.43	1.39	1.40	1.64	1.63	3.57	4.18

Address: 999 West Big Beaver Road, Troy, MI 48084
Telephone: 248-362-4444
Fax: 248-362-2258

Web Site: www.kellyservices.com
Officers: Terence E. Adderley - Chmn. Carl T. Camden - Pres., Acting C.E.O.

Auditors: PricewaterhouseCoopers LLP
Investor Contact: 248-244-5271
Transfer Agents: Mellon Investor Services, South Hackensack, NJ

KLA-TENCOR CORP.

Exchange	Symbol	Price	52Wk Range	Yield	P/E
NMS	KLAC	$43.91 (8/31/2006)	54.18-39.05	1.09	24.95

*7 Year Price Score 79.41 *NYSE Composite Index=100 *12 Month Price Score 85.97

Interim Earnings (Per Share)

Qtr.	Sep	Dec	Mar	Jun
2002-03	0.26	0.15	0.14	0.14
2003-04	0.18	0.22	0.33	0.48
2004-05	0.58	0.61	0.61	0.52
2005-06	0.38	0.38	0.48	...

Interim Dividends (Per Share)

Amt	Decl	Ex	Rec	Pay
0.12Q	9/27/2005	11/10/2005	11/15/2005	12/1/2005
0.12Q	1/24/2006	2/13/2006	2/15/2006	3/1/2006
0.12Q	5/5/2006	5/11/2006	5/15/2006	6/1/2006
0.12Q	8/3/2006	8/11/2006	8/15/2006	9/1/2006

Indicated Div: $0.48

Valuation Analysis

		Institutional Holding	
Forecast P/E	16.79	No of Institutions	
	(9/9/2006)	321	
Market Cap	$8.7 Billion	Shares	
Book Value	3.4 Billion		182,138,560
Price/Book	2.56	% Held	91.49
Price/Sales	4.41		

Business Summary: IT & Technology (MIC: 10.2 SIC: 3674 NAIC: 334413)

KLA-Tencor is a supplier of process control and yield management solutions for the semiconductor and related microelectronics industries. Co.'s portfolio of products, software, analysis, services and expertise is designed to help integrated circuit ("IC") manufacturers manage yield throughout the entire fabrication process-from research and development to final mass-production yield analysis. Co. operates in one operating segment for the design, manufacture and marketing of process control and yield management systems for the semiconductor and related microelectronics industry.

Recent Developments: For the quarter ended Mar 31 2006, net income decreased 20.3% to $98.1 million from $123.2 million in the year-earlier quarter. Revenues were $518.3 million, down 4.3% from $541.6 million the year before. Operating income was $87.3 million versus $154.8 million in the prior-year quarter, a decrease of 43.6%. Direct operating expenses rose 2.2% to $226.6 million from $221.8 million in the comparable period the year before. Indirect operating expenses increased 23.9% to $204.3 million from $164.9 million in the equivalent prior-year period.

Prospects: Co.'s outlook is supported by recent net order growth. Over the longer term, Co. expects process control to represent a higher percentage of its customers' capital spending. Co. believes this percentage increase in process control spending will be driven by the demand for more precise diagnostics capabilities to address multiple new defects as a result of further shrinking of device feature sizes, the transition to new materials, and fab process innovation. Key drivers for growth in the semiconductor equipment industry in calender year 2006 are expected to be the transition to 300 millimeter fabs, the increased demand for consumer electronics and the strength of the NAND flash market.

Financial Data
(US$ in Thousands)

	9 Mos	6 Mos	3 Mos	06/30/2005	06/30/2004	06/30/2003	06/30/2002	06/30/2001
Earnings Per Share	1.76	1.89	2.12	2.32	1.21	0.70	1.10	0.34
Cash Flow Per Share	1.68	2.05	2.16	2.58	1.79	1.30	1.51	2.19
Tang Book Value Per Share	16.79	16.16	15.67	15.19	13.24	11.45	10.70	9.38
Dividends Per Share	0.480	0.360	0.240	0.120	...	...	...	...
Dividend Payout %	27.27	19.05	11.32	5.17	...	...	...	...
Income Statement								
Total Revenue	1,490,086	971,830	483,860	2,085,153	1,496,718	1,323,049	1,637,282	2,103,757
EBITDA	344,879	223,680	112,728	652,584	387,802	227,886	357,046	568,233
Depn & Amortn	51,495	34,866	17,114	69,300	82,926	71,448	69,590	55,649
Income Before Taxes	293,384	188,814	95,614	620,317	324,716	180,518	287,456	512,584
Income Taxes	44,834	37,487	19,681	157,000	81,015	43,327	71,290	139,526
Net Income	251,470	153,327	76,678	466,695	243,701	137,191	216,166	66,683
Average Shares	204,818	203,345	202,715	201,014	201,799	194,785	196,594	193,435
Balance Sheet								
Total Assets	4,361,318	4,164,536	4,030,598	3,986,372	3,539,179	2,866,597	2,717,718	2,744,551
Current Liabilities	937,102	859,721	856,390	931,862	911,629	651,056	687,490	984,085
Total Liabilities	948,171	868,552	866,476	931,862	911,629	651,056	687,490	984,085
Stockholders' Equity	3,413,147	3,295,984	3,164,122	3,045,257	2,627,550	2,215,541	2,030,228	1,760,466
Shares Outstanding	199,085	199,527	197,411	196,624	196,836	191,733	189,752	187,779
Statistical Record								
Return on Assets %	8.57	9.62	11.21	12.40	7.59	4.91	7.91	2.70
Return on Equity %	11.16	12.44	14.60	16.45	10.04	6.46	11.41	3.84
EBITDA Margin %	23.14	23.02	23.30	31.30	25.91	17.22	21.81	27.01
Net Margin %	16.88	15.78	15.85	22.38	16.28	10.37	13.20	3.17
Asset Turnover	0.48	0.51	0.54	0.55	0.47	0.47	0.60	0.85
Current Ratio	3.76	3.89	3.76	3.44	2.40	2.77	2.36	1.93
Price Range	54.18-38.86	54.09-38.86	51.70-38.86	50.81-35.69	62.60-41.70	49.36-26.15	69.47-29.31	66.81-26.25
P/E Ratio	30.78-22.08	28.62-20.56	24.39-18.33	21.90-15.38	51.74-34.46	70.51-37.36	63.15-26.65	196.51-77.21
Average Yield %	0.99	0.76	0.52	0.28	...	...	...	...

Address: 160 Rio Robles, San Jose, CA 95134 **Telephone:** 408-875-3000 **Fax:** 408-434-4266	**Web Site:** www.kla-tencor.com **Officers:** Kenneth Levy - Chmn. Kenneth L. Schroeder - C.E.O.
Auditors: PricewaterhouseCoopers LLP **Investor Contact:** 408-875-3000 **Transfer Agents:** Equiserve LLP, Boston, Massachusetts	

LAM RESEARCH CORP.

Exchange	Symbol	Price	52Wk Range	Yield	P/E
NMS	LRCX	$42.73 (8/31/2006)	53.49-28.97	N/A	18.26

*7 Year Price Score 119.52 *NYSE Composite Index=100 *12 Month Price Score 100.27

Interim Earnings (Per Share)

Qtr.	Sep	Dec	Mar	Jun
2001-02	(0.07)	(0.41)	0.01	(0.24)
2002-03	(0.11)	0.01	0.01	0.03
2003-04	0.04	0.05	0.13	0.37
2004-05	0.64	0.59	0.41	0.46
2005-06	0.35	0.55	0.60	0.85

Interim Dividends (Per Share)
No Dividends Paid

Valuation Analysis
Forecast P/E 13.02 (9/9/2006)
Market Cap $5.5 Billion
Book Value 1.4 Billion
Price/Book 3.93
Price/Sales 3.34

Institutional Holding
No of Institutions 290
Shares 130,510,816
% Held 92.00

Business Summary: IT & Technology (MIC: 10.2 SIC: 3674 NAIC: 334413)
Lam Research designs, manufactures, markets, and services semiconductor processing equipment used in the fabrication of integrated circuits. Co.'s products selectively remove portions of various films from the wafer to create semiconductors. Co.'s plasma etch systems employ its TCP™ high density and Dual Frequency Confined™ medium density plasma sources. Co.'s product offerings include single-wafer plasma etch systems with a range of applications, wafer cleaning systems, and an array of services designed to optimize the use of these systems by its customers. Co. sells its products and services primarily to semiconductor manufacturers in the U.S., Europe, Japan, Korea and Asia Pacific.

Recent Developments: For the year ended June 25 2006, net income increased 12.2% to $335.8 million from $299.3 million in the prior year. Revenues were $1.64 billion, up 9.3% from $1.50 billion the year before. Operating income was $406.3 million versus $391.0 million in the prior year, an increase of 3.9%. Direct operating expenses rose 10.3% to $818.8 million from $738.4 million in the comparable period the year before. Indirect operating expenses increased 12.9% to $421.1 million from $373.1 million in the equivalent prior-year period.

Prospects: Looking ahead, Co. expects to continue to make substantial investments in research and development in order to meet customers products needs and enhance its competitive position. In addition, Co. expects its international sales to continue to account for a large portion of its total revenue, notably from the Asia region as a substantial amount of the worldwide capacity additions for semiconductor manufacturing continues to occur in this region. Separately, for the fiscal quarter ending Sept 24 2006, Co. projects revenue of $580.0 million to $600.0 million and new orders growth of 5.0% to 10.0% versus the prior quarter, along with gross margin as a percent of revenue of about 51.5%.

Financial Data
(US$ in Thousands)

	06/25/2006	06/26/2005	06/27/2004	06/29/2003	06/30/2002	06/24/2001	06/25/2000	06/30/1999
Earnings Per Share	2.34	2.10	0.59	(0.06)	(0.71)	0.39	1.53	(0.98)
Cash Flow Per Share	2.61	3.10	1.20	0.55	0.17	2.12	1.00	(0.32)
Tang Book Value Per Share	10.89	8.20	6.08	5.09	5.27	5.70	5.11	3.54
Income Statement								
Total Revenue	1,642,171	1,502,453	935,946	755,234	943,114	1,519,789	1,230,767	647,955
EBITDA	428,826	412,664	140,742	19,614	(69,175)	248,391	278,395	(64,631)
Depn & Amortn	24,683	29,666	35,373	44,967	64,338	58,727	46,015	50,924
Income Before Taxes	441,287	399,122	110,650	(15,645)	(127,995)	201,634	236,813	(112,913)
Income Taxes	105,532	99,781	27,662	(7,906)	(37,944)	60,497	32,057	...
Net Income	335,755	299,341	82,988	(7,739)	(90,051)	52,106	204,756	(112,913)
Average Shares	143,732	142,417	144,928	126,300	126,356	132,243	143,327	115,476
Balance Sheet								
Total Assets	2,313,344	1,448,815	1,198,626	1,198,275	1,632,291	1,871,775	1,244,837	979,451
Current Liabilities	566,226	379,133	376,606	216,982	597,544	499,684	287,756	243,995
Long-Term Obligations	350,000	2,786	9,554	332,209	359,691	659,718	321,657	326,500
Total Liabilities	917,195	381,919	386,160	549,191	957,235	1,159,402	609,413	570,495
Stockholders' Equity	1,396,149	1,066,896	812,466	649,084	675,056	712,373	635,424	408,956
Shares Outstanding	128,253	130,098	133,603	127,435	127,978	124,917	124,389	115,674
Statistical Record								
Return on Assets %	17.90	22.68	6.94	N.M.	N.M.	3.35	18.61	N.M.
Return on Equity %	27.34	31.94	11.39	N.M.	N.M.	7.75	39.65	N.M.
EBITDA Margin %	26.11	27.47	15.04	2.60	N.M.	16.34	22.62	N.M.
Net Margin %	20.45	19.92	8.87	N.M.	N.M.	3.43	16.64	N.M.
Asset Turnover	0.88	1.14	0.78	0.54	0.53	0.98	1.12	0.61
Current Ratio	3.01	3.28	2.38	4.02	2.27	3.16	3.55	3.03
Debt to Equity	0.25	N.M.	0.01	0.51	0.53	0.93	0.51	0.80
Price Range	53.49-28.15	31.98-19.80	35.40-18.26	19.29-6.72	30.60-16.00	40.25-13.69	55.56-14.27	15.56-2.94
P/E Ratio	22.86-12.03	15.23-9.43	60.00-30.95	...	...	103.21-35.10	36.32-9.33	...

Address: 4650 Cushing Parkway, Fremont, CA 94538
Telephone: 510-572-0200
Fax: 510-572-6454

Web Site: www.lamresearch.com
Officers: James W. Bagley - Chmn. Stephen G. Newberry - Pres., C.E.O.

Auditors: Ernst & Young LLP
Investor Contact: 510-572-4566
Transfer Agents: Mellon Investor Services LLC, Ridgefield Park, NJ

LAMAR ADVERTISING CO.

Exchange	Symbol	Price	52Wk Range	Yield	P/E
NMS	LAMR	$52.30 (8/31/2006)	59.04-39.65	N/A	153.82

*7 Year Price Score 95.16 *NYSE Composite Index=100 *12 Month Price Score 100.04

Interim Earnings (Per Share)

Qtr.	Mar	Jun	Sep	Dec
2002	(0.16)	0.00	(0.06)	(0.13)
2003	(0.32)	(0.02)	(0.06)	(0.06)
2004	(0.02)	0.08	0.08	0.00
2005	0.05	0.18	0.11	...

Interim Dividends (Per Share)

No Dividends Paid

Valuation Analysis

		Institutional Holding	
Forecast P/E	133.15	No of Institutions	
	(9/9/2006)	186	
Market Cap	$5.5 Billion	Shares	
Book Value	1.8 Billion	89,771,952	
Price/Book	3.02	% Held	
Price/Sales	5.61	88.02	

Business Summary: Advertising, Marketing & PR (MIC: 12.4 SIC: 7311 NAIC: 541810)

Lamar Advertising is engaged in the outdoor advertising business operating more than 151,000 outdoor billboard advertising displays in 44 states and Canada as of Dec 31 2005. Co. also operated over 98,000 logo advertising displays in 19 states and the province of Ontario, Canada, and operated about 31,330 transit advertising displays in 17 states and Canada. Co. satisfies billboard display requirements from ad copy production to placement and maintenance. Logo signs are erected on public rights-of-way near highway exits and deliver brand name information on available gas, food, lodging and camping services. Co. also provides transit advertising on bus shelters, benches and buses.

Recent Developments: For the quarter ended Sep 30 2005, net income increased 45.8% to $12.1 million from $8.3 million in the year-earlier quarter. Revenues were $265.6 million, up 14.7% from $231.6 million the year before. Operating income was $48.7 million versus $33.2 million in the prior-year quarter, an increase of 46.5%. Direct operating expenses rose 17.7% to $89.9 million from $76.4 million in the comparable period the year before. Indirect operating expenses increased 4.1% to $127.0 million from $122.0 million in the equivalent prior-year period.

Prospects: Co. is experiencing solid revenue growth reflecting both organic and acquisition-related increases. Billboard revenues are benefiting from increased sales of outdoor advertising, and higher logo sign revenue is being driven by growth across several markets within Co.'s logo signs program. Meanwhile, Co.'s transit revenue growth is mainly due to the acquisition of Obie Media Corporation. Separately, Co.'s capital expenditures are significantly higher as a result of the deployment of new digital billboards, as well as the reconstruction of inventory destroyed by the hurricanes of 2005. For the second quarter of 2006, Co. expects net revenues of approximately $284.0 million.

Financial Data (US$ in Thousands)	9 Mos	6 Mos	3 Mos	12/31/2004	12/31/2003	12/31/2002	12/31/2001	12/31/2000
Earnings Per Share	0.34	0.31	0.21	0.12	(0.46)	(0.36)	(1.11)	(1.04)
Cash Flow Per Share	3.18	3.18	2.99	3.10	2.53	2.34	1.93	1.94
Income Statement								
Total Revenue	763,166	497,572	232,829	883,510	810,139	775,682	729,050	687,319
EBITDA	347,625	226,873	99,700	399,430	313,706	328,214	327,442	332,768
Depn & Amortn	219,861	143,819	70,571	299,386	282,273	277,893	355,529	318,096
Income Before Taxes	61,986	41,150	8,719	24,460	(55,815)	(56,022)	(154,308)	(131,220)
Income Taxes	26,126	17,371	3,684	11,305	(20,643)	(19,694)	(45,674)	(37,115)
Net Income	35,860	23,779	5,035	13,155	(46,851)	(36,328)	(108,634)	(94,105)
Average Shares	106,279	106,031	104,945	104,571	102,686	101,089	98,566	91,164
Balance Sheet								
Total Assets	3,766,243	3,748,748	3,765,069	3,689,472	3,637,347	3,888,106	3,665,707	3,637,773
Current Liabilities	77,109	149,666	142,260	148,104	74,215	322,561	121,899	128,461
Long-Term Obligations	1,603,802	1,538,761	1,597,429	1,587,424	1,699,819	1,734,746	1,745,026	1,671,466
Total Liabilities	1,934,952	1,935,665	1,978,240	1,953,125	1,914,542	2,178,933	1,993,486	1,948,318
Stockholders' Equity	1,831,291	1,813,083	1,786,829	1,736,347	1,722,805	1,709,173	1,672,221	1,689,455
Shares Outstanding	105,912	105,732	105,513	104,414	103,413	101,494	99,511	97,101
Statistical Record								
Return on Assets %	0.99	0.89	0.62	0.36	N.M.	N.M.	N.M.	N.M.
Return on Equity %	2.06	1.84	1.31	0.76	N.M.	N.M.	N.M.	N.M.
EBITDA Margin %	45.55	45.60	42.82	45.21	38.72	42.31	44.91	48.42
Net Margin %	4.70	4.78	2.16	1.49	N.M.	N.M.	N.M.	N.M.
Asset Turnover	0.27	0.26	0.25	0.24	0.22	0.21	0.20	0.20
Current Ratio	2.80	1.35	1.33	1.23	1.94	1.30	1.17	1.53
Debt to Equity	0.88	0.85	0.89	0.91	0.99	1.01	1.04	0.99
Price Range	45.35-36.86	43.69-36.86	44.40-38.12	44.40-37.18	37.49-28.12	44.99-26.54	48.75-26.42	67.34-36.13
P/E Ratio	133.38-108.41	140.94-118.90	211.43-181.52	370.00-309.83	...	...	...	...

Address: 5551 Corporate Blvd., Baton Rouge, LA 70808 Telephone: 225-926-1000 Fax: 225-926-1005	Web Site: www.lamar.com Officers: Kevin P. Reilly Jr. - Chmn., Pres., C.E.O. Keith A. Istre - C.F.O., Treas.	Auditors: KPMG LLP Investor Contact: 225-926-1000 Transfer Agents: American Stock Transfer & Trust Company

LANCASTER COLONY CORP.

Exchange	Symbol	Price	52Wk Range	Yield	P/E	Div Acheiver
NMS	LANC	$44.14 (8/31/2006)	45.75-37.05	2.36	17.80	36 Years

*7 Year Price Score 88.19 *NYSE Composite Index=100 *12 Month Price Score 96.59

Interim Earnings (Per Share)

Qtr.	Sep	Dec	Mar	Jun
2001-02	0.55	0.47	0.78	0.69
2002-03	0.56	1.43	0.50	0.62
2003-04	0.55	0.74	0.45	0.50
2004-05	0.52	1.08	0.46	0.60
2005-06	0.53	0.89	0.35	0.70

Interim Dividends (Per Share)

Amt	Decl	Ex	Rec	Pay
0.26Q	11/21/2005	12/7/2005	12/9/2005	12/30/2005
0.26Q	2/22/2006	3/8/2006	3/10/2006	3/31/2006
0.26Q	5/24/2006	6/7/2006	6/9/2006	6/30/2006
0.26Q	8/23/2006	9/6/2006	9/8/2006	9/29/2006

Indicated Div: $1.04 (Div. Reinv. Plan)

Valuation Analysis
Forecast P/E   N/A
Market Cap $1.4 Billion
Book Value   494.4 Million
Price/Book   2.88
Price/Sales   1.21

Institutional Holding
No of Institutions   149
Shares   16,143,429
% Held   49.27

Business Summary: Food (MIC: 4.1 SIC: 2038 NAIC: 311412)

Lancaster Colony is a manufacturer and marketer of consumer products including specialty foods for the retail and foodservice markets; glassware and candles for the retail, floral, industrial and foodservice markets; and automotive accessories. Co. operates in three business segments – Specialty Foods manufactures and sells include salad dressings and sauces, fruit glazes, vegetable dips, fruit dips, frozen hearth-baked breads, and dry egg noodles, frozen noodles and pastas, croutons and candies; Glassware and Candles include candles, candle accessories and glass product; and Automotive manufactures and sells a line of rubber, vinyl and carpeted floor mats.

Recent Developments: For the year ended June 30 2006, net income decreased 10.9% to $83.0 million from $93.1 million in the prior year. Revenues were $1.18 billion, up 3.9% from $1.13 billion the year before. Operating income was $113.5 million versus $117.9 million in the prior year, a decrease of 3.8%. Direct operating expenses rose 5.4% to $960.9 million from $912.0 million in the comparable period the year before. Indirect operating expenses decreased 0.6% to $100.9 million from $101.6 million in the equivalent prior-year period.

Prospects: Co.'s earnings are being adversely affected by competitive market pressures on pricing and promotions as well as higher costs for freight, raw materials and energy. Moreover, results are being hampered by Co.'s planned, temporary idling of most manufacturing activities at its Oklahoma glassware facility that resulted in recognizing over $3.0 million in unabsorbed pretax costs. Notwithstanding, Co. is encouraged by improved sales in its Specialty Foods and Automotive segments. Looking ahead, Co. is positive that both its Specialty Foods and Automotive segments will continue to exhibit favorable sales growth towards the fourth fiscal quarter ending June 30 2006.

Financial Data (US$ in Thousands)	06/30/2006	06/30/2005	06/30/2004	06/30/2003	06/30/2002	06/30/2001	06/30/2000	06/30/1999
Earnings Per Share	2.48	2.67	2.24	3.11	2.49	2.37	2.51	2.28
Cash Flow Per Share	2.90	3.35	3.34	4.31	4.35	3.36	3.24	3.03
Tang Book Value Per Share	12.74	14.71	14.16	13.20	11.71	10.38	10.03	9.35
Dividends Per Share	3.030	0.980	0.890	0.780	0.710	0.670	0.630	0.590
Dividend Payout %	122.18	36.70	39.73	25.08	28.51	28.27	25.10	25.88
Income Statement								
Total Revenue	1,175,260	1,131,466	1,096,953	1,106,800	1,129,687	1,098,464	1,104,258	1,045,702
EBITDA	161,142	181,283	159,731	212,470	184,683	182,652	196,117	191,749
Depn & Amortn	32,341	33,262	31,267	31,669	35,287	35,528	34,340	35,569
Income Before Taxes	128,801	148,021	128,464	180,801	149,342	145,885	160,189	153,462
Income Taxes	45,847	54,933	48,462	68,255	57,402	55,649	60,925	58,333
Net Income	82,954	93,088	80,002	112,546	91,940	89,238	99,264	95,129
Average Shares	33,502	34,925	35,778	36,243	36,910	37,636	39,554	41,799
Balance Sheet								
Total Assets	628,021	731,278	712,887	667,716	618,705	571,937	531,844	550,014
Current Liabilities	103,500	103,846	92,731	84,923	89,304	92,294	96,475	116,217
Long-Term Obligations	...	...	...	...	...	1,095	3,040	3,575
Total Liabilities	133,600	143,552	126,102	120,051	117,428	112,036	116,361	135,159
Stockholders' Equity	494,421	587,726	586,785	547,665	501,277	459,901	415,483	414,855
Shares Outstanding	32,245	34,235	35,472	35,770	36,598	37,253	37,962	40,547
Statistical Record								
Return on Assets %	12.21	12.89	11.56	17.50	15.44	16.17	18.30	17.63
Return on Equity %	15.33	15.85	14.07	21.46	19.13	20.39	23.84	23.05
EBITDA Margin %	13.71	16.02	14.56	19.20	16.35	16.63	17.76	18.34
Net Margin %	7.06	8.23	7.29	10.17	8.14	8.12	8.99	9.10
Asset Turnover	1.73	1.57	1.58	1.72	1.90	1.99	2.04	1.94
Current Ratio	3.27	4.57	4.86	4.88	4.10	3.44	3.27	2.83
Debt to Equity	...	...	...	...	...	N.M.	0.01	0.01
Price Range	45.75-37.05	44.63-38.26	46.11-38.20	46.74-32.68	40.16-26.10	33.46-19.50	36.25-19.50	39.44-25.50
P/E Ratio	18.45-14.94	16.72-14.33	20.58-17.05	15.03-10.51	16.13-10.48	14.12-8.23	14.44-7.77	17.30-11.18
Average Yield %	7.39	2.32	2.15	2.00	2.06	2.46	2.06	1.91

Address: 37 West Broad Street, Columbus, OH 43215
Telephone: 614-224-7141
Fax: 614-469-8219

Web Site: www.lancastercolony.com
Officers: John B. Gerlach Jr. - Chmn., Pres., C.E.O.
John L. Boylan - V.P., C.F.O., Treas., Asst. Sec.

Auditors: Deloitte & Touche LLP
Transfer Agents: American Stock Transfer and Trust Company, New York, NY

LATTICE SEMICONDUCTOR CORP.

Exchange	Symbol	Price	52Wk Range	Yield	P/E
NMS	LSCC	$7.32 (8/31/2006)	7.32-4.04	N/A	N/A

*7 Year Price Score 32.20 *NYSE Composite Index=100 *12 Month Price Score 110.06

Interim Earnings (Per Share)

Qtr.	Mar	Jun	Sep	Dec
2003	(0.17)	(0.15)	(0.20)	(0.30)
2004	(0.51)	(0.14)	(0.06)	(0.12)
2005	(0.10)	(0.07)	(0.06)	(0.20)
2006	(0.01)	0.02	...	...

Interim Dividends (Per Share)
No Dividends Paid

Valuation Analysis

		Institutional Holding	
Forecast P/E	54.85	No of Institutions	
	(9/9/2006)	123	
Market Cap	$836.8 Million	Shares	
Book Value	504.5 Million	102,051,768	
Price/Book	1.66	% Held	
Price/Sales	3.68	89.43	

Business Summary: IT & Technology (MIC: 10.2 SIC: 3674 NAIC: 334413)

Lattice Semiconductor designs, develops and markets Field Programmable Gate Arrays and Programmable Logic Devices (PLD), including Field Programmable System Chips, Complex Programmable Logic Devices, Programmable Mixed-Signal Products and Programmable Digital Interconnect Devices, as well as related software. PLDs are widely-used semiconductor components that can be configured by end customers as specific logic circuits, and thus enable shorter design cycle times and reduced development costs. Co.'s products are sold worldwide primarily to original equipment manufacturer customers in the communications, computing, industrial, automotive, medical, consumer and military end markets.

Recent Developments: For the quarter ended June 30 2006, net income amounted to $2.1 million versus a net loss of $8.2 million in the year-earlier quarter. Revenues were $62.7 million, up 19.7% from $52.4 million the year before. Operating loss was $2.2 million versus a loss of $15.5 million in the prior-year quarter. Direct operating expenses rose 18.8% to $27.2 million from $22.9 million in the comparable period the year before. Indirect operating expenses decreased 16.2% to $37.7 million from $45.0 million in the equivalent prior-year period.

Prospects: Co.'s prospects appear constructive, reflecting recent solid revenue growth and improved margins that contributed to a return to profitability. Co.'s top line is also being strengthened by positive market acceptance for its new Field Programmable Gate Array products, which are upgrading its product portfolio. Separately, Co. continues to make significant investments in its research and development activities, of which it believes is essential to maintain product competitiveness and provide new product offerings. For the third quarter of 2006, Co. anticipates sequential revenue growth of flat to approximately 4.0%.

Financial Data
(US$ in Thousands)

	6 Mos	3 Mos	12/31/2005	12/31/2004	12/31/2003	12/31/2002	12/31/2001	12/31/2000
Earnings Per Share	(0.25)	(0.34)	(0.43)	(0.46)	(0.82)	(1.59)	(1.01)	1.47
Cash Flow Per Share	0.06	0.04	(0.18)	0.05	0.31	0.42	0.06	0.92
Tang Book Value Per Share	2.27	2.22	2.18	2.45	2.64	2.51	5.79	5.29
Income Statement								
Total Revenue	120,171	57,452	211,060	225,832	209,662	229,126	295,326	567,759
EBITDA	15,285	6,204	(27,743)	8,095	5,747	8,255	(71,198)	362,118
Depn & Amortn	13,581	6,822	29,611	64,149	99,902	94,375	106,539	102,213
Income Before Taxes	1,704	(618)	(48,886)	(51,661)	(97,660)	(93,369)	(173,966)	262,071
Income Taxes	445	189	233	318	(5,854)	81,866	(64,447)	94,184
Net Income	1,259	(807)	(49,119)	(51,979)	(91,806)	(175,235)	(109,519)	167,887
Average Shares	115,104	113,791	113,525	112,976	111,794	110,193	108,814	120,321
Balance Sheet								
Total Assets	709,078	702,405	715,857	810,906	851,628	941,263	1,173,980	1,295,884
Current Liabilities	62,937	60,110	63,887	72,560	39,101	45,722	59,109	164,704
Long-Term Obligations	123,500	123,500	133,500	169,000	184,000	208,061	260,000	260,000
Total Liabilities	204,605	201,380	217,773	268,315	245,516	280,128	334,210	440,229
Stockholders' Equity	504,473	501,025	498,084	542,591	606,112	661,135	839,770	855,655
Shares Outstanding	114,323	114,104	113,646	113,610	113,040	112,358	109,428	107,533
Statistical Record								
Return on Assets %	N.M.	N.M.	N.M.	N.M.	N.M.	N.M.	N.M.	15.14
Return on Equity %	N.M.	N.M.	N.M.	N.M.	N.M.	N.M.	N.M.	25.02
EBITDA Margin %	12.72	10.80	N.M.	3.58	2.74	3.60	N.M.	63.78
Net Margin %	1.05	N.M.	N.M.	N.M.	N.M.	N.M.	N.M.	29.57
Asset Turnover	0.31	0.30	0.28	0.27	0.23	0.22	0.24	0.51
Current Ratio	5.66	5.54	5.34	5.53	10.30	8.63	11.44	4.35
Debt to Equity	0.24	0.25	0.27	0.31	0.30	0.31	0.31	0.30
Price Range	7.12-4.04	6.66-4.04	5.70-4.04	12.39-4.03	10.05-6.56	22.88-4.34	27.16-14.74	41.34-15.88
P/E Ratio	...	...	...	...	...	...	...	28.13-10.80

Address: 5555 N.E. Moore Court, Hillsboro, OR 97124-6421 Telephone: 503-268-8000 Fax: 503-268-8347	Web Site: www.latticesemi.com Officers: Patrick S. Jones - Acting Chmn. Stephen A. Skaggs - Pres., Acting C.E.O., Sec.	Auditors: PricewaterhouseCoopers LLP Investor Contact: 503-681-8000

LAUREATE EDUCATION INC

Exchange	Symbol	Price	52Wk Range	Yield	P/E
NMS	LAUR	$48.02 (8/31/2006)	55.05-40.94	N/A	28.41

*7 Year Price Score 139.32 *NYSE Composite Index=100 *12 Month Price Score 89.71

Interim Earnings (Per Share)

Qtr.	Mar	Jun	Sep	Dec
2003	(0.39)	0.75	0.12	0.56
2004	(0.01)	0.43	0.19	0.67
2005	0.09	0.38	0.23	0.75
2006	(0.01)	0.72	...	...

Interim Dividends (Per Share)

No Dividends Paid

Valuation Analysis **Institutional Holding**

Forecast P/E	N/A	No of Institutions	189
Market Cap	$2.5 Billion	Shares	
Book Value	1.0 Billion	43,206,112	
Price/Book	2.37	% Held	
Price/Sales	2.43	84.07	

Business Summary: Vocational Education Services (MIC: 6.2 SIC: 8299 NAIC: 611519)

Laureate Education operates an international network of accredited campus-based and online universities and higher education institutions. Through this network, Co. offers career-oriented undergraduate and graduate degree programs as well as other services. Co.'s network of schools offers an education in a variety of disciplines, includuding international business, hotel management, health sciences, information technology and engineering. As of Mar 16 2006, Co. enrolled more than 217,000 students at its higher education institutions located throughout The Americas, Europe, and Asia. Co. has three segments: Campus Based – Latin America, Campus Based – Europe and Laureate Online Education.

Recent Developments: For the quarter ended June 30 2006, income from continuing operations increased 29.9% to $40.7 million from $31.3 million in the year-earlier quarter. Net income increased 76.1% to $38.0 million from $21.6 million in the year-earlier quarter. Revenues were $303.1 million, up 33.6% from $227.0 million the year before. Operating income was $57.0 million versus $44.6 million in the prior-year quarter, an increase of 27.7%. Direct operating expenses rose 32.9% to $234.7 million from $176.6 million in the comparable period the year before. Indirect operating expenses increased 96.9% to $11.4 million from $5.8 million in the equivalent prior-year period.

Prospects: Co.'s results continue to be driven by strong top-line growth and robust student enrollment. For instances, Co.'s enrollment in the South America region is higher, attributable to the strong enrollment growth in Peru and in its traditional universities in Chile. For the second quarter of 2006, Co. anticipates campus-based revenue of $225.0 million to $245.0 million, revenue in Latin America of $175.0 million to $190.0 million, revenue in Europe of $50.0 million to $55.0 million, and online revenue of $50.0 million to $55.0 million. In addition, Co. is targeting earnings of $0.68 to $0.73 per diluted share for the second quarter 2006, and $2.05 and $2.15 per diluted share for full-year 2006.

Financial Data
(US$ in Thousands)

	6 Mos	3 Mos	12/31/2005	12/31/2004	12/31/2003	12/31/2002	12/31/2001	12/31/2000
Earnings Per Share	1.69	1.35	1.45	1.29	1.05	(2.40)	(0.46)	7.02
Cash Flow Per Share	3.26	3.17	2.84	2.67	1.40	2.03	(1.19)	0.18
Tang Book Value Per Share	7.85	7.09	6.91	6.71	7.71	4.35	6.53	7.39
Income Statement								
Total Revenue	538,229	235,110	875,376	648,019	472,806	603,998	484,804	316,651
EBITDA	103,795	18,445	182,151	139,446	63,243	21,063	24,011	31,839
Depn & Amortn	29,775	14,807	50,765	41,558	30,921	31,037	37,968	30,442
Income Before Taxes	67,272	32	130,268	110,800	23,478	(18,365)	(23,126)	(5,925)
Income Taxes	12,367	233	19,667	6,798	(2,930)	(3,490)	(5,680)	(4,308)
Net Income	37,298	(675)	75,183	63,011	46,135	(95,943)	(17,446)	305,222
Average Shares	53,098	50,436	52,028	49,016	43,778	40,053	38,135	43,501
Balance Sheet								
Total Assets	1,835,166	1,842,396	1,782,943	1,530,710	1,149,914	965,275	910,236	1,016,963
Current Liabilities	533,515	600,373	561,413	456,094	312,967	224,643	168,719	293,714
Long-Term Obligations	143,797	142,358	146,683	116,007	105,041	154,055	124,474	128,575
Total Liabilities	704,284	768,703	731,555	614,537	434,713	405,334	307,400	430,820
Stockholders' Equity	1,041,602	999,648	978,709	878,635	669,150	485,928	545,855	553,263
Shares Outstanding	51,353	51,258	49,861	48,813	44,984	40,331	38,742	37,278
Statistical Record								
Return on Assets %	5.36	4.18	4.54	4.69	4.36	N.M.	N.M.	33.73
Return on Equity %	9.08	7.46	8.10	8.12	7.99	N.M.	N.M.	59.26
EBITDA Margin %	19.28	7.85	20.81	21.52	13.38	3.49	4.95	10.05
Net Margin %	6.93	N.M.	8.59	9.72	9.76	N.M.	N.M.	96.39
Asset Turnover	0.62	0.56	0.53	0.48	0.45	0.64	0.50	0.35
Current Ratio	0.73	0.75	0.73	0.84	0.86	1.20	1.71	1.54
Debt to Equity	0.14	0.14	0.15	0.13	0.16	0.32	0.23	0.23
Price Range	55.05-41.85	55.05-41.47	54.63-41.47	44.96-28.51	32.34-11.43	28.68-9.90	28.00-13.56	16.69-11.00
P/E Ratio	32.57-24.76	40.78-30.72	37.68-28.60	34.85-22.10	30.80-10.89	...	...	2.38-1.57

Address: 1001 Fleet Street, Baltimore, MD 21202
Telephone: 410-843-8000
Fax: 410-880-8817

Web Site: www.educate.com; www.sylvan.net
Officers: Douglas L. Becker - Chmn., C.E.O. Peter Cohen - Pres., C.O.O.

Auditors: Ernst & Young LLP

LEVEL 3 COMMUNICATIONS, INC.

Exchange	Symbol	Price	52Wk Range	Yield	P/E
NMS	LVLT	$4.43 (8/31/2006)	5.72-1.96	N/A	N/A

*7 Year Price Score 15.95 *NYSE Composite Index=100 *12 Month Price Score 104.92

Interim Earnings (Per Share)

Qtr.	Mar	Jun	Sep	Dec
2003	0.22	(0.95)	(0.38)	(0.15)
2004	(0.22)	(0.09)	(0.25)	(0.11)
2005	(0.11)	(0.27)	(0.29)	(0.24)
2006	(0.20)	(0.23)	...	...

Interim Dividends (Per Share)
No Dividends Paid

Valuation Analysis   **Institutional Holding**

Forecast P/E	N/A	No of Institutions	
	(9/9/2006)	240	
Market Cap	$4.4 Billion	Shares	
Book Value	N/A		681,754,368
Price/Book	N/A	% Held	58.13
Price/Sales	0.99		

Business Summary: Communications (MIC: 10.1 SIC: 4813 NAIC: 334210)
Level 3 Communications is mainly engaged in the communications and information services businesses, with additional operations in coal mining. As of Dec 31 2005, Co.'s network encompassed an intercity network covering about 48,000 miles in North America; leased or owned local networks in 110 North American markets; an intercity network covering about 3,600 miles across Europe; leased or owned local networks in about 20 European markets; about 6.7 million square feet of Gateway and transmission facilities in North America and Europe; and a 1.28 Terabyte per second (Tbps) transatlantic cable system.

Recent Developments: For the quarter ended June 30 2006, net loss amounted to $201.0 million versus a net loss of $188.0 million in the year-earlier quarter. Revenues were $1.53 billion, up 71.1% from $894.0 million the year before. Operating income was $4.0 million versus a loss of $65.0 million in the prior-year quarter. Direct operating expenses rose 78.1% to $1.03 billion from $576.0 million in the comparable period the year before. Indirect operating expenses increased 30.5% to $500.0 million from $383.0 million in the equivalent prior-year period.

Prospects: On Jul 20 2006, Co. signed a definitive agreement to sell its subsidiary, Software Spectrum to Insight Enterprises Inc., a provider of information technology products and services. Under the agreement, Co. will receive a total of $287.0 million payable in cash at closing, which is expected to occur in the third quarter of 2006. Separately, on Aug 3 2006, Co. acquired Looking Glass Networks Inc., a facilities-based provider of metropolitan transport services, for approximately 21.3 million unregistered shares of its common stock to Looking Glass security holders and approximately $8.7 million in cash, in addition to the assumption of $67.0 million in outstanding Looking Glass debt.

Financial Data
(US$ in Thousands)

	6 Mos	3 Mos	12/31/2005	12/31/2004	12/31/2003	12/31/2002	12/31/2001	12/31/2000
Earnings Per Share	(0.96)	(1.00)	(0.91)	(0.67)	(1.26)	(2.11)	(13.32)	(4.01)
Cash Flow Per Share	0.03	(0.14)	(0.17)	(0.09)	0.04	(1.05)	0.38	2.75
Tang Book Value Per Share	...	...	...	...	N.M.	...	...	12.37
Income Statement								
Total Revenue	2,797,000	1,267,000	3,613,000	3,637,000	4,026,000	3,148,000	1,533,000	1,185,000
EBITDA	274,000	154,000	473,000	715,000	605,000	139,000	(3,809,000)	(986,000)
Depn & Amortn	345,000	181,000	657,000	695,000	827,000	842,000	1,154,000	564,000
Income Before Taxes	(366,000)	(168,000)	(679,000)	(452,000)	(771,000)	(1,234,000)	(5,448,000)	(1,504,000)
Income Taxes	3,000	...	8,000	6,000	(50,000)	(121,000)	...	(49,000)
Net Income	(369,000)	(168,000)	(638,000)	(458,000)	(711,000)	(858,000)	(4,978,000)	(1,455,000)
Average Shares	881,155	821,918	699,589	683,846	565,931	407,317	373,792	362,539
Balance Sheet								
Total Assets	9,751,000	8,284,000	8,277,000	7,544,000	8,293,000	8,963,000	9,316,000	14,919,000
Current Liabilities	1,919,000	1,188,000	1,435,000	1,273,000	1,431,000	1,353,000	1,392,000	1,947,000
Long-Term Obligations	6,558,000	6,357,000	6,023,000	5,067,000	5,250,000	6,102,000	6,209,000	7,318,000
Total Liabilities	9,784,000	8,830,000	8,753,000	7,701,000	8,112,000	9,203,000	9,381,000	10,370,000
Stockholders' Equity	(33,000)	(546,000)	(476,000)	(157,000)	181,000	(240,000)	(65,000)	4,549,000
Shares Outstanding	1,000,173	844,059	817,767	686,496	677,828	443,556	384,704	367,600
Statistical Record								
EBITDA Margin %	9.80	12.15	13.09	19.66	15.03	4.42	N.M.	N.M.
Asset Turnover	0.51	0.50	0.46	0.46	0.47	0.34	0.13	0.10
Current Ratio	1.69	1.60	1.17	1.10	1.36	1.43	1.46	2.59
Debt to Equity	...	...	...	...	29.01	...	...	1.61
Price Range	5.72-1.90	5.60-1.62	3.90-1.62	6.82-2.50	7.46-4.45	7.06-2.22	49.69-1.98	130.19-26.88

Address: 1025 Eldorado Boulevard, Broomfield, CO 80021
Telephone: 720-888-1000
Fax: 720-888-5088

Web Site: www.level3.com
Officers: Walter Scott Jr. - Chmn. Charles C. Miller III - Vice-Chmn., Exec. V.P.

Auditors: KPMG LLP
Investor Contact: 877-585-8266
Transfer Agents: Wells Fargo Bank, Shareholders Services

LIFEPOINT HOSPITALS INC

Exchange	Symbol	Price	52Wk Range	Yield	P/E
NMS	LPNT	$34.05 (8/31/2006)	46.57-28.48	N/A	14.93

*7 Year Price Score 88.03   *NYSE Composite Index=100   *12 Month Price Score 92.10

Interim Earnings (Per Share)

Qtr.	Mar	Jun	Sep	Dec
2003	0.45	0.40	0.42	0.50
2004	0.60	0.48	0.50	0.59
2005	0.63	(0.13)	0.53	0.45
2006	0.68	0.62	...	...

Interim Dividends (Per Share)
No Dividends Paid

Valuation Analysis

		Institutional Holding	
Forecast P/E	14.74	No of Institutions	207
	(9/9/2006)		
Market Cap	$2.0 Billion	Shares	55,291,784
Book Value	1.4 Billion	% Held	96.50
Price/Book	1.42		
Price/Sales	0.86		

Business Summary: Hospitals & Health Care (MIC: 9.3 SIC: 8062 NAIC: 622110)

LifePoint Hospitals is a holding company that owns and operates general acute care hospitals in non-urban communities in the U.S. Co.'s subsidiaries own, lease and operate their respective facilities and other assets. As of Dec 31 2005, Co. operated 53 hospitals, including one hospital that was disposed of effective Jan 1 2006 and two hospitals that are part of discontinued operations not yet divested. Co.'s hospitals are geographically diversified across 20 states: Alabama, Arizona, California, Colorado, Florida, Indiana, Kansas, Kentucky, Louisiana, Mississippi, Nevada, New Mexico, Pennsylvania, South Carolina, Tennessee, Utah, Virginia, West Virginia and Wyoming.

Recent Developments: For the quarter ended June 30 2006, income from continuing operations was $36.4 million compared with a loss of $3.1 million in the year-earlier quarter. Net income amounted to $34.8 million versus a net loss of $7.1 million in the year-earlier quarter. Revenues were $569.2 million, up 22.6% from $464.4 million the year before. Operating income was $61.2 million versus $3.4 million in the prior-year quarter, an increase of. Indirect operating expenses increased 10.2% to $508.0 million from $461.0 million in the equivalent prior-year period.

Prospects: On Jul 20 2006, Co. signed a definitive agreement to acquire Havasu Surgery Center in Lake Havasu City, AZ, which had annual revenues of about $5.5 million. Concurrently, Co. also announced that its Havasu Regional Medical Center had entered into a partnership with the physicians affiliated with Havasu Surgery Center to operate a new venture between Havasu Regional Medical Center and Havasu Surgery Center. The transaction is expected to close in the third quarter of 2006. Following this transaction, Co. will not actively pursue any additional hospital acquisitions for the remainder of 2006, instead, it will continue to focus on the integration of its recent hospital acquisitions.

Financial Data
(US$ in Thousands)

	6 Mos	3 Mos	12/31/2005	12/31/2004	12/31/2003	12/31/2002	12/31/2001	12/31/2000
Earnings Per Share	2.28	1.53	1.43	2.17	1.76	1.10	0.90	0.54
Cash Flow Per Share	5.08	5.32	6.02	4.01	2.81	3.06	3.20	2.77
Tang Book Value Per Share	N.M.	N.M.	N.M.	9.15	6.71	7.20	5.99	2.15
Income Statement								
Total Revenue	1,158,800	589,600	1,855,100	996,900	907,100	743,600	619,400	557,100
EBITDA	167,700	89,500	299,600	203,500	172,100	...	118,800	97,900
Depn & Amortn	50,600	33,200	101,100	48,100	45,700	37,900	34,700	34,100
Income Before Taxes	117,100	56,300	138,200	142,800	113,600	...	66,000	33,100
Income Taxes	46,900	22,500	58,400	56,000	45,100	44,000	31,100	15,200
Net Income	72,900	38,100	72,900	85,700	68,500	41,500	33,300	17,900
Average Shares	56,200	56,100	53,200	42,800	43,300	41,900	37,100	30,000
Balance Sheet								
Total Assets	3,503,100	3,266,000	3,224,600	887,300	799,000	733,500	554,300	488,000
Current Liabilities	217,400	223,700	230,100	79,200	68,800	75,400	66,200	52,100
Long-Term Obligations	1,760,000	1,515,700	1,515,800	221,000	270,000	250,000	150,000	278,300
Total Liabilities	2,130,500	1,933,600	1,936,800	377,800	404,700	375,900	259,300	359,600
Stockholders' Equity	1,372,600	1,332,400	1,287,800	509,500	394,300	357,600	295,000	128,400
Shares Outstanding	57,299	57,487	55,904	38,924	37,885	39,550	39,276	34,709
Statistical Record								
Return on Assets %	3.81	4.04	3.55	10.14	8.94	6.45	6.39	3.93
Return on Equity %	9.81	9.02	8.11	18.91	18.22	12.72	15.73	16.68
EBITDA Margin %	14.47	15.18	16.15	20.41	18.97	...	19.18	17.57
Net Margin %	6.29	6.46	3.93	8.60	7.55	5.58	5.38	3.21
Asset Turnover	0.68	1.03	0.90	1.18	1.18	1.15	1.19	1.22
Current Ratio	2.06	2.06	1.83	2.88	2.49	1.90	2.25	2.26
Debt to Equity	1.28	1.14	1.18	0.43	0.68	0.70	0.51	2.17
Price Range	51.47-28.48	51.47-28.48	51.47-33.56	38.50-27.70	30.47-18.00	42.28-29.37	46.61-28.19	51.13-11.81
P/E Ratio	22.57-12.49	33.64-18.61	35.99-23.47	17.74-12.76	17.31-10.23	38.44-26.70	51.79-31.32	94.68-21.87

Address: 103 Powell Court, Suite 200, Brentwood, TN 37027
Telephone: 615-372-8500
Fax: 615-372-8575

Web Site: www.lifepointhospitals.com
Officers: Kenneth C. Donahey - Chmn., Pres., C.E.O.
Michael J. Culotta - Sr. V.P., C.F.O.

Auditors: Ernst & Young LLP
Transfer Agents: National City Bank, Cleveland, OH

LINCARE HOLDINGS INC.

Exchange	Symbol	Price	52Wk Range	Yield	P/E
NMS	LNCR	$37.03 (8/31/2006)	44.39-34.72	N/A	17.98

*7 Year Price Score 104.68 *NYSE Composite Index=100 *12 Month Price Score 88.87

Interim Earnings (Per Share)

Qtr.	Mar	Jun	Sep	Dec
2003	0.49	0.53	0.59	0.61
2004	0.62	0.66	0.69	0.63
2005	0.51	0.48	0.52	0.54
2006	0.48	0.52	...	...

Interim Dividends (Per Share)
No Dividends Paid

Valuation Analysis | **Institutional Holding**
Forecast P/E | 17.55 | No of Institutions
 | (9/9/2006) | 247
Market Cap | $3.5 Billion | Shares
Book Value | 1.2 Billion | 89,733,800
Price/Book | 2.97 | % Held
Price/Sales | 2.61 | 95.80

Business Summary: Diagnostic Services (MIC: 9.5 SIC: 8099 NAIC: 621999)

Lincare Holdings is a provider of oxygen and other respiratory therapy services to patients in the home. Co.'s customers typically suffer from chronic obstructive pulmonary disease (COPD), such as emphysema, chronic bronchitis or asthma, and require supplemental oxygen or other respiratory therapy services in order to alleviate the symptoms and discomfort of respiratory dysfunction. As of Dec 31 2005, Co. served approximately 625,000 customers in 47 states through 883 operating centers. Co. also provides a variety of durable medical equipment and home infusion therapies in certain geographic markets.

Recent Developments: For the quarter ended June 30 2006, net income increased 3.6% to $51.9 million from $50.1 million in the year-earlier quarter. Revenues were $350.1 million, up 11.1% from $315.2 million the year before. Operating income was $86.5 million versus $82.8 million in the prior-year quarter, an increase of 4.5%. Direct operating expenses rose 15.3% to $77.9 million from $67.6 million in the comparable period the year before. Indirect operating expenses increased 12.7% to $185.7 million from $164.8 million in the equivalent prior-year period.

Prospects: Co.'s near-term outlook appears encouraging, reflecting solid top-line growth. Specifically, Co.'s results are benefiting from internal growth, which it believes is primarily attributable to the underlying demographic growth in the markets for its products and gains in customer counts resulting from its sales and marketing efforts that emphasize enhanced equipment and customer service. Meanwhile, Co. continues to expand by opening denovo locations in new and contiguous geographic markets, while being selective regarding acquisitions of respiratory providers.

Financial Data (US$ in Thousands)	6 Mos	3 Mos	12/31/2005	12/31/2004	12/31/2003	12/31/2002	12/31/2001	12/31/2000
Earnings Per Share	2.06	2.02	2.06	2.60	2.22	1.73	1.23	1.08
Cash Flow Per Share	3.53	3.74	3.74	4.19	3.64	2.69	2.18	2.02
Tang Book Value Per Share	N.M.	0.12	N.M.	1.26	N.M.	0.47	0.40	0.32
Income Statement								
Total Revenue	683,718	333,591	1,266,627	1,268,531	1,147,356	960,904	812,442	702,484
EBITDA	216,619	104,788	447,460	543,878	464,344	383,841	308,685	272,480
Depn & Amortn	50,382	25,116	95,680	88,571	75,875	64,178	75,033	67,422
Income Before Taxes	162,691	77,851	343,066	440,403	371,264	305,662	218,004	188,802
Income Taxes	62,900	29,965	129,370	166,975	139,153	115,234	83,060	71,934
Net Income	99,791	47,886	213,696	273,428	232,111	190,428	134,944	116,868
Average Shares	101,751	102,876	106,306	107,223	104,565	109,770	110,071	108,302
Balance Sheet								
Total Assets	1,697,974	1,720,577	1,666,873	1,721,064	1,431,660	1,198,601	1,071,064	877,595
Current Liabilities	80,702	114,053	93,811	132,415	147,157	110,665	162,015	51,777
Long-Term Obligations	275,000	275,415	275,436	275,293	320,817	155,525	125,775	204,024
Total Liabilities	528,352	558,500	528,997	554,739	583,413	342,311	332,106	293,145
Stockholders' Equity	1,169,622	1,162,077	1,137,876	1,166,325	848,247	856,290	738,958	584,450
Shares Outstanding	93,669	95,620	96,118	101,241	99,012	105,798	107,743	106,635
Statistical Record								
Return on Assets %	12.07	11.87	12.62	17.30	17.65	16.78	13.85	14.62
Return on Equity %	17.77	17.71	18.55	27.07	27.23	23.87	20.39	21.77
EBITDA Margin %	31.68	31.41	35.33	42.87	40.47	39.95	37.99	38.79
Net Margin %	14.60	14.35	16.87	21.55	20.23	19.82	16.61	16.64
Asset Turnover	0.77	0.74	0.75	0.80	0.87	0.85	0.83	0.88
Current Ratio	2.54	2.22	2.12	2.85	1.27	1.39	1.00	2.63
Debt to Equity	0.24	0.24	0.24	0.24	0.38	0.18	0.17	0.35
Price Range	44.39-36.66	45.92-38.14	45.92-38.14	42.65-28.28	43.85-27.80	35.00-24.55	33.89-23.00	30.53-10.66
P/E Ratio	21.55-17.80	22.73-18.88	22.29-18.51	16.40-10.88	19.75-12.52	20.23-14.19	27.55-18.70	28.27-9.87

Address: 19387 US 19 North, Clearwater, FL 33764
Telephone: 727-530-7700
Fax: 727-532-9692

Web Site: www.lincare.com
Officers: John P. Byrnes - Pres., C.E.O. Shawn S. Schabel - C.O.O.

Auditors: KPMG LLP
Investor Contact: 727-530-7700
Transfer Agents: Computershare Investor Services

LINEAR TECHNOLOGY CORP.

Exchange	Symbol	Price	52Wk Range	Yield	P/E	Div Achiever
NMS	LLTC	$34.01 (8/31/2006)	39.26-30.01	1.76	24.82	13 Years

*7 Year Price Score 70.74 *NYSE Composite Index=100 *12 Month Price Score 88.34

Interim Earnings (Per Share)

Qtr.	Sep	Dec	Mar	Jun
2001-02	0.14	0.14	0.16	0.17
2002-03	0.17	0.18	0.19	0.21
2003-04	0.22	0.23	0.27	0.31
2004-05	0.33	0.33	0.39	0.34
2005-06	0.31	0.33	0.35	0.37

Interim Dividends (Per Share)

Amt	Decl	Ex	Rec	Pay
0.10Q	10/19/2005	10/26/2005	10/28/2005	11/16/2005
0.15Q	1/17/2006	1/25/2006	1/27/2006	2/15/2006
0.15Q	4/18/2006	4/26/2006	4/28/2006	5/17/2006
0.15Q	7/27/2006	8/2/2006	8/4/2006	8/23/2006

Indicated Div: $0.60

Valuation Analysis

Forecast P/E	17.96
	(9/9/2006)
Market Cap	$10.3 Billion
Book Value	2.1 Billion
Price/Book	4.90
Price/Sales	9.43

Institutional Holding

No of Institutions	421
Shares	278,294,400
% Held	91.66

Business Summary: IT & Technology (MIC: 10.2 SIC: 3674 NAIC: 334413)

Linear Technology designs, manufactures and markets a broad line of standard high performance linear integrated circuits. Applications for Co.'s products include telecommunications, cellular telephones, networking products, notebook computers, computer peripherals, video/multimedia, industrial instrumentation, security monitoring devices, high-end consumer products, complex medical devices, automotive electronics, factory automation, process control, and military and space systems. The principal product categories are: Amplifiers, High Speed Amplifiers, Voltage regulators, Voltage References, Interface, Data Converters, Radio Frequency Circuits, and Other.

Recent Developments: For the year ended July 2 2006, net income decreased 1.2% to $428.7 million from $434.0 million in the prior year. Revenues were $1.09 billion, up 4.1% from $1.05 billion the year before. Operating income was $564.0 million versus $589.6 million in the prior year, a decrease of 4.4%. Direct operating expenses rose 8.8% to $238.4 million from $219.2 million in the comparable period the year before. Indirect operating expenses increased 20.7% to $290.6 million from $240.9 million in the equivalent prior-year period.

Prospects: Co.'s recent good performance is attributable to strong products sales growth, reflecting robust return on sales including the effects of stock option accounting. Going forward, Co. anticipates fiscal first quarter ended Oct 2006 will be typically slow for industrial and communication businesses, but with growing strength in consumer oriented businesses as the build period for year-end holiday sales approaches. Moreover, Co. projects sales and profits for the first quarter of fiscal 2007 to be similar to the prior quarter as a result of the expected increased bookings, with most of the consumer related bookings increase will not be shipped until the fiscal second quarter ended Jan 2007.

Financial Data
(US$ in Thousands)

	07/02/2006	07/03/2005	06/27/2004	06/29/2003	06/30/2002	07/01/2001	07/02/2000	06/27/1999
Earnings Per Share	1.37	1.38	1.02	0.74	0.60	1.29	0.88	0.61
Cash Flow Per Share	1.68	1.58	1.47	0.91	0.81	1.77	1.40	0.92
Tang Book Value Per Share	6.94	6.55	5.87	5.80	5.63	5.59	4.20	2.95
Dividends Per Share	0.500	0.360	0.280	0.210	0.170	0.130	0.090	0.072
Dividend Payout %	36.50	26.09	27.45	28.38	28.33	10.08	10.23	11.89
Income Statement								
Total Revenue	1,092,977	1,049,694	807,281	606,573	512,282	972,625	705,917	506,669
EBITDA	613,222	638,466	485,475	340,414	271,360	582,073	399,354	279,898
Depn & Amortn	49,272	48,837	48,745	45,903	46,261	35,788	24,958	21,972
Income Before Taxes	616,808	619,964	462,213	333,226	278,350	610,651	417,254	285,727
Income Taxes	188,128	185,990	134,042	96,635	80,721	183,195	129,348	91,434
Net Income	428,680	433,974	328,171	236,591	197,629	427,456	287,906	194,293
Average Shares	313,285	315,067	321,456	321,375	328,538	332,527	328,002	317,888
Balance Sheet								
Total Assets	2,390,895	2,286,234	2,087,703	2,056,879	1,988,433	2,017,074	1,507,256	1,046,914
Current Liabilities	236,826	207,739	202,614	162,029	168,997	202,224	168,677	125,275
Total Liabilities	286,397	279,200	277,098	241,950	206,979	235,117	185,059	140,120
Stockholders' Equity	2,104,498	2,007,034	1,810,605	1,814,929	1,781,454	1,781,957	1,322,197	906,794
Shares Outstanding	303,092	306,587	308,548	312,706	316,150	318,908	315,167	307,462
Statistical Record								
Return on Assets %	18.38	19.52	15.88	11.73	9.89	24.32	22.18	20.09
Return on Equity %	20.91	22.37	18.15	13.19	11.12	27.62	25.42	23.43
EBITDA Margin %	56.11	60.82	60.14	56.12	52.97	59.85	56.57	55.24
Net Margin %	39.22	41.34	40.65	39.00	38.58	43.95	40.78	38.35
Asset Turnover	0.47	0.47	0.39	0.30	0.26	0.55	0.54	0.52
Current Ratio	8.77	9.66	9.04	10.96	10.22	8.54	7.77	7.23
Price Range	41.54-32.90	40.31-34.42	44.95-32.38	36.77-19.61	48.24-28.58	72.94-33.95	72.31-27.89	32.84-10.25
P/E Ratio	30.32-24.01	29.21-24.94	44.07-31.75	49.69-26.50	80.40-47.63	56.54-26.32	82.17-31.69	53.84-16.80
Average Yield %	1.37	0.96	0.71	0.71	0.42	0.24	0.21	0.35

Address: 1630 McCarthy Boulevard, Milpitas, CA 95035
Telephone: 408-432-1900
Fax: 408-434-0507

Web Site: www.linear.com
Officers: Robert H. Swanson Jr. - Chmn. David B. Bell - Pres.

Auditors: Ernst & Young LLP
Investor Contact: 408-432-1900
Transfer Agents: EquiServe Trust Company

LSI INDUSTRIES INC.

Exchange	Symbol	Price	52Wk Range	Yield	P/E	Div Acheiver
NMS	LYTS	$18.33 (8/31/2006)	19.02-12.08	2.62	26.57	12 Years

*7 Year Price Score 107.84 *NYSE Composite Index=100 *12 Month Price Score 94.39

Interim Earnings (Per Share)

Qtr.	Sep	Dec	Mar	Jun
2002-03	0.11	0.14	0.02	(0.81)
2003-04	0.13	0.20	0.05	0.05
2004-05	0.17	0.24	0.12	0.20
2005-06	0.18	0.19	0.12	...

Interim Dividends (Per Share)

Amt	Decl	Ex	Rec	Pay
0.12Q	10/27/2005	11/4/2005	11/8/2005	11/15/2005
0.12Q	1/26/2006	2/3/2006	2/7/2006	2/14/2006
0.12Q	4/27/2006	5/5/2006	5/9/2006	5/16/2006
0.12Q	8/23/2006	8/31/2006	9/5/2006	9/12/2006

Indicated Div: $0.48

Valuation Analysis

Forecast P/E	18.52
	(9/9/2006)
Market Cap	$366.7 Million
Book Value	142.1 Million
Price/Book	2.58
Price/Sales	1.31

Institutional Holding

No of Institutions	93
Shares	16,187,115
% Held	80.86

Business Summary: Electrical (MIC: 11.14 SIC: 3648 NAIC: 335129)

LSI Industries is a provider of corporate visual image products and services through the combination of extensive screen and digital graphics capabilities, a wide variety of high quality indoor and outdoor lighting products, and related professional services. Co. also provides graphics and lighting products and professional services on a stand-alone basis. Co. is a major provider of corporate visual image solutions to the petroleum/convenience store industry. Co.'s business is organized in two segments: the Lighting segment and the Graphics segment.

Recent Developments: For the quarter ended Mar 31 2006, net income was unchanged at $2.4 million versus $2.4 million the year-earlier quarter. Revenues were $64.5 million, down 4.9% from $67.8 million the year before. Operating income was $3.5 million versus $3.2 million in the prior-year quarter, an increase of 9.5%. Direct operating expenses declined 5.7% to $49.5 million from $52.4 million in the comparable period the year before. Indirect operating expenses decreased 5.2% to $11.5 million from $12.2 million in the equivalent prior-year period.

Prospects: Looking ahead to fiscal 2006, Co. expects net sales of $272.0 million to $279.0 million and earnings of $0.66 to $0.71 per diluted share. For fiscal 2007, Co. anticipates a favorable outlook for both its lighting and graphics business as it executes several major national programs. In addition, Co. plans to introduce several new energy efficient lighting products to the marketplace. On the graphics side, Co. expects to benefit from its recently installed third high-speed digital press which is part of its overall capacity expansion. Meanwhile, Co. is actively considering selective acquisitions as part of its core strategy of 'Lighting + Graphics + Technology = Complete Image Solutions'.

Financial Data
(US$ in Thousands)

	9 Mos	6 Mos	3 Mos	06/30/2005	06/30/2004	06/30/2003	06/30/2002	06/30/2001
Earnings Per Share	0.69	0.69	0.74	0.73	0.43	(0.54)	0.70	0.50
Cash Flow Per Share	1.39	1.67	1.76	1.39	0.61	0.67	1.39	(0.14)
Tang Book Value Per Share	6.05	6.04	5.94	5.87	5.41	5.20	4.95	4.37
Dividends Per Share	0.540	0.520	0.472	0.344	0.264	0.192	0.189	0.205
Dividend Payout %	78.26	75.36	63.78	47.12	61.40	...	26.89	40.96
Income Statement								
Total Revenue	208,726	144,222	70,900	282,440	241,405	213,133	259,261	233,940
EBITDA	20,465	15,275	7,444	30,000	19,959	17,068	29,480	22,852
Depn & Amortn	5,093	3,422	1,707	6,974	5,925	5,702	6,096	5,558
Income Before Taxes	15,696	12,025	5,823	22,873	13,797	11,247	22,860	17,317
Income Taxes	5,706	4,450	2,154	8,237	5,107	3,454	8,674	6,716
Net Income	9,990	7,575	3,669	14,636	8,690	(10,748)	14,186	9,878
Average Shares	20,393	20,457	20,344	20,087	20,038	19,922	20,058	19,730
Balance Sheet								
Total Assets	173,035	171,657	175,836	172,637	174,732	162,776	189,842	181,759
Current Liabilities	28,451	27,338	33,473	31,615	32,399	23,872	30,383	29,661
Long-Term Obligations	...	...	...	...	11,554	13,999	17,688	23,638
Total Liabilities	30,945	29,849	35,970	34,597	45,869	37,871	50,493	54,566
Stockholders' Equity	142,090	141,808	139,866	138,040	128,863	124,905	139,349	127,193
Shares Outstanding	20,006	19,990	19,974	19,869	19,733	19,702	19,720	19,572
Statistical Record								
Return on Assets %	8.26	8.13	8.48	8.43	5.14	N.M.	7.64	6.01
Return on Equity %	10.18	10.21	11.07	10.97	6.83	N.M.	10.64	8.05
EBITDA Margin %	9.80	10.59	10.50	10.62	8.27	8.01	11.37	9.77
Net Margin %	4.79	5.25	5.17	5.18	3.60	N.M.	5.47	4.22
Asset Turnover	1.65	1.64	1.61	1.63	1.43	1.21	1.40	1.42
Current Ratio	3.56	3.64	3.07	3.13	3.00	3.50	2.84	3.09
Debt to Equity	...	...	...	...	0.09	0.11	0.13	0.19
Price Range	19.02-10.95	19.02-10.05	19.00-9.57	14.26-8.49	14.37-8.73	14.79-6.54	17.29-10.77	14.29-7.87
P/E Ratio	27.57-15.87	27.57-14.57	25.68-12.93	19.53-11.63	33.42-20.30	...	24.70-15.39	28.58-15.73
Average Yield %	3.54	3.62	3.74	3.11	2.28	2.18	1.37	1.88

Address: 10000 Alliance Road, Cincinnati, OH 45242	**Auditors:** Grant Thornton LLP
Telephone: 513-793-3200	**Investor Contact:** 513-793-3200
Fax: 513-791-0813	**Transfer Agents:** Computershare Investor Services, LLC
Web Site: www.lsi-industries.com	
Officers: Robert J. Ready - Chmn., Pres., C.E.O. James P. Sferra - Exec. V.P., Manufacturing, Sec.	

LTX CORP.

Exchange	Symbol	Price	52Wk Range	Yield	P/E
NMS	LTXX	$5.07 (8/31/2006)	7.65-3.29	N/A	N/A

*7 Year Price Score 31.01 *NYSE Composite Index=100 *12 Month Price Score 106.48

Interim Earnings (Per Share)

Qtr.	Oct	Jan	Apr	Jul
2002-03	(0.46)	(0.46)	(0.36)	(1.63)
2003-04	(0.19)	(0.03)	0.07	0.16
2004-05	(1.01)	(0.31)	(0.75)	(0.10)
2005-06	(0.14)	(0.02)	0.13	

Interim Dividends (Per Share)
No Dividends Paid

Valuation Analysis

		Institutional Holding	
Forecast P/E	14.83	No of Institutions	
	(9/9/2006)	102	
Market Cap	$313.8 Million	Shares	
Book Value	103.6 Million		45,245,604
Price/Book	3.03	% Held	
Price/Sales	1.67		73.11

Business Summary: Instruments and Related Products (MIC: 11.15 SIC: 3823 NAIC: 334513)

LTX Corporation designs, manufactures and markets automatic semiconductor test equipment, used to test devices at different stages during the manufacturing process. These devices are used in numerous products including in wireless access points and interfaces, in cable as well as digital subscriber line modems, in personal communication products such as cell phones and personal digital assistants, in consumer products such as televisions, videogame systems, digital cameras and automobile electronics, as well as for power management in portable and automotive electronics. Co. also sells hardware and software support and maintenance services for its test systems.

Recent Developments: For the quarter ended Apr 30 2006, net income amounted to $8.1 million versus a net loss of $45.7 million in the year-earlier quarter. Revenues were $56.3 million, up 120.6% from $25.5 million the year before. Operating income was $8.9 million versus a loss of $45.6 million in the prior-year quarter. Direct operating expenses rose 43.7% to $26.9 million from $18.7 million in the comparable period the year before. Indirect operating expenses decreased 60.7% to $20.6 million from $52.4 million in the equivalent prior-year period.

Prospects: Co. is encouraged by the customer acceptance of its product strategy which, together with an improving business environment, continues to boost its current growth cycle. Moreover, Co.'s top-line growth is reflecting a continued upward trend in demand for its semiconductor test equipment as well as the increased demand for its Fusion CX, EX and MX products, driven by the communications system-on-a-chip (SOC), radio frequency wireless, automotive and mixed signal/converter end markets. Going forward into full-year fiscal 2006, Co. expects revenue to be in the range of $68.0 million to $70.0 million, while earnings are projected to range from $0.22 to $0.24 per share.

Financial Data
(US$ in Thousands)

	9 Mos	6 Mos	3 Mos	07/31/2005	07/31/2004	07/31/2003	07/31/2002	07/31/2001
Earnings Per Share	(0.13)	(1.01)	(1.30)	(2.17)	0.03	(2.92)	(3.08)	0.43
Cash Flow Per Share	0.16	(0.24)	(0.33)	(0.91)	0.21	(1.41)	(1.80)	0.30
Tang Book Value Per Share	1.42	1.26	1.28	1.41	3.59	1.63	4.59	7.64
Income Statement								
Total Revenue	149,093	92,754	44,951	134,531	255,801	119,449	121,273	330,030
EBITDA	...	...	...	...	24,136	(125,711)	(99,347)	50,119
Depn & Amortn	10,913	7,313	3,643	18,494	18,699	16,896	17,025	14,139
Income Before Taxes	...	...	...	...	1,961	(145,068)	(116,157)	43,874
Income Taxes	...	...	...	...	...	...	33,723	13,163
Net Income	(1,688)	(9,829)	(8,383)	(132,726)	1,961	(145,068)	(149,880)	21,145
Average Shares	62,088	61,566	61,535	61,144	58,057	49,614	48,693	49,634
Balance Sheet								
Total Assets	312,501	302,132	311,186	316,392	459,564	324,896	463,989	483,039
Current Liabilities	124,651	122,395	131,563	65,857	75,310	75,744	87,163	107,786
Long-Term Obligations	81,220	83,020	84,820	147,687	150,000	150,064	151,293	5,984
Total Liabilities	208,871	208,319	216,383	213,544	225,310	225,808	238,456	113,770
Stockholders' Equity	103,630	93,813	94,803	102,848	234,254	99,088	225,533	369,269
Shares Outstanding	61,888	61,707	61,543	61,531	60,903	51,633	49,184	48,355
Statistical Record								
Return on Assets %	N.M.	N.M.	N.M.	N.M.	0.50	N.M.	N.M.	4.50
Return on Equity %	N.M.	N.M.	N.M.	N.M.	1.17	N.M.	N.M.	5.97
EBITDA Margin %	...	...	...	...	9.44	N.M.	N.M.	15.19
Net Margin %	N.M.	N.M.	N.M.	N.M.	0.77	N.M.	N.M.	6.41
Asset Turnover	0.59	0.48	0.39	0.35	0.65	0.30	0.26	0.70
Current Ratio	2.04	1.97	1.87	3.78	4.89	3.06	4.27	3.73
Debt to Equity	0.78	0.88	0.89	1.44	0.64	1.51	0.67	0.02
Price Range	6.66-3.29	6.66-3.29	8.09-3.29	8.09-3.53	19.83-7.49	11.14-3.33	27.41-8.40	31.82-10.19
P/E Ratio	...	...	...	...	661.00-249.67	...	...	74.00-23.69

Address: 50 Rosemont Road, Westwood, MA 02090
Telephone: 781-461-1000

Web Site: www.ltx.com
Officers: Roger W. Blethen - Chmn., C.E.O. Mark J. Gallenberger - V.P., C.F.O., Treas.

Auditors: Ernst & Young LLP
Transfer Agents: EquiServe LP, Boston, MA

MACROVISION CORP.

Exchange	Symbol	Price	52Wk Range	Yield	P/E
NMS	MVSN	$23.28 (8/31/2006)	25.65-14.93	N/A	59.69

*7 Year Price Score 51.22 *NYSE Composite Index=100 *12 Month Price Score 103.31

Interim Earnings (Per Share)

Qtr.	Mar	Jun	Sep	Dec
2003	0.14	0.09	0.15	0.21
2004	0.21	0.18	0.03	0.31
2005	0.11	0.12	0.12	0.09
2006	0.06	0.12	...	...

Interim Dividends (Per Share)
No Dividends Paid

Valuation Analysis   **Institutional Holding**

Forecast P/E	20.96 (9/9/2006)	No of Institutions	142
Market Cap	$1.2 Billion	Shares	50,159,608
Book Value	468.0 Million	% Held	96.29
Price/Book	2.59		
Price/Sales	5.44		

Business Summary: IT & Technology (MIC: 10.2 SIC: 7373 NAIC: 541512)
Macrovision provides digital lifecycle value management services that enable the delivery and enhanced use of software and content. Co.'s services include anti-piracy and content protection technologies and services, embedded licensing technologies, usage monitoring for enterprises, and services from installation to update to back-office entitlement management. In addition, Co. markets the FLEXnet licensing platform and the InstallShield suite of software installation, repackaging, and update services. Co. also operates Trymedia Systems, a distribution network for downloadable personal computer games. Co.'s customers include motion picture studios, music labels, and software publishers.

Recent Developments: For the quarter ended June 30 2006, net income increased 2.9% to $6.2 million from $6.1 million in the year-earlier quarter. Revenues were $58.3 million, up 31.4% from $44.4 million the year before. Operating income was $4.2 million versus $8.5 million in the prior-year quarter, a decrease of 50.9%. Direct operating expenses rose 93.4% to $14.4 million from $7.5 million in the comparable period the year before. Indirect operating expenses increased 39.8% to $39.7 million from $28.4 million in the equivalent prior-year period.

Prospects: Co.'s top-line results are being primarily driven by solid organic growth of its existing software products due to increased market penetration and a growing customer base. In addition, Co. is benefiting from an increase in its software licensing revenue related to its Feb 2006 acquisition of eMeta Corp. Moreover, Co. is experiencing an increase in its service revenue as a result of its Jul 2005 acquisition of Trymedia Systems, Inc. and the acquisition of eMeta. In view of that, Co. continues to believe that its revenue will range between $239.0 million and $249.0 million in 2006, while it expects revenue to range from $56.0 million to $58.0 million for the third quarter of 2006.

Financial Data (US$ in Thousands)	6 Mos	3 Mos	12/31/2005	12/31/2004	12/31/2003	12/31/2002	12/31/2001	12/31/2000
Earnings Per Share	0.39	0.39	0.43	0.73	0.60	0.24	0.37	0.26
Cash Flow Per Share	1.40	1.18	1.09	1.20	1.21	1.10	0.70	0.75
Tang Book Value Per Share	5.74	5.33	5.61	5.83	6.03	5.29	5.68	4.79
Income Statement								
Total Revenue	115,367	57,018	203,230	182,099	128,346	102,262	98,813	80,116
EBITDA	26,987	14,930	51,630	63,827	55,571	26,597	55,426	51,762
Depn & Amortn	11,021	5,261	15,786	9,570	9,627	11,762	22,267	22,344
Income Before Taxes	15,966	9,669	41,603	57,390	49,494	21,916	33,159	29,418
Income Taxes	6,818	6,766	19,488	20,660	19,798	9,827	13,974	15,825
Net Income	9,148	2,903	22,115	36,730	29,696	12,089	19,185	13,593
Average Shares	53,090	52,543	51,373	50,619	49,518	50,602	51,746	51,386
Balance Sheet								
Total Assets	559,248	532,369	497,925	452,473	385,566	324,666	342,869	296,438
Current Liabilities	88,312	84,278	68,816	53,150	40,726	27,359	17,353	16,250
Long-Term Obligations	...	...	...	...	...	17	33	56
Total Liabilities	91,256	85,019	69,775	54,129	41,600	27,807	24,669	20,463
Stockholders' Equity	467,992	447,350	428,150	398,344	343,966	296,859	318,200	275,975
Shares Outstanding	52,090	51,706	51,368	50,194	49,098	48,424	50,818	49,818
Statistical Record								
Return on Assets %	3.83	3.94	4.65	8.74	8.36	3.62	6.00	6.39
Return on Equity %	4.48	4.58	5.35	9.87	9.27	3.93	6.46	7.15
EBITDA Margin %	23.39	26.18	25.40	35.05	43.30	26.01	56.09	64.61
Net Margin %	7.93	5.09	10.88	20.17	23.14	11.82	19.42	16.97
Asset Turnover	0.43	0.42	0.43	0.43	0.36	0.31	0.31	0.38
Current Ratio	3.37	3.53	4.35	4.91	4.14	8.01	9.34	8.62
Price Range	25.65-14.93	24.13-14.93	26.41-14.93	27.94-16.81	23.62-10.89	37.31-9.19	75.81-23.72	107.00-30.25
P/E Ratio	65.77-38.28	61.87-38.28	61.42-34.72	38.27-23.03	39.37-18.15	155.46-38.29	204.90-64.11	411.54-116.35

Address: 2830 De La Cruz Boulevard, Santa Clara, CA 95050 Telephone: 408-743-8600 Fax: 408-743-8610	Web Site: www.macrovision.com Officers: John O. Ryan - Chmn. William A. Krepick - Pres.	Auditors: KPMG LLP Investor Contact: 408-743-8600

MAF BANCORP, INC.

Exchange	Symbol	Price	52Wk Range	Yield	P/E	Div Acheiver
NMS	MAFB	$41.27 (8/31/2006)	44.79-39.37	2.42	13.10	11 Years

*7 Year Price Score 98.72 *NYSE Composite Index=100 *12 Month Price Score 95.74

Interim Earnings (Per Share)

Qtr.	Mar	Jun	Sep	Dec
2003	0.81	0.82	0.79	0.84
2004	0.73	0.77	0.77	0.74
2005	0.72	0.76	0.83	0.83
2006	0.74	0.75	...	...

Interim Dividends (Per Share)

Amt	Decl	Ex	Rec	Pay
0.23Q	10/28/2005	12/13/2005	12/15/2005	1/4/2006
0.25Q	1/25/2006	3/15/2006	3/17/2006	4/4/2006
0.25Q	5/10/2006	6/13/2006	6/15/2006	7/3/2006
0.25Q	9/13/2006	9/15/2006	9/15/2006	10/3/2006

Indicated Div: $1.00

Valuation Analysis

		Institutional Holding	
Forecast P/E	13.67 (9/9/2006)	No of Institutions	131
Market Cap	$1.4 Billion	Shares	18,408,336
Book Value	1.0 Billion	% Held	55.80
Price/Book	1.32		
Price/Sales	2.17		

Business Summary: Other Depository Banking (MIC: 8.5 SIC: 6035 NAIC: 522120)

MAF Bancorp is a holding company. Through its wholly-owned subsidiary, Mid America Bank, Co. offers a variety of checking, savings and other deposit accounts as well as investment services, general insurance services and other financial services targeted to individuals, families and small- to medium-sized businesses in its primary market areas of Illinois and Wisconsin. Co. also originates residential one- to four-family mortgage loans, home equity loans, and equity lines of credit. In addition, Co. targets multi-family mortgage and residential construction loans and commercial real estate, land development and commercial loans. As of Dec 31 2005, Co. had total assets of $10.49 billion.

Recent Developments: For the quarter ended June 30 2006, net income increased 2.5% to $25.7 million from $25.1 million in the year-earlier quarter. Net interest income decreased 0.2% to $66.9 million from $67.1 million in the year-earlier quarter. Non-interest income rose 19.5% to $22.0 million from $18.4 million, while non-interest expense advanced 3.7% to $48.8 million.

Prospects: Notwithstanding being restrained by a decline in net interest margin, Co.'s results are benefiting from an increase in its non-interest income, largely due to higher deposit account service fee income and brokerage commissions, increased yields on bank-owned life insurance investments, as well as gains from the sale of fixed assets and other real estate. Going forward, Co. expects further compression in its net interest margin due to the flat yield curve environment, continued pressure on funding costs from strong competition in its markets. Also, the softness in the residential real estate market is expected to negatively affect Co.'s real estate profit in the second half of 2006.

Financial Data (US$ in Thousands)	6 Mos	3 Mos	12/31/2005	12/31/2004	12/31/2003	12/31/2002	12/31/2001	12/31/2000
Earnings Per Share	3.15	3.16	3.13	3.01	3.26	3.11	2.56	2.40
Cash Flow Per Share	1.87	2.28	4.54	2.40	8.14	2.18	(3.68)	0.53
Tang Book Value Per Share	18.35	18.75	20.08	18.95	18.17	16.62	14.37	13.80
Dividends Per Share	0.960	0.940	0.920	0.840	0.720	0.600	0.460	0.390
Dividend Payout %	30.48	29.75	29.39	27.91	22.09	19.29	17.97	16.25
Income Statement								
Interest Income	291,652	141,515	478,656	421,173	316,430	329,490	345,736	343,103
Interest Expense	157,283	74,073	213,897	159,885	136,952	171,465	214,489	217,173
Net Interest Income	134,369	67,442	264,759	261,288	179,478	158,025	131,247	125,930
Provision for Losses	1,650	400	1,980	1,215	...	300	...	1,500
Non-Interest Income	42,699	20,707	81,176	76,286	71,633	56,363	47,118	37,443
Non-Interest Expense	98,455	49,668	186,074	184,048	120,197	99,342	83,424	73,003
Income Before Taxes	76,963	38,081	157,881	152,311	130,914	114,746	94,941	88,870
Income Taxes	26,196	13,001	54,528	50,789	47,481	40,775	35,466	32,311
Net Income	50,767	25,080	103,353	101,522	83,433	73,971	59,475	56,559
Average Shares	34,131	34,018	32,983	33,706	25,592	23,748	23,195	23,586
Balance Sheet								
Net Loans & Leases	7,955,098	8,026,515	7,174,742	6,842,259	6,324,596	4,363,152	4,286,470	4,287,040
Total Assets	11,450,336	11,534,062	10,487,504	9,681,384	8,933,585	5,937,181	5,595,039	5,195,588
Total Deposits	6,926,537	6,895,974	6,197,503	5,935,708	5,580,455	3,751,237	3,557,997	2,974,213
Total Liabilities	10,411,480	10,467,758	9,509,325	8,706,998	8,031,981	5,435,723	5,159,166	4,807,859
Stockholders' Equity	1,038,856	1,066,304	978,179	974,386	901,604	501,458	435,873	387,729
Shares Outstanding	33,101	33,854	32,066	33,273	33,063	23,252	22,982	23,110
Statistical Record								
Return on Assets %	0.98	0.98	1.02	1.09	1.12	1.28	1.10	1.14
Return on Equity %	10.55	10.33	10.59	10.79	11.89	15.78	14.44	15.23
Net Interest Margin %	44.58	47.66	55.31	62.04	56.72	47.96	37.96	36.70
Efficiency Ratio %	28.34	30.62	33.24	37.00	30.97	25.75	21.24	19.18
Loans to Deposits	1.15	1.16	1.16	1.15	1.13	1.16	1.20	1.44
Price Range	44.80-39.37	44.80-38.50	44.82-38.50	47.00-39.30	44.53-32.87	39.95-28.26	32.35-24.81	28.50-15.50
P/E Ratio	14.22-12.50	14.18-12.18	14.32-12.30	15.61-13.06	13.66-10.08	12.85-9.25	12.64-9.69	11.88-6.46
Average Yield %	2.24	2.21	2.17	1.95	1.91	1.76	1.63	1.94

Address: 55th Street & Holmes Avenue, Clarendon Hills, IL 60514-1500
Telephone: 630-325-7300
Fax: 630-325-1326

Web Site: www.mafbancorp.com
Officers: Allen H. Koranda - Chmn., C.E.O. Kenneth Koranda - Vice-Chmn., Pres.

Auditors: KPMG LLP
Investor Contact: 630-325-7300

MATTHEWS INTERNATIONAL CORP

Exchange	Symbol	Price	52Wk Range	Yield	P/E	Div Acheiver
NMS	MATW	$35.60 (8/31/2006)	40.23-31.87	0.56	18.26	11 Years

7 Year Price Score 113.60 *NYSE Composite Index=100* **12 Month Price Score 92.38**

Interim Earnings (Per Share)

Qtr.	Dec	Mar	Jun	Sep
2002-03	0.29	0.36	0.38	0.36
2003-04	0.35	0.42	0.44	0.51
2004-05	0.39	0.47	0.50	0.48
2005-06	0.40	0.52	0.55	...

Interim Dividends (Per Share)

Amt	Decl	Ex	Rec	Pay
0.05Q	10/18/2005	10/27/2005	10/31/2005	11/14/2005
0.05Q	1/19/2006	1/27/2006	1/31/2006	2/14/2006
0.05Q	4/25/2006	5/3/2006	5/5/2006	5/19/2006
0.05Q	7/20/2006	7/27/2006	7/31/2006	8/14/2006

Indicated Div: $0.20

Valuation Analysis

Forecast P/E	17.29
	(9/9/2006)
Market Cap	$1.1 Billion
Book Value	391.4 Million
Price/Book	2.90
Price/Sales	1.60

Institutional Holding

No of Institutions	107
Shares	22,930,272
% Held	71.89

Business Summary: Consumer Accessories (MIC: 4.6 SIC: 3995 NAIC: 339995)

Matthews International is engaged in the design, manufacture and marketing of memorialization products and brand solutions for the cemetery and funeral home industries. Memorialization products consist primarily of bronze memorials and memorialization products, caskets and cremation equipment for the cemetery and funeral home industries. Brand solutions include graphics imaging products and services, merchandising solutions, and marking products. Co.'s products and operations are comprised of six business segments: Bronze, Casket, Cremation, Graphics Imaging, Marking Products and Merchandising Solutions.

Recent Developments: For the quarter ended June 30 2006, net income increased 13.4% to $17.7 million from $15.6 million in the year-earlier quarter. Revenues were $181.8 million, up 14.4% from $159.0 million the year before. Operating income was $30.5 million versus $26.6 million in the prior-year quarter, an increase of 14.7%. Direct operating expenses rose 9.5% to $111.5 million from $101.9 million in the comparable period the year before. Indirect operating expenses increased 30.3% to $39.8 million from $30.5 million in the equivalent prior-year period.

Prospects: Co.'s near term outlook appears mixed. On the positive side, Co. is experiencing higher sales and improved operating profit, due principally to its acquisition of Milso Industries Corporation in July 2005 and sales gains in several of its businesses. Furthermore, Co. indicated that it is beginning to realize the benefits of some of its cost control initiatives in its businesses, particularly the Casket and Merchandising Solutions businesses. However, Co. cautioned that as it is still in the early stages of these trends, it continues to anticipate challenges over the near term.

Financial Data
(US$ in Thousands)

	9 Mos	6 Mos	3 Mos	09/30/2005	09/30/2004	09/30/2003	09/30/2002	09/30/2001
Earnings Per Share	1.95	1.90	1.85	1.84	1.72	1.39	1.10	1.01
Cash Flow Per Share	1.48	2.15	2.26	2.29	2.58	1.85	1.80	1.26
Tang Book Value Per Share	1.89	1.34	1.33	0.85	2.81	2.75	0.74	1.29
Dividends Per Share	0.195	0.190	0.185	0.180	0.160	0.110	0.105	0.100
Dividend Payout %	10.00	10.00	10.00	9.78	9.30	7.91	9.55	9.90
Income Statement								
Total Revenue	532,981	351,177	170,109	639,822	508,801	458,865	428,086	283,282
EBITDA	97,171	61,413	27,524	118,789	109,459	91,078	80,484	66,037
Depn & Amortn	16,165	10,706	5,400	19,893	15,628	14,872	13,856	12,932
Income Before Taxes	76,066	47,691	20,684	95,930	91,833	73,354	62,457	51,458
Income Taxes	28,601	17,932	7,777	36,106	35,638	28,461	24,225	19,859
Net Income	47,465	29,759	12,907	59,824	56,195	44,893	35,006	31,599
Average Shares	32,295	32,293	32,299	32,525	32,688	32,314	31,795	31,320
Balance Sheet								
Total Assets	706,819	687,114	655,611	662,067	530,542	436,741	422,601	288,952
Current Liabilities	117,742	119,627	130,318	145,577	111,572	76,323	87,186	66,539
Long-Term Obligations	133,708	136,757	115,696	118,952	54,389	57,023	96,487	40,726
Total Liabilities	315,451	318,931	307,188	327,706	218,292	180,513	241,226	145,236
Stockholders' Equity	391,368	368,183	348,423	334,361	312,250	256,228	181,375	143,716
Shares Outstanding	31,898	32,120	32,078	32,026	32,410	32,162	31,167	30,273
Statistical Record								
Return on Assets %	10.14	10.18	10.07	10.03	11.59	10.45	9.84	12.40
Return on Equity %	17.52	17.86	17.82	18.50	19.72	20.52	21.54	23.36
EBITDA Margin %	18.23	17.49	16.18	18.57	21.51	19.85	18.80	23.31
Net Margin %	8.91	8.47	7.59	9.35	11.04	9.78	8.18	11.15
Asset Turnover	1.14	1.13	1.11	1.07	1.05	1.07	1.20	1.11
Current Ratio	2.11	1.96	1.71	1.59	1.81	2.18	1.79	1.54
Debt to Equity	0.34	0.37	0.33	0.36	0.17	0.22	0.53	0.28
Price Range	41.57-33.57	41.57-31.64	41.57-31.64	41.57-31.64	36.08-26.33	28.46-21.71	28.67-21.23	22.30-13.06
P/E Ratio	21.32-17.22	21.88-16.65	22.47-17.10	22.59-17.20	20.98-15.31	20.47-15.62	26.06-19.30	22.08-12.93
Average Yield %	0.52	0.51	0.50	0.50	0.51	0.46	0.43	0.58

Address: Two Northshore Center, Pittsburgh, PA 15212-5851 **Telephone:** 412-442-8200 **Fax:** 412-442-8290	**Web Site:** www.matw.com **Officers:** David M. Kelly - Chmn., C.E.O. David J. DeCarlo - Vice-Chmn.	**Auditors:** PricewaterhouseCoopers LLP **Investor Contact:** 412-442-8200 **Transfer Agents:** Computershare Investor Services LLC, Chicago, IL

MAXIM INTEGRATED PRODUCTS, INC.

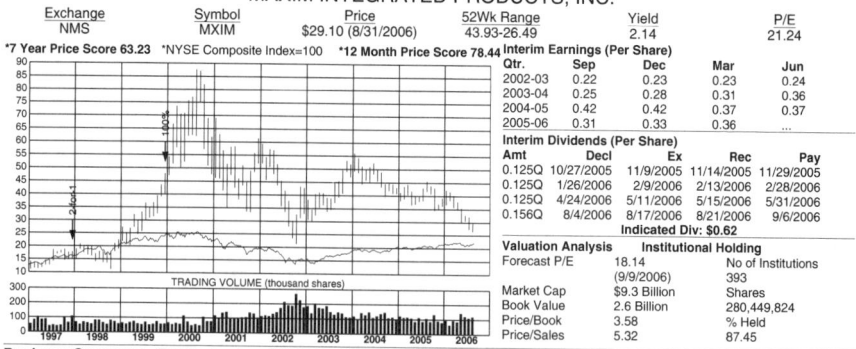

Exchange	Symbol	Price	52Wk Range	Yield	P/E
NMS	MXIM	$29.10 (8/31/2006)	43.93-26.49	2.14	21.24

*7 Year Price Score 63.23 *NYSE Composite Index=100 *12 Month Price Score 78.44

Interim Earnings (Per Share)

Qtr.	Sep	Dec	Mar	Jun
2002-03	0.22	0.23	0.23	0.24
2003-04	0.25	0.28	0.31	0.36
2004-05	0.42	0.42	0.37	0.37
2005-06	0.31	0.33	0.36	...

Interim Dividends (Per Share)

Amt	Decl	Ex	Rec	Pay
0.125Q	10/27/2005	11/9/2005	11/14/2005	11/29/2005
0.125Q	1/26/2006	2/9/2006	2/13/2006	2/28/2006
0.125Q	4/24/2006	5/11/2006	5/15/2006	5/31/2006
0.156Q	8/4/2006	8/17/2006	8/21/2006	9/6/2006

Indicated Div: $0.62

Valuation Analysis

Forecast P/E	18.14 (9/9/2006)
Market Cap	$9.3 Billion
Book Value	2.6 Billion
Price/Book	3.58
Price/Sales	5.32

Institutional Holding

No of Institutions	393
Shares	280,449,824
% Held	87.45

Business Summary: IT & Technology (MIC: 10.2 SIC: 3674 NAIC: 334413)

Maxim Integrated Products designs, develops, manufactures, and markets linear and mixed-signal integrated circuits. Co.'s products include data converters, interface circuits, microprocessor supervisors, operational amplifiers, power supplies, multiplexers, delay lines, real-time clocks, microcontrollers, switches, battery chargers, battery management circuits, RF circuits, fiber optic transceivers, hot-swap controllers, sensors, voltage references and T/E transmission products. Co.'s products are sold to customers in numerous markets, including automotive, communications, consumer, data processing, industrial control, instrumentation, and medical industries.

Recent Developments: For the quarter ended Mar 25 2006, net income decreased 4.2% to $120.3 million from $125.5 million in the year-earlier quarter. Revenues were $478.1 million, up 19.5% from $400.2 million the year before. Operating income was $168.3 million versus $180.4 million in the prior-year quarter, a decrease of 6.7%. Direct operating expenses rose 40.2% to $156.9 million from $111.9 million in the comparable period the year before. Indirect operating expenses increased 41.8% to $152.9 million from $107.9 million in the equivalent prior-year period.

Prospects: Results are being fueled by higher unit shipments, supported by strong gains in gross bookings of about $537.0 million, a 6.0% increase from the prior quarter's level of $506.0 million. Gross turns orders also grew by 7.0% from the $230.0 million received in the prior quarter. Fiscal third quarter ending backlog shippable within the next 12 months is approximately $401.0 million, including approximately $346.0 million requested for shipment in the fiscal fourth quarter 2006. Co.'s fiscal second quarter 2006 ended backlog shippable within the next 12 months was approximately $370.0 million, including about $329.0 million that was requested for shipment in the fiscal third quarter 2006.

Financial Data
(US$ in Thousands)

	9 Mos	6 Mos	3 Mos	06/25/2005	06/26/2004	06/28/2003	06/29/2002	06/30/2001
Earnings Per Share	1.37	1.38	1.47	1.58	1.20	0.91	0.73	0.93
Cash Flow Per Share	1.87	2.01	2.04	2.15	2.13	1.81	1.24	2.45
Tang Book Value Per Share	8.13	7.85	8.23	7.89	6.51	6.38	5.44	6.36
Dividends Per Share	0.450	0.425	0.400	0.380	0.320	0.080	...	0.020
Dividend Payout %	32.75	30.69	27.13	24.05	26.67	8.79	...	2.15
Income Statement								
Total Revenue	1,348,365	870,245	424,364	1,671,713	1,439,263	1,153,219	1,025,104	1,576,613
EBITDA	564,112	364,047	176,798	885,537	626,496	462,091	386,840	504,988
Depn & Amortn	61,300	40,000	20,000	75,900	...	...	...	...
Income Before Taxes	502,812	324,047	156,798	809,637	626,496	462,091	386,840	504,988
Income Taxes	164,577	106,121	51,430	268,800	206,744	152,490	127,657	170,049
Net Income	338,235	217,926	105,368	540,837	419,752	309,601	259,183	334,939
Average Shares	334,036	337,429	344,860	342,843	350,575	341,253	355,821	361,620
Balance Sheet								
Total Assets	3,041,556	2,957,033	3,154,224	3,004,071	2,549,462	2,367,962	2,010,812	2,430,531
Current Liabilities	323,287	322,791	328,272	285,203	318,745	215,917	229,027	325,377
Total Liabilities	433,546	441,427	456,468	419,889	437,144	297,550	269,661	329,377
Stockholders' Equity	2,608,010	2,515,606	2,697,756	2,584,182	2,112,318	2,070,412	1,741,151	2,101,154
Shares Outstanding	320,690	320,601	327,815	327,494	324,444	324,637	320,060	330,235
Statistical Record								
Return on Assets %	15.57	16.34	17.17	19.53	17.12	14.18	11.70	17.43
Return on Equity %	18.22	19.23	20.44	23.09	20.13	16.29	13.53	20.47
EBITDA Margin %	41.84	41.83	41.66	52.97	43.53	40.07	37.74	32.03
Net Margin %	25.08	25.04	24.83	32.35	29.16	26.85	25.28	21.24
Asset Turnover	0.59	0.58	0.57	0.60	0.59	0.53	0.46	0.82
Current Ratio	6.00	5.92	6.48	6.92	4.95	7.25	5.40	5.22
Price Range	45.65-34.60	45.65-34.60	45.65-36.60	52.42-36.60	55.99-34.10	43.38-21.35	61.42-33.40	87.69-34.92
P/E Ratio	33.32-25.26	33.08-25.07	31.05-24.90	33.18-23.16	46.66-28.42	47.67-23.46	84.14-45.75	94.29-37.55
Average Yield %	1.14	1.06	0.97	0.90	0.68	0.23	...	0.03

Address: 120 San Gabriel Drive, Sunnyvale, CA 94086
Telephone: 408-737-7600
Fax: 408-737-7194

Web Site: www.maxim-ic.com
Officers: John F. Gifford - Chmn., Pres., C.E.O. Tunc Doluca - Group Pres.

Auditors: DELOITTE & TOUCHE LLP
Investor Contact: 408-737-7600
Transfer Agents: EquiServe Trust Company, N.A. Boston, MA

MCDATA CORP

Exchange	Symbol	Price	52Wk Range	Yield	P/E
NMS	MCDT	$4.18 (8/31/2006)	5.04-2.85	N/A	N/A

*7 Year Price Score N/A *NYSE Composite Index=100 *12 Month Price Score 85.77

Interim Earnings (Per Share)

Qtr.	Apr	Jul	Oct	Jan
2003-04	0.05	0.08	(0.44)	(0.07)
2004-05	(0.09)	(0.05)	(0.05)	0.00
2005-06	(0.02)	(0.18)	(0.05)	0.04
2006-07	(0.06)	...	...	...

Interim Dividends (Per Share)
No Dividends Paid

Valuation Analysis

		Institutional Holding	
Forecast P/E	16.24	No of Institutions	
	(9/9/2006)	35	
Market Cap	$664.6 Million	Shares	
Book Value	546.6 Million		19,243,932
Price/Book	1.22	% Held	
Price/Sales	0.97	49.39	

Business Summary: IT & Technology (MIC: 10.2 SIC: 3669 NAIC: 334290)

McData provides storage area networking, metropolitan area networking and wide area networking products and services, including hardware and software, for connecting servers and storage devices throughout an enterprise's data infrastructure. Co.'s offerings also include hardware and software products, professional services and education that enable businesses to scale their operations globally. Co.'s sales and marketing approach is focused on an indirect sales model executed through original equipment manufacturers and large resellers, such as EMC, IBM, Hitachi Data Systems, Hewlett-Packard, StorageTechnology, Sun Microsystems, and Dell, and its distributors and system integrators.

Recent Developments: For the quarter ended Apr 30 2006, net loss amounted to $9.5 million versus a net loss of $2.9 million in the year-earlier quarter. Revenues were $168.3 million, up 70.2% from $98.9 million the year before. Operating loss was $8.5 million versus a loss of $3.4 million in the prior-year quarter. Direct operating expenses rose 100.5% to $91.1 million from $45.4 million in the comparable period the year before. Indirect operating expenses increased 50.8% to $85.7 million from $56.8 million in the equivalent prior-year period.

Prospects: Results are being driven by continued solid end-user interest for Co.'s products and applications, notably for its 4 gigabytes per second switching products and its Intrepid 10000 Director, and contributions from its Jul 2005 acquisition of Computer Network Technology. Meanwhile, Co. noted that the market for both its storage and wide area network products and applications remains competitive due to factors including the entrance of competitors into its markets and pricing pressures due to an increase in competitive products and applications. Hence, Co. anticipates continued elongated sales cycles and price declines that could negatively affect its revenue growth rate going forward.

Financial Data
(US$ in Thousands)

	3 Mos	01/31/2006	01/31/2005	01/31/2004	01/31/2003	12/31/2002	12/31/2001	12/31/2000
Earnings Per Share	(0.25)	(0.22)	(0.18)	(0.38)	(0.03)	(0.09)	(0.08)	0.28
Cash Flow Per Share	0.13	0.10	0.19	0.53	2.62	0.27	0.07	0.23
Tang Book Value Per Share	1.05	1.06	1.99	1.96	...	3.99	4.17	4.13
Income Statement								
Total Revenue	168,312	614,433	399,660	418,860	17,045	328,279	344,406	248,686
EBITDA	18,385	40,620	31,876	43,612	(2,779)	10,301	(11,540)	52,108
Depn & Amortn	26,500	71,410	49,673	44,589	2,527	25,524	16,383	8,689
Income Before Taxes	(7,880)	(30,170)	(19,130)	(3,737)	(5,323)	(15,516)	(13,740)	51,655
Income Taxes	1,663	431	362	38,412	(1,863)	(5,529)	(5,084)	20,891
Net Income	(9,543)	(30,601)	(20,872)	(43,133)	(3,460)	(9,987)	(8,656)	30,764
Average Shares	153,702	140,331	115,355	114,682	114,000	113,185	111,475	107,953
Balance Sheet								
Total Assets	1,152,513	1,146,709	818,235	830,968	...	555,191	513,953	511,369
Current Liabilities	390,719	264,288	219,346	219,103	...	66,032	43,373	55,932
Long-Term Obligations	167,517	289,421	170,751	173,242	...	1,540	789	1,624
Total Liabilities	605,951	594,486	421,011	413,326	...	80,686	44,162	57,556
Stockholders' Equity	546,562	552,223	397,224	417,642	...	474,505	469,791	453,813
Shares Outstanding	158,993	153,389	115,938	116,075	...	113,962	112,562	109,907
Statistical Record								
Return on Assets %	N.M.	N.M.	N.M.	...	...	N.M.	N.M.	10.96
Return on Equity %	N.M.	N.M.	N.M.	...	...	N.M.	N.M.	12.69
EBITDA Margin %	10.92	6.61	7.98	10.41	N.M.	3.14	N.M.	20.95
Net Margin %	N.M.	N.M.	N.M.	N.M.	N.M.	N.M.	N.M.	12.37
Asset Turnover	0.70	0.63	0.48	...	...	0.61	0.67	0.89
Current Ratio	1.45	2.06	1.94	1.89	...	5.30	7.30	8.23
Debt to Equity	0.31	0.52	0.43	0.41	...	N.M.	N.M.	N.M.
Price Range	5.04-2.86	5.04-2.86	8.31-3.69	15.67-7.17	9.83-7.03	33.11-4.35	69.25-7.75	133.00-43.00
P/E Ratio	...	...	...	...	...	...	...	475.00-153.57

Address: 380 Interlocken Crescent, Broomfield, CO 80021
Telephone: 720-558-8000
Fax: 720-558-3860

Web Site: www.mcdata.com
Officers: John A. Kelley Jr. - Chmn., Pres., C.E.O.
Thomas O. McGimpsey - Exec. V.P., Bus. Devel., Gen. Couns.

Auditors: Deloitte & Touche LLP
Investor Contact: 303-460-4474

MCGRATH RENTCORP

Exchange	Symbol	Price	52Wk Range	Yield	P/E	Div Achiever
NMS	MGRC	$22.80 (8/31/2006)	33.05-21.53	2.81	14.25	15 Years

*7 Year Price Score 142.90 *NYSE Composite Index=100 *12 Month Price Score 88.34

Interim Earnings (Per Share)
Qtr.	Mar	Jun	Sep	Dec
2003	0.20	0.20	0.25	0.28
2004	0.23	0.25	0.38	0.35
2005	0.29	0.38	0.48	0.47
2006	0.31	0.34	...	...

Interim Dividends (Per Share)
Amt	Decl	Ex	Rec	Pay
0.14Q	8/24/2005	10/12/2005	10/14/2005	10/31/2005
0.14Q	12/2/2005	1/11/2006	1/13/2006	1/31/2006
0.16Q	2/23/2006	4/11/2006	4/14/2006	4/28/2006
0.16Q	5/31/2006	7/12/2006	7/14/2006	7/31/2006

Indicated Div: $0.64

Valuation Analysis
Forecast P/E	16.16
	(9/9/2006)
Market Cap	$569.2 Million
Book Value	210.6 Million
Price/Book	2.70
Price/Sales	284.65

Institutional Holding
No of Institutions	115
Shares	17,548,888
% Held	70.30

Business Summary: General Construction Supplies & Services (MIC: 3.3 SIC: 7359 NAIC: 532490)

McGrath RentCorp is a rental company with two rental products; relocatable modular buildings and electronic test equipment. Co. operates through three business segments: Mobile Modular Management Corporation (MMMC), its modular building division, TRS-RenTelco, its electronic test equipment division, and Enviroplex, Inc., its majority-owned subsidiary classroom manufacturing business selling portable classrooms directly to California public school districts. MMMC rents and sells modular buildings and accessories to fulfill customers' temporary and permanent space needs in California, Texas and Florida. TRS-RenTelco rents and sells electronic test equipment nationally and internationally.

Recent Developments: For the quarter ended June 30 2006, net income decreased 8.4% to $8.7 million from $9.5 million in the year-earlier quarter. Revenues were $60.7 million, down 5.0% from $63.9 million the year before. Operating income was $15.5 million versus $17.2 million in the prior-year quarter, a decrease of 10.0%. Direct operating expenses declined 7.7% to $34.4 million from $37.2 million in the comparable period the year before. Indirect operating expenses increased 14.7% to $10.8 million from $9.4 million in the equivalent prior-year period.

Prospects: Co.'s results reflect a decline in modular and electronics equipment sales, and a reduction in gross profit on rents for modulars due to higher inventory center expenses. Offsetting these declines is an increase in Co.'s rental business activity across its product segments and markets, which it believes is reflective of an increasingly positive outlook for its test equipment rental business going forward. For the third quarter of 2006, Co. expects rental revenue growth to derive from classroom shipments and the increased level of commercial rental activity. For 2006, Co. is reducing its earnings guidance from $1.50 to $1.60 per diluted share to $1.42 to $1.49 per diluted share.

Financial Data
(US$ in Thousands)

	6 Mos	3 Mos	12/31/2005	12/31/2004	12/31/2003	12/31/2002	12/31/2001	12/31/2000
Earnings Per Share	1.60	1.64	1.61	1.21	0.93	0.50	1.07	1.10
Cash Flow Per Share	0.67	0.20	3.32	2.55	1.98	2.10	2.41	2.02
Tang Book Value Per Share	8.44	8.25	7.99	6.80	5.94	5.57	5.33	4.49
Dividends Per Share	0.580	0.560	0.530	0.430	0.390	0.340	0.310	0.270
Dividend Payout %	36.25	34.15	32.92	35.54	42.16	68.00	28.97	24.66
Income Statement								
Total Revenue	118,529	57,856	272	202,520	130,971	145,086	159,394	164,158
EBITDA	53,859	26,533	120	88,577	55,400	43,107	81,677	82,232
Depn & Amortn	23,223	11,384	46	34,501	14,692	17,872	29,632	25,716
Income Before Taxes	25,510	12,796	66	48,888	38,040	21,253	44,967	47,676
Income Taxes	9,069	4,991	25	18,843	15,178	8,459	17,807	19,762
Net Income	16,506	7,837	41	29,997	22,692	12,633	26,677	27,244
Average Shares	25,209	25,604	25	24,804	24,518	25,238	24,990	24,856
Balance Sheet								
Total Assets	570,740	548,613	542	474,280	323,858	313,134	354,884	357,246
Current Liabilities	238,759	220,505	52	39,460	28,695	29,889	30,745	37,012
Long-Term Obligations	...	...	163	151,888	47,266	55,523	104,140	126,876
Total Liabilities	360,136	343,630	344	307,392	179,880	174,115	223,289	248,288
Stockholders' Equity	210,604	204,983	198	166,888	143,978	139,019	131,595	108,958
Shares Outstanding	24,964	24,832	24	24,543	24,244	24,980	24,670	24,250
Statistical Record								
Return on Assets %	N.M.	0.14	0.02	7.50	7.12	3.78	7.49	8.30
Return on Equity %	N.M.	0.37	0.05	19.25	16.04	9.34	22.18	26.59
EBITDA Margin %	45.44	45.86	44.11	43.74	42.30	29.71	51.24	50.09
Net Margin %	13.93	13.55	15.00	14.81	17.33	8.71	16.74	16.60
Asset Turnover	0.00	0.01	0.00	0.51	0.41	0.43	0.45	0.50
Current Ratio	0.23	0.23	1.24	1.37	1.12	1.11	1.20	1.25
Debt to Equity	...	...	0.82	0.91	0.33	0.40	0.79	1.16
Price Range	33.05-22.35	33.05-21.05	29.69-20.65	22.75-13.63	14.88-10.90	18.82-9.40	18.77-9.06	9.94-7.00
P/E Ratio	20.66-13.97	20.15-12.84	18.44-12.82	18.80-11.26	16.00-11.73	37.64-18.80	17.54-8.47	9.03-6.36
Average Yield %	2.09	2.11	2.16	2.51	3.01	2.65	2.60	3.24

Address: 5700 Las Positas Road, Livermore, CA 94551-7800 **Telephone:** 925-606-9200 **Fax:** 925-276-3905	**Web Site:** www.mgrc.com **Officers:** Robert P. McGrath - Chmn. Dennis C. Kakures - Pres., C.E.O.	**Auditors:** Grant Thornton LLP **Investor Contact:** 206-652-9704 **Transfer Agents:** U.S. Stock Transfer, Glendale, CA

MEDIMMUNE, INC

Exchange	Symbol	Price	52Wk Range	Yield	P/E
NMS	MEDI	$27.64 (8/31/2006)	37.38-25.28	N/A	N/A

*7 Year Price Score 71.70 *NYSE Composite Index=100 *12 Month Price Score 80.51

Interim Earnings (Per Share)

Qtr.	Mar	Jun	Sep	Dec
2003	0.43	0.05	(0.07)	0.30
2004	0.44	(0.40)	(0.26)	0.20
2005	0.45	(0.18)	(0.26)	(0.09)
2006	0.18	(0.26)	...	...

Interim Dividends (Per Share)
No Dividends Paid

Valuation Analysis

Forecast P/E	155.78	Institutional Holding	
	(9/9/2006)	No of Institutions	321
Market Cap	$6.6 Billion	Shares	220,557,760
Book Value	1.3 Billion	% Held	92.12
Price/Book	5.01		
Price/Sales	5.44		

Business Summary: Biotechnology (MIC: 9.2 SIC: 2836 NAIC: 325414)

Medimmune is a biotechnology company focused on discovering, developing, manufacturing and commercializing products to treat or prevent infectious diseases, immune system disorders and cancer. Co.'s care competencies are in the areas of monoclonal antibodies and vaccines. Co. promotes three main products: Synagis® and FluMist™ to prevent two common respiratory tract diseases; and Ethyol®, to reduce undesired side effects of certain anti-cancer chemo- and radiotherapies. Co. operates five facilities in the U.S. and Europe. Co. also has clinical, research and development staff in the U.S., through which it is developing a pipeline of product candidates for potential commercialization.

Recent Developments: For the quarter ended June 30 2006, net loss amounted to $63.2 million versus a net loss of $44.2 million in the year-earlier quarter. Revenues were $72.9 million, down 17.6% from $88.5 million the year before. Operating loss was $125.6 million versus a loss of $82.6 million in the prior-year quarter. Direct operating expenses declined 50.0% to $14.0 million from $28.0 million in the comparable period the year before. Indirect operating expenses increased 28.9% to $184.5 million from $143.1 million in the equivalent prior-year period.

Prospects: Co. continues to further invest in research and development as it has completed multiple Phase 3 trials, filed three Investigational New Drug applications and added new initiatives to its portfolio. Meanwhile, revenues are benefiting from substantial worldwide reported sales of Co.'s key product, Synagis (palivizumab), offset by continuing fluctuating sales of frozen FluMist. Looking ahead, Co. will continue to focus on providing long-term value to its shareholders through the development of significant new drugs. For fiscal 2006, Co. expects total revenues growth of 10.0% year over year, or approximately $1.40 billion, and earnings in the range of $0.40 to $0.45 per diluted share.

Financial Data
(US$ in Thousands)

	6 Mos	3 Mos	12/31/2005	12/31/2004	12/31/2003	12/31/2002	12/31/2001	12/31/2000
Earnings Per Share	(0.43)	(0.35)	(0.07)	(0.02)	0.72	(4.40)	0.68	0.50
Cash Flow Per Share	0.06	0.13	0.45	0.58	1.43	1.06	1.18	0.82
Tang Book Value Per Share	4.37	5.59	5.05	6.59	6.57	6.16	4.87	3.99
Income Statement								
Total Revenue	570,900	498,000	1,243,900	1,141,100	1,054,334	847,739	618,679	540,495
EBITDA	17,700	127,700	48,200	(9,900)	298,057	(1,026,104)	199,640	184,844
Depn & Amortn	70,800	56,100	93,500	56,400	53,399	63,981	7,100	4,526
Income Before Taxes	(27,900)	84,600	7,500	(9,200)	291,177	(1,049,840)	228,466	209,413
Income Taxes	(11,700)	37,600	24,100	(5,400)	107,973	48,175	79,506	64,436
Net Income	(16,200)	47,000	(16,600)	(3,800)	183,204	(1,098,015)	148,960	111,156
Average Shares	245,900	260,000	246,900	248,600	253,817	249,600	220,101	220,428
Balance Sheet								
Total Assets	3,475,300	2,891,700	2,780,000	2,564,400	2,794,670	2,188,289	1,219,386	1,006,575
Current Liabilities	989,400	1,217,000	1,148,500	363,800	390,715	266,653	164,546	151,465
Long-Term Obligations	1,165,100	...	...	506,200	681,223	217,554	8,791	9,595
Total Liabilities	2,155,200	1,222,700	1,209,500	889,800	1,095,452	511,055	175,113	162,993
Stockholders' Equity	1,320,100	1,669,000	1,570,500	1,674,600	1,699,218	1,677,234	1,044,273	843,582
Shares Outstanding	239,400	248,800	247,000	248,500	241,797	251,262	214,484	211,347
Statistical Record								
Return on Assets %	N.M.	N.M.	N.M.	N.M.	7.35	N.M.	13.38	13.40
Return on Equity %	N.M.	N.M.	N.M.	N.M.	10.85	N.M.	15.78	16.06
EBITDA Margin %	3.10	25.64	3.87	N.M.	28.27	N.M.	32.27	34.20
Net Margin %	N.M.	9.44	N.M.	N.M.	17.38	N.M.	24.08	20.57
Asset Turnover	0.41	0.44	0.47	0.42	0.42	0.50	0.56	0.65
Current Ratio	1.74	1.06	0.90	1.91	2.82	2.79	3.61	4.54
Debt to Equity	0.88	...	...	0.30	0.40	0.13	0.01	0.01
Price Range	37.38-26.40	37.38-23.81	37.06-23.32	28.42-21.40	40.30-23.30	47.33-20.92	52.38-28.31	84.13-42.96
P/E Ratio	...	...	...	...	55.97-32.36	...	77.02-41.64	168.25-85.92

Address: One MedImmune Way, Gaithersburg, MD 20878
Telephone: 301-398-0000
Fax: 301-527-4200

Web Site: www.medimmune.com
Officers: Wayne T. Hockmeyer Ph.D. - Chmn. David M. Mott - Vice-Chmn., Pres., C.E.O.

Auditors: PricewaterhouseCoopers LLP
Investor Contact: 301-417-0770

MENTOR GRAPHICS CORP.

Exchange	Symbol	Price	52Wk Range	Yield	P/E
NMS	MENT	$14.50 (8/31/2006)	14.98-8.00	N/A	111.54

*7 Year Price Score 59.53   *NYSE Composite Index=100   *12 Month Price Score 119.87

Interim Earnings (Per Share)

Qtr.	Mar	Jun	Sep	Dec
2003	0.05	0.06	(0.19)	0.19
2004	0.03	(0.47)	(0.08)	0.23
2005	(0.06)	(0.09)	0.00	0.21
2006	(0.07)	(0.01)	...	...

Interim Dividends (Per Share)
No Dividends Paid

Valuation Analysis

		Institutional Holding	
Forecast P/E	20.70	No of Institutions	161
	(9/9/2006)	Shares	79,198,936
Market Cap	$1.2 Billion	% Held	97.41
Book Value	463.8 Million		
Price/Book	2.51		
Price/Sales	1.57		

Business Summary: IT & Technology (MIC: 10.2 SIC: 7373 NAIC: 541512)

Mentor Graphics develops, manufactures, markets, sells and supports electronic design automation products and provides related services, which are used by engineers to design, analyze, simulate, model, implement and verify the components of electronic systems. Co. markets its products and services mainly to large companies in the military/aerospace, communications, computer, consumer electronics, semiconductor, networking, multimedia and transportation industries. Customers use Co.'s products in the design of wire harness systems and semiconductors, such as microprocessors, field programmable gate arrays, and memory and application specific integrated circuits, and printed circuit boards.

Recent Developments: For the quarter ended June 30 2006, net loss amounted to $448,000 versus a net loss of $6.8 million in the year-earlier quarter. Revenues were $178.4 million, up 15.2% from $154.8 million the year before. Operating income was $1.1 million versus a loss of $16.3 million in the prior-year quarter. Direct operating expenses declined 0.3% to $27.8 million from $27.9 million in the comparable period the year before. Indirect operating expenses increased 4.4% to $149.5 million from $143.3 million in the equivalent prior-year period.

Prospects: Co.'s business continues to focus largely in its Integrated Circuit Design to Silicon product line, with recent solid bookings for total system and software. Looking ahead, Co. expects contract renewals to benefit from the increased research and development spending of its customers. Beyond the growth from its family of Calibre products, Co. believes the strength seen in Scalable Verification offers opportunities for growth. Co. also expects higher demand for electronic design automation products for non-traditional markets, such as automotive electronic design and embedded software. Taken together, Co. is targeting full year 2006 revenue of $763.0 million and earnings of $0.19 per share.

Financial Data
(US$ in Thousands)

	6 Mos	3 Mos	12/31/2005	12/31/2004	12/31/2003	12/31/2002	12/31/2001	12/31/2000
Earnings Per Share	0.13	0.05	0.07	(0.28)	0.11	(0.22)	0.46	0.81
Cash Flow Per Share	0.95	0.66	0.56	0.56	(0.22)	(0.07)	0.80	1.38
Tang Book Value Per Share	1.07	0.93	0.85	0.78	0.70	0.26	4.89	4.02
Income Statement								
Total Revenue	354,755	176,322	705,249	710,956	675,668	596,179	600,371	589,835
EBITDA	31,636	13,623	66,527	83,124	54,524	30,890	67,365	95,674
Depn & Amortn	22,462	10,964	44,069	43,720	41,850	37,811	28,494	25,178
Income Before Taxes	(11,291)	(11,048)	13,294	28,944	1,129	(18,617)	38,871	70,496
Income Taxes	(4,983)	(5,188)	7,487	49,494	(6,804)	(4,303)	7,767	15,509
Net Income	(6,308)	(5,860)	5,807	(20,550)	7,933	(14,314)	31,104	54,987
Average Shares	80,348	80,108	80,133	72,381	70,464	65,766	67,681	67,509
Balance Sheet								
Total Assets	1,032,735	1,005,638	1,020,937	1,021,907	940,688	804,848	523,475	530,914
Current Liabilities	281,235	256,456	273,783	285,111	253,002	244,949	177,634	204,447
Long-Term Obligations	271,855	276,996	282,188	283,983	286,768	177,685	5,100	6,100
Total Liabilities	568,947	549,910	572,797	588,192	562,931	441,909	192,100	211,694
Stockholders' Equity	463,788	455,728	448,140	433,715	374,366	359,720	328,462	316,537
Shares Outstanding	80,437	80,220	79,248	76,430	68,277	66,629	64,706	64,624
Statistical Record								
Return on Assets %	1.07	0.43	0.57	N.M.	0.91	N.M.	5.90	11.19
Return on Equity %	2.42	0.97	1.32	N.M.	2.16	N.M.	9.64	18.12
EBITDA Margin %	8.92	7.73	9.43	11.69	8.07	5.18	11.22	16.22
Net Margin %	N.M.	N.M.	0.82	N.M.	1.17	N.M.	5.18	9.32
Asset Turnover	0.74	0.72	0.69	0.72	0.77	0.90	1.14	1.20
Current Ratio	1.46	1.48	1.43	1.32	1.35	0.98	1.83	1.65
Debt to Equity	0.59	0.61	0.63	0.65	0.77	0.49	0.02	0.02
Price Range	13.75-8.00	13.70-8.00	15.29-8.00	18.06-10.38	20.97-7.52	26.85-4.08	33.63-13.11	28.88-11.75
P/E Ratio	105.77-61.54	274.00-160.00	218.43-114.29	...	190.64-68.36	...	73.10-28.50	35.65-14.51

Address: 8005 S.W. Boeckman Road, Wilsonville, OR 97070-7777
Telephone: 503-685-7000
Fax: 503-685-1202

Web Site: www.mentor.com
Officers: Walden C. Rhines - Chmn., C.E.O. Gregory K. Hinkley - Pres.

Auditors: KPMG LLP
Transfer Agents: American Stock Transfer & Trust Co.

MERCANTILE BANKSHARES CORP.

Exchange	Symbol	Price	52Wk Range	Yield	P/E	Div Acheiver
NMS	MRBK	$36.93 (8/31/2006)	39.95-34.43	3.03	15.78	29 Years

*7 Year Price Score 104.31 *NYSE Composite Index=100 *12 Month Price Score 93.70

Interim Earnings (Per Share)

Qtr.	Mar	Jun	Sep	Dec
2003	0.47	0.48	0.42	0.42
2004	0.46	0.47	0.47	0.51
2005	0.52	0.56	0.57	0.61
2006	0.57	0.59	...	...

Interim Dividends (Per Share)

Amt	Decl	Ex	Rec	Pay
0.253Q	12/13/2005	12/21/2005	12/23/2005	12/30/2005
50%	1/10/2006	1/30/2006	1/20/2006	1/27/2006
0.26Q	3/14/2006	3/22/2006	3/24/2006	3/31/2006
0.28Q	6/13/2006	6/21/2006	6/23/2006	6/30/2006

Indicated Div: $1.12 (Div. Reinv. Plan)

Valuation Analysis
Forecast P/E N/A

Institutional Holding
No of Institutions 231
Shares 51,145,888
% Held 40.80

Market Cap $4.6 Billion
Book Value 2.3 Billion
Price/Book 2.01
Price/Sales 3.93

Business Summary: Commercial Banking (MIC: 8.1 SIC: 6022 NAIC: 522110)

Mercantile Bankshares is a regional multibank-holding company with $16.42 billion in assets and $12.08 billion in deposits as of Dec 31 2005. Through its primary bank subsidiary, Mercantile-Safe Deposit and Trust Company (MSD&T), and 10 affiliated banks, Co. is engaged in providing retail banking services, small-businesses and commercial banking services, mortgage banking services, consumer insurance products, as well as a range of wealth management services. As of Dec 31 2005, MSD&T operated 40 offices in Maryland, 13 in Virginia, two in Washington, D.C., and one in Pennsylvania.

Recent Developments: For the quarter ended June 30 2006, net income increased 7.7% to $73.1 million from $67.9 million in the year-earlier quarter. Net interest income increased 5.9% to $161.4 million from $152.4 million in the year-earlier quarter. Non-interest income rose 7.3% to $64.5 million from $60.1 million, while non-interest expense advanced 5.3% to $109.4 million.

Prospects: Despite being challenged by the unfavorable interest rate and competitive environment within the banking industry, Co. is experiencing higher net interest income due to growth in its average earning asset. The increase in Co.'s total loans is primarily driven by growth in construction lending, commercial real estate and residential mortgages. Separately, on Jul 17 2006, Co. completed its acquisition of James Monroe Bancorp Inc. (Monroe), by which Monroe's shareholders were entitled to receive either cash in the amount of $23.50, without interest, for each share of the stock they held or 0.6033 shares of Co.'s stock for each such share, subject to the terms of the agreement.

Financial Data
(US$ in Thousands)

	6 Mos	3 Mos	12/31/2005	12/31/2004	12/31/2003	12/31/2002	12/31/2001	12/31/2000
Earnings Per Share	2.34	2.31	2.26	1.91	1.79	1.81	1.70	1.67
Cash Flow Per Share	2.32	2.59	2.40	2.09	1.81	3.22	0.88	2.05
Tang Book Value Per Share	12.49	12.23	12.02	11.45	10.56	11.76	10.68	10.02
Dividends Per Share	1.047	1.020	0.993	0.920	0.860	0.787	0.733	0.680
Dividend Payout %	44.73	44.16	43.95	48.08	48.13	43.38	43.14	40.64
Income Statement								
Interest Income	469,706	227,913	816,037	659,037	596,575	586,386	649,766	646,495
Interest Expense	149,983	69,600	198,911	113,256	117,245	144,582	231,525	237,110
Net Interest Income	319,723	158,313	617,126	545,781	479,330	441,804	418,241	409,385
Provision for Losses	...	...	1,576	7,221	12,105	16,378	13,434	17,231
Non-Interest Income	125,074	60,606	243,120	213,929	176,591	143,750	145,490	125,541
Non-Interest Expense	216,137	106,715	420,821	391,958	337,447	272,608	263,959	243,505
Income Before Taxes	228,660	112,204	437,849	360,531	306,369	296,568	286,338	274,190
Income Taxes	84,809	41,445	161,530	131,124	109,555	106,330	105,043	98,960
Net Income	143,851	70,759	276,319	229,407	196,814	190,238	181,295	175,230
Average Shares	124,324	124,294	122,390	119,781	110,131	105,100	106,798	104,578
Balance Sheet								
Net Loans & Leases	11,907,320	11,554,294	11,451,172	10,079,431	9,116,823	7,173,426	6,764,783	6,554,682
Total Assets	17,002,714	16,783,227	16,421,729	14,425,690	13,695,472	10,790,376	9,928,786	8,938,030
Total Deposits	12,444,022	12,573,556	12,077,350	10,799,199	10,262,553	8,260,940	7,447,372	6,796,541
Total Liabilities	14,737,669	14,554,308	14,227,007	12,508,007	11,854,031	9,466,018	8,698,580	7,764,729
Stockholders' Equity	2,265,045	2,228,919	2,194,722	1,917,683	1,841,441	1,324,358	1,230,206	1,173,301
Shares Outstanding	123,523	123,143	122,999	118,950	119,659	103,254	104,663	106,648
Statistical Record								
Return on Assets %	1.75	1.81	1.79	1.63	1.61	1.84	1.92	2.08
Return on Equity %	13.21	13.65	13.44	12.17	12.43	14.89	15.09	16.28
Net Interest Margin %	66.76	69.46	75.62	82.81	80.35	75.34	64.37	63.32
Efficiency Ratio %	35.73	36.99	39.73	44.90	43.64	37.34	33.19	31.54
Loans to Deposits	0.96	0.92	0.95	0.93	0.89	0.87	0.91	0.96
Price Range	39.95-34.35	39.95-32.65	39.95-32.35	35.27-27.00	30.39-21.83	30.13-21.77	29.16-22.71	29.79-15.90
P/E Ratio	17.07-14.68	17.29-14.13	17.68-14.31	18.46-14.14	16.98-12.20	16.65-12.03	17.15-13.36	17.84-9.52
Average Yield %	2.81	2.79	2.80	2.98	3.24	2.91	2.78	3.14

Address: Two Hopkins Plaza, Baltimore, MD 21203 Telephone: 410-237-5900 Fax: 410-347-8493	Web Site: www.mercantile.com Officers: Edward J. Kelly III - Chmn., Pres., C.E.O. Jay M. Wilson - Vice-Chmn.	Auditors: PricewaterhouseCoopers, LLP Transfer Agents: American Stock Transfer & Trust Company, New York, NY

MERCURY INTERACTIVE CORP.

Exchange	Symbol	Price	52Wk Range	Yield	P/E
NBB	MERQ	$50.39 (8/31/2006)	50.67-25.66	N/A	52.49

*7 Year Price Score 60.50 *NYSE Composite Index=100 *12 Month Price Score 125.97

Interim Earnings (Per Share)

Qtr.	Mar	Jun	Sep	Dec
2002	0.17	0.20	0.15	0.22
2003	0.20	0.19	(0.08)	0.14
2004	0.19	0.12	0.21	0.31
2005	0.32	...	...	...

Interim Dividends (Per Share)

Amt	Decl	Ex	Rec	Pay
100%	1/28/1999	3/1/1999	2/12/1999	2/26/1999
100%	1/13/2000	2/14/2000	1/28/2000	2/11/2000

Valuation Analysis **Institutional Holding**

Forecast P/E	35.60	No of Institutions	
	(9/9/2006)	66	
Market Cap	$4.4 Billion	Shares	
Book Value	656.9 Million	36,910,476	
Price/Book	6.64	% Held	
Price/Sales	6.00	42.62	

Business Summary: IT & Technology (MIC: 10.2 SIC: 7372 NAIC: 511210)

Mercury Interactive is a provider of software and services for the business technology optimization (BTO) marketplace. Co. has introduced a variety of BTO software and service offerings, including offerings in application delivery for testing software quality and performance in pre-production, application management for monitoring and managing application availability in production, and information technology (IT) governance for managing IT's portfolio of projects, processes, priorities, and resources. Co.'s BTO offerings are designed to help customers maximize the business value of IT by optimizing application quality and performance as well as managing IT costs, risks, and compliance.

Recent Developments: On Mar 17 2006, Co. announced that it continues to expect to complete its restated financial statements and file its amended 2004 Form 10-K and first quarter 2005 Form 10-Q with the U.S. Securities and Exchange Commission (SEC) in the second quarter of 2006, and to file all other required SEC filings in a timely fashion thereafter.

Prospects: On Feb 1 2006, Co. announced it has completed its acquisition of Systinet Corporation, a provider of service-oriented architecture (SOA) governance and lifecycle management software and services. Co. expects Systinet's technology, when combined with Mercury BTO Enterprise™ offerings, will help enable customers to improve the quality, performance and availability of SOA business services. Separately, on May 30 2006, Co. announced Mercury Business Availability Center™ 6.1 for SAP® solutions. This new product version is designed to help customers improve the performance and availability of business-critical SAP solutions built on an IT service management foundation.

Financial Data
(US$ in Thousands)

	3 Mos	12/31/2004	12/31/2003	12/31/2002	12/31/2001	12/31/2000	12/31/1999	12/31/1998
Earnings Per Share	0.96	0.83	0.45	0.74	0.38	0.70	0.39	0.28
Cash Flow Per Share	2.60	2.38	2.07	1.57	1.01	1.62	0.80	0.60
Tang Book Value Per Share	2.62	1.73	3.43	3.89	2.85	3.74	2.56	1.99
Income Statement								
Total Revenue	198,762	685,547	506,473	400,122	361,000	307,000	187,700	121,000
EBITDA	43,450	121,986	64,396	87,719	75,447	90,499	48,076	31,397
Depn & Amortn	9,683	33,163	21,870	17,079	45,101	9,624	6,063	4,141
Income Before Taxes	38,762	107,145	57,695	82,389	30,346	80,875	42,013	27,256
Income Taxes	7,323	22,545	16,182	17,185	12,504	16,175	8,869	5,451
Net Income	31,439	84,600	41,513	65,204	34,154	64,700	33,144	21,805
Average Shares	99,428	103,207	92,728	87,640	89,725	91,938	85,208	78,060
Balance Sheet								
Total Assets	2,074,659	2,019,950	1,970,510	1,075,734	927,625	976,375	297,218	203,576
Current Liabilities	515,938	526,698	390,266	289,546	195,800	173,343	97,687	57,987
Long-Term Obligations	799,654	804,483	811,159	316,972	377,480	500,000	...	...
Total Liabilities	1,417,746	1,438,964	1,270,141	630,566	573,280	673,343	97,687	57,987
Stockholders' Equity	656,913	580,986	700,369	445,168	354,345	303,032	199,531	145,589
Shares Outstanding	86,602	84,990	89,697	84,694	82,849	81,129	78,090	73,252
Statistical Record								
Return on Assets %	4.70	4.23	2.73	6.51	3.59	10.13	13.24	12.57
Return on Equity %	13.69	13.17	7.25	16.31	10.39	25.68	19.21	16.87
EBITDA Margin %	21.86	17.79	12.71	21.92	20.90	29.48	25.61	25.95
Net Margin %	15.82	12.34	8.20	16.30	9.46	21.07	17.66	18.02
Asset Turnover	0.35	0.34	0.33	0.40	0.38	0.48	0.75	0.70
Current Ratio	1.96	1.80	2.34	2.30	2.68	4.19	2.40	2.65
Debt to Equity	1.22	1.38	1.16	0.71	1.07	1.65	...	...
Price Range	50.60-32.36	54.00-32.36	51.92-29.65	41.58-15.73	97.00-18.71	156.75-40.72	54.69-10.81	15.81-6.03
P/E Ratio	52.71-33.71	65.06-38.99	115.38-65.89	56.19-21.26	255.26-49.24	223.93-58.17	140.22-28.04	56.47-21.54

Address: 379 North Whisman Road, Mountain View, CA 94043-3969 **Telephone:** 650-603-5200	**Web Site:** www.mercuryinteractive.com **Officers:** Giora Yaron - Chmn. Anthony Zingale - Pres., C.E.O., C.O.O.	**Auditors:** PricewaterhouseCoopers LLP **Investor Contact:** 408-822-5359

MERIDIAN BIOSCIENCE INC.

Exchange	Symbol	Price	52Wk Range	Yield	P/E	Div Acheiver
NMS	VIVO	$23.86 (8/31/2006)	27.55-17.00	1.93	36.15	13 Years

*7 Year Price Score 212.93 *NYSE Composite Index=100 *12 Month Price Score 95.72

Interim Earnings (Per Share)

Qtr.	Dec	Mar	Jun	Sep
2002-03	0.07	0.09	0.08	0.08
2003-04	0.08	0.10	0.09	0.13
2004-05	0.09	0.13	0.14	0.15
2005-06	0.15	0.18	0.18	...

Interim Dividends (Per Share)

Amt	Decl	Ex	Rec	Pay
0.08Q	11/10/2005	11/17/2005	11/21/2005	12/1/2005
0.115Q	1/19/2006	1/30/2006	2/1/2006	2/9/2006
0.115Q	4/20/2006	4/27/2006	5/1/2006	5/8/2006
0.115Q	7/20/2006	7/27/2006	7/31/2006	8/7/2006

Indicated Div: $0.46 (Div. Reinv. Plan)

Valuation Analysis

Forecast P/E	33.53
	(9/9/2006)
Market Cap	$622.9 Million
Book Value	92.1 Million
Price/Book	6.76
Price/Sales	5.94

Institutional Holding

No of Institutions	125
Shares	14,651,694
% Held	56.09

Business Summary: Biotechnology (MIC: 9.2 SIC: 2835 NAIC: 325413)

Meridian Bioscience is an integrated life science company whose principal businesses are the development, manufacture, sale and distribution of diagnostic test kits, primarily for certain respiratory, gastrointestinal, viral and parasitic infectious diseases; the manufacture and distribution of bulk antigens and reagents used by researchers and other diagnostic manufacturers; and the contract manufacture of proteins and other biologicals for use by biopharmaceutical and biotechnology companies engaged in research for new drugs and vaccines. Co. conducts its operations in three business segments: US Diagnostics, European Diagnostics, and Life Science.

Recent Developments: For the quarter ended June 30 2006, net income increased 39.0% to $4.9 million from $3.5 million in the year-earlier quarter. Revenues were $26.6 million, up 4.6% from $25.4 million for the quarter. Operating income was $6.9 million versus $5.7 million in the prior-year quarter, an increase of 20.8%. Direct operating expenses rose 5.1% to $10.2 million from $9.7 million in the comparable period the year before. Indirect operating expenses decreased 5.2% to $9.5 million from $10.0 million in the equivalent prior-year period.

Prospects: Looking ahead to fiscal 2007, Co. anticipates strong revenue and profit contributions from its diagnostics business units driven by higher unit demand for its upper gastrointestinal infections, especially its C. difficile products, as well as its products that aid in the diagnosis of peptic ulcers. In addition, new diagnostic tests are due for introduction throughout 2007 to support Co.'s organic growth. New contract business is also underway in Co.'s Life Science unit, which should further boost growth in the segment. Thus, Co. is projecting net sales for its fiscal year ending Sep 30 2007 in the range of $118.0 million to $123.0 million and earnings of $0.83 to $0.87 per diluted share.

Financial Data
(US$ in Thousands)

	9 Mos	6 Mos	3 Mos	09/30/2005	09/30/2004	09/30/2003	09/30/2002	09/30/2001
Earnings Per Share	0.66	0.62	0.58	0.52	0.40	0.31	0.23	(0.47)
Cash Flow Per Share	0.77	0.69	0.67	0.77	0.57	0.56	0.52	0.40
Tang Book Value Per Share	2.73	2.60	2.51	2.38	0.81	0.56	0.38	0.33
Dividends Per Share	0.390	0.355	0.320	0.307	0.260	0.227	0.183	0.170
Dividend Payout %	58.79	56.95	55.49	58.97	65.00	72.34	80.88	...
Income Statement								
Total Revenue	79,763	53,180	24,908	92,965	79,606	65,864	59,104	56,527
EBITDA	23,460	15,326	7,184	24,483	18,540	17,047	13,898	(7,780)
Depn & Amortn	3,294	2,208	1,106	4,160	3,819	3,780	3,719	4,746
Income Before Taxes	20,847	13,538	6,292	19,596	13,195	11,591	8,243	(14,906)
Income Taxes	7,300	4,853	2,330	7,031	4,010	4,573	3,212	(4,631)
Net Income	13,547	8,685	3,962	12,565	9,185	7,018	5,031	(10,275)
Average Shares	26,788	26,836	26,711	24,104	22,888	22,425	22,140	21,883
Balance Sheet								
Total Assets	114,836	109,565	110,974	110,569	69,322	66,420	65,095	65,982
Current Liabilities	16,636	14,343	17,963	19,791	16,650	15,330	15,249	16,368
Long-Term Obligations	1,823	1,833	1,968	2,684	17,093	21,505	23,626	24,349
Total Liabilities	22,696	20,362	23,932	26,801	36,390	38,936	40,714	43,038
Stockholders' Equity	92,140	89,203	87,042	83,768	32,932	27,484	24,381	22,944
Shares Outstanding	26,106	26,077	26,053	25,927	22,444	22,080	21,937	21,886
Statistical Record								
Return on Assets %	17.71	16.83	15.78	13.97	13.50	10.67	7.68	N.M.
Return on Equity %	24.53	23.81	23.23	21.53	30.32	27.06	21.26	N.M.
EBITDA Margin %	29.41	28.82	28.84	26.34	23.29	25.88	23.51	N.M.
Net Margin %	16.98	16.33	15.91	13.52	11.54	10.66	8.51	N.M.
Asset Turnover	1.07	1.09	1.08	1.03	1.17	1.00	0.90	0.75
Current Ratio	4.51	4.83	3.93	3.55	2.17	2.16	1.99	1.99
Debt to Equity	0.02	0.02	0.02	0.03	0.52	0.78	0.97	1.06
Price Range	27.55-12.63	26.98-9.11	22.90-9.11	20.70-8.70	8.88-6.51	7.37-3.74	5.03-3.03	5.25-1.54
P/E Ratio	41.74-19.14	43.52-14.69	39.48-15.70	39.81-16.73	22.20-16.27	23.78-12.07	21.88-13.16	...
Average Yield %	1.83	1.97	2.13	2.47	3.56	4.08	4.40	5.16

Address: 3471 River Hills Drive, Cincinnati, OH 45244	**Web Site:** www.meridianbioscience.com	**Auditors:** Grant Thornton LLP
Telephone: 513-271-3700	**Officers:** William J. Motto - Chmn., C.E.O. John A. Kraeutler - Pres., C.O.O.	**Investor Contact:** 513-271-3700
Fax: 513-271-3762		**Transfer Agents:** Computershare Investor Services LLC, OH

MGE ENERGY INC

Exchange	Symbol	Price	52Wk Range	Yield	P/E	Div Acheiver
NMS	MGEE	$33.61 (8/31/2006)	37.75-29.28	4.15	18.67	30 Years

*7 Year Price Score 94.45 *NYSE Composite Index=100 *12 Month Price Score 93.46

Interim Earnings (Per Share)

Qtr.	Mar	Jun	Sep	Dec
2003	0.53	0.33	0.56	0.29
2004	0.74	0.30	0.48	0.24
2005	0.40	0.31	0.48	0.42
2006	0.56	0.34	...	...

Interim Dividends (Per Share)

Amt	Decl	Ex	Rec	Pay
0.345Q	11/18/2005	11/29/2005	12/1/2005	12/15/2005
0.345Q	2/17/2006	2/27/2006	3/1/2006	3/15/2006
0.345Q	5/23/2006	5/30/2006	6/1/2006	6/15/2006
0.348Q	8/18/2006	8/30/2006	9/1/2006	9/15/2006

Indicated Div: $1.39 (Div. Reinv. Plan)

Valuation Analysis **Institutional Holding**
Forecast P/E N/A No of Institutions 70
Market Cap $690.9 Million Shares 5,158,264
Book Value 351.1 Million % Held 25.09
Price/Book 1.97
Price/Sales 1.30

Business Summary: Electricity (MIC: 7.1 SIC: 4931 NAIC: 221121)

MGE Energy is the holding company for Madison Gas & Electric, which is a public utility that generates and distributes electricity to nearly 136,000 customers in Dane County, WI as of Dec 31 2005. Co. also purchases, transports and distributes natural gas to nearly 137,000 customers in the Wisconsin cities of Elroy, Fitchburg, Lodi, Madison, Middleton, Monona, Prairie du Chien, Verona, and Viroqua; 24 villages and all or parts of 45 townships. Co. has a 22.0% ownership interest in two, 512-megawatt coal-burning units at the Columbia Energy Center in Columbia, WI. The units burn low-sulfur coal obtained from the Powder River Basin coal fields located in Wyoming and Montana.

Recent Developments: For the quarter ended June 30 2006, net income increased 29.6% to $7.1 million from $5.4 million in the year-earlier quarter. Revenues were $99.7 million, down 0.7% from $100.5 million the year before. Operating income was $13.8 million versus $10.7 million in the prior-year quarter, an increase of 28.8%. Direct operating expenses declined 5.0% to $82.1 million from $86.4 million in the comparable period the year before. Indirect operating expenses increased 15.0% to $3.8 million from $3.3 million in the equivalent prior-year period.

Prospects: Co.'s utility operations are benefiting from an increase in rates that became effective in January 2006. The increase in rates was implemented to cover forecasted increases in fuel costs and the costs of additional facilities, including MGE Power Elm Road and MGE Power West Campus. Meanwhile, Co.'s stated primary focus for the foreseeable future is its core utility customers at Madison Gas and Electric Company (MGE). As part of its effort of providing its customers with reliable power at competitive prices, Co. plans to build more efficient generation projects while continuing its efforts to control operational costs.

Financial Data
(US$ in Thousands)

	6 Mos	3 Mos	12/31/2005	12/31/2004	12/31/2003	12/31/2002	12/31/2001	12/31/2000
Earnings Per Share	1.80	1.77	1.57	1.77	1.71	1.69	1.62	1.67
Cash Flow Per Share	3.31	2.55	2.44	3.25	3.83	3.28	4.44	2.91
Tang Book Value Per Share	17.08	17.04	16.81	16.59	14.34	12.94	12.67	12.05
Dividends Per Share	1.380	1.377	1.373	1.360	1.348	1.338	1.328	1.318
Dividend Payout %	76.67	77.78	87.47	76.84	78.85	79.19	81.99	78.93
Income Statement								
Total Revenue	258,306	158,585	513,370	424,881	401,547	347,096	333,711	324,108
EBITDA	53,371	30,293	94,718	90,861	85,145	89,307	...	...
Depn & Amortn	15,636	7,736	29,308	24,931	22,828	28,842	36,459	36,548
Income Before Taxes	30,037	18,727	51,962	54,496	50,541	47,920	...	...
Income Taxes	11,470	7,211	19,871	20,656	19,901	18,727	2,105	...
Net Income	18,567	11,516	32,091	33,840	30,640	29,193	27,245	27,355
Average Shares	20,468	20,454	20,436	19,119	17,894	17,311	16,819	16,382
Balance Sheet								
Total Assets	901,707	899,655	916,907	827,371	721,687	628,895	541,451	571,604
Long-Term Obligations	222,339	222,325	222,312	202,257	202,204	192,149	157,600	183,437
Total Liabilities	550,638	551,153	573,024	489,174	458,617	401,525	325,159	371,292
Stockholders' Equity	351,069	348,502	343,883	338,197	263,070	227,370	216,292	200,312
Shares Outstanding	20,557	20,454	20,451	20,389	18,343	17,574	17,071	16,618
Statistical Record								
Return on Assets %	4.31	4.16	3.68	4.36	4.54	4.99	4.90	5.11
Return on Equity %	10.72	10.26	9.41	11.23	12.49	13.16	13.08	14.13
EBITDA Margin %	20.66	19.10	18.45	21.39	21.20	25.73	...	...
Net Margin %	7.19	7.26	6.25	7.96	7.63	8.41	8.16	8.44
PPE Turnover	0.81	0.82	0.81	0.74	0.80	0.81	0.79	0.77
Asset Turnover	0.62	0.63	0.59	0.55	0.59	0.59	0.60	0.61
Debt to Equity	0.63	0.64	0.65	0.60	0.77	0.85	0.73	0.92
Price Range	38.63-29.28	38.63-30.43	38.63-31.18	36.30-28.57	34.45-25.27	29.84-25.01	27.80-21.06	22.75-17.00
P/E Ratio	21.46-16.27	21.82-17.19	24.61-19.86	20.51-16.14	20.15-14.78	17.66-14.80	17.16-13.00	13.62-10.18
Average Yield %	4.07	3.96	3.90	4.28	4.50	4.97	5.53	6.70

Address: 133 South Blair Street, Madison, WI 53703 **Telephone:** 608-252-7000 **Fax:** 608-252-7098	**Web Site:** www.mgeenergy.com **Officers:** Gary J. Wolter - Chmn., Pres., C.E.O. David C. Mebane - Vice-Chmn.	**Auditors:** PricewaterhouseCoopers LLP **Investor Contact:** 608-252-7907 **Transfer Agents:** Continental Stock Transfer & Trust Company, New York, NY

MICREL, INC.

Exchange	Symbol	Price	52Wk Range	Yield	P/E
NMS	MCRL	$10.02 (8/31/2006)	15.78-8.30	N/A	24.44

*7 Year Price Score 45.23 *NYSE Composite Index=100 *12 Month Price Score 78.63

Interim Earnings (Per Share)

Qtr.	Mar	Jun	Sep	Dec
2003	0.00	(0.01)	0.02	0.04
2004	0.05	0.15	0.08	0.06
2005	0.07	0.01	0.09	0.11
2006	0.10	0.11	...	...

Interim Dividends (Per Share)

No Dividends Paid

Valuation Analysis   Institutional Holding

Forecast P/E	22.20	No of Institutions
	(9/9/2006)	161
Market Cap	$826.2 Million	Shares
Book Value	253.3 Million	60,969,464
Price/Book	3.26	% Held
Price/Sales	3.11	75.16

Business Summary: IT & Technology (MIC: 10.2 SIC: 3674 NAIC: 334413)

Micrel designs, develops, manufactures and markets analog power integrated circuits (ICs) and mixed-signal and digital ICs. At Dec 31 2005, Co. shipped over 2,500 standard products and derived most of its product revenue from sales of standard analog and high speed communications integrated circuits. These products address a range of end markets including cellular handsets, portable computing, enterprise and home networking, wide area and metropolitan area networks and industrial equipment. Co. also manufactures custom analog and mixed-signal circuits and provides wafer foundry services for customers who produce electronic systems for communications, consumer and military applications.

Recent Developments: For the quarter ended June 30 2006, net income increased 660.0% to $9.0 million from $1.2 million in the year-earlier quarter. Revenues were $70.2 million, up 13.1% from $62.1 million the year before. Operating income was $13.8 million versus $815,000 in the prior-year quarter, an increase of. Direct operating expenses was unchanged at $29.9 million versus the comparable period the year before. Indirect operating expenses decreased 15.7% to $26.4 million from $31.3 million in the equivalent prior-year period.

Prospects: Co.'s revenue growth is being driven by demand from customers serving the wireline communications and industrial end markets. Going forward, despite a variety of macroeconomic and industry-specific risks that appear to threaten the semiconductor cycle, Co. expects the industry to grow at previous rates in 2006 and 2007. However, Co. expects continued pricing pressure for its products in the future attributable to the increased concentration of electronics procurement and manufacturing in the Asia Pacific region by its customers. For the third quarter of 2006, based on current backlog and demand estimates, Co. expects revenues to be between $70.0 million and $72.0 million.

Financial Data
(US$ in Thousands)

	6 Mos	3 Mos	12/31/2005	12/31/2004	12/31/2003	12/31/2002	12/31/2001	12/31/2000
Earnings Per Share	0.41	0.31	0.29	0.34	0.05	(0.44)	0.01	0.82
Cash Flow Per Share	0.67	0.67	0.66	0.72	0.55	0.31	0.47	1.38
Tang Book Value Per Share	3.02	3.01	2.99	3.10	3.00	2.88	3.38	3.05
Income Statement								
Total Revenue	138,343	68,151	250,356	257,551	211,726	204,704	217,808	322,475
EBITDA	38,392	18,932	53,084	65,433	33,674	(38,295)	22,378	136,542
Depn & Amortn	8,535	4,235	19,952	24,828	28,649	33,910	32,373	25,062
Income Before Taxes	29,857	14,697	37,300	42,459	5,702	(70,690)	(4,982)	115,932
Income Taxes	12,165	5,996	11,942	11,206	855	(29,690)	(5,534)	38,261
Net Income	17,692	8,701	25,358	31,253	4,847	(41,000)	552	77,671
Average Shares	84,696	85,794	87,971	93,083	93,786	92,600	98,092	94,687
Balance Sheet								
Total Assets	320,244	322,325	319,540	334,267	337,439	330,675	354,813	332,894
Current Liabilities	66,509	66,213	61,379	47,212	45,651	37,819	36,283	57,901
Long-Term Obligations	...	...	...	83	3,280	10,983	1,299	5,327
Total Liabilities	66,967	66,671	61,854	49,380	53,830	57,056	41,483	67,069
Stockholders' Equity	253,277	255,654	257,686	284,887	283,609	273,619	313,330	265,825
Shares Outstanding	82,454	83,627	84,646	89,825	92,522	92,006	92,823	85,374
Statistical Record								
Return on Assets %	11.11	8.49	7.76	9.28	1.45	N.M.	0.16	28.90
Return on Equity %	13.64	10.34	9.35	10.96	1.74	N.M.	0.19	37.38
EBITDA Margin %	27.75	27.78	21.20	25.41	15.90	N.M.	10.27	42.34
Net Margin %	12.79	12.77	10.13	12.13	2.29	N.M.	0.25	24.09
Asset Turnover	0.84	0.80	0.77	0.76	0.63	0.60	0.63	1.20
Current Ratio	3.39	3.45	3.69	5.16	5.27	5.82	6.43	3.73
Debt to Equity	...	...	...	N.M.	0.01	0.04	N.M.	0.02
Price Range	15.78-9.55	14.82-8.07	13.27-8.07	19.20-8.40	18.02-8.02	29.52-4.57	48.94-18.15	76.44-27.19
P/E Ratio	38.49-23.29	47.81-26.03	45.76-27.83	56.47-24.71	360.40-160.40	...	N.M.	93.22-33.16

Address: 2180 Fortune Drive, San Jose, CA 95131
Telephone: 408-944-0800
Fax: 408-944-0970

Web Site: www.micrel.com
Officers: Raymond D. Zinn - Chmn., Pres., C.E.O.
Robert Whelton - Exec. V.P., Oper.

Auditors: PricewaterhouseCoopers LLP

MICROCHIP TECHNOLOGY, INC.

Exchange	Symbol	Price	52Wk Range	Yield	P/E
NMS	MCHP	$34.16 (8/31/2006)	38.15-27.30	2.75	28.47

*7 Year Price Score 102.38 *NYSE Composite Index=100 *12 Month Price Score 95.76

Interim Earnings (Per Share)

Qtr.	Jun	Sep	Dec	Mar
2003-04	0.06	0.17	0.19	0.22
2004-05	0.21	0.29	0.25	0.27
2005-06	0.29	0.31	0.19	0.35
2006-07	0.35	...	...	...

Interim Dividends (Per Share)

Amt	Decl	Ex	Rec	Pay
0.16Q	10/20/2005	11/1/2005	11/3/2005	11/18/2005
0.19Q	1/19/2006	1/31/2006	2/2/2006	2/16/2006
0.215Q	4/25/2006	5/5/2006	5/9/2006	5/23/2006
0.235Q	7/20/2006	8/1/2006	8/3/2006	8/17/2006

Indicated Div: $0.94

Valuation Analysis

Forecast P/E	19.15
	(9/9/2006)
Market Cap	$7.3 Billion
Book Value	1.8 Billion
Price/Book	4.10
Price/Sales	7.54

Institutional Holding

No of Institutions	315
Shares	190,914,896
% Held	88.83

Business Summary: IT & Technology (MIC: 10.2 SIC: 3674 NAIC: 334413)

Microchip Technology develops and manufactures specialized semiconductor products used by its customers for a variety of embedded control applications. Co.'s product portfolio comprises 8- and 16-bit PIC® microcontrollers and 16-bit dsPIC® digital signal controllers, which feature on-board Flash (reprogrammable) memory technology. In addition, Co. offers a spectrum of high-performance linear, mixed-signal, power management, thermal management, battery management and interface devices. Co. also makes serial EEPROMs and complementary microperipheral products.

Recent Developments: For the quarter ended June 30 2006, net income increased 26.2% to $77.0 million from $61.0 million in the year-earlier quarter. Revenues were $262.6 million, up 20.1% from $218.5 million the year before. Operating income was $89.7 million versus $73.0 million in the prior-year quarter, an increase of 22.8%. Direct operating expenses rose 14.3% to $104.1 million from $91.0 million in the comparable period the year before. Indirect operating expenses increased 26.3% to $68.8 million from $54.5 million in the equivalent prior-year period.

Prospects: Co.'s outlook appears encouraging, given favorable top- and bottom-line growth exhibited across all its product lines. In particular, Co.'s results are benefiting from an increase in demand for its microcontroller products in end markets, which includes the automotive, communications, computing, consumer and industrial control markets. For fiscal quarter ending Sep 30 2006, Co. expects net sales to be up about 4.0% from the prior quarter, with gross margins of approximately 60.6%. In addition, Co. is targeting earnings per diluted share of $0.37, including the effect of all share-based compensation expense.

Financial Data (US$ in Thousands)	3 Mos	03/31/2006	03/31/2005	03/31/2004	03/31/2003	03/31/2002	03/31/2001	03/31/2000
Earnings Per Share	1.20	1.13	1.01	0.65	0.42	0.45	0.69	0.56
Cash Flow Per Share	2.21	2.08	1.71	1.66	1.28	0.90	1.31	1.39
Tang Book Value Per Share	8.14	7.89	6.95	6.19	5.58	5.36	4.80	3.52
Dividends Per Share	0.690	0.570	0.208	0.113	0.040	...	...	...
Dividend Payout %	57.50	50.44	20.59	17.38	9.52	...	...	...
Income Statement								
Total Revenue	262,557	927,893	846,936	699,260	651,462	571,254	715,730	495,729
EBITDA	118,376	439,081	380,870	284,884	236,064	231,886	287,784	207,072
Depn & Amortn	28,519	110,682	120,466	111,627	111,076	109,039	104,326	68,472
Income Before Taxes	101,295	359,185	277,268	177,896	128,332	127,191	196,199	139,784
Income Taxes	24,311	116,816	63,483	40,634	28,657	32,377	53,363	37,740
Net Income	76,984	242,369	213,785	137,262	88,232	94,814	142,836	102,044
Average Shares	219,791	215,094	211,962	212,172	210,646	208,907	205,189	183,046
Balance Sheet								
Total Assets	2,294,691	2,350,596	1,817,554	1,622,143	1,428,275	1,275,600	1,161,349	812,411
Current Liabilities	494,699	608,969	306,665	270,051	215,130	167,965	194,623	168,500
Total Liabilities	506,882	624,407	331,820	301,626	249,326	199,821	218,501	188,115
Stockholders' Equity	1,787,809	1,726,189	1,485,734	1,320,517	1,178,949	1,075,779	942,848	624,296
Shares Outstanding	214,651	213,614	207,738	206,589	203,432	200,629	196,346	177,541
Statistical Record								
Return on Assets %	12.34	11.63	12.43	8.97	6.53	7.78	14.47	15.45
Return on Equity %	15.46	15.09	15.24	10.95	7.83	9.39	18.23	20.70
EBITDA Margin %	45.09	47.32	44.97	40.74	36.24	40.59	40.21	41.77
Net Margin %	29.32	26.12	25.24	19.63	13.54	16.60	19.96	20.58
Asset Turnover	0.46	0.45	0.49	0.46	0.48	0.47	0.73	0.75
Current Ratio	2.24	1.84	3.51	3.27	2.83	3.27	1.91	2.17
Price Range	38.15-27.30	37.74-24.60	32.63-24.28	36.03-18.15	33.07-15.36	28.81-14.96	32.33-13.33	32.11-9.98
P/E Ratio	31.79-22.75	33.40-21.77	32.31-24.04	55.43-27.92	78.74-36.57	64.03-33.24	46.86-19.32	57.34-17.82
Average Yield %	2.09	1.82	0.75	0.42	0.16	...	...	...

Address: 2355 W. Chandler Blvd., Chandler, AZ 85224-6199 **Telephone:** 480-792-7200 **Fax:** 480-792-7790	**Web Site:** www.microchip.com **Officers:** Steve Sanghi - Chmn., Pres., C.E.O. Steve Drehobl - V.P., Security, Microcontroller & Tech. Div.	**Auditors:** Ernst & Young LLP **Investor Contact:** 480-786-7761 **Transfer Agents:** Wells Fargo Bank Minnesota, N.A.

MICROSOFT CORPORATION

Exchange	Symbol	Price	52Wk Range	Yield	P/E
NMS	MSFT	$25.70 (8/31/2006)	28.16-21.51	1.40	21.42

*7 Year Price Score 68.97 *NYSE Composite Index=100 *12 Month Price Score 92.04

Interim Earnings (Per Share)

Qtr.	Sep	Dec	Mar	Jun
2001-02	0.12	0.20	0.25	0.00
2002-03	0.25	0.23	0.26	0.00
2003-04	0.24	0.14	0.12	0.25
2004-05	0.23	0.32	0.23	0.34
2005-06	0.29	0.34	0.29	0.28

Interim Dividends (Per Share)

Amt	Decl	Ex	Rec	Pay
0.08Q	9/23/2005	11/15/2005	11/17/2005	12/8/2005
0.09Q	12/14/2005	2/15/2006	2/17/2006	3/9/2006
0.09Q	3/27/2006	5/15/2006	5/17/2006	6/8/2006
0.09Q	6/22/2006	8/15/2006	8/17/2006	9/14/2006

Indicated Div: $0.36

Valuation Analysis

		Institutional Holding	
Forecast P/E	15.37	No of Institutions	
	(9/9/2006)	1439	
Market Cap	$258.6 Billion	Shares	5,783,955,456
Book Value	40.1 Billion	% Held	58.01
Price/Book	6.45		
Price/Sales	5.84		

Business Summary: IT & Technology (MIC: 10.2 SIC: 7372 NAIC: 511210)

Microsoft develops, manufactures, licenses, and supports a wide range of software products for many computing devices. Co.'s software products include operating systems for servers, PCs, and intelligent devices; server applications for distributed computing environments; information worker productivity applications; business solutions applications; and software development tools. Co. provides consulting and product support services, and trains and certifies system integrators and developers. Co. sells the Xbox video game console and games, PC games, and PC peripherals. Online communication and information services are delivered through Co.'s MSN portals and channels around the world.

Recent Developments: For the year ended June 30 2006, net income increased 2.8% to $12.60 billion from $12.25 billion in the prior year. Revenues were $44.28 billion, up 11.3% from $39.79 billion the year before. Operating income was $16.47 billion versus $14.56 billion in the prior year, an increase of 13.1%. Direct operating expenses rose 26.8% to $7.65 billion from $6.03 billion in the comparable period the year before. Indirect operating expenses increased 5.0% to $20.16 billion from $19.20 billion in the equivalent prior-year period.

Prospects: Co. is optimistic regarding its business outlook going forward. Robust top-line growth is being fueled by solid demand for Co.'s new consumer and business offerings, particularly in its Home and Entertainment segment stemming from strong demand for its Xbox 360™ system. As a result, Co. is accelerating its investments in the business to further drive growth. For the fourth quarter of fiscal 2006, Co. expects revenue to be in the range of $11.50 billion to $11.70 billion and earnings to be approximately $0.30 per diluted share. For full fiscal 2007, Co. expects revenue to be in the range of $49.50 billion to $50.50 billion, along with earnings of between $1.36 and $1.41 per diluted share.

Financial Data
(US$ in Thousands)

	06/30/2006	06/30/2005	06/30/2004	06/30/2003	06/30/2002	06/30/2001	06/30/2000	06/30/1999
Earnings Per Share	1.20	1.12	0.75	0.92	0.70	0.66	0.85	0.71
Cash Flow Per Share	1.38	1.53	1.35	1.47	1.34	1.26	1.34	1.00
Tang Book Value Per Share	3.55	4.14	6.55	5.34	4.71	4.39	3.92	2.69
Dividends Per Share	0.340	3.320	0.160	0.080	...	...	...	...
Dividend Payout %	28.33	296.43	21.33	8.70	...	...	...	...
Income Statement								
Total Revenue	44,282,000	39,788,000	36,835,000	32,187,000	28,365,000	25,296,000	22,956,000	19,747,000
EBITDA	18,262,000	16,628,000	9,009,000	13,149,000	11,818,000	11,561,000	11,093,000	10,088,000
Income Before Taxes	18,262,000	16,628,000	12,196,000	14,726,000	11,513,000	11,525,000	14,275,000	11,891,000
Income Taxes	5,663,000	4,374,000	4,028,000	4,733,000	3,684,000	3,804,000	4,854,000	4,106,000
Net Income	12,599,000	12,254,000	8,168,000	9,993,000	7,829,000	7,346,000	9,421,000	7,785,000
Average Shares	10,531,000	10,906,001	10,894,001	10,882,001	11,106,001	11,148,001	11,072,001	10,964,001
Balance Sheet								
Total Assets	69,597,000	70,815,000	92,389,000	79,571,000	67,646,000	59,257,000	52,150,000	37,156,000
Current Liabilities	22,442,000	16,877,000	14,969,000	13,974,000	12,744,000	11,132,000	9,755,000	8,718,000
Total Liabilities	29,493,000	22,700,000	17,564,000	18,551,000	15,466,000	11,968,000	10,782,000	8,718,000
Stockholders' Equity	40,104,000	48,115,000	74,825,000	61,020,000	52,180,000	47,289,000	41,368,000	28,438,000
Shares Outstanding	10,062,000	10,710,000	10,862,001	10,771,001	10,718,000	10,766,001	10,566,001	10,218,000
Statistical Record								
Return on Assets %	17.95	15.02	9.47	13.58	12.34	13.19	21.04	26.16
Return on Equity %	28.56	19.93	11.99	17.66	15.74	16.57	26.92	34.55
EBITDA Margin %	41.24	41.79	24.46	40.85	41.66	45.70	48.32	51.09
Net Margin %	28.45	30.80	22.17	31.05	27.60	29.04	41.04	39.42
Asset Turnover	0.63	0.49	0.43	0.44	0.45	0.45	0.51	0.66
Current Ratio	2.18	2.89	4.71	4.22	3.81	3.56	3.11	2.32
Price Range	28.16-21.51	29.98-23.92	29.96-24.15	29.12-21.41	36.29-24.31	41.00-20.75	59.56-30.72	47.47-22.81
P/E Ratio	23.47-17.93	26.77-21.36	39.95-32.20	31.65-23.28	51.84-34.73	62.12-31.44	70.07-36.14	66.86-32.11
Average Yield %	1.31	12.50	0.60	0.32	...	...	...	...

Address: One Microsoft Way, Redmond, WA 98052-6399	**Web Site:** www.microsoft.com	**Auditors:** Deloitte & Touche LLP
Telephone: 425-882-8080	**Officers:** William H. Gates III - Chmn., Chief Software Architect Steven A. Ballmer - C.E.O.	**Investor Contact:** 800-285-7772
Fax: 425-936-7329		**Transfer Agents:** Mellon Investor Services

MIDLAND CO.

Exchange	Symbol	Price	52Wk Range	Yield	P/E	Div Achiever
NMS	MLAN	$41.40 (8/31/2006)	43.81-31.22	0.59	14.58	19 Years

*7 Year Price Score 125.94 *NYSE Composite Index=100 *12 Month Price Score 101.80

Interim Earnings (Per Share)

Qtr.	Mar	Jun	Sep	Dec
2003	0.56	(0.60)	0.23	0.56
2004	0.90	0.58	0.12	1.23
2005	1.10	1.06	0.21	0.98
2006	1.15	0.50	...	...

Interim Dividends (Per Share)

Amt	Decl	Ex	Rec	Pay
0.056Q	10/28/2005	12/19/2005	12/21/2005	1/4/2006
0.061Q	1/27/2006	3/20/2006	3/22/2006	4/5/2006
0.061Q	4/27/2006	6/20/2006	6/22/2006	7/6/2006
0.061Q	7/27/2006	9/19/2006	9/21/2006	10/4/2006

Indicated Div: $0.25 (Div. Reinv. Plan)

Valuation Analysis

Forecast P/E	14.16 (9/9/2006)
Market Cap	$790.3 Million
Book Value	510.4 Million
Price/Book	1.55
Price/Sales	1.08

Institutional Holding

No of Institutions	75
Shares	8,286,376
% Held	43.39

Business Summary: Insurance (MIC: 8.2 SIC: 6399 NAIC: 524128)

Midland is a provider of specialty insurance products and services through its American Modern Insurance Group subsidiary. Co. also maintains an investment in a niche river transportation business. Co.'s residential property segment includes manufactured housing and site-built dwelling insurance products. Co.'s recreational casualty segment includes specialty insurance products such as motorcycle, watercraft, recreational vehicle, collector car and snowmobile. Co.'s financial institutions segment includes specialty insurance products such as mortgage fire and debt cancellation. The all other insurance segment includes products such as credit life, commercial, excess and surplus lines.

Recent Developments: For the quarter ended June 30 2006, net income decreased 52.1% to $9.8 million from $20.5 million in the year-earlier quarter. Revenues were $190.2 million, up 2.1% from $186.3 million the year before. Net premiums earned were $165.6 million versus $162.8 million in the prior-year quarter, an increase of 1.7%. Net investment income was unchanged at $10.2 million versus a year ago.

Prospects: For the second half of 2006, Co. is increasing its top line growth expectations to be in the high single digit to low double digit range, reflecting a mid-single digit organic growth rate, coupled with the expected benefit from the expansion of its strategic business alliance with Homesite Insurance Company and its pending acquisition of Southern Pioneer Life Insurance Company. At the same time, Co. will continue to focus on growing its underwriting and distribution platform. Overall, Co. believes that its earnings, exclusive of net capital gains or losses, will be toward the low end of its prior earnings guidance range of $2.90 to $3.20 per share.

Financial Data (US$ in Thousands)	6 Mos	3 Mos	12/31/2005	12/31/2004	12/31/2003	12/31/2002	12/31/2001	12/31/2000
Earnings Per Share	2.84	3.40	3.37	2.83	1.30	1.06	1.51	1.89
Cash Flow Per Share	1.11	1.76	1.44	4.76	4.42	2.46	2.79	4.01
Tang Book Value Per Share	26.74	26.61	25.54	22.98	20.18	17.59	16.53	15.73
Dividends Per Share	0.235	0.230	0.225	0.205	0.190	0.175	0.160	0.150
Dividend Payout %	8.27	6.76	6.68	7.24	14.62	16.51	10.56	7.94
Income Statement								
Premium Income	327,963	162,404	631,864	677,584	638,038	577,668	508,233	456,120
Total Revenue	377,105	186,932	733,430	783,841	718,187	636,690	586,543	534,422
Benefits & Claims	152,839	60,898	286,662	348,611	392,232	341,015	292,188	240,680
Income Before Taxes	44,821	32,113	92,901	77,104	30,232	25,741	36,704	50,669
Income Taxes	12,581	9,678	27,575	22,866	6,956	5,437	9,482	15,206
Net Income	32,240	22,435	65,326	54,238	23,276	18,841	27,222	35,463
Average Shares	19,585	19,511	19,407	19,190	17,937	17,789	17,990	18,758
Balance Sheet								
Total Assets	1,429,766	1,408,591	1,428,113	1,364,684	1,179,505	1,090,674	1,053,942	993,850
Total Liabilities	919,360	901,849	943,736	932,408	823,447	781,766	762,066	710,673
Stockholders' Equity	510,406	506,742	484,377	432,276	356,058	308,908	291,876	283,177
Shares Outstanding	19,089	19,040	18,964	18,807	17,643	17,566	17,660	18,000
Statistical Record								
Return on Assets %	3.90	4.83	4.68	4.25	2.05	1.76	2.66	3.76
Return on Equity %	11.30	13.99	14.25	13.72	7.00	6.27	9.47	13.07
Loss Ratio %	46.60	37.50	45.37	51.45	61.47	59.03	57.49	52.77
Net Margin %	8.55	12.00	8.91	6.92	3.24	2.96	4.64	6.63
Price Range	43.81-31.22	39.74-30.95	39.74-30.02	32.74-23.04	24.29-16.32	25.23-16.44	23.60-13.25	15.69-9.25
P/E Ratio	15.43-10.99	11.69-9.10	11.79-8.91	11.57-8.14	18.68-12.55	23.81-15.51	15.63-8.77	8.30-4.89
Average Yield %	0.65	0.66	0.66	0.76	0.91	0.84	0.86	1.21

Address: 7000 Midland Blvd., Amelia, OH 45102-2607
Telephone: 513-943-7100
Fax: 513-943-7111

Web Site: www.midlandcompany.com
Officers: John P. Hayden III - Chmn., C.O.O. John W. Hayden - Pres., C.E.O.

Auditors: Deloitte & Touche LLP
Investor Contact: 513-943-7100
Transfer Agents: National City Bank

MILLENNIUM PHARMACEUTICALS, INC.

Exchange	Symbol	Price	52Wk Range	Yield	P/E
NMS	MLNM	$10.84 (8/31/2006)	11.15-8.04	N/A	N/A

*7 Year Price Score 35.95 *NYSE Composite Index=100 *12 Month Price Score 98.53

Interim Earnings (Per Share)

Qtr.	Mar	Jun	Sep	Dec
2003	(0.47)	(0.36)	(0.31)	(0.49)
2004	(0.13)	(0.18)	(0.21)	(0.31)
2005	(0.12)	(0.14)	(0.24)	(0.14)
2006	(0.07)	(0.06)	...	...

Interim Dividends (Per Share)
No Dividends Paid

Valuation Analysis **Institutional Holding**

Forecast P/E	N/A	No of Institutions
		222
Market Cap	$3.4 Billion	Shares
Book Value	2.1 Billion	252,432,688
Price/Book	1.62	% Held
Price/Sales	6.03	80.05

Business Summary: Pharmaceuticals (MIC: 9.1 SIC: 2834 NAIC: 325412)

Millennium Pharmaceuticals is a biopharmaceutical company focused on developing and commercializing products in the areas of cancer, cardiovascular disease and inflammatory disease. Co.'s cancer product, VELCADE® (bortezomib) for Injection, is marketed as a treatment for patients with multiple myeloma, a type of blood cancer, who have received at least two prior therapies and demonstrated disease progression on their most recent therapy. In the U.S., Co. co-promotes its cardiovascular product, INTEGRILIN® (eptifibatide) Injection with Schering-Plough Corporation and Schering-Plough Ltd. In the European Union, GlaxoSmithKline plc exclusively markets INTEGRILIN under a license from Co.

Recent Developments: For the quarter ended June 30 2006, net loss amounted to $17.7 million versus a net loss of $44.1 million in the year-earlier quarter. Revenues were $120.1 million, up 8.6% from $110.6 million the year before. Operating loss was $20.7 million versus a loss of $56.5 million in the prior-year quarter. Direct operating expenses declined 15.5% to $14.1 million from $16.7 million in the comparable period the year before. Indirect operating expenses decreased 15.8% to $126.7 million from $150.5 million in the equivalent prior-year period.

Prospects: Looking ahead, Co. expects to see sales increase through the balance of 2006 with growth coming from increasing the average length of therapy used by patients and treating more patients with its Velcade®. Additionally, Co. expects to file a supplemental New Drug Application for Velcade® as a monotherapy for the treatment of relapsed and refractory mantle cell lymphoma during the second half of 2006. For full-year 2006, Co. expects Velcade® U.S. net product sales to be in the range of $225.0 million to $250.0 million, while royalties are expected to be in the range of $115.0 million to $125.0 million. Meanwhile, Co. expects a net loss of between $95.0 million and $115.0 million in 2006.

Financial Data
(US$ in Thousands)

	6 Mos	3 Mos	12/31/2005	12/31/2004	12/31/2003	12/31/2002	12/31/2001	12/31/2000
Earnings Per Share	(0.51)	(0.59)	(0.64)	(0.83)	(1.63)	(2.13)	(0.88)	(1.84)
Cash Flow Per Share	0.11	0.09	(0.18)	(0.57)	(0.74)	(1.27)	(0.72)	(0.56)
Tang Book Value Per Share	1.73	1.72	1.68	2.16	2.87	4.18	6.26	5.87
Income Statement								
Total Revenue	242,598	122,475	558,308	448,206	433,687	353,033	246,216	196,269
Depn & Amortn	33,252	16,442	76,300	93,412	107,000	86,504	100,115	79,346
Net Income	(38,508)	(20,841)	(198,249)	(252,297)	(483,687)	(590,193)	(192,005)	(309,619)
Average Shares	313,321	311,823	308,284	304,830	297,641	277,665	218,937	192,835
Balance Sheet								
Total Assets	2,476,062	2,505,106	2,527,632	2,757,031	3,010,263	3,997,607	1,907,734	1,811,922
Current Liabilities	226,405	243,117	164,595	240,861	255,758	949,547	203,163	136,174
Long-Term Obligations	75,641	75,935	175,797	185,913	193,350	144,663	118,432	125,296
Total Liabilities	369,084	394,059	425,954	484,037	508,737	1,095,914	339,497	349,639
Stockholders' Equity	2,106,978	2,111,047	2,101,678	2,272,994	2,501,526	2,901,693	1,568,237	1,462,283
Shares Outstanding	315,215	314,107	311,121	306,399	302,290	291,094	224,290	213,979
Statistical Record								
Asset Turnover	0.22	0.22	0.21	0.16	0.12	0.12	0.13	0.17
Current Ratio	3.18	3.02	4.50	3.74	4.36	2.04	7.46	10.91
Debt to Equity	0.04	0.04	0.08	0.08	0.08	0.05	0.08	0.09
Price Range	11.15-8.04	11.15-7.79	12.14-7.79	19.63-10.15	18.87-6.43	25.28-7.19	58.19-16.13	86.50-26.19

Address: 40 Landsdowne Street, Cambridge, MA 02139 **Telephone:** 617-679-7000 **Fax:** 617-374-9379	**Web Site:** www.mlnm.com **Officers:** Kenneth E. Weg - Chmn. Deborah Dunsire M.D. - Pres., C.E.O.	**Auditors:** Ernst & Young LLP **Investor Contact:** 617-679-7000 **Transfer Agents:** EquiServe Trust Company, Kansas City, MO

MILLER (HERMAN) INC.

Exchange	Symbol	Price	52Wk Range	Yield	P/E
NMS	MLHR	$28.24 (8/31/2006)	32.54-25.77	1.13	19.48

*7 Year Price Score 94.37 *NYSE Composite Index=100 *12 Month Price Score 91.19

Interim Earnings (Per Share)

Qtr.	Aug	Nov	Feb	May
2001-02	(0.04)	(0.30)	(0.15)	(0.25)
2002-03	0.13	0.16	0.04	(0.02)
2003-04	0.08	0.12	0.11	0.27
2004-05	0.20	0.22	0.24	0.31
2005-06	0.34	0.40	0.33	0.38

Interim Dividends (Per Share)

Amt	Decl	Ex	Rec	Pay
0.072Q	9/27/2005	11/30/2005	12/3/2005	1/15/2006
0.08Q	1/26/2006	3/1/2006	3/3/2006	4/15/2006
0.08Q	4/24/2006	5/31/2006	6/3/2006	7/15/2006
0.08Q	7/24/2006	8/30/2006	9/2/2006	10/15/2006

Indicated Div: $0.32

Valuation Analysis **Institutional Holding**
Forecast P/E   N/A   No of Institutions 185
Market Cap $1.9 Billion   Shares
Book Value   138.4 Million   50,051,888
Price/Book   13.47   % Held
Price/Sales   1.07   76.68

Business Summary: Furniture and Fixtures (MIC: 11.10 SIC: 2521 NAIC: 337211)

Herman Miller is engaged in the design and development of furniture and furniture systems. Co. has modular systems (including Action Office®, Q™ System, Ethospace®, and Resolve®). Co.also provides a broad array of seating (including Aeron®, Mirra®, Celle™, Equa®, Ergon®, and Ambi® office chairs), storage (including Meridian® filing products), wooden casegoods (including Geiger® products), and freestanding furniture products (including Passage® and Abak™). Co. introduced two additional furniture platforms during fiscal 2006: My Studio Environments™ and Vivo Interiors™. The Foray™ chair, an executive-task chair made by Co.'s Geiger subsidiary, and Leaf™, a light emitting diode desk lamp.

Recent Developments: For the year ended June 3 2006, net income increased 45.9% to $99.2 million from $68.0 million in the prior year. Revenues were $1.74 billion, up 14.6% from $1.52 billion the year before. Operating income was $157.7 million versus $121.9 million in the prior year, an increase of 29.4%. Direct operating expenses rose 13.3% to $1.16 billion from $1.03 billion in the comparable period the year before. Indirect operating expenses increased 13.4% to $417.1 million from $367.9 million in the equivalent prior-year period.

Prospects: Co.'s results appear solid, reflecting higher sales growth from gains in its North American and Non-North American Furniture Solutions business segments. Meanwhile, Co continues to focus on the development of new products and technologies and is confident that these new products will significantly benefit its businesses, while providing better options to expand into new markets and geographic areas of potential growth. As a result, Co. expects to attain double-digit growth rate in sales in fiscal 2007. For its fiscal first quarter ended Sep 2007, Co. expects revenue to be in the range of $435.0 million to $455.0 million and earnings per share to be in the range of $0.38 to $0.42.

Financial Data
(US$ in Thousands)

	06/03/2006	05/28/2005	05/29/2004	05/31/2003	06/01/2002	06/02/2001	06/03/2000	05/29/1999
Earnings Per Share	1.45	0.96	0.58	0.31	(0.74)	1.81	1.74	1.67
Cash Flow Per Share	2.18	1.56	1.14	1.96	0.72	2.77	2.50	2.47
Tang Book Value Per Share	1.39	1.78	2.08	2.00	3.45	4.62	3.76	2.63
Dividends Per Share	0.305	0.290	0.181	0.145	0.145	0.145	0.145	0.145
Dividend Payout %	21.03	30.21	31.25	46.77	...	...	8.01	8.33	8.68
Income Statement								
Total Revenue	1,737,200	1,515,600	1,338,300	1,336,500	1,468,700	2,236,200	1,938,000	1,766,239
EBITDA	203,200	169,100	120,500	44,900	33,900	327,500	305,900	292,133
Depn & Amortn	41,600	46,900	59,300	...	112,900	92,600	77,100	62,054
Income Before Taxes	147,600	112,800	51,600	35,800	(91,000)	225,100	221,800	229,912
Income Taxes	47,700	44,700	8,800	12,500	(35,000)	81,000	82,100	88,100
Net Income	99,200	68,000	42,300	23,300	(56,000)	140,600	139,700	141,812
Average Shares	68,501	70,829	73,072	74,479	75,873	77,647	80,531	84,831
Balance Sheet								
Total Assets	668,000	705,500	714,700	767,500	788,000	996,500	941,200	761,506
Current Liabilities	299,400	284,900	237,300	237,200	211,000	309,600	474,000	351,500
Long-Term Obligations	175,800	181,000	192,700	209,400	221,800	232,900	77,800	90,842
Total Liabilities	529,600	534,900	520,100	576,500	525,000	645,000	646,700	552,431
Stockholders' Equity	138,400	170,500	194,600	191,000	263,000	351,500	294,500	209,075
Shares Outstanding	66,034	69,585	71,750	72,829	76,158	76,019	78,298	79,565
Statistical Record								
Return on Assets %	14.21	9.60	5.72	3.00	N.M.	14.55	16.14	18.45
Return on Equity %	63.19	37.35	22.00	10.29	N.M.	43.65	54.59	64.80
EBITDA Margin %	11.70	11.16	9.00	3.36	2.31	14.65	15.78	16.54
Net Margin %	5.71	4.49	3.16	1.74	N.M.	6.29	7.21	8.03
Asset Turnover	2.49	2.14	1.81	1.72	1.65	2.31	2.24	2.30
Current Ratio	1.30	1.52	1.81	1.74	1.83	1.53	0.90	1.00
Debt to Equity	1.27	1.06	0.99	1.10	0.84	0.66	0.26	0.43
Price Range	32.91-26.88	31.60-22.40	29.73-19.38	23.77-14.58	26.91-18.25	32.81-22.63	29.75-19.88	30.31-15.81
P/E Ratio	22.70-18.54	32.92-23.33	51.26-33.41	76.68-47.03	...	18.13-12.50	17.10-11.42	18.15-9.47
Average Yield %	1.01	1.08	0.75	0.82	0.62	0.53	0.61	0.65

Address: 855 East Main Avenue, P.O. Box 302, Zeeland, MI 49464-0302
Telephone: 616-654-3000
Web Site: www.hermanmiller.com
Officers: Michael A. Volkema - Chmn Brian C. Walker - Pres., C.E.O.
Auditors: Ernst & Young LLP
Investor Contact: 616-654-3000

MOLEX INC

Exchange	Symbol	Price	52Wk Range	Yield	P/E
NMS	MOLX A	$31.46 (8/31/2006)	33.47-22.82	0.95	24.97

*7 Year Price Score 80.89   *NYSE Composite Index=100   *12 Month Price Score 99.62

Interim Earnings (Per Share)

Qtr.	Sep	Dec	Mar	Jun
2001-02	0.13	0.02	0.10	0.14
2002-03	0.15	0.15	0.13	0.01
2003-04	0.17	0.17	0.24	0.30
2004-05	0.29	0.27	0.24	0.03
2005-06	0.25	0.31	0.33	0.37

Interim Dividends (Per Share)

Amt	Decl	Ex	Rec	Pay
0.05Q	7/28/2005	9/28/2005	9/30/2005	10/25/2005
0.05Q	7/28/2005	12/28/2005	12/30/2005	1/25/2006
0.037Q	12/16/2005	12/28/2004	12/30/2004	1/25/2005
0.075Q	4/28/2006	6/28/2006	6/30/2006	7/25/2006

Indicated Div: $0.30

Valuation Analysis

Forecast P/E 19.34 (9/9/2006)
Market Cap $5.8 Billion
Book Value 2.3 Billion
Price/Book 2.53
Price/Sales 2.02

Institutional Holding

No of Institutions 159
Shares 64,217,452
% Held 76.31

Business Summary: Electrical (MIC: 11.14 SIC: 3678 NAIC: 334417)

Molex is engaged in the manufactures and sales of electronic components. Co.'s products are used by a large number of original equipment manufacturers (OEMs) throughout the world. Co. designs, manufactures and sells more than 100,000 products, including terminals, connectors, planar cables, cable assemblies, interconnection systems, backplanes, integrated products and mechanical and electronic switches. Co. also provides manufacturing services to integrate specific components into a customer's product. As of June 30 2006, Co. operated 54 manufacturing plants, located in 18 countries on five continents.

Recent Developments: For the year ended June 30 2006, net income increased 53.5% to $237.0 million from $154.4 million in the prior year. Revenues were $2.86 billion, up 12.3% from $2.55 billion the year before. Operating income was $311.1 million versus $197.3 million in the prior year, an increase of 57.6%. Direct operating expenses rose 11.2% to $1.86 billion from $1.68 billion in the comparable period the year before. Indirect operating expenses increased 1.7% to $687.7 million from $676.0 million in the equivalent prior-year period.

Prospects: On June 30 2006, Co. announced that it has signed a definitive agreement to acquire Woodhead Industries, Inc., a manufacturer of network and electrical infrastructure products, in which Co. will acquire Woodhead, in a cash transaction valued at about $256.0 million. For fiscal year ended June 30 2007, Co. plans to transition its business to a global organizational structure, with full implementation scheduled on Jul1 2007. The plan is expected to improve the efficiencies of its global operations, as well as to better capitalize on its low-cost production centers globally. Accordingly, Co. is targeting revenue of $3.00 billion to $3.30 billion and earnings per share of $1.60 to $1.70.

Financial Data
(US$ in Thousands)

	06/30/2006	06/30/2005	06/30/2004	06/30/2003	06/30/2002	06/30/2001	06/30/2000	06/30/1999
Earnings Per Share	1.26	0.81	0.92	0.44	0.39	1.03	0.90	0.91
Cash Flow Per Share	2.39	2.28	1.53	1.82	2.04	2.13	1.50	1.62
Tang Book Value Per Share	11.61	10.78	10.05	9.10	8.64	8.25	6.30	5.56
Dividends Per Share	0.225	0.150	0.100	0.100	0.100	0.100	0.090	0.048
Dividend Payout %	17.86	18.52	10.87	22.73	25.64	9.71	10.04	5.27
Income Statement								
Total Revenue	2,861,289	2,548,652	2,246,715	1,843,098	1,711,497	2,365,549	2,217,096	1,711,649
EBITDA	534,031	441,160	464,624	330,574	310,727	502,002	512,030	389,586
Depn & Amortn	214,657	230,722	228,480	228,698	223,492	217,440	195,753	168,255
Income Before Taxes	329,303	216,887	239,892	110,042	93,221	291,416	323,694	230,214
Income Taxes	92,205	62,463	63,571	24,762	16,684	87,424	100,810	52,363
Net Income	237,000	154,434	175,950	84,918	76,479	203,919	222,454	178,029
Average Shares	187,416	190,572	192,186	193,229	195,986	197,633	247,760	195,631
Balance Sheet								
Total Assets	2,973,241	2,727,672	2,572,346	2,334,890	2,253,920	2,213,627	2,247,106	1,902,012
Current Liabilities	594,812	469,504	428,464	356,148	359,593	374,106	475,449	342,441
Long-Term Obligations	8,815	9,975	14,039	16,868	17,849	25,465	21,593	20,148
Total Liabilities	692,551	559,408	506,352	438,322	426,268	447,987	541,302	401,475
Stockholders' Equity	2,280,690	2,168,264	2,065,994	1,896,568	1,827,652	1,765,640	1,705,804	1,500,537
Shares Outstanding	183,605	187,857	189,070	190,777	193,036	195,311	244,568	245,377
Statistical Record								
Return on Assets %	8.31	5.83	7.15	3.70	3.42	9.14	10.69	10.05
Return on Equity %	10.65	7.29	8.86	4.56	4.26	11.75	13.84	12.89
EBITDA Margin %	18.66	17.31	20.68	17.94	18.16	21.22	23.09	22.76
Net Margin %	8.28	6.06	7.83	4.61	4.47	8.62	10.03	10.40
Asset Turnover	1.00	0.96	0.91	0.80	0.77	1.06	1.07	0.97
Current Ratio	2.60	2.93	2.73	2.70	2.55	2.38	2.15	2.57
Debt to Equity	N.M.	N.M.	0.01	0.01	0.01	0.01	0.01	0.01
Price Range	33.47-22.82	27.46-21.75	30.30-22.05	28.40-17.23	33.45-22.92	42.69-25.25	44.75-22.00	27.70-18.00
P/E Ratio	26.56-18.11	33.90-26.85	32.93-23.97	64.55-39.16	85.77-58.77	41.44-24.51	49.72-24.44	30.44-19.78
Average Yield %	0.83	0.61	0.38	0.46	0.36	0.31	0.28	0.22

Address: 2222 Wellington Court, Lisle, IL 60532
Telephone: 630-969-4550
Fax: 630-969-1352

Web Site: www.molex.com
Officers: Frederick A. Krehbiel - Co-Chmn. John H. Krehbiel Jr. - Co-Chmn.

Auditors: Ernst & Young LLP
Transfer Agents: Computershare Investor Services LLP

MONSTER WORLDWIDE INC

Exchange	Symbol	Price	52Wk Range	Yield	P/E
NMS	MNST	$40.74 (8/31/2006)	59.28-28.86	N/A	39.94

*7 Year Price Score 95.50 *NYSE Composite Index=100 *12 Month Price Score 92.41

Interim Earnings (Per Share)

Qtr.	Mar	Jun	Sep	Dec
2003	(1.04)	0.08	0.11	0.12
2004	0.11	0.14	0.17	0.20
2005	0.17	0.16	0.25	0.29
2006	0.32	...	...	...

Interim Dividends (Per Share)

Amt	Decl	Ex	Rec	Pay
2-for-1	1/11/2000	3/1/2000	2/16/2000	2/29/2000
0.00U	3/17/2003	4/1/2003	3/14/2003	3/31/2003

Valuation Analysis Institutional Holding

Forecast P/E	N/A	No of Institutions	282
Market Cap	$5.2 Billion	Shares	
Book Value	1.0 Billion	119,752,936	
Price/Book	5.12	% Held	
Price/Sales	4.99	93.29	

Business Summary: Advertising, Marketing & PR (MIC: 12.4 SIC: 7311 NAIC: 541810)

Monster Worldwide is the parent company of Monster, a global online careers property. Co. also owns TMP Worldwide, a recruitment advertising agency network. Co.'s clients range from Fortune 100 companies to small and medium-sized enterprises and government agencies. Co. operates in two business segments: Monster and Advertising & Communications. Monster, a global online career property and Co.'s flagship brand, connects companies with the most qualified career-minded individuals and offers innovative technology and superior services that give employers more control over the recruiting process.

Recent Developments: For the quarter ended Mar 31 2006, income from continuing operations increased 58.0% to $37.4 million from $23.7 million in the year-earlier quarter. Net income increased 105.5% to $42.3 million from $20.6 million in the year-earlier quarter. Revenues were $291.7 million, up 27.7% from $228.5 million the year before. Operating income was $57.5 million versus $37.1 million in the prior-year quarter, an increase of 55.1%. Indirect operating expenses increased 22.4% to $234.3 million from $191.5 million in the equivalent prior-year period.

Prospects: On May 10 2006, Co. announced that it has completed its sale of its remaining TMP Worldwide Advertising & Communications businesses in Europe. The sale includes all of Co.'s advertising and communications businesses in the U.K and Ireland. In a separate transaction, Co. also sold its recruitment advertising agency in Spain. The net purchase price for these transactions was approximately $40.0 million. The sales of these businesses are consistent with Co.'s ongoing assessment of its operations to support the growth across local and international markets. Separately, on May 9 2006, Co. announced it has acquired PWP, LLC. , a publisher of directory websites in the educational field.

Financial Data
(US$ in Thousands)

	3 Mos	12/31/2005	12/31/2004	12/31/2003	12/31/2002	12/31/2001	12/31/2000	12/31/1999
Earnings Per Share	1.02	0.86	0.61	(0.72)	(4.80)	0.61	0.53	(0.09)
Cash Flow Per Share	2.02	1.82	0.78	0.15	(0.13)	1.75	1.84	1.18
Tang Book Value Per Share	2.14	1.47	0.27	0.18	2.02	2.61	5.16	0.16
Income Statement								
Total Revenue	291,747	986,917	845,519	679,640	1,114,622	1,448,057	1,291,737	765,805
EBITDA	71,514	216,405	151,339	52,396	(74,870)	189,798	155,927	49,647
Depn & Amortn	10,694	37,955	37,623	28,049	55,485	75,971	62,618	42,392
Income Before Taxes	60,820	182,646	113,023	23,621	(130,019)	124,994	114,019	(1,548)
Income Taxes	22,149	64,186	38,716	16,300	(21,281)	57,566	57,602	5,450
Net Income	42,262	107,432	73,104	(81,864)	(534,896)	69,020	56,859	(7,405)
Average Shares	130,619	125,038	120,075	114,087	111,339	113,426	107,903	79,836
Balance Sheet								
Total Assets	1,769,568	1,678,715	1,543,613	1,122,279	1,630,795	2,206,362	1,991,843	944,655
Current Liabilities	700,422	696,588	730,743	639,995	799,220	929,608	852,804	564,974
Long-Term Obligations	3,093	15,678	33,975	2,087	3,925	9,130	28,034	71,161
Total Liabilities	750,984	759,040	788,099	654,087	817,356	977,100	933,967	664,131
Stockholders' Equity	1,018,584	919,675	755,514	468,192	813,439	1,229,262	1,057,876	280,515
Shares Outstanding	128,072	125,465	120,532	113,051	111,310	110,943	103,972	81,383
Statistical Record								
Return on Assets %	7.85	6.67	5.47	N.M.	N.M.	3.29	3.86	N.M.
Return on Equity %	14.55	12.83	11.92	N.M.	N.M.	6.04	8.47	N.M.
EBITDA Margin %	24.51	21.93	17.90	7.71	N.M.	13.11	12.07	6.48
Net Margin %	14.49	10.89	8.65	N.M.	N.M.	4.77	4.40	N.M.
Asset Turnover	0.64	0.61	0.63	0.49	0.58	0.69	0.88	0.99
Current Ratio	1.19	1.11	0.96	0.89	1.01	1.08	1.46	0.99
Debt to Equity	N.M.	0.02	0.04	N.M.	N.M.	0.01	0.03	0.25
Price Range	50.92-22.92	41.36-22.92	33.83-17.93	29.19-7.55	44.23-7.96	62.19-25.52	86.55-43.51	75.10-18.27
P/E Ratio	49.92-22.47	48.09-26.65	55.46-29.39	...	...	101.95-41.84	163.30-82.09	...

Address: 622 Third Ave, New York, NY 10017
Telephone: 212-351-7000
Fax: 646-658-0540

Web Site: www.monsterworldwide.com
Officers: Andrew J. McKelvey - Chmn., C.E.O. Paul M. Camara - Exec. V.P., Creative, Sales, Mktg.

Auditors: BDO Seidman, LLP
Investor Contact: 212-351-7084

NASH FINCH CO

Exchange	Symbol	Price	52Wk Range	Yield	P/E
NMS	NAFC	$22.85 (8/31/2006)	42.85-19.42	3.15	N/A

*7 Year Price Score 103.17 *NYSE Composite Index=100 *12 Month Price Score 74.47

Interim Earnings (Per Share)

Qtr.	Mar	Jun	Sep	Dec
2003	0.27	0.61	0.95	1.06
2004	0.38	(1.26)	1.15	0.00
2005	0.54	0.75	0.83	2.84
2006	0.29	0.31	...	...

Interim Dividends (Per Share)

Amt	Decl	Ex	Rec	Pay
0.18Q	11/9/2005	11/16/2005	11/18/2005	12/2/2005
0.18Q	2/27/2006	3/1/2006	3/3/2006	3/17/2006
0.18Q	4/25/2006	5/17/2006	5/19/2006	6/2/2006
0.18Q	7/18/2006	8/16/2006	8/18/2006	9/1/2006

Indicated Div: $0.72

Valuation Analysis   **Institutional Holding**

Forecast P/E	11.09	No of Institutions
	(9/9/2006)	112
Market Cap	$304.8 Million	Shares
Book Value	328.1 Million	15,657,171
Price/Book	0.93	% Held
Price/Sales	N/A	N/A

Business Summary: Retail - Food & Beverage (MIC: 5.3 SIC: 5149 NAIC: 424410)

Nash Finch is a food distribution and retail company. Through its Food Distribution Segment, Co. sells and distributes numerous grocery and perishable food products from 17 distribution centers to approximately 2,000 grocery stores located in 26 states across the U.S. Co.'s military segment, Military Distributors of Virginia (MDV), distributes grocery products to over 200 U.S. commissaries and exchanges located in the continental U.S., Europe, Cuba, Puerto Rico, Iceland, the Azores and Honduras. Co.'s retail segment is made up of 78 corporate-owned stores which operate under the Econofoods, Sun Mart, Family Thrift Center, AVANZA and Wholesale Food Outlet banners as of Dec 31 2005.

Recent Developments: For the quarter ended June 17 2006, net income decreased 57.6% to $4.1 million from $9.7 million in the year-earlier quarter. Revenues were $1.07 billion, down 1.3% from $1.09 billion the year before. Direct operating expenses declined 0.8% to $974.2 million from $981.9 million in the comparable period the year before. Indirect operating expenses increased 2.4% to $82.7 million from $80.7 million in the equivalent prior-year period.

Prospects: Co.'s near-term outlook appears to be slightly unfavorable, given the continued competitive environment within the industry in which supercenters and other alternative formats are competing for price-conscious consumers. Within Co.'s Food Distribution segment, the decline in its organic sales is attributable to slower growth in new accounts and somewhat higher customer attrition. Nevertheless, the inclusion of results from Co.'s acquisitions of the Lima and Westville divisions in 2005 has managed to mitigate these setbacks. As such, Co. continues towards the proper integration of these acquisitions in an attempt to grow its food distribution business in a cost-effective manner.

Financial Data
(US$ in Thousands)

	6 Mos	3 Mos	12/31/2005	01/01/2005	01/03/2004	12/28/2002	12/29/2001	12/30/2000
Earnings Per Share	...	...	3.13	1.18	2.88	1.95	1.78	1.35
Cash Flow Per Share	...	...	4.75	8.21	9.32	4.85	7.72	7.59
Tang Book Value Per Share	3.88	3.55	3.19	10.00	8.80	6.15	5.62	6.18
Dividends Per Share	0.720	0.720	0.675	0.540	0.360	0.360	0.360	0.360
Dividend Payout %	...	...	21.57	45.76	12.50	18.46	20.22	26.67
Income Statement								
Total Revenue	2,105,523	1,034,759	4,555,507	3,897,074	3,971,502	3,874,672	4,107,434	4,015,541
EBITDA	46,939	22,719	138,735	88,745	130,864	122,543	117,196	108,001
Depn & Amortn	20,705	10,338	47,137	43,748	45,062	42,921	46,601	46,485
Income Before Taxes	14,047	6,314	66,866	19,199	51,933	50,132	36,292	27,499
Income Taxes	6,230	2,627	25,670	4,322	17,254	19,552	15,025	11,659
Net Income	7,986	3,856	41,252	14,932	35,092	23,620	21,267	15,471
Average Shares	13,377	13,374	13,185	12,657	12,195	12,114	11,959	11,495
Balance Sheet								
Total Assets	1,034,622	1,038,724	1,077,424	815,628	886,352	947,922	970,245	880,828
Current Liabilities	316,859	305,424	325,859	280,162	284,752	309,256	383,624	324,786
Long-Term Obligations	369,666	389,172	407,659	239,603	326,583	405,376	368,807	353,664
Total Liabilities	706,499	714,043	754,846	541,700	629,895	726,443	766,837	696,288
Stockholders' Equity	328,123	324,681	322,578	273,928	256,457	221,479	203,408	184,540
Shares Outstanding	13,337	13,328	13,306	12,646	12,117	11,942	11,758	11,485
Statistical Record								
Return on Assets %	...	...	4.37	1.76	3.76	2.47	2.30	1.78
Return on Equity %	...	...	13.87	5.65	14.45	11.15	10.99	8.69
EBITDA Margin %	2.23	2.20	3.05	2.28	3.30	3.16	2.85	2.69
Net Margin %	0.38	0.37	0.91	0.38	0.88	0.61	0.52	0.39
Asset Turnover	...	...	4.83	4.59	4.26	4.05	4.45	4.62
Current Ratio	1.55	1.58	1.57	1.43	1.46	1.51	1.25	1.33
Debt to Equity	1.13	1.20	1.26	0.87	1.27	1.83	1.81	1.92
Price Range	43.90-19.42	43.90-24.83	44.00-24.83	38.66-18.06	24.70-4.26	33.18-7.12	35.54-11.81	13.56-5.97
P/E Ratio	...	...	14.06-7.93	32.76-15.31	8.58-1.48	17.02-3.65	19.97-6.64	10.05-4.42
Average Yield %	2.24	2.07	1.83	2.01	2.65	1.58	1.55	3.86

Address: 7600 France Avenue South, P.O. Box 355, Minneapolis, MN 55440-0355 **Telephone:** 952-832-0534 **Fax:** 952-844-1236	**Web Site:** www.nashfinch.com **Officers:** Allister P. Graham - Chmn. Ron Marshall - C.E.O.	**Auditors:** Ernst & Young LLP **Investor Contact:** 952-844-1060 **Transfer Agents:** Wells Fargo Bank, N.A., South St. Paul, MN

NATIONAL INSTRUMENTS CORP.

Exchange	Symbol	Price	52Wk Range	Yield	P/E
NMS	NATI	$27.76 (8/31/2006)	36.57-23.38	0.86	34.70

*7 Year Price Score 88.50 *NYSE Composite Index=100 *12 Month Price Score 90.05

Interim Earnings (Per Share)

Qtr.	Mar	Jun	Sep	Dec
2003	0.09	0.09	0.10	0.14
2004	0.16	0.14	0.10	0.20
2005	0.14	0.19	0.18	0.26
2006	0.15	0.21	...	...

Interim Dividends (Per Share)

Amt	Decl	Ex	Rec	Pay
0.05Q	10/26/2005	11/3/2005	11/7/2005	11/28/2005
0.06Q	1/25/2006	2/2/2006	2/6/2006	2/27/2006
0.06Q	4/26/2006	5/4/2006	5/8/2006	5/30/2006
0.06Q	7/27/2006	8/3/2006	8/7/2006	8/28/2006

Indicated Div: $0.24

Valuation Analysis

Forecast P/E	31.80
	(9/9/2006)
Market Cap	$2.2 Billion
Book Value	554.8 Million
Price/Book	3.99
Price/Sales	3.59

Institutional Holding

No of Institutions	161
Shares	46,086,960
% Held	57.77

Business Summary: IT & Technology (MIC: 10.2 SIC: 7372 NAIC: 334119)

National Instruments offers a line of measurement and automation products which consist of application software products such as LabVIEW, LabVIEW Real-Time, LabVIEW FPGA, Measurement Studio, LabWindows/CVI, DIA dem, TestStand, MATRIXx and SignalExpress; and hardware and related driver software products such as data acquisition, Peripheral-Component-Interconnect Extensions for Instrumentation chassis and controllers, image acquisition, motion control, Distributed Input/Output, Modular Instruments and Embedded Control Hardware/Software, industrial communications interfaces, General-Purpose-Interface-Bus interfaces and Virtual-Machine-Environment-Extensions for Instrumentation Controllers.

Recent Developments: For the quarter ended June 30 2006, net income increased 13.3% to $17.0 million from $15.0 million in the year-earlier quarter. Revenues were $160.1 million, up 13.7% from $140.8 million the year before. Operating income was $20.9 million versus $19.1 million in the prior-year quarter, an increase of 9.5%. Direct operating expenses rose 11.3% to $40.9 million from $36.7 million in the comparable period the year before. Indirect operating expenses increased 15.7% to $98.4 million from $85.0 million in the equivalent prior-year period.

Prospects: Co.'s operating results are bolstered by robust revenue growth, indicative of the continued improvement in the test and measurement market. In addition, Co. is encouraged by the solid growth of its virtual instrumentation products, driven by the performance of new products particularly in the areas of software, data acquisition, Peripheral-Component-Interconnect extensions for instrumentation (PXI), modular instruments and distributed Input/Output connections. Looking ahead, Co. expects revenue to be in the range of $157.0 million to $164.0 million and earnings to range from $0.16 to $0.21 per diluted share for the third quarter of 2006.

Financial Data
(US$ in Thousands)

	6 Mos	3 Mos	12/31/2005	12/31/2004	12/31/2003	12/31/2002	12/31/2001	12/31/2000
Earnings Per Share	0.80	0.78	0.76	0.59	0.41	0.39	0.45	0.69
Cash Flow Per Share	1.12	1.11	1.12	0.83	0.81	0.64	0.75	0.73
Tang Book Value Per Share	5.77	5.49	5.14	5.74	5.19	5.04	4.77	4.23
Dividends Per Share	0.220	0.210	0.200	0.183	0.067	...	...	...
Dividend Payout %	27.50	26.92	26.32	31.07	16.13			
Income Statement								
Total Revenue	314,875	154,752	571,841	514,088	425,892	390,790	385,275	410,149
EBITDA	54,537	24,107	105,422	87,539	66,742	61,199	64,524	91,601
Depn & Amortn	17,930	8,478	28,500	25,600	24,700	20,748	16,802	16,345
Income Before Taxes	39,541	16,882	80,680	64,813	44,491	43,618	53,533	81,113
Income Taxes	9,918	4,280	19,163	16,203	11,123	12,213	17,131	25,956
Net Income	29,623	12,602	61,517	48,610	33,368	31,405	36,402	55,157
Average Shares	81,653	81,608	80,910	82,096	80,946	80,116	80,476	80,346
Balance Sheet								
Total Assets	673,010	634,956	608,336	582,415	525,151	458,714	424,619	389,350
Current Liabilities	101,376	89,229	87,620	82,669	75,795	66,513	53,922	64,351
Total Liabilities	118,242	106,095	104,486	95,966	85,699	72,251	58,455	68,327
Stockholders' Equity	554,768	528,861	503,850	486,449	439,452	386,463	366,164	321,023
Shares Outstanding	79,701	79,204	79,276	78,945	78,269	76,611	76,743	75,951
Statistical Record								
Return on Assets %	10.53	10.28	10.33	8.75	6.78	7.11	8.94	15.54
Return on Equity %	12.69	12.30	12.42	10.47	8.08	8.35	10.59	19.12
EBITDA Margin %	17.32	15.58	18.44	17.03	15.67	15.66	16.75	22.33
Net Margin %	9.41	8.14	10.76	9.46	7.83	8.04	9.45	13.45
Asset Turnover	1.00	0.97	0.96	0.93	0.87	0.88	0.95	1.16
Current Ratio	4.25	4.40	4.13	4.75	4.37	4.18	4.89	4.42
Price Range	36.57-21.20	36.57-21.17	33.00-21.17	34.56-24.54	31.29-19.57	28.41-13.33	37.42-16.91	37.83-22.00
P/E Ratio	45.71-26.50	46.88-27.14	43.42-27.86	58.58-41.59	76.31-47.74	72.85-34.19	83.15-37.59	54.83-31.88
Average Yield %	0.77	0.78	0.78	0.62	0.26			

Address: 11500 North MoPac Expressway, Austin, TX 78759 **Telephone:** 512-338-9119 **Fax:** 512-683-9300	**Web Site:** www.ni.com **Officers:** James J. Truchard - Chmn., Pres. Alexander M. Davern - Sr. V.P., IT & Mfg. Opers., C.F.O., Treas.	**Auditors:** PricewaterhouseCoopers LLP **Investor Contact:** 512-683-6873

NATIONAL PENN BANCSHARES INC (BOYERTOWN, PENN.)

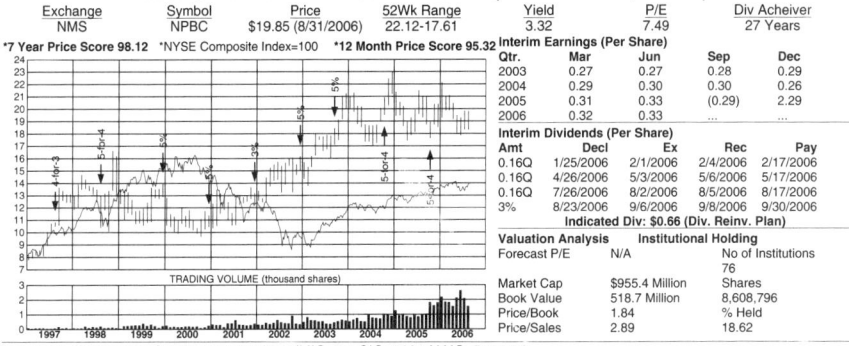

Exchange	Symbol	Price	52Wk Range	Yield	P/E	Div Acheiver
NMS	NPBC	$19.85 (8/31/2006)	22.12-17.61	3.32	7.49	27 Years

*7 Year Price Score 98.12 *NYSE Composite Index=100 *12 Month Price Score 95.32

Interim Earnings (Per Share)

Qtr.	Mar	Jun	Sep	Dec
2003	0.27	0.27	0.28	0.29
2004	0.29	0.30	0.30	0.26
2005	0.31	0.33	(0.29)	2.29
2006	0.32	0.33	...	...

Interim Dividends (Per Share)

Amt	Decl	Ex	Rec	Pay
0.16Q	1/25/2006	2/1/2006	2/4/2006	2/17/2006
0.16Q	4/26/2006	5/3/2006	5/6/2006	5/17/2006
0.16Q	7/26/2006	8/2/2006	8/5/2006	8/17/2006
3%	8/23/2006	9/6/2006	9/8/2006	9/30/2006

Indicated Div: $0.66 (Div. Reinv. Plan)

Valuation Analysis

Forecast P/E   N/A

Market Cap	$955.4 Million
Book Value	518.7 Million
Price/Book	1.84
Price/Sales	2.89

Institutional Holding

No of Institutions 76
Shares 8,608,796
% Held 18.62

Business Summary: Commercial Banking (MIC: 8.1 SIC: 6021 NAIC: 522110)

National Penn Bancshares is a bank holding company. Co. provides a diversified range of financial services, principally through its national bank subsidiary, National Penn Bank. In addition, Co. conducts business through Nittany Bank and various other direct or indirect subsidiaries. These other subsidiaries are engaged in activities related to the business of banking. At Dec 31 2005, Co. operated 73 community banking offices throughout nine counties in southeastern Pennsylvania and one community office in Cecil County, MD. At Dec 31 2005, Co. had total assets of $4.60 billion and total deposits of $3.31 billion.

Recent Developments: For the quarter ended June 30 2006, net income increased 11.8% to $16.1 million from $14.4 million in the year-earlier quarter. Net interest income increased 4.4% to $39.0 million from $37.4 million in the year-earlier quarter. Provision for loan losses was $460,000 versus $950,000 in the prior-year quarter, a decrease of 51.6%. Non-interest income rose 9.3% to $15.9 million from $14.5 million, while non-interest expense advanced 4.0% to $32.8 million.

Prospects: Co.'s results are benefiting from an increase in net interest income due primarily to the growth in the volume of interest earning assets. Conversely, Co.'s net interest margin is decreasing due to ongoing competitive pressures, the continuing effects of the flat yield curve and general overall margin compression between loan growth and higher-costing funding sources. Separately, on Apr 10 2006, Co. completed the acquisition of RESOURCES for Retirement, Inc. RESOURCES, which is a retirement plan advisory firm, operates as a division of National Penn Capital Advisors, Inc., a subsidiary of National Penn Bank.

Financial Data
(US$ in Thousands)

	6 Mos	3 Mos	12/31/2005	12/31/2004	12/31/2003	12/31/2002	12/31/2001	12/31/2000
Earnings Per Share	2.65	2.65	1.32	1.12	1.11	1.02	0.91	0.85
Cash Flow Per Share	1.64	1.49	1.51	1.62	2.06	1.73	1.32	0.97
Tang Book Value Per Share	4.88	4.88	5.39	5.03	5.29	6.36	5.53	5.19
Dividends Per Share	0.636	0.631	0.626	0.603	0.557	0.502	0.465	0.422
Dividend Payout %	23.99	23.84	47.43	53.89	50.40	49.28	50.94	49.45
Income Statement								
Interest Income	144,701	69,356	242,586	198,775	165,648	173,010	188,497	184,652
Interest Expense	67,171	30,874	93,937	60,493	51,099	63,446	92,512	99,702
Net Interest Income	77,530	38,482	148,649	138,282	114,549	109,564	95,985	84,950
Provision for Losses	1,140	680	3,200	4,800	9,371	14,000	9,000	5,600
Non-Interest Income	31,044	15,182	57,016	46,774	41,285	39,847	34,502	27,164
Non-Interest Expense	66,030	33,242	123,103	117,491	103,033	89,831	80,723	70,777
Income Before Taxes	41,404	19,742	79,362	62,765	43,430	45,580	40,764	35,737
Income Taxes	10,290	4,712	19,607	14,851	8,697	9,346	8,030	6,500
Net Income	31,114	15,030	59,755	47,914	43,354	36,234	32,734	29,237
Average Shares	48,887	47,223	45,369	42,939	39,286	35,571	35,882	34,334
Balance Sheet								
Net Loans & Leases	3,426,120	3,327,904	2,975,161	2,805,048	2,192,090	1,842,987	1,814,162	1,683,198
Total Assets	5,225,420	5,112,009	4,600,609	4,478,793	3,512,574	2,858,262	2,727,482	2,512,508
Total Deposits	3,786,748	3,616,965	3,309,046	3,143,193	2,435,296	2,112,640	2,076,795	1,814,253
Total Liabilities	4,706,681	4,593,769	4,155,721	4,050,668	3,194,761	2,635,902	2,531,800	2,335,080
Stockholders' Equity	518,739	518,240	444,888	428,125	317,813	222,360	195,682	177,428
Shares Outstanding	48,119	48,061	44,683	44,319	39,082	34,979	35,356	34,158
Statistical Record								
Return on Assets %	1.27	1.26	1.32	1.20	1.36	1.30	1.25	1.23
Return on Equity %	12.99	12.87	13.69	12.81	16.05	17.34	17.55	17.94
Net Interest Margin %	51.83	55.48	61.28	69.57	69.15	63.33	50.92	46.01
Efficiency Ratio %	35.95	39.32	41.09	47.85	49.79	42.20	36.20	33.41
Loans to Deposits	0.90	0.92	0.90	0.89	0.90	0.87	0.87	0.93
Price Range	22.12-17.61	22.12-17.41	21.51-17.41	23.01-17.03	21.25-13.75	16.16-12.40	13.68-10.33	13.09-9.64
P/E Ratio	8.35-6.65	8.35-6.57	16.30-13.19	20.55-15.20	19.14-12.39	15.84-12.16	15.03-11.35	15.40-11.34
Average Yield %	3.24	3.24	3.22	3.09	3.21	3.46	3.83	3.90

Address: Philadelphia and Reading Avenues, Boyertown, PA 19512 Telephone: 610-367-6001 Fax: 610-369-6349	Web Site: www.nationalpennbancshares.com Officers: Wayne R. Weidner - Chmn., C.E.O. Glenn E. Moyer - Pres.	Auditors: Grant Thornton LLP Investor Contact: 610-369-6291 Transfer Agents: Mellon Investor Services, L.L.C., Ridgefield Park, NJ

NETWORK APPLIANCE INC.

Exchange	Symbol	Price	52Wk Range	Yield	P/E
NMS	NTAP	$34.24 (8/31/2006)	37.79-22.92	N/A	51.10

*7 Year Price Score 78.65 *NYSE Composite Index=100 *12 Month Price Score 99.11

Interim Earnings (Per Share)

Qtr.	Jul	Oct	Jan	Apr
2003-04	0.08	0.13	0.11	0.10
2004-05	0.13	0.15	0.16	0.16
2005-06	0.16	0.18	0.20	0.15
2006-07	0.14	...	...	...

Interim Dividends (Per Share)
No Dividends Paid

Valuation Analysis | Institutional Holding

Forecast P/E	33.62	No of Institutions
	(9/9/2006)	325
Market Cap	$12.7 Billion	Shares
Book Value	1.9 Billion	319,553,824
Price/Book	6.80	% Held
Price/Sales	5.67	85.57

Business Summary: IT & Technology (MIC: 10.2 SIC: 3572 NAIC: 334112)

Network Appliance is engaged in the design, manufacturing, marketing and technical support of network data storage devices that provide file service for data-intensive network environments. Co. pioneered the concept of the "network appliance," an extension of the industry trend toward specialized products that perform a single function. Co.'s products consist of fabric-attached storage appliances, also known as filers, NearStore® systems, NetCache® content delivery appliances, the Data ONTAP™ operating system, the WAFL file management system, data management and content delivery software, and NetApp Global Services. Co.'s appliances are based primarily on commodity hardware.

Recent Developments: For the quarter ended July 28 2006, net income decreased 9.1% to $54.7 million from $60.1 million in the year-earlier quarter. Revenues were $621.3 million, up 38.6% from $448.4 million the year before. Operating income was $56.6 million versus $63.6 million in the prior-year quarter, a decrease of 11.0%. Direct operating expenses rose 41.9% to $248.2 million from $174.9 million in the comparable period the year before. Indirect operating expenses increased 50.8% to $316.5 million from $209.9 million in the equivalent prior-year period.

Prospects: Co.'s outlook appears mixed. Co. expects to experience further price declines per petabyte for its products, which may hamper future gross margins. Co.'s future gross margin could also be tempered by global service investment cost, competition, indirect sales and high disk content. Nevertheless, Co. believes that its new emerging products such as Decru®, Virtual Tape Library, and StoreVault™ S500 for the small and medium business market should further expand its market opportunity. For fiscal 2007 ending Apr 2007, Co. estimates revenue to be 32.0% to 33.0% higher than fiscal year 2006, along with earnings per share of $0.61 to $0.69, including the implementation of SFAS123R.

Financial Data
(US$ in Thousands)

	3 Mos	04/30/2006	04/30/2005	04/30/2004	04/30/2003	04/30/2002	04/30/2001	04/30/2000
Earnings Per Share	0.67	0.69	0.59	0.42	0.22	0.01	0.21	0.21
Cash Flow Per Share	1.56	1.49	1.28	0.89	0.58	0.43	0.68	0.39
Tang Book Value Per Share	3.53	3.62	3.67	3.06	2.75	2.39	2.21	1.54
Income Statement								
Total Revenue	621,288	2,066,456	1,598,131	1,170,310	892,068	798,369	1,006,186	579,300
EBITDA	81,226	391,832	317,603	216,203	143,011	67,823	153,065	119,268
Depn & Amortn	23,895	81,796	65,624	59,453	57,411	65,290	42,260	15,708
Income Before Taxes	70,116	350,272	276,228	170,454	97,815	2,533	133,009	114,406
Income Taxes	15,446	83,820	50,474	18,367	21,343	(500)	58,123	40,614
Net Income	54,670	266,452	225,754	152,087	76,472	3,033	74,886	73,792
Average Shares	391,319	388,381	380,412	366,195	350,122	350,498	359,824	345,171
Balance Sheet								
Total Assets	3,180,669	3,260,965	2,372,647	1,877,266	1,319,173	1,108,806	1,036,252	592,233
Current Liabilities	886,508	917,163	520,189	344,223	265,016	215,560	218,773	113,433
Long-Term Obligations	108,780	133,789	...	...	...	...	...	...
Total Liabilities	1,309,842	1,337,512	711,843	461,418	331,816	250,330	231,804	113,487
Stockholders' Equity	1,870,827	1,923,453	1,660,804	1,415,848	987,357	858,476	804,448	478,746
Shares Outstanding	371,695	375,998	366,943	357,482	340,668	335,135	328,746	311,803
Statistical Record								
Return on Assets %	9.38	9.46	10.62	9.49	6.30	0.28	9.20	15.68
Return on Equity %	14.69	14.87	14.68	12.62	8.29	0.36	11.67	19.00
EBITDA Margin %	13.07	18.96	19.87	18.47	16.03	8.50	15.21	20.59
Net Margin %	8.80	12.89	14.13	13.00	8.57	0.38	7.44	12.74
Asset Turnover	0.80	0.73	0.75	0.73	0.73	0.74	1.24	1.23
Current Ratio	2.18	2.22	3.03	3.16	3.22	3.15	2.90	4.70
Debt to Equity	0.06	0.07	...	...	...	...	...	...
Price Range	37.79-22.77	37.79-22.77	34.64-16.57	26.13-13.26	18.04-5.63	28.21-6.54	148.63-11.81	120.19-9.91
P/E Ratio	56.40-33.99	54.77-33.00	58.71-28.08	62.21-31.57	82.00-25.59	N.M.	707.74-56.25	572.32-47.17

Address: 495 East Java Drive, Sunnyvale, CA 94089
Telephone: 408-822-6000
Fax: 408-822-4501

Web Site: www.netapp.com
Officers: Donald T. Valentine - Chmn. Daniel J. Warmenhoven - C.E.O.

Auditors: Deloitte & Touche LLP
Investor Contact: 408-822-6428
Transfer Agents: Computershare Investor Services

NEUROCRINE BIOSCIENCES, INC.

Exchange	Symbol	Price	52Wk Range	Yield	P/E
NMS	NBIX	$11.59 (8/31/2006)	71.62-8.61	N/A	N/A

*7 Year Price Score 89.75 *NYSE Composite Index=100 *12 Month Price Score 21.51

Interim Earnings (Per Share)

Qtr.	Mar	Jun	Sep	Dec
2003	(0.43)	(0.33)	(0.31)	0.14
2004	(0.35)	(0.31)	(0.05)	(0.56)
2005	(0.51)	(0.15)	0.68	(0.65)
2006	(0.69)	(0.73)	...	...

Interim Dividends (Per Share)
No Dividends Paid

Valuation Analysis **Institutional Holding**

Forecast P/E	N/A	No of Institutions	180
Market Cap	$438.9 Million	Shares	
Book Value	361.8 Million		37,677,960
Price/Book	1.21	% Held	
Price/Sales	4.08		99.50

Business Summary: Biotechnology (MIC: 9.2 SIC: 2836 NAIC: 325414)

Neurocrine Biosciences discovers, develops and intends to commercialize drugs for the treatment of neurological and endocrine-related diseases and disorders. Co.'s product candidates address several pharmaceutical markets in the world including insomnia, anxiety, depression, various female and male health disorders, multiple sclerosis, diabetes and other neurological and endocrine related diseases and disorders. As of Dec 31 2005, Co. had nine programs in various stages of research and development including seven in clinical development, and had entered into collaborations for three of its programs. Co.'s key clinical development program, indiplon, is a drug for the treatment of insomnia.

Recent Developments: For the quarter ended June 30 2006, net loss amounted to $27.4 million versus a net loss of $5.6 million in the year-earlier quarter. Revenues were $9.2 million, down 72.1% from $33.2 million the year before. Operating loss was $29.3 million versus a loss of $6.3 million in the prior-year quarter. Indirect operating expenses decreased 2.3% to $38.5 million from $39.4 million in the equivalent prior-year period.

Prospects: On June 22 2006, Co. agreed to terminate its collaboration with Pfizer to develop and co-promote indiplon effective Dec 19 2006. As such, Co. will reacquire all worldwide rights for indiplon capsules and tablets, with reimbursement of certain indiplon expenses incurred or committed prior to June 22 2006, as well as certain ongoing expenses until the effective date of termination. Thereafter, Co. plans to review various business and commercial options to accelerate further commercialization of indiplon going forward, in addition to its expectations to report on several Phase II and proof of concept clinical trials for its other compounds in the clinical pipeline throughout 2006 and 2007.

Financial Data (US$ in Thousands)	6 Mos	3 Mos	12/31/2005	12/31/2004	12/31/2003	12/31/2002	12/31/2001	12/31/2000
Earnings Per Share	(1.39)	(0.81)	(0.60)	(1.26)	(0.93)	(3.10)	(1.42)	(1.30)
Cash Flow Per Share	(0.69)	(0.67)	(0.84)	(2.75)	1.15	(2.60)	(0.84)	(0.84)
Tang Book Value Per Share	9.55	10.18	10.51	10.78	11.08	7.31	10.22	6.43
Income Statement								
Total Revenue	28,720	19,476	123,889	85,176	139,078	18,045	41,242	14,588
EBITDA	...	...	(14,978)	(45,388)	(37,007)	(100,302)	(40,801)	(32,356)
Depn & Amortn	5,356	2,666	10,094	7,081	3,692	3,098	2,651	2,198
Income Before Taxes	...	...	(22,191)	(45,694)	(30,098)	(94,536)	(36,790)	(28,506)
Income Taxes	...	...	...	79	158	...	120	302
Net Income	(53,350)	(25,901)	(22,191)	(45,773)	(30,256)	(94,536)	(36,910)	(28,808)
Average Shares	37,764	37,355	36,763	36,201	32,374	30,488	26,028	22,124
Balance Sheet								
Total Assets	442,543	477,403	483,123	519,217	554,955	266,539	346,350	185,962
Current Liabilities	23,932	32,757	33,693	59,585	110,012	32,479	24,761	14,959
Long-Term Obligations	51,205	52,403	53,590	59,452	32,473	5,277	3,600	2,283
Total Liabilities	80,771	93,573	93,019	125,390	163,835	42,285	35,957	22,754
Stockholders' Equity	361,772	383,830	390,104	393,827	391,120	224,254	310,393	163,208
Shares Outstanding	37,866	37,711	37,132	36,532	35,311	30,662	30,347	25,314
Statistical Record								
Asset Turnover	0.23	0.27	0.25	0.16	0.34	...	...	0.10
Current Ratio	10.05	8.39	8.29	5.27	4.29	7.64	13.39	11.53
Debt to Equity	0.14	0.14	0.14	0.15	0.08	0.02	0.01	0.01
Price Range	71.62-9.85	71.62-34.02	64.25-34.02	69.02-40.85	57.64-38.10	51.31-24.53	53.46-15.38	45.44-16.63

Address: 12790 El Camino Real, San Diego, CA 92130 **Telephone:** 858-617-7600 **Fax:** 858-617-7601	**Web Site:** www.neurocrine.com **Officers:** Joseph A. Mollica - Chmn. Gary A. Lyons - Pres., C.E.O.	**Auditors:** Ernst & Young LLP **Transfer Agents:** American Stock Transfer

NEWPORT CORP.

Exchange	Symbol	Price	52Wk Range	Yield	P/E
NMS	NEWP	$17.63 (8/31/2006)	19.65-12.31	N/A	38.33

*7 Year Price Score 46.93 *NYSE Composite Index=100 *12 Month Price Score 101.79

Interim Earnings (Per Share)

Qtr.	Mar	Jun	Sep	Dec
2003	(0.15)	(0.06)	(0.08)	(0.05)
2004	0.03	0.07	(0.44)	(1.62)
2005	0.10	0.06	(0.05)	0.15
2006	0.14	0.22	...	...

Interim Dividends (Per Share)

Amt	Decl	Ex	Rec	Pay
0.01S	6/5/2001	6/13/2001	6/15/2001	7/10/2001

Valuation Analysis

		Institutional Holding	
Forecast P/E	21.47	No of Institutions	
	(9/9/2006)	133	
Market Cap	$718.9 Million	Shares	30,905,136
Book Value	397.4 Million	% Held	75.77
Price/Book	1.81		
Price/Sales	1.70		

Business Summary: Instruments and Related Products (MIC: 11.15 SIC: 3821 NAIC: 339111)
Newport is a global supplier of advanced technology lasers, components, instruments, subsystems and systems. Co.'s products are used in mission-critical applications in industries including microelectronics manufacturing, aerospace and defense/security, life and health sciences and industrial manufacturing. Co. also provides lasers, components, instruments and subsystems to commercial, academic and governmental research institutions worldwide. Co.'s operations are conducted through two divisions, its Lasers Division, and its Photonics and Precision Technologies Division.

Recent Developments: For the quarter ended July 1 2006, income from continuing operations increased 66.5% to $9.2 million from $5.6 million in the year-earlier quarter. Net income increased 223.5% to $9.2 million from $2.9 million in the year-earlier quarter. Revenues were $112.4 million, up 13.9% from $98.6 million the year before. Operating income was $11.0 million versus $7.1 million in the prior-year quarter, an increase of 54.2%. Direct operating expenses rose 8.9% to $62.6 million from $57.5 million in the comparable period the year before. Indirect operating expenses increased 13.9% to $38.8 million from $34.1 million in the equivalent prior-year period.

Prospects: Co.'s near-term outlook appears positive, reflecting double digit year-over-year growth in new orders, sales and profit. Co. also expects the microelectronics market to remain robust at least through the end of 2006, while expecting to benefit from the increasing use of ultrafast laser technology for biological studies worldwide. Coupled with its expectation of a seasonally strong fourth quarter sales level, Co. expects its full-year 2006 sales to meet or exceed the high end of its guidance range of $420.0 million to $440.0 million, and projects full-year 2006 earnings per diluted share, including stock option expense, to be near the high end of its guidance range of $0.65 to $0.78.

Financial Data
(US$ in Thousands)

	6 Mos	3 Mos	12/31/2005	01/01/2005	12/31/2003	12/31/2002	12/31/2001	12/31/2000
Earnings Per Share	0.46	0.30	0.27	(1.99)	(0.34)	(2.65)	(0.17)	0.86
Cash Flow Per Share	0.66	0.63	0.34	0.43	(0.25)	0.17	0.40	(0.79)
Tang Book Value Per Share	4.29	4.02	3.80	4.30	9.76	10.09	12.59	13.83
Dividends Per Share	...	...	...	...	...	...	0.010	0.020
Dividend Payout %	...	...	...	...	...	...	...	2.33
Income Statement								
Total Revenue	215,555	103,186	403,733	285,781	134,789	163,994	318,869	252,853
EBITDA	29,169	11,959	52,902	(63,203)	(924)	(45,779)	5,340	44,268
Depn & Amortn	9,621	4,707	19,746	17,167	10,238	11,119	14,701	10,805
Income Before Taxes	17,719	6,340	29,460	(82,196)	(11,367)	(56,898)	(9,361)	39,964
Income Taxes	2,140	10	3,746	(1,328)	(812)	14,011	(3,089)	12,145
Net Income	14,927	5,678	11,632	(81,436)	(13,160)	(100,618)	(6,272)	27,819
Average Shares	41,852	41,750	42,716	40,838	38,685	37,970	36,405	32,309
Balance Sheet								
Total Assets	545,012	534,913	529,406	578,468	468,219	486,338	543,877	531,712
Current Liabilities	81,305	82,438	87,168	98,572	27,291	38,317	50,803	53,629
Long-Term Obligations	51,711	51,472	51,295	46,716	1,612	1,230	3,409	7,173
Total Liabilities	147,625	148,280	152,823	161,383	29,810	39,821	54,870	61,477
Stockholders' Equity	397,387	386,633	376,583	415,509	438,409	446,517	489,007	470,235
Shares Outstanding	40,777	40,624	40,035	43,022	39,032	38,560	36,693	32,643
Statistical Record								
Return on Assets %	3.62	2.34	2.11	N.M.	N.M.	N.M.	N.M.	8.48
Return on Equity %	5.01	3.21	2.95	N.M.	N.M.	N.M.	N.M.	10.14
EBITDA Margin %	13.53	11.59	13.10	N.M.	N.M.	N.M.	1.67	17.51
Net Margin %	6.92	5.50	2.88	N.M.	N.M.	N.M.	N.M.	11.00
Asset Turnover	0.80	0.74	0.73	0.54	0.28	0.32	0.59	0.77
Current Ratio	3.10	2.94	2.73	2.82	12.90	9.65	8.66	8.72
Debt to Equity	0.13	0.13	0.14	0.11	N.M.	N.M.	0.01	0.02
Price Range	19.65-12.31	19.65-12.31	15.96-12.23	21.90-11.12	19.05-10.60	26.84-9.50	113.63-13.15	189.25-14.31
P/E Ratio	42.72-26.76	65.50-41.03	59.11-45.30	...	...	...	... 220.06-16.64	
Average Yield %	...	...	...	...	...	...	0.03	0.02

Address: 1791 Deere Avenue, Irvine, CA 92606
Telephone: 949-863-3144
Fax: 949-253-1671

Web Site: www.newport.com
Officers: Robert G. Deuster - Chmn., Pres., C.E.O.
Charles F. Cargile - V.P., C.F.O.

Auditors: ERNST & YOUNG LLP
Transfer Agents: Wells Fargo Bank, N.A.

NORDSON CORP.

Exchange	Symbol	Price	52Wk Range	Yield	P/E	Div Acheiver
NMS	NDSN	$40.04 (8/31/2006)	57.17-35.22	1.70	15.34	25 Years

*7 Year Price Score 114.26 *NYSE Composite Index=100 *12 Month Price Score 97.39

Interim Earnings (Per Share)

Qtr.	Jan	Apr	Jul	Oct
2002-03	0.15	0.24	0.26	0.39
2003-04	0.27	0.46	0.47	0.53
2004-05	0.39	0.47	0.50	0.78
2005-06	0.47	0.64	0.72	...

Interim Dividends (Per Share)

Amt	Decl	Ex	Rec	Pay
0.165Q	12/7/2005	12/15/2005	12/19/2005	1/4/2006
0.165Q	2/21/2006	3/3/2006	3/7/2006	3/21/2006
0.17Q	5/25/2006	6/2/2006	6/6/2006	6/20/2006
0.17Q	8/22/2006	9/1/2006	9/6/2006	9/20/2006

Indicated Div: $0.68 (Div. Reinv. Plan)

Valuation Analysis

Forecast P/E	15.22 (9/9/2006)
Market Cap	$1.3 Billion
Book Value	410.0 Million
Price/Book	3.29
Price/Sales	1.51

Institutional Holding

No of Institutions	160
Shares	20,328,090
% Held	60.23

Business Summary: Industrial Machinery and Equipment (MIC: 11.5 SIC: 3569 NAIC: 333999)

Nordson produces precision dispensing equipment that applies adhesives, sealants and coatings to a range of consumer and industrial products during manufacturing operations. Co. also produces technology-based systems for curing and surface-treatment processes, as well as life sciences applications. Co.'s products are marketed through a network of direct operations in 30 countries. In addition, Co.'s primary manufacturing facilities are located in Alabama, California, Florida, Georgia, New Jersey, Ohio and Rhode Island in the U.S., as well as in China, Germany, India, The Netherlands and the U.K.

Recent Developments: For the quarter ended July 31 2006, net income increased 33.5% to $24.8 million from $18.6 million in the year-earlier quarter. Revenues were $226.0 million, up 12.1% from $201.6 million the year before. Operating income was $34.0 million versus $27.9 million in the prior-year quarter, an increase of 21.7%. Direct operating expenses rose 12.1% to $98.3 million from $87.7 million in the comparable period the year before. Indirect operating expenses increased 9.0% to $93.6 million from $85.9 million in the equivalent prior-year period.

Prospects: Co.'s results for the third fiscal quarter of 2006 are reflecting robust growth in sales volumes, particularly within its Advanced Technology segment which continues to exhibit strong performance. On a geographic basis, Co. is encouraged by an overall increase in terms of sales volume across all areas, with a significant growth demonstrated within the Asia Pacific region. However, Co. is experiencing a deceleration of order growth, in contrast to its continuing orders that positively correspond to levels attained during comparable period in 2005. Given such trend, Co. expects to generate relatively flat sales for the fourth fiscal quarter of 2006.

Financial Data
(US$ in Thousands)

	9 Mos	6 Mos	3 Mos	10/30/2005	10/31/2004	11/02/2003	11/03/2002	10/28/2001
Earnings Per Share	2.61	2.40	2.21	2.14	1.73	1.04	0.66	0.74
Cash Flow Per Share	3.38	3.06	3.81	3.34	3.09	2.60	3.84	2.25
Tang Book Value Per Share	1.90	1.40	0.44	N.M.	1.50	N.M.	N.M.	N.M.
Dividends Per Share	0.665	0.655	0.650	0.645	0.625	0.605	0.570	0.560
Dividend Payout %	25.48	27.35	29.35	30.14	36.13	58.17	86.36	75.68
Income Statement								
Total Revenue	655,247	429,282	197,452	839,162	793,544	667,347	647,756	731,416
EBITDA	117,900	76,359	33,764	150,784	136,136	99,780	84,144	108,166
Depn & Amortn	18,506	12,294	6,062	25,683	26,876	29,240	29,487	40,961
Income Before Taxes	89,796	57,261	24,211	111,276	93,828	52,477	32,944	37,716
Income Taxes	26,984	19,263	8,144	32,938	30,494	17,317	10,872	13,106
Net Income	62,812	37,998	16,067	78,338	63,334	35,160	22,072	24,610
Average Shares	34,460	34,358	33,847	36,527	36,546	33,899	33,690	33,050
Balance Sheet								
Total Assets	799,226	824,476	776,981	788,526	839,387	766,806	764,472	862,453
Current Liabilities	179,104	224,324	212,294	250,074	195,749	211,662	252,647	355,653
Long-Term Obligations	97,130	101,420	101,420	106,351	152,479	176,725	174,895	191,773
Total Liabilities	389,227	430,918	415,753	457,614	436,054	466,697	495,582	598,727
Stockholders' Equity	409,999	393,558	361,228	330,912	403,333	300,109	268,890	263,726
Shares Outstanding	33,664	33,748	33,467	32,911	36,278	34,035	33,613	33,137
Statistical Record								
Return on Assets %	10.87	10.00	9.84	9.65	7.91	4.60	2.67	3.35
Return on Equity %	21.54	20.51	20.29	21.40	18.06	12.39	8.15	9.66
EBITDA Margin %	17.99	17.79	17.10	17.97	17.16	14.95	12.99	14.79
Net Margin %	9.59	8.85	8.14	9.34	7.98	5.27	3.41	3.36
Asset Turnover	1.07	1.03	1.04	1.03	0.99	0.87	0.78	1.00
Current Ratio	1.81	1.56	1.41	1.25	1.85	1.31	1.09	1.02
Debt to Equity	0.24	0.26	0.28	0.32	0.38	0.59	0.65	0.73
Price Range	57.17-31.96	53.45-29.96	46.02-29.96	40.46-29.96	43.74-28.23	28.11-20.72	33.32-21.45	31.75-21.14
P/E Ratio	21.90-12.25	22.27-12.48	20.82-13.56	18.91-14.00	25.28-16.32	27.03-19.92	50.48-32.50	42.91-28.57
Average Yield %	1.53	1.66	1.78	1.80	1.72	2.42	2.17	2.10

Address: 28601 Clemens Road, Westlake, OH 44145-4551 **Telephone:** 440-892-1580 **Fax:** 440-892-9507	**Web Site:** www.nordson.com **Officers:** Edward P. Campbell - Chmn., C.E.O. Peter S. Hellman - Pres., C.F.O., Chief Admin. Officer	**Auditors:** Ernst & Young LLP **Investor Contact:** 440-414-5344 **Transfer Agents:** National City Bank, Cleveland, OH

NORTHERN TRUST CORP.

Exchange	Symbol	Price	52Wk Range	Yield	P/E	Div Achiever
NMS	NTRS	$55.99 (8/31/2006)	59.74-48.07	1.64	19.71	20 Years

*7 Year Price Score 82.67 *NYSE Composite Index=100 *12 Month Price Score 101.84

Interim Earnings (Per Share)

Qtr.	Mar	Jun	Sep	Dec
2003	0.42	0.30	0.51	0.57
2004	0.57	0.59	0.52	0.60
2005	0.63	0.68	0.67	0.67
2006	0.74	0.76	...	...

Interim Dividends (Per Share)

Amt	Decl	Ex	Rec	Pay
0.23Q	11/15/2005	12/7/2005	12/9/2005	1/2/2006
0.23Q	2/21/2006	3/8/2006	3/10/2006	4/3/2006
0.23Q	4/18/2006	6/7/2006	6/9/2006	7/3/2006
0.23Q	7/18/2006	9/6/2006	9/8/2006	10/2/2006

Indicated Div: $0.92

Valuation Analysis **Institutional Holding**

Forecast P/E	18.20	No of Institutions
	(9/9/2006)	413
Market Cap	$12.2 Billion	Shares
Book Value	3.8 Billion	152,181,712
Price/Book	3.20	% Held
Price/Sales	3.03	69.84

Business Summary: Commercial Banking (MIC: 8.1 SIC: 6022 NAIC: 522110)

Northern Trust is a financial holding company. Through its primary bank subsidiary, The Northern Trust Company (the Bank), Co. provides banking and trust services to the public within and outside the U.S. In addition, Co. organizes its services globally around its two primary business units: Corporate and Institutional Services (C&IS); and Personal Financial Services (PFS), both of which are supported by two other business units: Northern Trust Global Investments (NTGI), which provides investment management; and Worldwide Operations and Technology (WWOT), which provides operating and systems support. As of Dec 31 2005, Co. had consolidated total assets of $53.4 billion.

Recent Developments: For the quarter ended June 30 2006, net income increased 11.9% to $167.9 million from $150.0 million in the year-earlier quarter. Net interest income increased 10.8% to $182.9 million from $165.1 million in the year-earlier quarter. Non-interest income rose 16.9% to $593.3 million from $507.6 million, while non-interest expense advanced 11.4% to $492.0 million.

Prospects: Co.'s near-term outlook appears to be optimistic, given the continuation of its solid earnings growth into the second quarter of 2006. Moreover, Co.'s strong operating results are driven by the combination of robust revenue growth and prudent expense management. Meanwhile, the growth in Co.'s total assets is fueled primarily through increases in both its interest- and non-interest-bearing deposits. Furthermore, Co. is encouraged by the increase in its assets-under-custody and assets-under-management, both of which are contributing towards robust growth in its non-interest income.

Financial Data
(US$ in Thousands)

	6 Mos	3 Mos	12/31/2005	12/31/2004	12/31/2003	12/31/2002	12/31/2001	12/31/2000
Earnings Per Share	2.84	2.76	2.64	2.27	1.80	1.97	2.11	2.08
Cash Flow Per Share	2.34	2.24	2.68	2.97	2.32	3.17	3.28	1.67
Tang Book Value Per Share	17.48	16.98	16.51	15.04	13.88	13.04	11.97	10.54
Dividends Per Share	0.900	0.880	0.860	0.780	0.700	0.680	0.635	0.560
Dividend Payout %	31.69	31.88	32.58	34.36	38.89	34.52	30.09	26.92
Income Statement								
Interest Income	1,017,900	477,100	1,590,600	1,118,200	1,055,700	1,238,300	1,681,500	2,011,100
Interest Expense	659,700	301,800	929,200	557,100	507,500	636,500	1,086,200	1,442,500
Net Interest Income	358,200	175,300	661,400	561,100	548,200	601,800	595,300	568,600
Provision for Losses	7,000	4,000	2,500	(15,000)	2,500	37,500	66,500	24,000
Non-Interest Income	1,145,700	552,400	1,963,800	1,710,900	1,542,200	1,536,800	1,580,000	1,537,000
Non-Interest Expense	965,300	473,300	1,734,900	1,532,500	1,456,800	1,432,100	1,376,900	1,351,500
Income Before Taxes	531,600	250,400	887,800	754,500	631,100	669,000	731,900	730,100
Income Taxes	200,700	87,400	303,400	249,700	207,800	221,900	244,400	245,000
Net Income	330,900	163,000	584,400	505,600	404,800	447,100	487,500	485,100
Average Shares	221,589	221,475	221,557	223,135	224,067	225,834	228,971	230,613
Balance Sheet								
Net Loans & Leases	21,297,200	20,040,600	19,843,100	17,812,000	17,664,600	17,902,600	17,818,300	17,981,700
Total Assets	53,325,900	50,195,300	53,413,600	45,276,700	41,450,200	39,478,200	39,664,500	36,022,300
Total Deposits	38,683,100	34,608,800	38,519,500	31,057,600	26,270,000	26,062,100	25,019,300	22,827,900
Total Liabilities	49,517,500	46,491,600	49,813,000	41,981,100	38,394,900	36,478,400	36,891,000	33,560,100
Stockholders' Equity	3,808,400	3,703,400	3,600,800	3,295,600	3,055,300	2,999,800	2,773,500	2,462,200
Shares Outstanding	217,914	218,046	218,128	219,067	220,118	220,800	221,647	222,232
Statistical Record								
Return on Assets %	1.26	1.24	1.18	1.16	1.00	1.13	1.29	1.49
Return on Equity %	17.26	17.22	16.95	15.88	13.37	15.49	18.62	20.87
Net Interest Margin %	33.82	36.74	41.58	50.18	51.93	48.60	35.40	28.27
Efficiency Ratio %	43.38	45.97	48.81	54.17	56.08	51.61	42.22	38.09
Loans to Deposits	0.55	0.58	0.52	0.57	0.67	0.69	0.71	0.79
Price Range	59.74-45.59	54.83-42.95	54.83-41.60	50.76-38.87	48.02-28.27	62.02-30.74	81.30-45.25	90.19-47.19
P/E Ratio	21.04-16.05	19.87-15.56	20.77-15.76	22.36-17.12	26.68-15.71	31.48-15.60	38.53-21.45	43.36-22.69
Average Yield %	1.72	1.77	1.80	1.76	1.77	1.47	1.02	0.78

Address: 50 South La Salle Street, Chicago, IL 60603 **Telephone:** 312-630-6000 **Fax:** 312-444-7843	**Web Site:** www.northerntrust.com **Officers:** William A. Osborn - Chmn., C.E.O. Federick H. Waddell - Pres., C.O.O., Pres. - C&IS	**Auditors:** KPMG LLP **Investor Contact:** 312-444-7811 **Transfer Agents:** Wells Fargo Shareowners Services, St. Paul, MN

NORTHWEST AIRLINES CORP.

Exchange	Symbol	Price	52Wk Range	Yield	P/E
NBB	NWAC Q	$0.54 (8/31/2006)	5.03-0.35	N/A	N/A

*7 Year Price Score 3.98 *NYSE Composite Index=100 *12 Month Price Score 79.53

Interim Earnings (Per Share)

Qtr.	Mar	Jun	Sep	Dec
2003	(4.62)	2.45	0.49	4.22
2004	(2.67)	(2.11)	(0.54)	(5.01)
2005	(5.28)	(2.69)	(5.45)	(15.03)
2006	(12.65)	(3.27)	...	...

Interim Dividends (Per Share)
No Dividends Paid

Valuation Analysis

		Institutional Holding	
Forecast P/E	N/A	No of Institutions	10
Market Cap	$47.1 Million	Shares	5,113,813
Book Value	N/A	% Held	5.86
Price/Book	N/A		
Price/Sales	0.00		

Business Summary: Aviation (MIC: 1.1 SIC: 4512 NAIC: 481111)
Northwest Airlines is a holding company. Co.'s principal subsidiary, Northwest Airlines, Inc., is engaged in the business of transporting passengers and cargo. Co.'s global airline network includes domestic hubs at Detroit, Minneapolis/St. Paul and Memphis, an extensive Pacific route system with a hub in Tokyo, a domestic and international alliance with Continental and Delta, a global airlines alliance with Continental, Delta, Air France, Alitalia, Aeroméxico, and Korean Air, and a cargo business that includes a fleet of 14 freighter aircraft that operate through hubs in Anchorage and Tokyo. As of Dec 31 2005, Co. served more than 248 cities in 23 countries in North America, Asia and Europe.

Recent Developments: For the quarter ended June 30 2006, net loss amounted to $285.0 million versus a net loss of $226.0 million in the year-earlier quarter. Revenues were $3.29 billion, up 3.0% from $3.20 billion the year before. Operating income was $295.0 million versus a loss of $190.0 million in the prior-year quarter. Indirect operating expenses decreased 11.5% to $3.00 billion from $3.39 billion in the equivalent prior-year period.

Prospects: Going forward, Co. continues to make progress on its restructuring goals, which include realizing permanent labor savings agreements with the International Association of Machinists and Aerospace Workers, the Air Line Pilots Association, Aircraft Technical Support Association, the Transport Workers Union of America, and the Northwest Airlines Meteorologists Association. In addition, Co. will focus on securing additional agreements towards its goal of $400.0 million in annual fleet savings. Furthermore, Co. intends to accelerate the replacement of its remaining 12 DC10-30 aircraft with Airbus A330 and Boeing 747-400 aircraft, while striving to deliver enhanced service to its customers.

Financial Data
(US$ in Thousands)

	6 Mos	3 Mos	12/31/2005	12/31/2004	12/31/2003	12/31/2002	12/31/2001	12/31/2000
Earnings Per Share	(36.40)	(35.82)	(29.36)	(10.32)	2.74	(9.32)	(5.03)	2.77
Cash Flow Per Share	3.47	...	(5.02)	3.13	4.37	(3.32)	7.66	10.78
Income Statement								
Total Revenue	6,181,000	2,890,000	12,286,000	11,279,000	9,510,000	9,489,000	9,905,000	11,415,000
EBITDA	(845,000)	(832,000)	(1,305,000)	405,000	1,294,000	110,000	385,000	1,406,000
Depn & Amortn	268,000	134,000	552,000	731,000	586,000	903,000	690,000	617,000
Income Before Taxes	(1,389,000)	(1,104,000)	(2,457,000)	(861,000)	218,000	(1,220,000)	(670,000)	435,000
Income Taxes	...	...	7,000	1,000	(30,000)	(422,000)	(247,000)	179,000
Net Income	(1,389,000)	(1,104,000)	(2,533,000)	(862,000)	248,000	(798,000)	(423,000)	256,000
Average Shares	87,000	87,000	87,003	86,403	86,363	85,655	84,280	92,255
Balance Sheet								
Total Assets	13,635,000	13,352,000	13,083,000	14,042,000	14,154,000	13,289,000	12,955,000	10,877,000
Long-Term Obligations	1,401,000	1,437,000	1,085,000	8,023,000	7,552,000	6,636,000	5,221,000	3,545,000
Total Liabilities	20,366,000	19,801,000	18,711,000	17,129,000	16,165,000	15,551,000	13,386,000	10,646,000
Stockholders' Equity	(7,010,000)	(6,728,000)	(5,628,000)	(3,087,000)	(2,011,000)	(2,262,000)	(431,000)	231,000
Shares Outstanding	87,286	87,272	87,255	87,106	86,006	85,799	85,208	110,088
Statistical Record								
Return on Assets %	N.M.	N.M.	N.M.	N.M.	1.81	N.M.	N.M.	2.38
Return on Equity %	...	...	...	...	...	...	...	285.25
EBITDA Margin %	N.M.	N.M.	N.M.	3.59	13.61	1.16	3.89	12.32
Net Margin %	(22.47)	(38.20)	(20.62)	(7.64)	2.61	(8.41)	(4.27)	2.24
Asset Turnover	0.89	0.91	0.91	0.80	0.69	0.72	0.83	1.06
Price Range	5.66-0.35	6.95-0.35	10.95-0.35	14.11-7.44	14.65-5.31	20.68-5.14	32.94-10.45	38.06-16.25
P/E Ratio	...	...	...	...	5.35-1.94	...	...	13.74-5.87

Address: 2700 Lone Oak Parkway, Eagan, MN 55121 **Telephone:** 612-726-2111 **Fax:** 612-726-3942	**Web Site:** www.nwa.com **Officers:** Gary L. Wilson - Chmn. Douglas M. Steenland - Pres., C.E.O.	**Auditors:** Ernst & Young LLP **Investor Contact:** 800-953-3332

NOVELL, INC.

Exchange	Symbol	Price	52Wk Range	Yield	P/E
NMS	NOVL	$6.68 (8/31/2006)	9.76-5.84	N/A	N/A

*7 Year Price Score 75.09 *NYSE Composite Index=100 *12 Month Price Score 81.64

Interim Earnings (Per Share)

Qtr.	Jan	Apr	Jul	Oct
2002-03	(0.03)	(0.08)	(0.03)	(0.30)
2003-04	0.03	(0.04)	0.06	0.03
2004-05	0.90	(0.04)	0.00	(0.02)
2005-06	0.00	0.01	...	...

Interim Dividends (Per Share)
No Dividends Paid

Valuation Analysis

		Institutional Holding	
Forecast P/E	46.50	No of Institutions	
	(9/9/2006)	250	
Market Cap	$2.4 Billion	Shares	
Book Value	1.2 Billion	281,395,136	
Price/Book	2.03	% Held	
Price/Sales	2.04	83.00	

Business Summary: IT & Technology (MIC: 10.2 SIC: 7372 NAIC: 511210)

Novell designs, develops, maintains, implements, and supports proprietary and open source software for use in business solutions. Co. provides security and identity management, resource management, desktop, workgroup, and data center applications for use on several operating systems, including Linux, NetWare®, Windows®, and Unix. Co. develops, maintains and delivers information solutions in the following categories: Identity-driven computing solutions; Linux and platform services solutions; Global services and support; and Celerant Consulting, Co.'s majority-owned subsidiary.

Recent Developments: For the quarter ended Apr 30 2006, net income amounted to $3.3 million versus a net loss of $15.6 million in the year-earlier quarter. Revenues were $278.3 million, down 6.3% from $297.1 million the year before. Operating loss was $2.5 million versus a loss of $6.4 million in the prior-year quarter. Direct operating expenses declined 11.0% to $104.4 million from $117.3 million in the comparable period the year before. Indirect operating expenses decreased 5.2% to $176.4 million from $186.1 million in the equivalent prior-year period.

Prospects: On Apr 19 2006, Co. announced its acquisition of e-Security, Inc. for $72.0 million. The purchase should allow Co. to provide a real-time view of security and compliance activities, while helping customers monitor, report, and respond automatically to network events across the enterprise. Co. expects the acquisition to positively affect revenues by approximately $20.0 million in the coming 12 months. Separately, on May 24 2006, Co. announced the sale of Celerant Consulting, its majority-owned management consulting subsidiary, to Celerant management and Caledonia Investments, for $77.0 million. For the third quarter of fiscal 2006, Co. expects revenue to be $239.0 million to $247.0 million.

Financial Data
(US$ in Thousands)

	6 Mos	3 Mos	10/31/2005	10/31/2004	10/31/2003	10/31/2002	10/31/2001	10/31/2000
Earnings Per Share	(0.01)	(0.06)	0.86	0.08	(0.44)	(0.68)	(0.82)	0.15
Cash Flow Per Share	0.20	0.19	1.32	0.31	0.15	0.14	0.28	1.04
Tang Book Value Per Share	1.88	2.53	2.42	1.39	1.89	2.31	2.98	3.80
Income Statement								
Total Revenue	552,724	274,408	1,197,696	1,165,917	1,105,496	1,134,320	1,040,097	1,161,735
EBITDA	46,407	24,699	522,403	128,456	6,048	(23,440)	(190,058)	152,581
Depn & Amortn	22,378	11,511	56,261	53,482	61,058	68,785	86,708	81,909
Income Before Taxes	24,029	13,188	466,142	74,974	(55,010)	(92,225)	(276,766)	70,672
Income Taxes	18,822	11,323	89,420	17,786	106,894	10,896	(14,944)	21,202
Net Income	5,207	1,865	376,722	57,188	(161,904)	(246,823)	(272,870)	49,470
Average Shares	385,320	394,534	440,585	390,879	370,545	363,569	332,582	335,034
Balance Sheet								
Total Assets	2,422,600	2,675,065	2,761,858	2,291,548	1,567,653	1,665,065	1,904,006	1,712,346
Current Liabilities	635,478	639,367	752,930	692,814	626,458	591,507	610,903	455,078
Long-Term Obligations	600,000	600,000	600,000	600,000	...	...	...	...
Total Liabilities	1,239,544	1,243,736	1,357,467	1,296,669	626,458	591,507	610,903	455,078
Stockholders' Equity	1,170,732	1,419,174	1,386,486	963,364	934,470	1,065,542	1,270,667	1,245,085
Shares Outstanding	355,043	388,880	385,820	377,874	376,460	367,537	362,341	327,618
Statistical Record								
Return on Assets %	0.09	N.M.	14.91	2.96	N.M.	N.M.	N.M.	2.70
Return on Equity %	0.19	N.M.	32.06	6.01	N.M.	N.M.	N.M.	3.60
EBITDA Margin %	8.40	9.00	43.62	11.02	0.55	N.M.	N.M.	13.13
Net Margin %	0.94	0.68	31.45	4.90	N.M.	N.M.	N.M.	4.26
Asset Turnover	0.46	0.44	0.47	0.60	0.68	0.64	0.58	0.63
Current Ratio	2.56	3.02	2.67	2.22	1.65	1.55	1.68	2.21
Debt to Equity	0.51	0.42	0.43	0.62	...	...	...	...
Price Range	9.76-5.74	9.74-5.21	7.67-5.21	14.06-5.78	6.35-2.15	5.58-1.58	9.34-3.10	43.06-7.72
P/E Ratio	...	...	8.92-6.06	175.75-72.25	...	...	...	287.08-51.46

Address: 404 Wyman Street, Suite 500, Waltham, MA 02451
Telephone: 781-464-8000

Web Site: www.novell.com
Officers: Jack L. Messman - Chmn., C.E.O. Ronald W. Hovsepian - Pres., C.O.O.

Auditors: PricewaterhouseCoopers LLP
Investor Contact: 800-317-3195
Transfer Agents: Mellon Investor Services, LLC

NOVELLUS SYSTEMS, INC.

Exchange	Symbol	Price	52Wk Range	Yield	P/E
NMS	NVLS	$27.92 (8/31/2006)	29.88-21.36	N/A	29.08

*7 Year Price Score 57.04   *NYSE Composite Index=100   *12 Month Price Score 97.94

Interim Earnings (Per Share)

Qtr.	Mar	Jun	Sep	Dec
2003	0.08	0.05	(0.64)	0.07
2004	0.11	0.25	0.45	0.27
2005	0.22	0.24	0.17	0.18
2006	0.19	0.42	...	...

Interim Dividends (Per Share)

No Dividends Paid

Valuation Analysis

		Institutional Holding	
Forecast P/E	16.21	No of Institutions	
	(9/9/2006)	262	
Market Cap	$3.4 Billion	Shares	
Book Value	1.7 Billion	109,142,688	
Price/Book	2.07	% Held	
Price/Sales	2.37	88.56	

Business Summary: Industrial Machinery and Equipment (MIC: 11.5 SIC: 3559 NAIC: 333298)

Novellus Systems is primarily a supplier of semiconductor manufacturing equipment used in the fabrication of integrated circuits. Co. manufactures, sells and supports equipment used in the fabrication of integrated circuits, which are commonly called microchips or chips. Co. focuses on a single aspect of the semiconductor device process, the deposition of conducting and insulating material films. Co.'s advanced deposition systems use chemical vapor deposition (CVD), physical vapor deposition (PVD) and electrochemical deposition (ECD) processes to form the interconnects in the device structure.

Recent Developments: For the quarter ended July 1 2006, net income increased 58.6% to $52.7 million from $33.2 million in the year-earlier quarter. Revenues were $410.1 million, up 24.4% from $329.6 million the year before. Operating income was $75.2 million versus $43.8 million in the prior-year quarter, an increase of 71.6%. Direct operating expenses rose 19.3% to $205.3 million from $172.0 million in the comparable period the year before. Indirect operating expenses increased 13.9% to $129.6 million from $113.8 million in the equivalent prior-year period.

Prospects: Co. remains cautiously optimistic regarding its prospects despite the cyclical conditions of the semiconductor manufacturing industry. Nevertheless, Co. continues to benefit from net order growth, driven primarily by increases in the utilization of its customer's production capacity. In addition, Co. noted that a significant portion of its net sales is generated in Asia, attributable to the fact that a substantial portion of the world's semiconductor manufacturing capacity is located there. Going forward, Co. plans to continue its focus on expanding its market presence in Asia, as it believes that significant additional growth potential exists in this region over the long term.

Financial Data (US$ in Thousands)	6 Mos	3 Mos	12/31/2005	12/31/2004	12/31/2003	12/31/2002	12/31/2001	12/31/2000
Earnings Per Share	0.96	0.78	0.80	1.06	(0.45)	0.15	0.97	1.12
Cash Flow Per Share	1.86	1.65	1.99	1.22	0.29	1.49	0.54	2.17
Tang Book Value Per Share	11.37	11.83	11.47	11.28	12.42	12.69	13.04	11.49
Income Statement								
Total Revenue	775,979	365,906	1,340,471	1,357,288	925,070	839,958	1,339,322	1,173,731
EBITDA	145,000	49,741	228,370	307,083	41,216	28,025	199,611	329,832
Depn & Amortn	36,959	19,298	86,985	93,337	72,899	45,936	53,385	41,922
Income Before Taxes	118,241	35,475	158,613	223,191	(15,320)	22,920	209,377	341,590
Income Taxes	41,767	11,706	48,506	66,501	(10,286)	...	64,907	105,893
Net Income	77,422	24,717	110,107	156,690	(67,814)	22,920	144,470	151,065
Average Shares	125,910	132,264	137,423	147,937	150,680	148,748	148,924	135,109
Balance Sheet								
Total Assets	2,217,133	2,276,953	2,290,249	2,401,832	2,338,900	2,493,994	3,009,662	2,015,472
Current Liabilities	385,552	344,798	344,344	324,030	221,082	381,610	1,137,668	504,760
Long-Term Obligations	127,911	126,963	124,858	161,103	...	...	...	...
Total Liabilities	556,609	515,594	510,966	539,998	267,040	438,306	1,137,668	504,760
Stockholders' Equity	1,660,524	1,761,359	1,779,283	1,861,834	2,071,860	2,055,688	1,871,994	1,510,712
Shares Outstanding	123,245	127,243	132,820	140,306	152,899	149,119	143,606	131,507
Statistical Record								
Return on Assets %	5.40	4.46	4.69	6.59	N.M.	0.83	5.75	10.30
Return on Equity %	7.03	5.72	6.05	7.94	N.M.	1.17	8.54	13.21
EBITDA Margin %	18.69	13.59	17.04	22.62	4.46	3.34	14.90	28.10
Net Margin %	9.98	6.76	8.21	11.54	N.M.	2.73	10.79	12.87
Asset Turnover	0.63	0.58	0.57	0.57	0.38	0.31	0.53	0.80
Current Ratio	3.38	3.97	3.96	4.23	7.11	4.28	2.21	3.62
Debt to Equity	0.08	0.07	0.07	0.09	...	...	...	...
Price Range	29.88-21.36	29.88-21.36	30.18-21.36	44.44-23.13	45.03-25.27	54.14-20.00	58.09-26.40	69.94-25.94
P/E Ratio	31.13-22.25	38.31-27.38	37.73-26.70	41.92-21.82	...	360.93-133.33	59.89-27.22	62.44-23.16

Address: 4000 North First Street, San Jose, CA 95134 Telephone: 408-943-9700 Fax: 408-570-2635	Web Site: www.novellus.com Officers: Richard S. Hill - Chmn., C.E.O. Sasson Somekh - Pres.	Auditors: Ernst & Young LLP

NVIDIA CORP

Exchange	Symbol	Price	52Wk Range	Yield	P/E
NMS	NVDA	$29.11 (8/31/2006)	31.28-15.10	N/A	33.08

*7 Year Price Score 125.88 *NYSE Composite Index=100 *12 Month Price Score 101.03

Interim Earnings (Per Share)

Qtr.	Apr	Jul	Oct	Jan
2003-04	0.06	0.07	0.02	0.07
2004-05	0.06	0.01	0.07	0.14
2005-06	0.18	0.20	0.18	0.26
2006-07	0.23	...	...	...

Interim Dividends (Per Share)

Amt	Decl	Ex	Rec	Pay
2-for-1	5/16/2000	6/27/2000	6/12/2000	6/26/2000
100%	8/14/2001	9/12/2001	8/28/2001	9/11/2001
100%	3/6/2006	4/7/2006	3/17/2006	4/6/2006

Valuation Analysis

		Institutional Holding	
Forecast P/E	20.84	No of Institutions	
	(9/9/2006)	372	
Market Cap	$10.3 Billion	Shares	258,488,480
Book Value	1.6 Billion	% Held	73.33
Price/Book	6.38		
Price/Sales	4.14		

Business Summary: IT & Technology (MIC: 10.2 SIC: 3674 NAIC: 334413)

NVIDIA is a worldwide provider of graphics and digital media processors designed to enhance the interactive experience on consumer and professional computing platforms. Co. designs, develops and markets graphics processing units, media and communications processors, wireless media processors, and related software. Co.'s products are used in a variety of visual computing platforms, including enterprise personal computers (PC), consumer PCs, professional workstations, notebook PCs, personal digital assistants, cellular phones, game consoles and digital media centers. Co.'s major product lines include NVIDIA GeForce™, nForce™, GeForce Go™, NVIDIA Quadro™ and NVIDIA GoForce™.

Recent Developments: For the quarter ended Apr 30 2006, net income increased 40.7% to $90.7 million from $64.4 million in the year-earlier quarter. Revenues were $681.8 million, up 16.8% from $583.8 million the year before. Operating income was $100.7 million versus $76.2 million in the prior-year quarter, an increase of 32.2%. Direct operating expenses rose 5.2% to $393.1 million from $373.7 million in the comparable period the year before. Indirect operating expenses increased 40.4% to $188.1 million from $134.0 million in the equivalent prior-year period.

Prospects: Co.'s near-term prospects remain optimistic, as it continues to intensify its focus towards improving its gross margin for the second half of fiscal year 2007. Co.'s top-line results are exhibiting robust improvement, reflecting positive growth in each of its businesses, namely graphics processing unit (GPU), media and communications processor (MCP), handheld GPU and consumer electronics. Notably, Co. is also encouraged by the potential growth exhibited by a number of its products, which include the adoption of Microsoft Vista, high-definition video and the launch of the Sony PlayStation 3.

Financial Data
(US$ in Thousands)

	3 Mos	01/29/2006	01/30/2005	01/25/2004	01/26/2003	01/27/2002	01/28/2001	01/30/2000
Earnings Per Share	0.88	0.82	0.28	0.22	0.27	0.52	0.31	0.13
Cash Flow Per Share	1.17	1.32	0.39	0.15	0.87	0.56	...	0.07
Tang Book Value Per Share	3.92	3.78	3.12	2.75	2.71	2.28	1.48	0.50
Income Statement								
Total Revenue	681,807	2,375,687	2,010,033	1,822,945	1,909,447	1,369,471	735,264	374,505
EBITDA	124,472	432,895	205,187	155,622	208,773	285,229	146,127	65,834
Depn & Amortn	24,031	93,300	91,000	75,500	58,216	43,497	15,836	9,668
Income Before Taxes	109,248	360,221	125,445	86,673	150,557	252,749	146,964	56,166
Income Taxes	18,572	57,635	25,089	12,254	59,758	75,825	47,027	18,068
Net Income	90,676	302,586	100,356	74,419	90,799	176,924	99,937	38,098
Average Shares	390,370	365,902	353,116	345,414	336,786	342,148	318,588	288,784
Balance Sheet								
Total Assets	2,161,453	1,915,299	1,628,536	1,399,344	1,617,015	1,503,174	1,016,427	202,250
Current Liabilities	534,386	438,659	421,156	334,112	379,448	433,494	110,335	76,225
Long-Term Obligations	...	...	...	856	304,880	305,861	300,378	1,462
Total Liabilities	552,802	457,543	450,268	348,159	684,328	739,355	610,713	77,687
Stockholders' Equity	1,608,651	1,457,756	1,178,268	1,051,185	932,687	763,819	405,714	124,563
Shares Outstanding	352,513	342,954	334,179	328,291	315,580	299,106	273,824	248,801
Statistical Record								
Return on Assets %	17.36	17.12	6.52	4.95	5.84	14.08	...	24.21
Return on Equity %	23.21	23.02	8.86	7.52	10.73	30.34	...	40.47
EBITDA Margin %	18.26	18.22	10.21	8.54	10.93	20.83	19.87	17.58
Net Margin %	13.30	12.74	4.99	4.08	4.76	12.92	13.59	10.17
Asset Turnover	1.31	1.34	1.31	1.21	1.23	1.09	...	2.38
Current Ratio	3.22	3.53	3.10	3.15	3.56	2.85	8.43	2.27
Debt to Equity	...	...	...	N.M.	0.33	0.40	0.74	0.01
Price Range	30.61-10.87	23.13-10.60	13.62-4.71	13.29-4.85	33.99-3.69	35.85-10.78	21.62-4.63	5.87-2.05
P/E Ratio	34.78-12.35	28.20-12.93	48.64-16.84	60.39-22.05	125.91-13.65	68.95-20.73	69.73-14.94	45.13-15.75

Address: 2701 San Tomas Expressway, Santa Clara, CA 95050 Telephone: 408-486-2000	Web Site: www.nvidia.com Officers: Jen-Hsun Huang - Pres., C.E.O. Jeffrey D. Fisher - Exec. V.P., Worldwide Sales	Auditors: PricewaterhouseCoopers LLP

NVR INC.

Exchange	Symbol	Price	52Wk Range	Yield	P/E
ASE	NVR	$513.65 (8/31/2006)	905.00-394.00	N/A	5.05

*7 Year Price Score 143.32 *NYSE Composite Index=100 *12 Month Price Score 66.36

Interim Earnings (Per Share)

Qtr.	Mar	Jun	Sep	Dec
2003	10.10	10.90	12.55	14.86
2004	12.58	14.82	19.04	20.06
2005	14.38	21.42	24.33	29.74
2006	19.48	28.08	...	...

Interim Dividends (Per Share)
No Dividends Paid

Valuation Analysis

		Institutional Holding	
Forecast P/E	5.21	No of Institutions	
	(9/9/2006)	171	
Market Cap	$3.0 Billion	Shares	
Book Value	1.0 Billion		4,710,482
Price/Book	2.95	% Held	
Price/Sales	0.49		81.86

Business Summary: Building & General Construction (MIC: 3.2 SIC: 1531 NAIC: 236117)
NVR is engaged in the homebuilding business, by which it conducts its homebuilding activities primarily in the eastern part of the U.S., with key focus in the Washington, D.C. and Baltimore, MD metropolitan areas. Co.'s homebuilding operations include the construction and sale of single-family detached homes, townhomes and condominium buildings under four trade names: Ryan Homes, NVHomes, Fox Ridge Homes, and Rymarc Homes. In addition to building and selling homes, Co. provides a number of mortgage-related services through its mortgage banking operations, which is operated primarily through a wholly-owned subsidiary, NVR Mortgage Finance Inc.

Recent Developments: For the quarter ended June 30 2006, net income increased 13.5% to $190.4 million from $167.6 million in the year-earlier quarter. Revenues were $1.75 billion, up 37.0% from $1.28 billion the year before. Direct operating expenses rose 43.7% to $1.30 billion from $907.3 million in the comparable period the year before. Indirect operating expenses increased 41.1% to $130.4 million from $92.4 million in the equivalent prior-year period.

Prospects: The decline in Co.'s sales particularly in Washington and Baltimore is attributable to the discouraging market conditions, by which has also resulted in downward pressure on its selling prices. Notwithstanding, Co.'s results are encouraged by the robust increase in its homebuilding revenues, stemming from growth in the number of units settled and growth in its average settlement price. Going forward, Co. will continue to experience challenges deriving from the pricing pressure in many of its markets throughout the second half of 2006. For the full-year 2006, Co. expects net income of approximately $690.0 million.

Financial Data
(US$ in Thousands)

	6 Mos	3 Mos	12/31/2005	12/31/2004	12/31/2003	12/31/2002	12/31/2001	12/31/2000
Earnings Per Share	101.63	94.97	89.61	66.42	48.39	36.05	24.86	14.98
Cash Flow Per Share	84.31	77.45	84.29	71.48	78.06	52.38	18.96	21.27
Tang Book Value Per Share	163.33	125.49	118.17	126.02	72.59	55.72	45.67	26.93
Income Statement								
Total Revenue	2,962,457	1,208,721	5,275,097	4,327,701	3,687,172	3,136,274	2,623,752	2,316,407
EBITDA	549,059	226,565	1,170,677	893,885	719,446	558,544	...	...
Depn & Amortn	6,322	3,011	10,690	8,858	8,427	7,657	15,162	13,840
Income Before Taxes	531,105	218,027	1,144,419	872,005	696,172	536,023	...	...
Income Taxes	208,193	85,467	446,860	348,801	276,381	204,553	157,864	108,608
Net Income	322,912	132,560	697,559	523,204	419,791	331,470	236,794	158,246
Average Shares	6,779	6,805	7,784	7,877	8,674	9,193	9,525	10,564
Balance Sheet								
Total Assets	2,527,826	2,347,703	2,269,588	1,777,967	1,363,105	1,182,288	995,047	841,260
Current Liabilities	566,248	779,162	794,762	540,179	422,953	361,186	281,823	233,802
Long-Term Obligations	371,388	281,654	463,141	213,803	257,859	259,160	238,970	173,655
Total Liabilities	1,527,619	1,573,809	1,592,426	942,972	868,237	779,043	645,929	528,752
Stockholders' Equity	1,000,207	773,894	677,162	834,995	494,868	403,245	349,118	247,480
Shares Outstanding	5,750	5,681	5,628	6,574	6,727	7,022	7,475	8,858
Statistical Record								
Return on Assets %	31.66	33.98	34.47	33.22	32.98	30.45	25.79	19.62
Return on Equity %	80.91	91.31	92.26	78.47	93.48	88.11	79.38	70.43
EBITDA Margin %	18.53	18.74	22.19	20.65	19.51	17.81	...	...
Net Margin %	10.90	10.97	13.22	12.09	11.39	10.57	9.03	6.83
Asset Turnover	2.59	2.64	2.61	2.75	2.90	2.88	2.86	2.87
Current Ratio	2.14	1.46	1.27	1.80	1.84	1.63	1.94	2.05
Debt to Equity	0.37	0.36	0.68	0.26	0.52	0.64	0.68	0.70
Price Range	938.00-486.00	938.00-660.00	938.00-660.00	769.40-410.00	539.20-302.75	388.25-193.95	205.75-109.40	124.60-42.25
P/E Ratio	9.23-4.78	9.88-6.95	10.47-7.37	11.58-6.17	11.14-6.26	10.77-5.38	8.28-4.40	8.32-2.82

Address: 7601 Lewinsville Road, Suite 300, McLean, VA 22102 Telephone: 703-761-2000 Fax: 800-758-5804	Web Site: www.nvrinc.com Officers: Dwight C. Schar - Chmn., Pres. Paul C. Saville - C.E.O.	Auditors: KPMG LLP Transfer Agents: EquiServe Trust Company, N.A.

OHIO CASUALTY CORP

Exchange	Symbol	Price	52Wk Range	Yield	P/E
NMS	OCAS	$25.95 (8/31/2006)	32.60-24.73	1.39	7.70

*7 Year Price Score 129.54 *NYSE Composite Index=100 *12 Month Price Score 90.79

Interim Earnings (Per Share)

Qtr.	Mar	Jun	Sep	Dec
2003	0.33	0.18	0.28	0.45
2004	0.31	0.52	0.31	0.75
2005	0.55	0.63	0.85	1.17
2006	0.80	0.55	...	...

Interim Dividends (Per Share)

Amt	Decl	Ex	Rec	Pay
0.06Q	11/17/2005	11/29/2005	12/1/2005	12/12/2005
0.09Q	2/16/2006	2/27/2006	3/1/2006	3/10/2006
0.09Q	5/18/2006	5/30/2006	6/1/2006	6/12/2006
0.09Q	8/17/2006	8/30/2006	9/1/2006	9/13/2006

Indicated Div: $0.36

Valuation Analysis

Forecast P/E	10.88 (9/9/2006)
Market Cap	$1.6 Billion
Book Value	1.4 Billion
Price/Book	1.16
Price/Sales	0.94

Institutional Holding

No of Institutions	183
Shares	50,862,588
% Held	82.79

Business Summary: Insurance (MIC: 8.2 SIC: 6331 NAIC: 524126)

Ohio Casualty is a holding company. Co. has six subsidiaries that are collectively known as the Ohio Casualty Group (the Group). The Group's primary products consist of insurance for personal auto, homeowners, commercial property, commercial auto, workers' compensation and other miscellaneous lines. The Group operates through the independent agency system in over 40 states, with 29.7% of its 2005 net premiums written generated in the states of New Jersey, Pennsylvania and Kentucky. The Group consists of: The Ohio Casualty Insurance Co., West American Insurance Co., Ohio Security Insurance Co., American Fire and Casualty Co., Avomark Insurance Co. and Ohio Casualty of New Jersey, Inc.

Recent Developments: For the quarter ended June 30 2006, net income decreased 15.4% to $35.6 million from $42.1 million in the year-earlier quarter. Revenues were $412.7 million, down 3.6% from $427.9 million the year before. Net premiums earned were $355.5 million versus $365.5 million in the prior-year quarter, a decrease of 2.7%.

Prospects: Co.'s results are being restrained by a decline in gross premiums written, due to lower in-force policy counts in its Personal and Specialty Lines, partially offset by an increase in new business premium production and improved policy renewal rates. Meanwhile, Co.'s net premiums written are being favorably affected by gains from its ceded premium on experienced based reinsurance contracts. Going forward, Co. will continue to monitor and control its expenses, while seeking additional opportunities to grow with adequately priced business. Co. believes that this strategy will continue to optimize its results and produce enhanced benefits for its policyholders and independent agents.

Financial Data
(US$ in Thousands)

	6 Mos	3 Mos	12/31/2005	12/31/2004	12/31/2003	12/31/2002	12/31/2001	12/31/2000
Earnings Per Share	3.37	3.45	3.19	1.89	1.24	(0.01)	1.64	(1.32)
Cash Flow Per Share	3.46	3.80	4.22	4.38	2.77	2.45	1.17	1.65
Tang Book Value Per Share	20.72	21.02	20.81	18.85	16.46	14.78	13.96	14.20
Dividends Per Share	0.300	0.270	0.180	...	...	...	...	0.590
Dividend Payout %	8.90	7.83	5.64	...	...	...	...	...
Income Statement								
Premium Income	713,200	357,700	...	...	...	...	...	...
Total Revenue	835,500	422,800	1,702,400	1,671,000	1,669,000	1,702,792	1,902,003	1,736,669
Benefits & Claims	388,300	189,000	907,300	936,300	1,027,400	1,129,812	1,204,034	1,294,165
Income Before Taxes	122,000	73,200	280,700	186,500	107,600	(6,706)	126,388	(129,702)
Income Taxes	34,500	21,300	68,000	56,500	31,800	(5,815)	27,808	(50,453)
Net Income	87,500	51,900	212,700	128,400	75,800	(891)	98,580	(79,249)
Average Shares	64,351	64,836	67,194	71,508	61,326	61,284	60,209	60,075
Balance Sheet								
Total Assets	5,679,800	5,759,900	5,763,100	5,715,000	5,168,900	4,778,994	4,524,619	4,489,365
Total Liabilities	4,304,600	4,318,100	4,336,700	4,420,100	4,023,100	3,720,291	3,444,587	3,372,774
Stockholders' Equity	1,375,200	1,441,800	1,426,400	1,294,900	1,145,800	1,058,703	1,080,032	1,116,591
Shares Outstanding	61,421	63,493	63,281	62,209	60,957	60,725	60,106	60,072
Statistical Record								
Return on Assets %	3.88	3.93	3.71	2.35	1.52	N.M.	2.19	N.M.
Return on Equity %	15.82	16.59	15.63	10.49	6.88	N.M.	8.98	N.M.
Loss Ratio %	54.44	52.84	...	...	...	...	...	...
Net Margin %	10.47	12.28	12.49	7.68	4.54	(0.05)	5.18	(4.56)
Price Range	32.60-24.17	31.97-22.68	29.85-22.56	23.48-17.25	17.64-11.57	22.07-11.22	16.05-8.38	17.88-6.34
P/E Ratio	9.67-7.17	9.27-6.57	9.36-7.07	12.42-9.13	14.23-9.33	...	9.79-5.11	...
Average Yield %	1.06	1.01	0.72	...	...	...	...	5.43

Address: 9450 Seward Road, Fairfield, OH 45014-5456 **Telephone:** 513-603-2400 **Fax:** 513-867-3215	**Web Site:** www.ocas.com **Officers:** Dan R. Carmichael - Pres., C.E.O. Donald F. McKee - Exec. V.P., C.F.O.	**Auditors:** Ernst & Young LLP **Transfer Agents:** EquiServe Trust Company

OLD SECOND BANCORP., INC. (AURORA, ILL.)

Exchange	Symbol	Price	52Wk Range	Yield	P/E	Div Acheiver
NMS	OSBC	$30.36 (8/31/2006)	33.64-28.57	1.84	15.18	11 Years

*7 Year Price Score 123.35 *NYSE Composite Index=100 *12 Month Price Score 95.17

Interim Earnings (Per Share)

Qtr.	Mar	Jun	Sep	Dec
2003	0.35	0.38	0.42	0.41
2004	0.45	0.41	0.46	0.62
2005	0.46	0.48	0.52	0.57
2006	0.45	0.46	...	...

Interim Dividends (Per Share)

Amt	Decl	Ex	Rec	Pay
0.13Q	9/20/2005	9/28/2005	9/30/2005	10/10/2005
0.13Q	12/20/2005	12/28/2005	12/30/2005	1/9/2006
0.13Q	3/21/2006	3/29/2006	3/31/2006	4/10/2006
0.14Q	6/20/2006	6/28/2006	6/30/2006	7/10/2006

Indicated Div: $0.56

Valuation Analysis

		Institutional Holding	
Forecast P/E	15.77	No of Institutions	61
	(9/9/2006)	Shares	4,049,737
Market Cap	$407.2 Million	% Held	30.19
Book Value	155.3 Million		
Price/Book	2.62		
Price/Sales	2.52		

Business Summary: Commercial Banking (MIC: 8.1 SIC: 6022 NAIC: 522110)

Old Second Bancorp is a bank holding company. Through its subsidiaries, Co. provides financial services through its twenty-three banking locations and four mortgage banking offices located in Kane, Kendall, DeKalb, DuPage, Lake and LaSalle counties in Illinois. Co.'s primary deposit products are checking, savings, and certificates of deposit, and its primary lending products are residential and commercial mortgages, construction lending, commercial and installment loans. A major portion of loans are secured by various forms of collateral including real estate, business assets, consumer property, and other items. As of Dec 31 2005, Co. had total assets of $2.24 billion.

Recent Developments: For the quarter ended June 30 2006, net income decreased 3.1% to $6.4 million from $6.6 million in the year-earlier quarter. Net interest income decreased 2.1% to $18.1 million from $18.5 million in the year-earlier quarter. Provision for loan losses was unchanged at $400,000 versus the prior-year quarter. Non-interest income rose 3.7% to $7.4 million from $7.1 million, while non-interest expense advanced 1.5% to $15.6 million.

Prospects: Co.'s results are being restrained by a lower net interest margin driven by decreased net interest income and slower growth in its earnings assets. Moreover, the decline in Co.'s mortgage banking income is due to higher cost of borrowing associated with an increase in interest rates. Nevertheless, Co. is experiencing robust growth in its loan portfolio, driven by significant growth in its commercial real estate and residential loans, while continuing to focus on delivering consistent growth in its core deposits to provide funding for further loan growth. Separately, on June 26 2006, Co. announced a new branch in Plano, IL, which is slated to be opened for business in the Fall of 2006.

Financial Data

(US$ in Thousands)	6 Mos	3 Mos	12/31/2005	12/31/2004	12/31/2003	12/31/2002	12/31/2001	12/31/2000
Earnings Per Share	2.00	2.02	2.03	1.94	1.55	1.35	1.11	0.86
Cash Flow Per Share	0.55	0.81	0.77	0.75	4.48	0.88	(0.03)	0.86
Tang Book Value Per Share	11.21	11.20	10.91	9.84	8.50	8.75	7.94	6.95
Dividends Per Share	0.530	0.520	0.510	0.460	0.400	0.375	0.281	0.225
Dividend Payout %	26.50	25.74	25.12	23.71	25.72	27.88	25.25	26.20
Income Statement								
Interest Income	68,750	33,492	120,223	97,398	87,844	85,491	84,791	77,141
Interest Expense	32,525	15,357	46,224	29,039	25,468	28,009	35,290	35,816
Net Interest Income	36,225	18,135	73,999	68,359	62,376	57,482	49,501	41,325
Provision for Losses	844	444	353	(2,900)	3,251	3,805	3,840	1,380
Non-Interest Income	14,440	7,075	28,149	25,914	29,227	25,276	22,301	16,568
Non-Interest Expense	31,795	16,148	60,500	57,608	54,175	48,056	41,476	37,088
Income Before Taxes	18,026	8,618	41,295	39,565	34,177	30,897	26,486	19,425
Income Taxes	5,555	2,513	13,612	13,278	12,069	10,751	9,263	5,954
Net Income	12,471	6,105	27,683	26,287	22,108	20,146	17,223	13,471
Average Shares	13,700	13,708	13,661	13,535	14,198	14,859	15,442	15,702
Balance Sheet								
Net Loans & Leases	1,730,443	1,723,155	1,689,053	1,493,581	1,301,237	1,046,098	883,142	720,042
Total Assets	2,423,139	2,364,399	2,367,830	2,102,266	1,838,844	1,608,087	1,333,348	1,149,442
Total Deposits	2,008,021	2,004,479	1,935,278	1,798,849	1,524,634	1,390,661	1,090,816	996,478
Total Liabilities	2,267,811	2,207,717	2,215,568	1,967,278	1,721,850	1,475,011	1,208,402	1,036,480
Stockholders' Equity	155,328	156,682	152,262	134,988	116,994	133,076	124,946	112,962
Shares Outstanding	13,412	13,559	13,520	13,424	13,387	14,786	15,215	15,552
Statistical Record								
Return on Assets %	1.18	1.21	1.24	1.33	1.28	1.37	1.39	1.25
Return on Equity %	18.27	18.74	19.27	20.81	17.68	15.62	14.48	12.40
Net Interest Margin %	51.31	54.15	61.55	70.19	71.01	67.24	58.38	53.57
Efficiency Ratio %	36.71	39.81	40.78	46.72	46.28	43.38	38.73	39.58
Loans to Deposits	0.86	0.86	0.87	0.83	0.85	0.75	0.81	0.72
Price Range	33.64-28.57	33.64-28.01	34.81-28.01	34.73-23.11	25.96-18.25	21.27-14.40	15.00-8.77	9.56-7.78
P/E Ratio	16.82-14.29	16.65-13.87	17.15-13.80	17.90-11.91	16.75-11.77	15.76-10.67	13.51-7.90	11.12-9.05
Average Yield %	1.71	1.69	1.66	1.70	1.90	2.14	2.35	2.69

Address: 37 South River Street, Aurora, IL 60507-4172	**Auditors:** ERNST & YOUNG LLP
Telephone: 630-892-0202	**Investor Contact:** 708-892-0202
Web Site: www.o2bancorp.com	**Transfer Agents:** Old Second Bancorp, Inc.
Officers: William B. Skoglund - Chmn., Pres., C.E.O. J. Douglas Cheatham - Sr. V.P., C.F.O.	

ORACLE CORP.

Exchange	Symbol	Price	52Wk Range	Yield	P/E
NMS	ORCL	$15.66 (8/31/2006)	15.81-11.98	N/A	24.47

*7 Year Price Score 64.97 *NYSE Composite Index=100 *12 Month Price Score 108.30

Interim Earnings (Per Share)

Qtr.	Aug	Nov	Feb	May
2001-02	0.09	0.10	0.09	0.12
2002-03	0.06	0.10	0.11	0.16
2003-04	0.08	0.12	0.12	0.18
2004-05	0.10	0.16	0.10	0.19
2005-06	0.10	0.15	0.14	0.24

Interim Dividends (Per Share)

Amt	Decl	Ex	Rec	Pay
2-for-1	12/20/1999	1/19/2000	12/30/1999	1/18/2000
2-for-1	9/14/2000	10/13/2000	9/25/2000	10/12/2000

Valuation Analysis

Forecast P/E 15.10 (9/9/2006)
Market Cap $81.9 Billion
Book Value 15.0 Billion
Price/Book 5.46
Price/Sales 5.70

Institutional Holding

No of Institutions 813
Shares 2,783,114,240
% Held 53.13

Business Summary: IT & Technology (MIC: 10.2 SIC: 6719 NAIC: 551112)

Oracle is a holding company. Through its subsidiaries, Co. develops, manufactures, markets, distributes and services database, middleware and applications software that helps organizations manage and grow their businesses. Database and middleware software is used for developing and deploying applications on the internet and on corporate intranets. Applications software can be used to automate business processes and to provide business intelligence. Co. also offers software license updates and product support and other services including consulting, On Demand and education.

Recent Developments: For the year ended May 31 2006, net income increased 17.2% to $3.38 billion from $2.89 billion in the prior year. Revenues were $14.38 billion, up 21.9% from $11.80 billion the year before.

Prospects: For fiscal 2006, Co. expects its consulting revenues to increase, largely due to greater application implementations related to acquired products. Accordingly, Co. will continue to invest in its On Demand product services to support future revenue growth. Co. also anticipates higher education revenues, largely due to an increase in customer training on the use of its application products. Separately, on Dec 14 2005, Co. announced that it has completed its acquisition of Citigroup's 43.0% interest in i-flex Solutions Ltd., a provider of software solutions and services to the financial services industry, for about $605.0 million.

Financial Data
(US$ in Thousands)

	05/31/2006	05/31/2005	05/31/2004	05/31/2003	05/31/2002	05/31/2001	05/31/2000	05/31/1999
Earnings Per Share	0.64	0.55	0.50	0.43	0.39	0.44	1.05	0.22
Cash Flow Per Share	0.87	0.69	0.61	0.57	0.59	0.39	0.51	0.31
Tang Book Value Per Share	0.13	0.09	1.55	1.21	1.13	1.12	1.15	0.63
Income Statement								
Total Revenue	14,380,000	11,799,000	10,156,000	9,475,000	9,673,000	10,859,672	10,130,128	8,827,252
EBITDA	5,615,000	4,426,000	4,082,000	3,639,000	3,625,000	4,052,642	10,391,349	2,260,400
Depn & Amortn	806,000	425,000	234,000	327,000	363,000	346,896	390,925	375,384
Income Before Taxes	4,810,000	4,051,000	3,945,000	3,425,000	3,408,000	3,971,230	10,123,434	1,982,078
Income Taxes	1,429,000	1,165,000	1,264,000	1,118,000	1,184,000	1,410,134	3,826,631	692,320
Net Income	3,381,000	2,886,000	2,681,000	2,307,000	2,224,000	2,561,096	6,296,803	1,289,758
Average Shares	5,286,999	5,230,999	5,325,999	5,417,999	5,688,999	5,864,805	5,995,841	5,936,899
Balance Sheet								
Total Assets	29,029,000	20,687,000	12,763,000	11,064,000	10,800,000	11,030,160	13,076,779	7,259,654
Current Liabilities	6,930,000	8,063,000	4,272,000	4,158,000	3,960,000	3,916,619	5,862,238	3,046,423
Long-Term Obligations	5,735,000	159,000	163,000	175,000	298,000	300,847	300,770	304,140
Total Liabilities	14,017,000	9,850,000	4,768,000	4,744,000	4,683,000	4,752,389	6,615,316	3,564,387
Stockholders' Equity	15,012,000	10,837,000	7,995,000	6,320,000	6,117,000	6,277,771	6,461,463	3,695,267
Shares Outstanding	5,231,999	5,144,999	5,170,999	5,232,999	5,430,999	5,592,360	5,615,143	5,724,531
Statistical Record								
Return on Assets %	13.60	17.26	22.44	21.10	20.38	21.25	61.76	19.72
Return on Equity %	26.16	30.65	37.35	37.10	35.89	40.21	123.65	38.77
EBITDA Margin %	39.05	37.51	40.19	38.41	37.48	37.32	102.58	25.61
Net Margin %	23.51	24.46	26.40	24.35	22.99	23.58	62.16	14.61
Asset Turnover	0.58	0.71	0.85	0.87	0.89	0.90	0.99	1.35
Current Ratio	1.73	1.05	2.65	2.22	2.20	2.29	1.86	1.79
Debt to Equity	0.38	0.01	0.02	0.03	0.05	0.05	0.05	0.08
Price Range	14.93-11.98	14.63-9.86	14.89-11.23	13.26-7.32	19.77-7.92	46.31-13.25	44.22-6.28	10.13-3.18
P/E Ratio	23.33-18.72	26.60-17.93	29.78-22.46	30.84-17.03	50.69-20.31	105.26-30.11	42.11-5.98	46.02-14.44

Address: 500 Oracle Parkway, Redwood City, CA 94065
Telephone: 650-506-7000
Fax: 650-506-7200

Web Site: www.oracle.com
Officers: Jeffrey O. Henley - Chmn. Safra A. Catz - Pres., C.F.O.

Auditors: Ernst & Young LLP
Investor Contact: 650-506-4184

O'REILLY AUTOMOTIVE, INC.

Exchange	Symbol	Price	52Wk Range	Yield	P/E
NMS	ORLY	$29.69 (8/31/2006)	37.20-26.11	N/A	19.15

*7 Year Price Score 139.16 *NYSE Composite Index=100 *12 Month Price Score 90.96

Interim Earnings (Per Share)

Qtr.	Mar	Jun	Sep	Dec
2003	0.19	0.25	0.27	0.22
2004	0.25	0.29	0.30	0.42
2005	0.29	0.38	0.42	0.35
2006	0.35	0.43	...	...

Interim Dividends (Per Share)

Amt	Decl	Ex	Rec	Pay
100%	5/24/2005	6/16/2005	5/31/2005	6/15/2005

Valuation Analysis   **Institutional Holding**

Forecast P/E	18.77	No of Institutions
	(9/9/2006)	242
Market Cap	$3.4 Billion	Shares
Book Value	1.3 Billion	90,242,480
Price/Book	2.67	% Held
Price/Sales	1.54	79.58

Business Summary: Retail - Automotive (MIC: 5.7 SIC: 5531 NAIC: 441310)

O'Reilly Automotive is a specialty retailer of automotive aftermarket parts, tools, supplies, equipment and accessories. Co. sells its products to both do-it-yourself (DIY) customers and professional installers. At Dec 31 2005, Co. operated 1,470 stores in Alabama, Arkansas, Florida, Georgia, Illinois, Indiana, Iowa, Kansas, Kentucky, Louisiana, Minnesota, Mississippi, Missouri, Montana, Nebraska, North Carolina, North Dakota, Oklahoma, South Carolina, South Dakota, Tennessee, Texas, Virginia, Wisconsin and Wyoming. Co.'s stores on average carry approximately 21,000 stock keeping units (SKUs) and average approximately 6,700 total square feet in size.

Recent Developments: For the quarter ended June 30 2006, net income increased 14.9% to $49.3 million from $42.9 million in the year-earlier quarter. Revenues were $591.2 million, up 13.4% from $521.2 million the year before. Operating income was $78.2 million versus $68.1 million in the prior-year quarter, an increase of 14.8%. Direct operating expenses rose 13.0% to $330.3 million from $292.2 million in the comparable period the year before. Indirect operating expenses increased 13.6% to $182.7 million from $160.8 million in the equivalent prior-year period.

Prospects: Co.'s near term outlook appears positive, reflecting the recent increase in revenues and earnings aided by comparable store sales growth. Co. believes the comparable store sales increase is primarily attributable to its offering of a broader selection of products in most stores, an increased promotional and advertising effort through a variety of media and localized promotional events, continued improvement in the merchandising and store layouts of most stores, and compensation programs for all store team members that provide incentives for performance. Meanwhile, Co. plans to open 85 to 90 additional stores during the second half of 2006.

Financial Data
(US$ in Thousands)

	6 Mos	3 Mos	12/31/2005	12/31/2004	12/31/2003	12/31/2002	12/31/2001	12/31/2000
Earnings Per Share	1.55	1.50	1.45	1.25	0.92	0.77	0.63	0.50
Cash Flow Per Share	1.87	1.83	1.91	2.05	1.60	0.98	0.48	0.06
Tang Book Value Per Share	11.13	10.66	10.19	8.56	7.17	6.09	5.26	4.50
Income Statement								
Total Revenue	1,127,746	536,547	2,045,318	1,721,241	1,511,816	1,312,490	1,092,112	890,421
EBITDA	142,912	64,514	311,777	245,861	208,982	176,148	145,001	115,894
Depn & Amortn	...	...	57,228	54,325	42,374	36,907	30,544	24,812
Income Before Taxes	142,912	64,514	251,069	187,737	160,042	130,982	106,727	83,159
Income Taxes	53,035	23,950	86,803	70,063	59,955	48,990	40,375	31,451
Net Income	89,877	40,564	164,266	139,566	100,087	81,992	66,352	51,708
Average Shares	115,196	114,615	113,385	111,422	109,060	107,384	105,572	103,456
Balance Sheet								
Total Assets	1,916,326	1,802,994	1,713,899	1,432,357	1,187,592	1,009,419	856,859	715,995
Current Liabilities	486,818	508,567	485,681	333,815	245,868	147,422	121,136	152,932
Long-Term Obligations	100,678	25,436	25,461	100,322	120,977	190,470	165,618	90,463
Total Liabilities	654,624	596,522	568,130	484,540	403,307	358,895	300,568	252,264
Stockholders' Equity	1,261,702	1,206,472	1,145,769	947,817	784,285	650,524	556,291	463,731
Shares Outstanding	113,394	113,199	112,389	110,754	109,329	106,742	105,701	103,089
Statistical Record								
Return on Assets %	10.10	10.38	10.44	10.62	9.11	8.79	8.44	7.78
Return on Equity %	15.44	15.63	15.69	16.07	13.95	13.59	13.01	11.90
EBITDA Margin %	12.67	12.02	15.24	14.28	13.82	13.42	13.28	13.02
Net Margin %	7.97	7.56	8.03	8.11	6.62	6.25	6.08	5.81
Asset Turnover	1.24	1.28	1.30	1.31	1.38	1.41	1.39	1.34
Current Ratio	2.09	1.89	1.88	2.44	2.80	4.28	4.55	2.94
Debt to Equity	0.08	0.02	0.02	0.11	0.15	0.29	0.30	0.20
Price Range	37.20-26.11	37.20-23.34	32.41-22.18	23.38-18.39	22.41-11.51	18.23-12.31	19.09-8.91	13.38-4.63
P/E Ratio	24.00-16.85	24.80-15.56	22.35-15.30	18.70-14.71	24.35-12.51	23.68-15.98	30.31-14.14	26.75-9.25

Address: 233 South Patterson, Springfield, MO 65802
Telephone: 417-862-6708

Web Site: www.oreillyauto.com
Officers: David E. O'Reilly - Co.-Chmn., C.E.O.
Lawrence P. O'Reilly - Co.-Chmn., C.O.O.

Auditors: ERNST & YOUNG LLP
Investor Contact: 417-862-6708

OTTER TAIL CORP.

Exchange	Symbol	Price	52Wk Range	Yield	P/E	Div Achiever
NMS	OTTR	$30.15 (8/31/2006)	31.75-25.95	3.81	15.87	30 Years

*7 Year Price Score 88.63 *NYSE Composite Index=100 *12 Month Price Score 95.94

Interim Earnings (Per Share)

Qtr.	Mar	Jun	Sep	Dec
2003	0.38	0.32	0.46	0.36
2004	0.31	0.30	0.42	0.55
2005	0.33	0.76	0.59	0.43
2006	0.50	0.38	...	...

Interim Dividends (Per Share)

Amt	Decl	Ex	Rec	Pay
0.28Q	10/31/2005	11/10/2005	11/15/2005	12/10/2005
0.287Q	2/6/2006	2/13/2006	2/15/2006	3/10/2006
0.287Q	4/10/2006	5/11/2006	5/15/2006	6/10/2006
0.287Q	8/1/2006	8/11/2006	8/15/2006	9/9/2006

Indicated Div: $1.15 (Div. Reinv. Plan)

Valuation Analysis
Forecast P/E 17.55 (9/9/2006)
Market Cap $888.4 Million
Book Value 476.4 Million
Price/Book 1.86
Price/Sales 0.80

Institutional Holding
No of Institutions 101
Shares 10,342,849
% Held 35.10

Business Summary: Electricity (MIC: 7.1 SIC: 4911 NAIC: 221121)

Otter Tail operates through six business segments. Co.'s Electric segment consists of the production, transmission, distribution and sale of electric energy. Plastics consists of businesses producing polyvinyl chloride and polyethylene pipe. Manufacturing activities include the production of waterfront equipment; wind towers; material and handling trays and horticultural containers; contract machining; and metal parts stamping and fabrication. Health Services includes the sale of diagnostic medical equipment, patient monitoring equipment and related supplies and accessories. Food Ingredient Processing consists of Idaho Pacific Holdings, Inc. Co. also operates various other businesses.

Recent Developments: For the quarter ended June 30 2006, income from continuing operations increased 1.7% to $11.1 million from $11.0 million in the year-earlier quarter. Net income decreased 48.9% to $11.4 million from $22.3 million in the year-earlier quarter. Revenues were $279.9 million, up 13.9% from $245.8 million the year before. Operating income was $22.1 million versus $20.8 million in the prior-year quarter, an increase of 6.3%. Direct operating expenses rose 15.1% to $242.8 million from $211.0 million in the comparable period the year before. Indirect operating expenses increased 6.9% to $14.9 million from $14.0 million in the equivalent prior-year period.

Prospects: For full-year 2006, Co. has raised its earnings from continuing operations estimate to $1.55 to $1.75 per diluted share, due primarily to the continued strong earnings performance and high prices for PVC resin at its plastics segment, and the significant improvement in short-term coal supply at its electric segment. Co. also expects net income in its manufacturing segment to increase due to several factors including market expansion. However, Co. expects lower earnings from its health services segment due to lower results in the first half of 2006, and a net loss of $1.60 million to $3.40 million in its food processing business stemming from the ongoing shortage of raw potato supplies.

Financial Data
(US$ in Thousands)

	6 Mos	3 Mos	12/31/2005	12/31/2004	12/31/2003	12/31/2002	12/31/2001	12/31/2000
Earnings Per Share	1.90	2.28	2.11	1.58	1.51	1.79	1.68	1.60
Cash Flow Per Share	3.13	2.44	3.28	2.29	3.00	3.05	3.15	2.52
Tang Book Value Per Share	12.14	11.96	11.74	10.95	9.88	9.51	9.31	9.06
Dividends Per Share	1.135	1.127	1.120	1.100	1.080	1.060	1.040	1.020
Dividend Payout %	59.74	49.45	53.08	69.62	71.52	59.22	61.90	63.75
Income Statement								
Total Revenue	537,711	278,778	1,046,408	882,324	753,239	710,116	654,132	559,445
EBITDA	75,200	40,250	145,838	119,600	118,414	126,652	121,777	112,571
Depn & Amortn	24,603	12,224	46,458	44,344	45,962	42,613	42,100	38,249
Income Before Taxes	41,053	23,532	80,822	56,984	54,586	66,189	63,686	57,739
Income Taxes	15,061	8,572	27,967	17,004	14,930	20,061	20,083	17,515
Net Income	26,354	14,960	62,551	42,195	39,656	46,128	43,603	40,224
Average Shares	29,766	29,676	29,348	26,207	25,826	25,397	24,832	23,928
Balance Sheet								
Total Assets	1,233,101	1,214,967	1,181,496	1,134,148	986,423	878,736	782,541	722,115
Long-Term Obligations	256,850	257,553	258,260	261,810	265,193	258,229	227,360	191,493
Total Liabilities	756,682	743,699	701,566	689,438	637,036	549,771	487,733	429,236
Stockholders' Equity	476,419	471,268	479,930	444,710	349,387	328,965	294,808	292,879
Shares Outstanding	29,465	29,446	29,401	28,976	25,723	25,592	24,653	23,852
Statistical Record								
Return on Assets %	4.67	5.67	5.40	3.97	4.25	5.55	5.80	5.72
Return on Equity %	12.25	14.91	13.53	10.60	11.69	14.79	14.84	14.02
EBITDA Margin %	13.99	14.44	13.94	13.56	15.72	17.84	18.62	20.12
Net Margin %	4.90	5.37	5.98	4.78	5.26	6.50	6.67	7.19
PPE Turnover	1.60	1.57	1.52	1.34	1.23	1.26	1.24	1.10
Asset Turnover	0.92	0.92	0.90	0.83	0.81	0.85	0.87	0.80
Debt to Equity	0.54	0.55	0.54	0.59	0.76	0.78	0.77	0.65
Price Range	31.75-25.95	31.75-24.13	31.75-24.13	27.36-23.85	28.50-24.00	34.12-23.80	30.69-23.88	29.00-17.81
P/E Ratio	16.71-13.66	13.93-10.58	15.05-11.44	17.32-15.09	18.87-15.89	19.06-13.30	18.27-14.21	18.13-11.13
Average Yield %	3.90	3.96	4.24	4.02	3.70	3.76	4.72

Address: 215 South Cascade Street, P.O. Box 496, Fergus Falls, MN 56538-0496
Telephone: 866-410-8780
Fax: 218-998-3165

Web Site: www.ottertail.com
Officers: John C. MacFarlane - Chmn. John D. Erickson - Pres., C.E.O.

Auditors: Deloitte & Touche LLP
Transfer Agents: Wells Fargo Bank, Minnesota, N.A., St. Paul, MN

OWENS CORNING

Exchange	Symbol	Price	52Wk Range	Yield	P/E
OTC	OWEN Q	$0.90 (8/31/2006)	5.38-0.90	N/A	0.14

*7 Year Price Score N/A *NYSE Composite Index=100 *12 Month Price Score 45.82

Interim Earnings (Per Share)

Qtr.	Mar	Jun	Sep	Dec
2003	(0.02)	0.30	0.92	0.72
2004	0.09	0.55	1.57	1.20
2005	(76.59)	1.13	(4.82)	6.11
2006	1.05	4.19	...	...

Interim Dividends (Per Share)
Dividend Payment Suspended

Valuation Analysis

		Institutional Holding	
Forecast P/E	N/A	No of Institutions	8
Market Cap	$49.8 Million	Shares	665,600
Book Value	N/A	% Held	1.20
Price/Book	N/A		
Price/Sales	0.01		

Business Summary: General Construction Supplies & Services (MIC: 3.3 SIC: 5039 NAIC: 423390)

Owens Corning provides consumers and industrial customers with building materials systems and composites systems through two business segments: Building Materials Systems, which products and systems are used in residential remodeling and repair, commercial improvement, new residential and commercial construction, and other related markets; and Composite Solutions, which products and systems are used in end-use markets such as building construction, automotive, telecommunications, marine, aerospace, energy, appliance, packaging and electronics. Many of Co.'s products are marketed under registered trademarks such as Cultured Stone®, Propink®, Advantex®, and the color PINK.

Recent Developments: For the quarter ended June 30 2006, net income increased 274.6% to $251.0 million from $67.0 million in the year-earlier quarter. Revenues were $1.72 billion, up 8.3% from $1.59 billion the year before. Operating income was $168.0 million versus $169.0 million in the prior-year quarter, a decrease of 0.6%. Direct operating expenses rose 11.6% to $1.43 billion from $1.28 billion in the comparable period the year before. Indirect operating expenses decreased 10.5% to $128.0 million from $143.0 million in the equivalent prior-year period.

Prospects: On Jul 25 2006, Co. signed a purchase agreement to acquire The Modulo™/ParMur Group, a producer and distributor of manufactured stone veneer in Europe for approximately $32.0 million. The acquisition, which is expected to close in September 2006, will further the global expansion of Co.'s Cultured Stone® business in the European building products market. Separately, on Jul 27 2006, Co. announced its intention to combine its Reinforcements Business with the Reinforcement and Composites Businesses of Saint-Gobain Group, by which the partnership is projected to establish a global company in reinforcements and composite fabrics products with worldwide revenues of approximately $1.80 billion.

Financial Data
(US$ in Thousands)

	6 Mos	3 Mos	12/31/2005	12/31/2004	12/31/2003	12/31/2002	12/31/2001	12/31/2000
Earnings Per Share	6.53	3.47	(74.08)	3.40	1.92	(51.02)	0.66	(8.71)
Cash Flow Per Share	13.94	13.22	13.49	8.10	5.91	6.48	8.68	(3.46)
Dividends Per Share	...	...	...	...	...	...	...	0.150
Income Statement								
Total Revenue	3,323,000	1,601,000	6,323,000	5,675,000	4,996,000	4,872,000	4,762,000	4,940,000
EBITDA	407,000	175,000	(3,509,000)	658,000	473,000	(2,124,000)	339,000	(588,000)
Depn & Amortn	124,000	60,000	234,000	231,000	206,000	205,000	237,000	203,000
Income Before Taxes	132,000	50,000	(4,482,000)	439,000	259,000	(2,329,000)	102,000	(791,000)
Income Taxes	(179,000)	(10,000)	(387,000)	227,000	145,000	31,000	57,000	(312,000)
Net Income	314,000	63,000	(4,099,000)	204,000	115,000	(2,809,000)	39,000	(478,000)
Average Shares	59,900	59,900	55,300	59,900	59,900	55,100	59,900	54,800
Balance Sheet								
Total Assets	9,219,000	8,733,000	8,735,000	7,639,000	7,358,000	6,920,000	7,041,000	6,912,000
Current Liabilities	1,919,000	1,724,000	1,786,000	951,000	864,000	861,000	849,000	609,000
Long-Term Obligations	42,000	35,000	36,000	38,000	73,000	71,000	5,000	7,000
Total Liabilities	17,046,000	16,828,000	16,882,000	11,719,000	11,686,000	11,388,000	8,658,000	8,311,000
Stockholders' Equity	(7,827,000)	(8,095,000)	(8,147,000)	(4,080,000)	(4,328,000)	(4,468,000)	(1,617,000)	(1,399,000)
Shares Outstanding	55,300	55,300	55,300	55,300	55,300	55,200	55,300	55,400
Statistical Record								
Return on Assets %	4.53	2.45	N.M.	2.71	1.61	N.M.	0.56	N.M.
EBITDA Margin %	12.25	10.93	N.M.	11.59	9.47	N.M.	7.12	N.M.
Net Margin %	9.45	3.94	N.M.	3.59	2.30	N.M.	0.82	N.M.
Asset Turnover	0.78	0.80	0.77	0.75	0.70	0.70	0.68	0.73
Current Ratio	1.51	1.54	1.51	2.24	2.19	2.06	1.94	2.57
Price Range	5.53-0.93	5.53-1.15	5.53-1.81	4.84-0.50	...	...	...	...
P/E Ratio	0.85-0.14	1.59-0.33	...	1.42-0.15	...	...	...	...

Address: One Owens Corning Parkway, Toledo, OH 43659
Telephone: 419-248-8000
Fax: 419-248-8445

Web Site: www.owenscorning.com
Officers: Michael H. Thaman - Chmn., C.F.O. Sheree L. Bargabos - V.P., Pres., Exterior Systems Business

Auditors: PricewaterhouseCoopers LLP

PACCAR INC.

Exchange	Symbol	Price	52Wk Range	Yield	P/E
NMS	PCAR	$54.67 (8/31/2006)	58.31-42.72	1.46	10.45

*7 Year Price Score 134.45 *NYSE Composite Index=100 *12 Month Price Score 108.82

Interim Earnings (Per Share)

Qtr.	Mar	Jun	Sep	Dec
2003	0.42	0.47	0.50	0.60
2004	0.69	0.89	0.94	0.92
2005	1.04	0.93	1.19	1.22
2006	1.35	1.47	...	...

Interim Dividends (Per Share)

Amt	Decl	Ex	Rec	Pay
1.333Q	12/6/2005	12/15/2005	12/19/2005	1/5/2006
0.20Q	4/25/2006	5/16/2006	5/18/2006	6/5/2006
50%	7/11/2006	8/11/2006	7/27/2006	8/10/2006
0.20Q	7/11/2006	8/16/2006	8/18/2006	9/5/2006

Indicated Div: $0.80

Valuation Analysis

		Institutional Holding	
Forecast P/E	9.27 (9/9/2006)	No of Institutions	342
Market Cap	$13.6 Billion	Shares	122,384,568
Book Value	4.4 Billion	% Held	49.09
Price/Book	3.08		
Price/Sales	0.90		

Business Summary: Automotive (MIC: 15.1 SIC: 3711 NAIC: 336120)

Paccar designs and manufactures heavy- and medium-duty diesel trucks which are marketed under the Peterbilt, Kenworth, DAF and Foden nameplates. Co. operates in two principal industry segments: the manufacture of trucks and related parts, and finance and leasing services provided to customers and dealers. Co. competes in the truck parts aftermarket primarily through its dealer network. Co.'s finance and leasing activities are principally related to company products and associated equipment and are conducted by its PACCAR Financial Services companies. Co. also manufactures winches under the Braden, Gearmatic and Carco nameplates.

Recent Developments: For the quarter ended June 30 2006, net income increased 53.2% to $369.9 million from $241.5 million in the year-earlier quarter. Revenues were $4.17 billion, up 17.2% from $3.56 billion the year before. Direct operating expenses rose 16.5% to $3.36 billion from $2.89 billion in the comparable period the year before. Indirect operating expenses increased 19.3% to $275.1 million from $230.6 million in the equivalent prior-year period.

Prospects: During 2006, Co. is increasing capital expenditures and intends to concentrate investments on three main business segments of power-train development, new product introductions and customer service. Meanwhile, truck market expansion in North America is being driven by a strong general economy, increasing freight volume and continuing fleet growth. Consequently, U.S. and Canadian Class 8 industry truck retail sales are estimated to range from 290,000 to 310,000 units as customers continue updating and expanding their fleets to satisfy the demands of a growing economy. Similarly, industry truck sales in Western Europe above 15 tonnes are expected to remain between 245,000 and 265,000 units.

Financial Data
(US$ in Thousands)

	6 Mos	3 Mos	12/31/2005	12/31/2004	12/31/2003	12/31/2002	12/31/2001	12/31/2000
Earnings Per Share	5.23	4.68	4.37	3.44	1.99	1.42	0.67	1.70
Cash Flow Per Share	5.62	5.08	3.83	3.39	3.12	3.06	2.42	2.00
Tang Book Value Per Share	17.73	16.29	15.40	14.42	12.36	9.97	8.69	8.72
Dividends Per Share	2.007	1.947	1.913	1.833	0.916	0.667	0.430	0.652
Dividend Payout %	38.39	41.60	43.75	53.29	45.93	46.88	64.16	38.38
Income Statement								
Total Revenue	8,019,700	3,851,700	14,057,400	11,396,300	8,194,000	7,218,600	6,088,800	7,919,400
EBITDA	1,257,100	600,900	2,143,700	1,683,200	1,073,000	792,300	435,200	820,600
Depn & Amortn	208,200	100,200	370,100	315,000	267,500	218,200	179,900	155,500
Income Before Taxes	1,048,900	500,700	1,773,600	1,368,200	805,500	574,100	255,300	665,100
Income Taxes	337,000	158,700	640,400	461,400	279,000	202,100	81,700	223,300
Net Income	711,900	342,000	1,133,200	906,800	526,500	372,000	173,600	441,800
Average Shares	251,400	253,650	259,200	263,550	264,150	261,900	259,650	260,417
Balance Sheet								
Total Assets	14,741,900	14,142,400	13,715,400	12,228,000	9,939,600	8,702,500	7,913,900	8,270,900
Current Liabilities	5,878,200	6,090,200	2,351,100	2,299,400	1,609,100	1,384,300	1,230,800	1,360,600
Long-Term Obligations	3,112,800	2,715,800	6,246,300	4,816,400	3,819,800	3,561,500	3,466,900	3,928,600
Total Liabilities	10,320,800	10,066,700	9,814,300	8,465,600	6,693,200	6,101,800	5,661,300	6,021,800
Stockholders' Equity	4,421,100	4,075,700	3,901,100	3,762,400	3,246,400	2,600,700	2,252,600	2,249,100
Shares Outstanding	249,300	250,200	253,350	260,850	262,650	260,775	259,200	257,850
Statistical Record								
Return on Assets %	9.71	9.07	8.74	8.16	5.65	4.48	2.15	5.44
Return on Equity %	32.03	30.00	29.57	25.81	18.01	15.33	7.71	20.21
EBITDA Margin %	15.68	15.60	15.25	14.77	13.09	10.98	7.15	10.36
Net Margin %	8.88	8.88	8.06	7.96	6.42	5.15	2.85	5.58
Asset Turnover	1.11	1.10	1.08	1.03	0.88	0.87	0.75	0.97
Current Ratio	0.66	0.62	1.49	1.45	1.62	1.52	1.49	1.37
Debt to Equity	0.70	0.67	1.60	1.28	1.18	1.37	1.54	1.75
Price Range	54.92-42.72	50.53-42.72	53.65-42.72	53.65-33.33	38.67-18.92	23.47-13.75	20.11-12.89	15.63-10.98
P/E Ratio	10.50-8.17	10.80-9.13	12.28-9.78	15.60-9.69	19.43-9.51	16.53-9.68	30.02-19.24	9.19-6.46
Average Yield %	4.21	4.17	4.06	4.47	3.07	3.50	2.74	5.08

Address: 777 - 106th Ave. N.E., Bellevue, WA 98004
Telephone: 425-468-7400
Fax: 425-468-8216

Web Site: www.paccar.com
Officers: Mark C. Pigott - Chmn., C.E.O. Michael A. Tembreull - Vice-Chmn.

Auditors: Ernst & Young LLP
Transfer Agents: Wells Fargo Bank Minnesota, N.A., St. Paul, MN

PACIFIC CAPITAL BANCORP (NEW)

Exchange	Symbol	Price	52Wk Range	Yield	P/E	Div Achiever
NMS	PCBC	$27.96 (8/31/2006)	38.23-27.83	3.15	12.65	36 Years

*7 Year Price Score 115.66 *NYSE Composite Index=100 *12 Month Price Score 84.62

Interim Earnings (Per Share)

Qtr.	Mar	Jun	Sep	Dec
2003	0.79	0.29	0.29	0.28
2004	0.93	0.36	0.32	0.31
2005	1.29	0.31	0.31	0.23
2006	1.43	0.24	...	...

Interim Dividends (Per Share)

Amt	Decl	Ex	Rec	Pay
0.20Q	10/3/2005	10/14/2005	10/18/2005	11/8/2005
0.22Q	1/3/2006	1/20/2006	1/24/2006	2/14/2006
0.22Q	4/1/2006	4/21/2006	4/25/2006	5/16/2006
0.22Q	7/3/2006	7/20/2006	7/24/2006	8/15/2006

Indicated Div: $0.88

Valuation Analysis

Forecast P/E	N/A
Market Cap	$1.3 Billion
Book Value	597.9 Million
Price/Book	2.19
Price/Sales	1.92

Institutional Holding

No of Institutions 123
Shares 17,992,246
% Held 38.09

Business Summary: Commercial Banking (MIC: 8.1 SIC: 6022 NAIC: 522110)

Pacific Capital Bancorp is the parent of Pacific Capital Bank, N.A., a nationally chartered bank with four brands: Santa Barbara Bank & Trust, First National Bank of Central California, South Valley National Bank First, Bank of San Luis Obispo, San Benito Bank and Pacific Capital Bank. Co. provides commercial banking services to households, professionals, and small- to medium-sized businesses. Co. also offers products related to income tax returns filed electronically. Pacific Capital Bank, N.A. is a 48 branch community bank network serving several California central coast counties. As of Dec 31 2005, Co. had assets of $6.88 billion and deposits of $5.02 billion.

Recent Developments: For the quarter ended June 30 2006, net income decreased 20.2% to $11.5 million from $14.4 million in the year-earlier quarter. Net interest income increased 12.5% to $69.4 million from $61.7 million in the year-earlier quarter. Provision for loan losses was $6.0 million versus $7.9 million in the prior-year quarter, a decrease of 24.6%. Non-interest income rose 24.0% to $22.3 million from $18.0 million, while non-interest expense advanced 41.6% to $68.4 million.

Prospects: On Jul 3 2006, Co. announced that it has completed its acquisition of Morton Capital Management, a registered investment advisor, for an initial payment in cash of about $7.0 million, and future payments based upon the financial performance of the acquired business over a specific period following the closing on Jul 1 2006. Moving forward, Co. remains focused on reducing its expense levels. Also, Co.'s loan pipeline remains promising as it develops new relationships within its traditional markets and generates lending opportunities through its business development efforts in adjacent markets. For full year 2006, Co. continues to expect fully diluted earnings per share of $2.15 to $2.20.

Financial Data
(US$ in Thousands)

	6 Mos	3 Mos	12/31/2005	12/31/2004	12/31/2003	12/31/2002	12/31/2001	12/31/2000
Earnings Per Share	2.21	2.28	2.14	1.92	1.64	1.61	1.19	1.09
Cash Flow Per Share	4.17	4.26	3.85	2.48	2.66	1.94	2.05	1.01
Tang Book Value Per Share	9.60	9.64	8.47	7.54	8.08	7.31	6.99	6.29
Dividends Per Share	0.840	0.820	0.780	0.690	0.600	0.517	0.495	0.450
Dividend Payout %	38.01	35.96	36.45	35.94	36.53	32.24	41.71	41.45
Income Statement								
Interest Income	330,297	217,091	426,157	326,181	272,189	266,746	291,108	290,916
Interest Expense	85,731	41,953	111,505	69,211	53,933	62,799	97,226	110,526
Net Interest Income	244,566	175,138	314,652	256,970	218,256	203,947	193,882	180,390
Provision for Losses	54,102	48,146	53,873	12,809	18,286	19,727	26,671	14,440
Non-Interest Income	126,186	103,891	111,923	75,635	81,745	73,784	65,726	49,388
Non-Interest Expense	191,437	123,014	214,405	179,906	163,702	143,288	143,150	131,957
Income Before Taxes	125,213	107,869	158,297	139,890	118,013	114,716	89,787	83,381
Income Taxes	46,325	40,501	59,012	51,946	42,342	39,865	33,676	31,925
Net Income	78,888	67,368	99,285	87,944	75,671	74,851	56,111	51,456
Average Shares	47,091	47,096	46,358	45,911	46,082	46,653	47,358	47,304
Balance Sheet								
Net Loans & Leases	5,176,666	4,923,163	4,841,688	4,008,317	3,131,329	2,965,999	2,750,220	2,481,979
Total Assets	7,182,740	6,970,124	6,876,519	6,024,785	4,859,630	4,219,213	3,960,929	3,677,625
Total Deposits	4,842,139	5,223,940	5,017,866	4,512,290	3,854,717	3,516,077	3,365,575	3,102,819
Total Liabilities	6,584,876	6,370,327	6,330,903	5,565,103	4,460,582	3,848,138	3,635,053	3,381,364
Stockholders' Equity	597,864	599,809	545,256	459,682	399,048	371,075	325,876	296,261
Shares Outstanding	46,790	46,689	46,631	45,719	45,284	46,066	46,590	47,077
Statistical Record								
Return on Assets %	1.56	1.63	1.54	1.61	1.67	1.83	1.47	1.57
Return on Equity %	18.58	19.42	19.76	20.43	19.65	21.48	18.04	19.33
Net Interest Margin %	61.33	80.67	73.83	78.78	80.19	76.46	66.60	62.01
Efficiency Ratio %	50.50	38.32	39.85	44.77	46.25	42.08	40.12	38.78
Loans to Deposits	1.07	0.94	0.96	0.89	0.81	0.84	0.82	0.80
Price Range	39.36-29.86	39.36-26.64	39.36-26.64	34.54-25.87	28.66-19.03	21.75-15.37	17.13-14.31	17.30-13.18
P/E Ratio	17.81-13.51	17.26-11.68	18.39-12.45	17.99-13.47	17.48-11.60	13.51-9.55	14.39-12.02	15.87-12.10
Average Yield %	2.42	2.40	2.38	2.37	2.47	2.81	3.12	2.96

Address: 1021 Anacapa Street, 3rd Floor, Santa Barbara, CA 93101
Telephone: 805-564-6300
Fax: 805-564-6293

Web Site: www.pcbancorp.com
Officers: David W. Spainhour - Chmn. D. Vernon Horton - Vice-Chmn.

Auditors: PricewaterhouseCoopers LLP
Investor Contact: 805-564-6298
Transfer Agents: Norwest Shareowner Services, South St. Paul, MN

PACIFIC SUNWEAR OF CALIFORNIA, INC.

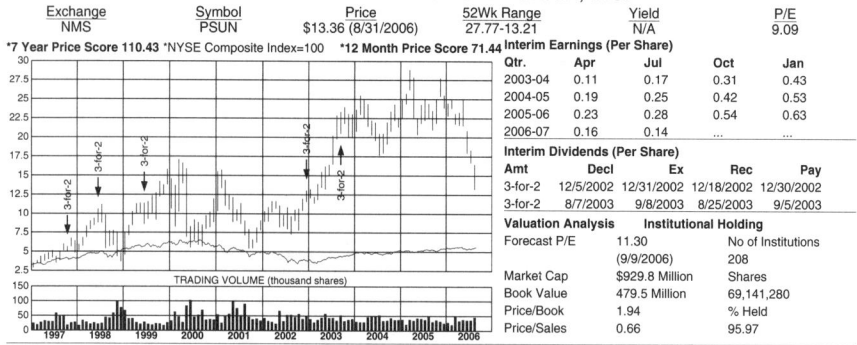

Exchange	Symbol	Price	52Wk Range	Yield	P/E
NMS	PSUN	$13.36 (8/31/2006)	27.77-13.21	N/A	9.09

*7 Year Price Score 110.43 *NYSE Composite Index=100 *12 Month Price Score 71.44

Interim Earnings (Per Share)

Qtr.	Apr	Jul	Oct	Jan
2003-04	0.11	0.17	0.31	0.43
2004-05	0.19	0.25	0.42	0.53
2005-06	0.23	0.28	0.54	0.63
2006-07	0.16	0.14	...	...

Interim Dividends (Per Share)

Amt	Decl	Ex	Rec	Pay
3-for-2	12/5/2002	12/31/2002	12/18/2002	12/30/2002
3-for-2	8/7/2003	9/8/2003	8/25/2003	9/5/2003

Valuation Analysis   **Institutional Holding**

Forecast P/E	11.30 (9/9/2006)	No of Institutions	208
Market Cap	$929.8 Million	Shares	69,141,280
Book Value	479.5 Million	% Held	95.97
Price/Book	1.94		
Price/Sales	0.66		

Business Summary: Retail - Apparel and Accessory Stores (MIC: 5.8 SIC: 5699 NAIC: 448150)

Pacific Sunwear of California is a specialty retailer of everyday casual apparel, accessories and footwear designed to meet the needs of active teens and young adults. Co. operates three nationwide, primarily mall-based chains of retail stores under the names Pacific Sunwear (also PacSun), Pacific Sunwear Outlet (PacSun Outlet), and d.e.m.o. As of Jan 28 2006, Co. leased and operated a total of 1,105 stores among all 50 states and Puerto Rico, comprising 811 stores under the PacSun name, 96 stores under the PacSun Outlet name and 198 stores under d.e.m.o. name.

Recent Developments: For the quarter ended July 29 2006, net income decreased 54.0% to $9.7 million from $21.1 million in the year-earlier quarter. Revenues were $313.7 million, up 1.5% from $309.1 million the year before. Operating income was $14.6 million versus $32.8 million in the prior-year quarter, a decrease of 55.5%. Direct operating expenses rose 8.8% to $216.3 million from $198.7 million in the comparable period the year before. Indirect operating expenses increased 6.8% to $82.9 million from $77.6 million in the equivalent prior-year period.

Prospects: Co. remains cautious regarding its near-term outlook. Co.'s lackluster results for the second quarter ended Jul 29 2006 are reflective of overall declines in its comparable store net sales throughout the first half and into the third quarter of fiscal year 2006. Specifically, Co. noted a slight decrease in the average sale transaction per comparable store, while average retail prices were exhibiting a modest increase. Assuming a further continuation of this unfavorable trend in comparable store net sales, Co. is maintaining its earnings estimates for the third quarter of fiscal 2006 to be in the range of $0.22 to $0.30 per diluted share.

Financial Data
(US$ in Thousands)

	6 Mos	3 Mos	01/28/2006	01/29/2005	01/31/2004	02/01/2003	02/02/2002	02/04/2001
Earnings Per Share	1.47	1.61	1.67	1.38	1.02	0.66	0.37	0.54
Cash Flow Per Share	1.49	2.08	2.47	1.89	1.99	1.04	0.75	0.69
Tang Book Value Per Share	6.89	7.28	7.41	6.03	5.39	3.99	3.27	2.83
Income Statement								
Total Revenue	613,570	299,888	1,391,473	1,229,762	1,040,294	846,393	684,840	589,438
EBITDA	66,299	34,248	260,434	221,698	164,495	113,691	71,428	83,895
Depn & Amortn	34,385	16,905	63,161	51,685	36,246	32,453	27,146	19,872
Income Before Taxes	34,799	19,138	202,946	171,902	128,981	80,644	44,752	64,967
Income Taxes	13,223	7,273	76,734	64,998	48,768	30,967	17,186	25,213
Net Income	21,576	11,865	126,212	106,904	80,213	49,677	27,566	39,754
Average Shares	71,866	73,711	75,713	77,464	78,849	75,146	74,488	73,233
Balance Sheet								
Total Assets	759,667	772,790	807,561	677,778	575,261	399,743	355,441	277,453
Current Liabilities	143,045	111,178	122,471	95,310	110,544	73,328	65,931	47,799
Long-Term Obligations	...	...	...	403	1,455	3,338	25,329	1,103
Total Liabilities	280,142	245,567	260,771	219,744	146,499	97,352	107,485	64,321
Stockholders' Equity	479,525	527,223	546,790	458,034	428,762	302,391	247,955	213,131
Shares Outstanding	69,595	72,386	73,751	74,916	78,351	74,233	73,733	72,993
Statistical Record								
Return on Assets %	14.09	16.35	17.04	17.11	16.50	13.19	8.76	16.07
Return on Equity %	22.45	23.80	25.19	24.18	22.00	18.10	12.02	20.86
EBITDA Margin %	10.81	11.42	18.72	18.03	15.81	13.43	10.43	14.17
Net Margin %	3.52	3.96	9.07	8.69	7.71	5.87	4.03	6.74
Asset Turnover	1.83	1.92	1.88	1.97	2.14	2.25	2.18	2.38
Current Ratio	2.39	3.34	3.48	3.70	3.20	2.49	2.20	2.67
Debt to Equity	...	...	...	N.M.	N.M.	0.01	0.10	0.01
Price Range	27.77-17.17	27.77-20.35	28.90-20.35	25.50-17.65	23.97-11.39	13.23-7.28	15.75-5.42	17.11-5.53
P/E Ratio	18.89-11.68	17.25-12.64	17.31-12.19	18.48-12.79	23.50-11.16	20.05-11.04	42.57-14.65	31.69-10.24

Address: 3450 E. Miraloma Avenue, Anaheim, CA 92806-2101 **Telephone:** 714-414-4000	**Web Site:** www.pacsun.com **Officers:** Greg H. Weaver - Chmn., C.E.O. Timothy M. Harmon - Pres., Chief Merchandising Officer	**Auditors:** Deloitte & Touche LLP

PARAMETRIC TECHNOLOGY CORP

Exchange	Symbol	Price	52Wk Range	Yield	P/E
NMS	PMTC	$16.11 (8/31/2006)	17.68-11.73	N/A	34.28

*7 Year Price Score 63.21   *NYSE Composite Index=100   *12 Month Price Score 93.32

Interim Earnings (Per Share)

Qtr.	Dec	Mar	Jun	Sep
2002-03	(0.10)	(0.15)	(0.33)	(0.35)
2003-04	(0.25)	0.03	0.15	0.40
2004-05	0.17	0.18	0.25	0.15
2005-06	0.07	0.09	0.15	...

Interim Dividends (Per Share)
No Dividends Paid

Valuation Analysis

Forecast P/E	17.81
	(9/9/2006)
Market Cap	$1.8 Billion
Book Value	393.0 Million
Price/Book	4.57
Price/Sales	2.23

Institutional Holding

No of Institutions	221
Shares	96,700,336
% Held	86.61

Business Summary: IT & Technology (MIC: 10.2 SIC: 7372 NAIC: 511210)
Parametric Technology develops, markets and supports product lifecycle management (PLM) and enterprise content management (ECM) software and related services that are designed to help companies improve their processes for developing physical and information products. Co.'s products and services include a suite of mechanical computer-aided design and document authoring tools (Desktop Solutions), and a range of Internet-based collaboration, content and process management, and publishing technologies (Enterprise Solutions). Co.'s software is complemented by its services and technical support organizations, as well as third-party resellers and other strategic partners.

Recent Developments: For the quarter ended July 1 2006, net income decreased 36.7% to $16.9 million from $26.7 million in the year-earlier quarter. Revenues were $216.7 million, up 20.2% from $180.3 million the year before. Operating income was $13.5 million versus $26.5 million in the prior-year quarter, a decrease of 49.2%. Direct operating expenses rose 31.6% to $68.6 million from $52.1 million in the comparable period the year before. Indirect operating expenses increased 32.4% to $134.7 million from $101.7 million in the equivalent prior-year period.

Prospects: Co.'s top-line growth is being driven by organic license and service revenue across both its Desktop and Enterprise Solutions categories, as well as revenue attributable to the acquired businesses of Arbortext and Mathsoft. Looking ahead, Co. believes that the Asia-Pacific region presents an important growth opportunity as global manufacturing companies continues to invest in that region. For the fourth quarter of fiscal 2006, Co. expects revenue to range from $217.0 million to $225.0 million and earnings from $0.15 to $0.19 per share. For the fiscal year ending Sep 30 2006, Co. expects revenue to range from $826.0 million to $834.0 million and earnings from $0.46 to $0.50 per share.

Financial Data
(US$ in Thousands)

	9 Mos	6 Mos	3 Mos	09/30/2005	09/30/2004	09/30/2003	09/30/2002	09/30/2001
Earnings Per Share	0.47	0.57	0.66	0.75	0.33	(0.93)	(0.90)	(0.07)
Cash Flow Per Share	0.57	0.77	0.71	1.18	0.94	0.06	(0.22)	0.48
Tang Book Value Per Share	0.58	0.88	0.66	0.59	1.72	1.34	2.24	2.94
Income Statement								
Total Revenue	609,416	392,712	192,518	720,719	660,029	671,940	741,957	934,606
EBITDA	67,379	44,393	20,438	110,319	68,655	(44,052)	(5,789)	55,460
Depn & Amortn	24,809	16,124	8,061	25,885	35,100	41,637	72,625	76,370
Income Before Taxes	42,570	28,269	12,377	91,312	37,039	(82,429)	(74,339)	(10,861)
Income Taxes	7,427	10,002	4,861	7,720	2,226	15,851	19,282	(2,647)
Net Income	35,143	18,267	7,516	83,592	34,813	(98,280)	(93,621)	(8,214)
Average Shares	112,871	113,403	112,666	111,980	109,273	105,659	104,360	105,776
Balance Sheet								
Total Assets	851,954	829,301	772,058	786,623	666,382	577,690	674,959	797,838
Current Liabilities	346,244	351,743	315,178	344,762	332,665	297,500	315,697	359,636
Total Liabilities	458,906	465,845	430,556	462,779	424,431	382,532	385,031	398,136
Stockholders' Equity	393,048	363,456	341,502	323,844	241,951	195,158	289,928	399,702
Shares Outstanding	111,464	111,330	110,991	110,029	107,803	106,553	105,033	104,215
Statistical Record								
Return on Assets %	6.56	7.90	9.77	11.51	5.58	N.M.	N.M.	N.M.
Return on Equity %	14.85	19.02	23.64	29.55	15.89	N.M.	N.M.	N.M.
EBITDA Margin %	11.06	11.30	10.62	15.31	10.40	N.M.	N.M.	5.93
Net Margin %	5.77	4.65	3.90	11.60	5.27	N.M.	N.M.	N.M.
Asset Turnover	1.00	0.97	1.01	0.99	1.06	1.07	1.01	1.09
Current Ratio	1.18	1.30	1.25	1.23	1.57	1.40	1.59	1.43
Price Range	17.93-11.73	17.93-12.10	17.93-12.10	17.93-12.07	13.35-7.67	10.03-4.13	23.85-4.50	41.56-11.50
P/E Ratio	38.14-24.96	31.45-21.23	27.16-18.33	23.90-16.10	40.45-23.26	...	...	...

Address: 140 Kendrick Street, Needham, MA 02494 Telephone: 781-370-5000	Web Site: www.ptc.com Officers: Noel G. Posternak - Chmn. C. Richard Harrison - Pres., C.E.O.	Auditors: PricewaterhouseCoopers LLP Investor Contact: 718-398-5000

PARK NATIONAL CORP. (NEWARK, OH)

Exchange	Symbol	Price	52Wk Range	Yield	P/E	Div Achiever
ASE	PRK	$103.61 (8/31/2006)	117.21-92.36	3.55	15.49	18 Years

*7 Year Price Score 84.12 *NYSE Composite Index=100 *12 Month Price Score 93.51

Interim Earnings (Per Share)

Qtr.	Mar	Jun	Sep	Dec
2003	1.60	1.72	1.39	1.26
2004	1.58	1.67	1.63	1.44
2005	1.61	1.72	1.69	1.61
2006	1.69	1.70	...	...

Interim Dividends (Per Share)

Amt	Decl	Ex	Rec	Pay
0.92Q	11/21/2005	12/16/2005	12/20/2005	1/3/2006
0.92Q	1/17/2006	2/17/2006	2/22/2006	3/10/2006
0.92Q	4/17/2006	5/19/2006	5/23/2006	6/9/2006
0.92Q	7/17/2006	8/18/2006	8/22/2006	9/8/2006

Indicated Div: $3.68 (Div. Reinv. Plan)

Valuation Analysis

Forecast P/E	14.82
	(9/9/2006)
Market Cap	$1.4 Billion
Book Value	539.5 Million
Price/Book	2.68
Price/Sales	3.74

Institutional Holding

No of Institutions	80
Shares	4,166,272
% Held	30.01

Business Summary: Commercial Banking (MIC: 8.1 SIC: 6021 NAIC: 522110)

Park National is a bank holding company engaged in the commercial banking and trust business, generally in small and medium population Ohio communities. At Dec 31 2005, Co.'s subsidiary banks operated 126 financial service offices and a network of 137 automated teller machines. These financial service offices cover 29 Ohio counties including Ashland, Athens, Butler, Champaign, Clark, Clermont, Coshocton, Crawford, Darke, Delaware, Fairfield, Fayette, Franklin, Greene, Hamilton, Hocking, Holmes, Knox, Licking, Madison, Marion, Mercer, Miami, Montgomery, Morrow, Muskingum, Perry, Richland and Tuscarawas. As of Dec 31 2005, Co. had total assets of $5.44 billion.

Recent Developments: For the quarter ended June 30 2006, net income decreased 3.6% to $23.9 million from $24.8 million in the year-earlier quarter. Net interest income decreased 2.9% to $53.8 million from $55.4 million in the year-earlier quarter. Provision for loan losses was $1.5 million versus $1.3 million in the prior-year quarter, an increase of 10.7%. Non-interest income rose 5.0% to $16.3 million from $15.6 million, while non-interest expense advanced 1.5% to $34.9 million.

Prospects: During the second half of 2006, Co. expects total loans to increase by $40.0 million to $60.0 million, but expects annual growth rate for 2006 to be less than 3.0%. Co. also expects the average yield on its loan portfolio to continue to gradually rise as adjustable rate loans reprice at higher interest rate. Further, Co. expects the average balance of interest earning assets in the second half of 2006 to remain below the same period in 2005 until further investment securities are purchased. For full-year 2006, Co. expects net interest income to be about 0.5% to 1.0% less than 2005, with net interest margin of about 4.4%. Co. also projects average total deposits growth of 1.0% to 2.0%.

Financial Data
(US$ in Thousands)

	6 Mos	3 Mos	12/31/2005	12/31/2004	12/31/2003	12/31/2002	12/31/2001	12/31/2000
Earnings Per Share	6.69	6.71	6.64	6.32	5.97	5.86	5.31	4.86
Cash Flow Per Share	6.15	5.91	5.68	6.03	6.86	10.94	6.67	5.11
Tang Book Value Per Share	33.85	34.01	34.72	39.28	37.57	35.17	32.00	28.25
Dividends Per Share	3.660	3.640	3.620	3.414	3.210	2.962	2.752	2.533
Dividend Payout %	54.71	54.25	54.52	54.02	53.75	50.57	51.79	52.16
Income Statement								
Interest Income	163,894	80,596	314,459	270,993	264,629	287,920	320,348	249,332
Interest Expense	56,653	27,177	93,895	58,702	61,992	82,588	127,404	110,437
Net Interest Income	107,241	53,419	220,564	212,291	202,637	205,332	192,944	138,895
Provision for Losses	1,467	...	5,407	8,600	12,595	15,043	13,059	8,729
Non-Interest Income	31,721	15,393	59,705	51,848	55,523	50,850	45,238	29,691
Non-Interest Expense	69,868	35,012	139,438	126,290	122,376	119,964	114,207	82,919
Income Before Taxes	67,627	33,800	135,424	129,249	123,189	121,175	110,916	76,938
Income Taxes	19,934	9,993	43,079	40,210	38,829	37,883	35,893	23,538
Net Income	47,693	23,807	95,238	91,507	86,878	85,579	78,362	55,405
Average Shares	14,010	14,095	14,348	14,486	14,551	14,605	14,753	11,420
Balance Sheet								
Net Loans & Leases	3,298,397	3,248,619	3,258,418	3,052,280	2,667,661	2,630,159	2,735,849	2,229,259
Total Assets	5,412,447	5,444,445	5,436,048	5,412,584	5,034,956	4,446,625	4,569,515	3,211,068
Total Deposits	3,849,076	3,833,939	3,757,757	3,689,861	3,414,249	3,495,135	3,314,203	2,415,575
Total Liabilities	4,872,968	4,899,484	4,877,618	4,850,023	4,491,915	3,937,333	4,101,169	2,891,316
Stockholders' Equity	539,479	544,961	558,430	562,561	543,041	509,292	468,346	319,752
Shares Outstanding	13,932	14,008	14,092	14,320	14,455	14,481	14,637	11,317
Statistical Record								
Return on Assets %	1.72	1.72	1.76	1.75	1.83	3.77	2.01	1.89
Return on Equity %	17.00	17.38	16.99	16.51	16.51	34.73	19.89	19.76
Net Interest Margin %	64.61	66.28	70.14	78.34	76.57	71.32	60.23	55.71
Efficiency Ratio %	34.99	36.48	37.27	39.12	38.22	35.41	31.24	29.72
Loans to Deposits	0.86	0.85	0.87	0.83	0.78	0.75	0.83	0.92
Price Range	118.20-92.36	118.20-99.04	135.50-99.04	141.25-105.33	114.29-88.86	97.24-80.01	97.62-71.52	98.93-74.76
P/E Ratio	17.67-13.81	17.62-14.76	20.41-14.92	22.35-16.67	19.14-14.88	16.59-13.65	18.38-13.47	20.36-15.38
Average Yield %	3.47	3.39	3.27	2.92	3.11	3.22	3.24	2.88

Address: 50 North Third Street, Newark, OH 43055 Telephone: 740-349-8451 Fax: 740-349-3765	Web Site: www.parknationalcorp.com Officers: C. Daniel DeLawder - Chmn., C.E.O. Harry O. Egger - Vice Chmn.	Auditors: Ernst & Young LLP Investor Contact: 740-349-8451 Transfer Agents: First-Knox National Bank, Mount Vernon, OH

PATHMARK STORES INC. (NEW)

Exchange	Symbol	Price	52Wk Range	Yield	P/E
NMS	PTMK	$9.71 (8/31/2006)	12.28-7.90	N/A	N/A

*7 Year Price Score N/A *NYSE Composite Index=100 *12 Month Price Score 86.12

Interim Earnings (Per Share)

Qtr.	Apr	Jul	Oct	Jan
2003-04	0.03	0.21	(0.01)	0.31
2004-05	(0.06)	(0.05)	(0.12)	(10.03)
2005-06	(0.07)	(0.12)	(0.36)	(0.30)
2006-07	(0.10)	(0.17)	...	...

Interim Dividends (Per Share)
No Dividends Paid

Valuation Analysis
Forecast P/E: N/A
Market Cap: $505.9 Million
Book Value: 161.6 Million
Price/Book: 3.13
Price/Sales: 0.13

Institutional Holding
No of Institutions: 96
Shares: 28,694,004
% Held: 55.14

Business Summary: Retail - Miscellaneous (MIC: 5.11 SIC: 5411 NAIC: 445110)

Pathmark Stores is a supermarket chain in the New York-New Jersey and Philadelphia metropolitan areas, with its stores designed to provide customers with "one-stop" shopping that offers an assortment of foods and general merchandise, as well as a host of additional conveniences that includes 128 in-store full-service pharmacies and an array of financial services offered by its in-store banks. As of Jan 28 2006, Co. operated 141 supermarkets that were either freestanding stores or located in shopping centers, of which 65 stores were located in New Jersey, 55 stores in New York, 17 stores in Pennsylvania and 4 in Delaware.

Recent Developments: For the quarter ended July 29 2006, net loss amounted to $8.8 million versus a net loss of $5.1 million in the year-earlier quarter. Revenues were $1.00 billion, unchanged from the year before. Operating income was $700,000 versus $8.7 million in the prior-year quarter, a decrease of 92.0%. Direct operating expenses rose 0.4% to $718.0 million from $714.8 million in the comparable period the year before. Indirect operating expenses increased 2.5% to $284.2 million from $277.2 million in the equivalent prior-year period.

Prospects: For the remainder of fiscal 2006, Co. expects to improve its gross margin as its merchandising initiatives continues to yield higher average order sizes. On the cost side, Co. expects its other efforts will aid in mitigating the overall anticipated increase in expenses. Meanwhile, Co. expects to complete ten store renovations in the third fiscal quarter of 2006, and one renovation in the subsequent fiscal quarter. Correspondingly, these renovations will constitute a part of Co.'s projected capital expenditures for the full-fiscal year 2006 of approximately $70.0 million.

Financial Data
(US$ in Thousands)

	6 Mos	3 Mos	01/28/2006	01/29/2005	01/31/2004	02/01/2003	02/02/2002	02/03/2001
Earnings Per Share	(0.93)	(0.88)	(0.92)	(10.26)	0.54	0.44	(8.07)	(2.58)
Cash Flow Per Share	0.17	0.39	0.63	3.37	3.02	3.06	2.76	3.49
Tang Book Value Per Share	0.32	0.45	N.M.	N.M.	N.M.	N.M.	11.46	19.57
Income Statement								
Total Revenue	2,001,400	998,500	3,977,000	3,978,500	3,991,300	3,937,700	3,963,300	1,493,693
EBITDA	58,800	32,200	92,800	(158,100)	189,500	178,400	189,600	90,363
Depn & Amortn	51,400	25,500	93,800	92,800	88,700	86,400	344,500	125,484
Income Before Taxes	(23,500)	(8,800)	(65,700)	(317,900)	28,300	26,900	(220,200)	(62,851)
Income Taxes	(9,300)	(3,400)	(25,600)	(9,300)	11,800	13,000	18,500	14,640
Net Income	(14,200)	(5,400)	(40,100)	(308,600)	16,500	13,300	(242,000)	(77,491)
Average Shares	52,100	52,000	43,500	30,100	30,400	30,400	30,000	30,000
Balance Sheet								
Total Assets	1,225,700	1,240,800	1,254,600	1,253,400	1,520,900	1,522,600	1,495,500	1,725,441
Current Liabilities	287,000	284,100	280,500	314,100	260,100	267,300	274,500	268,801
Long-Term Obligations	587,800	589,900	592,300	622,900	600,200	622,300	613,400	618,354
Total Liabilities	1,064,100	1,072,800	1,083,300	1,188,200	1,145,900	1,165,800	1,151,100	1,136,468
Stockholders' Equity	161,600	168,000	171,300	65,200	375,000	356,800	344,400	588,973
Shares Outstanding	52,097	52,034	52,012	30,071	30,071	30,071	30,054	30,098
Statistical Record								
Return on Assets %	N.M.	N.M.	N.M.	N.M.	1.09	0.88	N.M.	...
Return on Equity %	N.M.	N.M.	N.M.	N.M.	4.52	3.80	N.M.	...
EBITDA Margin %	2.94	3.22	2.33	N.M.	4.75	4.53	4.78	6.05
Net Margin %	N.M.	N.M.	N.M.	N.M.	0.41	0.34	N.M.	N.M.
Asset Turnover	3.13	3.19	3.18	2.88	2.63	2.62	2.47	...
Current Ratio	1.23	1.30	1.33	1.09	1.27	1.22	1.25	1.36
Debt to Equity	3.64	3.51	3.46	9.55	1.60	1.74	1.78	1.05
Price Range	12.28-7.90	12.28-7.72	12.28-4.48	9.19-3.50	9.07-4.53	24.70-2.98	25.92-16.00	17.00-11.75
P/E Ratio	...	...	...	...	16.80-8.39	56.14-6.77	...	...

Address: 200 Milik Street, Carteret, NJ 07008
Telephone: 732-499-3000

Web Site: www.pathmark.com
Officers: Steven L. Volla - Chmn. Frank G. Vitrano - Pres., C.F.O., Treas.

Auditors: Deloitte & Touche LLP

PATTERSON COMPANIES INC

Exchange	Symbol	Price	52Wk Range	Yield	P/E
NMS	PDCO	$30.82 (8/31/2006)	42.93-30.82	N/A	21.70

*7 Year Price Score 107.25 *NYSE Composite Index=100 *12 Month Price Score 90.30

Interim Earnings (Per Share)

Qtr.	Jul	Oct	Jan	Apr
2003-04	0.22	0.26	0.29	0.33
2004-05	0.29	0.31	0.36	0.36
2005-06	0.31	0.32	0.39	0.41
2006-07	0.30	...	...	...

Interim Dividends (Per Share)

Amt	Decl	Ex	Rec	Pay
100%	6/13/2000	7/24/2000	6/30/2000	7/21/2000
100%	9/14/2004	10/25/2004	10/8/2004	10/22/2004

Valuation Analysis

Forecast P/E	17.62 (9/9/2006)
Market Cap	$4.3 Billion
Book Value	1.3 Billion
Price/Book	3.32
Price/Sales	1.60

Institutional Holding

No of Institutions	310
Shares	102,461,648
% Held	73.80

Business Summary: Medical Instruments & Equipment (MIC: 9.6 SIC: 5047 NAIC: 423450)

Co. provides consumable products such as x-ray film, restorative materials, hand instruments and sterilization products, technology dental equipment, practice management and clinical software, patient education systems, and office forms and stationery for the North American dental supply market. In addition, Co. offers products used for the diagnosis, treatment and/or prevention of diseases in companion pets and equine animals for the U.S. companion-pet and equine veterinary supply market. Co. also supplies a range of distributed and self-manufactured rehabilitation products to health care professionals for the worldwide rehabilitation and non-wheelchair assistive products supply markets.

Recent Developments: For the quarter ended July 29 2006, net income decreased 3.0% to $41.6 million from $42.9 million in the year-earlier quarter. Revenues were $655.5 million, up 10.0% from $595.8 million the year before. Operating income was $68.5 million versus $69.5 million in the prior-year quarter, a decrease of 1.4%. Direct operating expenses rose 11.4% to $433.1 million from $388.6 million in the comparable period the year before. Indirect operating expenses increased 11.7% to $153.9 million from $137.7 million in the equivalent prior-year period.

Prospects: For full-fiscal year 2007, Co. has reduced its earnings guidance by $0.03 to a range of $1.58 to $1.61 per diluted share to reflect the uncertainty over the sales of its CEREC 3D® (CEREC) dental restorative systems. Nonetheless, Co. remains optimistic regarding CEREC's potential as a viable technology for use in future dental restorative procedures, along with prospective growth within both its veterinarian and rehabilitation supply businesses. Meanwhile, Co. is forecasting earnings to be in the range of $0.33 to $0.35 per diluted share for the second quarter of fiscal 2007.

Financial Data
(US$ in Thousands)

	3 Mos	04/29/2006	04/30/2005	04/24/2004	04/26/2003	04/27/2002	04/28/2001	04/29/2000
Earnings Per Share	1.42	1.43	1.32	1.09	0.88	0.70	0.56	0.47
Cash Flow Per Share	1.36	1.19	1.49	1.46	0.64	0.67	0.60	0.50
Tang Book Value Per Share	3.76	2.73	1.95	0.76	3.66	2.85	2.64	2.08
Income Statement								
Total Revenue	655,488	2,615,123	2,421,457	1,969,349	1,656,956	1,415,515	1,156,455	1,040,348
EBITDA	76,746	354,024	335,450	268,588	199,244	166,615	133,396	113,321
Depn & Amortn	6,244	23,676	26,862	19,441	12,776	14,283	11,077	10,190
Income Before Taxes	66,696	316,973	293,447	239,520	186,402	152,223	122,196	102,999
Income Taxes	25,112	118,548	109,749	90,055	70,082	56,933	45,721	38,527
Net Income	41,584	198,425	183,698	149,465	119,692	95,290	76,475	64,472
Average Shares	139,168	139,234	138,873	137,768	136,894	136,402	135,526	135,088
Balance Sheet								
Total Assets	1,950,257	1,911,718	1,685,301	1,588,957	823,978	718,376	549,180	451,976
Current Liabilities	407,484	409,647	322,288	263,688	184,024	198,007	132,715	112,906
Long-Term Obligations	205,010	210,014	301,530	479,556	...	...	...	...
Total Liabilities	660,696	669,197	670,229	787,199	190,292	200,644	136,408	116,364
Stockholders' Equity	1,289,561	1,242,521	1,015,072	801,758	633,686	514,360	408,515	330,470
Shares Outstanding	138,954	138,751	137,834	136,900	136,169	136,249	134,978	134,726
Statistical Record								
Return on Assets %	10.77	11.06	11.04	12.42	15.56	15.08	15.32	15.37
Return on Equity %	16.82	17.63	19.89	20.88	20.91	20.71	20.75	21.30
EBITDA Margin %	11.71	13.54	13.85	13.64	12.02	11.77	11.53	10.89
Net Margin %	6.34	7.59	7.59	7.59	7.22	6.73	6.61	6.20
Asset Turnover	1.46	1.46	1.46	1.64	2.15	2.24	2.32	2.48
Current Ratio	2.16	2.07	2.48	2.95	3.29	2.67	3.34	3.11
Debt to Equity	0.16	0.17	0.30	0.60	...	...	...	...
Price Range	44.60-31.69	53.58-32.20	51.86-34.92	39.31-19.54	27.20-17.81	23.56-15.15	17.00-10.63	12.39-8.22
P/E Ratio	31.41-22.32	37.47-22.52	39.29-26.45	36.06-17.92	30.90-20.24	33.66-21.65	30.36-18.97	26.36-17.49

Address: 1031 Mendota Heights Road, St. Paul, MN 55120-1419 **Telephone:** 651-686-1600 **Fax:** 651-686-9331	**Web Site:** www.pattersoncompanies.com **Officers:** Peter L. Frechette - Chmn. James W. Wiltz - Pres., C.E.O.	**Auditors:** Ernst & Young LLP **Investor Contact:** 651-686-1600 **Transfer Agents:** Wells Fargo Bank Minnesota, N.A.

PATTERSON-UTI ENERGY INC.

Exchange	Symbol	Price	52Wk Range	Yield	P/E
NMS	PTEN	$27.40 (8/31/2006)	38.33-22.55	1.17	8.40

*7 Year Price Score 142.71 *NYSE Composite Index=100 *12 Month Price Score 81.60

Interim Earnings (Per Share)

Qtr.	Mar	Jun	Sep	Dec
2003	0.04	0.07	0.11	0.12
2004	0.13	0.12	0.18	0.22
2005	0.35	0.45	0.63	0.72
2006	0.91	1.00	...	...

Interim Dividends (Per Share)

Amt	Decl	Ex	Rec	Pay
0.04Q	10/27/2005	11/10/2005	11/15/2005	12/1/2005
0.04Q	3/2/2006	3/13/2006	3/15/2006	3/30/2006
0.08Q	5/3/2006	6/13/2006	6/15/2006	6/30/2006
0.08Q	8/3/2006	9/12/2006	9/14/2006	9/29/2006

Indicated Div: $0.32

Valuation Analysis

		Institutional Holding	
Forecast P/E	6.37	No of Institutions	
	(9/9/2006)	326	
Market Cap	$4.5 Billion	Shares	
Book Value	1.5 Billion	135,384,592	
Price/Book	3.06	% Held	
Price/Sales	2.04	81.53	

Business Summary: Oil and Gas (MIC: 14.2 SIC: 1381 NAIC: 213111)
Patterson-UTI Energy provides onshore contract drilling services to oil and natural gas operators in Texas, New Mexico, Oklahoma, Louisiana, Mississippi, Colorado, Utah, Wyoming, and Western Canada. As of Dec 31 2005, Co. owned 403 drilling rigs. Co. provides pressure pumping services to oil and natural gas operators mainly in the Appalachian Basin. Co. provides drilling fluids, completion fluids, and related services to oil and natural gas operators in Texas, Southeastern New Mexico, South Texas, Oklahoma, the Gulf Coast region off Louisiana, and the Gulf of Mexico. Co. is also engaged in the development, exploration, acquisition, and production of oil and natural gas.

Recent Developments: For the quarter ended June 30 2006, net income increased 131.9% to $171.7 million from $74.0 million in the year-earlier quarter. Revenues were $636.8 million, up 63.3% from $389.9 million the year before. Operating income was $268.9 million versus $116.7 million in the prior-year quarter, an increase of 130.5%. Direct operating expenses rose 39.3% to $305.3 million from $219.1 million in the comparable period the year before. Indirect operating expenses increased 15.6% to $62.7 million from $54.2 million in the equivalent prior-year period.

Prospects: Co. is seeing growth in revenues and direct operating costs due to increased numbers of operating days, as well as an increase in the average revenue and average direct operating costs per operating day. Furthermore, Co. stated that the demand for its drilling services continues to exceed the supply of available rigs, resulting in continuing improvement in pricing. However, recent gas storage levels have moderated the rate of increase. As a result for continuing solid demand, Co. noted that it is maintaining its program of refurbishing approximately 30 drilling rigs during 2006, including 17 that have already been completed so far in 2006.

Financial Data
(US$ in Thousands)

	6 Mos	3 Mos	12/31/2005	12/31/2004	12/31/2003	12/31/2002	12/31/2001	12/31/2000
Earnings Per Share	3.26	2.71	2.15	0.64	0.34	0.01	1.03	0.33
Cash Flow Per Share	3.89	3.55	2.70	1.33	1.00	0.83	1.66	0.71
Tang Book Value Per Share	8.37	8.24	7.35	5.38	4.75	4.29	4.13	3.55
Dividends Per Share	0.200	0.160	0.160	0.060	...	...	...	...
Dividend Payout %	6.13	5.90	7.44	9.38				
Income Statement								
Total Revenue	1,234,546	597,733	1,740,455	1,000,769	776,170	527,957	989,975	307,901
EBITDA	605,685	289,232	740,942	277,549	178,367	94,477	353,716	75,130
Depn & Amortn	91,030	43,549	159,218	106,100	91,034	91,216	86,159	33,133
Income Before Taxes	519,173	247,976	584,759	171,894	88,157	3,839	266,495	37,999
Income Taxes	188,914	89,407	212,019	63,161	32,362	1,670	102,333	14,244
Net Income	330,946	159,256	372,740	108,733	55,326	2,169	164,162	23,755
Average Shares	171,522	174,313	173,767	169,211	164,572	162,504	158,394	71,506
Balance Sheet								
Total Assets	1,942,195	2,029,210	1,795,781	1,322,911	1,075,830	942,509	869,642	410,586
Current Liabilities	270,033	327,761	255,409	150,076	108,447	75,152	89,286	56,878
Long-Term Obligations	...	...	...	...	...	...	...	19,939
Total Liabilities	453,545	507,172	428,770	315,372	255,759	204,953	182,500	107,780
Stockholders' Equity	1,488,650	1,522,038	1,367,011	1,007,539	820,071	737,556	687,142	302,806
Shares Outstanding	166,055	172,652	172,441	168,512	161,953	160,140	153,912	74,354
Statistical Record								
Return on Assets %	32.74	27.25	23.90	9.04	5.48	0.24	25.65	7.32
Return on Equity %	42.54	36.40	31.39	11.87	7.10	0.30	33.17	10.40
EBITDA Margin %	49.06	48.39	42.57	27.73	22.98	17.89	35.73	24.40
Net Margin %	26.81	26.64	21.42	10.86	7.13	0.41	16.58	7.72
Asset Turnover	1.29	1.15	1.12	0.83	0.77	0.58	1.55	0.95
Current Ratio	2.31	2.45	2.50	2.58	2.84	3.23	2.23	2.95
Debt to Equity	...	...	...	...	...	...	...	0.07
Price Range	38.33-25.51	38.33-23.03	36.31-17.58	20.21-14.67	18.30-12.79	17.06-9.54	20.22-5.84	19.09-6.19
P/E Ratio	11.76-7.83	14.14-8.50	16.89-8.18	31.58-22.92	53.82-37.60	N.M.	19.63-5.67	57.86-18.75
Average Yield %	0.63	0.52	0.57	0.34				

Address: 4510 Lamesa Highway, P.O. Drawer 1416, Snyder, TX 79549 Telephone: 915-574-6300 Fax: 915-573-0281	Web Site: www.patenergy.com Officers: Mark S. Siegel - Chmn. A. Glenn Patterson - Pres., C.O.O.	Auditors: PricewaterhouseCoopers LLP

PAYCHEX INC

Exchange	Symbol	Price	52Wk Range	Yield	P/E	Div Achiever
NMS	PAYX	$35.95 (8/31/2006)	43.18-32.80	1.78	29.47	17 Years

*7 Year Price Score 88.06 *NYSE Composite Index=100 *12 Month Price Score 90.55

Interim Earnings (Per Share)

Qtr.	Aug	Nov	Feb	May
2001-02	0.19	0.18	0.18	0.19
2002-03	0.20	0.20	0.19	0.19
2003-04	0.21	0.21	0.21	0.16
2004-05	0.23	0.23	0.24	0.27
2005-06	0.30	0.30	0.30	0.32

Interim Dividends (Per Share)

Amt	Decl	Ex	Rec	Pay
0.16Q	10/12/2005	10/28/2005	11/1/2005	11/15/2005
0.16Q	1/13/2006	1/30/2006	2/1/2006	2/15/2006
0.16Q	4/13/2006	4/27/2006	5/1/2006	5/15/2006
0.16Q	7/13/2006	7/28/2006	8/1/2006	8/15/2006

Indicated Div: $0.64 (Div. Reinv. Plan)

Valuation Analysis **Institutional Holding**

Forecast P/E	21.98	No of Institutions
	(9/9/2006)	471
Market Cap	$13.7 Billion	Shares
Book Value	1.7 Billion	249,733,280
Price/Book	8.26	% Held
Price/Sales	8.16	65.66

Business Summary: Accounting & Management Consulting Services (MIC: 12.2 SIC: 8721 NAIC: 541214)
Paychex provides payroll and integrated human resource and employee benefits outsourcing solutions for small- to medium-sized businesses in the U.S. Co. offers a comprehensive portfolio of payroll, payroll-related, and human resource products and services to meet the diverse needs of Co.'s client base. These include: payroll processing, payroll tax administration services, employee payment services, regulatory compliance services, comprehensive human resource administrative services, retirement services administration, workers' compensation insurance administration, employee benefits administration, time and attendance solutions, and other human resource products and services.

Recent Developments: For the year ended May 31 2006, net income increased 26.0% to $464.9 million from $368.8 million in the prior year. Revenues were $1.67 billion, up 15.9% from $1.45 billion the year before. Operating income was $649.6 million versus $533.8 million in the prior year, an increase of 21.7%. Indirect operating expenses increased 12.5% to $1.03 billion from $911.4 million in the equivalent prior-year period.

Prospects: For the full fiscal year ending May 31 2006, Co. is projecting total revenue growth of 14.0% to 16.0%, with payroll service revenue growth in the range of 9.0% to 11.0%, human resource services revenue growth in the range of 26.0% to 28.0% and service revenue growth of 12.0% to 14.0%. Additionally, Co. is projecting net income growth of between 24.0% and 26.0% for fiscal 2006, based on an effective income tax rate of approximately 31.5%. Lastly, Co. anticipates purchases of property and equipment for fiscal 2006 to be in the range of $75.0 million to $80.0 million, including anticipated purchases for printing equipment, communication system upgrades and branch expansions.

Financial Data
(US$ in Thousands)

	05/31/2006	05/31/2005	05/31/2004	05/31/2003	05/31/2002	05/31/2001	05/31/2000	05/31/1999
Earnings Per Share	1.22	0.97	0.80	0.78	0.73	0.68	0.51	0.37
Cash Flow Per Share	1.50	1.24	1.03	0.99	0.81	0.82	0.67	0.47
Tang Book Value Per Share	3.12	2.40	1.88	1.55	2.43	2.00	1.50	1.17
Dividends Per Share	0.610	0.510	0.470	0.440	0.420	0.330	0.220	0.147
Dividend Payout %	50.00	52.58	58.75	56.41	57.53	48.53	43.14	39.29
Income Statement								
Total Revenue	1,674,596	1,445,143	1,294,347	1,099,079	954,910	869,857	728,119	597,296
EBITDA	743,985	625,630	516,106	465,596	411,086	375,841	295,377	220,473
Depn & Amortn	94,414	91,855	82,791	64,555	47,392	39,139	36,484	32,911
Income Before Taxes	674,766	546,166	449,784	431,544	395,009	363,981	275,372	200,143
Income Taxes	209,852	177,317	146,834	138,092	120,478	109,112	85,365	61,044
Net Income	464,914	368,849	302,950	293,452	274,531	254,869	190,007	139,099
Average Shares	381,351	379,763	379,524	378,083	378,002	377,510	375,081	373,182
Balance Sheet								
Total Assets	5,549,302	4,379,116	3,950,203	3,690,783	2,953,075	2,907,196	2,455,577	1,873,101
Current Liabilities	3,838,372	2,941,824	2,721,903	2,587,525	2,023,406	2,143,842	1,886,945	1,432,336
Total Liabilities	3,894,459	2,993,441	2,750,230	2,613,412	2,029,094	2,149,354	1,892,145	1,437,301
Stockholders' Equity	1,654,843	1,385,675	1,199,973	1,077,371	923,981	757,842	563,432	435,800
Shares Outstanding	380,303	378,629	377,968	376,698	375,859	373,647	371,769	369,489
Statistical Record								
Return on Assets %	9.37	8.86	7.91	8.83	9.37	9.51	8.75	8.13
Return on Equity %	30.58	28.53	26.53	29.33	32.65	38.58	37.93	36.35
EBITDA Margin %	44.43	43.29	39.87	42.36	43.05	43.21	40.57	36.91
Net Margin %	27.76	25.52	23.41	26.70	28.75	29.30	26.10	23.29
Asset Turnover	0.34	0.35	0.34	0.33	0.33	0.32	0.34	0.35
Current Ratio	1.16	1.25	1.21	1.17	1.39	1.30	1.25	1.25
Price Range	43.18-28.88	38.84-28.88	40.14-28.52	35.00-20.55	42.00-29.28	59.69-31.44	36.88-16.58	24.06-16.53
P/E Ratio	35.39-23.67	40.04-29.77	50.17-35.65	44.87-26.35	57.53-40.11	87.78-46.24	72.30-32.52	65.02-44.67
Average Yield %	1.63	1.60	1.33	1.61	1.14	0.75	0.84	0.72

Address: 911 Panorama Trail South, Rochester, NY 14625-2396
Telephone: 585-385-6666
Fax: 585-383-3428

Web Site: www.paychex.com
Officers: B. Thomas Golisano - Chmn. Jonathan J. Judge - Pres., C.E.O.

Auditors: Ernst & Young LLP
Investor Contact: 585-383-3406
Transfer Agents: American Stock Transfer & Trust Co. New York. NY

PDL BIOPHARMA INC

Exchange	Symbol	Price	52Wk Range	Yield	P/E
NMS	PDLI	$19.70 (8/31/2006)	32.80-16.51	N/A	N/A

*7 Year Price Score 91.00 *NYSE Composite Index=100 *12 Month Price Score 67.56

Interim Earnings (Per Share)

Qtr.	Mar	Jun	Sep	Dec
2003	0.05	(0.45)	(0.20)	(0.78)
2004	(0.13)	(0.13)	(0.14)	(0.15)
2005	(0.87)	(0.03)	(0.37)	(0.36)
2006	(0.23)	(0.06)	...	...

Interim Dividends (Per Share)
No Dividends Paid

Valuation Analysis

Forecast P/E	118.06		
	(9/9/2006)		
Market Cap	$2.2 Billion		
Book Value	538.2 Million		
Price/Book	4.17		
Price/Sales	6.27		

Institutional Holding

No of Institutions	243
Shares	104,352,608
% Held	90.86

Business Summary: Biotechnology (MIC: 9.2 SIC: 2836 NAIC: 325414)

PDL BioPharma is a biopharmaceutical company focused on discovering, developing and commercializing therapies for severe or life-threatening illnesses. Co. markets its products in the acute-care hospital setting in the U.S. and Canada and generates royalties through licensing agreements with biotechnology and pharmaceutical companies based on its antibody humanization technology. Co. has also entered into collaborations with other pharmaceutical companies for joint development, manufacture and commercialization of certain of its investigational compounds. Co.'s research platform is focused on the discovery and development of antibodies for the treatment of cancer and autoimmune diseases.

Recent Developments: For the quarter ended June 30 2006, net loss amounted to $7.4 million versus a net loss of $3.4 million in the year-earlier quarter. Revenues were $104.3 million, up 28.8% from $81.0 million the year before. Operating loss was $8.2 million versus a loss of $2.5 million in the prior-year quarter. Direct operating expenses rose 6.7% to $21.5 million from $20.1 million in the comparable period the year before. Indirect operating expenses increased 43.7% to $91.0 million from $63.4 million in the equivalent prior-year period.

Prospects: Increases in both product sales and royalty revenue are driving substantial growth in Co.'s overall revenue. Looking forward, Co. is optimistic that sales revenue growth through at least 2008 will be driven in large part by the growth of sales of Cardene product lines. Meanwhile, despite results from its terlipressin phase 3 study that did not meet its primary endpoint in the treatment of type 1 hepatorenal syndrome (HRS), Co. is advancing its other clinical programs and is working to expand the pipeline with its antibody discovery and development activities.

Financial Data
(US$ in Thousands)

	6 Mos	3 Mos	12/31/2005	12/31/2004	12/31/2003	12/31/2002	12/31/2001	12/31/2000
Earnings Per Share	(1.02)	(0.99)	(1.60)	(0.56)	(1.40)	(0.16)	0.03	0.01
Cash Flow Per Share	0.68	0.38	0.30	(0.29)	(0.25)	(0.06)	0.03	0.08
Tang Book Value Per Share	0.92	0.79	0.63	3.98	4.43	6.11	6.31	6.13
Income Statement								
Total Revenue	195,536	90,460	279,654	96,024	66,686	46,373	79,535	63,056
EBITDA	10,652	(4,221)	(138,032)	(33,833)	(110,831)	(25,902)	...	...
Depn & Amortn	38,236	19,244	17,500	14,300	9,140	6,162	5,503	4,198
Income Before Taxes	(33,356)	(26,115)	(165,709)	(53,161)	(129,741)	(14,512)	...	...
Income Taxes	233	115	868	80	73	42	...	...
Net Income	(33,589)	(26,230)	(166,577)	(53,241)	(129,814)	(14,554)	2,647	647
Average Shares	113,539	112,472	104,326	94,982	92,478	88,865	92,889	88,562
Balance Sheet								
Total Assets	1,180,422	1,173,344	1,166,001	713,732	742,030	717,818	729,898	704,980
Current Liabilities	72,039	67,815	74,899	43,454	35,176	14,626	12,563	11,512
Long-Term Obligations	507,207	507,244	507,294	257,467	258,523	158,426	158,892	159,324
Total Liabilities	642,204	640,007	639,936	301,222	293,699	173,052	171,455	170,836
Stockholders' Equity	538,218	533,337	526,065	412,510	448,331	544,766	558,443	534,144
Shares Outstanding	113,891	113,469	112,062	95,857	93,886	89,179	88,499	87,152
Statistical Record								
Return on Assets %	N.M.	N.M.	N.M.	N.M.	N.M.	N.M.	0.37	0.15
Return on Equity %	N.M.	N.M.	N.M.	N.M.	N.M.	N.M.	0.48	0.18
EBITDA Margin %	5.45	N.M.	N.M.	N.M.	N.M.	N.M.	...	...
Net Margin %	N.M.	N.M.	N.M.	N.M.	N.M.	N.M.	3.33	1.03
Asset Turnover	0.32	0.30	0.30	0.13	0.09	0.06	0.11	0.14
Current Ratio	6.36	5.87	5.10	9.21	14.31	41.97	52.09	57.61
Debt to Equity	0.94	0.95	0.96	0.62	0.58	0.29	0.28	0.30
Price Range	32.80-17.10	32.80-15.14	29.92-13.85	27.14-15.10	18.92-6.98	32.80-7.40	45.20-17.38	81.81-14.88

Address: 34801 Campus Drive, Fremont, CA 94555 **Telephone:** 510-574-1400 **Fax:** 510-574-1500	**Web Site:** www.pdl.com **Officers:** Max Link - Chmn. Mark McDade - C.E.O.	**Auditors:** ERNST & YOUNG LLP

PEOPLE'S BANK (BRIDGEPORT, CT)

Exchange	Symbol	Price	52Wk Range	Yield	P/E	Div Achiever
NMS	PBCT	$36.15 (8/31/2006)	37.10-28.47	2.77	36.52	12 Years

*7 Year Price Score 151.65 *NYSE Composite Index=100 *12 Month Price Score 106.27

Interim Earnings (Per Share)

Qtr.	Mar	Jun	Sep	Dec
2003	0.12	0.11	0.11	0.12
2004	0.85	0.18	0.19	0.20
2005	0.22	0.26	0.24	0.25
2006	0.24	...	...	...

Interim Dividends (Per Share)

Amt	Decl	Ex	Rec	Pay
0.22Q	10/20/2005	10/28/2005	11/1/2005	11/15/2005
0.22Q	1/20/2006	1/30/2006	2/1/2006	2/15/2006
0.25Q	4/20/2006	4/27/2006	5/1/2006	5/15/2006
0.25Q	7/20/2006	7/28/2006	8/1/2006	8/15/2006

Indicated Div: $1.00 (Div. Reinv. Plan)

Valuation Analysis

		Institutional Holding	
Forecast P/E	37.08	No of Institutions	
	(9/9/2006)	144	
Market Cap	$5.1 Billion	Shares	34,196,132
Book Value	1.3 Billion	% Held	24.74
Price/Book	3.92		
Price/Sales	7.30		

Business Summary: Commercial Banking (MIC: 8.1 SIC: 6022 NAIC: 522110)

People's Bank is a state-chartered stock savings bank offering a range of financial services to individual, corporate and municipal customers, primarily in Connecticut. Co. provides traditional banking services of accepting deposits and originating loans, as well as specialized financial services through its subsidiaries, including: brokerage, financial advisory services and life insurance; equipment leasing and financing; asset management; and insurance services. As of Dec 31 2005, Co.'s operations included eight financial centers, 67 traditional branches, 70 supermarket branches, and eight limited-service branches. As of Dec 31 2005, Co. had total assets of $10.93 billion.

Recent Developments: For the quarter ended Mar 31 2006, income from continuing operations increased 13.8% to $33.9 million from $29.8 million in the year-earlier quarter. Net income increased 10.8% to $34.8 million from $31.4 million in the year-earlier quarter. Net interest income increased 3.1% to $94.0 million from $91.2 million in the year-earlier quarter. Credit for loan losses was $2.3 million versus a provision for loan losses of $1.3 million in the prior-year quarter. Non-interest income rose 12.1% to $41.8 million from $37.3 million, while non-interest expense advanced 7.0% to $87.0 million.

Prospects: On May 26 2006, Co. announced that it intends to switch from a state-charted savings bank to a federally-chartered savings bank. The federal charter positions Co. more competitively to pursue business expansion across state lines. Concurrently, Co. announced plans to open at least 15 branches in Westchester County, NY in the next three years at locations to be announced. Meanwhile, Co. continues to generate loan growth across its core lending businesses and its net interest margin is benefiting from a combination of its asset sensitive position and ongoing substitution of securities with higher-yielding loans.

Financial Data
(US$ in Thousands)

	3 Mos	12/31/2005	12/31/2004	12/31/2003	12/31/2002	12/31/2001	12/31/2000	12/31/1999
Earnings Per Share	0.99	0.97	1.42	0.46	0.40	0.55	0.79	0.80
Cash Flow Per Share	0.69	0.66	2.94	1.05	0.26	0.67	1.56	1.27
Tang Book Value Per Share	8.47	8.35	7.74	6.37	5.95	5.92	5.49	4.71
Dividends Per Share	0.880	0.853	0.753	0.680	0.631	0.596	0.533	0.458
Dividend Payout %	88.89	87.97	53.05	148.54	157.78	108.94	67.80	56.91
Income Statement								
Interest Income	137,800	507,900	437,200	514,700	614,200	727,100	766,800	666,800
Interest Expense	43,800	138,200	110,100	194,300	263,000	373,100	381,700	328,900
Net Interest Income	94,000	369,700	327,100	320,400	351,200	354,000	385,100	337,900
Provision for Losses	(2,300)	8,600	13,300	48,600	77,700	101,100	59,900	54,500
Non-Interest Income	41,800	171,800	150,700	251,000	247,900	320,500	293,000	300,800
Non-Interest Expense	87,000	342,900	478,700	435,900	441,000	440,500	452,700	413,800
Income Before Taxes	51,100	190,000	(14,200)	86,900	80,400	132,900	165,500	170,400
Income Taxes	17,200	64,100	(8,600)	23,100	25,000	46,200	57,100	58,400
Net Income	34,800	137,100	199,700	63,800	55,400	75,800	108,400	112,000
Average Shares	142,000	141,700	140,850	139,275	138,825	138,600	138,150	139,500
Balance Sheet								
Net Loans & Leases	8,685,300	8,497,900	7,860,900	8,121,800	7,336,200	6,931,000	7,344,700	6,969,600
Total Assets	11,081,400	10,932,500	10,717,900	11,671,500	12,260,600	11,890,600	11,570,900	10,738,100
Total Deposits	9,252,400	9,082,600	8,862,000	8,714,000	8,426,100	7,983,400	7,761,300	7,191,100
Total Liabilities	9,774,700	9,643,900	9,518,100	10,669,500	11,321,000	10,955,600	10,689,100	9,956,400
Stockholders' Equity	1,306,400	1,288,600	1,199,800	1,002,000	939,600	935,000	881,800	781,700
Shares Outstanding	141,700	141,600	140,850	139,500	138,825	138,375	137,925	137,475
Statistical Record								
Return on Assets %	1.28	1.27	1.78	0.53	0.46	0.65	0.97	1.08
Return on Equity %	11.14	11.02	18.09	6.57	5.91	8.34	13.00	13.71
Net Interest Margin %	68.21	72.79	74.82	62.25	57.18	48.69	50.22	50.67
Efficiency Ratio %	48.44	50.45	81.43	56.93	51.15	42.05	42.72	42.77
Loans to Deposits	0.94	0.94	0.89	0.93	0.87	0.87	0.95	0.97
Price Range	33.61-26.43	33.36-24.33	29.50-14.47	15.06-10.88	12.40-9.22	12.56-9.74	11.92-7.56	14.19-8.89
P/E Ratio	33.95-26.70	34.39-25.09	20.77-10.19	32.74-23.66	31.00-23.06	22.83-16.98	15.08-9.56	17.74-11.11
Average Yield %	2.88	2.94	3.54	5.34	5.83	5.61	5.86	3.80

Address: 850 Main Street, Bridgeport, CT 06604 Telephone: 203-338-7171 Fax: 203-338-2545	Web Site: www.peoples.com Officers: John A. Klein - Chmn., Pres., C.E.O. Jacinta A. Coleman - Exec. V.P., Chief Info. Off.	Auditors: KPMG LLP Investor Contact: 203-338-4114 Transfer Agents: Mellon Investor Services, LLC, Ridgefield Park, NJ

PERFORMANCE FOOD GROUP CO.

Exchange	Symbol	Price	52Wk Range	Yield	P/E
NMS	PFGC	$24.61 (8/31/2006)	33.44-24.29	N/A	16.52

*7 Year Price Score 83.93 *NYSE Composite Index=100 *12 Month Price Score 91.09

Interim Earnings (Per Share)

Qtr.	Mar	Jun	Sep	Dec
2003	0.35	0.49	0.44	0.26
2004	0.16	0.39	0.37	0.18
2005	0.29	4.28	0.27	0.66
2006	0.16	0.35	...	...

Interim Dividends (Per Share)

Amt	Decl	Ex	Rec	Pay
100%	4/11/2001	5/1/2001	4/23/2001	4/30/2001

Valuation Analysis

		Institutional Holding	
Forecast P/E	20.06	No of Institutions	
	(9/9/2006)	173	
Market Cap	$856.8 Million	Shares	
Book Value	763.5 Million	38,581,408	
Price/Book	1.12	% Held	
Price/Sales	0.15	N/A	

Business Summary: Retail - Food & Beverage (MIC: 5.3 SIC: 5141 NAIC: 424420)

Performance Food Group markets and distributes national and private label food and food-related products to foodservice customers. Co.'s Broadline distribution segment markets and distributes more than 63,000 national and proprietary brand food and non-food products to more than 43,000 customers, including street customers, such as independent restaurants, and certain corporate-owned and franchisee locations of chains such as Burger King, Church's, Compass, Popeye's and Subway. Co.'s Customized distribution segment focuses on serving casual and family dining chain restaurants such as Cracker Barrel Old Country Store, Outback Steakhouse, Ruby Tuesday and T.G.I. Friday's.

Recent Developments: For the quarter ended July 1 2006, income from continuing operations was unchanged at $12.2 million compared with the year-earlier quarter. Net income decreased 94.0% to $12.2 million from $203.8 million in the year-earlier quarter. Revenues were $1.45 billion, down 0.6% from $1.46 billion the year before. Operating income was $21.5 million versus $22.0 million in the prior-year quarter, a decrease of 1.9%. Direct operating expenses declined 1.0% to $1.25 billion from $1.27 billion in the comparable period the year before. Indirect operating expenses increased 2.5% to $171.7 million from $167.4 million in the equivalent prior-year period.

Prospects: Going forward, Co. intends to be aggressive in implementing its strategy to grow higher margin street business while maintaining its focus on improving productivity by utilizing new technologies and standardization programs, as well as implementing its procurement initiatives. Based on current business trends, Co. expects net earnings to be in the range of $0.32 to $0.36 per diluted share for the third quarter of 2006. For full-year 2006, Co. projects net earnings to be in the range of $1.22 to $1.30 per diluted share, which reflects its anticipated stock compensation expense for the year of about $5.0 million to $5.5 million, or approximately $0.09 to $0.10 per share.

Financial Data
(US$ in Thousands)

	6 Mos	3 Mos	12/31/2005	01/01/2005	01/03/2004	12/28/2002	12/29/2001	12/30/2000
Earnings Per Share	1.49	5.37	5.64	1.11	1.54	1.42	1.03	0.91
Cash Flow Per Share	0.48	1.24	1.77	2.51	2.74	2.66	4.36	0.52
Tang Book Value Per Share	10.27	9.84	10.36	2.20	0.52	N.M.	0.09	3.34
Income Statement								
Total Revenue	2,917,520	1,469,493	5,721,372	6,148,923	5,519,811	4,438,383	3,237,248	2,605,468
EBITDA	42,922	16,035	92,705	161,587	191,397	169,987	106,083	67,826
Depn & Amortn	14,016	6,863	27,018	60,082	52,611	44,862	31,981	17,877
Income Before Taxes	29,044	9,290	67,092	84,676	119,663	106,362	65,295	43,356
Income Taxes	11,202	3,616	25,328	32,118	45,472	39,886	24,812	16,475
Net Income	17,824	5,642	247,138	52,558	74,191	66,476	40,483	26,881
Average Shares	34,797	34,919	43,795	47,181	53,002	52,047	39,328	29,538
Balance Sheet								
Total Assets	1,293,226	1,299,443	1,312,290	1,827,765	1,736,468	1,617,717	1,277,791	709,696
Current Liabilities	482,278	504,599	489,124	561,095	468,924	448,064	348,034	227,786
Long-Term Obligations	2,961	3,105	3,250	278,584	353,919	370,095	270,594	114,492
Total Liabilities	529,680	552,360	535,773	953,452	932,653	902,848	669,594	351,979
Stockholders' Equity	763,546	747,083	776,517	874,313	803,815	714,869	608,197	357,717
Shares Outstanding	34,816	34,569	35,581	46,770	45,862	45,275	43,768	35,480
Statistical Record								
Return on Assets %	3.22	15.13	15.78	2.96	4.35	4.60	4.08	4.60
Return on Equity %	5.34	29.20	30.02	6.28	9.61	10.08	8.41	9.85
EBITDA Margin %	1.47	1.09	1.62	2.63	3.47	3.83	3.28	2.60
Net Margin %	0.61	0.38	4.32	0.85	1.34	1.50	1.25	1.03
Asset Turnover	3.74	3.66	3.65	3.46	3.24	3.07	3.27	4.46
Current Ratio	1.25	1.22	1.29	1.15	1.24	1.18	1.20	1.42
Debt to Equity	N.M.	N.M.	N.M.	0.32	0.44	0.52	0.44	0.32
Price Range	33.44-25.65	32.26-25.65	31.53-23.97	37.92-21.04	41.15-26.06	38.80-29.19	36.10-22.44	28.38-9.78
P/E Ratio	22.44-17.21	6.01-4.78	5.59-4.25	34.16-18.95	26.72-16.92	27.32-20.56	35.05-21.78	31.18-10.75

Address: 12500 West Creek Parkway, Richmond, VA 23238 **Telephone:** 804-484-7700 **Fax:** 804-484-7701	**Web Site:** www.pfgc.com **Officers:** Robert C. Sledd - Chmn., Pres., C.E.O. John D. Austin - Sr. V.P., C.F.O.	**Auditors:** KPMG LLP **Investor Contact:** 804-484-7700 **Transfer Agents:** American Stock Transfer & Trust Company

PERRIGO COMPANY

Exchange	Symbol	Price	52Wk Range	Yield	P/E
NMS	PRGO	$16.14 (8/31/2006)	16.84-12.86	1.05	21.24

*7 Year Price Score 91.52 *NYSE Composite Index=100 *12 Month Price Score 99.34

Interim Earnings (Per Share)

Qtr.	Sep	Dec	Mar	Jun
2001-02	0.17	0.22	0.26	0.02
2002-03	0.28	0.24	0.20	0.06
2003-04	0.23	0.53	0.24	0.10
2004-05	0.24	0.22	(5.15)	0.24
2005-06	0.14	0.27	0.22	0.13

Interim Dividends (Per Share)

Amt	Decl	Ex	Rec	Pay
0.043Q	10/28/2005	11/22/2005	11/25/2005	12/20/2005
0.043Q	2/15/2006	2/22/2006	2/24/2006	3/21/2006
0.043Q	5/12/2006	5/24/2006	5/26/2006	6/20/2006
0.043Q	8/11/2006	8/23/2006	8/25/2006	9/19/2006

Indicated Div: $0.17

Valuation Analysis

Forecast P/E 15.45 (9/9/2006)
Market Cap $1.5 Billion
Book Value 640.7 Million
Price/Book 2.34
Price/Sales 1.10

Institutional Holding

No of Institutions 135
Shares 65,442,812
% Held 70.60

Business Summary: Pharmaceuticals (MIC: 9.1 SIC: 2834 NAIC: 325412)

Perrigo is a global healthcare supplier and a manufacturer of over-the-counter pharmaceutical and nutritional products for the store brand market. Co. also develops and manufactures generic prescription (Rx) drugs, active pharmaceutical ingredients (API) and consumer products. Co.'s primary markets and locations of manufacturing and logistics operations are the United States, Israel, Mexico and the United Kingdom. Co. has three reportable segments, aligned primarily by product: Consumer Healthcare, Rx Pharmaceuticals and API. Additionally, Co. has an Other category that includes two operating segments.

Recent Developments: For the year ended July 1 2006, net income amounted to $71.4 million versus a net loss of $353.0 million in the prior year. Revenues were $1.37 billion, up 33.5% from $1.02 billion the year before. Operating income was $111.3 million versus a loss of $330.5 million in the prior year. Direct operating expenses rose 26.9% to $969.1 million from $763.7 million in the comparable period the year before. Indirect operating expenses decreased 51.5% to $286.4 million from $590.9 million in the equivalent prior-year period.

Prospects: During fiscal 2007, Co. expects increased pricing and margin pressure in the market on some of its existing core products. Going forward, investment for new product research and development is expected to increase focusing on complex, high-barrier niche products that will be key growth driver of Co.'s business. For the fiscal year ending Jul 2007, Co. expects sales for its generic prescription pharmaceuticals, active pharmaceutical ingredients and Other Israeli businesses to increase to about $400.0 million while sales for its consumer healthcare could exceed $1.00 billion. Co. also expects operating earnings of $0.86 to $0.91 per share, excluding $0.02 per share of restructuring costs.

Financial Data
(US$ in Thousands)

	07/01/2006	06/25/2005	06/26/2004	06/28/2003	06/29/2002	06/30/2001	07/01/2000	07/03/1999
Earnings Per Share	0.76	(4.57)	1.11	0.76	0.67	0.37	0.26	0.02
Cash Flow Per Share	1.34	1.01	1.69	1.15	1.43	0.93	1.61	(0.21)
Tang Book Value Per Share	3.83	3.12	7.06	5.89	5.24	4.57	4.54	...
Dividends Per Share	0.168	0.155	0.130	0.050	...	...	...	...
Dividend Payout %	22.04	...	11.71	6.58	...	...	...	...
Income Statement								
Total Revenue	1,366,821	1,024,098	898,204	825,987	826,322	753,488	738,555	877,587
EBITDA	177,746	(295,880)	134,435	112,384	113,967	66,881	52,730	25,170
Depn & Amortn	56,604	34,813	28,452	26,126	25,613	23,022	22,245	21,156
Income Before Taxes	105,935	(330,693)	105,983	86,258	88,354	43,859	30,485	4,014
Income Taxes	34,535	22,290	25,416	32,210	38,157	16,203	11,187	2,468
Net Income	71,400	(352,983)	80,567	54,048	50,197	27,656	19,298	1,546
Average Shares	94,105	77,313	72,289	71,158	75,113	74,566	73,593	73,707
Balance Sheet								
Total Assets	1,750,624	1,704,976	759,094	643,970	593,787	575,912	486,064	615,858
Current Liabilities	371,431	340,542	187,486	166,542	154,934	171,759	113,920	133,170
Long-Term Obligations	621,717	656,128	...	...	...	...	...	135,026
Total Liabilities	1,109,880	1,114,139	222,862	195,546	177,643	190,037	134,304	283,439
Stockholders' Equity	640,744	590,837	536,232	448,424	416,144	385,875	351,760	332,419
Shares Outstanding	92,922	93,903	70,882	70,034	72,550	74,072	73,489	...
Statistical Record								
Return on Assets %	4.07	N.M.	11.52	8.76	8.61	5.22	3.51	0.25
Return on Equity %	11.41	N.M.	16.41	12.54	12.55	7.52	5.66	0.45
EBITDA Margin %	13.00	N.M.	14.97	13.61	13.79	8.88	7.14	2.87
Net Margin %	5.22	N.M.	8.97	6.54	6.07	3.67	2.61	0.18
Asset Turnover	0.78	0.83	1.28	1.34	1.42	1.42	1.34	1.44
Current Ratio	1.77	1.79	2.52	2.28	2.21	1.82	2.36	2.87
Debt to Equity	0.97	1.11	...	...	...	...	...	0.41
Price Range	16.84-12.86	21.48-13.90	23.19-12.73	16.26-9.47	18.29-10.80	16.69-5.94	9.06-5.16	10.13-7.25
P/E Ratio	22.16-16.92	...	20.89-11.47	21.39-12.46	27.30-16.12	45.11-16.05	34.86-19.83	506.25-362.50
Average Yield %	1.12	0.86	0.77	0.41	...	...	...	...

Address: 515 Eastern Avenue, Allegan, MI 49010
Telephone: 269-673-8451
Fax: 269-673-7535

Web Site: www.perrigo.com
Officers: David T. Gibbons - Chmn., Pres., C.E.O.
Moshe Arkin - Vice-Chmn., Gen. Mgr.

Auditors: BDO SEIDMAN, LLP

PETSMART, INC.

Exchange	Symbol	Price	52Wk Range	Yield	P/E
NMS	PETM	$25.10 (8/31/2006)	29.18-21.31	0.48	20.08

*7 Year Price Score 117.78 *NYSE Composite Index=100 *12 Month Price Score 93.85

Interim Earnings (Per Share)

Qtr.	Apr	Jul	Oct	Jan
2003-04	0.17	0.19	0.21	0.39
2004-05	0.24	0.23	0.24	0.43
2005-06	0.30	0.24	0.21	0.49
2006-07	0.30	0.25	...	...

Interim Dividends (Per Share)

Amt	Decl	Ex	Rec	Pay
0.03Q	9/21/2005	10/27/2005	10/31/2005	11/18/2005
0.03Q	12/15/2005	1/25/2006	1/27/2006	2/10/2006
0.03Q	3/30/2006	4/26/2006	4/28/2006	5/12/2006
0.03Q	7/7/2006	7/26/2006	7/28/2006	8/11/2006

Indicated Div: $0.12

Valuation Analysis

		Institutional Holding	
Forecast P/E	16.62	No of Institutions	278
	(9/9/2006)		
Market Cap	$3.5 Billion	Shares	119,365,976
Book Value	1.0 Billion	% Held	85.20
Price/Book	3.42		
Price/Sales	0.88		

Business Summary: Retail - Miscellaneous (MIC: 5.11 SIC: 5999 NAIC: 453910)

PETsMART is engaged in the business of providing products and services for pets, including grooming, pet training, boarding and day camp. Co. also manages its direct marketing channels via online, which includes PetSmart.com, as well as an e-commerce site specifically for equine products and an equine catalog. In addition, Co. has PetPerks loyalty campaign that allows it to target various offers directly to its customers. As of Jan 29 2006, Co. operated 826 retail stores in North America, of which 525 of its stores had full-service veterinary care, operated in partnership with Banfield, The Pet Hospital.

Recent Developments: For the quarter ended July 30 2006, net income decreased 3.1% to $34.6 million from $35.7 million in the year-earlier quarter. Revenues were $1.02 billion, up 13.5% from $899.1 million in the year before. Operating income was $62.0 million versus $61.1 million in the prior-year quarter, an increase of 1.4%. Direct operating expenses rose 15.9% to $715.8 million from $617.4 million in the comparable period the year before. Indirect operating expenses increased 10.1% to $242.9 million from $220.6 million in the equivalent prior-year period.

Prospects: Co. has recently announced a plan to accelerate certain investments originally scheduled for fiscal 2007 and fiscal 2008, into fiscal 2006 ending Jan 2007. These investments are focused on building a robust infrastructure and enhancing Co.'s ability to grow and gain additional market presence. Looking ahead to the fiscal year ending Jan 2007, Co. expects comparable store sales growth in the mid-single digits, along with earnings per share of $1.30 to $1.33. In addition, Co. expects to open 45 to 48 net new stores, 15 net new PetsHotels and one Doggie Day Camp during the remainder of the fiscal year ending Jan 2007.

Financial Data
(US$ in Thousands)

	6 Mos	3 Mos	01/29/2006	01/30/2005	02/01/2004	02/02/2003	02/03/2002	01/28/2001
Earnings Per Share	1.25	1.24	1.25	1.14	0.95	0.63	0.35	(0.28)
Cash Flow Per Share	2.57	2.07	2.44	1.97	1.74	1.67	1.67	1.00
Tang Book Value Per Share	7.22	6.95	6.65	6.42	5.73	4.75	2.89	2.52
Dividends Per Share	0.120	0.120	0.120	0.120	0.040	...	...	...
Dividend Payout %	9.58	9.65	9.60	10.53	4.21	...	...	...
Income Statement								
Total Revenue	2,032,138	1,011,529	3,760,499	3,363,452	2,996,051	2,695,184	2,501,012	2,224,222
EBITDA	213,494	112,563	451,005	393,627	339,876	249,114	128,191	32,394
Depn & Amortn	76,835	37,884	139,625	112,648	95,948	77,268	58,709	44,943
Income Before Taxes	120,606	67,946	289,209	264,444	227,832	153,813	44,053	(33,165)
Income Taxes	44,212	26,182	106,719	93,216	88,283	64,958	7,496	851
Net Income	76,394	41,764	182,490	171,228	139,549	88,855	39,567	(30,904)
Average Shares	141,237	141,088	145,577	149,652	147,255	141,682	114,067	111,494
Balance Sheet								
Total Assets	2,011,699	1,930,543	1,863,691	1,655,454	1,376,695	1,158,856	961,103	782,147
Current Liabilities	476,438	450,338	462,730	350,921	339,814	288,464	276,174	235,277
Long-Term Obligations	401,246	384,306	351,564	244,150	165,738	159,443	329,688	242,804
Total Liabilities	984,176	941,808	922,941	704,460	537,540	477,657	635,297	498,668
Stockholders' Equity	1,027,523	988,735	940,750	950,994	839,155	681,199	325,806	280,579
Shares Outstanding	140,179	140,061	138,997	145,430	143,407	139,914	112,609	111,403
Statistical Record								
Return on Assets %	9.37	9.93	10.40	11.33	11.04	8.41	4.47	N.M.
Return on Equity %	17.86	18.83	19.35	19.18	18.41	17.70	12.84	N.M.
EBITDA Margin %	10.51	11.13	11.99	11.70	11.34	9.24	5.13	1.46
Net Margin %	3.76	4.13	4.85	5.09	4.66	3.30	1.58	N.M.
Asset Turnover	2.10	2.14	2.14	2.22	2.37	2.55	2.82	2.76
Current Ratio	1.91	1.92	1.82	2.34	2.02	2.02	1.73	1.83
Debt to Equity	0.39	0.39	0.37	0.26	0.20	0.23	1.01	0.87
Price Range	29.57-21.31	32.96-21.31	32.96-21.31	35.90-23.36	28.59-10.53	20.92-10.30	10.96-2.66	5.00-2.38
P/E Ratio	23.66-17.05	26.58-17.19	26.37-17.05	31.49-20.49	30.09-11.08	33.21-16.35	31.31-7.59	...
Average Yield %	0.47	0.45	0.44	0.40	0.20	...	...	...

Address: 19601 North 27th Avenue, Phoenix, AZ 85027
Telephone: 623-580-6100
Fax: 623-395-6517
Web Site: www.petsmart.com
Officers: Philip L. Francis - Chmn., C.E.O. Robert F. Moran - Pres., C.O.O.
Auditors: Deloitte & Touche LLP
Investor Contact: 623-587-2025
Transfer Agents: Wells Fargo Shareowner Services, St. Paul, MN

PHARMACEUTICAL PRODUCT DEVELOPMENT INC.

Exchange	Symbol	Price	52Wk Range	Yield	P/E
NMS	PPDI	$38.12 (8/31/2006)	39.99-27.50	0.26	29.78

*7 Year Price Score 163.85 *NYSE Composite Index=100 *12 Month Price Score 110.04

Interim Earnings (Per Share)

Qtr.	Mar	Jun	Sep	Dec
2003	0.19	0.15	0.22	(0.15)
2004	0.22	0.20	0.22	0.23
2005	0.31	0.20	0.33	0.29
2006	0.35	0.31	...	...

Interim Dividends (Per Share)

Amt	Decl	Ex	Rec	Pay
2-for-1	2/8/2006	3/1/2006	2/17/2006	2/28/2006
0.025Q	2/23/2006	3/9/2006	3/13/2006	3/27/2006
0.025Q	5/18/2006	6/12/2006	6/14/2006	6/28/2006
0.025Q	8/25/2006	9/12/2006	9/14/2006	9/28/2006

Indicated Div: $0.10

Valuation Analysis

Forecast P/E	27.25
	(9/9/2006)
Market Cap	$4.5 Billion
Book Value	850.2 Million
Price/Book	5.25
Price/Sales	3.86

Institutional Holding

No of Institutions	242
Shares	90,044,536
% Held	76.97

Business Summary: Biotechnology (MIC: 9.2 SIC: 8731 NAIC: 541710)

Pharmaceutical Product Development is a global contract research organization that operates in two segments: The Discovery Sciences Group focuses on the discovery research segment of the biopharmaceutical research and development outsourcing market. The Development Group provides development services, either individually or as an integrated package, to meet clients' needs. In addition, for marketed drugs, biologics and devices, Co. offers support services, such as product launch services, medical information, patient compliance programs, patient and disease registry programs, product safety and pharmacovigilance, Phase IV monitored studies and prescription-to-over-the-counter programs.

Recent Developments: For the quarter ended June 30 2006, net income increased 75.1% to $36.4 million from $20.8 million in the year-earlier quarter. Revenues were $309.0 million, up 26.0% from $245.1 million the year before. Operating income was $49.0 million versus $29.1 million in the prior-year quarter, an increase of 68.4%. Direct operating expenses rose 26.1% to $167.6 million from $132.9 million in the comparable period the year before. Indirect operating expenses increased 11.1% to $92.3 million from $83.1 million in the equivalent prior-year period.

Prospects: Co.'s prospects appear promising, reflecting the continuing strength in its market and its performance across the continuum of global drug development markets and service segments. With current backlog of more than $2.00 billion as of Jun 30 2006 and the continued progress of the Phase III development program for the Takeda DPP4 compound, Co. remains confident in driving value through its platform of drug discovery and development services going forward. Furthermore, Co. expects continuing growth in its Latin American and European Phase II and IV units for the remaining of 2006 and continues to plan expansions and new services for its GMP laboratory facilities over the next two years.

Financial Data
(US$ in Thousands)

	6 Mos	3 Mos	12/31/2005	12/31/2004	12/31/2003	12/31/2002	12/31/2001	12/31/2000
Earnings Per Share	1.28	1.18	1.13	0.87	0.41	0.36	0.47	0.32
Cash Flow Per Share	1.78	1.48	1.66	1.59	0.12	0.97	0.98	0.62
Tang Book Value Per Share	5.44	5.13	4.57	3.99	2.97	2.63	2.79	2.22
Dividends Per Share	0.575	0.550	0.525	...	...	...	...	...
Dividend Payout %	44.92	46.81	46.46	...	...	...	...	...
Income Statement								
Total Revenue	608,322	299,369	1,037,090	841,256	726,983	608,657	431,541	345,318
EBITDA	133,841	72,073	231,231	177,698	98,725	100,929	93,808	62,761
Depn & Amortn	22,706	11,296	41,231	29,854	28,968	24,480	20,747	17,233
Income Before Taxes	117,437	63,887	197,729	149,845	71,245	78,647	78,006	50,831
Income Taxes	39,177	22,041	66,246	50,957	24,935	38,645	28,747	18,521
Net Income	78,260	41,846	131,483	98,888	46,310	39,897	49,167	32,310
Average Shares	118,418	117,973	116,434	113,808	112,572	110,686	104,988	100,708
Balance Sheet								
Total Assets	1,320,674	1,232,676	1,151,148	975,201	775,467	692,120	465,400	344,915
Current Liabilities	397,369	361,291	355,246	317,960	241,345	227,798	157,376	106,830
Long-Term Obligations	39,315	29,543	22,695	6,371	6,281	6,649	1,871	1,353
Total Liabilities	470,507	422,090	408,924	339,891	262,946	251,783	162,765	110,972
Stockholders' Equity	850,167	810,586	742,224	635,310	512,521	440,337	302,635	233,943
Shares Outstanding	116,985	116,628	115,998	113,236	112,100	110,872	105,860	101,339
Statistical Record								
Return on Assets %	12.66	12.23	12.37	11.27	6.31	6.89	12.14	10.17
Return on Equity %	19.33	18.56	19.09	17.18	9.72	10.74	18.33	15.11
EBITDA Margin %	22.00	24.07	22.30	21.12	13.58	16.58	21.74	18.17
Net Margin %	12.86	13.98	12.68	11.75	6.37	6.55	11.39	9.36
Asset Turnover	0.97	0.97	0.98	0.96	0.99	1.05	1.07	1.09
Current Ratio	2.00	2.03	1.92	1.81	1.65	1.82	1.97	2.00
Debt to Equity	0.05	0.04	0.03	0.01	0.01	0.02	0.01	0.01
Price Range	37.75-23.43	35.82-22.11	32.08-20.02	21.70-13.48	15.69-11.90	17.52-8.40	18.95-8.84	13.97-2.94
P/E Ratio	29.49-18.30	30.36-18.73	28.38-17.72	24.94-15.50	38.26-29.01	48.67-23.33	40.31-18.82	43.65-9.18
Average Yield %	1.82	1.91	2.04	...	...	...	...	...

| Address: 3151 South 17th Street, Wilmington, NC 28412
Telephone: 910-251-0081
Fax: 910-762-5820 | Web Site: www.PPDI.com
Officers: Fredric N. Eshelman Ph. D. - Vice-Chmn., C.E.O. Fred B. Davenport Jr. - Pres., Asst. Sec. | Auditors: Deloitte & Touche LLP
Investor Contact: 910-251-0081
Transfer Agents: Wachovia Bank, N.A. |

PLEXUS CORP.

Exchange	Symbol	Price	52Wk Range	Yield	P/E
NMS	PLXS	$19.82 (8/31/2006)	46.91-16.23	N/A	13.48

*7 Year Price Score 95.72 *NYSE Composite Index=100 *12 Month Price Score 87.32

Interim Earnings (Per Share)

Qtr.	Dec	Mar	Jun	Sep
2002-03	(1.05)	(0.12)	(0.35)	(0.09)
2003-04	0.06	0.08	(0.02)	(0.86)
2004-05	0.07	(0.10)	(0.50)	0.24
2005-06	0.31	0.40	0.53	...

Interim Dividends (Per Share)
No Dividends Paid

Valuation Analysis
Forecast P/E	10.95
	(9/9/2006)
Market Cap	$915.6 Million
Book Value	437.0 Million
Price/Book	2.09
Price/Sales	0.66

Institutional Holding
No of Institutions	179
Shares	40,597,928
% Held	87.86

Business Summary: Electrical (MIC: 11.14 SIC: 3672 NAIC: 334412)
Plexus is a participant in the Electronics Manufacturing Services industry. Co. provides product realization services to original equipment manufacturers, and other technology companies in the wireline/networking, wireless infrastructure, medical, industrial/commercial, and defense/security/aerospace industries and high technology manufacturing and test services. Co. offers its customers the ability to outsource all stages of product realization, including development and design, materials procurement and management, prototyping and new product introduction, testing, manufacturing, product configuration, direct order fulfillment, logistics and test/repair.

Recent Developments: For the quarter ended July 1 2006, net income amounted to $25.1 million versus a net loss of $21.5 million in the year-earlier quarter. Revenues were $397.4 million, up 26.7% from $313.7 million the year before. Operating income was $24.0 million versus a loss of $19.8 million in the prior-year quarter. Direct operating expenses rose 22.8% to $351.9 million from $286.6 million in the comparable period the year before. Indirect operating expenses decreased 54.1% to $21.6 million from $46.9 million in the equivalent prior-year period.

Prospects: Based on expected demand and estimates of new program wins, including the new program in its defense/security/ aerospace sector, Co projects revenues of $390.0 million to $405.0 million for the fourth fiscal quarter ending Sep 2006; providing top-line growth of 18.3% to 19.5% for fiscal 2006. Co. also projects diluted earnings per share of $0.46 to $0.50, before any restructuring or special items but including charges related to stock-based compensation and the effect of the FIN 47. Separately, on Jul 18 2006, Co. announced a new operating lease for an extension to its existing production facility in China, allowing it to meet the expected needs of existing and new global customers.

Financial Data
(US$ in Thousands)

	9 Mos	6 Mos	3 Mos	10/01/2005	09/30/2004	09/30/2003	09/30/2002	09/30/2001
Earnings Per Share	1.47	0.45	(0.05)	(0.29)	(0.74)	(1.61)	(0.10)	0.91
Cash Flow Per Share	2.05	2.83	2.37	1.88	(0.50)	(0.47)	3.11	2.90
Tang Book Value Per Share	9.30	8.55	7.94	7.61	7.35	7.95	8.70	8.53
Income Statement								
Total Revenue	1,063,615	666,217	328,306	1,228,882	1,040,858	807,837	883,603	1,062,304
EBITDA	73,580	43,298	20,676	16,363	36,140	(41,772)	34,599	101,704
Depn & Amortn	17,189	11,493	5,836	23,890	25,449	27,135	36,604	29,890
Income Before Taxes	57,965	32,547	14,010	(10,998)	7,611	(71,724)	(5,826)	65,366
Income Taxes	579	253	253	1,419	39,191	(27,228)	(1,753)	26,216
Net Income	57,386	32,294	13,757	(12,417)	(31,580)	(67,978)	(4,073)	39,150
Average Shares	47,274	46,347	45,099	43,373	42,961	42,284	41,895	43,230
Balance Sheet								
Total Assets	775,038	687,123	628,588	600,468	545,708	553,054	583,945	602,525
Current Liabilities	304,894	258,246	235,351	222,598	159,087	148,068	121,957	101,754
Long-Term Obligations	21,666	21,623	21,959	22,310	23,160	23,502	25,356	70,016
Total Liabilities	338,000	294,012	271,959	260,453	194,295	182,038	153,256	175,673
Stockholders' Equity	437,038	393,111	356,629	340,015	351,413	371,016	430,689	426,852
Shares Outstanding	46,195	45,170	44,048	43,752	43,184	42,607	42,030	41,757
Statistical Record								
Return on Assets %	10.11	3.42	N.M.	N.M.	N.M.	N.M.	N.M.	7.00
Return on Equity %	17.72	5.70	N.M.	N.M.	N.M.	N.M.	N.M.	12.31
EBITDA Margin %	6.92	6.50	6.30	1.33	3.47	N.M.	3.92	9.57
Net Margin %	5.40	4.85	4.19	N.M.	N.M.	N.M.	N.M.	3.69
Asset Turnover	2.08	2.10	2.11	2.14	1.89	1.42	1.49	1.90
Current Ratio	2.06	2.09	2.06	2.08	2.35	2.42	2.80	3.72
Debt to Equity	0.05	0.06	0.06	0.07	0.07	0.06	0.06	0.16
Price Range	46.91-13.77	38.55-10.09	23.26-10.09	17.26-10.09	24.46-10.00	18.31-7.59	36.25-9.25	73.00-20.63
P/E Ratio	31.91-9.37	85.67-22.42	...	...	...	...	...	80.22-22.66

Address: 55 Jewelers Park Drive, Neenah, WI 54957-0156	**Web Site:** www.plexus.com
Telephone: 920-722-3451	**Officers:** John L. Nussbaum - Chmn. Dean A. Foate - Pres., C.E.O.

Auditors: PricewaterhouseCoopers LLP
Investor Contact: 920-722-3451

PMC-SIERRA INC.

Exchange	Symbol	Price	52Wk Range	Yield	P/E
NMS	PMCS	$6.86 (8/31/2006)	13.57-4.86	N/A	N/A

*7 Year Price Score 18.71 *NYSE Composite Index=100 *12 Month Price Score 70.24

Interim Earnings (Per Share)

Qtr.	Mar	Jun	Sep	Dec
2003	(0.07)	(0.05)	0.02	0.05
2004	0.09	0.08	0.03	0.07
2005	0.02	0.00	0.03	0.10
2006	(0.08)	(0.16)	...	...

Interim Dividends (Per Share)
No Dividends Paid

Valuation Analysis **Institutional Holding**

Forecast P/E	18.20	No of Institutions
	(9/9/2006)	224
Market Cap	$1.4 Billion	Shares
Book Value	599.2 Million	186,673,776
Price/Book	2.39	% Held
Price/Sales	3.97	89.32

Business Summary: IT & Technology (MIC: 10.2 SIC: 3674 NAIC: 334413)

PMC-Sierra designs, develops, markets and supports communications semiconductors, storage semiconductors and microprocessors primarily for the communications service provider, storage, and enterprise markets. Co. has more than 250 different semiconductor devices that are sold to equipment and design manufacturers. Co.'s networking products comprise communications semiconductors, including microprocessors that are used in many different types of equipment throughout the network infrastructure: Co.'s networking products are sold primarily into five areas of the worldwide network infrastructure: access, metro, storage, enterprise, and customer premise markets.

Recent Developments: For the quarter ended July 2 2006, net income amounted to $31.8 million versus net income of $529,000 in the year-earlier quarter. Revenues were $118.8 million, up 66.0% from $71.5 million the year before. Operating loss was $24.0 million versus a loss of $359,000 in the prior-year quarter. Direct operating expenses rose 103.8% to $43.6 million from $21.4 million in the comparable period the year before. Indirect operating expenses increased 96.3% to $99.2 million from $50.5 million in the equivalent prior-year period.

Prospects: For the third quarter of 2006, Co. projects revenue of $122.0 million to $124.0 million, assuming that it achieves 37.0% to 39.0% of its revenues from orders placed and shipped during the same quarter. In addition, Co. expects to see a continued decline in its gross profit as a percentage of revenues, as most of its acquired products sell at overall lower gross margins, particularly the Fiber To The Home (FTTH) products acquired in May 2006; while the proportion of its revenues to be derived from its FTTH products increases in future quarters. As a result, Co. expects gross margins to be approximately 68.0% before stock-based compensation and acquisition-related costs.

Financial Data
(US$ in Thousands)

	6 Mos	3 Mos	12/31/2005	12/31/2004	12/31/2003	12/31/2002	12/30/2001	12/31/2000
Earnings Per Share	(0.11)	0.05	0.15	0.27	(0.05)	(0.38)	(3.80)	0.41
Cash Flow Per Share	0.21	0.20	0.28	0.32	(0.42)	(0.12)	(0.32)	1.12
Tang Book Value Per Share	N.M.	N.M.	1.86	1.60	1.25	1.14	1.59	3.24
Income Statement								
Total Revenue	206,561	87,781	291,411	297,383	249,483	218,093	322,738	694,684
EBITDA	(18,069)	(1,326)	29,895	58,811	10,895	(47,971)	(558,802)	251,891
Depn & Amortn	19,382	5,412	11,907	15,312	26,940	40,847	98,015	74,181
Income Before Taxes	(32,618)	(3,172)	30,094	48,358	(15,843)	(83,865)	(656,817)	177,710
Income Taxes	13,549	11,161	2,108	(3,323)	(7,852)	(18,858)	(17,763)	102,412
Net Income	(46,167)	(14,333)	27,986	51,681	(7,991)	(65,007)	(639,054)	75,298
Average Shares	203,067	187,218	189,132	188,903	173,568	170,107	167,967	181,891
Balance Sheet								
Total Assets	1,016,842	757,369	732,949	507,024	552,956	728,716	855,341	1,126,090
Current Liabilities	146,776	140,344	121,450	175,176	146,951	247,261	279,755	230,017
Long-Term Obligations	225,000	225,000	225,000	...	175,000	275,000	275,000	564
Total Liabilities	417,670	397,264	375,540	203,253	322,140	525,025	577,797	268,405
Stockholders' Equity	599,172	360,105	354,047	299,337	226,297	198,639	272,227	851,318
Shares Outstanding	208,762	186,081	183,306	178,510	174,289	167,400	165,702	162,284
Statistical Record								
Return on Assets %	N.M.	1.72	4.51	9.72	N.M.	N.M.	N.M.	10.23
Return on Equity %	N.M.	3.11	8.57	19.61	N.M.	N.M.	N.M.	13.82
EBITDA Margin %	N.M.	N.M.	10.26	19.78	4.37	N.M.	N.M.	36.26
Net Margin %	N.M.	N.M.	9.60	17.38	N.M.	N.M.	N.M.	10.84
Asset Turnover	0.49	0.52	0.47	0.56	0.39	0.27	0.33	0.94
Current Ratio	2.37	2.17	5.66	1.87	3.16	1.93	1.77	2.48
Debt to Equity	0.38	0.62	0.64	...	0.77	1.38	1.01	N.M.
Price Range	13.57-6.34	12.45-6.34	11.25-6.34	24.51-8.26	22.47-4.77	25.98-2.72	105.94-9.87	245.44-62.75
P/E Ratio	...	249.00-126.80	75.00-42.27	90.78-30.59	...	...	...	598.63-153.05

Address: 3975 Freedom Circle, Santa Clara, CA 95054
Telephone: 408-239-8000
Fax: 408-492-9192

Web Site: www.pmc-sierra.com
Officers: Alexandre Balkanski - Chmn. James V. Diller - Vice-Chmn.

Auditors: Deloitte & Touche LLP
Investor Contact: 408-988-8276

POLYCOM INC.

Exchange	Symbol	Price	52Wk Range	Yield	P/E
NMS	PLCM	$23.79 (8/31/2006)	24.52-14.46	N/A	38.37

*7 Year Price Score 65.58 *NYSE Composite Index=100 *12 Month Price Score 112.39

Interim Earnings (Per Share)

Qtr.	Mar	Jun	Sep	Dec
2003	(0.02)	0.02	0.10	0.14
2004	0.03	0.13	0.11	0.08
2005	0.16	0.20	0.18	0.11
2006	0.16	0.17	...	...

Interim Dividends (Per Share)
No Dividends Paid

Valuation Analysis

		Institutional Holding	
Forecast P/E	23.13	No of Institutions	
	(9/9/2006)	188	
Market Cap	$2.1 Billion	Shares	
Book Value	871.1 Million	87,075,176	
Price/Book	2.40	% Held	
Price/Sales	3.35	98.73	

Business Summary: Communications (MIC: 10.1 SIC: 3661 NAIC: 334210)

Polycom is a global provider of a line of communications equipment that enables enterprise users to conduct video, voice, data and web communications. Co.'s business operates in three segments: Communications segment, which includes videoconferencing collaboration products and voice communications products; Network Systems segment, which includes its MGC™ and ReadiVoice® series of media servers, its ReadiManager™ network management product, its PathNavigator™ call processing server, and its other network management and scheduling software; and Services segment, which includes a range of professional service and support offerings to its resellers and directly to some end-user customers.

Recent Developments: For the quarter ended June 30 2006, income from continuing operations decreased 24.5% to $15.0 million from $19.9 million in the year-earlier quarter. Net income decreased 25.0% to $15.0 million from $20.0 million in the year-earlier quarter. Revenues were $165.0 million, up 15.6% from $142.7 million the year before. Operating income was $17.6 million versus $19.3 million in the prior-year quarter, a decrease of 9.1%. Direct operating expenses rose 18.2% to $63.4 million from $53.7 million in the comparable period the year before. Indirect operating expenses increased 20.4% to $84.0 million from $69.7 million in the equivalent prior-year period.

Prospects: Co.'s near-term outlook appears optimistic, reflecting significant advancements with its partners in the second quarter of 2006. For instance, Co. announced Cisco Skinny Client Control Protocol video products, along with its new Communicator for wideband voice over Internet Protocol (VoIP) with Skype, and the support for its 2007 launch of Microsoft's Unified Communications platform with its VoIP endpoints. These integrated applications should augment Co.'s positions with other architectures, such as Alcatel, Avaya, and Nortel. Looking ahead, Co. will continue to launch new products to fulfill the demand for its Internet Protocol-based unified collaborative communications applications.

Financial Data
(US$ in Thousands)

	6 Mos	3 Mos	12/31/2005	12/31/2004	12/31/2003	12/31/2002	12/31/2001	12/31/2000
Earnings Per Share	0.62	0.65	0.65	0.35	0.23	0.27	(0.33)	0.64
Cash Flow Per Share	1.61	1.53	1.23	0.80	1.02	0.82	0.90	0.65
Tang Book Value Per Share	5.64	5.28	5.38	5.90	6.29	5.77	3.26	4.73
Income Statement								
Total Revenue	322,668	157,713	580,659	540,252	420,423	465,959	383,189	331,302
EBITDA	48,992	23,765	104,990	82,335	56,647	59,098	(1,440)	75,313
Depn & Amortn	13,526	6,740	20,755	40,706	33,174	31,680	24,275	8,675
Income Before Taxes	43,992	20,943	97,083	48,908	31,924	36,910	(12,960)	73,475
Income Taxes	14,957	6,911	34,722	14,332	8,958	10,150	14,740	24,247
Net Income	29,035	14,032	62,745	35,349	22,823	26,760	(27,700)	49,228
Average Shares	89,761	89,346	97,014	102,018	100,752	100,696	85,123	77,507
Balance Sheet								
Total Assets	1,103,097	1,055,852	1,071,400	1,154,641	1,103,790	1,076,874	821,165	431,869
Current Liabilities	206,796	192,914	191,498	174,153	145,678	135,135	150,600	67,129
Total Liabilities	232,013	218,184	214,531	190,027	174,511	173,131	177,179	67,129
Stockholders' Equity	871,084	837,668	856,869	964,614	929,279	903,743	643,986	364,740
Shares Outstanding	87,824	87,122	88,755	99,116	99,349	98,987	91,112	75,625
Statistical Record								
Return on Assets %	4.91	5.49	5.64	3.12	2.09	2.82	N.M.	16.46
Return on Equity %	6.06	6.72	6.89	3.72	2.49	3.46	N.M.	20.54
EBITDA Margin %	15.18	15.07	18.08	15.24	13.47	12.68	N.M.	22.73
Net Margin %	9.00	8.90	10.81	6.54	5.43	5.74	N.M.	14.86
Asset Turnover	0.55	0.55	0.52	0.48	0.39	0.49	0.61	1.11
Current Ratio	2.73	2.39	2.29	1.98	2.31	2.50	2.34	5.25
Price Range	22.58-14.07	22.24-14.07	23.32-14.07	23.87-16.97	21.80-7.99	38.11-6.79	41.64-11.25	70.81-26.54
P/E Ratio	36.42-22.69	34.22-21.65	35.88-21.65	68.20-48.49	94.78-34.74	141.15-25.15	...	110.64-41.47

Address: 4750 Willow Road, Pleasanton, CA 94588 **Telephone:** 925-924-6000	**Web Site:** www.polycom.com **Officers:** Robert C. Hagerty - Chmn., Pres., C.E.O. Michael R. Kourey - Sr. V.P., Fin., Admin., C.F.O., Sec.	**Auditors:** PricewaterhouseCoopers LLP **Investor Contact:** 408-474-2907

POPULAR INC.

Exchange	Symbol	Price	52Wk Range	Yield	P/E	Div Acheiver
NMS	BPOP	$19.05 (8/31/2006)	27.52-17.41	3.36	11.55	13 Years

*7 Year Price Score 91.37 *NYSE Composite Index=100 *12 Month Price Score 86.48

Interim Earnings (Per Share)

Qtr.	Mar	Jun	Sep	Dec
2003	0.37	0.50	0.48	0.39
2004	0.44	0.47	0.42	0.47
2005	0.60	0.48	0.42	0.47
2006	0.42	0.34	...	...

Interim Dividends (Per Share)

Amt	Decl	Ex	Rec	Pay
0.16Q	11/16/2005	12/7/2005	12/9/2005	1/2/2006
0.16Q	2/15/2006	3/8/2006	3/10/2006	4/3/2006
0.16Q	5/17/2006	6/7/2006	6/9/2006	7/3/2006
0.16Q	8/16/2006	9/6/2006	9/8/2006	10/2/2006

Indicated Div: $0.64 (Div. Reinv. Plan)

Valuation Analysis

Forecast P/E	12.76
	(9/9/2006)
Market Cap	$5.3 Billion
Book Value	3.5 Billion
Price/Book	1.53
Price/Sales	1.44

Institutional Holding

No of Institutions	134
Shares	80,288,528
% Held	28.82

Business Summary: Commercial Banking (MIC: 8.1 SIC: 6022 NAIC: 522110)

Popular is a financial holding company which provides various financial services primarily in Puerto Rico, the U.S., the Caribbean and Latin America. Co. offers retail and commercial banking services through its principal banking subsidiary, Banco Popular de Puerto Rico, as well as investment banking, auto and equipment leasing and financing, mortgage loans, consumer lending, insurance and information processing through specialized subsidiaries. In the U.S., Co. operates the Hispanic-owned financial services franchise, Banco Popular North America, providing financial services in the communities it serves. As of Dec 31 2005, Co. had total assets of $48.62 billion.

Recent Developments: For the quarter ended June 30 2006, net income decreased 26.4% to $97.4 million from $132.4 million in the year-earlier quarter. Net interest income increased 2.3% to $365.8 million from $357.4 million in the year-earlier quarter. Provision for loan losses was $67.1 million versus $49.9 million in the prior-year quarter, an increase of 34.4%. Non-interest income fell 3.4% to $184.0 million from $190.5 million, while non-interest expense advanced 12.0% to $363.0 million.

Prospects: Co.'s results are being adversely affected by a flattening yield curve, as well as less than robust economic environment and higher delinquencies in the Puerto Rica market. Nevertheless, Co. continues to focus on generating sound loan growth while maintaining adequate asset quality and underwriting standards. Loan growth has been notably strong in both Co.'s commercial loan and construction loan categories. Going forward, Co. expects to continue countering the challenges by proceeding with the restructuring of its mortgage business in the U.S., while increasing deposits and loan originations across the markets that it serves.

Financial Data
(US$ in Thousands)

	6 Mos	3 Mos	12/31/2005	12/31/2004	12/31/2003	12/31/2002	12/31/2001	12/31/2000
Earnings Per Share	1.65	1.79	1.97	1.79	1.74	1.30	1.09	0.98
Cash Flow Per Share	(1.91)	3.65	4.00	0.54	2.12	1.43	1.62	1.51
Tang Book Value Per Share	8.46	8.53	9.05	9.26	8.84	8.28	7.02	5.93
Dividends Per Share	0.640	0.640	0.640	0.615	0.505	0.400	0.380	0.320
Dividend Payout %	38.79	35.75	32.49	34.36	29.11	30.65	35.02	32.49
Income Statement								
Interest Income	1,504,247	742,210	2,665,859	2,216,265	2,034,238	2,023,797	2,095,862	2,150,157
Interest Expense	778,704	382,446	1,241,652	840,754	749,550	843,468	1,018,877	1,167,396
Net Interest Income	725,543	359,764	1,424,207	1,375,511	1,284,688	1,180,329	1,076,985	982,761
Provision for Losses	116,043	48,947	195,272	178,657	195,939	205,570	213,250	194,640
Non-Interest Income	412,819	228,833	785,275	608,771	626,010	523,678	465,516	465,098
Non-Interest Expense	746,234	383,254	1,328,200	1,171,012	1,113,083	1,029,002	920,137	877,471
Income Before Taxes	276,085	156,396	686,010	634,613	601,676	469,435	409,114	375,748
Income Taxes	60,201	37,893	148,915	144,705	130,326	117,255	105,280	100,797
Net Income	215,884	118,503	540,702	489,908	470,915	351,932	304,538	276,103
Average Shares	278,636	278,415	267,839	266,674	265,595	267,830	272,476	271,814
Balance Sheet								
Net Loans & Leases	31,126,197	30,426,345	30,549,319	27,554,452	21,922,058	18,116,395	16,892,431	14,942,531
Total Assets	48,399,514	48,591,703	48,623,668	44,401,576	36,434,715	33,660,352	30,744,676	28,057,051
Total Deposits	23,449,520	23,411,812	22,638,005	20,593,160	18,097,828	17,614,740	16,370,042	14,804,907
Total Liabilities	44,936,409	45,104,033	45,174,306	41,296,853	33,680,193	31,248,311	28,470,949	26,062,480
Stockholders' Equity	3,462,993	3,487,557	3,449,247	3,104,621	2,754,417	2,410,879	2,272,818	1,993,644
Shares Outstanding	278,293	278,072	275,955	266,582	265,783	264,878	272,724	271,997
Statistical Record								
Return on Assets %	0.98	1.06	1.16	1.21	1.34	1.09	1.04	1.03
Return on Equity %	13.70	15.15	16.50	16.68	18.23	15.03	14.28	15.07
Net Interest Margin %	48.00	48.47	53.42	62.06	63.15	58.32	51.39	45.71
Efficiency Ratio %	38.37	39.47	38.49	41.45	41.84	40.39	35.92	33.55
Loans to Deposits	1.33	1.30	1.35	1.34	1.21	1.03	1.03	1.01
Price Range	27.52-18.53	27.52-19.54	28.83-20.10	28.87-20.04	23.79-15.98	17.93-13.75	18.13-12.63	13.97-9.31
P/E Ratio	16.68-11.23	15.37-10.92	14.63-10.20	16.13-11.20	13.67-9.18	13.79-10.58	16.63-11.58	14.25-9.50
Average Yield %	2.91	2.78	2.60	2.62	2.62	2.55	2.54	2.79

Address: Popular Center Building, 209 Munoz Rivera Avenue, Hato Rey, San Juan, PR 00918 **Telephone:** 809-765-9800 **Fax:** 809-759-7803	**Web Site:** www.popularinc.com **Officers:** Richard L. Carrion - Chmn., Pres., C.E.O. Antonion Luis Ferre - Vice-Chmn.
Auditors: PricewaterhouseCoopers LLP **Investor Contact:** 787-765-9800x6102 **Transfer Agents:** Banco Popular de Puerto Rico, San Juan, Puerto Rico	

POWER-ONE, INC.

Exchange	Symbol	Price	52Wk Range	Yield	P/E
NMS	PWER	$6.79 (8/31/2006)	7.98-4.31	N/A	169.75

*7 Year Price Score 34.80 *NYSE Composite Index=100 *12 Month Price Score 98.56

Interim Earnings (Per Share)

Qtr.	Mar	Jun	Sep	Dec
2003	(0.04)	(0.01)	(0.04)	(0.12)
2004	(0.03)	(0.05)	(0.06)	(0.11)
2005	(0.34)	(0.17)	0.02	0.04
2006	(0.06)	0.04	...	...

Interim Dividends (Per Share)
No Dividends Paid

Valuation Analysis

		Institutional Holding	
Forecast P/E	219.33	No of Institutions	
	(9/9/2006)	92	
Market Cap	$586.3 Million	Shares	
Book Value	229.7 Million	46,946,164	
Price/Book	2.55	% Held	
Price/Sales	2.13	54.37	

Business Summary: Electrical (MIC: 11.14 SIC: 3679 NAIC: 334419)

Power-One is a designer and manufacturer of power conversion products, primarily for the technology and communications infrastructure markets. Co.'s products are used to convert, process and manage electrical energy to the high levels of quality, reliability and precise levels of direct current (DC) voltage required by communications infrastructure and other equipment. Co.'s products include: alternating current (AC)/DC power supplies, DC/DC converters, DC power systems, DC/DC point-of-load converters, and a new digital power management architecture, Z-One™ system, and related digital products that integrate conversion, communications, and control for a digital board-level solution.

Recent Developments: For the quarter ended June 30 2006, net income amounted to $3.1 million versus a net loss of $14.8 million in the year-earlier quarter. Revenues were $78.6 million, up 24.0% from $63.4 million the year before. Operating income was $919,000 versus a loss of $15.1 million in the prior-year quarter. Direct operating expenses rose 10.1% to $52.3 million from $47.5 million in the comparable period the year before. Indirect operating expenses decreased 17.8% to $25.4 million from $30.9 million in the equivalent prior-year period.

Prospects: Co. continues to focus on customer growth, as well as reducing material cost and improving its margins on its new program. Also, Co. is managing increasing component lead time and improving its design capabilities, notably in low-cost conditions to meet customer demands. Meanwhile, Co. is promoting its Z-One™ suite of digital power management products, with more emphasis on tier-one customers and higher volume programs. For the third quarter of 2006, Co. expects the broad growth in new customers and programs to offset the seasonally lower third quarter revenue, and projects net sales of $74.0 million to $78.0 million, with net income in the range of breakeven to $0.02 per share.

Financial Data
(US$ in Thousands)

	6 Mos	3 Mos	12/31/2005	12/31/2004	12/31/2003	12/31/2002	12/31/2001	12/31/2000
Earnings Per Share	0.04	(0.17)	(0.45)	(0.25)	(0.22)	(2.62)	(2.36)	0.56
Cash Flow Per Share	(0.13)	(0.04)	(0.06)	(0.01)	(0.10)	0.39	(0.01)	(1.06)
Tang Book Value Per Share	2.06	1.97	2.01	2.52	2.62	2.86	4.06	6.00
Income Statement								
Total Revenue	143,210	64,580	261,557	280,279	256,334	230,656	363,727	510,955
EBITDA	1,937	(1,159)	(23,664)	(2,871)	(3,726)	(202,969)	(151,672)	93,718
Depn & Amortn	6,195	3,073	14,949	16,396	16,049	20,900	36,500	24,190
Income Before Taxes	(3,164)	(3,683)	(36,462)	(18,090)	(19,173)	(223,244)	(186,852)	66,386
Income Taxes	(1,502)	1,127	1,820	3,100	(969)	(12,240)	(949)	22,495
Net Income	(1,662)	(4,810)	(38,282)	(21,190)	(18,204)	(211,004)	(185,903)	43,891
Average Shares	88,152	85,558	84,991	83,757	82,539	80,396	78,759	77,871
Balance Sheet								
Total Assets	300,059	286,963	285,673	327,053	349,877	360,863	520,235	782,317
Current Liabilities	69,618	64,386	59,940	55,384	72,628	71,959	54,849	126,279
Long-Term Obligations	...	...	...	...	...	8,900	7,598	9,412
Total Liabilities	70,366	65,571	61,178	57,016	74,558	81,717	70,032	148,589
Stockholders' Equity	229,693	221,392	224,495	270,037	275,319	279,138	450,203	633,728
Shares Outstanding	86,346	85,843	85,588	84,252	83,308	79,898	78,912	78,497
Statistical Record								
Return on Assets %	1.11	N.M.	N.M.	N.M.	N.M.	N.M.	N.M.	8.22
Return on Equity %	1.45	N.M.	N.M.	N.M.	N.M.	N.M.	N.M.	10.12
EBITDA Margin %	1.35	N.M.	N.M.	N.M.	N.M.	N.M.	N.M.	18.34
Net Margin %	N.M.	N.M.	N.M.	N.M.	N.M.	N.M.	N.M.	8.59
Asset Turnover	0.93	0.88	0.85	0.83	0.72	0.52	0.56	0.96
Current Ratio	2.57	2.57	2.72	3.11	3.13	3.09	4.95	3.98
Debt to Equity	...	...	...	...	...	0.03	0.02	0.01
Price Range	7.98-4.31	7.20-4.18	8.92-4.18	14.26-6.08	12.46-4.25	12.51-2.40	49.80-5.57	87.38-11.17
P/E Ratio	199.50-107.75	...	...	...	...	...	...	... 156.03-19.94

Address: 740 Calle Plano, Camarillo, CA 93012
Telephone: 805-987-8741
Fax: 805-388-0476

Web Site: www.power-one.com
Officers: Steven J. Goldman - Chmn., C.E.O. William T. Yeates - Pres., C.O.O.

Auditors: Deloitte & Touche LLP

POWERWAVE TECHNOLOGIES INC.

Exchange	Symbol	Price	52Wk Range	Yield	P/E
NMS	PWAV	$7.58 (8/31/2006)	15.33-6.29	N/A	22.29

*7 Year Price Score 57.55   *NYSE Composite Index=100   *12 Month Price Score 64.68

Interim Earnings (Per Share)

Qtr.	Mar	Jun	Sep	Dec
2003	(0.16)	(0.23)	(0.09)	(0.03)
2004	(0.05)	(0.33)	0.03	(0.45)
2005	0.05	0.11	0.11	0.15
2006	(0.02)	0.10	...	...

Interim Dividends (Per Share)
No Dividends Paid

Valuation Analysis
Forecast P/E	20.26
	(9/9/2006)
Market Cap	$850.5 Million
Book Value	626.9 Million
Price/Book	1.36
Price/Sales	0.94

Institutional Holding
No of Institutions	221
Shares	93,889,568
% Held	83.43

Business Summary: Communications (MIC: 10.1 SIC: 3663 NAIC: 334220)

Powerwave Technologies' primary business consists of the design, manufacture and marketing and sale of products to improve coverage, capacity and data speed in wireless communications networks, including antennas, boosters, combiners, filters, radio frequency power amplifiers, repeaters, tower-mounted amplifiers, and advanced coverage services. Co. sells such products to both original equipment manufacturers, who incorporate Co.'s products into their proprietary base stations, and directly to individual wireless network operators for deployment into their existing networks. Co. also manufactures and sells advanced industrial components, primarily for the automotive and food industries.

Recent Developments: For the quarter ended July 2 2006, net income decreased 3.0% to $12.6 million from $13.0 million in the year-earlier quarter. Revenues were $232.4 million, up 24.7% from $186.3 million the year before. Operating income was $13.1 million versus $11.1 million in the prior-year quarter, an increase of 18.0%. Direct operating expenses rose 29.8% to $180.0 million from $138.7 million in the comparable period the year before. Indirect operating expenses increased 7.4% to $39.2 million from $36.5 million in the equivalent prior-year period.

Prospects: On June 12 2006, Co. agreed to acquire majority of Filtronic plc's Wireless Infrastructure division business for a combination of 20.7 million newly issued shares of Co.'s common stock and $150.0 million in cash. The transaction, which is expected to close in the third quarter of calendar 2006, will be immediately accretive to Co.'s earnings. Moreover, Co. believes that combined revenues in calendar year 2007 will exceed $1.40 billion, while the transaction will be accretive to its fiscal year 2007 earnings per share in the range of $0.08 to $0.12. Also, Co. estimates that it will realize over $10.0 million in annual cost savings following the integration of the acquisition.

Financial Data
(US$ in Thousands)

	6 Mos	3 Mos	01/01/2006	01/02/2005	12/28/2003	12/29/2002	12/30/2001	12/31/2000
Earnings Per Share	0.34	0.35	0.42	(0.80)	(0.51)	0.06	(0.33)	0.71
Cash Flow Per Share	(0.32)	0.04	0.12	(0.15)	0.11	0.61	0.10	0.93
Tang Book Value Per Share	2.22	2.01	2.09	1.74	4.23	4.88	4.77	4.81
Income Statement								
Total Revenue	425,459	193,065	825,078	473,914	239,069	384,889	300,293	447,422
EBITDA	37,210	10,879	101,519	11,687	(34,216)	27,176	(6,128)	89,789
Depn & Amortn	24,998	13,017	47,565	37,555	19,214	21,303	25,922	19,009
Income Before Taxes	12,517	(2,005)	53,879	(26,809)	(53,430)	5,873	(32,050)	70,780
Income Taxes	2,175	275	3,233	45,313	(20,571)	1,762	(11,538)	25,127
Net Income	10,342	(2,280)	50,646	(72,122)	(32,859)	4,111	(20,512)	45,653
Average Shares	144,007	111,660	135,906	90,212	64,667	66,230	64,197	65,313
Balance Sheet								
Total Assets	1,188,170	1,140,363	1,130,250	1,020,771	466,257	369,173	363,017	393,797
Current Liabilities	215,921	208,868	215,215	170,524	65,101	43,429	46,475	77,247
Long-Term Obligations	330,000	330,000	330,000	330,000	130,000	...	239	42
Total Liabilities	561,243	549,243	548,989	505,159	195,220	43,512	46,782	77,525
Stockholders' Equity	626,927	591,120	581,261	515,612	271,037	325,661	316,235	316,272
Shares Outstanding	112,207	112,130	111,138	99,411	63,257	65,707	65,081	63,509
Statistical Record								
Return on Assets %	3.94	4.04	4.72	N.M.	N.M.	1.13	N.M.	14.84
Return on Equity %	7.81	7.94	9.26	N.M.	N.M.	1.28	N.M.	18.84
EBITDA Margin %	8.75	5.63	12.30	2.47	N.M.	7.06	N.M.	20.07
Net Margin %	2.43	N.M.	6.14	N.M.	N.M.	1.07	N.M.	10.20
Asset Turnover	0.83	0.81	0.77	0.63	0.57	1.05	0.80	1.45
Current Ratio	2.95	2.88	2.79	3.02	5.30	6.03	5.01	3.55
Debt to Equity	0.53	0.56	0.57	0.64	0.48	...	N.M.	N.M.
Price Range	15.33-8.95	15.33-6.88	13.78-6.76	10.95-4.88	10.64-3.12	20.10-2.75	58.75-9.00	73.81-15.42
P/E Ratio	45.09-26.32	43.80-19.66	32.81-16.10	...	...	335.00-45.83	...	103.96-21.71

Address: 1801 E. St. Andrew Place, Santa Ana, CA 92705
Telephone: 714-466-1000
Fax: 714-466-1001

Web Site: www.powerwave.com
Officers: John L. Clendenin - Chmn. Bruce C. Edwards - Pres., C.E.O.

Auditors: Deloitte & Touche
Investor Contact: 949-757-0530

QLOGIC CORP.

Exchange	Symbol	Price	52Wk Range	Yield	P/E
NMS	QLGC	$18.38 (8/31/2006)	21.08-14.11	N/A	11.49

*7 Year Price Score 59.41 *NYSE Composite Index=100 *12 Month Price Score 94.29

Interim Earnings (Per Share)

Qtr.	Jun	Sep	Dec	Mar
2003-04	0.17	0.17	0.18	0.17
2004-05	0.17	0.19	0.23	0.25
2005-06	0.23	0.24	1.02	0.21
2006-07	0.13	...	...	...

Interim Dividends (Per Share)
No Dividends Paid

Valuation Analysis

		Institutional Holding	
Forecast P/E	21.72	No of Institutions	
(9/9/2006)		270	
Market Cap	$3.0 Billion	Shares	128,611,960
Book Value	858.6 Million	% Held	80.72
Price/Book	3.44		
Price/Sales	5.71		

Business Summary: IT & Technology (MIC: 10.2 SIC: 3674 NAIC: 334413)
QLogic is engaged in designing and developing storage network infrastructure components. Co. produces host bus adapters, Fibre Channel blade switches, Fibre Channel stackable switches and other fabric switches. In addition, Co. designs and develops storage routers for bridging Fibre Channel and Internet Small Computer Systems Interface networks and storage services platforms and Original Equipment Manufacturer storage management software that has been ported to the platform. Co. also designs and develop InfiniBand® Host Channel Adapters that provide connectivity infrastructure for clustered server fabrics. Finally, Co. designs and produces management controller chips.

Recent Developments: For the quarter ended July 2 2006, income from continuing operations decreased 25.5% to $21.1 million from $28.3 million in the year-earlier quarter. Net income decreased 49.6% to $21.1 million from $41.8 million in the year-earlier quarter. Revenues were $136.7 million, up 18.4% from $115.4 million the year before. Operating income was $27.7 million versus $42.0 million in the prior-year quarter, a decrease of 34.0%. Direct operating expenses rose 27.4% to $43.3 million from $34.0 million in the comparable period the year before. Indirect operating expenses increased 66.3% to $65.7 million from $39.5 million in the equivalent prior-year period.

Prospects: Co. is seeing volume shipment growth for its storage area network (SAN) Infrastructure Products as the global market for SANs continues to expand in response to the information storage requirements of enterprise business environments and the emerging market for SAN-based applications for small and medium-sized businesses. Thus, Co. believes it is well-positioned for continued growth in its existing core business and expects its emerging markets to provide an opportunity for future revenue growth. Conversely, Co. continues to expect downward pressure on its gross profit percentage due to changes in product and technology mix, declining average selling prices and high manufacturing costs.

Financial Data
(US$ in Thousands)

	3 Mos	04/02/2006	04/03/2005	03/28/2004	03/30/2003	03/31/2002	04/01/2001	04/02/2000
Earnings Per Share	1.60	1.63	0.84	0.69	0.55	0.37	0.36	0.35
Cash Flow Per Share	0.73	0.78	0.97	0.84	0.83	0.81	0.54	0.49
Tang Book Value Per Share	4.54	5.10	5.18	4.61	4.00	3.33	2.84	1.64
Income Statement								
Total Revenue	136,692	494,077	571,903	523,860	440,809	344,189	357,542	203,143
EBITDA	36,930	192,564	239,993	231,626	175,829	120,580	127,743	86,566
Depn & Amortn	9,027	17,898	16,164	16,025	16,610	15,040	10,806	4,799
Income Before Taxes	34,541	200,484	242,359	215,601	159,219	105,540	116,937	81,748
Income Taxes	13,465	78,653	84,763	81,928	55,746	34,814	48,168	27,795
Net Income	21,076	283,588	157,596	133,673	103,473	70,726	68,769	53,953
Average Shares	162,897	173,467	187,314	192,492	190,708	190,252	190,278	154,994
Balance Sheet								
Total Assets	953,546	937,707	1,026,340	928,515	817,419	670,015	571,497	267,156
Current Liabilities	89,575	78,353	68,821	60,797	66,684	51,032	47,795	24,187
Total Liabilities	94,958	78,353	70,157	60,797	66,684	51,032	47,795	24,187
Stockholders' Equity	858,588	859,354	956,183	867,718	750,735	618,983	523,702	242,969
Shares Outstanding	160,561	162,092	184,418	188,220	187,708	186,058	184,648	148,585
Statistical Record								
Return on Assets %	26.51	28.96	15.86	15.35	13.95	11.42	16.44	24.12
Return on Equity %	29.12	31.33	17.00	16.56	15.15	12.41	17.99	26.83
EBITDA Margin %	27.02	38.97	41.96	44.22	39.89	35.03	35.73	42.61
Net Margin %	15.42	57.40	27.56	25.52	23.47	20.55	19.23	26.56
Asset Turnover	0.52	0.50	0.58	0.60	0.59	0.56	0.85	0.91
Current Ratio	8.03	10.45	13.65	14.04	11.22	11.50	10.26	7.33
Price Range	21.08-14.11	20.79-14.11	21.51-10.83	29.22-18.57	26.35-9.98	32.23-8.99	64.13-11.25	95.22-7.63
P/E Ratio	13.17-8.82	12.75-8.66	25.61-12.89	42.34-26.91	47.91-18.15	87.09-24.31	178.13-31.25	272.05-21.79

Address: 26650 Aliso Viejo Parkway, Aliso Viejo, CA 92656
Telephone: 949-389-6000

Web Site: www.qlogic.com
Officers: H. K. Desai - Chmn., Pres., C.E.O. Anthony J. Massetti - Sr. V.P., C.F.O.

Auditors: KPMG LLP
Transfer Agents: Computershare Investor Services

QUALCOMM, INC.

Exchange	Symbol	Price	52Wk Range	Yield	P/E
NMS	QCOM	$37.67 (8/31/2006)	52.74-33.31	1.27	27.30

*7 Year Price Score 107.37 *NYSE Composite Index=100 *12 Month Price Score 79.83

Interim Earnings (Per Share)

Qtr.	Dec	Mar	Jun	Sep
2002-03	0.15	0.07	0.12	0.17
2003-04	0.22	0.29	0.29	0.23
2004-05	0.30	0.31	0.33	0.31
2005-06	0.36	0.34	0.37	...

Interim Dividends (Per Share)

Amt	Decl	Ex	Rec	Pay
0.09Q	10/10/2005	12/5/2005	12/7/2005	1/4/2006
0.09Q	1/12/2006	2/22/2006	2/24/2006	3/24/2006
0.12Q	4/7/2006	5/24/2006	5/26/2006	6/23/2006
0.12Q	7/7/2006	8/23/2006	8/25/2006	9/22/2006

Indicated Div: $0.48

Valuation Analysis
Forecast P/E 22.82 (9/9/2006)
Market Cap $62.4 Billion
Book Value 13.0 Billion
Price/Book 4.80
Price/Sales 8.78

Institutional Holding
No of Institutions 870
Shares 1,183,725,952
% Held 71.66

Business Summary: Communications (MIC: 10.1 SIC: 3669 NAIC: 334290)

Qualcomm is engaged in the development and commercialization of Code Division Multiple Access (CDMA) technology, which is one of the key technologies currently used in digital wireless communications networks. Co. owns significant intellectual property, including patents, patent applications and trade secrets, portions of which it licenses to other companies and implements in its own products. As of Sep 25 2005, Co. had been granted more than 1,540 U.S. patents and had over 2,500 patent applications pending in the U.S., with the majority of such patents and patent applications relate to its CDMA digital wireless communications technology.

Recent Developments: For the quarter ended June 25 2006, net income increased 14.8% to $643.0 million from $560.0 million in the year-earlier quarter. Revenues were $1.95 billion, up 43.7% from $1.36 billion the year before. Operating income was $704.0 million versus $560.0 million in the prior-year quarter, an increase of 25.7%. Direct operating expenses rose 43.7% to $559.0 million from $389.0 million in the comparable period the year before. Indirect operating expenses increased 68.2% to $688.0 million from $409.0 million in the equivalent prior-year period.

Prospects: Co.'s results are driven by continued customer demand for its chipsets, as demonstrated by the increased shipments of its Wideband Code Division Multiple Access (WCDMA) handsets and Mobile Station Modem™ units, as well as its cell site modem voice-equivalent channel elements. Therefore, Co. is raising its full-year 2006 guidance for revenues to range from $7.40 billion to $7.50 billion and earnings of $1.40 to $1.42 per diluted share, over its previous ranges of $7.10 billion to $7.40 billion for revenues and $1.31 to $1.35 for diluted earnings per share. For the fourth quarter of 2006, Co. expects revenues of $1.88 billion to $1.98 billion and earnings of $0.33 to $0.35 per diluted share.

Financial Data
(US$ in Thousands)

	9 Mos	6 Mos	3 Mos	09/25/2005	09/26/2004	09/30/2003	09/30/2002	09/30/2001
Earnings Per Share	1.38	1.34	1.31	1.26	1.03	0.51	0.22	(0.36)
Cash Flow Per Share	1.94	1.78	1.76	1.64	1.55	1.13	0.63	1.83
Tang Book Value Per Share	7.10	7.40	6.91	6.43	5.69	4.54	3.24	2.82
Dividends Per Share	0.390	0.360	0.340	0.320	0.190	0.085	...	...
Dividend Payout %	28.19	26.80	25.89	25.40	18.45	16.83	...	...
Income Statement								
Total Revenue	5,527,000	3,575,000	1,741,000	5,673,000	4,880,000	3,970,636	3,039,560	2,679,786
EBITDA	2,539,000	1,644,000	795,000	2,756,000	2,278,000	1,495,550	881,113	(96,259)
Depn & Amortn	190,000	121,000	58,000	200,000	138,000	179,694	394,257	319,811
Income Before Taxes	2,346,000	1,521,000	736,000	2,809,000	2,313,000	1,285,147	461,125	(426,305)
Income Taxes	490,000	308,000	116,000	666,000	588,000	457,706	101,448	104,501
Net Income	1,856,000	1,213,000	620,000	2,143,000	1,720,000	827,441	359,677	(548,743)
Average Shares	1,728,000	1,721,000	1,702,000	1,694,000	1,675,000	1,635,510	1,618,658	1,511,938
Balance Sheet								
Total Assets	14,713,000	14,859,000	13,429,000	12,479,000	10,820,000	8,822,436	6,509,521	5,747,133
Current Liabilities	1,336,000	1,142,000	1,160,000	1,070,000	894,000	808,202	674,986	520,989
Long-Term Obligations	...	...	...	...	...	123,302	94,288	...
Total Liabilities	1,715,000	1,459,000	1,457,000	1,360,000	1,156,000	1,223,814	1,073,025	851,431
Stockholders' Equity	12,998,000	13,400,000	11,972,000	11,119,000	9,664,000	7,598,572	5,391,956	4,889,815
Shares Outstanding	1,656,000	1,673,000	1,650,000	1,640,000	1,635,000	1,596,706	1,557,098	1,526,578
Statistical Record								
Return on Assets %	18.26	17.37	18.05	18.45	17.66	10.79	5.87	N.M.
Return on Equity %	20.47	19.37	20.22	20.68	20.09	12.74	7.00	N.M.
EBITDA Margin %	45.94	45.99	45.66	48.58	46.68	37.67	28.99	N.M.
Net Margin %	33.58	33.93	35.61	37.78	35.25	20.84	11.83	N.M.
Asset Turnover	0.54	0.49	0.48	0.49	0.50	0.52	0.50	1.82
Current Ratio	5.44	7.58	7.24	7.28	8.08	7.36	5.84	5.86
Debt to Equity	...	...	...	...	...	0.02	0.02	...
Price Range	52.74-33.01	50.77-32.52	46.23-32.52	44.76-32.52	40.90-20.84	22.86-13.81	31.23-11.88	52.22-21.94
P/E Ratio	38.22-23.92	37.89-24.27	35.29-24.82	35.52-25.81	39.71-20.23	44.83-27.08	141.98-53.98	...
Average Yield %	0.87	0.87	0.87	0.83	0.62	0.47	...	...

Address: 5775 Morehouse Drive, San Diego, CA 92121-1714
Telephone: 858-587-1121
Fax: 858-658-2100

Web Site: www.qualcomm.com
Officers: Irwin Mark Jacobs - Chmn. Steven R. Altman - Pres.

Auditors: PricewaterhouseCoopers LLP
Investor Contact: 619-658-4844

QUIXOTE CORP.

Exchange	Symbol	Price	52Wk Range	Yield	P/E	Div Acheiver
NMS	QUIX	$16.92 (8/31/2006)	24.75-15.51	2.25	338.40	12 Years

*7 Year Price Score 83.36 *NYSE Composite Index=100 *12 Month Price Score 78.43

Interim Earnings (Per Share)

Qtr.	Sep	Dec	Mar	Jun
2002-03	0.22	0.19	0.20	0.56
2003-04	0.27	0.05	0.05	(2.36)
2004-05	(0.03)	(0.12)	(0.08)	0.16
2005-06	0.03	(0.04)	(0.10)	...

Interim Dividends (Per Share)

Amt	Decl	Ex	Rec	Pay
0.18S	11/19/2004	11/24/2004	11/29/2004	1/3/2005
0.18S	5/18/2005	6/2/2005	6/6/2005	7/6/2005
0.18S	11/16/2005	12/27/2005	11/29/2005	1/4/2006
0.19S	5/18/2006	6/2/2006	6/6/2006	7/6/2006

Indicated Div: $0.38

Valuation Analysis

Forecast P/E 25.00 (9/9/2006)
Market Cap $149.8 Million
Book Value 58.7 Million
Price/Book 2.55
Price/Sales 0.96

Institutional Holding

No of Institutions 44
Shares 7,824,833
% Held 88.17

Business Summary: Construction - Public Infrastructure (MIC: 3.1 SIC: 1611 NAIC: 237310)

Quixote develops, manufactures and markets highway and transportation safety products to protect, direct and inform motorists and highway workers in both domestic and international markets. These products include energy-absorbing highway crash cushions, flexible post delineators, electronic wireless measuring and sensing devices, weather information systems and forecasting services, variable message signs, highway advisory radios, intelligent intersection control devices, automated enforcement systems, video detection equipment and other highway and transportation safety devices.

Recent Developments: For the quarter ended Mar 31 2006, net loss amounted to $878,000 versus a net loss of $741,000 in the year-earlier quarter. Revenues were $37.5 million, up 7.2% from $35.0 million the year before. Operating loss was $178,000 versus a loss of $231,000 in the prior-year quarter. Direct operating expenses rose 15.2% to $26.4 million from $22.9 million in the comparable period the year before. Indirect operating expenses decreased 8.3% to $11.2 million from $12.2 million in the equivalent prior-year period.

Prospects: Going forward, Co. plans to consolidate several of the facilities and at the same time, eliminate low-margin and non-core products in its Intersection Control business, as part of its restructuring efforts to counteract the continuing under-performance of the business. Moreover, Co. expects these restructuring efforts to be completed by the end of second quarter of fiscal 2007. Meanwhile, Co. remains optimistic regarding the business outlook for its Inform Group as well as its Protect and Direct Group, given the potential growth exhibited by these businesses. For the fourth quarter of fiscal 2006, Co. anticipates earnings of between $0.10 and $0.15 per diluted share.

Financial Data
(US$ in Thousands)

	9 Mos	6 Mos	3 Mos	06/30/2005	06/30/2004	06/30/2003	06/30/2002	06/30/2001
Earnings Per Share	0.05	0.07	(0.01)	(0.07)	(1.99)	1.17	0.84	1.35
Cash Flow Per Share	0.51	(0.05)	0.25	0.39	1.01	2.06	1.65	1.47
Tang Book Value Per Share	2.55	2.56	2.71	2.84	2.99	2.23	3.17	3.36
Dividends Per Share	0.360	0.360	0.360	0.360	0.340	0.330	0.320	0.300
Dividend Payout %	720.00	514.29	...	...	...	28.21	38.10	22.22
Income Statement								
Total Revenue	116,047	78,577	39,391	146,353	150,290	114,310	89,694	93,554
EBITDA	6,786	5,558	3,222	7,833	(19,294)	19,132	13,858	22,815
Depn & Amortn	4,849	3,443	1,595	5,666	6,520	3,978	3,539	3,916
Income Before Taxes	(1,589)	(173)	445	(1,097)	(27,928)	14,352	9,213	17,488
Income Taxes	(604)	(66)	169	(447)	(10,901)	4,880	3,316	6,645
Net Income	(985)	(107)	276	(650)	(17,027)	9,472	6,824	10,843
Average Shares	8,839	8,820	9,061	8,800	8,567	8,062	8,121	8,049
Balance Sheet								
Total Assets	139,922	141,428	138,272	136,790	139,882	150,825	100,044	88,029
Current Liabilities	21,424	24,552	21,538	24,304	28,268	30,999	12,171	13,542
Long-Term Obligations	58,770	56,984	55,384	49,587	47,014	39,789	24,772	21,526
Total Liabilities	81,247	82,596	77,971	74,944	75,975	75,270	40,818	37,423
Stockholders' Equity	58,675	58,832	60,301	61,846	63,907	75,555	59,226	50,606
Shares Outstanding	8,854	8,828	8,812	8,884	8,756	8,305	7,776	7,517
Statistical Record								
Return on Assets %	0.30	0.39	N.M.	N.M.	N.M.	7.55	7.26	13.45
Return on Equity %	0.68	0.90	N.M.	N.M.	N.M.	14.06	12.43	23.14
EBITDA Margin %	5.85	7.07	8.18	5.35	N.M.	16.74	15.45	24.39
Net Margin %	N.M.	N.M.	0.70	N.M.	N.M.	8.29	7.61	11.59
Asset Turnover	1.13	1.12	1.07	1.06	1.03	0.91	0.95	1.16
Current Ratio	3.40	3.02	3.25	2.77	2.41	2.16	3.54	3.29
Debt to Equity	1.00	0.97	0.92	0.80	0.74	0.53	0.42	0.43
Price Range	24.75-18.34	24.07-17.50	24.07-17.50	22.54-17.50	28.18-19.40	26.05-14.75	27.83-15.82	28.61-13.00
P/E Ratio	495.00-366.80	343.86-250.00	...	...	...	22.26-12.61	33.13-18.83	21.19-9.63
Average Yield %	1.72	1.78	1.80	1.83	1.47	1.77	1.53	1.51

Address: 35 East Wacker Drive, Suite 1100, Chicago, IL 60601
Telephone: 312-467-6755
Fax: 312-467-1356

Web Site: www.quixotecorp.com
Officers: Leslie J. e - Chmn., Pres., C.E.O. Daniel P. Gorey - V.P., C.F.O., Treas.

Auditors: PricewaterhouseCoopers LLP
Investor Contact: 312-467-6755
Transfer Agents: EquiServe Trust Company, N.A., Providence, RI

RADIO ONE, INC.

Exchange	Symbol	Price	52Wk Range	Yield	P/E
NMS	ROIA	$6.18 (8/31/2006)	14.08-5.70	N/A	19.31

*7 Year Price Score 48.00 *NYSE Composite Index=100 *12 Month Price Score 70.81

Interim Earnings (Per Share)

Qtr.	Mar	Jun	Sep	Dec
2003	0.02	0.10	0.11	0.09
2004	0.04	0.12	0.11	0.13
2005	0.07	0.19	0.11	0.10
2006	0.03	0.08	...	...

Interim Dividends (Per Share)
No Dividends Paid

Valuation Analysis   **Institutional Holding**
Forecast P/E   22.11   No of Institutions
                (9/9/2006)   50
Market Cap $610.0 Million   Shares
Book Value   1.0 Billion   8,274,185
Price/Book   0.59   % Held
Price/Sales   1.64   N/A

Business Summary: Media (MIC: 13.1 SIC: 4832 NAIC: 515111)
Radio One owns and/or operates 70 radio stations in 22 markets throughout the United States, as of Dec 31 2005. Co. owns and operates radio stations in markets that include Atlanta, Washington, D.C., Philadelphia, Detroit, Los Angeles, Miami, Houston, Dallas, Baltimore, St. Louis, Cleveland, Charlotte and Richmond. Co. targets stations in urban areas with high concentrations of African-Americans with increasing income and affluence. Additionally, Co. owns 51.0% of the common stock of Reach Media, Inc., which operates a nationally syndicated radio show, a weekly syndicated television show and related businesses.

Recent Developments: For the quarter ended June 30 2006, net income decreased 59.2% to $8.1 million from $19.8 million in the year-earlier quarter. Revenues were $97.8 million, down 3.6% from $101.5 million the year before. Operating income was $34.9 million versus $46.1 million in the prior-year quarter, a decrease of 24.3%. Indirect operating expenses increased 13.6% to $62.9 million from $55.4 million in the equivalent prior-year period.

Prospects: The ongoing softness in the radio industry is hampering Co.'s results in a number of its markets, primarily Los Angeles, Washington, DC, Atlanta, Dallas, Cleveland and Cincinnati. These declines are more than offsetting gains from its Houston, Philadelphia, Richmond and St. Louis markets, as well as higher net broadcast revenue from Reach Media. Thus, Co. is taking strategic steps to address these challenges, from which it believes it is well-positioned to benefit. Separately, on Aug 21 2006, Co. announced that it has agreed to sell the assets of radio station WILD-FM, located in the Boston, MA metropolitan area, for about $30.0 million in cash, to Entercom Communications Corporation.

Financial Data
(US$ in Thousands)

	6 Mos	3 Mos	12/31/2005	12/31/2004	12/31/2003	12/31/2002	12/31/2001	12/31/2000
Earnings Per Share	0.32	0.43	0.46	0.39	0.32	(0.13)	(0.83)	(0.16)
Cash Flow Per Share	0.87	0.96	0.98	1.18	1.05	0.70	0.66	0.66
Income Statement								
Total Revenue	179,917	82,083	371,134	319,761	303,150	295,851	243,804	155,666
EBITDA	66,490	26,742	161,745	156,042	147,457	141,020	120,565	95,006
Depn & Amortn	10,282	5,006	20,761	18,636	19,774	19,694	131,797	66,046
Income Before Taxes	21,403	4,787	79,401	100,319	86,245	62,183	(74,590)	(3,447)
Income Taxes	9,668	1,520	27,003	38,717	32,462	25,282	(24,550)	804
Net Income	10,697	2,593	50,530	61,602	53,783	7,054	(55,247)	(4,251)
Average Shares	98,710	98,743	103,893	105,429	105,071	101,821	90,295	84,540
Balance Sheet								
Total Assets	2,239,450	2,197,941	2,201,380	2,111,141	2,017,871	1,984,360	1,923,915	1,765,218
Current Liabilities	59,557	47,250	55,841	118,346	105,900	100,609	62,082	36,506
Long-Term Obligations	964,500	952,509	952,512	550,020	545,035	597,501	780,022	646,956
Total Liabilities	1,202,242	1,168,671	1,177,983	782,696	739,452	740,337	870,968	708,149
Stockholders' Equity	1,036,254	1,025,740	1,020,541	1,328,445	1,278,419	1,244,023	1,052,947	1,057,069
Shares Outstanding	98,710	98,710	98,703	105,010	104,740	94,214	94,214	87,034
Statistical Record								
Return on Assets %	1.43	1.99	2.34	2.98	2.69	0.36	N.M.	N.M.
Return on Equity %	3.02	4.17	4.30	4.71	4.26	0.61	N.M.	N.M.
EBITDA Margin %	36.96	32.58	43.58	48.80	48.64	47.67	49.45	61.03
Net Margin %	5.95	3.16	13.62	19.27	17.74	2.38	N.M.	N.M.
Asset Turnover	0.17	0.17	0.17	0.15	0.15	0.15	0.13	0.14
Current Ratio	1.65	1.92	1.68	0.78	1.44	1.58	1.58	2.16
Debt to Equity	0.93	0.93	0.93	0.41	0.43	0.48	0.74	0.61
Price Range	14.49-6.89	14.99-7.48	16.29-10.27	20.20-13.09	19.77-12.42	24.65-11.08	23.00-9.94	29.56-5.75
P/E Ratio	45.28-21.53	34.86-17.40	35.41-22.33	51.79-33.56	61.78-38.81	...	...	...

Address: 5900 Princess Garden Parkway, 7th Floor, Lanham, MD 20706
Telephone: 301-306-1111
Fax: 301-306-9426

Web Site: www.radio-one.com
Officers: Catherine L. Hughes - Chmn., Sec. Alfred C. Liggins III - Pres., C.E.O., Treas.

Auditors: Ernst & Young LLP
Transfer Agents: American Stock Transfer and Trust Company

RAMBUS INC. (DE)

Exchange	Symbol	Price	52Wk Range	Yield	P/E
NMS	RMBS	$15.87 (8/31/2006)	46.80-10.26	N/A	52.90

*7 Year Price Score 78.18   *NYSE Composite Index=100   *12 Month Price Score 69.73

Interim Earnings (Per Share)

Qtr.	Mar	Jun	Sep	Dec
2003	0.05	0.04	0.05	0.08
2004	0.07	0.08	0.10	0.06
2005	0.04	0.05	0.14	0.09
2006	0.02	...	...	...

Interim Dividends (Per Share)
No Dividends Paid

Valuation Analysis

		Institutional Holding	
Forecast P/E	48.55	No of Institutions	
	(9/9/2006)	111	
Market Cap	$1.6 Billion	Shares	
Book Value	339.9 Million	33,774,456	
Price/Book	4.79	% Held	
Price/Sales	9.87	32.87	

Business Summary: IT & Technology (MIC: 10.2 SIC: 3674 NAIC: 334413)
Rambus creates chip-to-chip interface technologies designed to improve the time-to-market, performance and cost-effectiveness of its customers' semiconductor and system products. Co.'s products are used in a range of computing, consumer electronics and communications applications. Co. licenses its portfolio of patented inventions to semiconductor and system companies for use in the development and manufacture of their own products. Co. also develops industry standard and custom chip interface designs that it provides to customers under license for incorporation into their products. In addition, Co. offers engineering services to integrate interface technologies into customers' products.

Recent Developments: For the first quarter ended Mar 31 2006, net income decreased 59.1% to $1.8 million compared with $4.4 million in the corresponding year-earlier quarter. Revenues advanced 19.3% to $47.2 million from $39.6 million the year before. Operating loss was $464,000 versus an income of $4.9 million in the prior-year quarter. Direct operating expenses rose 20.7% to $6.8 million from $5.6 million in the comparable period the year before. Indirect operating expenses increased 40.8% to $40.9 million from $29.1 million in the equivalent prior-year period.

Prospects: Co.'s operating results are being tempered by higher research and development expenses, reflecting its long-term plan to invest in research and development capability in the U.S. and Bangalore. Nevertheless, Co. is encouraged with its revenue growth, driven by increased royalty fees received as a result of the Advanced Micro Devices and Fujitsu agreements. Going forward, Co. expects XDR and FlexIO royalties to increase due to the expected launch of the Sony PlayStation®3 product in the second half of 2006. Additionally, Co. expects to recognize a total of $41.6 million of royalty revenues in fiscal 2006 from its recent patent license agreement with Fujitsu.

Financial Data

(US$ in Thousands)	3 Mos	12/31/2005	12/31/2004	12/31/2003	12/31/2002	09/30/2002	09/30/2001	09/30/2000
Earnings Per Share	0.30	0.32	0.30	0.22	0.06	0.24	0.29	(1.10)
Cash Flow Per Share	0.44	0.33	0.43	0.24	0.15	0.33	0.31	0.36
Tang Book Value Per Share	3.07	2.70	3.05	2.29	2.01	2.01	1.91	1.66
Income Statement								
Total Revenue	47,245	157,198	144,874	118,203	25,704	96,565	117,160	72,311
EBITDA	7,288	65,757	54,831	39,790	9,435	43,296	54,382	(135,306)
Depn & Amortn	4,307	9,165	6,946	5,643	1,304	5,290	4,735	3,488
Income Before Taxes	2,981	56,592	47,885	34,147	8,131	38,006	49,647	(138,794)
Income Taxes	1,164	22,915	14,326	10,926	2,602	13,302	18,376	(32,667)
Net Income	1,817	33,677	33,559	23,221	5,529	24,704	31,271	(106,127)
Average Shares	109,332	103,993	110,050	106,544	100,209	102,100	105,966	96,487
Balance Sheet								
Total Assets	535,638	485,519	376,724	293,086	232,959	232,959	237,790	219,631
Current Liabilities	26,479	20,607	36,711	34,984	21,566	21,566	22,375	33,187
Long-Term Obligations	160,000	160,000	...	...	...	...	...	...
Total Liabilities	195,765	190,516	41,267	53,006	37,467	37,467	46,433	57,309
Stockholders' Equity	339,873	295,003	335,457	240,080	195,492	195,492	191,357	162,322
Shares Outstanding	102,505	99,397	102,971	99,154	97,271	97,271	100,287	97,490
Statistical Record								
Return on Assets %	5.43	7.81	9.99	8.83	1.88	10.50	13.67	N.M.
Return on Equity %	10.22	10.68	11.63	10.66	2.28	12.77	17.68	N.M.
EBITDA Margin %	15.43	41.83	37.85	33.66	36.71	44.84	46.42	N.M.
Net Margin %	3.85	21.42	23.16	19.65	21.51	25.58	26.69	N.M.
Asset Turnover	0.29	0.36	0.43	0.45	0.09	0.41	0.51	0.43
Current Ratio	10.69	8.24	4.28	2.73	4.45	4.45	6.40	4.31
Debt to Equity	0.47	0.54	...	...	...	...	...	...
Price Range	39.81-10.29	23.00-10.29	35.20-12.69	30.70-6.71	9.42-3.98	11.72-3.33	83.25-4.86	117.38-15.66
P/E Ratio	132.70-34.30	71.88-32.16	117.33-42.30	139.55-30.50	157.00-66.33	48.83-13.88	287.07-16.76	...

Address: 4440 El Camino Real, Los Altos, CA 94022
Telephone: 650-947-5000
Fax: 650-947-5001

Web Site: www.rambus.com
Officers: Geoff Tate - Chmn. Harold Hughes - Pres., C.E.O.

Auditors: PricewaterhouseCoopers LLP
Investor Contact: 650-947-5050
Transfer Agents: EquiServe Trust Company, N.A.

RAVEN INDUSTRIES, INC.

Exchange	Symbol	Price	52Wk Range	Yield	P/E	Div Acheiver
NMS	RAVN	$27.93 (8/31/2006)	41.73-25.64	1.29	20.69	18 Years

*7 Year Price Score 200.70 *NYSE Composite Index=100 *12 Month Price Score 87.97

Interim Earnings (Per Share)

Qtr.	Apr	Jul	Oct	Jan
2003-04	0.23	0.17	0.21	0.14
2004-05	0.29	0.20	0.28	0.20
2005-06	0.39	0.26	0.37	0.29
2006-07	0.41	0.28	...	...

Interim Dividends (Per Share)

Amt	Decl	Ex	Rec	Pay
0.07Q	11/18/2005	12/21/2005	12/23/2005	1/13/2006
0.09Q	3/13/2006	3/23/2006	3/27/2006	4/14/2006
0.09Q	5/23/2006	6/22/2006	6/26/2006	7/14/2006
0.09Q	8/24/2006	9/21/2006	9/25/2006	10/13/2006

Indicated Div: $0.36 (Div. Reinv. Plan)

Valuation Analysis
Forecast P/E   N/A

Institutional Holding
No of Institutions 84
Shares 10,235,686
% Held 56.56

Market Cap $504.8 Million
Book Value 92.7 Million
Price/Book 5.45
Price/Sales 2.32

Business Summary: Miscellaneous (MIC: 8.11 SIC: 3672 NAIC: 334412)

Raven Industries is an industrial manufacturing company that operates through four business segments consisting of three Co. divisions and one subsidiary. The Engineered Films Division produces rugged reinforced plastic sheeting and high-altitude research balloons for public and commercial research. The Electronics Systems Division provides electronic manufacturing services. The Flow Controls Division develops global positioning systems-based control systems, computerized control hardware and software for precision farming, and systems for the precision application of insecticides, fertilizer and road de-icers. Aerostar International Inc. produces custom-shaped advertising inflatables.

Recent Developments: For the quarter ended July 31 2006, net income increased 7.4% to $5.1 million from $4.8 million in the year-earlier quarter. Revenues were $50.4 million, up 11.2% from $45.3 million the year before. Operating income was $7.9 million versus $7.3 million in the prior-year quarter, an increase of 7.9%. Direct operating expenses rose 11.0% to $38.2 million from $34.4 million in the comparable period the year before. Indirect operating expenses increased 20.3% to $4.3 million from $3.6 million in the equivalent prior-year period.

Prospects: Co. remains optimistic about attaining its target of double-digit earnings growth for full-year fiscal 2006, bolstered by solid performance within its Engineered Films Division (EFD). Furthermore, Co. believes that EFD will continue to benefit from strong demand related to oilfield activity, construction and disaster-related films, supported by its recent capital investments in expanding both its plastic film capacity and product capabilities. As such, Co. expects capital expenditures for fiscal year 2006 to be over $17.0 million, with $13.0 million of these expenditures is expected to be invested towards supporting EFD with extrusion equipment and facilities capacity.

Financial Data
(US$ in Thousands)

	6 Mos	3 Mos	01/31/2006	01/31/2005	01/31/2004	01/31/2003	01/31/2002	01/31/2001
Earnings Per Share	1.35	1.33	1.32	0.97	0.75	0.60	0.47	0.31
Cash Flow Per Share	1.40	1.35	1.17	1.04	1.09	0.70	0.99	0.46
Tang Book Value Per Share	4.64	4.52	4.19	3.33	3.26	2.83	2.82	2.53
Dividends Per Share	0.320	0.300	0.280	0.845	0.170	0.140	0.128	0.117
Dividend Payout %	23.70	22.56	21.21	87.11	22.67	23.33	27.42	37.63
Income Statement								
Total Revenue	108,846	58,465	204,528	168,086	142,727	120,903	118,515	132,858
EBITDA	22,261	12,904	42,680	31,831	25,931	21,283	16,839	14,849
Depn & Amortn	2,709	1,289	5,151	3,841	4,145	3,966	3,145	3,667
Income Before Taxes	19,552	11,615	37,494	27,955	21,716	17,254	13,565	10,924
Income Taxes	6,923	4,113	13,232	10,064	7,880	6,069	4,718	4,513
Net Income	12,629	7,502	24,262	17,891	13,836	11,185	8,847	6,411
Average Shares	18,284	18,349	18,314	18,410	18,489	18,695	18,983	20,675
Balance Sheet								
Total Assets	111,281	114,344	106,157	88,509	79,508	72,816	67,836	65,656
Current Liabilities	16,690	21,883	20,050	20,950	11,895	13,167	13,810	13,935
Long-Term Obligations	5	9	9	...	57	151	280	2,013
Total Liabilities	18,624	23,699	21,768	22,427	13,037	14,580	15,804	17,667
Stockholders' Equity	92,657	90,645	84,389	66,082	66,471	58,236	52,032	47,989
Shares Outstanding	18,072	18,127	18,072	17,999	18,041	18,132	18,422	18,956
Statistical Record								
Return on Assets %	24.49	23.88	24.93	21.24	18.17	15.90	13.25	9.15
Return on Equity %	29.76	30.30	32.25	26.92	22.19	20.29	17.69	12.47
EBITDA Margin %	20.45	22.07	20.87	18.94	18.17	17.60	14.21	11.18
Net Margin %	11.60	12.83	11.86	10.64	9.69	9.25	7.46	4.83
Asset Turnover	2.13	2.06	2.10	2.00	1.87	1.72	1.78	1.90
Current Ratio	4.14	3.42	3.56	2.94	4.68	3.75	3.28	3.75
Debt to Equity	N.M.	N.M.	N.M.	...	N.M.	N.M.	0.01	0.04
Price Range	41.73-21.76	41.65-19.16	32.75-17.08	26.56-13.54	15.07-7.84	9.00-4.89	5.88-3.02	3.04-1.85
P/E Ratio	30.91-16.12	31.32-14.40	24.81-12.94	27.38-13.75	20.09-10.45	15.00-8.15	12.50-6.43	9.81-5.98
Average Yield %	1.02	1.02	1.11	4.60	1.52	2.08	2.99	4.69

Address: 205 East 6th Street, P.O. Box 5107, Sioux Falls, SD 57117-5107
Telephone: 605-336-2750
Fax: 605-335-0268

Web Site: www.ravenind.com
Officers: Ronald M. Moquist – Pres., C.E.O. Thomas Iacarella - V.P., C.F.O., Treas., Sec.

Auditors: PricewaterhouseCoopers LLP
Investor Contact: 605-336-2750
Transfer Agents: Wells Fargo Bank N.A., St. Paul, MN

RED HAT INC

Exchange	Symbol	Price	52Wk Range	Yield	P/E
NMS	RHAT	$23.20 (8/31/2006)	32.27-14.20	N/A	55.24

*7 Year Price Score 106.57 *NYSE Composite Index=100 *12 Month Price Score 89.80

Interim Earnings (Per Share)

Qtr.	May	Aug	Nov	Feb
2003-04	0.01	0.02	0.02	0.03
2004-05	0.06	0.06	0.06	0.07
2005-06	0.07	0.09	0.12	0.14
2006-07	0.07	...	...	...

Interim Dividends (Per Share)
No Dividends Paid

Valuation Analysis **Institutional Holding**

Forecast P/E	37.18	No of Institutions
	(9/9/2006)	240
Market Cap	$4.3 Billion	Shares
Book Value	512.2 Million	186,015,200
Price/Book	8.33	% Held
Price/Sales	14.15	97.57

Business Summary: IT & Technology (MIC: 10.2 SIC: 7372 NAIC: 511210)
Red Hat provides open source software systems to the enterprise, including its core enterprise operating system platform, Red Hat Enterprise Linux (Enterprise Linux), as well as other enterprise technologies. Co. offers a choice of operating system platforms: Enterprise Linux AS, Enterprise Linux ES, Enterprise Linux WS and Red Hat Desktop for application areas, including the data center, edge-of-the-network applications, information technology infrastructure, corporate desktop and technical/developer workstation. Co. also provides other infrastructure enterprise technologies such as technologies for the development and deployment of JAVA-based web applications, among others.

Recent Developments: For the quarter ended May 31 2006, net income increased 10.6% to $13.8 million from $12.4 million in the year-earlier quarter. Revenues were $84.0 million, up 38.2% from $60.8 million the year before. Operating income was $12.6 million versus $7.6 million in the prior-year quarter, an increase of 64.9%. Direct operating expenses rose 6.5% to $13.4 million from $12.6 million in the comparable period the year before. Indirect operating expenses increased 43.1% to $57.9 million from $40.5 million in the equivalent prior-year period.

Prospects: For fiscal 2007, Co. is maintaining its focus on gaining further acceptance and deployment of Enterprise Linux as a significant computing platform by its key enterprise customers. In addition, Co. will concentrate on generating higher subscription revenue on a per installed system basis by renewing subscriptions and providing additional value to its customers, as well as by growing the number of enterprise technologies that comprise its open source architecture. Meanwhile, Co. expects to further capitalize upon its recent international expansion and acquisitions in order to obtain several new opportunities in key international geographies such as India and South America going forward.

Financial Data
(US$ in Thousands)

	3 Mos	02/28/2006	02/28/2005	02/29/2004	02/28/2003	02/28/2002	02/28/2001	02/29/2000
Earnings Per Share	0.42	0.41	0.24	0.08	(0.04)	(0.83)	(0.53)	(0.40)
Cash Flow Per Share	1.10	1.05	0.67	0.35	(0.00)	(0.04)	(0.24)	...
Tang Book Value Per Share	2.32	2.12	1.54	1.87	1.73	1.72	1.88	2.19
Income Statement								
Total Revenue	84,002	278,330	196,466	126,084	90,926	78,910	103,429	42,428
EBITDA	28,410	106,625	62,274	...	...	...	(52,482)	(37,971)
Depn & Amortn	5,096	18,490	10,897	6,864	6,519	59,720	54,997	5,941
Income Before Taxes	21,830	82,016	44,941	...	...	...	(86,447)	(39,548)
Income Taxes	8,077	2,331	(485)	...	...	...	267	294
Net Income	13,753	79,685	45,426	13,998	(6,599)	(140,216)	(86,714)	(39,842)
Average Shares	214,325	207,815	215,882	182,913	170,158	169,451	164,659	100,610
Balance Sheet								
Total Assets	1,379,975	1,314,241	1,134,036	1,109,619	390,339	369,865	505,251	423,535
Current Liabilities	221,431	200,922	139,199	83,570	47,143	36,975	40,691	29,857
Long-Term Obligations	570,077	570,213	600,097	600,538	1,393	1,563	277	231
Total Liabilities	867,732	836,683	772,365	700,412	53,918	42,316	40,969	30,088
Stockholders' Equity	512,243	477,558	361,671	409,207	336,421	327,549	464,283	393,447
Shares Outstanding	183,979	183,115	176,740	181,665	170,779	169,721	168,485	153,333
Statistical Record								
Return on Assets %	6.38	6.51	4.05	1.86	N.M.	N.M.	N.M.	...
Return on Equity %	18.25	18.99	11.79	3.74	N.M.	N.M.	N.M.	...
EBITDA Margin %	33.82	38.31	31.70	...	...	...	N.M.	N.M.
Net Margin %	16.37	28.63	23.12	11.10	N.M.	N.M.	N.M.	N.M.
Asset Turnover	0.24	0.23	0.18	0.17	0.24	0.18	0.22	...
Current Ratio	4.59	4.39	2.77	7.87	2.55	3.21	4.42	9.38
Debt to Equity	1.11	1.19	1.66	1.47	N.M.	N.M.	N.M.	N.M.
Price Range	32.27-11.97	30.82-10.46	28.73-10.49	21.23-5.43	7.32-3.75	9.00-3.02	75.81-5.13	143.13-26.03
P/E Ratio	76.83-28.50	75.17-25.51	119.71-43.71	265.38-67.88	...	...	...	...

Address: 1801 Varsity Drive, Raleigh, NC 27606 Telephone: 919-754-3700	Web Site: www.redhat.com Officers: Matthew J. Szulik - Chmn., Pres., C.E.O. Alex Pinchev - Exec. V.P., Worldwide Sales	Auditors: PricewaterhouseCoopers LLP

RENT-A-CENTER INC.

Exchange	Symbol	Price	52Wk Range	Yield	P/E
NMS	RCII	$27.10 (8/31/2006)	28.18-15.85	N/A	15.31

*7 Year Price Score 89.40 *NYSE Composite Index=100 *12 Month Price Score 112.07

Interim Earnings (Per Share)

Qtr.	Mar	Jun	Sep	Dec
2003	0.57	0.39	0.52	0.61
2004	0.63	0.62	0.07	0.60
2005	0.63	0.55	0.15	0.49
2006	0.57	0.56	...	...

Interim Dividends (Per Share)

Amt	Decl	Ex	Rec	Pay
150%	7/28/2003	9/2/2003	8/15/2003	8/29/2003

Valuation Analysis

		Institutional Holding	
Forecast P/E	12.63	No of Institutions	
	(9/9/2006)	190	
Market Cap	$1.9 Billion	Shares	
Book Value	915.8 Million	70,211,360	
Price/Book	2.06	% Held	
Price/Sales	0.80	N/A	

Business Summary: General Construction Supplies & Services (MIC: 3.3 SIC: 7359 NAIC: 532210)

Rent-A-Center is a large operator in the U.S. rent-to-own industry. As of Dec 31 2005, Co. operated 2,760 company-owned stores nationwide and in Puerto Rico, including 21 stores in Wisconsin operated by its subsidiary, Get It Now. Co. offers goods such as home electronics, appliances, computers, and furniture and accessories to consumers under flexible rental purchase arrangements that allow the customer to obtain ownership of the merchandise at the conclusion of an agreed upon rental period. Co.'s subsidiary, ColorTyme, Inc. is a national franchiser of 296 rent-to-own stores, 288 of which operated under the ColorTyme name and eight operated under the Rent-A-Center name.

Recent Developments: For the quarter ended June 30 2006, net income decreased 4.5% to $39.8 million from $41.7 million in the year-earlier quarter. Revenues were $583.6 million, up 0.5% from $580.6 million the year before. Operating income was $75.2 million versus $73.0 million in the prior-year quarter, an increase of 3.0%. Direct operating expenses rose 0.2% to $486.2 million from $485.1 million in the comparable period the year before. Indirect operating expenses decreased 1.1% to $22.2 million from $22.4 million in the equivalent prior-year period.

Prospects: On Aug 8 2006, Co. announced that it has entered into a definitive agreement under which it will acquire Rent-Way, a rental purchase company, for about $567.0 million, including the purchase of all outstanding common stock and options, net debt and other liabilities of Rent-Way, and the redemption of all outstanding convertible preferred stock. Including the amortization of intangible assets related to the customer and non-compete agreements, Co. expects the transaction to be about $0.01 to $0.02 accretive to earnings per diluted share in 2007, accelerating to $0.20 and $0.35 per diluted share in 2008 and 2009, respectively. The transaction should close in the fourth quarter of 2006.

Financial Data
(US$ in Thousands)

	6 Mos	3 Mos	12/31/2005	12/31/2004	12/31/2003	12/31/2002	12/31/2001	12/31/2000
Earnings Per Share	1.77	1.76	1.83	1.94	2.08	1.90	0.71	1.18
Cash Flow Per Share	2.40	2.33	2.57	4.22	4.07	4.01	2.72	3.13
Tang Book Value Per Share	N.M.	N.M.	N.M.	N.M.	N.M.	1.13	N.M.	N.M.
Income Statement								
Total Revenue	1,190,598	606,975	2,339,107	2,313	2,228	2,010,044	1,808,528	1,601,614
EBITDA	402,847	200,583	759,540	793	823	777,253	595,887	627,758
Depn & Amortn	252,170	125,099	509,769	506	489	426,804	411,301	360,745
Income Before Taxes	127,212	63,921	209,068	251	291	288,443	124,806	194,395
Income Taxes	47,041	23,593	73,330	96	109	116,270	58,589	91,368
Net Income	80,171	40,328	135,738	156	181	172,173	66,217	103,027
Average Shares	70,640	70,250	74,108	80	87	90,865	92,698	87,030
Balance Sheet								
Total Assets	2,006,846	1,982,356	1,948,664	1,968	1,831	1,616,052	1,619,920	1,486,910
Current Liabilities	373,941	447,650	279,978	302	206	166,178	220,126	155,256
Long-Term Obligations	717,155	667,625	724,050	708	698	521,330	702,506	741,051
Total Liabilities	1,091,096	1,115,275	1,125,232	1,174	1,036	773,650	922,632	896,307
Stockholders' Equity	915,750	867,081	823,432	794	795	842,400	405,378	309,371
Shares Outstanding	69,686	69,312	69,187	74	80	87,346	63,754	61,774
Statistical Record								
Return on Assets %	6.43	6.47	13.92	8.18	0.02	10.64	4.26	6.91
Return on Equity %	14.02	14.98	32.94	19.56	0.04	27.60	18.53	39.82
EBITDA Margin %	33.84	33.05	32.47	34.26	36.95	38.67	32.95	39.20
Net Margin %	6.73	6.64	5.80	6.74	8.15	8.57	3.66	6.43
Asset Turnover	1.19	1.18	2.40	1.21	0.00	1.24	1.16	1.07
Current Ratio	2.43	2.01	3.11	2.99	4.45	4.61	3.64	4.45
Debt to Equity	0.78	0.77	0.88	0.89	0.88	0.62	1.73	2.40
Price Range	28.18-15.85	27.63-15.85	27.71-15.85	33.50-23.46	34.59-18.36	25.40-12.40	21.04-7.72	14.25-5.60
P/E Ratio	15.92-8.95	15.70-9.01	15.14-8.66	17.27-12.09	16.63-8.82	13.37-6.52	29.63-10.88	12.08-4.75

Address: 5700 Tennyson Parkway, Suite 100, Plano, TX 75024
Telephone: 972-801-1100
Fax: 972-701-0360

Web Site: www.rentacenter.com
Officers: Mark E. Speese - Chmn., C.E.O. Mitchell E. Fadel - Pres., C.O.O.

Auditors: Grant Thornton LLP
Investor Contact: 972-801-1214
Transfer Agents: Mellon Investor Services LLC, Ridgefield Park, NJ

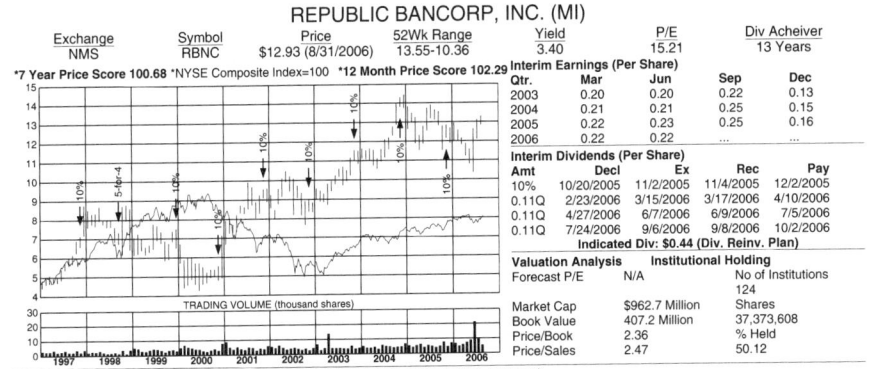

REPUBLIC BANCORP, INC. (MI)

Exchange	Symbol	Price	52Wk Range	Yield	P/E	Div Acheiver
NMS	RBNC	$12.93 (8/31/2006)	13.55-10.36	3.40	15.21	13 Years

*7 Year Price Score 100.68 *NYSE Composite Index=100 *12 Month Price Score 102.29

Interim Earnings (Per Share)

Qtr.	Mar	Jun	Sep	Dec
2003	0.20	0.20	0.22	0.13
2004	0.21	0.21	0.25	0.15
2005	0.22	0.23	0.25	0.16
2006	0.22	0.22	...	...

Interim Dividends (Per Share)

Amt	Decl	Ex	Rec	Pay
10%	10/20/2005	11/2/2005	11/4/2005	12/2/2005
0.11Q	2/23/2006	3/15/2006	3/17/2006	4/10/2006
0.11Q	4/27/2006	6/7/2006	6/9/2006	7/5/2006
0.11Q	7/24/2006	9/6/2006	9/8/2006	10/2/2006

Indicated Div: $0.44 (Div. Reinv. Plan)

Valuation Analysis
Forecast P/E   N/A
Market Cap $962.7 Million
Book Value   407.2 Million
Price/Book   2.36
Price/Sales 2.47

Institutional Holding
No of Institutions 124
Shares 37,373,608
% Held 50.12

Business Summary: Commercial Banking (MIC: 8.1 SIC: 6021 NAIC: 522110)

Republic Bancorp is a bank holding company. Through its wholly-owned subsidiary, Republic Bank, Co. provides commercial, retail and mortgage banking products and services. Republic Bank is headquartered in Lansing, MI. As of Dec 31 2005, Republic Bank operated 92 offices and 91 ATMs in seven market areas in Michigan, the greater Cleveland, Ohio area and Indianapolis, IN. In addition, Republic Bank operates a retail mortgage loan production office in Massachusetts. As of Dec 31 2005, Co. had total assets of $6.08 billion and total deposits of $3.14 billion.

Recent Developments: For the quarter ended June 30 2006, net income decreased 6.2% to $16.4 million from $17.5 million in the year-earlier quarter. Net interest income decreased 3.3% to $37.5 million from $38.8 million in the year-earlier quarter. Provision for loan losses was $1.8 million versus $1.4 million in the prior-year quarter, an increase of 25.0%. Non-interest income fell 10.4% to $8.0 million from $8.9 million, while non-interest expense declined 5.6% to $20.1 million.

Prospects: On June 27 2006, Co. and Citizens Banking Corporation announced that they have agreed to merge Co. into Citizens in a transaction valued at about $1.05 billion in stock and cash. Under the agreement, in which Co. will be acquired by Citizens, Co. shareholders will have the right to elect to receive either cash or Citizens common stock, subject to pro-ration if either is oversubscribed. At closing, each Co. shareholder will receive, in exchange for each share of Republic common stock they hold, cash or Citizens common stock, in either case having a value equal to $2.08 in cash plus 0.4378 shares of Citizens common stock. The transaction is projected to close in the fourth quarter of 2006.

Financial Data
(US$ in Thousands)

	6 Mos	3 Mos	12/31/2005	12/31/2004	12/31/2003	12/31/2002	12/31/2001	12/31/2000
Earnings Per Share	0.85	0.86	0.90	0.85	0.79	0.72	0.59	0.57
Cash Flow Per Share	1.91	0.78	1.51	1.05	7.39	1.72	(6.32)	1.49
Tang Book Value Per Share	5.47	5.44	5.39	5.29	4.81	4.35	3.89	3.05
Dividends Per Share	0.430	0.420	0.410	0.348	0.278	0.238	0.216	0.197
Dividend Payout %	50.59	48.99	45.56	40.72	35.36	33.60	36.42	34.44
Income Statement								
Interest Income	181,014	88,399	326,200	282,379	265,680	284,704	333,376	348,328
Interest Expense	104,865	49,711	172,164	132,529	123,183	137,024	189,767	213,680
Net Interest Income	76,149	38,688	154,036	149,850	142,497	147,680	143,609	134,648
Provision for Losses	3,150	1,400	5,800	8,500	12,000	16,000	8,700	6,500
Non-Interest Income	15,238	7,279	43,304	47,319	60,779	56,027	71,384	70,838
Non-Interest Expense	41,049	20,972	93,261	94,075	104,654	100,515	132,213	127,641
Income Before Taxes	47,188	23,595	98,279	94,594	86,622	87,192	74,080	71,345
Income Taxes	14,375	7,178	29,098	27,910	25,896	24,687	22,515	22,945
Net Income	32,813	16,417	69,181	66,684	60,726	62,505	51,565	48,400
Average Shares	75,116	75,552	77,074	78,400	77,647	78,562	80,554	80,364
Balance Sheet								
Net Loans & Leases	4,786,364	4,704,628	4,586,136	4,422,157	4,117,243	3,620,466	3,429,224	3,743,226
Total Assets	6,346,590	6,243,670	6,081,766	5,713,977	5,353,688	4,778,195	4,740,605	4,610,641
Total Deposits	3,061,447	3,083,975	3,142,943	3,046,211	2,815,269	2,788,272	2,753,468	2,728,526
Total Liabilities	5,939,406	5,837,183	5,677,307	5,304,339	4,984,268	4,395,467	4,356,969	4,287,058
Stockholders' Equity	407,184	406,487	404,459	409,638	369,420	332,728	304,917	294,864
Shares Outstanding	74,451	74,684	74,976	77,467	76,867	76,453	77,840	79,597
Statistical Record								
Return on Assets %	1.08	1.12	1.17	1.20	1.20	1.31	1.10	1.08
Return on Equity %	16.47	16.83	17.00	17.07	17.30	19.60	17.19	17.20
Net Interest Margin %	40.45	43.77	47.22	53.07	53.63	51.87	43.08	38.66
Efficiency Ratio %	19.96	21.92	25.24	28.53	32.06	29.50	32.66	30.45
Loans to Deposits	1.56	1.53	1.46	1.45	1.46	1.30	1.25	1.37
Price Range	13.90-10.36	13.90-11.53	13.90-11.53	14.45-10.58	11.55-8.72	10.48-7.68	9.92-6.67	7.14-4.27
P/E Ratio	16.35-12.19	16.16-13.40	15.44-12.81	17.01-12.45	14.62-11.03	14.56-10.66	16.81-11.31	12.53-7.49
Average Yield %	3.50	3.34	3.21	2.88	2.77	2.60	2.56	3.72

Address: 1070 East Main Street, P.O. Box 70, Owosso, MI 48867
Telephone: 989-725-7337
Fax: 989-723-8762
Web Site: www.republicbancorp.com
Officers: Jerry D. Campbell - Chmn. George J. Butvilas - Vice-Chmn.
Auditors: Ernst & Young LLP
Investor Contact: 989-725-7337
Transfer Agents: EquiServe Trust Company, N.A., Providence, RI

RESEARCH FRONTIERS INC.

Exchange	Symbol	Price	52Wk Range	Yield	P/E
NAS	REFR	$4.20 (8/31/2006)	6.10-2.81	N/A	N/A

*7 Year Price Score 30.98 *NYSE Composite Index=100 *12 Month Price Score 92.56

Interim Earnings (Per Share)

Qtr.	Mar	Jun	Sep	Dec
2003	(0.11)	(0.09)	(0.07)	(0.11)
2004	(0.10)	(0.08)	(0.07)	(0.08)
2005	(0.07)	(0.07)	(0.07)	(0.06)
2006	(0.07)	(0.06)	...	...

Interim Dividends (Per Share)

No Dividends Paid

Valuation Analysis

		Institutional Holding	
Forecast P/E	N/A	No of Institutions	16
Market Cap	$58.0 Million	Shares	992,645
Book Value	1.9 Million	% Held	7.19
Price/Book	30.59		
Price/Sales	385.11		

Business Summary: Biotechnology (MIC: 9.2 SIC: 8731 NAIC: 541710)

Research Frontiers develops and licenses suspended particle device (SPD) technology used in light-control glass and plastic products. Co.'s SPD technology has numerous product applications including SPD-Smart™ windows, sunshades, skylights and interior partitions for homes and buildings, automotive and aircraft windows, sunroofs, sun visors and rear-view mirrors, instrument panels and navigation systems, variable light transmission eyewear, including sunglasses and goggles, and flat panel information displays for use in billboards, scoreboards, point-of-purchase advertising displays, traffic signs, computers, televisions, telephones, PDAs and other electronic instruments.

Recent Developments: For the quarter ended June 30 2006, net loss amounted to $831,699 versus a net loss of $962,104 in the year-earlier quarter. Revenues were $63,889, up 72.7% from $36,992 the year before. Operating loss was $856,973 versus a loss of $999,180 in the prior-year quarter. Indirect operating expenses decreased 11.1% to $920,862 from $1.0 million in the equivalent prior-year period.

Prospects: Co. attributes the recent gain in fee income from licensing activities to the timing and amount of minimum annual royalties paid, and the date of receipt of such payment on certain license agreements, by end- product licensees. Certain license fees, which are paid in advance, resulting in the recognition of deferred revenue for the current accounting period however, will be recognized as fee income in future periods. Separately, based upon existing levels of cash expenditures, existing cash reserves and budgeted revenues, Co. believes that it will not require additional funding until the first quarter of 2007.

Financial Data (US$ in Thousands)	6 Mos	3 Mos	12/31/2005	12/31/2004	12/31/2003	12/31/2002	12/31/2001	12/31/2000
Earnings Per Share	(0.26)	(0.27)	(0.27)	(0.33)	(0.38)	(0.33)	(0.38)	(0.63)
Cash Flow Per Share	(0.25)	(0.28)	(0.29)	(0.28)	(0.33)	(0.30)	(0.41)	(0.27)
Tang Book Value Per Share	0.14	0.20	0.26	0.19	0.43	0.49	0.75	1.22
Income Statement								
Total Revenue	90	26	139	201	258	218	142	334
Depn & Amortn	17	8	46	83	112	114	119	109
Net Income	(1,750)	(918)	(3,746)	(4,261)	(4,772)	(3,951)	(4,541)	(7,568)
Average Shares	13,812	13,812	13,692	12,792	12,436	12,152	12,085	12,096
Balance Sheet								
Total Assets	2,188	2,965	3,957	2,861	5,690	6,267	9,325	15,729
Current Liabilities	291	237	311	468	221	293	275	991
Total Liabilities	291	237	311	468	221	293	275	991
Stockholders' Equity	1,896	2,728	3,646	2,392	5,469	5,974	9,050	14,738
Shares Outstanding	13,812	13,812	13,812	12,812	12,683	12,215	12,108	12,103
Statistical Record								
Asset Turnover	0.04	0.02	0.04	0.05	0.04	0.03	...	0.03
Current Ratio	7.03	11.97	12.29	5.80	24.10	18.09	30.08	15.50
Price Range	6.10-2.78	6.10-2.78	6.46-2.78	13.61-5.43	16.00-4.55	19.80-7.15	29.41-10.00	38.63-14.85

Address: 240 Crossways Park Drive, Woodbury, NY 11797-2033
Telephone: 516-364-1902
Fax: 516-364-3798

Web Site: www.SmartGlass.com
Officers: Robert L. Saxe - Chmn. Joseph M. Harary - Pres., Treas.

Auditors: BDO SEIDMAN, LLP
Investor Contact: 516-364-1902
Transfer Agents: Continental Stock Transfer & Trust Company, New York, NY

RESEARCH IN MOTION, LTD.

Exchange	Symbol	Price	52Wk Range	Yield	P/E
NMS	RIMM	$82.50 (8/31/2006)	88.71-57.40	N/A	41.88

*7 Year Price Score 149.81 *NYSE Composite Index=100 *12 Month Price Score 97.17

Interim Earnings (Per Share)

Qtr.	May	Aug	Nov	Feb
2002-03	(0.07)	(0.09)	(0.60)	(0.20)
2003-04	(0.06)	0.01	0.10	0.22
2004-05	0.28	0.36	0.46	(0.01)
2005-06	0.67	0.56	0.61	0.12
2006-07	0.68	...	...	...

Interim Dividends (Per Share)

Amt	Decl	Ex	Rec	Pay
100%	4/7/2004	6/7/2004	5/27/2004	6/4/2004

Valuation Analysis | **Institutional Holding**

Forecast P/E	20.77	No of Institutions
	(9/9/2006)	242
Market Cap	$15.3 Billion	Shares
Book Value	2.0 Billion	129,098,904
Price/Book	7.68	% Held
Price/Sales	7.43	69.21

Business Summary: Communications (MIC: 10.1 SIC: 4899 NAIC: 517212)
Research in Motion is a designer, manufacturer and marketer of wireless applications and products for the worldwide mobile communications market. Through the development of integrated hardware, software and services that support multiple wireless network standards, Co. provides platforms and applications for seamless access to e-mail, phone, SMS (short message service) messaging, Internet and intranet-based applications. Co. also licenses its technology to handset and software vendors to enable these companies to offer wireless data services using the BlackBerry™ Enterprise Server and BlackBerry™ Internet Service.

Recent Developments: For the quarter ended June 3 2006, net income slipped 2.1% to $129.8 million compared with $132.5 million in the corresponding period of the previous year. Results for 2005 included a pre-tax litigation expense of $6.5 million. Revenues jumped 35.1% to $613.1 million from $453.9 million in the year-earlier quarter. Gross margin advanced 35.0% to $337.8 million from $250.2 million in the prior-year period. Income from operations increased 19.8% to $163.0 million versus $136.1 million the year before. During the first quarter, Co. added approximately 680,000 new BlackBerry subscriber accounts.

Prospects: Co. is benefiting from solid revenue and earnings results, boosted by an increase in sales for handhelds, service and software. In addition, Co. is pleased with its subscriber results, which increased by approximately 680,000 to 5.5 total subscriber accounts. Meanwhile, Co. will look to continue its competitive focus on driving strong growth in existing markets and fueling meaningful international expansion. Separately, Co. announced that BlackBerry ISV Alliance members will continue to build upon the BlackBerry® platform with a range of new products and services expected to help customers extend their wireless data strategies beyond wireless email.

Financial Data (US$ in Thousands)	03/04/2006	02/26/2005	02/28/2004	03/01/2003	03/02/2002	02/28/2001	02/29/2000	02/28/1999
Earnings Per Share	1.96	1.09	0.28	(0.95)	(0.18)	(0.04)	0.07	0.07
Cash Flow Per Share	0.78	1.49	0.40	0.02	0.11	...	...	...
Tang Book Value Per Share	10.13	9.87	8.78	4.03	5.37	5.77	2.19	1.25
Income Statement								
Total Revenue	2,065,845	1,350,447	594,616	306,732	294,053	221,327	84,967	70,483
EBITDA	571,930	137,921	102,158	(85,958)	(20,602)	12,165	20,719	17,028
Depn & Amortn	85,873	66,760	54,529	31,600	17,740	8,645	4,683	4,144
Income Before Taxes	486,057	71,161	47,629	(117,558)	(38,342)	3,520	16,036	12,884
Income Taxes	103,979	(142,226)	(4,200)	31,106	(9,863)	9,731	5,538	3,343
Net Income	382,078	213,387	51,829	(148,664)	(28,479)	(6,211)	10,498	9,541
Average Shares	194,942	196,439	163,868	155,272	156,934	147,110	145,992	...
Balance Sheet								
Current Assets	1,256,579	1,544,248	1,355,405	424,937	737,318	857,065	294,382	153,177
Total Assets	2,312,156	2,620,994	1,931,378	859,609	948,157	970,063	337,227	175,527
Current Liabilities	278,680	630,814	208,875	149,099	59,538	60,802	19,310	15,473
Long-Term Obligations	6,851	6,504	6,240	5,776	11,874	6,328	6,526	...
Total Liabilities	313,389	637,318	215,115	154,875	71,412	67,130	25,836	15,473
Stockholders' Equity	1,998,767	1,983,676	1,716,263	704,734	876,745	902,933	311,391	160,054
Shares Outstanding	186,001	189,484	184,830	154,344	157,582	156,541	142,272	128,518
Statistical Record								
Return on Assets %	15.24	9.40	3.72	N.M.	N.M.	N.M.	...	5.80
Return on Equity %	18.88	11.57	4.29	N.M.	N.M.	N.M.	...	6.15
EBITDA Margin %	27.69	10.21	17.18	N.M.	N.M.	N.M.	24.38	24.16
Net Margin %	18.49	15.80	8.72	N.M.	N.M.	N.M.	12.36	13.54
Asset Turnover	0.82	0.59	0.43	0.34	0.30	0.34	...	0.43
Current Ratio	4.51	2.45	6.49	2.85	12.38	14.10	15.25	9.90
Debt to Equity	N.M.	N.M.	N.M.	0.01	0.01	0.01	0.02	...
Price Range	83.82-57.40	93.96-43.01	49.45-5.50	14.65-4.21	23.25-7.08	78.06-12.56	73.88-3.81	5.77-4.44
P/E Ratio	42.77-29.29	86.20-39.46	176.61-19.66	...	...	...	N.M.	82.48-63.39

Address: 295 Phillip Street, Waterloo, N2L 3W8
Telephone: 519-888-7465
Fax: 519-888-6906

Web Site: www.rim.com
Officers: James L. Balsillie - Chmn., Co-C.E.O.
Michael Lazaridis - Pres., Co-C.E.O.

Auditors: Ernst & Young LLP
Transfer Agents: Computershare Trust Company of Canada, Toronto, Ontario

RESPIRONICS, INC.

Exchange	Symbol	Price	52Wk Range	Yield	P/E
NMS	RESP	$36.91 (8/31/2006)	42.62-33.39	N/A	28.39

*7 Year Price Score 142.36 *NYSE Composite Index=100 *12 Month Price Score 93.37

Interim Earnings (Per Share)

Qtr.	Sep	Dec	Mar	Jun
2002-03	0.13	0.14	0.20	0.22
2003-04	0.16	0.23	0.26	0.28
2004-05	0.21	0.28	0.34	0.34
2005-06	0.25	0.33	0.38	...

Interim Dividends (Per Share)
No Dividends Paid

Valuation Analysis

		Institutional Holding	
Forecast P/E	22.05 (9/9/2006)	No of Institutions	243
Market Cap	$2.7 Billion	Shares	
Book Value	727.4 Million		62,304,924
Price/Book	3.69	% Held	78.21
Price/Sales	2.64		

Business Summary: Medical Instruments & Equipment (MIC: 9.6 SIC: 3842 NAIC: 339113)
Respironics is a designer, developer, manufacturer and marketer of medical devices used primarily for the treatment of patients suffering from sleep and respiratory disorders. Co.'s main product lines are: Homecare products, including sleep apnea products, respiratory devices, invasive portable volume ventilation products used in the home, and home oxygen products; Hospital products, including therapeutic devices that assist or control a patient's ventilation, cardio-respiratory monitoring products that provide information about a patient's condition, and respiratory drug delivery products; and other emerging product lines, including infant management and developmental care products.

Recent Developments: For the third quarter ended Mar 31 2006, net income increased 14.1% to $27.9 million compared with $24.4 million in the corresponding year-earlier quarter. Revenues were $267.3 million, up 13.0% from $236.5 million the year before. Direct operating expenses rose 13.5% to $120.6 million from $106.3 million in the comparable period the year before. Indirect operating expenses increased 13.6% to $102.1 million from $89.9 million in the equivalent prior-year period.

Prospects: Co. recently launched the REMstar® Plus unit from its new M-Series platform and it expects favorable results from the market introduction of the remaining continuous positive airway pressure devices in this new product family by the end of fiscal 2006. Additionally, Co. continues to receive positive market feedback about its ComfortLite™ II patient interface device which was recently released to the marketplace. Meanwhile, Co. remains committed to exploring opportunities to invest in and strengthen its presence in various international markets. For fiscal 2006, Co. expects earnings in the range of $1.46 to $1.48 per share and revenue of approximately $1.05 billion.

Financial Data
(US$ in Thousands)

	9 Mos	6 Mos	3 Mos	06/30/2005	06/30/2004	06/30/2003	06/30/2002	06/30/2001
Earnings Per Share	1.30	1.26	1.21	1.17	0.92	0.68	0.60	0.55
Cash Flow Per Share	1.30	1.60	1.79	1.91	2.04	1.85	1.40	0.89
Tang Book Value Per Share	7.63	7.09	6.78	6.43	5.85	4.68	3.96	2.89
Income Statement								
Total Revenue	765,435	498,124	240,222	911,497	759,550	629,817	494,919	422,438
EBITDA	152,896	90,532	39,677	180,414	147,728	121,842	98,268	84,246
Depn & Amortn	39,781	22,005	9,776	44,695	42,493	46,952	34,232	28,338
Income Before Taxes	113,115	68,527	29,901	135,719	105,234	74,890	64,036	55,908
Income Taxes	42,623	25,898	11,324	51,363	40,214	28,308	25,619	22,337
Net Income	70,492	42,629	18,576	84,356	65,020	46,581	38,417	33,571
Average Shares	73,704	73,540	73,341	72,254	70,618	68,688	64,016	61,772
Balance Sheet								
Total Assets	979,145	939,523	903,854	878,446	711,139	582,196	547,450	367,948
Current Liabilities	206,341	202,160	196,736	201,128	151,581	127,229	110,886	52,625
Long-Term Obligations	27,849	28,322	29,924	29,241	26,897	16,513	59,502	80,055
Total Liabilities	251,700	253,073	248,022	250,801	192,086	155,327	179,729	132,680
Stockholders' Equity	727,445	686,450	655,832	627,646	519,053	426,869	367,720	235,268
Shares Outstanding	72,668	72,295	72,054	71,698	69,966	67,914	66,586	60,749
Statistical Record								
Return on Assets %	10.47	10.63	10.71	10.61	10.03	8.25	8.39	9.31
Return on Equity %	14.30	14.63	14.71	14.71	13.71	11.72	12.74	15.75
EBITDA Margin %	19.98	18.17	16.52	19.79	19.45	19.35	19.86	19.94
Net Margin %	9.21	8.56	7.73	9.25	8.56	7.40	7.76	7.95
Asset Turnover	1.12	1.14	1.16	1.15	1.17	1.12	1.08	1.17
Current Ratio	3.02	2.91	2.85	2.67	2.99	2.67	2.79	4.27
Debt to Equity	0.04	0.04	0.05	0.05	0.05	0.04	0.16	0.34
Price Range	42.62-29.14	42.62-26.27	42.18-22.90	36.97-22.90	29.38-18.61	19.73-13.90	18.50-12.13	17.38-8.00
P/E Ratio	32.78-22.41	33.83-20.85	34.86-18.92	31.60-19.57	31.93-20.23	29.01-20.44	30.83-20.22	31.59-14.55

Address: 1010 Murry Ridge Lane, Murrysville, PA 15668-8525
Telephone: 724-387-5180

Web Site: www.respironics.com
Officers: Gerald E. McGinnis - Chmn. James W. Liken - Vice-Chmn.

Auditors: Ernst & Young LLP
Investor Contact: 412-731-2100
Transfer Agents: Mellon Investor Services LLC

RF MICRO DEVICES, INC.

Exchange	Symbol	Price	52Wk Range	Yield	P/E
NMS	RFMD	$6.62 (8/31/2006)	9.44-5.00	N/A	41.38

*7 Year Price Score 32.97 *NYSE Composite Index=100 *12 Month Price Score 89.47

Interim Earnings (Per Share)

Qtr.	Jun	Sep	Dec	Mar
2003-04	(0.04)	0.06	0.13	(0.01)
2004-05	0.02	(0.04)	0.00	(0.33)
2005-06	(0.01)	0.03	0.07	(0.01)
2006-07	0.07	...	...	...

Interim Dividends (Per Share)
No Dividends Paid

Valuation Analysis

		Institutional Holding	
Forecast P/E	15.29	No of Institutions	
	(9/9/2006)	189	
Market Cap	$1.3 Billion	Shares	
Book Value	623.7 Million	137,936,448	
Price/Book	2.03	% Held	
Price/Sales	1.49	72.08	

Business Summary: IT & Technology (MIC: 10.2 SIC: 3674 NAIC: 334413)

RF Micro Devices designs and manufactures high-performance radio frequency (RF) components and systems for mobile communications. Co.'s power amplifiers (PAs), transmit modules, cellular transceivers and transceiver modules and system-on-chip (SoC) systems enable worldwide mobility, provide connectivity and support advanced functionality in mobile devices, cellular base stations, wireless local area networks (WLANs), wireless personal area networks (WPANs) and global positioning systems (GPS). Co. offers standard and custom-designed RF components and system-level programs.

Recent Developments: For the quarter ended June 30 2006, net income amounted to $13.9 million versus a net loss of $2.7 million in the year-earlier quarter. Revenues were $238.3 million, up 49.5% from $159.4 million the year before. Operating income was $14.0 million versus a loss of $2.3 million in the prior-year quarter. Direct operating expenses rose 51.0% to $158.7 million from $105.1 million in the comparable period the year before. Indirect operating expenses increased 16.0% to $65.6 million from $56.6 million in the equivalent prior-year period.

Prospects: Co. expects continued growth in the shipment of its POLARIS™ TOTAL RADIO™ transceiver and transmit modules, while it continues to grow its existing product portfolios for handsets and selectively introduce products for additional wireless markets. Co. also expects to complete its wafer fabrication facility expansion in the fiscal quarter ending Dec 2006, and raise its wafer manufacturing capacity by 40.0%. For the quarter ending Sept 2006, Co. anticipates revenue of $240.0 million to $250.0 million, with net income of $0.08 to $0.09 per share, including estimated non-cash share-based compensation expense and non-cash amortization of intangibles of about $4.0 million in total.

Financial Data
(US$ in Thousands)

	3 Mos	03/31/2006	03/31/2005	03/31/2004	03/31/2003	03/31/2002	03/31/2001	03/31/2000
Earnings Per Share	0.16	0.08	(0.35)	0.15	(0.05)	(0.12)	0.20	0.29
Cash Flow Per Share	0.42	0.28	0.30	0.63	0.30	0.42	0.35	...
Tang Book Value Per Share	2.59	2.48	2.22	2.38	2.12	2.05	2.23	1.81
Income Statement								
Total Revenue	238,335	770,247	634,204	651,379	507,819	369,308	335,364	288,960
EBITDA	31,371	86,770	8,671	118,381	67,839	20,235	79,362	94,197
Depn & Amortn	17,159	66,725	71,647	78,786	58,036	42,619	32,672	15,729
Income Before Taxes	14,983	20,211	(65,464)	30,193	(9,085)	(27,413)	52,409	77,068
Income Taxes	1,049	3,881	581	485	250	(6,829)	17,435	26,974
Net Income	13,934	16,330	(66,045)	29,708	(9,335)	(20,584)	34,974	50,094
Average Shares	225,706	192,781	186,985	213,272	172,706	165,827	173,216	171,668
Balance Sheet								
Total Assets	983,977	935,443	859,746	988,016	932,825	729,000	720,931	344,612
Current Liabilities	106,498	103,032	79,652	55,884	77,540	34,918	28,999	27,540
Long-Term Obligations	247,983	226,876	226,168	324,686	296,476	294,417	295,963	8,203
Total Liabilities	360,324	336,086	311,696	384,878	375,425	339,315	344,433	41,459
Stockholders' Equity	623,653	599,357	548,050	603,138	557,400	389,685	376,498	303,153
Shares Outstanding	191,443	190,280	188,063	186,257	183,958	167,768	163,710	160,208
Statistical Record								
Return on Assets %	3.60	1.82	N.M.	3.08	N.M.	N.M.	6.56	...
Return on Equity %	5.64	2.85	N.M.	5.11	N.M.	N.M.	10.29	...
EBITDA Margin %	13.16	11.27	1.37	18.17	13.36	5.48	23.66	32.60
Net Margin %	5.85	2.12	N.M.	4.56	N.M.	N.M.	10.43	17.34
Asset Turnover	0.93	0.86	0.69	0.68	0.61	0.51	0.63	...
Current Ratio	4.07	3.91	4.10	8.64	5.06	13.06	16.98	6.17
Debt to Equity	0.40	0.38	0.41	0.54	0.53	0.76	0.79	0.03
Price Range	9.44-5.00	8.73-3.81	8.90-4.81	12.43-4.67	20.35-5.19	36.60-9.06	68.00-10.88	87.50-9.97
P/E Ratio	59.00-31.25	109.13-47.63	...	82.87-31.13	...	...	340.00-54.38	301.72-34.38

Address: 7628 Thorndike Road, Greensboro, NC 27409-9421	**Web Site:** www.rfmd.com	**Auditors:** Ernst & Young LLP
Telephone: 336-664-1233	**Officers:** Albert E. Paladino - Chmn. Robert A. Bruggeworth - Pres., C.E.O.	**Investor Contact:** 336-664-1233
Fax: 336-664-0839		

ROBINSON (C.H.) WORLDWIDE, INC.

Exchange	Symbol	Price	52Wk Range	Yield	P/E
NMS	CHRW	$45.82 (8/31/2006)	54.79-30.20	1.13	33.94

*7 Year Price Score 162.09 *NYSE Composite Index=100 *12 Month Price Score 109.75

Interim Earnings (Per Share)

Qtr.	Mar	Jun	Sep	Dec
2003	0.16	0.17	0.17	0.17
2004	0.17	0.19	0.22	0.23
2005	0.24	0.28	0.31	0.33
2006	0.33	0.38	...	...

Interim Dividends (Per Share)

Amt	Decl	Ex	Rec	Pay
0.13Q	11/18/2005	12/7/2005	12/9/2005	1/3/2006
0.13Q	2/16/2006	3/8/2006	3/10/2006	4/3/2006
0.13Q	5/18/2006	6/7/2006	6/9/2006	7/3/2006
0.13Q	8/17/2006	9/6/2006	9/8/2006	10/2/2006

Indicated Div: $0.52

Valuation Analysis

Forecast P/E N/A

Market Cap $7.9 Billion
Book Value 877.9 Million
Price/Book 9.05
Price/Sales 1.27

Institutional Holding

No of Institutions 263
Shares 123,262,720
% Held 71.09

Business Summary: Misc. Transportation Services (MIC: 15.4 SIC: 4731 NAIC: 488510)

Robinson (C.H.) Worldwide is a party logistics company in North America that provides freight transportation services through its relationships with approximately 40,000 transportation companies, including motor carriers, railroads, air freight and ocean carriers. Co. also provides a range of logistics services such as supply chain analysis, freight consolidation, core carrier program management and information reporting. Additionally, Co. operates through a network of 196 branches in North America, South America, Europe and Asia. As of Dec 31 2005, Co. handled approximately 4.4 million shipments for more than 20,500 customers.

Recent Developments: For the quarter ended June 30 2006, net income increased 35.0% to $66.6 million from $49.3 million in the year-earlier quarter. Revenues were $1.70 billion, up 21.1% from $1.41 billion the year before. Operating income was $103.9 million versus $80.3 million in the prior-year quarter, an increase of 29.4%. Direct operating expenses rose 20.2% to $1.43 billion from $1.19 billion in the comparable period the year before. Indirect operating expenses increased 23.4% to $166.7 million from $135.1 million in the equivalent prior-year period.

Prospects: Co.'s solid results are driven by robust growth across all of its business lines. In particular, the increase in Co.'s Transportation segment is attributable primarily to the mix of services constituting this business line, led by significant growth in both its air transportation and miscellaneous transportation management services. Meanwhile, both of Co.'s Sourcing and Information Services segments are benefiting from robust transaction volume growth in each respective business lines. Based on such favorable performance, Co. is optimistic regarding its ability to reach its long-term compounded annual growth target of 15.0% for gross profits, income from operations and earnings per share.

Financial Data
(US$ in Thousands)

	6 Mos	3 Mos	12/31/2005	12/31/2004	12/31/2003	12/31/2002	12/31/2001	12/31/2000
Earnings Per Share	1.35	1.25	1.16	0.80	0.67	0.56	0.49	0.41
Cash Flow Per Share	1.55	1.52	1.35	0.92	0.65	0.68	0.44	0.44
Tang Book Value Per Share	3.57	3.51	3.11	2.60	2.10	1.59	1.23	0.84
Dividends Per Share	0.465	0.410	0.355	0.255	0.180	0.130	0.105	0.085
Dividend Payout %	34.44	32.67	30.60	32.08	27.07	23.21	21.43	20.48
Income Statement								
Total Revenue	3,200,112	1,499,115	5,688,948	4,341,538	3,613,645	3,294,473	3,090,072	2,882,175
EBITDA	213,441	100,666	344,945	235,028	194,918	171,943	157,509	135,076
Depn & Amortn	11,547	5,567	18,500	11,814	10,992	14,029	19,136	17,318
Income Before Taxes	201,894	95,099	332,753	226,038	186,172	157,914	138,373	117,758
Income Taxes	77,186	36,985	129,395	88,784	72,049	61,589	54,381	46,516
Net Income	124,708	58,114	203,358	137,254	114,123	96,325	83,992	71,242
Average Shares	175,198	175,267	174,698	173,144	172,138	171,514	171,548	171,434
Balance Sheet								
Total Assets	1,527,450	1,426,439	1,395,068	1,080,696	908,149	777,151	683,490	644,207
Current Liabilities	648,301	584,292	612,483	452,819	381,201	343,474	323,528	346,251
Total Liabilities	649,544	585,530	615,031	459,840	391,119	351,321	327,675	347,191
Stockholders' Equity	877,906	840,909	780,037	620,856	517,030	425,830	355,815	297,016
Shares Outstanding	173,344	173,592	173,029	170,480	170,608	169,012	168,914	169,242
Statistical Record								
Return on Assets %	17.00	17.01	16.43	13.76	13.54	13.19	12.65	12.18
Return on Equity %	29.89	29.11	29.03	24.06	24.21	24.65	25.73	26.13
EBITDA Margin %	6.67	6.72	6.06	5.41	5.39	5.22	5.10	4.69
Net Margin %	3.90	3.88	3.57	3.16	3.16	2.92	2.72	2.47
Asset Turnover	4.50	4.62	4.60	4.35	4.29	4.51	4.65	4.93
Current Ratio	1.81	1.90	1.77	1.87	1.88	1.71	1.56	1.33
Price Range	53.30-28.98	49.60-23.65	41.48-23.65	28.18-18.62	21.26-13.75	17.52-13.06	15.97-11.79	16.25-8.75
P/E Ratio	39.48-21.47	39.68-18.92	35.76-20.39	35.23-23.28	31.73-20.52	31.28-23.32	32.59-24.06	39.63-21.34
Average Yield %	1.19	1.21	1.18	1.15	1.00	0.85	0.74	0.67

Address: 8100 Mitchell Road, Eden Prairie, MN 55344 **Telephone:** 952-937-8500 **Fax:** 952-937-6714	**Web Site:** www.chrobinson.com **Officers:** D. R. Verdoorn - Chmn. John P. Wiehoff - Pres., C.E.O.	**Auditors:** Deloitte & Touche LLP

ROSS STORES, INC.

Exchange	Symbol	Price	52Wk Range	Yield	P/E	Div Acheiver
NMS	ROST	$24.49 (8/31/2006)	30.64-22.71	0.98	16.66	11 Years

*7 Year Price Score 109.69 *NYSE Composite Index=100 *12 Month Price Score 89.25

Interim Earnings (Per Share)

Qtr.	Apr	Jul	Oct	Jan
2003-04	0.32	0.35	0.33	0.47
2004-05	0.32	0.22	0.26	0.34
2005-06	0.34	0.29	0.25	0.49
2006-07	0.41	0.32	...	...

Interim Dividends (Per Share)

Amt	Decl	Ex	Rec	Pay
0.06Q	11/15/2005	12/5/2005	12/7/2005	1/3/2006
0.06Q	1/25/2006	2/22/2006	2/24/2006	3/31/2006
0.06Q	5/18/2006	6/8/2006	6/12/2006	6/30/2006
0.06Q	8/17/2006	8/30/2006	9/1/2006	10/2/2006

Indicated Div: $0.24

Valuation Analysis

Forecast P/E	13.33
	(9/9/2006)
Market Cap	$3.5 Billion
Book Value	857.0 Million
Price/Book	4.03
Price/Sales	0.66

Institutional Holding

No of Institutions	245
Shares	129,839,400
% Held	90.88

Business Summary: Retail - Apparel and Accessory Stores (MIC: 5.8 SIC: 5651 NAIC: 448140)

Ross Stores operates two chains of off-price retail apparel and home accessories stores, which target men and women between the ages of 25 and 54, primarily in middle income households. Co. provides its customers with an assortment of brand-name apparel, accessories, footwear and home fashions for the entire family at everyday savings of 20.0% to 60.0% below regular department and specialty store prices. As of Jan 28 2006, Co. operated 734 stores, of which 714 were Ross stores in 26 U.S. states and 20 were dd's DISCOUNTS stores all located in California.

Recent Developments: For the quarter ended July 29 2006, net income increased 7.3% to $45.4 million from $42.3 million in the year-earlier quarter. Revenues were $1.31 billion, up 11.6% from $1.17 billion the year before. Direct operating expenses rose 11.4% to $1.02 billion from $919.2 million in the comparable period the year before. Indirect operating expenses increased 14.2% to $209.1 million from $183.1 million in the equivalent prior-year period.

Prospects: Co.'s near-term outlook appears to be somewhat mixed. Co.'s sales are benefiting primarily from the addition of new stores into its operations during the second fiscal quarter ended Jul 29 2006. However, Co. expects to experience compression in its gross margin in the third fiscal quarter ending Oct 28 2006, given its entry into the fall season with residual inventory and clearance levels. Notwithstanding, Co.'s same store sales for the third fiscal quarter are expected to increase by 1.0% to 3.0% over comparable period in 2005, while earnings are projected to be in the range of $0.24 to $0.27 per share.

Financial Data
(US$ in Thousands)

	6 Mos	3 Mos	01/28/2006	01/29/2005	01/31/2004	02/01/2003	02/02/2002	02/03/2001
Earnings Per Share	1.47	1.44	1.36	1.13	1.47	1.26	0.95	0.91
Cash Flow Per Share	2.88	2.73	2.61	2.03	2.08	2.13	1.52	0.85
Tang Book Value Per Share	6.07	6.02	5.80	5.22	5.00	4.15	3.45	2.90
Dividends Per Share	0.230	0.220	0.210	0.170	0.115	0.095	0.085	0.075
Dividend Payout %	15.61	15.24	15.44	15.04	7.82	7.54	8.90	8.24
Income Statement								
Total Revenue	2,599,728	1,291,676	4,944,179	4,239,990	3,920,583	3,531,349	2,986,596	2,709,039
EBITDA	223,313	121,818	436,292	374,493	451,028	396,797	320,378	307,715
Depn & Amortn	50,915	24,261	110,848	94,593	76,739	66,176	62,621	55,063
Income Before Taxes	172,398	97,557	328,342	278,985	374,551	330,342	254,589	249,186
Income Taxes	67,804	38,340	128,710	109,083	146,465	129,164	99,544	97,432
Net Income	104,594	59,217	199,632	169,902	228,102	201,178	155,045	151,754
Average Shares	142,698	144,193	146,532	150,380	155,151	159,492	162,420	166,674
Balance Sheet								
Total Assets	1,936,147	1,973,637	1,938,738	1,735,999	1,657,210	1,361,345	1,082,725	975,047
Current Liabilities	860,591	890,487	878,983	711,561	711,844	626,684	489,588	434,065
Long-Term Obligations	...	...	...	50,000	50,000	25,000	...	30,000
Total Liabilities	1,079,098	1,112,915	1,102,566	970,430	901,791	718,157	538,270	507,500
Stockholders' Equity	857,049	860,722	836,172	765,569	755,419	643,188	544,455	467,547
Shares Outstanding	141,106	142,872	144,112	146,717	151,208	154,982	157,920	161,054
Statistical Record								
Return on Assets %	11.13	10.86	10.89	10.04	15.15	16.51	15.11	15.53
Return on Equity %	25.49	25.10	25.00	22.40	32.71	33.97	30.73	31.73
EBITDA Margin %	8.59	9.43	8.82	8.83	11.50	11.24	10.73	11.36
Net Margin %	4.02	4.58	4.04	4.01	5.82	5.70	5.19	5.60
Asset Turnover	2.76	2.66	2.70	2.51	2.60	2.90	2.91	2.77
Current Ratio	1.31	1.42	1.40	1.58	1.57	1.47	1.46	1.45
Debt to Equity	...	...	...	0.07	0.07	0.04	...	0.06
Price Range	30.64-22.71	30.64-22.71	30.50-22.71	32.85-21.15	28.79-16.45	23.44-16.38	18.16-9.04	12.03-6.38
P/E Ratio	20.84-15.45	21.28-15.77	22.43-16.70	29.07-18.72	19.59-11.21	18.60-13.00	19.12-9.52	13.22-7.01
Average Yield %	0.85	0.80	0.77	0.64	0.51	0.48	0.65	0.87

Address: 8333 Central Ave., Newark, CA 94560-3433
Telephone: 510-505-4400
Fax: 510-505-4174

Web Site: www.rossstores.com
Officers: Norman A. Ferber - Chmn. Lawrence M. Higby - Chmn. Emeritus

Auditors: Deloitte & Touche LLP
Transfer Agents: Bank of New York

RSA SECURITY INC

Exchange	Symbol	Price	52Wk Range	Yield	P/E
NMS	RSAS	$27.85 (8/31/2006)	27.85-10.73	N/A	58.02

*7 Year Price Score 71.90 *NYSE Composite Index=100 *12 Month Price Score 155.83

Interim Earnings (Per Share)

Qtr.	Mar	Jun	Sep	Dec
2003	0.03	0.05	0.06	0.10
2004	0.10	0.12	0.13	0.16
2005	0.10	0.12	0.21	0.16
2006	0.07	0.04	...	...

Interim Dividends (Per Share)

Amt	Decl	Ex	Rec	Pay
50%	2/1/2001	3/26/2001	3/9/2001	3/23/2001

Valuation Analysis   **Institutional Holding**

Forecast P/E	45.46	No of Institutions
	(9/9/2006)	177
Market Cap	$2.1 Billion	Shares
Book Value	586.3 Million	66,702,816
Price/Book	3.59	% Held
Price/Sales	6.19	86.83

Business Summary: Office Equipment Supplies (MIC: 11.12 SIC: 3577 NAIC: 334119)

RSA Security is engaged in protecting online identities and digital assets. Co.'s Authentication and Credential Management unit allows organizations to develop and manage trusted identities through authentication and password management. Co.'s Access Management unit allows organizations to provide various groups of users with access to the resources while securing those resources from unauthorized access. Co.'s Data Protection unit helps organizations ensure that their sensitive customer and partner information remains private and their critical business transactions remain trusted and secure. Co. also provides online security and anti-fraud solutions to financial institutions.

Recent Developments: For the quarter ended June 30 2006, net income decreased 67.4% to $2.8 million from $8.5 million in the year-earlier quarter. Revenues were $94.4 million, up 23.4% from $76.5 million the year before. Operating income was $2.1 million versus $8.5 million in the prior-year quarter, a decrease of 75.1%. Direct operating expenses rose 34.8% to $21.9 million from $16.3 million in the comparable period the year before. Indirect operating expenses increased 35.9% to $70.4 million from $51.8 million in the equivalent prior-year period.

Prospects: On June 29 2006, Co. announced that it had entered into a definitive agreement to be acquired by EMC Corp., one of the providers of information management and storage services. Under the terms of the agreement, EMC will pay $28 per share in cash in exchange for each of Co.'s shares and the assumption of outstanding options, for an aggregate purchase price of slightly less than $2.10 billion. The acquisition is expected to be consummated late in the third quarter or early in the fourth quarter of 2006, subject to customary closing conditions and regulatory approvals.

Financial Data
(US$ in Thousands)

	6 Mos	3 Mos	12/31/2005	12/31/2004	12/31/2003	12/31/2002	12/31/2001	12/31/2000
Earnings Per Share	0.48	0.56	0.58	0.51	0.24	(1.71)	(0.04)	3.21
Cash Flow Per Share	0.88	0.88	0.79	0.82	1.39	0.74	(0.14)	0.06
Tang Book Value Per Share	3.53	3.48	3.25	4.24	1.96	1.26	2.31	8.56
Income Statement								
Total Revenue	181,918	87,507	310,115	307,507	259,866	232,084	282,720	280,191
EBITDA	18,821	10,938	59,123	59,533	33,384	(110,164)	31,484	326,882
Depn & Amortn	8,783	4,072	13,749	11,682	14,828	26,536	29,636	9,971
Income Before Taxes	10,038	6,866	45,374	43,651	18,556	(136,700)	48	329,775
Income Taxes	1,950	1,536	2,940	8,669	3,720	(39,876)	2,555	124,012
Net Income	8,088	5,330	42,434	34,982	14,836	(96,824)	(2,507)	205,763
Average Shares	76,599	73,667	73,074	68,638	62,304	56,621	56,259	64,027
Balance Sheet								
Total Assets	751,976	671,287	657,784	624,827	529,577	484,400	509,114	589,514
Current Liabilities	135,563	120,546	125,069	128,556	194,895	114,582	79,599	108,510
Long-Term Obligations	...	...	...	...	...	77,477	...	...
Total Liabilities	165,652	144,039	150,924	148,295	220,802	220,966	79,599	108,510
Stockholders' Equity	586,324	527,248	506,860	476,532	308,775	263,434	353,413	481,004
Shares Outstanding	75,498	72,732	71,026	71,567	60,870	57,066	56,409	56,166
Statistical Record								
Return on Assets %	5.09	6.33	6.62	6.04	2.93	N.M.	N.M.	19.53
Return on Equity %	6.57	8.10	8.63	8.88	5.19	N.M.	N.M.	37.58
EBITDA Margin %	10.35	12.50	19.06	19.36	12.85	N.M.	11.14	116.66
Net Margin %	4.45	6.09	13.68	11.38	5.71	N.M.	N.M.	73.44
Asset Turnover	0.50	0.50	0.48	0.53	0.51	0.47	0.51	0.27
Current Ratio	2.23	2.30	2.10	2.81	1.36	1.84	1.84	3.82
Debt to Equity	...	...	...	...	...	0.29	...	...
Price Range	27.10-10.73	17.98-10.07	20.06-10.07	23.81-14.25	17.02-5.00	19.02-2.23	43.17-7.56	60.17-26.21
P/E Ratio	56.46-22.35	32.11-17.98	34.59-17.36	46.69-27.94	70.92-20.83	...	...	18.74-8.16

Address: 174 Middlesex Turnpike, Bedford, MA 01730 Telephone: 781-515-5000 Fax: 781-515-5170	Web Site: www.rsasecurity.com Officers: James K. Sims - Chmn. Arthur W. Coviello Jr. - Pres., C.E.O.	Auditors: DELOITTE & TOUCHE LLP Investor Contact: 781-301-5139

S & T BANCORP, INC. (INDIANA, PA.)

Exchange	Symbol	Price	52Wk Range	Yield	P/E	Div Acheiver
NMS	STBA	$31.07 (8/31/2006)	39.47-29.84	3.73	15.08	16 Years

*7 Year Price Score 101.34 *NYSE Composite Index=100 *12 Month Price Score 86.01

Interim Earnings (Per Share)

Qtr.	Mar	Jun	Sep	Dec
2003	0.47	0.48	0.50	0.49
2004	0.48	0.51	0.50	0.54
2005	0.51	0.58	0.54	0.55
2006	0.54	0.43	...	...

Interim Dividends (Per Share)

Amt	Decl	Ex	Rec	Pay
0.28Q	9/19/2005	9/28/2005	9/30/2005	10/25/2005
0.29Q	12/20/2005	12/28/2005	12/30/2005	1/25/2006
0.29Q	3/20/2006	3/29/2006	3/31/2006	4/25/2006
0.29Q	6/20/2006	6/28/2006	6/30/2006	7/25/2006

Indicated Div: $1.16

Valuation Analysis

Forecast P/E	13.93
	(9/9/2006)
Market Cap	$798.2 Million
Book Value	337.6 Million
Price/Book	2.36
Price/Sales	3.48

Institutional Holding

No of Institutions	66
Shares	8,423,813
% Held	32.92

Business Summary: Commercial Banking (MIC: 8.1 SIC: 6022 NAIC: 522110)
S&T Bancorp is a bank holding company with two wholly owned subsidiaries, S&T Bank and 9th Street Holdings, Inc. Co. owns a 50.0% interest in Commonwealth Trust Credit Life Insurance Company. S&T Bank provides service to its customers through a branch network of 51 offices located in Allegheny, Armstrong, Blair, Butler, Cambria, Clarion, Clearfield, Indiana, Jefferson and Westmoreland counties of Pennsylvania. S&T Bank's services include accepting time and demand deposit accounts, originating commercial and consumer loans, offering discount brokerage services, personal financial planning and credit card services. At Dec 31 2005, Co. had total assets of $3.19 billion.

Recent Developments: For the quarter ended June 30 2006, net income decreased 27.5% to $11.2 million from $15.5 million in the year-earlier quarter. Net interest income decreased 0.8% to $28.1 million from $28.4 million in the year-earlier quarter. Provision for loan losses was $5.7 million versus a credit for loan losses of $300,000 in the prior-year quarter. Non-interest income rose 12.5% to $10.3 million from $9.2 million, while non-interest expense advanced 11.5% to $17.3 million.

Prospects: Co.'s results are being hampered by an increase in its provision for loan losses due to the deterioration in the credit quality of three commercial loan relationships. Moreover, the effect of rising short-term interest rates in combination with a flat yield curve is resulting in a decline in Co.'s net interest income. However, Co. remains encouraged regarding its outlook as it is experiencing an increase in non-interest income, driven by increases in its service charges on deposit accounts, wealth management fees, and insurance commissions. Going forward, Co. will focus on its business strategy, while continuing to expand its core deposit funding for further commercial lending growth.

Financial Data
(US$ in Thousands)

	6 Mos	3 Mos	12/31/2005	12/31/2004	12/31/2003	12/31/2002	12/31/2001	12/31/2000
Earnings Per Share	2.06	2.21	2.18	2.03	1.94	1.81	1.75	1.66
Cash Flow Per Share	1.95	2.07	1.97	2.34	1.92	1.89	2.85	1.58
Tang Book Value Per Share	11.01	11.31	11.34	11.12	10.48	9.47	11.01	10.28
Dividends Per Share	1.150	1.140	1.130	1.070	1.020	0.970	0.920	0.840
Dividend Payout %	55.83	51.58	51.83	52.71	52.58	53.59	52.57	50.60
Income Statement								
Interest Income	98,841	47,884	172,122	148,638	151,460	151,160	166,702	176,184
Interest Expense	42,640	19,810	59,514	40,890	47,066	56,300	76,713	86,141
Net Interest Income	56,201	28,074	112,608	107,748	104,394	94,860	89,989	90,043
Provision for Losses	7,200	1,500	5,000	4,400	7,300	7,800	5,000	4,000
Non-Interest Income	20,818	10,507	37,568	34,202	36,204	32,680	31,230	22,154
Non-Interest Expense	34,213	16,963	62,646	60,191	60,658	51,766	46,972	45,658
Income Before Taxes	35,606	20,118	82,530	77,359	72,640	67,974	69,247	62,539
Income Taxes	10,132	5,881	24,287	23,001	20,863	19,370	20,062	17,566
Net Income	25,474	14,237	58,243	54,358	51,777	48,604	47,298	44,973
Average Shares	26,039	26,449	26,688	26,799	26,723	26,784	27,051	27,073
Balance Sheet								
Net Loans & Leases	2,584,471	2,510,274	2,454,934	2,253,089	2,069,142	1,968,755	1,615,842	1,577,629
Total Assets	3,301,896	3,250,246	3,194,979	2,989,034	2,900,272	2,823,867	2,357,874	2,310,290
Total Deposits	2,496,909	2,470,151	2,418,884	2,176,263	1,962,253	1,926,119	1,611,317	1,525,332
Total Liabilities	2,964,298	2,900,350	2,842,558	2,639,905	2,567,554	2,517,753	2,064,547	2,033,193
Stockholders' Equity	337,598	349,896	352,421	349,129	332,718	306,114	293,327	277,097
Shares Outstanding	25,690	26,083	26,270	26,600	26,652	26,584	26,646	26,947
Statistical Record								
Return on Assets %	1.70	1.87	1.88	1.84	1.81	1.88	2.03	1.99
Return on Equity %	15.99	16.83	16.60	15.90	16.21	16.22	16.58	17.36
Net Interest Margin %	55.20	58.63	65.42	72.49	68.93	62.75	53.98	51.11
Efficiency Ratio %	28.18	29.05	29.88	32.92	32.32	28.16	23.73	23.02
Loans to Deposits	1.04	1.02	1.01	1.04	1.05	1.02	1.00	1.03
Price Range	40.25-32.27	40.25-33.32	40.25-33.32	38.40-28.42	31.25-25.05	28.03-23.30	25.30-20.31	23.44-16.75
P/E Ratio	19.54-15.67	18.21-15.08	18.46-15.28	18.92-14.00	16.11-12.91	15.49-12.87	14.46-11.61	14.12-10.09
Average Yield %	3.14	3.10	3.06	3.27	3.63	3.80	4.00	4.43

Address: 43 South Ninth Street, Indiana, PA 15701	**Web Site:** www.stbank.com	**Auditors:** ERNST & YOUNG LLP
Telephone: 724-465-1466	**Officers:** James C. Miller - Chmn., C.E.O. Todd C. Brice - Pres.	**Investor Contact:** 724-465-1466
Fax: 724-465-1488		**Transfer Agents:** American Stock Transfer & Trust Company, New York, NY

SAFECO CORPORATION

Exchange	Symbol	Price	52Wk Range	Yield	P/E
NMS	SAFC	$57.71 (8/31/2006)	58.61-49.12	2.08	10.14

*7 Year Price Score 114.59 *NYSE Composite Index=100 *12 Month Price Score 99.09

Interim Earnings (Per Share)

Qtr.	Mar	Jun	Sep	Dec
2003	0.65	0.81	(0.21)	1.19
2004	1.70	1.77	(0.76)	1.38
2005	1.65	1.46	0.80	1.52
2006	1.69	1.68	...	...

Interim Dividends (Per Share)

Amt	Decl	Ex	Rec	Pay
0.25Q	11/2/2005	1/4/2006	1/6/2006	1/23/2006
0.25Q	2/1/2006	4/5/2006	4/7/2006	4/24/2006
0.30Q	5/3/2006	7/5/2006	7/7/2006	7/24/2006
0.30Q	8/11/2006	10/4/2006	10/6/2006	10/23/2006

Indicated Div: $1.20

Valuation Analysis

		Institutional Holding	
Forecast P/E	9.35	No of Institutions	322
	(9/9/2006)	Shares	83,569,096
Market Cap	$6.7 Billion	% Held	71.82
Book Value	3.9 Billion		
Price/Book	1.70		
Price/Sales	1.07		

Business Summary: Insurance (MIC: 8.2 SIC: 6331 NAIC: 524126)

Safeco sells property and casualty insurance to drivers, homeowners and owners of small- and mid-sized businesses through independent agents and brokers. Co.'s four business segments include: Safeco Personal Insurance, which provides auto, property and specialty insurance products for individuals; Safeco Business Insurance, which provides business owner policies, commercial auto, commercial multi-peril, workers compensation, commercial property and general liability policies; Surety, which provides surety bonds primarily for construction and commercial businesses; and Property and Casualty Other, which includes runoff of assumed reinsurance and large-commercial business accounts in runoff.

Recent Developments: For the quarter ended June 30 2006, net income increased 6.6% to $199.7 million from $187.3 million in the year-earlier quarter. Revenues were $1.54 billion, down 3.4% from $1.59 billion the year before. Net premiums earned were $1.41 billion versus $1.46 billion in the prior-year quarter, a decrease of 2.9%. Net investment income rose 4.7% to $125.5 million from $119.9 million a year ago.

Prospects: Going forward, Co. is exploring opportunities to bolster its distribution network and reach clients who are not buying insurance through the independent agency channel. Moreover, Co. is continuing its expense-savings activities, and expects to attain savings of $75.0 million in its expense run rate by the end of 2006, while greater reduction is anitpcated to occur in 2007. Meanwhile, Co. intends to sell its home office building complex in the second half of 2006, following its plan to relocate its corporate headquarters to leased space in downtown Seattle, WA. Separately, on May 31 2006, Co. completed the sale of its Redmond office campus and recognized a gain of $21.3 million.

Financial Data
(US$ in Thousands)

	6 Mos	3 Mos	12/31/2005	12/31/2004	12/31/2003	12/31/2002	12/31/2001	12/31/2000
Earnings Per Share	5.69	5.47	5.43	4.16	2.44	2.33	(7.75)	0.90
Cash Flow Per Share	6.91	7.68	8.11	7.36	11.31	6.62	4.14	5.14
Tang Book Value Per Share	33.92	33.57	33.37	30.88	34.92	30.69	27.71	26.54
Dividends Per Share	1.000	0.970	0.940	0.775	0.740	0.740	0.925	1.480
Dividend Payout %	17.57	17.73	17.31	18.63	30.33	31.76	...	164.44
Income Statement								
Premium Income	2,836,700	1,421,900	5,805,400	5,529,100	5,769,900	5,299,600	5,109,800	5,066,100
Total Revenue	3,097,500	1,561,500	6,351,100	6,195,400	7,358,100	7,065,100	6,862,500	7,118,400
Benefits & Claims	1,640,800	837,300	3,635,000	3,495,200	4,808,000	4,685,500	5,199,100	4,987,600
Income Before Taxes	590,200	304,100	985,700	892,900	441,100	462,500	(1,413,200)	158,600
Income Taxes	182,300	95,900	294,600	272,700	101,900	116,600	(412,800)	(800)
Net Income	407,900	208,200	691,100	562,400	339,200	301,100	(989,200)	114,600
Average Shares	119,000	123,000	127,200	135,200	138,900	129,300	127,700	127,800
Balance Sheet								
Total Assets	14,338,300	14,426,600	14,887,000	14,586,100	35,845,100	34,656,000	30,092,500	31,511,500
Total Liabilities	10,393,500	10,424,900	10,762,400	10,665,200	30,821,800	29,380,600	25,614,500	25,972,700
Stockholders' Equity	3,944,800	4,001,700	4,124,600	3,920,900	5,023,300	4,431,600	3,634,600	4,695,800
Shares Outstanding	116,300	119,200	123,584	126,958	138,600	138,195	127,733	127,649
Statistical Record								
Return on Assets %	4.78	4.75	4.69	2.22	0.96	0.93	N.M.	0.37
Return on Equity %	17.12	17.20	17.18	12.54	7.18	7.47	N.M.	2.54
Loss Ratio %	57.84	58.89	62.61	63.21	83.33	88.41	101.75	98.45
Net Margin %	13.17	13.33	10.88	9.08	4.61	4.26	(14.41)	1.61
Price Range	58.61-49.12	58.61-47.73	57.85-45.44	52.24-38.23	39.17-32.35	36.55-26.31	32.79-21.75	35.69-18.56
P/E Ratio	10.30-8.63	10.71-8.73	10.65-8.37	12.56-9.19	16.05-13.26	15.69-11.29	...	39.65-20.63
Average Yield %	1.85	1.81	1.79	1.72	2.07	2.27	3.24	6.14

Address: Safeco Plaza, Seattle, WA 98185 **Telephone:** 206-545-5000 **Fax:** 206-545-5995	**Web Site:** www.safeco.com/ir **Officers:** Michael S. McGavick - Chmn. Christine B. Mead - Sr. V.P., C.F.O., Sec.	**Auditors:** Ernst & Young LLP **Investor Contact:** 206-545-3399 **Transfer Agents:** The Bank of New York, New York, NY

SANDISK CORP.

Exchange	Symbol	Price	52Wk Range	Yield	P/E
NMS	SNDK	$58.87 (8/31/2006)	77.22-37.51	N/A	31.48

*7 Year Price Score 170.57 *NYSE Composite Index=100 *12 Month Price Score 84.77

Interim Earnings (Per Share)

Qtr.	Mar	Jun	Sep	Dec
2003	0.17	0.26	0.09	0.51
2004	0.34	0.38	0.29	0.42
2005	0.39	0.37	0.55	0.68
2006	0.17	0.47	...	...

Interim Dividends (Per Share)

Amt	Decl	Ex	Rec	Pay
100%	1/21/2004	2/19/2004	2/3/2004	2/18/2004

Valuation Analysis   **Institutional Holding**

Forecast P/E	25.30	No of Institutions
	(9/9/2006)	325
Market Cap	$11.5 Billion	Shares
Book Value	3.2 Billion	165,538,992
Price/Book	3.64	% Held
Price/Sales	4.29	84.48

Business Summary: IT & Technology (MIC: 10.2 SIC: 3572 NAIC: 334112)

SanDisk is engaged in designing, manufacturing and marketing flash storage card products that are used in a variety of consumer electronics. Co.'s products include flash cards, Universal Serial Bus (USB) flash drives and digital audio players. Co.'s flash card and USB flash drive products focus on digital consumer devices like digital cameras, feature phones, personal digital assistants (PDAs), personal computers, portable digital audio players and digital video recorders, as well as industrial devices, like communication routers and switches. Co. also sells digital audio players with embedded flash memory.

Recent Developments: For the quarter ended July 2 2006, net income increased 35.7% to $95.6 million from $70.5 million in the year-earlier quarter. Revenues were $719.2 million, up 39.7% from $514.9 million the year before. Operating income was $128.5 million versus $106.0 million in the prior-year quarter, an increase of 21.2%. Direct operating expenses rose 43.0% to $430.2 million from $300.8 million in the comparable period the year before. Indirect operating expenses increased 48.5% to $160.5 million from $108.1 million in the equivalent prior-year period.

Prospects: On Jul 30 2006, Co. entered into definitive agreements for it to acquire M-Systems Ltd. in an all stock transaction. In the transaction, each msystems ordinary share will be converted into 0.76368 of a share of its common stock. The transaction combines both flash memory companies with complementary products, customers, channels and technology and manufacturing base. The transaction also better positions Co. to serve the growing storage needs of handset manufacturers and mobile network operators, and will be a catalyst in the development of upcoming flash enabled consumer applications. Co. expects the deal to close in the fourth quarter of 2006, subject to certain regulatory approvals.

Financial Data
(US$ in Thousands)

	6 Mos	3 Mos	01/01/2006	01/02/2005	12/28/2003	12/31/2002	12/31/2001	12/31/2000
Earnings Per Share	1.87	1.77	2.00	1.44	1.02	0.26	(2.19)	2.06
Cash Flow Per Share	2.04	2.07	2.63	1.37	1.88	0.77	(0.53)	0.63
Tang Book Value Per Share	14.82	13.63	13.41	10.78	9.33	4.54	4.93	6.40
Income Statement								
Total Revenue	1,342,445	623,260	2,306,069	1,777,055	1,079,801	541,273	366,301	601,812
EBITDA	246,083	87,509	636,845	447,686	262,766	60,205	(433,662)	485,334
Depn & Amortn	57,666	26,397	65,800	38,900	23,000	22,201	20,548	15,928
Income Before Taxes	226,944	76,389	613,307	423,200	241,881	39,979	(441,944)	492,192
Income Taxes	96,188	41,274	226,923	156,584	73,022	3,739	(144,000)	193,520
Net Income	130,756	35,115	386,384	266,616	168,859	36,240	(297,944)	298,672
Average Shares	202,980	201,892	193,016	188,837	171,614	142,460	136,296	145,302
Balance Sheet								
Total Assets	4,840,609	3,450,733	3,120,187	2,320,180	2,023,514	976,179	932,348	1,107,907
Current Liabilities	480,642	483,305	571,137	353,454	346,834	172,880	127,061	171,357
Long-Term Obligations	1,150,000	...	...	...	150,000	150,000	125,000	...
Total Liabilities	1,671,492	519,341	596,396	380,030	522,826	348,459	256,969	244,849
Stockholders' Equity	3,169,117	2,931,392	2,523,791	1,940,150	1,500,688	627,720	675,379	863,058
Shares Outstanding	195,956	195,331	188,221	179,964	160,914	138,312	136,928	134,850
Statistical Record								
Return on Assets %	10.04	11.79	14.24	12.08	11.35	3.80	N.M.	33.74
Return on Equity %	14.15	14.03	17.36	15.25	16.00	5.56	N.M.	41.51
EBITDA Margin %	18.33	14.04	27.62	25.19	24.33	11.12	N.M.	80.65
Net Margin %	9.74	5.63	16.76	15.00	15.64	6.70	N.M.	49.63
Asset Turnover	0.72	0.84	0.85	0.80	0.73	0.57	0.36	0.68
Current Ratio	6.69	5.34	4.51	5.32	4.97	4.38	4.27	4.07
Debt to Equity	0.36	...	...	...	0.10	0.24	0.19	...
Price Range	77.22-23.76	77.22-23.64	65.14-21.45	36.23-19.61	42.49-7.58	13.99-4.88	23.09-4.50	81.00-13.88
P/E Ratio	41.29-12.71	43.63-13.36	32.57-10.73	25.16-13.62	41.66-7.43	53.83-18.77	...	39.32-6.74

Address: 140 Caspian Court, Sunnyvale, CA 94089
Telephone: 408-542-0500
Fax: 408-542-0503

Web Site: www.sandisk.com
Officers: Irwin Federman - Chmn. Eli Harari - Pres., C.E.O.

Auditors: Ernst & Young LLP

SANDY SPRING BANCORP

Exchange	Symbol	Price	52Wk Range	Yield	P/E	Div Achiever
NMS	SASR	$36.49 (8/31/2006)	38.48-31.75	2.41	16.00	10 Years

*7 Year Price Score 98.23 *NYSE Composite Index=100 *12 Month Price Score 97.41

Interim Earnings (Per Share)

Qtr.	Mar	Jun	Sep	Dec
2003	0.56	0.60	0.56	0.46
2004	0.50	0.43	0.44	(0.39)
2005	0.53	0.53	0.64	0.54
2006	0.56	0.54	...	...

Interim Dividends (Per Share)

Amt	Decl	Ex	Rec	Pay
0.22Q	11/18/2005	11/23/2005	11/28/2005	12/8/2005
0.22Q	2/27/2006	2/28/2006	2/27/2006	3/6/2006
0.22Q	6/1/2006	6/8/2006	6/12/2006	6/22/2006
0.22Q	8/31/2006	9/7/2006	9/11/2006	9/21/2006

Indicated Div: $0.88

Valuation Analysis

		Institutional Holding	
Forecast P/E	15.64	No of Institutions	
	(9/9/2006)	56	
Market Cap	$539.5 Million	Shares	
Book Value	226.7 Million	3,875,707	
Price/Book	2.38	% Held	
Price/Sales	3.05	26.18	

Business Summary: Commercial Banking (MIC: 8.1 SIC: 6021 NAIC: 522110)

Sandy Spring Bancorp is the holding company for Sandy Spring Bank and its principal subsidiaries, Sandy Spring Insurance Corporation and The Equipment Leasing Company. Co. is a community banking organization that focuses its lending and other services on businesses and consumers in the local market area. As of Dec 31 2005, Co. offered a range of commercial banking, retail banking and trust services through 31 community offices and 67 ATMs located in Anne Arundel, Frederick, Howard, Montgomery, and Prince George's counties in Maryland. As of Dec 31 2005, Co. had total assets of $2.46 billion and total deposits of $1.80 billion.

Recent Developments: For the quarter ended June 30 2006, net income increased 3.8% to $8.1 million from $7.8 million in the year-earlier quarter. Net interest income increased 10.8% to $23.9 million from $21.5 million in the year-earlier quarter. Provision for loan losses was $1.0 million versus $900,000 in the prior-year quarter, an increase of 16.1%. Non-interest income rose 3.8% to $9.4 million from $9.1 million, while non-interest expense advanced 8.7% to $20.8 million.

Prospects: Results are benefiting from higher net interest income due largely to continued loan growth, as well as higher non-interest income due to growth in most of Co.'s business line. However, net interest margin is declining due to the slowing growth in non-interest bearing deposits and increased short-term borrowings within a flat yield curve environment. Meanwhile, Co. continues to be challenged by the need to fund the growth of its loan portfolio with alternative sources of fund, given the rising interest rate environment and its effect on core deposit gathering. Going forward, Co. will focus on cost control across while making selected investments that will grow and enhance its position.

Financial Data
(US$ in Thousands)

	6 Mos	3 Mos	12/31/2005	12/31/2004	12/31/2003	12/31/2002	12/31/2001	12/31/2000
Earnings Per Share	2.28	2.27	2.24	0.98	2.18	2.08	1.59	1.31
Cash Flow Per Share	3.08	2.91	2.89	1.25	3.41	0.22	0.75	0.77
Tang Book Value Per Share	13.78	13.46	13.21	12.16	12.03	10.81	8.73	7.25
Dividends Per Share	0.870	0.860	0.840	0.780	0.740	0.690	0.607	0.540
Dividend Payout %	38.16	37.89	37.50	79.59	33.94	33.17	38.16	41.33
Income Statement								
Interest Income	73,050	35,177	122,160	109,390	112,467	122,722	127,870	118,680
Interest Expense	26,021	12,000	33,982	34,768	37,432	43,900	61,043	61,260
Net Interest Income	47,029	23,177	88,178	74,622	75,035	78,822	66,827	57,420
Provision for Losses	1,995	950	2,600	...	...	2,865	2,470	2,690
Non-Interest Income	19,241	9,846	36,909	30,769	33,736	29,729	21,836	17,528
Non-Interest Expense	41,184	20,356	77,194	92,703	67,226	63,961	54,618	47,601
Income Before Taxes	23,091	11,717	45,293	12,688	41,545	41,725	31,575	24,657
Income Taxes	6,656	3,377	12,195	(1,679)	9,479	11,012	8,429	5,887
Net Income	16,435	8,340	33,098	14,367	32,066	30,713	23,146	18,770
Average Shares	14,921	14,925	14,767	14,709	14,708	14,722	14,558	14,403
Balance Sheet								
Net Loans & Leases	1,763,054	1,726,488	1,667,493	1,430,871	1,138,548	1,048,817	983,266	956,287
Total Assets	2,586,353	2,499,577	2,459,616	2,309,343	2,333,342	2,307,404	2,081,834	1,773,001
Total Deposits	1,818,347	1,839,355	1,803,210	1,732,501	1,561,830	1,492,212	1,387,459	1,242,927
Total Liabilities	2,359,615	2,276,615	2,241,733	2,114,260	2,139,893	2,128,712	1,931,161	1,645,443
Stockholders' Equity	226,738	222,962	217,883	195,083	193,449	178,692	150,673	127,558
Shares Outstanding	14,785	14,801	14,793	14,628	14,495	14,536	14,483	14,329
Statistical Record								
Return on Assets %	1.37	1.40	1.39	0.62	1.38	1.40	1.20	1.11
Return on Equity %	15.76	15.93	16.03	7.38	17.23	18.65	16.64	15.84
Net Interest Margin %	62.98	65.89	72.18	68.22	66.72	64.23	52.26	48.38
Efficiency Ratio %	44.06	45.21	48.53	66.14	45.98	41.96	36.48	34.95
Loans to Deposits	0.97	0.94	0.92	0.83	0.73	0.70	0.71	0.77
Price Range	38.48-31.75	38.48-30.61	38.52-30.61	38.50-31.14	40.25-30.33	35.19-27.90	32.82-15.17	18.00-12.79
P/E Ratio	16.88-13.93	16.95-13.48	17.20-13.67	39.29-31.78	18.46-13.91	16.92-13.41	20.64-9.54	13.74-9.76
Average Yield %	2.46	2.49	2.46	2.23	2.18	2.17	2.68	3.69

Address: 17801 Georgia Avenue, Olney, MD 20832 Telephone: 301-774-6400 Fax: 301-774-8434	Web Site: www.ssnb.com Officers: W. Drew Stabler - Chmn. Hunter R. Hollar - Pres., C.E.O.	Auditors: McGladrey & Pullen LLP

SANMINA-SCI CORP

Exchange	Symbol	Price	52Wk Range	Yield	P/E
NMS	SANM	$3.37 (8/31/2006)	5.72-3.08	N/A	N/A

*7 Year Price Score 22.85 *NYSE Composite Index=100 *12 Month Price Score 84.92

Interim Earnings (Per Share)

Qtr.	Dec	Mar	Jun	Sep
2002-03	(0.01)	(0.06)	(0.02)	(0.17)
2003-04	0.03	(0.09)	0.02	0.01
2004-05	0.05	(1.99)	0.00	0.01
2005-06	0.05	(0.20)	...	...

Interim Dividends (Per Share)

Amt	Decl	Ex	Rec	Pay
100%	12/13/2000	1/9/2001	12/18/2000	1/8/2001

Valuation Analysis **Institutional Holding**

Forecast P/E	N/A	No of Institutions	269
Market Cap	$1.8 Billion	Shares	
Book Value	2.3 Billion	401,945,888	
Price/Book	0.78	% Held	
Price/Sales	0.16	75.44	

Business Summary: Electrical (MIC: 11.14 SIC: 3672 NAIC: 334412)
Sanmina-SCI is an independent global provider of customized, integrated electronics manufacturing services, or EMS. Co. provides these services to original equipment manufacturers, or OEMs, primarily in the communications, computing, multimedia, industrial and semiconductor capital equipment, defense and aerospace, medical and automotive industries. Co.'s services consist primarily of product design and engineering, including initial development, detailed design and services in connection with preproduction, volume manufacturing of complete systems, components and subassemblies, final system assembly and test, direct order fulfillment and after-market product service and support.

Recent Developments: For the second quarter ended Apr 1 2006, net loss amounted to $103.4 million compared with a net loss of $1.04 billion in the equivalent year-earlier quarter. Revenues were $2.67 billion, down 7.5% from $2.89 billion the year before. Operating income was $44.6 million versus a loss of $604.1 million in the prior-year quarter. Direct operating expenses declined 8.5% to $2.50 billion from $2.74 billion in the comparable period the year before. Indirect operating expenses decreased 84.1% to $120.0 million from $754.2 million in the equivalent prior-year period.

Prospects: Results reflect an improving economy and increasing demand in Co.'s core electronics manufacturing services, printed circuit board fabrication and backplane businesses. Also, Co. is experiencing a continuing rise in its gross margins, due to increased operating efficiencies and a shift in product mix to its higher margin core business. These positive market trends are expected to strengthen throughout fiscal 2006. For the third quarter of fiscal 2006, Co. expects revenue of $2.70 billion to $2.80 billion. Meanwhile, on Apr 4 2006, Co. entered into a joint development agreement with Shocking Technologies, Inc. to develop embedded Electrostatic Discharge protection in printed circuit boards.

Financial Data
(US$ in Thousands)

	6 Mos	3 Mos	10/01/2005	10/02/2004	09/27/2003	09/28/2002	09/29/2001	09/30/2000
Earnings Per Share	(0.16)	(1.93)	(1.93)	(0.02)	(0.27)	(5.60)	0.12	0.62
Cash Flow Per Share	0.17	0.57	0.80	0.37	1.08	1.71	1.26	0.30
Tang Book Value Per Share	1.14	1.34	1.24	2.10	2.15	2.50	4.85	4.54
Income Statement								
Total Revenue	5,530,215	2,861,797	11,734,674	12,204,607	10,361,434	8,761,630	4,054,048	3,911,559
EBITDA	37,884	70,416	(296,695)	282,742	136,956	(2,492,779)	246,470	487,495
Depn & Amortn	71,601	35,170	177,385	190,904	222,600	249,572	180,793	157,256
Income Before Taxes	(89,938)	6,923	(593,863)	(15,581)	(198,207)	(2,814,892)	82,792	330,239
Income Taxes	(6,398)	(12,957)	412,139	(600)	(61,050)	(118,139)	42,346	132,946
Net Income	(78,788)	24,632	(1,006,002)	(11,398)	(137,157)	(2,696,753)	40,446	192,334
Average Shares	525,256	524,703	520,574	515,803	510,102	481,985	330,229	310,076
Balance Sheet								
Total Assets	5,770,835	6,318,203	6,241,775	7,546,636	7,450,256	7,518,057	3,640,331	3,639,470
Current Liabilities	2,351,312	2,132,119	2,074,218	2,786,059	2,036,053	2,053,989	492,337	712,495
Long-Term Obligations	978,768	1,635,847	1,644,666	1,311,377	1,925,630	1,975,331	1,218,608	1,143,942
Total Liabilities	3,461,402	3,920,740	3,862,757	4,191,925	4,127,002	4,103,342	1,799,351	1,937,988
Stockholders' Equity	2,309,433	2,397,463	2,379,018	3,354,711	3,323,254	3,414,715	1,840,980	1,701,482
Shares Outstanding	532,831	531,206	526,837	522,478	511,199	506,152	318,819	304,518
Statistical Record								
Return on Assets %	N.M.	N.M.	N.M.	N.M.	N.M.	N.M.	1.11	7.97
Return on Equity %	N.M.	N.M.	N.M.	N.M.	N.M.	N.M.	2.29	16.57
EBITDA Margin %	0.69	2.46	N.M.	2.32	1.32	N.M.	6.08	12.46
Net Margin %	N.M.	0.86	N.M.	N.M.	N.M.	N.M.	1.00	4.92
Asset Turnover	1.82	1.63	1.71	1.60	1.39	1.57	1.12	1.62
Current Ratio	1.43	1.84	1.81	1.53	2.05	2.02	5.25	3.63
Debt to Equity	0.42	0.68	0.69	0.39	0.58	0.58	0.66	0.67
Price Range	5.99-3.53	8.47-3.53	9.29-3.79	15.31-6.37	10.78-1.61	25.60-2.51	57.81-12.59	59.00-18.98
P/E Ratio	...	...	...	...	...	...	481.77-104.92	95.16-30.62

Address: 2700 North First Street, San Jose, CA 95134 **Telephone:** 408-964-3500 **Fax:** 408-964-3636	**Web Site:** www.sanmina-sci.com **Officers:** Jure Sola - Chmn., C.E.O. David L. White - Exec. V.P., C.F.O.
Auditors: KPMG LLP **Investor Contact:** 408-964-3500 **Transfer Agents:** Wells Fargo Bank Minnesota, N.A., South St. Paul, MN	

SCHEIN (HENRY), INC.

Exchange	Symbol	Price	52Wk Range	Yield	P/E
NMS	HSIC	$49.87 (8/31/2006)	50.55-38.15	N/A	32.59

*7 Year Price Score 138.84 *NYSE Composite Index=100 *12 Month Price Score 103.56

Interim Earnings (Per Share)

Qtr.	Mar	Jun	Sep	Dec
2003	0.28	0.37	0.50	1.03
2004	0.32	0.43	0.35	0.33
2005	0.37	0.45	0.29	0.58
2006	0.18	0.50	...	...

Interim Dividends (Per Share)
No Dividends Paid

Valuation Analysis | **Institutional Holding**

Forecast P/E	N/A	No of Institutions
		291
Market Cap	$4.4 Billion	Shares
Book Value	1.4 Billion	73,574,864
Price/Book	3.25	% Held
Price/Sales	0.92	83.44

Business Summary: Specialist Equipment Supplies (MIC: 12.10 SIC: 5047 NAIC: 423450)

Henry Schein is a distributor of healthcare products and services primarily to office-based healthcare practitioners in the combined North American and European markets. Co. customers include dental practices and laboratories, physician practices and veterinary clinics, as well as government and other institutions. Co.'s healthcare distribution segment aggregates its dental, medical and international operating segments. Products distributed include consumable products, laboratory products, branded and generic pharmaceuticals, vaccines, surgical products, diagnostic tests, infection control products and vitamins. Co.'s technology group provides software, technology and other services.

Recent Developments: For the quarter ended July 1 2006, income from continuing operations increased 19.7% to $45.2 million from $37.8 million in the year-earlier quarter. Net income increased 22.4% to $45.2 million from $37.0 million in the year-earlier quarter. Revenues were $1.22 billion, up 10.5% from $1.10 billion the year before. Operating income was $76.7 million versus $67.1 million in the prior-year quarter, an increase of 14.5%. Direct operating expenses rose 9.9% to $860.9 million from $783.1 million in the comparable period the year before. Indirect operating expenses increased 11.2% to $282.7 million from $254.3 million in the equivalent prior-year period.

Prospects: On Jul 13 2006, Co. announced that it will acquire Island Dental Co., Inc., Darby Medical Supply Co. and Darby Dental Laboratory Supply Co., Inc. from Darby Group Companies for about $51.5 million; allowing deeper penetration into Co.'s Dental and Medical divisions. The purchase should be slightly accretive to Co.'s 2006 diluted earnings per share (EPS), and add about $0.01 to $0.03 to its 2007 diluted EPS. The dealings should close during the third quarter of 2006, and Co. expects to realize operational efficiencies upon integration. Meanwhile, Co has raised full-year 2006 diluted EPS guidance to $2.10 to $2.16, including the impact of stock-based compensation expense per FAS No. 123®.

Financial Data
(US$ in Thousands)

	6 Mos	3 Mos	12/31/2005	12/25/2004	12/27/2003	12/28/2002	12/29/2001	12/30/2000
Earnings Per Share	1.53	1.47	1.70	1.43	1.53	1.31	1.00	0.68
Cash Flow Per Share	2.15	2.71	3.00	2.20	1.48	1.55	2.26	1.82
Tang Book Value Per Share	5.64	5.47	5.51	4.03	6.49	6.26	4.60	3.43
Income Statement								
Total Revenue	2,382,141	1,161,781	4,635,929	4,060,266	3,353,805	2,825,001	2,558,243	2,381,721
EBITDA	167,706	75,491	343,092	264,755	272,141	226,215	183,239	144,426
Depn & Amortn	30,158	14,352	60,345	51,300	36,800	28,272	35,642	33,762
Income Before Taxes	131,377	58,301	264,554	203,374	225,776	190,429	140,351	96,534
Income Taxes	47,601	21,222	97,002	75,404	84,378	70,510	51,930	36,150
Net Income	61,477	16,259	151,326	128,183	137,510	117,987	87,373	56,749
Average Shares	89,822	89,241	89,186	89,462	89,975	89,744	87,090	84,014
Balance Sheet								
Total Assets	2,650,053	2,566,944	2,583,120	2,433,670	1,819,370	1,558,052	1,385,428	1,231,068
Current Liabilities	672,084	649,075	724,114	693,899	519,188	423,330	437,062	364,857
Long-Term Obligations	486,014	488,214	489,520	525,682	247,100	242,561	242,169	266,224
Total Liabilities	1,277,952	1,253,809	1,341,223	1,315,179	803,720	690,087	698,185	644,012
Stockholders' Equity	1,354,848	1,298,877	1,229,544	1,106,053	1,004,118	861,217	680,457	579,050
Shares Outstanding	88,160	88,256	87,092	86,650	87,523	87,958	85,365	83,767
Statistical Record								
Return on Assets %	5.42	5.37	5.94	6.04	8.17	8.04	6.70	4.59
Return on Equity %	10.95	10.85	12.75	12.18	14.78	15.35	13.91	10.18
EBITDA Margin %	7.04	6.50	7.40	6.52	8.11	8.01	7.16	6.06
Net Margin %	2.58	1.40	3.26	3.16	4.10	4.18	3.42	2.38
Asset Turnover	1.88	1.91	1.82	1.91	1.99	1.92	1.96	1.92
Current Ratio	2.27	2.30	2.19	2.06	2.23	2.43	2.12	2.16
Debt to Equity	0.36	0.38	0.40	0.48	0.25	0.28	0.36	0.46
Price Range	49.01-38.15	48.75-35.74	45.48-32.99	39.60-28.80	34.41-17.48	27.78-17.91	20.10-14.06	17.91-6.00
P/E Ratio	32.03-24.93	33.16-24.31	26.75-19.41	27.70-20.14	22.49-11.43	21.21-13.67	20.10-14.06	26.33-8.82

Address: 135 Duryea Road, Melville, NY 11747 Telephone: 631-843-5500 Fax: 631-843-5665	Web Site: www.henryschein.com; www.sullivanschein.com Officers: Stanley M. Bergman - Chmn., C.E.O. James P. Breslawski - Pres., C.O.O.	Auditors: BDO Seidman, LLP Investor Contact: 631-843-5562 Transfer Agents: Continental Stock Transfer & Trust Company

SCHOLASTIC CORP.

Exchange	Symbol	Price	52Wk Range	Yield	P/E
NMS	SCHL	$30.06 (8/31/2006)	37.42-25.23	N/A	18.44

*7 Year Price Score 68.83 *NYSE Composite Index=100 *12 Month Price Score 92.28

Interim Earnings (Per Share)

Qtr.	Aug	Nov	Feb	May
2001-02	(1.05)	1.69	0.31	1.29
2002-03	(1.14)	1.85	(0.01)	0.72
2003-04	(0.63)	1.67	(0.15)	0.56
2004-05	(1.27)	1.80	(0.02)	1.04
2005-06	(0.52)	1.59	(0.37)	0.90

Interim Dividends (Per Share)

Amt	Decl	Ex	Rec	Pay
2-for-1	12/14/2000	1/17/2001	12/29/2000	1/16/2001

Valuation Analysis

		Institutional Holding	
Forecast P/E	12.67	No of Institutions	
	(9/9/2006)	170	
Market Cap	$1.3 Billion	Shares	35,148,680
Book Value	1.0 Billion	% Held	83.94
Price/Book	1.20		
Price/Sales	0.55		

Business Summary: Non-Media Publishing (MIC: 13.3 SIC: 2731 NAIC: 511130)
Scholastic is a global children's publishing, education and media company. Co. creates educational and entertaining materials and products for use in school and at home including children's books, textbooks, magazines, children's reference and non-fiction materials, teacher materials, and television programming, film, videos and toys. Co. distributes its products and services through school-based book clubs and book fairs, school-based and direct-to-home continuity programs, retail stores, the internet and television networks. Co.'s operating segments include Children's Book Publishing and Distribution; Educational Publishing; Media, Licensing and Advertising; and International.

Recent Developments: For the year ended May 31 2006, net income increased 6.7% to $68.6 million from $64.3 million in the prior year. Revenues were $2.28 billion, up 9.8% from $2.08 billion the year before. Operating income was $139.3 million versus $134.9 million in the prior year, an increase of 3.3%. Direct operating expenses rose 12.7% to $1.10 billion from $979.7 million in the comparable period the year before. Indirect operating expenses increased 7.8% to $1.04 billion from $966.0 million in the equivalent prior-year period.

Prospects: Co. continues to control costs and improve margins through several efforts including reducing overhead spending by $40.0 million annually by fiscal 2008, with about two thirds of the savings expected to be realized in fiscal 2007. For the fiscal year ending May 2007, Co. expects total revenues of about $2.10 billion to $2.20 billion and earnings of $1.55 to $1.85 per diluted share, due to several factors including expected revenue growth in its Educational Publishing segment based on its 2005 investment in sales and support; continued revenue growth in its International segment with improved profitability; and ongoing implementation of its cost savings plan to lower overhead spending.

Financial Data
(US$ in Thousands)

	05/31/2006	05/31/2005	05/31/2004	05/31/2003	05/31/2002	05/31/2001	05/31/2000	05/31/1999
Earnings Per Share	1.63	1.58	1.46	1.46	2.38	1.01	1.48	1.10
Cash Flow Per Share	5.67	6.17	5.37	4.58	4.49	5.73	4.37	3.59
Tang Book Value Per Share	17.12	14.83	13.31	11.52	10.21	5.95	11.24	9.28
Income Statement								
Total Revenue	2,283,800	2,079,900	2,233,800	1,958,300	1,917,000	1,962,300	1,402,500	1,154,700
EBITDA	272,900	265,700	176,500	228,700	271,500	209,900	170,400	151,500
Depn & Amortn	133,600	130,800	53,500	107,100	86,800	111,200	71,400	73,600
Income Before Taxes	107,600	99,700	90,500	90,100	153,300	57,100	80,400	58,900
Income Taxes	39,000	35,400	32,100	31,500	54,600	20,800	29,000	22,100
Net Income	68,600	64,300	58,400	58,600	93,500	36,300	51,400	36,800
Average Shares	42,200	40,800	40,100	40,100	40,100	36,100	37,200	33,400
Balance Sheet								
Total Assets	2,052,200	1,931,400	1,755,800	1,801,000	1,636,700	1,501,800	983,200	842,300
Current Liabilities	689,000	374,800	357,400	477,700	330,200	374,900	285,800	211,800
Long-Term Obligations	234,600	539,900	985,000	964,400	525,800	585,300	241,100	248,000
Total Liabilities	1,002,900	994,300	899,800	1,028,400	917,800	1,008,100	553,200	480,900
Stockholders' Equity	1,049,300	937,100	856,000	772,600	718,900	493,700	430,000	361,400
Shares Outstanding	41,938	40,732	39,587	39,264	39,073	35,288	32,352	31,290
Statistical Record								
Return on Assets %	3.44	3.49	3.27	3.41	5.96	2.92	5.62	4.58
Return on Equity %	6.91	7.17	7.15	7.86	15.42	7.86	12.95	10.83
EBITDA Margin %	11.95	12.77	7.90	11.68	14.16	10.70	12.15	13.12
Net Margin %	3.00	3.09	2.61	2.99	4.88	1.85	3.66	3.19
Asset Turnover	1.15	1.13	1.25	1.14	1.22	1.58	1.53	1.44
Current Ratio	1.57	2.51	2.36	1.85	2.42	2.05	1.89	2.05
Debt to Equity	0.22	0.58	1.15	1.25	0.73	1.19	0.56	0.69
Price Range	39.50-26.00	38.62-26.35	35.39-26.65	48.89-23.00	56.40-36.00	48.56-26.59	34.88-19.81	29.38-18.31
P/E Ratio	24.23-15.95	24.44-16.68	24.24-18.25	33.49-15.75	23.70-15.13	48.08-26.33	23.56-13.39	26.70-16.65

Address: 557 Broadway, New York, NY 10012
Telephone: 212-343-6100

Web Site: www.scholastic.com
Officers: Richard Robinson - Chmn., Pres., C.E.O.
Mary A. Winston - Exec. V.P., C.F.O.

Auditors: Ernst & Young LLP
Investor Contact: 212-343-6741

SEARS HOLDINGS CORP

Exchange	Symbol	Price	52Wk Range	Yield	P/E
NMS	SHLD	$144.11 (8/31/2006)	164.19-113.52	N/A	19.01

*7 Year Price Score N/A *NYSE Composite Index=100 *12 Month Price Score 106.71

Interim Earnings (Per Share)

Qtr.	Apr	Jul	Oct	Jan
2003-04	...	...	...	2.84
2004-05	0.94	1.54	5.45	3.07
2005-06	(0.07)	0.98	0.35	4.20
2006-07	1.14	1.88	...	...

Interim Dividends (Per Share)
No Dividends Paid

Valuation Analysis
Forecast P/E N/A
Market Cap $22.5 Billion
Book Value 11.6 Billion
Price/Book 1.94
Price/Sales 0.42

Institutional Holding
No of Institutions 362
Shares 140,610,416
% Held 89.89

Business Summary: Retail - General (MIC: 5.2 SIC: 5331 NAIC: 452990)

Sears Holdings is a broadline retailer and parent company of Kmart Holding Corporation (Kmart) and Sears, Roebuck and Co. (Sears). As of Jan 28 2006, Co. operated a total of 3,410 stores in the U.S. through Kmart and Sears as well as about 123 full-line and 252 specialty retail stores in Canada through Sears Canada Inc., its 54%-owned subsidiary. Co.'s brands include KENMORE®, CRAFTSMAN®, DIEHARD® and LANDS END®. Co.'s trademarks and service marks include THE GREAT INDOORS®, OSH®, CANYON RIVER BLUES®, COVINGTON®, and ATHLETECH®. Co. also has the right to sell an exclusive line of Martha Stewart Everyday® products in its Kmart locations, as well as within Sears Canada stores.

Recent Developments: For the quarter ended July 29 2006, net income increased 82.6% to $294.0 million from $161.0 million in the year-earlier quarter. Revenues were $12.79 billion, down 3.1% from $13.19 billion the year before. Operating income was $517.0 million versus $324.0 million in the prior-year quarter, an increase of 59.6%. Direct operating expenses declined 4.0% to $9.16 billion from $9.54 billion in the comparable period the year before. Indirect operating expenses decreased 6.5% to $3.11 billion from $3.33 billion in the equivalent prior-year period.

Prospects: Co.'s near-term outlook appears somewhat mixed. On one hand, Co.'s domestic comparable stores sales are exhibiting a decline within both Sears Domestic and Kmart. Nevertheless, Co. is also experiencing growth in operating income within both these segments, supported by lower expenses as a result of realizing merger integration and improved expense management. Separately, on Mar 20 2006, Co. acquired 10,161,968 common shares of Sears Canada following its take-over bid, resulting in approximately 63.2% in its ownership of Sears Canada's outstanding shares. Going forward, Co. remains optimistic that it will gain full-ownership of Sears Canada by December 2006.

Financial Data
(US$ in Thousands)

	6 Mos	3 Mos	01/28/2006	01/26/2005	01/28/2004	04/30/2003	01/29/2003	01/30/2002
Earnings Per Share	7.58	6.67	5.59	11.00	2.52	(1.65)	(6.36)	(4.89)
Cash Flow Per Share	12.95	13.16	14.99	11.99	10.98	0.88	0.17	2.02
Tang Book Value Per Share	40.21	39.26	40.49	50.95	24.47	...	...	6.87
Income Statement								
Total Revenue	24,783,000	11,998,000	49,124,000	19,701,000	17,072,000	6,181,000	29,352,000	36,151,000
EBITDA	1,452,000	632,000	3,134,000	1,952,000	536,000	(624,000)	(1,903,000)	...
Depn & Amortn	565,000	289,000	932,000	69,000	31,000	177,000	737,000	824,000
Income Before Taxes	798,000	296,000	1,965,000	1,775,000	400,000	(858,000)	(2,795,000)	...
Income Taxes	319,000	118,000	716,000	669,000	152,000	(6,000)	(24,000)	(115,000)
Net Income	474,000	180,000	858,000	1,106,000	248,000	(862,000)	(3,219,000)	(2,418,000)
Average Shares	156,500	158,000	153,600	101,400	99,300	522,700	506,400	494,100
Balance Sheet								
Total Assets	30,061,000	29,891,000	30,573,000	8,651,000	6,084,000	6,660,000	11,238,000	14,298,000
Current Liabilities	9,895,000	9,982,000	10,350,000	2,086,000	1,776,000	2,763,000	2,120,000	624,000
Long-Term Obligations	3,475,000	3,510,000	3,268,000	367,000	477,000	523,000	623,000	1,187,000
Total Liabilities	18,450,000	18,517,000	18,962,000	4,182,000	3,892,000	4,947,000	2,924,000	1,890,000
Stockholders' Equity	11,611,000	11,374,000	11,611,000	4,469,000	2,192,000	1,713,000	(301,000)	3,459,000
Shares Outstanding	156,000	156,000	160,000	87,708	89,590	...	519,124	503,294
Statistical Record								
Return on Assets %	3.91	3.46	4.35	15.05	5.20	N.M.	N.M.	N.M.
Return on Equity %	10.32	9.29	10.61	33.30	16.98	N.M.	N.M.	N.M.
EBITDA Margin %	5.86	5.27	6.38	9.91	3.14	N.M.	N.M.	...
Net Margin %	1.91	1.50	1.75	5.61	1.45	N.M.	N.M.	N.M.
Asset Turnover	1.76	1.77	2.49	2.68	3.58	0.47	2.31	2.51
Current Ratio	1.50	1.46	1.47	3.62	3.27	2.37	2.88	12.63
Debt to Equity	0.30	0.31	0.28	0.08	0.22	0.31	...	0.34
Price Range	164.19-113.52	163.11-113.52	163.11-90.33	109.00-26.52	32.74-12.85	15.00-15.00	...	...
P/E Ratio	21.66-14.98	24.45-17.02	29.18-16.16	9.91-2.41	12.99-5.10		...	...

Address: 3333 Beverly Road, Hoffman Estates, IL 60179 **Telephone:** 847-286-2500	**Web Site:** www.searsholdings.com **Officers:** Edward S. Lampert - Chmn. Alan J. Lacy - Vice-Chmn.	**Auditors:** DELOITTE & TOUCHE LLP **Investor Contact:** 248-643-1040

SEI INVESTMENTS CO.

Exchange	Symbol	Price	52Wk Range	Yield	P/E	Div Acheiver
NMS	SEIC	$51.04 (8/31/2006)	52.49-35.12	0.47	24.30	14 Years

*7 Year Price Score 100.15 *NYSE Composite Index=100 *12 Month Price Score 112.95

Interim Earnings (Per Share)

Qtr.	Mar	Jun	Sep	Dec
2003	0.32	0.32	0.33	0.35
2004	0.37	0.39	0.43	0.41
2005	0.42	0.43	0.48	0.51
2006	0.54	0.57	...	...

Interim Dividends (Per Share)

Amt	Decl	Ex	Rec	Pay
0.10S	12/14/2004	12/31/2004	1/4/2005	1/21/2005
0.11S	5/25/2005	6/6/2005	6/8/2005	6/24/2005
0.11S	12/14/2005	12/29/2005	1/3/2006	1/20/2006
0.12S	5/24/2006	6/6/2006	6/8/2006	6/22/2006
		Indicated Div: $0.24		

Valuation Analysis

Forecast P/E	22.91
	(9/9/2006)
Market Cap	$5.0 Billion
Book Value	494.8 Million
Price/Book	10.14
Price/Sales	5.23

Institutional Holding

No of Institutions	262
Shares	49,692,480
% Held	50.45

Business Summary: Finance Intermediaries & Services (MIC: 8.7 SIC: 6211 NAIC: 523120)
SEI Investments provides investment processing, fund processing, and investment management business outsourcing solutions to corporations, financial institutions, investment managers, and affluent families in the U.S., Canada, the U.K., continental Europe. Investment processing solutions use Co.'s proprietary software system to track investment activities in multiple types of investment accounts, including trust and non-trust investment accounts, allowing banks and trust companies to outsource trust and investment related activities. Co. also offers administration and distribution support services to mutual funds, collective trust funds, hedge funds, fund of funds and private equity funds.

Recent Developments: For the quarter ended June 30 2006, net income increased 31.1% to $57.9 million from $44.2 million in the year-earlier quarter. Revenues were $285.0 million, up 49.9% from $190.1 million the year before. Operating income was $120.0 million versus $50.4 million in the prior-year quarter, an increase of 138.0%. Indirect operating expenses increased 18.2% to $165.1 million from $139.7 million in the equivalent prior-year period.

Prospects: Co.'s significant revenue growth is being driven principally by the consolidation of the accounts of LSV Asset Management (LSV) into its financial statements beginning in 2006 due to the Guaranty and Collateral Agreement in Jan 2006. Co. is also seeing growth in its assets under management, primarily owing to LSV. Additionally, Co. is benefiting from increased net income and earnings, as well as constructive growth across all its business segments. Meanwhile, Co. continues to make significant expenditures for the development of its Global Wealth Platform as it is progressing through the development phase, and expects to incur significant development costs for the rest of 2006 and 2007.

Financial Data
(US$ in Thousands)

	6 Mos	3 Mos	12/31/2005	12/31/2004	12/31/2003	12/31/2002	12/31/2001	12/31/2000
Earnings Per Share	2.10	1.96	1.83	1.60	1.32	1.25	1.09	0.87
Cash Flow Per Share	3.19	2.93	2.14	1.80	1.69	1.62	1.61	1.39
Tang Book Value Per Share	2.56	2.31	3.09	3.41	3.27	2.54	2.38	1.70
Dividends Per Share	0.230	0.220	0.220	0.290	0.070	0.170	0.090	0.073
Dividend Payout %	10.95	11.22	12.02	18.13	5.30	13.60	8.26	8.43
Income Statement								
Total Revenue	562,151	277,133	773,007	692,269	636,233	620,819	658,013	598,806
EBITDA	179,748	90,689	305,332	278,322	238,823	238,171	213,178	172,797
Depn & Amortn	10,919	5,448	16,966	15,624	16,599	18,060	19,650	17,305
Income Before Taxes	171,978	86,740	295,209	265,131	224,284	223,048	198,324	159,618
Income Taxes	59,161	31,834	106,865	96,110	81,303	82,528	73,380	60,655
Net Income	112,817	54,906	188,344	169,021	142,981	140,520	124,944	98,963
Average Shares	101,263	101,311	103,138	105,866	108,137	112,803	114,810	113,820
Balance Sheet								
Total Assets	871,301	839,576	657,147	615,475	592,629	464,147	460,916	375,582
Current Liabilities	147,187	151,519	167,470	163,569	193,474	134,247	144,343	146,453
Long-Term Obligations	74,039	77,800	9,000	14,389	23,944	33,500	43,055	27,000
Total Liabilities	376,486	380,740	235,459	211,533	228,856	174,140	190,323	178,161
Stockholders' Equity	494,815	458,836	421,688	403,942	363,773	290,007	270,593	197,421
Shares Outstanding	98,330	98,239	98,580	102,175	104,869	109,180	109,180	108,560
Statistical Record								
Return on Assets %	29.50	28.05	29.60	27.90	27.06	30.38	29.87	31.36
Return on Equity %	47.67	46.29	45.62	43.91	43.74	50.13	53.39	71.41
EBITDA Margin %	31.98	32.72	39.50	40.20	37.54	38.36	32.40	28.86
Net Margin %	20.07	19.81	24.37	24.42	22.47	22.63	18.99	16.53
Asset Turnover	1.33	1.22	1.21	1.14	1.20	1.34	1.57	1.90
Current Ratio	3.03	2.77	1.83	2.17	1.82	1.95	1.84	1.70
Debt to Equity	0.15	0.17	0.02	0.04	0.07	0.12	0.16	0.14
Price Range	48.88-35.12	42.44-32.15	42.10-32.15	43.09-27.40	35.92-22.90	45.75-19.03	51.31-27.90	61.72-14.89
P/E Ratio	23.28-16.72	21.65-16.40	23.01-17.57	26.93-17.13	27.21-17.35	36.60-15.22	47.07-25.60	70.94-17.11
Average Yield %	0.57	0.58	0.59	0.87	0.24	0.53	0.23	0.26

Address: 1 Freedom Valley Drive, Oaks, PA 19456-1100 **Telephone:** 610-676-1000 **Fax:** 610-676-1105	**Web Site:** www.seic.com **Officers:** Alfred P. West Jr. - Chmn., C.E.O. Carmen V. Romeo - Exec. V.P.	**Auditors:** PricewaterhouseCoopers LLP **Investor Contact:** 610-676-1000 **Transfer Agents:** American Stock Transfer & Trust Co., New York, NY

SEMTECH CORP.

Exchange	Symbol	Price	52Wk Range	Yield	P/E
NMS	SMTC	$13.07 (8/31/2006)	21.00-11.09	N/A	22.93

*7 Year Price Score 56.47 *NYSE Composite Index=100 *12 Month Price Score 73.86

Interim Earnings (Per Share)

Qtr.	Apr	Jul	Oct	Jan
2001-02	0.17	(0.07)	0.12	0.11
2002-03	0.13	0.14	0.17	0.00
2003-04	0.11	0.03	0.12	0.16
2004-05	0.19	0.22	0.19	0.15
2005-06	0.14	0.10	0.15	0.18

Interim Dividends (Per Share)

No Dividends Paid

Valuation Analysis   **Institutional Holding**

Forecast P/E	15.81	No of Institutions
	(9/9/2006)	149
Market Cap	$950.1 Million	Shares
Book Value	438.5 Million	70,077,136
Price/Book	2.17	% Held
Price/Sales	3.97	96.79

Business Summary: IT & Technology (MIC: 10.2 SIC: 3674 NAIC: 334413)

Semtech designs, produces and markets a range of analog and mixed-signal semiconductor products that are sold principally to customers in the computer, communications and industrial markets. Co.'s products are designed into a variety of end applications, including notebook and desktop computers, personal digital assistants, cellular phones, wireline networks, consumer devices and semiconductor test platforms. Co.'s end customers are primarily original equipment manufacturers and their suppliers, including Apple, Cisco, Compal Electronics, Curitel Communications, Dell, Hewlett Packard, Intel, LG Electronics, Motorola, Nortel, Panasonic, Quanta Computer and Samsung.

Recent Developments: For the year ended Jan 29 2006, net income decreased 27.0% to $43.0 million from $58.9 million in the prior year. Revenues were $239.4 million, down 5.6% from $253.6 million the year before. Operating income was $47.4 million versus $70.0 million in the prior year, a decrease of 32.3%. Direct operating expenses declined 0.7% to $105.0 million from $105.7 million in the comparable period the year before. Indirect operating expenses increased 11.7% to $87.0 million from $77.9 million in the equivalent prior-year period.

Prospects: Despite the decline in its Power Management product line sales, Co.'s top-line growth is being driven by continuing robust shipment of Co.'s Protection Products as well as solid sales growth in its test and measurement products used in automated test equipment (ATE). Going forward, Co. is optimistic regarding the prospective improvements towards its new product introductions and design wins in the second half of fiscal year 2007. For the first quarter of fiscal year 2007, Co. projects growth in its net sales to be in the range of 1.0% to 3.0% and earnings of between $0.13 and $0.14 cents per diluted share.

Financial Data

(US$ in Thousands)	01/29/2006	01/30/2005	01/25/2004	01/26/2003	01/27/2002	01/28/2001	01/30/2000	01/31/1999
Earnings Per Share	0.57	0.75	0.42	0.44	0.33	0.79	0.41	0.20
Cash Flow Per Share	0.89	0.93	0.49	0.86	0.93	1.30	0.60	0.36
Tang Book Value Per Share	5.50	5.75	5.12	4.67	4.14	3.56	1.96	1.31
Income Statement								
Total Revenue	239,405	253,612	192,079	192,958	191,210	256,685	173,768	114,519
EBITDA	58,572	79,839	47,842	52,650	37,348	85,531	47,076	22,299
Depn & Amortn	11,752	9,836	8,371	9,581	10,327	8,837	4,118	3,723
Income Before Taxes	54,656	76,270	42,718	46,084	33,832	86,028	44,104	19,362
Income Taxes	11,671	17,382	10,252	11,903	9,473	25,808	14,709	6,467
Net Income	42,985	58,888	32,466	34,181	26,003	60,220	29,395	12,895
Average Shares	75,992	78,124	77,504	77,789	77,747	76,527	70,630	63,568
Balance Sheet								
Total Assets	473,765	457,925	408,473	620,546	690,401	677,288	149,350	92,556
Current Liabilities	26,121	29,018	28,863	37,536	27,286	34,701	23,737	12,728
Long-Term Obligations	...	...	...	241,570	364,320	400,000	...	...
Total Liabilities	35,306	33,559	28,863	279,106	391,606	434,931	23,868	12,785
Stockholders' Equity	438,459	424,366	379,610	341,440	298,795	242,357	125,482	79,771
Shares Outstanding	72,693	73,845	74,120	73,165	72,148	68,116	64,096	60,776
Statistical Record								
Return on Assets %	9.25	13.37	6.33	5.23	3.81	14.61	24.37	16.19
Return on Equity %	9.99	14.41	9.03	10.71	9.64	32.83	28.72	19.24
EBITDA Margin %	24.47	31.48	24.91	27.29	19.53	33.32	27.09	19.47
Net Margin %	17.95	23.22	16.90	17.71	13.60	23.46	16.92	11.26
Asset Turnover	0.52	0.58	0.37	0.30	0.28	0.62	1.44	1.44
Current Ratio	10.02	8.63	8.52	12.21	15.77	16.30	5.07	6.17
Debt to Equity	...	...	...	0.71	1.22	1.65	...	...
Price Range	21.00-14.57	26.25-16.47	27.14-11.90	39.00-9.05	43.38-23.44	59.22-15.38	34.00-6.19	9.78-2.59
P/E Ratio	36.84-25.56	35.00-21.96	64.62-28.33	88.64-20.57	131.45-71.02	74.96-19.46	82.93-15.09	48.91-12.97

Address: 200 Flynn Road, Camarillo, CA 93012-8790
Telephone: 805-498-2111
Fax: 805-498-3804

Web Site: www.semtech.com
Officers: John D. Poe - Chmn. Rock N. Hankin - Vice-Chmn.

Auditors: Ernst & Young LLP

SEPRACOR INC.

Exchange	Symbol	Price	52Wk Range	Yield	P/E
NMS	SEPR	$47.01 (8/31/2006)	60.26-42.93	N/A	90.40

*7 Year Price Score 90.39 *NYSE Composite Index=100 *12 Month Price Score 92.36

Interim Earnings (Per Share)

Qtr.	Mar	Jun	Sep	Dec
2003	(0.35)	(0.40)	(0.45)	(0.40)
2004	(0.59)	(0.93)	(1.40)	(0.24)
2005	(0.22)	(0.07)	(0.02)	0.35
2006	0.09	0.10	...	...

Interim Dividends (Per Share)
No Dividends Paid

Valuation Analysis

		Institutional Holding	
Forecast P/E	43.00	No of Institutions	
	(9/9/2006)	285	
Market Cap	$4.9 Billion	Shares	
Book Value	N/A	107,958,432	
Price/Book	N/A	% Held	
Price/Sales	4.62	98.81	

Business Summary: Instruments and Related Products (MIC: 11.15 SIC: 3826 NAIC: 334516)

Sepracor is pharmaceutical company engaged in the discovery, development and commercialization of differentiated products that are prescribed principally by primary care physicians. Co. manufactures and sells three products: XOPENEX® Inhalation Solution, a short-acting bronchodilator for the treatment or prevention of bronchospasm in patients with reversible obstructive airway disease; XOPENEX HFA™ Inhalation Aerosol, a hydrofluoroalkane (HFA), metered-dose inhaler (MDI) for the treatment or prevention of bronchospasm in adults, adolescents and children of four years of age and older with reversible obstructive airway disease, and LUNESTA™ for the treatment of insomnia.

Recent Developments: For the quarter ended June 30 2006, net income amounted to $11.0 million versus a net loss of $7.7 million in the year-earlier quarter. Revenues were $264.4 million, up 42.9% from $185.1 million the year before. Operating income was $6.4 million versus a loss of $7.0 million in the prior-year quarter. Direct operating expenses rose 43.1% to $21.0 million from $14.7 million in the comparable period the year before. Indirect operating expenses increased 33.6% to $237.1 million from $177.4 million in the equivalent prior-year period.

Prospects: Co.'s product sales are benefiting from higher LUNESTA™ and XOPENEX® Inhalation Solution revenue. Co. attributed the increase sales of LUNESTA™ to a higher number of units sold and a climb in the net selling price per unit. Conversely, Co. continues to experience a decline in royalties earned on the sales of ALLEGRA, with the majority of the decrease occurring in the U.S. Separately, during the second-quarter of 2006, Co. filed an Investigational New Drug Application for SEP-227162, a serotonin and norepinephrine reuptake inhibitor (SNRI), and expects to begin a Phase I trial of SEP-227162 for the treatment of depression and/or anxiety during the third quarter of 2006.

Financial Data
(US$ in Thousands)

	6 Mos	3 Mos	12/31/2005	12/31/2004	12/31/2003	12/31/2002	12/31/2001	12/31/2000
Earnings Per Share	0.52	0.35	0.04	(3.21)	(1.61)	(3.34)	(2.89)	(2.80)
Cash Flow Per Share	0.08	0.11	(0.22)	(1.99)	(1.23)	(2.98)	(2.69)	(2.34)
Income Statement								
Total Revenue	550,084	285,678	820,928	380,877	344,040	238,968	152,095	85,245
EBITDA	22,654	11,095	18,182	...	...	...	...	...
Depn & Amortn	10,723	4,968	17,154	18,706	19,551	18,561	13,048	11,536
Income Before Taxes	21,621	10,370	5,122	...	...	...	...	...
Income Taxes	541	111	151	...	...	...	...	...
Net Income	21,080	10,259	4,971	(295,658)	(135,936)	(276,490)	(224,015)	(204,017)
Average Shares	115,371	115,470	118,162	92,017	84,639	82,899	77,534	72,757
Balance Sheet								
Total Assets	1,277,485	1,283,787	1,274,497	1,039,118	1,020,225	727,113	1,093,531	750,958
Current Liabilities	665,051	249,456	277,906	204,110	598,428	136,441	145,837	104,179
Long-Term Obligations	721,893	1,161,984	1,162,080	1,163,349	1,040,789	982,852	1,261,396	853,916
Total Liabilities	1,386,944	1,411,440	1,439,986	1,370,233	1,639,436	1,119,293	1,407,233	958,573
Stockholders' Equity	(109,459)	(127,653)	(165,489)	(331,115)	(619,211)	(392,180)	(313,702)	(214,674)
Shares Outstanding	104,936	104,468	104,093	103,376	85,025	84,356	78,059	73,829
Statistical Record								
Return on Assets %	4.59	3.35	0.43	N.M.	N.M.	N.M.	N.M.	N.M.
EBITDA Margin %	4.12	3.88	2.21	...	...	...	...	...
Net Margin %	3.83	3.59	0.61	N.M.	N.M.	N.M.	N.M.	N.M.
Asset Turnover	0.87	0.87	0.71	0.37	0.39	0.26	0.16	0.15
Current Ratio	1.55	4.14	3.77	4.12	1.43	4.03	5.99	6.04
Price Range	60.26-42.93	63.24-47.91	65.70-49.06	59.80-23.93	32.10-9.67	57.06-4.00	76.56-24.54	137.39-47.25
P/E Ratio	115.88-82.56	180.69-136.89	N.M.	...	...	...	...	...

Address: 84 Waterford Drive, Marlborough, MA 01752 **Telephone:** 508-481-6700 **Fax:** 508-357-7499	**Web Site:** www.sepracor.com **Officers:** Timothy J. Barberich - Chmn., C.E.O. William J. O'Shea - Pres., C.O.O.	**Auditors:** PricewaterhouseCoopers LLP **Investor Contact:** 508-481-6700 **Transfer Agents:** EquiServe Trust Company, N.A. Providence, RI

SIGMA-ALDRICH CORP.

Exchange	Symbol	Price	52Wk Range	Yield	P/E	Div Achiever
NMS	SIAL	$72.63 (8/31/2006)	73.43-60.14	1.16	19.11	24 Years

*7 Year Price Score 107.11 *NYSE Composite Index=100 *12 Month Price Score 103.77

Interim Earnings (Per Share)

Qtr.	Mar	Jun	Sep	Dec
2003	0.72	0.67	0.66	0.66
2004	0.89	0.85	0.81	0.79
2005	1.07	0.91	0.94	0.84
2006	0.98	1.04	...	...

Interim Dividends (Per Share)

Amt	Decl	Ex	Rec	Pay
0.19Q	11/8/2005	11/29/2005	12/1/2005	12/15/2005
0.21Q	2/14/2006	2/27/2006	3/1/2006	3/15/2006
0.21Q	5/2/2006	5/30/2006	6/1/2006	6/15/2006
0.21Q	8/8/2006	8/30/2006	9/1/2006	9/15/2006

Indicated Div: $0.84

Valuation Analysis

		Institutional Holding	
Forecast P/E	18.03	No of Institutions	
	(9/9/2006)	347	
Market Cap	$4.8 Billion	Shares	
Book Value	1.3 Billion	52,403,680	
Price/Book	3.63	% Held	
Price/Sales	2.81	78.95	

Business Summary: Biotechnology (MIC: 9.2 SIC: 5169 NAIC: 424690)

Sigma-Aldrich develops, manufactures and distributes a range of biochemicals and organic chemicals. These chemical products and kits are used in scientific and genomic research, biotechnology, pharmaceutical development, the diagnosis of disease, and chemical manufacturing. Co. consists of three business units: Scientific Research, Biotechnology and Fine Chemicals. The Scientific Research unit sells biochemicals, organic chemicals, and reagents. The Biotechnology unit supplies immunochemical, cell culture, molecular biology, cell signaling and neuroscience biochemicals. The Fine Chemicals unit supplies organic chemicals and biochemicals.

Recent Developments: For the quarter ended June 30 2006, net income increased 12.5% to $70.3 million from $62.5 million in the year-earlier quarter. Revenues were $448.5 million, up 1.0% from $444.0 million the year before. Direct operating expenses declined 3.3% to $214.0 million from $221.2 million in the comparable period the year before. Indirect operating expenses increased 1.9% to $137.4 million from $134.8 million in the equivalent prior-year period.

Prospects: On Aug 9 2006, Co. announced that it has acquired Pharmorphix Limited, a privately held firm based in Cambridge, U.K., offering solid-form research services to the pharmaceutical and biotech markets. The acquisition, which will broaden Co.'s SAFC Pharma's manufacturing services customer base and enhance its technology services offering for existing customers, is expected to allow it to meet its growth goals over the next several years. For 2006, Co. expects organic sales growth of 8.0%, of which approximately 1.0% is derived from its Feb 2005 acquisition of the JRH industrial cell culture business. Additionally, Co. is raising its earnings forecast to $3.90 to $4.00 per diluted share.

Financial Data
(US$ in Thousands)

	6 Mos	3 Mos	12/31/2005	12/31/2004	12/31/2003	12/31/2002	12/31/2001	12/31/2000
Earnings Per Share	3.80	3.67	3.76	3.34	2.71	1.78	1.87	3.83
Cash Flow Per Share	4.35	3.87	4.13	4.68	4.38	4.83	2.13	1.38
Tang Book Value Per Share	12.87	12.04	11.42	15.34	12.83	10.90	9.34	9.72
Dividends Per Share	0.800	0.780	0.760	0.680	0.500	0.345	0.333	0.315
Dividend Payout %	21.05	21.25	20.21	20.36	18.45	19.38	17.78	8.22
Income Statement								
Total Revenue	891,600	443,100	1,666,500	1,409,200	1,298,146	1,206,982	1,179,447	1,096,270
EBITDA	238,900	119,700	451,500	392,400	352,216	352,302	289,548	277,043
Depn & Amortn	43,800	21,700	90,100	73,400	69,267	66,326	71,373	67,563
Income Before Taxes	195,100	98,000	343,300	311,800	272,823	272,139	201,633	202,909
Income Taxes	58,300	31,500	85,000	78,900	82,393	85,404	60,928	63,859
Net Income	136,800	66,500	258,300	232,900	193,102	130,714	140,705	320,198
Average Shares	67,600	68,000	68,700	69,800	71,126	73,412	75,175	83,585
Balance Sheet								
Total Assets	2,343,500	2,214,900	2,131,300	1,745,000	1,548,242	1,389,656	1,439,802	1,347,707
Current Liabilities	598,800	534,000	460,700	230,900	257,378	265,653	397,563	335,280
Long-Term Obligations	255,600	253,400	283,200	177,100	176,259	176,805	177,700	100,846
Total Liabilities	1,014,100	944,200	897,900	533,300	548,981	507,482	630,087	488,432
Stockholders' Equity	1,329,400	1,270,700	1,233,400	1,211,700	999,261	882,174	809,715	859,275
Shares Outstanding	66,400	66,900	67,200	68,700	69,101	71,253	73,014	76,216
Statistical Record								
Return on Assets %	11.33	11.27	13.33	14.11	13.15	9.24	10.10	22.98
Return on Equity %	20.59	19.82	21.13	21.01	20.53	15.45	16.86	30.14
EBITDA Margin %	26.79	27.01	27.09	27.85	27.13	29.19	24.55	25.27
Net Margin %	15.34	15.01	15.50	16.53	14.88	10.83	11.93	29.21
Asset Turnover	0.75	0.77	0.86	0.85	0.88	0.85	0.85	0.79
Current Ratio	1.84	1.90	2.06	3.87	3.17	2.62	1.83	2.13
Debt to Equity	0.19	0.20	0.23	0.15	0.18	0.20	0.22	0.12
Price Range	72.80-55.99	66.67-55.72	66.67-55.72	61.34-53.92	57.46-41.17	52.51-39.41	51.21-37.10	40.25-20.75
P/E Ratio	19.16-14.73	18.17-15.18	17.73-14.82	18.37-16.14	21.20-15.19	29.50-22.14	27.39-19.84	10.51-5.42
Average Yield %	1.24	1.26	1.24	1.19	0.98	0.73	0.77	1.01

Address: 3050 Spruce Street, St. Louis, MO 63103	**Web Site:** www.sigma-aldrich.com	**Auditors:** KPMG LLP
Telephone: 314-771-5765	**Officers:** David R. Harvey - Chmn., C.E.O. Jai P. Nagarkatti - Pres., C.O.O.	**Investor Contact:** 314-286-8004
Fax: 314-286-7874		**Transfer Agents:** Computershare Investor Services, Chicago, IL

SILICON LABORATORIES INC

Exchange	Symbol	Price	52Wk Range	Yield	P/E
NMS	SLAB	$35.27 (8/31/2006)	59.77-26.68	N/A	55.11

*7 Year Price Score N/A *NYSE Composite Index=100 *12 Month Price Score 83.81

Interim Earnings (Per Share)

Qtr.	Mar	Jun	Sep	Dec
2003	(0.02)	0.21	0.26	0.40
2004	0.36	0.41	0.39	0.23
2005	0.31	0.28	(0.01)	0.28
2006	0.19	0.18	...	...

Interim Dividends (Per Share)
No Dividends Paid

Valuation Analysis

		Institutional Holding	
Forecast P/E	22.16	No of Institutions	
(9/9/2006)		194	
Market Cap	$2.0 Billion	Shares	
Book Value	582.1 Million	48,710,380	
Price/Book	3.39	% Held	
Price/Sales	4.36	87.00	

Business Summary: IT & Technology (MIC: 10.2 SIC: 3674 NAIC: 334413)
Silicon Laboratories designs and develops proprietary, analog-intensive, mixed-signal integrated circuits (ICs) which typically use standard complementary metal oxide semiconductor (CMOS) technology for a range of applications. Co.'s Co. also designs and develops mixed-signal 8-bit microcontrollers (MCUs) which are incorporated in a range of applications in a variety of markets including automotive, communications, consumer, industrial, medical and power management. As of Dec 31 2005, Co. had more than 600 issued or pending U.S. patents in the IC field.

Recent Developments: For the quarter ended July 1 2006, net income decreased 35.1% to $10.1 million from $15.6 million in the year-earlier quarter. Revenues were $123.5 million, up 15.3% from $107.2 million the year before. Operating income was $11.3 million versus $17.9 million in the prior-year quarter, a decrease of 37.0%. Direct operating expenses rose 9.1% to $53.0 million from $48.6 million in the comparable period the year before. Indirect operating expenses increased 45.6% to $59.2 million from $40.7 million in the equivalent prior-year period.

Prospects: Co. is optimistic upon attaining further growth through its portfolio expansion, access to new markets as well as the potential of its research and development pipeline. Moreover, Co.'s outlook appears to be exemplified through its acquisition on May 15 2006 of Silembia, a private company in France that develops semiconductor intellectual property for digital demodulation and channel decoding, for approximately $20.0 million. Similarly, on Jul 20 2006, Co. acquired StackCom, a private company developing wireless protocol software stacks for GSM and GPRS mobile applications for approximately $7.0 million. For the third quarter of 2006, Co. expects revenue of $122.0 million to $127.0 million.

Financial Data
(US$ in Thousands)

	6 Mos	3 Mos	12/31/2005	01/01/2005	01/03/2004	12/28/2002	12/29/2001	12/30/2000
Earnings Per Share	0.64	0.74	0.86	1.39	0.86	0.41	(0.99)	0.29
Cash Flow Per Share	1.51	1.82	1.95	1.88	1.45	0.83	0.26	0.59
Tang Book Value Per Share	8.75	8.49	7.71	6.42	4.56	3.18	2.57	2.56
Income Statement								
Total Revenue	238,044	114,540	425,689	456,225	325,305	182,016	74,065	103,103
EBITDA	33,092	16,905	78,208	132,576	89,032	47,929	(33,075)	36,881
Depn & Amortn	10,542	5,677	20,530	23,743	24,155	17,587	18,174	13,834
Income Before Taxes	28,976	14,255	65,641	111,576	66,196	31,307	(48,376)	25,849
Income Taxes	7,775	3,191	18,135	34,883	21,480	10,590	(2,803)	11,832
Net Income	21,201	11,064	47,506	76,693	44,716	20,717	(45,573)	14,017
Average Shares	57,858	57,656	55,485	54,983	52,288	50,811	45,914	48,788
Balance Sheet								
Total Assets	712,690	673,274	613,003	484,402	378,095	197,065	145,021	184,840
Current Liabilities	115,244	113,342	107,537	82,348	80,928	40,394	15,797	16,764
Long-Term Obligations	...	...	...	...	...	...	1,363	3,390
Total Liabilities	130,621	125,008	114,955	84,918	90,890	41,343	19,614	21,889
Stockholders' Equity	582,069	548,266	498,048	399,484	287,205	155,722	125,407	162,951
Shares Outstanding	55,987	55,491	54,530	52,508	51,237	48,903	48,640	48,117
Statistical Record								
Return on Assets %	5.66	7.01	8.68	17.83	15.30	12.15	N.M.	12.39
Return on Equity %	6.87	8.54	10.62	22.40	19.86	14.78	N.M.	16.44
EBITDA Margin %	13.90	14.76	18.37	29.06	27.37	26.33	N.M.	35.77
Net Margin %	8.91	9.66	11.16	16.81	13.75	11.38	N.M.	13.60
Asset Turnover	0.71	0.74	0.78	1.06	1.11	1.07	0.45	0.91
Current Ratio	4.77	4.74	4.43	4.58	3.50	4.03	7.75	7.16
Debt to Equity	...	...	...	...	...	...	0.01	0.02
Price Range	59.77-25.75	55.88-24.88	41.02-24.88	58.83-27.88	57.05-19.08	38.02-17.05	40.06-11.00	98.00-10.50
P/E Ratio	93.39-40.23	75.51-33.62	47.70-28.93	42.32-20.06	66.34-22.19	92.73-41.59	...	337.93-36.21

Address: 4635 Boston Lane, Austin, TX 78735 **Telephone:** 512-416-8500 **Fax:** 512-464-9444	**Web Site:** www.silabs.com **Officers:** Navdeep S. Sooch - Chmn. Daniel A. Artusi - Pres., C.E.O.	**Auditors:** Ernst & Young LLP

SIRIUS SATELLITE RADIO INC

Exchange	Symbol	Price	52Wk Range	Yield	P/E
NMS	SIRI	$4.08 (8/31/2006)	7.87-3.65	N/A	N/A

*7 Year Price Score 36.07 *NYSE Composite Index=100 *12 Month Price Score 72.46

Interim Earnings (Per Share)

Qtr.	Mar	Jun	Sep	Dec
2003	0.16	(0.12)	(0.11)	(0.16)
2004	(0.12)	(0.11)	(0.14)	(0.20)
2005	(0.15)	(0.13)	(0.14)	(0.23)
2006	(0.33)	(0.17)	...	...

Interim Dividends (Per Share)
No Dividends Paid

Valuation Analysis

		Institutional Holding	
Forecast P/E	N/A	No of Institutions	279
Market Cap	$5.7 Billion	Shares	429,969,120
Book Value	N/A	% Held	30.60
Price/Book	N/A		
Price/Sales	13.53		

Business Summary: Media (MIC: 13.1 SIC: 4832 NAIC: 515111)

Sirius Satellite Radio is a provider of satellite radio service. As of Dec 31 2005, Co. offered over 133 channels, including 69 channels of commercial-free music and over 64 channels of sports, news, talk, entertainment, traffic and weather programming to subscribers throughout the continental U.S. Co.'s commercial-free music channels are produced principally at its national broadcast studio in New York City and covers virtually every genre of music. Co.'s non-music streams include programming from CNN, FOX News, ESPN, NPR, The Weather Channel, traffic for America's top 20 markets and a number of other talk and entertainment channels. At Dec 31 2005, Co. had 3.3 million subscribers.

Recent Developments: For the quarter ended June 30 2006, net loss amounted to $237.8 million versus a net loss of $177.5 million in the year-earlier quarter. Revenues were $150.1 million, up 187.5% from $52.2 million the year before. Operating loss was $230.5 million versus a loss of $174.6 million in the prior-year quarter. Direct operating expenses rose 198.3% to $112.6 million from $37.7 million in the comparable period the year before. Indirect operating expenses increased 41.8% to $268.0 million from $189.0 million in the equivalent prior-year period.

Prospects: While earnings are being hurt by higher subscriber acquisition costs and programming and content expenses, Co. is seeing strong revenue fueled by higher subscriber revenue due to an increase in subscribers, as well as higher net advertising revenue. For full-year 2006, Co. has raised its total revenue guidance to $615.0 million, and expects to have 6.3 million subscribers by the end of 2006. Going forward, Co. expects advertising revenue to grow as its subscribers increase and it continues to improve brand awareness and content. Co. also expects equipment revenue to increase as it continues to introduce new products and as sales through its direct to consumer distribution channel grow.

Financial Data (US$ in Thousands)	6 Mos	3 Mos	12/31/2005	12/31/2004	12/31/2003	12/31/2002	12/31/2001	12/31/2000
Earnings Per Share	(0.87)	(0.83)	(0.65)	(0.57)	(0.38)	(6.13)	(5.30)	(4.72)
Cash Flow Per Share	(0.26)	(0.23)	(0.21)	(0.27)	(0.34)	(4.20)	(2.84)	(1.76)
Tang Book Value Per Share	...	0.04	0.18	0.72	1.09	N.M.	4.16	4.92
Income Statement								
Total Revenue	276,742	126,664	242,245	66,854	12,872	805	...	...
EBITDA	(611,586)	(415,734)	(743,648)	(580,918)	...	...	(159,459)	(123,282)
Depn & Amortn	50,671	24,933	98,555	95,370	95,353	94,658	8,997	2,352
Income Before Taxes	(695,041)	(457,791)	(860,686)	(707,961)	...	...	(241,076)	(134,744)
Income Taxes	1,331	753	2,311	4,201	...	...	...	...
Net Income	(696,372)	(458,544)	(862,997)	(712,162)	(226,215)	(422,481)	(235,763)	(134,744)
Average Shares	1,404,022	1,386,982	1,325,739	1,238,585	827,186	76,394	42,427	38,889
Balance Sheet								
Total Assets	1,811,396	1,908,104	2,085,362	1,957,613	1,617,317	1,340,940	1,527,605	1,323,582
Current Liabilities	681,512	591,769	606,967	269,514	82,003	48,320	60,313	54,367
Long-Term Obligations	1,083,929	1,083,929	1,084,437	656,274	194,803	670,357	589,990	472,602
Total Liabilities	1,868,519	1,773,401	1,760,394	956,980	292,123	772,941	719,788	590,087
Stockholders' Equity	(57,123)	134,703	324,968	1,000,633	1,325,194	36,846	322,649	290,483
Shares Outstanding	1,404,780	1,401,964	1,346,226	1,276,922	1,137,758	77,454	57,455	42,107
Statistical Record								
Asset Turnover	0.24	0.17	0.12	0.04	0.01	0.00	...	...
Current Ratio	1.10	1.45	1.67	3.01	7.07	4.13	5.69	3.65
Debt to Equity	...	8.05	3.34	0.66	0.15	18.19	1.83	1.63
Price Range	7.87-3.68	7.87-4.45	7.87-4.67	9.01-2.05	3.16-0.41	11.63-0.52	35.00-2.29	66.50-21.50

Address: 1221 Avenue of the Americas, 36th Floor, New York, NY 10020 Telephone: 212-584-5100	Web Site: www.sirius.com Officers: Joseph P. Clayton - Chmn. Mel Karmazin - C.E.O.	Auditors: Ernst & Young LLP Investor Contact: 212-584-5100

SKY FINANCIAL GROUP, INC.

Exchange	Symbol	Price	52Wk Range	Yield	P/E	Div Acheiver
NMS	SKYF	$24.62 (8/31/2006)	29.81-23.31	3.74	13.60	11 Years

*7 Year Price Score 95.77 *NYSE Composite Index=100 *12 Month Price Score 90.66

Interim Earnings (Per Share)

Qtr.	Mar	Jun	Sep	Dec
2003	0.41	0.42	0.46	0.44
2004	0.62	0.43	0.43	0.46
2005	0.29	0.45	0.47	0.47
2006	0.46	0.41	...	...

Interim Dividends (Per Share)

Amt	Decl	Ex	Rec	Pay
0.23Q	11/18/2005	12/13/2005	12/15/2005	1/3/2006
0.23Q	2/27/2006	3/13/2006	3/15/2006	4/3/2006
0.23Q	5/17/2006	6/13/2006	6/15/2006	7/3/2006
0.23Q	9/1/2006	9/13/2006	9/15/2006	10/2/2006

Indicated Div: $0.92

Valuation Analysis

Forecast P/E	12.88 (9/9/2006)
Market Cap	$2.7 Billion
Book Value	1.6 Billion
Price/Book	1.70
Price/Sales	2.44

Institutional Holding

No of Institutions 145
Shares 38,292,888
% Held 35.19

Business Summary: Commercial Banking (MIC: 8.1 SIC: 6021 NAIC: 522110)

Sky Financial Group is a financial holding company that owns and operates Sky Bank, which is primarily engaged in the commercial and consumer banking business that includes the acceptance of a variety of demand, savings and time deposits and the extension of commercial and consumer loans. Co. also operates businesses relating to insurance, trust and other financial-related services. As of Dec 31 2005, Co. operated over 290 financial centers and over 300 ATMs serving Ohio, western Pennsylvania, southern Michigan, eastern Indiana and northern West Virginia. As of Dec 31 2005, Co. had total assets of $15.68 billion and total deposits of $10.76 billion.

Recent Developments: For the quarter ended June 30 2006, net income decreased 5.7% to $45.1 million from $47.8 million in the year-earlier quarter. Net interest income increased 4.1% to $133.2 million from $128.0 million in the year-earlier quarter. Provision for loan losses was $9.5 million versus $5.9 million in the prior-year quarter, an increase of 60.8%. Non-interest income fell 10.8% to $46.0 million from $51.5 million, while non-interest expense declined 0.1% to $101.9 million.

Prospects: Results are benefiting from growth in Co.'s key fee-based businesses and net interest margin management, while expense and credit losses remain well-controlled. For the remainder of 2006, Co. will continue to focus on its core strategies to achieve earnings growth as well as expanding its franchise into the Indianapolis, Indiana market with the ongoing integration of its pending Feb 2006 acquisition of Union Federal Bank of Indianapolis and its parent company, Waterfield Mortgage Company, Inc., in the third quarter of 2006. Meanwhile, Co. maintains its full-year 2006 guidance for earnings per diluted share on a core operating basis of $1.90 to $1.95 per diluted share.

Financial Data

(US$ in Thousands)	6 Mos	3 Mos	12/31/2005	12/31/2004	12/31/2003	12/31/2002	12/31/2001	12/31/2000
Earnings Per Share	1.81	1.85	1.69	1.93	1.73	1.52	1.45	1.35
Cash Flow Per Share	2.56	2.72	2.59	2.37	3.02	2.10	0.59	1.61
Tang Book Value Per Share	9.11	9.01	8.91	8.65	8.24	7.81	7.92	7.31
Dividends Per Share	0.910	0.900	0.890	0.850	0.810	0.770	0.740	0.725
Dividend Payout %	50.28	48.65	52.66	44.04	46.82	50.66	51.03	53.74
Income Statement								
Interest Income	477,190	234,044	830,224	661,943	662,935	625,906	642,376	626,015
Interest Expense	211,134	101,208	315,572	210,632	242,732	264,221	316,779	322,219
Net Interest Income	266,056	132,836	514,652	451,311	420,203	361,685	325,597	303,796
Provision for Losses	16,630	7,154	52,249	37,660	42,712	43,577	34,635	22,250
Non-Interest Income	102,614	56,659	184,040	176,553	156,135	115,890	96,780	90,006
Non-Interest Expense	208,099	106,178	400,047	356,524	323,769	276,814	237,220	235,407
Income Before Taxes	143,941	76,163	273,738	260,544	235,072	191,175	179,982	168,097
Income Taxes	48,228	25,523	91,547	85,344	78,455	63,368	59,319	53,724
Net Income	95,713	50,640	182,563	194,355	156,617	127,807	120,663	114,373
Average Shares	109,266	109,287	107,973	100,568	90,404	84,096	83,028	84,967
Balance Sheet								
Net Loans & Leases	11,073,433	10,950,535	11,004,761	10,464,729	9,240,279	7,764,149	6,370,466	5,822,837
Total Assets	15,751,002	15,658,551	15,683,291	14,944,423	12,896,494	11,013,943	9,220,228	8,386,802
Total Deposits	11,091,721	11,002,998	10,755,676	10,351,591	8,514,852	7,615,420	6,542,177	5,891,932
Total Liabilities	14,176,489	14,091,980	14,129,414	13,473,468	11,897,918	10,181,510	8,571,784	7,777,112
Stockholders' Equity	1,574,513	1,566,571	1,553,877	1,470,955	998,576	832,433	648,444	609,690
Shares Outstanding	108,783	108,705	108,308	106,839	92,443	87,056	81,847	83,407
Statistical Record								
Return on Assets %	1.28	1.32	1.19	1.39	1.31	1.26	1.37	1.39
Return on Equity %	12.92	13.57	12.07	15.70	17.11	17.26	19.18	19.40
Net Interest Margin %	54.79	56.76	61.99	68.18	63.39	57.79	50.69	48.53
Efficiency Ratio %	35.25	36.52	39.44	42.52	39.53	37.32	32.09	32.88
Loans to Deposits	1.00	1.00	1.02	1.01	1.09	1.02	0.97	0.99
Price Range	29.81-23.31	29.81-25.44	29.81-25.83	29.01-23.23	25.95-19.03	23.52-17.71	20.80-15.69	18.30-12.67
P/E Ratio	16.47-12.88	16.11-13.75	17.64-15.28	15.03-12.04	15.00-11.00	15.47-11.65	14.34-10.82	13.55-9.39
Average Yield %	3.36	3.25	3.18	3.29	3.67	3.74	3.90	4.70

Address: 221 South Church Street, P.O. Box 428, Bowling Green, OH 43402 **Telephone:** 419-327-6402	**Web Site:** www.skyfi.com **Officers:** Marty E. Adams - Chmn., Pres., C.E.O. Kevin T. Thompson - Exec. V.P., C.F.O.	**Auditors:** Deloitte & Touche LLP **Investor Contact:** 800-576-5007 **Transfer Agents:** The Bank of New York, New York, NY

SMURFIT-STONE CONTAINER CORP

Exchange	Symbol	Price	52Wk Range	Yield	P/E
NMS	SSCC	$11.39 (8/31/2006)	14.96-9.16	N/A	N/A

*7 Year Price Score 63.59   *NYSE Composite Index=100   *12 Month Price Score 86.50

Interim Earnings (Per Share)

Qtr.	Mar	Jun	Sep	Dec
2003	(0.13)	(0.03)	(0.30)	(0.38)
2004	(0.26)	(0.04)	0.11	(0.04)
2005	(0.07)	0.00	(0.90)	(0.36)
2006	(0.25)	(0.17)	...	...

Interim Dividends (Per Share)

No Dividends Paid

Valuation Analysis

Forecast P/E	217.75
	(9/9/2006)
Market Cap	$2.9 Billion
Book Value	1.8 Billion
Price/Book	1.63
Price/Sales	0.36

Institutional Holding

No of Institutions	207
Shares	218,138,848
% Held	85.65

Business Summary: Paper Products (MIC: 11.11 SIC: 2631 NAIC: 322130)

Smurfit-Stone Container is a holding company. Co. has one reportable segment, Containerboard and Corrugated Containers. The Containerboard and Corrugated Containers segment includes a system of mills and plants that produces a full line of containerboard that is converted into corrugated containers. It also provides single source full merchandising services to retailers and consumer packaging companies. Corrugated containers are used to transport such diverse products as home appliances, electric motors, small machinery, grocery products, produce, books, tobacco and furniture.

Recent Developments: For the quarter ended June 30 2006, loss from continuing operations was $44.0 million compared with a loss of $10.0 million in the year-earlier quarter. Net loss amounted to $41.0 million versus net income of $4.0 million in the year-earlier quarter. Revenues were $1.77 billion, up 0.3% from $1.76 billion the year before. Operating income was $70.0 million versus $69.0 million in the prior-year quarter, an increase of 1.4%. Direct operating expenses declined 0.7% to $1.51 billion from $1.52 billion in the comparable period the year before. Indirect operating expenses increased 9.0% to $182.0 million from $167.0 million in the equivalent prior-year period.

Prospects: On June 30 2006, Co. announced that it has completed the sale of its Consumer Packaging division to a company formed by Texas Pacific Group, for approximately $1.04 billion. Net proceeds from the sale will be applied to debt reduction, providing Co. with additional financial flexibility to execute its strategic initiatives. Co. expects the sale to result in a pre-tax gain of about $170.0 million and an after-tax loss of approximately $4.0 million, subject to the finalization of certain post-closing adjustments. Separately, Co. expects solid product demand and low containerboard inventory levels to drive continuing average price improvement for the balance of 2006.

Financial Data
(US$ in Thousands)

	6 Mos	3 Mos	12/31/2005	12/31/2004	12/31/2003	12/31/2002	12/31/2001	12/31/2000
Earnings Per Share	(1.68)	(1.51)	(1.33)	(0.23)	(0.85)	0.22	0.27	0.96
Cash Flow Per Share	0.52	0.67	0.87	1.08	0.66	2.06	2.45	3.45
Income Statement								
Total Revenue	3,494,000	2,125,000	8,396,000	8,291,000	7,722,000	7,483,000	8,377,000	8,796,000
EBITDA	204,000	96,000	229,000	661,000	428,000	891,000	1,135,000	1,403,000
Depn & Amortn	204,000	102,000	417,000	427,000	425,000	410,000	489,000	442,000
Income Before Taxes	(188,000)	(98,000)	(534,000)	(109,000)	(338,000)	126,000	191,000	434,000
Income Taxes	(73,000)	(37,000)	(207,000)	(63,000)	(140,000)	47,000	107,000	206,000
Net Income	(102,000)	(61,000)	(327,000)	(46,000)	(197,000)	65,000	77,000	225,000
Average Shares	255,000	255,000	255,000	253,000	246,000	246,000	245,000	234,000
Balance Sheet								
Total Assets	8,053,000	9,062,000	9,114,000	9,725,000	10,102,000	10,805,000	10,652,000	11,280,000
Current Liabilities	1,011,000	1,086,000	1,188,000	1,116,000	1,171,000	1,375,000	1,240,000	1,250,000
Long-Term Obligations	3,785,000	4,682,000	4,536,000	4,479,000	4,610,000	4,918,000	4,754,000	5,298,000
Total Liabilities	6,272,000	7,245,000	7,232,000	7,466,000	7,832,000	8,485,000	8,167,000	8,752,000
Stockholders' Equity	1,781,000	1,817,000	1,882,000	2,259,000	2,270,000	2,320,000	2,485,000	2,528,000
Shares Outstanding	255,264	255,035	254,652	254,238	250,547	244,578	243,902	243,567
Statistical Record								
Return on Assets %	N.M.	N.M.	N.M.	N.M.	N.M.	0.61	0.70	2.12
Return on Equity %	N.M.	N.M.	N.M.	N.M.	N.M.	2.71	3.07	10.26
EBITDA Margin %	5.84	4.52	2.73	7.97	5.54	11.91	13.55	15.95
Net Margin %	N.M.	N.M.	N.M.	N.M.	N.M.	0.87	0.92	2.56
Asset Turnover	0.91	0.90	0.89	0.83	0.74	0.70	0.76	0.83
Current Ratio	1.02	1.10	1.00	1.26	1.24	1.43	1.20	1.38
Debt to Equity	2.13	2.58	2.41	1.98	2.03	2.12	1.91	2.10
Price Range	14.96-9.16	15.47-9.16	18.68-9.16	19.95-16.04	18.57-12.16	18.00-11.53	17.95-12.15	24.88-9.63
P/E Ratio	...	...	...	...	...	81.82-52.41	66.48-45.00	25.91-10.03

Address: 150 North Michigan Avenue, Chicago, IL 60601
Telephone: 312-346-6600

Web Site: www.smurfit-stone.com
Officers: Patrick J. Moore - Chmn., Pres., C.E.O.
James E. Burdiss - Sr. V.P., Chief Info. Officer

Auditors: ERNST & YOUNG LLP
Investor Contact: 314-746-1254

SOUTH FINANCIAL GROUP INC (THE)

Exchange	Symbol	Price	52Wk Range	Yield	P/E	Div Acheiver
NMS	TSFG	$27.03 (8/31/2006)	29.85-25.14	2.52	32.96	11 Years

*7 Year Price Score 97.08 *NYSE Composite Index=100 *12 Month Price Score 95.39

Interim Earnings (Per Share)

Qtr.	Mar	Jun	Sep	Dec
2003	0.42	0.48	0.50	0.50
2004	0.53	0.49	0.44	0.34
2005	0.47	0.38	0.28	(0.22)
2006	0.37	0.39	...	...

Interim Dividends (Per Share)

Amt	Decl	Ex	Rec	Pay
0.17Q	12/14/2005	1/11/2006	1/15/2006	2/1/2006
0.17Q	2/28/2006	4/11/2006	4/15/2006	5/1/2006
0.17Q	5/19/2006	7/12/2006	7/15/2006	8/1/2006
0.17Q	8/17/2006	10/11/2006	10/15/2006	11/1/2006

Indicated Div: $0.68

Valuation Analysis

Forecast P/E	16.91
	(9/9/2006)
Market Cap	$2.0 Billion
Book Value	1.5 Billion
Price/Book	1.37
Price/Sales	2.32

Institutional Holding

No of Institutions	149
Shares	39,754,476
% Held	52.92

Business Summary: Commercial Banking (MIC: 8.1 SIC: 6022 NAIC: 522110)

The South Financial Group is a financial holding company that offers a range of financial products and services, including mortgage, trust, investment, and insurance services to consumers and commercial customers. At Dec 31 2005, Co. operated through 80 branch offices in South Carolina, 66 in Florida, and 26 in North Carolina. In South Carolina, the branches are mainly located in the largest metropolitan areas. The Florida operations are mainly concentrated in the Jacksonville, Orlando, Tampa Bay, Southeast Florida, and Gainesville areas. The North Carolina branches are primarily located in the Hendersonville, Asheville and Wilmington areas. At Dec 31 2005, Co. had assets of $14.32 billion.

Recent Developments: For the quarter ended June 30 2006, net income decreased 31.3% to $29.3 million from $42.7 million in the year-earlier quarter. Net interest income increased 0.8% to $103.1 million from $102.3 million in the year-earlier quarter. Provision for loan losses was $7.5 million versus $9.9 million in the prior-year quarter, a decrease of 24.7%. Non-interest income fell 36.6% to $32.0 million from $50.5 million, while non-interest expense advanced 4.4% to $83.1 million.

Prospects: Despite being challenged by an unfavorable environment, Co. is seeing growth in operating revenue and continued lower net loan charge-offs. In addition, Co. is benefiting from its fee income and customer deposit initiatives. Moving forward, Co. plans to continue its focus on growing low-cost customer deposits. Specifically, Co. attempts to enhance its deposit mix by working to attract lower-cost transaction accounts through actions such as new transaction account opening goals, differentiating pricing for promotions and specific markets. Moreover, Co. is focusing on loan growth with strong risk-adjusted returns, double digit fee income growth, and cost control.

Financial Data (US$ in Thousands)	6 Mos	3 Mos	12/31/2005	12/31/2004	12/31/2003	12/31/2002	12/31/2001	12/31/2000
Earnings Per Share	0.82	0.81	0.94	1.80	1.89	1.38	0.98	0.16
Cash Flow Per Share	3.11	3.15	2.97	3.54	3.73	7.14	3.84	1.15
Tang Book Value Per Share	10.60	10.58	10.64	11.08	10.61	8.55	8.76	8.51
Dividends Per Share	0.660	0.650	0.640	0.600	0.560	0.480	0.440	0.400
Dividend Payout %	80.49	80.25	68.09	33.33	29.63	34.78	44.90	250.00
Income Statement								
Interest Income	421,079	205,367	754,297	542,232	414,128	353,739	382,548	389,032
Interest Expense	215,045	102,455	345,241	175,504	141,537	135,487	197,324	214,403
Net Interest Income	206,034	102,912	409,056	366,728	272,591	218,252	185,224	174,629
Provision for Losses	17,398	9,911	40,592	34,987	20,581	22,266	22,045	23,378
Non-Interest Income	61,340	29,320	55,210	94,767	95,490	59,640	53,827	49,348
Non-Interest Expense	162,893	79,834	328,053	250,244	207,170	162,840	148,504	189,859
Income Before Taxes	87,083	42,487	95,621	176,264	140,330	92,786	68,502	10,740
Income Taxes	29,933	14,680	25,404	56,657	43,260	28,972	23,571	3,751
Net Income	57,150	27,807	69,821	119,117	95,058	59,158	41,892	6,989
Average Shares	75,505	75,339	74,595	66,235	50,328	42,714	42,823	43,550
Balance Sheet								
Net Loans & Leases	9,330,450	9,609,672	9,368,799	8,032,141	5,688,537	4,430,954	3,692,176	3,692,158
Total Assets	14,077,083	14,361,925	14,319,285	13,789,814	10,719,401	7,941,010	6,029,442	5,220,554
Total Deposits	9,240,319	9,178,682	9,234,437	7,665,537	6,028,649	4,592,510	3,605,255	3,894,662
Total Liabilities	12,592,094	12,877,820	12,832,378	12,389,211	9,739,532	7,207,799	5,534,245	4,751,901
Stockholders' Equity	1,484,989	1,484,105	1,486,907	1,400,603	979,869	646,799	458,174	468,653
Shares Outstanding	75,033	74,907	74,721	71,252	59,064	47,347	41,228	42,460
Statistical Record								
Return on Assets %	0.43	0.42	0.50	0.97	1.02	0.85	0.74	0.16
Return on Equity %	4.11	4.24	4.84	9.98	11.69	10.71	9.04	1.59
Net Interest Margin %	47.81	50.11	54.23	67.63	65.82	61.70	48.42	44.89
Efficiency Ratio %	33.53	34.02	40.53	39.28	40.65	39.39	34.03	43.31
Loans to Deposits	1.01	1.05	1.01	1.05	0.94	0.96	1.02	0.95
Price Range	30.16-25.14	30.54-25.52	32.53-25.86	32.53-26.00	29.25-19.46	23.46-17.61	19.95-12.25	18.25-9.25
P/E Ratio	36.77-30.66	37.70-31.51	34.61-27.51	18.07-14.44	15.48-10.30	17.00-12.76	20.36-12.50	114.06-57.81
Average Yield %	2.39	2.35	2.22	2.06	2.32	2.31	2.71	3.00

Address: 102 South Main Street, Greenville, SC 29601 Telephone: 864-255-7900 Fax: 864-239-6401	Web Site: www.thesouthgroup.com Officers: William R. Timmons Jr. - Chmn. William S. Hummers III - Vice-Chmn., Exec. V.P., C.F.O.	Auditors: KPMG LLP Investor Contact: 800-951-2699*54919

SOUTHWEST BANCORP, INC. (OK)

Exchange	Symbol	Price	52Wk Range	Yield	P/E	Div Achiever
NMS	OKSB	$26.55 (8/31/2006)	26.97-19.74	1.24	16.49	11 Years

*7 Year Price Score 131.53 *NYSE Composite Index=100 *12 Month Price Score 108.71

Interim Earnings (Per Share)

Qtr.	Mar	Jun	Sep	Dec
2003	0.29	0.33	0.28	0.32
2004	0.34	0.36	0.39	0.39
2005	0.43	0.40	0.41	0.31
2006	0.44	0.45	...	...

Interim Dividends (Per Share)

Amt	Decl	Ex	Rec	Pay
0.075Q	11/17/2005	12/15/2005	12/19/2005	1/3/2006
0.083Q	2/23/2006	3/15/2006	3/17/2006	4/3/2006
0.083Q	5/30/2006	6/15/2006	6/19/2006	7/3/2006
0.083Q	8/24/2006	9/14/2006	9/18/2006	10/2/2006

Indicated Div: $0.33

Valuation Analysis

Forecast P/E	19.75 (12/7/2005)
Market Cap	$376.3 Million
Book Value	182.7 Million
Price/Book	2.06
Price/Sales	2.20

Institutional Holding

No of Institutions	85
Shares	8,744,042
% Held	61.54

Business Summary: Other Depository Banking (MIC: 8.5 SIC: 6035 NAIC: 522120)

Southwest Bancorp is the financial holding company for the Stillwater National Bank and Trust Company, SNB Bank of Wichita, Business Consulting Group, Inc., and Healthcare Strategic Support, Inc. Through its subsidiaries, Co. offers commercial and consumer lending, deposit and investment services, and specialized cash management, consulting and other financial services from offices in Oklahoma City, Stillwater, Tulsa, and Chickasha, OK; Austin, Dallas and San Antonio, TX; and Kansas City and Wichita, KS, and on the Internet, through SNB DirectBanker®. As of Dec 31 2005, Co. had total assets of $2.10 billion.

Recent Developments: For the quarter ended June 30 2006, net income increased 26.7% to $6.6 million from $5.2 million in the year-earlier quarter. Net interest income increased 9.4% to $22.9 million from $20.9 million in the year-earlier quarter. Provision for loan losses was $3.3 million versus $3.0 million in the prior-year quarter, an increase of 11.1%. Non-interest income rose 7.8% to $4.5 million from $4.2 million, while non-interest expense advanced 0.5% to $13.9 million.

Prospects: Co.'s results are benefiting from the increase in net interest income that is being fueled by growth of interest and fees on loans, and also an increase in other income due mainly to higher service charges on deposit accounts. In addition, Co. is experiencing improvement in its asset quality and a healthy net interest margin, as well as growth in its non-interest income. Separately, on Jul 28 2006, Co. announced that it has closed its acquisition of McMullen Bank. Consequently, this transaction resulted in two additional Texas branches and additional assets of approximately $35.0 million.

Financial Data
(US$ in Thousands)

	6 Mos	3 Mos	12/31/2005	12/31/2004	12/31/2003	12/31/2002	12/31/2001	12/31/2000
Earnings Per Share	1.61	1.56	1.55	1.48	1.22	1.12	1.00	0.88
Cash Flow Per Share	7.19	3.30	0.19	(9.15)	(8.03)	1.54	1.35	0.88
Tang Book Value Per Share	12.88	12.52	12.16	10.41	9.20	8.35	6.95	6.44
Dividends Per Share	0.315	0.308	0.300	0.280	0.250	0.220	0.160	0.147
Dividend Payout %	19.57	19.71	19.35	18.92	20.49	19.73	16.00	16.67
Income Statement								
Interest Income	81,220	39,408	137,344	104,723	84,079	76,495	90,400	97,274
Interest Expense	36,117	17,166	52,238	32,246	28,611	30,606	48,867	57,155
Net Interest Income	45,103	22,242	85,106	72,477	55,468	45,889	41,533	40,119
Provision for Losses	5,992	2,676	15,785	12,982	8,522	5,443	4,000	3,550
Non-Interest Income	8,473	3,968	17,406	14,085	14,500	12,646	10,741	8,489
Non-Interest Expense	27,042	13,190	51,873	44,412	38,448	33,319	31,165	29,615
Income Before Taxes	20,542	10,344	34,854	29,168	22,998	19,773	17,109	15,443
Income Taxes	7,637	4,065	13,840	10,539	8,106	6,354	5,357	5,238
Net Income	12,905	6,279	21,014	18,629	14,892	13,419	11,752	10,205
Average Shares	14,470	14,406	13,563	12,548	12,159	12,052	11,728	11,585
Balance Sheet								
Net Loans & Leases	1,431,364	1,367,057	1,328,621	1,249,374	1,074,566	1,078,586	906,814	900,425
Total Assets	2,188,102	2,145,839	2,099,639	1,912,834	1,580,725	1,349,768	1,216,495	1,203,566
Total Deposits	1,764,774	1,699,212	1,657,820	1,500,058	1,204,125	1,021,757	904,796	945,102
Total Liabilities	2,005,402	1,968,894	1,929,195	1,786,850	1,470,790	1,253,396	1,131,370	1,130,327
Stockholders' Equity	182,700	176,945	170,444	125,984	109,935	96,372	85,125	73,239
Shares Outstanding	14,173	14,133	14,021	12,104	11,955	11,546	12,243	11,370
Statistical Record								
Return on Assets %	1.10	1.06	1.05	1.06	1.02	1.05	0.97	0.88
Return on Equity %	13.49	14.29	14.18	15.75	14.44	14.79	14.84	14.80
Net Interest Margin %	54.68	56.44	61.97	69.21	65.97	59.99	45.94	41.24
Efficiency Ratio %	29.91	30.41	33.52	37.38	39.00	37.38	30.81	28.00
Loans to Deposits	0.81	0.80	0.80	0.83	0.89	1.06	1.00	0.95
Price Range	25.50-19.74	24.12-17.11	24.83-17.11	26.85-16.22	18.90-11.25	13.62-8.80	9.57-5.58	7.00-4.50
P/E Ratio	15.84-12.26	15.46-10.97	16.02-11.04	18.14-10.96	15.49-9.22	12.16-7.86	9.57-5.58	7.95-5.11
Average Yield %	1.40	1.44	1.42	1.44	1.75	1.87	2.03	2.64

Address: 608 South Main Street, Stillwater, OK 74074
Telephone: 405-372-2230
Fax: 405-377-3846

Web Site: www.oksb.com
Officers: Robert B. Rodgers - Chmn. Rick J. Green - Vice-Chmn., Pres., C.E.O.

Auditors: Ernst & Young LLP
Investor Contact: 405-372-2230

SOUTHWEST WATER CO.

Exchange	Symbol	Price	52Wk Range	Yield	P/E	Div Acheiver
NMS	SWWC	$12.97 (8/31/2006)	19.03-10.85	1.62	40.53	10 Years

*7 Year Price Score 112.59 *NYSE Composite Index=100 *12 Month Price Score 85.78

Interim Earnings (Per Share)

Qtr.	Mar	Jun	Sep	Dec
2003	(0.01)	0.12	0.20	0.12
2004	0.00	0.14	0.12	(0.03)
2005	(0.01)	(0.09)	0.14	0.06
2006	0.03	0.08	...	...

Interim Dividends (Per Share)

Amt	Decl	Ex	Rec	Pay
0.052Q	11/11/2005	12/28/2005	12/30/2005	1/20/2006
0.052Q	3/9/2006	3/28/2006	3/30/2006	4/20/2006
0.052Q	5/17/2006	6/28/2006	6/30/2006	7/20/2006
0.052Q	8/18/2006	9/27/2006	9/30/2006	10/20/2006

Indicated Div: $0.21

Valuation Analysis   **Institutional Holding**

Forecast P/E	35.53	No of Institutions
(9/9/2006)		72
Market Cap	$296.4 Million	Shares
Book Value	152.4 Million	8,315,421
Price/Book	1.94	% Held
Price/Sales	1.88	36.30

Business Summary: Water Utilities (MIC: 7.2 SIC: 4941 NAIC: 221310)
Southwest Water provides a range of services including water production, treatment and distribution; wastewater collection and treatment; utility billing and collection; utility infrastructure construction management; and public works services. Co. owns regulated public utilities and also serves cities, utility districts and private companies under contract. At Dec 31 2005, Co. provided services to more than 2.0 million people. Within its Utility Group, Co. owns and manages the operations of rate-regulated public water and wastewater utilities in California, New Mexico, Oklahoma and Texas, under which it sells water to residential and commercial customers. Co. also operates a Services Group.

Recent Developments: For the quarter ended June 30 2006, income from continuing operations decreased 40.4% to $1.8 million from $3.0 million in the year-earlier quarter. Net income amounted to $1.8 million versus a net loss of $1.7 million in the year-earlier quarter. Revenues were $55.4 million, up 8.0% from $51.3 million in the year before. Operating income was $5.0 million versus $6.5 million in the prior-year quarter, a decrease of 23.6%. Direct operating expenses rose 8.4% to $40.5 million from $37.4 million in the comparable period the year before. Indirect operating expenses increased 33.0% to $9.9 million from $7.4 million in the equivalent prior-year period.

Prospects: Despite being restrained by one time costs for execution relocation, and reduced consumption at its California utility from cooler temperatures and higher rainfall, Co. is experiencing improved revenue growth in its Utility Group due to the acquisition of an Alabama wastewater treatment facility in the third quarter of 2005 and increased connections in Texas and New Mexico. Co. is also benefiting from growth in its Services Group due to higher contract operations, maintenance and construction work. Hence, for 2006, Co. expects net income will be at the low end of its 10.0% to 15.0% growth, while it invests in infrastructure with capital expenditure expected to approximate $30.0 million.

Financial Data
(US$ in Thousands)

	6 Mos	3 Mos	12/31/2005	12/31/2004	12/31/2003	12/31/2002	12/31/2001	12/31/2000
Earnings Per Share	0.32	0.15	0.11	0.23	0.44	0.40	0.42	0.38
Cash Flow Per Share	1.18	1.05	1.18	0.87	0.57	1.55	0.29	(0.04)
Tang Book Value Per Share	5.06	4.91	4.91	4.15	3.45	4.29	3.85	3.45
Dividends Per Share	0.205	0.200	0.195	0.181	0.161	0.148	0.140	0.128
Dividend Payout %	64.97	133.77	177.49	79.37	36.32	37.51	33.15	33.46
Income Statement								
Total Revenue	...	50,802	203,181	187,952	172,974	130,800	115,547	104,741
EBITDA	13,324	5,841	30,732	23,299	22,999	19,824	18,854	17,190
Depn & Amortn	5,358	2,685	12,600	11,500	7,549	6,380	6,060	5,264
Income Before Taxes	3,969	1,106	11,362	7,098	11,217	9,215	9,755	8,541
Income Taxes	1,452	405	4,061	2,564	4,024	3,213	3,512	3,160
Net Income	2,588	772	2,399	4,534	7,193	6,002	6,243	5,381
Average Shares	23,451	23,307	21,611	19,413	16,163	15,031	14,738	13,927
Balance Sheet								
Total Assets	464,000	449,645	444,725	404,809	296,222	268,744	225,186	196,652
Long-Term Obligations	122,490	122,577	117,603	115,827	73,102	80,985	58,063	46,351
Total Liabilities	311,570	300,653	299,472	278,611	216,555	206,907	170,231	148,041
Stockholders' Equity	152,430	148,992	145,253	126,198	79,667	61,837	54,955	48,611
Shares Outstanding	22,855	22,667	22,185	20,364	16,169	14,310	14,138	13,957
Statistical Record								
Return on Assets %	1.59	0.79	0.56	1.29	2.55	2.43	2.96	3.16
Return on Equity %	5.03	2.49	1.77	4.39	10.17	10.28	12.06	12.05
EBITDA Margin %	...	11.50	15.13	12.40	13.30	15.16	16.32	16.41
Net Margin %	...	1.52	1.18	2.41	4.16	4.59	5.40	5.14
PPE Turnover	0.47	0.63	0.63	0.72	0.82	0.70	0.70	0.77
Asset Turnover	0.36	0.48	0.48	0.53	0.61	0.53	0.55	0.62
Debt to Equity	0.80	0.82	0.81	0.92	0.92	1.31	1.06	0.95
Price Range	19.03-10.85	19.03-9.43	15.08-9.43	14.07-10.51	11.10-8.22	12.30-8.28	9.74-6.96	8.29-5.13
P/E Ratio	59.47-33.91	126.87-62.86	137.09-85.71	61.17-45.71	25.22-18.68	30.74-20.70	23.20-16.57	21.81-13.51
Average Yield %	1.47	1.53	1.62	1.54	1.71	1.51	1.67	1.97

Address: One Wilshire Building, 624 South Grand Avenue, Suite 2900, Los Angeles, CA 90017-3782 **Telephone:** 213-929-1800 **Fax:** 213-929-1888	**Web Site:** www.swwc.com **Officers:** Anton C. Garnier - Chmn., Pres., C.E.O. Shelley A. Farnham - V.P., H.R., Sec.	**Auditors:** KPMG LLP **Transfer Agents:** Mellon Investor Services LLC

SPARTAN STORES INC

Exchange	Symbol	Price	52Wk Range	Yield	P/E
NMS	SPTN	$18.03 (8/31/2006)	18.44-8.93	N/A	20.97

*7 Year Price Score N/A *NYSE Composite Index=100 *12 Month Price Score 120.89

Interim Earnings (Per Share)

Qtr.	Jun	Sep	Dec	Mar
2003-04	(0.31)	0.09	(0.20)	0.09
2004-05	0.08	0.34	0.22	0.28
2005-06	0.12	0.32	0.16	0.26
2006-07	0.12	...	...	...

Interim Dividends (Per Share)

No Dividends Paid

Valuation Analysis

	Institutional Holding	
Forecast P/E	14.25	No of Institutions
	(9/9/2006)	90
Market Cap	$384.4 Million	Shares
Book Value	147.9 Million	12,827,256
Price/Book	2.60	% Held
Price/Sales	0.18	60.18

Business Summary: Retail - Food & Beverage (MIC: 5.3 SIC: 5141 NAIC: 424410)

Spartan Stores is a regional grocery distributor and grocery retailer, operating in Michigan, Ohio and Indiana. Co. operates in two business segments: Distribution segment, which provides a selection of about 42,000 stock-keeping units, including dry groceries, produce, dairy products, meat, deli, bakery, frozen food, floral products, general merchandise, pharmacy, and health and beauty care items to over 350 independent grocery stores and its 89 corporate-owned stores, as well as provides about 2,800 private label grocery and general merchandise items; and Retail segment, which operates 70 retail supermarkets and 19 deep-discount food and drug stores predominantly in Michigan and Ohio.

Recent Developments: For the quarter ended June 17 2006, income from continuing operations decreased 7.0% to $2.6 million from $2.8 million in the year-earlier quarter. Net income was unchanged at $2.7 million versus $2.7 million the year-earlier quarter. Revenues were $528.0 million, up 15.0% from $459.3 million the year before. Operating income was $6.9 million versus $6.0 million in the prior-year quarter, an increase of 14.3%. Direct operating expenses rose 13.7% to $424.5 million from $373.5 million in the comparable period the year before. Indirect operating expenses increased 21.1% to $96.6 million from $79.8 million in the equivalent prior-year period.

Prospects: Looking ahead, Co. remains optimistic regarding its sales and profit growth prospects for fiscal 2007. Notably, Co. expects that its distribution sales will continue to benefit from the addition of new stores in late fiscal 2006, and expects to further increase sales penetration with certain existing customers. Moreover, Co.'s retail division will cycle the remaining competitive stores that opened in fiscal 2006 in the fiscal second quarter ended Sep 2007 and should benefit from its market rationalization efforts as well as its new fuel center sales. In addition, Co. anticipates that its fiscal 2007 retail comparable store sales growth rate will be in the low to mid single digits.

Financial Data
(US$ in Thousands)

	3 Mos	03/25/2006	03/26/2005	03/27/2004	03/29/2003	03/30/2002	03/31/2001	03/25/2000
Earnings Per Share	0.86	0.86	0.91	(0.33)	(6.15)	0.50	1.35	1.28
Cash Flow Per Share	2.45	2.64	2.97	1.38	1.24	1.75	3.31	4.07
Tang Book Value Per Share	0.29	3.47	2.59	1.67	2.04	3.86	3.25	2.50
Dividends Per Share	0.100	0.050	...	...	...	...	0.013	0.050
Dividend Payout %	11.61	5.81	...	...	...	...	0.93	3.91
Income Statement								
Total Revenue	528,016	2,039,926	2,043,187	2,054,977	2,148,067	3,501,153	3,505,923	3,030,917
EBITDA	12,082	60,490	60,442	32,117	(4,383)	90,026	103,449	80,509
Depn & Amortn	5,194	22,152	22,582	28,433	30,262	48,551	39,445	32,063
Income Before Taxes	4,031	30,669	28,545	(9,107)	(52,074)	16,948	36,960	25,644
Income Taxes	1,413	10,307	8,682	(3,187)	(18,087)	5,610	13,925	9,653
Net Income	2,689	18,172	18,826	(6,698)	(122,332)	9,847	23,442	17,194
Average Shares	21,542	21,174	20,743	20,016	19,896	19,690	17,333	13,439
Balance Sheet								
Total Assets	489,600	378,597	384,457	392,511	556,306	746,540	810,845	570,573
Current Liabilities	161,354	146,959	141,190	136,170	226,633	183,533	258,474	168,332
Long-Term Obligations	129,895	64,015	91,946	124,616	183,817	295,185	306,632	266,071
Total Liabilities	341,702	233,180	259,047	286,844	446,674	515,048	592,432	444,566
Stockholders' Equity	147,898	145,417	125,410	105,667	109,632	231,492	218,413	126,007
Shares Outstanding	21,322	21,023	20,524	20,092	19,999	19,766	19,262	9,919
Statistical Record								
Return on Assets %	4.21	4.78	4.86	N.M.	N.M.	1.27	3.34	3.11
Return on Equity %	13.20	13.46	16.34	N.M.	N.M.	4.39	13.39	13.96
EBITDA Margin %	2.29	2.97	2.96	1.56	N.M.	2.57	2.95	2.66
Net Margin %	0.51	0.89	0.92	N.M.	N.M.	0.28	0.67	0.57
Asset Turnover	4.88	5.36	5.27	4.34	3.31	4.51	4.99	5.48
Current Ratio	1.16	1.14	1.21	1.25	1.39	1.62	1.27	1.53
Debt to Equity	0.88	0.44	0.73	1.18	1.68	1.28	1.40	2.11
Price Range	15.35-8.93	15.35-8.93	11.14-3.05	5.71-2.22	8.52-1.28	16.78-6.09	11.19-5.00	...
P/E Ratio	17.85-10.38	17.85-10.38	12.24-3.35	...	...	33.56-12.18	8.29-3.70	...
Average Yield %	0.85	0.44	...	...	...	...	0.16	...

Address: 850 76th Street S.W., P.O. Box 8700, Grand Rapids, MI 49518-8700
Telephone: 616-878-2000
Fax: 616-878-8092

Web Site: www.spartanstores.com
Officers: James B. Meyer - Chmn. Craig C. Sturken - Pres., C.E.O.

Auditors: Deloitte & Touche LLP
Transfer Agents: LaSalle Bank N.A. Trust & Asset Management

STAPLES INC

Exchange	Symbol	Price	52Wk Range	Yield	P/E
NMS	SPLS	$22.56 (8/31/2006)	26.98-20.69	0.98	19.12

*7 Year Price Score 120.34 *NYSE Composite Index=100 *12 Month Price Score 94.91

Interim Earnings (Per Share)

Qtr.	Apr	Jul	Oct	Jan
2003-04	0.03	0.12	0.22	0.28
2004-05	0.17	0.16	0.27	0.33
2005-06	0.21	0.20	0.32	0.39
2006-07	0.25	0.22	...	...

Interim Dividends (Per Share)

Amt	Decl	Ex	Rec	Pay
0.133A	3/4/2004	4/22/2004	4/26/2004	5/17/2004
3-for-2	2/24/2005	4/18/2005	3/29/2005	4/15/2005
0.167A	2/24/2005	3/23/2005	3/28/2005	4/14/2005
0.22A	2/28/2006	3/29/2006	3/31/2006	4/20/2006

Indicated Div: $0.22

Valuation Analysis

Forecast P/E 15.92 (9/9/2006)
Market Cap $16.4 Billion
Book Value 4.5 Billion
Price/Book 3.63
Price/Sales 0.97

Institutional Holding

No of Institutions 550
Shares 623,393,216
% Held 85.81

Business Summary: Retail - Miscellaneous (MIC: 5.11 SIC: 5112 NAIC: 424120)

Staples operates office superstores that provide small and medium-sized businesses with brand name office products, supplies and accessories including business machines and computers and related items and office furniture. Co.'s North American Retail segment operates office products stores in the U.S. and Canada. Co.'s North American Delivery segment sells and delivers office products and services directly to customers in the U.S. and Canada, and includes Staples Business Delivery, Quill and its contract operations. The International Operations segment operates office products stores and sells and delivers office products and services in 19 countries in Europe, South America and Asia.

Recent Developments: For the quarter ended July 29 2006, net income increased 19.2% to $161.2 million from $135.2 million in the year-earlier quarter. Revenues were $3.88 billion, up 11.8% from $3.47 billion the year before. Operating income was $252.3 million versus $213.8 million in the prior-year quarter, an increase of 18.0%. Direct operating expenses rose 12.1% to $2.78 billion from $2.48 billion in the comparable period the year before. Indirect operating expenses increased 8.9% to $844.3 million from $775.6 million in the equivalent prior-year period.

Prospects: Co.'s solid results are reflecting improvements within both its North America and International operations. In particular, Co.'s North American business are benefiting primarily from robust customer traffic as well as continued strength in categories such as mobile computing and accessories, core office supplies, copy and print, ink and toner. Looking ahead, Co. anticipates sales growth to be in the low double-digit and earnings per share to grow by 15.0% to 20.0% for the third quarter of 2006. For full-year 2006, Co. projects earnings to be at the high end of its 15.0% to 20.0% targeted growth range. Additionally, Co. expects to open approximately 85 new stores in the second half of 2006.

Financial Data
(US$ in Thousands)

	6 Mos	3 Mos	01/28/2006	01/29/2005	01/31/2004	02/01/2003	02/02/2002	02/03/2001
Earnings Per Share	1.18	1.16	1.12	0.93	0.66	0.63	0.27	...
Cash Flow Per Share	1.47	1.71	1.69	1.59	1.41	1.31	1.12	1.00
Tang Book Value Per Share	4.00	3.92	3.84	3.45	3.01	1.74	2.63	2.19
Dividends Per Share	0.220	0.220	0.167	0.133	...	...	...	...
Dividend Payout %	18.61	18.93	14.88	14.29	...	...	...	...
Income Statement								
Total Revenue	8,118,320	4,237,646	16,078,852	14,448,378	13,181,222	11,596,075	10,744,373	10,673,671
EBITDA	699,812	365,190	1,615,235	1,403,263	1,081,099	949,881	707,029	520,723
Depn & Amortn	162,495	79,704	303,900	278,845	282,811	267,209	248,965	231,380
Income Before Taxes	542,185	290,347	1,314,499	1,115,572	778,112	662,063	430,845	244,185
Income Taxes	195,187	104,525	479,792	407,184	287,901	215,963	165,875	184,473
Net Income	347,251	186,074	834,409	708,388	490,211	446,100	264,970	59,712
Average Shares	744,068	744,304	747,218	758,733	740,236	709,042	699,736	691,186
Balance Sheet								
Total Assets	7,561,763	7,657,086	7,676,589	7,071,448	6,503,046	5,721,388	4,093,035	3,989,413
Current Liabilities	2,255,974	2,406,395	2,479,906	2,196,861	2,123,234	2,175,326	1,595,699	1,711,276
Long-Term Obligations	514,642	516,470	761,032	736,077	709,349	836,903	436,424	514,304
Total Liabilities	3,040,514	3,192,811	3,251,118	2,956,252	2,840,146	3,062,496	2,038,861	2,225,583
Stockholders' Equity	4,521,249	4,464,275	4,425,471	4,115,196	3,662,900	2,658,892	2,054,174	1,763,830
Shares Outstanding	728,151	728,313	730,441	744,501	748,791	709,660	695,991	695,970
Statistical Record								
Return on Assets %	12.08	11.88	11.35	10.47	8.04	9.12	6.57	1.50
Return on Equity %	20.50	20.41	19.59	18.26	15.55	18.98	13.92	3.27
EBITDA Margin %	8.62	8.62	10.05	9.71	8.20	8.19	6.58	4.88
Net Margin %	4.28	4.39	5.19	4.90	3.72	3.85	2.47	0.56
Asset Turnover	2.32	2.27	2.19	2.13	2.16	2.37	2.67	2.68
Current Ratio	1.71	1.67	1.67	1.72	1.64	1.25	1.51	1.38
Debt to Equity	0.11	0.12	0.17	0.18	0.19	0.31	0.21	0.29
Price Range	26.98-20.69	26.64-19.07	23.93-18.64	22.47-15.97	18.51-10.89	14.76-7.95	12.80-7.71	18.71-7.17
P/E Ratio	22.86-17.53	22.97-16.44	21.37-16.64	24.16-17.18	28.05-16.51	23.43-12.61	47.41-28.54	...
Average Yield %	0.94	0.97	0.76	0.70	...	...	...	...

Address: Five Hundred Staples Drive, Framingham, MA 01702
Telephone: 508-253-5000
Fax: 508-370-8955

Web Site: www.staples.com
Officers: Thomas G. Stemberg - Chmn., Basil L. Anderson - Vice-Chmn.

Auditors: ERNST & YOUNG LLP

STARBUCKS CORP.

Exchange	Symbol	Price	52Wk Range	Yield	P/E
NMS	SBUX	$31.01 (8/31/2006)	39.63-23.08	N/A	43.07

*7 Year Price Score 154.70 *NYSE Composite Index=100 *12 Month Price Score 100.19

Interim Earnings (Per Share)

Qtr.	Dec	Mar	Jun	Sep
2002-03	0.10	0.07	0.09	0.09
2003-04	0.14	0.10	0.12	0.13
2004-05	0.17	0.12	0.16	0.16
2005-06	0.22	0.16	0.18	...

Interim Dividends (Per Share)

Amt	Decl	Ex	Rec	Pay
2-for-1	9/21/2005	10/24/2005	10/3/2005	10/21/2005

Valuation Analysis

		Institutional Holding	
Forecast P/E	42.70	No of Institutions	
	(9/9/2006)	567	
Market Cap	$23.8 Billion	Shares	
Book Value	2.5 Billion	516,432,192	
Price/Book	9.51	% Held	
Price/Sales	3.19	68.31	

Business Summary: Food (MIC: 4.1 SIC: 2095 NAIC: 311920)

Starbucks purchases and roasts whole bean coffees and sells them, along with brewed coffees, Italian-style espresso beverages, cold blended beverages, complementary food items, coffee-related accessories and equipment, a selection of teas and a line of compact discs, primarily through Company-operated retail stores. Co. sells coffee and tea products through other channels, and, through certain of its equity investees, it also produces and sells bottled Frappuccino® and Starbucks DoubleShot™ coffee drinks and a line of ice creams. As of Oct 2 2005, Co. operated a total of 10,241 stores, including 6,000 Company-operated stores and 4,241 licensed stores.

Recent Developments: For the quarter ended July 2 2006, net income increased 15.9% to $145.5 million from $125.5 million in the year-earlier quarter. Revenues were $1.96 billion, up 22.6% from $1.60 billion the year before. Operating income was $214.6 million versus $199.6 million in the prior-year quarter, an increase of 7.5%. Direct operating expenses rose 23.9% to $804.9 million from $649.8 million in the comparable period the year before. Indirect operating expenses increased 25.5% to $944.2 million from $752.4 million in the equivalent prior-year period.

Prospects: For its fiscal year ending Oct 2006, Co. now expects to open at least 2,000 net new stores on a global basis, 200 higher than its previous target. Co. continues to target total net revenue growth of about 20.0% and comparable store sales growth in the range of 3.0% to 7.0% percent, with monthly anomalies. Co. is now targeting earnings per share in the range of $0.72 to $0.73 for fiscal 2006. For fiscal 2007, Co. expects to open about 2,400 net new stores on a global basis. Co. is targeting total net revenue growth of about 20.0% and comparable store sales growth in the range of 3.0% to 7.0%, with monthly anomalies. Co. is targeting earnings per share of $0.87 to $0.89 for fiscal 2007.

Financial Data
(US$ in Thousands)

	9 Mos	6 Mos	3 Mos	10/02/2005	10/03/2004	09/28/2003	09/29/2002	09/30/2001
Earnings Per Share	0.72	0.70	0.66	0.61	0.47	0.34	0.27	0.23
Cash Flow Per Share	1.43	1.46	1.47	1.17	0.98	0.73	0.62	0.61
Tang Book Value Per Share	3.00	2.87	2.76	2.56	3.01	2.53	2.20	1.78
Income Statement								
Total Revenue	5,783,587	3,819,914	1,934,092	6,369,300	5,294,247	4,075,522	3,288,908	2,648,980
EBITDA	1,009,606	684,994	378,518	1,163,651	929,077	695,606	562,527	466,009
Depn & Amortn	304,853	199,842	98,289	367,207	304,820	259,271	221,141	177,087
Income Before Taxes	704,753	485,152	280,229	796,444	624,257	436,335	341,386	288,922
Income Taxes	257,783	183,680	106,039	301,977	232,482	167,989	126,313	107,712
Net Income	446,970	301,472	174,190	494,467	391,775	268,346	215,073	181,210
Average Shares	798,259	794,613	792,949	815,417	822,930	803,296	795,052	788,698
Balance Sheet								
Total Assets	4,052,442	3,817,699	3,711,505	3,514,065	3,328,168	2,729,746	2,292,736	1,851,039
Current Liabilities	1,322,780	1,187,123	1,270,708	1,226,996	782,980	608,703	537,490	445,264
Long-Term Obligations	2,300	2,491	2,681	2,870	3,618	4,354	5,076	5,786
Total Liabilities	1,547,347	1,399,790	1,478,713	1,423,431	841,413	647,319	566,098	475,112
Stockholders' Equity	2,505,095	2,417,909	2,232,792	2,090,634	2,486,755	2,082,427	1,726,638	1,375,927
Shares Outstanding	768,376	769,274	763,710	767,442	794,811	787,385	776,457	760,088
Statistical Record								
Return on Assets %	15.50	14.87	13.95	14.49	12.73	10.72	10.41	10.87
Return on Equity %	23.93	21.97	20.88	21.66	16.87	14.13	13.90	14.40
EBITDA Margin %	17.46	17.93	19.57	18.27	17.55	17.07	17.10	17.59
Net Margin %	7.73	7.89	9.01	7.76	7.40	6.58	6.54	6.84
Asset Turnover	2.02	1.91	1.79	1.87	1.72	1.63	1.59	1.59
Current Ratio	1.04	1.07	1.06	0.99	1.75	1.52	1.58	1.33
Price Range	39.63-23.08	37.63-22.78	31.96-22.78	31.93-22.78	23.94-14.40	15.10-9.90	12.82-7.28	12.50-7.00
P/E Ratio	55.04-32.06	53.76-32.54	48.42-34.52	52.35-37.34	50.94-30.64	44.40-29.12	47.46-26.96	54.35-30.43

Address: 2401 Utah Avenue South, Seattle, WA 98134
Telephone: 206-447-1575
Fax: 206-447-0828

Web Site: www.starbucks.com
Officers: Howard Schultz - Chmn., Chief Global Strategist Orin C. Smith - Pres., C.E.O.

Auditors: Deloitte & Touche LLP
Investor Contact: 206-447-1575

STATE AUTO FINANCIAL CORP.

Exchange	Symbol	Price	52Wk Range	Yield	P/E	Div Acheiver
NMS	STFC	$31.34 (8/31/2006)	39.54-28.53	1.28	14.31	14 Years

*7 Year Price Score 127.42 *NYSE Composite Index=100 *12 Month Price Score 88.51

Interim Earnings (Per Share)

Qtr.	Mar	Jun	Sep	Dec
2003	0.53	0.21	0.38	0.46
2004	0.80	0.85	0.12	0.93
2005	1.00	0.94	0.41	0.71
2006	0.97	0.10	...	...

Interim Dividends (Per Share)

Amt	Decl	Ex	Rec	Pay
0.09Q	11/11/2005	12/13/2005	12/15/2005	12/31/2005
0.09Q	3/3/2006	3/13/2006	3/15/2006	3/31/2006
0.09Q	5/18/2006	6/13/2006	6/15/2006	6/30/2006
0.10Q	8/18/2006	9/13/2006	9/15/2006	9/29/2006

Indicated Div: $0.40 (Div. Reinv. Plan)

Valuation Analysis **Institutional Holding**

Forecast P/E	11.35	No of Institutions
	(9/9/2006)	99
Market Cap	$1.3 Billion	Shares
Book Value	786.9 Million	8,843,771
Price/Book	1.62	% Held
Price/Sales	1.14	21.59

Business Summary: Insurance (MIC: 8.2 SIC: 6331 NAIC: 524126)

State Auto Financial, through its principal insurance subsidiaries, State Auto Property and Casualty Insurance, Milbank Insurance, Farmers Casualty Insurance and State Auto Insurance, provides personal and commercial insurance. Co.'s principal lines of business include personal and commercial auto, homeowners, commercial multi-peril, workers' compensation, general liability and fire insurance. As of Dec 31 2005, Co. marketed its products through about 22,100 independent insurance agents associated with 3,050 agencies in 27 states. Co.'s products are marketed primarily in the central and eastern U.S., excluding New York, New Jersey and the New England States.

Recent Developments: For the quarter ended June 30 2006, net income decreased 89.4% to $4.1 million from $38.8 million in the year-earlier quarter. Revenues were $280.0 million, down 1.5% from $284.2 million the year before. Net premiums earned were $256.7 million versus $263.7 million in the prior-year quarter, a decrease of 2.7%. Net investment income rose 6.7% to $20.6 million from $19.3 million a year ago.

Prospects: Co.'s near term outlook appears mixed. Co. noted that its standard personal auto premiums are being affected by an extremely competitive personal auto marketplace, which have not only have affected new business production but also put downward pressures on existing rates. On the positive side, Co. anticipates that the continued roll out of its new CustomFit auto program, which uses a multi-variate rating approach that broadens the underwriting and eligibility guidelines for new clients, will have a positive affect on net written premiums. Meanwhile, Co.'s standard homeowners' business has shown modest growth in 2006, while standard commercial business new premiums have increased modestly.

Financial Data

(US$ in Thousands)	6 Mos	3 Mos	12/31/2005	12/31/2004	12/31/2003	12/31/2002	12/31/2001	12/31/2000
Earnings Per Share	2.19	3.03	3.06	2.70	1.58	0.93	0.52	1.21
Cash Flow Per Share	3.19	4.28	5.62	3.69	3.51	3.25	1.64	2.28
Tang Book Value Per Share	19.29	19.57	18.85	16.41	13.71	11.89	10.23	9.95
Dividends Per Share	0.360	0.315	0.270	0.170	0.150	0.135	0.125	0.115
Dividend Payout %	16.44	10.40	8.82	6.30	9.49	14.52	24.04	9.50
Income Statement								
Premium Income	512,800	256,100	1,050,300	1,006,800	960,568	896,595	555,207	397,967
Total Revenue	556,800	276,800	1,139,500	1,092,400	1,041,696	967,479	623,272	462,774
Benefits & Claims	321,300	127,300	613,400	619,200	651,223	653,474	427,074	272,167
Income Before Taxes	56,500	56,700	172,000	151,600	83,277	37,790	17,976	61,444
Income Taxes	12,200	16,500	46,100	41,600	19,655	795	(2,639)	13,730
Net Income	44,300	40,200	125,900	110,000	63,622	36,995	20,615	47,714
Average Shares	41,600	41,500	41,100	40,800	40,153	39,743	39,681	39,120
Balance Sheet								
Total Assets	2,198,200	2,295,800	2,274,900	2,023,700	1,836,667	1,592,995	1,367,496	898,106
Total Liabilities	1,411,300	1,499,200	1,511,400	1,365,500	1,294,376	1,129,226	967,303	512,047
Stockholders' Equity	786,900	796,600	763,500	658,200	542,291	463,769	400,193	386,059
Shares Outstanding	40,800	40,700	40,500	40,100	39,559	39,001	38,937	38,554
Statistical Record								
Return on Assets %	4.12	5.65	5.86	5.68	3.71	2.50	1.82	5.74
Return on Equity %	11.87	16.98	17.71	18.28	12.65	8.56	5.24	13.52
Loss Ratio %	62.66	49.71	58.40	61.50	67.80	72.88	76.92	68.39
Net Margin %	7.96	14.52	11.05	10.07	6.11	3.82	3.31	10.31
Price Range	39.54-28.99	39.54-25.50	36.69-24.47	30.93-22.68	26.82-15.33	17.19-13.10	17.67-12.50	18.00-7.19
P/E Ratio	18.05-13.24	13.05-8.42	11.99-8.00	11.46-8.40	16.97-9.70	18.48-14.09	33.98-24.04	14.88-5.94
Average Yield %	1.08	0.99	0.91	0.62	0.70	0.87	0.81	1.03

Address: 518 East Broad Street, Columbus, OH 43215-3976 Telephone: 614-464-5000	Web Site: www.STFC.com Officers: Robert H. Moone - Chmn., Pres., C.E.O. Mark A. Blackburn - Sr. V.P.	Auditors: Ernst & Young LLP Investor Contact: 614-464-5078 Transfer Agents: National City Bank, Cleveland, OH

STERICYCLE INC.

Exchange	Symbol	Price	52Wk Range	Yield	P/E
NMS	SRCL	$66.69 (8/31/2006)	69.00-54.36	N/A	42.21

*7 Year Price Score 136.36 *NYSE Composite Index=100 *12 Month Price Score 102.63

Interim Earnings (Per Share)

Qtr.	Mar	Jun	Sep	Dec
2003	0.32	0.34	0.37	0.40
2004	0.42	0.41	0.46	0.41
2005	0.48	0.51	0.52	(0.02)
2006	0.52	0.56	...	...

Interim Dividends (Per Share)

Amt	Decl	Ex	Rec	Pay
100%	5/16/2002	6/3/2002	5/16/2002	5/31/2002

Valuation Analysis

Forecast P/E	28.15
	(9/9/2006)
Market Cap	$2.9 Billion
Book Value	574.4 Million
Price/Book	5.14
Price/Sales	4.23

Institutional Holding

No of Institutions	277
Shares	36,998,896
% Held	83.91

Business Summary: Sanitation Services (MIC: 7.3 SIC: 4953 NAIC: 562211)

Stericycle is a regulated medical waste management company serving about 333,000 customers throughout the U.S., Puerto Rico, Canada, Mexico and the U.K., at Dec 31 2005. Co.'s network includes 45 treatment/collection centers and 105 additional transfer and collection sites. Co.'s treatment technologies include its proprietary electro-thermal-deactivation system as well as autoclaving and incineration. Co.'s main customer groups include about 325,000 small medical waste generators such as outpatient clinics, medical and dental offices and long-term and sub-acute care facilities and about 7,700 large medical waste generators such as hospitals, blood banks and pharmaceutical manufacturers.

Recent Developments: For the quarter ended June 30 2006, net income increased 9.5% to $25.2 million from $23.0 million in the year-earlier quarter. Revenues were $198.4 million, up 33.0% from $149.1 million the year before. Operating income was $50.0 million versus $42.0 million in the prior-year quarter, an increase of 19.0%. Direct operating expenses rose 32.6% to $105.9 million from $79.9 million in the comparable period the year before. Indirect operating expenses increased 56.0% to $42.6 million from $27.3 million in the equivalent prior-year period.

Prospects: Co.'s top-line results continues to benefit from the acquisitions completed during both 2005 and 2006, coupled with Co.'s continued strategy of focusing on sales to higher-margin small quantity customers. Additionally, Co. is seeing increasing revenue growth in its base internal for small quantity customers as well as from the large quantity customers as it continues to increase its number of Bio Systems customers. Meanwhile, Co. is seeing an increase in gross margins on its domestic business as it continues to realize improvements from its ongoing programs to improve margins on its large quantity business.

Financial Data
(US$ in Thousands)

	6 Mos	3 Mos	12/31/2005	12/31/2004	12/31/2003	12/31/2002	12/31/2001	12/31/2000
Earnings Per Share	1.58	1.53	1.48	1.69	1.43	1.01	0.35	0.36
Cash Flow Per Share	2.30	2.03	2.13	2.58	2.92	2.56	2.03	0.35
Income Statement								
Total Revenue	377,673	179,249	609,457	516,228	453,225	401,519	359,024	323,722
EBITDA	105,485	50,511	145,658	160,995	138,282	111,666	97,033	86,512
Depn & Amortn	13,008	6,295	21,431	21,803	17,255	14,981	25,234	23,469
Income Before Taxes	79,825	38,566	111,980	128,564	108,729	75,577	36,748	23,816
Income Taxes	31,132	15,041	44,826	50,386	42,948	29,853	14,729	9,305
Net Income	48,693	23,525	67,154	78,178	65,781	45,724	14,710	14,511
Average Shares	45,310	45,155	45,310	46,195	46,097	45,113	42,200	40,185
Balance Sheet								
Total Assets	1,235,405	1,212,411	1,047,660	834,141	707,462	667,095	614,530	597,982
Current Liabilities	116,690	111,564	98,760	83,238	68,994	53,754	63,379	43,113
Long-Term Obligations	456,825	473,930	348,841	190,431	163,016	224,124	267,365	345,104
Total Liabilities	660,997	668,593	526,026	338,769	278,698	312,317	337,148	391,845
Stockholders' Equity	574,408	543,818	521,634	495,372	407,820	326,729	232,510	134,700
Shares Outstanding	44,230	44,232	44,149	44,732	41,868	40,437	37,079	30,417
Statistical Record								
Return on Assets %	6.62	6.71	7.14	10.11	9.57	7.14	2.43	2.42
Return on Equity %	13.12	13.37	13.21	17.26	17.91	16.35	8.01	11.45
EBITDA Margin %	27.93	28.18	23.90	31.19	30.51	27.81	27.03	26.72
Net Margin %	12.89	13.12	11.02	15.14	14.51	11.39	4.10	4.48
Asset Turnover	0.65	0.63	0.65	0.67	0.66	0.63	0.59	0.54
Current Ratio	1.49	1.54	1.46	1.39	1.42	1.76	1.55	2.11
Debt to Equity	0.80	0.87	0.67	0.38	0.40	0.69	1.15	2.56
Price Range	69.00-53.42	67.62-43.92	63.52-43.92	53.06-41.79	51.34-32.38	40.15-26.50	31.22-14.31	19.56-7.69
P/E Ratio	43.67-31.85	44.20-28.71	42.92-29.68	31.40-24.73	35.90-22.64	39.75-26.23	89.20-40.89	54.34-21.35

Address: 28161 North Keith Drive, Lake Forest, IL 60045
Telephone: 847-367-5910

Web Site: www.stericycle.com
Officers: Jack W. Schuler - Chmn. Mark C. Miller - Pres., C.E.O.

Auditors: Ernst & Young LLP
Transfer Agents: LaSalle Bank N.A., Chicago, Illinois

STERLING BANCSHARES, INC. (TX)

Exchange	Symbol	Price	52Wk Range	Yield	P/E	Div Acheiver
NMS	SBIB	$20.74 (8/31/2006)	20.76-13.67	1.35	23.04	12 Years

*7 Year Price Score 105.45 *NYSE Composite Index=100 *12 Month Price Score 112.59

Interim Earnings (Per Share)

Qtr.	Mar	Jun	Sep	Dec
2003	0.25	0.10	0.61	0.13
2004	0.12	0.16	0.14	0.13
2005	0.17	0.19	0.19	0.24
2006	0.22	0.25	...	...

Interim Dividends (Per Share)

Amt	Decl	Ex	Rec	Pay
0.06Q	10/31/2005	11/8/2005	11/11/2005	11/25/2005
0.07Q	1/30/2006	2/8/2006	2/10/2006	2/24/2006
0.07Q	4/24/2006	5/3/2006	5/5/2006	5/19/2006
0.07Q	8/1/2006	8/9/2006	8/11/2006	8/25/2006

Indicated Div: $0.28

Valuation Analysis
Forecast P/E N/A
Market Cap $941.8 Million
Book Value 344.0 Million
Price/Book 2.74
Price/Sales 3.68

Institutional Holding
No of Institutions 131
Shares 30,884,288
% Held 67.45

Business Summary: Commercial Banking (MIC: 8.1 SIC: 6022 NAIC: 522110)

Sterling Bancshares is a bank holding company that provides commercial and retail banking to small- to mid-sized businesses and consumers primarily in the Houston, Dallas and San Antonio metropolitan areas through 40 banking offices of Sterling Bank. Co.'s commercial and consumer banking services include demand, savings and time deposits; commercial, real estate and consumer loans; merchant credit card services; letters of credit; and cash and asset management services. In addition, Co. facilitates sales of brokerage, mutual fund, alternative financing and insurance products through third party vendors. As of Dec 31 2005, Co. had total assets of $3.73 billion and deposits of $2.84 billion.

Recent Developments: For the quarter ended June 30 2006, net income increased 32.3% to $11.3 million from $8.5 million in the year-earlier quarter. Net interest income increased 17.2% to $42.8 million from $36.5 million in the year-earlier quarter. Provision for loan losses was $1.8 million versus $3.2 million in the prior-year quarter, a decrease of 43.0%. Non-interest income rose 38.1% to $9.0 million from $6.5 million, while non-interest expense advanced 20.8% to $33.2 million.

Prospects: On Jul 26 2006, Co. announced that it has entered into a definitive agreement to acquire BOTH, Inc., and its subsidiary, Bank of the Hills; expanding its presence in the San Antonio/Kerrville area. The deal, valued at a total of about $72.5 million, should close in the fourth quarter of 2006. Meanwhile, Co. noted that its earnings continue to benefit from favorable trends in its asset quality, loan growth and net interest margin. Co. is also seeing growth opportunities in all three of the markets it serves. During 2006, Co. will introduce new products and services such as free checking in order to help deepen its customer relationships and capitalize on opportunities for future growth.

Financial Data (US$ in Thousands)	6 Mos	3 Mos	12/31/2005	12/31/2004	12/31/2003	12/31/2002	12/31/2001	12/31/2000
Earnings Per Share	0.90	0.84	0.79	0.55	1.10	0.82	0.71	0.67
Cash Flow Per Share	1.85	1.39	1.45	2.88	18.84	(10.91)	(5.39)	(0.78)
Tang Book Value Per Share	5.63	5.54	5.42	5.52	5.09	3.67	3.27	3.89
Dividends Per Share	0.260	0.250	0.240	0.200	0.180	0.160	0.147	0.133
Dividend Payout %	28.89	29.76	30.38	36.36	16.36	19.51	20.66	20.00
Income Statement								
Interest Income	120,097	57,912	204,603	166,097	171,383	176,391	173,053	156,430
Interest Expense	36,592	17,220	54,373	30,713	26,769	29,719	50,052	58,109
Net Interest Income	83,505	40,692	150,230	135,384	144,614	146,672	123,001	98,321
Provision for Losses	3,163	1,326	14,371	12,250	17,698	14,018	11,684	9,100
Non-Interest Income	15,509	6,490	26,959	30,922	33,078	94,510	66,171	39,567
Non-Interest Expense	64,151	30,958	110,646	119,609	117,603	172,352	130,677	89,927
Income Before Taxes	31,700	14,898	52,172	34,447	42,391	54,812	46,811	38,861
Income Taxes	10,399	4,866	15,950	9,484	14,037	18,139	16,410	12,281
Net Income	21,301	10,032	36,222	24,963	49,110	36,551	30,401	26,580
Average Shares	45,868	45,794	45,761	45,278	44,648	44,756	43,044	39,832
Balance Sheet								
Net Loans & Leases	2,848,994	2,727,612	2,668,132	2,314,745	2,126,317	1,882,944	1,643,861	1,213,288
Total Assets	3,789,920	3,745,578	3,726,859	3,336,070	3,204,405	3,582,745	2,778,090	1,925,131
Total Deposits	2,984,275	2,959,980	2,838,143	2,443,967	2,418,369	2,532,902	2,268,980	1,577,735
Total Liabilities	3,445,906	3,405,297	3,392,387	3,022,898	2,831,809	3,248,344	2,498,989	1,735,195
Stockholders' Equity	344,014	340,281	334,472	313,172	292,596	249,327	217,369	159,134
Shares Outstanding	45,410	45,445	45,333	45,068	44,642	43,982	43,769	39,345
Statistical Record								
Return on Assets %	1.12	1.07	1.03	0.76	1.45	1.15	1.29	1.36
Return on Equity %	12.32	11.75	11.19	8.22	18.12	15.66	16.15	18.05
Net Interest Margin %	68.85	70.27	73.43	81.51	84.38	83.15	71.08	62.85
Efficiency Ratio %	46.62	48.07	47.78	60.71	57.52	63.62	54.63	45.88
Loans to Deposits	0.95	0.92	0.94	0.94	0.88	0.74	0.72	0.77
Price Range	18.75-13.67	18.05-12.87	16.16-12.87	15.00-11.92	14.00-11.12	15.30-10.60	16.15-10.83	13.42-5.81
P/E Ratio	20.83-15.19	21.49-15.32	20.46-16.29	27.27-21.67	12.73-10.11	18.66-12.93	22.74-15.26	20.02-8.68
Average Yield %	1.61	1.64	1.64	1.49	1.46	1.21	1.17	1.58

Address: 2550 North Loop West, Suite 600, Houston, TX 77092 **Telephone:** 713-466-8300 **Fax:** 713-466-3117	**Web Site:** www.banksterling.com **Officers:** J. Downey Bridgwater - Chmn., Pres., C.E.O. Stephen C. Raffaele - Exec. V.P., C.F.O.
Auditors: DELOITTE & TOUCHE LLP **Investor Contact:** 888-577-7242 **Transfer Agents:** American Stock Transfer & Trust Company, New York, NY	

STERLING FINANCIAL CORP. (PA)

Exchange	Symbol	Price	52Wk Range	Yield	P/E	Div Achiever
NMS	SLFI	$22.39 (8/31/2006)	22.46-18.47	2.68	16.11	18 Years

*7 Year Price Score 107.05 *NYSE Composite Index=100 *12 Month Price Score 100.33

Interim Earnings (Per Share)

Qtr.	Mar	Jun	Sep	Dec
2003	0.25	0.26	0.28	0.29
2004	0.28	0.30	0.30	0.32
2005	0.32	0.33	0.34	0.35
2006	0.35	0.35	...	...

Interim Dividends (Per Share)

Amt	Decl	Ex	Rec	Pay
0.14Q	11/16/2005	12/13/2005	12/15/2005	1/3/2006
0.14Q	2/28/2006	3/13/2006	3/15/2006	4/3/2006
0.14Q	5/24/2006	6/13/2006	6/15/2006	7/3/2006
0.15Q	8/22/2006	9/13/2006	9/15/2006	10/2/2006

Indicated Div: $0.60 (Div. Reinv. Plan)

Valuation Analysis

Forecast P/E 14.79 (9/9/2006)
Market Cap $646.0 Million
Book Value 302.4 Million
Price/Book 2.14
Price/Sales 2.49

Institutional Holding

No of Institutions 61
Shares 4,531,690
% Held 15.55

Business Summary: Commercial Banking (MIC: 8.1 SIC: 6021 NAIC: 522110)

Sterling Financial is a multi-bank financial holding company with $2.96 billion in assets as of Dec 31 2005. Co. provides a broad range of financial services to individuals and businesses through its banking and nonbanking subsidiaries, including personal and business banking, leasing, insurance and wealth management. As of Dec 31 2005, Co. operated 63 branch banking offices in south central Pennsylvania, northern Maryland and northern Delaware through its subsidiary banks, Bank of Lancaster County, N.A., Bank of Hanover and Trust Company, Pennsylvania State Bank, First National Bank of North East and Delaware Sterling Bank & Trust Company.

Recent Developments: For the quarter ended June 30 2006, net income increased 6.2% to $10.3 million from $9.7 million in the year-earlier quarter. Net interest income increased 7.4% to $30.4 million from $28.3 million in the year-earlier quarter. Provision for loan losses was $1.3 million versus $1.1 million in the prior-year quarter, an increase of 13.9%. Non-interest income rose 8.4% to $18.6 million from $17.1 million, while non-interest expense advanced 6.6% to $32.8 million.

Prospects: Co. is experiencing an increase in net interest income, driven by strong organic growth in loans, particularly in the commercial and finance receivable portfolios. Looking ahead, although it has experienced some recent modest compression in its net interest margin, Co.'s results could benefit from its efforts to achieve revenue growth by delivering a variety of complementary financial services through its banks and financial services group companies. Meanwhile, Co. plans to manage its net interest margin through a combination of managing pricing on loans and deposits as well as improving its mix of interest earning assets.

Financial Data
(US$ in Thousands)

	6 Mos	3 Mos	12/31/2005	12/31/2004	12/31/2003	12/31/2002	12/31/2001	12/31/2000
Earnings Per Share	1.39	1.37	1.34	1.21	1.08	0.94	0.83	0.68
Cash Flow Per Share	2.90	2.51	2.41	1.94	2.40	2.28	0.93	1.51
Tang Book Value Per Share	7.02	7.12	7.06	6.52	6.79	6.76	6.22	5.69
Dividends Per Share	0.560	0.550	0.538	0.496	0.448	0.422	0.399	0.384
Dividend Payout %	40.20	40.03	40.15	40.99	41.48	44.90	48.15	56.82
Income Statement								
Interest Income	97,542	47,444	172,210	137,682	127,074	123,591	115,916	113,319
Interest Expense	37,403	17,701	57,921	40,265	41,156	48,617	57,274	58,501
Net Interest Income	60,139	29,743	114,289	97,417	85,918	74,974	58,642	54,818
Provision for Losses	2,423	1,125	4,383	4,438	3,697	2,095	1,217	605
Non-Interest Income	36,550	17,952	67,836	59,296	49,721	44,806	43,925	37,508
Non-Interest Expense	65,042	32,246	123,380	107,086	92,568	85,922	75,172	70,203
Income Before Taxes	29,224	14,324	54,362	45,189	39,374	31,763	26,178	21,518
Income Taxes	8,786	4,167	15,095	11,860	10,315	7,018	5,844	4,951
Net Income	20,438	10,157	39,267	33,329	29,059	24,745	20,334	16,567
Average Shares	29,273	29,283	29,317	27,651	26,810	26,285	24,570	24,524
Balance Sheet								
Net Loans & Leases	2,217,959	2,142,993	2,083,083	1,888,380	1,481,369	1,283,075	1,087,102	1,021,499
Total Assets	3,094,126	3,013,840	2,965,737	2,742,762	2,343,517	2,156,309	1,861,439	1,726,138
Total Deposits	2,353,591	2,274,905	2,226,287	2,015,394	1,778,587	1,702,302	1,535,649	1,420,300
Total Liabilities	2,791,769	2,715,427	2,667,651	2,460,818	2,123,506	1,959,476	1,709,328	1,586,791
Stockholders' Equity	302,357	298,413	298,086	281,944	220,011	196,833	152,111	139,347
Shares Outstanding	28,854	28,903	29,055	29,100	27,146	26,407	24,437	24,504
Statistical Record								
Return on Assets %	1.38	1.39	1.38	1.31	1.29	1.23	1.13	1.19
Return on Equity %	13.76	13.90	13.54	13.24	13.94	14.18	13.95	14.41
Net Interest Margin %	60.67	62.69	66.37	70.76	67.61	60.66	50.59	48.37
Efficiency Ratio %	47.74	49.31	51.40	54.36	52.36	51.02	47.03	46.55
Loans to Deposits	0.94	0.94	0.94	0.94	0.83	0.75	0.71	0.72
Price Range	23.52-18.47	23.52-18.47	23.52-18.47	24.31-17.76	18.84-13.91	17.11-11.52	12.95-7.74	14.43-6.57
P/E Ratio	16.92-13.29	17.17-13.48	17.55-13.78	20.09-14.68	17.44-12.88	18.20-12.26	15.61-9.33	21.22-9.67
Average Yield %	2.66	2.62	2.55	2.43	2.77	2.93	3.67	4.54

Address: 101 North Pointe Boulevard, Lancaster, PA 17601-4133 **Telephone:** 717-581-6030 **Fax:** 717-735-5608	**Web Site:** www.sterlingfi.com **Officers:** Glenn R. Walz - Chmn. W. Garth Sprecher - Vice-Chmn.	**Auditors:** Ernst & Young LLP **Investor Contact:** 717-735-5602 **Transfer Agents:** American Stock Transfer and Trust Company, New York, NY

SUFFOLK BANCORP

Exchange	Symbol	Price	52Wk Range	Yield	P/E	Div Acheiver
NMS	SUBK	$34.84 (8/31/2006)	37.00-27.40	2.53	16.06	16 Years

*7 Year Price Score 95.30 *NYSE Composite Index=100 *12 Month Price Score 95.78

Interim Earnings (Per Share)

Qtr.	Mar	Jun	Sep	Dec
2003	0.47	0.46	0.49	0.50
2004	0.44	0.46	0.48	0.53
2005	0.48	0.50	0.56	0.56
2006	0.50	0.55	...	...

Interim Dividends (Per Share)

Amt	Decl	Ex	Rec	Pay
0.20Q	11/28/2005	12/13/2005	12/15/2005	1/3/2006
0.22Q	2/28/2006	3/13/2006	3/15/2006	4/3/2006
0.22Q	5/22/2006	6/13/2006	6/15/2006	7/3/2006
0.22Q	8/28/2006	9/13/2006	9/15/2006	10/2/2006

Indicated Div: $0.88

Valuation Analysis
Forecast P/E N/A
Market Cap $357.1 Million
Book Value 100.1 Million
Price/Book 3.57
Price/Sales 3.88

Institutional Holding
No of Institutions 52
Shares 2,688,042
% Held 26.22

Business Summary: Commercial Banking (MIC: 8.1 SIC: 6021 NAIC: 522110)
Suffolk Bancorp is a bank holding company. Co. does commercial banking through its wholly-owned subsidiary, Suffolk County National Ban (SCNB), a full-service, nationally chartered commercial bank. SCNB operates 26 full-service offices throughout Suffolk County, NY. Most of SCNB's business is retail, and includes loans to individual consumers, to professionals, and to small and medium-sized commercial enterprises. Co. has special expertise in indirect retail lending, evaluating and buying loans generated from automobile dealers. The Bank also makes loans for automobiles in Nassau and Queens Counties, NY. and lends to small manufacturers, wholesalers, builders, farmers, and retailers.

Recent Developments: For the quarter ended June 30 2006, net income increased 5.9% to $5.6 million from $5.3 million in the year-earlier quarter. Net interest income increased 4.8% to $16.7 million from $15.9 million in the year-earlier quarter. Provision for loan losses was $300,000 versus $375,000 in the prior-year quarter, a decrease of 20.0%. Non-interest income rose 9.2% to $2.7 million from $2.5 million, while non-interest expense advanced 6.1% to $10.0 million.

Prospects: Results are benefiting from Co.'s efforts to redirect flow of investments from the consumer portfolio, comprised primarily of indirect automobile paper to the commercial and commercial real estate portfolios, as well as residential mortgages and construction loans. Meanwhile, results are also being positively affected by increased capital management and continuing emphasis on both personal and commercial demand deposits. However, Co. indicated that its consumer loans continue to come under increasing pressure with regard to term, rate, and volume in the face of the incentive programs of the major manufacturers.

Financial Data
(US$ in Thousands)

	6 Mos	3 Mos	12/31/2005	12/31/2004	12/31/2003	12/31/2002	12/31/2001	12/31/2000
Earnings Per Share	2.17	2.12	2.09	1.91	1.92	1.82	1.58	1.35
Cash Flow Per Share	2.75	2.66	3.17	2.74	2.99	2.33	1.39	1.93
Tang Book Value Per Share	9.68	9.62	9.72	9.72	9.07	9.40	9.59	9.86
Dividends Per Share	0.840	0.820	0.790	0.760	0.760	0.660	0.560	0.460
Dividend Payout %	38.71	38.68	37.80	39.79	39.58	36.26	35.44	34.07
Income Statement								
Interest Income	42,356	20,539	75,673	67,984	70,995	78,428	79,565	76,853
Interest Expense	9,532	4,384	11,312	7,379	9,801	16,088	24,342	24,348
Net Interest Income	32,824	16,155	64,361	60,605	61,193	62,340	55,223	52,505
Provision for Losses	600	300	1,575	1,973	932	1,380	1,544	1,200
Non-Interest Income	5,105	2,386	10,145	12,294	11,311	10,074	9,548	7,814
Non-Interest Expense	19,899	9,860	37,453	36,622	36,190	35,744	32,307	31,977
Income Before Taxes	17,430	8,381	35,478	34,305	35,382	35,289	30,920	27,116
Income Taxes	6,567	3,157	13,376	13,430	14,046	14,020	12,235	10,883
Net Income	10,863	5,224	22,102	20,875	21,336	21,269	18,685	16,232
Average Shares	10,321	10,390	10,600	10,913	11,090	11,700	11,839	12,030
Balance Sheet								
Net Loans & Leases	912,538	914,106	895,209	817,220	830,510	779,862	787,285	768,248
Total Assets	1,443,104	1,424,910	1,408,283	1,348,218	1,328,757	1,272,717	1,164,947	1,049,580
Total Deposits	1,181,288	1,133,803	1,158,707	1,197,592	1,187,496	1,142,582	1,051,712	942,436
Total Liabilities	1,343,013	1,323,993	1,306,282	1,242,007	1,228,587	1,163,924	1,068,111	961,527
Stockholders' Equity	100,091	100,917	102,001	106,212	100,170	108,793	96,837	88,053
Shares Outstanding	10,251	10,406	10,406	10,842	10,949	11,489	10,010	8,810
Statistical Record								
Return on Assets %	1.57	1.59	1.60	1.56	1.64	1.75	1.69	1.59
Return on Equity %	22.21	22.20	21.23	20.17	20.42	20.69	20.21	19.58
Net Interest Margin %	76.40	78.66	85.05	89.15	86.19	79.49	69.41	68.32
Efficiency Ratio %	40.92	43.01	43.64	45.62	43.97	40.39	36.25	37.77
Loans to Deposits	0.77	0.81	0.77	0.68	0.70	0.68	0.75	0.82
Price Range	37.00-27.40	37.00-25.99	37.00-25.99	36.06-29.83	37.33-30.30	36.50-27.00	27.90-15.31	15.69-12.88
P/E Ratio	17.05-12.63	17.45-12.26	17.70-12.44	18.88-15.62	19.44-15.78	20.05-14.84	17.66-9.69	11.62-9.54
Average Yield %	2.60	2.55	2.48	2.34	2.29	2.11	2.66	3.36

Address: 4 West Second Street, Riverhead, NY 11901 **Telephone:** 631-727-5667 **Fax:** 631-727-3214	**Web Site:** www.scnb.com **Officers:** Edward J. Merz - Chmn. Thomas S. Kohlmann - Pres., C.E.O.	**Auditors:** Grant Thornton LLP **Investor Contact:** 631-727-5667 **Transfer Agents:** American Stock Transfer & Trust Co., New York, NY

SUN MICROSYSTEMS INC

Exchange	Symbol	Price	52Wk Range	Yield	P/E
NMS	SUNW	$4.99 (8/31/2006)	5.25-3.66	N/A	N/A

*7 Year Price Score 25.75 *NYSE Composite Index=100 *12 Month Price Score 97.56

Interim Earnings (Per Share)

Qtr.	Sep	Dec	Mar	Jun
2001-02	(0.06)	(0.13)	(0.01)	0.02
2002-03	(0.04)	(0.72)	0.00	(0.32)
2003-04	(0.09)	(0.04)	(0.23)	0.24
2004-05	(0.04)	0.01	0.00	0.01
2005-06	(0.04)	(0.07)	(0.06)	(0.09)

Interim Dividends (Per Share)

Amt	Decl	Ex	Rec	Pay
2-for-1	9/17/1999	12/8/1999	11/11/1999	12/7/1999
100%	8/17/2000	12/6/2000	11/9/2000	12/5/2000

Valuation Analysis

Forecast P/E 51.58
(9/12/2006)
Market Cap $17.5 Billion
Book Value 6.3 Billion
Price/Book 2.76
Price/Sales 1.34

Institutional Holding

No of Institutions 485
Shares 2,140,995,840
% Held 61.8

Business Summary: IT & Technology (MIC: 10.2 SIC: 3571 NAIC: 334111)

Sun Microsystems is focused on providing network computing products and services. Co.'s products consist of computer systems and storage product lines, and a variety of software and services related to both systems and storage. Co.'s systems power the infrastructure underlying a range of business and technical processes from webserving to technical computing to enterprise-wide resource planning, customer relationship management and database management, in a range of industries, including telecommunications, government, financial services, manufacturing, education, retail, life sciences, media and entertainment, transportation, energy/utilities and healthcare.

Recent Developments: For the year ended June 30 2006, net loss amounted to $864.0 million versus a net loss of $107.0 million in the prior year. Revenues were $13.07 billion, up 18.0% from $11.07 billion the year before. Operating loss was $870.0 million versus a loss of $377.0 million in the prior year. Direct operating expenses rose 14.8% to $7.44 billion from $6.48 billion in the comparable period the year before. Indirect operating expenses increased 30.9% to $6.50 billion from $4.97 billion in the equivalent prior-year period.

Prospects: Co.'s top-line growth is being driven by recent acquisitions, coupled with the growing acceptance of its Solaris™ 10 Operating System and the recent introduction of several of its products, including UltraSPARC T1®. In addition, Co. is benefiting from increased bookings and improved backlog. Separately, on Jul 17 2006, Co. and Avnet Technology Solutions, an operating group of Avnet, Inc. announced an expanded relationship to offer the complete line of its Sun StorageTek™ products to Avnet partners. Going forward, Co. expects the addition of its Sun StorageTek™ products to Avnet's offerings will help boost partner opportunities to capitalize on the position of its existing products.

Financial Data
(US$ in Thousands)

	06/30/2006	06/30/2005	06/30/2004	06/30/2003	06/30/2002	06/30/2001	06/30/2000	06/30/1999
Earnings Per Share	(0.25)	(0.03)	(0.12)	(1.07)	(0.18)	0.27	0.55	0.32
Cash Flow Per Share	0.19	0.11	0.68	0.33	0.27	0.65	1.19	0.82
Tang Book Value Per Share	0.80	1.80	1.77	1.88	2.32	2.63	2.29	1.55
Income Statement								
Total Revenue	13,068,000	11,070,000	11,185,000	11,434,000	12,496,000	18,250,000	15,721,000	11,726,297
EBITDA	96,000	386,000	992,000	(1,748,000)	(141,000)	2,450,000	3,377,000	2,148,711
Depn & Amortn	771,000	570,000	655,000	1,028,000	1,092,000	1,229,000	776,000	626,946
Income Before Taxes	(675,000)	(184,000)	437,000	(2,653,000)	(1,048,000)	1,584,000	2,771,000	1,605,689
Income Taxes	189,000	(77,000)	825,000	776,000	(461,000)	603,000	917,000	574,355
Net Income	(864,000)	(107,000)	(388,000)	(3,429,000)	(587,000)	927,000	1,854,000	1,031,334
Average Shares	3,437,000	3,368,000	3,277,000	3,190,000	3,242,000	3,417,000	3,378,000	3,256,964
Balance Sheet								
Total Assets	15,082,000	14,190,000	14,503,000	12,985,000	16,522,000	18,181,000	14,152,000	8,420,352
Current Liabilities	6,165,000	4,766,000	5,113,000	4,129,000	5,057,000	5,146,000	4,759,000	3,226,977
Long-Term Obligations	575,000	1,123,000	1,175,000	1,531,000	1,449,000	1,705,000	1,720,000	...
Total Liabilities	8,738,000	7,516,000	8,065,000	6,494,000	6,721,000	7,595,000	6,843,000	3,608,572
Stockholders' Equity	6,344,000	6,674,000	6,438,000	6,491,000	9,801,000	10,586,000	7,309,000	4,811,780
Shares Outstanding	3,503,000	3,408,000	3,336,000	3,236,000	3,234,000	3,248,000	3,194,000	3,109,344
Statistical Record								
Return on Assets %	N.M.	N.M.	N.M.	N.M.	N.M.	5.73	16.38	14.60
Return on Equity %	N.M.	N.M.	N.M.	N.M.	N.M.	10.36	30.51	24.78
EBITDA Margin %	0.73	3.49	8.87	N.M.	N.M.	13.42	21.48	18.32
Net Margin %	N.M.	N.M.	N.M.	N.M.	N.M.	5.08	11.79	8.80
Asset Turnover	0.89	0.77	0.81	0.78	0.72	1.13	1.39	1.66
Current Ratio	1.34	1.51	1.43	1.64	1.54	1.54	1.45	1.90
Debt to Equity	0.09	0.17	0.18	0.24	0.15	0.16	0.24	...
Price Range	5.25-3.59	5.55-3.31	5.82-3.20	5.80-2.42	18.17-4.71	64.31-13.04	52.50-16.80	17.88-4.95
P/E Ratio	...	...	...	...	...	238.19-48.30	95.45-30.54	55.86-15.48

Address: 4150 Network Circle, Santa Clara, CA 95054
Telephone: 650-960-1300
Fax: 650-336-0646

Web Site: www.sun.com
Officers: Scott G. McNealy - Chmn., C.E.O. Jonathan I Schwartz - Pres., C.O.O.

Auditors: Ernst & Young LLP
Investor Contact: 650-336-2238
Transfer Agents: Computershare Investor Services

SUSQUEHANNA BANCSHARES, INC

Exchange	Symbol	Price	52Wk Range	Yield	P/E	Div Acheiver
NMS	SUSQ	$24.47 (8/31/2006)	25.93-22.11	3.92	14.14	35 Years

*7 Year Price Score 89.50 *NYSE Composite Index=100 *12 Month Price Score 96.69

Interim Earnings (Per Share)

Qtr.	Mar	Jun	Sep	Dec
2003	0.40	0.41	0.40	0.35
2004	0.40	0.40	0.40	0.41
2005	0.33	0.40	0.38	0.59
2006	0.38	0.38	...	...

Interim Dividends (Per Share)

Amt	Decl	Ex	Rec	Pay
0.24Q	10/19/2005	10/27/2005	10/31/2005	11/18/2005
0.24Q	1/18/2006	1/30/2006	2/1/2006	2/17/2006
0.24Q	4/19/2006	4/27/2006	5/1/2006	5/19/2006
0.24Q	7/19/2006	7/28/2006	8/1/2006	8/18/2006

Indicated Div: $0.96

Valuation Analysis
Forecast P/E 14.76 (9/9/2006)
Market Cap $1.3 Billion
Book Value 904.9 Million
Price/Book 1.40
Price/Sales 2.31

Institutional Holding
No of Institutions 121
Shares 21,836,008
% Held 42.15

Business Summary: Commercial Banking (MIC: 8.1 SIC: 6021 NAIC: 522110)
Susquehanna Bancshares is a financial holding company that provides a range of retail and commercial banking and financial services through its subsidiaries in the mid-Atlantic region. In addition to its commercial banks that included an aggregate of 153 branches as of Dec 31 2005, Co. operates a trust and investment company, an asset management company, a property and casualty insurance brokerage company, a commercial leasing company and a vehicle leasing company. As of Dec 31 2005, Co. had total assets of $7.47 billion and deposits of $5.31 billion.

Recent Developments: For the quarter ended June 30 2006, net income increased 3.4% to $19.3 million from $18.7 million in the year-earlier quarter. Net interest income increased 10.4% to $66.1 million from $59.9 million in the year-earlier quarter. Provision for loan losses was $1.3 million versus $2.5 million in the prior-year quarter, a decrease of 48.6%. Non-interest income rose 6.1% to $32.1 million from $30.2 million, while non-interest expense advanced 13.9% to $68.4 million.

Prospects: Despite a difficult interest rate environment, Co. is progressing toward its goals for 2006, notably in the area of loan growth and improvement in its net interest margin. Moreover, Co.'s results are benefiting from its Apr 2006 acquisition of Minotola National Bank. Meanwhile, Co. plans to relocate its Baltimore-area corporate offices from Towson to Hunt Valley, MD. In addition, in June 2006, developers commenced construction on the Camden, NJ, waterfront building that will house the new headquarters for Susquehanna Patriot Bank. Construction on the project is expected to be completed in 2007.

Financial Data
(US$ in Thousands)

	6 Mos	3 Mos	12/31/2005	12/31/2004	12/31/2003	12/31/2002	12/31/2001	12/31/2000
Earnings Per Share	1.73	1.75	1.70	1.60	1.56	1.55	1.41	1.40
Cash Flow Per Share	2.63	5.87	1.36	1.83	2.50	2.13	1.74	1.35
Tang Book Value Per Share	10.66	11.30	11.23	10.71	12.14	11.96	12.54	11.56
Dividends Per Share	0.950	0.940	0.930	0.890	0.860	0.810	0.770	0.700
Dividend Payout %	54.91	53.71	54.71	55.63	55.13	52.26	54.61	50.00
Income Statement								
Interest Income	219,255	103,962	387,020	321,759	286,020	316,713	341,295	353,416
Interest Expense	93,408	44,225	144,775	107,741	99,014	129,473	169,051	188,464
Net Interest Income	125,847	59,737	242,245	214,018	187,006	187,240	172,244	164,952
Provision for Losses	3,950	2,675	12,335	10,020	10,222	10,664	7,310	3,726
Non-Interest Income	61,929	29,850	125,078	114,590	101,750	94,150	84,166	74,010
Non-Interest Expense	129,354	60,957	242,550	219,042	189,430	181,663	167,763	155,581
Income Before Taxes	54,472	25,955	112,438	99,546	89,104	89,063	81,337	79,655
Income Taxes	17,431	8,254	32,875	29,366	26,731	27,342	25,621	24,693
Net Income	37,041	17,701	79,563	70,180	62,373	61,721	55,716	54,962
Average Shares	50,820	47,029	46,919	43,872	40,037	39,932	39,593	39,365
Balance Sheet								
Net Loans & Leases	5,683,721	4,988,756	5,164,945	5,198,915	4,220,600	3,791,282	3,481,800	3,396,423
Total Assets	8,256,165	7,378,067	7,466,007	7,475,073	5,953,107	5,544,647	5,051,092	4,792,856
Total Deposits	5,917,311	5,355,616	5,309,187	5,130,682	4,134,467	3,831,315	3,484,331	3,249,013
Total Liabilities	7,351,236	6,593,454	6,685,537	6,723,379	5,405,725	5,010,792	4,557,556	4,339,419
Stockholders' Equity	904,929	784,613	780,470	751,694	547,382	533,855	493,536	453,437
Shares Outstanding	51,798	46,927	46,853	46,592	39,861	39,638	39,344	39,221
Statistical Record								
Return on Assets %	1.06	1.12	1.07	1.04	1.08	1.17	1.13	1.20
Return on Equity %	9.92	10.70	10.39	10.78	11.54	12.02	11.77	12.78
Net Interest Margin %	57.34	57.46	62.59	66.52	65.38	59.12	50.47	46.67
Efficiency Ratio %	46.41	45.55	47.36	50.20	48.85	44.21	39.43	36.40
Loans to Deposits	0.96	0.93	0.97	1.01	1.02	0.99	1.00	1.05
Price Range	27.24-22.11	27.24-21.03	27.24-21.03	26.89-22.44	27.80-20.20	25.97-18.41	22.80-15.75	17.50-12.25
P/E Ratio	15.75-12.78	15.57-12.02	16.02-12.37	16.81-14.03	17.82-12.95	16.75-11.88	16.17-11.17	12.50-8.75
Average Yield %	3.91	3.87	3.82	3.58	3.60	3.60	4.00	4.97

Address: 26 North Cedar St., Lititz, PA 17543
Telephone: 717-626-4721
Fax: 717-626-1874

Web Site: www.susquehanna.net
Officers: William J. Reuter - Chmn., Pres., C.E.O.
Gregory A. Duncan - Exec. V.P., C.O.O.

Auditors: PricewaterhouseCoopers LLP
Investor Contact: 717-625-6305
Transfer Agents: The Bank of New York, New York, NY

SVB FINANCIAL GROUP

Exchange	Symbol	Price	52Wk Range	Yield	P/E
NMS	SIVB	$45.19 (8/31/2006)	54.64-44.04	N/A	20.45

*7 Year Price Score 115.35 *NYSE Composite Index=100 *12 Month Price Score 90.95

Interim Earnings (Per Share)

Qtr.	Mar	Jun	Sep	Dec
2003	0.26	(0.02)	0.49	(0.40)
2004	0.38	0.43	0.43	0.50
2005	0.62	0.54	0.60	0.67
2006	0.58	0.36	...	...

Interim Dividends (Per Share)

No Dividends Paid

Valuation Analysis   **Institutional Holding**

Forecast P/E	17.01	No of Institutions
	(9/9/2006)	182
Market Cap	$1.6 Billion	Shares
Book Value	568.1 Million	34,728,940
Price/Book	2.77	% Held
Price/Sales	3.30	N/A

Business Summary: Commercial Banking (MIC: 8.1 SIC: 6022 NAIC: 522110)

SVB Financial Group is a bank holding company and a financial holding company whose principal subsidiary is Silicon Valley Bank (the Bank), a California-chartered bank. The Bank serves its clients through its 27 regional offices in the U.S. and three subsidiaries outside the U.S.. The Bank has 13 offices throughout California and operates regional offices across the country in Arizona, Colorado, Georgia, Illinois, Massachusetts, Minnesota, New York, North Carolina, Oregon, Pennsylvania, Texas, Virginia, and Washington. The three international offices are located in Bangalore, India; Shanghai, China; and London, England. As of Dec 31 2005, Co. had total assets of $5.54 billion.

Recent Developments: For the quarter ended June 30 2006, net income decreased 34.9% to $13.6 million from $20.9 million in the year-earlier quarter. Net interest income increased 20.1% to $85.8 million from $71.4 million in the year-earlier quarter. Provision for loan losses was $4.6 million versus $814,000 in the prior-year quarter, an increase of 465.4%. Non-interest income rose 34.8% to $41.0 million from $30.4 million, while non-interest expense advanced 41.2% to $93.6 million.

Prospects: Co.'s net interest income is benefiting from rising average loans, particularly commercial loans, and improving yields being generated from these loans. Similarly, non-interest income is experiencing higher client investment fees, net gains on investment securities and net gains on derivative instruments, partially offset by a decline in corporate finance fees. Looking ahead, Co. expects third quarter 2006 earnings to be between $0.66 and $0.72 per diluted common share. Co. also expects higher average loan growth in the third quarter versus the second quarter, modest growth in total client funds, and lower noninterest income related to net derivative gains versus the second quarter.

Financial Data
(US$ in Thousands)

	6 Mos	3 Mos	12/31/2005	12/31/2004	12/31/2003	12/31/2002	12/31/2001	12/31/2000
Earnings Per Share	2.21	2.39	2.40	1.74	0.32	1.18	1.79	3.23
Cash Flow Per Share	3.15	3.04	3.23	2.61	2.14	2.32	2.36	2.16
Tang Book Value Per Share	15.80	15.53	15.20	13.81	11.69	12.07	11.70	12.54
Income Statement								
Interest Income	182,535	89,405	316,459	246,139	202,337	212,584	300,326	386,760
Interest Expense	12,894	5,526	17,166	11,391	13,453	17,876	37,341	56,912
Net Interest Income	169,641	83,879	299,293	234,748	188,884	194,708	262,985	329,848
Provision for Losses	2,128	(2,474)	237	(9,901)	(6,223)	3,882	16,724	54,602
Non-Interest Income	64,379	23,401	117,495	106,033	75,060	67,858	70,833	189,630
Non-Interest Expense	164,326	70,688	259,860	242,486	262,093	184,144	180,188	195,061
Income Before Taxes	61,508	38,822	153,295	105,117	15,169	80,077	141,152	266,975
Income Taxes	25,835	16,743	60,758	39,741	3,192	26,719	52,998	107,907
Net Income	35,865	22,271	92,537	65,376	11,977	53,358	88,154	159,068
Average Shares	37,991	38,447	38,489	37,595	37,321	44,897	49,155	49,220
Balance Sheet								
Net Loans & Leases	2,912,719	2,721,998	2,806,568	2,274,530	1,924,729	2,015,580	1,694,663	1,642,749
Total Assets	5,471,651	5,446,268	5,541,715	5,153,600	4,465,370	4,183,181	4,172,077	5,626,775
Total Deposits	3,913,304	4,148,506	4,252,730	4,219,514	3,666,876	3,436,127	3,380,977	4,862,259
Total Liabilities	4,750,497	4,721,785	4,852,958	4,550,658	3,967,621	3,510,201	3,477,646	4,943,397
Stockholders' Equity	568,121	586,118	569,301	532,268	447,005	590,350	627,515	614,121
Shares Outstanding	34,858	35,446	35,103	35,970	35,028	40,578	45,390	48,977
Statistical Record								
Return on Assets %	1.57	1.75	1.73	1.36	0.28	1.28	1.80	3.10
Return on Equity %	15.36	16.66	16.80	13.32	2.31	8.76	14.20	32.28
Net Interest Margin %	92.09	93.82	94.58	95.37	93.35	91.59	87.57	85.28
Efficiency Ratio %	69.82	62.66	59.88	68.85	94.48	65.66	48.55	33.84
Loans to Deposits	0.74	0.66	0.66	0.54	0.52	0.59	0.50	0.34
Price Range	54.64-44.07	53.47-43.26	51.91-41.08	44.99-31.02	37.00-15.75	33.87-14.58	38.00-16.67	64.06-17.00
P/E Ratio	24.72-19.94	22.37-18.10	21.63-17.12	25.86-17.83	115.63-49.22	28.70-12.36	21.23-9.31	19.83-5.26

Address: 3003 Tasman Drive, Santa Clara, CA 95054-1191 **Telephone:** 408-654-7400 **Fax:** 408-496-2405	**Web Site:** www.svb.com. **Officers:** Alex W. Hart - Chmn. Kenneth P. Wilcox - Pres., C.E.O.
Auditors: KPMG LLP **Investor Contact:** 408-654-7282 **Transfer Agents:** Wells Fargo Bank, N.A., St. Paul, MN	

SWIFT TRANSPORTATION CO., INC.

Exchange	Symbol	Price	52Wk Range	Yield	P/E
NMS	SWFT	$23.19 (8/31/2006)	33.62-16.70	N/A	12.88

*7 Year Price Score 96.82 *NYSE Composite Index=100 *12 Month Price Score 111.32

Interim Earnings (Per Share)

Qtr.	Mar	Jun	Sep	Dec
2003	0.10	0.23	0.29	0.32
2004	0.08	0.43	0.32	0.48
2005	0.26	0.40	0.17	0.53
2006	0.50	0.60	...	...

Interim Dividends (Per Share)
No Dividends Paid

Valuation Analysis   **Institutional Holding**

Forecast P/E	10.90	No of Institutions
	(9/9/2006)	181
Market Cap	$1.7 Billion	Shares
Book Value	966.1 Million	51,476,692
Price/Book	1.80	% Held
Price/Sales	0.54	68.93

Business Summary: Road Transport (MIC: 15.2 SIC: 4213 NAIC: 484121)
Swift Transportation is a publicly-held, national truckload carrier that operates primarily throughout the continental U.S., combining regional operations with a transcontinental van operation. The principal types of freight transported by Co. include retail and discount department store merchandise, manufactured goods, paper products, non-perishable and perishable food, beverages and beverage containers and building materials. In addition to its domestic operations, Co. has a cross border operation that primarily ships through commercial border crossings from Laredo, TX westward to California. As of Dec 31 2005, Co. had 14,465 tractors and 51,997 trailers owned and leased.

Recent Developments: For the quarter ended June 30 2006, net income increased 52.7% to $45.5 million from $29.8 million in the year-earlier quarter. Revenues were $813.1 million, up 1.9% from $798.3 million the year before. Operating income was $80.0 million versus $56.5 million in the prior-year quarter, an increase of 41.6%. Direct operating expenses rose 5.4% to $383.0 million from $363.3 million in the comparable period the year before. Indirect operating expenses decreased 7.5% to $350.2 million from $378.4 million in the equivalent prior-year period.

Prospects: Despite being challenged by the availability of drivers, Co. is experiencing top- and bottom-line growth. Specifically, Co.'s results reflect the progress it is making in its performance improvement plan, which includes improving profitability through its focus on increasing asset utilization, reducing deadhead, controlling costs, increasing fuel surcharge recovery and increasing its revenue per loaded mile. Looking ahead, Co. anticipates that the tight driver market will further deteriorate in the third quarter of 2006 before improving in the fourth quarter of 2006. As such, Co. is actively exploring alternatives to address the recruiting and retention of its drivers and owner operators.

Financial Data (US$ in Thousands)	6 Mos	3 Mos	12/31/2005	12/31/2004	12/31/2003	12/31/2002	12/31/2001	12/31/2000
Earnings Per Share	1.80	1.60	1.37	1.29	0.94	0.69	0.32	0.82
Cash Flow Per Share	5.54	5.41	5.00	4.58	3.45	3.12	3.14	1.52
Tang Book Value Per Share	11.67	11.02	10.53	8.91	9.29	9.02	8.46	6.81
Income Statement								
Total Revenue	1,576,139	763,012	3,197,455	2,826,201	2,397,655	2,101,472	2,112,221	1,258,671
EBITDA	148,513	67,127	203,262	370,200	303,703	264,235	221,541	166,160
Depn & Amortn	1,376	224	13,993	192,228	160,289	148,501	143,979	66,173
Income Before Taxes	134,984	60,635	164,350	159,949	127,982	96,108	45,369	84,856
Income Taxes	51,971	23,088	63,223	56,467	48,611	36,520	18,148	32,255
Net Income	83,013	37,547	101,127	103,482	79,371	59,588	27,221	52,601
Average Shares	75,867	75,564	73,823	80,176	84,727	86,928	85,778	64,062
Balance Sheet								
Total Assets	2,218,220	2,183,657	2,218,530	2,030,158	1,820,943	1,654,482	1,556,096	960,211
Long-Term Obligations	285,000	310,000	364,000	366,787	257,894	183,470	223,486	169,240
Total Liabilities	1,252,116	1,273,108	1,348,486	1,291,889	976,328	888,704	820,893	523,487
Stockholders' Equity	966,104	910,549	870,044	738,269	844,615	765,778	735,203	436,724
Shares Outstanding	74,838	74,098	73,640	71,897	83,941	83,945	85,891	63,231
Statistical Record								
Return on Assets %	6.22	5.61	4.76	5.36	4.57	3.71	2.16	5.98
Return on Equity %	15.28	14.26	12.58	13.04	9.86	7.94	4.65	12.63
EBITDA Margin %	9.42	8.80	6.36	13.10	12.67	12.57	10.49	13.20
Net Margin %	5.27	4.92	3.16	3.66	3.31	2.84	1.29	4.18
Asset Turnover	1.49	1.51	1.51	1.46	1.38	1.31	1.68	1.43
Price Range	32.63-16.70	25.55-16.70	25.94-16.70	22.00-14.83	25.06-14.98	25.05-15.05	24.00-14.63	22.25-12.06
P/E Ratio	18.13-9.28	15.97-10.44	18.93-12.19	17.05-11.50	26.66-15.94	36.30-21.81	75.00-45.70	27.13-14.71

Address: 2200 South 75th Avenue, Phoenix, AZ 85043
Telephone: 602-269-9700
Fax: 623-907-7380

Web Site: www.swifttrans.com
Officers: Robert W. Cunningham - Pres., C.E.O. William F. Riley III - Sr. Exec. V.P., Sec.

Auditors: KPMG LLP
Investor Contact: 602-269-9700
Transfer Agents: Mellon Investor Services, Los Angeles, CA

SYMANTEC CORP.

Exchange	Symbol	Price	52Wk Range	Yield	P/E
NMS	SYMC	$18.62 (8/31/2006)	24.00-14.89	N/A	266.00

*7 Year Price Score 108.57 *NYSE Composite Index=100 *12 Month Price Score 92.12

Interim Earnings (Per Share)

Qtr.	Jun	Sep	Dec	Mar
2003-04	0.09	0.12	0.16	0.17
2004-05	0.17	0.18	0.22	0.16
2005-06	0.27	(0.21)	0.08	0.11
2006-07	0.09	...	...	...

Interim Dividends (Per Share)

Amt	Decl	Ex	Rec	Pay
100%	12/17/2001	2/1/2002	1/17/2002	1/31/2002
100%	10/22/2003	11/20/2003	11/5/2003	11/19/2003
2-for-1	10/20/2004	12/1/2004	11/11/2004	11/30/2004

Valuation Analysis | **Institutional Holding**
Forecast P/E | 15.30 | No of Institutions
 | (9/9/2006) | 557
Market Cap | $18.4 Billion | Shares
Book Value | 12.9 Billion | 833,675,456
Price/Book | 1.42 | % Held
Price/Sales | 3.91 | 84.28

Business Summary: IT & Technology (MIC: 10.2 SIC: 7372 NAIC: 334611)
Symantec provides services to help individuals and enterprises assure the security, availability, and integrity of their digital assets. Co. provides Internet security and problem-solving products for individual users, home offices, and small businesses; endpoint security, messaging management, compliance, archiving, Windows back-up solutions, security response and managed security services, storage and server management, data protection, and application performance management solutions for enterprise and large enterprise customers; and, consulting and educational services. Co. operates in five segments: Consumer, Data Center Management, Security and Data Management, Services, and Other.

Recent Developments: For the quarter ended June 30 2006, net income decreased 52.3% to $94.8 million from $198.6 million in the year-earlier quarter. Revenues were $1.26 billion, up 79.9% from $699.9 million the year before. Operating income was $134.3 million versus $232.3 million in the prior-year quarter, a decrease of 42.2%. Direct operating expenses rose 157.5% to $300.8 million from $116.8 million in the comparable period the year before. Indirect operating expenses increased 134.9% to $824.1 million from $350.8 million in the equivalent prior-year period.

Prospects: Co.'s results reflect solid sales of its Norton Internet Security, Storage Foundation and enterprise messaging services, along with contributions from its services organization. Results are being further affected by Co.'s Jul 2005 acquisition of Veritas Software Corporation and the continued awareness of Internet-related threats around the world. Given its diversified business model and long-standing relationships with consumers and enterprises around the world, Co. anticipates revenue for fiscal 2007 in the range of $5.10 billion to $5.30 billion and earnings of $0.46 to $0.56 per diluted share.

Financial Data (US$ in Thousands)	3 Mos	03/31/2006	03/31/2005	03/31/2004	03/31/2003	03/31/2002	03/31/2001	03/31/2000
Earnings Per Share	0.07	0.15	0.74	0.54	0.39	(0.05)	0.12	0.34
Cash Flow Per Share	1.63	1.54	1.83	1.47	1.00	0.89	0.63	0.48
Tang Book Value Per Share	0.06	0.63	3.07	1.96	1.44	1.26	0.97	1.04
Income Statement								
Total Revenue	1,259,086	4,143,392	2,582,849	1,870,129	1,406,946	1,071,438	853,554	745,725
EBITDA	355,139	706,245	950,430	599,992	407,987	261,725	212,252	286,800
Depn & Amortn	193,246	325,526	79,979	74,863	60,894	239,027	104,729	42,895
Income Before Taxes	155,217	362,723	858,128	542,222	363,631	45,498	140,780	257,291
Income Taxes	60,426	205,871	321,969	171,603	115,193	73,649	76,844	87,143
Net Income	94,791	156,852	536,159	370,619	248,438	(28,151)	63,936	170,148
Average Shares	1,048,833	1,025,856	738,245	719,110	682,872	574,416	545,896	497,712
Balance Sheet								
Total Assets	18,988,731	17,913,183	5,614,221	4,456,498	3,265,730	2,502,605	1,791,581	846,027
Current Liabilities	3,416,139	3,477,567	1,701,023	1,287,040	894,624	579,098	412,717	226,517
Long-Term Obligations	2,100,000	24,916	4,408	606,019	406,727	603,631	2,363	1,553
Total Liabilities	6,050,963	4,244,712	1,908,768	2,030,290	1,501,351	1,182,729	415,080	228,070
Stockholders' Equity	12,937,768	13,668,471	3,705,453	2,426,208	1,764,379	1,319,876	1,376,501	617,957
Shares Outstanding	987,549	1,040,885	710,522	623,708	595,140	574,236	576,048	482,472
Statistical Record								
Return on Assets %	0.43	1.33	10.65	9.57	8.61	N.M.	4.85	24.08
Return on Equity %	0.63	1.81	17.49	17.64	16.11	N.M.	6.41	35.24
EBITDA Margin %	28.21	17.05	36.80	32.08	29.00	24.45	24.87	38.46
Net Margin %	7.53	3.79	20.76	19.82	17.66	N.M.	7.49	22.82
Asset Turnover	0.38	0.35	0.51	0.48	0.49	0.50	0.65	1.06
Current Ratio	1.46	1.12	2.17	2.21	2.22	2.70	1.89	2.41
Debt to Equity	0.16	N.M.	N.M.	0.25	0.34	0.46	N.M.	N.M.
Price Range	24.34-15.16	24.34-15.49	33.48-20.00	23.63-9.41	11.98-6.92	10.60-4.33	9.39-3.73	10.10-1.63
P/E Ratio	347.71-216.57	162.27-103.27	45.24-27.03	43.76-17.43	30.72-17.74	...	78.26-31.05	29.71-4.78

Address: 20330 Stevens Creek Blvd., Cupertino, CA 95014-2132
Telephone: 408-517-8000
Fax: 408-253-6060

Web Site: www.symantec.com
Officers: John W. Thompson - Chmn., C.E.O. Gary Bloom - Vice-Chmn., Co-Pres.

Auditors: KPMG LLP
Investor Contact: 408-517-8324
Transfer Agents: EquiServe Trust Company

SYNOPSYS INC

Exchange	Symbol	Price	52Wk Range	Yield	P/E
NMS	SNPS	$18.96 (8/31/2006)	22.96-17.18	N/A	N/A

*7 Year Price Score 68.41 *NYSE Composite Index=100 *12 Month Price Score 88.40

Interim Earnings (Per Share)

Qtr.	Jan	Apr	Jul	Oct
2002-03	0.23	0.14	0.30	0.28
2003-04	0.19	0.18	0.26	(0.17)
2004-05	(0.10)	(0.03)	0.12	(0.10)
2005-06	0.01	0.04	0.05	...

Interim Dividends (Per Share)

Amt	Decl	Ex	Rec	Pay
100%	8/20/2003	9/24/2003	9/2/2003	9/23/2003

Valuation Analysis   **Institutional Holding**

Forecast P/E	25.01	No of Institutions	
	(9/9/2006)	230	
Market Cap	$2.7 Billion	Shares	
Book Value	1.2 Billion	121,388,400	
Price/Book	2.30	% Held	
Price/Sales	2.49	84.59	

Business Summary: IT & Technology (MIC: 10.2 SIC: 7372 NAIC: 511210)

Synopsys is a provider of electronic design automation software and related services for semiconductor design. Co. provides technology semiconductor design and verification software platforms and integrated circuit manufacturing software products to the global electronics market, enabling the development and production of complex systems-on-chips. Also, Co. provides intellectual property and design services to simplify the design process, and accelerate time-to-market for its customers, and provides software and services to help customers prepare their designs for manufacturing.

Recent Developments: For the quarter ended July 31 2006, net income decreased 56.3% to $7.6 million from $17.3 million in the year-earlier quarter. Revenues were $277.2 million, up 10.2% from $251.5 million the year before. Operating income was $13.2 million versus a loss of $7.6 million in the prior-year quarter. Direct operating expenses declined 6.7% to $55.4 million from $59.4 million in the comparable period the year before. Indirect operating expenses increased 4.5% to $208.6 million from $199.7 million in the equivalent prior-year period.

Prospects: Co. remains focused on improving its customers' economics of design by providing more fully integrated design software. Accordingly, on Aug 16 2006, Co. announced that it has completed the acquisition of SIGMA-C™ Software AG, a provider of simulation software, for $20.5 million. The purchase should enable a tighter integration between design and manufacturing tools, allowing Co.'s customers to perform more accurate design layout analysis with 3D lithography simulation and understand yield issues for enhanced design for manufacturing implementation. For fiscal 2006 ending Oct 2006, Co. expects revenues to be about $1.08 billion to $1.09 billion, with earnings per share of $0.11 to $0.15.

Financial Data
(US$ in Thousands)

	9 Mos	6 Mos	3 Mos	10/31/2005	10/31/2004	10/31/2003	10/31/2002	10/31/2001
Earnings Per Share	...	0.07	...	(0.11)	0.46	0.95	(1.50)	0.44
Cash Flow Per Share	1.27	1.29	1.01	1.86	1.70	2.59	(1.35)	2.44
Tang Book Value Per Share	2.13	2.36	2.03	2.58	3.21	3.85	2.20	3.79
Income Statement								
Total Revenue	812,176	534,968	260,189	991,931	1,092,104	1,176,983	906,534	680,350
EBITDA	103,258	63,799	29,757	157,725	278,392	403,099	(172,840)	148,695
Depn & Amortn	85,546	57,974	29,729	175,057	192,774	184,110	116,100	65,162
Income Before Taxes	27,743	12,169	3,026	(7,789)	91,592	218,989	(288,940)	83,533
Income Taxes	13,121	5,097	1,329	7,689	17,255	69,265	(88,947)	26,731
Net Income	14,622	7,072	1,697	(15,478)	74,337	149,724	(199,993)	56,802
Average Shares	143,964	146,010	146,969	144,970	159,991	158,326	133,616	129,318
Balance Sheet								
Total Assets	2,065,381	2,131,760	2,070,031	2,141,476	2,092,187	2,307,353	1,978,714	1,128,907
Current Liabilities	787,859	818,687	794,214	816,680	741,155	804,959	777,369	626,127
Long-Term Obligations	...	...	...	...	...	...	...	73
Total Liabilities	908,842	933,285	900,174	922,540	827,138	873,943	865,233	643,251
Stockholders' Equity	1,156,539	1,198,475	1,169,857	1,218,936	1,265,049	1,433,410	1,113,481	485,656
Shares Outstanding	140,409	143,833	142,680	134,638	147,378	155,175	147,124	118,856
Statistical Record								
Return on Assets %	0.05	0.51	0.03	N.M.	3.37	6.99	N.M.	5.21
Return on Equity %	0.10	0.92	0.05	N.M.	5.49	11.76	N.M.	9.72
EBITDA Margin %	12.71	11.93	11.44	15.90	25.49	34.25	N.M.	21.86
Net Margin %	1.80	1.32	0.65	N.M.	6.81	12.72	N.M.	8.35
Asset Turnover	0.51	0.49	0.48	0.47	0.50	0.55	0.58	0.62
Current Ratio	0.99	1.15	1.09	1.16	1.23	1.54	1.20	1.26
Price Range	22.96-16.98	22.96-16.61	22.27-16.44	19.55-16.44	37.36-14.65	34.50-18.29	29.85-16.32	31.38-17.06
P/E Ratio	N.M.	328.00-237.29	N.M.	...	81.22-31.85	36.32-19.21	...	71.31-38.78

Address: 700 East Middlefield Road, Mountain View, CA 94043	Web Site: www.synopsys.com	Auditors: KPMG LLP
Telephone: 650-584-5000	Officers: Aart J. de Geus - Chmn., C.E.O. Chi-Foon Chan - Pres., C.O.O.	Investor Contact: 650-584-4257
Fax: 650-965-8637		

T ROWE PRICE GROUP INC.

Exchange	Symbol	Price	52Wk Range	Yield	P/E	Div Acheiver
NMS	TROW	$44.06 (8/31/2006)	44.06-30.45	1.27	13.19	19 Years

*7 Year Price Score 130.23 *NYSE Composite Index=100 *12 Month Price Score 105.16

Interim Earnings (Per Share)
Qtr.	Mar	Jun	Sep	Dec
2003	0.16	0.21	0.26	1.15
2004	0.29	0.30	0.31	1.61
2005	0.34	0.38	0.42	2.00
2006	0.42	0.49	...	...

Interim Dividends (Per Share)
Amt	Decl	Ex	Rec	Pay
0.14Q	3/10/2006	3/22/2006	3/24/2006	4/7/2006
2-for-1	6/8/2006	6/26/2006	6/19/2006	6/23/2006
0.14Q	6/8/2006	6/22/2006	6/26/2006	7/11/2006
0.14Q	9/7/2006	9/26/2006	9/28/2006	10/12/2006

Indicated Div: $0.56

Valuation Analysis
Forecast P/E: N/A

Institutional Holding
No of Institutions: 408
Shares: 158,730,560
% Held: 60.66

Market Cap: $11.6 Billion
Book Value: 2.1 Billion
Price/Book: 5.38
Price/Sales: 6.91

Business Summary: Wealth Management (MIC: 8.8 SIC: 6282 NAIC: 523930)

T. Rowe Price Group is a financial services holding company with total assets under management of $269.50 billion as of Dec 31 2005. Through its subsidiaries, Co. is engaged in providing investment advisory services to individual and institutional investors through the sponsored T. Rowe Price mutual funds and other investment portfolios. Co.'s assets under management are sourced approximately 20.0% to 30.0% from each of the following: third-party financial intermediaries that distribute its managed investment portfolios in the U.S. and foreign countries, individual U.S. investors, U.S. defined contribution retirement plans, and institutional investors in the U.S. and foreign countries.

Recent Developments: For the quarter ended June 30 2006, net income increased 32.1% to $135.7 million from $102.7 million in the year-earlier quarter. Revenues were $446.0 million, up 22.7% from $363.5 million the year before. Operating income was $192.9 million versus $155.5 million in the prior-year quarter, an increase of 24.0%. Indirect operating expenses increased 21.7% to $253.1 million from $208.0 million in the equivalent prior-year period.

Prospects: Co.'s operating results are benefiting from higher investment advisory revenues, reflecting an increase in its average asset under management. Going forward, Co. remains optimistic about the remainder of 2006 and believes that the financial markets can make moderate progress, despite investors less willing to take risks, coupled with several headwinds such as increased tension in the Middle East and rising global interest rates that could create a more challenging investment environment. However, Co. anticipates that equity investing may be less rewarding in the near-term. Also, Co. projects its advertising and promotion expenditures for 2006 to be about 10.0% higher than in 2005.

Financial Data
(US$ in Thousands)

	6 Mos	3 Mos	12/31/2005	12/31/2004	12/31/2003	12/31/2002	12/31/2001	12/31/2000
Earnings Per Share	3.34	3.23	3.15	2.51	1.77	1.52	1.52	2.08
Cash Flow Per Share	2.28	2.16	4.14	2.93	2.41	2.19	2.36	2.66
Tang Book Value Per Share	5.63	5.68	10.41	7.96	5.31	3.82	3.35	2.42
Dividends Per Share	0.535	0.510	0.485	0.400	0.350	0.325	0.305	0.270
Dividend Payout %	16.04	15.81	15.40	15.94	19.77	21.38	20.07	12.98
Income Statement								
Total Revenue	875,316	429,321	1,515,815	1,280,349	998,855	925,829	1,027,496	1,212,327
Income Before Taxes	402,492	186,082	679,391	533,783	365,516	309,604	330,589	458,192
Income Taxes	150,087	69,388	248,462	196,523	138,029	115,350	135,078	174,818
Net Income	252,405	116,694	430,929	337,260	227,487	194,254	195,868	269,029
Average Shares	279,684	277,962	136,598	134,135	128,289	127,706	129,045	129,600
Balance Sheet								
Total Assets	2,498,226	2,494,324	2,310,546	1,928,825	1,546,577	1,370,433	1,313,115	1,469,459
Total Liabilities	352,348	322,916	274,444	231,525	217,497	236,593	235,290	478,394
Stockholders' Equity	2,145,878	2,171,408	2,036,102	1,697,300	1,329,080	1,133,840	1,077,825	991,065
Shares Outstanding	262,168	265,078	131,678	129,607	124,932	122,648	123,088	122,439
Statistical Record								
Return on Assets %	21.30	20.16	20.33	19.36	15.60	14.48	14.08	21.75
Return on Equity %	24.64	23.10	23.09	22.23	18.47	17.57	18.93	30.47
Price Range	43.01-30.45	39.55-27.41	37.37-27.41	31.57-22.34	23.70-12.15	21.00-10.73	21.34-12.85	24.31-15.09
P/E Ratio	12.88-9.12	12.24-8.49	11.86-8.70	12.58-8.90	13.39-6.86	13.81-7.06	14.04-8.45	11.69-7.26
Average Yield %	1.49	1.52	1.54	1.54	1.94	2.02	1.76	1.34

Address: 100 East Pratt Street, Baltimore, MD 21202
Telephone: 410-345-2000
Fax: 410-752-3477

Web Site: www.troweprice.com
Officers: George A. Roche - Chmn., Pres., Interim C.F.O. James S. Riepe - Vice-Chmn., V.P.

Auditors: KPMG LLP
Investor Contact: 410-345-2124
Transfer Agents: Wells Fargo Bank Minnesota, N.A., St. Paul, MN

TD AMERITRADE HOLDING CORP

Exchange	Symbol	Price	52Wk Range	Yield	P/E
NMS	AMTD	$17.52 (8/31/2006)	26.10-13.64	N/A	18.06

7 Year Price Score 130.58 *NYSE Composite Index=100* **12 Month Price Score 79.39**

Interim Earnings (Per Share)

Qtr.	Dec	Mar	Jun	Sep
2002-03	0.05	0.02	0.12	0.13
2003-04	0.17	0.19	0.15	0.14
2004-05	0.22	0.17	0.18	0.24
2005-06	0.21	0.30	0.23	...

Interim Dividends (Per Share)
No Dividends Paid

Valuation Analysis / Institutional Holding

Forecast P/E	18.59	No of Institutions
(9/9/2006)		203
Market Cap	$10.7 Billion	Shares
Book Value	1.6 Billion	232,535,296
Price/Book	6.48	% Held
Price/Sales	5.79	38.07

Business Summary: Finance Intermediaries & Services (MIC: 8.7 SIC: 6211 NAIC: 523120)

TD Ameritrade Holding is a holding company. Co. is engaged in the business of providing securities brokerage services and technology-based financial services to retail investors and business partners, predominantly through the Internet. Co.'s customers include retail investors, traders, financial planners and institutions. Co. provides the following products and services to retail clients: touch-tone trading; trading over the Internet; unlimited, streaming, free real-time quotes; extended trading hours; direct access; and commitment to the speed of execution.

Recent Developments: For the quarter ended June 30 2006, net income increased 67.3% to $139.8 million from $83.6 million in the year-earlier quarter. Revenues were $638.9 million, up 134.0% from $273.0 million the year before. Direct operating expenses rose 171.2% to $124.4 million from $45.9 million in the comparable period the year before. Indirect operating expenses increased 166.5% to $279.2 million from $104.8 million in the equivalent prior-year period.

Prospects: Looking ahead to fiscal 2006, Co.'s earnings guidance has been tightened to $0.87 to $0.93 per share, excluding a one-time gain realized on the sale of its investment in Knight Capital Group, Inc. In addition, Co. is increasing its earnings projections for fiscal 2007 to range from $0.99 to $1.21 per share. Furthermore, Co. anticipates that the investments in its technology and brand throughout 2007 will enhance its growth and strengthen its market position going into 2008. Meanwhile, Co. continues to focus on completing the integration of its Jan 2006 acquisition of TD Waterhouse Group, Inc., while focusing on growth in its long-term investor segment.

Financial Data
(US$ in Thousands)

	9 Mos	6 Mos	3 Mos	09/30/2005	09/24/2004	09/26/2003	09/27/2002	09/28/2001
Earnings Per Share	0.97	0.92	0.80	0.82	0.64	0.32	(0.13)	(0.49)
Cash Flow Per Share	0.37	0.73	0.81	0.80	0.79	0.07	0.39	(0.26)
Tang Book Value Per Share	N.M.	N.M.	1.48	1.21	0.48	0.61	0.31	0.68
Dividends Per Share	6.000	6.000	...	...	...	...	...	...
Dividend Payout %	621.56	653.50	...	...	...	...	...	...

Income Statement

Total Revenue	1,543,811	904,889	327,015	1,144,552	921,974	731,065	443,053	498,677
Income Before Taxes	655,588	422,509	...	553,492	441,157	227,357	(18,517)	(146,392)
Income Taxes	256,939	163,677	54,303	213,739	168,810	90,715	10,446	(55,215)
Net Income	398,649	258,832	85,997	339,753	272,347	136,642	(28,963)	(91,177)
Average Shares	619,707	566,710	417,063	413,167	426,972	432,480	227,327	185,830

Balance Sheet

Total Assets	22,318,210	22,953,216	15,776,079	16,417,110	15,277,021	14,404,268	9,800,841	3,653,871
Total Liabilities	20,668,893	21,504,715	14,148,731	14,898,243	14,066,113	13,168,494	8,702,442	3,282,438
Stockholders' Equity	1,649,317	1,448,501	1,627,348	1,518,867	1,210,908	1,235,774	1,098,399	371,433
Shares Outstanding	609,901	601,422	406,994	406,058	407,210	429,784	432,106	215,178

Statistical Record

Return on Assets %	2.54	2.19	2.03	2.11	1.84	1.13	N.M.	N.M.
Return on Equity %	32.37	31.20	23.05	24.49	22.32	11.74	N.M.	N.M.
Price Range	26.10-14.32	26.10-10.20	24.65-10.17	22.01-10.17	17.26-9.39	13.00-3.42	6.90-3.11	17.75-3.51
P/E Ratio	26.91-14.76	28.37-11.09	30.81-12.71	26.84-12.40	26.97-14.67	40.63-10.69	...	...
Average Yield %	29.25	31.04	...	...	...	...	...	...

Address: 4211 South 102nd Street, Omaha, NE 68127
Telephone: 402-331-7856
Fax: 402-597-7789

Web Site: www.amtd.com
Officers: J. Joe Ricketts - Chmn. J. Peter Ricketts - Vice-Chmn., C.O.O., Exec. V.P., Sec.

Auditors: Deloitte & Touche LLP
Investor Contact: 402-597-5658

TECH DATA CORP.

Exchange	Symbol	Price	52Wk Range	Yield	P/E
NMS	TECD	$34.89 (8/31/2006)	42.55-34.02	N/A	N/A

*7 Year Price Score 84.20 *NYSE Composite Index=100 *12 Month Price Score 93.97

Interim Earnings (Per Share)

Qtr.	Apr	Jul	Oct	Jan
2003-04	0.38	0.30	0.46	0.67
2004-05	0.59	0.52	0.64	0.99
2005-06	0.56	(1.02)	0.40	0.50
2006-07	0.23	(2.81)	...	...

Interim Dividends (Per Share)
No Dividends Paid

Valuation Analysis | **Institutional Holding**
Forecast P/E	17.85	No of Institutions
	(9/9/2006)	183
Market Cap	$1.9 Billion	Shares
Book Value	1.6 Billion	51,272,960
Price/Book	1.18	% Held
Price/Sales	0.09	92.31

Business Summary: IT & Technology (MIC: 10.2 SIC: 5045 NAIC: 423430)
Tech Data is a distributor of information technology (IT) products, logistics management and other value-added services worldwide. Co. offers more than 100,000 products of these products to over 90,000 value-added resellers (VARs), direct marketers, retailers and corporate resellers in more than 100 countries throughout the U.S., Europe, Canada, Latin America, the Caribbean, and the Middle East and Africa (EMEA). As of Jan 31 2006, Co. operated a total of 28 logistics centers, 13 of which were located in the Americas and 15 in the EMEA to provide the delivery of its products to customers.

Recent Developments: For the quarter ended July 31 2006, net loss amounted to $155.5 million versus a net loss of $59.4 million in the year-earlier quarter. Revenues were $4.94 billion, up 2.7% from $4.81 billion the year before. Operating loss was $130.8 million versus an income of $12.8 million in the prior-year quarter. Direct operating expenses rose 3.1% to $4.72 billion from $4.57 billion in the comparable period the year before. Indirect operating expenses increased 56.9% to $356.5 million from $227.1 million in the equivalent prior-year period.

Prospects: Co.'s results are being hindered by challenging market conditions in the EMEA (Europe, Middle East and Africa) regions, coupled with distractions resulting from EMEA's restructuring program in May 2006. Nevertheless, Co. remains optimistic regarding the potential viability of this restructuring program in positively aligning EMEA's operating cost structure with the existing business environment and improving its overall operating capabilities over the long-term. For the third fiscal quarter ending Oct 31 2006, Co. anticipates net sales to be in the range of $5.10 billion to $5.25 billion.

Financial Data
(US$ in Thousands)

	6 Mos	3 Mos	01/31/2006	01/31/2005	01/31/2004	01/31/2003	01/31/2002	01/31/2001
Earnings Per Share	(1.68)	0.11	0.45	2.74	1.81	(3.55)	1.98	3.14
Cash Flow Per Share	7.44	6.39	4.46	1.83	5.34	2.22	17.95	(1.86)
Tang Book Value Per Share	29.60	29.89	28.94	30.14	26.29	23.65	17.87	16.65
Income Statement								
Total Revenue	9,887,407	4,944,126	20,482,851	19,790,333	17,406,340	15,738,945	17,197,511	20,427,679
EBITDA	(80,497)	39,278	209,720	293,945	222,593	(58,796)	286,747	430,562
Depn & Amortn	26,436	13,009	53,744	55,472	55,084	49,849	63,488	63,922
Income Before Taxes	(120,239)	19,273	131,980	215,606	150,943	(132,690)	167,840	274,355
Income Taxes	26,345	10,328	109,013	53,146	46,796	67,128	57,063	96,033
Net Income	(142,638)	12,891	26,586	162,460	104,147	(199,818)	110,777	177,983
Average Shares	55,307	56,265	58,414	59,193	57,501	56,256	60,963	53,234
Balance Sheet								
Total Assets	4,004,675	4,288,579	4,404,634	4,557,736	4,167,886	3,248,018	3,458,330	4,615,545
Current Liabilities	2,322,065	2,438,581	2,591,351	2,567,872	2,154,872	1,578,835	1,585,610	3,098,985
Long-Term Obligations	14,243	14,521	14,378	17,215	307,934	314,498	612,335	320,757
Total Liabilities	2,374,955	2,491,613	2,644,327	2,630,265	2,509,397	1,909,488	2,197,945	3,419,742
Stockholders' Equity	1,629,720	1,796,966	1,760,307	1,927,471	1,658,489	1,338,530	1,259,933	1,195,314
Shares Outstanding	54,962	55,527	56,191	58,984	57,717	56,483	55,454	53,796
Statistical Record								
Return on Assets %	N.M.	0.13	0.59	3.71	2.81	N.M.	2.74	4.06
Return on Equity %	N.M.	0.32	1.44	9.04	6.95	N.M.	9.02	16.07
EBITDA Margin %	N.M.	0.79	1.02	1.49	1.28	N.M.	1.67	2.11
Net Margin %	N.M.	0.26	0.13	0.82	0.60	N.M.	0.64	0.87
Asset Turnover	5.03	4.61	4.57	4.52	4.69	4.69	4.26	4.66
Current Ratio	1.60	1.59	1.54	1.58	1.71	1.89	1.87	1.31
Debt to Equity	0.01	0.01	0.01	0.01	0.19	0.23	0.49	0.27
Price Range	42.55-34.39	42.55-34.39	43.50-33.90	45.67-33.27	42.63-19.50	51.17-24.10	50.52-26.19	54.31-20.94
P/E Ratio	...	386.82-312.64	96.67-75.33	16.67-12.14	23.55-10.77	...	25.52-13.23	17.30-6.67

Address: 5350 Tech Data Drive, Clearwater, FL 33760 **Telephone:** 727-539-7429 **Fax:** 727-538-7808	**Web Site:** www.techdata.com **Officers:** Steven A. Raymund - Chmn., C.E.O. Jeffery P. Howells - Exec. V.P., C.F.O.	**Auditors:** ERNST & YOUNG LLP **Investor Contact:** 800-292-7906

TECUMSEH PRODUCTS CO.

Exchange	Symbol	Price	52Wk Range	Yield	P/E
NMS	TECU B	$14.32 (8/31/2006)	26.21-13.70	N/A	N/A

*7 Year Price Score 40.73 *NYSE Composite Index=100 *12 Month Price Score 79.71

Interim Earnings (Per Share)

Qtr.	Mar	Jun	Sep	Dec
2003	0.13	(0.35)	1.03	(0.80)
2004	0.34	0.22	0.67	(0.71)
2005	(0.67)	(6.63)	(1.77)	(3.02)
2006	(0.52)	1.82	...	...

Interim Dividends (Per Share)

Amt	Decl	Ex	Rec	Pay
0.32Q	8/25/2004	9/8/2004	9/10/2004	9/24/2004
0.32Q	11/19/2004	12/1/2004	12/3/2004	12/17/2004
0.32Q	2/23/2005	3/9/2005	3/11/2005	3/25/2005
0.32Q	5/26/2005	6/8/2005	6/10/2005	6/24/2005

Valuation Analysis

Forecast P/E	N/A
Market Cap	$264.6 Million
Book Value	860.9 Million
Price/Book	0.31
Price/Sales	0.15

Institutional Holding

No of Institutions	28
Shares	4,718,384
% Held	92.92

Business Summary: Purpose Machinery (MIC: 11.13 SIC: 3585 NAIC: 333415)

Tecumseh Products is a full-line global manufacturer of hermetic compressors for residential and commercial refrigerators, freezers, water coolers, dehumidifiers, window air conditioning units and residential and commercial central system air conditioners and heat pumps. In addition, Co. manufactures electric motors and components, gasoline engines and power trains for lawn mowers, lawn and garden tractors, garden tillers, string trimmers, snow throwers, industrial and agricultural applications and recreational vehicles. Co. also produces a line of pump products such as centrifugal pumps, sump pumps and small submersible pumps for industrial, commercial, marine and agricultural applications.

Recent Developments: For the quarter ended June 30 2006, loss from continuing operations was $29.1 million compared with a loss of $124.3 million in the year-earlier quarter. Net income amounted to $33.7 million versus a net loss of $122.5 million in the year-earlier quarter. Revenues were $456.3 million, up 5.4% from $432.8 million the year before. Operating loss was $25.3 million versus a loss of $120.1 million in the prior-year quarter. Direct operating expenses rose 7.5% to $432.3 million from $402.2 million in the comparable period the year before. Indirect operating expenses decreased 67.3% to $49.3 million from $150.7 million in the equivalent prior-year period.

Prospects: Co.'s outlook for the remainder of 2006 appears to be somewhat unfavorable, reflecting the continued rise in key commodity costs particularly copper, aluminum and steel. Nevertheless, Co. also expects results for 2006 to reflect its initiatives implemented across all business segments. For instance, Co.'s Compressor and Electrical Components groups introduced both price increases and commodity surcharges effective June and July 2006 as an attempt to mitigate rising commodity prices. Additionally, Co. will continue its focus on further improvement of its worldwide operations, potentially through additional production relocation and consolidation initiatives during 2006 and/or 2007.

Financial Data
(US$ in Thousands)

	6 Mos	3 Mos	12/31/2005	12/31/2004	12/31/2003	12/31/2002	12/31/2001	12/31/2000
Earnings Per Share	(3.49)	(11.94)	(12.09)	0.55	0.01	2.76	2.30	3.44
Cash Flow Per Share	(1.21)	2.10	0.87	0.28	4.65	7.12	9.30	6.95
Tang Book Value Per Share	36.82	43.82	34.02	38.55	37.19	38.34	50.47	50.24
Dividends Per Share	...	0.320	0.640	1.280	1.280	1.280	1.280	1.280
Dividend Payout %	...	...	...	232.73	12,800.00	46.38	55.65	37.21
Income Statement								
Total Revenue	902,400	446,100	1,847,000	1,911,700	1,819,000	1,343,800	1,398,900	1,649,900
EBITDA	(28,700)	(6,300)	(72,900)	141,000	119,800	154,700	136,500	185,800
Depn & Amortn	...	...	92,300	102,900	97,600	65,100	72,000	71,200
Income Before Taxes	(48,100)	(14,700)	(196,300)	15,400	(600)	83,800	60,400	107,900
Income Taxes	(9,900)	(5,600)	27,200	5,300	(700)	29,700	17,600	41,800
Net Income	24,100	(9,600)	(223,500)	10,100	100	51,000	42,800	66,100
Average Shares	18,480	18,480	18,479	18,479	18,479	18,479	18,607	20,276
Balance Sheet								
Total Assets	1,863,900	1,870,600	1,800,500	2,062,800	2,105,800	2,063,000	1,519,800	1,553,100
Current Liabilities	485,700	473,900	405,100	421,500	434,600	451,400	253,800	280,300
Long-Term Obligations	221,400	281,800	283,000	317,300	327,600	298,200	13,700	14,200
Total Liabilities	1,003,000	1,047,400	986,100	1,044,500	1,101,000	1,084,100	542,100	557,700
Stockholders' Equity	860,900	823,200	814,400	1,018,300	1,004,800	978,900	977,700	995,400
Shares Outstanding	18,479	14,631	18,479	18,479	18,479	18,479	18,479	18,880
Statistical Record								
Return on Assets %	N.M.	N.M.	N.M.	0.48	0.00	2.85	2.79	4.24
Return on Equity %	N.M.	N.M.	N.M.	1.00	0.01	5.21	4.34	6.56
EBITDA Margin %	N.M.	N.M.	N.M.	7.38	6.59	11.51	9.76	11.26
Net Margin %	2.67	N.M.	N.M.	0.53	0.01	3.80	3.06	4.01
Asset Turnover	0.96	0.94	0.96	0.91	0.87	0.75	0.91	1.06
Current Ratio	1.66	1.78	1.99	2.20	2.26	2.12	3.39	3.15
Debt to Equity	0.26	0.34	0.35	0.31	0.33	0.30	0.01	0.01
Price Range	30.40-15.87	39.99-17.81	45.77-17.81	48.12-35.40	47.50-33.82	51.99-35.50	50.50-36.63	45.75-34.50
P/E Ratio	...	...	...	87.49-64.36	N.M.	18.84-12.86	21.96-15.92	13.30-10.03
Average Yield %	...	1.32	2.21	3.05	3.27	2.85	2.85	3.15

Address: 100 East Patterson Street, Tecumseh, MI 49286	**Web Site:** www.tecumseh.com	**Auditors:** PricewaterhouseCoopers LLP
Telephone: 517-423-8411	**Officers:** Todd W. Herrick - Chmn., Pres., C.E.O.	**Investor Contact:** 517-423-8455
Fax: 517-423-8760	Michael R. Forman - V.P., Corp. Dir., Human Res.	

TELLABS, INC.

Exchange	Symbol	Price	52Wk Range	Yield	P/E
NMS	TLAB	$10.19 (8/31/2006)	17.09-8.58	N/A	19.23

*7 Year Price Score 45.55 *NYSE Composite Index=100 *12 Month Price Score 84.19

Interim Earnings (Per Share)

Qtr.	Mar	Jun	Sep	Dec
2003	(0.10)	(0.22)	(0.16)	(0.05)
2004	0.03	0.12	0.11	(0.33)
2005	0.00	0.09	0.09	0.21
2006	0.11	0.12	...	...

Interim Dividends (Per Share)
No Dividends Paid

Valuation Analysis | **Institutional Holding**
Forecast P/E | 18.00 | No of Institutions
 | (9/9/2006) | 364
Market Cap | $4.6 Billion | Shares
Book Value | 2.9 Billion | 324,224,224
Price/Book | 1.57 | % Held
Price/Sales | 2.22 | 72.36

Business Summary: Communications (MIC: 10.1 SIC: 3661 NAIC: 334210)
Tellabs is engaged in the designing and marketing of communications equipment to telecommunications service providers around the world. Co.'s products and services help deliver wireline services, wireless services and broadband data networking for business and residential customers and bundled voice, video and high-speed Internet/data services. Co.'s customer base includes incumbent local exchange carriers, wireless service operators, post telephone and telegraph administrations, independent operating companies, original equipment manufacturers, cable and multiple system operators, competitive local exchange carriers, system integrators and alternate service providers.

Recent Developments: For the quarter ended June 30 2006, net income increased 30.2% to $53.5 million from $41.1 million in the year-earlier quarter. Revenues were $549.3 million, up 18.8% from $462.5 million the year before. Operating income was $79.9 million versus $46.1 million in the prior-year quarter, an increase of 73.3%. Direct operating expenses rose 15.6% to $295.1 million from $255.3 million in the comparable period the year before. Indirect operating expenses increased 8.2% to $174.3 million from $161.1 million in the equivalent prior-year period.

Prospects: Looking ahead, Co. expects the migration of its customers to the "triple-play" of voice, data and video wireless services such as mobile video and Internet to drive further growth in its transport business. Moreover, Co. plans to extend fiber access technology to an additional 3 million homes in 2006. For the 2006 third quarter, Co. projects revenue in the range of $510.0 million to $535.0 million, which represents a growth of 10.0% to 15.0% above the third quarter of 2005. Co. also expects margin, excluding equity based compensation expense, to be in the range of 46.0% to 47.0% depending on product and services mix. Further, Co. targets operating expenses to be flat to slightly down.

Financial Data (US$ in Thousands)	6 Mos	3 Mos	12/30/2005	12/31/2004	01/02/2004	12/27/2002	12/28/2001	12/29/2000
Earnings Per Share	0.53	0.50	0.39	(0.07)	(0.58)	(0.76)	(0.44)	1.75
Cash Flow Per Share	0.61	0.58	0.58	0.51	0.36	0.43	1.03	1.04
Tang Book Value Per Share	3.78	3.60	3.53	3.34	3.76	4.45	5.55	6.26
Income Statement								
Total Revenue	1,064,000	514,700	1,883,400	1,231,800	980,400	1,317,000	2,199,747	3,387,435
EBITDA	194,800	96,300	327,200	51,700	(156,000)	(207,100)	(133,611)	1,170,134
Depn & Amortn	51,600	25,600	142,400	88,800	121,400	153,100	157,509	116,209
Income Before Taxes	165,100	81,200	213,100	(10,200)	(244,700)	(327,800)	(244,755)	1,109,426
Income Taxes	59,200	28,800	37,300	19,600	(3,100)	(14,700)	(62,779)	349,469
Net Income	105,900	52,400	175,800	(29,800)	(241,600)	(313,100)	(181,976)	730,796
Average Shares	458,500	460,000	454,500	420,200	413,100	411,400	409,569	418,385
Balance Sheet								
Total Assets	3,646,000	3,558,900	3,514,900	3,522,500	2,607,500	2,622,800	2,865,785	3,073,067
Current Liabilities	554,200	542,900	525,200	524,200	207,800	257,300	319,545	412,345
Long-Term Obligations	...	...	...	...	...	...	3,390	2,850
Total Liabilities	736,100	720,900	700,200	725,300	388,200	332,500	400,170	445,483
Stockholders' Equity	2,909,900	2,838,000	2,814,700	2,797,200	2,219,300	2,290,300	2,465,615	2,627,584
Shares Outstanding	447,687	448,087	449,384	463,660	414,609	412,190	410,247	408,182
Statistical Record								
Return on Assets %	6.81	6.54	5.01	N.M.	N.M.	N.M.	N.M.	27.01
Return on Equity %	8.63	8.29	6.28	N.M.	N.M.	N.M.	N.M.	31.34
EBITDA Margin %	18.31	18.71	17.37	4.20	N.M.	N.M.	N.M.	34.54
Net Margin %	9.95	10.18	9.33	N.M.	N.M.	N.M.	N.M.	21.57
Asset Turnover	0.58	0.57	0.54	0.40	0.37	0.48	0.74	1.25
Current Ratio	3.60	3.53	3.57	3.47	7.21	5.96	6.09	5.63
Price Range	17.09-8.58	15.95-6.66	11.23-6.66	11.00-7.44	9.54-5.57	17.19-4.07	67.00-9.30	74.94-40.63
P/E Ratio	32.25-16.19	31.90-13.32	28.79-17.08	...	...	...	...	42.82-23.21

Address: One Tellabs Center, 1415 West Diehl Road, Naperville, IL 60563
Telephone: 630-798-8800
Web Site: www.tellabs.com
Officers: Michael J. Birck - Chmn. Krish A. Prabhu - Pres., C.E.O.
Auditors: ERNST & YOUNG LLP
Transfer Agents: ComputerShare Investor Services, Chicago, IL

TEVA PHARMACEUTICAL INDUSTRIES LTD

Exchange	Symbol	Price	52Wk Range	Yield	P/E
NMS	TEVA	$34.76 (8/31/2006)	45.53-29.76	0.69	21.86

*7 Year Price Score 133.12 *NYSE Composite Index=100 *12 Month Price Score 84.05

Interim Earnings (Per Share)
No earnings information available

Interim Dividends (Per Share)

Amt	Decl	Ex	Rec	Pay
0.052Q	...	11/10/2005	11/15/2005	12/7/2005
0.061Q	...	3/6/2006	3/8/2006	3/30/2006
0.063Q	...	5/12/2006	5/16/2006	6/7/2006
0.064Q	...	8/11/2006	8/15/2006	9/8/2006

Indicated Div: $0.24

Valuation Analysis

Forecast P/E	N/A	**Institutional Holding**
Market Cap	$22.5 Billion	No of Institutions 614
Book Value	6.0 Billion	Shares 467,933,632
Price/Book	3.72	% Held 72.36
Price/Sales	4.28	

Business Summary: Pharmaceuticals (MIC: 9.1 SIC: 2834 NAIC: 325412)

Teva Pharmaceutical Industries is a global pharmaceutical company. Co. operates a global pharmaceutical operation focused on supplying generic drugs and proprietary branded products for specific niche categories, such as its branded drug Copaxone® for multiple sclerosis. Co.'s active pharmaceutical ingredients business is engaged in sales to third party manufacturers and the timely delivery of significant raw materials. Co.'s operations are conducted directly and through subsidiaries in Israel, Europe, North America and several other jurisdictions.

Recent Developments: For the quarter ended June 30 2006, net income more than doubled to $488.4 million compared with $241.2 million in the equivalent period of the previous year. Results for 2006 included a pre-tax charge of $27.8 million for impairment and restructuring expenses. Net sales advanced 77.0% to $2.17 billion from $1.23 billion in the year-earlier quarter. Gross profit increased to $1.17 billion, or 53.9% of net sales, from $581.8 million, or 47.4% of net sales, the year before. Operating income more than doubled to $647.4 million versus $308.6 million in the prior-year period.

Prospects: Co. is pleased with its performance, particularly the launch of Simvastatin. The launch demonstrated Co.'s business model, the flexibility of its global supply chain, and its strategy execution. As a result, Co. is well-positioned to continue to capitalize on its strengths and address the opportunities of its global marketplace. Meanwhile, Co. is making progress on the IVAX integration, which is accretive to earnings. Going forward, Co. expects full-year 2006 sales to reach approximately $8.50 billion. In addition, Co. is increasing its previously announced 2006 earnings per share range from $2.02 to $2.15 to a range of $2.15 to $2.25.

Financial Data
(US$ in Thousands)

	12/31/2005	12/31/2004	12/31/2003	12/31/2002	12/31/2001	12/31/2000	12/31/1999	12/31/1998
Earnings Per Share	1.59	0.50	1.16	0.76	0.51	0.28	...	...
Cash Flow Per Share	2.22	2.03	1.17	0.67	0.52	0.32	...	...
Tang Book Value Per Share	5.54	4.49	4.76	2.41	1.55	1.05	0.90	0.98
Income Statement								
Total Revenue	5,250,400	4,798,900	3,276,400	2,518,600	2,077,370	1,749,854	1,282,406	1,115,928
EBITDA	1,555,600	798,200	1,005,800	620,900	477,766	350,146	192,127	122,173
Depn & Amortn	242,700	220,400	128,400	96,900	109,844	95,770	...	...
Income Before Taxes	1,308,600	603,700	872,400	499,400	340,357	208,361	161,962	98,845
Income Taxes	236,200	267,200	181,500	84,800	63,650	59,568	44,335	30,888
Net Income	1,072,300	331,800	691,000	410,300	278,212	148,417	117,833	68,830
Average Shares	680,800	688,000	608,800	561,600	561,844	527,356	503,520	501,208
Balance Sheet								
Total Assets	10,387,400	9,632,000	5,915,900	4,626,800	3,460,152	2,855,618	1,714,019	1,435,998
Current Liabilities	2,260,100	2,203,900	1,694,900	1,524,200	738,121	783,755	537,572	537,645
Long-Term Obligations	1,313,900	1,513,400	449,900	810,000	910,000	550,000	...	...
Total Liabilities	4,337,100	4,232,200	2,619,800	2,792,500	2,077,311	1,702,635	971,719	776,411
Stockholders' Equity	6,042,300	5,388,900	3,289,400	1,829,400	1,380,677	1,151,346	742,283	658,806
Shares Outstanding	646,700	626,800	555,400	526,400	512,344	511,668	500,108	498,216
Statistical Record								
Return on Assets %	10.71	4.26	13.11	10.15	8.81	6.48	7.48	5.25
Return on Equity %	18.76	7.63	27.00	25.56	21.98	15.63	16.82	10.83
EBITDA Margin %	29.63	16.63	30.70	24.65	23.00	20.01	14.98	10.95
Net Margin %	20.42	6.91	21.09	16.29	13.39	8.48	9.19	6.17
Asset Turnover	0.52	0.62	0.62	0.62	0.66	0.76	0.81	0.85
Current Ratio	2.44	1.91	2.19	1.90	2.95	2.05	1.69	1.44
Debt to Equity	0.22	0.28	0.14	0.44	0.66	0.48	...	...
Price Range	45.53-26.89	34.27-23.65	30.66-17.34	19.78-12.98	18.26-12.72	19.50-8.03	8.96-4.98	6.25-4.02
P/E Ratio	28.64-16.91	68.55-47.30	26.44-14.95	26.03-17.07	35.81-24.94	69.64-28.68	...	...

Address: 5 Basel St., P.O. Box 3190, Petach Tikva, 49131	**Web Site:** www.tevapharm.com
Telephone: 392-672-67	**Officers:** Israel Makov - Pres., C.E.O. George S. Barrett - Grp. V.P., North America, Pres., C.E.O., Teva North America
Fax: 392-340-50	
	Auditors: Kesselman & Kesselman
	Investor Contact: 972-392-67554

TEXAS REGIONAL BANCSHARES, INC.

Exchange	Symbol	Price	52Wk Range	Yield	P/E	Div Achiever
NMS	TRBS	$38.27 (8/31/2006)	38.27-24.49	1.46	26.03	11 Years

*7 Year Price Score 121.44 *NYSE Composite Index=100 *12 Month Price Score 124.17

Interim Earnings (Per Share)

Qtr.	Mar	Jun	Sep	Dec
2003	0.32	0.47	0.32	0.33
2004	0.34	0.52	0.36	0.39
2005	0.44	0.40	0.36	0.42
2006	0.42	0.27	...	...

Interim Dividends (Per Share)

Amt	Decl	Ex	Rec	Pay
0.109Q	12/13/2005	12/28/2005	12/30/2005	1/13/2006
10%	3/14/2006	3/29/2006	3/31/2006	4/13/2006
0.14Q	3/14/2006	3/29/2006	3/31/2006	4/13/2006
0.14Q	6/11/2006	6/28/2006	6/30/2006	7/14/2006

Indicated Div: $0.56

Valuation Analysis

Forecast P/E N/A

Market Cap $2.1 Billion
Book Value 656.2 Million
Price/Book 3.19
Price/Sales 4.41

Institutional Holding

No of Institutions 140
Shares 31,583,850
% Held 57.63

Business Summary: Commercial Banking (MIC: 8.1 SIC: 6022 NAIC: 522110)

Texas Regional Bancshares is a holding company. Through its subsidiaries, Co. provides community banking services to individuals and businesses in Texas, including checking accounts, savings accounts, certificates of deposits, and individual retirement accounts; short-term loans for working capital purposes, construction financing, commercial and residential mortgage loans, term loans for fixed asset and expansion needs, and consumer loans; travelers' checks, money orders, and safe deposit facilities; internet banking, international banking, and trust services; and, general line insurance products, title insurance products, mortgage banking services and full service broker-dealer services.

Recent Developments: For the quarter ended June 30 2006, net income decreased 32.7% to $14.8 million from $21.9 million in the year-earlier quarter. Net interest income increased 8.2% to $62.9 million from $58.1 million in the year-earlier quarter. Provision for loan losses was $16.7 million versus $5.8 million in the prior-year quarter, an increase of 188.7%. Non-interest income fell 2.4% to $20.4 million from $20.9 million, while non-interest expense advanced 13.8% to $44.6 million.

Prospects: On June 12 2006, Co. announced that it has signed a definitive agreement under which it will be acquired by Banco Bilbao Vizcaya Argentaria, S.A. (BBVA). According to the terms of the agreement, Co. will become a wholly-owned subsidiary of BBVA, which operates in 32 countries and is based in Spain. Under the terms of the definitive agreement, the all cash transaction is valued at over $2.16 billion, based upon a purchase price of $38.90 per share of Texas Regional common stock. The transaction is subject to the approval of Texas Regional's shareholders and regulatory approval in both the U.S. and Spain. It is expected to close during the fourth quarter of 2006.

Financial Data
(US$ in Thousands)

	6 Mos	3 Mos	12/31/2005	12/31/2004	12/31/2003	12/31/2002	12/31/2001	12/31/2000
Earnings Per Share	1.47	1.60	1.61	1.45	1.27	1.13	0.89	0.80
Cash Flow Per Share	2.04	2.30	2.44	2.25	2.50	1.45	1.21	1.21
Tang Book Value Per Share	8.04	8.02	7.76	7.15	7.74	6.87	5.19	4.28
Dividends Per Share	0.498	0.467	0.418	0.333	0.291	0.246	0.220	0.195
Dividend Payout %	33.85	29.17	25.99	23.06	22.86	21.79	24.69	24.28
Income Statement								
Interest Income	208,163	100,816	355,327	272,057	208,777	201,705	183,302	181,537
Interest Expense	83,655	39,176	118,817	67,807	60,385	71,986	83,776	86,513
Net Interest Income	124,508	61,640	236,510	204,250	148,392	129,719	99,526	95,024
Provision for Losses	21,620	4,871	26,071	20,583	13,155	12,331	8,667	8,927
Non-Interest Income	40,217	19,776	83,849	67,880	39,415	35,218	27,717	21,562
Non-Interest Expense	86,331	41,736	161,163	142,810	91,890	76,159	59,344	53,544
Income Before Taxes	56,774	34,809	133,923	114,592	93,602	81,232	60,728	54,127
Income Taxes	19,004	11,798	45,555	37,934	31,293	27,385	21,306	18,825
Net Income	37,770	23,011	88,368	76,658	62,309	53,847	39,422	35,302
Average Shares	55,191	54,936	54,873	53,189	49,002	47,657	36,084	43,962
Balance Sheet								
Net Loans & Leases	4,113,188	4,053,716	4,059,588	3,705,495	2,488,460	2,239,414	1,688,951	1,568,369
Total Assets	6,846,144	6,633,994	6,588,319	5,839,347	4,217,936	3,835,187	2,590,812	2,426,097
Total Deposits	5,478,860	5,606,576	5,393,311	4,760,840	3,516,435	3,132,191	2,235,877	2,109,748
Total Liabilities	6,189,989	5,977,474	5,945,827	5,245,289	3,796,205	3,457,732	2,325,553	2,198,393
Stockholders' Equity	656,155	656,520	642,492	594,058	421,731	377,455	265,259	227,704
Shares Outstanding	54,766	54,764	54,683	54,508	48,626	48,075	44,203	43,806
Statistical Record								
Return on Assets %	1.23	1.38	1.42	1.52	1.55	1.68	1.57	1.55
Return on Equity %	12.59	13.93	14.29	15.05	15.59	16.76	15.99	16.93
Net Interest Margin %	58.57	61.14	66.56	75.08	71.08	64.31	54.30	52.34
Efficiency Ratio %	34.90	34.61	36.70	42.01	37.02	32.15	28.12	26.36
Loans to Deposits	0.75	0.72	0.75	0.78	0.71	0.71	0.76	0.74
Price Range	38.03-24.49	29.49-24.49	29.75-24.49	32.62-22.05	22.90-17.27	19.97-13.26	14.80-10.47	12.26-7.43
P/E Ratio	25.87-16.66	18.43-15.31	18.48-15.21	22.50-15.21	18.03-13.60	17.67-11.73	16.63-11.76	15.32-9.29
Average Yield %	1.77	1.74	1.56	1.25	1.42	1.43	1.67	2.18

Address: 3900 North 10th Street, 11th Floor, McAllen, TX 78502-5910 **Telephone:** 956-631-5400	**Web Site:** www.trbsinc.com **Officers:** Glen E. Roney - Chmn., Pres., C.E.O. Paul S. Moxley - Sr. Exec. V.P.	**Auditors:** KPMG LLP **Investor Contact:** 956-632-7608 **Transfer Agents:** Computershare Investor Services, LLC

3COM CORP.

Exchange	Symbol	Price	52Wk Range	Yield	P/E
NMS	COMS	$4.44 (8/31/2006)	5.62-3.39	N/A	N/A

7 Year Price Score 56.72 *NYSE Composite Index=100 *12 Month Price Score 102.71

Interim Earnings (Per Share)
Qtr.	Aug	Nov	Feb	May
2001-02	(0.67)	(0.30)	(0.67)	(0.06)
2002-03	(0.09)	(0.19)	(0.22)	(0.11)
2003-04	(0.29)	(0.37)	(0.22)	(0.04)
2004-05	(0.09)	(0.13)	(0.14)	(0.15)
2005-06	(0.11)	(0.03)	(0.08)	(0.04)

Interim Dividends (Per Share)
Amt	Decl	Ex	Rec	Pay
0.00U	5/8/2000	7/28/2000	7/11/2000	7/27/2000

Valuation Analysis / Institutional Holding
Forecast P/E	30.01	
	(9/9/2006)	No of Institutions 236
Market Cap	$1.7 Billion	Shares
Book Value	1.2 Billion	262,859,872
Price/Book	1.45	% Held
Price/Sales	2.20	66.70

Business Summary: IT & Technology (MIC: 10.2 SIC: 3577 NAIC: 334119)

3Com is engaged in providing secure, converged networking solutions, as well as maintenance and support services, for enterprises and public sector organizations of all sizes. Co. is organized in two reportable segments: Secured Converged Networking SCN and H-3C. The SCN reportable segment was comprised of all business activities outside of the joint venture in China. The H-3C segment was comprised of operations of Co.'s joint venture in China. Co.'s products and services can generally be classified in the following categories: Security; IP Telephony; Networking; and Services.

Recent Developments: For the year ended May 31 2006, loss from continuing operations was $100.7 million compared with a loss of $195.7 million a year earlier. Net loss amounted to $100.7 million versus a net loss of $195.7 million in the prior year. Revenues were $794.8 million, up 22.0% from $651.2 million the year before. Operating loss was $157.1 million versus a loss of $203.5 million in the prior year. Direct operating expenses rose 12.0% to $466.7 million from $416.9 million in the comparable period the year before. Indirect operating expenses increased 10.8% to $485.2 million from $437.8 million in the equivalent prior-year period.

Prospects: In an effort to create a business model that Co. believes supports long-term profitability and growth, Co. is implementing a multi-faceted restructuring plan. The plan focuses on reducing components of Co.'s secure and converged netowrking (SCN) segment cost structure in order to achieve future profitability. The plan includes the closure of approximately 21 facilities around the world, a reduction in workforce of about 250 employees, and focusing its sales, marketing and services efforts. As a result of the realignment, Co. expects to record restructuring charges of approximately $10.0 million to $13.0 million. These actions are expected to be substantially completed by Dec 31 2006.

Financial Data
(US$ in Thousands)

	05/31/2006	05/31/2005	05/28/2004	05/30/2003	05/31/2002	06/01/2001	06/02/2000	05/28/1999
Earnings Per Share	(0.26)	(0.51)	(0.92)	(0.79)	(1.71)	(2.80)	1.88	1.09
Cash Flow Per Share	(0.22)	(0.35)	(0.46)	0.22	(0.40)	(2.89)	2.72	3.25
Tang Book Value Per Share	1.87	2.33	3.80	4.64	5.34	6.85	11.05	8.74
Income Statement								
Total Revenue	794,807	651,244	698,884	932,866	1,477,932	2,820,881	4,333,942	5,772,149
EBITDA	(99,850)	(154,828)	(239,946)	(104,942)	(237,831)	(948,787)	1,266,269	860,133
Depn & Amortn	44,685	51,852	109,407	159,323	266,820	277,415	304,415	275,641
Income Before Taxes	(115,450)	(185,274)	(332,819)	(240,615)	(504,651)	(1,226,202)	961,854	584,492
Income Taxes	(14,833)	3,490	(3,135)	(10,522)	91,299	(257,641)	341,672	181,719
Net Income	(100,675)	(195,686)	(349,263)	(283,754)	(595,950)	(965,376)	674,303	403,874
Average Shares	386,801	382,309	379,766	360,520	349,489	345,027	357,883	369,361
Balance Sheet								
Total Assets	1,861,361	1,592,967	1,820,818	2,062,360	2,526,792	3,452,802	6,492,954	4,495,389
Current Liabilities	471,281	309,560	306,569	339,168	503,222	936,845	1,182,476	1,198,562
Long-Term Obligations	...	...	...	...	68,404	2,385	14,740	30,405
Total Liabilities	485,069	318,044	321,704	343,763	576,587	947,381	2,449,890	1,298,934
Stockholders' Equity	1,202,362	1,274,923	1,499,114	1,718,597	1,950,205	2,505,421	4,043,064	3,196,455
Shares Outstanding	393,442	385,242	392,738	367,796	365,449	365,711	365,825	365,805
Statistical Record								
Return on Assets %	N.M.	N.M.	N.M.	N.M.	N.M.	N.M.	12.07	9.50
Return on Equity %	N.M.	N.M.	N.M.	N.M.	N.M.	N.M.	18.33	13.57
EBITDA Margin %	N.M.	N.M.	N.M.	N.M.	N.M.	N.M.	29.22	14.90
Net Margin %	N.M.	N.M.	N.M.	N.M.	N.M.	N.M.	15.56	7.00
Asset Turnover	0.46	0.38	0.36	0.41	0.50	0.57	0.78	1.36
Current Ratio	2.65	3.16	4.96	4.87	3.30	2.49	4.59	2.85
Debt to Equity	...	...	...	...	0.04	N.M.	N.M.	0.01
Price Range	5.62-3.27	6.86-2.96	9.09-4.61	5.73-3.87	6.85-3.45	20.69-4.55	19.01-4.19	8.88-3.67
P/E Ratio	...	...	...	...	...	...	10.11-2.23	8.14-3.37

Address: 350 Campus Drive, Marlborough, MA 01752
Telephone: 508-323-1000

Web Site: www.3com.com
Officers: Eric A. Benhamou - Chmn. Bruce L. Claflin - Pres., C.E.O.

Auditors: Deloitte & Touche LLP

TRANSACTION SYSTEMS ARCHITECTS INC

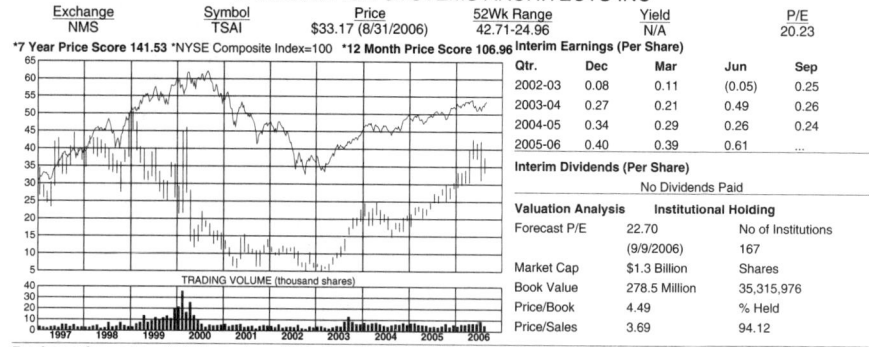

Exchange	Symbol	Price	52Wk Range	Yield	P/E
NMS	TSAI	$33.17 (8/31/2006)	42.71-24.96	N/A	20.23

*7 Year Price Score 141.53 *NYSE Composite Index=100 *12 Month Price Score 106.96

Interim Earnings (Per Share)

Qtr.	Dec	Mar	Jun	Sep
2002-03	0.08	0.11	(0.05)	0.25
2003-04	0.27	0.21	0.49	0.26
2004-05	0.34	0.29	0.26	0.24
2005-06	0.40	0.39	0.61	...

Interim Dividends (Per Share)
No Dividends Paid

Valuation Analysis — **Institutional Holding**

Forecast P/E	22.70	No of Institutions
	(9/9/2006)	167
Market Cap	$1.3 Billion	Shares
Book Value	278.5 Million	35,315,976
Price/Book	4.49	% Held
Price/Sales	3.69	94.12

Business Summary: IT & Technology (MIC: 10.2 SIC: 7372 NAIC: 511210)

Transaction Systems Architects develops, markets, installs and supports a line of software products and services primarily focused on facilitating electronic payments (e-payments) through three business units: ACI Worldwide; Insession Technologies; and IntraNet Worldwide. In addition, Co. distributes or acts as a sales agent for, software developed by third parties. These products and services are used primarily by financial institutions, retailers and e-payment processors, both domestically and internationally. Most of Co.'s products are sold and supported through distribution networks covering three geographic regions: the Americas; Europe/Middle East/Africa (EMEA) and Asia/Pacific.

Recent Developments: For the quarter ended June 30 2006, net income increased 133.2% to $23.3 million from $10.0 million in the year-earlier quarter. Revenues were $84.8 million, up 8.7% from $78.0 million the year before. Operating income was $15.5 million versus $15.2 million in the prior-year quarter, an increase of 2.2%. Direct operating expenses rose 32.2% to $27.3 million from $20.6 million in the comparable period the year before. Indirect operating expenses decreased 0.5% to $42.0 million from $42.2 million in the equivalent prior-year period.

Prospects: As part of the objective in refining its global infrastructure towards further significant growth, Co. has recently launched a globalization strategy slated to improve its supply chain and provide low-cost centers of expertise to support a growing international customer base. In this respect, Co. established a new subsidiary in Ireland to serve as the focal point for certain international product development and commercialization efforts such as those in Romania. For fiscal 2006, Co. has revised its diluted earnings per share estimate from a range of $1.51 to $1.63 to a range of $1.78 to $1.90, while its revenue guidance remains at the $348.0 million to $360.0 million range.

Financial Data
(US$ in Thousands)

	9 Mos	6 Mos	3 Mos	09/30/2005	09/30/2004	09/30/2003	09/30/2002	09/30/2001
Earnings Per Share	1.64	1.29	1.19	1.12	1.23	0.40	0.43	(1.26)
Cash Flow Per Share	1.40	1.77	1.39	1.41	1.57	1.07	2.24	0.67
Tang Book Value Per Share	4.27	4.36	3.79	3.54	3.69	2.05	1.17	2.95
Income Statement								
Total Revenue	259,672	174,908	85,075	313,237	292,784	277,291	282,829	299,801
EBITDA	56,976	39,608	16,062	67,954	63,679	44,438	57,526	(25,375)
Depn & Amortn	5,978	3,903	1,913	5,180	6,571	9,039	15,885	21,829
Income Before Taxes	57,026	40,102	17,047	66,107	57,435	33,612	37,712	(44,811)
Income Taxes	3,542	9,926	1,857	22,861	10,750	19,287	22,443	(1,794)
Net Income	53,484	30,176	15,190	43,246	46,685	14,325	15,269	(43,017)
Average Shares	38,454	38,065	38,026	38,501	38,076	35,707	35,572	34,116
Balance Sheet								
Total Assets	427,336	390,795	362,306	363,380	325,458	263,900	266,519	327,453
Current Liabilities	129,640	122,390	116,288	124,018	119,892	113,420	113,186	94,357
Long-Term Obligations	...	...	58	154	2,327	9,444	24,866	761
Total Liabilities	148,839	144,673	137,506	146,262	138,497	141,026	163,661	108,785
Stockholders' Equity	278,497	246,122	224,800	217,118	186,961	122,874	102,858	218,668
Shares Outstanding	37,685	37,392	37,155	37,384	37,629	36,184	35,411	36,687
Statistical Record								
Return on Assets %	16.27	13.19	12.88	12.56	15.80	5.40	5.14	N.M.
Return on Equity %	25.93	21.43	21.18	21.40	30.05	12.69	9.50	N.M.
EBITDA Margin %	21.94	22.65	18.88	21.69	21.75	16.03	20.34	N.M.
Net Margin %	20.60	17.25	17.85	13.81	15.95	5.17	5.40	N.M.
Asset Turnover	0.88	0.89	0.90	0.91	0.99	1.05	0.95	0.91
Current Ratio	2.05	2.24	2.10	1.97	2.03	1.71	1.44	1.67
Debt to Equity	...	...	N.M.	N.M.	0.01	0.08	0.24	N.M.
Price Range	42.71-24.63	34.03-20.33	30.48-17.78	28.72-16.36	24.74-14.76	17.67-5.00	14.08-6.20	16.47-5.86
P/E Ratio	26.04-15.02	26.38-15.76	25.61-14.94	25.64-14.61	20.11-12.00	44.18-12.50	32.74-14.42	...

Address: 224 South 108th Avenue, Omaha, NE 68154
Telephone: 402-334-5101
Fax: 402-390-8077

Web Site: www.tsainc.com
Officers: Harlan F. Seymour - Chmn. Gregory D. Derkacht - Pres., C.E.O.

Auditors: KPMG LLP
Transfer Agents: Wells Fargo Shareowner Services, South St. Paul, Minnesota

TRIQUINT SEMICONDUCTOR, INC.

Exchange	Symbol	Price	52Wk Range	Yield	P/E
NMS	TQNT	$4.93 (8/31/2006)	5.96-3.35	N/A	49.30

*7 Year Price Score 26.36 *NYSE Composite Index=100 *12 Month Price Score 94.09

Interim Earnings (Per Share)

Qtr.	Mar	Jun	Sep	Dec
2003	(0.12)	(0.45)	(0.04)	0.07
2004	0.00	0.00	(0.03)	(0.18)
2005	(0.06)	0.04	0.02	0.02
2006	0.02	0.04	...	...

Interim Dividends (Per Share)

No Dividends Paid

Valuation Analysis

	Institutional Holding	
Forecast P/E	24.56	No of Institutions
	(9/9/2006)	144
Market Cap	$688.6 Million	Shares
Book Value	455.1 Million	94,173,568
Price/Book	1.51	% Held
Price/Sales	2.00	67.71

Business Summary: IT & Technology (MIC: 10.2 SIC: 3674 NAIC: 334413)

TriQuint Semiconductor is engaged in the design, manufacture and marketing of modules, components and foundry services to communications companies. Co.'s wholly owned subsidiaries include TFR Technologies, Inc., TriQuint Semiconductor Texas LP, TriQuint Semiconductor GmbH, Sawtek, Inc. and Sawtek SRL. Its products are designed on various wafer substrates, including compound semiconductor materials, such as gallium arsenide (GaAs) and piezoelectric crystals, such as lithium tantalate (LiTaO3). Co. sells its products and services to communication and military equipment companies worldwide.

Recent Developments: For the quarter ended June 30 2006, income from continuing operations was $5.6 million compared with a loss of $1.5 million in the year-earlier quarter. Net income decreased 9.0% to $5.6 million from $6.2 million in the year-earlier quarter. Revenues were $96.3 million, up 41.8% from $67.9 million the year before. Operating income was $3.9 million versus a loss of $5.8 million in the prior-year quarter. Direct operating expenses rose 34.1% to $65.4 million from $48.8 million in the comparable period the year before. Indirect operating expenses increased 8.2% to $27.0 million from $25.0 million in the equivalent prior-year period.

Prospects: Co. continues to experience solid bookings. Looking ahead, Co. expects revenues for the third quarter of 2006 to increase 4.0% to 8.0% from the second quarter of 2006, while projecting earnings to range from $0.04 to $0.06 per diluted share. For full-year 2006, Co. is raising its earnings per share to a range of $0.13 to $0.18, including equity compensation expense. Separately, on Jul 10 2006, Co. announced that the Office of Naval Research (ONR) has awarded it a 20-month, $3.1 million contract to improve manufacturing methods of producing high-power, high-voltage S-band gallium arsenide (GaAs) amplifiers.

Financial Data
(US$ in Thousands)

	6 Mos	3 Mos	12/31/2005	12/31/2004	12/31/2003	12/31/2002	12/31/2001	12/31/2000
Earnings Per Share	0.10	0.10	0.03	(0.21)	(0.54)	(1.20)	(0.21)	0.83
Cash Flow Per Share	0.06	0.08	0.10	0.30	(0.21)	0.23	1.13	1.42
Tang Book Value Per Share	3.23	3.19	3.16	3.18	3.40	3.95	5.21	5.38
Income Statement								
Total Revenue	184,221	87,880	294,787	347,005	312,272	267,313	334,972	300,749
EBITDA	21,311	8,970	24,476	16,088	(29,132)	(85,192)	(32,954)	107,767
Depn & Amortn	15,888	7,735	33,847	41,113	39,516	38,312	29,782	11,606
Income Before Taxes	7,923	2,361	(7,776)	(28,629)	(74,522)	(124,319)	(49,944)	114,258
Income Taxes	29	115	(3,573)	425	(1,544)	34,241	(18,093)	42,847
Net Income	7,894	2,246	3,980	(29,054)	(72,978)	(158,560)	(26,211)	71,411
Average Shares	140,703	141,282	139,566	136,936	133,920	131,969	129,784	86,251
Balance Sheet								
Total Assets	739,515	731,022	728,741	722,400	792,800	840,666	1,020,873	825,416
Current Liabilities	280,685	276,143	56,401	56,642	55,717	39,689	41,240	47,738
Long-Term Obligations	...	...	218,755	223,755	268,755	268,755	296,859	346,991
Total Liabilities	284,418	279,508	278,131	281,013	332,679	314,994	338,099	394,729
Stockholders' Equity	455,097	451,514	450,610	441,387	460,121	525,672	682,774	430,687
Shares Outstanding	139,675	140,080	141,080	138,773	135,403	133,162	131,141	80,098
Statistical Record								
Return on Assets %	1.85	1.93	0.55	N.M.	N.M.	N.M.	N.M.	12.22
Return on Equity %	2.99	3.16	0.89	N.M.	N.M.	N.M.	N.M.	19.44
EBITDA Margin %	11.57	10.21	8.30	4.64	N.M.	N.M.	N.M.	35.83
Net Margin %	4.29	2.56	1.35	N.M.	N.M.	N.M.	N.M.	23.74
Asset Turnover	0.48	0.44	0.41	0.46	0.38	0.29	0.36	0.51
Current Ratio	1.86	1.76	7.35	5.79	8.04	10.50	14.59	11.53
Debt to Equity	...	...	0.49	0.51	0.58	0.51	0.43	0.81
Price Range	5.96-3.33	5.03-2.91	4.97-2.91	9.83-3.25	8.50-2.82	13.37-2.77	47.69-10.38	65.37-23.81
P/E Ratio	59.60-33.30	50.30-29.10	165.67-97.00	...	...	...	...	78.76-28.69

Address: 2300 N.E. Brookwood Parkway, Hillsboro, OR 97124 **Telephone:** 503-615-9000 **Fax:** 503-615-8900	**Web Site:** www.tqs.com **Officers:** Steven J. Sharp - Chmn. Ralph G. Quinsey - Pres., C.E.O.	**Auditors:** KPMG LLP **Investor Contact:** 503-615-9414

TRUSTMARK CORP.

Exchange	Symbol	Price	52Wk Range	Yield	P/E	Div Acheiver
NMS	TRMK	$31.57 (8/31/2006)	32.60-24.41	2.66	15.63	32 Years

*7 Year Price Score 93.39 *NYSE Composite Index=100 *12 Month Price Score 102.41

Interim Earnings (Per Share)

Qtr.	Mar	Jun	Sep	Dec
2003	0.41	0.53	0.55	0.52
2004	0.46	0.57	0.48	0.49
2005	0.47	0.39	0.46	0.49
2006	0.52	0.55	...	...

Interim Dividends (Per Share)

Amt	Decl	Ex	Rec	Pay
0.21Q	10/18/2005	11/29/2005	12/1/2005	12/15/2005
0.21Q	1/17/2006	2/27/2006	3/1/2006	3/15/2006
0.21Q	4/19/2006	5/30/2006	6/1/2006	6/15/2006
0.21Q	7/19/2006	8/30/2006	9/1/2006	9/15/2006

Indicated Div: $0.84

Valuation Analysis

Forecast P/E	14.66
	(9/9/2006)
Market Cap	$1.7 Billion
Book Value	761.3 Million
Price/Book	2.29
Price/Sales	2.90

Institutional Holding

No of Institutions	94
Shares	14,840,369
% Held	26.87

Business Summary: Commercial Banking (MIC: 8.1 SIC: 6021 NAIC: 522110)
Trustmark is a multi-bank holding company. Through its subsidiaries, Co. operates as a financial services organization providing banking and financial services to corporate, institutional and individual customers predominantly within the states of Florida, Mississippi, Tennessee, and Texas. Co.'s General Banking division provides traditional banking products and services, including loans and deposits. Co.'s Wealth Management division provides guidance and advice for accumulating, preserving, and transferring wealth. Co.'s Insurance division provides a range of retail insurance products. As of Dec 31 2005, Co. had total assets of $8.39 billion.

Recent Developments: For the quarter ended June 30 2006, net income increased 38.6% to $30.8 million from $22.2 million in the year-earlier quarter. Net interest income increased 2.5% to $69.6 million from $67.9 million in the year-earlier quarter. Credit for loan losses was $2.0 million versus a provision for loan losses of $1.4 million in the prior-year quarter. Non-interest income rose 40.9% to $39.4 million from $28.0 million, while non-interest expense advanced 5.8% to $63.8 million.

Prospects: Co. is progressing with the repositioning of its balance sheet, reflecting a more favorable mix of earning assets, and an improvement in its interest rate risk profile and net interest margin. Going forward, Co. expects borrowing activity to accelerate at areas affected by Hurricane Katrina, in line with rebuilding activities. Meanwhile, Co. continues to progress with its initiative to build additional banking centers in higher-growth markets within its four state franchise, and plans to open two additional banking centers in 2006 and eight banking centers in 2007. Separately, Co. expects its acquisition of Republic Bancshares of Texas, Inc. to be completed in the third quarter of 2006.

Financial Data
(US$ in Thousands)

	6 Mos	3 Mos	12/31/2005	12/31/2004	12/31/2003	12/31/2002	12/31/2001	12/31/2000
Earnings Per Share	2.02	1.86	1.81	2.00	2.00	1.94	1.72	1.50
Cash Flow Per Share	2.22	1.87	1.50	2.77	3.39	1.10	3.75	(1.76)
Tang Book Value Per Share	9.56	9.45	9.27	9.14	8.96	9.25	8.93	8.70
Dividends Per Share	0.830	0.820	0.810	0.770	0.685	0.615	0.555	0.510
Dividend Payout %	41.09	44.09	44.75	38.50	34.25	31.70	32.27	34.00
Income Statement								
Interest Income	226,769	110,633	415,697	364,355	359,388	405,952	477,820	488,759
Interest Expense	88,910	42,392	139,256	88,738	89,558	113,766	209,242	255,196
Net Interest Income	137,859	68,241	276,441	275,617	269,830	292,186	268,578	233,563
Provision for Losses	(4,948)	(2,984)	19,541	(3,055)	9,771	14,107	13,200	10,401
Non-Interest Income	76,073	36,690	143,107	124,028	157,543	141,870	131,990	124,540
Non-Interest Expense	127,264	63,512	243,276	225,309	236,120	233,841	215,941	189,377
Income Before Taxes	91,616	44,403	156,731	177,391	181,482	186,108	171,427	158,325
Income Taxes	31,523	15,084	53,780	60,682	62,952	64,968	60,146	54,124
Net Income	60,093	29,319	102,951	116,709	118,530	121,140	111,281	101,737
Average Shares	55,834	56,035	56,743	58,273	59,244	62,416	64,876	67,928
Balance Sheet								
Net Loans & Leases	5,934,090	5,871,361	5,816,748	5,265,298	4,845,776	4,542,595	4,448,832	4,078,083
Total Assets	8,234,588	8,237,688	8,389,750	8,052,957	7,914,321	7,138,706	7,180,339	6,886,988
Total Deposits	6,363,313	6,321,032	6,282,814	5,450,093	5,089,459	4,686,296	4,613,365	4,058,418
Total Liabilities	7,473,313	7,482,003	7,648,287	7,302,561	7,224,748	6,459,172	6,494,895	6,257,347
Stockholders' Equity	761,275	755,685	741,463	750,396	689,573	679,534	685,444	629,641
Shares Outstanding	55,262	55,680	55,771	57,858	58,246	60,516	63,705	64,755
Statistical Record								
Return on Assets %	1.40	1.29	1.25	1.46	1.57	1.69	1.58	1.49
Return on Equity %	15.15	14.19	13.80	16.17	17.31	17.75	16.92	15.79
Net Interest Margin %	59.95	61.68	66.50	75.65	75.08	71.98	56.21	47.79
Efficiency Ratio %	40.99	43.11	43.54	46.13	45.68	42.69	35.41	30.88
Loans to Deposits	0.93	0.93	0.93	0.97	0.95	0.97	0.96	1.00
Price Range	32.08-24.41	32.00-24.41	31.07-24.41	32.42-26.10	29.82-22.74	26.90-20.49	24.70-19.56	21.61-15.31
P/E Ratio	15.88-12.08	17.20-13.12	17.17-13.49	16.21-13.05	14.91-11.37	13.87-10.56	14.36-11.37	14.41-10.21
Average Yield %	2.85	2.87	2.87	2.60	2.61	2.53	2.48	2.72

Address: 248 East Capitol Street, Jackson, MS 39201 Telephone: 601-208-5111 Fax: 601-354-5053	Web Site: www.trustmark.com Officers: Richard G. Hickson - Chmn., Pres., C.E.O. Louis E. Greer - Chief Acctg. Officer	Auditors: KPMG LLP Investor Contact: 601-949-6898 Transfer Agents: Trustmark National Bank, Jackson, MS

UNITED BANKSHARES, INC.

Exchange	Symbol	Price	52Wk Range	Yield	P/E	Div Acheiver
NMS	UBSI	$37.27 (8/31/2006)	38.48-32.80	2.90	15.73	24 Years

*7 Year Price Score 99.80   *NYSE Composite Index=100   *12 Month Price Score 96.51

Interim Earnings (Per Share)

Qtr.	Mar	Jun	Sep	Dec
2003	0.53	0.54	0.55	0.23
2004	0.53	0.55	0.56	0.58
2005	0.57	0.57	0.59	0.60
2006	0.58	0.60	...	...

Interim Dividends (Per Share)

Amt	Decl	Ex	Rec	Pay
0.27Q	11/22/2005	12/7/2005	12/9/2005	1/3/2006
0.27Q	1/26/2006	3/8/2006	3/10/2006	4/1/2006
0.27Q	5/16/2006	6/7/2006	6/9/2006	7/3/2006
0.27Q	7/21/2006	9/6/2006	9/8/2006	10/2/2006

Indicated Div: $1.08 (Div. Reinv. Plan)

Valuation Analysis

		Institutional Holding	
Forecast P/E	15.06	No of Institutions	131
	(9/9/2006)		
Market Cap	$1.5 Billion	Shares	16,697,977
Book Value	635.0 Million	% Held	40.32
Price/Book	2.44		
Price/Sales	3.56		

Business Summary: Commercial Banking (MIC: 8.1 SIC: 6021 NAIC: 522110)
United Bankshares is a bank holding company with total assets of $6.73 billion and total deposits of $4.62 billion as of Dec 31 2005. Co. has two banking subsidiaries "doing business" under the name of United Bank. These engage primarily in community banking. Banking services include the acceptance of deposits; the making and servicing of personal, commercial, floor plan and student loans; and the making of construction and real estate loans. Co. also owns non-bank subsidiaries which engage in other community banking services such as asset management, real property title insurance, investment banking, financial planning, and brokerage services.

Recent Developments: For the quarter ended June 30 2006, net income increased 3.9% to $25.5 million from $24.5 million in the year-earlier quarter. Net interest income increased 4.0% to $55.6 million from $53.5 million in the year-earlier quarter. Provision for loan losses was $348,000 versus $504,000 in the prior-year quarter, a decrease of 31.0%. Non-interest income rose 8.0% to $14.4 million from $13.4 million, while non-interest expense advanced 5.2% to $32.2 million.

Prospects: Co.'s bottom line results are being driven primarily by increased net interest income, attributable mainly to growth in average loans. Also, the average yield on earning assets has benefited from higher interest rates. Co.'s net interest margin for both the second quarter of 2006 and 2005 was 3.88%. However, as a result of the higher interest rates, Co.'s average cost of funds has risen. Co. noted that a sustained flat yield curve between short-term and long-term interest rates has resulted in a lesser increase in yields on earning assets while the upward trend in the general market interest rates has resulted in a more significant increase to funding costs.

Financial Data
(US$ in Thousands)

	6 Mos	3 Mos	12/31/2005	12/31/2004	12/31/2003	12/31/2002	12/31/2001	12/31/2000
Earnings Per Share	2.37	2.34	2.33	2.22	1.85	2.06	1.90	1.40
Cash Flow Per Share	2.75	2.83	2.66	2.17	11.70	(2.28)	(1.38)	0.02
Tang Book Value Per Share	11.26	11.26	11.13	10.80	10.20	10.73	11.80	10.32
Dividends Per Share	1.070	1.060	1.050	1.020	1.000	0.950	0.910	0.840
Dividend Payout %	45.15	45.30	45.06	45.95	54.05	46.12	47.89	60.00
Income Statement								
Interest Income	196,042	95,581	345,278	293,350	297,508	339,478	360,610	377,847
Interest Expense	85,441	40,560	124,451	88,914	104,151	132,557	175,507	197,766
Net Interest Income	110,601	55,021	220,827	204,436	193,357	206,921	185,103	180,081
Provision for Losses	598	250	5,618	4,520	7,475	7,937	12,833	15,745
Non-Interest Income	28,087	13,662	52,625	54,231	103,316	73,479	62,205	33,786
Non-Interest Expense	64,351	32,188	121,160	137,061	176,678	144,130	115,745	110,422
Income Before Taxes	73,739	36,245	146,674	117,086	112,520	128,333	118,730	87,700
Income Taxes	23,670	11,635	46,265	33,771	33,755	39,400	38,739	28,724
Net Income	50,069	24,610	100,409	97,762	78,765	88,933	79,991	58,976
Average Shares	42,084	42,379	43,024	43,978	42,620	43,113	42,064	42,260
Balance Sheet								
Net Loans & Leases	4,762,798	4,649,194	4,605,691	4,374,911	4,045,587	3,525,774	3,454,926	3,151,962
Total Assets	6,717,873	6,706,832	6,728,492	6,435,971	6,378,999	5,792,019	5,631,715	4,904,547
Total Deposits	4,755,480	4,703,268	4,617,452	4,297,563	4,182,372	3,900,848	3,787,793	3,391,449
Total Liabilities	6,082,846	6,068,225	6,093,287	5,804,464	5,763,808	5,250,480	5,125,246	4,473,677
Stockholders' Equity	635,027	638,607	635,205	631,507	615,191	541,539	506,529	430,870
Shares Outstanding	41,512	41,848	42,008	43,008	43,689	42,031	42,926	41,765
Statistical Record								
Return on Assets %	1.53	1.54	1.53	1.52	1.29	1.56	1.52	1.18
Return on Equity %	15.92	15.85	15.85	15.64	13.62	16.97	17.07	14.23
Net Interest Margin %	55.32	57.56	63.96	69.69	64.99	60.95	51.33	47.66
Efficiency Ratio %	28.00	29.46	30.45	39.43	44.08	34.90	27.37	26.83
Loans to Deposits	1.00	0.99	1.00	1.02	0.97	0.90	0.91	0.93
Price Range	38.48-32.80	38.48-30.00	38.48-30.00	39.18-29.35	31.53-26.97	32.01-26.24	28.86-20.19	23.88-16.44
P/E Ratio	16.24-13.84	16.44-12.82	16.52-12.88	17.65-13.22	17.04-14.58	15.54-12.74	15.19-10.63	17.05-11.74
Average Yield %	2.94	2.98	3.01	3.11	3.38	3.23	3.65	4.25

Address: 300 United Center, 500 Virginia Street East, Charleston, WV 25301	**Web Site:** www.ubsi-wv.com **Officers:** Richard M. Adams - Chmn., C.E.O. Steven E. Wilson - C.F.O., Chief Acctg. Officer
Telephone: 304-424-8800 **Fax:** 304-424-8758	**Auditors:** Ernst & Young LLP **Investor Contact:** 304-424-8704 **Transfer Agents:** Mellon Investor Services LLC, Ridgefield Park, NJ

UNITED STATIONERS INC.

Exchange	Symbol	Price	52Wk Range	Yield	P/E
NMS	USTR	$45.83 (8/31/2006)	56.01-43.42	N/A	13.72

*7 Year Price Score 108.33 *NYSE Composite Index=100 *12 Month Price Score 95.60

Interim Earnings (Per Share)

Qtr.	Mar	Jun	Sep	Dec
2003	0.39	0.46	0.69	0.64
2004	0.68	0.62	0.78	0.57
2005	0.80	0.62	0.77	0.72
2006	0.56	1.29	...	...

Interim Dividends (Per Share)

No Dividends Paid

Valuation Analysis   **Institutional Holding**

Forecast P/E	15.77	No of Institutions
	(9/9/2006)	152
Market Cap	$1.4 Billion	Shares
Book Value	757.9 Million	31,980,096
Price/Book	1.85	% Held
Price/Sales	0.31	N/A

Business Summary: Retail - General (MIC: 5.2 SIC: 5111 NAIC: 424110)

United Stationers is a wholesale distributor of business products. Through 68 distribution centers, Co. offers nearly 50,000 items to approximately 20,000 resellers including office products dealers and contract stationers, national mega-dealers, office products superstores, computer products resellers, office furniture dealers, mass merchandisers, mail order companies, sanitary supply distributors, drug and grocery store chains, and e-commerce merchants. Co. also provides marketing and logistics services to resellers. Co.'s products include computer consumables, traditional office products, office furniture, janitorial/sanitation supplies, business machines and presentation products.

Recent Developments: For the quarter ended June 30 2006, income from continuing operations increased 91.8% to $41.5 million from $21.6 million in the year-earlier quarter. Net income increased 98.1% to $41.4 million from $20.9 million in the year-earlier quarter. Revenues were $1.11 billion, up 6.2% from $1.05 billion the year before. Operating income was $71.5 million versus $36.9 million in the prior-year quarter, an increase of 93.8%. Direct operating expenses rose 2.8% to $921.4 million from $896.1 million in the comparable period the year before. Indirect operating expenses increased 4.3% to $118.2 million from $113.3 million in the equivalent prior-year period.

Prospects: Looking ahead to full-year 2006, Co. is focusing its efforts on increasing its sales growth rate, including introducing its mid-year catalog which should drive sales, as well as its Reseller Technology Solution (RTS), which should help enhance its relationship with the independent dealer channel. Additionally, Co. believes that it has further opportunities to improve its operating results in the long term through its margin initiatives and by extending its War on Waste (WOW) initiatives to other areas of the business to reduce its cost structure. Separately, on Jun 9 2006, Co. completed the sale of certain net assets of its Canadian division to SYNNEX Canada Ltd., for $14.0 million.

Financial Data
(US$ in Thousands)

	6 Mos	3 Mos	12/31/2005	12/31/2004	12/31/2003	12/31/2002	12/31/2001	12/31/2000
Earnings Per Share	3.34	2.67	2.90	2.65	2.18	1.78	1.68	2.65
Cash Flow Per Share	3.36	7.92	6.63	1.40	5.06	3.18	5.70	1.13
Tang Book Value Per Share	16.39	16.34	14.75	16.50	14.47	11.66	10.67	8.87
Income Statement								
Total Revenue	2,259,323	1,148,230	4,408,546	3,991,190	3,847,722	3,701,564	3,925,936	3,944,862
EBITDA	121,683	43,996	191,624	173,513	166,530	147,689	157,285	224,198
Depn & Amortn	18,244	8,907	32,749	27,812	32,433	34,625	39,851	32,853
Income Before Taxes	100,757	33,686	156,089	142,800	127,605	96,369	93,641	164,116
Income Taxes	38,409	12,820	58,588	52,829	48,495	36,141	36,663	65,473
Net Income	59,401	18,040	97,501	89,971	73,002	60,228	56,978	92,167
Average Shares	32,120	32,316	33,612	33,985	33,439	33,783	33,928	34,775
Balance Sheet								
Total Assets	1,527,044	1,502,773	1,542,201	1,407,240	1,295,010	1,349,229	1,339,587	1,447,027
Current Liabilities	627,811	641,013	664,862	590,870	538,456	566,310	537,332	559,031
Long-Term Obligations	60,100	7,300	21,000	18,000	17,300	165,345	218,735	369,594
Total Liabilities	769,146	731,690	773,689	676,037	622,032	790,345	800,906	968,588
Stockholders' Equity	757,898	771,083	768,512	731,203	672,978	558,884	538,681	478,439
Shares Outstanding	30,640	31,559	31,877	33,141	33,903	32,479	33,603	33,445
Statistical Record								
Return on Assets %	7.39	6.07	6.61	6.64	5.52	4.48	4.09	6.74
Return on Equity %	14.16	11.57	13.00	12.78	11.85	10.97	11.20	20.78
EBITDA Margin %	5.39	3.83	4.35	4.35	4.33	3.99	4.01	5.68
Net Margin %	2.63	1.57	2.21	2.25	1.90	1.63	1.45	2.34
Asset Turnover	3.07	3.08	2.99	2.95	2.91	2.75	2.82	2.89
Current Ratio	1.71	1.63	1.61	1.78	1.72	1.71	1.77	1.89
Debt to Equity	0.08	0.01	0.03	0.02	0.03	0.30	0.41	0.77
Price Range	56.01-43.42	53.62-41.45	53.62-41.45	49.25-36.30	42.37-18.00	42.40-23.60	34.95-22.00	37.81-21.50
P/E Ratio	16.77-13.00	20.08-15.52	18.49-14.29	18.58-13.70	19.44-8.26	23.82-13.26	20.80-13.10	14.27-8.11

Address: 2200 East Golf Road, Des Plaines, IL 60016-1267
Telephone: 847-699-5000
Fax: 847-699-4716

Web Site: www.unitedstationers.com
Officers: Frederick B. Hegi Jr. - Chmn. Richard W. Gochnauer - Pres., C.E.O.

Auditors: ERNST & YOUNG LLP
Investor Contact: 847-699-5000x2321

UNIVERSAL FOREST PRODUCTS INC.

Exchange	Symbol	Price	52Wk Range	Yield	P/E	Div Acheiver
NMS	UFPI	$48.76 (8/31/2006)	79.96-47.82	0.23	12.19	12 Years

*7 Year Price Score 167.06 *NYSE Composite Index=100 *12 Month Price Score 87.12

Interim Earnings (Per Share)

Qtr.	Mar	Jun	Sep	Dec
2003	0.25	0.94	0.66	0.33
2004	0.30	1.06	0.78	0.46
2005	0.49	1.20	1.00	0.84
2006	0.82	1.41	...	...

Interim Dividends (Per Share)

Amt	Decl	Ex	Rec	Pay
0.05S	10/22/2004	11/29/2004	12/1/2004	12/15/2004
0.05S	4/22/2005	5/27/2005	6/1/2005	6/15/2005
0.055S	10/18/2005	11/29/2005	12/1/2005	12/15/2005
0.055S	4/19/2006	5/30/2006	6/1/2006	6/15/2006

Indicated Div: $0.11

Valuation Analysis
Forecast P/E 11.34 (9/9/2006)
Market Cap $918.4 Million
Book Value 487.7 Million
Price/Book 1.88
Price/Sales 0.33

Institutional Holding
No of Institutions 148
Shares 14,555,201
% Held 77.27

Business Summary: Wood Products (MIC: 11.9 SIC: 2421 NAIC: 321113)
Universal Forest Products engineers, manufactures, treats, distributes and installs lumber, composite wood, plastic and other building products to the do-it-yourself/retail, site-built construction, manufactured housing, and industrial markets. Co.'s principal products include preservative-treated wood, remanufactured lumber, lattice, fence panels, deck components, specialty packaging, engineered trusses, wall panels, and other building products. As of Dec 31 2005, Co. had approximately 105 facilities located throughout the United States, Canada, and Mexico.

Recent Developments: For the quarter ended July 1 2006, net income increased 19.9% to $27.3 million from $22.8 million in the year-earlier quarter. Revenues were $826.8 million, up 6.1% from $779.6 million the year before. Operating income was $49.6 million versus $41.7 million in the prior-year quarter, an increase of 18.9%. Direct operating expenses rose 4.1% to $706.4 million from $678.3 million in the comparable period the year before. Indirect operating expenses increased 18.9% to $70.8 million from $59.5 million in the equivalent prior-year period.

Prospects: Co. remains optimistic about the future of its business, markets and strategies. For instance, Co. appears to be well-positioned in the highly fragmented site-build construction and industrial markets and could grow its manufactured housing business through proprietary products and a focus on modular customers. Co. is also focusing on expanding its Do-It-Yourself/retail market by aggressively pursing new business and by executing its plan to introduce products through its new Consumer Products Division. Thus, on Apr 17 2006, Co. raised its annual target for net earnings growth to 15.0% to 20.0% from 10.0% to 15.0%, and reaffirmed its unit sales targets 10.0% to 15.0%.

Financial Data
(US$ in Thousands)

	6 Mos	3 Mos	12/31/2005	12/25/2004	12/27/2003	12/28/2002	12/29/2001	12/30/2000
Earnings Per Share	4.00	3.78	3.53	2.59	2.18	1.97	1.63	1.49
Cash Flow Per Share	6.62	7.04	3.97	2.79	3.97	0.93	3.96	3.28
Tang Book Value Per Share	18.04	16.80	15.72	12.50	9.71	7.45	6.06	6.60
Dividends Per Share	0.110	0.105	0.105	0.100	0.095	0.090	0.085	0.080
Dividend Payout %	2.75	2.78	2.97	3.86	4.36	4.57	5.21	5.37
Income Statement								
Total Revenue	1,492,456	665,609	2,691,522	2,453,281	1,898,830	1,639,899	1,530,353	1,389,443
EBITDA	98,371	39,372	159,656	128,532	107,563	97,832	90,233	84,084
Depn & Amortn	18,881	9,590	34,811	30,853	27,547	24,639	24,476	21,462
Income Before Taxes	72,728	26,412	110,772	83,059	65,792	62,115	54,300	50,375
Income Taxes	27,641	9,756	41,050	31,462	24,325	22,983	19,612	19,218
Net Income	43,180	15,866	67,373	48,603	40,119	36,637	33,142	30,438
Average Shares	19,432	19,278	19,106	18,771	18,379	18,619	20,377	20,477
Balance Sheet								
Total Assets	939,342	914,969	876,920	762,360	684,757	634,794	551,209	485,320
Current Liabilities	248,426	224,209	204,151	183,865	141,878	108,841	110,895	80,038
Long-Term Obligations	170,192	204,010	209,039	185,109	205,049	235,319	154,370	150,807
Total Liabilities	451,668	460,522	445,068	405,591	380,008	371,794	284,347	249,551
Stockholders' Equity	487,674	454,447	431,852	356,769	304,749	263,000	230,862	235,769
Shares Outstanding	18,836	18,626	18,402	18,002	17,813	17,741	17,787	19,719
Statistical Record								
Return on Assets %	8.47	8.13	8.09	6.74	6.10	6.20	6.41	6.28
Return on Equity %	17.58	17.60	16.81	14.73	14.17	14.88	14.24	13.30
EBITDA Margin %	6.59	5.92	5.93	5.24	5.66	5.97	5.90	6.05
Net Margin %	2.89	2.38	2.50	1.98	2.11	2.23	2.17	2.19
Asset Turnover	3.09	3.10	3.23	3.40	2.89	2.77	2.96	2.87
Current Ratio	2.24	2.41	2.46	2.21	2.34	2.70	2.12	2.50
Debt to Equity	0.35	0.45	0.48	0.52	0.67	0.89	0.67	0.64
Price Range	79.96-41.45	64.42-37.37	60.40-37.37	43.50-26.69	31.74-15.23	26.86-16.08	23.00-13.00	16.13-10.63
P/E Ratio	19.99-10.36	17.04-9.89	17.11-10.59	16.80-10.31	14.56-6.99	13.63-8.16	14.11-7.98	10.82-7.13
Average Yield %	0.19	0.20	0.23	0.28	0.31	0.42	0.42	0.48	0.62

Address: 2801 East Beltline N.E., Grand Rapids, MI 49525 **Telephone:** 616-364-6161 **Fax:** 616-361-7534	**Web Site:** www.ufpi.com **Officers:** William G. Currie - Vice-Chmn., C.E.O. Michael R. Cole - C.F.O., Treas.	**Auditors:** ERNST & YOUNG LLP **Transfer Agents:** American Stock Transfer & Trust Company, New York, NY

URBAN OUTFITTERS, INC.

Exchange	Symbol	Price	52Wk Range	Yield	P/E
NMS	URBN	$15.69 (8/31/2006)	33.43-14.01	N/A	21.49

*7 Year Price Score 197.51 *NYSE Composite Index=100 *12 Month Price Score 63.97

Interim Earnings (Per Share)

Qtr.	Apr	Jul	Oct	Jan
2003-04	0.04	0.06	0.09	0.12
2004-05	0.10	0.13	0.16	0.16
2005-06	0.16	0.18	0.22	0.21
2006-07	0.12	...	...	...

Interim Dividends (Per Share)

Amt	Decl	Ex	Rec	Pay
100%	8/14/2003	9/22/2003	9/5/2003	9/19/2003
100%	6/1/2004	7/12/2004	6/22/2004	7/9/2004
2-for-1	8/17/2005	9/26/2005	9/6/2005	9/23/2005

Valuation Analysis

Forecast P/E	14.47 (9/9/2006)
Market Cap	$2.6 Billion
Book Value	585.8 Million
Price/Book	4.42
Price/Sales	2.29

Institutional Holding

No of Institutions	254
Shares	108,203,304
% Held	65.48

Business Summary: Retail - Apparel and Accessory Stores (MIC: 5.8 SIC: 5651 NAIC: 448140)

Urban Outfitters is a lifestyle merchandising company engaged in specialty retail stores under the Urban Outfitters, Anthropologie and Free People brands, and a wholesale division under the Free People brand. Co.'s retail stores offer a variety of fashion apparel, accessories, home goods and store settings. Co. distributes wholesale apparel to about 1,500 better specialty retailers worldwide. As of Jan 31 2006, Co. operated 175 stores in the U.S., Canada, the U.K. and Ireland. Co.'s trademarks include Urban Outfitters, Anthropologie, Urban Renewal, Free People, Co-Operative, Ecote, Field Flower, Hei-Hei, Fink, Lucky Penny, Nap Time, 365 Days, Stapleford, Character Hero, Idra and Urbn.com.

Recent Developments: For the quarter ended Apr 30 2006, net income decreased 26.0% to $20.3 million from $27.4 million in the year-earlier quarter. Revenues were $270.0 million, up 16.7% from $231.3 million the year before. Operating income was $31.6 million versus $44.8 million in the prior-year quarter, a decrease of 29.5%. Direct operating expenses rose 29.6% to $173.2 million from $133.7 million in the comparable period the year before. Indirect operating expenses increased 23.4% to $65.2 million from $52.8 million in the equivalent prior-year period.

Prospects: Co.'s sales are being led by higher retail segment sales from increased non-comparable and new store sales, and favorable gains in its direct to consumer sales. Co is also benefiting from continuing improvements in its inventories due to the acquisition of inventory to stock new retail stores. For the rest of fiscal 2007, Co. plans to open an additional 27 to 30 stores. Subsequently, Co. plans to open about 35 to 38 stores in fiscal 2007, including three to five new Free People stores. Co.'s goal thereafter is to grow net sales by about 20.0% annually through new stores opening, growing comparable store sales and continuing the growth of its direct-to-consumer and wholesale operations.

Financial Data
(US$ in Thousands)

	3 Mos	01/31/2006	01/31/2005	01/31/2004	01/31/2003	01/31/2002	01/31/2001	01/31/2000
Earnings Per Share	0.73	0.77	0.54	0.30	0.18	0.11	0.08	0.13
Cash Flow Per Share	1.02	0.91	0.93	0.44	0.28	0.24	0.17	0.17
Tang Book Value Per Share	3.55	3.40	2.47	1.82	1.45	1.05	0.94	0.87
Income Statement								
Total Revenue	270,007	1,092,107	827,750	548,361	422,754	348,958	295,333	276,106
EBITDA	44,900	246,251	179,473	102,195	62,784	40,366	29,303	41,725
Depn & Amortn	11,937	39,340	31,858	22,415	18,208	15,462	11,997	8,667
Income Before Taxes	32,963	212,397	150,192	81,304	46,073	25,222	17,787	34,849
Income Taxes	12,664	81,601	59,703	32,928	18,660	10,215	7,292	16,169
Net Income	20,299	130,796	90,489	48,376	27,413	15,007	10,495	18,680
Average Shares	168,020	169,936	167,303	161,662	155,107	139,507	138,198	142,754
Balance Sheet								
Total Assets	798,935	769,205	556,684	359,595	277,996	195,102	168,716	153,501
Current Liabilities	135,109	133,508	98,271	57,762	43,072	40,830	33,318	28,072
Total Liabilities	213,126	208,325	154,440	69,465	53,611	49,214	39,104	32,585
Stockholders' Equity	585,809	560,880	402,244	290,130	224,385	145,888	129,612	120,916
Shares Outstanding	165,137	164,831	162,894	159,553	155,053	138,823	138,027	138,865
Statistical Record								
Return on Assets %	17.83	19.73	19.70	15.17	11.59	8.25	6.50	13.02
Return on Equity %	24.12	27.16	26.07	18.80	14.81	10.89	8.36	16.52
EBITDA Margin %	16.63	22.55	21.68	18.64	14.85	11.57	9.92	15.11
Net Margin %	7.52	11.98	10.93	8.82	6.48	4.30	3.55	6.77
Asset Turnover	1.63	1.65	1.80	1.72	1.79	1.92	1.83	1.92
Current Ratio	2.79	2.89	2.93	3.04	3.36	2.01	1.95	2.35
Price Range	33.43-22.00	33.43-20.55	23.55-10.07	10.19-2.13	4.59-2.36	3.27-1.11	1.87-0.87	3.78-1.53
P/E Ratio	45.79-30.14	43.42-26.69	43.60-18.66	33.98-7.08	25.53-13.10	29.70-10.09	23.34-10.84	29.09-11.78

Address: 1809 Walnut Street, Philadelphia, PA 19103 Telephone: 215-564-2313 Fax: 215-568-1549	Web Site: www.urbn.com Officers: Richard A. Hayne - Chmn., Pres. John E. Kyees - C.F.O.	Auditors: KPMG LLP Investor Contact: 215-564-2313

UTSTARCOM INC

Exchange	Symbol	Price	52Wk Range	Yield	P/E
NMS	UTSI	$8.21 (8/31/2006)	8.91-5.26	N/A	N/A

*7 Year Price Score N/A *NYSE Composite Index=100 *12 Month Price Score 104.24

Interim Earnings (Per Share)

Qtr.	Mar	Jun	Sep	Dec
2003	0.33	0.33	0.46	0.52
2004	0.40	0.33	0.04	(0.22)
2005	0.29	(0.65)	(3.40)	(0.37)
2006	(0.09)	(0.18)	...	...

Interim Dividends (Per Share)
No Dividends Paid

Valuation Analysis Institutional Holding

Forecast P/E	N/A	No of Institutions	144
Market Cap	$990.3 Million	Shares	75,210,504
Book Value	907.1 Million	% Held	62.24
Price/Book	1.09		
Price/Sales	0.40		

Business Summary: Communications (MIC: 10.1 SIC: 3669 NAIC: 517910)
UTStarcom designs, manufactures and sells telecommunications infrastructure, handsets and customer premise equipment and provide services associated with their installation, operation and maintenance. Co.'s products are sold primarily to telecommunications service providers or operators, and are designed to enable voice, data and video services for its worldwide operator customers and consumers. Co.'s products and services are being deployed and implemented in markets including China, Japan, India, the Central and Latin American, European, Middle Eastern, African, North American regions, as well as the Southeast and North Asia regions.

Recent Developments: For the quarter ended June 30 2006, net loss amounted to $21.4 million versus a net loss of $73.9 million in the year-earlier quarter. Revenues were $549.1 million, down 23.7% from $719.8 million the year before. Operating loss was $24.7 million versus a loss of $79.1 million in the prior-year quarter. Direct operating expenses declined 27.6% to $439.9 million from $607.6 million in the comparable period the year before. Indirect operating expenses decreased 29.9% to $134.0 million from $191.2 million in the equivalent prior-year period.

Prospects: Co. is experiencing decline in its sales across all of its operating segments, particularly in its Broadband segment. Geographically, Co. has shifted its market concentration previously from China towards the U.S., as it noted the continued softening in the Chinese market due to competitive pricing pressure that resulted in lower average selling prices. Notwithstanding, Co. strives to develop and enhance the features of its existing products, which will enable it to offer such products at a higher average selling price level to its customers. For the third quarter of 2006, Co. expects total revenues of $590.0 million to $625.0 million and a loss of $0.23 to $0.33 per share.

Financial Data
(US$ in Thousands)

	6 Mos	3 Mos	12/31/2005	12/31/2004	12/31/2003	12/31/2002	12/31/2001	12/31/2000
Earnings Per Share	(4.04)	(4.51)	(4.16)	0.56	1.64	0.94	0.52	0.27
Cash Flow Per Share	3.62	3.77	1.87	(0.83)	0.49	1.44	0.40	(0.58)
Tang Book Value Per Share	6.95	7.04	7.05	9.49	7.03	6.71	5.88	4.13
Income Statement								
Total Revenue	1,145,717	596,571	2,929,343	2,703,581	1,964,332	981,806	626,840	368,646
EBITDA	8,456	9,092	(262,226)	135,433	313,456	154,436	91,969	44,931
Depn & Amortn	34,653	17,476	92,800	71,400	42,600	22,435	18,533	9,494
Income Before Taxes	(25,385)	(8,352)	(364,699)	63,289	269,769	136,272	78,099	44,321
Income Taxes	7,508	2,839	117,889	(9,841)	67,442	27,254	19,823	14,021
Net Income	(32,078)	(10,635)	(487,359)	73,415	202,251	107,862	56,954	27,013
Average Shares	120,608	120,600	117,034	135,541	124,909	114,407	108,612	101,867
Balance Sheet								
Total Assets	2,316,818	2,375,516	2,366,052	3,316,005	2,226,958	1,305,552	1,005,880	591,837
Current Liabilities	1,099,719	1,139,642	1,133,309	1,534,953	944,707	539,157	305,372	161,514
Long-Term Obligations	274,900	274,900	274,900	410,655	402,500	...	12,048	12,048
Total Liabilities	1,402,089	1,445,485	1,429,167	1,945,608	1,347,207	539,157	317,420	173,562
Stockholders' Equity	907,136	922,179	928,547	1,365,372	879,191	766,395	681,887	412,319
Shares Outstanding	120,618	120,607	120,585	114,486	104,272	106,787	109,302	95,032
Statistical Record								
Return on Assets %	N.M.	N.M.	N.M.	2.64	11.45	9.33	7.13	6.24
Return on Equity %	N.M.	N.M.	N.M.	6.52	24.58	14.90	10.41	9.32
EBITDA Margin %	0.74	1.52	N.M.	5.01	15.96	15.73	14.67	12.19
Net Margin %	N.M.	N.M.	N.M.	2.72	10.30	10.99	9.09	7.33
Asset Turnover	0.95	0.96	1.03	0.97	1.11	0.85	0.78	0.85
Current Ratio	1.79	1.78	1.77	1.73	1.94	2.05	2.94	3.29
Debt to Equity	0.30	0.30	0.30	0.30	0.46	...	0.02	0.03
Price Range	9.09-5.26	11.11-5.26	22.20-5.26	41.34-13.71	45.36-17.00	33.95-12.57	30.43-12.56	87.50-12.50
P/E Ratio	...	...	...	73.82-24.48	27.66-10.37	36.12-13.37	58.52-24.16	324.07-46.30

Address: 1275 Harbor Bay Parkway, Alameda, CA 94502	**Web Site:** www.utstar.com
Telephone: 510-864-8800	**Officers:** Hong Liang Lu - Chmn., Pres., C.E.O. Francis P. Barton - Exec. V.P., C.F.O.
	Auditors: PricewaterhouseCoopers LLP **Investor Contact:** 510-749-1510 **Transfer Agents:** EquiServe

VARIAN, INC.

Exchange	Symbol	Price	52Wk Range	Yield	P/E
NMS	VARI	$46.68 (8/31/2006)	47.85-33.50	N/A	28.99

*7 Year Price Score 91.95 *NYSE Composite Index=100 *12 Month Price Score 105.24

Interim Earnings (Per Share)

Qtr.	Dec	Mar	Jun	Sep
2002-03	0.36	0.40	0.31	0.33
2003-04	0.38	0.41	0.43	0.44
2004-05	0.42	2.29	0.43	0.49
2005-06	0.30	0.36	0.46	...

Interim Dividends (Per Share)
No Dividends Paid

Valuation Analysis

		Institutional Holding	
Forecast P/E	24.00 (9/9/2006)	No of Institutions	168
Market Cap	$1.4 Billion	Shares	28,669,120
Book Value	532.9 Million	% Held	92.62
Price/Book	2.71		
Price/Sales	1.77		

Business Summary: Instruments and Related Products (MIC: 11.15 SIC: 3826 NAIC: 334516)

Varian and its subsidiaries are engaged in designing, developing, manufacturing, marketing, selling and servicing scientific instruments and vacuum products. Co.'s Scientific Instruments include chromatography and optical spectroscopy instruments, dissolution testing equipment, mass spectroscopy instruments, Nuclear Magnetic Resonance (NMR) spectroscopy systems, MR imaging systems, NMR, MR imaging and other superconducting magnets, and related software and consumable products. Co. also offers various products used to create, control, measure, and test vacuum environments in life science, industrial, and scientific applications, where ultra-clean, high-vacuum environments are needed.

Recent Developments: For the quarter ended June 30 2006, income from continuing operations increased 37.4% to $14.5 million from $10.5 million in the year-earlier quarter. Net income was unchanged at $14.5 million versus $14.5 million the year-earlier quarter. Revenues were $209.7 million, up 12.3% from $186.8 million the year before. Operating income was $18.9 million versus $11.9 million in the prior-year quarter, an increase of 58.8%. Direct operating expenses rose 11.6% to $115.2 million from $103.2 million in the comparable period the year before. Indirect operating expenses increased 5.6% to $75.6 million from $71.6 million in the equivalent prior-year period.

Prospects: Co. is benefiting from its balanced approach of focusing on a broad array of applications, product lines and geographies. In particular, Co. is seeing significant increases in life sciences and industrial applications for both its Scientific Instruments and Vacuum Technologies segments. Products with high demand are, for instance, Co.'s Magnetic Resonance imaging systems, mass spectrometers and other analytical instruments as well as its turbomolecular pumps. Consequently, Co. has increased its earnings per share guidance for its fiscal year ending Sep 30 2006 to $1.55, plus or minus $0.04.

Financial Data
(US$ in Thousands)

	9 Mos	6 Mos	3 Mos	09/30/2005	10/01/2004	10/03/2003	09/27/2002	09/28/2001
Earnings Per Share	1.61	1.61	3.51	3.67	1.66	1.40	1.48	1.07
Cash Flow Per Share	2.14	2.44	2.43	2.36	2.69	3.53	2.41	1.94
Tang Book Value Per Share	10.11	9.21	9.32	10.36	10.75	9.20	7.41	9.19
Income Statement								
Total Revenue	615,108	405,363	195,737	772,795	915,963	847,739	779,893	749,201
EBITDA	70,311	43,958	20,994	...	116,404	100,687	104,403	95,352
Depn & Amortn	19,807	12,388	6,344	26,249	25,481	24,082	21,331	21,503
Income Before Taxes	51,731	32,504	15,208	...	91,585	75,610	81,167	72,628
Income Taxes	16,339	11,603	5,549	16,766	32,055	26,463	29,540	28,325
Net Income	35,392	20,901	9,659	125,957	59,530	49,147	51,627	36,848
Average Shares	31,315	31,412	31,713	34,355	35,773	35,057	34,928	34,470
Balance Sheet								
Total Assets	817,265	787,896	784,247	795,995	830,665	737,052	634,604	559,257
Current Liabilities	229,746	233,172	228,425	241,148	249,356	220,343	199,178	201,611
Long-Term Obligations	25,000	26,250	26,250	27,500	30,000	36,273	37,635	39,656
Total Liabilities	284,360	286,822	284,829	296,473	303,454	279,483	254,883	253,986
Stockholders' Equity	532,905	501,074	499,418	499,522	527,211	457,569	379,721	305,271
Shares Outstanding	30,897	30,717	31,044	31,016	34,838	34,181	33,951	33,223
Statistical Record								
Return on Assets %	6.12	5.87	14.40	15.53	7.62	7.05	8.67	6.90
Return on Equity %	9.51	9.10	22.64	24.60	12.12	11.55	15.12	13.16
EBITDA Margin %	11.43	10.84	10.73	...	12.71	11.88	13.39	12.73
Net Margin %	5.75	5.16	4.93	16.30	6.50	5.80	6.62	4.92
Asset Turnover	1.00	0.91	0.93	0.95	1.17	1.22	1.31	1.40
Current Ratio	2.05	1.92	2.01	2.10	2.21	2.14	1.99	1.86
Debt to Equity	0.05	0.05	0.05	0.06	0.06	0.08	0.10	0.13
Price Range	45.91-33.50	43.10-33.17	43.10-33.17	43.05-33.17	45.93-33.75	36.50-25.81	39.23-22.99	45.06-22.63
P/E Ratio	28.52-20.81	26.77-20.60	12.28-9.45	11.73-9.04	27.67-20.33	26.07-18.44	26.51-15.53	42.11-21.14

Address: 3120 Hansen Way, Palo Alto, CA 94304-1030 Telephone: 650-213-8000	Web Site: www.varianinc.com Officers: Allen J. Lauer - Chmn. Garry W. Rogerson - Pres., C.E.O.	Auditors: PricewaterhouseCoopers LLP

VERISIGN INC.

Exchange	Symbol	Price	52Wk Range	Yield	P/E
NMS	VRSN	$20.24 (8/31/2006)	25.39-17.06	N/A	14.15

*7 Year Price Score 38.28 *NYSE Composite Index=100 *12 Month Price Score 85.47

Interim Earnings (Per Share)

Qtr.	Mar	Jun	Sep	Dec
2003	(0.22)	(0.60)	(0.13)	(0.13)
2004	0.04	0.09	0.16	0.44
2005	0.19	0.15	0.17	1.03
2006	0.08	...	...	...

Interim Dividends (Per Share)
No Dividends Paid

Valuation Analysis

		Institutional Holding	
Forecast P/E	20.09	No of Institutions	
	(9/9/2006)	310	
Market Cap	$5.0 Billion	Shares	198,516,800
Book Value	2.0 Billion	% Held	
Price/Book	2.44		80.98
Price/Sales	3.13		

Business Summary: IT & Technology (MIC: 10.2 SIC: 7371 NAIC: 541511)
Verisign is a provider of critical infrastructure services that enable Web site owners, enterprises, communications service providers, electronic commerce service providers and individuals to engage in secure digital commerce and communications. Co. is organized into two customer-focused lines of business: the Internet Services Group and the Communication Services Group. The Internet Services Group consists of two business units: Security Services and Naming and Directory Services. The Communication Services Group provides network, directory and application services, intelligent data base, and billing and payment services to wireline and wireless telecommunications carriers.

Recent Developments: For the quarter ended Mar 31 2006, income from continuing operations decreased 57.9% to $19.0 million from $45.2 million in the year-earlier quarter. Net income decreased 59.8% to $19.8 million from $49.2 million in the year-earlier quarter. Revenues were $373.6 million, down 3.5% from $387.3 million the year before. Operating income was $15.5 million versus $55.4 million in the prior-year quarter, a decrease of 72.1%. Direct operating expenses rose 13.5% to $138.9 million from $122.4 million in the comparable period the year before. Indirect operating expenses increased 4.7% to $219.2 million from $209.4 million in the equivalent prior-year period.

Prospects: Co.'s Internet Services Group revenues are benefiting from increasing information services revenues due to increasing number of active domain names ending in .com and .net under management. Similarly, Co.'s security services revenues are being positively affected by increasing managed security services revenues and higher installed base of digital certificates. Co. expects this segment's revenues will continue to benefit from increased demand for information and security services. Separately, on May 1 2006, Co. announced that it has completed its acquisition of m-Qube for about $250.0 million in cash. Co. expects the acquisition will be neutral to earnings for 2006.

Financial Data
(US$ in Thousands)

	3 Mos	12/31/2005	12/31/2004	12/31/2003	12/31/2002	12/31/2001	12/31/2000	12/31/1999
Earnings Per Share	1.43	1.54	0.72	(1.08)	(20.97)	(65.64)	(19.57)	0.03
Cash Flow Per Share	2.16	1.98	1.45	1.49	1.01	1.12	1.20	0.15
Tang Book Value Per Share	2.35	2.98	2.85	3.16	1.89	3.48	4.10	2.88
Income Statement								
Total Revenue	373,604	1,609,494	1,166,455	1,054,780	1,221,668	983,564	474,766	84,776
EBITDA	88,441	308,813	302,582	(114,661)	(4,826,068)	203,023	104,387	8,627
Depn & Amortn	52,444	95,621	88,777	121,865	124,438	13,636,318	3,218,527	5,508
Income Before Taxes	43,620	243,233	213,805	(236,526)	(4,950,506)	(13,433,295)	(3,114,140)	3,119
Income Taxes	24,627	104,655	27,580	23,353	10,375	(77,922)	...	...
Net Income	19,771	406,461	186,225	(259,879)	(4,961,297)	(13,355,952)	(3,115,474)	3,955
Average Shares	248,905	264,513	257,992	239,780	236,552	203,478	159,169	114,610
Balance Sheet								
Total Assets	3,209,835	3,172,899	2,592,874	2,100,217	2,391,318	7,537,508	19,195,222	341,166
Current Liabilities	956,735	938,133	699,595	555,206	665,345	833,845	665,479	42,679
Total Liabilities	1,138,384	1,099,739	864,600	687,735	811,893	1,031,434	724,614	42,807
Stockholders' Equity	2,029,817	2,031,675	1,691,997	1,383,653	1,579,425	6,506,074	18,470,608	298,359
Shares Outstanding	244,790	246,418	253,341	241,979	237,510	234,358	198,639	103,482
Statistical Record								
Return on Assets %	12.75	14.10	7.91	N.M.	N.M.	N.M.	N.M.	1.95
Return on Equity %	19.92	21.83	12.08	N.M.	N.M.	N.M.	N.M.	2.33
EBITDA Margin %	23.67	19.19	25.94	N.M.	N.M.	20.64	21.99	10.18
Net Margin %	5.29	25.25	15.97	N.M.	N.M.	N.M.	N.M.	4.67
Asset Turnover	0.53	0.56	0.50	0.47	0.25	0.07	0.05	0.42
Current Ratio	1.18	1.31	1.44	1.59	0.91	1.31	1.78	4.28
Price Range	32.95-19.53	33.60-19.53	35.96-15.04	17.25-7.09	38.06-4.13	91.94-28.00	253.00-68.13	190.63-14.78
P/E Ratio	23.04-13.66	21.82-12.68	49.94-20.89	...	...	...	...	N.M.

Address: 487 East Middlefield Road, Mountain View, CA 94043
Telephone: 650-961-7500
Fax: 650-961-7300

Web Site: www.verisign-grs.com
Officers: Stratton D. Sclavos - Chmn., Pres., C.E.O.
D. James Bidzos - Vice-Chmn.

Auditors: KPMG LLP
Investor Contact: 650-429-3512

VERTEX PHARMACEUTICALS, INC.

Exchange	Symbol	Price	52Wk Range	Yield	P/E
NMS	VRTX	$34.45 (8/31/2006)	44.20-17.90	N/A	N/A

*7 Year Price Score 98.35 *NYSE Composite Index=100 *12 Month Price Score 105.33

Interim Earnings (Per Share)

Qtr.	Mar	Jun	Sep	Dec
2003	0.27	(1.17)	(1.12)	(0.53)
2004	(0.52)	(0.56)	(0.49)	(0.55)
2005	(0.56)	(0.50)	(0.84)	(0.35)
2006	(0.47)	(0.72)	...	...

Interim Dividends (Per Share)
No Dividends Paid

Valuation Analysis	**Institutional Holding**
Forecast P/E N/A	No of Institutions 212
Market Cap $3.8 Billion	Shares
Book Value 175.0 Million	98,652,312
Price/Book 21.77	% Held
Price/Sales 22.58	88.24

Business Summary: Pharmaceuticals (MIC: 9.1 SIC: 2834 NAIC: 325412)
Vertex Pharmaceuticals is engaged in discovering, developing, and commercializing small molecule drugs. Co.'s candidates target serious diseases, including HIV infection, chronic hepatitis C virus (HCV) infection, inflammatory and autoimmune disorders, cancer, pain and bacterial infection. Co.'s pipeline of potential products includes several drug candidates targeting chronic HCV infection, inflammatory and autoimmune diseases such as rheumatoid arthritis and psoriasis, and cancer. Co.'s first product approved, Agenerase®, is an HIV protease inhibitor which is co-promoted with GlaxoSmithKline. Co. has collaborations with Novartis Pharma, GlaxoSmithKline, Merck & Co. and other companies.

Recent Developments: For the quarter ended June 30 2006, net loss amounted to $77.7 million versus a net loss of $41.0 million in the year-earlier quarter. Revenues were $29.7 million, down 8.0% from $32.3 million the year before. Operating loss was $79.2 million versus a loss of $38.6 million in the prior-year quarter. Indirect operating expenses increased 53.6% to $108.9 million from $70.9 million in the equivalent prior-year period.

Prospects: Looking ahead, Co. intends to expand and increase its investment into VX-950, its investigational hepatitis C virus protease inhibitor, to support the global Phase 2b clinical development program. Accordingly, in June 2006, Co. signed a major collaboration with Janssen Pharmaceutica for the development and commercialization of VX-950 in Europe and other regions. The collaboration should enhance the commercial potential of VX-950 going forward. For full-year 2006, Co. anticipates a net loss of between $222.0 million and $237.0 million, revenues in the range of $210.0 million to $235.0 million while research and development expenses to range between $375.0 million and $395.0 million.

Financial Data
(US$ in Thousands)

	6 Mos	3 Mos	12/31/2005	12/31/2004	12/31/2003	12/31/2002	12/31/2001	12/31/2000
Earnings Per Share	(2.38)	(2.16)	(2.28)	(2.12)	(2.56)	(1.43)	(0.89)	(0.73)
Cash Flow Per Share	(1.69)	(1.66)	(1.93)	(1.80)	(2.18)	(1.05)	(0.11)	(0.31)
Tang Book Value Per Share	1.58	2.12	2.21	0.44	2.47	4.96	6.33	6.49
Income Statement								
Total Revenue	68,813	39,087	160,890	102,717	69,141	161,085	167,490	78,127
Depn & Amortn	13,059	6,250	27,289	29,640	23,438	25,432	17,964	9,148
Net Income	(127,745)	(50,087)	(203,417)	(166,247)	(196,767)	(108,621)	(66,233)	(39,658)
Average Shares	108,523	107,440	89,241	78,571	77,004	75,749	74,464	54,322
Balance Sheet								
Total Assets	625,478	524,658	548,998	545,453	724,411	815,720	925,131	772,881
Current Liabilities	108,735	82,243	100,243	153,745	139,067	64,597	91,553	38,671
Long-Term Obligations	180,092	180,097	180,097	334,997	333,460	315,000	315,000	347,313
Total Liabilities	450,482	291,746	309,822	510,012	531,566	437,139	449,780	385,984
Stockholders' Equity	174,996	232,912	239,176	35,441	192,845	378,581	475,351	386,897
Shares Outstanding	110,600	109,873	108,153	80,764	78,025	76,357	75,055	59,612
Statistical Record								
Asset Turnover	0.28	0.34	0.29	0.16	0.09	0.19	0.20	0.16
Current Ratio	4.16	4.50	3.84	2.65	4.27	10.16	8.48	10.43
Debt to Equity	1.03	0.77	0.75	9.45	1.73	0.83	0.66	0.90
Price Range	44.20-15.53	44.20-8.83	28.92-8.83	11.91-8.17	16.40-8.00	31.61-12.95	74.19-16.48	97.25-16.75

Address: 130 Waverly Street, Cambridge, MA 02139-4242
Telephone: 617-444-6100
Fax: 617-444-6680

Web Site: www.vrtx.com
Officers: Joshua S. Boger Ph.D. - Chmn., Pres., C.E.O. Victor A. Hartmann M.D. - Exec. V.P., Strategic & Corp. Devel.

Auditors: PricewaterhouseCoopers LLP
Investor Contact: 617-444-6100
Transfer Agents: Equiserve Trust Company, N.A., Canton, MA

WASHINGTON FEDERAL INC.

Exchange	Symbol	Price	52Wk Range	Yield	P/E	Div Acheiver
NMS	WFSL	$22.22 (8/31/2006)	24.88-21.31	3.69	13.63	22 Years

*7 Year Price Score 97.22 *NYSE Composite Index=100 *12 Month Price Score 93.94

Interim Earnings (Per Share)

Qtr.	Dec	Mar	Jun	Sep
2002-03	0.48	0.45	0.43	0.40
2003-04	0.42	0.37	0.40	0.35
2004-05	0.41	0.47	0.39	0.40
2005-06	0.41	0.42	0.40	...

Interim Dividends (Per Share)

Amt	Decl	Ex	Rec	Pay
0.20Q	9/26/2005	10/5/2005	10/7/2005	10/21/2005
0.20Q	12/19/2005	12/28/2005	12/30/2005	1/13/2006
0.20Q	3/20/2006	3/29/2006	3/31/2006	4/14/2006
0.205Q	6/19/2006	6/28/2006	6/30/2006	7/14/2006

Indicated Div: $0.82

Valuation Analysis

Forecast P/E	13.57
	(9/9/2006)
Market Cap	$1.9 Billion
Book Value	1.2 Billion
Price/Book	1.59
Price/Sales	3.74

Institutional Holding

No of Institutions	177
Shares	50,282,036
% Held	57.62

Business Summary: Other Depository Banking (MIC: 8.5 SIC: 6035 NAIC: 522120)
Washington Federal is a non-diversified unitary savings and loan holding company with total assets of $8.23 billion, as of Sep 30 2005. Co. conducts its operations through its federally insured savings and loan association subsidiary, Washington Federal Savings and Loan Association. Co.'s business consists primarily of attracting savings deposits from the general public and investing these funds in loans secured by first mortgage liens on single-family dwellings, including loans for the construction of such dwellings, and loans on multi-family dwellings. As of Sep 30 2005, Co. operated 122 offices located in seven states in the western United States.

Recent Developments: For the quarter ended June 30 2006, net income increased 3.1% to $35.3 million from $34.3 million in the year-earlier quarter. Net interest income increased 1.4% to $63.6 million from $62.8 million in the year-earlier quarter. Provision for loan losses was $100,000 versus a credit for loan losses of $134,000 in the prior-year quarter. Non-interest income rose 56.0% to $4.0 million from $2.6 million, while non-interest expense advanced 8.0% to $13.8 million.

Prospects: Co.'s near-term outlook appears satisfactory, reflecting recent moderate bottom line gains, despite the strong increase in deposit costs and the softening of the housing market environment. Specifically, Co. is benefiting from the growth in its net interest income, which is being driven by increases in the volume of earning assets and liabilities, as well as the rate earned on those assets or the rate paid on those liabilities. Going forward, Co. believes its strong net worth position will help protect earnings against interest rate risk and enable it to compete more effectively for controlled growth through acquisitions, de novo expansion and increased customer deposits.

Financial Data
(US$ in Thousands)

	9 Mos	6 Mos	3 Mos	09/30/2005	09/30/2004	09/30/2003	09/30/2002	09/30/2001
Earnings Per Share	1.63	1.62	1.67	1.67	1.51	1.71	1.69	1.33
Cash Flow Per Share	1.63	1.64	1.48	1.65	1.60	1.42	1.61	1.47
Tang Book Value Per Share	13.33	13.29	13.12	13.00	12.26	11.56	10.94	10.89
Dividends Per Share	0.805	0.800	0.790	0.772	0.736	0.701	0.666	0.631
Dividend Payout %	49.39	49.38	47.31	46.22	48.80	40.97	39.39	47.41
Income Statement								
Interest Income	388,103	253,221	124,562	461,901	413,772	450,185	507,317	536,410
Interest Expense	194,959	123,682	60,500	195,260	169,753	194,884	234,941	320,120
Net Interest Income	193,144	129,539	64,062	266,641	244,019	255,301	272,376	216,290
Provision for Losses	185	85	...	(134)	(231)	1,500	7,000	1,850
Non-Interest Income	10,798	6,796	3,391	6,409	5,143	15,017	8,088	9,736
Non-Interest Expense	39,982	26,186	12,669	52,319	46,264	44,059	51,228	49,113
Income Before Taxes	163,959	110,208	54,923	222,308	203,712	224,565	222,354	175,464
Income Taxes	56,136	37,722	18,777	76,419	71,844	79,021	78,400	61,850
Net Income	107,823	72,486	36,146	145,889	131,868	145,544	143,954	113,614
Average Shares	87,502	87,363	87,285	87,478	87,130	84,981	85,333	85,258
Balance Sheet								
Net Loans & Leases	6,815,713	6,543,126	6,264,599	5,937,675	4,982,836	4,606,726	4,292,003	4,207,769
Total Assets	8,803,135	8,587,552	8,305,301	8,234,450	7,169,205	7,535,975	7,392,441	7,026,743
Total Deposits	5,255,882	5,130,275	5,057,434	5,002,172	4,569,245	4,520,051	4,452,250	4,251,113
Total Liabilities	7,583,910	7,372,112	7,106,662	7,047,142	6,049,017	6,480,379	6,431,723	6,152,734
Stockholders' Equity	1,219,225	1,215,440	1,198,639	1,187,308	1,120,188	1,055,596	960,718	874,009
Shares Outstanding	87,225	87,187	87,017	86,933	86,547	86,119	84,572	77,013
Statistical Record								
Return on Assets %	1.70	1.75	1.84	1.89	1.79	1.95	2.00	1.65
Return on Equity %	11.88	11.94	12.49	12.64	12.09	14.44	15.69	13.91
Net Interest Margin %	47.16	50.89	51.43	57.73	58.97	56.71	53.69	40.32
Efficiency Ratio %	9.93	10.23	9.90	11.17	11.04	9.47	9.94	8.99
Loans to Deposits	1.30	1.28	1.24	1.19	1.09	1.02	0.96	0.99
Price Range	24.88-21.31	24.88-21.31	24.72-21.31	25.08-22.03	23.96-20.24	21.83-15.15	20.59-15.03	18.88-12.30
P/E Ratio	15.26-13.07	15.36-13.15	14.80-12.76	15.02-13.19	15.87-13.40	12.76-9.07	12.19-8.89	14.19-9.25
Average Yield %	3.43	3.43	3.40	3.31	3.27	3.74	3.64	3.80

Address: 425 Pike Street, Seattle, WA 98101
Telephone: 206-624-7930
Fax: 206-624-2334

Web Site: www.washingtonfederal.com
Officers: Guy C. Pinkerton - Chmn. Roy M. Whitehead - Vice Chmn., Pres., C.E.O.

Auditors: Deloitte & Touche LLP
Investor Contact: 206-624-7930
Transfer Agents: American Stock Transfer & Trust Company, New York, NY

WERNER ENTERPRISES, INC.

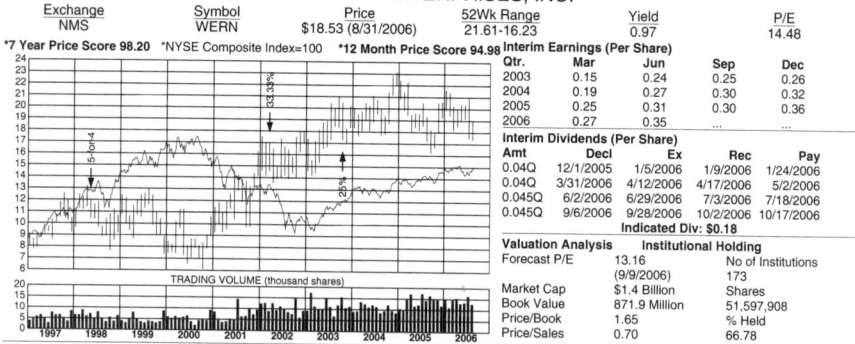

Exchange	Symbol	Price	52Wk Range	Yield	P/E
NMS	WERN	$18.53 (8/31/2006)	21.61-16.23	0.97	14.48

*7 Year Price Score 98.20 *NYSE Composite Index=100 *12 Month Price Score 94.98

Interim Earnings (Per Share)

Qtr.	Mar	Jun	Sep	Dec
2003	0.15	0.24	0.25	0.26
2004	0.19	0.27	0.30	0.32
2005	0.25	0.31	0.30	0.36
2006	0.27	0.35	...	...

Interim Dividends (Per Share)

Amt	Decl	Ex	Rec	Pay
0.04Q	12/1/2005	1/5/2006	1/9/2006	1/24/2006
0.04Q	3/31/2006	4/12/2006	4/17/2006	5/2/2006
0.045Q	6/2/2006	6/29/2006	7/3/2006	7/18/2006
0.045Q	9/6/2006	9/28/2006	10/2/2006	10/17/2006

Indicated Div: $0.18

Valuation Analysis

Forecast P/E	13.16 (9/9/2006)
Market Cap	$1.4 Billion
Book Value	871.9 Million
Price/Book	1.65
Price/Sales	0.70

Institutional Holding

No of Institutions	173
Shares	51,597,908
% Held	66.78

Business Summary: Road Transport (MIC: 15.2 SIC: 4213 NAIC: 484121)

Werner Enterprises is a transportation company engaged primarily in hauling truckload shipments of general commodities in both interstate and intrastate commerce as well as providing logistics services. Co. operates throughout the contiguous U.S. and in the ten provinces of Canada and provides trailer services for customers doing business in and out of Mexico. The principal types of freight transported by Co. include retail store merchandise, consumer products, manufactured products, and grocery products. As of Dec 31 2005, Co. had a fleet of 25,210 trailers and 8,750 tractors, of which 7,920 were owned by it, and 830 were owned and operated by owner-operators (independent contractors).

Recent Developments: For the quarter ended June 30 2006, net income increased 10.8% to $28.0 million from $25.3 million in the year-earlier quarter. Revenues were $528.9 million, up 8.9% from $485.8 million the year before. Operating income was $46.4 million versus $42.1 million in the prior-year quarter, an increase of 10.0%. Direct operating expenses rose 20.2% to $141.8 million from $118.0 million in the comparable period the year before. Indirect operating expenses increased 4.6% to $340.7 million from $325.7 million in the equivalent prior-year period.

Prospects: Co. continues to keep its fleet as new as possible due to the new engine emission requirements for newly manufactured trucks starting in Jan 2007. As such, Co. will be taking delivery of a substantial number of new trucks in the second half of 2006, while continuing to sell its oldest van trailers and replacing them with new ones. Meanwhile, Co. believes that there continues to be several inflationary cost pressures that are affecting truckload carriers, including driver pay and driver-related costs due to a difficult driver market, and rising diesel fuel prices. Thus, Co. will be seeking freight rate increases during its contract renewal period in the second half of 2006.

Financial Data
(US$ in Thousands)

	6 Mos	3 Mos	12/31/2005	12/31/2004	12/31/2003	12/31/2002	12/31/2001	12/31/2000
Earnings Per Share	1.28	1.24	1.22	1.08	0.90	0.75	0.59	0.61
Cash Flow Per Share	2.85	2.63	2.17	2.85	2.60	2.84	2.87	2.16
Tang Book Value Per Share	11.21	11.00	10.86	9.76	8.90	8.12	7.42	6.84
Dividends Per Share	0.165	0.155	0.150	0.120	0.081	0.063	0.060	0.060
Dividend Payout %	12.89	12.50	12.30	11.11	9.00	8.38	10.14	9.80
Income Statement								
Total Revenue	1,020,811	491,922	1,971,847	1,678,043	1,457,766	1,341,456	1,270,519	1,214,628
EBITDA	165,220	77,882	326,812	285,665	134,568	220,823	193,581	192,082
Depn & Amortn	82,173	41,101	162,462	144,535	135,168	121,702	116,043	109,107
Income Before Taxes	84,986	37,503	167,059	143,697	...	98,604	76,391	77,456
Income Taxes	34,936	15,474	68,525	56,387	44,249	36,977	28,647	29,433
Net Income	50,050	22,029	98,534	87,310	73,727	61,627	47,744	48,023
Average Shares	79,689	80,963	80,701	80,868	81,668	81,521	80,183	78,761
Balance Sheet								
Total Assets	1,348,251	1,342,850	1,385,762	1,225,775	1,121,527	1,062,878	964,014	927,207
Long-Term Obligations	...	...	...	...	...	...	20,000	105,000
Total Liabilities	476,377	476,169	523,311	452,606	412,416	415,235	373,965	391,123
Stockholders' Equity	871,874	866,681	862,451	773,169	709,111	647,643	590,049	536,084
Shares Outstanding	77,810	78,777	79,420	79,197	79,714	79,726	79,546	78,398
Statistical Record								
Return on Assets %	7.88	7.70	7.55	7.42	6.75	6.08	5.05	5.25
Return on Equity %	12.25	12.13	12.05	11.75	10.87	9.96	8.48	9.29
EBITDA Margin %	16.19	15.83	16.57	17.02	9.23	16.46	15.24	15.81
Net Margin %	4.90	4.48	5.00	5.20	5.06	4.59	3.76	3.95
Asset Turnover	1.56	1.54	1.51	1.43	1.33	1.32	1.34	1.33
Price Range	21.61-16.23	21.61-16.23	22.64-16.23	23.14-17.65	20.98-14.24	18.05-13.56	16.25-9.26	11.25-6.15
P/E Ratio	16.88-12.68	17.43-13.09	18.56-13.30	21.43-16.34	23.31-15.82	24.06-18.08	27.54-15.70	18.44-10.08
Average Yield %	0.86	0.81	0.78	0.61	0.46	0.40	0.49	0.72

Address: 14507 Frontier Road, P.O. Box 45308, Omaha, NE 68145-0308
Telephone: 402-895-6640
Fax: 402-894-3821
Web Site: www.werner.com
Officers: Clarence L. Werner - Chmn., C.E.O. Gary L. Werner - Vice-Chmn.
Auditors: KPMG LLP
Investor Contact: 402-894-3036
Transfer Agents: Wells Fargo Bank, N.A., St. Paul, MN

WESBANCO, INC.

Exchange	Symbol	Price	52Wk Range	Yield	P/E	Div Acheiver
NMS	WSBC	$30.33 (8/31/2006)	32.81-26.63	3.49	17.95	20 Years

*7 Year Price Score 94.63 *NYSE Composite Index=100 *12 Month Price Score 94.95

Interim Earnings (Per Share)

Qtr.	Mar	Jun	Sep	Dec
2003	0.44	0.38	0.49	0.49
2004	0.49	0.48	0.50	0.43
2005	0.48	0.50	0.44	0.48
2006	0.25	0.52	...	...

Interim Dividends (Per Share)

Amt	Decl	Ex	Rec	Pay
0.26Q	11/16/2005	12/7/2005	12/9/2005	1/3/2006
0.265Q	2/23/2006	3/8/2006	3/10/2006	4/1/2006
0.265Q	5/17/2006	6/7/2006	6/9/2006	7/1/2006
0.265Q	8/25/2006	9/6/2006	9/8/2006	10/2/2006

Indicated Div: $1.06 (Div. Reinv. Plan)

Valuation Analysis   **Institutional Holding**

Forecast P/E	15.34	No of Institutions
	(9/9/2006)	71
Market Cap	$660.7 Million	Shares
Book Value	416.6 Million	7,071,275
Price/Book	1.59	% Held
Price/Sales	2.52	32.46

Business Summary: Commercial Banking (MIC: 8.1 SIC: 6021 NAIC: 522110)

WesBanco is a bank holding company, with total assets of $4.42 billion and total deposits of $3.03 billion as of Dec 31 2005. Through its subsidiaries, Co. offers financial services including retail banking, corporate banking, personal and corporate trust services, brokerage services, mortgage banking and insurance. Co. offers these services through two reportable segments, community banking and trust and investment services. As of Dec 31 2005, Co. operated a commercial bank, WesBanco Bank, through 85 offices, two loan production offices and 125 ATMs located in West Virginia, Ohio, and Western Pennsylvania. Co. also serves investment adviser to the WesMark Funds mutual fund family.

Recent Developments: For the quarter ended June 30 2006, net income was unchanged at $11.3 million versus $11.3 million the year-earlier quarter. Net interest income decreased 8.9% to $30.9 million from $33.9 million in the year-earlier quarter. Provision for loan losses was $2.3 million versus $1.9 million in the prior-year quarter, an increase of 17.9%. Non-interest income rose 14.1% to $11.3 million from $9.9 million, while non-interest expense declined 1.8% to $27.0 million.

Prospects: Co.'s results are reflecting improvement in its net interest margin, stemming from its recent balance sheet repositioning as part of its ongoing efforts to increase certain portfolio loans, while utilizing assets with lower yields to reduce exposure to higher-rate interest-bearing liabilities as well as money market deposits. Additionally, Co.'s continued focus in its marketing efforts have generated in a significant number of new non-interest bearing accounts and customers, aided by savings deriving from its branch-optimization project and cost-containment initiatives. Collectively, these initiatives are believed to bode well with Co.'s target for long-term profitability.

Financial Data
(US$ in Thousands)

	6 Mos	3 Mos	12/31/2005	12/31/2004	12/31/2003	12/31/2002	12/31/2001	12/31/2000
Earnings Per Share	1.69	1.67	1.90	1.90	1.80	1.70	1.60	1.41
Cash Flow Per Share	3.56	2.46	2.00	2.38	2.77	2.32	2.02	2.01
Tang Book Value Per Share	12.41	12.28	12.19	13.74	13.20	13.02	14.46	12.31
Dividends Per Share	1.050	1.045	1.040	1.000	0.960	0.935	0.920	0.895
Dividend Payout %	62.13	62.57	54.74	52.63	53.33	55.00	57.50	63.48
Income Statement								
Interest Income	112,441	56,447	224,745	169,436	165,516	176,155	163,939	163,079
Interest Expense	50,594	25,464	92,434	60,212	62,512	72,555	76,354	79,552
Net Interest Income	61,847	30,983	132,311	109,224	103,004	103,600	87,585	83,527
Provision for Losses	4,903	2,640	8,045	7,735	9,612	9,359	5,995	3,225
Non-Interest Income	16,757	5,414	39,133	35,541	33,230	27,852	24,588	23,376
Non-Interest Expense	53,800	26,812	108,920	89,872	81,810	76,647	64,894	64,483
Income Before Taxes	20,948	6,945	54,479	47,158	44,812	45,446	41,284	39,195
Income Taxes	4,103	1,361	11,722	8,976	8,682	10,620	12,282	12,271
Net Income	16,845	5,584	42,757	38,182	36,130	34,826	29,002	26,924
Average Shares	21,946	21,998	22,528	20,083	20,056	20,459	18,123	19,092
Balance Sheet								
Net Loans & Leases	2,879,708	2,897,176	2,881,120	2,455,880	1,905,562	1,791,081	1,513,387	1,568,281
Total Assets	4,089,003	4,347,310	4,422,115	4,011,399	3,445,006	3,297,231	2,474,454	2,310,137
Total Deposits	2,969,164	2,992,023	3,028,324	2,725,934	2,482,082	2,399,956	1,913,458	1,870,361
Total Liabilities	3,672,372	3,931,139	4,006,885	3,641,218	3,126,570	2,972,060	2,216,253	2,051,631
Stockholders' Equity	416,631	416,171	415,230	370,181	318,436	325,171	258,201	258,506
Shares Outstanding	21,783	21,925	21,955	20,837	19,741	20,461	17,854	20,996
Statistical Record								
Return on Assets %	0.87	0.84	1.01	1.02	1.07	1.21	1.21	1.17
Return on Equity %	8.91	8.87	10.89	11.06	11.23	11.94	11.23	10.17
Net Interest Margin %	55.12	54.89	58.87	64.46	62.23	58.81	53.43	51.22
Efficiency Ratio %	40.08	43.34	41.28	43.84	41.16	37.57	34.42	34.58
Loans to Deposits	0.97	0.97	0.95	0.90	0.77	0.75	0.79	0.84
Price Range	32.81-26.63	32.81-24.87	32.39-24.87	32.75-25.88	28.74-21.99	25.86-19.42	26.10-17.69	26.00-19.13
P/E Ratio	19.41-15.76	19.65-14.89	17.05-13.09	17.24-13.62	15.97-12.22	15.21-11.42	16.31-11.05	18.44-13.56
Average Yield %	3.46	3.50	3.57	3.44	3.85	4.02	4.23	3.93

Address: 1 Bank Plaza, Wheeling, WV 26003	**Web Site:** www.wesbanco.com	**Auditors:** ERNST & YOUNG LLP
Telephone: 304-234-9000	**Officers:** Edward M. George - Chmn. Paul M. Limbert - Pres., C.E.O.	**Investor Contact:** 304-234-9000
Fax: 304-234-9450		**Transfer Agents:** WesBanco, Inc. c/o Corporate Trust Services, Cincinnati, OH

WESCO FINANCIAL CORP.

Exchange	Symbol	Price	52Wk Range	Yield	P/E	Div Acheiver
ASE	WSC	$420.55 (8/31/2006)	421.36-337.14	0.35	9.85	34 Years

*7 Year Price Score 93.42 *NYSE Composite Index=100 *12 Month Price Score 101.52

Interim Earnings (Per Share)

Qtr.	Mar	Jun	Sep	Dec
2003	1.76	6.45	1.00	1.28
2004	1.71	1.49	1.27	2.19
2005	2.59	2.69	2.51	33.58
2006	3.29	3.33	...	...

Interim Dividends (Per Share)

Amt	Decl	Ex	Rec	Pay
0.365Q	1/19/2006	1/30/2006	2/1/2006	3/2/2006
0.365Q	3/3/2006	5/2/2006	5/4/2006	6/8/2006
0.365Q	7/20/2006	8/1/2006	8/3/2006	9/7/2006
0.365Q	9/7/2006	10/31/2006	11/2/2006	12/7/2006

Indicated Div: $1.46

Valuation Analysis
Forecast P/E N/A
Market Cap $3.0 Billion
Book Value 2.3 Billion
Price/Book 1.31
Price/Sales 3.25

Institutional Holding
No of Institutions 76
Shares 6,299,866
% Held 88.48

Business Summary: Insurance (MIC: 8.2 SIC: 6411 NAIC: 524210)

Wesco Financial is engaged in three principal businesses: the insurance business, through Wesco-Financial Insurance Company, which engages in the property and casualty insurance business, and The Kansas Bankers Surety Company, which provides specialized insurance coverages for banks; the furniture rental business, through CORT Business Services Corporation, a provider of rental furniture, accessories and related services; and the steel service center business, through Precision Steel Warehouse, Inc. Co.'s operations also include, through MS Property Company, the ownership and management of commercial real estate property, and the development and liquidation of foreclosed real estate.

Recent Developments: For the quarter ended June 30 2006, net income increased 23.8% to $23.7 million from $19.2 million in the year-earlier quarter. Revenues were $151.2 million, up 8.8% from $139.0 million the year before. Net premiums earned were $13.3 million versus $12.7 million in the prior-year quarter, an increase of 5.0%.

Prospects: Notwithstanding the recent decrease in primary insurance premiums written, due to restructuring of The Kansas Bankers Surety Company's reinsurance program at the beginning of 2006, and intensified price competition, Co.'s near term outlook appears satisfactory. For instance, Co. is experiencing an increase in investment income earned by its insurance businesses, attributable primarily to increased interest rates on short-term investments. In addition, Co.'s furniture rental business is exhibiting positive improvement due primarily to the increase in furniture rental revenues as well as a continued focus on managing operating expenses.

Financial Data
(US$ in Thousands)

	6 Mos	3 Mos	12/31/2005	12/31/2004	12/31/2003	12/31/2002	12/31/2001	12/31/2000
Earnings Per Share	42.71	42.07	41.37	6.66	10.49	7.40	7.38	129.56
Cash Flow Per Share	12.41	13.93	14.24	17.29	17.28	26.47	23.11	(38.03)
Tang Book Value Per Share	282.88	280.03	275.83	259.89	254.44	237.64	231.46	241.16
Dividends Per Share	1.440	1.430	1.420	1.380	1.340	1.300	1.260	1.220
Dividend Payout %	3.37	3.40	3.43	20.72	12.77	17.57	17.07	0.94
Income Statement								
Total Revenue	304,798	153,550	888,290	509,313	614,317	575,677	561,079	1,823,964
EBITDA	71,900	35,641	474,691	104,708	152,370	132,831	146,892	1,465,595
Depn & Amortn	...	...	38,887	36,473	44,114	51,914	65,564	47,203
Income Before Taxes	71,900	35,641	435,804	68,235	108,256	80,917	81,328	1,418,392
Income Taxes	24,738	12,226	141,225	20,808	34,852	28,199	28,792	495,922
Net Income	47,162	23,415	294,579	47,427	74,711	52,718	52,536	922,470
Average Shares	7,119	7,119	7,119	7,119	7,119	7,119	7,119	7,119
Balance Sheet								
Total Assets	2,815,771	2,785,257	2,728,511	2,571,535	2,538,395	2,406,975	2,319,693	2,460,915
Current Liabilities	310,066	307,911	343,202	323,506	296,172	272,086	262,459	339,056
Long-Term Obligations	51,900	41,800	42,300	29,225	12,679	32,481	33,649	56,035
Total Liabilities	535,081	524,859	498,079	454,592	460,205	448,813	407,296	483,881
Stockholders' Equity	2,280,690	2,260,398	2,230,432	2,116,943	2,078,190	1,958,162	1,912,397	1,977,034
Shares Outstanding	7,119	7,119	7,119	7,119	7,119	7,119	7,119	7,119
Statistical Record								
Return on Assets %	11.12	11.10	11.12	1.85	3.02	2.23	2.20	35.98
Return on Equity %	13.67	13.59	13.55	2.25	3.70	2.72	2.70	47.51
EBITDA Margin %	23.59	23.21	53.44	20.56	24.80	23.07	26.18	80.35
Net Margin %	15.47	15.25	33.16	9.31	12.16	9.16	9.36	50.58
Asset Turnover	0.34	0.34	0.34	0.20	0.25	0.24	0.23	0.71
Current Ratio	4.03	3.91	3.64	3.73	3.76	1.53	0.63	0.57
Debt to Equity	0.02	0.02	0.02	0.01	0.01	0.02	0.02	0.03
Price Range	410.00-337.14	410.00-337.14	405.00-337.14	429.75-332.00	370.01-286.00	334.00-298.00	347.90-273.00	290.00-205.00
P/E Ratio	9.60-7.89	9.75-8.01	9.79-8.15	64.53-49.85	35.27-27.26	45.14-40.27	47.14-36.99	2.24-1.58
Average Yield %	0.39	0.39	0.39	0.37	0.42	0.42	0.41	0.50

Address: 301 East Colorado Boulevard, Suite 300, Pasadena, CA 91101-1901
Telephone: 626-585-6700

Web Site: www.wescofinancial.com
Officers: Charles T. Munger - Chmn., C.E.O. Robert H. Bird - Pres.

Auditors: Deloitte & Touche LLP
Transfer Agents: Mellon Investor Services, South Hackensack, NJ

WEST CORP.

Exchange	Symbol	Price	52Wk Range	Yield	P/E
NMS	WSTC	$48.18 (8/31/2006)	49.52-36.11	N/A	21.90

*7 Year Price Score 126.15 *NYSE Composite Index=100 *12 Month Price Score 107.89

Interim Earnings (Per Share)

Qtr.	Mar	Jun	Sep	Dec
2003	0.30	0.30	0.35	0.33
2004	0.40	0.39	0.41	0.44
2005	0.47	0.53	0.53	0.58
2006	0.57	0.52	...	...

Interim Dividends (Per Share)
No Dividends Paid

Valuation Analysis

Forecast P/E	21.26 (9/9/2006)
Market Cap	$3.4 Billion
Book Value	1.1 Billion
Price/Book	3.14
Price/Sales	2.03

Institutional Holding

No of Institutions	151
Shares	29,080,684
% Held	41.10

Business Summary: Miscellaneous Business Services (MIC: 12.8 SIC: 7389 NAIC: 561421)

West is a provider of business process outsourcing services focused on helping its clients communicate well with their customers. As of Dec 31 2005, Co. delivered its services through three segments: Communication Services segment, which provides its clients with a portfolio of voice services through the following offerings: dedicated agent, shared agent, business services and automated services; Conferencing Services segment, which provides its clients with an integrated, global suite of audio, web and video conferencing options; and Receivables Management segment, which assists its clients in collecting and managing their receivables.

Recent Developments: For the quarter ended June 30 2006, net income increased 0.8% to $37.8 million from $37.5 million in the year-earlier quarter. Revenues were $461.7 million, up 24.8% from $369.8 million the year before. Operating income was $76.5 million versus $66.1 million in the prior-year quarter, an increase of 15.7%. Direct operating expenses rose 21.1% to $200.1 million from $165.3 million in the comparable period the year before. Indirect operating expenses increased 33.7% to $185.1 million from $138.4 million in the equivalent prior-year period.

Prospects: Co.'s top-line results are being driven by organic growth, its June 2005 acquisition of Sprint conferencing assets, as well as its Apr 2006 acquisitions of Intrado Inc. and Raindance Communications, Inc. Separately, on May 31 2006, Co. announced that it has entered into a definitive agreement to be acquired by Omaha Acquisition Corp., a newly-formed corporation whose private equity funds are sponsored by Thomas H. Lee Partners, L.P. and Quadrangle Group LLC, in transaction valued at about $4.10 billion. Under the terms of the agreement, all stockholders except Co. founders Gary and Mary West will receive $48.75 per share in cash. The transaction is expected to be completed by Dec 31 2005.

Financial Data
(US$ in Thousands)

	6 Mos	3 Mos	12/31/2005	12/31/2004	12/31/2003	12/31/2002	12/31/2001	12/31/2000
Earnings Per Share	2.20	2.21	2.11	1.63	1.28	1.01	1.11	1.03
Cash Flow Per Share	4.26	4.08	4.05	3.28	2.89	1.78	1.57	1.73
Tang Book Value Per Share	N.M.	2.57	1.63	1.70	1.57	6.05	6.54	5.19
Income Statement								
Total Revenue	886,416	424,738	1,523,923	1,217,383	988,341	820,665	780,159	724,505
EBITDA	212,702	99,562	374,983	285,956	229,349	169,753	169,596	154,756
Depn & Amortn	63,996	27,956	107,628	95,947	84,747	61,514	50,353	45,167
Income Before Taxes	133,443	67,724	253,496	181,523	139,820	108,648	120,922	110,922
Income Taxes	48,005	24,084	87,736	65,762	51,779	39,706	44,633	40,663
Net Income	78,814	41,064	150,349	113,171	87,876	68,642	75,786	70,259
Average Shares	72,932	72,420	71,310	69,469	68,617	68,129	68,130	67,950
Balance Sheet								
Total Assets	2,105,829	1,533,295	1,498,662	1,271,206	1,015,863	670,822	591,435	553,907
Current Liabilities	272,801	243,394	206,295	160,755	121,621	66,322	93,592	132,659
Long-Term Obligations	704,197	175,758	233,245	238,354	169,500	17,155	20,893	21,775
Total Liabilities	1,011,419	501,624	526,794	481,751	359,625	121,230	123,276	175,782
Stockholders' Equity	1,084,435	1,031,671	971,868	789,455	656,238	549,592	468,159	378,125
Shares Outstanding	70,686	70,315	69,718	68,380	67,255	66,156	65,200	64,445
Statistical Record								
Return on Assets %	8.81	11.26	10.86	9.87	10.42	10.88	13.23	14.55
Return on Equity %	16.20	17.01	17.07	15.61	14.58	13.49	17.91	20.91
EBITDA Margin %	24.00	23.44	24.61	23.49	23.21	20.68	21.74	21.36
Net Margin %	8.89	9.67	9.87	9.30	8.89	8.36	9.71	9.70
Asset Turnover	0.94	1.13	1.10	1.06	1.17	1.30	1.36	1.50
Current Ratio	1.41	1.44	1.53	1.75	1.66	4.37	3.51	2.14
Debt to Equity	0.65	0.17	0.24	0.30	0.26	0.03	0.04	0.06
Price Range	49.52-36.11	45.02-31.17	42.20-31.17	35.45-23.23	28.30-13.45	33.01-11.99	30.81-18.71	30.00-18.13
P/E Ratio	22.51-16.41	20.37-14.10	20.00-14.77	21.75-14.25	22.11-10.51	32.68-11.87	27.76-16.86	29.13-17.60

Address: 11808 Miracle Hills Drive, Omaha, NE 68154 **Telephone:** 402-963-1200	**Web Site:** www.west.com **Officers:** Gary L. West - Chmn. Mary E. West - Vice-Chmn., Sec.	**Auditors:** Deloitte & Touche LLP **Investor Contact:** 402-963-1200

WESTAMERICA BANCORPORATION

Exchange	Symbol	Price	52Wk Range	Yield	P/E	Div Acheiver
NMS	WABC	$47.83 (8/31/2006)	55.36-46.14	2.68	14.41	16 Years

*7 Year Price Score 95.50 *NYSE Composite Index=100 *12 Month Price Score 90.43

Interim Earnings (Per Share)

Qtr.	Mar	Jun	Sep	Dec
2003	0.69	0.71	0.72	0.73
2004	0.74	0.76	0.78	0.65
2005	0.70	0.84	0.89	0.85
2006	0.81	0.77	...	...

Interim Dividends (Per Share)

Amt	Decl	Ex	Rec	Pay
0.32Q	10/27/2005	11/3/2005	11/7/2005	11/18/2005
0.32Q	1/26/2006	2/2/2006	2/6/2006	2/17/2006
0.32Q	4/27/2006	5/4/2006	5/8/2006	5/19/2006
0.32Q	7/27/2006	8/3/2006	8/7/2006	8/18/2006

Indicated Div: $1.28 (Div. Reinv. Plan)

Valuation Analysis
Forecast P/E 15.18 (9/9/2006)
Market Cap $1.5 Billion
Book Value 421.7 Million
Price/Book 3.54
Price/Sales 4.85

Institutional Holding
No of Institutions 143
Shares 16,339,912
% Held 52.39

Business Summary: Commercial Banking (MIC: 8.1 SIC: 6021 NAIC: 522110)
Westamerica Bancorporation is a bank holding company. Co. provides a full range of banking services to individual and corporate customers in Northern and Central California through its subsidiary bank, Westamerica Bank. The principal communities served are located in Northern and Central California, from Mendocino, Lake and Nevada Counties in the North to Kern County in the South. In addition, Co. also owns 100.0% of the capital stock of Community Banker Services Corporation, a company engaged in providing Co. and its subsidiaries data processing services and other support functions. As of Dec 31 2005, Co. had total assets of $5.15 billion.

Recent Developments: For the quarter ended June 30 2006, net income decreased 11.6% to $24.5 million from $27.7 million in the year-earlier quarter. Net interest income decreased 10.1% to $45.6 million from $50.7 million in the year-earlier quarter. Provision for loan losses was $150,000 versus $300,000 in the prior-year quarter, a decrease of 50.0%. Non-interest income fell 9.2% to $14.1 million from $15.5 million, while non-interest expense declined 2.7% to $26.3 million.

Prospects: Rising short-term interest rates are slowing the growth of Co.'s lower-costing deposit products, placing more reliance on higher-cost certificates of deposit and wholesale funding, which is leading to an increase in cost of funds. Nevertheless, Co. is benefiting from its accumulation of non-interest bearing demand deposits and money market checking balances from small business customers, which are less sensitive to interest rates changes. Going forward, Co. believes the competitive loan pricing and loosened underwriting standards in the banking industry are limiting the opportunity to originate commercial loans which will remain profitable throughout the duration of the loans.

Financial Data
(US$ in Thousands)

	6 Mos	3 Mos	12/31/2005	12/31/2004	12/31/2003	12/31/2002	12/31/2001	12/31/2000
Earnings Per Share	3.32	3.39	3.27	2.93	2.85	2.55	2.36	2.16
Cash Flow Per Share	4.08	3.80	3.70	3.56	3.51	2.69	2.80	2.55
Tang Book Value Per Share	8.84	8.96	8.74	11.33	10.54	10.22	9.19	9.32
Dividends Per Share	1.260	1.240	1.220	1.100	1.000	0.900	0.820	0.740
Dividend Payout %	37.95	36.58	37.31	37.54	35.09	35.29	34.75	34.26
Income Statement								
Interest Income	124,344	62,467	242,797	216,337	223,493	237,633	257,056	269,516
Interest Expense	30,796	14,512	43,649	21,106	27,197	39,182	68,887	88,614
Net Interest Income	93,548	47,955	199,148	195,231	196,296	198,451	188,169	180,902
Provision for Losses	300	150	900	2,700	3,300	3,600	3,600	3,675
Non-Interest Income	27,701	13,639	54,540	38,583	42,916	36,551	42,655	41,130
Non-Interest Expense	51,829	25,483	104,856	98,751	101,703	103,323	102,651	100,198
Income Before Taxes	69,120	35,961	147,932	132,363	134,209	128,079	124,573	118,159
Income Taxes	18,509	9,844	40,491	37,145	39,146	40,941	40,294	38,380
Net Income	50,611	26,117	107,441	95,218	95,063	87,138	84,279	79,779
Average Shares	31,932	32,276	32,897	32,461	33,369	34,225	35,748	36,936
Balance Sheet								
Net Loans & Leases	2,524,928	2,584,200	2,616,372	2,246,078	2,269,420	2,440,411	2,432,371	2,429,880
Total Assets	4,906,886	5,055,553	5,149,209	4,737,268	4,576,385	4,224,867	3,927,967	4,031,381
Total Deposits	3,647,047	3,739,186	3,846,101	3,583,619	3,463,991	3,294,065	3,234,635	3,236,744
Total Liabilities	4,485,155	4,626,181	4,722,495	4,378,659	4,236,014	3,883,368	3,613,608	3,693,634
Stockholders' Equity	421,731	429,372	426,714	358,609	340,371	341,499	314,359	337,747
Shares Outstanding	31,201	31,544	31,882	31,640	32,287	33,411	34,220	36,251
Statistical Record								
Return on Assets %	2.13	2.16	2.17	2.04	2.16	2.14	2.12	2.01
Return on Equity %	24.94	25.57	27.36	27.17	27.88	26.57	25.85	24.93
Net Interest Margin %	73.68	76.77	82.02	90.24	87.83	83.51	73.20	67.12
Efficiency Ratio %	34.69	33.48	35.27	38.74	38.18	37.68	34.25	32.25
Loans to Deposits	0.69	0.69	0.68	0.63	0.66	0.74	0.75	0.75
Price Range	56.25-47.56	56.25-48.16	58.31-48.16	61.05-47.58	53.28-38.70	45.67-35.57	42.00-32.55	43.75-21.00
P/E Ratio	16.94-14.33	16.59-14.21	17.83-14.73	20.84-16.24	18.69-13.58	17.91-13.95	17.80-13.79	20.25-9.72
Average Yield %	2.40	2.35	2.31	2.10	2.26	2.19	2.16	2.54

Address: 1108 Fifth Avenue, San Rafael, CA 94901
Telephone: 707-863-8000

Web Site: www.westamerica.com
Officers: David L. Payne - Chmn., Pres., C.E.O.
Robert W. Entwisle - Sr. V.P., Banking Division

Auditors: KPMG LLP
Transfer Agents: Computershare Investor Services LLC

WHITNEY HOLDING CORP.

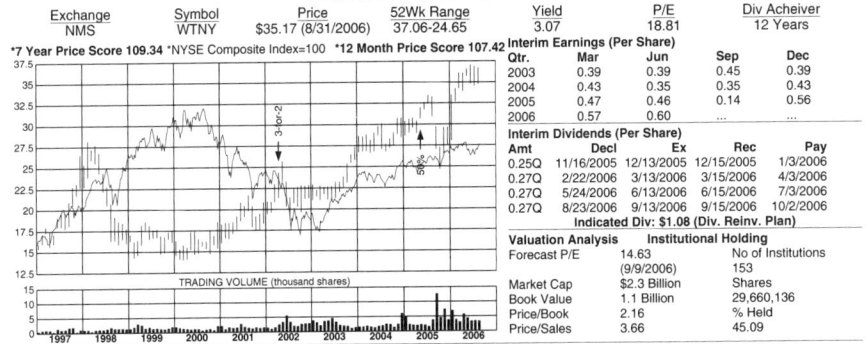

Exchange	Symbol	Price	52Wk Range	Yield	P/E	Div Acheiver
NMS	WTNY	$35.17 (8/31/2006)	37.06-24.65	3.07	18.81	12 Years

*7 Year Price Score 109.34 *NYSE Composite Index=100 *12 Month Price Score 107.42

Interim Earnings (Per Share)
Qtr.	Mar	Jun	Sep	Dec
2003	0.39	0.39	0.45	0.39
2004	0.43	0.35	0.35	0.43
2005	0.47	0.46	0.14	0.56
2006	0.57	0.60	...	...

Interim Dividends (Per Share)
Amt	Decl	Ex	Rec	Pay
0.25Q	11/16/2005	12/13/2005	12/15/2005	1/3/2006
0.27Q	2/22/2006	3/13/2006	3/15/2006	4/3/2006
0.27Q	5/24/2006	6/13/2006	6/15/2006	7/3/2006
0.27Q	8/23/2006	9/13/2006	9/15/2006	10/2/2006

Indicated Div: $1.08 (Div. Reinv. Plan)

Valuation Analysis
Forecast P/E	14.63 (9/9/2006)
Market Cap	$2.3 Billion
Book Value	1.1 Billion
Price/Book	2.16
Price/Sales	3.66

Institutional Holding
No of Institutions	153
Shares	29,660,136
% Held	45.09

Business Summary: Commercial Banking (MIC: 8.1 SIC: 6021 NAIC: 522110)

Whitney Holding is a bank holding company. Co., through its banking subsidiaries, engages in commercial and retail banking and in the trust business, including the taking of deposits, the making of secured and unsecured loans, the financing of commercial transactions, the issuance of credit cards, the delivery of corporate, pension and personal trust services, investment services and safe deposit rentals. As of Dec 31 2005, Co. operated 45 offices in south Louisiana, seven offices in south Alabama, and a foreign branch on Grand Cayman in the British West Indies. As of Dec 31 2005, Co. had total assets of $3.15 billion.

Recent Developments: For the quarter ended June 30 2006, net income increased 34.4% to $39.4 million from $29.3 million in the year-earlier quarter. Net interest income increased 28.2% to $121.2 million from $94.6 million in the year-earlier quarter. Provision for loan losses was $1.0 million versus $1.5 million in the prior-year quarter, a decrease of 33.3%. Non-interest income fell 4.4% to $21.2 million from $22.2 million, while non-interest expense advanced 14.2% to $82.7 million.

Prospects: Co.'s net interest income is being driven by increasing average earning assets and a wider net interest margin. Specifically, Co.'s net interest margin is benefiting from rising rates for the large variable-rate segment of its loan portfolio in the overall asset yield despite increasing percentage of lower-yielding short-term investments in the earning asset mix, prompted by the deployment of a significant influx of deposit funds following the two hurricanes that struck parts of Co.'s market area. Recent loan portfolio growth, excluding the Apr 2006 acquisition of 1st National Bancshares, reflects advances on existing credits and newly originated loans, offset by pay-downs and payoffs.

Financial Data
(US$ in Thousands)

	6 Mos	3 Mos	12/31/2005	12/31/2004	12/31/2003	12/31/2002	12/31/2001	12/31/2000
Earnings Per Share	1.87	1.73	1.63	1.57	1.63	1.59	1.27	1.31
Cash Flow Per Share	3.32	2.61	1.83	2.44	2.44	2.51	2.08	2.02
Tang Book Value Per Share	11.43	11.85	11.54	12.31	12.32	11.69	10.32	10.20
Dividends Per Share	1.040	1.020	0.983	0.893	0.820	0.740	0.684	0.640
Dividend Payout %	55.61	58.96	60.33	57.02	50.41	46.64	54.04	48.98
Income Statement								
Interest Income	298,191	141,992	468,085	360,772	338,069	370,909	441,145	417,687
Interest Expense	63,705	28,755	80,986	40,682	43,509	75,701	161,349	170,574
Net Interest Income	234,486	113,237	387,099	320,090	294,560	295,208	279,796	247,113
Provision for Losses	3,000	2,000	37,000	2,000	(3,500)	7,500	19,500	10,000
Non-Interest Income	42,419	21,176	82,235	82,523	89,504	85,185	91,209	71,625
Non-Interest Expense	161,793	79,100	286,978	260,278	242,923	230,926	239,104	208,903
Income Before Taxes	112,112	53,313	145,356	140,335	144,641	141,967	112,401	99,835
Income Taxes	36,550	17,164	43,007	43,198	46,099	46,644	36,581	32,807
Net Income	75,562	36,149	102,349	97,137	98,542	95,323	75,820	67,028
Average Shares	66,197	63,950	62,953	62,083	60,594	60,182	59,754	51,384
Balance Sheet								
Net Loans & Leases	6,780,031	6,399,430	6,470,569	5,571,931	4,823,135	4,389,297	4,482,905	4,245,501
Total Assets	10,427,716	10,301,742	10,109,006	8,222,624	7,754,982	7,097,881	7,243,650	6,242,076
Total Deposits	8,623,661	8,683,776	8,604,836	6,612,607	6,158,575	5,782,879	5,950,160	4,960,177
Total Liabilities	9,354,952	9,320,987	9,147,963	7,317,859	6,914,669	6,297,398	6,525,762	5,619,116
Stockholders' Equity	1,072,764	980,755	961,043	904,765	840,313	800,483	717,888	622,960
Shares Outstanding	65,753	63,491	63,340	62,101	60,671	60,101	59,500	52,541
Statistical Record								
Return on Assets %	1.24	1.18	1.12	1.21	1.33	1.33	1.12	1.14
Return on Equity %	11.82	11.86	10.97	11.10	12.01	12.56	11.31	11.33
Net Interest Margin %	77.62	79.75	82.70	88.72	87.13	79.59	63.42	59.16
Efficiency Ratio %	46.60	48.48	52.15	58.71	56.81	50.63	44.91	42.69
Loans to Deposits	0.79	0.74	0.75	0.84	0.78	0.76	0.75	0.86
Price Range	37.06-24.65	36.11-24.65	33.44-24.65	30.79-26.63	27.33-21.08	25.68-18.65	21.71-16.60	18.53-14.00
P/E Ratio	19.82-13.18	20.87-14.25	20.52-15.12	19.61-16.96	16.76-12.93	16.15-11.73	17.09-12.60	14.14-10.69
Average Yield %	3.27	3.32	3.28	3.16	3.55	3.39	3.68	4.09

Address: 228 St. Charles Avenue, New Orleans, LA 70130
Telephone: 504-586-7272
Fax: 504-586-3658

Web Site: www.whitneybank.com
Officers: William L. Marks - Chmn., C.E.O. R. King Milling - Pres.

Auditors: PricewaterhouseCoopers LLP
Investor Contact: 504-552-4591
Transfer Agents: American Stock Transfer & Trust Company, New York, NY

WHOLE FOODS MARKET, INC.

Exchange	Symbol	Price	52Wk Range	Yield	P/E
NMS	WFMI	$53.62 (8/31/2006)	79.10-47.37	1.12	46.22

*7 Year Price Score 165.30 *NYSE Composite Index=100 *12 Month Price Score 82.46

Interim Earnings (Per Share)

Qtr.	Jan	Apr	Jun	Sep
2002-03	0.21	0.20	0.23	0.19
2003-04	0.30	0.27	0.25	0.23
2004-05	0.34	0.30	0.30	0.03
2005-06	0.40	0.36	0.37	...

Interim Dividends (Per Share)

Amt	Decl	Ex	Rec	Pay
2-for-1	11/9/2005	12/28/2005	12/12/2005	12/27/2005
0.15Q	11/9/2005	1/11/2006	1/13/2006	1/23/2006
0.15Q	4/5/2006	4/11/2006	4/14/2006	4/24/2006
0.15Q	6/14/2006	7/12/2006	7/14/2006	7/24/2006

Indicated Div: $0.60

Valuation Analysis

Forecast P/E 37.36 (9/9/2006)
Market Cap $7.6 Billion
Book Value 1.4 Billion
Price/Book 5.25
Price/Sales 1.39

Institutional Holding

No of Institutions 436
Shares 112,742,816
% Held 79.86

Business Summary: Retail - Food & Beverage (MIC: 5.3 SIC: 5411 NAIC: 445110)

Whole Foods Market is engaged in owning and operating a chain of natural and organic foods supermarkets. Co.'s stores are supported by distribution centers, bakehouse facilities, commissary kitchens, seafood-processing facilities, produce procurement centers and a coffee roasting operation. Co. offers a product selection with an emphasis on perishable foods designed to appeal to both natural foods and gourmet shoppers. Most of Co's products are from natural food vendors; however, Co. does sell a limited selection of national brands that meet Co.'s standards. As of Sep 25 2005, Co. operated 175 stores: 165 stores in U.S. states; 3 stores in Canada; and 7 stores in the United Kingdom.

Recent Developments: For the quarter ended July 2 2006, net income increased 33.5% to $53.9 million from $40.4 million in the year-earlier quarter. Revenues were $1.34 billion, up 18.1% from $1.13 billion the year before. Operating income was $84.3 million versus $64.6 million in the prior-year quarter, an increase of 30.4%. Direct operating expenses rose 17.9% to $1.20 billion from $1.02 billion in the comparable period the year before. Indirect operating expenses increased 7.1% to $51.8 million from $48.4 million in the equivalent prior-year period.

Prospects: Based on its strong sales trends and its 3.6 million square feet under development, Co. expects to continue to produce similar results on average over the next five years and is therefore raising its 2010 sales goal from $10.00 billion to $12.00 billion. Also, Co. anticipates it will continue to produce strong cash flow from operations and stock option exercises in excess of its capital expenditure needs. Separately, top-line results are being positively affected by weighted average square footage growth and comparable-store sales growth, while Co. estimates the negative sales impact from Hurricane Katrina to range between $5.0 million to $6.0 million.

Financial Data
(US$ in Thousands)

	9 Mos	6 Mos	3 Mos	09/25/2005	09/26/2004	09/28/2003	09/29/2002	09/30/2001
Earnings Per Share	1.16	1.09	1.03	0.99	1.04	0.83	0.70	0.60
Cash Flow Per Share	2.90	2.69	2.75	3.17	2.69	2.37	2.04	1.59
Tang Book Value Per Share	9.16	8.68	8.17	9.06	6.82	5.57	4.21	2.98
Dividends Per Share	2.550	2.525	2.525	0.420	0.225	...	...	...
Dividend Payout %	220.10	231.94	244.41	42.42	21.53			
Income Statement								
Total Revenue	4,316,359	2,978,473	1,666,953	4,701,289	3,864,950	3,148,593	2,690,475	2,272,231
EBITDA	392,037	264,860	143,598	373,115	347,662	278,913	237,071	192,169
Depn & Amortn	118,648	81,308	46,399	133,759	111,891	97,986	85,869	78,823
Income Before Taxes	273,378	183,549	97,196	237,133	228,522	172,813	140,818	95,455
Income Taxes	109,351	73,420	38,878	100,782	91,409	69,126	56,327	38,182
Net Income	164,027	110,129	58,318	136,351	137,113	103,687	84,491	67,880
Average Shares	145,925	145,546	145,317	139,950	135,454	130,660	126,680	112,370
Balance Sheet								
Total Assets	2,078,805	1,944,282	2,094,260	1,889,296	1,519,793	1,196,820	943,201	829,171
Current Liabilities	520,863	481,294	719,620	418,383	331,262	239,584	176,298	156,336
Long-Term Obligations	8,538	9,487	9,400	12,932	164,770	162,909	161,952	250,705
Total Liabilities	636,965	591,232	824,720	523,620	531,354	420,644	354,115	419,814
Stockholders' Equity	1,441,840	1,353,050	1,269,540	1,365,676	988,439	776,176	589,086	409,357
Shares Outstanding	141,181	140,084	138,928	135,908	124,814	120,140	115,478	109,540
Statistical Record								
Return on Assets %	8.65	8.49	7.94	8.02	10.12	9.72	9.56	8.40
Return on Equity %	12.27	12.39	12.54	11.62	15.58	15.23	16.97	18.64
EBITDA Margin %	9.08	8.89	8.61	7.94	9.00	8.86	8.81	8.46
Net Margin %	3.80	3.70	3.50	2.90	3.55	3.29	3.14	2.99
Asset Turnover	2.78	2.83	2.70	2.77	2.85	2.95	3.04	2.81
Current Ratio	1.43	1.41	1.18	1.61	1.46	1.52	0.98	0.93
Debt to Equity	0.01	0.01	0.01	0.01	0.17	0.21	0.27	0.61
Price Range	79.10-59.06	79.10-48.09	79.10-44.30	69.69-40.16	48.17-27.60	30.89-20.60	25.59-15.62	17.78-9.84
P/E Ratio	68.19-50.91	72.57-44.12	76.80-43.00	70.40-40.57	46.32-26.54	37.21-24.82	36.55-22.31	29.63-16.41
Average Yield %	3.78	3.87	4.12	0.79	0.60	...	...	...

Address: 550 Bowie Street, Austin, TX 78703
Telephone: 512-477-4455
Fax: 512-477-1069

Web Site: www.wholefoodsmarket.com
Officers: John P. Mackey - Chmn., C.E.O. A. C. Gallo - Co-Pres., C.O.O.

Auditors: Ernst & Young LLP
Investor Contact: 512-477-5566ex8000
Transfer Agents: Securities Transfer Corporation, Frisco, TX

WIND RIVER SYSTEMS, INC.

Exchange	Symbol	Price	52Wk Range	Yield	P/E
NMS	WIND	$10.17 (8/31/2006)	15.87-7.91	N/A	36.32

*7 Year Price Score 58.56 *NYSE Composite Index=100 *12 Month Price Score 71.28

Interim Earnings (Per Share)

Qtr.	Apr	Jul	Oct	Jan
2003-04	(0.14)	(0.12)	(0.09)	0.03
2004-05	(0.05)	0.04	0.03	0.07
2005-06	0.02	0.06	0.06	0.18
2006-07	(0.02)	...	...	...

Interim Dividends (Per Share)
No Dividends Paid

Valuation Analysis **Institutional Holding**

Forecast P/E	21.47	No of Institutions
	(9/9/2006)	151
Market Cap	$872.5 Million	Shares
Book Value	306.9 Million	70,132,648
Price/Book	2.84	% Held
Price/Sales	3.24	81.71

Business Summary: IT & Technology (MIC: 10.2 SIC: 7371 NAIC: 541511)

Wind River Systems is engaged in device software optimization, or DSO. Co.'s software is used to optimize the development and functionality of devices such as digital imaging products, automobile braking systems, Internet routers, avionics control panels and factory automation equipment. Co. aids its customers' process of programming for these devices by providing integrated software development and runtime platforms targeted to specific markets, as well as off-the-shelf device software, programming tools and hardware. Co.'s customers include end-users, distributors, original equipment manufacturers, system integrators and value-added resellers.

Recent Developments: For the quarter ended Apr 30 2006, net loss amounted to $2.1 million compared with net income of $1.8 million in the corresponding year-earlier quarter. Revenues were $65.0 million, up 5.2% from $61.8 million the year before. Operating loss was $3.9 million versus an income of $1.7 million in the prior-year quarter. Direct operating expenses rose 16.5% to $15.5 million from $13.3 million in the comparable period the year before. Indirect operating expenses increased 14.1% to $53.4 million from $46.8 million in the equivalent prior-year period.

Prospects: Co.'s operating results are being hampered by an increase in operating expenses, reflecting investments in marketing and sales. Nevertheless, Co. is seeing its revenue growth being driven by an increase in subscription revenues earned under its enterprise licensing model, partially offset by a reduction in its product revenues, due to the transition of some of customers to Wind River Platform subscriptions. Looking ahead to the second quarter of fiscal 2007, Co. expects a loss of $0.01 to $0.02 per share, along with revenue of between $66.0 million and $68.0 million. For fiscal 2007, Co. estimates earnings to be $0.12 to $0.17 per share, and revenue of $290.0 million and $300.0 million.

Financial Data
(US$ in Thousands)

	3 Mos	01/31/2006	01/31/2005	01/31/2004	01/31/2003	01/31/2002	01/31/2001	01/31/2000
Earnings Per Share	0.28	0.33	0.09	(0.31)	(1.35)	(4.84)	(1.05)	0.50
Cash Flow Per Share	0.60	0.58	0.49	(0.11)	(0.49)	0.34	0.34	0.78
Tang Book Value Per Share	2.26	2.45	1.94	1.81	1.98	3.05	3.96	4.77
Income Statement								
Total Revenue	64,976	266,323	235,400	204,119	249,121	351,072	437,984	171,110
EBITDA	(1,341)	31,705	23,007	(3,763)	(79,655)	(283,857)	34,408	40,837
Depn & Amortn	2,650	8,918	10,900	19,821	30,501	100,845	112,273	10,523
Income Before Taxes	(2,652)	26,063	10,416	(22,164)	(104,857)	(373,823)	(64,036)	36,580
Income Taxes	(532)	(3,232)	2,251	2,400	2,007	1,811	12,355	14,109
Net Income	(2,120)	29,295	8,165	(24,564)	(106,864)	(375,634)	(76,391)	22,471
Average Shares	85,773	89,939	86,062	80,056	79,035	77,544	72,467	44,778
Balance Sheet								
Total Assets	486,806	483,244	452,254	502,552	490,454	607,620	1,003,505	423,210
Current Liabilities	163,120	163,029	108,274	79,536	88,529	106,484	147,763	67,219
Long-Term Obligations	...	...	75,000	150,000	150,000	150,000	140,007	140,000
Total Liabilities	179,934	179,797	196,309	269,536	238,529	259,479	296,758	219,627
Stockholders' Equity	306,872	303,447	255,945	233,016	251,925	348,141	706,747	202,705
Shares Outstanding	85,796	85,762	83,366	80,807	79,539	78,586	76,589	42,453
Statistical Record								
Return on Assets %	5.49	6.26	1.71	N.M.	N.M.	N.M.	N.M.	5.99
Return on Equity %	8.92	10.47	3.33	N.M.	N.M.	N.M.	N.M.	12.76
EBITDA Margin %	N.M.	11.90	9.77	N.M.	N.M.	N.M.	7.86	23.87
Net Margin %	N.M.	11.00	3.47	N.M.	N.M.	N.M.	N.M.	13.13
Asset Turnover	0.58	0.57	0.49	0.41	0.45	0.44	0.61	0.46
Current Ratio	1.13	1.12	1.12	1.32	1.32	2.19	1.98	2.34
Debt to Equity	...	...	0.29	0.64	0.60	0.43	0.20	0.69
Price Range	17.54-11.34	17.54-11.34	14.46-7.90	9.36-2.82	18.05-2.09	38.00-10.00	60.50-28.13	42.88-11.88
P/E Ratio	62.64-40.50	53.15-34.36	160.67-87.78	...	...	...	...	85.75-23.75

Address: 500 Wind River Way, Alameda, CA 94501
Telephone: 510-748-4100
Fax: 510-749-2010

Web Site: www.windriver.com
Officers: Kenneth R. Klein - Chmn., Pres., C.E.O. Michael W. Zellner - Sr. V.P., Fin. & Admin., C.F.O., Sec.

Auditors: PricewaterhouseCoopers LLP
Investor Contact: 866-296-5361

WYNN RESORTS LTD

Exchange	Symbol	Price	52Wk Range	Yield	P/E
NMS	WYNN	$77.41 (8/31/2006)	78.90-42.18	N/A	N/A

*7 Year Price Score N/A *NYSE Composite Index=100 *12 Month Price Score 107.00

Interim Earnings (Per Share)

Qtr.	Mar	Jun	Sep	Dec
2003	(0.12)	(0.16)	(0.18)	(0.16)
2004	(0.16)	(0.49)	(0.26)	(1.45)
2005	(0.38)	(0.36)	(0.14)	(0.03)
2006	(0.12)	(0.20)	...	...

Interim Dividends (Per Share)
No Dividends Paid

Valuation Analysis	**Institutional Holding**
Forecast P/E	150.16	(9/9/2006)	No of Institutions 150
Market Cap	$7.8 Billion	Shares
Book Value	1.6 Billion	62,169,764
Price/Book	4.97	% Held
Price/Sales	7.28	61.63

Business Summary: Hospitality & Tourism (MIC: 5.1 SIC: 7011 NAIC: 721120)

Wynn Resorts is a developer, owner and operator of destination casino resorts. Co. owns and operates Wynn Las Vegas, a destination casino resort in Las Vegas, NV, and is constructing and will own and operate Wynn Macau, a casino resort development located in the Macau Special Administrative Region of the People's Republic of China which is scheduled to open to the public in the third quarter of 2006. Co. is also are developing an expansion of Wynn Las Vegas named Encore at Wynn Las Vegas. In addition, Co. continues to explore opportunities to develop additional gaming or related businesses in other domestic and international markets.

Recent Developments: For the quarter ended June 30 2006, net loss amounted to $20.1 million versus a net loss of $41.8 million in the year-earlier quarter. Revenues were $273.4 million, up 35.9% from $201.1 million the year before. Operating income was $1.7 million versus a loss of $15.8 million in the prior-year quarter. Direct operating expenses rose 47.7% to $159.6 million from $108.0 million in the comparable period the year before. Indirect operating expenses increased 2.9% to $112.1 million from $108.9 million in the equivalent prior-year period.

Prospects: Looking forward, Co. anticipates the first phase of Wynn Macau to be open in September 2006 while the second phase is expected to be completed and will be fully open to the public in the fourth-quarter of 2007. Accordingly, Co. expects that Wynn Macau's pre-opening costs will continue to increase in the third quarter of 2006 as construction and development continue toward opening, similar to the trend experienced with Wynn Las Vegas in 2005, prior to its opening. Separately, as the Encore development progresses in 2006, Co. expects associated pre-opening expenses to increase, but not to the same level as it experienced with Wynn Las Vegas.

Financial Data
(US$ in Thousands)

	6 Mos	3 Mos	12/31/2005	12/31/2004	12/31/2003	12/31/2002	12/31/2001	12/31/2000
Earnings Per Share	(0.49)	(0.65)	(0.92)	(2.37)	(0.62)	(0.68)	(86.27)	(53.08)
Cash Flow Per Share	1.08	0.89	0.49	(1.32)	(0.27)	(0.21)	(0.02)	...
Tang Book Value Per Share	14.89	15.13	15.13	16.54	12.10	12.46	...	...
Income Statement								
Total Revenue	550,595	277,225	721,981	195	1,018	1,159	1,157	87
EBITDA	130,184	...	...	...	...	...	...	...
Depn & Amortn	90,129	41,785	108,020	10,408	21,941	9,246	8,163	5,510
Income Before Taxes	(31,195)	...	...	...	...	...	...	...
Income Taxes	309	...	...	...	...	...	...	...
Net Income	(31,504)	(11,434)	(90,836)	(205,586)	(48,892)	(31,713)	(17,726)	(10,616)
Average Shares	99,830	98,736	98,308	86,778	79,429	48,706	205,479	200,000
Balance Sheet								
Total Assets	4,101,465	4,009,387	3,945,283	3,464,212	1,733,323	1,398,601	388,543	387,084
Current Liabilities	230,682	241,606	269,779	169,953	71,176	20,652	4,022	4,802
Long-Term Obligations	2,279,617	2,180,146	2,110,064	1,627,968	635,432	382,153	291	326
Total Liabilities	2,531,698	2,437,357	2,382,388	1,819,921	730,454	402,805	4,313	5,128
Stockholders' Equity	1,569,767	1,572,030	1,562,895	1,644,291	1,001,815	991,613	384,230	381,956
Shares Outstanding	100,706	100,069	99,331	98,983	82,168	78,972	...	...
Statistical Record								
EBITDA Margin %	23.64	...	...	...	...	...	...	...
Asset Turnover	0.27	0.25	0.19	0.00	0.00	0.00	0.00	...
Current Ratio	2.61	2.87	2.54	2.66	5.65	43.82	10.35	11.78
Debt to Equity	1.45	1.39	1.35	0.99	0.63	0.39	N.M.	N.M.
Price Range	78.90-42.18	76.94-42.18	74.45-42.18	70.38-27.59	28.18-13.00	13.74-11.09	...	...

Address: 3131 Las Vegas Boulevard South, Las Vegas, NV 89109
Telephone: 702-770-7555
Web Site: www.wynnresorts.com
Officers: Stephen A. Wynn - Chmn., C.E.O. Kazuo Okada - Vice-Chmn.
Auditors: DELOITTE & TOUCHE LLP
Investor Contact: 702-770-7555
Transfer Agents: American Stock Transfer & Trust Co.

XILINX, INC.

Exchange	Symbol	Price	52Wk Range	Yield	P/E
NMS	XLNX	$22.87 (8/31/2006)	29.79-19.60	1.57	22.20

7 Year Price Score 55.51 *NYSE Composite Index=100 *12 Month Price Score 81.48

Interim Earnings (Per Share)

Qtr.	Jun	Sep	Dec	Mar
2003-04	0.13	0.16	0.19	0.36
2004-05	0.26	0.24	0.18	0.19
2005-06	0.21	0.24	0.23	0.32
2006-07	0.24	...	...	...

Interim Dividends (Per Share)

Amt	Decl	Ex	Rec	Pay
0.07Q	10/20/2005	11/15/2005	11/17/2005	12/1/2005
0.07Q	1/19/2006	2/6/2006	2/8/2006	3/1/2006
0.09Q	4/26/2006	5/8/2006	5/10/2006	5/31/2006
0.09Q	7/25/2006	8/14/2006	8/16/2006	9/6/2006

Indicated Div: $0.36

Valuation Analysis

		Institutional Holding	
Forecast P/E	17.26	No of Institutions	
	(9/9/2006)	338	
Market Cap	$7.8 Billion	Shares	
Book Value	2.7 Billion	299,189,664	
Price/Book	2.86	% Held	
Price/Sales	4.30	88.03	

Business Summary: IT & Technology (MIC: 10.2 SIC: 3674 NAIC: 334413)

Xilinx designs, develops and markets complete programmable logic solutions, including advanced integrated circuits, software design tools, predefined system functions delivered as intellectual property cores, design services, customer training, field engineering and technical support. The programmable logic devices include field programmable gate arrays and complex programmable logic devices. These devices are standard products that Co.'s customers program to perform desired logic functions. Co.'s products are designed to provide high integration and quick time-to-market for electronic equipment manufacturers in the communications, storage, server, consumer, industrial and other markets.

Recent Developments: For the quarter ended July 1 2006, net income increased 7.4% to $82.5 million from $76.8 million in the year-earlier quarter. Revenues were $481.4 million, up 18.7% from $405.4 million the year before. Operating income was $93.1 million versus $90.5 million in the prior-year quarter, an increase of 2.9%. Direct operating expenses rose 21.2% to $192.1 million from $158.5 million in the comparable period the year before. Indirect operating expenses increased 25.4% to $196.2 million from $156.4 million in the equivalent prior-year period.

Prospects: Co. remains focused on long-term revenue growth as well as end-market expansion, and will continue to further enhance new products development to expand its market opportunities in fiscal 2007. Accordingly, Co. plans to continue to invest in research and development efforts in a wide variety of areas such as 65-nanometer and more advanced process development, Internet Protocol cores, digital signal processing, embedded processing and the development of new design and layout software. For the fiscal quarter ending Sept 2006, Co. expects revenues to be flat to down 5.0% sequentially and growth margins to be 61.0% to 62.0%, including about $3.0 million of stock-based compensation charges.

Financial Data
(US$ in Thousands)

	3 Mos	04/01/2006	04/02/2005	04/03/2004	03/29/2003	03/30/2002	03/31/2001	03/31/2000
Earnings Per Share	1.03	1.00	0.87	0.85	0.36	(0.34)	0.10	1.90
Cash Flow Per Share	1.44	1.41	0.79	1.25	1.03	0.84	1.15	1.07
Tang Book Value Per Share	7.56	7.53	7.24	6.79	5.40	5.26	5.82	5.46
Dividends Per Share	0.300	0.280	0.200	...	...	...	...	...
Dividend Payout %	29.06	28.00	22.99	...	...	...	...	...
Income Statement								
Total Revenue	481,362	1,726,250	1,573,233	1,397,846	1,155,977	1,015,579	1,659,358	1,020,993
EBITDA	122,151	516,878	459,112	422,234	248,712	(75,819)	154,719	1,068,472
Depn & Amortn	14,684	60,276	58,568	71,690	78,840	117,078	93,451	44,191
Income Before Taxes	107,467	456,602	400,544	350,544	169,872	(192,954)	61,103	1,024,272
Income Taxes	24,976	102,453	87,821	47,555	44,167	(79,347)	25,845	378,006
Net Income	82,491	354,149	312,723	302,989	125,705	(113,607)	35,258	652,450
Average Shares	348,988	355,065	358,230	354,551	348,622	333,556	353,345	343,479
Balance Sheet								
Total Assets	3,129,693	3,173,547	3,039,196	2,937,473	2,421,676	2,335,360	2,502,196	2,348,639
Current Liabilities	308,513	345,024	298,394	381,130	313,834	195,840	350,410	244,712
Total Liabilities	414,557	444,662	365,688	454,411	470,937	431,620	583,880	571,984
Stockholders' Equity	2,715,136	2,728,885	2,673,508	2,483,062	1,950,739	1,903,740	1,918,316	1,776,655
Shares Outstanding	339,873	342,618	350,161	346,962	339,005	336,188	329,740	325,512
Statistical Record								
Return on Assets %	11.59	11.43	10.49	11.12	5.30	N.M.	1.45	38.06
Return on Equity %	13.29	13.15	12.16	13.45	6.54	N.M.	1.91	49.00
EBITDA Margin %	25.38	29.94	29.18	30.21	21.52	N.M.	9.32	104.65
Net Margin %	17.14	20.52	19.88	21.68	10.87	N.M.	2.12	63.90
Asset Turnover	0.58	0.56	0.53	0.51	0.49	0.42	0.68	0.60
Current Ratio	5.42	4.78	4.91	3.41	3.74	5.10	2.94	4.25
Price Range	29.79-21.94	29.96-21.94	40.22-25.44	42.90-23.41	43.84-13.75	50.00-21.64	97.94-35.13	86.81-20.28
P/E Ratio	28.92-21.30	29.96-21.94	46.23-29.24	50.47-27.54	121.78-38.19	...	..979.38-351.25	45.69-10.67
Average Yield %	1.13	1.04	0.65	...	...	...	...	...

Address: 2100 Logic Drive, San Jose, CA 95124-3400	**Web Site:** www.xilinx.com	**Auditors:** Ernst & Young LLP
Telephone: 408-559-7778	**Officers:** Willem P. Roelandts - Chmn., Pres., C.E.O. Richard W. Sevcik - Exec. V.P., Gen. Mgr.	**Investor Contact:** 800-836-4002
Fax: 408-559-7114		**Transfer Agents:** Equiserve L.P., Boston, MA

XM SATELLITE RADIO HOLDINGS INC

Exchange	Symbol	Price	52Wk Range	Yield	P/E
NMS	XMSR	$12.95 (8/31/2006)	36.41-10.36	N/A	N/A

*7 Year Price Score N/A *NYSE Composite Index=100 *12 Month Price Score 52.57

Interim Earnings (Per Share)

Qtr.	Mar	Jun	Sep	Dec
2003	(1.26)	(1.38)	(1.12)	(1.08)
2004	(0.96)	(0.84)	(0.59)	(0.93)
2005	(0.58)	(0.70)	(0.60)	(1.19)
2006	(0.60)	(0.87)	...	...

Interim Dividends (Per Share)
No Dividends Paid

Valuation Analysis | **Institutional Holding**
Forecast P/E | N/A | No of Institutions 293
Market Cap | $3.5 Billion | Shares
Book Value | N/A | 257,973,504
Price/Book | N/A | % Held
Price/Sales | 4.53 | 96.19

Business Summary: Media (MIC: 13.1 SIC: 4832 NAIC: 517410)

XM Satellite Radio Holdings is a satellite radio service company, providing music, news, talk, information, entertainment and sports programming for reception by vehicle, home and portable radios nationwide and over the Internet to more than 6.0 million subscribers as of Dec 31 2005. Co.'s full channel lineup as of Jan 31 2006 included over 160 channels, featuring 67 commercial-free music channels; 34 news, talk and entertainment channels; 39 sports channels; and 21 Instant Traffic & Weather channels. Commercial-free music channels include the genres Decades, Country, Pop & Hits, Christian, Rock, Hip-Hop/Urban, Jazz & Blues, Lifestyle, Dance, Latin, World and Classical.

Recent Developments: For the quarter ended June 30 2006, net loss amounted to $229.1 million versus a net loss of $146.6 million in the year-earlier quarter. Revenues were $227.9 million, up 81.6% from $125.5 million the year before. Operating loss was $101.7 million versus a loss of $127.1 million in the prior-year quarter. Direct operating expenses rose 55.9% to $146.8 million from $94.2 million in the comparable period the year before. Indirect operating expenses increased 15.4% to $182.7 million from $158.3 million in the equivalent prior-year period.

Prospects: Co.'s top-line results are being driven by continuing year over year subscriber growth, and increases in average revenue per subscriber. Meanwhile, Co. plans to launch Oprah and Friends in Sep 2006. The three year, $55.0 million agreement will feature original daily programming of The Oprah Winfrey Show and O, The Oprah Magazine on a variety of topics, including self-improvement, nutrition, fitness, health, home and current events. Looking forward, Co. projects full-year 2006 total subscriber guidance of between 7.7 million and 8.2 million, and expects to achieve positive cash flow from operations for the fourth quarter of 2006 and the full-year of 2007.

Financial Data
(US$ in Thousands)

	6 Mos	3 Mos	12/31/2005	12/31/2004	12/31/2003	12/31/2002	12/31/2001	12/31/2000
Earnings Per Share	(3.26)	(3.09)	(3.07)	(3.30)	(4.83)	(5.95)	(5.13)	(4.15)
Cash Flow Per Share	(1.94)	(0.94)	(0.77)	(0.43)	(1.96)	(3.39)	(3.39)	(0.77)
Tang Book Value Per Share	...	N.M.	N.M.	0.90	2.38	4.78	10.17	18.40
Income Statement								
Total Revenue	435,852	207,966	558,266	244,443	91,781	20,181	533	...
EBITDA	(230,594)	(71,298)	(404,132)	(369,844)	...	...	...	...
Depn & Amortn	100,177	52,128	176,048	165,689	175,726	123,911	42,422	3,369
Income Before Taxes	(380,375)	(150,089)	(664,385)	(615,051)	...	...	...	...
Income Taxes	(2,045)	(868)	2,330	27,317	...	...	...	...
Net Income	(378,330)	(149,221)	(666,715)	(642,368)	(584,535)	(495,012)	(284,379)	(51,873)
Average Shares	266,098	253,213	219,620	197,317	125,176	86,735	59,920	48,508
Balance Sheet								
Total Assets	2,147,594	2,010,969	2,223,661	1,821,635	1,526,782	1,160,280	1,456,203	1,293,218
Current Liabilities	732,368	686,152	764,158	411,456	183,140	132,962	114,878	67,829
Long-Term Obligations	1,341,066	995,165	1,089,485	987,652	767,175	423,158	411,520	262,665
Total Liabilities	2,333,532	1,999,594	2,142,713	1,485,472	993,894	567,969	529,552	337,266
Stockholders' Equity	(185,938)	11,375	80,948	336,163	532,888	592,311	926,651	955,952
Shares Outstanding	268,193	258,364	240,701	208,249	160,665	91,706	74,482	50,631
Statistical Record								
Asset Turnover	0.35	0.34	0.28	0.15	0.07	0.02	0.00	...
Current Ratio	0.92	1.10	1.23	1.95	2.61	0.63	2.37	4.85
Debt to Equity	...	87.49	13.46	2.94	1.44	0.71	0.44	0.27
Price Range	36.93-13.23	36.93-20.17	37.62-26.53	40.45-21.45	26.72-2.67	18.36-1.75	19.63-4.13	45.94-13.13

Address: 1500 Eckington Place NE, Suite 57, Washington, DC 20002-2194
Telephone: 202-380-4000
Fax: 202-380-4500

Web Site: www.xmradio.com
Officers: Gary M. Parsons - Chmn. Hugh Panero - Pres., C.E.O.

Auditors: KPMG LLP

YAHOO! INC.

Exchange	Symbol	Price	52Wk Range	Yield	P/E
NMS	YHOO	$28.83 (8/31/2006)	43.42-25.20	N/A	33.92

*7 Year Price Score 95.39 *NYSE Composite Index=100 *12 Month Price Score 83.14

Interim Earnings (Per Share)

Qtr.	Mar	Jun	Sep	Dec
2003	0.04	0.04	0.05	0.06
2004	0.07	0.08	0.17	0.26
2005	0.14	0.51	0.17	0.46
2006	0.11	0.11	...	...

Interim Dividends (Per Share)

Amt	Decl	Ex	Rec	Pay
2-for-1	...	5/12/2004	4/26/2004	5/11/2004

Valuation Analysis

Forecast P/E	56.86
	(9/9/2006)
Market Cap	$40.8 Billion
Book Value	8.7 Billion
Price/Book	4.69
Price/Sales	6.83

Institutional Holding

No of Institutions	570
Shares	1,028,308,928
% Held	74.45

Business Summary: IT & Technology (MIC: 10.2 SIC: 7373 NAIC: 541512)

Yahoo! is a global Internet communications, commerce and media company that helps Internet users navigate the World Wide Web. Under the Yahoo! brand, Co. provides context-based guides to on-line content to individuals each month worldwide, Web search capabilities, aggregated third-party content, e-mail, and community and personalization features. Co.'s basic products and service offerings are available without charge to its users. Co. also offers a variety of fee-based premium services that provide its users access to its value-added content or services. In addition, Co. sells marketing and advertising services to businesses across the majority of its properties and services.

Recent Developments: For the quarter ended June 30 2006, net income decreased 78.2% to $164.3 million from $754.7 million in the year-earlier quarter. Revenues were $1.58 billion, up 25.8% from $1.25 billion the year before. Operating income was $229.6 million versus $261.4 million in the prior-year quarter, a decrease of 12.2%. Direct operating expenses rose 29.1% to $645.8 million from $500.2 million in the comparable period the year before. Indirect operating expenses increased 42.5% to $700.5 million from $491.5 million in the equivalent prior-year period.

Prospects: Co.'s top line is benefiting from higher marketing services revenues, led by an increase in its user base and activity levels on the Yahoo! Properties, resulting in a higher volume of search queries, page views and click-throughs. Looking forward, Co. believes that the deeper engagement of new and existing users, coupled with growth of the Internet as an advertising medium should increase its revenues for the remainder of 2006 over 2005. Accordingly, for the third quarter of 2006, Co. expects revenues to range from $1.12 billion to $1.23 billion while full-year 2006 revenues are projected to be between $4.60 billion to $4.85 billion, excluding traffic acquisition costs.

Financial Data
(US$ in Thousands)

	6 Mos	3 Mos	12/31/2005	12/31/2004	12/31/2003	12/31/2002	12/31/2001	12/31/2000
Earnings Per Share	0.85	1.25	1.28	0.58	0.19	0.04	(0.08)	0.06
Cash Flow Per Share	1.24	1.21	1.22	0.80	0.35	0.25	0.09	0.46
Tang Book Value Per Share	3.72	3.55	3.59	2.94	1.60	1.47	1.71	1.69
Income Statement								
Total Revenue	3,142,909	1,567,055	5,257,668	3,574,517	1,625,097	953,067	717,422	1,110,178
EBITDA	754,526	361,262	2,940,724	1,496,065	544,591	287,614	48,750	327,923
Depn & Amortn	252,201	124,614	397,142	311,041	159,688	109,389	130,575	69,102
Income Before Taxes	502,325	236,648	2,543,582	1,185,024	384,903	178,225	(81,825)	258,821
Income Taxes	225,630	102,932	767,816	437,966	147,024	71,290	10,963	188,045
Net Income	324,189	159,859	1,896,230	839,553	237,879	42,815	(92,788)	70,776
Average Shares	1,476,642	1,493,307	1,485,591	1,452,499	1,284,162	1,220,120	1,139,448	1,221,356
Balance Sheet								
Total Assets	11,190,562	10,825,408	10,831,834	9,178,201	5,931,654	2,790,181	2,379,346	2,269,576
Current Liabilities	1,422,891	1,309,429	1,204,052	1,180,707	707,796	411,814	358,517	311,834
Long-Term Obligations	749,971	749,993	749,995	750,000	750,000	...	...	...
Total Liabilities	2,492,900	2,380,306	2,265,419	2,076,755	1,568,164	527,911	412,329	372,662
Stockholders' Equity	8,697,662	8,445,102	8,566,415	7,101,446	4,363,490	2,262,270	1,967,017	1,896,914
Shares Outstanding	1,414,422	1,414,422	1,430,162	1,383,584	1,321,408	1,189,720	1,151,040	1,123,302
Statistical Record								
Return on Assets %	12.09	18.40	18.95	11.08	5.45	1.66	N.M.	3.78
Return on Equity %	15.40	23.65	24.21	14.61	7.18	2.02	N.M.	4.47
EBITDA Margin %	24.01	23.05	55.93	41.85	33.51	30.18	6.80	29.54
Net Margin %	10.31	10.20	36.07	23.49	14.64	4.49	N.M.	6.38
Asset Turnover	0.57	0.56	0.53	0.47	0.37	0.37	0.31	0.59
Current Ratio	2.57	2.57	2.86	3.46	2.43	2.36	2.93	4.15
Debt to Equity	0.09	0.09	0.09	0.11	0.17	...	...	...
Price Range	43.42-29.00	43.42-30.07	42.50-30.87	39.14-20.82	22.52-8.18	10.25-4.50	21.44-4.75	118.75-12.81
P/E Ratio	51.08-34.12	34.74-24.06	33.20-24.12	67.48-35.91	118.50-43.03	256.25-112.50	...	N.M.

Address: 701 First Avenue, Sunnyvale, CA 94089
Telephone: 408-349-3300
Fax: 408-349-3301

Web Site: www.yahoo.com
Officers: Terry S. Semel - Chmn., C.E.O. Susan L. Decker - Exec. V.P., Fin. & Admin., C.F.O.

Auditors: PricewaterhouseCoopers LLP
Transfer Agents: quiServeTrustCompany,N.A

ZEBRA TECHNOLOGIES CORP.

Exchange	Symbol	Price	52Wk Range	Yield	P/E
NMS	ZBRA	$33.84 (8/31/2006)	46.51-29.58	N/A	21.55

*7 Year Price Score 96.95 *NYSE Composite Index=100 *12 Month Price Score 78.66

Interim Earnings (Per Share)

Qtr.	Mar	Jun	Sep	Dec
2003	0.31	0.31	0.32	0.33
2004	0.39	0.41	0.43	0.44
2005	0.37	0.37	0.41	0.40
2006	0.37	0.39	...	...

Interim Dividends (Per Share)

Amt	Decl	Ex	Rec	Pay
50%	7/24/2003	8/22/2003	8/7/2003	8/21/2003
3-for-2	7/15/2004	8/26/2004	7/29/2004	8/25/2004

Valuation Analysis

Forecast P/E	22.02 (9/9/2006)
Market Cap	$2.4 Billion
Book Value	921.1 Million
Price/Book	2.60
Price/Sales	3.33

Institutional Holding

No of Institutions	251
Shares	64,168,916
% Held	90.60

Business Summary: Industrial Machinery and Equipment (MIC: 11.5 SIC: 3569 NAIC: 333999)

Zebra Technologies designs, manufactures and distributes specialty printing devices that print variable information on demand at the point of issuance. These devices are used by manufacturers, service organizations and governments for automatic identification, data collection and personal identification in applications that improve productivity, deliver better customer service and provide more effective security. Co.'s product range consists of direct thermal and thermal transfer label and receipt printers, radio frequency identification (RFID) printer/encoders, dye sublimation card printers, and digital photo printers.

Recent Developments: For the quarter ended July 1 2006, net income increased 8.7% to $27.7 million from $25.4 million in the year-earlier quarter. Revenues were $187.4 million, up 6.1% from $176.6 million the year before. Operating income was $37.8 million versus $35.4 million in the prior-year quarter, an increase of 6.9%. Direct operating expenses rose 11.9% to $97.9 million from $87.5 million in the comparable period the year before. Indirect operating expenses decreased 3.8% to $51.7 million from $53.8 million in the equivalent prior-year period.

Prospects: Co. is benefiting from improved sales growth in its Europe, Middle East and Africa region, spurred in particular by growth in unit shipments, partially offset by lower average unit prices. Going forward, Co. will be capturing more opportunities in healthcare, route accounting, retail and other vertical market applications. With a more improved business across its core products, channels and markets, Co. is optimistic about its growth prospects and is estimating net sales for the third quarter of 2006 to be in the range of $180.0 million to $190.0 million and earnings to be in the range of $0.34 to $0.39 per diluted share.

Financial Data
(US$ in Thousands)

	6 Mos	3 Mos	12/31/2005	12/31/2004	12/31/2003	12/31/2002	12/31/2001	12/31/2000
Earnings Per Share	1.57	1.55	1.55	1.66	1.28	1.02	0.88	1.02
Cash Flow Per Share	1.54	1.37	1.30	1.55	1.48	(0.19)	0.20	1.93
Tang Book Value Per Share	11.74	11.31	10.82	10.16	8.18	6.79	5.57	4.48
Income Statement								
Total Revenue	363,235	175,814	702,271	663,054	536,397	475,611	450,008	481,569
EBITDA	87,587	41,696	181,648	196,847	147,726	114,056	100,394	120,029
Depn & Amortn	7,300	3,669	13,104	12,255	11,580	2,854	4,024	6,998
Income Before Taxes	80,056	37,809	168,465	184,548	135,992	110,883	96,139	111,911
Income Taxes	27,612	13,037	56,862	63,905	44,296	39,288	34,610	40,289
Net Income	53,763	26,091	111,603	120,643	91,696	71,595	61,529	71,622
Average Shares	71,229	71,119	72,022	72,539	71,494	70,346	69,482	70,098
Balance Sheet								
Total Assets	985,848	952,476	912,199	862,222	701,611	573,088	479,556	418,896
Current Liabilities	58,210	57,996	54,348	59,576	45,602	36,904	33,828	46,887
Long-Term Obligations	...	...	...	117	452	605	408	513
Total Liabilities	64,779	64,466	61,685	64,568	49,696	38,933	34,549	47,608
Stockholders' Equity	921,069	888,010	850,514	797,654	651,915	534,155	445,007	371,288
Shares Outstanding	70,813	70,761	70,451	71,819	71,098	70,128	69,264	68,597
Statistical Record								
Return on Assets %	11.74	11.96	12.58	15.39	14.39	13.60	13.70	17.56
Return on Equity %	12.56	12.92	13.54	16.60	15.46	14.62	15.08	19.82
EBITDA Margin %	24.11	23.72	25.87	29.69	27.54	23.98	22.31	24.92
Net Margin %	14.80	14.84	15.89	18.20	17.09	15.05	13.67	14.87
Asset Turnover	0.76	0.77	0.79	0.85	0.84	0.90	1.00	1.18
Current Ratio	7.13	7.12	13.48	12.16	12.80	12.59	10.77	6.48
Price Range	47.39-32.91	47.94-35.30	56.28-35.30	61.89-41.71	44.25-24.12	29.76-20.73	25.08-15.19	30.94-17.19
P/E Ratio	30.18-20.96	30.93-22.77	36.31-22.77	37.28-25.13	34.57-18.84	29.18-20.33	28.50-17.27	30.34-16.86

Address: 333 Corporate Woods Pkwy, Vernon Hills, IL 60061
Telephone: 847-634-6700
Fax: 847-913-8766

Web Site: www.zebra.com
Officers: Edward L. Kaplan - Chmn., Pres., C.E.O.
Gerhard Cless - Exec. V.P., Sec.

Auditors: KPMG LLP
Investor Contact: 847-634-6700

ZIONS BANCORPORATION

Exchange	Symbol	Price	52Wk Range	Yield	P/E
NMS	ZION	$78.99 (8/31/2006)	85.04-67.72	1.82	14.93

*7 Year Price Score 106.76 *NYSE Composite Index=100 *12 Month Price Score 100.01

Interim Earnings (Per Share)
Qtr.	Mar	Jun	Sep	Dec
2003	0.97	1.02	0.68	1.05
2004	1.10	1.09	1.13	1.16
2005	1.20	1.30	1.34	1.32
2006	1.28	1.35	...	...

Interim Dividends (Per Share)
Amt	Decl	Ex	Rec	Pay
0.36Q	10/28/2005	11/7/2005	11/9/2005	11/23/2005
0.36Q	1/30/2006	2/6/2006	2/8/2006	2/22/2006
0.36Q	5/1/2006	5/8/2006	5/10/2006	5/24/2006
0.36Q	7/25/2006	8/7/2006	8/9/2006	8/23/2006

Indicated Div: $1.44

Valuation Analysis
Forecast P/E	13.84
	(9/9/2006)
Market Cap	$8.4 Billion
Book Value	4.4 Billion
Price/Book	1.89
Price/Sales	2.95

Institutional Holding
No of Institutions	337
Shares	55,296,444
% Held	52.11

Business Summary: Commercial Banking (MIC: 8.1 SIC: 6021 NAIC: 522110)
Zions Bancorporation is a bank holding company with total assets of $42.78 billion and total deposits of $32.64 billion as of Dec 31 2005. Co. owns and operates eight commercial banks with a total of 475 offices. Co. provides banking and related services through its banking and other subsidiaries, primarily in Utah, California, Texas, Arizona, Nevada, Colorado, Idaho, Washington, and Oregon. In addition, Co. is an active participant in Small Business Administration lending, public finance advisory services, agricultural finance and electronic bond trading. Co. also controls four venture capitals that provide early-stage capital, primarily for start-up companies in the western U.S.

Recent Developments: For the quarter ended June 30 2006, net income increased 22.3% to $145.3 million from $118.8 million in the year-earlier quarter. Net interest income increased 31.8% to $436.3 million from $330.9 million in the year-earlier quarter. Provision for loan losses was $17.0 million versus $11.4 million in the prior-year quarter, an increase of 49.1%. Non-interest income rose 30.0% to $137.8 million from $105.9 million, while non-interest expense advanced 37.7% to $333.3 million.

Prospects: Co.'s earnings are being driven primarily by strong loan growth, notably in the commercial and commercial real estate categories as economic activity remains strong throughout most of the markets in the West and Southwest; and to a lesser extent, a relatively stable net interest margin and continued solid credit quality. Looking ahead, Co. expects the conversion of the Amegy Bank systems as a result of its Jul 2005 merger with Amegy Bancorporation in Texas will improve its operating capabilities. Accordingly, Co. believes that the addition of Texas to its market portfolio will provide it with a market which is expected to grow at a rate of 108.0% greater than the national average.

Financial Data
(US$ in Thousands)	6 Mos	3 Mos	12/31/2005	12/31/2004	12/31/2003	12/31/2002	12/31/2001	12/31/2000
Earnings Per Share	5.29	5.24	5.16	4.47	3.72	2.78	3.07	1.86
Cash Flow Per Share	7.89	6.69	8.27	7.37	4.89	3.01	9.25	4.03
Tang Book Value Per Share	22.40	21.41	20.45	23.29	20.23	17.21	15.19	13.06
Dividends Per Share	1.440	1.440	1.440	1.260	1.020	0.800	0.800	0.890
Dividend Payout %	27.22	27.48	27.91	28.19	27.42	28.78	26.06	47.85
Income Statement								
Interest Income	1,324,671	638,070	1,910,256	1,505,138	1,399,388	1,455,919	1,591,952	1,626,183
Interest Expense	465,497	215,223	548,906	330,642	303,894	420,777	642,163	822,805
Net Interest Income	859,174	422,847	1,361,350	1,174,496	1,095,494	1,035,142	949,789	803,378
Provision for Losses	31,534	14,512	43,023	44,067	69,940	71,879	73,191	31,811
Non-Interest Income	266,247	129,931	438,843	417,863	490,095	376,814	418,706	192,164
Non-Interest Expense	657,731	325,898	1,014,681	923,299	893,862	858,928	855,123	720,827
Income Before Taxes	436,156	212,368	741,887	624,391	546,159	481,149	440,181	242,904
Income Taxes	154,079	75,258	263,418	220,126	213,751	167,702	157,800	79,661
Net Income	282,943	137,633	480,121	405,987	337,823	256,278	283,020	161,709
Average Shares	107,883	107,725	92,994	90,882	90,734	92,079	92,174	87,120
Balance Sheet								
Net Loans & Leases	32,333,860	30,799,065	29,788,537	22,356,004	19,651,855	18,760,250	17,050,355	14,182,498
Total Assets	45,142,086	43,318,029	42,779,639	31,469,834	28,558,238	26,565,689	24,304,164	21,939,443
Total Deposits	33,254,210	32,872,708	32,642,408	23,292,261	20,896,695	20,131,980	17,841,690	15,069,983
Total Liabilities	40,666,137	38,945,318	38,514,824	28,656,496	25,998,439	24,169,169	22,006,973	20,120,742
Stockholders' Equity	4,447,330	4,343,816	4,237,264	2,789,979	2,540,023	2,373,843	2,280,869	1,778,844
Shares Outstanding	106,611	106,070	105,147	89,829	89,840	90,717	92,208	87,100
Statistical Record								
Return on Assets %	1.37	1.35	1.29	1.35	1.23	1.01	1.22	0.76
Return on Equity %	14.46	14.17	13.66	15.19	13.75	11.01	13.94	9.38
Net Interest Margin %	63.55	66.27	71.27	78.03	78.28	71.10	59.66	49.40
Efficiency Ratio %	40.43	42.43	43.19	48.01	47.31	46.87	42.53	39.64
Loans to Deposits	0.97	0.94	0.91	0.96	0.94	0.93	0.96	0.94
Price Range	85.04-67.72	85.04-66.40	76.85-63.56	69.25-54.55	63.50-39.35	59.40-34.45	61.94-42.45	62.75-36.44
P/E Ratio	16.08-12.80	16.23-12.67	14.89-12.32	15.49-12.20	17.07-10.58	21.37-12.39	20.18-13.83	33.74-19.59
Average Yield %	1.88	1.95	2.03	2.06	1.96	1.62	1.48	1.83

Address: One South Main Street, Suite 1134, Salt Lake City, UT 84111 **Telephone:** 801-524-4787 **Fax:** 801-524-4796	**Web Site:** www.zionsbancorporation.com **Officers:** Harris H. Simmons - Chmn., Pres., C.E.O. Doyle L. Arnold - Vice-Chmn., C.F.O., Sec.	**Auditors:** Ernst & Young LLP **Investor Contact:** 801-524-4787 **Transfer Agents:** Zions First National Bank